Econometric Modelling with Time Series

This book provides a general framework for specifying, estimating and testing time series econometric models. Special emphasis is given to estimation by maximum likelihood, but other methods are also discussed, including quasi-maximum likelihood estimation, generalized method of moments estimation, nonparametric estimation and estimation by simulation. An important advantage of adopting the principle of maximum likelihood as the unifying framework for the book is that many of the estimators and test statistics proposed in econometrics can be derived within a likelihood framework, thereby providing a coherent vehicle for understanding their properties and interrelationships. In contrast to many existing econometric textbooks, which deal mainly with the theoretical properties of estimators and test statistics through a theorem-proof presentation, this book squarely addresses issues of implementation to provide a direct conduit between theory and applied work. The comprehensive website accompanying this text may be found at www.cambridge.org/econmodelling.

Vance Martin is Professor of Econometrics at the University of Melbourne, Australia, a position he has held since 2000. He graduated with a PhD from Monash University in 1990. He was appointed a Lecturer at University of Melbourne in 1985 and became a Senior Lecturer in 1990.

Stan Hurn is Professor of Economics and Finance at Queensland University of Technology, Australia, a position he has held since 1998. He graduated with a DPhil in Economics from St. Edmund Hall, Oxford, in 1992. He was appointed as a Lecturer at University of Glasgow in 1988 and became a Senior Lecturer in 1993 before being named Official Fellow in Economics at Brasenose College, Oxford, in 1996.

David Harris is Professor of Econometrics at Monash University, Australia. He was awarded his PhD in Econometrics from Monash University in 1995. He was lecturer in econometrics from 1995 to 1997 at Monash University and from 1998 to 2010 at the University of Melbourne.

Themes in Modern Econometrics

Managing Editor
ERIC GHYSELS, *University of North Carolina, Chapel Hill*
RICHARD J. SMITH, *University of Cambridge*

Series Editor
PETER C. B. PHILLIPS, *Yale University*

Themes in Modern Econometrics is designed to service the large and growing need for explicit teaching tools in econometrics. It provides an organized sequence of textbooks in econometrics aimed squarely at the student population, and is the first series in the discipline to have this as its express aim. Written at a level accessible to students with an introductory course in econometrics behind them, each book addresses topics or themes that students and researchers encounter daily. Although each book is designed to stand alone as an authoritative survey in its own right, the distinct emphasis throughout is on pedagogic excellence.

Titles in Series
Statistics and Econometric Models: Volumes 1 and 2 CHRISTIAN
    GOURIEROUX *and* ALAIN MONFORT *Translated by* QUANG VUONG
Time Series and Dynamic Models CHRISTIAN GOURIEROUX *and* ALAIN
    MONFORT *Translated and edited by* GIAMPIERO GALLO
Unit Roots, Cointegration, and Structural Change G. S. MADDALA *and*
    IN-MOO KIM
Generalized Method of Moments Estimation Edited by LÁSZLÓ MÁTYÁS
Nonparametric Econometrics ADRIAN PAGAN *and* AMAN ULLAH
Econometrics of Qualitative Dependent Variables CHRISTIAN GOURIEROUX
    Translated by PAUL B. KLASSEN
The Econometric Analysis of Seasonal Time Series ERIC GHYSELS *and*
    DENISE R. OSBORN
Semiparametric Regression for the Applied Econometrician ADONIS
    YATCHEW
Applied Time Series Econometrics HELMUT LÜTKEPOHL *and* MARKUS
    KRÄTZIG
Introduction to the Mathematical and Statistical Foundations of Econometrics
    HERMAN J. BIERENS
Economic Modeling and Inference JEAN-PIERRE FLORENS, VELAYOUDOM
    MARIMOUTOU, *and* ANNE PEGUIN-FEISSOLLE *Translated by* JOSEF
    PERKTOLD *and* MARINE CARRASCO

ECONOMETRIC MODELLING WITH TIME SERIES

Specification, Estimation and Testing

VANCE MARTIN
University of Melbourne, Australia

STAN HURN
Queensland University of Technology, Australia

DAVID HARRIS
Monash University, Australia

CAMBRIDGE
UNIVERSITY PRESS

CAMBRIDGE
UNIVERSITY PRESS

32 Avenue of the Americas, New York NY 10013-2473, USA

Cambridge University Press is part of the University of Cambridge.

It furthers the University's mission by disseminating knowledge in the pursuit of education, learning and research at the highest international levels of excellence.

www.cambridge.org
Information on this title: www.cambridge.org/9780521139816

© Vance Martin, Stan Hurn and David Harris 2013

First published 2013

A catalogue record for this publication is available from the British Library

Library of Congress Cataloguing in Publication data

Martin, Vance, 1955–
Econometric modelling with time series : specification, estimation and testing /
Vance Martin, University of Melbourne, Australia, Stan Hurn, Queensland University
of Technology, Australia, David Harris, Monash University, Australia.
    p. cm. – (Themes in modern econometrics)
Includes bibliographical references and index.
ISBN 978-0-521-19660-4 (hardback) – ISBN 978-0-521-13981-6 (paperback)
1. Econometric models.   2. Time-series analysis.   I. Hurn, Stan.   II. Harris,
David, 1969–   III. Title.
HB141.M3555   2012
330.01'51955–dc23   2012004347

ISBN 978-0-521-19660-4 Hardback
ISBN 978-0-521-13981-6 Paperback

Additional resources for this publication at www.cambridge.org/econmodelling

In memory of

Tim Monks (1961–1999), engineer, and

Simon Monks (1958–2007), physician. (S.H.)

Contents

List of Illustrations   *page* xxi
Computer Code Used in the Examples   xxv
Preface   xxxi

PART ONE   Maximum Likelihood

1 The Maximum Likelihood Principle   3
  1.1   Introduction   3
  1.2   Motivating Examples   3
  1.3   Joint Probability Distributions   9
  1.4   Maximum Likelihood Framework   11
    1.4.1   The Log-Likelihood Function   12
    1.4.2   Gradient   17
    1.4.3   Hessian   19
  1.5   Applications   22
    1.5.1   Stationary Distribution of the Vasicek Model   23
    1.5.2   Transitional Distribution of the Vasicek Model   24
  1.6   Exercises   27

2 Properties of Maximum Likelihood Estimators   33
  2.1   Introduction   33
  2.2   Preliminaries   33
    2.2.1   Properties of Stochastic Time Series   34
    2.2.2   Weak Law of Large Numbers   38
    2.2.3   Rates of Convergence   42
    2.2.4   Central Limit Theorems   45
  2.3   Regularity Conditions   53
  2.4   Properties of the Likelihood Function   54
    2.4.1   The Population Likelihood Function   54

		2.4.2	Moments of the Gradient	55
		2.4.3	The Information Matrix	58
	2.5	Asymptotic Properties		60
		2.5.1	Consistency	60
		2.5.2	Normality	63
		2.5.3	Efficiency	65
	2.6	Finite-Sample Properties		68
		2.6.1	Unbiasedness	69
		2.6.2	Sufficiency	70
		2.6.3	Invariance	71
		2.6.4	Non-Uniqueness	72
	2.7	Applications		72
		2.7.1	Portfolio Diversification	74
		2.7.2	Bimodal Likelihood	76
	2.8	Exercises		78
3	**Numerical Estimation Methods**			**87**
	3.1	Introduction		87
	3.2	Newton Methods		88
		3.2.1	Newton-Raphson	89
		3.2.2	Method of Scoring	90
		3.2.3	BHHH Algorithm	92
		3.2.4	Comparative Examples	94
	3.3	Quasi-Newton Methods		96
	3.4	Line Searching		98
	3.5	Optimisation Based on Function Evaluation		100
	3.6	Computing Standard Errors		101
	3.7	Hints for Practical Optimisation		104
		3.7.1	Concentrating the Likelihood	104
		3.7.2	Parameter Constraints	105
		3.7.3	Choice of Algorithm	106
		3.7.4	Numerical Derivatives	107
		3.7.5	Starting Values	108
		3.7.6	Convergence Criteria	108
	3.8	Applications		109
		3.8.1	Stationary Distribution of the CIR Model	109
		3.8.2	Transitional Distribution of the CIR Model	111
	3.9	Exercises		112
4	**Hypothesis Testing**			**119**
	4.1	Introduction		119
	4.2	Overview		119
	4.3	Types of Hypotheses		121

		4.3.1 Simple and Composite Hypotheses	121
		4.3.2 Linear Hypotheses	122
		4.3.3 Nonlinear Hypotheses	123
	4.4	Likelihood Ratio Test	124
	4.5	Wald Test	128
		4.5.1 Linear Hypotheses	129
		4.5.2 Nonlinear Hypotheses	130
	4.6	Lagrange Multiplier Test	131
	4.7	Distribution Theory	133
		4.7.1 Asymptotic Distribution of the Wald Statistic	133
		4.7.2 Asymptotic Relationships Among the Tests	136
		4.7.3 Finite Sample Relationships	138
	4.8	Size and Power Properties	139
		4.8.1 Size of a Test	139
		4.8.2 Power of a Test	140
	4.9	Applications	141
		4.9.1 Exponential Regression Model	142
		4.9.2 Gamma Regression Model	144
	4.10	Exercises	147

PART TWO   Regression Models

5	**Linear Regression Models**		157
	5.1	Introduction	157
	5.2	Specification	158
		5.2.1 Model Classification	158
		5.2.2 Structural and Reduced Forms	160
	5.3	Estimation	162
		5.3.1 Single Equation: Ordinary Least Squares	162
		5.3.2 Multiple Equations: FIML	167
		5.3.3 Identification	171
		5.3.4 Instrumental Variables	173
		5.3.5 Seemingly Unrelated Regression (SUR) Models	176
	5.4	Testing	177
	5.5	Applications	183
		5.5.1 Linear Taylor Rule	183
		5.5.2 The Klein Model of the United States Economy	184
	5.6	Exercises	187
6	**Nonlinear Regression Models**		194
	6.1	Introduction	194
	6.2	Specification	194
	6.3	Maximum Likelihood Estimation	196

6.4	Gauss-Newton		202
	6.4.1	Relationship to Nonlinear Least Squares	206
	6.4.2	Relationship to Ordinary Least Squares	207
	6.4.3	Asymptotic Distributions	207
6.5	Testing		208
	6.5.1	LR, Wald and LM Tests	208
	6.5.2	Non-nested Tests	212
6.6	Applications		215
	6.6.1	Robust Estimation of the CAPM	215
	6.6.2	Stochastic Frontier Models	218
6.7	Exercises		222

7 Autocorrelated Regression Models — 228

7.1	Introduction		228
7.2	Specification		228
7.3	Maximum Likelihood Estimation		230
	7.3.1	Exact Maximum Likelihood	230
	7.3.2	Conditional Maximum Likelihood	232
7.4	Alternative Estimators		235
	7.4.1	Gauss-Newton	235
	7.4.2	Zig-Zag Algorithms	238
	7.4.3	Cochrane-Orcutt	240
7.5	Distribution Theory		242
	7.5.1	Maximum Likelihood Estimator	243
	7.5.2	Least Squares Estimator	247
7.6	Lagged Dependent Variables		251
7.7	Testing		252
	7.7.1	Alternative LM Test I	255
	7.7.2	Alternative LM Test II	256
	7.7.3	Alternative LM Test III	257
7.8	Autocorrelation in Systems of Equations		258
	7.8.1	Estimation	259
	7.8.2	Testing	260
7.9	Applications		261
	7.9.1	Illiquidity and Hedge Funds	261
	7.9.2	Beach-MacKinnon Simulation Study	262
7.10	Exercises		263

8 Heteroskedastic Regression Models — 272

8.1	Introduction	272
8.2	Specification	272
8.3	Estimation	276

8.3.1	Maximum Likelihood	276
8.3.2	Relationship with Weighted Least Squares	279
8.4	Distribution Theory	281
8.5	Testing	282
8.6	Heteroskedasticity in Systems of Equations	288
8.6.1	Specification	288
8.6.2	Estimation	289
8.6.3	Testing	291
8.6.4	Heteroskedastic and Autocorrelated Disturbances	292
8.7	Applications	294
8.7.1	The Great Moderation	294
8.7.2	Finite Sample Properties of the Wald Test	295
8.8	Exercises	297

PART THREE   Other Estimation Methods

9	**Quasi-Maximum Likelihood Estimation**	307
9.1	Introduction	307
9.2	Misspecification	308
9.3	The Quasi-Maximum Likelihood Estimator	312
9.4	Asymptotic Distribution	314
9.4.1	Misspecification and the Information Equality	317
9.4.2	Independent and Identically Distributed Data	320
9.4.3	Dependent Data and Martingale Difference Score	322
9.4.4	Dependent Data and Score	322
9.5	Variance Estimation	324
9.6	Quasi-Maximum Likelihood and Linear Regression	326
9.6.1	Misspecification: Non-normality	329
9.6.2	Misspecification: Heteroskedasticity	329
9.6.3	Misspecification: Autocorrelation	331
9.6.4	The White Variance Estimator	332
9.6.5	The Newey-West Variance Estimator	334
9.7	Testing	338
9.8	Applications	339
9.8.1	Autoregressive Models for Count Data	339
9.8.2	The CKLS Model of Interest Rates	342
9.9	Exercises	345

10	**Generalised Method of Moments**	352
10.1	Introduction	352
10.2	Motivating Examples	353

	10.2.1 Population Moments	353
	10.2.2 Empirical Moments	354
	10.2.3 GMM Models from Conditional Expectations	358
	10.2.4 GMM and Maximum Likelihood	361
10.3	Estimation	362
	10.3.1 The GMM Objective Function	362
	10.3.2 Asymptotic Properties	364
	10.3.3 Estimation Strategies	369
10.4	Over-identification Testing	373
10.5	Applications	378
	10.5.1 Monte Carlo Evidence	378
	10.5.2 Levels Effect in Interest Rates	381
10.6	Exercises	384

11 Nonparametric Estimation — 392
11.1	Introduction	392
11.2	The Kernel Density Estimator	393
11.3	Properties of the Kernel Density Estimator	397
	11.3.1 Finite Sample Properties	397
	11.3.2 Optimal Bandwidth Selection	398
	11.3.3 Asymptotic Properties	401
	11.3.4 Dependent Data	403
11.4	Semi-parametric Density Estimation	404
11.5	The Nadaraya-Watson Kernel Regression Estimator	406
11.6	Properties of Kernel Regression Estimators	410
11.7	Bandwidth Selection for Kernel Regression	413
11.8	Multivariate Kernel Regression	416
11.9	Semi-parametric Regression of the Partial Linear Model	418
11.10	Applications	419
	11.10.1 Derivatives of a Nonlinear Production Function	420
	11.10.2 Drift and Diffusion Functions of SDEs	422
11.11	Exercises	424

12 Estimation by Simulation — 432
12.1	Introduction	432
12.2	Motivating Example	433
12.3	Indirect Inference	435
	12.3.1 Estimation	436
	12.3.2 Relationship with Indirect Least Squares	439
12.4	Efficient Method of Moments (EMM)	441
	12.4.1 Estimation	441
	12.4.2 Relationship with Instrumental Variables	442

12.5	Simulated Generalised Method of Moments (SMM)	444
12.6	Estimating Continuous-Time Models	445
	12.6.1 Brownian Motion	448
	12.6.2 Geometric Brownian Motion	451
	12.6.3 Stochastic Volatility	454
12.7	Applications	456
	12.7.1 Finite Sample Properties	457
	12.7.2 Empirical Properties	459
12.8	Exercises	460

PART FOUR Stationary Time Series

13	**Linear Time Series Models**	**467**
13.1	Introduction	467
13.2	Time Series Properties of Data	468
13.3	Specification	470
	13.3.1 Univariate Model Classification	471
	13.3.2 Multivariate Model Classification	474
13.4	Stationarity	476
	13.4.1 The Stationarity Condition	476
	13.4.2 Wold's Representation Theorem	477
	13.4.3 Transforming a VAR to a VMA	478
13.5	Invertibility	481
	13.5.1 The Invertibility Condition	481
	13.5.2 Transforming a VMA to a VAR	481
13.6	Estimation	482
13.7	Optimal Choice of Lag Order	486
13.8	Distribution Theory	488
13.9	Testing	489
13.10	Analysing Vector Autoregressions	491
	13.10.1 Granger Causality Testing	492
	13.10.2 Impulse Response Functions	493
	13.10.3 Variance Decompositions	498
13.11	Applications	500
	13.11.1 Barro's Rational Expectations Model	501
	13.11.2 The Campbell-Shiller Present Value Model	502
13.12	Exercises	504
14	**Structural Vector Autoregressions**	**512**
14.1	Introduction	512
14.2	Specification	513
	14.2.1 Short-Run Restrictions	516
	14.2.2 Long-Run Restrictions	519

	14.2.3 Short-Run and Long-Run Restrictions	522
	14.2.4 Sign Restrictions	524
14.3	Estimation	527
14.4	Identification	531
14.5	Testing	533
14.6	Applications	535
	14.6.1 Peersman's Model of Oil Price Shocks	535
	14.6.2 A Portfolio SVAR Model of Australia	537
14.7	Exercises	539

15 Latent Factor Models 544
15.1	Introduction	544
15.2	Motivating Examples	545
	15.2.1 Empirical	545
	15.2.2 Theoretical	547
15.3	The Recursions of the Kalman Filter	548
	15.3.1 Univariate	548
	15.3.2 Multivariate	554
15.4	Extensions	557
	15.4.1 Intercepts	557
	15.4.2 Dynamics	557
	15.4.3 Nonstationary Factors	558
	15.4.4 Exogenous and Predetermined Variables	559
15.5	Factor Extraction	560
15.6	Estimation	561
	15.6.1 Identification	561
	15.6.2 Maximum Likelihood	562
	15.6.3 Principal Components Estimator	564
15.7	Relationship to VARMA Models	566
15.8	Applications	567
	15.8.1 The Hodrick-Prescott Filter	567
	15.8.2 A Factor Model of Spreads with Money Shocks	571
15.9	Exercises	573

PART FIVE   Nonstationary Time Series

16 Nonstationary Distribution Theory 583
16.1	Introduction	583
16.2	Specification	584
	16.2.1 Models of Trends	584
	16.2.2 Integration	586
16.3	Estimation	588
	16.3.1 Stationary Case	588

16.3.2 Nonstationary Case: Stochastic Trends 591
16.3.3 Nonstationary Case: Deterministic Trends 594
16.4 Asymptotics for Integrated Processes 596
16.4.1 Brownian Motion 597
16.4.2 Functional Central Limit Theorem 598
16.4.3 Continuous Mapping Theorem 602
16.4.4 Stochastic Integrals 603
16.5 Multivariate Analysis 606
16.6 Applications 609
16.6.1 Least Squares Estimator of the AR(1) Model 609
16.6.2 Trend Estimation in the Presence of a Random
Walk 611
16.7 Exercises 613

17 Unit Root Testing 619
17.1 Introduction 619
17.2 Specification 619
17.3 Detrending 621
17.3.1 Ordinary Least Squares (OLS) 623
17.3.2 First Differences 624
17.3.3 Generalised Least Squares (GLS) 625
17.4 Testing 626
17.4.1 Dickey-Fuller Tests 626
17.4.2 M Tests 627
17.5 Distribution Theory 629
17.5.1 Ordinary Least Squares Detrending 631
17.5.2 Generalised Least Squares Detrending 632
17.5.3 Simulating Critical Values 634
17.6 Power 636
17.6.1 Near Integration 637
17.6.2 Asymptotic Local Power 639
17.6.3 Point Optimal Tests 639
17.6.4 Asymptotic Power Envelope 641
17.7 Autocorrelation 642
17.7.1 Dickey-Fuller Test with Autocorrelation 642
17.7.2 M Tests with Autocorrelation 643
17.8 Structural Breaks 645
17.8.1 Known Break Point 647
17.8.2 Unknown Break Point 651
17.9 Applications 652
17.9.1 Power and the Initial Value 652
17.9.2 Nelson-Plosser Data Revisited 653
17.10 Exercises 655

18 Cointegration   662
    18.1 Introduction   662
    18.2 Long-Run Economic Models   663
    18.3 Specification of a VECM   665
        18.3.1 Bivariate Models   665
        18.3.2 Multivariate Models   667
        18.3.3 Cointegration   668
        18.3.4 Deterministic Components   670
    18.4 Estimation   672
        18.4.1 Full-Rank Case   673
        18.4.2 Reduced-Rank Case: Iterative Estimator   674
        18.4.3 Reduced-Rank Case: Johansen Estimator   675
        18.4.4 Zero-Rank Case   681
    18.5 Identification   682
        18.5.1 Triangular Restrictions   682
        18.5.2 Structural Restrictions   683
    18.6 Distribution Theory   684
        18.6.1 Asymptotic Distribution of the Eigenvalues   684
        18.6.2 Asymptotic Distribution of the Parameters   686
    18.7 Testing   689
        18.7.1 Cointegrating Rank   690
        18.7.2 Cointegrating Vector   693
        18.7.3 Exogeneity   695
    18.8 Dynamics   696
        18.8.1 Impulse Responses   696
        18.8.2 Cointegrating Vector Interpretation   697
    18.9 Applications   698
        18.9.1 Rank Selection Based on Information Criteria   698
        18.9.2 Effects of Heteroskedasticity on the Trace Test 700
    18.10 Exercises   701

PART SIX   Nonlinear Time Series

19 Nonlinearities in Mean   715
    19.1 Introduction   715
    19.2 Motivating Examples   715
    19.3 Threshold Models   720
        19.3.1 Specification   720
        19.3.2 Estimation   722
        19.3.3 Testing   723
    19.4 Artificial Neural Networks   726
        19.4.1 Specification   726
        19.4.2 Estimation   728

19.4.3 Testing 731
19.5 Bilinear Time Series Models 732
19.5.1 Specification 732
19.5.2 Estimation 733
19.5.3 Testing 734
19.6 Markov Switching Model 734
19.7 Nonparametric Autoregression 738
19.8 Nonlinear Impulse Responses 740
19.9 Applications 744
19.9.1 A Multiple Equilibrium Model of Unemployment 744
19.9.2 Bivariate Threshold Models of G7 Countries 745
19.10 Exercises 748

20 Nonlinearities in Variance 758
20.1 Introduction 758
20.2 Statistical Properties of Asset Returns 758
20.3 The ARCH Model 762
20.3.1 Specification 762
20.3.2 Estimation 763
20.3.3 Testing 767
20.4 Univariate Extensions 769
20.4.1 GARCH 769
20.4.2 Integrated GARCH 774
20.4.3 Additional Variables 775
20.4.4 Asymmetries 776
20.4.5 Garch-in-Mean 777
20.4.6 Diagnostics 779
20.5 Conditional Non-normality 780
20.5.1 Parametric 780
20.5.2 Semi-parametric 782
20.5.3 Nonparametric 783
20.6 Multivariate GARCH 786
20.6.1 VECH 787
20.6.2 BEKK 788
20.6.3 DCC 791
20.6.4 DECO 797
20.7 Applications 798
20.7.1 DCC and DECO Models of United States Yields 798
20.7.2 A Time-Varying Volatility SVAR Model 799
20.8 Exercises 802

21 Discrete Time Series Models 812
21.1 Introduction 812

21.2   Motivating Examples   812
21.3   Qualitative Data   815
       21.3.1 Specification   815
       21.3.2 Estimation   819
       21.3.3 Testing   822
       21.3.4 Binary Autoregressive Models   824
21.4   Ordered Data   826
21.5   Count Data   828
       21.5.1 The Poisson Regression Model   830
       21.5.2 Integer Autoregressive Models   831
21.6   Duration Data   835
21.7   Applications   837
       21.7.1 An ACH Model of United States Airline Trades   837
       21.7.2 EMM Estimator of Integer Models   840
21.8   Exercises   842

Appendix A: Change of Variable in Density Functions   849

Appendix B: The Lag Operator   850
       B.1   Basics   850
       B.2   Polynomial Convolution   850
       B.3   Polynomial Inversion   851
       B.4   Polynomial Decomposition   852

Appendix C: FIML Estimation of a Structural Model   854
       C.1   Log-Likelihood Function   854
       C.2   First-Order Conditions   854
       C.3   Solution   855

Appendix D: Additional Nonparametric Results   857
       D.1   Mean   857
       D.2   Variance   859
       D.3   Mean Square Error   861
       D.4   Roughness   862
             D.4.1 Roughness Results for the Gaussian Distribution 862
             D.4.2 Roughness Results for the Gaussian Kernel   863

References   865
Author Index   877
Subject Index   881

List of Illustrations

1.1	Probability distributions of y_t for various models	*page* 5
1.2	Probability distributions of y_t for various models	7
1.3	Log-likelihood function for Poisson distribution	13
1.4	Log-likelihood function for exponential distribution	14
1.5	Log-likelihood function for the normal distribution	16
1.6	Eurodollar interest rates	22
1.7	Stationary density of Eurodollar interest rates	24
1.8	Transitional density of Eurodollar interest rates	26
2.1	Demonstration of the weak law of large numbers	39
2.2	Demonstration of the Lindeberg-Levy central limit theorem	46
2.3	Convergence of log-likelihood function	61
2.4	Consistency of sample mean for normal distribution	62
2.5	Consistency of median for Cauchy distribution	63
2.6	Illustrating asymptotic normality	65
2.7	Bivariate normal distribution	73
2.8	Scatterplot of returns on Apple and Ford stocks	74
2.9	Gradient of the bivariate normal model	77
3.1	Stationary density of Eurodollar interest rates: CIR model	110
3.2	Estimated variance function of CIR model	112
4.1	Illustrating the LR and Wald tests	120
4.2	Illustrating the LM test	120
4.3	Simulated and asymptotic distributions of the Wald test	136
5.1	Simulating a bivariate regression model	162
5.2	Sampling distribution of a weak instrument	175
5.3	United States data on the Taylor Rule	183
6.1	Simulated exponential models	196
6.2	Scatterplot of Martin Marietta returns data	216
6.3	Stochastic frontier disturbance distribution	219
7.1	Simulated models with autocorrelated disturbances	230

7.2	Distribution of maximum likelihood estimator in an autocorrelated regression model	246
8.1	Simulated data from heteroskedastic models	275
8.2	The Great Moderation	294
8.3	Sampling distribution of Wald test	296
8.4	Power of Wald test	297
9.1	Comparison of the true and misspecified log-likelihood functions	309
9.2	United States Dollar/British Pound exchange rates	336
9.3	Estimated variance function of CKLS model	344
10.1	Consistency of GMM	366
11.1	Bias and variance of the kernel estimate of density	398
11.2	Kernel estimate of distribution of stock index returns	400
11.3	Bivariate normal density	401
11.4	Semi-parametric density estimator	405
11.5	Parametric conditional mean estimates	406
11.6	Nadaraya-Watson nonparametric kernel regression	410
11.7	Effect of bandwidth on kernel regression	411
11.8	Bandwidth selection and cross-validation	416
11.9	Two-dimensional product kernel	417
11.10	Semi-parametric regression	419
11.11	Nonparametric production function	421
11.12	Nonparametric estimates of the drift and diffusion functions	423
12.1	Simulated AR(1) model	435
12.2	Illustrating Brownian motion	446
13.1	United States macroeconomic data	469
13.2	Plots of simulated stationary time series	472
13.3	Choice of optimal lag order	488
14.1	Bivariate SVAR model	516
14.2	Bivariate SVAR with short-run restrictions	519
14.3	Bivariate SVAR with long-run restrictions	521
14.4	Bivariate SVAR with short- and long-run restrictions	523
14.5	Bivariate SVAR with sign restrictions	526
14.6	Impulse responses of Peersman's model	537
15.1	Daily United States zero coupon rates	546
15.2	Alternative priors for latent factors in the Kalman filter	559
15.3	Factor loadings of a term structure model	565
15.4	Hodrick-Prescott filter of real United States GDP	571
16.1	Nelson-Plosser data	585
16.2	Simulated distribution of AR(1) parameter	591
16.3	Continuous-time processes	600
16.4	Functional Central Limit Theorem	602
16.5	Distribution of a stochastic integral	606

16.6	Mixed normal distribution	609
17.1	Real United States GDP	620
17.2	Detrending	626
17.3	Near unit root process	637
17.4	Asymptotic power curve of ADF tests	640
17.5	Asymptotic power envelope of ADF tests	642
17.6	Structural breaks in United States GDP	647
17.7	Union of rejections approach	653
18.1	Permanent income hypothesis	663
18.2	Long-run money demand	664
18.3	Term structure of United States yields	665
18.4	Error correction phase diagram	666
19.1	Properties of an AR(2) model	716
19.2	Limit cycle	717
19.3	Strange attractor	718
19.4	Nonlinear error correction model	719
19.5	United States unemployment	719
19.6	Threshold functions	722
19.7	Decomposition of an ANN	727
19.8	Simulated bilinear time series models	733
19.9	Markov switching model of United States output	738
19.10	Nonparametric estimate of a TAR(1) model	740
19.11	Simulated TAR models for G7 countries	747
20.1	Statistical properties of FTSE returns	759
20.2	Distribution of FTSE returns	762
20.3	News impact curve	763
20.4	ACF of GARCH(1,1) models	772
20.5	Conditional variance of FTSE returns	774
20.6	BEKK model of United States zero coupon bonds	790
20.7	DECO model of interest rates	800
20.8	SVAR model of United Kingdom LIBOR spread	802
21.1	United States Federal funds target rate from 1984 to 2009	814
21.2	Money demand equation with a floor interest rate	815
21.3	Duration descriptive statistics for AMR	838

Computer Code Used in the Examples

Code is written in GAUSS (*.g) , MATLAB (*.m) and in R (*.R)

1.1	basic_sample.*	4
1.2	basic_sample.*	5
1.3	basic_sample.*	6
1.4	basic_sample.*	6
1.5	basic_sample.*	6
1.6	basic_sample.*	7
1.7	basic_sample.*	8
1.8	basic_sample.*	8
1.10	basic_poisson.*	13
1.11	basic_exp.*	14
1.12	basic_normal_like.*	15
1.14	basic_poisson.*	17
1.15	basic_exp.*	18
1.16	basic_normal_like.*	18
1.17	basic_poisson.*	20
1.18	basic_exp.*	21
1.19	basic_normal.*	21
2.5	prop_wlln1.*	39
2.6	prop_wlln2.*	40
2.8	prop_moment.*	43
2.10	prop_lindlevy.*	45
2.21	prop_consistency.*	61
2.22	prop_normal.*	62
2.23	prop_cauchy.*	62
2.25	prop_asymnorm.*	64
2.28	prop_edgeworth.*	68
2.29	prop_bias.*	70
3.2	max_exp.*	89
3.3	max_exp.*	91
3.4	max_exp.*	93

3.6	max_weibull.*	95
3.7	max_exp.*	97
3.8	max_exp.*	99
3.9	max_exp.*	102
4.3	test_weibull.*	127
4.5	test_weibull.*	130
4.7	test_weibull.*	133
4.10	test_asymptotic.*	135
4.11	text_size.*	139
4.12	test_power.*	140
4.13	test_power.*	141
5.6	linear_simulation.*	161
5.7	linear_estimate.*	165
5.9	linear_fiml.*	170
5.11	linear_weak.*	174
5.15	linear_estimate.*	178
5.16	linear_fiml.*	181
6.3	nls_simulate.*	195
6.5	nls_exponential.*	200
6.7	nls_consumption_estimate.*	204
6.8	nls_contest.*	208
6.11	nls_money.*	214
7.1	auto_simulate.*	229
7.5	auto_invest.*	234
7.8	auto_distribution.*	245
7.11	auto_test.*	253
7.12	auto_system.*	260
7.13	auto_system.*	260
8.1	hetero_event.*	273
8.2	hetero_simulate.*	274
8.4	hetero_estimate.*	277
8.7	hetero_test.*	286
8.9	hetero_system.*	290
8.10	hetero_system.*	291
8.11	hetero_general.*	293
9.1	qmle_graph.*	308
9.3	qmle_graph.*	309
9.19	qmle_ar1reg.*	334
9.20	qmle_sf.*	335
9.21	qmle_sf.*	339
10.1	gmm_table.*	356
10.2	gmm_table.*	357
10.3	gmm_table.*	358

10.8	gmm_consistency.*	365
10.10	gmm_gamma.*	372
10.11	gmm_ccapm.*	373
10.16	gmm_ccapm.*	377
11.1	npd_kernel.*	395
11.2	npd_property.*	398
11.3	npd_ftse.*	400
11.4	npd_bivariate.*	401
11.5	npd_seminonlin.*	405
11.6	npr_parametric.*	406
11.7	npr_nadwatson.*	409
11.8	npr_property.*	410
11.9	npr_crossvalid.*	415
11.10	npr_bivariate.*	417
11.11	npr_semi.*	419
12.1	sim_mom.*	435
12.3	sim_accuracy.*	437
12.4	sim_ma1indirect.*	439
12.5	sim_ma1emm.*	441
12.6	sim_ma1overid.*	445
12.7	sim_brownind.*, sim_brownemm.*	450
13.1	stsm_simulate.*	471
13.8	stsm_root.*	477
13.9	stsm_root.*	477
13.17	stsm_varma.*	484
13.19	stsm_recursive.*	485
13.20	stsm_laglength.*	487
13.24	stsm_recursive.*	492
13.25	stsm_recursive.*	497
13.26	stsm_recursive.*	499
14.2	svar_bivariate.*	515
14.5	svar_bivariate.*	518
14.7	svar_bivariate.*	520
14.10	svar_bivariate.*	522
14.12	svar_bivariate.*	526
14.13	svar_shortrun.*	528
14.14	svar_longrun.*	530
14.15	svar_recursive.*	531
14.17	svar_test.*	533
14.18	svar_test.*	534
15.1	lfac_termfig.*	545
15.5	lfac_uni.*	553
15.6	lfac_multi.*	555

15.8	lfac_smooth.*	561
15.9	lfac_uni.*	562
15.10	lfac_term.*	563
15.11	lfac_fvar.*	564
15.12	lfac_panic.*	565
16.1	nts_nelplos.*	584
16.2	nts_nelplos.*	584
16.3	nts_nelplos.*	586
16.4	nts_moment.*, nts_distribution.*	590
16.5	nts_moment.*	592
16.6	nts_distribution.*	593
16.7	nts_yts.*	599
16.8	nts_fclt.*	601
16.10	nts_stochint.*	604
16.11	nts_stochint.*	605
16.13	nts_mixednormal.*	608
17.1	unit_qusgdp.*	625
17.2	unit_qusgdp.*	635
17.3	unit_asypower.*	639
17.4	unit_asypowerenv.*	642
17.5	unit_maicsim.*	644
17.6	unit_qusgdp.*	646
17.7	unit_breakeffect.*	646
17.8	unit_qusgdp.*	650
17.9	unit_qusgdp.*	651
18.1	coint_lrgraphs.*	663
18.2	coint_lrgraphs.*	663
18.3	coint_lrgraphs.*	664
18.4	coint_lrgraphs.*	668
18.6	coint_bivterm.*	673
18.7	coint_bivterm.*	674
18.8	coint_bivterm.*	679
18.9	coint_permincome.*	680
18.10	coint_bivterm.*	681
18.11	coint_triterm.*	682
18.13	coint_simevals.*	685
18.14	coint_bivterm.*	691
18.15	coint_triterm.*	692
18.16	coint_bivterm.*	693
18.17	coint_bivterm.*	695
19.1	nlm_features.*	715
19.2	nlm_features.*	716
19.3	nlm_features.*	717

19.4	nlm_features.*	717
19.5	nlm_usrate.*	718
19.6	nlm_tarsim.*	725
19.7	nlm_annfig.*	727
19.8	nlm_bilinear.*	732
19.9	nlm_bcycle.*	737
19.10	nlm_tar.*	739
19.11	nlm_girf.*	743
20.1	garch_nic.*	763
20.2	garch_estimate.*	766
20.3	garch_test.*	769
20.4	garch_simulate.*	771
20.5	garch_estimate.*	772
20.6	garch_seasonality.*	775
20.7	garch_m.*	778
20.8	garch_studt.*	785
20.9	mgarch_bekk.*	790
21.2	discrete_mpol.*	814
21.3	discrete_floor.*	814
21.4	discrete_simulation.*	818
21.7	discrete_probit.*	821
21.8	discrete_probit.*	824
21.9	discrete_ordered.*	827
21.11	discrete_thinning.*	832
21.12	discrete_poissonauto.*	833

Code Disclaimer Information

Note that the computer code is provided for illustrative purposes only and although care has been taken to ensure that it works properly, it has not been thoroughly tested under all conditions and on all platforms. The authors and Cambridge University Press cannot guarantee or imply reliability, serviceability or function of this computer code. All code is therefore provided 'as is' without any warranties of any kind.

Preface

This book provides a general framework for specifying, estimating and testing time series econometric models. Special emphasis is given to estimation by maximum likelihood, but other methods are also discussed, including quasi-maximum likelihood estimation, generalised method of moments, nonparametrics and estimation by simulation. An important advantage of adopting the principle of maximum likelihood as the unifying framework for the book is that many of the estimators and test statistics proposed in econometrics can be derived within a likelihood framework, thereby providing a coherent vehicle for understanding their properties and interrelationships.

In contrast to many existing econometric textbooks, which deal mainly with the theoretical properties of estimators and test statistics through a theorem-proof presentation, this book is very concerned with implementation issues in order to provide a fast track between theory and applied work. Consequently many of the econometric methods discussed in the book are illustrated by means of a suite of programs written in GAUSS, MATLAB® and R.[1] The computer code emphasises the computational side of econometrics and follows the notation in the book as closely as possible, thereby reinforcing the principles presented in the text. More generally, the computer code also helps to bridge the gap between theory and practice by enabling the reproduction of both theoretical and empirical results published in recent journal articles. The reader, as a result, may build on the code and tailor it to more involved applications.

Organization of the Book

Part ONE of the book is an exposition of the basic maximum likelihood framework. To implement this approach, three conditions are required: the probability

[1] GAUSS is a registered trademark of Aptech Systems, Inc. www.aptech.com, MATLAB® is a registered trademark of The MathWorks, Inc. www.mathworks.com and R www.r-project.org is a free software environment for statistical computation and graphics which is part of the GNU Project.

distribution of the stochastic process must be known and specified correctly, the parametric specifications of the moments of the distribution must be known and specified correctly and the likelihood must be tractable. The properties of maximum likelihood estimators are presented and three fundamental testing procedures – the Likelihood Ratio test, the Wald test and the Lagrange Multiplier test – are discussed in detail. There is also a comprehensive treatment of iterative algorithms to compute maximum likelihood estimators when no analytical expressions are available.

Part TWO is the usual regression framework taught in standard econometric courses but presented within the maximum likelihood framework. Both nonlinear regression models and non-spherical models exhibiting either autocorrelation or heteroskedasticity or both, are presented. A further advantage of the maximum likelihood strategy is that it provides a mechanism for deriving new estimators and new test statistics, which are designed specifically for non-standard problems.

Part THREE provides a coherent treatment of a number of alternative estimation procedures which are applicable when the conditions to implement maximum likelihood estimation are not satisfied. For the case where the probability distribution is incorrectly specified, quasi-maximum likelihood is appropriate. If the joint probability distribution of the data is treated as unknown, then a generalised method of moments estimator is adopted. This estimator has the advantage of circumventing the need to specify the distribution and hence avoids any potential misspecification from an incorrect choice of the distribution. An even less restrictive approach is not to specify either the distribution or the parametric form of the moments of the distribution and to use nonparametric procedures to model either the distribution of variables or the relationships between variables. Simulation estimation methods are used for models where the likelihood is intractable arising, for example, from the presence of latent variables. Indirect inference, efficient methods of moments and simulated methods of moments are presented and compared.

Part FOUR examines stationary time series models with a special emphasis on using maximum likelihood methods to estimate and test these models. Both single equation models, including the autoregressive moving average class of models, and multiple equation models, including vector autoregressions and structural vector autoregressions, are dealt with in detail. Also discussed are linear factor models where the factors are treated as latent. The presence of the latent factor means that the full likelihood is generally not tractable. However, if the models are specified in terms of the normal distribution with moments based on linear parametric representations, a Kalman filter is used to rewrite the likelihood in terms of the observable variables, making estimation and testing by maximum likelihood feasible.

Part FIVE focusses on nonstationary time series models and in particular tests for unit roots and cointegration. Some important asymptotic results for nonstationary time series are presented, followed by a comprehensive discussion of testing for unit roots. Cointegration is tackled from the perspective that the well-known Johansen estimator may be usefully interpreted as a maximum likelihood estimator based on the assumption of a normal distribution applied to a system of equations that is subject to a set of cross-equation restrictions arising from the assumption of common long-run relationships. Further, the trace and maximum eigenvalue tests of cointegration are shown to be likelihood ratio tests.

Part SIX is concerned with nonlinear time series models. Models that are nonlinear in mean include the threshold class of model, bilinear models and also artificial neural network modelling, which, contrary to many existing treatments, is again addressed from the econometric perspective of estimation and testing based on maximum likelihood methods. Nonlinearities in variance are dealt with in terms of the GARCH class of models. The final chapter focusses on models that deal with discrete or truncated time series data.

Even in a project of this size and scope, sacrifices have had to be made to keep the length of the book manageable. Accordingly, there are a number of important topics that are omitted.

(i) Although Bayesian methods are increasingly being used in many areas of statistics and econometrics, no material on Bayesian econometrics is included. This is an important field in its own right and the interested reader is referred to recent books by Koop (2003), Geweke (2005), Koop, Poirier and Tobias (2007) and Greenberg (2008), *inter alia*. Where appropriate, references to Bayesian methods are provided in the body of the text.

(ii) With great reluctance a chapter on bootstrapping was not included because of space issues. A good place to start reading is the introductory text by Efron and Tibshirani (1993) and the useful surveys by Horowitz (1997), Maddala and Li (1996) and Li and Maddala (1996).

(iii) In Part SIX, in the chapter dealing with modelling the variance of time series, there are important recent developments in stochastic volatility and realised volatility that would have been worthy of inclusion. For stochastic volatility, there is an excellent volume of readings edited by Shephard (2005), while the seminal articles in the area of realised volatility are those by Anderson et al. (2001, 2003).

The fact that these areas have not been covered should not be regarded as a value judgement about their relative importance. Instead, the subject matter chosen for inclusion reflects a balance between the interests of the authors and purely operational decisions aimed at preserving the flow and continuity of the book.

Computer Code

Computer code written in GAUSS (*.g), MATLAB (*.m) and R (*.R) is available from a companion website to reproduce relevant examples in the text, figures in the text that are not part of an example and the applications presented in the final section of each chapter, and to complete the exercises. Where applicable, the time series data used in these examples, applications and exercises are also available in a number of different formats.

Presenting the numerical results of the examples in the text immediately gives rise to two important issues concerning numerical precision.

(1) In all of the examples listed in the front of the book where computer code has been used, the numbers appearing in the text are rounded versions of those generated by the code. Accordingly, the rounded numbers should be interpreted as such and **not** be used independently of the computer code to try and reproduce the numbers reported in the text.

(2) In many of the examples, simulation has been used to demonstrate a concept. Since GAUSS, MATLAB and R all have different random number generators, the results generated by the different sets of code will not be identical to one another. For consistency we have always used the GAUSS output for reporting purposes.

Although GAUSS, MATLAB and R are very similar high-level programming languages, there are some important differences that require explanation. Probably the most important difference is one of programming style. GAUSS programs are script files that allow calls to both inbuilt GAUSS and user-defined *procedures*. MATLAB and R, on the other hand, do not support the use of user-defined *functions* in script files. Furthermore, the MATLAB programming style favours writing user-defined functions in separate files and then calling them as if they were in-built functions. This style of programming does not suit the learning-by-doing environment that the book tries to create. Consequently, the MATLAB and R programs are written mainly as function files with a main function and with all of the required user-defined functions required to implement the procedure in the same file. The only exception to this rule is that a few utility files are provided as separate stand-alone MATLAB and R function files. Finally, all the figures in the text were created using MATLAB together with a utility file `laprint.m` written by Arno Linnemann of the University of Kessel.[2]

Acknowledgements

Creating a manuscript of this scope and magnitude is a daunting task and there are many people to whom we are indebted. In particular, we would like to thank Kenneth Lindsay, Adrian Pagan, Russell Davidson, Tony Hall and Andy Tremayne for their careful reading of various chapters of the manuscript and for many helpful comments and suggestions. Frank Diebold, together with

---

[2] A user guide is available at www.uni-kassel.de/fb16/rat/matlab/laprint/laprintdoc.ps.

Molin Zhong and Minchul Shin, provided useful feedback on an earlier version of the book. Gael Martin helped with compiling a suitable list of references to Bayesian econometric methods. Ayesha Scott compiled the index, a painstaking task for a manuscript of this size. Ahmad Bahir assisted with the compilation of the R code. Many others have commented on earlier drafts of chapters and we are grateful to the following individuals: our colleagues, Gunnar Bårdsen, Ralf Becker, Adam Clements, Vlad Pavlov, Anke Leroux, Annastiina Silvennoinen and Joseph Jeisman; and our graduate students, Tim Christensen, Christopher Coleman-Fenn, Andrew McClelland, Andrea La Nauze, Jessie Wang and Vivianne Vilar.

We also wish to express our deep appreciation to the team at Cambridge University Press, particularly Peter C. B. Phillips for his encouragement and support throughout the long gestation period of the book as well as for reading and commenting on earlier drafts. Scott Parris, with his energy and enthusiasm for the project, was a great help in sustaining the authors during the long slog of completing the manuscript. Our thanks are also due to our Cambridge University Press readers who provided detailed and constructive feedback at various stages in the compilation of the final document. Michael Erkelenz of Fine Line Writers edited the entire manuscript, helped to smooth out the prose and provided particular assistance with the correct use of adjectival constructions in the passive voice.

It is fair to say that writing this book was an immense task that involved the consumption of copious quantities of chillies, champagne and port over a protracted period of time. The biggest debt of gratitude we owe, therefore, is to our respective families. To Gael, Sarah and David; Catherine, Iain, Robert and Tim; and Fiona and Caitlin: thank you for your patience, your good humour in putting up with and cleaning up after many a pizza night, your stoicism in enduring yet another vacant stare during an important conversation and, ultimately, for making it all worthwhile.

Vance Martin, Stan Hurn and David Harris
June 2012

PART ONE

Maximum Likelihood

1   The Maximum Likelihood Principle

1.1 Introduction

Maximum likelihood estimation is a general method for estimating the parameters of econometric models from observed data. The principle of maximum likelihood plays a central role in the exposition of this book, since a number of estimators used in econometrics can be derived within this framework. Examples include ordinary least squares, generalised least squares and full-information maximum likelihood. In deriving the maximum likelihood estimator, a key concept is the joint probability density function (pdf) of the observed random variables, y_t. Maximum likelihood estimation requires that the following conditions are satisfied.

(1) The form of the joint pdf of y_t is known.
(2) The specifications of the moments of the joint pdf are known.
(3) The joint pdf can be evaluated for all values of the parameters, θ.

Parts ONE and TWO of this book deal with models in which all these conditions are satisfied. Part THREE investigates models in which these conditions are not satisfied and considers four important cases. First, if the distribution of y_t is misspecified, resulting in both conditions 1 and 2 being violated, estimation is by quasi-maximum likelihood (Chapter 9). Second, if condition 1 is not satisfied, a generalised method of moments estimator (Chapter 10) is required. Third, if condition 2 is not satisfied, estimation relies on nonparametric methods (Chapter 11). Fourth, if condition 3 is violated, simulation-based estimation methods are used (Chapter 12).

1.2 Motivating Examples

This section emphasises the link between observed sample data and the probability distribution from which they are drawn. This relationship is illustrated with a number of simulation examples in which samples of size $T = 5$ are

Table 1.1. *Realisations of y_t from alternative models: $t = 1, 2, \cdots, 5$*

Model	t=1	t=2	t=3	t=4	t=5
Time Invariant	−2.720	2.470	0.495	0.597	−0.960
Count	2.000	4.000	3.000	4.000	0.000
Linear Regression	0.493	2.538	4.827	9.830	12.517
Exponential Regression	0.033	2.938	2.679	2.423	5.464
Autoregressive	−0.783	0.608	0.232	1.164	−3.127
Bilinear	0.820	−3.277	3.395	3.233	−2.617
Auto-Heteroskedasticity	0.535	0.975	0.321	−1.523	−1.067
ARCH	0.095	3.290	7.975	8.092	12.778

drawn from a range of alternative models. The realisations of these draws for each model are listed in Table 1.1.

Example 1.1 Time Invariant Model
Consider the model

$$y_t = \sigma z_t ,$$

in which z_t is a disturbance term and σ is a parameter. Let z_t be a standardised normal distribution, $N(0, 1)$, defined by

$$f(z_t) = \frac{1}{\sqrt{2\pi}} \exp\left[-\frac{z_t^2}{2}\right] .$$

The distribution of y_t is obtained from the distribution of z_t using the change of variable technique (see Appendix A for details)

$$f(y_t ; \theta) = f(z_t) \left| \frac{\partial z_t}{\partial y_t} \right| ,$$

with $\theta = \{\sigma^2\}$. Applying this rule, and recognising that $z_t = y_t/\sigma$, yields

$$f(y_t ; \theta) = \frac{1}{\sqrt{2\pi}} \exp\left[-\frac{(y_t/\sigma)^2}{2}\right] \left| \frac{1}{\sigma} \right| = \frac{1}{\sqrt{2\pi\sigma^2}} \exp\left[-\frac{y_t^2}{2\sigma^2}\right] ,$$

or $y_t \sim N(0, \sigma^2)$. In this model, the distribution of y_t is time invariant because neither the mean nor the variance depend on time. This distribution is shown in panel (a) of Figure 1.1 in which the parameter is $\sigma = 2$. For comparative purposes the distributions of both y_t and z_t are given. As $y_t = 2z_t$, the distribution of y_t is flatter than the distribution of z_t.   □

As the distribution of y_t in Example 1.1 does not depend on lagged values y_{t-i}, y_t is independently distributed. In addition, since the distribution of y_t is the same at each t, y_t is identically distributed. These two properties are

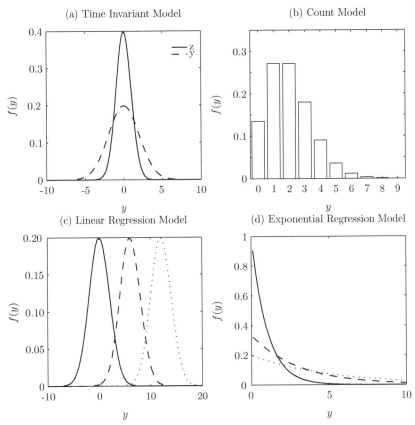

Figure 1.1. Probability distributions of y generated from the time invariant, count, linear regression and exponential regression models. Except for the time invariant and count models, the solid line represents the density at $t = 1$, the dashed line represents the density at $t = 3$ and the dotted line represents the density at $t = 5$.

abbreviated as iid. Conversely, the distribution is dependent if y_t depends on its own lagged values and non-identical if it changes over time.

Example 1.2 Count Model
Consider a time series of counts modelled as a series of iid draws from a Poisson distribution given by

$$f(y_t; \theta) = \frac{\theta^{y_t} \exp[-\theta]}{y_t!}, \qquad y_t = 0, 1, 2, \cdots,$$

in which $\theta > 0$ is an unknown parameter. A sample of $T = 5$ realisations of y_t, given in Table 1.1, is drawn from the Poisson probability distribution in panel (b) of Figure 1.1 for $\theta = 2$. By assumption, this distribution is the same at each point in time. In contrast to the data in the previous example in which the random variable is continuous, the data here are discrete as they are positive integers that measure counts. □

Example 1.3 Linear Regression Model

Consider the regression model

$$y_t = \beta x_t + \sigma z_t, \qquad z_t \sim iid \ N(0, 1),$$

in which x_t is an explanatory variable that is independent of z_t and $\theta = \{\beta, \sigma^2\}$. The distribution of y_t conditional on x_t is

$$f(y_t \mid x_t; \theta) = \frac{1}{\sqrt{2\pi\sigma^2}} \exp\left[-\frac{(y_t - \beta x_t)^2}{2\sigma^2}\right],$$

which is a normal distribution with conditional mean βx_t and variance σ^2, or $y_t \sim N(\beta x_t, \sigma^2)$. This distribution is illustrated in panel (c) of Figure 1.1 with $\beta = 3$, $\sigma = 2$ and explanatory variable $x_t = \{0, 1, 2, 3, 4\}$. The effect of x_t is to shift the distribution of y_t over time into the positive region, resulting in the draws of y_t given in Table 1.1 becoming increasingly positive. As the variance at each point in time is constant, the spread of the distributions of y_t is the same for all t. □

Example 1.4 Exponential Regression Model

Consider the exponential regression model

$$f(y_t \mid x_t; \theta) = \frac{1}{\mu_t} \exp\left[-\frac{y_t}{\mu_t}\right],$$

in which $\mu_t = \beta_0 + \beta_1 x_t$ is the time-varying conditional mean, x_t is an explanatory variable and $\theta = \{\beta_0, \beta_1\}$. This distribution is displayed in panel (d) of Figure 1.1 with $\beta_0 = 1$, $\beta_1 = 1$ and $x_t = \{0, 1, 2, 3, 4\}$. As $\beta_1 > 0$, the effect of x_t is to cause the distribution of y_t to become more positively skewed over time. □

Example 1.5 Autoregressive Model

An example of a first-order autoregressive model, denoted AR(1), is

$$y_t = \rho y_{t-1} + u_t, \qquad u_t \sim iid \ N(0, \sigma^2),$$

with $|\rho| < 1$ and $\theta = \{\rho, \sigma^2\}$. The distribution of y_t, conditional on y_{t-1}, is

$$f(y_t \mid y_{t-1}; \theta) = \frac{1}{\sqrt{2\pi\sigma^2}} \exp\left[-\frac{(y_t - \rho y_{t-1})^2}{2\sigma^2}\right],$$

which is a normal distribution with conditional mean ρy_{t-1} and variance σ^2, or $y_t \sim N(\rho y_{t-1}, \sigma^2)$. If $0 < \rho < 1$, then a large positive (negative) value of

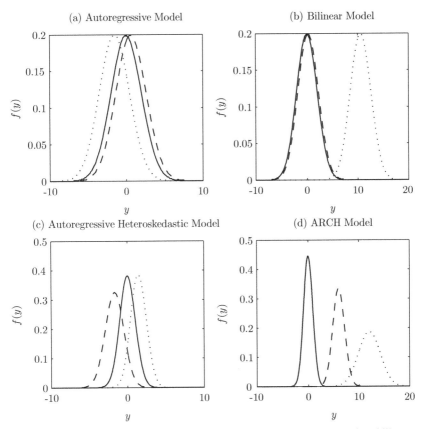

Figure 1.2. Probability distributions of y generated from the autoregressive, bilinear, autoregressive with heteroskedasticity and ARCH models. The solid line represents the density at $t = 1$, the dashed line represents the density at $t = 3$ and the dotted line represents the density at $t = 5$.

y_{t-1} shifts the distribution into the positive (negative) region for y_t, raising the probability that the next draw from this distribution is also positive (negative). This property of the autoregressive model is illustrated in panel (a) of Figure 1.2 with $\rho = 0.8$, $\sigma = 2$ and initial value $y_0 = 0$. □

Example 1.6 Bilinear Time Series Model

The autoregressive model discussed previously specifies a linear relationship between y_t and y_{t-1}. The bilinear model

$$y_t = \rho y_{t-1} + \gamma y_{t-1} u_{t-1} + u_t, \qquad u_t \sim iid\ N(0, \sigma^2),$$

is an example of a nonlinear time series model, in which $y_{t-1}u_{t-1}$ represents the bilinear term and $\theta = \{\rho, \gamma, \sigma^2\}$. The distribution of y_t conditional on y_{t-1} is

$$f(y_t \mid y_{t-1}; \theta) = \frac{1}{\sqrt{2\pi\sigma^2}} \exp\left[-\frac{(y_t - \mu_t)^2}{2\sigma^2}\right],$$

which is a normal distribution with conditional mean $\mu_t = \rho y_{t-1} + \gamma y_{t-1} u_{t-1}$ and variance σ^2. To demonstrate the nonlinear property of the model, substitute out u_{t-1} in the equation for the mean

$$\mu_t = \rho y_{t-1} + \gamma y_{t-1}(y_{t-1} - \rho y_{t-2} - \gamma y_{t-2} u_{t-2})$$
$$= \rho y_{t-1} + \gamma y_{t-1}^2 - \gamma \rho y_{t-1} y_{t-2} - \gamma^2 y_{t-1} y_{t-2} u_{t-2},$$

which shows that the mean is a nonlinear function of y_{t-1}. Setting $\gamma = 0$ yields the linear AR(1) model of Example 1.5. The distribution of the bilinear model is illustrated in panel (b) of Figure 1.2 with $\rho = 0.8$, $\gamma = 0.4$, $\sigma = 2$ and initial value $y_0 = 0$. □

Example 1.7 Autoregressive Model with Heteroskedasticity

An example of an AR(1) model with heteroskedasticity is

$$y_t = \rho y_{t-1} + \sigma_t z_t$$
$$\sigma_t^2 = \alpha_0 + \alpha_1 w_t$$
$$z_t \sim iid\ N(0, 1),$$

in which $\theta = \{\rho, \alpha_0, \alpha_1\}$ and w_t is an explanatory variable. The distribution of y_t conditional on y_{t-1} and w_t is

$$f(y_t \mid y_{t-1}, w_t; \theta) = \frac{1}{\sqrt{2\pi\sigma_t^2}} \exp\left[-\frac{(y_t - \rho y_{t-1})^2}{2\sigma_t^2}\right],$$

which is a normal distribution with conditional mean ρy_{t-1} and conditional variance $\alpha_0 + \alpha_1 w_t$. For this model, the distribution shifts because of the dependence on y_{t-1} and the spread of the distribution changes because of w_t. These features are highlighted in panel (c) of Figure 1.2 with $\rho = 0.8$, $\alpha_0 = 0.8$, $\alpha_1 = 0.8$, w_t is defined as a uniform random number on the unit interval and the initial value is $y_0 = 0$. □

Example 1.8 Autoregressive Conditional Heteroskedasticity

The autoregressive conditional heteroskedasticity (ARCH) class of models is a special case of the heteroskedastic regression model where w_t in Example 1.7 is expressed in terms of lagged values of the disturbance term squared. An example of a regression model as in Example 1.3 with ARCH is

$$y_t = \beta x_t + u_t$$
$$u_t = \sigma_t z_t$$
$$\sigma_t^2 = \alpha_0 + \alpha_1 u_{t-1}^2$$
$$z_t \sim iid \ N(0, 1),$$

in which x_t is an explanatory variable and $\theta = \{\beta, \alpha_0, \alpha_1\}$. The distribution of y_t conditional on y_{t-1}, x_t and x_{t-1} is

$$f(y_t \mid y_{t-1}, x_t, x_{t-1}; \theta) = \frac{1}{\sqrt{2\pi \left(\alpha_0 + \alpha_1 (y_{t-1} - \beta x_{t-1})^2\right)}}$$
$$\times \exp\left[-\frac{(y_t - \beta x_t)^2}{2\left(\alpha_0 + \alpha_1 (y_{t-1} - \beta x_{t-1})^2\right)}\right].$$

For this model, a large shock, represented by a large value of u_t, results in an increased variance in the next period if $\alpha_1 > 0$. The distribution from which y_t is drawn in the next period will therefore have a larger variance. The distribution of this model is shown in panel (d) of Figure 1.2 with $\beta = 3, \alpha_0 = 0.8, \alpha_1 = 0.8$ and $x_t = \{0, 1, 2, 3, 4\}$. □

1.3 Joint Probability Distributions

The motivating examples of the previous section focus on the distribution of y_t at time t which is generally a function of its own lags and the current and lagged values of explanatory variables x_t. The derivation of the maximum likelihood estimator of the model parameters requires using all of the information $t = 1, 2, \cdots, T$ by defining the joint probability density function (pdf). In the case where both y_t and x_t are stochastic, the joint probability pdf for a sample of T observations is

$$f(y_1, y_2, \cdots, y_T, x_1, x_2, \cdots, x_T; \psi), \tag{1.1}$$

in which ψ is a vector of parameters. An important feature of the previous examples is that y_t depends on the explanatory variable x_t. To capture this conditioning, the joint distribution in (1.1) is expressed as

$$f(y_1, y_2, \cdots, y_T, x_1, x_2, \cdots, x_T; \psi) = f(y_1, y_2, \cdots, y_T \mid x_1, x_2, \cdots, x_T; \psi)$$
$$\times f(x_1, x_2, \cdots, x_T; \psi), \tag{1.2}$$

in which the first term on the right-hand side of (1.2) represents the conditional distribution of $\{y_1, y_2, \cdots, y_T\}$ on $\{x_1, x_2, \cdots, x_T\}$ and the second term is the marginal distribution of $\{x_1, x_2, \cdots, x_T\}$. Assuming that the parameter vector

ψ can be decomposed into $\{\theta, \theta_x\}$, expression (1.2) becomes

$$f(y_1, y_2, \cdots, y_T, x_1, x_2, \cdots, x_T; \psi) = f(y_1, y_2, \cdots, y_T \mid x_1, x_2, \cdots, x_T; \theta)$$
$$\times f(x_1, x_2, \cdots, x_T; \theta_x). \qquad (1.3)$$

In these circumstances, the maximum likelihood estimation of the parameters θ is based on the conditional distribution without loss of information from the exclusion of the marginal distribution $f(x_1, x_2, \cdots, x_T; \theta_x)$.

The conditional distribution on the right-hand side of expression (1.3) simplifies further in the presence of additional restrictions.

Independent and identically distributed (*iid*)
In the simplest case, $\{y_1, y_2, \cdots, y_T\}$ is independent of $\{x_1, x_2, \cdots, x_T\}$ and y_t is *iid* with density function $f(y_t; \theta)$. The conditional pdf in equation (1.3) is then

$$f(y_1, y_2, \cdots, y_T \mid x_1, x_2, \cdots, x_T; \theta) = \prod_{t=1}^{T} f(y_t; \theta). \qquad (1.4)$$

Examples of this case are the time invariant model (Example 1.1) and the count model (Example 1.2).

If both y_t and x_t are *iid* and y_t is dependent on x_t then the decomposition in equation (1.3) implies that inference can be based on

$$f(y_1, y_2, \cdots, y_T \mid x_1, x_2, \cdots, x_T; \theta) = \prod_{t=1}^{T} f(y_t \mid x_t; \theta). \qquad (1.5)$$

Examples include the regression models in Examples 1.3 and 1.4 if sampling is *iid*.

Dependent
Now assume that $\{y_1, y_2, \cdots, y_T\}$ depends on its own lags but is independent of the explanatory variable $\{x_1, x_2, \cdots, x_T\}$. The joint pdf is expressed as a sequence of conditional distributions where conditioning is based on lags of y_t. By using standard rules of probability the distributions for the first three observations are, respectively,

$$f(y_1; \theta) = f(y_1; \theta)$$
$$f(y_1, y_2; \theta) = f(y_2 \mid y_1; \theta) f(y_1; \theta)$$
$$f(y_1, y_2, y_3; \theta) = f(y_3 \mid y_2, y_1; \theta) f(y_2 \mid y_1; \theta) f(y_1; \theta),$$

in which y_1 is the initial value with marginal probability density.

Extending this sequence to a sample of T observations, yields the joint pdf

$$f(y_1, y_2, \cdots, y_T; \theta) = f(y_1; \theta) \prod_{t=2}^{T} f(y_t \mid y_{t-1}, \cdots, y_1; \theta). \qquad (1.6)$$

Examples of this general case are the AR model (Example 1.5), the bilinear model (Example 1.6) and the ARCH model (Example 1.8). Extending the model to allow for dependence on explanatory variables, x_t, gives

$$f(y_1, y_2, \cdots, y_T \mid x_1, x_2, \cdots, x_T; \theta)$$
$$= f(y_1 \mid x_1; \theta) \prod_{t=2}^{T} f(y_t \mid y_{t-1}, \cdots, y_1, x_t, x_{t-1}, \cdots x_1; \theta). \quad (1.7)$$

An example is the autoregressive model with heteroskedasticity (Example 1.7).

Example 1.9 Autoregressive Model
The joint pdf for the AR(1) model in Example 1.5 is

$$f(y_1, y_2, \cdots, y_T; \theta) = f(y_1; \theta) \prod_{t=2}^{T} f(y_t \mid y_{t-1}; \theta),$$

where the conditional distribution is given by

$$f(y_t \mid y_{t-1}; \theta) = \frac{1}{\sqrt{2\pi\sigma^2}} \exp\left[-\frac{(y_t - \rho y_{t-1})^2}{2\sigma^2}\right],$$

and the marginal distribution is

$$f(y_1; \theta) = \frac{1}{\sqrt{2\pi\sigma^2/(1-\rho^2)}} \exp\left[-\frac{y_1^2}{2\sigma^2/(1-\rho^2)}\right].$$

which has unconditional mean $E[y_t] = 0$ and variance $\sigma^2/(1-\rho^2)$. □

Non-stochastic explanatory variables
In the case of non-stochastic explanatory variables, because x_t is deterministic its probability mass is degenerate. Explanatory variables of this form are also referred to as fixed in repeated samples. The joint probability in expression (1.3) simplifies to

$$f(y_1, y_2, \cdots, y_T, x_1, x_2, \cdots, x_T; \psi) = f(y_1, y_2, \cdots, y_T \mid x_1, x_2, \cdots, x_T; \theta).$$

Now $\psi = \theta$ and there is no potential loss of information from using the conditional distribution to estimate θ.

1.4 Maximum Likelihood Framework

As emphasised previously, a time series of data represents the observed realisation of draws from a joint pdf. The maximum likelihood principle makes use of this result by providing a general framework for estimating the unknown parameters, θ, from the observed time series data, $\{y_1, y_2, \cdots, y_T\}$.

1.4.1   The Log-Likelihood Function

The standard interpretation of the joint pdf in (1.7) is that f is a function of y_t for given parameters, θ. In defining the maximum likelihood estimator this interpretation is reversed, so that f is taken as a function of θ for given y_t. The motivation behind this change in the interpretation of the arguments of the pdf is to regard $\{y_1, y_2, \cdots, y_T\}$ as a realised data set which is no longer random. The maximum likelihood estimator is then obtained by finding the value of θ which is 'most likely' to have generated the observed data. Here the phrase 'most likely' is loosely interpreted in a probability sense.

It is important to remember that the likelihood function is simply a redefinition of the joint pdf in equation (1.7). For many problems it is simpler to work with the logarithm of this joint density function. The log-likelihood function is defined as

$$
\ln L_T(\theta) = \frac{1}{T} \ln f(y_1 \mid x_1; \theta)
$$
$$
+ \frac{1}{T} \sum_{t=2}^{T} \ln f(y_t \mid y_{t-1}, \cdots, y_1, x_t, x_{t-1}, \cdots x_1; \theta), \tag{1.8}
$$

where, for notational economy, θ is the sole argument. The T subscript indicates that the log-likelihood is an average over the sample of the logarithm of the density evaluated at y_t. It is worth emphasising that the term log-likelihood function, used here without any qualification, is also known as the average log-likelihood function. This convention is also used by, among others, Newey and McFadden (1994) and White (1994). This definition of the log-likelihood function is consistent with the theoretical development of the properties of maximum likelihood estimators discussed in Chapter 2, particularly Sections 2.3 and 2.5.1.

For the special case where y_t is *iid*, the log-likelihood function is based on the joint pdf in (1.4) and is

$$
\ln L_T(\theta) = \frac{1}{T} \sum_{t=1}^{T} \ln f(y_t; \theta).
$$

In all cases, the log-likelihood function, $\ln L_T(\theta)$, is a scalar that represents a summary measure of the data for given θ.

The maximum likelihood estimator of θ is defined as that value of θ, denoted as $\widehat{\theta}$, that maximises the log-likelihood function. In a large number of cases, this may be achieved using standard calculus. Chapter 3 discusses numerical approaches to the problem of finding maximum likelihood estimates when no analytical solutions exist, or are difficult to derive.

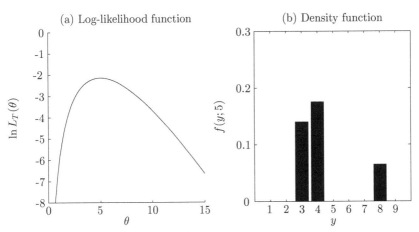

Figure 1.3. Plot of $\ln L_T(\theta)$ and $f(y; \widehat{\theta} = 5)$ for the Poisson distribution example with a sample size of $T = 3$.

Example 1.10 Poisson Distribution

Let $\{y_1, y_2, \cdots, y_T\}$ be *iid* observations from a Poisson distribution

$$f(y; \theta) = \frac{\theta^{y_t} \exp[-\theta]}{y_t!},$$

in which $\theta > 0$. The log-likelihood function for the sample is

$$\ln L_T(\theta) = \frac{1}{T} \sum_{t=1}^{T} \ln f(y_t; \theta) = \frac{1}{T} \sum_{t=1}^{T} y_t \ln \theta - \theta - \frac{\ln(y_1! y_2! \cdots y_T!)}{T}.$$

Consider the following $T = 3$ observations, $y_t = \{8, 3, 4\}$. The log-likelihood function is

$$\ln L_T(\theta) = \frac{15}{3} \ln \theta - \theta - \frac{\ln(8!3!4!)}{3} = 5 \ln \theta - \theta - 5.191.$$

A plot of the log-likelihood function is given in panel (a) of Figure 1.3 for values of θ ranging from 0 to 15. Even though the Poisson distribution is a discrete distribution in terms of the random variable y_t, the log-likelihood function is continuous in the unknown parameter θ. Inspection shows that a maximum occurs at $\widehat{\theta} = 5$ with a log-likelihood value of

$$\ln L_T(5) = 5 \times \ln 5 - 5 - 5.191 = -2.144.$$

The contribution to the log-likelihood function at the first observation $y_1 = 8$, evaluated at $\widehat{\theta} = 5$, is

$$\ln f(y_1; 5) = y_1 \ln 5 - 5 - \ln(y_1!) = 8 \times \ln 5 - 5 - \ln(8!) = -2.729.$$

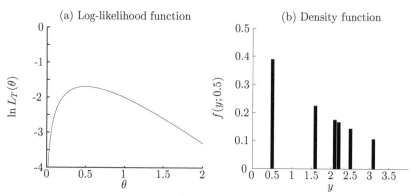

Figure 1.4. Plot of $\ln L_T(\theta)$ and $f(y; \widehat{\theta} = 0.5)$ for the exponential distribution example with a sample size of $T = 6$.

For the other two observations, the contributions are $\ln f(y_2; 5) = -1.963$, $\ln f(y_3; 5) = -1.740$. The probabilities $f(y_t; \theta)$ are between 0 and 1 by definition and therefore all of the contributions are negative because they are computed as the logarithm of $f(y_t; \theta)$. The average of these $T = 3$ contributions is $\ln L_T(5) = -2.144$, which corresponds to the value given earlier. A plot of $f(y; \widehat{\theta} = 5)$ in panel (b) of Figure 1.3 shows that observations closer to $\widehat{\theta} = 5$ have a relatively higher probability thereby having a relatively greater contribution to the log-likelihood function than observations further away. □

Example 1.11 Exponential Distribution

Let $\{y_1, y_2, \cdots, y_T\}$ be *iid* drawings from an exponential distribution

$$f(y_t; \theta) = \theta \exp[-\theta y_t],$$

in which $\theta > 0$. The log-likelihood function for the sample is

$$\ln L_T(\theta) = \frac{1}{T} \sum_{t=1}^{T} \ln f(y_t; \theta) = \frac{1}{T} \sum_{t=1}^{T} (\ln \theta - \theta y_t) = \ln \theta - \theta \frac{1}{T} \sum_{t=1}^{T} y_t.$$

Consider the following $T = 6$ observations, $y_t = \{2.1, 2.2, 3.1, 1.6, 2.5, 0.5\}$. The log-likelihood function is

$$\ln L_T(\theta) = \ln \theta - \theta \frac{1}{T} \sum_{t=1}^{T} y_t = \ln \theta - 2\theta.$$

A plot of the log-likelihood function, $\ln L_T(\theta)$, in panel (a) of Figure 1.4, shows that a maximum occurs at $\widehat{\theta} = 0.5$. Table 1.2 provides details of the calculations. Let the log-likelihood function at each observation evaluated at the maximum likelihood estimate be denoted as $\ln l_t(\theta) = \ln f(y_t; \theta)$. The second

Table 1.2. *Maximum likelihood calculations for the exponential distribution example. The maximum likelihood estimate is $\widehat{\theta} = 0.5$*

y_t	$\ln l_t(0.5)$	$g_t(0.5)$	$h_t(0.5)$
2.1	-1.743	-0.100	-4.000
2.2	-1.793	-0.200	-4.000
3.1	-2.243	-1.100	-4.000
1.6	-1.493	0.400	-4.000
2.5	-1.943	-0.500	-4.000
0.5	-0.943	1.500	-4.000
	$\ln L_T(0.5) = -1.693$	$G_T(0.5) = 0.000$	$H_T(0.5) = -4.000$

column shows $\ln l_t(\theta)$ evaluated at $\widehat{\theta} = 0.5$

$$\ln l_t(0.5) = \ln(0.5) - 0.5 y_t ,$$

resulting in a maximum value of the log-likelihood function of

$$\ln L_T(0.5) = \frac{1}{6} \sum_{t=1}^{6} \ln l_t(0.5) = \frac{-10.159}{6} = -1.693 .$$

In panel (b) of Figure 1.4, a plot of the ordinates of density corresponding to each observation y_t, evaluated at $\widehat{\theta} = 0.5$, shows that observations closer to $\widehat{\theta} = 0.5$ have a relatively higher probability than observations further away and therefore make a larger contribution to the log-likelihood function. ☐

Example 1.12 Normal Distribution
Let $\{y_1, y_2, \cdots, y_T\}$ be *iid* observations drawn from a normal distribution

$$f(y_t; \theta) = \frac{1}{\sqrt{2\pi\sigma^2}} \exp\left[-\frac{(y_t - \mu)^2}{2\sigma^2}\right] ,$$

with unknown parameters $\theta = \{\mu, \sigma^2\}$. The log-likelihood function is

$$\ln L_T(\theta) = \frac{1}{T} \sum_{t=1}^{T} \ln f(y_t; \theta)$$

$$= \frac{1}{T} \sum_{t=1}^{T} \left(-\frac{1}{2}\ln 2\pi - \frac{1}{2}\ln\sigma^2 - \frac{(y_t - \mu)^2}{2\sigma^2}\right)$$

$$= -\frac{1}{2}\ln 2\pi - \frac{1}{2}\ln\sigma^2 - \frac{1}{2\sigma^2 T}\sum_{t=1}^{T}(y_t - \mu)^2 .$$

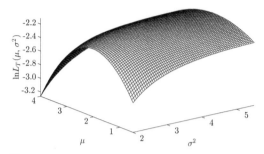

Figure 1.5. Plot of $\ln L_T(\theta)$ for the normal distribution example.

Consider the following $T = 6$ observations, $y_t = \{5, -1, 3, 0, 2, 3\}$. The log-likelihood function is

$$\ln L_T(\theta) = -\frac{1}{2}\ln 2\pi - \frac{1}{2}\ln \sigma^2 - \frac{1}{12\sigma^2}\sum_{t=1}^{6}(y_t - \mu)^2 .$$

A plot of this function in Figure 1.5 shows that a maximum occurs at $\hat{\mu} = 2$ and $\hat{\sigma}^2 = 4$. ☐

Example 1.13 Autoregressive Model

From Example 1.9, the log-likelihood function for the AR(1) model is

$$\ln L_T(\theta) = \frac{1}{T}\left(\frac{1}{2}\ln\left(1 - \rho^2\right) - \frac{1}{2\sigma^2}\left(1 - \rho^2\right)y_1^2\right)$$

$$-\frac{1}{2}\ln 2\pi - \frac{1}{2}\ln \sigma^2 - \frac{1}{2\sigma^2 T}\sum_{t=2}^{T}(y_t - \rho y_{t-1})^2 .$$

As the contribution of the first term disappears asymptotically

$$\lim_{T\longrightarrow\infty}\frac{1}{T}\left(\frac{1}{2}\ln\left(1 - \rho^2\right) - \frac{1}{2\sigma^2}\left(1 - \rho^2\right)y_1^2\right) = 0,$$

it is commonly excluded from $\ln L_T(\theta)$. ☐

As the aim of maximum likelihood estimation is to find the value of θ that maximises the log-likelihood function, a natural way to do this is to use the rules of calculus. This involves computing the first derivatives and second derivatives of the log-likelihood function with respect to the parameter vector θ.

1.4.2 Gradient

Differentiating $\ln L_T(\theta)$, with respect to a $(K \times 1)$ parameter vector, θ, yields a $(K \times 1)$ gradient vector, also known as the score, given by

$$
G_T(\theta) = \frac{\partial \ln L_T(\theta)}{\partial \theta} = \begin{bmatrix} \dfrac{\partial \ln L_T(\theta)}{\partial \theta_1} \\ \dfrac{\partial \ln L_T(\theta)}{\partial \theta_2} \\ \vdots \\ \dfrac{\partial \ln L_T(\theta)}{\partial \theta_K} \end{bmatrix} = \frac{1}{T} \sum_{t=1}^{T} g_t(\theta), \tag{1.9}
$$

in which the subscript T emphasises that the gradient is the sample average of the individual gradients

$$
g_t(\theta) = \frac{\partial \ln l_t(\theta)}{\partial \theta} .
$$

The maximum likelihood estimator of θ, denoted $\widehat{\theta}$, is obtained by setting the gradients equal to zero and solving the resultant K first-order conditions. The maximum likelihood estimator, $\widehat{\theta}$, therefore satisfies the condition

$$
G_T(\widehat{\theta}) = \frac{\partial \ln L_T(\theta)}{\partial \theta}\bigg|_{\theta=\widehat{\theta}} = 0 . \tag{1.10}
$$

Example 1.14 Poisson Distribution
From Example 1.10, the first derivative of $\ln L_T(\theta)$ with respect to θ is

$$
G_T(\theta) = \frac{1}{T\theta} \sum_{t=1}^{T} y_t - 1 .
$$

The maximum likelihood estimator is the solution of the first-order condition

$$
\frac{1}{T\widehat{\theta}} \sum_{t=1}^{T} y_t - 1 = 0 ,
$$

which yields the sample mean as the maximum likelihood estimator

$$
\widehat{\theta} = \frac{1}{T} \sum_{t=1}^{T} y_t = \overline{y} .
$$

Using the data for y_t in Example 1.10, the maximum likelihood estimate is $\widehat{\theta} = 15/3 = 5$. Evaluating the gradient at $\widehat{\theta} = 5$ verifies that it is zero at the maximum likelihood estimate

$$G_T(\widehat{\theta}) = \frac{1}{T\widehat{\theta}} \sum_{t=1}^{T} y_t - 1 = \frac{15}{3 \times 5} - 1 = 0.$$

□

Example 1.15 Exponential Distribution

From Example 1.11, the first derivative of $\ln L_T(\theta)$ with respect to θ is

$$G_T(\theta) = \frac{1}{\theta} - \frac{1}{T} \sum_{t=1}^{T} y_t .$$

Setting $G_T(\widehat{\theta}) = 0$ and solving the resultant first-order condition yields

$$\widehat{\theta} = \frac{T}{\sum_{t=1}^{T} y_t} = \frac{1}{\overline{y}},$$

which is the reciprocal of the sample mean. Using the same observed data for y_t as in Example 1.11, the maximum likelihood estimate is $\widehat{\theta} = 6/12 = 0.5$.

The third column of Table 1.2 gives the gradients at each observation evaluated at $\widehat{\theta} = 0.5$

$$g_t(0.5) = \frac{1}{0.5} - y_t .$$

The gradient is

$$G_T(0.5) = \frac{1}{6} \sum_{t=1}^{6} g_t(0.5) = 0 ,$$

which follows from the properties of the maximum likelihood estimator.   □

Example 1.16 Normal Distribution

From Example 1.12, the first derivatives of the log-likelihood function are

$$\frac{\partial \ln L_T(\theta)}{\partial \mu} = \frac{1}{\sigma^2 T} \sum_{t=1}^{T} (y_t - \mu),$$

$$\frac{\partial \ln L_T(\theta)}{\partial (\sigma^2)} = -\frac{1}{2\sigma^2} + \frac{1}{2\sigma^4 T} \sum_{t=1}^{T} (y_t - \mu)^2,$$

yielding the gradient vector

$$G_T(\theta) = \begin{bmatrix} \dfrac{1}{\sigma^2 T} \sum_{t=1}^{T} (y_t - \mu) \\[4ex] -\dfrac{1}{2\sigma^2} + \dfrac{1}{2\sigma^4 T} \sum_{t=1}^{T} (y_t - \mu)^2 \end{bmatrix}.$$

Evaluating the gradient at $\widehat{\theta}$ and setting $G_T(\widehat{\theta}) = 0$, gives

$$
G_T(\widehat{\theta}) = \begin{bmatrix} \dfrac{1}{\widehat{\sigma}^2 T} \sum_{t=1}^{T} (y_t - \widehat{\mu}) \\[2ex] -\dfrac{1}{2\widehat{\sigma}^2} + \dfrac{1}{2\widehat{\sigma}^4 T} \sum_{t=1}^{T} (y_t - \widehat{\mu})^2 \end{bmatrix} = \begin{bmatrix} 0 \\[2ex] 0 \end{bmatrix} .
$$

Solving for $\widehat{\theta} = \{\widehat{\mu}, \widehat{\sigma}^2\}$, the maximum likelihood estimators are

$$
\widehat{\mu} = \frac{1}{T} \sum_{t=1}^{T} y_t = \overline{y}, \qquad \widehat{\sigma}^2 = \frac{1}{T} \sum_{t=1}^{T} (y_t - \overline{y})^2 .
$$

Using the data from Example 1.12, the maximum likelihood estimates are

$$
\widehat{\mu} = \frac{5 - 1 + 3 + 0 + 2 + 3}{6} = 2
$$
$$
\widehat{\sigma}^2 = \frac{(5 - 2)^2 + (-1 - 2)^2 + (3 - 2)^2 + (0 - 2)^2 + (2 - 2)^2 + (3 - 2)^2}{6} = 4,
$$

which agree with the values given in Example 1.12. □

1.4.3 Hessian

To establish that $\widehat{\theta}$ maximises the log-likelihood function, it is necessary to determine that the Hessian

$$
H_T(\theta) = \frac{\partial^2 \ln L_T(\theta)}{\partial \theta \, \partial \theta'}, \tag{1.11}
$$

associated with the log-likelihood function is negative definite. As θ is a $(K \times 1)$ vector, the Hessian is the $(K \times K)$ symmetric matrix

$$
H_T(\theta) = \begin{bmatrix} \dfrac{\partial^2 \ln L_T(\theta)}{\partial \theta_1 \partial \theta_1} & \dfrac{\partial^2 \ln L_T(\theta)}{\partial \theta_1 \partial \theta_2} & \cdots & \dfrac{\partial^2 \ln L_T(\theta)}{\partial \theta_1 \partial \theta_K} \\[2ex] \dfrac{\partial^2 \ln L_T(\theta)}{\partial \theta_2 \partial \theta_1} & \dfrac{\partial^2 \ln L_T(\theta)}{\partial \theta_2 \partial \theta_2} & \cdots & \dfrac{\partial^2 \ln L_T(\theta)}{\partial \theta_2 \partial \theta_K} \\[2ex] \vdots & \vdots & \vdots & \vdots \\[2ex] \dfrac{\partial^2 \ln L_T(\theta)}{\partial \theta_K \partial \theta_1} & \dfrac{\partial^2 \ln L_T(\theta)}{\partial \theta_K \partial \theta_2} & \cdots & \dfrac{\partial^2 \ln L_T(\theta)}{\partial \theta_K \partial \theta_K} \end{bmatrix} = \frac{1}{T} \sum_{t=1}^{T} h_t(\theta),
$$

in which the subscript T emphasises that the Hessian is the sample average of the individual elements

$$h_t(\theta) = \frac{\partial^2 \ln l_t(\theta)}{\partial \theta \partial \theta'}.$$

The second-order condition for a maximum requires that the Hessian matrix evaluated at $\widehat{\theta}$,

$$H_T(\widehat{\theta}) = \frac{\partial^2 \ln L_T(\theta)}{\partial \theta \partial \theta'}\bigg|_{\theta=\widehat{\theta}}, \qquad (1.12)$$

is negative definite. The conditions for negative definiteness are

$$|H_{11}| < 0, \quad \begin{vmatrix} H_{11} & H_{12} \\ H_{21} & H_{22} \end{vmatrix} > 0, \quad \begin{vmatrix} H_{11} & H_{12} & H_{13} \\ H_{21} & H_{22} & H_{23} \\ H_{31} & H_{32} & H_{33} \end{vmatrix} < 0, \quad \cdots$$

in which H_{ij} is the ij^{th} element of $H_T(\widehat{\theta})$. In the case of $K = 1$, the condition is

$$H_{11} < 0. \qquad (1.13)$$

For the case of $K = 2$, the condition is

$$H_{11} < 0, \quad H_{11} H_{22} - H_{12} H_{21} > 0. \qquad (1.14)$$

Example 1.17 Poisson Distribution

From Examples 1.10 and 1.14, the second derivative of $\ln L_T(\theta)$ with respect to θ is

$$H_T(\theta) = -\frac{1}{\theta^2 T} \sum_{t=1}^{T} y_t.$$

Evaluating the Hessian at the maximum likelihood estimator, $\widehat{\theta} = \bar{y}$, yields

$$H_T(\widehat{\theta}) = -\frac{1}{\widehat{\theta}^2 T} \sum_{t=1}^{T} y_t = -\frac{1}{\bar{y}^2 T} \sum_{t=1}^{T} y_t = -\frac{1}{\bar{y}} < 0.$$

As $\bar{y}$ is always positive because it is the mean of a sample of positive integers, the Hessian is negative and a maximum is achieved. Using the data for y_t in Example 1.10, verifies that the Hessian at $\widehat{\theta} = 5$ is negative

$$H_T(\widehat{\theta}) = -\frac{1}{\widehat{\theta}^2 T} \sum_{t=1}^{T} y_t = -\frac{15}{5^2 \times 3} = -0.200. \qquad \square$$

Example 1.18 Exponential Distribution

From Examples 1.11 and 1.15, the second derivative of $\ln L_T(\theta)$ with respect to θ is

$$H_T(\theta) = -\frac{1}{\theta^2} \, .$$

Evaluating the Hessian at the maximum likelihood estimator yields

$$H_T(\widehat{\theta}) = -\frac{1}{\widehat{\theta}^2} < 0 \, .$$

As this term is negative for any $\widehat{\theta}$, the condition in equation (1.13) is satisfied and a maximum is achieved. The last column of Table 1.2 shows that the Hessian at each observation evaluated at the maximum likelihood estimate is constant. The value of the Hessian is

$$H_T(0.5) = \frac{1}{6} \sum_{t=1}^{6} h_t(0.5) = \frac{-24.000}{6} = -4 \, ,$$

which is negative confirming that a maximum has been reached. $\square$

Example 1.19 Normal Distribution

From Examples 1.12 and 1.16, the second derivatives of $\ln L_T(\theta)$ with respect to θ are

$$\frac{\partial^2 \ln L_T(\theta)}{\partial \mu^2} = -\frac{1}{\sigma^2}$$

$$\frac{\partial^2 \ln L_T(\theta)}{\partial \mu \partial \sigma^2} = -\frac{1}{\sigma^4 T} \sum_{t=1}^{T}(y_t - \mu)$$

$$\frac{\partial^2 \ln L_T(\theta)}{\partial (\sigma^2)^2} = \frac{1}{2\sigma^4} - \frac{1}{\sigma^6 T} \sum_{t=1}^{T}(y_t - \mu)^2 \, ,$$

so that the Hessian is

$$H_T(\theta) = \begin{bmatrix} -\dfrac{1}{\sigma^2} & -\dfrac{1}{\sigma^4 T} \displaystyle\sum_{t=1}^{T}(y_t - \mu) \\[4mm] -\dfrac{1}{\sigma^4 T} \displaystyle\sum_{t=1}^{T}(y_t - \mu) & \dfrac{1}{2\sigma^4} - \dfrac{1}{\sigma^6 T} \displaystyle\sum_{t=1}^{T}(y_t - \mu)^2 \end{bmatrix} \, .$$

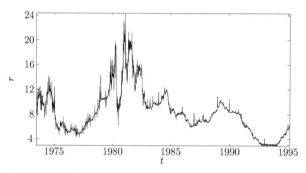

Figure 1.6. Daily seven-day Eurodollar interest rates, r_t, from the 1 June 1973 to 25 February 1995 expressed as a percentage.

Given that $G_T(\widehat{\theta}) = 0$, from Example 1.16 it follows that $\sum_{t=1}^{T}(y_t - \widehat{\mu}) = 0$ and therefore

$$H_T(\widehat{\theta}) = \begin{bmatrix} -\dfrac{1}{\widehat{\sigma}^2} & 0 \\ 0 & -\dfrac{1}{2\widehat{\sigma}^4} \end{bmatrix}.$$

From equation (1.14)

$$H_{11} = -\frac{T}{\widehat{\sigma}^2} < 0, \qquad H_{11} H_{22} - H_{12} H_{21} = -\Big(\frac{T}{\widehat{\sigma}^2}\Big)\Big(-\frac{T}{2\widehat{\sigma}^4}\Big) - 0^2 > 0,$$

establishing that the second-order condition for a maximum is satisfied. Using the maximum likelihood estimates from Example 1.16, the Hessian is

$$H_T(\widehat{\mu}, \widehat{\sigma}^2) = \begin{bmatrix} -\dfrac{1}{4} & 0 \\ 0 & -\dfrac{1}{2 \times 4^2} \end{bmatrix} = \begin{bmatrix} -0.250 & 0.000 \\ 0.000 & -0.031 \end{bmatrix}.$$

□

1.5   Applications

Two applications of maximum likelihood estimation are presented that focus on estimating the discrete time version of the Vasicek (1977) model of interest rates, r_t. The first application is based on the marginal (stationary) distribution while the second focusses on the conditional (transitional) distribution that gives the distribution of r_t conditional on r_{t-1}. The interest rate data used are from Aït-Sahalia (1996). The data, plotted in Figure 1.6, consists of daily seven-day Eurodollar rates (expressed as percentages) for the period 1 June 1973 to the 25 February 1995, a total of $T = 5505$ observations.

The Vasicek model imposes absence of arbitrage on a system of interest rates. It begins with the dynamics of a short-maturity interest rate, r_t, which are assumed to be first-order autoregressive according to

$$r_t - r_{t-1} = \alpha + \beta r_{t-1} + u_t, \qquad u_t \sim iid \, N\left(0, \sigma^2\right), \qquad (1.15)$$

in which $\theta = \{\alpha, \beta, \sigma^2\}$ are unknown parameters and $\beta < 0$.

1.5.1 Stationary Distribution of the Vasicek Model

As a preliminary step to estimating the parameters of the Vasicek model in equation (1.15), consider the alternative model where the level of the interest rate is independent of previous interest rates

$$r_t = \mu_s + v_t, \qquad v_t \sim iid \, N(0, \sigma_s^2).$$

The stationary distribution of r_t for this model is

$$f(r_t; \mu_s, \sigma_s^2) = \frac{1}{\sqrt{2\pi\sigma_s^2}} \exp\left[-\frac{(r_t - \mu_s)^2}{2\sigma_s^2}\right]. \qquad (1.16)$$

The relationship between the parameters of the stationary distribution and the parameters of the model in equation (1.15) is

$$\mu_s = -\frac{\alpha}{\beta}, \qquad \sigma_s^2 = -\frac{\sigma^2}{\beta(2+\beta)}. \qquad (1.17)$$

which are obtained as the unconditional mean and variance of (1.15).

The log-likelihood function based on the stationary distribution in equation (1.16) for a sample of T observations is

$$\ln L_T(\theta) = -\frac{1}{2}\ln 2\pi - \frac{1}{2}\ln \sigma_s^2 - \frac{1}{2\sigma_s^2 T}\sum_{t=1}^{T}(r_t - \mu_s)^2,$$

with $\theta = \{\mu_s, \sigma_s^2\}$. Maximising $\ln L_T(\theta)$ with respect to θ gives

$$\widehat{\mu_s} = \frac{1}{T}\sum_{t=1}^{T} r_t, \qquad \widehat{\sigma}_s^2 = \frac{1}{T}\sum_{t=1}^{T}(r_t - \widehat{\mu_s})^2. \qquad (1.18)$$

Using the Eurodollar interest rates, the maximum likelihood estimates are

$$\widehat{\mu_s} = 8.362, \qquad \widehat{\sigma}_s^2 = 12.893. \qquad (1.19)$$

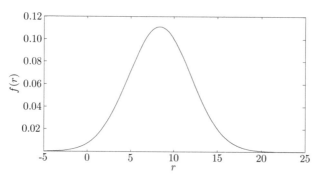

Figure 1.7. Estimated stationary distribution of the Vasicek model based on evaluating (1.16) at the maximum likelihood estimates (1.19), using daily Eurodollar rates, r_t, from the 1 June 1973 to 25 February 1995.

The stationary distribution is estimated by evaluating equation (1.16) at the maximum likelihood estimates in (1.19) and is given by

$$
f\left(r_t; \widehat{\mu}_s, \widehat{\sigma}_s^2\right) = \frac{1}{\sqrt{2\pi\widehat{\sigma}_s^2}} \exp\left[-\frac{\left(r_t - \widehat{\mu}_s\right)^2}{2\widehat{\sigma}_s^2}\right]
$$

$$
= \frac{1}{\sqrt{2\pi \times 12.893}} \exp\left[-\frac{(r_t - 8.362)^2}{2 \times 12.893}\right], \qquad (1.20)
$$

which is presented in Figure 1.7.

Inspection of the estimated distribution shows a potential problem with the Vasicek stationary distribution, namely that the support of the distribution is not restricted to being positive. The probability of negative values for the interest rate is

$$
\Pr(r < 0) = \int_{-\infty}^{0} \frac{1}{\sqrt{2\pi \times 12.893}} \exp\left[-\frac{(r - 8.362)^2}{2 \times 12.893}\right] dr = 0.0099.
$$

To avoid this problem, alternative models of interest rates are specified where the stationary distribution is just defined over the positive region. A well known example is the CIR interest rate model (Cox, Ingersoll and Ross, 1985) which is discussed in Chapters 2, 3 and 12.

1.5.2   Transitional Distribution of the Vasicek Model

In contrast to the stationary model specification of the previous section, the full dynamics of the Vasicek model in equation (1.15) are now used by specifying the transitional distribution

$$f\left(r_t \mid r_{t-1}; \alpha, \rho, \sigma^2\right) = \frac{1}{\sqrt{2\pi\sigma^2}} \exp\left[-\frac{(r_t - \alpha - \rho r_{t-1})^2}{2\sigma^2}\right],$$

(1.21)

in which $\theta = \{\alpha, \rho, \sigma^2\}$ and the substitution $\rho = 1 + \beta$ is made for convenience. This distribution is now of the same form as the conditional distribution of the AR(1) model in Examples 1.5, 1.9 and 1.13.

The log-likelihood function based on the transitional distribution in equation (1.21) is

$$\ln L_T(\theta) = -\frac{1}{2}\ln 2\pi - \frac{1}{2}\ln\sigma^2 - \frac{1}{2\sigma^2(T-1)}\sum_{t=2}^{T}(r_t - \alpha - \rho r_{t-1})^2,$$

where the sample size is reduced by one observation as a result of the lagged term r_{t-1}. This form of the log-likelihood function does not contain the marginal distribution $f(r_1; \theta)$, a point that is made in Example 1.13. The first derivatives of the log-likelihood function are

$$\frac{\partial \ln L(\theta)}{\partial \alpha} = \frac{1}{\sigma^2(T-1)}\sum_{t=2}^{T}(r_t - \alpha - \rho r_{t-1})$$

$$\frac{\partial \ln L(\theta)}{\partial \rho} = \frac{1}{\sigma^2(T-1)}\sum_{t=2}^{T}(r_t - \alpha - \rho r_{t-1})r_{t-1}$$

$$\frac{\partial \ln L(\theta)}{\partial(\sigma^2)} = -\frac{1}{2\sigma^2} + \frac{1}{2\sigma^4(T-1)}\sum_{t=2}^{T}(r_t - \alpha - \rho r_{t-1})^2.$$

Setting these derivatives to zero yields the maximum likelihood estimators

$$\widehat{\alpha} = \overline{r}_t - \widehat{\rho}\,\overline{r}_{t-1}$$

$$\widehat{\rho} = \frac{\displaystyle\sum_{t=2}^{T}(r_t - \overline{r}_t)(r_{t-1} - \overline{r}_{t-1})}{\displaystyle\sum_{t=2}^{T}(r_{t-1} - \overline{r}_{t-1})^2}$$

$$\widehat{\sigma}^2 = \frac{1}{T-1}\sum_{t=2}^{T}(r_t - \widehat{\alpha} - \widehat{\rho} r_{t-1})^2,$$

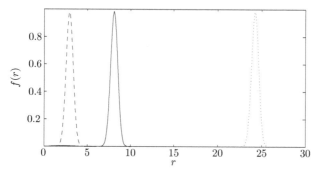

Figure 1.8. Estimated transitional distribution of the Vasicek model, based on evaluating (1.23) at the maximum likelihood estimates in (1.22) using Eurodollar rates from 1 June 1973 to 25 February 1995. The dashed line is the transitional density for the minimum (2.9%), the solid line is the transitional density for the median (8.1%) and the dotted line is the transitional density for the maximum (24.3%) Eurodollar rate.

where

$$\bar{r}_t = \frac{1}{T-1} \sum_{t=2}^{T} r_t, \qquad \bar{r}_{t-1} = \frac{1}{T-1} \sum_{t=2}^{T} r_{t-1}.$$

The maximum likelihood estimates for the Eurodollar interest rates are

$$\widehat{\alpha} = 0.053, \qquad \widehat{\rho} = 0.994, \qquad \widehat{\sigma}^2 = 0.165. \tag{1.22}$$

An estimate of β is obtained by using the relationship $\rho = 1 + \beta$. Rearranging for β and evaluating at $\widehat{\rho}$ gives $\widehat{\beta} = \widehat{\rho} - 1 = -0.006$.

The estimated transitional distribution is obtained by evaluating (1.21) at the maximum likelihood estimates in (1.22)

$$f\left(r_t \mid r_{t-1}; \widehat{\alpha}, \widehat{\rho}, \widehat{\sigma}^2\right) = \frac{1}{\sqrt{2\pi\widehat{\sigma}^2}} \exp\left[-\frac{(r_t - \widehat{\alpha} - \widehat{\rho}r_{t-1})^2}{2\widehat{\sigma}^2}\right]. \tag{1.23}$$

Plots of this distribution are given in Figure 1.8 for three values of the conditioning variable r_{t-1}, corresponding to the minimum (2.9%), median (8.1%) and maximum (24.3%) interest rates in the sample.

The location of the three transitional distributions changes over time, while the spread of each distribution remains constant at $\widehat{\sigma}^2 = 0.165$. A comparison of the estimates of the variances of the stationary and transitional distributions, in equations (1.19) and (1.22), respectively, shows that $\widehat{\sigma}^2 < \widehat{\sigma}_s^2$. This result is a reflection of the property that by conditioning on information, in this case r_{t-1}, the transitional distribution is better at tracking the time series behaviour of the interest rate, r_t, than the stationary distribution where there is no conditioning on lagged dependent variables.

Having obtained the estimated transitional distribution using the maximum likelihood estimates in (1.22), it is also possible to use these estimates to re-estimate the stationary interest rate distribution in (1.20) by using the expressions in (1.17). The alternative estimates of the mean and variance of the stationary distribution are

$$\tilde{\mu}_s = -\frac{\hat{\alpha}}{\hat{\beta}} = \frac{0.053}{0.006} = 8.308,$$

$$\tilde{\sigma}_s^2 = -\frac{\hat{\sigma}^2}{\hat{\beta}\left(2 + \hat{\beta}\right)} = \frac{0.165}{0.006\,(2 - 0.006)} = 12.967.$$

As these estimates are based on the transitional distribution, which incorporates the full dynamic specification of the Vasicek model, they represent the maximum likelihood estimates of the parameters of the stationary distribution. This relationship between the maximum likelihood estimators of the transitional and stationary distributions is based on the invariance property of maximum likelihood estimators which is discussed in Chapter 2. While the parameter estimates of the stationary distribution derived from the estimates of the transitional distribution are numerically close to those reported in Section 1.5.1, the latter are obtained from a misspecified model because the stationary model excludes the dynamic structure in equation (1.15). Issues relating to misspecified models are discussed in Chapter 9.

1.6   Exercises

(1) Sampling Data

Program files   basic_sample.*

This exercise reproduces the simulation results in Figures 1.1 and 1.2. For each model, simulate $T = 5$ draws of y_t and plot the corresponding distribution at each point in time. Where applicable the explanatory variable in these exercises is $x_t = \{0, 1, 2, 3, 4\}$ and w_t are iid draws from a uniform distribution on the unit circle.

(a) Time invariant model

$$y_t = 2z_t, \qquad z_t \sim iid\, N(0, 1).$$

(b) Count model

$$f(y_t; 2) = \frac{2^{y_t}\exp[-2]}{y_t!}, \qquad y_t = 0, 1, \cdots.$$

(c) Linear regression model

$$y_t = 3x_t + 2z_t , \qquad z_t \sim iid\ N(0, 1).$$

(d) Exponential regression model

$$f(y_t; \theta) = \frac{1}{\mu_t} \exp\left[-\frac{y}{\mu_t}\right], \qquad \mu_t = 1 + x_t .$$

(e) Autoregressive model

$$y_t = 0.8y_{t-1} + 2z_t , \qquad z_t \sim iid\ N(0, 1).$$

(f) Bilinear time series model

$$y_t = 0.8y_{t-1} + 0.4y_{t-1}u_{t-1} + 2z_t , \qquad z_t \sim iid\ N(0, 1).$$

(g) Autoregressive model with heteroskedasticity

$$y_t = 0.8y_{t-1} + \sigma_t z_t , \qquad z_t \sim iid\ N(0, 1)$$
$$\sigma_t^2 = 0.8 + 0.8w_t .$$

(h) The ARCH regression model

$$y_t = 3x_t + u_t$$
$$u_t = \sigma_t z_t$$
$$\sigma_t^2 = 0.8 + 0.8u_{t-1}^2$$
$$z_t \sim iid\ N(0, 1).$$

(2) Poisson Distribution

Program files   `basic_poisson.*`

A sample of $T = 4$ observations, $y_t = \{6, 2, 3, 1\}$, is drawn from the Poisson distribution

$$f(y_t; \theta) = \frac{\theta^{y_t} \exp[-\theta]}{y_t!} .$$

(a) Derive the log-likelihood function, $\ln L_T(\theta)$, the gradient $G_T(\theta)$, and the Hessian $H_T(\theta)$.
(b) Derive and interpret the maximum likelihood estimator, $\widehat{\theta}$.
(c) Compute the maximum likelihood estimate, $\widehat{\theta}$.
(d) Compute $\ln l_t(\widehat{\theta})$, $g_t(\widehat{\theta})$ and $h_t(\widehat{\theta})$ for each observation.
(e) Compute $\ln L_T(\widehat{\theta})$, $G_T(\widehat{\theta})$ and $H_T(\widehat{\theta})$.

(3) Exponential Distribution

Program files   basic_exp.*

A sample of $T = 4$ observations, $y_t = \{5.5, 2.0, 3.5, 5.0\}$, is drawn from the exponential distribution

$$f(y_t; \theta) = \theta \exp[-\theta y_t].$$

(a) Derive the log-likelihood function, $\ln L_T(\theta)$, the gradient $G_T(\theta)$, and the Hessian $H_T(\theta)$.
(b) Derive and interpret the maximum likelihood estimator, $\widehat{\theta}$.
(c) Compute the maximum likelihood estimate, $\widehat{\theta}$ for the given data.
(d) Compute $\ln l_t(\widehat{\theta})$, $g_t(\widehat{\theta})$ and $h_t(\widehat{\theta})$ for each observation.
(e) Compute $\ln L_T(\widehat{\theta})$, $G_T(\widehat{\theta})$ and $H_T(\widehat{\theta})$.
(f) An alternative form of the exponential distribution is

$$f(y_t; \theta) = \frac{1}{\theta} \exp\left[-\frac{y_t}{\theta}\right].$$

Derive the maximum likelihood estimator of θ and compare the result with that obtained in part (b).

(4) Normal Distribution

Program files   basic_normal.*, basic_normal_like.*

A sample of $T = 5$ observations consisting of the values $\{1, 2, 5, 1, 2\}$ is drawn from the normal distribution

$$f(y_t; \theta) = \frac{1}{\sqrt{2\pi\sigma^2}} \exp\left[-\frac{(y_t - \mu)^2}{2\sigma^2}\right],$$

with parameters μ and σ^2.

(a) Assume that the variance is known $\sigma^2 = 1$ and the unknown parameter is $\theta = \{\mu\}$.
   (i) Derive the log-likelihood function, $\ln L_T(\theta)$, the gradient $G_T(\theta)$ and the Hessian $H_T(\theta)$.
   (ii) Derive and interpret the maximum likelihood estimator, $\widehat{\theta}$.
   (iii) Compute the maximum likelihood estimate, $\widehat{\theta}$.
   (iv) Compute $\ln l_t(\widehat{\theta})$, $g_t(\widehat{\theta})$ and $h_t(\widehat{\theta})$ for each observation.
   (v) Compute $\ln L_T(\widehat{\theta})$, $G_T(\widehat{\theta})$ and $H_T(\widehat{\theta})$.
(b) Repeat part (a) for the case where the variance is unknown, $\theta = \{\sigma^2\}$ and the mean is known with a value of $\mu = 2$.

(c) Repeat part (a) for the case where both the mean and the variance are unknown, $\theta = \{\mu, \sigma^2\}$.

(5) A Model of the Number of Strikes

Program files	basic_count.*
Data files	strike.*

The data are the number of strikes per annum, y_t, in the United States from 1968 to 1976, taken from Kennan (1985). The number of strikes is specified as an iid Poisson-distributed random variable with unknown parameter θ

$$f(y_t; \theta) = \frac{\theta^{y_t} \exp[-\theta]}{y_t!}.$$

(a) Derive the log-likelihood function for a sample of T observations.
(b) Derive and interpret the maximum likelihood estimator of θ.
(c) Estimate θ and interpret the result.
(d) Use the estimate of θ from part (c), to plot the distribution of the number of strikes $f(y_t; \widehat{\theta})$ and interpret its shape.
(e) Compute the empirical distribution of y_t using a histogram and compare its shape with the estimated distribution in part (d).

(6) A Model of the Duration of Strikes

Program files	basic_strike.*
Data files	strike.*

The data are 62 observations, taken from the same source as Exercise 5, of the duration of strikes in the United States per annum expressed in days, y_t. Durations are assumed to have an exponential distribution with unknown parameter θ

$$f(y_t; \theta) = \frac{1}{\theta} \exp\left[-\frac{y_t}{\theta}\right].$$

(a) Derive the log-likelihood function for a sample of T observations.
(b) Derive and interpret the maximum likelihood estimator of θ.
(c) Use the data on strike durations to estimate θ. Interpret the result.
(d) Use the estimate of θ from part (c) to plot the distribution of strike durations $f(y_t; \widehat{\theta})$ and interpret this plot.
(e) Compute the empirical distribution of y_t using a histogram and compare its shape with the estimated distribution in part (d).

(7) Asset Prices

Program files	basic_assetprices.*
Data files	assetprices.*

The data consist of the Australian, Singapore and NASDAQ stock market indexes for the period 3 January 1989 to 31 December 2009, a total of $T = 5478$ observations. Consider the following model of asset prices, p_t, that is commonly adopted in the financial econometrics literature

$$\ln p_t - \ln p_{t-1} = \alpha + u_t, \qquad u_t \sim iid\ N(0, \sigma^2),$$

in which $\theta = \{\alpha, \sigma^2\}$ are unknown parameters.

(a) Use the transformation of variable technique to show that the conditional distribution of p_t is the log-normal distribution

$$f(p_t \mid p_{t-1}; \theta) = \frac{1}{\sqrt{2\pi\sigma^2}\, p_t} \exp\left[-\frac{\ln p_t - \ln p_{t-1} - \alpha}{2\sigma^2}\right].$$

(b) For a sample of size T, construct the log-likelihood function and derive the maximum likelihood estimator of $\theta = \{\alpha, \sigma^2\}$ based on the conditional distribution of p_t.

(c) Use the results in part (b) to compute $\widehat{\theta}$ for the three stock indexes.

(d) Estimate the asset price distribution for each index using the maximum likelihood parameter estimates obtained in part (c), conditional on p_{t-1} equaling the sample mean of p_t.

(e) Letting $r_t = \ln p_t - \ln p_{t-1}$ represent the return on an asset, derive the maximum likelihood estimator of θ based on the distribution of r_t. Compute $\widehat{\theta}$ for the three stock market indexes and compare the estimates to those obtained in part (c).

(8) Stationary Distribution of the Vasicek Model

Program files	basic_stationary.*
Data files	eurodata.*

The data are daily 7-day Eurodollar rates, expressed as percentages, from 1 June 1973 to the 25 February 1995, a total of $T = 5505$ observations. The Vasicek discrete time model of interest rates, r_t, is

$$r_t - r_{t-1} = \alpha + \beta r_{t-1} + u_t, \qquad u_t \sim iid\ N(0, \sigma^2),$$

in which $\theta = \{\alpha, \beta, \sigma^2\}$ are unknown parameters and $\beta < 0$.

(a) Show that the mean and variance of the stationary distribution are given by

$$\mu_s = -\frac{\alpha}{\beta}, \qquad \sigma_s^2 = -\frac{\sigma^2}{\beta(2+\beta)},$$

respectively.

(b) Derive the maximum likelihood estimators of the parameters of the stationary distribution.

(c) Compute the maximum likelihood estimates of the parameters of the stationary distribution using the Eurodollar interest rates.

(d) Use the estimates from part (c) to plot the stationary distribution and interpret its properties.

(9) **Transitional Distribution of the Vasicek Model**

Program files	basic_transitional.*
Data files	eurodata.*

The data are the same daily 7-day Eurodollar rates, expressed in percentages, as used in Exercise 8. The Vasicek discrete time model of interest rates, r_t, is

$$r_t - r_{t-1} = \alpha + \beta r_{t-1} + u_t, \qquad u_t \sim iid\ N(0, \sigma^2),$$

in which $\theta = \{\alpha, \beta, \sigma^2\}$ are unknown parameters and $\beta < 0$.

(a) Derive the maximum likelihood estimators of the parameters of the transitional distribution.

(b) Compute the maximum likelihood estimates of the parameters of the transitional distribution using the Eurodollar interest rates.

(c) Use the estimates from part (b) to plot the transitional distribution where conditioning is based on the minimum, median and maximum interest rates in the sample. Interpret the properties of the three transitional distributions.

(d) Use the results in part (b) to estimate the mean and the variance of the stationary distribution and compare these values to the estimates obtained in part (c) of Exercise 8.

2 Properties of Maximum Likelihood Estimators

2.1 Introduction

Under certain conditions known as regularity conditions, the maximum likelihood estimator introduced in Chapter 1 possesses a number of important statistical properties and the aim of this chapter is to derive these properties. In large samples, the maximum likelihood estimator is consistent, efficient and normally distributed. In small samples, it satisfies an invariance property, is a function of sufficient statistics and in some, but not all, cases, is unbiased and unique. As the derivation of analytical expressions for the finite-sample distributions of the maximum likelihood estimator is generally complicated, computationally intensive methods based on Monte Carlo simulations or series expansions are used to examine some of these properties.

The maximum likelihood estimator encompasses many other estimators often used in econometrics, including ordinary least squares and instrumental variables (Chapter 5), nonlinear least squares (Chapter 6), the Cochrane-Orcutt method for the autocorrelated regression model (Chapter 7), weighted least squares estimation of heteroskedastic regression models (Chapter 8) and the Johansen procedure for cointegrated nonstationary time series models (Chapter 18).

2.2 Preliminaries

Before deriving the formal properties of the maximum likelihood estimator, four important preliminary concepts are reviewed. The first presents some stochastic models of time series and briefly discusses their properties. The second is concerned with the convergence of a sample average to its population mean as $T \to \infty$, known as the weak law of large numbers. The third identifies the scaling factor ensuring convergence of scaled random variables to non-degenerate distributions. The fourth focusses on the form of the distribution of the sample average around its population mean as $T \to \infty$, known as the central limit theorem. Four central limit theorems are discussed: the Lindeberg-Levy central limit theorem, the Lindeberg-Feller central limit theorem, the martingale difference sequence central limit theorem and a mixing central limit theorem. These central limit theorems are extended to allow for nonstationary dependence using the functional central limit theorem in Chapter 16.

2.2.1 Properties of Stochastic Time Series

In this section various classes of time series models and their properties are introduced. These stochastic processes and the behaviour of the moments of their probability distribution functions are particularly important in the establishment of a range of convergence results and central limit theorems that enable the derivation of the properties of maximum likelihood estimators.

Stationarity

A variable y_t is stationary if its distribution, or some important aspect of its distribution, is constant over time. There are two commonly used definitions of stationarity known as weak (or covariance) and strong (or strict) stationarity. A variable that is not stationary is said to be nonstationary, a class of models that is discussed in detail in Part FIVE.

Weak Stationarity

The variable y_t is weakly stationary if the first two unconditional moments of the joint distribution function $F(y_1, y_2, \cdots, y_j)$ do not depend on t for all finite j. This definition is summarised by the following three properties:

$$
\begin{aligned}
&\text{Property 1:} \quad \mathrm{E}[y_t] = \mu < \infty \\
&\text{Property 2:} \quad \mathrm{var}(y_t) = \mathrm{E}[(y_t - \mu)^2] = \sigma^2 < \infty \\
&\text{Property 3:} \quad \mathrm{cov}(y_t y_{t-k}) = \mathrm{E}[(y_t - \mu)(y_{t-k} - \mu)] = \gamma_k, \quad k > 0.
\end{aligned}
$$

These properties require that the mean, μ, is constant and finite, that the variance, σ^2, is constant and finite and that the covariance between y_t and y_{t-k}, γ_k, is a function of the time between the two points, k, and is not a function of time, t. Consider two snapshots of a time series of equal length which are s periods apart, a situation which can be represented schematically as follows:

$$y_1, \quad y_2, \quad \cdots \quad y_s, \quad y_{s+1}, \quad \cdots \quad y_j, \quad y_{j+1}, \quad \cdots \quad y_{j+s} \quad y_{j+s+1} \quad \cdots$$

$$\underbrace{\hspace{5cm}}$$
$$\text{Period 1 } (Y_1^j)$$

$$\underbrace{\hspace{5cm}}$$
$$\text{Period 2 } (Y_{s+1}^{j+s})$$

Here Y_1^j and Y_{s+1}^{j+s} represent the time series of the two sub-periods. An implication of weak stationarity is that Y_1^j and Y_{s+1}^{j+s} are governed by the same parameters μ, σ^2 and γ_k.

Example 2.1 Stationary AR(1) Model

Consider the AR(1) process

$$y_t = \alpha + \rho y_{t-1} + u_t, \qquad u_t \sim iid\,(0, \sigma^2),$$

with $|\rho| < 1$. This process is stationary since

$$\mu = E[y_t] = \frac{\alpha}{1 - \rho}$$

$$\sigma^2 = E[(y_t - \mu)^2] = \frac{\sigma^2}{1 - \rho^2}$$

$$\gamma_k = E[(y_t - \mu)(y_{t-k} - \mu)] = \frac{\sigma^2 \rho^k}{1 - \rho^2}.$$

are all constant and finite. $\qquad\qquad\square$

Many time series are weakly stationary including stationary ARMA models which are discussed in detail in Chapter 13.

Strict Stationarity

The variable y_t is strictly stationary if the joint distribution function given by $F(y_1, y_2, \cdots, y_j)$ does not depend on t for all finite j. Strict stationarity requires that the joint distribution function of two time series s periods apart is invariant with respect to an arbitrary time shift. That is,

$$F(y_1, y_2, \cdots, y_j) = F(y_{1+s}, y_{2+s}, \cdots, y_{j+s}).$$

As strict stationarity requires that all the moments of y_t, if they exist, are independent of t, it follows that higher-order moments such as

$$E[(y_t - \mu)(y_{t-k} - \mu)] = E[(y_{t+s} - \mu)(y_{t+s-k} - \mu)]$$
$$E[(y_t - \mu)(y_{t-k} - \mu)^2] = E[(y_{t+s} - \mu)(y_{t+s-k} - \mu)^2]$$
$$E[(y_t - \mu)^2(y_{t-k} - \mu)^2] = E[(y_{t+s} - \mu)^2(y_{t+s-k} - \mu)^2],$$

must be functions of k only.

Strict stationarity does not require the existence of the first two moments of the joint distribution of y_t. For the special case in which the first two moments do exist and are finite, $\mu, \sigma^2 < \infty$, and the joint distribution function is a normal distribution, weak and strict stationarity are equivalent. In the case where the first two moments of the joint distribution do not exist, y_t can be strictly stationary, but not weakly stationary. An example is where y_t is *iid* with a Cauchy distribution, which is strictly stationary but has no finite moments and is therefore not weakly stationary. Another example is an IGARCH model discussed in Chapter 20, which is strictly stationary but not weakly stationary because the unconditional variance does not exist. An implication of the definition of strict stationarity is that if y_t is stationary then any function of a stationary process is also stationary, such as higher-order terms y_t^2, y_t^3 and y_t^4.

Martingale Difference Sequence

A martingale difference sequence (mds) is defined in terms of its first conditional moment having the property

$$E_{t-1}[y_t] = E[y_t | y_{t-1}, y_{t-2}, \cdots] = 0. \tag{2.1}$$

This condition shows that information at time $t - 1$ cannot be used to forecast y_t. Two important properties of a mds arising from (2.1) are

Property 1 : $E[y_t] = E[E_{t-1}[y_t]] = E[0] = 0$

Property 2 : $E[E_{t-1}[y_t y_{t-k}]] = E[y_{t-k} E_{t-1}[y_t]] = E[y_{t-k} \times 0] = 0, \quad k > 0.$

The first property is that the unconditional mean of a mds is zero which follows by using the law of iterated expectations. The second property shows that a mds is uncorrelated with past values of y_t. The condition in (2.1) does not, however, rule out higher-order moment dependence.

Example 2.2 Nonlinear Time Series

Consider the nonlinear time series model

$$y_t = u_t u_{t-1}, \qquad u_t \sim iid\,(0, \sigma^2).$$

The process y_t is a mds because

$$E_{t-1}[y_t] = E_{t-1}[u_t u_{t-1}] = E_{t-1}[u_t] u_{t-1} = 0,$$

since $E_{t-1}[u_t] = E[u_t] = 0$. The process y_t nonetheless exhibits dependence in the higher-order moments. For example,

$$
\begin{aligned}
\text{cov}(y_t^2, y_{t-1}^2) &= E[y_t^2 y_{t-1}^2] - E[y_t^2] E[y_{t-1}^2] \\
&= E[u_t^2 u_{t-1}^4 u_{t-2}^2] - E[u_t^2 u_{t-1}^2] E[u_{t-1}^2 u_{t-2}^2] \\
&= E[u_t^2] E[u_{t-1}^4] E[u_{t-2}^2] - E[u_t^2] E[u_{t-1}^2]^2 E[u_{t-2}^2] \\
&= \sigma^4 (E[u_{t-1}^4] - \sigma^4) \neq 0.
\end{aligned}
$$

$\square$

Example 2.3 Autoregressive Conditional Heteroskedasticity

Consider the ARCH model from Example 1.8 in Chapter 1 given by

$$y_t = z_t \sqrt{\alpha_0 + \alpha_1 y_{t-1}^2}, \qquad z_t \sim iid\, N(0, 1).$$

Now y_t is a mds because

$$E_{t-1}[y_t] = E_{t-1}\left[z_t\sqrt{\alpha_0 + \alpha_1 y_{t-1}^2}\right] = E_{t-1}[z_t]\sqrt{\alpha_0 + \alpha_1 y_{t-1}^2} = 0,$$

since $E_{t-1}[z_t] = 0$. The process y_t nonetheless exhibits dependence in the second moment because

$$E_{t-1}[y_t^2] = E_{t-1}[z_t^2(\alpha_0 + \alpha_1 y_{t-1}^2)] = E_{t-1}\left[z_t^2\right](\alpha_0 + \alpha_1 y_{t-1}^2) = \alpha_0 + \alpha_1 y_{t-1}^2,$$

by using the property $E_{t-1}[z_t^2] = E[z_t^2] = 1$. $\qquad\qquad\square$

In contrast to the properties of stationary time series, a function of a mds is not necessarily a mds.

White Noise
For a process to be white noise, its first and second unconditional moments must satisfy the following three properties:

Property 1 : $\quad E[y_t] = 0$
Property 2 : $\quad E[y_t^2] = \sigma^2 < \infty$
Property 3 : $\quad E[y_t y_{t-k}] = 0, \qquad k > 0.$

White noise is a special case of a weakly stationary process with mean zero, constant and finite variance, σ^2, and zero covariance between y_t and y_{t-k}. A mds with finite and constant variance is also a white noise process since the first two unconditional moments exist and the process is not correlated. If a mds has infinite variance, then it is not white noise. Similarly, a white noise process is not necessarily a mds, as demonstrated by the following example.

Example 2.4 Bilinear Time Series
Consider the bilinear time series model

$$y_t = u_t + \delta u_{t-1} u_{t-2}, \qquad u_t \sim iid\ (0, \sigma^2),$$

in which δ is a parameter. The process y_t is white noise since

$$E[y_t] = E[u_t + \delta u_{t-1} u_{t-2}] = E[u_t] + \delta E[u_{t-1}]E[u_{t-2}] = 0,$$
$$E[y_t^2] = E[(u_t + \delta u_{t-1} u_{t-2})^2]$$
$$= E[u_t^2 + \delta^2 u_{t-1}^2 u_{t-2}^2 + 2\delta u_t u_{t-1} u_{t-2}] = \sigma^2(1 + \delta^2 \sigma^2) < \infty$$
$$E[y_t y_{t-k}] = E[(u_t + \delta u_{t-1} u_{t-2})(u_{t-k} + \delta u_{t-1-k} u_{t-2-k})]$$
$$= E[u_t u_{t-k} + \delta u_{t-1} u_{t-2} u_{t-k}$$
$$+ \delta u_t u_{t-1} u_{t-2-k} + \delta^2 u_{t-1} u_{t-2} u_{t-1-k} u_{t-2-k}] = 0,$$

where the last step follows from the property that every term contains at least two disturbances occurring at different points in time. However, y_t is not a mds because

$$E_{t-1}[y_t] = E_{t-1}[u_t + \delta u_{t-1} u_{t-2}] = E_{t-1}[u_t] + E_{t-1}[\delta u_{t-1} u_{t-2}]$$
$$= \delta u_{t-1} u_{t-2} \neq 0.$$

$\square$

Mixing

As martingale difference sequences are uncorrelated, it is important also to consider alternative processes that exhibit autocorrelation. Consider two sub-periods of a time series s periods apart

First sub-period   Second sub-period

$$\underbrace{\cdots, y_{t-2}, y_{t-1}, y_t}_{Y^t_{-\infty}} \quad y_{t+1}, y_{t+2}, \cdots, y_{t+s-1} \quad \underbrace{y_{t+s}, y_{t+s+1}, y_{t+s+2}, \cdots}_{Y^\infty_{t+s}}$$

in which $Y^s_t = \{y_t, y_{t+1}, \cdots, y_s\}$. If

$$\text{cov}\left(g\left(Y^t_{-\infty}\right), h\left(Y^\infty_{t+s}\right)\right) \to 0 \text{ as } s \to \infty, \tag{2.2}$$

where $g(\cdot)$ and $h(\cdot)$ are arbitrary functions, then as $Y^t_{-\infty}$ and Y^∞_{t+s} become more widely separated in time, they behave like independent sets of random variables. A process satisfying (2.2) is known as mixing (technically α-mixing or strong mixing). The concepts of strong stationarity and mixing have the convenient property that if they apply to y_t then they also apply to functions of y_t. A more formal treatment of mixing is provided by White (1984) and in Chapters 13 and 14 of Davidson (1994).

An *iid* process is mixing because all the covariances are zero and the mixing condition (2.2) is satisfied trivially. As will become apparent from the results for stationary time series models presented in Chapter 13, a moving average process with q lags, MA(q), with *iid* disturbances is mixing because it has finite dependence so that condition (2.2) is satisfied for $k > q$. Provided that the additional assumption is made that u_t in Example 2.1 is normally distributed, the AR(1) process is mixing since the covariance between y_t and y_{t-k} decays at an exponential rate as k increases, which implies that (2.2) is satisfied. If u_t does not have a continuous distribution then y_t may no longer be mixing (Andrews, 1984).

2.2.2   Weak Law of Large Numbers

The stochastic time series models discussed in the previous section are defined in terms of probability distributions with moments defined in terms of the parameters of these distributions. As maximum likelihood estimators are sample statistics of the data in samples of size T, it is of interest to identify the relationship between the population parameters and the sample statistics as $T \to \infty$.

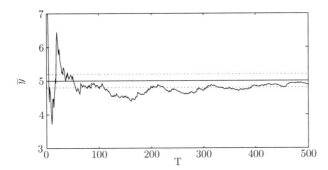

Figure 2.1. The weak law of large numbers for sample means based on progressively increasing sample sizes drawn from the exponential distribution with mean $\mu = 5$. The dotted lines represent $\mu \pm r$ with $r = 0.2$.

Let $\{y_1, y_2, \cdots, y_T\}$ represent a set of T *iid* random variables from a distribution with a finite mean μ. Consider the statistic based on the sample mean

$$\overline{y} = \frac{1}{T} \sum_{t=1}^{T} y_t. \tag{2.3}$$

The weak law of large numbers is about determining what happens to $\overline{y}$ as the sample size T increases without limit, $T \to \infty$.

Example 2.5 Exponential Distribution

Figure 2.1 gives the results of a simulation experiment from computing sample means of progressively larger samples of size $T = 1, 2, \cdots, 500$, comprising *iid* draws from the exponential distribution

$$f(y_t; \mu) = \frac{1}{\mu} \exp\left[-\frac{y_t}{\mu}\right], \qquad y_t > 0,$$

with population mean $\mu = 5$. For relatively small sample sizes, $\overline{y}$ is quite volatile, but settles down as T increases. The distance between $\overline{y}$ and μ eventually lies within a 'small' band of length $r = 0.2$, that is $|\overline{y} - \mu| < r$, as represented by the dotted lines. □

An important feature of Example 2.5 is that $\overline{y}$ is a random variable the value of which in any single sample need not necessarily equal μ in any deterministic sense, but is simply 'close enough' to the value of μ with probability approaching 1 as $T \to \infty$. This property is written formally as

$$\lim_{T \to \infty} \Pr(|\overline{y} - \mu| < r) = 1, \text{ for any } r > 0,$$

or, more compactly, as $\text{plim}(\bar{y}) = \mu$, where the notation plim represents the limit in a probability sense. This is the weak law of large numbers (WLLN), which states that the sample mean converges in probability to the population mean

$$\frac{1}{T} \sum_{t=1}^{T} y_t \xrightarrow{p} E[y_t] = \mu, \tag{2.4}$$

in which p denotes the convergence in probability or plim. This result also extends to higher order moments

$$\frac{1}{T} \sum_{t=1}^{T} y_t^i \xrightarrow{p} E[y_t^i], \qquad i > 0. \tag{2.5}$$

A necessary condition needed for the weak law of large numbers to be satisfied is that μ is finite (Stuart and Ord, 1994, p310). A sufficient condition is that $E[\bar{y}] \to \mu$ and $\text{var}(\bar{y}) \to 0$ as $T \to \infty$, so that the sampling distribution of $\bar{y}$ converges to a degenerate distribution with all its probability mass concentrated at the population mean μ.

Example 2.6 Uniform Distribution
Assume that y_t has a uniform distribution

$$f(y_t) = 1, \qquad -0.5 < y < 0.5.$$

The first four population moments are

$$\int_{-0.5}^{0.5} y f(y) dy = 0, \quad \int_{-0.5}^{0.5} y^2 f(y) dy = \frac{1}{12}, \quad \int_{-0.5}^{0.5} y^3 f(y) dy = 0,$$

$$\int_{-0.5}^{0.5} y^4 f(y) dy = \frac{1}{80}.$$

Table 2.1 gives the mean and the variance of simulated samples of size $T = \{50, 100, 200, 400, 800\}$ for the first four moments given in equation (2.5). The results demonstrate the two key properties of the weak law of large numbers: the means of the sample moments converge to their population means and their variances all converge to zero, with the variance roughly halving as T is doubled. $\square$

Some important properties of plims are as follows. Let $\bar{y}_1$ and $\bar{y}_2$ be the means of two samples of size T, from distributions with respective population means, μ_1 and μ_2, and let $c(\cdot)$ be a continuous function that is not dependent on T, then

Property 1: $\text{plim}(\bar{y}_1 \pm \bar{y}_2) = \text{plim}(\bar{y}_1) \pm \text{plim}(\bar{y}_2) = \mu_1 \pm \mu_2$

Property 2: $\text{plim}(\bar{y}_1 \bar{y}_2) = \text{plim}(\bar{y}_1)\text{plim}(\bar{y}_2) = \mu_1 \mu_2$

Table 2.1. *Properties of the moments of y_t simulated from samples of size T drawn from the uniform distribution $(-0.5, 0.5)$. The number of replications is 50000 and the moments have been scaled by 10^4*

	$\frac{1}{T}\sum_{t=1}^{T} y_t$		$\frac{1}{T}\sum_{t=1}^{T} y_t^2$		$\frac{1}{T}\sum_{t=1}^{T} y_t^3$		$\frac{1}{T}\sum_{t=1}^{T} y_t^4$	
T	Mean	Var.	Mean	Var.	Mean	Var.	Mean	Var.
50	−1.380	16.828	833.960	1.115	−0.250	0.450	125.170	0.056
100	0.000	8.384	833.605	0.555	−0.078	0.224	125.091	0.028
200	0.297	4.207	833.499	0.276	0.000	0.112	125.049	0.014
400	−0.167	2.079	833.460	0.139	−0.037	0.056	125.026	0.007
800	0.106	1.045	833.347	0.070	0.000	0.028	125.004	0.003

Property 3: $\quad \text{plim}\left(\dfrac{\bar{y}_1}{\bar{y}_2}\right) = \dfrac{\text{plim}(\bar{y}_1)}{\text{plim}(\bar{y}_2)} = \dfrac{\mu_1}{\mu_2} \quad (\mu_2 \neq 0)$

Property 4: $\quad \text{plim}\, c(\bar{y}) = c(\text{plim}(\bar{y}))$.

Property 4 is known as Slutsky's theorem (see also Exercise 3). These results generalise to the vector case, where the plim is taken with respect to each element separately.

The WLLN holds under weaker conditions than the assumption of an *iid* process. Assuming only that $\text{var}(y_t) < \infty$ for all t, the variance of $\bar{y}$ can always be written as

$$\text{var}(\bar{y}) = \frac{1}{T^2} \sum_{t=1}^{T} \sum_{s=1}^{T} \text{cov}(y_t, y_s)$$

$$= \frac{1}{T^2} \sum_{t=1}^{T} \text{var}(y_t) + \frac{1}{T^2} \sum_{t=2}^{T} \sum_{s=1}^{t-1} \text{cov}(y_t, y_s) + \frac{1}{T^2} \sum_{t=1}^{T-1} \sum_{s=t+1}^{T} \text{cov}(y_t, y_s)$$

$$= \frac{1}{T^2} \sum_{t=1}^{T} \text{var}(y_t) + \frac{1}{T^2} \sum_{t=2}^{T} \sum_{s=1}^{t-1} \text{cov}(y_t, y_s) + \frac{1}{T^2} \sum_{s=2}^{T} \sum_{t=1}^{s-1} \text{cov}(y_t, y_s)$$

$$= \frac{1}{T^2} \sum_{t=1}^{T} \text{var}(y_t) + \frac{2}{T^2} \sum_{t=2}^{T} \sum_{s=1}^{t-1} \text{cov}(y_t, y_s)$$

$$= \frac{1}{T^2} \sum_{t=1}^{T} \text{var}(y_t) + \frac{2}{T^2} \sum_{t=2}^{T} \sum_{s=1}^{t-1} \text{cov}(y_t, y_{t-s})$$

$$= \frac{1}{T^2} \sum_{t=1}^{T} \text{var}(y_t) + \frac{2}{T^2} \sum_{s=1}^{T-1} \sum_{t=s+1}^{T} \text{cov}(y_t, y_{t-s}).$$

If y_t is weakly stationary, $\text{cov}(y_t, y_s) = \gamma_s$, and this simplifies to

$$\text{var}(\bar{y}) = \frac{1}{T}\gamma_0 + \frac{2}{T}\sum_{s=1}^{T}\left(1 - \frac{s}{T}\right)\gamma_s, \tag{2.6}$$

where $\gamma_s = \text{cov}(y_t, y_{t-s})$ are the autocovariances of y_t for $s = 0, 1, 2, \cdots$.

If y_t is either *iid* or a mds or white noise, then $\gamma_s = 0$ for all $s \geq 1$. In that case (2.6) simplifies to

$$\text{var}(\bar{y}) = \frac{1}{T}\gamma_0 \rightarrow 0$$

as $T \rightarrow \infty$ and the WLLN holds. If y_t is autocorrelated then a sufficient condition for the WLLN is that $|\gamma_s| \rightarrow 0$ as $s \rightarrow \infty$. To show why this works, consider the second term on the right-hand side of (2.6). It follows from the triangle inequality that

$$\left|\frac{1}{T}\sum_{s=1}^{T}\left(1 - \frac{s}{T}\right)\gamma_s\right| \leq \frac{1}{T}\sum_{s=1}^{T}\left(1 - \frac{s}{T}\right)|\gamma_s| \leq \frac{1}{T}\sum_{s=1}^{T}|\gamma_s| \rightarrow 0, \quad T \rightarrow \infty.$$

since $1 - s/T < 1$. The last step uses Cesaro summation, which states that if a sequence a_t satisfies $a_t \rightarrow a$ as $t \rightarrow \infty$ then $T^{-1}\sum_{t=1}^{T}a_t \rightarrow a$ as $T \rightarrow \infty$. This implies that $\text{var}(\bar{y})$ given in (2.6) disappears as $T \rightarrow \infty$. Thus, any weakly stationary time series whose autocovariances satisfy $|\gamma_s| \rightarrow 0$ as $s \rightarrow \infty$ will obey the WLLN (2.4). If y_t is weakly stationary and strong mixing, then $|\gamma_s| \rightarrow 0$ as $s \rightarrow \infty$ follows by definition, so the WLLN applies to this general class of processes as well.

Example 2.7 WLLN for an AR(1) Model

In the stationary AR(1) model from Example 2.1, since $|\rho| < 1$ it follows that

$$\gamma_s = \frac{\sigma^2\rho^s}{1 - \rho^2},$$

so that the condition $|\gamma_s| \rightarrow 0$ as $s \rightarrow \infty$ is clearly satisfied. This shows the WLLN applies to a stationary AR(1) process. $\square$

2.2.3   Rates of Convergence

The weak law of large numbers in (2.4) involves computing statistics based on averaging random variables over a sample of size T. Establishing many of the results of the maximum likelihood estimator requires choosing the correct scaling factor to ensure that the relevant statistics have non-degenerate distributions.

Table 2.2. *Simulation properties of the moments of the linear regression model using alternative scale factors. The parameters are* $\theta_0 = \{\beta = 1.0, \sigma_u^2 = 2.0\}$, *the number of replications is* 50000, u_t *is drawn from* $N(0, 2)$ *and the stochastic regressor* x_t *is drawn from a uniform distribution with support* $(-0.5, 0.5)$

	$\dfrac{1}{T^{1/4}} \displaystyle\sum_{t=1}^{T} x_t u_t$		$\dfrac{1}{T^{1/2}} \displaystyle\sum_{t=1}^{T} x_t u_t$		$\dfrac{1}{T^{3/4}} \displaystyle\sum_{t=1}^{T} x_t u_t$		$\dfrac{1}{T} \displaystyle\sum_{t=1}^{T} x_t u_t$	
T	Mean	Var.	Mean	Var.	Mean	Var.	Mean	Var.
50	−0.001	1.177	0.000	0.166	0.000	0.024	0.000	0.003
100	−0.007	1.670	−0.002	0.167	−0.001	0.017	0.000	0.002
200	−0.014	2.378	−0.004	0.168	−0.001	0.012	0.000	0.001
400	−0.001	3.373	0.000	0.169	0.000	0.008	0.000	0.000
800	0.007	4.753	0.001	0.168	0.000	0.006	0.000	0.000

Example 2.8 Linear Regression with Stochastic Regressors

Consider the linear regression model

$$y_t = \beta x_t + u_t, \qquad u_t \sim iid\ N(0, \sigma_u^2),$$

in which x_t is an *iid* drawing from the uniform distribution on the interval $(-0.5, 0.5)$ with variance σ_x^2 and x_t and u_t are independent, $E[x_t u_t] = 0$. The maximum likelihood estimator of β is

$$\widehat{\beta} = \left[\sum_{t=1}^{T} x_t^2\right]^{-1} \sum_{t=1}^{T} x_t y_t = \beta + \left[\sum_{t=1}^{T} x_t^2\right]^{-1} \sum_{t=1}^{T} x_t u_t,$$

where the last term is obtained by substituting for y_t. This expression shows that the relevant moments to consider are $\sum_{t=1}^{T} x_t u_t$ and $\sum_{t=1}^{T} x_t^2$. The appropriate scaling of the first moment to ensure that it has a non-degenerate distribution follows from

$$E\left[T^{-k} \sum_{t=1}^{T} x_t u_t\right] = 0$$

$$\text{var}\left(T^{-k} \sum_{t=1}^{T} x_t u_t\right) = T^{-2k}\,\text{var}\left(\sum_{t=1}^{T} x_t u_t\right) = T^{1-2k}\sigma_u^2\sigma_x^2,$$

which hold for any k. Consequently, the appropriate choice of scaling factor is $k = 1/2$ because $T^{-1/2}$ stabilises the variance and thus prevents it approaching 0 ($k > 1/2$) or ∞ ($k < 1/2$). This property is demonstrated in Table 2.2 which gives simulated moments for alternative scale factors using the model parameters $\beta = 1$, $\sigma_u^2 = 2$ and $\sigma_x^2 = 1/12$.

The variances in Table 2.2 demonstrate that only with the scale factor $T^{-1/2}$ does $\sum_{t=1}^{T} x_t u_t$ have a non-degenerate distribution with mean converging to 0 and variance converging to

$$\text{var}(x_t u_t) = \text{var}(u_t) \times \text{var}(x_t) = 2 \times \frac{1}{12} = 0.167.$$

Since

$$\frac{1}{T} \sum_{t=1}^{T} x_t^2 \xrightarrow{p} \sigma_x^2,$$

by the WLLN, it follows that the distribution of $\sqrt{T}(\hat{\beta} - \beta)$ is non-degenerate because the variance of both terms on the right-hand side of

$$\sqrt{T}(\hat{\beta} - \beta) = \left[\frac{1}{T} \sum_{t=1}^{T} x_t^2 \right]^{-1} \left[\frac{1}{\sqrt{T}} \sum_{t=1}^{T} x_t u_t \right],$$

converge to finite non-zero values.   □

Determining the correct scaling factors for derivatives of the log-likelihood function is important to establishing the asymptotic distribution of the maximum likelihood estimator in Section 2.5.2, as the following example illustrates.

Example 2.9 Higher-Order Derivatives
The log-likelihood function associated with an *iid* sample $\{y_1, y_2, \cdots, y_T\}$ from the exponential distribution is

$$\ln L_T(\theta) = \ln \theta - \frac{\theta}{T} \sum_{t=1}^{T} y_t.$$

The first four derivatives are

$$\frac{d \ln L_T(\theta)}{d\theta} = \theta^{-1} - \frac{1}{T} \sum_{t=1}^{T} y_t \qquad \frac{d^2 \ln L_T(\theta)}{d\theta^2} = -\theta^{-2}$$

$$\frac{d^3 \ln L_T(\theta)}{d\theta^3} = 2\theta^{-3} \qquad \frac{d^4 \ln L_T(\theta)}{d\theta^4} = -6\theta^{-4}.$$

The first derivative $G_T(\theta) = \theta^{-1} - T^{-1} \sum_{t=1}^{T} y_t$ is an average of *iid* random variables, $g_t(\theta) = \theta^{-1} - y_t$. The scaled first derivative

$$\sqrt{T} G_T(\theta) = \frac{1}{\sqrt{T}} \sum_{t=1}^{T} g_t(\theta),$$

has zero mean and finite variance because

$$\text{var}\left(\sqrt{T} G_T(\theta)\right) = \frac{1}{T} \sum_{t=1}^{T} \text{var}(\theta^{-1} - y_t) = \frac{1}{T} \sum_{t=1}^{T} \theta^{-2} = \theta^{-2},$$

by using the *iid* assumption and the fact that $E[(y_t - \theta^{-1})^2] = \theta^{-2}$ for the exponential distribution. All the other derivatives already have finite limits as they are independent of T. $\qquad\qquad\qquad\qquad\qquad\qquad\qquad\qquad\qquad\qquad\Box$

2.2.4 Central Limit Theorems

The previous section established the appropriate scaling factor needed to ensure that a statistic has a non-degenerate distribution. The aim of this section is to identify the form of this distribution as $T \to \infty$, referred to as the asymptotic distribution. The results are established in a series of four central limit theorems.

Lindeberg-Levy Central Limit Theorem
Let $\{y_1, y_2, \cdots, y_T\}$ represent a set of T *iid* random variables from a distribution with finite mean μ and finite variance $\sigma^2 > 0$. The Lindeberg-Levy central limit theorem for the scalar case states that

$$\sqrt{T}(\bar{y} - \mu) \overset{d}{\to} N(0, \sigma^2), \tag{2.7}$$

where $\overset{d}{\to}$ represents convergence of the distribution as $T \to \infty$. In terms of standardised random variables, the central limit theorem is

$$z = \sqrt{T}\frac{(\bar{y} - \mu)}{\sigma} \overset{d}{\to} N(0, 1). \tag{2.8}$$

Alternatively, the asymptotic distribution is given by rearranging (2.7) as

$$\bar{y} \overset{a}{\sim} N(\mu, \frac{\sigma^2}{T}), \tag{2.9}$$

where $\overset{a}{\sim}$ signifies convergence to the asymptotic distribution. The fundamental difference between (2.7) and (2.9) is that the former represents a normal distribution with zero mean and constant variance in the limit, whereas the latter represents a normal distribution with mean μ, but with a variance that approaches zero as T grows, resulting in all of its mass concentrated at μ in the limit.

Example 2.10 Uniform Distribution
Let $\{y_1, y_2, \cdots, y_T\}$ represent a set of T *iid* random variables from the uniform distribution

$$f(y_t) = 1, \qquad 0 < y_t < 1.$$

The conditions of the Lindeberg-Levy central limit theorem are satisfied, because the random variables are *iid* with finite mean and variance given by $\mu = 1/2$ and $\sigma^2 = 1/12$, respectively. Based on 5000 draws, the sampling distribution of

$$z_i = \sqrt{T}\frac{(\bar{y}_i - \mu)}{\sigma} = \sqrt{T}\frac{(\bar{y}_i - 1/2)}{\sqrt{12}}, \qquad i = 1, 2, \cdots, 5000,$$

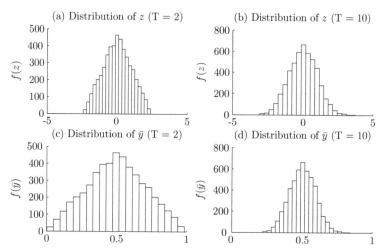

Figure 2.2. Demonstration of the Lindeberg-Levy Central Limit Theorem. Population distribution is the uniform distribution.

for samples of size $T = 2$ and $T = 10$, are shown in panels (a) and (b) of Figure 2.2, respectively. Despite the population distribution being non-normal, the sampling distributions approach the standardised normal distribution very quickly. Also shown are the corresponding asymptotic distributions of $\bar{y}$ in panels (c) and (d), which become more compact around $\mu = 1/2$ as T increases.

□

Example 2.11 Linear Regression with *iid* Regressors

Assume that the joint distribution of y_t and x_t is *iid* and

$$y_t = \beta x_t + u_t, \qquad u_t \sim iid\,(0, \sigma_u^2),$$

in which $E[u_t | x_t] = 0$ and $E[u_t^2 | x_t] = \sigma_u^2$. From Example 2.8 the least squares estimator $\widehat{\beta}$ is expressed as

$$\sqrt{T}(\widehat{\beta} - \beta) = \Big[\frac{1}{T}\sum_{t=1}^{T} x_t^2\Big]^{-1}\Big[\frac{1}{\sqrt{T}}\sum_{t=1}^{T} x_t u_t\Big].$$

To establish the asymptotic distribution of $\widehat{\beta}$, the following results are required

$$\frac{1}{T}\sum_{t=1}^{T} x_t^2 \xrightarrow{p} \sigma_x^2, \qquad \frac{1}{\sqrt{T}}\sum_{t=1}^{T} x_t u_t \xrightarrow{d} N(0, \sigma_u^2\sigma_x^2),$$

where the first result follows from the WLLN and the second result is an application of the Lindeberg-Levy central limit theorem. Combining these two results yields

$$\sqrt{T}(\hat{\beta} - \beta) \xrightarrow{d} \sigma_x^{-2} \times N(0, \sigma_u^2 \sigma_x^2) = N(0, \sigma_u^2 \sigma_x^{-2}).$$

This is the usual expression for the asymptotic distribution of the maximum likelihood (least squares) estimator. □

The Lindeberg-Levy central limit theorem generalises to the case where y_t is a vector with mean μ and covariance matrix V

$$\sqrt{T}(\bar{y} - \mu) \xrightarrow{d} N(0, V). \tag{2.10}$$

Lindeberg-Feller Central Limit Theorem
The Lindeberg-Feller central limit theorem is applicable to models based on independent and non-identically distributed random variables, in which y_t has time-varying mean μ_t and time-varying covariance matrix V_t. For the scalar case, let $\{y_1, y_2, \cdots, y_T\}$ represent a set of T independent and non-identically distributed random variables from a distribution with finite time-varying means $E[y_t] = \mu_t < \infty$, finite time-varying variances $\text{var}(y_t) = \sigma_t^2 < \infty$ and finite higher-order moments. The Lindeberg-Feller central limit theorem gives necessary and sufficient conditions for

$$\sqrt{T}\left(\frac{\bar{y} - \bar{\mu}}{\bar{\sigma}}\right) \xrightarrow{d} N(0, 1), \tag{2.11}$$

where

$$\bar{\mu} = \frac{1}{T}\sum_{t=1}^{T}\mu_t, \qquad \bar{\sigma}^2 = \frac{1}{T}\sum_{t=1}^{T}\sigma_t^2. \tag{2.12}$$

A sufficient condition for the Lindeberg-Feller central limit theorem is given by

$$E[|y_t - \mu_t|^{2+\delta}] < \infty, \qquad \delta > 0, \tag{2.13}$$

uniformly in t. This is known as the Lyapunov condition, which operates on moments higher than the second moment. This requirement is in fact a stricter condition than is needed to satisfy this theorem, but it is more intuitive and tends to be an easier condition to demonstrate than the conditions initially proposed by Lindeberg and Feller. Although this condition is applicable to all moments marginally higher than the second, namely $2 + \delta$, considering the first integer moment to which the condition applies, namely the third moment by setting $\delta = 1$ in (2.13), is of practical interest. The condition now becomes

$$E[|y_t - \mu_t|^3] < \infty, \tag{2.14}$$

which represents a restriction on the standardised third moment, or skewness, of y_t.

Example 2.12 Bernoulli Distribution

Let $\{y_1, y_2, \cdots, y_T\}$ represent a set of T independent random variables with time-varying probabilities θ_t from a Bernoulli distribution

$$f(y_t; \theta_t) = \theta_t^{y_t} (1 - \theta_t)^{1-y_t}, \qquad 0 < \theta_t < 1.$$

From the properties of the Bernoulli distribution, the mean and the variance are time-varying since $\mu_t = \theta_t$ and $\sigma_t^2 = \theta_t (1 - \theta_t)$. As $0 < \theta_t < 1$ then

$$E\left[|y_t - \mu_t|^3\right] = \theta_t (1 - \theta_t)^3 + (1 - \theta_t)\theta_t^3 = \sigma_t^2 \left((1 - \theta_t)^2 - \theta_t^2\right) \leq \sigma_t^2,$$

so the third moment is bounded.   □

Example 2.13 Linear Regression with Bounded Fixed Regressors

Consider the linear regression model

$$y_t = \beta x_t + u_t, \qquad u_t \sim iid\,(0, \sigma_u^2),$$

in which u_t has finite third moment $E[u_t^3] = \kappa_3$. The variable x_t is a uniformly bounded fixed regressor, such as a constant, a level shift dummy variable or seasonal dummy variables, but not a time trend which is a fixed regressor that is not uniformly bounded in t. From Example 2.8 the least squares estimator of $\widehat{\beta}$ is

$$\sqrt{T}(\widehat{\beta} - \beta) = \left[\frac{1}{T}\sum_{t=1}^{T}x_t^2\right]^{-1}\frac{1}{\sqrt{T}}\sum_{t=1}^{T}x_t u_t.$$

The Lindeberg-Feller central limit theorem based on the Lyapunov condition applies to the product $x_t u_t$, because the terms are independent for all t, with mean, variance and uniformly bounded third moment, respectively,

$$\overline{\mu} = 0, \quad \overline{\sigma}^2 = \frac{1}{T}\sum_{t=1}^{T}var(x_t u_t) = \sigma_u^2\frac{1}{T}\sum_{t=1}^{T}x_t^2, \quad E[x_t^3 u_t^3] = x_t^3\kappa_3 < \infty.$$

Thus

$$\frac{(\sum_{t=1}^{T}x_t^2)^{1/2}}{\sigma_u}(\widehat{\beta} - \beta) = \sqrt{T}\frac{T^{-1}\sum_{t=1}^{T}x_t u_t}{\overline{\sigma}} \xrightarrow{d} N(0, 1),$$

where the convergence in distribution follows from (2.11).   □

As in the case of the Lindeberg-Levy central limit theorem, the Lindeberg-Feller central limit theorem generalises to independent and non-identically distributed vector random variables with time-varying vector mean μ_t and time-varying positive definite covariance matrix V_t. The theorem states that

$$\sqrt{T}\,\overline{V}^{-1/2}(\overline{y} - \overline{\mu}) \xrightarrow{d} N(0, I), \tag{2.15}$$

where

$$\bar{\mu} = \frac{1}{T} \sum_{t=1}^{T} \mu_t, \qquad \bar{V} = \frac{1}{T} \sum_{t=1}^{T} V_t, \tag{2.16}$$

and $\bar{V}^{1/2}$ represents the square root of the matrix $\bar{V}$.

Martingale Difference Central Limit Theorem

The martingale difference central limit theorem is essentially the Lindeberg-Levy central limit theorem, but with the assumption that $y_t = \{y_1, y_2, \cdots, y_T\}$ represents a set of T iid random variables being replaced with the more general assumption that y_t is a mds. If y_t is a mds with sample mean and average variance given by

$$\bar{y} = \frac{1}{T} \sum_{t=1}^{T} y_t, \qquad \bar{\sigma}^2 = \frac{1}{T} \sum_{t=1}^{T} \sigma_t^2,$$

and provided that higher-order moments are bounded,

$$E[|y_t|^{2+\delta}] < \infty, \qquad \delta > 0, \tag{2.17}$$

and

$$\frac{1}{T} \sum_{t=1}^{T} y_t^2 - \bar{\sigma}^2 \xrightarrow{p} 0, \tag{2.18}$$

then the martingale difference central limit theorem states

$$\sqrt{T} \left(\frac{\bar{y} - \bar{\mu}}{\bar{\sigma}} \right) = \sqrt{T} \left(\frac{\bar{y}}{\bar{\sigma}} \right) \xrightarrow{d} N(0, 1). \tag{2.19}$$

The martingale difference property weakens the iid assumption, but the assumptions that the sample variance must consistently estimate the average variance and the boundedness of higher moments in (2.17) are stronger than those required for the Lindeberg-Levy central limit theorem.

More detail on martingale central limit theory can be found in section V.5 of White (1984), section 24.2 of Davidson (1994) and Chapter 3 of Hall and Heyde (1980).

Example 2.14 Linear AR(1) Model

Consider the autoregressive model from Example 1.5 in Chapter 1, where for convenience the sample contains $T + 1$ observations, $y_t = \{y_0, y_1, \cdots y_T\}$.

$$y_t = \rho y_{t-1} + u_t, \qquad u_t \sim iid\,(0, \sigma^2),$$

with finite fourth moment $E[u_t^4] = \kappa_4 < \infty$ and $|\rho| < 1$. The least squares estimator of $\hat{\rho}$ is

$$\hat{\rho} = \frac{\sum_{t=1}^{T} y_t y_{t-1}}{\sum_{t=1}^{T} y_{t-1}^2}.$$

Rearranging and introducing the scale factor $\sqrt{T}$ gives

$$\sqrt{T}(\hat{\rho} - \rho) = \left[\frac{1}{T}\sum_{t=1}^{T} y_{t-1}^2\right]^{-1} \left[\frac{1}{\sqrt{T}}\sum_{t=1}^{T} u_t y_{t-1}\right].$$

To use the mds central limit theorem to find the asymptotic distribution of $\hat{\rho}$, it is necessary to establish that $u_t y_{t-1}$ satisfies the conditions of the theorem and also that $T^{-1}\sum_{t=2}^{T} y_{t-1}^2$ satisfies the WLLN.

The product $u_t y_{t-1}$ is a mds because

$$E_{t-1}[u_t y_{t-1}] = E_{t-1}[u_t] y_{t-1} = 0,$$

since $E_{t-1}[u_t] = 0$. To establish that the conditions of the mds central limit theorem are satisfied, define

$$\bar{\mu} = \frac{1}{T}\sum_{t=1}^{T} u_t y_{t-1}$$

$$\bar{\sigma}^2 = \frac{1}{T}\sum_{t=1}^{T} \sigma_t^2 = \frac{1}{T}\sum_{t=1}^{T} \mathrm{var}(u_t y_{t-1}) = \frac{1}{T}\sum_{t=1}^{T} \frac{\sigma^4}{1-\rho^2} = \frac{\sigma^4}{1-\rho^2}.$$

To establish the boundedness condition in (2.17), choose $\delta = 2$, so that

$$E[|u_t y_{t-1}|^4] = E[u_t^4]E[y_{t-1}^4] = \kappa_4 E[y_{t-1}^4] < \infty,$$

because $\kappa_4 < \infty$ and it can be shown that $E[y_{t-1}^4] < \infty$ provided that $|\rho| < 1$. To establish (2.18), write

$$\frac{1}{T}\sum_{t=1}^{T} u_t^2 y_{t-1}^2 = \frac{1}{T}\sum_{t=1}^{T}(u_t^2 - \sigma^2)y_{t-1}^2 + \sigma^2 \frac{1}{T}\sum_{t=1}^{T} y_{t-1}^2.$$

The first term is the sample mean of a mds, which has mean zero, so the weak law of large numbers gives

$$\frac{1}{T}\sum_{t=1}^{T}(u_t^2 - \sigma^2)y_{t-1}^2 \xrightarrow{p} 0.$$

The second term is the sample mean of a stationary process and the weak law of large numbers gives

$$\frac{1}{T} \sum_{t=1}^{T} y_{t-1}^2 \overset{p}{\to} E[y_{t-1}^2] = \frac{\sigma^2}{1 - \rho^2} .$$

Thus, as required by (2.18)

$$\frac{1}{T} \sum_{t=1}^{T} u_t^2 y_{t-1}^2 \overset{p}{\to} \frac{\sigma^4}{1 - \rho^2} .$$

Therefore, from the statement of the mds central limit theorem in (2.19) it follows that

$$\frac{1}{\sqrt{T}} \sum_{t=1}^{T} u_t y_{t-1} \overset{d}{\to} N\left(0, \frac{\sigma^4}{1 - \rho^2}\right) .$$

The asymptotic distribution of $\hat{\rho}$ is therefore

$$\sqrt{T}(\hat{\rho} - \rho) \overset{d}{\to} \left(\frac{\sigma^2}{1 - \rho^2}\right)^{-1} \times N\left(0, \frac{\sigma^4}{1 - \rho^2}\right)$$

$$= N(0, 1 - \rho^2) .$$

$\square$

The martingale difference central limit theorem also applies to vector processes with covariance matrix V_t

$$\sqrt{T} \overline{V}^{-1/2} \overline{\mu} \overset{d}{\to} N(0, I), \tag{2.20}$$

where

$$\overline{V} = \frac{1}{T} \sum_{t=1}^{T} V_t .$$

Mixing Central Limit Theorem

As will become apparent in Chapter 9, in some situations it is necessary to have a central limit theorem that applies for autocorrelated processes. This is particularly pertinent to situations in which models do not completely specify the dynamics of the dependent variable.

If y_t has zero mean, $E |y_t|^\delta < \infty$ uniformly in t for some $\delta > 2$, and y_t is mixing at a sufficiently fast rate then the following central limit theorem applies

$$\frac{1}{\sqrt{T}} \sum_{t=1}^{T} y_t \overset{d}{\to} N(0, J), \tag{2.21}$$

where

$$J = \lim_{T \to \infty} \frac{1}{T} \mathrm{E}\left[\left(\sum_{t=1}^{T} y_t\right)^2\right],$$

assuming this limit exists. If y_t is also weakly stationary, the expression for J simplifies to

$$J = \mathrm{E}[y_t^2] + 2\sum_{j=1}^{\infty} \mathrm{E}[y_t y_{t-j}]$$

$$= \mathrm{var}(y_t) + 2\sum_{j=1}^{\infty} \mathrm{cov}(y_t, y_{t-j}), \tag{2.22}$$

which shows that the asymptotic variance of the sample mean depends on the variance and all autocovariances of y_t. See Theorem 5.19 of White (1984) for further details of the mixing central limit theorem and section 24.4 of Davidson (1994) for generalisations.

Example 2.15 Sample Moments of an AR(1) Model
  Consider the AR(1) model

$$y_t = \rho y_{t-1} + u_t, \qquad u_t \sim iid\, N(0, \sigma^2),$$

and $|\rho| < 1$. The asymptotic distribution of the sample mean and variance of y_t are obtained as follows. Since y_t is stationary, mixing, has mean zero and all moments finite (by normality), the mixing central limit theorem in (2.21) applies to the standardised sample mean $\sqrt{T}\bar{y} = T^{-1/2}\sum_{t=1}^{T} y_t$ with variance given in (2.22). In the case of the sample variance, since y_t has zero mean, an estimator of its variance $\sigma^2/(1 - \rho^2)$ is $T^{-1}\sum_{t=1}^{T} y_t^2$. The function

$$z_t = y_t^2 - \frac{\sigma^2}{1 - \phi^2},$$

has mean zero and inherits strict stationarity and mixing from y_t, so that

$$\frac{1}{\sqrt{T}}\sum_{t=1}^{T}\left(y_t^2 - \frac{\sigma^2}{1 - \phi^2}\right) \overset{d}{\to} N(0, J),$$

in which

$$J = \mathrm{var}(z_t) + 2\sum_{j=1}^{\infty}\mathrm{cov}(z_t, z_{t-j}),$$

demonstrating that the sample variance is also asymptotically normal.   □

2.3   Regularity Conditions

This section sets out a number of assumptions, known as regularity conditions, that are used in the derivation of the properties of the maximum likelihood estimator. Let the true population parameter value be represented by θ_0 and assume that the distribution $f(y; \theta)$ is specified correctly. The following regularity conditions apply to *iid*, stationary, mds and white noise processes as discussed in Section 2.2.1. For simplicity, many of the regularity conditions are presented for the *iid* case.

R1: Existence
The expectation

$$E\left[\ln f(y_t; \theta)\right] = \int_{-\infty}^{\infty} \ln f(y_t; \theta)\, f(y_t; \theta_0) dy_t \,, \qquad (2.23)$$

exists.

R2: Convergence
The log-likelihood function converges in probability to its expectation

$$\ln L_T(\theta) = \frac{1}{T} \sum_{t=1}^{T} \ln f(y_t; \theta) \xrightarrow{p} E\left[\ln f(y_t; \theta)\right] \,, \qquad (2.24)$$

uniformly in θ.

R3: Continuity
The log-likelihood function, $\ln L_T(\theta)$, is continuous in θ.

R4: Differentiability
The log-likelihood function, $\ln L_T(\theta)$, is at least twice continuously differentiable in an open interval around θ_0.

R5: Interchangeability
The order of differentiation and integration of $\ln L_T(\theta)$ is interchangeable.

Condition R1 is a statement of the existence of the population log-likelihood function. Condition R2 is a statement of how the sample log-likelihood function converges to the population value by virtue of the WLLN, provided that this expectation exists in the first place, as given by the existence condition (R1). The continuity condition (R3) is a necessary condition for the differentiability condition (R4). The requirement that the log-likelihood function is at least twice differentiable naturally arises from the discussion in Chapter 1 where the first two derivatives are used to derive the maximum likelihood estimator and establish that a maximum is reached. Even when the likelihood is not differentiable everywhere, the maximum likelihood estimator can, in some instances, still be obtained. An example is given by the Laplace distribution in which the median is the maximum likelihood estimator (see Section 6.6.1

of Chapter 6). Finally, the interchangeability condition (R5) is used in the derivation of many of the properties of the maximum likelihood estimator.

Example 2.16 Likelihood Function of the Normal Distribution

Assume that y_t has a normal distribution with unknown mean $\theta = \{\mu\}$ and known variance σ_0^2 given by

$$f(y_t; \theta) = \frac{1}{\sqrt{2\pi\sigma_0^2}} \exp\left[-\frac{(y_t - \mu)^2}{2\sigma_0^2}\right].$$

If the population parameter is defined as $\theta_0 = \{\mu_0\}$, the existence regularity condition (R1) becomes

$$
\begin{aligned}
E[\ln f(y_t; \theta)] &= -\frac{1}{2}\ln\left(2\pi\sigma_0^2\right) - \frac{1}{2\sigma_0^2}E[(y_t - \mu)^2] \\
&= -\frac{1}{2}\ln\left(2\pi\sigma_0^2\right) - \frac{1}{2\sigma_0^2}E[(y_t - \mu_0)^2 + (\mu_0 - \mu)^2 \\
&\quad + 2(y_t - \mu_0)(\mu_0 - \mu)] \\
&= -\frac{1}{2}\ln\left(2\pi\sigma_0^2\right) - \frac{1}{2\sigma_0^2}\left(\sigma_0^2 + (\mu_0 - \mu)^2\right) \\
&= -\frac{1}{2}\ln\left(2\pi\sigma_0^2\right) - \frac{1}{2} - \frac{(\mu_0 - \mu)^2}{2\sigma_0^2},
\end{aligned}
$$

which exists because $0 < \sigma_0^2 < \infty$.   □

2.4   Properties of the Likelihood Function

This section establishes various features of the log-likelihood function used in the derivation of the properties of the maximum likelihood estimator.

2.4.1   The Population Likelihood Function

Given that the existence condition (R1) is satisfied, an important property of this expectation is

$$\theta_0 = \underset{\theta}{\arg\max}\ E[\ln f(y_t; \theta)]. \tag{2.25}$$

The principle of maximum likelihood requires that the maximum likelihood estimator, $\widehat{\theta}$, maximises the sample log-likelihood function by replacing the expectation in equation (2.25) by the sample average. This property represents the population analogue of the maximum likelihood principle in which θ_0 maximises $E[\ln f(y_t; \theta)]$.

Proof: Consider

$$E[\ln f(y_t; \theta)] - E[\ln f(y_t; \theta_0)] = E\left[\ln \frac{f(y_t; \theta)}{f(y_t; \theta_0)}\right] < \ln E\left[\frac{f(y_t; \theta)}{f(y_t; \theta_0)}\right],$$

in which $\theta \neq \theta_0$ and the inequality follows from Jensen's inequality.[1] Working with the term on the right-hand side yields

$$\ln E\left[\frac{f(y_t; \theta)}{f(y_t; \theta_0)}\right] = \ln \int_{-\infty}^{\infty} \frac{f(y_t; \theta)}{f(y_t; \theta_0)} f(y_t; \theta_0) dy_t = \ln \int_{-\infty}^{\infty} f(y_t; \theta) dy_t = \ln 1 = 0,$$

as $f(y_t; \theta)$ is a probability distribution it satisfies the condition

$$\int_{-\infty}^{\infty} f(y_t; \theta) dy_t = 1.$$

It follows immediately that $E[\ln f(y_t; \theta)] < E[\ln f(y_t; \theta_0)]$, for arbitrary θ, which establishes that the maximum occurs just for θ_0. □

Example 2.17 Population Likelihood of the Normal Distribution

From Example 2.16, the population log-likelihood function based on a normal distribution with unknown mean, μ, and known variance, σ_0^2, is

$$E[\ln f(y_t; \theta)] = -\frac{1}{2} \ln \left(2\pi\sigma_0^2\right) - \frac{1}{2} - \frac{(\mu_0 - \mu)^2}{2\sigma_0^2},$$

which clearly has its maximum at $\mu = \mu_0$. □

2.4.2 Moments of the Gradient

The gradient function at observation t, introduced in Chapter 1, is defined as

$$g_t(\theta) = \frac{\partial \ln f(y_t; \theta)}{\partial \theta}. \tag{2.26}$$

This function has two important properties that are fundamental to maximum likelihood estimation. These properties are also used in Chapter 3 to devise numerical algorithms for computing maximum likelihood estimators, in Chapter 4 to construct test statistics, and in Chapter 9 to derive the quasi-maximum likelihood estimator.

Mean of the Gradient

The first property is

$$E[g_t(\theta_0)] = 0. \tag{2.27}$$

---

[1] If $g(y)$ is a concave function in the random variable y, Jensen's inequality states that $E[g(y)] < g(E[y])$. This condition is satisfied here since $g(y) = \ln(y)$ is concave.

Proof: As $f(y_t; \theta)$ is a probability distribution, it has the property

$$\int_{-\infty}^{\infty} f(y_t; \theta) dy_t = 1.$$

Now differentiating both sides with respect to θ gives

$$\frac{\partial}{\partial \theta} \left(\int_{-\infty}^{\infty} f(y_t; \theta) dy_t \right) = 0.$$

Using the interchangeability regularity condition (R5) and the property of natural logarithms

$$\frac{\partial f(y_t; \theta)}{\partial \theta} = \frac{\partial \ln f(y_t; \theta)}{\partial \theta} f(y_t; \theta) = g_t(\theta) f(y_t; \theta),$$

the left-hand side expression is rewritten as

$$\int_{-\infty}^{\infty} g_t(\theta) f(y_t; \theta) dy_t.$$

Evaluating this expression at $\theta = \theta_0$ means that the relevant integral is evaluated using the population density function, $f(y_t; \theta_0)$, thereby enabling it to be interpreted as an expectation. This yields

$$E[g_t(\theta_0)] = 0,$$

which proves the result. $\qquad\qquad\qquad\qquad\qquad\qquad\qquad\qquad \square$

Variance of the Gradient

The second property is

$$\text{cov}(g_t(\theta_0)) = E[g_t(\theta_0) g_t(\theta_0)'] = -E[h_t(\theta_0)], \qquad (2.28)$$

where the first equality uses the result from expression (2.27) that $g_t(\theta_0)$ has zero mean. This expression links the first and second derivatives of the likelihood function and establishes that the expectation of the square of the gradient is equal to the negative of the expectation of the Hessian.

Proof: Differentiating

$$\int_{-\infty}^{\infty} f(y_t; \theta) dy_t = 1,$$

twice with respect to θ and using the same regularity conditions to establish the first property of the gradient, gives

$$\int_{-\infty}^{\infty} \left[\frac{\partial \ln f(y_t;\theta)}{\partial\theta} \frac{\partial f(y_t;\theta)}{\partial\theta'} + \frac{\partial^2 \ln f(y_t;\theta)}{\partial\theta\,\partial\theta'} f(y_t;\theta) \right] dy_t = 0$$

$$\int_{-\infty}^{\infty} \left[\frac{\partial \ln f(y_t;\theta)}{\partial\theta} \frac{\partial \ln f(y_t;\theta)}{\partial\theta'} f(y_t;\theta) + \frac{\partial^2 \ln f(y_t;\theta)}{\partial\theta\,\partial\theta'} f(y_t;\theta) \right] dy_t = 0$$

$$\int_{-\infty}^{\infty} [g_t(\theta)g_t(\theta)' + h_t(\theta)] f(y_t;\theta) dy_t = 0.$$

Once again, evaluating this expression at $\theta = \theta_0$ gives

$$E[g_t(\theta_0)g_t(\theta_0)'] + E[h_t(\theta_0)] = 0,$$

which proves the result. □

The properties of the gradient function in equations (2.27) and (2.28) are completely general, because they hold for any arbitrary distribution.

Example 2.18 Gradient Properties and the Poisson Distribution

The first and second derivatives of the log-likelihood function of the Poisson distribution, given in Examples 1.14 and 1.17 in Chapter 1, are, respectively,

$$g_t(\theta) = \frac{y_t}{\theta} - 1, \qquad h_t(\theta) = -\frac{y_t}{\theta^2}.$$

To establish the first property of the gradient, take expectations and evaluate at $\theta = \theta_0$

$$E[g_t(\theta_0)] = E\left[\frac{y_t}{\theta_0} - 1\right] = \frac{E[y_t]}{\theta_0} - 1 = \frac{\theta_0}{\theta_0} - 1 = 0,$$

because $E[y_t] = \theta_0$ for the Poisson distribution.

To establish the second property of the gradient, consider

$$E\left[g_t(\theta_0)g_t(\theta_0)'\right] = E\left[\left(\frac{y_t}{\theta_0} - 1\right)^2\right] = \frac{1}{\theta_0^2} E[(y_t - \theta_0)^2] = \frac{\theta_0}{\theta_0^2} = \frac{1}{\theta_0},$$

since $E\left[(y_t - \theta_0)^2\right] = \theta_0$ for the Poisson distribution. Alternatively

$$E[h_t(\theta_0)] = E\left[-\frac{y_t}{\theta_0^2}\right] = -\frac{E[y_t]}{\theta_0^2} = -\frac{\theta_0}{\theta_0^2} = -\frac{1}{\theta_0},$$

and hence

$$E[g_t(\theta_0)g_t(\theta_0)'] = -E[h_t(\theta_0)] = \frac{1}{\theta_0}. \qquad \square$$

The relationship between the gradient and the Hessian is presented more compactly by defining

$$J(\theta_0) = \mathrm{E}[g_t(\theta_0)g_t(\theta_0)']$$
$$H(\theta_0) = \mathrm{E}[h_t(\theta_0)],$$

in which case

$$J(\theta_0) = -H(\theta_0).\tag{2.29}$$

The matrix $J(\theta_0)$ is referred to as the outer product of the gradients matrix. In the more general case in which y_t is dependent and g_t is a mds, $J(\theta_0)$ and $H(\theta_0)$ in equation (2.29) become, respectively,

$$J(\theta_0) = \lim_{T\to\infty} \frac{1}{T} \sum_{t=1}^{T} \mathrm{E}[g_t(\theta_0)g_t(\theta_0)']\tag{2.30}$$

$$H(\theta_0) = \lim_{T\to\infty} \frac{1}{T} \sum_{t=1}^{T} \mathrm{E}[h_t(\theta_0)].\tag{2.31}$$

2.4.3   The Information Matrix

The definition of the outer product of the gradients matrix in equation (2.29) is commonly referred to as the information matrix

$$I(\theta_0) = J(\theta_0).\tag{2.32}$$

Given the relationship between $J(\theta_0)$ and $H(\theta_0)$ in equation (2.29) it immediately follows that

$$I(\theta_0) = J(\theta_0) = -H(\theta_0).\tag{2.33}$$

Equation (2.33) represents the well-known information equality. An important assumption underlying this result is that the distribution used to construct the log-likelihood function is correctly specified. This assumption is relaxed in Chapter 9 on quasi-maximum likelihood estimation.

The information matrix represents a measure of the quality of the information in the sample to locate the population parameter θ_0. For log-likelihood functions that are relatively flat, the information in the sample is dispersed thereby providing imprecise information on the location of θ_0. For samples that are less diffuse the log-likelihood function is more concentrated providing more precise information on the location of θ_0. Interpreting information this way follows from the expression of the information matrix in equation (2.33) where the quantity of information in the sample is measured by the curvature of the log-likelihood function, as given by $-H(\theta)$. For relatively flat log-likelihood functions the curvature of $\ln L(\theta)$ means that $-H(\theta)$ is relatively small around θ_0. For log-likelihood functions exhibiting stronger curvature, the second derivative is correspondingly larger.

If $-h_t(\theta)$ represents the information available from the data at time t, it follows from (2.31) that the total information available from a sample of size T is

$$TI(\theta_0) = -\sum_{t=1}^{T} E[h_t] . \qquad (2.34)$$

Example 2.19 Information Matrix of the Bernoulli Distribution

Let $\{y_1, y_2, \cdots, y_T\}$ be *iid* observations from a Bernoulli distribution

$$f(y_t; \theta) = \theta^{y_t}(1 - \theta)^{1-y_t} ,$$

in which $0 < \theta < 1$. The log-likelihood function at observation t is

$$\ln l_t(\theta) = y_t \ln \theta + (1 - y_t) \ln(1 - \theta) .$$

The first and second derivatives are, respectively, given by

$$g_t(\theta) = \frac{y_t}{\theta} - \frac{1 - y_t}{1 - \theta} , \quad h_t(\theta) = -\frac{y_t}{\theta^2} - \frac{1 - y_t}{(1 - \theta)^2} .$$

The information matrix is

$$I(\theta_0) = -E[h_t(\theta_0)] = \frac{E[y_t]}{\theta_0^2} - \frac{E[1 - y_t]}{(1 - \theta_0)^2} = \frac{\theta_0}{\theta_0^2} + \frac{(1 - \theta_0)}{(1 - \theta_0)^2} = \frac{1}{\theta_0(1 - \theta_0)} ,$$

because $E[y_t] = \theta_0$ for the Bernoulli distribution. The total amount of information in the sample is

$$TI(\theta_0) = \frac{T}{\theta_0(1 - \theta_0)} .$$

$\square$

Example 2.20 Information Matrix of the Normal Distribution

Let $\{y_1, y_2, \ldots, y_T\}$ be *iid* observations drawn from the normal distribution

$$f(y_t; \theta) = \frac{1}{\sqrt{2\pi\sigma^2}} \exp\left[-\frac{(y_t - \mu)^2}{2\sigma^2}\right] ,$$

where $\theta = \{\mu, \sigma^2\}$. From Example 1.12 in Chapter 1, the log-likelihood function at observation t is

$$\ln l_t(\theta) = -\frac{1}{2} \ln 2\pi - \frac{1}{2} \ln \sigma^2 - \frac{1}{2\sigma^2}(y_t - \mu)^2 ,$$

and the gradient and Hessian are, respectively,

$$
g_t(\theta) = \begin{bmatrix} \dfrac{y_t - \mu}{\sigma^2} \\[2mm] -\dfrac{1}{2\sigma^2} + \dfrac{(y_t - \mu)^2}{2\sigma^4} \end{bmatrix}, \quad h_t(\theta) = \begin{bmatrix} -\dfrac{1}{\sigma^2} & -\dfrac{y_t - \mu}{\sigma^4} \\[2mm] -\dfrac{y_t - \mu}{\sigma^4} & \dfrac{1}{2\sigma^4} - \dfrac{(y_t - \mu)^2}{\sigma^6} \end{bmatrix}.
$$

Taking expectations of the negative Hessian, evaluating at $\theta = \theta_0$ and scaling the result by T gives the total information matrix

$$
TI(\theta_0) = -T \, \mathrm{E}[h_t(\theta_0)] = \begin{bmatrix} \dfrac{T}{\sigma_0^2} & 0 \\[2mm] 0 & \dfrac{T}{2\sigma_0^4} \end{bmatrix}.
$$

$\square$

2.5   Asymptotic Properties

Assuming that the regularity conditions (R1) to (R5) in Section 2.3 are satisfied, the results in Section 2.4 are now used to study the relationship between the maximum likelihood estimator, $\widehat{\theta}$, and the population parameter, θ_0, as $T \to \infty$. Three properties are investigated, namely, consistency, asymptotic normality and asymptotic efficiency. The first property focusses on the distance $\widehat{\theta} - \theta_0$, the second looks at the distribution of $\widehat{\theta} - \theta_0$ and the third examines the variance of this distribution.

2.5.1   Consistency

A desirable property of an estimator $\widehat{\theta}$ is that additional information obtained by increasing the sample size, T, yields more reliable estimates of the population parameter, θ_0. Formally this result is stated as

$$
\mathrm{plim}(\widehat{\theta}) = \theta_0 \,. \tag{2.35}
$$

An estimator satisfying this property is a consistent estimator.

Given the regularity conditions in Section 2.3, all maximum likelihood estimators are consistent. To derive this result, consider a sample of T observations, $\{y_1, y_2, \cdots, y_T\}$. By definition the maximum likelihood estimator satisfies the condition

$$
\widehat{\theta} = \arg\max_{\theta} \frac{1}{T} \sum_{t=1}^{T} \ln f(y_t; \theta) \,.
$$

From the convergence regularity condition (R2)

$$
\frac{1}{T} \sum_{t=1}^{T} \ln f(y_t; \theta) \xrightarrow{p} \mathrm{E}\left[\ln f(y_t; \theta)\right] ,
$$

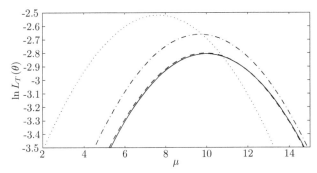

Figure 2.3. Log-likelihood functions for samples of size $T = 5$ (dotted line), $T = 20$ (dot-dashed line) and $T = 500$ (dashed line), simulated from the population distribution $N(10, 16)$. The bold line is the population log-likelihood $E[\ln f(y_t; \theta)]$ given by Example 2.16.

which implies that the two functions are converging asymptotically. But, given the result in equation (2.25), it is possible to write

$$\arg\max_{\theta} \frac{1}{T} \sum_{t=1}^{T} \ln f(y_t; \theta) \xrightarrow{p} \arg\max_{\theta} E[\ln f(y_t; \theta)] \ .$$

So the maxima of these two functions, $\widehat{\theta}$ and θ_0, respectively, must also be converging as $T \to \infty$, in which case (2.35) holds.

This is a heuristic proof of the consistency property of the maximum likelihood estimator initially given by Wald (1949); see also Theorems 2.1 and 2.5 in Newey and McFadden (1994, pp2111–2245). The proof highlights that consistency requires:

i convergence of the sample log-likelihood function to the population log-likelihood function; and

ii convergence of the maximum of the sample log-likelihood function to the maximum of the population log-likelihood function.

These two features of the consistency proof are demonstrated in the following simulation experiment.

Example 2.21 Demonstration of Consistency
Figure 2.3 gives plots of the log-likelihood functions for samples of size $T = \{5, 20, 500\}$ simulated from the population distribution $N(10, 16)$. Also plotted is the population log-likelihood function, $E[\ln f(y_t; \theta)]$, given in Example 2.16. The consistency of the maximum likelihood estimator is first demonstrated with the sample log-likelihood functions approaching the population log-likelihood function $E[\ln f(y_t; \theta)]$ as T increases. The second demonstration of the consistency property is given by the maximum likelihood

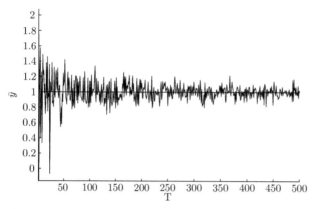

Figure 2.4. Demonstration of the consistency properties of the sample mean when samples of increasing size $T = 1, 2, \cdots, 500$ are drawn from a $N(1, 2)$ distribution.

estimates, in this case the sample means, of the three samples

$$\bar{y}(T = 5) = 7.6586, \quad \bar{y}(T = 20) = 9.6894, \quad \bar{y}(T = 500) = 9.9524,$$

which approach the population mean $\mu_0 = 10$ as $T \to \infty$. □

A further implication of consistency is that an estimator should exhibit decreasing variability around the population parameter θ_0 as T increases.

Example 2.22 Normal Distribution
   Consider the normal distribution

$$f(y_t; \theta) = \frac{1}{\sqrt{2\pi\sigma^2}} \exp\left[-\frac{(y_t - \mu)^2}{2\sigma^2}\right].$$

From Example 1.16 in Chapter 1, the sample mean, $\bar{y}$, is the maximum likelihood estimator of μ_0. Figure 2.4 shows that for the population distribution $N(1, 2)$ this estimator converges to $\mu_0 = 1$ for increasing samples of size T while simultaneously exhibiting decreasing variability. □

Example 2.23 Cauchy Distribution
   The sample mean, $\bar{y}$, and the sample median, $\bar{m}$, are computed from increasing samples of size $T = 1, 2, \cdots, 500$, drawn from a Cauchy distribution

$$f(y_t; \theta) = \frac{1}{\pi} \frac{1}{1 + (y_t - \theta)^2},$$

with location parameter $\theta_0 = 1$. A comparison of panels (a) and (b) in Figure 2.5 suggests that $\bar{y}$ is an inconsistent estimator of θ because its sampling variability does not decrease as T increases. By contrast, the sampling variability of $\bar{m}$ does decrease, suggesting that it is a consistent estimator. The failure of $\bar{y}$ to

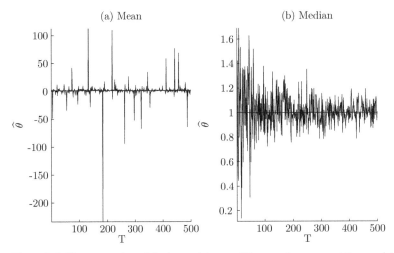

Figure 2.5. Demonstration of the inconsistency of the sample mean and the consistency of the sample median as estimators of the location parameter of a Cauchy distribution with $\theta_0 = 1$, for samples of increasing size $T = 1, 2, \cdots, 500$.

be a consistent estimator stems from the property that the mean of a Cauchy distribution does not exist and therefore represents a violation of the conditions needed for the weak law of large numbers to hold. In this example, neither $\bar{y}$ nor $\bar{m}$ are the maximum likelihood estimators. The maximum likelihood estimator of the location parameter of the Cauchy distribution is derived in Chapter 3. ☐

2.5.2 Normality

To establish the asymptotic distribution of the maximum likelihood estimator, $\widehat{\theta}$, consider the first-order condition

$$G_T(\widehat{\theta}) = \frac{1}{T} \sum_{t=1}^{T} g_t(\widehat{\theta}) = 0. \tag{2.36}$$

A mean value expansion of this condition around the true value θ_0, gives

$$0 = \frac{1}{T} \sum_{t=1}^{T} g_t(\widehat{\theta}) = \frac{1}{T} \sum_{t=1}^{T} g_t(\theta_0) + \left[\frac{1}{T} \sum_{t=1}^{T} h_t(\theta^*)\right](\widehat{\theta} - \theta_0), \tag{2.37}$$

in which θ^* lies between $\widehat{\theta}$ and θ_0, and hence $\theta^* \overset{p}{\to} \theta_0$ if $\widehat{\theta} \overset{p}{\to} \theta_0$. Rearranging and multiplying both sides by $\sqrt{T}$ shows that

$$\sqrt{T}(\widehat{\theta} - \theta_0) = \left[-\frac{1}{T} \sum_{t=1}^{T} h_t(\theta^*)\right]^{-1} \left[\frac{1}{\sqrt{T}} \sum_{t=1}^{T} g_t(\theta_0)\right]. \tag{2.38}$$

Now

$$\frac{1}{T} \sum_{t=1}^{T} h_t(\theta^*) \xrightarrow{p} H(\theta_0)$$

$$\frac{1}{\sqrt{T}} \sum_{t=1}^{T} g_t(\theta_0) \xrightarrow{d} N(0, J(\theta_0)), \qquad (2.39)$$

where

$$H(\theta_0) = \lim_{T \to \infty} \frac{1}{T} \sum_{t=1}^{T} E[h_t(\theta_0)]$$

$$J(\theta_0) = \lim_{T \to \infty} E\left[\left(\frac{1}{\sqrt{T}} \sum_{t=1}^{T} g_t(\theta_0) \right) \left(\frac{1}{\sqrt{T}} \sum_{t=1}^{T} g_t'(\theta_0) \right) \right].$$

The first condition in (2.39) follows from the uniform WLLN and the second condition is based on applying the appropriate central limit theorem based on the time series properties of $g_t(\theta)$. Combining equations (2.38) and (2.39) yields the asymptotic distribution

$$\sqrt{T}(\hat{\theta} - \theta_0) \xrightarrow{d} N\left(0, H^{-1}(\theta_0)J(\theta_0)H^{-1}(\theta_0)\right).$$

Using the information matrix equality in equation (2.33) simplifies the asymptotic distribution to

$$\sqrt{T}(\hat{\theta} - \theta_0) \xrightarrow{d} N\left(0, \Omega(\theta_0)\right), \qquad \Omega(\theta_0) = I^{-1}(\theta_0). \qquad (2.40)$$

or

$$\hat{\theta} \stackrel{a}{\sim} N\left(\theta_0, \frac{1}{T}\Omega(\theta_0)\right). \qquad (2.41)$$

This establishes that the maximum likelihood estimator has an asymptotic normal distribution with mean equal to the population parameter, θ_0, and covariance matrix, $T^{-1}\Omega(\theta_0)$. The asymptotic variances of $\hat{\theta}$ are obtained from the diagonal elements of the normalised covariance matrix $T^{-1}\Omega(\theta_0)$.

Example 2.24 Asymptotic Normality of the Poisson Parameter
From Example 2.18, equation (2.40) becomes

$$\sqrt{T}(\hat{\theta} - \theta_0) \xrightarrow{d} N(0, \theta_0),$$

because $H(\theta_0) = -1/\theta_0 = -I(\theta_0)$, then $I^{-1}(\theta_0) = \theta_0$. ☐

Example 2.25 Simulating Asymptotic Normality
Figure 2.6 gives the results of sampling *iid* random variables from an exponential distribution with $\theta_0 = 1$ for samples of size $T = 5$ and $T = 100$, using 5000 replications. The sample means are standardised using the population

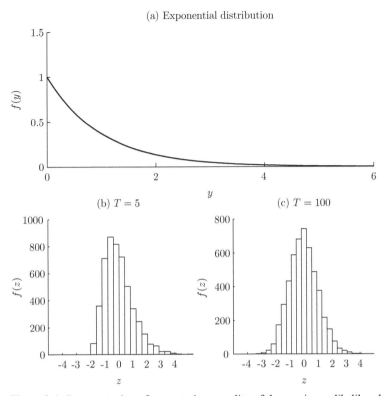

Figure 2.6. Demonstration of asymptotic normality of the maximum likelihood estimator based on samples of size $T = 5$ and $T = 100$ from an exponential distribution, $f(y; \theta_0)$, with mean $\theta_0 = 1$, for 5000 replications.

mean ($\theta_0 = 1$) and the population variance ($\theta_0^2 / T = 1^2 / T$) as

$$z_i = \frac{\bar{y}_i - 1}{\sqrt{1^2 / T}}, \qquad i = 1, 2, \cdots, 5000.$$

The sampling distribution of z is skewed to the right for $T = 5$ thus mimicking the positive skewness characteristic of the population distribution. Increasing the sample size to $T = 100$, reduces the skewness in the sampling distribution, which is now approximately normally distributed. □

2.5.3   Efficiency

Asymptotic efficiency concerns the limiting value of the variance of any estimator, say $\tilde{\theta}$, around θ_0 as the sample size increases. The Cramér-Rao lower bound provides a bound on the efficiency of this estimator.

Cramér-Rao Lower Bound: Single Parameter Case

Suppose θ_0 is a single parameter and $\widetilde{\theta}$ is any consistent estimator of θ_0 with asymptotic distribution of the form

$$\sqrt{T}(\widetilde{\theta} - \theta_0) \xrightarrow{d} N(0, \Omega).$$

The Cramér-Rao inequality states that

$$\Omega \geq \frac{1}{I(\theta_0)}. \tag{2.42}$$

Proof: An outline of the proof is as follows. A consistent estimator is asymptotically unbiased, so $E[\widetilde{\theta} - \theta_0] \to 0$ as $T \to \infty$, which can be expressed as

$$\int_{-\infty}^{\infty} \cdots \int_{-\infty}^{\infty} (\widetilde{\theta} - \theta_0) f(y_1, y_2, \cdots, y_T; \theta_0) dy_1 dy_2 \cdots dy_T \to 0.$$

Differentiating both sides with respect to θ_0 and using the interchangeability regularity condition (R4) gives

$$-\int_{-\infty}^{\infty} \cdots \int_{-\infty}^{\infty} f(y_1, y_2, \cdots, y_T; \theta_0) dy_1 dy_2 \cdots dy_T$$

$$+ \int_{-\infty}^{\infty} \cdots \int_{-\infty}^{\infty} (\widetilde{\theta} - \theta_0) \frac{\partial f(y_1, y_2, \cdots, y_T; \theta_0)}{\partial \theta_0} dy_1 dy_2 \cdots dy_T \to 0.$$

The first term on the right-hand side integrates to 1, since f is a probability density function. Thus

$$\int_{-\infty}^{\infty} \cdots \int_{-\infty}^{\infty} (\widetilde{\theta} - \theta_0) \frac{\partial \ln f(y_1, y_2, \cdots, y_T; \theta_0)}{\partial \theta_0} f(y_1, y_2, \cdots, y_T; \theta_0)$$

$$\times \, dy_1 dy_2 \cdots dy_T \to 1. \tag{2.43}$$

Using

$$\frac{\partial \ln f(y_1, y_2, \cdots, y_T; \theta_0)}{\partial \theta_0} = T G_T(\theta_0),$$

equation (2.43) is expressed as

$$\text{cov}(\sqrt{T}(\widetilde{\theta} - \theta_0), \sqrt{T} G_T(\theta_0)) \to 1,$$

since the gradient, $G_T(\theta_0)$, has mean zero.

The squared correlation between $\sqrt{T}(\widetilde{\theta} - \theta_0)$ and $G_T(\theta_0)$ satisfies

$$\text{cor}(\sqrt{T}(\widetilde{\theta} - \theta_0), \sqrt{T} G_T(\theta_0))^2 = \frac{\text{cov}(\sqrt{T}(\widetilde{\theta} - \theta_0), \sqrt{T} G_T(\theta_0))^2}{\text{var}(\sqrt{T}(\widetilde{\theta} - \theta_0)) \text{var}(\sqrt{T} G_T(\theta_0))} \leq 1$$

and rearranging gives

$$\text{var}(\sqrt{T}(\widetilde{\theta} - \theta_0)) \geq \frac{\text{cov}(\sqrt{T}(\widetilde{\theta} - \theta_0), \sqrt{T} G_T(\theta_0))^2}{\text{var}(\sqrt{T} G_T(\theta_0))}.$$

Taking limits on both sides of this inequality gives Ω on the left-hand side, 1 in the numerator on the right-hand side and $I(\theta_0)$ in the denominator, which gives the Cramér-Rao inequality in (2.42) as required. $\square$

Cramér-Rao Lower Bound: Multiple Parameter Case

For a vector parameter the Cramér-Rao inequality (2.42) becomes

$$\Omega \geq I^{-1}(\theta_0), \tag{2.44}$$

where this matrix inequality is understood to mean that $\Omega - I^{-1}(\theta_0)$ is a positive semi-definite matrix. Since equation (2.41) shows that the maximum likelihood estimator, $\widehat{\theta}$, has asymptotic covariance matrix $I^{-1}(\theta_0)$, the maximum likelihood estimator achieves the Cramér-Rao lower bound and is, therefore, asymptotically efficient. Moreover, since $T I(\theta_0)$ represents the total information available in a sample of size T, the inverse of this quantity provides a measure of the precision of the information in the sample, as given by the variance of $\widehat{\theta}$.

Example 2.26 Lower Bound for the Normal Distribution

From Example 2.20, the log-likelihood function is

$$\ln L_T(\theta) = -\frac{1}{2} \ln 2\pi - \frac{1}{2} \ln \sigma^2 - \frac{1}{2\sigma^2 T} \sum_{t=1}^{T} (y_t - \mu)^2,$$

with information matrix

$$I(\theta) = -\text{E}[H_T(\theta)] = \begin{bmatrix} \dfrac{1}{\sigma^2} & 0 \\ 0 & \dfrac{1}{2\sigma^4} \end{bmatrix}.$$

Evaluating this expression at $\theta = \theta_0$ gives

$$\frac{1}{T}\Omega = \frac{1}{T} I^{-1}(\theta_0) = \begin{bmatrix} \dfrac{\sigma_0^2}{T} & 0 \\ 0 & \dfrac{2\sigma_0^4}{T} \end{bmatrix},$$

so the asymptotic variances are $\text{var}(\widehat{\mu}) = \sigma_0^2 / T$ and $\text{var}(\widehat{\sigma}^2) = 2\sigma_0^4 / T$. $\square$

Example 2.27 Relative Efficiency of the Mean and Median

The sample mean, $\overline{y}$, and sample median, $\overline{m}$, are both consistent estimators of the population mean, μ, in samples drawn from a normal distribution, with $\overline{y}$ being the maximum likelihood estimator of μ. From Example 2.26 the variance of $\bar{y}$ is $\text{var}(\bar{y}) = \sigma_0^2 / T$. The variance of $\bar{m}$ is approximately (Stuart and Ord, 1994, p358)

$$\text{var}(\bar{m}) = \frac{1}{4Tf^2},$$

in which $f = f(m)$ is the value of the pdf evaluated at the population median (m). In the case of normality with known variance σ_0^2, $f(m)$ is

$$f(m) = \frac{1}{\sqrt{2\pi\sigma_0^2}} \exp\left[-\frac{(m-\mu)^2}{2\sigma_0^2}\right] = \frac{1}{\sqrt{2\pi\sigma_0^2}},$$

since $m = \mu$ because of symmetry. The variance of $\bar{m}$ is then

$$\text{var}(\bar{m}) = \frac{\pi\sigma_0^2}{2T} > \text{var}(\bar{y}),$$

because $\pi/2 > 1$, establishing that the maximum likelihood estimator has a smaller variance than another consistent estimator, $\bar{m}$.   □

2.6   Finite-Sample Properties

The properties of the maximum likelihood estimator established in the previous section are asymptotic properties. An important application of the asymptotic distribution is to approximate the finite sample distribution of the maximum likelihood estimator, $\widehat{\theta}$. There are a number of methods available to approximate the finite sample distribution, including simulating the sampling distribution by Monte Carlo methods or using an Edgeworth expansion.

Example 2.28 Edgeworth Expansion Approximations
As illustrated in Example 2.25, the asymptotic distribution of the maximum likelihood estimator of the parameter of an exponential population distribution is

$$z = \sqrt{T}\frac{(\widehat{\theta} - \theta_0)}{\theta_0} \xrightarrow{d} N(0, 1),$$

which has asymptotic distribution function given by the normal distribution function

$$F_a(s) = \Phi(s) = \frac{1}{\sqrt{2\pi}} \int_{-\infty}^{s} e^{-v^2/2} dv.$$

The Edgeworth expansion of the distribution function is

$$F_e(s) = \Phi(s) - \phi(s)\left[\left(1 + \frac{2}{3}H_2(s)\right)\frac{1}{\sqrt{T}} + \left(\frac{5}{2} + \frac{11}{12}H_3(s) + \frac{9}{2}H_5(s)\right)\frac{1}{T}\right],$$

Table 2.3. *Comparison of the finite sample,*
Edgeworth expansion and asymptotic
distribution functions of the standardised statistic
$z = \sqrt{T}\theta_0^{-1}(\widehat{\theta} - \theta_0)$, *for a sample of size*
$T = 5$ *draws from the exponential distribution*

s	Finite	Edgeworth	Asymptotic
-2	0.000	-0.019	0.023
-1	0.053	0.147	0.159
0	0.440	0.441	0.500
1	0.734	0.636	0.841
2	0.872	0.874	0.977

in which $H_2(s) = s^2 - 1$, $H_3(s) = s^3 - 3s$ and $H_5(s) = s^5 - 10s^3 + 15s$ are the probabilists' Hermite polynomials and $\phi(s)$ is the standard normal probability density (Severini, 2005, p144). The first term of this expansion is the asymptotic distribution function $\Phi(s)$. The finite sample distribution function is available in this case and is given by the complement of the gamma distribution function

$$F(s) = 1 - \frac{1}{\Gamma(s)} \int_0^w e^{-v} v^{s-1} dv, \qquad w = T / \left(1 + s/\sqrt{T}\right).$$

Table 2.3 shows that the Edgeworth approximation, $F_e(s)$, improves upon the asymptotic approximation, $F_a(s)$, although the former can yield negative probabilities in the tails of the distribution. □

As the previous example demonstrates, even for simple situations the finite sample distribution approximation of the maximum likelihood estimator is complicated. For this reason asymptotic approximations are commonly employed. However, some other important finite sample properties will now be discussed, namely, unbiasedness, sufficiency, invariance and non-uniqueness.

2.6.1 Unbiasedness

Not all maximum likelihood estimators are unbiased. Examples of unbiased maximum likelihood estimators are the sample mean in the normal and Poisson examples. Even in samples known to be normally distributed but with unknown mean, the sample standard deviation is an example of a biased estimator since $E[\widehat{\sigma}] \neq \sigma_0$. This result follows from the fact that Slutsky's theorem (see Section 2.2.2) does not hold for the expectations operator. Consequently

$$E[\tau(\widehat{\theta})] \neq \tau(E[\widehat{\theta}]),$$

in which $\tau(\cdot)$ is a monotonic function. This result contrasts with the property of consistency that uses probability limits, because Slutsky's theorem does apply to plims.

Example 2.29 Sample Variance of a Normal Distribution

The maximum likelihood estimator, $\widehat{\sigma}^2$, and an unbiased estimator, $\widetilde{\sigma}^2$, of the variance of a normal distribution with unknown mean, μ, are, respectively,

$$\widehat{\sigma}^2 = \frac{1}{T} \sum_{t=1}^{T} (y_t - \overline{y})^2, \qquad \widetilde{\sigma}^2 = \frac{1}{T-1} \sum_{t=1}^{T} (y_t - \overline{y})^2.$$

As $E[\widetilde{\sigma}^2] = \sigma_0^2$, the maximum likelihood estimator underestimates σ_0^2 in finite samples. To estimate the size of this bias, 20000 samples of size $T = 5$ are drawn from a $N(1, 2)$ distribution. The simulated expectations of the two statistics are

$$E[\widehat{\sigma}^2] \simeq \frac{1}{20000} \sum_{i=1}^{20000} \widehat{\sigma}_i^2 = 1.593, \qquad E[\widetilde{\sigma}^2] \simeq \frac{1}{20000} \sum_{i=1}^{20000} \widetilde{\sigma}_i^2 = 1.991,$$

showing a $100(1.593/2 - 1) = -20.35\%$ underestimation of $\sigma_0^2 = 2$.   □

2.6.2 Sufficiency

Let $\{y_1, y_2, \cdots, y_T\}$ be *iid* drawings from the joint pdf $f(y_1, y_2, \cdots, y_T; \theta)$. Any statistic computed using the observed sample, such as the sample mean or variance, is a way of summarising the data. Preferably, the statistics should summarise the data in such a way as not to lose any of the information contained by the entire sample. A sufficient statistic for the population parameter, θ_0, is a statistic that uses all of the information in the sample. Formally, this means that the joint pdf can be factorised into two components

$$f(y_1, y_2, \cdots, y_T; \theta) = c(\widetilde{\theta}; \theta) d(y_1, \cdots, y_T), \qquad (2.45)$$

in which $\widetilde{\theta}$ represents a sufficient statistic for θ.

If a sufficient statistic exists, the maximum likelihood estimator is a function of it. To demonstrate this result, use equation (2.45) to rewrite the log-likelihood function as

$$\ln L_T(\theta) = \frac{1}{T} \ln c(\widetilde{\theta}; \theta) + \frac{1}{T} \ln d(y_1, \cdots, y_T). \qquad (2.46)$$

Differentiating with respect to θ gives

$$\frac{\partial \ln L_T(\theta)}{\partial \theta} = \frac{1}{T} \frac{\partial \ln c(\widetilde{\theta}; \theta)}{\partial \theta}. \qquad (2.47)$$

The maximum likelihood estimator, $\widehat{\theta}$, is given as the solution of

$$\frac{\partial \ln c(\widetilde{\theta}; \widehat{\theta})}{\partial \theta} = 0. \tag{2.48}$$

Rearranging shows that $\widehat{\theta}$ is a function of the sufficient statistic $\widetilde{\theta}$.

Example 2.30 Sufficient Statistic of the Geometric Distribution
If $\{y_1, y_2, \cdots, y_T\}$ are *iid* observations from a geometric distribution

$$f(y_t; \theta) = (1 - \theta)^{y_t} \theta, \qquad 0 < \theta < 1,$$

the joint pdf is

$$\prod_{t=1}^{T} f(y_t; \theta) = (1 - \theta)^{\widetilde{\theta}} \theta^T,$$

where $\widetilde{\theta}$ is the sufficient statistic

$$\widetilde{\theta} = \sum_{t=1}^{T} y_t.$$

Defining $c(\widetilde{\theta}; \theta) = (1 - \theta)^{\widetilde{\theta}} \theta^T$ and $d(y_1, \cdots, y_T) = 1$, equation (2.48) becomes

$$\frac{d \ln c(\widehat{\theta}; \widehat{\theta})}{d\theta} = -\frac{\widetilde{\theta}}{1 - \widehat{\theta}} + \frac{T}{\widehat{\theta}} = 0,$$

showing that $\widehat{\theta} = T/(T + \widetilde{\theta})$ is a function of the sufficient statistic $\widetilde{\theta}$. □

2.6.3 Invariance

If $\widehat{\theta}$ is the maximum likelihood estimator of θ_0, then for any arbitrary nonlinear function, $\tau(\cdot)$, the maximum likelihood estimator of $\tau(\theta_0)$ is given by $\tau(\widehat{\theta})$. The invariance property is particularly useful in situations when an analytical expression for the maximum likelihood estimator is not available.

Example 2.31 Invariance Property and the Normal Distribution
Consider the following normal distribution with known mean μ_0

$$f(y_t; \sigma^2) = \frac{1}{\sqrt{2\pi\sigma^2}} \exp\left[-\frac{(y - \mu_0)^2}{2\sigma^2}\right].$$

As shown in Example 1.16, for a sample of size T the maximum likelihood estimator of the variance is $\widehat{\sigma}^2 = T^{-1} \sum_{t=1}^{T} (y_t - \mu_0)^2$. Using the invariance property, the maximum likelihood estimator of σ is

$$\hat{\sigma} = \sqrt{\frac{1}{T} \sum_{t=1}^{T} (y_t - \mu_0)^2},$$

which immediately follows by defining $\tau(\theta) = \sqrt{\theta}$.   □

Example 2.32 Vasicek Interest Rate Model

From the Vasicek model of interest rates in Section 1.5 of Chapter 1, the relationship between the parameters of the transitional distribution $\theta = \{\alpha, \beta, \sigma^2\}$ and the parameters of the stationary distribution μ_s, σ_s^2, is

$$\mu_s = -\frac{\alpha}{\beta}, \qquad \sigma_s^2 = -\frac{\sigma^2}{\beta(2+\beta)}.$$

Given the maximum likelihood estimator of the model parameters $\hat{\theta} = \{\hat{\alpha}, \hat{\beta}, \hat{\sigma}^2\}$, the maximum likelihood estimators of the parameters of the stationary distribution are

$$\hat{\mu}_s = -\frac{\hat{\alpha}}{\hat{\beta}}, \qquad \hat{\sigma}_s^2 = -\frac{\hat{\sigma}^2}{\hat{\beta}(2+\hat{\beta})}.$$

□

2.6.4   Non-Uniqueness

The maximum likelihood estimator of θ is obtained by solving

$$G_T(\hat{\theta}) = 0. \tag{2.49}$$

The problems considered so far have a unique and, in most cases, closed-form solution. However, there are examples where there are several solutions to equation (2.49). An example is the bivariate normal distribution, which is explored in Section 2.7.2.

2.7   Applications

Some of the key results from this chapter are now applied to the bivariate normal distribution. The first application is motivated by the portfolio diversification problem in finance. The second application is more theoretical and illustrates the non-uniqueness problem sometimes encountered in the context of maximum likelihood estimation.

Let $y_{1,t}$ and $y_{2,t}$ be jointly *iid* random variables with means $\mu_i = E[y_i]$, variances $\sigma_i^2 = E[(y_{i,t} - \mu_i)^2]$, covariance $\sigma_{1,2} = E[(y_{1,t} - \mu_1)(y_{2,t} - \mu_2)]$ and

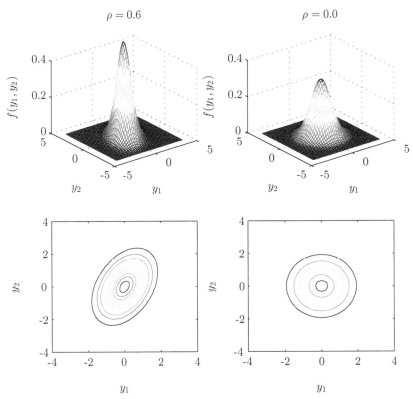

Figure 2.7. Bivariate normal distribution, based on $\mu_1 = \mu_2 = 0$, $\sigma_1^2 = \sigma_2^2 = 1$ and $\rho = 0.6$ (left-hand column) and $\rho = 0$ (right-hand column).

correlation $\rho = \sigma_{1,2}/\sigma_1 \sigma_2$. The bivariate normal distribution is

$$
f(y_{1,t}, y_{2,t}; \theta) = \frac{1}{2\pi \sqrt{\sigma_1^2 \sigma_2^2 \left(1 - \rho^2\right)}} \exp\left[-\frac{1}{2\left(1 - \rho^2\right)} \left(\left(\frac{y_{1,t} - \mu_1}{\sigma_1}\right)^2 \right. \right.
$$
$$
\left. \left. - 2\rho \left(\frac{y_{1,t} - \mu_1}{\sigma_1}\right) \left(\frac{y_{2,t} - \mu_2}{\sigma_2}\right) + \left(\frac{y_{2,t} - \mu_2}{\sigma_2}\right)^2 \right) \right],
$$

(2.50)

in which $\theta = \{\mu_1, \mu_{2,} \sigma_1^2, \sigma_2^2, \rho\}$ are the unknown parameters.

The shape of the bivariate normal distribution is shown in Figure 2.7 for the case of positive correlation $\rho = 0.6$ (left-hand column) and zero correlation $\rho = 0$ (right-hand column), with $\mu_1 = \mu_2 = 0$ and $\sigma_1^2 = \sigma_2^2 = 1$. The contour plots show that the effect of $\rho > 0$ is to make the contours ellipsoidal, which stretch the mass of the distribution over the quadrants with $y_{1,t}$ and

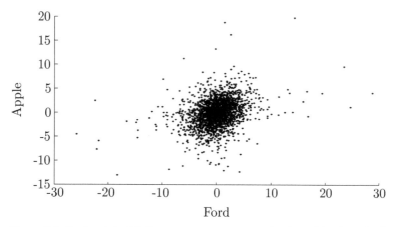

Figure 2.8. Scatterplot of daily percentage returns on Apple and Ford stocks from 2 January 2001 to 6 August 2010.

$y_{2,t}$ having the same signs. The contours are circular for $\rho = 0$, showing that the distribution is evenly spread across all quadrants. In this special case the joint distribution of $y_{1,t}$ and $y_{2,t}$ reduces to the product of the two marginal distributions

$$f\left(y_{1,t}, y_{2,t}; \mu_1, \mu_2, \sigma_1^2, \sigma_2^2, \rho = 0\right) = f_1\left(y_{1,t}; \mu_1, \sigma_1^2\right) f_2\left(y_{2,t}; \mu_2, \sigma_2^2\right),$$
(2.51)

where $f_i(\cdot)$ is the univariate normal distribution.

2.7.1 Portfolio Diversification

A fundamental result in finance is that the risk of a portfolio can be reduced by diversification when the correlation between the returns on the assets in the portfolio is $\rho < 1$. In the extreme case of $\rho = 1$, all assets move in exactly the same way and there are no gains to diversification. Figure 2.8 gives a scatterplot of the daily percentage returns on Apple and Ford stocks from 2 January 2001 to 6 August 2010. The cluster of returns exhibits positive, but less than perfect, correlation, suggesting gains to diversification.

A common assumption underlying portfolio diversification models is that returns are normally distributed. In the case of two assets, the returns $y_{1,t}$ (Apple) and $y_{2,t}$ (Ford) are assumed to be *iid* with the bivariate normal distribution in (2.50). For $t = 1, 2, \cdots , T$ pairs of observations, the log-likelihood

function is

$$\ln L_T(\theta) = -\ln 2\pi - \frac{1}{2}\left(\ln \sigma_1^2 + \ln \sigma_2^2 + \ln(1 - \rho^2)\right)$$

$$-\frac{1}{2(1-\rho^2)T}\sum_{t=1}^{T}(z_{1,t}^2 - 2\rho z_{1,t}z_{2,t} + z_{2,t}^2),$$

(2.52)

in which

$$z_{i,t} = \frac{y_{i,t} - \mu_i}{\sigma_i}, \qquad i = 1, 2.$$

To find the maximum likelihood estimator, $\widehat{\theta}$, the first-order derivatives of the log-likelihood function in equation (2.52) are

$$\frac{\partial \ln L_T(\theta)}{\partial \mu_i} = \frac{1}{\sigma_i \left(1 - \rho^2\right)} \frac{1}{T} \sum_{t=1}^{T}(z_{i,t} - \rho z_{j,t})$$

$$\frac{\partial \ln L_T(\theta)}{\partial \sigma_i^2} = -\frac{1}{2\sigma_i^2(1 - \rho^2)}\left((1 - \rho^2) - \frac{1}{T}\sum_{t=1}^{T}z_{i,t}^2 + \frac{\rho}{T}\sum_{t=1}^{T}z_{i,t}z_{j,t}\right)$$

$$\frac{\partial \ln L_T(\theta)}{\partial \rho} = \frac{\rho}{1 - \rho^2} - \frac{1}{\left(1 - \rho^2\right)^2}\frac{1}{T}\sum_{t=1}^{T}\left(\rho z_{1,t}^2 + \rho z_{2,t} + \frac{1 + \rho^2}{\left(1 - \rho^2\right)^2} z_{1,t}z_{2,t}\right),$$

for $i, j = 1, 2$ and where $i \neq j$. Setting these derivatives to zero and rearranging yields the maximum likelihood estimators

$$\widehat{\mu}_i = \frac{1}{T}\sum_{t=1}^{T}y_{i,t}, \qquad \widehat{\sigma}_i^2 = \frac{1}{T}\sum_{t=1}^{T}(y_{i,t} - \widehat{\mu}_i)^2, \qquad i = 1, 2,$$

$$\widehat{\rho} = \frac{1}{T\widehat{\sigma}_1\widehat{\sigma}_2}\sum_{t=1}^{T}(y_{1,t} - \widehat{\mu}_1)(y_{2,t} - \widehat{\mu}_2).$$

Evaluating these expressions using the data in Figure 2.8 gives

$$\widehat{\mu}_1 = -0.147, \quad \widehat{\mu}_2 = 0.017, \quad \widehat{\sigma}_1^2 = 7.764, \quad \widehat{\sigma}_2^2 = 10.546, \quad \widehat{\rho} = 0.301,$$

(2.53)

while the estimate of the covariance is

$$\widehat{\sigma}_{1,2} = \widehat{\rho}_{1,2}\widehat{\sigma}_1\widehat{\sigma}_1 = 0.301 \times \sqrt{7.764} \times \sqrt{10.546} = 2.724.$$

The estimate of the correlation $\widehat{\rho} = 0.301$ confirms the positive ellipsoidal shape of the scatterplot in Figure 2.8.

To demonstrate the potential advantages of portfolio diversification, define the return on the portfolio of the two assets Apple and Ford as

$$r_t = w_1 y_{1,t} + w_2 y_{2,t} \,,$$

in which w_1 and w_2 are the respective weights on Apple and Ford in the portfolio, with the property that $w_1 + w_2 = 1$. The risk of this portfolio is

$$\sigma^2 = E[(r_t - E[r_t])^2] = w_1^2 \sigma_1^2 + w_2^2 \sigma_2^2 + 2 w_1 w_2 \sigma_{1,2} \,.$$

For the minimum variance portfolio, w_1 and w_2 are the solutions of

$$\arg\min_{w_1, w_2} \sigma^2 \quad \text{s.t.} \quad w_1 + w_2 = 1 \,.$$

The optimal weight on Apple is

$$w_1 = \frac{\sigma_2^2 - \sigma_{1,2}}{\sigma_1^2 + \sigma_2^2 - 2\sigma_{1,2}} \,.$$

Using the sample estimates in (2.53), the estimate of this weight is

$$\widehat{w}_1 = \frac{\widehat{\sigma}_2^2 - \widehat{\sigma}_{1,2}}{\widehat{\sigma}_1^2 + \widehat{\sigma}_2^2 - 2\widehat{\sigma}_{1,2}} = \frac{10.546 - 2.724}{7.764 + 10.546 - 2 \times 2.724} = 0.608 \,.$$

On Ford it is $\widehat{w}_2 = 1 - \widehat{w}_1 = 0.392$. An estimate of the risk of the optimal portfolio is

$$\widehat{\sigma}^2 = 0.608^2 \times 7.764 + 0.392^2 \times 10.546 + 2 \times 0.608 \times 0.392 \times 2.724$$
$$= 5.789 \,.$$

From the invariance property the estimates of the portfolio weights $\widehat{w}_1$ and $\widehat{w}_2$ and the estimate of the risk of the portfolio $\widehat{\sigma}^2$ are maximum likelihood estimates of the population parameters. The risk on the optimal portfolio is less than the individual risks on Apple ($\widehat{\sigma}_1^2 = 7.764$) and Ford ($\widehat{\sigma}_2^2 = 10.546$) stocks, which proves the advantage of portfolio diversification.

2.7.2 Bimodal Likelihood

Consider the bivariate normal distribution in (2.50) with $\mu_1 = \mu_2 = 0$ and $\sigma_1^2 = \sigma_2^2 = 1$ and in which ρ is the only unknown parameter. The log-likelihood function in (2.52) reduces to

$$\ln L_T(\rho) = -\ln 2\pi - \frac{\ln(1 - \rho^2)}{2} - \frac{1}{2(1 - \rho^2)T}$$
$$\times \left(\sum_{t=1}^{T} y_{1,t}^2 - 2\rho \sum_{t=1}^{T} y_{1,t} y_{2,t} + \sum_{t=1}^{T} y_{2,t}^2 \right).$$

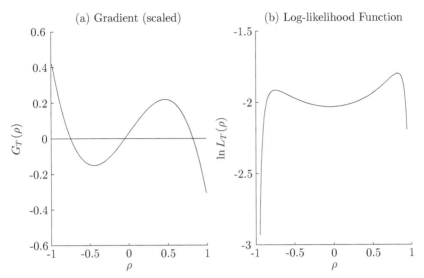

Figure 2.9. Gradient and log-likelihood function of the bivariate normal model with respect to the parameter ρ for sample size $T = 4$.

The gradient is

$$\frac{d \ln L_T(\rho)}{d\rho} = \frac{\rho}{1 - \rho^2} + \frac{1}{(1 - \rho^2)T} \sum_{t=1}^{T} y_{1,t} y_{2,t}$$

$$- \frac{\rho}{(1 - \rho^2)^2 T} \left(\sum_{t=1}^{T} y_{1,t}^2 - 2\rho \sum_{t=1}^{T} y_{1,t} y_{2,t} + \sum_{t=1}^{T} y_{2,t}^2 \right).$$

Setting the gradient to zero with $\rho = \hat{\rho}$ and simplifying the resulting expression by multiplying both sides by $(1 - \rho^2)^2$, shows that the maximum likelihood estimator is the solution of the cubic equation

$$\hat{\rho}(1 - \hat{\rho}^2) + (1 + \hat{\rho}^2)\frac{1}{T} \sum_{t=1}^{T} y_{1,t} y_{2,t} - \hat{\rho} \left(\frac{1}{T} \sum_{t=1}^{T} y_{1,t}^2 + \frac{1}{T} \sum_{t=1}^{T} y_{2,t}^2 \right) = 0.$$

$$(2.54)$$

This equation can have at most three real roots and so the maximum likelihood estimator may not be uniquely defined by the first-order conditions in this case.

An example of multiple roots is given in Figure 2.9. The data are $T = 4$ simulated bivariate normal draws $y_{1,t} = \{-0.6030, -0.0983, -0.1590, -0.6534\}$

and $y_{2,t} = \{0.1537, -0.2297, 0.6682, -0.4433\}$, with parameters

$$\theta = \{\mu_1 = 0, \mu_2 = 0, \sigma_1^2 = 1, \sigma_2^2 = 1, \rho = 0.6\}.$$

Computing the sample moments yields

$$\frac{1}{T}\sum_{t=1}^{T} y_{1,t} y_{2,t} = 0.0283, \quad \frac{1}{T}\sum_{t=1}^{T} y_{1,t}^2 = 0.2064, \quad \frac{1}{T}\sum_{t=1}^{T} y_{2,t}^2 = 0.1798.$$

Using (2.54), the scaled gradient function is

$$G_T(\rho) = \rho(1 - \rho^2) + (1 + \rho^2)(0.0283) - \rho(0.2064 + 0.1798),$$

which is plotted in panel (a) of Figure 2.9 together with the corresponding log-likelihood function in panel (b). The function $G_T(\rho)$ has three real roots located at -0.745, -0.045 and 0.815, with the middle root corresponding to a minimum. The global maximum occurs at $\rho = 0.815$, so this is the maximum likelihood estimate. It also happens to be the closest root to the true value of $\rho = 0.6$. The solution to the non-uniqueness problem suggested by this example is to evaluate the log-likelihood function at all possible solution values and choose the parameter estimate corresponding to the global maximum.

2.8   Exercises

(1) WLLN (Necessary Condition)

Program files   prop_wlln1.*

(a) Compute the sample mean of progressively larger samples of size $T = 1, 2, \cdots, 500$, comprising *iid* draws from the exponential distribution

$$f(y_t; \mu) = \frac{1}{\mu} \exp\left[-\frac{y_t}{\mu}\right], \qquad y_t > 0,$$

with population mean $\mu_0 = 5$. For each sample of size T, compute the sample mean $\bar{y}$ and show that the WLLN holds and hence compare the results with Figure 2.1.

(b) Repeat part (a) using the Student t distribution with $\mu_0 = 5$ and degrees of freedom parameter $\nu_0 = \{4, 3, 2, 1\}$. Show that the WLLN holds for all cases except $\nu_0 = 1$. Discuss.

(2) WLLN (Sufficient Condition)

Program files   prop_wlln2.*g

(a) A sufficient condition for the WLLN to hold is that $E[\bar{y}] \to \mu$ and $\text{var}(\bar{y}) \to 0$ as $T \to \infty$. Compute the sample moments

$m_i = T^{-1} \sum_{t=1}^{T} y_t^i$, $i = 1, 2, 3, 4$, for $T = \{50, 100, 200, 400, 800\}$ iid draws from the uniform distribution

$$f(y_t) = 1, \qquad -0.5 < y_t < 0.5.$$

Illustrate by simulation that the WLLN holds and compare the results with Table 2.1.

(b) Repeat part (a) using the Student t distribution, with $\mu_0 = 2$, degrees of freedom parameter $\nu_0 = 3$ and where the first two population moments are

$$E[y] = \mu_0, \qquad E[y^2] = \frac{\nu_0}{\nu_0 - 2} + \mu_0^2.$$

Confirm that the WLLN holds only for the sample moments m_1 and m_2, but not m_3 and m_4.

(c) Repeat part (b) for $\nu_0 = 4$ and show that the WLLN now holds for m_3 but not for m_4.

(d) Repeat part (b) for $\nu_0 = 5$ and show that the WLLN now holds for m_1, m_2, m_3 and m_4.

(3) Slutsky's Theorem

Program files   `prop_slutsky.*`

(a) Consider the sample moment given by the square of the standardised mean

$$m = \left(\frac{\bar{y}}{s} \right)^2,$$

in which $\bar{y} = T^{-1} \sum_{t=1}^{T} y_t$ and $s^2 = T^{-1} \sum_{t=1}^{T} (y_t - \bar{y})^2$. Simulate this statistic 5000 times for samples of size $T = \{10, 100, 1000\}$ comprising iid draws from the exponential distribution

$$f(y_t; \mu) = \frac{1}{\mu} \exp \left[-\frac{y_t}{\mu} \right], \qquad y_t > 0,$$

with mean $\mu_0 = 2$ and variance $\mu_0^2 = 4$. Given that

$$\text{plim} \left(\frac{\bar{y}}{s} \right)^2 = \frac{(\text{plim}\,\bar{y})^2}{\text{plim}\,s^2} = \frac{\mu^2}{\mu^2} = 1,$$

demonstrate Slutsky's theorem in this case.

(b) Show that Slutsky's theorem does not hold for the statistic

$$m = \left(\sqrt{T}\bar{y} \right)^2$$

by repeating the simulation experiment in part (a). Discuss why the theorem fails in this case.

(4) Properties of the Gradient Function

Program files   prop_gradient.*

(a) Consider a random sample of size T, $\{y_1, y_2, \cdots, y_T\}$, of *iid* random variables from the normal distribution with unknown mean θ and known variance $\sigma_0^2 = 1$

$$f(y_t; \theta) = \frac{1}{\sqrt{2\pi}} \exp\left[-\frac{(y_t - \theta)^2}{2}\right].$$

Derive expressions for the log-likelihood at t, $\ln l_t(\theta)$, the gradient at t, $g_t(\theta)$, and the Hessian at t, $h_t(\theta)$. Prove that

$$\mathrm{E}\left[\frac{d \ln l_t}{d\theta}\right] = 0, \quad \mathrm{E}\left[\left(\frac{d \ln l_t}{d\theta}\right)^2\right] = -\mathrm{E}\left[\frac{d^2 \ln l_t}{d\theta^2}\right].$$

Verify this result by simulating the normal distribution $N(1, 1)$ for a sample size of $T = 5000$ and computing the statistics

$$\frac{1}{5000}\sum_{t=1}^{5000} g_t, \qquad \frac{1}{5000}\sum_{i=1}^{5000} g_t^2, \qquad \frac{1}{5000}\sum_{i=1}^{5000} h_t.$$

(b) Derive the information matrix $I(\theta) = -E[\theta]$. Hence derive the Cramér-Rao lower bound and the asymptotic distribution of $\widehat{\theta}$.

(c) Repeat parts (a) and (b) where the random sample is from the exponential distribution

$$f(y_t; \theta) = \theta \exp[-\theta y_t],$$

with parameter $\theta_0 = 2$.

(5) Graphical Demonstration of Consistency

Program files   prop_consistency.*

(a) Simulate samples of size $T = \{5, 20, 500\}$ from the normal distribution with mean $\mu_0 = 10$ and variance $\sigma_0^2 = 16$. For each sample, plot the log-likelihood function

$$\ln L_T(\mu, \sigma_0^2) = \frac{1}{T} \sum_{t=1}^{T} f(y_t; \mu, \sigma_0^2),$$

over the range $\mu = \{0.0, 0.2, \cdots, 15\}$. Compare $\ln L_T(\mu, \sigma_0^2)$ with the population log-likelihood function $E[\ln f(y_t; \mu, \sigma_0^2)]$ and discuss the consistency property of the maximum likelihood estimator of μ.

(b) Repeat part (a) for samples of size $T = \{50, 500, 5000\}$, except now plot the sample log-likelihood function $\ln L_T(\mu_0, \sigma^2)$ over the range $\sigma^2 = \{10, 11, \cdots, 30\}$. Compare $\ln L_T(\mu_0, \sigma^2)$ with the population log-likelihood function $E[\ln f(y_t; \mu_0, \sigma^2)]$. Discuss the consistency property of the maximum likelihood estimator of σ^2.

(6) Consistency of the Sample Mean Assuming Normality

Program files   `prop_normal.*`

This exercise demonstrates the consistency property of the maximum likelihood estimator of the population mean of a normal distribution.

(a) Generate sample means for increasing samples of size $T = \{1, 2, \cdots, 500\}$, from a $N(1, 2)$ distribution. Plot the sample means for each T and compare the result with Figure 2.4. Interpret the results.
(b) Repeat part (a) using the $N(1, 20)$ distribution.
(c) Repeat parts (a) and (b) taking the largest sample to be $T = 5000$.

(7) Inconsistency of the Sample Mean of a Cauchy Distribution

Program files   `prop_cauchy.*`

This exercise shows that the sample mean is an inconsistent estimator of the population mean of a Cauchy distribution, while the median is a consistent estimator.

(a) Generate the sample mean and median of the Cauchy distribution with parameter $\mu_0 = 1$ for increasing samples of size $T = \{1, 2, \cdots, 500\}$. Plot the sample statistics for each T and compare the result with Figure 2.5. Interpret the results.
(b) Repeat part (a) using the Student t distribution with mean $\mu_0 = 1$ and $\nu_0 = 2$ degrees of freedom. Compare the two results.

(8) Efficiency Property of Maximum Likelihood Estimators

Program files   `prop_efficiency.*`

This exercise demonstrates the efficiency property of the maximum likelihood estimator of the population mean of a normal distribution.

(a) Generate 10000 samples of size $T = 100$ from a normal distribution with mean $\mu_0 = 1$ and variance $\sigma_0^2 = 2$.
(b) For each of the 10000 replications compute the sample mean $\bar{y}_i$ and the sample median $\bar{m}_i$.

(c) Compute the variance of the sample means around $\mu_0 = 1$ as

$$\text{var}(\bar{y}) = \frac{1}{10000} \sum_{i=1}^{10000} (\bar{y}_i - \mu_0)^2 \,,$$

and compare the result with the theoretical solution $\text{var}(\bar{y}) = \sigma_0^2 / T$.

(d) Compute the variance of the sample medians around $\mu_0 = 1$ as

$$\text{var}(\bar{m}) = \frac{1}{10000} \sum_{i=1}^{10000} (\bar{m}_i - \mu_0)^2 \,,$$

and compare the result with the theoretical solution $\text{var}(\bar{m}) = \pi \sigma_0^2 / 2T$.

(e) Use the results in parts (c) and (d) to show that $\text{var}(\bar{y}) < \text{var}(\bar{m})$.

(9) Asymptotic Normality (Exponential Distribution)

Program files   prop_asymnorm.*

This exercise demonstrates the asymptotic normality of the maximum likelihood estimator of the parameter (sample mean) of the exponential distribution.

(a) Generate 5000 samples of size $T = 5$ from the exponential distribution with parameter $\theta_0 = 1$,

$$f(y_t; \theta) = \frac{1}{\theta} \exp \left[-\frac{y_t}{\theta} \right] \,,$$

and compute the maximum likelihood estimates

$$\widehat{\theta}_i = \bar{y}_i, \qquad i = 1, 2, \cdots, 5000.$$

(b) Using the property that an exponential distribution has mean θ_0 and variance θ_0^2, compute the standardised statistic

$$z_i = \sqrt{T} \frac{(\bar{y}_i - \theta_0)}{\sqrt{\theta_0^2}}, \qquad i = 1, 2, \cdots, 5000.$$

Plot the empirical distribution of z using a histogram and interpret its shape.

(c) Repeat parts (a) and (b) for $T = \{50, 100, 500\}$, and interpret the results.

(10) Asymptotic Normality (Chi Square Distribution)

Program files   prop_chisq.*

This exercise demonstrates the asymptotic normality of the sample mean where the population distribution is a chi-square distribution with ν degrees of freedom.

(a) Generate 5000 samples of size $T = 5$ from the chi-square distribution with $\nu_0 = 1$ degrees of freedom. For each replication compute the sample mean.

(b) Using the property that a chi-square distribution has mean ν_0 and variance $2\nu_0$, compute the standardised statistic

$$z_i = \sqrt{T}\frac{(\bar{y}_i - \nu_0)}{\sqrt{2\nu_0}}, \qquad i = 1, 2, \cdots, 5000.$$

Plot the empirical distribution of z using a histogram and interpret its shape.

(c) Repeat parts (a) and (b) for $T = \{50, 100, 500\}$, and interpret the results.

(11) Central Limit Theorem – Student t Distribution

Program files   `prop_clt_student.*`

This exercise investigates the moment conditions required for the Lindeberg-Levy central limit theorem to hold when the population follows a Student t distribution.

(a) Generate 5000 samples of size $T = 10$ from the Student t distribution with $\nu = \{1, 2, 3\}$ degrees of freedom and for each draw compute the standardised statistic

$$z_i = \frac{\sqrt{T}\bar{y}_i}{\hat{\sigma}_i}, \qquad i = 1, 2, \cdots, 5000.$$

Plot the sampling distribution of z for each value of ν and interpret its shape.

(b) Repeat part (a) for samples of size $T = \{100, 1000\}$. Discuss whether the Lindeberg-Levy central limit theorem holds for each value of ν. *Hint: the Student t distribution with $\nu = 1$ degrees of freedom is the Cauchy distribution.*

(12) Edgeworth Expansions

Program files   `prop_edgeworth.*`

Assume that y_t is *iid* exponential with mean θ_0. Define the standardised statistic

$$z = \sqrt{T}\frac{(\hat{\theta} - \theta_0)}{\theta_0},$$

where $\widehat{\theta} = \bar{y}$ is the maximum likelihood estimator.

(a) For a sample of size $T = 5$, compute the Edgeworth, asymptotic and finite sample distribution functions of z at $s = \{-3, -2, \cdots, 3\}$.

(b) Repeat part (a) for $T = \{10, 100\}$.

(c) Discuss the ability of the Edgeworth expansion and the asymptotic distribution to approximate the finite sample distribution.

(13) Bias of the Sample Variance

Program files   prop_bias.*

This exercise demonstrates by simulation that the maximum likelihood estimator of the population variance of a normal distribution with unknown mean is biased.

(a) Generate 20000 samples of size $T = 5$ from a normal distribution with mean $\mu_0 = 1$ and variance $\sigma_0^2 = 2$. For each replication compute the maximum likelihood estimator of σ_0^2 and the unbiased estimator, respectively, as

$$\widehat{\sigma}_i^2 = \frac{1}{T} \sum_{t=1}^{T} (y_t - \bar{y}_i)^2, \qquad \widetilde{\sigma}_i^2 = \frac{1}{T-1} \sum_{t=1}^{T} (y_t - \bar{y}_i)^2 .$$

(b) Compute the average of the maximum likelihood estimates and the unbiased estimates, respectively, as

$$E\left[\widehat{\sigma}_T^2\right] \simeq \frac{1}{20000} \sum_{i=1}^{20000} \widehat{\sigma}_i^2, \qquad E\left[\widetilde{\sigma}_T^2\right] \simeq \frac{1}{20000} \sum_{i=1}^{20000} \widetilde{\sigma}_i^2 .$$

Compare the computed simulated expectations with the population value $\sigma_0^2 = 2$.

(c) Repeat parts (a) and (b) for $T = \{10, 50, 100, 500\}$. Hence show that the maximum likelihood estimator is asymptotically unbiased.

(d) Repeat parts (a) and (b) for known μ_0. Hence show that the maximum likelihood estimator of the population variance is now unbiased even in finite samples.

(14) Portfolio Diversification

Program files   prop_diversify.*
Data files   apple.csv, ford.csv, diversify.*

The data files contain daily share prices of Apple and Ford from 2 January 2001 to 6 August 2010, a total of $T = 2413$ observations.

(a) Compute the daily percentage returns on Apple, $y_{1,t}$, and Ford, $y_{2,t}$. Draw a scatterplot of the two returns and interpret the graph.

(b) Assume that the returns are *iid* from a bivariate normal distribution with means $\mu_1 = \mu_2 = 1$, variances $\sigma_1^2 = \sigma_2^2 = 4$, and correlation ρ. Plot the bivariate normal distribution for the following values of the correlation parameter

$$\rho = \{-0.8, -0.6, -0.4, -0.2, 0.0, 0.2, 0.4, 0.6, 0.8\}.$$

Interpret the shape of each distribution.
(c) Derive the maximum likelihood estimators of $\theta = \{\mu_1, \mu_2, \sigma_1^2, \sigma_2^2, \rho\}$.
(d) Use the data on returns to compute the maximum likelihood estimates.
(e) Let the return on a portfolio containing Apple and Ford be

$$r_t = w_1 y_{1,t} + w_2 y_{2,t},$$

in which w_1 and w_2 are the respective weights.
   (i) Derive an expression of the risk of the portfolio $\mathrm{var}(r_t)$.
   (ii) Derive expressions of the weights, w_1 and w_2, that minimise $\mathrm{var}(r_t)$.
   (iii) Use the sample moments in part (d) to estimate the optimal weights and the risk of the portfolio. Compare the estimate of $\mathrm{var}(r_t)$ with the individual sample variances.

(15) Bimodal Likelihood

Program files   `prop_bimodal.*`

(a) Simulate a sample of size $T = 4$ from a bivariate normal distribution with zero means, unit variances and correlation $\rho_0 = 0.6$. Plot the log-likelihood function

$$\ln L_T(\rho) = -\ln 2\pi - \frac{1}{2}\ln(1 - \rho^2)$$

$$-\frac{1}{2(1 - \rho^2)}\left(\frac{1}{T}\sum_{t=1}^{T} y_{1,t}^2 - 2\rho\frac{1}{T}\sum_{t=1}^{T} y_{1,t}y_{2,t} + \frac{1}{T}\sum_{t=1}^{T} y_{2,t}^2\right),$$

and the scaled gradient function

$$G_T(\rho) = \rho(1 - \rho^2) + (1 + \rho^2)\frac{1}{T}\sum_{t=1}^{T} y_{1,t}y_{2,t}$$

$$-\rho\left(\frac{1}{T}\sum_{t=1}^{T} y_{1,t}^2 + \frac{1}{T}\sum_{t=1}^{T} y_{2,t}^2\right),$$

for values of $\rho = \{-0.99, -0.98, \cdots, 0.99\}$. Interpret the result and compare the graphs of $\ln L_T(\rho)$ and $G_T(\rho)$ with Figure 2.9.
(b) Repeat part (a) for $T = \{10, 50, 100\}$, and compare the results with part (a) for the case of $T = 4$. Hence demonstrate that for the case of

multiple roots, the likelihood converges to a global maximum resulting in the maximum likelihood estimator being unique asymptotically (see Stuart, Ord and Arnold, 1999, pp50–52, for a more formal treatment of this property).

(16) Nonlinear Regression

Program files   `prop_nonlinear.*`

Consider the following regression model that is nonlinear in the parameters

$$y_t = \beta_0 + \beta_1 x_{1,t} + \beta_1^2 x_{2,t} + u_t, \qquad u_t \sim iid\ N(0, \sigma^2),$$

in which y_t is the dependent variable, $x_{1,t} \sim U(0, 1)$ and $x_{2,t} \sim U(0, 1)$ are the explanatory variables and the population parameters are $\theta_0 = \{\beta_0 = 2.5, \beta_1 = -1.0, \sigma^2 = 1.0\}$. The nonlinearity arises because the parameter on the variable $x_{1,t}$ is the square of the parameter on the variable $x_{2,t}$.

(a) Derive the log-likelihood function, $\ln L_T(\theta)$, and the gradient vector, $G_T(\theta)$.

(b) Simulate the model for samples of size $T = \{100, 500, 1000\}$ observations and use the simulated data to evaluate and plot $\ln L_T(\theta)$ and $G_T(\theta)$ for a grid of values for β_1. The remaining parameters should be set at the values $\beta_0 = 2.5$ and $\sigma^2 = 1.0$. Interpret the results.

3 Numerical Estimation Methods

3.1 Introduction

The maximum likelihood estimator is the solution of a set of equations obtained by evaluating the gradient of the log-likelihood function at zero. For many of the examples considered in the previous chapters, a closed-form solution is available. Typical examples consist of the sample mean, or some function of it, the sample variance and the least squares estimator. There are, however, many cases in which the specified model yields a likelihood function that does not admit closed-form solutions for the maximum likelihood estimators.

Example 3.1 Cauchy Distribution
Let $\{y_1, y_2, \cdots, y_T\}$ be T *iid* realised values from the Cauchy distribution

$$f(y_t; \theta) = \frac{1}{\pi} \frac{1}{1 + (y_t - \theta)^2},$$

in which θ is the unknown parameter. The log-likelihood function is

$$\ln L_T(\theta) = -\ln \pi - \frac{1}{T} \sum_{t=1}^{T} \ln \left[1 + (y_t - \theta)^2 \right],$$

resulting in the gradient

$$\frac{d \ln L_T(\theta)}{d\theta} = \frac{2}{T} \sum_{t=1}^{T} \frac{y_t - \theta}{1 + (y_t - \theta)^2}.$$

The maximum likelihood estimator, $\widehat{\theta}$, is the solution of

$$\frac{2}{T} \sum_{t=1}^{T} \frac{y_t - \widehat{\theta}}{1 + (y_t - \widehat{\theta})^2} = 0.$$

This is a nonlinear function of $\widehat{\theta}$ for which no analytical solution exists. □

To obtain the maximum likelihood estimator where no analytical solution is available, numerical optimisation algorithms must be used. These algorithms begin by assuming starting values for the unknown parameters and then proceed iteratively until a convergence criterion is satisfied. A general form for the kth iteration is

$$\theta_{(k)} = F(\theta_{(k-1)}),$$

where the form of the function $F(\cdot)$ is governed by the choice of the numerical algorithm. Convergence of the algorithm is achieved when the log-likelihood function cannot be further improved, a situation in which $\theta_{(k)} \simeq \theta_{(k-1)}$, resulting in $\theta_{(k)}$ being the maximum likelihood estimator of θ.

3.2   Newton Methods

From Chapter 1, the gradient and Hessian are defined, respectively, as

$$G_T(\theta) = \frac{\partial \ln L_T(\theta)}{\partial \theta} = \frac{1}{T} \sum_{t=1}^{T} g_t, \qquad H_T(\theta) = \frac{\partial^2 \ln L_T(\theta)}{\partial \theta \partial \theta'} = \frac{1}{T} \sum_{t=1}^{T} h_t.$$

A first-order Taylor series expansion of the gradient function around the true parameter vector θ_0 is

$$G_T(\theta) \simeq G_T(\theta_0) + H_T(\theta_0)(\theta - \theta_0), \tag{3.1}$$

where higher-order terms are excluded in the expansion and $G_T(\theta_0)$ and $H_T(\theta_0)$ are, respectively, the gradient and Hessian evaluated at the true parameter value, θ_0.

As the maximum likelihood estimator, $\widehat{\theta}$, is the solution to the equation $G_T(\widehat{\theta}) = 0$, the maximum likelihood estimator satisfies

$$G_T(\widehat{\theta}) = 0 = G_T(\theta_0) + H_T(\theta_0)(\widehat{\theta} - \theta_0), \tag{3.2}$$

where, for convenience, the equation is now written as an equality. This is a linear equation in $\widehat{\theta}$ with solution

$$\widehat{\theta} = \theta_0 - H_T^{-1}(\theta_0) G_T(\theta_0). \tag{3.3}$$

As it stands, this equation is of little practical use because it expresses the maximum likelihood estimator as a function of the unknown parameter that it seeks to estimate, namely θ_0. This suggests, however, that a natural way to proceed is to replace θ_0 with a starting value and use (3.3) as an updating scheme. This is indeed the basis of Newton methods. Three algorithms are discussed, differing only in the way that the Hessian, $H_T(\theta)$, is evaluated.

3.2.1 Newton-Raphson

Let $\theta_{(k)}$ be the value of the unknown parameters at the kth iteration. The Newton-Raphson algorithm is given by replacing θ_0 in (3.3) by $\theta_{(k-1)}$ to yield the updated parameter $\theta_{(k)}$ according to

$$\theta_{(k)} = \theta_{(k-1)} - H_{(k-1)}^{-1} G_{(k-1)},\qquad(3.4)$$

where

$$G_{(k)} = \left.\frac{\partial \ln L_T(\theta)}{\partial \theta}\right|_{\theta=\theta_{(k)}}, \qquad H_{(k)} = \left.\frac{\partial^2 \ln L_T(\theta)}{\partial \theta \, \partial \theta'}\right|_{\theta=\theta_{(k)}}.$$

The algorithm proceeds until $\theta_{(k)} \simeq \theta_{(k-1)}$, subject to some tolerance level, which is discussed in more detail later. From (3.4), convergence occurs when

$$\theta_{(k)} - \theta_{(k-1)} = -H_{(k-1)}^{-1} G_{(k-1)} \simeq 0,$$

which can only be satisfied if

$$G_{(k)} \simeq G_{(k-1)} \simeq 0,$$

because both $H_{(k-1)}^{-1}$ and $H_{(k)}^{-1}$ are negative definite. But this is exactly the condition that defines the maximum likelihood estimator, $\widehat{\theta}$ so that $\theta_{(k)} \simeq \widehat{\theta}$ at the final iteration.

To implement the Newton-Raphson algorithm, both the first and second derivatives of the log-likelihood function, $G(\cdot)$ and $H(\cdot)$, respectively, are needed at each iteration. The Newton-Raphson algorithm is used to estimate the parameter of an exponential distribution. As an analytical solution is available for this example, the accuracy and convergence properties of the numerical procedure can be assessed.

Example 3.2 Exponential Distribution: Newton-Raphson
   Let $y_t = \{3.5,\ 1.0,\ 1.5\}$ be *iid* drawings from the exponential distribution

$$f(y_t; \theta) = \frac{1}{\theta} \exp\left[-\frac{y_t}{\theta}\right],$$

in which $\theta > 0$. The log-likelihood function is

$$\ln L_T(\theta) = \frac{1}{T} \sum_{t=1}^{T} \ln f(y_t; \theta) = -\ln(\theta) - \frac{1}{\theta T} \sum_{t=1}^{T} y_t = -\ln(\theta) - \frac{2}{\theta}.$$

The first and second derivatives are, respectively,

$$G_T(\theta) = -\frac{1}{\theta} + \frac{1}{\theta^2 T} \sum_{t=1}^{T} y_t = -\frac{1}{\theta} + \frac{2}{\theta^2},$$

$$H_T(\theta) = \frac{1}{\theta^2} - \frac{2}{\theta^3 T} \sum_{t=1}^{T} y_t = \frac{1}{\theta^2} - \frac{4}{\theta^3}.$$

Setting $G_T(\widehat{\theta}) = 0$ gives the analytical solution

$$\widehat{\theta} = \frac{1}{T} \sum_{t=1}^{T} y_t = \frac{6}{3} = 2.$$

Let the starting value for the Newton-Raphson algorithm be $\theta_{(0)} = 1$. Then the starting values for the gradient and Hessian are, respectively,

$$G_{(0)} = -\frac{1}{1} + \frac{2}{1^2} = 1, \qquad H_{(0)} = \frac{1}{1^2} - \frac{4}{1^3} = -3.$$

The updated parameter value is computed using (3.4) and is given by

$$\theta_{(1)} = \theta_{(0)} - H_{(0)}^{-1} G_{(0)} = 1 - \left(-\frac{1}{3}\right) \times 1 = 1.333.$$

As $\theta_{(1)} \neq \theta_{(0)}$, the iterations continue. For the next iteration the gradient and Hessian are re-evaluated at $\theta_{(1)} = 1.333$ to give, respectively,

$$G_{(1)} = -\frac{1}{1.333} + \frac{2}{1.333^2} = 0.375, \quad H_{(1)} = \frac{1}{1.333^2} - \frac{4}{1.333^3} = -1.126,$$

yielding the updated value

$$\theta_{(2)} = \theta_{(1)} - H_{(1)}^{-1} G_{(1)} = 1.333 - \left(-\frac{1}{1.126}\right) \times 0.375 = 1.667.$$

As $G_{(1)} = 0.375 < G_{(0)} = 1$, the algorithm is converging to the maximum likelihood estimator where $G_{(k)} \simeq 0$. The calculations for successive iterations are reported in the first block of results in Table 3.1. Using a convergence tolerance of 0.00001, the Newton-Raphson algorithm converges in $k = 7$ iterations to $\widehat{\theta} = 2.0$, which is also the analytical solution.   □

3.2.2   Method of Scoring

The method of scoring uses the information matrix equality in equation (2.33) of Chapter 2 from which it follows that

$$I(\theta_0) = -E[h_t(\theta_0)].$$

By replacing the expectation by the sample average an estimate of $I(\theta_0)$ is the negative of the Hessian

$$-H_T(\theta_0) = -\frac{1}{T} \sum_{t=1}^{T} h_t(\theta_0),$$

which is used in the Newton-Raphson algorithm. This suggests that another variation of (3.3) is to replace $-H_T(\theta_0)$ by the information matrix evaluated at $\theta_{(k-1)}$. The iterative scheme of the method of scoring is

$$\theta_{(k)} = \theta_{(k-1)} + I_{(k-1)}^{-1} G_{(k-1)}, \tag{3.5}$$

where $I_{(k)} = E[h_t(\theta_{(k)})]$.

Example 3.3 Exponential Distribution: Method of Scoring

From Example 3.2 the Hessian at time t is

$$h_t(\theta) = \frac{1}{\theta^2} - \frac{2}{\theta^3} y_t.$$

The information matrix is then

$$I(\theta_0) = -E[h_t] = -E\left[\frac{1}{\theta_0^2} - \frac{2}{\theta_0^3} y_t\right] = -\frac{1}{\theta_0^2} + \frac{2}{\theta_0^3} E[y_t] = -\frac{1}{\theta_0^2} + \frac{2\theta_0}{\theta_0^3} = \frac{1}{\theta_0^2},$$

in which the result $E[y_t] = \theta_0$ for the exponential distribution is used. Evaluating the gradient and the information matrix at the starting value $\theta_{(0)} = 1$ gives, respectively,

$$G_{(0)} = -\frac{1}{1} + \frac{2}{1^2} = 1, \qquad I_{(0)} = \frac{1}{1^2} = 1.$$

The updated parameter value, computed using equation (3.5), is

$$\theta_{(1)} = \theta_{(0)} + I_{(0)}^{-1} G_{(0)} = 1 + \left(\frac{1}{1}\right) \times 1 = 2.$$

The sequence of iterations is in the second block of results in Table 3.1. For this algorithm, convergence is achieved in $k = 1$ iterations since $G_{(1)} = 0$ and $\theta_{(1)} = 2$, which is also the analytical solution. □

As demonstrated by Example 3.3, the method of scoring requires potentially fewer iterations than the Newton-Raphson algorithm to achieve convergence. This is because the scoring algorithm, by replacing the Hessian with the information matrix, uses more information about the structure of the model than does Newton-Raphson. However, for many econometric models the calculation of the information matrix can be difficult, making this algorithm problematic to implement in general.

Table 3.1. *Newton-Raphson, scoring and BHHH iterations to compute the maximum likelihood estimate of the parameter of the exponential distribution*

Iteration	$\theta_{(k-1)}$	$G_{(k-1)}$	$M_{(k-1)}$	$\ln L_{(k-1)}$	$\theta_{(k)}$
	Newton-Raphson: $M_{(k-1)} = H_{(k-1)}$				
k = 1	1.0000	1.0000	−3.0000	−2.0000	1.3333
k = 2	1.3333	0.3750	−1.1250	−1.7877	1.6667
k = 3	1.6667	0.1200	−0.5040	−1.7108	1.9048
k = 4	1.9048	0.0262	−0.3032	−1.6944	1.9913
k = 5	1.9913	0.0022	−0.2544	−1.6932	1.9999
k = 6	1.9999	0.0000	−0.2500	−1.6931	2.0000
k = 7	2.0000	0.0000	−0.2500	−1.6931	2.0000
	Scoring: $M_{(k-1)} = I_{(k-1)}$				
k = 1	1.0000	1.0000	1.0000	−2.0000	2.0000
k = 2	2.0000	0.0000	0.2500	−1.6931	2.0000
	BHHH: $M_{(k-1)} = J_{(k-1)}$				
k = 1	1.0000	1.0000	2.1667	−2.0000	1.4615
k = 2	1.4615	0.2521	0.3192	−1.7479	2.2512
k = 3	2.2512	−0.0496	0.0479	−1.6999	1.2161
k = 4	1.2161	0.5301	0.8145	−1.8403	1.8669
k = 5	1.8669	0.0382	0.0975	−1.6956	2.2586
k = 6	2.2586	−0.0507	0.0474	−1.7002	1.1892
k = 7	1.1892	0.5734	0.9121	−1.8551	1.8178

3.2.3   BHHH Algorithm

The BHHH algorithm (Berndt, Hall, Hall and Hausman, 1974) uses the information matrix equality in equation (2.33) to express the information matrix as

$$I(\theta_0) = J(\theta_0) = \mathrm{E}\left[g_t(\theta_0)g_t'(\theta_0)\right]. \tag{3.6}$$

Replacing the expectation by the sample average yields an alternative estimate of $I(\theta_0)$ given by

$$J_T(\theta_0) = \frac{1}{T}\sum_{t=1}^{T} g_t(\theta_0)g_t'(\theta_0), \tag{3.7}$$

which is the sample analogue of the outer product of gradients matrix. The BHHH algorithm is obtained by replacing $-H_T(\theta_0)$ in equation (3.3) by $J_T(\theta_0)$ evaluated at $\theta_{(k-1)}$ to give

$$\theta_{(k)} = \theta_{(k-1)} + J_{k-1}^{-1} G_{(k-1)}, \tag{3.8}$$

where

$$J_{(k)} = \frac{1}{T} \sum_{t=1}^{T} g_t(\theta_{(k)}) g_t'(\theta_{(k)}) \,.$$

Example 3.4 Exponential Distribution: BHHH

To estimate the parameter of the exponential distribution using the BHHH algorithm, the gradient must be evaluated at each observation. From Example 3.2 the gradient at time t is

$$g_t(\theta) = \frac{\partial \ln l_t}{\partial \theta} = -\frac{1}{\theta} + \frac{y_t}{\theta^2} \,.$$

The outer product of gradients matrix in equation (3.7) is

$$
\begin{aligned}
J_T(\theta) &= \frac{1}{3} \sum_{t=1}^{3} g_t g_t' = \frac{1}{3} \sum_{t=1}^{3} g_t^2 \\
&= \frac{1}{3} \left(-\frac{1}{\theta} + \frac{3.5}{\theta^2} \right)^2 + \frac{1}{3} \left(-\frac{1}{\theta} + \frac{1.0}{\theta^2} \right)^2 + \frac{1}{3} \left(-\frac{1}{\theta} + \frac{1.5}{\theta^2} \right)^2 \,.
\end{aligned}
$$

Using $\theta_{(0)} = 1$ as the starting value gives

$$
\begin{aligned}
J_{(0)} &= \frac{1}{3} \left(-\frac{1}{1} + \frac{3.5}{1^2} \right)^2 + \frac{1}{3} \left(-\frac{1}{1} + \frac{1.0}{1^2} \right)^2 + \frac{1}{3} \left(-\frac{1}{1} + \frac{1.5}{1^2} \right)^2 \\
&= \frac{2.5^2 + 0.0^2 + 0.5^2}{3} = 2.1667 \,.
\end{aligned}
$$

The gradient vector evaluated at $\theta_{(0)} = 1$ immediately follows as

$$G_{(0)} = \frac{1}{3} \sum_{t=1}^{3} g_t = \frac{2.5 + 0.0 + 0.5}{3} = 1.0 \,.$$

The updated parameter value, computed using equation (3.8), is

$$\theta_{(1)} = \theta_{(0)} + J_{(0)}^{-1} G_{(0)} = 1 + (2.1667)^{-1} \times 1 = 1.4615 \,.$$

The remaining iterations of the BHHH algorithm are contained in the third block of results in Table 3.1. Inspection of these results reveals that the algorithm has still not converged after $k = 7$ iterations with the estimate at this iteration being $\theta_{(7)} = 1.8178$. It is also apparent that successive values of the log-likelihood function at each iteration do not increase monotonically. For iteration $k = 2$, the log-likelihood is $\ln L_{(2)} = -1.6999$, but, for $k = 3$, it decreases to $\ln L_{(3)} = -1.8403$. This problem is addressed in Section 3.4 by using a line-search procedure during the iterations of the algorithm. $\square$

The BHHH algorithm only requires the computation of the gradient of the log-likelihood function and is therefore relatively easy to implement. A potential advantage of this algorithm is that the outer product of the gradients matrix is always guaranteed to be positive semi-definite. The cost of using this algorithm, however, is that it may require more iterations than either the Newton-Raphson or the scoring algorithms do, because information is lost due to the approximation of the information matrix by the outer product of the gradients matrix.

A useful way to think about the structure of the BHHH algorithm is as follows. Let the $(T \times K)$ matrix, X, and the $(T \times 1)$ vector, Y, be given by

$$X = \begin{bmatrix} \dfrac{\partial \ln l_1(\theta)}{\partial \theta_1} & \dfrac{\partial \ln l_1(\theta)}{\partial \theta_2} & \cdots & \dfrac{\partial \ln l_1(\theta)}{\partial \theta_K} \\[2ex] \dfrac{\partial \ln l_2(\theta)}{\partial \theta_1} & \dfrac{\partial \ln l_2(\theta)}{\partial \theta_2} & \cdots & \dfrac{\partial \ln l_2(\theta)}{\partial \theta_K} \\[2ex] \vdots & \vdots & \ddots & \vdots \\[2ex] \dfrac{\partial \ln l_T(\theta)}{\partial \theta_1} & \dfrac{\partial \ln l_T(\theta)}{\partial \theta_2} & \cdots & \dfrac{\partial \ln l_T(\theta)}{\partial \theta_K} \end{bmatrix} \, , \quad Y = \begin{bmatrix} 1 \\ 1 \\ \vdots \\ 1 \end{bmatrix} \, .$$

An iteration of the BHHH algorithm is now written as

$$\theta_{(k)} = \theta_{(k-1)} + (X'_{(k-1)} X_{(k-1)})^{-1} X'_{(k-1)} Y \, , \tag{3.9}$$

where

$$J_{(k-1)} = \frac{1}{T} X'_{(k-1)} X_{(k-1)} \, , \qquad G_{(k-1)} = \frac{1}{T} X'_{(k-1)} Y \, .$$

The second term on the right-hand side of equation (3.9) represents an ordinary least squares regression, where the dependent variable Y is regressed on the explanatory variables given by the matrix of gradients, $X_{(k-1)}$, evaluated at $\theta_{(k-1)}$.

3.2.4 Comparative Examples

To compare the Newton-Raphson, scoring and BHHH algorithms, some additional examples are now presented.

Example 3.5 Cauchy Distribution

Let $\{y_1, y_2, \cdots, y_T\}$ be T *iid* realised values from the Cauchy distribution. From Example 3.1, the log-likelihood function is

$$\ln L_T(\theta) = -\ln \pi - \frac{1}{T} \sum_{t=1}^{T} \ln \left[1 + (y_t - \theta)^2 \right] \, .$$

Define

$$G_T(\theta) = \frac{2}{T} \sum_{t=1}^{T} \left[\frac{y_t - \theta}{1 + (y_t - \theta)^2} \right]$$

$$H_T(\theta) = \frac{2}{T} \sum_{t=1}^{T} \frac{(y_t - \theta)^2 - 1}{(1 + (y_t - \theta)^2)^2}$$

$$J_T(\theta) = \frac{4}{T} \sum_{t=1}^{T} \frac{(y_t - \theta)^2}{(1 + (y_t - \theta)^2)^2}$$

$$I(\theta) = - \int_{-\infty}^{\infty} \frac{2}{T} \sum_{t=1}^{T} \frac{(y - \theta)^2 - 1}{(1 + (y - \theta)^2)^2} f(y) dy = \frac{1}{2},$$

where the information matrix is as given by Kendall and Stuart (1973, Vol. 2). Given the starting value, $\theta_{(0)}$, the first iteration of the Newton-Raphson, scoring and BHHH algorithms are, respectively,

$$\theta_{(1)} = \theta_{(0)} - \left[\frac{2}{T} \sum_{t=1}^{T} \frac{(y_t - \theta_{(0)})^2 - 1}{(1 + (y_t - \theta_{(0)})^2)^2} \right]^{-1} \left[\frac{2}{T} \sum_{t=1}^{T} \frac{y_t - \theta_{(0)}}{1 + (y_t - \theta_{(0)})^2} \right]$$

$$\theta_{(1)} = \theta_{(0)} + \frac{4}{T} \sum_{t=1}^{T} \frac{y_t - \theta_{(0)}}{(1 + (y_t - \theta_{(0)})^2)}$$

$$\theta_{(1)} = \theta_{(0)} + \frac{1}{2} \left[\frac{1}{T} \sum_{t=1}^{T} \frac{(y_t - \theta_{(0)})^2}{(1 + (y_t - \theta_{(0)})^2)^2} \right]^{-1} \left[\frac{1}{T} \sum_{t=1}^{T} \frac{y_t - \theta_{(0)}}{(1 + (y_t - \theta_{(0)})^2)} \right].$$

$\square$

Example 3.6 Weibull Distribution
Consider $T = 20$ independent realisations

$$y_t = \{0.293, 0.589, 1.374, 0.954, 0.608, 1.199, 1.464, 0.383, 1.743, 0.022$$
$$0.719, 0.949, 1.888, 0.754, 0.873, 0.515, 1.049, 1.506, 1.090, 1.644\},$$

drawn from the Weibull distribution

$$f(y_t; \theta) = \alpha \beta y_t^{\beta - 1} \exp\left[-\alpha y_t^{\beta} \right],$$

with unknown parameters $\theta = \{\alpha, \beta\}$. The log-likelihood function is

$$\ln L_T(\alpha, \beta) = \ln \alpha + \ln \beta + (\beta - 1) \frac{1}{T} \sum_{t=1}^{T} \ln y_t - \alpha \frac{1}{T} \sum_{t=1}^{T} (y_t)^{\beta}.$$

Define

$$
G_T(\theta) =
\begin{bmatrix}
\dfrac{1}{\alpha} - \dfrac{1}{T} \sum_{t=1}^{T} y_t^{\beta} \\[2mm]
\dfrac{1}{\beta} + \dfrac{1}{T} \sum_{t=1}^{T} \ln y_t - \alpha \dfrac{1}{T} \sum_{t=1}^{T} (\ln y_t) y_t^{\beta}
\end{bmatrix}
$$

$$
H_T(\theta) =
\begin{bmatrix}
-\dfrac{1}{\alpha^2} & -\dfrac{1}{T} \sum_{t=1}^{T} (\ln y_t) y_t^{\beta} \\[2mm]
-\dfrac{1}{T} \sum_{t=1}^{T} (\ln y_t) y_t^{\beta} & -\dfrac{1}{\beta^2} - \alpha \dfrac{1}{T} \sum_{t=1}^{T} (\ln y_t)^2 y_t^{\beta}
\end{bmatrix}
$$

$$
J_T(\theta) =
\begin{bmatrix}
\dfrac{1}{T} \sum_{t=1}^{T} \left(\dfrac{1}{\alpha} - y_t^{\beta} \right)^2 & \dfrac{1}{T} \sum_{t=1}^{T} \left(\dfrac{1}{\alpha} - y_t^{\beta} \right) g_{2,t} \\[2mm]
\dfrac{1}{T} \sum_{t=1}^{T} g_{2,t} \left(\dfrac{1}{\alpha} - y_t^{\beta} \right) & \dfrac{1}{T} \sum_{t=1}^{T} g_{2,t}^2
\end{bmatrix},
$$

in which $g_{2,t} = \beta^{-1} + \ln y_t - \alpha (\ln y_t) y_t^{\beta}$. Only the iterations of the Newton-Raphson and BHHH algorithms are presented because in this case the information matrix is intractable. Choosing the starting values $\theta_{(0)} = \{0.5, 1.5\}$ yields a log-likelihood function value of $\ln L_{(0)} = -0.959$ and

$$
G_{(0)} = \begin{bmatrix} 0.931 \\ 0.280 \end{bmatrix}, \quad
H_{(0)} = \begin{bmatrix} -4.000 & -0.228 \\ -0.228 & -0.547 \end{bmatrix}, \quad
J_{(0)} = \begin{bmatrix} 1.403 & -0.068 \\ -0.068 & 0.800 \end{bmatrix}.
$$

The Newton-Raphson and the BHHH updates are, respectively,

$$
\begin{bmatrix} \alpha_{(1)} \\ \beta_{(1)} \end{bmatrix} =
\begin{bmatrix} 0.5 \\ 1.5 \end{bmatrix} -
\begin{bmatrix} -4.000 & -0.228 \\ -0.228 & -0.547 \end{bmatrix}^{-1}
\begin{bmatrix} 0.931 \\ 0.280 \end{bmatrix} =
\begin{bmatrix} 0.708 \\ 1.925 \end{bmatrix}
$$

$$
\begin{bmatrix} \alpha_{(1)} \\ \beta_{(1)} \end{bmatrix} =
\begin{bmatrix} 0.5 \\ 1.5 \end{bmatrix} +
\begin{bmatrix} 1.403 & -0.068 \\ -0.068 & 0.800 \end{bmatrix}^{-1}
\begin{bmatrix} 0.931 \\ 0.280 \end{bmatrix} =
\begin{bmatrix} 1.183 \\ 1.908 \end{bmatrix}.
$$

Evaluating the log-likelihood function at the updated parameter estimates gives $\ln L_{(1)} = -0.782$ for Newton-Raphson and $\ln L_{(1)} = -0.829$ for BHHH. Both algorithms, therefore, show an improvement in the value of the log-likelihood function after one iteration. □

3.3 Quasi-Newton Methods

The distinguishing feature of the Newton-Raphson algorithm is that it computes the Hessian directly. An alternative approach is to build up an estimate of the Hessian at each iteration, starting from an initial estimate known to be negative definite, usually the negative of the identity matrix. This type of algorithm is known as quasi-Newton. The general form for the updating sequence of the Hessian is

$$H_{(k)} = H_{(k-1)} + U_{(k-1)}, \qquad (3.10)$$

where $H_{(k)}$ is the estimate of the Hessian at the kth iteration and $U_{(k)}$ is an update matrix. Quasi-Newton algorithms differ only in their choice of this update matrix. One of the more important variants is the BFGS algorithm (Broyden, 1970; Fletcher, 1970; Goldfarb, 1970; Shanno, 1970) where the updating matrix $U_{(k-1)}$ in equation (3.10) is

$$U_{(k-1)} = -\frac{H_{(k-1)}\Delta_\theta\Delta_G' + \Delta_G\Delta_\theta' H_{(k-1)}}{\Delta_G'\Delta_\theta} + \left(1 + \frac{\Delta_\theta' H_{(k-1)}\Delta_\theta}{\Delta_G'\Delta_\theta}\right)\frac{\Delta_G\Delta_G'}{\Delta_G'\Delta_\theta},$$

in which

$$\Delta_\theta = \theta_{(k)} - \theta_{(k-1)}, \qquad \Delta_G = G_{(k)} - G_{(k-1)},$$

represent the changes in the parameter values and the gradients between iterations, respectively.

In the case where all terms are scalars, the BFGS scheme for updating the Hessian reduces to

$$U_{(k-1)} = -2H_{(k-1)} + \left(1 + \frac{\Delta_\theta H_{(k-1)}}{\Delta_G}\right)\frac{\Delta_G}{\Delta_\theta},$$

so that the approximation to the Hessian in equation (3.10) is

$$H_{(k)} = H_{(k-1)} - 2H_{(k-1)} + \left(1 + \frac{\Delta_\theta H_{(k-1)}}{\Delta_G}\right)\frac{\Delta_G}{\Delta_\theta} = \frac{\Delta_G}{\Delta_\theta} = \frac{G_{(k)} - G_{(k-1)}}{\theta_{(k)} - \theta_{(k-1)}}.$$

This equation represents a numerical approximation to the first derivative of the gradient based on a step length equal to the change in θ across iterations (see Section 3.7.4). For the early iterations of the BFGS algorithm, the numerical approximation is expected to be crude because the size of the step, Δ_θ, is potentially large. As the iterations progress, this step interval diminishes, resulting in an improvement in the accuracy of the numerical derivatives as the algorithm approaches the maximum likelihood estimate.

Example 3.7 Exponential Distribution Using BFGS

Continuing the example of the exponential distribution, let the initial value of the Hessian be $H_{(0)} = -1$, and the starting value of the parameter be $\theta_{(0)} = 1.5$. The gradient at $\theta_{(0)}$ is

$$G_{(0)} = -\frac{1}{1.5} + \frac{2}{1.5^2} = 0.2222,$$

and the updated parameter value is

$$\theta_{(1)} = \theta_{(0)} - H_{(0)}^{-1}G_{(0)} = 1.5 - (-1) \times 0.2222 = 1.7222.$$

Table 3.2. *Demonstration of the use of the BFGS algorithm to compute the maximum likelihood estimate of the parameter of the exponential distribution*

Iteration	$\theta_{(k-1)}$	$G_{(k-1)}$	$H_{(k-1)}$	$\ln L_{(k-1)}$	$\theta_{(k)}$
$k=1$	1.5000	0.2222	-1.0000	-1.7388	1.7222
$k=2$	1.7222	0.0937	-0.5786	-1.7049	1.8841
$k=3$	1.8841	0.0327	-0.3768	-1.6950	1.9707
$k=4$	1.9707	0.0075	-0.2899	-1.6933	1.9967
$k=5$	1.9967	0.0008	-0.2583	-1.6931	1.9999
$k=6$	1.9999	0.0000	-0.2508	-1.6931	2.0000
$k=7$	2.0000	0.0000	-0.2500	-1.6931	2.0000

The gradient evaluated at $\theta_{(1)}$ is

$$G_{(1)} = -\frac{1}{1.7222} + \frac{2}{1.7222^2} = 0.0937 \,,$$

and

$$\Delta_\theta = \theta_{(1)} - \theta_{(0)} = 1.7222 - 1.5 = 0.2222$$
$$\Delta_G = G_{(1)} - G_{(0)} = 0.0937 - 0.2222 = -0.1285 \,.$$

The updated value of the Hessian is

$$H_{(1)} = \frac{G_{(1)} - G_{(0)}}{\theta_{(1)} - \theta_{(0)}} = -\frac{0.1285}{0.2222} = -0.5786 \,,$$

so that for iteration $k = 2$

$$\theta_{(2)} = \theta_{(1)} - H_{(1)}^{-1} G_{(1)} = 1.7222 - (-0.5786)^{-1} \times 0.0937 = 1.8841.$$

The remaining iterations are given in Table 3.2. By iteration $k = 6$, the algorithm has converged to the analytical solution $\widehat{\theta} = 2$. Moreover, the computed value of the Hessian using the BFGS updating algorithm is equal to its analytical solution of -0.75.   □

3.4   Line Searching

One problem with the simple updating scheme in equation (3.3) is that the updated parameter estimates are not guaranteed to improve the log-likelihood, as in Example 3.4. To ensure that the log-likelihood function increases at each iteration, the algorithm is now augmented by a parameter, λ, that controls the size of updating at each step according to

$$\theta_{(k)} = \theta_{(k-1)} - \lambda H_{(k-1)}^{-1} G_{(k-1)} \,, \qquad 0 \leq \lambda \leq 1. \tag{3.11}$$

For $\lambda = 1$, the full step is taken so updating is as before; for smaller values of λ, updating is not based on the full step. Determining the optimal value of λ at each iteration is a one-dimensional optimisation problem known as line searching.

The simplest way to choose λ is to perform a coarse grid search over possible values for λ known as squeezing. Potential choices of λ follow the order

$$\lambda = 1, \lambda = \frac{1}{2}, \lambda = \frac{1}{3}, \lambda = \frac{1}{4}, \cdots$$

The strategy is to calculate $\theta_{(k)}$ for $\lambda = 1$ and check to see if $\ln L_{(k)} > \ln L_{(k-1)}$. If this condition is not satisfied, choose $\lambda = 1/2$ and test to see if the log-likelihood function improves. If it does not, then choose $\lambda = 1/3$ and repeat the function evaluation. Once a value of λ is chosen and an updated parameter value is computed, the procedure begins again at the next step with $\lambda = 1$.

Example 3.8 BHHH with Squeezing

In this example, the convergence problems experienced by the BHHH algorithm in Example 3.4 and shown in Table 3.1 are solved by allowing for squeezing. Inspection of Table 3.1 shows that for the simple BHHH algorithm, at iteration $k = 3$, the value of θ changes from $\theta_{(2)} = 2.2512$ to $\theta_{(3)} = 1.2161$ with the value of the log-likelihood function falling from $\ln L_{(2)} = -1.6999$ to $\ln L_{(3)} = -1.8403$. Now squeeze the step interval by $\lambda = 1/2$ so that the updated value of θ at the third iteration is

$$\theta_{(3)} = \theta_{(2)} + \frac{1}{2} J_{(2)}^{-1} G_{(2)} = 2.2512 + \frac{1}{2} \times (0.0479)^{-1}(-0.0496) = 1.7335 .$$

Evaluating the log-likelihood function at the new value for $\theta_{(3)}$ gives

$$\ln L_{(3)}(\lambda = 1/2) = -\ln(1.7335) - \frac{2}{1.7335} = -1.7039 ,$$

which represents an improvement on -1.8403, but is still lower than $\ln L_{(2)} = -1.6999$.

By again squeezing the step interval $\lambda = 1/3$, the updated value of θ is

$$\theta_{(3)} = \theta_{(2)} + \frac{1}{3} J_{(2)}^{-1} G_{(2)} = 2.2512 + \frac{1}{3} \times (0.0479)^{-1}(-0.0496) = 1.9061 .$$

Evaluating the log-likelihood function at this value gives

$$\ln L_{(3)}(\lambda = 1/3) = -\ln(1.9061) - \frac{2}{1.9061} = -1.6943 .$$

As this value is an improvement on $\ln L_{(2)} = -1.6999$, the value of θ at the third iteration is taken to be $\theta_{(3)} = 1.9061$. Inspection of the log-likelihood function at each iteration in Table 3.3 shows that the improvement in the log-likelihood function is now monotonic. $\square$

Table 3.3. *Demonstration of the use of the BHHH algorithm with squeezing to compute the maximum likelihood estimate of the parameter of the exponential distribution*

Iteration	$\theta_{(k-1)}$	$G_{(k-1)}$	$J_{(k-1)}$	$\ln L_{(k-1)}$	$\theta_{(k)}$
$k=1$	1.0000	1.0000	2.1667	-1.7479	1.4615
$k=2$	1.4615	0.2521	0.3192	-1.6999	2.2512
$k=3$	2.2512	-0.0496	0.0479	-1.6943	1.9061
$k=4$	1.9061	0.0258	0.0890	-1.6935	2.0512
$k=5$	2.0512	-0.0122	0.0661	-1.6934	1.9591
$k=6$	1.9591	0.0107	0.0793	-1.6932	2.0263
$k=7$	2.0263	-0.0064	0.0692	-1.6932	1.9801
$k=8$	1.9801	0.0051	0.0759	-1.6932	2.0136
$k=9$	2.0136	-0.0033	0.0710	-1.6932	1.9900
$k=10$	1.9900	0.0025	0.0744	-1.6932	2.0070

3.5   Optimisation Based on Function Evaluation

Practical optimisation problems frequently generate log-likelihood functions with irregular surfaces. In particular, if the gradient is nearly flat in several dimensions, numerical errors can cause a gradient algorithm to misbehave. Consequently, many iterative algorithms are based solely on function evaluation, including the simplex method of Nelder and Mead (1965) and other more sophisticated schemes such as simulated annealing and genetic search algorithms. These procedures are all fairly robust, but they are more inefficient than gradient-based methods and normally require many more function evaluations to locate the optimum. Because of its popularity in practical work and its simplicity, the simplex algorithm is only briefly described here. For a more detailed account, see Gill, Murray and Wright (1981). This algorithm is usually presented in terms of function minimisation rather than the maximising framework adopted in this chapter. This situation is easily accommodated by recognising that maximising the log-likelihood function with respect to θ is identical to minimising the negative log-likelihood function with respect to θ.

The simplex algorithm employs a simple sequence of moves based solely on function evaluations. Consider the negative log-likelihood function $-\ln L_T(\theta)$, which is to be minimised with respect to the parameter vector θ. The algorithm is initialised by evaluating the function for $n+1$ different starting choices, in which $n = \dim(\theta)$, and the function values are ordered so that $-\ln L(\theta_{n+1})$ is the current worst estimate and $-\ln L(\theta_1)$ is the best current estimate, that is $-\ln L(\theta_{n+1}) \geq -\ln L(\theta_n) \geq \cdots \geq -\ln L(\theta_1)$. Define

$$\bar{\theta} = \frac{1}{n} \sum_{i=1}^{n} \theta_i \,,$$

as the mean (centroid) of the best n vertices, $(\theta_1, \theta_2 \cdots, \theta_n)$. In a two-dimensional problem, $\overline{\theta}$ is the midpoint of the line joining the two best vertices of the current simplex. The basic iteration of the simplex algorithm consists of the following sequence of steps.

Reflect: Reflect the worst vertex through the opposite face of the simplex

$$\theta_r = \overline{\theta} + \alpha(\overline{\theta} - \theta_{n+1}), \qquad \alpha > 0.$$

If the reflection is successful, $-\ln L(\theta_r) < -\ln L(\theta_n)$, start the next iteration by replacing θ_{n+1} with θ_r.

Expand: If θ_r is also better than θ_1, $-\ln L(\theta_r) < -\ln L(\theta_1)$, compute

$$\theta_e = \overline{\theta} + \beta(\theta_r - \overline{\theta}), \qquad \beta > 1.$$

If $-\ln L(\theta_e) < -\ln L(\theta_r)$, start the next iteration by replacing θ_{n+1} with θ_e.

Contract: If θ_r is not successful, $-\ln L(\theta_r) > -\ln L(\theta_n)$, contract the simplex as follows

$$\theta_c = \begin{cases} \overline{\theta} + \gamma(\theta_r - \overline{\theta}) & \text{if} \quad -\ln L(\theta_r) < -\ln L(\theta_{n+1}) \\ \overline{\theta} + \gamma(\theta_{n+1} - \overline{\theta}) & \text{if} \quad -\ln L(\theta_r) \geq -\ln L(\theta_{n+1}), \end{cases}$$

for $0 < \gamma < 1$.

Shrink: If the contraction is not successful, shrink the vertices of the simplex half-way toward the current best point and start the next iteration.

To make the simplex algorithm operational, values for the reflection, α, expansion, β, and contraction, γ, parameters are required. Common choices of these parameters are $\alpha = 1$, $\beta = 2$ and $\gamma = 0.5$ (see, for example, Gill, Murray and Wright, 1981).

3.6 Computing Standard Errors

From Chapter 2, the asymptotic distribution of the maximum likelihood estimator is

$$\sqrt{T}(\hat{\theta} - \theta_0) \xrightarrow{d} N(0, I^{-1}(\theta_0)).$$

The asymptotic covariance matrix of the maximum likelihood estimator is estimated by replacing θ_0 by $\hat{\theta}$ and inverting the information matrix

$$\hat{\Omega} = I^{-1}(\hat{\theta}). \tag{3.12}$$

In most practical situations, the information matrix is not easily evaluated. A more common approach, therefore, is simply to use the negative of the inverse of the Hessian evaluated at $\hat{\theta}$

$$\hat{\Omega} = -H_T^{-1}(\hat{\theta}). \tag{3.13}$$

A popular alternative is to use the outer product of gradients matrix, $J_T(\widehat{\theta})$ from equation (3.7), instead of the negative of the Hessian

$$\widehat{\Omega} = J_T^{-1}(\widehat{\theta}).$$
(3.14)

Standard errors of $\widehat{\theta}$, denoted se$(\widehat{\theta})$, are computed as the square roots of the diagonal elements of the normalised covariance matrix

$$\text{cov}(\widehat{\theta}) = \frac{1}{T}\widehat{\Omega}.$$
(3.15)

Example 3.9 Exponential Distribution Standard Errors
The values of the Hessian and the information matrix, taken from Table 3.1, and the outer product of gradients matrix, taken from Table 3.3, are given by

$$H_T(\widehat{\theta}) = -0.250, \quad I(\widehat{\theta}) = 0.250, \quad J_T(\widehat{\theta}) = 0.074,$$

respectively. As $T = 3$ the standard errors are

Hessian : $se(\widehat{\theta}) = \sqrt{-\dfrac{1}{T}H_T^{-1}(\widehat{\theta})} = \sqrt{-\tfrac{1}{3}(-0.250)^{-1}} = 1.547$

Information : $se(\widehat{\theta}) = \sqrt{\dfrac{1}{T}I^{-1}(\widehat{\theta})} = \sqrt{\tfrac{1}{3}(0.250)^{-1}} = 1.547$

Outer Product : $se(\widehat{\theta}) = \sqrt{\dfrac{1}{T}J_T^{-1}(\widehat{\theta})} = \sqrt{\tfrac{1}{3}(0.074)^{-1}} = 2.122.$

The standard errors based on the Hessian and information matrices yield the same values, while the estimate based on the outer product of gradients matrix is nearly 40% larger. One reason for this difference is that the outer product of the gradients matrix may not always provide a good approximation to the information matrix. Another reason is that the information and outer product of the gradients matrices may not converge to the same value as T increases. This occurs when the distribution used to construct the log-likelihood function is misspecified (see Chapter 9). □

Estimating the covariance matrix of a nonlinear function of the maximum likelihood estimators, say $C(\theta)$, is a situation that often arises in practice. There are two approaches to dealing with this problem. The first approach, known as the substitution method, simply imposes the nonlinearity and then uses the constrained log-likelihood function to compute standard errors. The second approach, called the delta method, uses a mean value expansion of $C(\widehat{\theta})$ around the true parameter θ_0

$$C(\widehat{\theta}) = C(\theta_0) + D(\theta^*)(\widehat{\theta} - \theta_0),$$

in which

$$D(\theta) = \frac{\partial C(\theta)}{\partial \theta'},$$

and θ^* is an intermediate value between $\widehat{\theta}$ and θ_0. As $T \to \infty$ the mean value expansion gives

$$\sqrt{T}(C(\widehat{\theta}) - C(\theta_0)) = D(\theta^*)\sqrt{T}(\widehat{\theta} - \theta_0)$$
$$\xrightarrow{d} D(\theta_0) \times N(0, I(\theta_0)^{-1})$$
$$= N(0, D(\theta_0)I(\theta_0)^{-1}D(\theta_0)'),$$

or

$$C(\widehat{\theta}) \overset{a}{\sim} N(C(\theta_0), \frac{1}{T}D(\theta_0)I^{-1}(\theta_0)D(\theta_0)'),$$

from which it follows that

$$\text{cov}(C(\widehat{\theta})) = \frac{1}{T}D(\theta_0)I^{-1}(\theta_0)D(\theta_0)' = D(\theta_0)\text{cov}(\theta_0)D(\theta_0)'.$$

Standard errors are computed by taking the square roots of the diagonal elements of this matrix with θ_0 evaluated at $\widehat{\theta}$. This involves replacing $D(\theta_0)$ with $D(\widehat{\theta})$ and $I^{-1}(\theta_0)$ with $\widehat{\Omega}$ from any of equations (3.12), (3.13) or (3.14).

Example 3.10 Standard Errors of Nonlinear Functions

Consider the problem of finding the standard error for $\overline{y}^2$ where observations are drawn from a normal distribution with known variance σ_0^2.

(1) Substitution Method

Consider the log-likelihood function for the unconstrained problem

$$\ln L_T(\theta) = -\frac{1}{2}\ln(2\pi) - \frac{1}{2}\ln(\sigma_0^2) - \frac{1}{2\sigma_0^2 T}\sum_{t=1}^{T}(y_t - \theta)^2.$$

Now define $\psi = \theta^2$ so that the constrained log-likelihood function is

$$\ln L_T(\psi) = -\frac{1}{2}\ln(2\pi) - \frac{1}{2}\ln(\sigma_0^2) - \frac{1}{2\sigma_0^2 T}\sum_{t=1}^{T}(y_t - \psi^{1/2})^2.$$

The first and second derivatives are

$$\frac{d \ln L_T(\psi)}{d\psi} = \frac{1}{2\sigma_0^2 T}\sum_{t=1}^{T}(y_t - \psi^{1/2})\psi^{-1/2}$$

$$\frac{d^2 \ln L_T(\psi)}{d\psi^2} = -\frac{1}{2\sigma_0^2 T}\sum_{t=1}^{T}\left(\frac{1}{2\psi} + (y_t - \psi^{1/2})\frac{1}{2}\psi^{-3/2}\right).$$

Recognising that $E[y_t - \psi_0^{1/2}] = 0$, the information matrix is

$$I(\psi_0) = -E\left[\frac{d^2 \ln l_t}{d\psi^2}\right] = \frac{1}{2\sigma_0^2}\frac{1}{2\psi_0} = \frac{1}{4\sigma_0^4\psi_0} = \frac{1}{4\sigma_0^2\theta_0^2}.$$

The standard error with θ_0 evaluated at $\widehat{\theta}$ is then

$$\text{se}(\widehat{\psi}) = \sqrt{\frac{1}{T}I^{-1}(\widehat{\theta})} = \sqrt{\frac{4\sigma_0^2\widehat{\theta}^2}{T}} .$$

(2) *Delta Method*

For a normal distribution, the variance of the maximum likelihood estimator $\widehat{\theta} = \bar{y}$ is σ_0^2/T. Define $C(\theta) = \theta^2$ so that $D(\theta) = 2\theta$ and $D(\theta_0) = 2\theta_0$. Evaluating $\text{var}(\theta_0)$ and $D(\theta_0)$ at $\widehat{\theta}$ yields the standard error

$$\text{se}(\widehat{\psi}) = \sqrt{D(\widehat{\theta})^2\text{var}(\widehat{\theta})} = \sqrt{\frac{(2\widehat{\theta})^2\sigma_0^2}{T}} = \sqrt{\frac{4\sigma_0^2\widehat{\theta}^2}{T}} ,$$

which equals the variance obtained using the substitution method.   □

3.7   Hints for Practical Optimisation

This section provides an eclectic collection of strategies that may be used in the implementation of the optimisation methods discussed previously.

3.7.1   *Concentrating the Likelihood*

For certain problems, the dimension of the parameter vector to be estimated may be reduced. Such a reduction is known as concentrating the likelihood function and it arises when the gradient can be rearranged to express an unknown parameter as a function of another unknown parameter.

Consider a log-likelihood function that is a function of two unknown parameter vectors $\theta = \{\theta_1, \theta_2\}$, with dimensions $\dim(\theta_1) = K_1$ and $\dim(\theta_2) = K_2$, respectively. The first-order conditions to find the maximum likelihood estimators are

$$\frac{\partial \ln L_T(\theta)}{\partial \theta_1}\bigg|_{\theta=\widehat{\theta}} = 0, \qquad \frac{\partial \ln L_T(\theta)}{\partial \theta_2}\bigg|_{\theta=\widehat{\theta}} = 0,$$

which is a nonlinear system of $K_1 + K_2$ equations in $K_1 + K_2$ unknowns. If it is possible to write

$$\widehat{\theta}_2 = g(\widehat{\theta}_1), \tag{3.16}$$

then the problem is reduced to a K_1 dimensional problem. The log-likelihood function is now maximised with respect to θ_1 to yield $\widehat{\theta}_1$. Once the algorithm has converged, $\widehat{\theta}_1$ is substituted into (3.16) to yield $\widehat{\theta}_2$. The estimator of θ_2 is a maximum likelihood estimator because of the invariance property of maximum likelihood estimators discussed in Chapter 2. Standard errors are obtained from evaluating the full log-likelihood function containing all parameters. An alternative way of reducing the dimension of the problem is to compute the profile log-likelihood function (see Exercise 9).

Example 3.11 Weibull Distribution

Let $y_t = \{y_1, y_2, \ldots, y_T\}$ be *iid* observations drawn from the Weibull distribution given by

$$f(y_t; \alpha, \beta) = \beta \alpha y_t^{\beta-1} \exp(-\alpha y_t^{\beta}).$$

The log-likelihood function is

$$\ln L_T(\theta) = \ln \alpha + \ln \beta + (\beta - 1)\frac{1}{T} \sum_{t=1}^{T} \ln y_t - \alpha \frac{1}{T} \sum_{t=1}^{T} y_t^{\beta},$$

and the unknown parameters are $\theta = \{\alpha, \beta\}$. The first-order conditions are

$$0 = \frac{1}{\widehat{\alpha}} - \frac{1}{T} \sum_{t=1}^{T} y_t^{\widehat{\beta}}$$

$$0 = \frac{1}{\widehat{\beta}} + \frac{1}{T} \sum_{t=1}^{T} \ln y_t - \widehat{\alpha} \frac{1}{T} \sum_{t=1}^{T} (\ln y_t) y_t^{\widehat{\beta}},$$

which are two nonlinear equations in $\widehat{\theta} = \{\widehat{\alpha}, \widehat{\beta}\}$. The first equation gives

$$\widehat{\alpha} = \frac{T}{\sum_{t=1}^{T} y_t^{\widehat{\beta}}},$$

which is used to substitute for $\widehat{\alpha}$ in the equation for $\widehat{\beta}$. The maximum likelihood estimate for $\widehat{\beta}$ is then found using numerical methods with $\widehat{\alpha}$ evaluated at the last step. □

3.7.2 Parameter Constraints

In some econometric applications, the values of the parameters need to be constrained to lie within certain intervals. Some examples are as follows: an estimate of the variance is required to be positive ($\theta > 0$); the marginal propensity to consume is constrained to be positive but less than unity ($0 < \theta < 1$); for a MA(1) process to be invertible, the moving average parameter must lie within the unit interval ($-1 < \theta < 1$); and the degrees of freedom parameter in the Student t distribution must be greater than two, to ensure that the variance of the distribution exists.

Consider the case of estimating a single parameter $\theta \in (a, b)$. The approach is to transform the parameter θ by means of a nonlinear bijective (one-to-one) mapping, $\phi = c(\theta)$, between the constrained interval (a, b) and the real line. Thus each and every value of ϕ corresponds to a unique value of θ, satisfying

Table 3.4. *Some useful transformations for imposing constraints on θ*

Constraint	Transform $\phi = c(\theta)$	Inverse Transform $\theta = c^{-1}(\phi)$	Jacobian $dc(\theta)/d\theta$
$(0, \infty)$	$\phi = \ln\theta$	$\theta = e^{\phi}$	$\dfrac{1}{\theta}$
$(-\infty, 0)$	$\phi = \ln(-\theta)$	$\theta = -e^{\phi}$	$\dfrac{1}{\theta}$
$(0, 1)$	$\phi = \ln\left(\dfrac{\theta}{1-\theta}\right)$	$\theta = \dfrac{1}{1+e^{-\phi}}$	$\dfrac{1}{\theta(1-\theta)}$
$(0, b)$	$\phi = \ln\left(\dfrac{\theta}{b-\theta}\right)$	$\theta = \dfrac{b}{1+e^{-\phi}}$	$\dfrac{b}{\theta(b-\theta)}$
(a, b)	$\phi = \ln\left(\dfrac{\theta-a}{b-\theta}\right)$	$\theta = \dfrac{b+ae^{-\phi}}{1+e^{-\phi}}$	$\dfrac{b-a}{(\theta-a)(b-\theta)}$
$(-1, 1)$	$\phi = \operatorname{atanh}(\theta)$	$\theta = \tanh(\phi)$	$\dfrac{1}{1-\theta^2}$
$(-1, 1)$	$\phi = \dfrac{\theta}{1-|\theta|}$	$\theta = \dfrac{\phi}{1+|\phi|}$	$\dfrac{1}{(1-|\theta|)^2}$
$(-1, 1)$	$\phi = \tan\left(\dfrac{\pi\theta}{2}\right)$	$\theta = \dfrac{2}{\pi}\tan^{-1}\phi$	$\dfrac{\pi}{2}\sec^2\left(\dfrac{\pi\theta}{2}\right)$

the desired constraint, and is obtained by applying the inverse transform $\theta = c^{-1}(\phi)$. When the numerical algorithm returns $\widehat{\phi}$, from the invariance property of maximum likelihood estimators, the associated estimator of θ is given by $\widehat{\theta} = c^{-1}(\widehat{\phi})$, which is also the maximum likelihood estimator. Some useful one-dimensional transformations, their associated inverse functions and the gradients of the transformations are presented in Table 3.4.

The convenience of using an unconstrained algorithm on what is essentially a constrained problem has a price: the standard errors of the constrained model parameters are in terms of $\widehat{\phi}$ and not $\widehat{\theta}$. A straightforward way to compute standard errors of $\widehat{\theta}$ is the method of substitution discussed in Section 3.6 where the objective function is re-expressed in terms of the original parameters, θ. The gradient vector and Hessian matrix can then be computed numerically at the maximum of the log-likelihood function using the estimated values of the parameters. Alternatively, the delta method can be used.

3.7.3   Choice of Algorithm

In theory, there is little to choose between the gradient algorithms discussed in this chapter, because in the vicinity of a maximum each should enjoy quadratic convergence, which means that

$$\|\theta_{(k+1)} - \theta\| < \kappa \|\theta_{(k)} - \theta\|^2, \qquad \kappa > 0.$$

If $\theta_{(k)}$ is accurate to two decimal places, then it is anticipated that $\theta_{(k+1)}$ will be accurate to four decimal places and that $\theta_{(k+2)}$ will be accurate to eight decimal places and so on. In choosing an algorithm, however, there are a few practical considerations to bear in mind.

(1) The Newton-Raphson and the method of scoring require the first two derivatives of the log-likelihood function. Because the information matrix is the expected value of the negative Hessian matrix, it is problem specific and typically not easy to compute. Consequently, the method of scoring is largely of theoretical interest.
(2) Close to the maximum, Newton-Raphson converges quadratically, but, further away from the maximum, the Hessian matrix may not be negative definite and this may cause the algorithm to become unstable.
(3) BHHH ensures that the outer product of the gradients matrix is positive semi-definite making it a popular choice of algorithm for econometric problems.
(4) The current consensus seems to be that quasi-Newton algorithms are the preferred choice. The Hessian update of the BFGS algorithm is particularly robust and is, therefore, the default choice in many practical settings.
(5) A popular practical strategy is to use the simplex method to start the numerical optimisation process. After a few iterations, the BFGS algorithm is employed to speed up convergence.

3.7.4 Numerical Derivatives

For problems where deriving analytical derivatives is difficult, numerical derivatives can be used instead. A first-order numerical derivative is computed simply as

$$\left. \frac{\partial \ln L_T(\theta)}{\partial \theta} \right|_{\theta=\theta_{(k)}} \simeq \frac{\ln L(\theta_{(k)} + s) - \ln L(\theta_{(k)})}{s},$$

in which s is a suitably small step size. A second-order derivative is computed as

$$\left. \frac{\partial^2 \ln L_T(\theta)}{\partial \theta^2} \right|_{\theta=\theta_{(k)}} \simeq \frac{\ln L(\theta_{(k)} + s) - 2 \ln L(\theta_{(k)}) + \ln L(\theta_{(k)} - s)}{s^2}.$$

In general, the numerical derivatives are accurate enough to enable the maximum likelihood estimators to be computed with sufficient precision and most good optimisation routines will automatically select an appropriate value for the step size, s.

One computational advantage of using numerical derivatives is that it is then necessary to program only the log-likelihood function. A cost of using numerical derivatives is computational time, since the algorithm is slower than if analytical derivatives are used, although the absolute time difference is nonetheless very small given current computer hardware. Gradient algorithms based on numerical derivatives can also be thought of as a form of algorithm based solely on function evaluation, which differs from the simplex algorithm only in the way in which this information is used to update the parameter estimate.

3.7.5   Starting Values

All numerical algorithms require starting values, $\theta_{(0)}$, for the parameter vector. There are a number of strategies to choose starting values.

(1) *Arbitrary choice:* This method only works well if the log-likelihood function is globally concave. As a word of caution, in some cases $\theta_{(0)} = \{0\}$ is a bad choice of starting value because it can lead to multicollinearity problems causing the algorithm to break down.
(2) *Consistent estimator:* This approach is only feasible if a consistent estimator of the parameter vector is available. An advantage of this approach is that one iteration of a Newton algorithm yields an asymptotically efficient estimator (Harvey, 1990, p142). An example of a consistent estimator of the location parameter of the Cauchy distribution is given by the median (see Example 2.23 in Chapter 2).
(3) *Restricted model:* A restricted model is specified in which closed-form expressions are available for the remaining parameters.
(4) *Historical precedent:* Previous empirical work of a similar nature may provide guidance on the choice of reasonable starting values.

3.7.6   Convergence Criteria

A number of convergence criteria are employed in identifying when the maximum likelihood estimates are reached. Given a convergence tolerance of ε, say equal to 0.00001, some of the more commonly adopted convergence criteria are as follows:

(1) *Objective function*: $\ln L(\theta_{(k)}) - \ln L(\theta_{(k-1)}) < \varepsilon$.
(2) *Gradient function*: $G(\theta_{(k)})' G(\theta_{(k)}) < \varepsilon$.
(3) *Parameter values*: $(\theta_{(k)})'(\theta_{(k)}) < \varepsilon$.
(4) *Updating function*: $G(\theta_{(k)}) H(\theta_{(k)})^{-1} G(\theta_{(k)}) < \varepsilon$.

In specifying the termination rule, there is a trade-off between the precision of the estimates, which requires a stringent convergence criterion, and the precision with which the objective function and gradients can be computed. Too slack a termination criterion is almost sure to produce convergence, but the maximum likelihood estimator is likely to be imprecisely estimated in these situations.

3.8 Applications

In this section, two applications are presented which focus on estimating the continuous-time model of interest rates, r_t, known as the CIR model (Cox, Ingersoll and Ross, 1985) by maximum likelihood. Estimation of continuous-time models using simulation-based estimation are discussed in more detail in Chapter 12. The CIR model is one in which the interest rate evolves over time in steps of dt in accordance with

$$dr = \alpha(\mu - r)dt + \sigma \sqrt{r} \, dB , \tag{3.17}$$

in which $dB \sim N(0, dt)$ is the disturbance term over dt and $\theta = \{\alpha, \mu, \sigma\}$ are model parameters. This model requires the interest rate to revert to its mean, μ, at a speed given by α, with variance $\sigma^2 r$. As long as the condition $2\alpha\mu \geq \sigma^2$ is satisfied, interest rates are never negative.

As in Section 1.5 of Chaper 1, the data for these applications are the daily seven-day Eurodollar interest rates used by Aït-Sahalia (1996) for the period 1 June 1973 to 25 February 1995, $T = 5505$ observations, except that now the data are expressed in raw units rather than percentages. The first application is based on the stationary (unconditional) distribution while the second focusses on the transitional (conditional) distribution.

3.8.1 Stationary Distribution of the CIR Model

The stationary distribution of the interest rate, r_t whose evolution is governed by equation (3.17), is shown by Cox, Ingersoll and Ross (1985) to be a gamma distribution

$$f(r_t; \theta) = \frac{\omega^\nu}{\Gamma(\nu)} r_t^{\nu-1} e^{-\omega r_t} , \tag{3.18}$$

in which $\Gamma(\cdot)$ is the gamma function and $\theta = \{\nu, \omega\}$ are unknown parameters. The log-likelihood function is

$$\ln L_T(\theta) = (\nu - 1)\frac{1}{T} \sum_{t=1}^{T} \ln(r_t) + \nu \ln \omega - \ln \Gamma(\nu) - \omega \frac{1}{T} \sum_{t=1}^{T} r_t .$$

$$\tag{3.19}$$

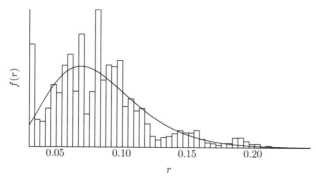

Figure 3.1. Estimated stationary gamma distribution of Eurodollar interest rates from 1 June 1973 to 25 February 1995.

The relationship between the parameters of the stationary gamma distribution and the model parameters of the CIR equation (3.17) is

$$\omega = \frac{2\alpha}{\sigma^2}, \qquad \nu = \frac{2\alpha\mu}{\sigma^2}. \tag{3.20}$$

As there is no closed-form solution for the maximum likelihood estimator, $\widehat{\theta}$, an iterative algorithm is needed. The maximum likelihood estimates obtained by using the BFGS algorithm are

$$\widehat{\omega} = \frac{67.634}{(1.310)}, \qquad \widehat{\nu} = \frac{5.656}{(0.105)}, \tag{3.21}$$

with standard errors based on the inverse Hessian shown in parentheses. An estimate of the mean from equation (3.20) is

$$\widehat{\mu} = \frac{\widehat{\nu}}{\widehat{\omega}} = \frac{5.656}{67.634} = 0.084,$$

or 8.4% per annum.

Figure 3.1 plots the gamma distribution in equation (3.18) evaluated at the maximum likelihood estimates $\widehat{\theta} = \{\widehat{\nu}, \widehat{\omega}\}$ given in equation (3.21). The results cast some doubt on the appropriateness of the CIR model for these data, because the gamma density does not capture the bunching effect at very low interest rates and also underestimates the peak of the distribution. The upper tail of the gamma distribution, however, does provide a reasonable fit to the observed Eurodollar interest rates.

The three parameters of the CIR model cannot all be uniquely identified from the two parameters of the stationary distribution. This distribution can identify only the ratio α/σ^2 and the parameter μ using equation (3.20). Identifying all three parameters of the CIR model requires using the transitional distribution of the process.

3.8.2 Transitional Distribution of the CIR Model

To estimate the parameters of the CIR model in equation (3.17), the transitional distribution must be used to construct the log-likelihood function. The transitional distribution of r_t given r_{t-1} is

$$f(r_t \mid r_{t-1}; \theta) = ce^{-u-v} \left(\frac{v}{u}\right)^{\frac{q}{2}} I_q(2\sqrt{uv}), \tag{3.22}$$

in which $I_q(x)$ is the modified Bessel function of the first kind of order q (see, for example, Abramowitz and Stegun, 1965) and

$$c = \frac{2\alpha}{\sigma^2(1 - e^{-\alpha\Delta})}, \quad u = cr_{t-1}e^{-\alpha\Delta}, \quad v = cr_t, \quad q = \frac{2\alpha\mu}{\sigma^2} - 1,$$

where the parameter Δ is a time step defined to be $1/252$ because the data are daily. Cox, Ingersoll and Ross (1985) show that the transformed variable $2cr_t$ is distributed as a non-central chi-square random variable with $2q + 2$ degrees of freedom and non-centrality parameter $2u$.

In constructing the log-likelihood function there are two equivalent approaches. The first is to construct the log-likelihood function for r_t directly from (3.22). In this instance care must be exercised in the computation of the modified Bessel function, $I_q(x)$, because it can be numerically unstable (Hurn, Jeisman and Lindsay, 2007). It is advisable to work with a scaled version of this function

$$I_q^s(2\sqrt{uv}) = e^{-2\sqrt{uv}} I_q(2\sqrt{uv}),$$

so that the log-likelihood function at observation t is

$$\ln l_t(\theta) = \log c - u - v + \frac{q}{2} \log\left(\frac{v}{u}\right) + \log(I_q^s(2\sqrt{uv})) + 2\sqrt{uv}, \tag{3.23}$$

with $\theta = \{\alpha, \mu, \sigma\}$. The second approach is to use the non-central chi-square distribution for the variable $2cr_t$ and then use the transformation of variable technique to obtain the density for r_t. These methods are equivalent and produce identical results. As with the stationary distribution of the CIR model, no closed-form solution for the maximum likelihood estimator, $\widehat{\theta}$, exists and an iterative algorithm must be used.

To obtain starting values, a discrete version of equation (3.17)

$$r_t - r_{t-1} = \alpha(\mu - r_{t-1})\Delta + \sigma\sqrt{r_{t-1}}e_t, \quad e_t \sim iid\ N(0, \Delta), \tag{3.24}$$

is used. Transforming equation (3.24) into

$$\frac{r_t - r_{t-1}}{\sqrt{r_{t-1}}} = \frac{\alpha\mu\Delta}{\sqrt{r_{t-1}}} - \alpha\sqrt{r_{t-1}}\Delta + \sigma e_t,$$

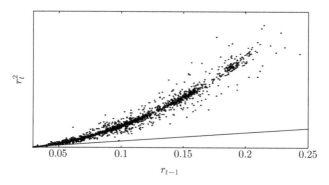

Figure 3.2. Scatterplot of r_t^2 on r_{t-1} together with the model predicted value, $\widehat{\sigma}^2 r_{t-1}$ (solid line).

allows estimates of $\alpha\mu$ and α to be obtained by an ordinary least squares regression of $(r_t - r_{t-1})/\sqrt{r_{t-1}}$ on $\Delta/\sqrt{r_{t-1}}$ and $\sqrt{r_{t-1}}\Delta$. A starting value for σ is obtained as the standard deviation of the ordinary least squares residuals.

Maximum likelihood estimates, obtained using the BFGS algorithm, are

$$\widehat{\alpha} = \frac{1.267}{(0.340)}, \qquad \widehat{\mu} = \frac{0.083}{(0.009)}, \qquad \widehat{\sigma} = \frac{0.191}{(0.002)}, \qquad (3.25)$$

with standard errors based on the inverse Hessian shown in parentheses. The mean interest rate is 0.083, or 8.3% per annum, and the estimate of the variance is $0.191^2 r_{t-1}$. While the estimates of μ and σ appear to be plausible, the estimate of α appears to be somewhat higher than usually found in models of this kind. The solution to this conundrum is to be found in the specification of the variance in this model. Figure 3.2 shows a scatterplot of r_t^2 on r_{t-1} and superimposes on it the predicted value in terms of the CIR model, $\widehat{\sigma}^2 r_{t-1}$. It appears that the variance specification of the CIR model is not dynamic enough to capture the dramatic increases in r_t^2 as r_{t-1} increases. This problem is explored further in Chapter 9 in the context of quasi-maximum likelihood estimation and in Chapter 12 dealing with estimation by simulation.

3.9 Exercises

(1) Maximum Likelihood Estimation using Graphical Methods

Program files   max_graph.*

Consider the regression model

$$y_t = \beta x_t + u_t, \qquad u_t \sim iid\ N(0, \sigma^2),$$

in which x_t is an explanatory variable given by $x_t = \{1, 2, 4, 5, 8\}$.

(a) Simulate the model for $T = 5$ observations using the parameter values $\theta_0 = \{\beta = 1, \sigma^2 = 4\}$.
(b) Compute the log-likelihood function, $\ln L_T(\theta)$, for:

 (i) $\beta = \{0.0, 0.1, \cdots, 1.9, 2.0\}$ and $\sigma^2 = 4$;
 (ii) $\beta = \{0.0, 0.1, \cdots, 1.9, 2.0\}$ and $\sigma^2 = 3.5$;
 (iii) plot $\ln L_T(\theta)$ against β for parts (i) and (ii).

(c) Compute the log-likelihood function, $\ln L_T(\theta)$, for:

 (i) $\beta = \{1.0\}$ and $\sigma^2 = \{1.0, 1.5, \cdots, 10.5, 11\}$;
 (ii) $\beta = \{0.9\}$ and $\sigma^2 = \{1.0, 1.5, \cdots, 10.5, 11\}$;
 (iii) plot $\ln L_T(\theta)$ against σ^2 for parts (i) and (ii).

(2) Maximum Likelihood Estimation using Grid Searching

Program files   `max_grid.*`

Consider the regression model set out in Exercise 1.

(a) Simulate the model for $T = 5$ observations using the parameter values $\theta_0 = \{\beta = 1, \sigma^2 = 4\}$.
(b) Derive an expression for the gradient with respect to β, $G_T(\beta)$.
(c) Choosing $\sigma^2 = 4$ perform a grid search of β over $G_T(\beta)$ with $\beta = \{0.5, 0.6, \cdots, 1.5\}$ and thus find the maximum likelihood estimate of β conditional on $\sigma^2 = 4$.
(d) Repeat part (c) except set $\sigma^2 = 3.5$. Find the maximum likelihood estimate of β conditional on $\sigma^2 = 3.5$.

(3) Maximum Likelihood Estimation using Newton-Raphson

Program files   `max_nr.*, max_iter.*`

Consider the regression model set out in Example 1.

(a) Simulate the model for $T = 5$ observations using the parameter values $\theta_0 = \{\beta = 1, \sigma^2 = 4\}$.
(b) Find the log-likelihood function, $\ln L_T(\theta)$, the gradient, $G_T(\theta)$, and the Hessian, $H_T(\theta)$.
(c) Evaluate $\ln L_T(\theta)$, $G_T(\theta)$ and $H_T(\theta)$ at $\theta_{(0)} = \{1, 4\}$.
(d) Update the value of the parameter vector using the Newton-Raphson update scheme

$$\theta_{(1)} = \theta_{(0)} - H_{(0)}^{-1} G_{(0)},$$

and re-compute $\ln L_T(\theta)$ at $\theta_{(1)}$. Compare this value with that obtained in part (c).

(e) Continue the iterations in (d) until convergence and compare these values to those obtained from the maximum likelihood estimators

$$\hat{\beta} = \frac{\sum_{t=1}^{T} x_t y_t}{\sum_{t=1}^{T} x_t^2}, \qquad \hat{\sigma}^2 = \frac{1}{T} \sum_{t=1}^{T} (y_t - \hat{\beta} x_t)^2.$$

(4) Exponential Distribution

Program files   max_exp.*

The aim of this exercise is to reproduce the convergence properties of the different algorithms in Table 3.1. Suppose that the following observations {3.5, 1.0, 1.5} are taken from the exponential distribution

$$f(y_t; \theta) = \frac{1}{\theta} \exp\left[-\frac{y_t}{\theta}\right], \qquad \theta > 0.$$

(a) Derive the log-likelihood function $\ln L_T(\theta)$ and also analytical expressions for the gradient, $G_T(\theta)$, the Hessian, $H_T(\theta)$, and the outer product of gradients matrix, $J_T(\theta)$.
(b) Using $\theta_{(0)} = 1$ as the starting value, compute ten iterations of the Newton-Raphson algorithm, the scoring algorithm, and the BHHH algorithm with and without squeezing.
(c) Redo (b) with $G_T(\theta)$ and $H_T(\theta)$ based on numerical derivatives.
(d) Using $\theta_{(0)} = 1.5$ as the starting value, compute ten iterations of the BFGS algorithm.
(e) Letting $\hat{\theta}$ be the maximum likelihood estimate, compute se($\hat{\theta}$) based on $H_T(\hat{\theta})$ and $J_T(\hat{\theta})$.

(5) Cauchy Distribution

Program files   max_cauchy.*

An *iid* random sample of size $T = 5$, $y_t = \{2, 5, -2, 3, 3\}$, is drawn from a Cauchy distribution

$$f(y_t; \theta) = \frac{1}{\pi} \frac{1}{1 + (y_t - \theta)^2}.$$

(a) Write the log-likelihood function at the tth observation as well as the log-likelihood function for the sample.
(b) Choosing the median, m, as a starting value for the parameter θ, update the value of θ with one iteration of the Newton-Raphson, scoring and BHHH algorithms.
(c) Show that the maximum likelihood estimator converges to $\hat{\theta} = 2.841$ by computing $G_T(\hat{\theta})$. Also show that $\ln L_T(\hat{\theta}) > \ln L_T(m)$.
(d) Compute se($\hat{\theta}$) based on $H_T(\hat{\theta})$ and $J_T(\hat{\theta})$.

(6) Weibull Distribution

Program files   `max_weibull.*`

(a) Simulate $T = 20$ observations with $\theta_0 = \{\alpha = 1, \beta = 2\}$ from the Weibull distribution

$$f(y_t; \theta) = \alpha \beta y_t^{\beta-1} \exp\left[-\alpha y_t^{\beta}\right].$$

(b) Derive $\ln L_T(\theta)$, $G_T(\theta)$, $H_T(\theta)$ and $J_T(\theta)$.

(c) Choose as starting values $\theta_{(0)} = \{\alpha_{(0)} = 0.5, \beta_{(0)} = 1.5\}$ and evaluate $G(\theta_{(0)})$, $H(\theta_{(0)})$ and $J(\theta_{(0)})$ for the data generated in part (a). Check the analytical results using numerical derivatives.

(d) Compute the update $\theta_{(1)}$ using the Newton-Raphson and BHHH algorithms.

(e) Continue the iterations in part (d) until convergence. Discuss the numerical performances of the two algorithms.

(f) Compute the covariance matrix, $\widehat{\Omega}$, using the Hessian and also the outer product of the gradients matrix.

(g) Repeat parts (d) and (e) where the log-likelihood function is concentrated with respect to $\widehat{\beta}$. Compare the parameter estimates of α and β with the estimates obtained using the full log-likelihood function.

(h) Suppose that the Weibull distribution is re-expressed as

$$f(y_t; \theta) = \frac{\beta}{\lambda} \left(\frac{y_t}{\lambda}\right)^{\beta-1} \exp\left[-\left(\frac{y_t}{\lambda}\right)^{\beta}\right],$$

with $\lambda = \alpha^{-1/\beta}$. Compute $\widehat{\lambda}$ and $\text{se}(\widehat{\lambda})$ for $T = 20$ observations by the substitution method and also by the delta method using the maximum likelihood estimates obtained previously.

(7) Leptokurtosis in the Distribution of Asset Returns

Program files   `max_returns.*`
Data files   `apple.csv, ford.csv, diversify.*`

The empirical distribution of asset returns tends to be leptokurtic because it exhibits fatter tails and a sharper peak than the normal distribution. To capture this feature a Student t distribution is often used to model the distribution of asset returns. The standardised Student t distribution is given by

$$f(y_t; \theta) = \frac{\Gamma\left(\dfrac{v+1}{2}\right)}{\sqrt{\pi(v-2)\sigma^2}\,\Gamma\left(\dfrac{v}{2}\right)} \left(1 + \frac{(y_t - \mu)^2}{(v-2)\sigma^2}\right)^{-\left(\frac{v+1}{2}\right)},$$

where y_t is the asset return, μ is the mean, σ^2 is the variance, ν is the degrees of freedom and $\Gamma(\cdot)$ is the gamma function. The data are daily share prices of Apple and Ford from 2 January 2001 to 6 August 2010, a total of $T = 2413$ observations.

(a) Compute the daily percentage returns on Apple and Ford. For each asset return compute sample statistics of the first four moments and plot the distribution of the standardised returns.

(b) Estimate $\theta = \{\mu, \sigma^2, \nu\}$ by maximum likelihood for each asset return using the descriptive statistics in part (a) as starting values for μ and σ^2 and choosing alternative starting values for $\nu > 2$. Interpret the parameter estimates.

(c) Repeat part (b) subject to the restrictions $\nu = \{10, 50, 100\}$. Interpret these restrictions and compare the log-likelihood values with the unrestricted values obtained in part (b) for each asset return.

(8) Simplex Algorithm

Program files   max_simplex.*

Suppose that the observations $y_t = \{3.5, 1.0, 1.5\}$ are *iid* drawings from the exponential distribution

$$f(y_t; \theta) = \frac{1}{\theta} \exp\left[-\frac{y_t}{\theta}\right], \qquad \theta > 0.$$

(a) Based on the negative of the log-likelihood function for this exponential distribution, compute the maximum likelihood estimator, $\widehat{\theta}$, using the starting vertices $\theta_1 = 1$ and $\theta_2 = 3$.

(b) Which move would the first iteration of the simplex algorithm choose?

(9) Profile Log-likelihood Function

Program files   max_profile.*
Data files   apple.csv, ford.csv, diversify.*

The data files contain daily share prices of Apple and Ford from 2 January 2001 to 6 August 2010, a total of $T = 2413$ observations. Let $\theta = \{\theta_1, \theta_2\}$ where θ_1 contains the parameters of interest. The profile log-likelihood function is defined as

$$\ln L_T(\theta_1, \widehat{\theta}_2) = \arg\max_{\theta_2} \ln L_T(\theta),$$

in which $\widehat{\theta}_2$ is the maximum likelihood solution of θ_2. A plot of $\ln L_T(\theta_1, \widehat{\theta}_2)$ over θ_1 provides information on θ_1.

(a) Assume that the returns on the two assets are *iid* drawings from a bivariate normal distribution with means μ_1 and μ_2, variances σ_1^2 and

σ_2^2, and correlation ρ. Defining $\theta_1 = \{\rho\}$ and $\theta_2 = \{\mu_1, \mu_2, \sigma_1^2, \sigma_2^2\}$, plot $\ln L_T(\theta_1, \widehat{\theta}_2)$ over $(-1, 1)$, where $\widehat{\theta}_2$ is the maximum likelihood estimate obtained from the returns data.

(b) Interpret the plot obtained in part (a).

(10) Stationary Distribution of the CIR Model

Program files	max_stationary.*
Data files	eurodollar.*

The data are daily seven-day Eurodollar rates from 1 June 1973 to 25 February 1995, a total of $T = 5505$ observations. The CIR model of interest rates, r_t, for time steps dt is

$$dr = \alpha(\mu - r)dt + \sigma\sqrt{r}\, dB,$$

in which $dB \sim N(0, dt)$. The stationary distribution of the CIR interest rate is the gamma distribution

$$f(r_t; v, \omega) = \frac{\omega^v}{\Gamma(v)} r_t^{v-1} e^{-\omega r_t},$$

where $\Gamma(\cdot)$ is the gamma function and $\theta = \{v, \omega\}$ are unknown parameters.

(a) Compute the maximum likelihood estimates of v and ω and their standard errors based on the Hessian.

(b) Use the results in part (a) to compute the maximum likelihood estimate of $\mu = v/\omega$ and its standard error using both the delta and the substitution methods.

(c) Use the estimates from part (a) to plot the stationary distribution and interpret its properties.

(d) Suppose that it is known that $v = 1$. Using the property of the gamma function that $\Gamma(1) = 1$, estimate ω and re-compute the mean interest rate.

(11) Transitional Distribution of the CIR Model

Program files	max_transitional.*
Data files	eurodollar.*

The data are the same seven-day Eurodollar rates used in Exercise 10.

(a) The transitional distribution of r_t given r_{t-1} for the CIR model in Exercise 10 is

$$f(r_t \mid r_{t-1}; \theta) = ce^{-u-v}\left(\frac{v}{u}\right)^{\frac{q}{2}} I_q(2\sqrt{uv}),$$

in which $I_q(x)$ is the modified Bessel function of the first kind of order q, $\Delta = 1/250$ is the time step and

$$c = \frac{2\alpha}{\sigma^2(1 - e^{-\alpha\Delta})}, \quad u = cr_{t-1}e^{-\alpha\Delta}, \quad v = cr_t, \quad q = \frac{2\alpha\mu}{\sigma^2} - 1.$$

Estimate the CIR model parameters, $\theta = \{\alpha, \mu, \sigma\}$, by maximum likelihood. Compute the standard errors based on the Hessian.

(b) Use the result that the transformed variable $2cr_t$ is distributed as a non-central chi-square random variable with $2q + 2$ degrees of freedom and non-centrality parameter $2u$ to obtain the maximum likelihood estimates of θ based on the non-central chi-square probability density function. Compute the standard errors based on the Hessian. Compare the results with those obtained in part (a).

(12) **Stationary and Transitional Distributions of a TAR Model**

Program files   max_tar.*

Consider the threshold autoregressive model (TAR)

$$y_t = \theta \, |y_{t-1}| + u_t, \quad u_t \sim iid \, N(0, 1),$$

with parameter $|\theta| < 1$. The stationary distribution is a skewed-normal distribution and the transitional distribution is a normal distribution given by

$$f(y_t) = \frac{2}{\sqrt{2\pi/(1 - \theta^2)}} \exp\left[-\frac{y_t^2}{2/(1 - \theta^2)}\right] \int_{-\infty}^{\theta y_t} \frac{1}{\sqrt{2\pi}} \exp\left[-\frac{s^2}{2}\right] ds$$

$$f(y_t | y_{t-1}) = \frac{1}{\sqrt{2\pi}} \exp\left[-\frac{(y_t - \theta \, |y_{t-1}|)^2}{2}\right],$$

respectively. See Chapter 19 for more on TAR models and Andel and Barton (1986) and Zhao (2010) for details on the stationary and transitional distributions.

(a) Simulate the TAR model for $\theta = 0.5$ with $T = 250$ and starting value $y_0 = 0.0$.

(b) Estimate θ by least squares by regressing y_t on $|y_{t-1}|$.

(c) Estimate θ by maximum likelihood using the stationary distribution with the starting value based on the estimate in part (b).

(d) Estimate θ by maximum likelihood using the transitional distribution with the starting value based on the estimate in part (b).

(e) Compare the estimates in parts (b) to (d).

(f) Repeat parts (a) to (e) for $T = \{500, 1000, 5000\}$.

4 Hypothesis Testing

4.1 Introduction

The discussion of maximum likelihood estimation has focussed on deriving estimators that maximise the likelihood function. In all of these cases, the potential values that the maximum likelihood estimator, $\widehat{\theta}$, can take are unrestricted. Now the discussion is extended to determining if the population parameter has a certain hypothesised value, θ_0. If this value differs from $\widehat{\theta}$, then by definition, it must correspond to a lower value of the log-likelihood function and the crucial question is then how significant this decrease is. Determining the significance of this reduction of the log-likelihood function represents the basis of hypothesis testing. That is, hypothesis testing is concerned about determining if the reduction in the value of the log-likelihood function brought about by imposing the restriction $\theta = \theta_0$ is severe enough to warrant rejecting it. If, however, it is concluded that the decrease in the log-likelihood function is not too severe, the restriction is interpreted as being consistent with the data and it is not rejected. The likelihood ratio test (LR), the Wald test and the Lagrange multiplier test (LM) are three general procedures used in developing statistics to test hypotheses in a likelihood framework. These tests encompass many of the test statistics used in econometrics, as demonstrated in Part TWO of the book. They also offer the advantage of providing a general framework to develop new classes of test statistics that are designed for specific models.

4.2 Overview

Suppose θ is a single parameter and consider the hypotheses

$$H_0 : \theta = \theta_0, \quad H_1 : \theta \neq \theta_0.$$

A natural test is based on a comparison of the log-likelihood function evaluated at the maximum likelihood estimator $\widehat{\theta}$ and at the null value θ_0. A statistic of

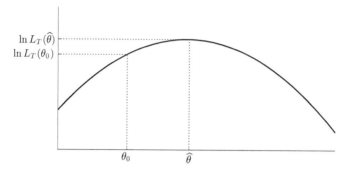

Figure 4.1. Comparison of the value of the log-likelihood function under the null hypothesis, θ_0, and under the alternative hypothesis, $\widehat{\theta}$.

the form

$$\ln L_T(\widehat{\theta}) - \ln L_T(\theta_0) = \frac{1}{T} \sum_{t=1}^{T} \ln f(y_t; \widehat{\theta}) - \frac{1}{T} \sum_{t=1}^{T} \ln f(y_t; \theta_0),$$

measures the distance between the maximised log-likelihood $\ln L_T(\widehat{\theta})$ and
the log-likelihood $\ln L_T(\theta_0)$ restricted by the null hypothesis. This distance is
measured on the vertical axis of Figure 4.1 and the test which uses this measure
in its construction is known as the likelihood ratio (LR) test.

The distance $(\widehat{\theta} - \theta_0)$, illustrated on the horizontal axis of Figure 4.1, is an
alternative measure of the difference between $\widehat{\theta}$ and θ_0. A test based on this
measure is known as a Wald test. The Lagrange multiplier (LM) test is the
hypothesis test based on the gradient of the log-likelihood function at the null
value θ_0, $G_T(\theta_0)$. The gradient at the maximum likelihood estimator, $G_T(\widehat{\theta})$, is
zero by definition (see Chapter 1). The LM statistic is therefore the distance on
the vertical axis in Figure 4.2 between $G_T(\theta_0)$ and $G_T(\widehat{\theta}) = 0$.

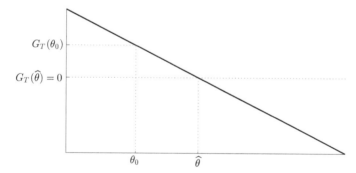

Figure 4.2. Comparison of the value of the gradient of the log-likelihood function under
the null hypothesis, θ_0, and under the alternative hypothesis, $\widehat{\theta}$.

The intuition behind the construction of these tests for a single parameter can be carried over to provide likelihood-based testing of general hypotheses, which are discussed next.

4.3 Types of Hypotheses

This section presents detailed examples of types of hypotheses encountered in econometrics, beginning with simple and composite hypotheses and progressing to linear and nonlinear hypotheses.

4.3.1 Simple and Composite Hypotheses

Consider a model based on the distribution $f(y_t; \theta)$ where θ is an unknown scalar parameter. The simplest form of hypothesis test is based on testing whether or not a parameter takes one of two specific values, θ_0 or θ_1. The null and alternative hypotheses are, respectively, given by

$$H_0 : \theta = \theta_0 , \qquad H_1 : \theta = \theta_1 ,$$

in which θ_0 represents the value of the parameter under the null hypothesis and θ_1 is the value under the alternative. In Chapter 2, θ_0 represents the true parameter value. In hypothesis testing, since the null and alternative hypotheses are distinct, θ_0 still represents the true value, but now interpreted to be under the null hypothesis. Both of these hypotheses represent simple hypotheses because as the parameter value in each case is given the distribution of y_t under both the null and alternative hypothesis is fully specified.

If the hypothesis is constructed in such a way that the distribution of y_t cannot be inferred fully, the hypothesis is referred to as being composite. An example is

$$H_0 : \theta = \theta_0 , \qquad H_1 : \theta \neq \theta_0 ,$$

where the alternative hypothesis is a composite hypothesis because the distribution of y_t under the alternative is not fully specified, whereas the null hypothesis is still a simple hypothesis. Another example of a composite hypothesis is where just some of the parameters of θ are specified uniquely, leaving the remaining parameters unspecified. The difference in the number of parameters of the two sets is known as the degrees of freedom.

For the alternative hypothesis in $\theta \neq \theta_0$ the parameter θ can take any value on either side of θ_0. This form of hypothesis test is referred to as a two-sided test. Restricting the range under the alternative to be just one side, $\theta > \theta_0$ or $\theta < \theta_0$, would change the test to a one-sided test. In both of these cases the alternative hypothesis is still a composite hypothesis.

4.3.2 *Linear Hypotheses*

Suppose that there are K unknown parameters, $\theta = \{\beta_1, \beta_2, \cdots, \beta_K\}$, so θ is a $(K \times 1)$ vector, and M linear hypotheses are to be tested simultaneously. The full set of M hypotheses is expressed as

$$H_0 : R\theta = Q, \qquad H_1 : R\theta \neq Q,$$

in which R and Q are $(M \times K)$ and $(M \times 1)$ matrices, respectively. The following cases give some examples of R and Q.

(1) $K = 1$, $M = 1$, $\theta = \{\beta_1\}$:
   The null and alternative hypotheses are

$$H_0 : \beta_1 = 0, \qquad H_1 : \beta_1 \neq 0,$$

with

$$R = [1], \qquad Q = [0].$$

(2) $K = 2$, $M = 1$, $\theta = \{\beta_1, \beta_2\}$:
   The null and alternative hypotheses are

$$H_0 : \beta_2 = 0, \qquad H_1 : \beta_2 \neq 0,$$

with

$$R = [0 \quad 1], \qquad Q = [0].$$

This corresponds to the usual example of performing a t test on the importance of an explanatory variable by testing to see if the pertinent parameter is zero.

(3) $K = 3$, $M = 1$, $\theta = \{\beta_1, \beta_2, \beta_3\}$:
   The null and alternative hypotheses are

$$H_0 : \beta_1 + \beta_2 + \beta_3 = 0, \qquad H_1 : \beta_1 + \beta_2 + \beta_3 \neq 0,$$

with

$$R = [1 \quad 1 \quad 1], \qquad Q = [0].$$

(4) $K = 4$, $M = 3$, $\theta = \{\beta_1, \beta_2, \beta_3, \beta_4\}$:
   The null and alternative hypotheses are

$$H_0 : \beta_1 = \beta_2, \ \beta_2 = \beta_3, \ \beta_3 = \beta_4$$
$$H_1 : \text{at least one restriction does not hold},$$

with

$$R = \begin{bmatrix} 1 & -1 & 0 & 0 \\ 0 & 1 & -1 & 0 \\ 0 & 0 & 1 & -1 \end{bmatrix}, \qquad Q = \begin{bmatrix} 0 \\ 0 \\ 0 \end{bmatrix}.$$

These restrictions arise in models of the term structure of interest rates.

(5) $K = 4$, $M = 3$, $\theta = \{\beta_1, \beta_2, \beta_3, \beta_4\}$:

The hypotheses are

$$H_0 : \beta_1 = \beta_2, \ \beta_3 = \beta_4, \ \beta_1 = 1 + \beta_3 - \beta_4$$
$$H_1 : \text{at least one restriction does not hold},$$

with

$$R = \begin{bmatrix} 1 & -1 & 0 & 0 \\ 0 & 0 & 1 & -1 \\ 1 & 0 & -1 & 1 \end{bmatrix}, \qquad Q = \begin{bmatrix} 0 \\ 0 \\ 1 \end{bmatrix}.$$

4.3.3 Nonlinear Hypotheses

The set of hypotheses entertained is now further extended to allow for nonlinearities. The full set of M nonlinear hypotheses is expressed as

$$H_0 : C(\theta) = Q, \qquad H_1 : C(\theta) \neq Q,$$

in which $C(\theta)$ is a $(M \times 1)$ matrix of nonlinear restrictions and Q is a $(M \times 1)$ matrix of constants. In the special case where the hypotheses are linear, $C(\theta) = R\theta$. To illustrate the construction of these matrices, consider the following cases.

(1) $K = 2$, $M = 1$, $\theta = \{\beta_1, \beta_2\}$:

The null and alternative hypotheses are

$$H_0 : \beta_1\beta_2 = 1, \qquad H_1 : \beta_1\beta_2 \neq 1,$$

with

$$C(\theta) = \begin{bmatrix} \beta_1\beta_2 \end{bmatrix}, \qquad Q = \begin{bmatrix} 1 \end{bmatrix}.$$

(2) $K = 2$, $M = 1$, $\theta = \{\beta_1, \beta_2\}$:

The null and alternative hypotheses are

$$H_0 : \frac{\beta_1}{1 - \beta_2} = 1, \qquad H_1 : \frac{\beta_1}{1 - \beta_2} \neq 1,$$

with

$$C(\theta) = \begin{bmatrix} \beta_1 \\ 1 - \beta_2 \end{bmatrix}, \qquad Q = [1].$$

This form of restriction often arises in dynamic time series models where restrictions on the value of the long-run multiplier are often imposed.

(3) $K = 3$, $M = 2$, $\theta = \{\beta_1, \beta_2, \beta_3\}$:

The null and alternative hypotheses are

$$H_0 : \beta_1\beta_2 = \beta_3, \quad \frac{\beta_1}{1 - \beta_2} = 1$$

$$H_1 : \text{at least one restriction does not hold},$$

and

$$C(\theta) = \begin{bmatrix} \beta_1\beta_2 - \beta_3 \\ \beta_1(1 - \beta_2)^{-1} \end{bmatrix}, \qquad Q = \begin{bmatrix} 0 \\ 1 \end{bmatrix}.$$

4.4   Likelihood Ratio Test

The LR test requires estimating the model under both the null and alternative hypotheses. The resulting estimators are denoted

$$\widehat{\theta}_0 = \text{restricted maximum likelihood estimator},$$
$$\widehat{\theta}_1 = \text{unrestricted maximum likelihood estimator}.$$

The unrestricted estimator $\widehat{\theta}_1$ is the usual maximum likelihood estimator. The restricted estimator $\widehat{\theta}_0$ is obtained by first imposing the null hypothesis on the model and then estimating any remaining unknown parameters. If the null hypothesis completely specifies the parameter, that is $H_0 : \theta = \theta_0$, then the restricted estimator is automatically given by $\widehat{\theta}_0 = \theta_0$. In most cases, however, a null hypothesis will specify only some of the parameters of the model, leaving the remaining parameters to be estimated in order to find $\widehat{\theta}_0$.

Let

$$\ln L_T(\widehat{\theta}_0) = \frac{1}{T} \sum_{t=1}^{T} \ln f(y_t; \widehat{\theta}_0), \qquad \ln L_T(\widehat{\theta}_1) = \frac{1}{T} \sum_{t=1}^{T} \ln f(y_t; \widehat{\theta}_1),$$

be the maximised log-likelihood functions under the null and alternative hypotheses, respectively. The general form of the LR statistic is

$$LR = -2T\left(\ln L_T(\widehat{\theta}_0) - \ln L_T(\widehat{\theta}_1)\right). \tag{4.1}$$

As the maximum likelihood estimator maximises the log-likelihood function, the term in brackets is non-positive as the restrictions under the null hypothesis at least correspond to a region of lower probability. This loss of probability is illustrated on the vertical axis of Figure 4.1, which gives the term in brackets. The range of LR is $0 \le LR < \infty$. For values of the statistic near $LR = 0$, the restrictions under the null hypothesis are consistent with the data since there is no serious loss of information from imposing these restrictions. For larger values of LR the restrictions under the null hypothesis are not consistent with the data since a serious loss of information caused by imposing these restrictions now results. In the former case, there is a failure to reject the null, whereas in the latter case the null is rejected in favour of the alternative hypothesis. It is shown in Section 4.7, that LR in equation (4.1) is asymptotically distributed as χ^2_M under the null hypothesis where M is the number of restrictions from which the appropriate p-value may be calculated.

Example 4.1 Univariate Normal Distribution

The log-likelihood function of a normal distribution with unknown mean and variance, $\theta = \{\mu, \sigma^2\}$, is

$$\ln L_T(\theta) = -\frac{1}{2}\ln 2\pi - \frac{1}{2}\ln \sigma^2 - \frac{1}{2\sigma^2 T}\sum_{t=1}^{T}(y_t - \mu)^2 .$$

A test of the mean is based on the null and alternative hypotheses

$$H_0 : \mu = \mu_0 , \qquad H_1 : \mu \neq \mu_0 .$$

The unrestricted maximum likelihood estimators are

$$\widehat{\mu}_1 = \frac{1}{T}\sum_{t=1}^{T} y_t = \overline{y}, \qquad \widehat{\sigma}_1^2 = \frac{1}{T}\sum_{t=1}^{T}(y_t - \overline{y})^2 ,$$

and the log-likelihood function evaluated at $\widehat{\theta}_1 = \{\widehat{\mu}_1, \widehat{\sigma}_1^2\}$ is

$$\ln L_T(\widehat{\theta}_1) = -\frac{1}{2}\ln 2\pi - \frac{1}{2}\ln \widehat{\sigma}_1^2 - \frac{1}{2\widehat{\sigma}_1^2 T}\sum_{t=1}^{T}(y_t - \widehat{\mu}_1)^2$$

$$= -\frac{1}{2}\ln 2\pi - \frac{1}{2}\ln \widehat{\sigma}_1^2 - \frac{1}{2} .$$

The restricted maximum likelihood estimators are

$$\widehat{\mu}_0 = \mu_0 , \qquad \widehat{\sigma}_0^2 = \frac{1}{T}\sum_{t=1}^{T}(y_t - \mu_0)^2 ,$$

and the log-likelihood function evaluated at $\widehat{\theta}_0 = \{\widehat{\mu}_0, \widehat{\sigma}_0^2\}$ is

$$\ln L_T(\widehat{\theta}_0) = -\frac{1}{2}\ln 2\pi - \frac{1}{2}\ln \widehat{\sigma}_0^2 - \frac{1}{2\widehat{\sigma}_0^2 T}\sum_{t=1}^{T}(y_t - \widehat{\mu}_0)^2$$

$$= -\frac{1}{2}\ln 2\pi - \frac{1}{2}\ln \widehat{\sigma}_0^2 - \frac{1}{2} .$$

Using equation (4.1), the LR statistic is

$$LR = -2T \left(\ln L_T(\widehat{\theta}_0) - \ln L_T(\widehat{\theta}_1) \right)$$

$$= -2T \left[\left(-\frac{1}{2} \ln 2\pi - \frac{1}{2} \ln \widehat{\sigma}_0^2 - \frac{1}{2} \right) - \left(-\frac{1}{2} \ln 2\pi - \frac{1}{2} \ln \widehat{\sigma}_1^2 - \frac{1}{2} \right) \right]$$

$$= T \ln \left(\frac{\widehat{\sigma}_0^2}{\widehat{\sigma}_1^2} \right).$$

Under the null hypothesis, the LR statistic is distributed asymptotically as χ_1^2. This expression shows that the LR test is equivalent to comparing the variances of the data under the null and alternative hypotheses. If $\widehat{\sigma}_0^2$ is close to $\widehat{\sigma}_1^2$, the restriction is consistent with the data, resulting in a small value of LR. In the extreme case where no loss of information from imposing the restrictions occurs, $\widehat{\sigma}_0^2 = \widehat{\sigma}_1^2$ and $LR = 0$. For values of $\widehat{\sigma}_0^2$ that are not statistically close to $\widehat{\sigma}_1^2$, LR is a large positive value.   □

Example 4.2 Multivariate Normal Distribution

The multivariate normal distribution of dimension N at time t is

$$f(y_t; \theta) = \left(\frac{1}{2\pi} \right)^{N/2} |V|^{-1/2} \exp \left[-\frac{1}{2} u_t' V^{-1} u_t \right],$$

in which $y_t = [y_{1,t}, y_{2,t}, \cdots, y_{N,t}]'$ is a $(N \times 1)$ vector of dependent variables at time t, $u_t = y_t - \beta x_t$ is a $(N \times 1)$ vector of disturbances with covariance matrix V, and x_t is a $(K \times 1)$ vector of explanatory variables and β is a $(N \times K)$ parameter matrix. The log-likelihood function is

$$\ln L_T(\theta) = \frac{1}{T} \sum_{t=1}^{T} \ln f(y_t; \theta) = -\frac{N}{2} \ln 2\pi - \frac{1}{2} \ln |V| - \frac{1}{2T} \sum_{t=1}^{T} u_t' V^{-1} u_t,$$

with $\theta = \{\beta, V\}$. Consider testing M restrictions on β. The unrestricted maximum likelihood estimator of V is

$$\widehat{V}_1 = \frac{1}{T} \sum_{t=1}^{T} \widehat{u}_t \widehat{u}_t',$$

in which $\widehat{u}_t = y_t - \widehat{\beta}_1 x_t$ and $\widehat{\beta}_1$ is the unrestricted estimator of β. The log-likelihood function evaluated at the unrestricted estimator is

$$\ln L_T(\widehat{\theta}_1) = -\frac{N}{2} \ln 2\pi - \frac{1}{2} \ln \left| \widehat{V}_1 \right| - \frac{1}{2T} \sum_{t=1}^{T} \widehat{u}_t' \widehat{V}_1^{-1} \widehat{u}_t$$

$$= -\frac{N}{2} \ln 2\pi - \frac{1}{2} \ln \left| \widehat{V}_1 \right| - \frac{N}{2}$$

$$= -\frac{N}{2} (1 + \ln 2\pi) - \frac{1}{2} \ln \left| \widehat{V}_1 \right|,$$

which uses the result

$$\sum_{t=1}^{T} \widehat{u}_t' \widehat{V}_1^{-1} \widehat{u}_t = \text{trace}\left(\sum_{t=1}^{T} \widehat{u}_t' \widehat{V}_1^{-1} \widehat{u}_t \right) = \text{trace}\left(\widehat{V}_1^{-1} \sum_{t=1}^{T} \widehat{u}_t \widehat{u}_t' \right)$$

$$= \text{trace}(\widehat{V}_1^{-1} T \widehat{V}_1) = \text{trace}(T I_N) = T N.$$

Now consider estimating the model subject to a set of restrictions on β. The restricted maximum likelihood estimator of V is

$$\widehat{V}_0 = \frac{1}{T} \sum_{t=1}^{T} \widehat{v}_t \widehat{v}_t' ,$$

in which $\widehat{v}_t = y_t - \widehat{\beta}_0 x_t$ and $\widehat{\beta}_0$ is the restricted estimator of β. The log-likelihood function evaluated at the restricted estimator is

$$\ln L_T(\widehat{\theta}_0) = -\frac{N}{2} \ln 2\pi - \frac{1}{2} \ln |\widehat{V}_0| - \frac{1}{2T} \sum_{t=1}^{T} \widehat{v}_t' \widehat{V}_0^{-1} \widehat{v}_t$$

$$= -\frac{N}{2} \ln 2\pi - \frac{1}{2} \ln |\widehat{V}_0| - \frac{N}{2}$$

$$= -\frac{N}{2}(1 + \ln 2\pi) - \frac{1}{2} \ln |\widehat{V}_0| .$$

The LR statistic is

$$LR = -2T\left(\ln L_T(\widehat{\theta}_0) - \ln L_T(\widehat{\theta}_1) \right) = T \ln\left(\frac{|\widehat{V}_0|}{|\widehat{V}_1|} \right),$$

which is distributed asymptotically under the null hypothesis as χ_M^2. This is the multivariate analogue of Example 4.1 that is commonly adopted when testing hypotheses within multivariate normal models. It should be stressed that this form of the likelihood ratio test is appropriate only for models based on the assumption of normality. □

Example 4.3 Weibull Distribution

Consider the $T = 20$ independent realisations, given in Example 3.6 in Chapter 3, drawn from the Weibull distribution

$$f(y_t; \theta) = \alpha \beta y_t^{\beta-1} \exp\left[-\alpha y_t^{\beta} \right],$$

with unknown parameters $\theta = \{\alpha, \beta\}$. A special case of the Weibull distribution is the exponential distribution that occurs when $\beta = 1$. To test that the data are drawn from the exponential distribution, the null and alternative hypotheses are, respectively,

$$H_0 : \beta = 1, \qquad H_1 : \beta \neq 1.$$

The unrestricted and restricted log-likelihood functions are

$$\ln L_T(\widehat{\theta}_1) = \ln \widehat{\alpha}_1 + \ln \widehat{\beta}_1 + (\widehat{\beta}_1 - 1)\frac{1}{T}\sum_{t=1}^{T} \ln y_t - \frac{1}{T}\sum_{t=1}^{T} \widehat{\alpha}_1 y_t^{\widehat{\beta}_1}$$

$$\ln L_T(\widehat{\theta}_0) = \ln \widehat{\alpha}_0 - \frac{1}{T}\sum_{t=1}^{T} \widehat{\alpha}_0 y_t,$$

respectively. Maximising the two log-likelihood functions yields

Unrestricted :	$\widehat{\alpha}_1 = 0.856$	$\widehat{\beta}_1 = 1.868$	$\ln L_T(\widehat{\theta}_1) = -0.766642,$
Restricted :	$\widehat{\alpha}_0 = 1.020$	$\widehat{\beta}_0 = 1.000$	$\ln L_T(\widehat{\theta}_0) = -0.980529.$

The LR statistic is computed using equation (4.1)

$$LR = -2T\left(\ln L_T(\widehat{\theta}_0) - \ln L_T(\widehat{\theta}_1)\right) = -2 \times 20(-0.980529 + 0.766642)$$
$$= 8.555.$$

Using the χ_1^2 distribution, the p-value is 0.003 resulting in a rejection of the null hypothesis at the 5% significance level that the data are drawn from an exponential distribution. □

4.5   Wald Test

The LR test requires estimating both the restricted and unrestricted models. The Wald test, on the other hand, requires estimation of just the unrestricted model, a property that is important in practice, especially in those cases where estimating the model under the null hypothesis is more difficult than under the alternative hypothesis.

The Wald test statistic for the null hypothesis $H_0 : \theta = \theta_0$, a hypothesis which completely specifies the parameter, is

$$W = (\widehat{\theta}_1 - \theta_0)'[\text{cov}(\widehat{\theta}_1 - \theta_0)]^{-1}(\widehat{\theta}_1 - \theta_0).$$

This test statistic is distributed asymptotically as χ_M^2, with M being the number of restrictions under the null hypothesis. The variance of $\widehat{\theta}_1$ is

$$\text{cov}(\widehat{\theta}_1 - \theta_0) = \text{cov}(\widehat{\theta}_1) = \frac{1}{T}\Omega(\theta_0).$$

To implement the test, $\Omega(\theta_0)$ is replaced by a consistent estimator evaluated under the alternative hypothesis, $\widehat{\Omega}(\widehat{\theta}_1)$, resulting in the Wald statistic

$$W = T(\widehat{\theta}_1 - \theta_0)'\widehat{\Omega}^{-1}(\widehat{\theta}_1)(\widehat{\theta}_1 - \theta_0). \tag{4.2}$$

The aim of the Wald test is to compare the unrestricted value $(\widehat{\theta}_1)$ with the value under the null hypothesis (θ_0). If the two values are considered to be close, then W is small. To determine the significance of this difference, the deviation $(\widehat{\theta}_1 - \theta_0)$ is scaled by the increase of the pertinent standard deviation.

4.5.1 Linear Hypotheses

For M linear hypotheses of the form $R\theta = Q$, the Wald statistic is

$$W = [R\widehat{\theta}_1 - Q]'[\text{cov}(R\widehat{\theta}_1 - Q)]^{-1}[R\widehat{\theta}_1 - Q].$$

The covariance matrix is

$$\text{cov}(R\widehat{\theta}_1 - Q) = \text{cov}(R\widehat{\theta}_1) = R\frac{1}{T}\Omega(\theta)R', \tag{4.3}$$

which gives the general form of the Wald test of linear restrictions as

$$W = T[R\widehat{\theta}_1 - Q]'[R\,\widehat{\Omega}(\widehat{\theta}_1)R']^{-1}[R\widehat{\theta}_1 - Q]. \tag{4.4}$$

Under the null hypothesis, the Wald statistic is asymptotically distributed as χ^2_M where M is the number of restrictions.

The covariance matrix can be based on the information matrix $I(\theta)$, the Hessian matrix $H_T(\theta)$ and the outer product of gradients matrix $J_T(\theta)$, which are all asymptotically equivalent under the null hypothesis. This suggests that the Wald statistic has the following asymptotically equivalent forms

$$W_I = T[R\widehat{\theta}_1 - Q]'[R\,I^{-1}(\widehat{\theta}_1)\,R']^{-1}[R\widehat{\theta}_1 - Q], \tag{4.5}$$

$$W_H = T[R\widehat{\theta}_1 - Q]'[R\,(-H_T^{-1}(\widehat{\theta}_1))\,R']^{-1}[R\widehat{\theta}_1 - Q], \tag{4.6}$$

$$W_J = T[R\widehat{\theta}_1 - Q]'[R\,J_T^{-1}(\widehat{\theta}_1)\,R']^{-1}[R\widehat{\theta}_1 - Q]. \tag{4.7}$$

Example 4.4 Normal Distribution

Consider the normal distribution example again where the null and alternative hypotheses are given by

$$H_0 : \mu = \mu_0 \qquad H_1 : \mu \neq \mu_0,$$

respectively, with $R = [\,1 \;\; 0\,]$ and $Q = [\,\mu_0\,]$. The unrestricted maximum likelihood estimators are

$$\widehat{\theta}_1 = [\,\widehat{\mu}_1 \;\; \widehat{\sigma}_1^2\,]' = \left[\,\overline{y} \quad \frac{1}{T}\sum_{t=1}^{T}(y_t - \overline{y})^2\,\right]'.$$

When evaluated at $\widehat{\theta}_1$ the information matrix is

$$I(\widehat{\theta}_1) = \begin{bmatrix} \dfrac{1}{\widehat{\sigma}_1^2} & 0 \\[2ex] 0 & \dfrac{1}{2\widehat{\sigma}_1^4} \end{bmatrix}.$$

Since $[R\widehat{\theta}_1 - Q] = [\bar{y} - \mu_0]$, it follows that

$$[R\,I^{-1}(\widehat{\theta}_1)R'] = \begin{bmatrix} 1 \\ 0 \end{bmatrix}' \begin{bmatrix} \dfrac{1}{\widehat{\sigma}_1^2} & 0 \\ 0 & \dfrac{1}{2\widehat{\sigma}_1^4} \end{bmatrix}^{-1} \begin{bmatrix} 1 \\ 0 \end{bmatrix} = \widehat{\sigma}_1^2 \,.$$

The Wald statistic in equation (4.5) then becomes

$$W = T\frac{(\bar{y} - \mu_0)^2}{\widehat{\sigma}_1^2} \,,$$

which is distributed asymptotically as χ_1^2. This form of the Wald statistic is equivalent to the square of the standard t statistic applied to the mean of a normal distribution. □

Example 4.5 Weibull Distribution

Consider a Wald test of $\beta = 1$ in the Weibull distribution in Example 4.3 where the covariance matrix of the unrestricted maximum likelihood estimator is computed using the Hessian. The unrestricted maximum likelihood estimates are $\widehat{\theta}_1 = \{\widehat{\alpha}_1 = 0.865, \widehat{\beta}_1 = 1.868\}$ and the Hessian evaluated at $\widehat{\theta}_1$ using numerical derivatives is

$$H_T(\widehat{\theta}_1) = \frac{1}{20}\begin{bmatrix} -27.266 & -6.136 \\ -6.136 & -9.573 \end{bmatrix} = \begin{bmatrix} -1.363 & -0.307 \\ -0.307 & -0.479 \end{bmatrix}.$$

Define $R = [\,0\ \ 1\,]$ and $Q = [\,1\,]$ so that

$$R\,(-H_T^{-1}(\widehat{\theta}_1))\,R' = \begin{bmatrix} 0 \\ 1 \end{bmatrix}' \begin{bmatrix} -1.363 & -0.307 \\ -0.307 & -0.479 \end{bmatrix}^{-1} \begin{bmatrix} 0 \\ 1 \end{bmatrix} = 2.441\,.$$

The Wald statistic, given in equation (4.6), is

$$W = 20(1.868 - 1)(2.441)^{-1}(1.868 - 1) = \frac{20(1.868 - 1.000)^2}{2.441} = 6.174\,.$$

Using the χ_1^2 distribution, the p-value of the Wald statistic is 0.013, resulting in the rejection of the null hypothesis at the 5% significance level that the data come from an exponential distribution. □

4.5.2 Nonlinear Hypotheses

For M nonlinear hypotheses of the form

$$H_0 : C(\theta) = Q, \qquad H_1 : C(\theta) \neq Q,$$

the Wald statistic is

$$W = [C(\widehat{\theta}_1) - Q]'\text{cov}(C(\widehat{\theta}_1))^{-1}[C(\widehat{\theta}_1) - Q]. \tag{4.8}$$

To compute the covariance matrix, $\text{cov}(C(\widehat{\theta}_1))$ the delta method discussed in Chapter 3 is used. There it is shown that

$$\text{cov}(C(\widehat{\theta}_1)) = \frac{1}{T} D(\theta_0)\Omega(\theta_0)D(\theta_0)',$$

in which

$$D(\theta) = \frac{\partial C(\theta)}{\partial \theta'}.$$

This expression for the covariance matrix depends on θ, which is estimated by the unrestricted maximum likelihood estimator $\widehat{\theta}_1$. The general form of the Wald statistic in the case of nonlinear restrictions is then

$$W = T[C(\widehat{\theta}_1) - Q]'[D(\widehat{\theta}_1)\,\widehat{\Omega}(\widehat{\theta}_1)D(\widehat{\theta}_1)']^{-1}[C(\widehat{\theta}_1) - Q],$$

which takes the asymptotically equivalent forms

$$W_I = T[C(\widehat{\theta}_1) - Q]'[D(\widehat{\theta}_1)\,I^{-1}(\widehat{\theta}_1)D(\widehat{\theta}_1)']^{-1}[C(\widehat{\theta}_1) - Q] \tag{4.9}$$

$$W_H = T[C(\widehat{\theta}_1) - Q]'[D(\widehat{\theta}_1)\,(-H_T^{-1}(\widehat{\theta}_1))D(\widehat{\theta}_1)']^{-1}[C(\widehat{\theta}_1) - Q] \tag{4.10}$$

$$W_J = T[C(\widehat{\theta}_1) - Q]'[D(\widehat{\theta}_1)\,J_T^{-1}(\widehat{\theta}_1)D(\widehat{\theta}_1)']^{-1}[C(\widehat{\theta}_1) - Q]. \tag{4.11}$$

Under the null hypothesis, the Wald statistic is asymptotically distributed as χ_M^2 where M is the number of restrictions. If the restrictions are linear, that is $C(\theta) = R\,\theta$, then

$$\frac{\partial C(\theta)}{\partial \theta'} = R,$$

and equations (4.9), (4.10) and (4.11) reduce to the forms given in equations (4.5), (4.6) and (4.7), respectively.

4.6 Lagrange Multiplier Test

The LM test is based on the property that the gradient, evaluated at the unrestricted maximum likelihood estimator, satisfies $G_T(\widehat{\theta}_1) = 0$. Assuming that the log-likelihood function has a unique maximum, evaluating the gradient under the null means that $G_T(\widehat{\theta}_0) \neq 0$. This suggests that if the null hypothesis is inconsistent with the data, the value of $G_T(\widehat{\theta}_0)$ represents a significant deviation from the unrestricted value of the gradient vector, $G_T(\widehat{\theta}_1) = 0$. A natural test statistic, therefore, is to compute the squared difference between the sample quantity under the null hypothesis, $G_T(\widehat{\theta}_0)$, and the theoretical value under the alternative, $G_T(\widehat{\theta}_1) = 0$ and scale the result by the increase of the covariance matrix, $I(\theta_0)/T$. Evaluating all terms at $\widehat{\theta}_0$, the general form of LM statistic is

$$LM = T[G_T'(\widehat{\theta}_0) - 0]'I^{-1}(\widehat{\theta}_0)[G_T'(\widehat{\theta}_0) - 0] = T G_T'(\widehat{\theta}_0)I^{-1}(\widehat{\theta}_0)G_T(\widehat{\theta}_0). \tag{4.12}$$

This statistic is distributed asymptotically as χ^2_M where M is the number of restrictions under the null hypothesis. This general form of the LM test is similar to that of the Wald test, where the test statistic is compared to a population value under the null hypothesis and standardised by the appropriate variance.

As in the computation of the Wald statistic, the covariance matrix can be based on the information matrix, $T(\theta)$, the Hessian matrix, $H_T(\theta)$, and the outer product of gradients matrix, $J_T(\theta)$, which are all asymptotically equivalent under the null hypothesis. It follows that the LM statistic has the following asymptotically equivalent forms:

$$LM_I = TG'_T(\widehat{\theta}_0)I^{-1}(\widehat{\theta}_0)G_T(\widehat{\theta}_0), \tag{4.13}$$

$$LM_H = TG'_T(\widehat{\theta}_0)(-H_T^{-1}(\widehat{\theta}_0))G_T(\widehat{\theta}_0), \tag{4.14}$$

$$LM_J = TG'_T(\widehat{\theta}_0)J_T^{-1}(\widehat{\theta}_0)G_T(\widehat{\theta}_0). \tag{4.15}$$

Example 4.6 Normal Distribution

Consider again the normal distribution in Examples 4.1 and 4.4 where the null and alternative hypotheses are, respectively,

$$H_0 : \mu = \mu_0, \qquad H_1 : \mu \neq \mu_0.$$

The restricted maximum likelihood estimators are

$$\widehat{\theta}_0 = \begin{bmatrix} \widehat{\mu}_0 & \widehat{\sigma}_0^2 \end{bmatrix}' = \begin{bmatrix} \mu_0 & \frac{1}{T}\sum_{t=1}^T (y_t - \mu_0)^2 \end{bmatrix}'.$$

The gradient and information matrix evaluated at $\widehat{\theta}_0$ are, respectively,

$$G_T(\widehat{\theta}_0) = \begin{bmatrix} \dfrac{1}{\widehat{\sigma}_0^2 T}\sum_{t=1}^T (y_t - \mu_0) \\[2ex] -\dfrac{1}{2\widehat{\sigma}_0^2} + \dfrac{1}{2\widehat{\sigma}_0^4 T}\sum_{t=1}^T (y_t - \mu_0)^2 \end{bmatrix} = \begin{bmatrix} \dfrac{1}{\widehat{\sigma}_0^2}(\overline{y} - \mu_0) \\[2ex] 0 \end{bmatrix},$$

and

$$I(\widehat{\theta}_0) = \begin{bmatrix} \dfrac{1}{\widehat{\sigma}_0^2} & 0 \\[2ex] 0 & \dfrac{1}{2\widehat{\sigma}_0^4} \end{bmatrix}.$$

The LM statistic based on the information matrix is

$$LM = T\begin{bmatrix} \dfrac{1}{\widehat{\sigma}_0^2}(\overline{y} - \mu_0) \\[2ex] 0 \end{bmatrix}' \begin{bmatrix} \dfrac{1}{\widehat{\sigma}_0^2} & 0 \\[2ex] 0 & \dfrac{1}{2\widehat{\sigma}_0^4} \end{bmatrix}^{-1} \begin{bmatrix} \dfrac{1}{\widehat{\sigma}_0^2}(\overline{y} - \mu_0) \\[2ex] 0 \end{bmatrix} = \dfrac{T(\overline{y} - \mu_0)^2}{\widehat{\sigma}_0^2},$$

which is distributed asymptotically as χ_1^2. This statistic is of a similar form to the Wald statistic in Example 4.4, except that now the variance in the denominator is based on the restricted estimator, $\widehat{\sigma}_0^2$, whereas in the Wald statistic it is based on the unrestricted estimator, $\widehat{\sigma}_1^2$. □

Example 4.7 Weibull Distribution

Re-consider the Weibull distribution testing problem in Examples 4.3 and 4.5. The null hypothesis is $\beta = 1$, which is to be tested using a LM test based on the outer product of gradients matrix. The gradient vector evaluated at $\widehat{\theta}_0$ using numerical derivatives is

$$G_T(\widehat{\theta}_0) = [0.000, 0.599]' .$$

The outer product of gradients matrix using numerical derivatives and evaluated at $\widehat{\theta}_0$ is

$$J_T(\widehat{\theta}_0) = \begin{bmatrix} 0.248 & -0.176 \\ -0.176 & 1.002 \end{bmatrix} .$$

From equation (4.15), the LM statistic is

$$LM_J = 20 \begin{bmatrix} 0.000 \\ 0.599 \end{bmatrix}' \begin{bmatrix} 0.248 & -0.176 \\ -0.176 & 1.002 \end{bmatrix}^{-1} \begin{bmatrix} 0.000 \\ 0.599 \end{bmatrix} = 8.175 .$$

Using the χ_1^2 distribution, the p-value is 0.004, which leads to a rejection of the null hypothesis at the 5% significance level that the data are drawn from an exponential distribution. This result is consistent with those obtained using the LR and Wald tests in Examples 4.3 and 4.5, respectively. □

4.7 Distribution Theory

The asymptotic distributions of the LR, Wald and LM tests under the null hypothesis have all been stated to be simply χ_M^2, where M is the number of restrictions being tested. To show this result formally, the asymptotic distribution of the Wald statistic is derived initially and then used to establish the asymptotic relationships between the three test statistics.

4.7.1 Asymptotic Distribution of the Wald Statistic

To derive the asymptotic distribution of the Wald statistic, the crucial link to be drawn is that between the normal distribution and the chi-square distribution. The chi-square distribution with M degrees of freedom is

$$f(y) = \frac{1}{\Gamma(M/2) 2^{M/2}} y^{M/2-1} \exp[-y/2] . \tag{4.16}$$

Consider the simple case of the distribution of $y = z^2$, in which $z \sim N(0, 1)$. Note that the standard normal variable z has as its domain the entire real line, while the transformed variable y is constrained to be positive. This change of domain means that the inverse function is given by $z = \pm\sqrt{y}$. To express the probability distribution of y in terms of the given probability distribution of z, use the change of variable technique (see Appendix A)

$$f(y) = f(z) \left| \frac{dz}{dy} \right|,$$

in which $dz/dy = \pm y^{-1/2}/2$ is the Jacobian of the transformation. The probability of every y therefore has contributions from both $f(-z)$ and $f(z)$

$$f(y) = f(z) \left| \frac{dz}{dy} \right|_{z=-\sqrt{y}} + f(z) \left| \frac{dz}{dy} \right|_{z=\sqrt{y}}. \tag{4.17}$$

Upon substituting the standard normal distribution in equation (4.17) yields

$$f(y) = \frac{1}{\sqrt{2\pi}} \exp\left[-\frac{z^2}{2} \right] \left| \frac{1}{2z} \right|_{z=-\sqrt{y}} + \frac{1}{\sqrt{2\pi}} \exp\left[-\frac{z^2}{2} \right] \left| \frac{1}{2z} \right|_{z=+\sqrt{y}}$$

$$= \frac{y^{-1/2}}{\sqrt{2\pi}} \exp\left[-\frac{z^2}{2} \right]$$

$$= \frac{y^{-1/2}}{\Gamma(1/2)\sqrt{2}} \exp\left[-\frac{y}{2} \right], \tag{4.18}$$

where the last step follows from the property of the gamma function that $\Gamma(1/2) = \sqrt{\pi}$. This is the chi-square distribution in (4.16) with $M = 1$ degrees of freedom.

Example 4.8 Single Restriction Case
Consider the hypotheses

$$H_0 : \mu = \mu_0, \qquad H_1 : \mu \neq \mu_0,$$

to be tested by means of the simple t statistic

$$z = \sqrt{T} \frac{\widehat{\mu} - \mu_0}{\widehat{\sigma}},$$

in which $\widehat{\mu}$ is the sample mean and $\widehat{\sigma}^2$ is the sample variance. From the Lindeberg-Levy central limit theorem in Chapter 2, $z \xrightarrow{d} N(0, 1)$ under H_0, so that from equation (4.18) it follows that z^2 is distributed as χ_1^2. But from equation (4.4), the statistic $z^2 = T(\widehat{\mu} - \mu_0)^2/\widehat{\sigma}^2$ corresponds to the Wald test of the restriction. The Wald statistic is, therefore, asymptotically distributed as a χ_1^2 random variable. $\qquad\square$

The relationship between the normal distribution and the chi-square distribution may be generalised to the case of multiple random variables. If $z_1, z_2, \cdots, z_M$ are M independent standard normal random variables, the transformed random variable,

$$y = z_1^2 + z_2^2 + \cdots z_M^2, \tag{4.19}$$

is χ_M^2, which follows from the additivity property of chi-square random variables.

Example 4.9 Multiple Restriction Case

Consider the Wald statistic given in equation (4.5)

$$W = T[R\widehat{\theta}_1 - Q]'[R\, I^{-1}(\widehat{\theta}_1)\, R']^{-1}[R\widehat{\theta}_1 - Q].$$

Using the Choleski decomposition, it is possible to write

$$R I^{-1}(\widehat{\theta}_1) R' = SS',$$

in which S is a lower triangular matrix that has the property

$$[R I^{-1}(\widehat{\theta}_1) R']^{-1} = (SS')^{-1} = S^{-1'} S^{-1}.$$

It is now possible to write the Wald statistic as

$$W = T[R\widehat{\theta}_1 - Q]' S^{-1'} S^{-1}[R\widehat{\theta}_1 - Q] = z'z = \sum_{i=1}^{M} z_i^2,$$

where

$$z = \sqrt{T} S^{-1}[R\widehat{\theta}_1 - Q] \xrightarrow{d} N(0_M, I_M).$$

Using the additive property of chi-square variables given in (4.19), it follows immediately that $W \xrightarrow{d} \chi_M^2$. $\qquad \square$

The following simulation experiment illustrates the theoretical results concerning the asymptotic distribution of the Wald statistic.

Example 4.10 Simulating the Distribution of the Wald Statistic

The multiple regression model

$$y_t = \beta_0 + \beta_1 x_{1,t} + \beta_2 x_{2,t} + \beta_3 x_{3,t} + u_t, \qquad u_t \sim iid\, N(0, \sigma^2),$$

is simulated 10000 times with a sample size of $T = 1000$ with explanatory variables $x_{1,t} \sim U(0, 1)$, $x_{2,t} \sim N(0, 1)$, $x_{3,t} \sim N(0, 1)^2$, which are fixed in repeated samples, and population parameter values $\theta_0 = \{\beta_0 = 1, \beta_1 = 0, \beta_2 = 0, \beta_3 = 0, \sigma^2 = 0.1\}$. The Wald statistic is constructed to test the hypotheses

$$H_0 : \beta_1 = \beta_2 = \beta_3 = 0, \quad H_1 : \text{ at least one restriction does not hold.}$$

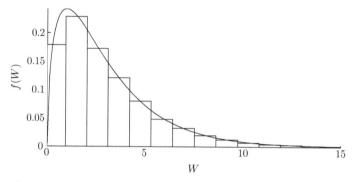

Figure 4.3. Simulated distribution of the Wald statistic (bars) and the asymptotic distribution (solid line) based on a χ^2_3 distribution.

As there are $M = 3$ restrictions, the asymptotic distribution under the null hypothesis of the Wald test is χ^2_3. Figure 4.3 shows that the simulated distribution (bar chart) of the test statistic matches its asymptotic distribution (continuous line). □

4.7.2 Asymptotic Relationships Among the Tests

The previous section establishes that the Wald test statistic is asymptotically distributed as χ^2_M under H_0, where M is the number of restrictions being tested. The relationships among the LR, Wald and LM tests are now used to demonstrate that all three test statistics have the same asymptotic distribution under the null hypothesis.

Suppose the null hypothesis $H_0 : \theta = \theta_0$ is true. Expanding $\ln L_T(\theta)$ in a second-order Taylor series expansion around $\widehat{\theta}_1$ and evaluating at $\theta = \theta_0$ gives

$$\ln L_T(\theta_0) \simeq \ln L_T(\widehat{\theta}_1) + (\theta_0 - \widehat{\theta}_1)' G_T(\widehat{\theta}_1) + \frac{1}{2}(\theta_0 - \widehat{\theta}_1)' H_T(\widehat{\theta}_1)(\theta_0 - \widehat{\theta}_1),$$

$$(4.20)$$

where

$$G_T(\widehat{\theta}_1) = \left. \frac{\partial \ln L_T(\theta)}{\partial \theta} \right|_{\theta = \widehat{\theta}_1}, \qquad H_T(\widehat{\theta}_1) = \left. \frac{\partial^2 \ln L_T(\theta)}{\partial \theta \, \partial \theta'} \right|_{\theta = \widehat{\theta}_1}.$$

$$(4.21)$$

The remainder in this Taylor series expansion is asymptotically negligible because $\widehat{\theta}_1$ is a $\sqrt{T}$-consistent estimator of θ_0. The first-order conditions of a maximum likelihood estimator require $G_T(\widehat{\theta}_1) = 0$ so that equation (4.20) reduces to

$$\ln L_T(\theta_0) \simeq \ln L_T(\widehat{\theta}_1) + \frac{1}{2}(\theta_0 - \widehat{\theta}_1)' H_T(\widehat{\theta}_1)(\theta_0 - \widehat{\theta}_1).$$

Multiplying both sides by T and rearranging gives

$$-2T\left(\ln L_T(\theta_0) - \ln L_T(\widehat{\theta}_1)\right) \simeq -T(\theta_0 - \widehat{\theta}_1)' H_T(\widehat{\theta}_1)(\theta_0 - \widehat{\theta}_1).$$

The left-hand side of this equation is the LR statistic and the right-hand side is the Wald statistic based on the Hessian. It follows directly, therefore, that the LR and Wald tests are asymptotically equivalent under H_0.

To show the relationship between the LM and Wald tests, expand

$$G_T(\theta) = \frac{\partial \ln L_T(\theta)}{\partial \theta},$$

in terms of a first-order Taylor series expansion around $\widehat{\theta}_1$ and evaluate at $\theta = \theta_0$ to get

$$G_T(\theta_0) \simeq G_T(\widehat{\theta}_1) + H_T(\widehat{\theta}_1)(\theta_0 - \widehat{\theta}_1),$$

where $G_T(\widehat{\theta}_1)$ and $H_T(\widehat{\theta}_1)$ are as defined in (4.21). Using the first-order conditions of the maximum likelihood estimator simplifies the expression as

$$G_T(\theta_0) \simeq H_T(\widehat{\theta}_1)(\theta_0 - \widehat{\theta}_1).$$

Substituting this expression into the LM statistic based on the Hessian gives

$$LM \simeq T(\widehat{\theta}_1 - \theta_0)' H_T(\widehat{\theta}_1)(-H_T^{-1}(\theta_0))H_T(\widehat{\theta}_1)'(\widehat{\theta}_1 - \theta_0).$$

As $H_T(\widehat{\theta}_0)$ and $H_T(\widehat{\theta}_1)$ are asymptotically equivalent under the null hypothesis this expression simplifies further to

$$LM \simeq T(\widehat{\theta}_1 - \theta_0)'(-H_T(\theta_0))(\widehat{\theta}_1 - \theta_0),$$

where the right-hand side is the Wald statistic based on the Hessian. This demonstrates that the LM and Wald tests are asymptotically equivalent under the null hypothesis.

As the LR, W and LM test statistics have the same asymptotic distribution, the choice of which to use is governed by convenience. When it is easier to estimate the unrestricted (restricted) model, the Wald (LM) test is the most convenient to compute. The LM test tends to dominate diagnostic analysis of regression models with normally distributed disturbances because the model under the null hypothesis is often estimated using a least squares estimation procedure. These features of the LM test are developed in Part TWO.

4.7.3   Finite Sample Relationships

The discussion of the LR, Wald and LM test statistics so far is based on asymptotic distribution theory. In general, the finite sample distribution of the test statistics is unknown and is commonly approximated by the asymptotic distribution. In situations where the asymptotic distribution does not provide an accurate approximation of the finite sample distribution, three possible solutions exist.

(1) *Second-order approximations*
   The asymptotic results are based on a first-order Taylor series expansion of the gradient of the log-likelihood function. In some cases, extending the expansions to higher-order terms by using Edgeworth expansions for example (see Example 2.28), will generally provide a more accurate approximation to the sampling distribution of the maximum likelihood estimator. However, this is more easily said than done, because deriving the sampling distribution of nonlinear functions is much more difficult than deriving sampling distributions of linear functions.

(2) *Monte Carlo methods*
   To circumvent the analytical problems associated with deriving the sampling distribution of the maximum likelihood estimator for finite samples using second-order or even higher-order expansions, a more convenient approach is to use Monte Carlo methods. The approach is to simulate the finite sample distribution of the test statistic for particular values of the sample size, T, by running the simulation for these sample sizes and computing the corresponding critical values from the simulated values.

(3) *Transformations*
   A final approach is to transform the statistic so that the asymptotic distribution provides a better approximation to the finite sample distribution. A well-known example is the distribution of the test of the correlation coefficient, which is asymptotically normally distributed, although convergence is relatively slow as T increases (Stuart and Ord, 1994, p567).

When testing linear restrictions of the coefficients in a normal linear regression model, the three test statistics satisfy the finite sample inequalities

$$W \geq LR \geq LM \,.$$

This result implies that the LM test tends to be a more conservative test in finite samples because the Wald statistic tends to reject the null hypothesis more frequently than the LR statistic, which, in turn, tends to reject the null hypothesis more frequently than the LM statistic. This relationship is highlighted by the Wald and LM tests of the normal distribution in Examples 4.4 and 4.6, respectively, because $\hat{\sigma}_1^2 \leq \hat{\sigma}_0^2$, it follows that

$$W = T \frac{(\bar{y} - \theta_0)^2}{\hat{\sigma}_1^2} \geq LM = T \frac{(\bar{y} - \theta_0)^2}{\hat{\sigma}_0^2} .$$

4.8 Size and Power Properties

4.8.1 Size of a Test

The probability of rejecting the null hypothesis when it is true (a Type-1 error) is usually denoted α and called the level of significance or the size of a test. For a test with size $\alpha = 0.05$, therefore, the null is rejected for p-values of less than 0.05. Equivalently, the null is rejected where the test statistic falls within a rejection region, ω, in which case the size of the test is expressed conveniently (in the case of the Wald test) as

$$\text{Size} = P(W \in \omega | H_0) . \tag{4.22}$$

In a simulation experiment, the size is computed by simulating the model under the null hypothesis, H_0, that is when the restrictions are true, and computing the proportion of simulated values of the test statistic that are greater than the critical value obtained from the asymptotic distribution. The asymptotic distribution of the LR, W and LM tests is χ^2 with M degrees of freedom under the null hypothesis; so in this case the critical value is $\chi_M^2(0.05)$.

Subject to some simulation error, the simulated and asymptotic sizes should match. In finite samples, however, this may not be true. In the case where the simulated size is greater than 0.05, the test is oversized with the null hypothesis being rejected more often than predicted by asymptotic theory. In the case where the simulated size is less than 0.05, the test is undersized (conservative) with the null hypothesis being rejected less often than predicted by asymptotic theory.

Example 4.11 Computing the Size of a Test by Simulation
Consider testing the hypotheses

$$H_0 : \beta_1 = 0, \qquad H_1 : \beta_1 \neq 0,$$

in the exponential regression model

$$f(y_t | x_t; \theta) = \mu_t^{-1} \exp\left[-\mu_t^{-1} y_t\right] ,$$

in which $\mu_t = \exp[\beta_0 + \beta_1 x_t]$ and $\theta = \{\beta_0, \beta_1\}$. Computing the size of the test requires simulating the model 10000 times under the null hypothesis $\beta_1 = 0$ for samples of size $T = \{5, 10, 25, 100\}$ with $x_t \sim iid\ N(0, 1)$, which is fixed in repeated samples, and the intercept is $\beta_0 = 1$. For each simulation, the Wald statistic

$$W = \frac{(\widehat{\beta}_1 - 0)^2}{\text{var}(\widehat{\beta}_1)} \, .$$

is computed. The size of the Wald test is computed as the proportion of the 10000 statistics with values greater than $\chi_1^2(0.05) = 3.841$. The results are as follows:

T:	5	10	25	100
Size:	0.066	0.053	0.052	0.051
Critical value (Simulated, 5%):	4.288	3.975	3.905	3.873

The test is slightly oversized for $T = 5$ since $0.066 > 0.05$, but the empirical size approaches the asymptotic size of 0.05 very quickly for $T \geq 10$. Also given are the simulated critical values corresponding to the value of the test statistic, which is exceeded by 5% of the simulated values. The fact that the test is oversized results in critical values in excess of the asymptotic critical value of 3.841. □

4.8.2 Power of a Test

The probability of rejecting the null hypothesis when it is false is called the 'power' of a test. A second type of error that occurs in hypothesis testing is failing to reject the null hypothesis when it is false (a Type-2 error). The power of a test is expressed formally (in the case of the Wald test) as

$$\text{Power} = P\left(W \in \omega \mid H_1\right), \tag{4.23}$$

so that $1 - \text{Power}$ is the probability of committing a Type-2 error.

In a simulation experiment, the power is computed by simulating the model under the alternative hypothesis, H_1; that is, when the restrictions stated in the null hypothesis, H_0, are false. The proportion of simulated values of the test statistic greater than the critical value then gives the power of the test. Here the critical value is not the one obtained from the asymptotic distribution, but rather from simulating the distribution of the statistic under the null hypothesis and then choosing the value that has a fixed size of, say, 0.05. As the size is fixed at a certain level in computing the power of a test, the power is then referred to as a size-adjusted power.

Example 4.12 Computing the Power of a Test by Simulation
Consider again the exponential regression model of Example 4.11 with the null hypothesis given by $\beta_1 = 0$. The power of the Wald test is computed for

10000 samples of size $T = 5$ with intercept $\beta_0 = 1$ and with the slope given by $\beta_1 = \{-4, -3, -2, -1, 0, 1, 2, 3, 4\}$. For each value of β_1, the size-adjusted power of the test is computed as the proportion of the 10000 statistics with values greater than 4.288, the critical value from Example 4.11 corresponding to a size of 0.05 for $T = 5$. The results are as follows:

β_1 :	-4	-3	-2	-1	0	1	2	3	4
Power:	0.99	0.98	0.86	0.38	0.05	0.42	0.89	0.99	0.99

The power of the Wald test at $\beta_1 = 0$ is 0.05 by construction as the powers are size-adjusted. The size-adjusted power of the test increases monotonically as the value of the parameter β_1 moves further and further away from its value under the null hypothesis with a maximum power of 99% attained at $\beta_1 = \pm 4$. $\square$

An important property of any test is that, as the sample increases, the probability of rejecting the null hypothesis when it is false, or the power of the test, approaches unity in the limit

$$\lim_{T \to \infty} P(W \in \omega | H_1) = 1. \tag{4.24}$$

A test having this property is known as a consistent test.

Example 4.13 Illustrating the Consistency of a Test by Simulation
The testing problem in the exponential regression model introduced in Examples 4.11 and 4.12 is now developed. The power of the Wald test, with respect to testing the null hypothesis $H_0 : \beta_1 = 0$, is computed for 10000 samples using parameter values $\beta_0 = 1$ and $\beta_1 = 1$. The results obtained for increasing sample sizes are given in the following table.

T:	5	10	25	100
Power:	0.420	0.647	0.993	1.000
Critical value (Simulated, 5%):	4.288	3.975	3.905	3.873

In computing the power for each sample size, a different critical value is used to ensure that the size of the test is 0.05 and, therefore, that the power values reported are size-adjusted. The results show that the Wald test is consistent because Power $\to 1$ as T is increased. $\square$

4.9   Applications

Two applications of LR, Wald and LM tests are now presented. The first involves performing tests of the parameters of an exponential regression model. The second extends the exponential regression example by generalising the distribution to a gamma distribution. Further applications of the three testing procedures to regression models are discussed in Part TWO of the book.

4.9.1   *Exponential Regression Model*

Consider the exponential regression model where y_t is assumed to be independent, but not identically distributed, from an exponential distribution with time-varying mean

$$E[y_t] = \mu_t = \beta_0 + \beta_1 x_t, \tag{4.25}$$

where x_t is the explanatory variable held fixed in repeated samples. The aim is to test the hypotheses

$$H_0 : \beta_1 = 0, \qquad H_1 : \beta_1 \neq 0. \tag{4.26}$$

Under the null hypothesis, the mean of y_t is simply β_0, which implies that y_t is an *iid* random variable. The parameters under the null and alternative hypotheses are, respectively, $\theta_0 = \{\beta_0, 0\}$ and $\theta_1 = \{\beta_0, \beta_1\}$.

As the distribution of y_t is exponential with mean μ_t, the log-likelihood function is

$$\ln L_T(\theta) = \frac{1}{T} \sum_{t=1}^{T} \left(-\ln(\mu_t) - \frac{y_t}{\mu_t} \right)$$

$$= -\frac{1}{T} \sum_{t=1}^{T} \ln(\beta_0 + \beta_1 x_t) - \frac{1}{T} \sum_{t=1}^{T} \frac{y_t}{\beta_0 + \beta_1 x_t}.$$

The gradient vector is

$$G_T(\theta) = \begin{bmatrix} \dfrac{1}{T} \sum_{t=1}^{T} (-\mu_t^{-1} + \mu_t^{-2} y_t) \\[2mm] \dfrac{1}{T} \sum_{t=1}^{T} (-\mu_t^{-1} + \mu_t^{-2} y_t) x_t \end{bmatrix},$$

and the Hessian matrix is

$$H_T(\theta) = \begin{bmatrix} \dfrac{1}{T} \sum_{t=1}^{T} (\mu_t^{-2} - 2\mu_t^{-3} y_t) & \dfrac{1}{T} \sum_{t=1}^{T} (\mu_t^{-2} - 2\mu_t^{-3} y_t) x_t \\[2mm] \dfrac{1}{T} \sum_{t=1}^{T} (\mu_t^{-2} - 2\mu_t^{-3} y_t) x_t & \dfrac{1}{T} \sum_{t=1}^{T} (\mu_t^{-2} - 2\mu_t^{-3} y_t) x_t^2 \end{bmatrix}.$$

Taking expectations and changing the sign gives the information matrix

$$I(\theta) = \begin{bmatrix} \dfrac{1}{T}\displaystyle\sum_{t=1}^{T}\mu_t^{-2} & \dfrac{1}{T}\displaystyle\sum_{t=1}^{T}\mu_t^{-2}x_t \\ \dfrac{1}{T}\displaystyle\sum_{t=1}^{T}\mu_t^{-2}x_t & \dfrac{1}{T}\displaystyle\sum_{t=1}^{T}\mu_t^{-2}x_t^2 \end{bmatrix}.$$

A sample of $T = 2000$ observations on y_t and x_t is generated from the following exponential regression model

$$f(y_t;\theta) = \frac{1}{\mu_t}\exp\left[-\frac{y_t}{\mu_t}\right], \qquad \mu_t = \beta_0 + \beta_1 x_t,$$

with parameters $\theta = \{\beta_0, \beta_1\}$. The parameters are set at $\beta_0 = 1$ and $\beta_1 = 2$ and $x_t \sim U(0, 1)$. The unrestricted parameter estimates, the gradient and log-likelihood function value are respectively given by

$$\widehat{\theta}_1 = [1.101, 1.760]', \quad G_T(\widehat{\theta}_1) = [0.000, 0.000]', \quad \ln L_T(\widehat{\theta}_1) = -1.653.$$

Evaluating the Hessian, information and outer product of gradient matrices at the unrestricted parameter estimates gives, respectively,

$$H_T(\widehat{\theta}_1) = \begin{bmatrix} -0.315 & -0.110 \\ -0.110 & -0.062 \end{bmatrix}$$

$$I(\widehat{\theta}_1) = \begin{bmatrix} 0.315 & 0.110 \\ 0.110 & 0.062 \end{bmatrix} \tag{4.27}$$

$$J_T(\widehat{\theta}_1) = \begin{bmatrix} 0.313 & 0.103 \\ 0.103 & 0.057 \end{bmatrix}.$$

The restricted parameter estimates, the gradient and log-likelihood function value are, respectively

$$\widehat{\theta}_0 = [1.989, 0.000]', \quad G_T(\widehat{\theta}_0) = [0.000, 0.037]', \quad \ln L_T(\widehat{\theta}_0) = -1.688.$$

Evaluating the Hessian, information and outer product of gradients matrices at the restricted parameter estimates gives, respectively,

$$H_T(\widehat{\theta}_0) = \begin{bmatrix} -0.377 & -0.092 \\ -0.092 & -0.038 \end{bmatrix}$$

$$I(\widehat{\theta}_0) = \begin{bmatrix} 0.253 & 0.128 \\ 0.128 & 0.086 \end{bmatrix} \tag{4.28}$$

$$J_T(\widehat{\theta}_0) = \begin{bmatrix} 0.265 & 0.165 \\ 0.165 & 0.123 \end{bmatrix}.$$

To test the hypotheses in (4.26), compute the LR statistic as

$$LR = -2T(\ln L_T(\widehat{\theta}_0) - \ln L_T(\widehat{\theta}_1)) = -2 \times 20(-1.688 + 1.653) = 138.425.$$

Using the χ_1^2 distribution, the p-value is 0.000 indicating a rejection of the null hypothesis that $\beta_1 = 0$ at conventional significance levels, a result that is consistent with the data-generating process.

To perform the Wald test, define $R = [0\ 1]$ and $Q = [0]$. Three Wald statistics are computed using the Hessian, information and outer product of gradients matrices in (4.27) are

$$
\begin{aligned}
W_H &= T[R\widehat{\theta}_1 - Q]'[R(-H^{-1}(\widehat{\theta}_1))\,R']^{-1}[R\widehat{\theta}_1 - Q] = 145.545 \\
W_I &= T[R\widehat{\theta}_1 - Q]'[R\,I^{-1}(\widehat{\theta}_1)\,R']^{-1}[R\widehat{\theta}_1 - Q] \quad = 147.338 \\
W_J &= T[R\widehat{\theta}_1 - Q]'[R\,J^{-1}(\widehat{\theta}_1)\,R']^{-1}[R\widehat{\theta}_1 - Q] \quad = 139.690\,.
\end{aligned}
$$

Using the χ_1^2 distribution, all p-values are 0.000, showing that the null hypothesis that $\beta_1 = 0$ is rejected at the 5% significance level for all three versions of the Wald test.

Finally, three Lagrange multiplier statistics are computed using the Hessian, information and outer product of gradients matrices, as in (4.28)

$$
LM_H = TG_T'(\widehat{\theta}_0)(-H_T^{-1}(\widehat{\theta}_0))G_T(\widehat{\theta}_0)
$$

$$
= 2000 \begin{bmatrix} 0.000 \\ 0.037 \end{bmatrix}' \begin{bmatrix} 0.377 & 0.092 \\ 0.092 & 0.038 \end{bmatrix}^{-1} \begin{bmatrix} 0.000 \\ 0.037 \end{bmatrix}
$$

$$
= 169.698\,,
$$

$$
LM_I = TG_T'(\widehat{\theta}_0)I^{-1}(\widehat{\theta}_0)G_T(\widehat{\theta}_0)
$$

$$
= 2000 \begin{bmatrix} 0.000 \\ 0.037 \end{bmatrix}' \begin{bmatrix} 0.253 & 0.128 \\ 0.128 & 0.086 \end{bmatrix}^{-1} \begin{bmatrix} 0.000 \\ 0.037 \end{bmatrix}
$$

$$
= 127.482\,,
$$

$$
LM_J = TG_T'(\widehat{\theta}_0)J_T^{-1}(\widehat{\theta}_0)G_T(\widehat{\theta}_0)
$$

$$
= 2000 \begin{bmatrix} 0.000 \\ 0.037 \end{bmatrix}' \begin{bmatrix} 0.265 & 0.165 \\ 0.165 & 0.123 \end{bmatrix}^{-1} \begin{bmatrix} 0.000 \\ 0.037 \end{bmatrix}
$$

$$
= 129.678\,.
$$

Using the χ_1^2 distribution, all p-values are 0.000, showing that the null hypothesis that $\beta_1 = 0$ is rejected at the 5% significance level for all three LM tests.

4.9.2 Gamma Regression Model

Consider the gamma regression model where y_t is assumed to be independent but not identically distributed from a gamma distribution with time-varying mean

$$E[y_t] = \mu_t = \beta_0 + \beta_1 x_t,$$

where x_t is the explanatory variable. The gamma distribution is given by

$$f(y_t|x_t;\theta) = \frac{1}{\Gamma(\rho)}\left(\frac{1}{\mu_t}\right)^\rho y_t^{\rho-1} \exp\left[-\frac{y_t}{\mu_t}\right], \qquad \Gamma(\rho) = \int_0^\infty s^{\rho-1}e^{-s}ds,$$

with $\theta = \{\beta_0, \beta_1, \rho\}$. As the gamma distribution nests the exponential distribution when $\rho = 1$, a natural hypothesis to test is

$$H_0 : \rho = 1, \qquad H_1 : \rho \neq 1.$$

The log-likelihood function is

$$\ln L_T(\theta) = -\ln \Gamma(\rho) - \frac{\rho}{T}\sum_{t=1}^{T}\ln(\beta_0 + \beta_1 x_t) + \frac{\rho-1}{T}\sum_{t=1}^{T}\ln y_t$$
$$- \frac{1}{T}\sum_{t=1}^{T}\frac{y_t}{\beta_0 + \beta_1 x_t}.$$

As the gamma function, $\Gamma(\rho)$, appears in the likelihood function, it is convenient to use numerical derivatives to calculate the maximum likelihood estimates and the test statistics.

The following numerical illustration uses the data from the previous application on the exponential regression model. The unrestricted maximum likelihood parameter estimates and log-likelihood function value are given by

$$\hat{\theta}_1 = [1.061, 1.698, 1.037]', \qquad \ln L_T(\hat{\theta}_1) = -1.65258,$$

respectively. The corresponding restricted values, which are also the unrestricted estimates of the exponential model of the previous application, are

$$\hat{\theta}_0 = [1.101, 1.760, 1.000]', \qquad \ln L_T(\hat{\theta}_0) = -1.65300.$$

The LR statistic is

$$LR = -2T(\ln L_T(\hat{\theta}_0) - \ln L_T(\hat{\theta}_1)) = -2 \times 2000(-1.65300 + 1.65258)$$
$$= 1.674.$$

Using the χ_1^2 distribution, the p-value is 0.196, which means that the null hypothesis that the distribution is exponential cannot be rejected at the 5% significance level, a result that is consistent with the data-generating process in Section 4.9.1.

The Wald statistic is computed with standard errors based on the Hessian evaluated at the unrestricted estimates. The Hessian matrix is

$$H_T(\widehat{\theta}_1) = \begin{bmatrix} -0.351 & -0.123 & -0.560 \\ -0.123 & -0.069 & -0.239 \\ -0.560 & -0.239 & -1.560 \end{bmatrix}.$$

Defining $R = [\,0\ 0\ 1\,]$ and $Q = [\,1\,]$, the Wald statistic is

$$
\begin{aligned}
W &= T[R\,\widehat{\theta}_1 - Q]'[R(-H_T^{-1}(\widehat{\theta}_1))R']^{-1}[R\,\widehat{\theta}_1 - Q] \\
&= \frac{(1.037 - 1.000)^2}{0.001} = 1.631\,.
\end{aligned}
$$

Using the χ_1^2 distribution, the p-value is 0.202, which also shows that the null hypothesis that the distribution is exponential cannot be rejected at the 5% significance level.

The LM statistic is based on the outer product of gradients matrix. To calculate the LM statistic, the gradient is evaluated at the restricted parameter estimates

$$G_T(\widehat{\theta}_0) = [\,0.000,\ 0.000,\ 0.023\,]'\,.$$

The outer product of gradients matrix evaluated at $\widehat{\theta}_0$ is

$$J_T(\widehat{\theta}_0) = \begin{bmatrix} 0.313 & 0.103 & 0.524 \\ 0.103 & 0.057 & 0.220 \\ 0.524 & 0.220 & 1.549 \end{bmatrix},$$

with inverse

$$J_T^{-1}(\widehat{\theta}_0) = \begin{bmatrix} 9.755 & -11.109 & -1.728 \\ -11.109 & 51.696 & -3.564 \\ -1.728 & -3.564 & 1.735 \end{bmatrix}.$$

The LM test statistic is

$$
\begin{aligned}
LM &= T\,G(\widehat{\theta}_0)'\,J_T^{-1}(\widehat{\theta}_0)\,G(\widehat{\theta}_0) \\
&= 2000 \begin{bmatrix} 0.000 \\ 0.000 \\ 0.023 \end{bmatrix}' \begin{bmatrix} 9.755 & -11.109 & -1.728 \\ -11.109 & 51.696 & -3.564 \\ -1.728 & -3.564 & 1.735 \end{bmatrix} \begin{bmatrix} 0.000 \\ 0.000 \\ 0.023 \end{bmatrix} \\
&= 1.853\,.
\end{aligned}
$$

Consistent with the results reported for the LR and Wald tests, using the χ_1^2 distribution the p-value of the LM test is 0.173 indicating that the null hypothesis cannot be rejected at the 5% level.

4.10   Exercises

(1) The Linear Regression Model

Program files   `test_regress.*`

Consider the regression model

$$y_t = \beta x_t + u_t, \qquad u_t \sim N(0, \sigma^2),$$

in which the explanatory variable is $x_t = \{1, 2, 4, 5, 8\}$. The aim is to test the hypotheses $H_0 : \beta = 1$, $H_1 : \beta \neq 1$.

(a) Simulate the model for $T = 5$ observations using the parameters $\beta = 1$, $\sigma^2 = 4$.

(b) Estimate the restricted model and unrestricted models and compute the corresponding values of the log-likelihood function. Perform a LR test choosing $\alpha = 0.05$ as the size of the test and interpret the result.

(c) Perform a Wald test choosing $\alpha = 0.05$ as the size of the test and interpret the result.

(d) Compute the gradient and Hessian of the unrestricted model, but evaluated at the restricted estimates $\widehat{\theta}_0$. Perform a LM test choosing $\alpha = 0.05$ as the size of the test and interpret the result.

(e) Repeat parts (b) to (d) where the hypothesis tests are based on the null hypothesis $H_0 : \beta = 0$. Interpret the results.

(f) Repeat parts (b) to (d) where the hypothesis tests are based on the null hypothesis $H_0 : \beta = 2$. Interpret the results.

(2) The Weibull Distribution

Program files   `test_weibull.*`

Generate $T = 20$ observations from the Weibull distribution

$$f(y_t; \theta) = \alpha \beta y_t^{\beta - 1} \exp \left[-\alpha y_t^{\beta} \right],$$

with $\theta = \{\alpha = 1, \beta = 2\}$.

(a) Compute the unrestricted maximum likelihood estimates, $\widehat{\theta}_1 = \{\widehat{\alpha}_1, \widehat{\beta}_1\}$ and the value of the log-likelihood function.

(b) A special case of the Weibull distribution is the exponential distribution where $\beta = 1$. Compute the restricted maximum likelihood estimates, $\widehat{\theta}_0 = \{\widehat{\alpha}_0, \widehat{\beta}_0 = 1\}$ and the value of the log-likelihood function.

(c) Test the hypotheses $H_0 : \beta = 1$, $H_1 : \beta \neq 1$ using a LR test, a Wald test and a LM test, and interpret the results.

(d) Test the hypotheses $H_0 : \beta = 2$, $H_1 : \beta \neq 2$ using a LR test, a Wald test and a LM test, and interpret the results.

(3) A Gamma Model of Interest Rates

Program files	`test_interest.*`
Data files	`eurodollar.*`

The data are daily seven-day Eurodollar rates from 1 June 1973 to 25 February 1995, a total of $T = 5505$ observations. In Chapter 3 the stationary distribution of the interest rate r_t, is assumed to have a gamma distribution

$$f(r_t; v, \omega) = \frac{\omega^v}{\Gamma(v)} r_t^{v-1} \exp[-\omega r_t],$$

where $\Gamma(\cdot)$ is the Gamma function and $\theta = \{v, \omega\}$ are unknown parameters.
(a) Compute the maximum likelihood estimates of v and ω, and the Hessian.
(b) The mean of the gamma distribution is given by

$$\mu = \frac{v}{\omega}.$$

Use the results of part (a) to compute $\widehat{\mu}$ and its standard error $se(\widehat{\mu})$. Perform a Wald test of the hypotheses

$$H_0 : \mu = 0.1 \quad H_1 : \mu \neq 0.1,$$

and interpret the results.
(c) The variance of the gamma distribution is given by

$$\sigma^2 = \frac{v}{\omega^2}.$$

Use the results of part (a) to compute $\widehat{\sigma}^2$ and its standard error $se(\widehat{\sigma}^2)$. Perform a Wald test of the hypotheses

$$H_0 : \sigma^2 = 0.1 \quad H_1 : \sigma^2 \neq 0.1,$$

and interpret the results.
(d) The skewness of the gamma distribution is given by

$$\kappa_3 = \frac{2}{\sqrt{v}}.$$

Use the results of part (a) to compute $\widehat{\kappa}_3$ and its standard error $se(\kappa_3)$. Perform a Wald test of the hypotheses

$$H_0 : \kappa_3 = 0 \quad H_1 : \kappa_3 \neq 0,$$

and interpret the results.
(e) The kurtosis of the gamma distribution is given by

$$\kappa_4 = 3 + \frac{6}{v}.$$

Use the results of part (a) to compute $\widehat{\kappa}_4$ and its standard error $\mathrm{se}(\kappa_4)$. Perform a Wald test of the hypotheses

$$H_0 : \kappa_4 = 3 \quad H_1 : \kappa_4 \neq 3,$$

and interpret the results.

(4) **Simulating the Distribution of the Wald Statistic**

Program files	`test_asymptotic.*`

Simulate the following multiple regression model 10000 times with a sample size of $T = 1000$

$$y_t = \beta_0 + \beta_1 x_{1,t} + \beta_2 x_{2,t} + \beta_3 x_{3,t} + u_t, \qquad u_t \sim iid \, N(0, \sigma^2),$$

where the explanatory variables are $x_{1,t} \sim U(0, 1)$, $x_{2,t} \sim N(0, 1)$, $x_{3,t} \sim N(0, 1)^2$, which are fixed in repeated samples, and $\theta_0 = \{\beta_0 = 1, \beta_1 = 0, \beta_2 = 0, \beta_3 = 0, \sigma^2 = 0.1\}$.

(a) For each simulation, compute the Wald test of the null hypothesis $H_0 : \beta_1 = 0$, and compare the simulated distribution to the asymptotic distribution given by the χ^2 distribution with 1 degree of freedom.

(b) For each simulation, compute the Wald test of the joint null hypothesis $H_0 : \beta_1 = \beta_2 = 0$, and compare the simulated distribution to the asymptotic distribution given by the χ^2 distribution with 2 degrees of freedom.

(c) For each simulation, compute the Wald test of the joint null hypothesis $H_0 : \beta_1 = \beta_2 = \beta_3 = 0$, and compare the simulated distribution to the asymptotic distribution given by the χ^2 distribution with 3 degrees of freedom.

(d) Repeat parts (a) to (c) for $T = \{10, 20\}$ and compare the simulated finite sample distribution of the Wald statistic with the asymptotic distribution given by the χ^2 distribution.

(5) **Simulating the Size and Power of the Wald Statistic**

Program files	`test_size.*, test_power.*`

Consider testing the hypotheses

$$H_0 : \beta_1 = 0, \qquad H_1 : \beta_1 \neq 0,$$

in the exponential regression model

$$f(y_t | x_t; \theta) = \mu_t^{-1} \exp\left[-\mu_t^{-1} y_t\right],$$

in which $\mu_t = \exp[\beta_0 + \beta_1 x_t]$, $x_t \sim iid \, N(0, 1)$, which is fixed in repeated samples, and $\theta_0 = \{\beta_0 = 1, \beta_1 = 0\}$.

(a) Compute the sampling distribution of the Wald test by simulating the model under the null hypothesis 10000 times for increasing samples of size $T = \{5, 10, 25, 100, 500\}$. Using the 0.05 critical value from the asymptotic distribution of the test statistic, compute the size of the test. Also, compute the critical value from the simulated distribution corresponding to a simulated size of 0.05. Interpret the results of the simulations.

(b) Compute the power of the Wald test for increasing samples of size $T = \{5, 10, 25, 100, 500\}$ and for $\beta_1 = \{-4, -3, -2, -1, 0, 1, 2, 3, 4\}$ with fixed $\beta_0 = 1$. Interpret the results of the simulations.

(6) Exponential Regression Model

Program files   test_expreg.*, test_gammareg.*

Generate a sample of size $T = 2000$ observations from the following exponential regression model

$$f(y_t \mid x_t; \theta) = \frac{1}{\mu_t} \exp\left[-\frac{y_t}{\mu_t}\right],$$

in which $\mu_t = \beta_0 + \beta_1 x_t$, $x_t \sim iid\, U(0, 1)$, which is fixed in repeated samples, and the parameter values are $\beta_0 = 1$ and $\beta_1 = 2$.

(a) Compute the unrestricted maximum likelihood estimates, $\widehat{\theta}_1 = \{\widehat{\beta}_0, \widehat{\beta}_1\}$ and the value of the log-likelihood function, $\ln L_T(\widehat{\theta}_1)$.

(b) Re-estimate the model subject to the restriction that $\beta_1 = 0$ and re-compute the value of the log-likelihood function, $\ln L_T(\widehat{\theta}_0)$.

(c) Use LR, Wald and LM statistics to test the following hypotheses

$$H_0 : \beta_1 = 0, \qquad H_1 : \beta_1 \neq 0.$$

In performing the Wald and LM tests, compare the results using the Hessian, information and outer product of gradients matrices, based on both analytical and numerical derivatives. Interpret the results.

(d) Now assume that the true distribution is gamma

$$f(y_t \mid x_t; \theta) = \frac{1}{\Gamma(\rho)} \left(\frac{1}{\mu_t}\right)^{\rho} y_t^{\rho-1} \exp\left(-\frac{y_t}{\mu_t}\right),$$

with $\theta = \{\beta_1, \beta_2, \rho\}$. Use LR, Wald and LM statistics to test the following hypotheses

$$H_0 : \rho = 1, \qquad H_1 : \rho \neq 1.$$

In performing the Wald and LM tests, compare the results using the Hessian, information and outer product of gradients matrices, based on both analytical and numerical derivatives. Interpret the results.

(7) Neyman's Smooth Goodness of Fit Test

Program files   `test_smooth.*`

Let $y_{1,t}, y_{2,t}, \cdots, y_T$, be *iid* random variables with unknown distribution function F. A test that the distribution function is known and equal to F_0 is given by the respective null and alternative hypotheses

$$H_0 : F = F_0, \qquad H_1 : F \neq F_0.$$

The Neyman (1937) smooth goodness of fit test (see also Bera, Ghosh and Xiao, 2010 for a recent application) is based on the property that the random variable

$$u_t = F_0(y_t) = \int_{-\infty}^{y_t} f_0(s)ds,$$

is uniformly distributed under the null hypothesis. The approach is to specify the generalised uniform distribution

$$g(u_t) = c(\theta)\exp[1 + \theta_1\phi_1(u_t) + \theta_2\phi_2(u_t) + \theta_3\phi_3(u_t) + \theta_4\phi_4(u_t)],$$

in which $c(\theta)$ is the normalising constant given by

$$c(\theta)^{-1} = \int_0^1 \exp[1 + \theta_1\phi_1(u) + \theta_2\phi_2(u) + \theta_3\phi_3(u) + \theta_4\phi_4(u)]du,$$

which ensures that $g(u)$ is a proper density function. The terms $\phi_i(u)$ are the Legendre orthogonal polynomials given by

$$\phi_1(u) = 2\sqrt{3}\left(u - \frac{1}{2}\right)$$

$$\phi_2(u) = \sqrt{5}\left(6\left(u - \frac{1}{2}\right)^2 - \frac{1}{2}\right)$$

$$\phi_3(u) = \sqrt{7}\left(20\left(u - \frac{1}{2}\right)^3 - 3\left(u - \frac{1}{2}\right)\right)$$

$$\phi_4(u) = 3\left(70\left(u - \frac{1}{2}\right)^4 - 15\left(u - \frac{1}{2}\right)^2 + \frac{3}{8}\right),$$

satisfying the orthogonality property

$$\int_0^1 \phi_i(u)\phi_j(u)du = \begin{cases} 1 & : \quad i = j \\ 0 & : \quad i \neq j. \end{cases}$$

A test of the null and alternative hypotheses is

$$H_0 : \theta_1 = \theta_2 = \theta_3 = \theta_4 = 0 \,, \qquad H_1 : \text{at least one restriction fails} \,,$$

as the distribution of u under H_0 is uniform.

(a) Derive the log-likelihood function, $\ln L_T(\theta)$, in terms of u_t where

$$u_t = F_0(y_t) = \int_{-\infty}^{y_t} f_0(s)ds \,,$$

as well as the gradient vector $G_T(\theta)$ and the information matrix $I(\theta)$. In writing out the log-likelihood function, it is necessary to use the expression of the Legendre polynomials $\phi_i(u)$.

(b) Derive the LR and Wald tests of the hypotheses. Show that a LM test is based on the statistic

$$LM = \sum_{i=1}^{4} \left(\frac{1}{\sqrt{T}} \sum_{t=1}^{T} \phi_i(u_t) \right)^2 \,.$$

(c) To examine the performance of the three testing procedures in part (b) under the null hypothesis, assume that F_0 is the normal distribution and that $T = 1000$ observations are drawn from $N(0, 1)$.

(d) To examine the performance of the three testing procedures in part (b) under the alternative hypothesis, assume that F_0 is the normal distribution and that $T = 1000$ observations are drawn from χ_1^2.

(8) **A Copula Model of Asset Returns**

Program files	`test_copula.*`
Data files	`apple.csv, ford.csv, diversify.*`

A copula expresses a multivariate distribution in terms of the marginal distributions. For a bivariate, $N = 2$, Gaussian copula with Gaussian marginals, the joint distribution function is

$$
\begin{aligned}
F(y_1, y_2) &= \Phi_{1,2}(\Phi(y_1; \mu_1, \sigma_1^2), \Phi(y_2; \mu_1, \sigma_1^2); \rho), \\
&= \Phi_{1,2}(\Phi^{-1}(u_1; \mu_1, \sigma_1^2), \Phi^{-1}(u_2; \mu_1, \sigma_1^2); \rho),
\end{aligned}
$$

in which the copula is the bivariate normal distribution function $\Phi_{1,2}(\cdot)$ with dependence parameter ρ. The marginals are normal distribution functions $\Phi(y_i; \mu_i, \sigma_i^2)$ with mean μ_i and variance σ_i^2. The joint distribution function, $F(y_1, y_2)$, is first expressed in terms of y_i and then in terms of the uniform random variable $u_i = \Phi(y_i; \mu_i, \sigma_i^2)$. For an introduction to copulas, see Nelsen (1999).

(a) Derive the copula joint density function given by

$$f(y_1, y_2) = \frac{\partial^2 F(y_1, y_2)}{\partial y_1 \partial y_2}.$$

(b) Use the density function in part (a) to derive the log-likelihood function and show that it may be written as

$$\ln L_T(\theta) = \ln L_{1,T}(\mu_1, \sigma_1^2) + \ln L_{2,T}(\mu_2, \sigma_2^2)$$
$$+ \ln L_{3,T}(\mu_1, \sigma_1^2, \mu_2, \sigma_2^2, \rho)$$

in which $\theta = \{\mu_1, \sigma_1^2, \mu_2, \sigma_2^2, \rho\}$.

(c) Using daily share prices of Apple and Ford from 2 January 2001 to 6 August 2010, compute daily returns (y_1, y_2) and estimate the parameters of the copula distribution by maximum likelihood. Test the independence restriction $\rho = 0$, and interpret the results. Compare the parameter estimates to the estimates obtained in Excercise 14 of Chapter 2.

PART TWO

Regression Models

5 Linear Regression Models

5.1 Introduction

The maximum likelihood framework set out in Part ONE is now applied to estimating and testing regression models. This chapter focusses on linear models, where the conditional mean of a dependent variable is specified to be a linear function of a set of exogenous variables. Extensions to this basic model are investigated in Chapter 6 (nonlinear regression), Chapter 7 (autocorrelation) and Chapter 8 (heteroskedasticity).

Single equation models include the linear regression model and the constant mean model. For single equation regression models, the maximum likelihood estimator has an analytical solution that is equivalent to the ordinary least squares estimator. The class of multiple equation models includes simultaneous equation models with multiple dependent and exogenous variables, seemingly unrelated systems and recursive models. In this instance, the maximum likelihood estimator is known as the full information maximum likelihood (FIML) estimator because the entire system is used to estimate all of the model parameters jointly. The FIML estimator is related to the instrumental variable estimator commonly used to estimate simultaneous models and, in some cases, the two estimators are equivalent. Unlike linear single equation models, analytical solutions of the maximum likelihood estimator for systems of linear equations are only available in certain special cases.

Many of the examples considered in Part ONE specify the distribution of the observable random variable, y_t. Regression models, by contrast, specify the distribution of the unobservable disturbance, u_t, which means that maximum likelihood estimation cannot be used directly because this method requires evaluating the log-likelihood function at the observed values of the data. This problem is circumvented by using the transformation of variable technique (Appendix A), which transforms the distribution of the unobservable u_t to that of the observable, y_t. Another important feature of regression models is that the distribution of u_t is often chosen to be the normal distribution. One of the gains in adopting this assumption is that it simplifies the computation of the maximum likelihood estimators so that they can be obtained simply by means of least squares regressions.

5.2   Specification

The different types of linear regression models can usefully be illustrated by means of examples which are all similar in the sense that each model includes: one or more endogenous or dependent variables, $y_{i,t}$, that are simultaneously determined by an interrelated series of equations; exogenous variables, $x_{i,t}$, that are assumed to be determined outside the model; and predetermined or lagged dependent variables, $y_{i,t-j}$, $j \geq 1$.

5.2.1   Model Classification

Example 5.1 Univariate Regression Model
    Consider a linear relationship between a single dependent (endogenous) variable, y_t, and a single exogenous variable, x_t, given by

$$y_t = \alpha x_t + u_t, \qquad u_t \sim iid\ N(0, \sigma^2),$$

in which u_t is the disturbance term. By definition, x_t is independent of the disturbance term, $E[x_t u_t] = 0$. ☐

Example 5.2 Constant Mean Model
    A special case of the univariate regression model in Example 5.1 is the constant mean model where the exogenous variable x_t is a constant

$$y_t = \alpha + u_t, \qquad u_t \sim iid\ N\left(0, \sigma^2\right).$$

This model is used in finance to model returns, where α represents the average return of an asset and σ^2 represents the volatility of returns. ☐

Example 5.3 Seemingly Unrelated Regression Model
    An extension of the univariate equation containing two dependent variables, $y_{1,t}$ and $y_{2,t}$, and one exogenous variable, x_t, is

$$y_{1,t} = \alpha_1 x_t + u_{1,t}$$
$$y_{2,t} = \alpha_2 x_t + u_{2,t},$$

with disturbance term $u_t = [u_{1,t}, u_{2,t}]'$ that has the properties

$$u_t \sim iid\ N\left(\begin{bmatrix} 0 \\ 0 \end{bmatrix}, \begin{bmatrix} \sigma_{1,1} & \sigma_{1,2} \\ \sigma_{1,2} & \sigma_{2,2} \end{bmatrix}\right).$$

This system is commonly known as a seemingly unrelated regression model (SUR). An important feature of the SUR model is that the dependent variables are expressed only in terms of the exogenous variable(s). □

Example 5.4 Simultaneous System of Equations

Systems of equations in which the dependent variables are functions of other dependent variables, and not just exogenous variables, are referred to as simultaneous systems of equations. Consider the bivariate system of equations

$$y_{1,t} = \beta_1 y_{2,t} + u_{1,t}$$
$$y_{2,t} = \beta_2 y_{1,t} + \alpha x_t + u_{2,t},$$

with disturbance term $u_t = [u_{1,t}, u_{2,t}]'$ that has the properties

$$u_t \sim iid\ N \left(\begin{bmatrix} 0 \\ 0 \end{bmatrix}, \begin{bmatrix} \sigma_{1,1} & 0 \\ 0 & \sigma_{2,2} \end{bmatrix} \right).$$

This system is characterised by the dependent variables $y_{1,t}$ and $y_{2,t}$ being functions of each other, with $y_{2,t}$ also being a function of the exogenous variable x_t. A slightly more general example is where each equation has its own exogenous variables and the disturbance covariance matrix is not diagonal

$$y_{1,t} = \beta_1 y_{2,t} + \alpha_1 x_{1,t} + u_{1,t}$$
$$y_{2,t} = \beta_2 y_{1,t} + \alpha_2 x_{2,t} + u_{2,t},$$

where the disturbance vector $u_t = [u_{1,t}, u_{2,t}]'$ is now given by

$$u_t \sim iid\ N \left(\begin{bmatrix} 0 \\ 0 \end{bmatrix}, \begin{bmatrix} \sigma_{1,1} & \sigma_{1,2} \\ \sigma_{2,1} & \sigma_{2,2} \end{bmatrix} \right),$$

where $\sigma_{1,2} = \sigma_{2,1}$. □

Example 5.5 Recursive System

A special case of the simultaneous model is the recursive model. An example of a trivariate recursive model is

$$
\begin{aligned}
y_{1,t} &= & & & & \alpha_1 x_{1,t} & + & u_{1,t} \\
y_{2,t} &= & \beta_1 y_{1,t} & & + & \alpha_2 x_{2,t} & + & u_{2,t} \\
y_{3,t} &= & \beta_2 y_{1,t} & + & \beta_3 y_{2,t} & + & \alpha_3 x_{3,t} & + & u_{3,t},
\end{aligned}
$$

with disturbance term $u_t = [u_{1,t}, u_{2,t}, u_{3,t}]'$ that has the properties

$$u_t \sim iid\ N \left(\begin{bmatrix} 0 \\ 0 \\ 0 \end{bmatrix}, \begin{bmatrix} \sigma_{1,1} & 0 & 0 \\ 0 & \sigma_{2,2} & 0 \\ 0 & 0 & \sigma_{3,3} \end{bmatrix} \right).$$

□

5.2.2   *Structural and Reduced Forms*

Before generalising the previous examples to many dependent variables and many exogenous variables, it is helpful to introduce some matrix notation. Consider rewriting the first simultaneous model in Example 5.4 as

$$y_{1,t} - \beta_1 y_{2,t} = u_{1,t}$$
$$-\beta_2 y_{1,t} + y_{2,t} - \alpha x_t = u_{2,t}.$$

This system is expressed more compactly as

$$By_t + Ax_t = u_t, \tag{5.1}$$

in which

$$y_t = \begin{bmatrix} y_{1,t} \\ y_{2,t} \end{bmatrix}, \quad B = \begin{bmatrix} 1 & -\beta_1 \\ -\beta_2 & 1 \end{bmatrix}, \quad A = \begin{bmatrix} 0 \\ -\alpha \end{bmatrix}, \quad u_t = \begin{bmatrix} u_{1,t} \\ u_{2,t} \end{bmatrix},$$

and the covariance matrix of the disturbances is

$$V = E\left[u_t u_t'\right] = E\begin{bmatrix} u_{1,t}^2 & u_{1,t} u_{2,t} \\ u_{1,t} u_{2,t} & u_{2,t}^2 \end{bmatrix} = \begin{bmatrix} \sigma_{1,1} & 0 \\ 0 & \sigma_{2,2} \end{bmatrix}.$$

Equation (5.1) is known as the structural form where y_t represents the endogenous variables and x_t the exogenous variables.

The bivariate system of equations in (5.1) is easily generalised to a system of N equations with K exogenous variables by simply extending the dimensions of the pertinent matrices. For example, the dependent and exogenous variables become

$$y_t = \begin{bmatrix} y_{1,t} & y_{2,t} & \cdots & y_{N,t} \end{bmatrix}'$$
$$x_t = \begin{bmatrix} x_{1,t} & x_{2,t} & \cdots & x_{K,t} \end{bmatrix}',$$

and the disturbance terms become

$$u_t = \begin{bmatrix} u_{1,t} & u_{2,t} & \cdots & u_{N,t} \end{bmatrix}',$$

so that in equation (5.1) B is now $(N \times N)$, A is $(N \times K)$ and V is a $(N \times N)$ covariance matrix of the disturbances.

An alternative way to write the system of equations in (5.1) is to express the system in terms of y_t,

$$y_t = -B^{-1} A x_t + B^{-1} u_t$$
$$= \Pi x_t + v_t, \tag{5.2}$$

where

$$\Pi = -B^{-1} A, \qquad v_t = B^{-1} u_t, \tag{5.3}$$

and the disturbance term v_t has the properties

$$E\left[v_t\right] = E\left[B^{-1}u_t\right] = B^{-1}E\left[u_t\right] = 0,$$
$$E\left[v_tv_t'\right] = E\left[B^{-1}u_tu_t'(B^{-1})'\right] = B^{-1}E\left[u_tu_t'\right](B^{-1})' = B^{-1}V(B^{-1})'.$$

Equation (5.2) is known as the reduced form. The reduced form of a set of structural equations serves a number of important purposes.

(1) It forms the basis for simulating a system of equations.
(2) It can be used as an alternative way to estimate a structural model. A popular approach is estimating structural vector autoregression models, which is discussed in Chapter 14.
(3) The reduced form is used to compute forecasts and perform experiments on models.

Example 5.6 Simulating a Simultaneous Model
Consider simulating $T = 500$ observations from the bivariate model

$$y_{1,t} = \beta_1 y_{2,t} + \alpha_1 x_{1,t} + u_{1,t}$$
$$y_{2,t} = \beta_2 y_{1,t} + \alpha_2 x_{2,t} + u_{2,t},$$

with parameters $\beta_1 = 0.6$, $\alpha_1 = 0.4$, $\beta_2 = 0.2$, $\alpha_2 = -0.5$ and covariance matrix of u_t

$$V = \begin{bmatrix} \sigma_{1,1} & \sigma_{1,2} \\ \sigma_{1,2} & \sigma_{2,2} \end{bmatrix} = \begin{bmatrix} 1 & 0.5 \\ 0.5 & 1 \end{bmatrix}.$$

Define the structural parameter matrices

$$B = \begin{bmatrix} 1 & -\beta_1 \\ -\beta_2 & 1 \end{bmatrix} = \begin{bmatrix} 1.000 & -0.600 \\ -0.200 & 1.000 \end{bmatrix}$$
$$A = \begin{bmatrix} -\alpha_1 & 0 \\ 0 & -\alpha_2 \end{bmatrix} = \begin{bmatrix} -0.400 & 0.000 \\ 0.000 & 0.500 \end{bmatrix}.$$

From equation (5.3) the reduced form parameter matrix is

$$\begin{aligned} \Pi &= -B^{-1}A \\ &= -\begin{bmatrix} 1.000 & -0.600 \\ -0.200 & 1.000 \end{bmatrix}^{-1} \begin{bmatrix} -0.400 & 0.000 \\ 0.000 & 0.500 \end{bmatrix} \\ &= -\begin{bmatrix} 1.136 & 0.681 \\ 0.227 & 1.136 \end{bmatrix} \begin{bmatrix} -0.400 & 0.000 \\ 0.000 & 0.500 \end{bmatrix} \\ &= \begin{bmatrix} 0.454 & -0.341 \\ 0.091 & -0.568 \end{bmatrix}. \end{aligned}$$

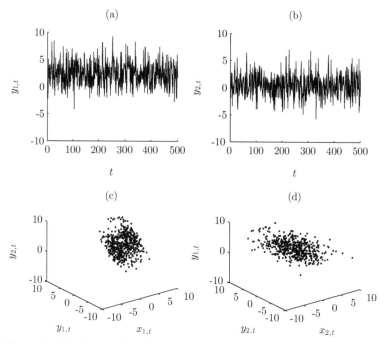

Figure 5.1. Simulating a bivariate simultaneous equations model with a sample of size $T = 500$.

The reduced form at time t is

$$\begin{bmatrix} y_{1,t} \\ y_{2,t} \end{bmatrix} = \begin{bmatrix} 0.454 & -0.341 \\ 0.091 & -0.568 \end{bmatrix} \begin{bmatrix} x_{1,t} \\ x_{2,t} \end{bmatrix} + \begin{bmatrix} v_{1,t} \\ v_{2,t} \end{bmatrix},$$

where the reduced form disturbances are given by equation (5.3)

$$\begin{bmatrix} v_{1,t} \\ v_{2,t} \end{bmatrix} = \begin{bmatrix} 1.136 & 0.681 \\ 0.227 & 1.136 \end{bmatrix} \begin{bmatrix} u_{1,t} \\ u_{2,t} \end{bmatrix}.$$

The simulated series of $y_{1,t}$ and $y_{2,t}$ are given in Figure 5.1, together with scatterplots corresponding to the two equations, where the exogenous variables are chosen as $x_{1,t} \sim iid\ U[0, 10]$ and $x_{2,t} \sim iid\ N(0, 9)$ with $x_{1,t}$ and $x_{2,t}$ independent of each other. ☐

5.3   Estimation

5.3.1   Single Equation: Ordinary Least Squares

Consider the linear regression model

$$y_t = \beta_0 + \beta_1 x_{1,t} + \beta_2 x_{2,t} + u_t, \qquad u_t \sim iid\ N(0, \sigma^2), \qquad (5.4)$$

in which y_t is the dependent variable, $x_{1,t}$ and $x_{2,t}$ are the exogenous variables and u_t is the disturbance term. To estimate the parameters $\theta = \{\beta_0, \beta_1, \beta_2, \sigma^2\}$ by maximum likelihood, it is necessary to use the transformation of variable technique to transform the distribution of the unobservable disturbance, u_t, into the distribution of y_t.

From equation (5.4) the pdf of u_t is

$$f(u_t) = \frac{1}{\sqrt{2\pi\sigma^2}} \exp\left[-\frac{u_t^2}{2\sigma^2}\right].$$

Using the transformation of variable technique, the pdf of y_t is

$$f(y_t) = f(u_t)\left|\frac{\partial u_t}{\partial y_t}\right| = \frac{1}{\sqrt{2\pi\sigma^2}} \exp\left[-\frac{(y_t - \beta_0 - \beta_1 x_{1,t} - \beta_2 x_{2,t})^2}{2\sigma^2}\right],$$

$$(5.5)$$

in which $\partial u_t / \partial y_t$ is

$$\frac{\partial u_t}{\partial y_t} = \frac{\partial}{\partial y_t}\left[y_t - \beta_0 - \beta_1 x_{1,t} - \beta_2 x_{2,t}\right] = 1.$$

Given the distribution of y_t in (5.5), the log-likelihood function at time t is

$$\ln l_t(\theta) = -\frac{1}{2}\ln(2\pi) - \frac{1}{2}\ln\sigma^2 - \frac{1}{2\sigma^2}(y_t - \beta_0 - \beta_1 x_{1,t} - \beta_2 x_{2,t})^2.$$

For a sample of $t = 1, 2, \cdots, T$ observations the log-likelihood function is

$$\ln L_T(\theta) = -\frac{1}{2}\ln(2\pi) - \frac{1}{2}\ln\sigma^2 - \frac{1}{2\sigma^2 T}\sum_{t=1}^{T}(y_t - \beta_0 - \beta_1 x_{1,t} - \beta_2 x_{2,t})^2.$$

Differentiating $\ln L_T(\theta)$ with respect to θ yields

$$\frac{\partial \ln L_T(\theta)}{\partial \beta_0} = \frac{1}{\sigma^2 T}\sum_{t=1}^{T}(y_t - \beta_0 - \beta_1 x_{1,t} - \beta_2 x_{2,t})$$

$$\frac{\partial \ln L_T(\theta)}{\partial \beta_1} = \frac{1}{\sigma^2 T}\sum_{t=1}^{T}(y_t - \beta_0 - \beta_1 x_{1,t} - \beta_2 x_{2,t})x_{1,t}$$

$$\frac{\partial \ln L_T(\theta)}{\partial \beta_2} = \frac{1}{\sigma^2 T}\sum_{t=1}^{T}(y_t - \beta_0 - \beta_1 x_{1,t} - \beta_2 x_{2,t})x_{2,t}$$

$$\frac{\partial \ln L_T(\theta)}{\partial \sigma^2} = -\frac{1}{2\sigma^2} + \frac{1}{2\sigma^4 T}\sum_{t=1}^{T}(y_t - \beta_0 - \beta_1 x_{1,t} - \beta_2 x_{2,t})^2. \qquad (5.6)$$

Setting these derivatives to zero

$$\frac{1}{\widehat{\sigma}^2 T} \sum_{t=1}^{T}(y_t - \widehat{\beta}_0 - \widehat{\beta}_1 x_{1,t} - \widehat{\beta}_2 x_{2,t}) \qquad = 0$$

$$\frac{1}{\widehat{\sigma}^2 T} \sum_{t=1}^{T}(y_t - \widehat{\beta}_0 - \widehat{\beta}_1 x_{1,t} - \widehat{\beta}_2 x_{2,t})x_{1,t} \qquad = 0$$

$$\frac{1}{\widehat{\sigma}^2 T} \sum_{t=1}^{T}(y_t - \widehat{\beta}_0 - \widehat{\beta}_1 x_{1,t} - \widehat{\beta}_2 x_{2,t})x_{2,t} \qquad = 0 \qquad (5.7)$$

$$-\frac{1}{2\widehat{\sigma}^2} + \frac{1}{2\widehat{\sigma}^4 T} \sum_{t=1}^{T}(y_t - \widehat{\beta}_0 - \widehat{\beta}_1 x_{1,t} - \widehat{\beta}_2 x_{2,t})^2 = 0\,,$$

and solving for $\widehat{\theta} = [\widehat{\beta}_0, \widehat{\beta}_1, \widehat{\beta}_2, \widehat{\sigma}^2]'$ yields the maximum likelihood estimators. For the system of equations in (5.7) an analytical solution exists. To derive this solution, first notice that the first three equations can be written independently of $\widehat{\sigma}^2$ by multiplying both sides by $T\widehat{\sigma}^2$ to give

$$\sum_{t=1}^{T}(y_t - \widehat{\beta}_0 - \widehat{\beta}_1 x_{1,t} - \widehat{\beta}_2 x_{2,t}) \quad = 0$$

$$\sum_{t=1}^{T}(y_t - \widehat{\beta}_0 - \widehat{\beta}_1 x_{1,t} - \widehat{\beta}_2 x_{2,t})x_{1,t} = 0$$

$$\sum_{t=1}^{T}(y_t - \widehat{\beta}_0 - \widehat{\beta}_1 x_{1,t} - \widehat{\beta}_2 x_{2,t})x_{2,t} = 0\,,$$

which is a system of three equations and three unknowns. Writing this system in matrix form gives

$$\begin{bmatrix} \sum_{t=1}^{T} y_t \\ \sum_{t=1}^{T} y_t x_{1,t} \\ \sum_{t=1}^{T} y_t x_{2,t} \end{bmatrix} - \begin{bmatrix} T & \sum_{t=1}^{T} x_{1,t} & \sum_{t=1}^{T} x_{2,t} \\ \sum_{t=1}^{T} x_{1,t} & \sum_{t=1}^{T} x_{1,t}^2 & \sum_{t=1}^{T} x_{1,t}x_{2,t} \\ \sum_{t=1}^{T} x_{2,t} & \sum_{t=1}^{T} x_{1,t}x_{2,t} & \sum_{t=1}^{T} x_{2,t}^2 \end{bmatrix} \begin{bmatrix} \widehat{\beta}_0 \\ \widehat{\beta}_1 \\ \widehat{\beta}_2 \end{bmatrix} = \begin{bmatrix} 0 \\ 0 \\ 0 \end{bmatrix}\,,$$

and solving for $[\,\widehat{\beta}_0, \widehat{\beta}_1, \widehat{\beta}_2\,]'$ gives

$$\begin{bmatrix} \widehat{\beta}_0 \\ \widehat{\beta}_1 \\ \widehat{\beta}_2 \end{bmatrix} = \begin{bmatrix} T & \sum_{t=1}^{T} x_{1,t} & \sum_{t=1}^{T} x_{2,t} \\ \sum_{t=1}^{T} x_{1,t} & \sum_{t=1}^{T} x_{1,t}^2 & \sum_{t=1}^{T} x_{1,t}x_{2,t} \\ \sum_{t=1}^{T} x_{2,t} & \sum_{t=1}^{T} x_{1,t}x_{2,t} & \sum_{t=1}^{T} x_{2,t}^2 \end{bmatrix}^{-1} \begin{bmatrix} \sum_{t=1}^{T} y_t \\ \sum_{t=1}^{T} x_{1,t} y_t \\ \sum_{t=1}^{T} x_{2,t} y_t \end{bmatrix}\,,$$

which is the ordinary least squares estimator (OLS) of $[\beta_0, \beta_1, \beta_2]'$. Once $[\widehat{\beta}_0, \widehat{\beta}_1, \widehat{\beta}_2]'$ is computed, the ordinary least squares estimator of the variance, $\widehat{\sigma}^2$, is obtained by rearranging the last equation in (5.7) to give

$$\widehat{\sigma}^2 = \frac{1}{T} \sum_{t=1}^{T} (y_t - \widehat{\beta}_0 - \widehat{\beta}_1 x_{1,t} - \widehat{\beta}_2 x_{2,t})^2 . \tag{5.8}$$

This result establishes the relationship between the maximum likelihood estimator and the ordinary least squares estimator in the case of the single equation linear regression model. In computing $\widehat{\sigma}^2$ in equation (5.8) it is common to express the denominator in terms of the degrees of freedom, $T - K - 1$, instead of merely T, where K is the number of explanatory variables excluding the constant.

Expressing $\widehat{\sigma}^2$ analytically in terms of the $\widehat{\beta}_0$, $\widehat{\beta}_1$ and $\widehat{\beta}_2$ in (5.8) means that $\widehat{\sigma}^2$ can be concentrated out of the log-likelihood function. Standard errors can be computed from the negative of the inverse of the Hessian. If estimation is based on the concentrated log-likelihood function, the estimated variance of $\widehat{\sigma}^2$ is

$$\text{var}(\widehat{\sigma}^2) = \frac{2\widehat{\sigma}^4}{T} .$$

Example 5.7 Estimating a Regression Model
Consider simulating the model

$$y_t = \beta_0 + \beta_1 x_{1,t} + \beta_2 x_{2,t} + u_t , \qquad u_t \sim iid\ N(0, \sigma^2) ,$$

for a sample of size $T = 200$, in which the parameters are $\theta_0 = \{\beta_0 = 1.0,\ \beta_1 = 0.7,\ \beta_2 = 0.3,\ \sigma^2 = 4\}$ and $x_{1,t}$ and $x_{2,t}$ are independently generated as $iid\ N(0, 1)$. The maximum likelihood parameter estimates without concentrating the log-likelihood function are

$$\widehat{\theta} = \{\widehat{\beta}_0 = 1.129,\ \widehat{\beta}_1 = 0.719,\ \widehat{\beta}_2 = 0.389,\ \widehat{\sigma}^2 = 3.862\},$$

with covariance matrix based on the Hessian

$$\text{cov}(\widehat{\theta}) = \begin{bmatrix} 0.019 & 0.001 & -0.001 & 0.000 \\ 0.001 & 0.018 & 0.000 & 0.000 \\ -0.001 & 0.000 & 0.023 & 0.000 \\ 0.000 & 0.000 & 0.000 & 0.149 \end{bmatrix} .$$

Maximising the concentrated log-likelihood function with respect to the parameters $\beta = \{\beta_0, \beta_1, \beta_2\}$ gives the estimates

$$\widehat{\theta}_{conc} = \left\{ \widehat{\beta}_0 = 1.129,\ \widehat{\beta}_1 = 0.719,\ \widehat{\beta}_2 = 0.389 \right\},$$

with covariance matrix based on the Hessian given by

$$
\text{cov}(\widehat{\beta}) =
\begin{bmatrix}
0.019 & 0.001 & -0.001 \\
0.001 & 0.018 & 0.000 \\
-0.001 & 0.000 & 0.023
\end{bmatrix}.
$$

The residuals at the second stage are computed as

$$
\widehat{u}_t = y_t - 1.129 - 0.719 x_{1,t} - 0.389 x_{2,t} .
$$

The residual variance is computed as

$$
\widehat{\sigma}^2 = \frac{1}{T} \sum_{t=1}^{T} \widehat{u}_t^2 = \frac{1}{200} \sum_{t=1}^{200} \widehat{u}_t^2 = 3.862,
$$

with variance

$$
\text{var}(\widehat{\sigma}^2) = \frac{2\widehat{\sigma}^4}{T} = \frac{2 \times 3.862^2}{200} = 0.149,
$$

which agrees with the estimate using the full log-likelihood function. □

For the case of K exogenous variables, the linear regression model is

$$
y_t = \beta_0 + \beta_1 x_{1,t} + \beta_2 x_{2,t} + \cdots + \beta_K x_{K,t} + u_t .
$$

This equation can also be written in matrix form,

$$
Y = X\beta + u , \qquad E[u] = 0 , \qquad \text{cov}(u) = E[uu'] = \sigma^2 I_T ,
$$

where I_T is the $T \times T$ identity matrix and

$$
Y =
\begin{bmatrix}
y_1 \\ y_2 \\ y_3 \\ \vdots \\ y_T
\end{bmatrix}, \quad
X =
\begin{bmatrix}
1 & x_{1,1} & \cdots & x_{K,1} \\
1 & x_{1,2} & \cdots & x_{K,2} \\
1 & x_{1,3} & \cdots & x_{K,3} \\
\vdots & \vdots & \cdots & \vdots \\
1 & x_{1,T} & \cdots & x_{K,T}
\end{bmatrix}, \quad
\beta =
\begin{bmatrix}
\beta_0 \\ \beta_1 \\ \beta_2 \\ \vdots \\ \beta_K
\end{bmatrix}
\text{ and } u =
\begin{bmatrix}
u_1 \\ u_2 \\ u_3 \\ \vdots \\ u_T
\end{bmatrix}.
$$

Referring to the $K = 2$ case solved previously, the matrix solution is

$$
\widehat{\beta} = (X'X)^{-1} X'Y . \tag{5.9}
$$

Once $\widehat{\beta}$ has been computed, an estimate of the variance $\widehat{\sigma}^2$ is

$$
\widehat{\sigma}^2 = \frac{\widehat{u}'\widehat{u}}{T} ,
$$

in which $\widehat{u} = Y - X\widehat{\beta}$. Alternatively, the denominator can also be expressed in terms of the degrees of freedom, $T - K - 1$.

5.3.2 Multiple Equations: FIML

Consider the system of equations in (5.1). For a system of N equations, the density of u_t is assumed to be the multivariate normal distribution

$$f(u_t) = \left(\frac{1}{\sqrt{2\pi}}\right)^N |V|^{-1/2} \exp\left[-\frac{1}{2}u_t'V^{-1}u_t\right].$$

Using the transformation of variable technique, the density of y_t becomes

$$f(y_t|x_t) = f(u_t)\left|\frac{\partial u_t}{\partial y_t}\right|$$

$$= \left(\frac{1}{\sqrt{2\pi}}\right)^N |V|^{-1/2} \exp\left[-\frac{1}{2}(By_t + Ax_t)'V^{-1}(By_t + Ax_t)\right]|B|,$$

because, from equation (5.1), $\partial u_t/\partial y_t = B'$. Given $t = 1, 2, \cdots, T$ observations, the log-likelihood function is

$$\ln L_T(\theta) = -\frac{N}{2}\ln(2\pi) - \frac{1}{2}\ln|V| + \ln|B|$$

$$-\frac{1}{2T}\sum_{t=1}^{T}(By_t + Ax_t)'V^{-1}(By_t + Ax_t). \tag{5.10}$$

The FIML estimator of the parameters of the model is obtained by differentiating $\ln L_T(\theta)$ with respect to θ, setting these derivatives to zero and solving to find $\widehat{\theta}$. As in the estimation of the single equation model, estimation can be simplified by concentrating the likelihood with respect to the estimated covariance matrix $\widehat{V}$. The residual covariance matrix is

$$\widehat{V} = \frac{1}{T}\begin{bmatrix} \sum_{t=1}^{T}\widehat{u}_{1,t}^2 & \sum_{t=1}^{T}\widehat{u}_{1,t}\widehat{u}_{2,t} & \cdots & \sum_{t=1}^{T}\widehat{u}_{1,t}\widehat{u}_{N,t} \\ \sum_{t=1}^{T}\widehat{u}_{2,t}\widehat{u}_{1,t} & \sum_{t=1}^{T}\widehat{u}_{2,t}^2 & & \sum_{t=1}^{T}\widehat{u}_{2,t}\widehat{u}_{N,t} \\ \vdots & \vdots & & \vdots \\ \sum_{t=1}^{T}\widehat{u}_{N,t}\widehat{u}_{1,t} & \sum_{t=1}^{T}\widehat{u}_{N,t}\widehat{u}_{2,t} & \cdots & \sum_{t=1}^{T}\widehat{u}_{N,t}^2 \end{bmatrix},$$

where $\widehat{u}_t = \widehat{B}y_t + \widehat{A}x_t$ and $\widehat{V}$ can be substituted for V in equation (5.10). This eliminates the need to estimate the variance parameters directly, thus reducing the dimensionality of the estimation problem. Note that this approach is appropriate for simultaneous models based on normality. For other models based on non-normal distributions, all the parameters may need to be estimated jointly. Further, if standard errors of $\widehat{V}$ are also required then these can be conveniently obtained by estimating all the parameters.

Example 5.8 FIML Estimation of a Structural Model

Consider the first bivariate model in Example 5.4, where the unknown parameters are $\theta = \{\beta_1, \beta_2, \alpha, \sigma_{1,1}, \sigma_{2,2}\}$. The log-likelihood function is

$$
\ln L_T(\theta) = -\frac{N}{2} \ln(2\pi) - \frac{1}{2} \ln |\sigma_{1,1}\sigma_{2,2}| + \ln |1 - \beta_1\beta_2|
$$
$$
- \frac{1}{2\sigma_{1,1}T} \sum_{t=1}^{T} (y_{1,t} - \beta_1 y_{2,t})^2 - \frac{1}{2\sigma_{2,2}T} \sum_{t=1}^{T} (y_{2,t} - \beta_2 y_{1,t} - \alpha x_t)^2.
$$

The first-order derivatives of $\ln L_T(\theta)$ with respect to θ are

$$
\frac{\partial \ln L_T(\theta)}{\partial \beta_1} = -\frac{\beta_2}{1 - \beta_1\beta_2} + \frac{1}{\sigma_{1,1}T} \sum_{t=1}^{T} (y_{1,t} - \beta_1 y_{2,t})y_{2,t}
$$

$$
\frac{\partial \ln L_T(\theta)}{\partial \beta_2} = -\frac{\beta_1}{1 - \beta_1\beta_2} + \frac{1}{\sigma_{2,2}T} \sum_{t=1}^{T} (y_{2,t} - \beta_2 y_{1,t} - \alpha x_t)y_{1,t}
$$

$$
\frac{\partial \ln L_T(\theta)}{\partial \alpha} = \frac{1}{\sigma_{2,2}T} \sum_{t=1}^{T} (y_{2,t} - \beta_2 y_{1,t} - \alpha x_t)x_t
$$

$$
\frac{\partial \ln L_T(\theta)}{\partial \sigma_{1,1}} = -\frac{1}{2\sigma_{1,1}} + \frac{1}{2\sigma_{1,1}^2 T} \sum_{t=1}^{T} (y_{1,t} - \beta_1 y_{2,t})^2
$$

$$
\frac{\partial \ln L_T(\theta)}{\partial \sigma_{2,2}} = -\frac{1}{2\sigma_{2,2}} + \frac{1}{2\sigma_{2,2}^2 T} \sum_{t=1}^{T} (y_{2,t} - \beta_2 y_{1,t} - \alpha x_t)^2.
$$

Setting these derivatives to zero yields

$$
-\frac{\widehat{\beta}_2}{1 - \widehat{\beta}_1\widehat{\beta}_2} + \frac{1}{\widehat{\sigma}_{1,1}T} \sum_{t=1}^{T} (y_{1,t} - \widehat{\beta}_1 y_{2,t})y_{2,t} = 0
$$

$$
-\frac{\widehat{\beta}_1}{1 - \widehat{\beta}_1\widehat{\beta}_2} + \frac{1}{\widehat{\sigma}_{2,2}T} \sum_{t=1}^{T} (y_{2,t} - \widehat{\beta}_2 y_{1,t} - \widehat{\alpha} x_t)y_{1,t} = 0
$$

$$
\frac{1}{\widehat{\sigma}_{2,2}T} \sum_{t=1}^{T} (y_{2,t} - \widehat{\beta}_2 y_{1,t} - \widehat{\alpha} x_t)x_t = 0
$$

$$
-\frac{1}{2\widehat{\sigma}_{1,1}} + \frac{1}{2\widehat{\sigma}_{1,1}^2 T} \sum_{t=1}^{T} (y_{1,t} - \widehat{\beta}_1 y_{2,t})^2 = 0
$$

$$
-\frac{1}{2\widehat{\sigma}_{2,2}} + \frac{1}{2\widehat{\sigma}_{2,2}^2 T} \sum_{t=1}^{T} (y_{2,t} - \widehat{\beta}_2 y_{1,t} - \widehat{\alpha} x_t)^2 = 0,
$$

and solving for $\widehat{\theta} = \{\widehat{\beta}_1, \widehat{\beta}_2, \widehat{\alpha}, \widehat{\sigma}_{1,1}, \widehat{\sigma}_{2,2}\}$ gives the maximum likelihood estimators

$$\widehat{\beta}_1 = \frac{\sum_{t=1}^{T} y_{1,t} x_t}{\sum_{t=1}^{T} y_{2,t} x_t}$$

$$\widehat{\beta}_2 = \frac{\sum_{t=1}^{T} y_{2,t} \widehat{u}_{1,t}}{\sum_{t=1}^{T} y_{1,t} \widehat{u}_{1,t}}$$

$$\widehat{\alpha} = \frac{\sum_{t=1}^{T} y_{2,t} \widehat{u}_{1,t} - \widehat{\beta}_2 \sum_{t=1}^{T} y_{1,t} \widehat{u}_{1,t}}{\sum_{t=1}^{T} x_t \widehat{u}_{1,t}}$$

$$\widehat{\sigma}_{1,1} = \frac{1}{T} \sum_{t=1}^{T} (y_{1,t} - \widehat{\beta}_1 y_{2,t})^2$$

$$\widehat{\sigma}_{2,2} = \frac{1}{T} \sum_{t=1}^{T} (y_{2,t} - \widehat{\beta}_2 y_{1,t} - \widehat{\alpha} x_t)^2 \,,$$

in which

$$\widehat{u}_{1,t} = y_{1,t} - \widehat{\beta}_1 y_{2,t}$$
$$\widehat{u}_{2,t} = y_{2,t} - \widehat{\beta}_2 y_{1,t} - \widehat{\alpha} x_t.$$

Full details of the derivation of these equations are given in Appendix C. Note that $\widehat{\sigma}_{1,1}$ and $\widehat{\sigma}_{2,2}$ are obtained having already computed the estimators $\widehat{\beta}_1$, $\widehat{\beta}_2$ and $\widehat{\alpha}$. This suggests that a further simplification can be achieved by concentrating the variances of $\widehat{u}_t$ out of the log-likelihood function and then maximising $\ln L_T(\theta)$ with respect to $\widehat{\beta}_1$, $\widehat{\beta}_2$, and $\widehat{\alpha}$ with

$$\widehat{V} = \frac{1}{T} \begin{bmatrix} \sum_{t=1}^{T} \widehat{u}_{1,t}^2 & 0 \\ 0 & \sum_{t=1}^{T} \widehat{u}_{2,t}^2 \end{bmatrix}.$$

$\square$

The key result from Section 5.3.1 is that an analytical solution for the maximum likelihood estimator exists for a single linear regression model. It does not necessarily follow, however, that an analytical solution always exists for systems of linear equations. While Example 5.8 is an exception, such exceptions are rare and an iterative algorithm, as discussed in Chapter 3, must usually be used to obtain the maximum likelihood estimates.

Example 5.9 FIML Estimation Based on Iteration

This example uses the $T = 500$ simulated data given in Figure 5.1 based on the model specified in Example 5.6. The steps to estimate the parameters of this model by FIML are as follows.

Step 1: Starting values are chosen at random to be

$$\theta_{(0)} = \{\beta_1 = 0.712, \ \alpha_1 = 0.290, \ \beta_2 = 0.122, \ \alpha_2 = 0.198\}.$$

Step 2: Evaluate the parameter matrices at the starting values

$$B_{(0)} = \begin{bmatrix} 1 & -\beta_1 \\ -\beta_2 & 1 \end{bmatrix} = \begin{bmatrix} 1 & -0.712 \\ -0.122 & 1 \end{bmatrix}$$

$$A_{(0)} = \begin{bmatrix} -\alpha_1 & 0 \\ 0 & -\alpha_2 \end{bmatrix} = \begin{bmatrix} -0.290 & 0.000 \\ 0.000 & -0.198 \end{bmatrix}.$$

Step 3: Compute the residuals at the starting values

$$\widehat{u}_{1,t} = y_{1,t} - 0.712\, y_{2,t} - 0.290\, x_{1,t}$$
$$\widehat{u}_{2,t} = y_{2,t} - 0.122\, y_{1,t} - 0.198\, x_{2,t}.$$

Step 4: Compute the residual covariance matrix at the starting estimates

$$V_{(0)} = \frac{1}{500} \begin{bmatrix} \displaystyle\sum_{t=1}^{T} \widehat{u}_{1,t}^2 & \displaystyle\sum_{t=1}^{T} \widehat{u}_{1,t}\widehat{u}_{2,t} \\ \displaystyle\sum_{t=1}^{T} \widehat{u}_{1,t}\widehat{u}_{2,t} & \displaystyle\sum_{t=1}^{T} \widehat{u}_{2,t}^2 \end{bmatrix} = \begin{bmatrix} 1.213 & 0.162 \\ 0.162 & 5.572 \end{bmatrix}.$$

Step 5: Compute the log-likelihood function for each observation at the starting values

$$\ln l_t(\theta) = -\frac{N}{2} \ln(2\pi) - \frac{1}{2} \ln|V_{(0)}| + \ln|B_{(0)}|$$
$$-\frac{1}{2}(B_{(0)}y_t + A_{(0)}x_t)'V_{(0)}^{-1}(B_{(0)}y_t + A_{(0)}x_t).$$

Step 6: Iterate until convergence using a gradient algorithm with the derivatives computed numerically. The residual covariance matrix is computed using the final estimates as follows

$$\widehat{V} = \frac{1}{500} \begin{bmatrix} \displaystyle\sum_{t=1}^{T} \widehat{u}_{1,t}^2 & \displaystyle\sum_{t=1}^{T} \widehat{u}_{1,t}\widehat{u}_{2,t} \\ \displaystyle\sum_{t=1}^{T} \widehat{u}_{1,t}\widehat{u}_{2,t} & \displaystyle\sum_{t=1}^{T} \widehat{u}_{2,t}^2 \end{bmatrix} = \begin{bmatrix} 0.952 & 0.444 \\ 0.444 & 0.967 \end{bmatrix}.$$

Table 5.1. *FIML estimates of the bivariate model.*
Standard errors are based on the Hessian

Population	Estimate	se	t stat.
$\beta_1 = 0.6$	0.592	0.027	21.920
$\alpha_1 = 0.4$	0.409	0.008	50.889
$\beta_2 = 0.2$	0.209	0.016	12.816
$\alpha_2 = -0.5$	−0.483	0.016	−30.203

The FIML estimates are given in Table 5.1 with standard errors based on the Hessian. The parameter estimates are in good agreement with their population counterparts given in Example 5.6. ☐

5.3.3 Identification

The set of first-order conditions in Example 5.8 is a system of five equations and five unknowns $\widehat{\theta} = \{\widehat{\beta}_1, \widehat{\beta}_2, \widehat{\alpha}, \widehat{\sigma}_{1,1}, \widehat{\sigma}_{2,2}\}$. The issue as to whether there is a unique solution is commonly referred to as the identification problem. There exist two conditions for identification.

(1) A necessary condition for identification is that there are at least as many equations as there are unknowns. This is commonly known as the order condition.
(2) A necessary and sufficient condition for the system of equations to have a solution is that the Jacobian of this system needs to be nonsingular, which is equivalent to the Hessian or information matrix being nonsingular. This is known as the rank condition for identification.

An alternative way to understand the identification problem is to note that the structural system in (5.1) and the reduced form system in (5.2) are alternative representations of the same system of equations bound by the relationships

$$\Pi = -B^{-1}A,$$
$$E\left[v_t v_t'\right] = B^{-1}V(B^{-1})',$$

(5.11)

where the dimensions of the relevant parameter matrices are as follows

Reduced form: Π is $(N \times (K+1))$ $\qquad$ $E[v_t v_t']$ is $(N(N+1)/2)$
Structural form: A is $(N \times (K+1))$, B is $(N \times N)$ $\quad$ V is $(N(N+1)/2)$.

This equivalence implies that estimation can proceed directly via the structural form to compute A, B and V directly, or indirectly via the reduced form with these parameter matrices being recovered from Π and $E[v_t v_t']$. For this latter step to be feasible, the system of equations in (5.11) needs to have a solution.

The total number of parameters in the reduced form is $N(K+1) + N(N+1)/2$, while the structural system has at most $N^2 + N(K+1) + N(N+1)/2$ parameters. This means that there are potentially

$$(N(K+1) + N^2 + N(N+1)/2) - (N(K+1) + N(N+1)/2) = N^2,$$

more parameters in the structural form than in the reduced form. In order to obtain unique estimates of the structural parameters from the reduced form parameters, it is necessary to reduce the number of unknown structural parameters by at least N^2. Normalisation of the system, by designating $y_{i,t}$ as the dependent variable in the ith equation for $i = 1, \cdots, N$, imposes N restrictions leaving a further $N^2 - N$ restrictions yet to be imposed. These additional restrictions can take several forms, including zero restrictions, cross-equation restrictions and restrictions on the covariance matrix of the disturbances, V. Restrictions on the covariance matrix of the disturbances are fundamental to identification of structural vector autoregression models, which are discussed in Chapter 14.

Example 5.10 Identification in a Bivariate Simultaneous System

Consider the bivariate simultaneous system introduced in Example 5.4 and developed in Example 5.8 where the structural parameter matrices are

$$B = \begin{bmatrix} 1 & -\beta_1 \\ -\beta_2 & 1 \end{bmatrix}, \quad A = \begin{bmatrix} 0 \\ -\alpha \end{bmatrix}, \quad V = \begin{bmatrix} \sigma_{1,1} & 0 \\ 0 & \sigma_{2,2} \end{bmatrix}.$$

The system of equations to be solved consists of the two equations

$$\Pi = -B^{-1}A = -\begin{bmatrix} 1 & -\beta_1 \\ -\beta_2 & 1 \end{bmatrix}^{-1} \begin{bmatrix} 0 \\ -\alpha \end{bmatrix} = \begin{bmatrix} \dfrac{\alpha\beta_1}{1-\beta_1\beta_2} & \dfrac{\alpha}{1-\beta_1\beta_2} \end{bmatrix},$$

and three unique equations obtained from the covariance restrictions

$$
\begin{aligned}
E\left[v_t v_t'\right] &= B^{-1}V\left(B^{-1}\right)' \\[4pt]
&= \begin{bmatrix} 1 & -\beta_1 \\ -\beta_2 & 1 \end{bmatrix}^{-1} \begin{bmatrix} \sigma_{1,1} & 0 \\ 0 & \sigma_{2,2} \end{bmatrix} \begin{bmatrix} 1 & -\beta_2 \\ -\beta_1 & 1 \end{bmatrix}^{-1} \\[4pt]
&= \begin{bmatrix} \dfrac{\sigma_{1,1} + \beta_1^2\sigma_{2,2}}{(1-\beta_1\beta_2)^2} & \dfrac{\beta_2\sigma_{1,1} + \beta_1\sigma_{2,2}}{(1-\beta_1\beta_2)^2} \\[10pt] \dfrac{\beta_2\sigma_{1,1} + \beta_1\sigma_{2,2}}{(1-\beta_1\beta_2)^2} & \dfrac{\sigma_{2,2} + \beta_2^2\sigma_{1,1}}{(1-\beta_1\beta_2)^2} \end{bmatrix}.
\end{aligned}
$$

As this system of five equations has five unknowns $\theta = \{\beta_1, \beta_2, \alpha, \sigma_{1,1}, \sigma_{2,2}\}$, the order condition is therefore satisfied.   □

If the number of parameters in the reduced form and the structural model are equal, the system is just identified resulting in a unique solution. If the reduced form has more parameters than the structural model, the system is over-identified. In this case, the system (5.11) has more equations than unknowns yielding non-unique solutions, unless the restrictions of the model are imposed. The system (5.11) is under-identified if the number of reduced form parameters is less than the number of structural parameters. A solution of the system of first-order conditions of the log-likelihood function now does not exist. This means that the Jacobian of this system, which of course is also the Hessian of the log-likelihood function, is singular. Any attempt to estimate an under-identified model using the iterative algorithms from Chapter 3 will be characterised by a lack of convergence and an inability to compute standard errors since it is not possible to invert the Hessian or information matrix.

5.3.4 Instrumental Variables

Instrumental variables estimation is another method that is important in estimating the parameters of simultaneous systems of equations. The ordinary least squares estimator of the structural parameter β_1 in the set of equations

$$
\begin{aligned}
y_{1,t} &= \beta_1 y_{2,t} + u_{1,t} \\
y_{2,t} &= \beta_2 y_{1,t} + \alpha x_t + u_{2,t},
\end{aligned}
\tag{5.12}
$$

is obtained by ignoring the second equation in the system

$$
\widehat{\beta}_1^{LS} = \frac{\sum_{t=1}^{T} y_{1,t} y_{2,t}}{\sum_{t=1}^{T} y_{2,t} y_{2,t}}.
$$

This estimator, however, is not a consistent estimator of β_1 because $y_{2,t}$ is not independent of the disturbance term $u_{1,t}$ if $\sigma_{1,2} \neq 0.0$.

From Example 5.8, the FIML estimator of β_1 is

$$
\widehat{\beta}_1 = \frac{\sum_{t=1}^{T} y_{1,t} x_t}{\sum_{t=1}^{T} y_{2,t} x_t},
\tag{5.13}
$$

which from the properties of the FIML estimator is a consistent estimator. The estimator in (5.13) is also known as an instrumental variable (IV) estimator. While the variable x_t is not included as an exogenous variable in the first structural equation in (5.12), it nonetheless is used to correct the dependence between $y_{2,t}$ and $u_{1,t}$ by acting as an instrument for $y_{2,t}$. A quick way to see this is to multiply both sides of the structural equation by x_t and take expectations

$$
E\left[y_{1,t} x_t\right] = \beta_1 E\left[y_{2,t} x_t\right] + E\left[u_{1,t} x_t\right].
$$

As x_t is exogenous in the system of equations, $E\left[u_{1,t} x_t\right] = 0$ and rearranging gives $\beta_1 = E\left[y_{1,t} x_t\right] / E\left[y_{2,t} x_t\right]$. Replacing the expectations in this expression by the corresponding sample moments gives the instrumental variables estimator in (5.13).

The FIML estimator of all of the structural parameters of the bivariate simultaneous system derived in Example 5.8 can be interpreted in an instrumental variables context. To demonstrate this point, rearrange the first-order conditions with respect to β_1, β_2 and α from Example 5.8 as

$$\sum_{t=1}^{T} \left(y_{1,t} - \widehat{\beta}_1 y_{2,t} \right) x_t = 0$$

$$\sum_{t=1}^{T} \left(y_{2,t} - \widehat{\beta}_2 y_{1,t} \right) \widehat{u}_{1,t} = 0 \qquad (5.14)$$

$$\sum_{t=1}^{T} \left(y_{2,t} - \widehat{\beta}_2 y_{1,t} - \widehat{\alpha} x_t \right) x_t = 0.$$

The first equation shows that β_1 is estimated by using x_t as an instrument for $y_{2,t}$. The second equation shows that β_2 is estimated by using $\widehat{u}_{1,t} = y_{1,t} - \widehat{\beta}_1 y_{2,t}$ as an instrument for $y_{1,t}$ and $\widehat{u}_{1,t}$ is obtained as the residuals from the first instrumental variables regression. The third equation shows that x_t acts as its own instrument. Thus, the FIML estimator is equivalent to using an instrumental variables estimator applied to each equation separately. This equivalence is explored in a numerical simulation in Exercise 6.

There are two key properties that an instrumental variable needs to satisfy; namely, that the instruments are correlated with the variables they are instrumenting and the instruments are uncorrelated with the disturbance term. The choice of the instrument x_t in (5.13) naturally arises from having specified the full model in the first place. Moreover, the construction of the other instrument $\widehat{u}_{1,t}$ also naturally arises from the first-order conditions in (5.14) to derive the FIML estimator. In many applications, however, only the single equation is specified leaving the choice of the instrument(s) x_t to the discretion of the researcher. Whilst the properties that a candidate instrument needs to satisfy in theory are transparent, whether a candidate instrument satisfies the two properties in practice is less transparent.

If the instruments are correlated with the variables they are instrumenting, the distribution of the instrumental variable (and FIML) estimators are asymptotically normal. In this example, the focus is on understanding the properties of the sampling distribution of the estimator where this requirement is not satisfied. This is known as the weak instrument problem.

Example 5.11 Weak Instruments
Consider the model

$$y_{1,t} = \beta y_{2,t} + u_{1,t}$$
$$y_{2,t} = \alpha x_t + u_{2,t},$$

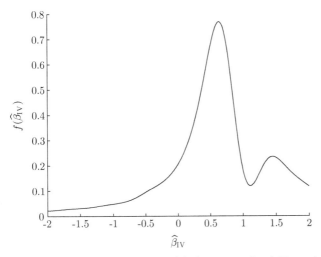

Figure 5.2. Sampling distribution of the instrumental variables estimator in the presence of a weak instrument. The distribution is approximated using a Gaussian kernel density estimator with bandwidth $h = 0.07$.

where

$$u_t \sim iid \, N \left(\begin{bmatrix} 0 \\ 0 \end{bmatrix}, \begin{bmatrix} \sigma_{1,1} & \sigma_{1,2} \\ \sigma_{1,2} & \sigma_{2,2} \end{bmatrix} \right) ,$$

in which $y_{1,t}$ and $y_{2,t}$ are the dependent variables and x_t is an exogenous variable. The parameter $\sigma_{1,2}$ controls the strength of the simultaneity bias, where a value of $\sigma_{1,2} = 0$ means that an ordinary least squares regression of $y_{1,t}$ on $y_{2,t}$ results in a consistent estimator of β that is asymptotically normal. The parameter α controls the strength of the instrument. A value of $\alpha = 0$ means that there is no correlation between $y_{2,t}$ and x_t, in which case x_t is not a valid instrument. The weak instrument problem occurs when the value of α is 'small' relative to $\sigma_{2,2}$, the variance of $u_{2,t}$.

Let the parameter values be $\beta = 0$, $\alpha = 0.25$, $\sigma_{1,1} = 1$, $\sigma_{2,2} = 1$ and $\sigma_{1,2} = 0.99$. Assume further that $x_t \sim iid \, N(0, 1)$. The sampling distribution of the instrumental variable estimator, computed by Monte Carlo methods for a sample of size $T = 5$ with 10000 replications, is given in Figure 5.2. The sampling distribution is far from being normal or centered on the true value of $\beta = 0$. In fact, the sampling distribution is bimodal with neither of the two modes being located near the true value of β. Hillier (2006), Forchini (2006) and Phillips (2006) provide some exact theory underlying this bimodality. By improving the quality of the instrument, as represented by higher values of α, the sampling distribution of the instrumental variable estimator approaches normality with its mean located at the true value of $\beta = 0$. $\qquad\square$

A necessary condition for instrumental variable estimation is that there are at least as many instruments, K, as variables requiring to be instrumented, M. From the discussion of the identification problem in Section 5.3.3, the model is just-identified when $K = M$, is over-identified when $K > M$ and is under-identified when $K < M$. Let X represent a $(T \times K)$ matrix containing the K instruments, Y_1 a $(T \times M)$ matrix of dependent variables and Y_2 a $(T \times M)$ matrix containing the M variables to be instrumented. In matrix notation, the instrumental variables estimator of a single equation is

$$\widehat{\theta}_{IV} = (Y_2'X(X'X)^{-1}X'Y_2)^{-1}(Y_2'X(X'X)^{-1}X'Y_1), \qquad (5.15)$$

with covariance matrix

$$\mathrm{cov}(\widehat{\theta}_{IV}) = \widehat{\sigma}^2(Y_2'X(X'X)^{-1}X'Y_2)^{-1}, \qquad (5.16)$$

in which $\widehat{\sigma}^2$ is the residual variance. For the case of a just-identified model, $M = K$, and the instrumental variable estimator reduces to

$$\widehat{\theta}_{IV} = (X'Y_2)^{-1}X'Y_1, \qquad (5.17)$$

which is the multiple regression version of (5.13) expressed in matrix notation.

Example 5.12 Modelling Contagion

Favero and Giavazzi (2002) propose the following bivariate model to test for contagion

$$y_{1,t} = \beta_1 y_{2,t} + \alpha_1 y_{1,t-1} + \alpha_2 d_{1,t} + \alpha_3 d_{2,t} + u_{1,t}$$
$$y_{2,t} = \beta_2 y_{1,t} + \alpha_4 y_{2,t-1} + \alpha_5 d_{1,t} + \alpha_6 d_{2,t} + u_{2,t},$$

in which $y_{1,t}$ and $y_{2,t}$ are the returns in two asset markets and $d_{1,t}$ and $d_{2,t}$ are dummy variables representing an outlier in the returns of the ith asset. A test of contagion from asset market 2 to asset market 1 is based on the null hypothesis $\alpha_3 = 0$. As each equation includes an endogenous explanatory variable the model is estimated by FIML, which, in this case, is equivalent to the instrumental variable estimator with instruments $y_{1,t-1}$ and $y_{2,t-1}$ because the model is just-identified. However, the autocorrelation in returns is likely to be relatively small and potentially zero from an efficient-markets point of view, resulting in a weak instrument problem.   □

5.3.5 Seemingly Unrelated Regression (SUR) Models

An important special case of the simultaneous equations model is the seemingly unrelated regression model (SUR) where each dependent variable only occurs in one equation, so that the structural coefficient matrix B in equation (5.1) is an $(N \times N)$ identity matrix.

Example 5.13 Trivariate SUR Model

An example of a trivariate SUR model is

$$y_{1,t} = \alpha_1 x_{1,t} + u_{1,t}$$
$$y_{2,t} = \alpha_2 x_{2,t} + u_{2,t}$$
$$y_{3,t} = \alpha_3 x_{3,t} + u_{3,t},$$

with disturbance term $u_t = [u_{1,t}, u_{2,t}, u_{3,t}]'$ that has the properties

$$u_t \sim iid \ N \left(\begin{bmatrix} 0 \\ 0 \\ 0 \end{bmatrix}, \begin{bmatrix} \sigma_{1,1} & \sigma_{1,2} & \sigma_{1,3} \\ \sigma_{1,2} & \sigma_{2,2} & \sigma_{2,3} \\ \sigma_{1,3} & \sigma_{2,3} & \sigma_{3,3} \end{bmatrix} \right).$$

In matrix notation, this system is written as

$$y_t + Ax_t = u_t,$$

in which $y_t = [y_{1,t}, y_{2,t}, y_{3,t}]'$ and $x_t = [x_{1,t}, x_{2,t}, x_{3,t}]'$ and A is a diagonal matrix

$$A = \begin{bmatrix} -\alpha_1 & 0 & 0 \\ 0 & -\alpha_2 & 0 \\ 0 & 0 & -\alpha_3 \end{bmatrix}.$$

The log-likelihood function is

$$\ln L_T(\theta) = -\frac{N}{2} \ln(2\pi) - \frac{1}{2} \ln|V| - \frac{1}{2T} \sum_{t=1}^{T} (y_t + Ax_t)' V^{-1} (y_t + Ax_t),$$

with $N = 3$. This expression is maximised by differentiating $\ln L_T(\theta)$ with respect to the parameters $\theta = \{\alpha_1, \alpha_2, \alpha_3, \sigma_{1,1}, \sigma_{2,1}, \sigma_{2,2}, \sigma_{3,1}, \sigma_{3,2}, \sigma_{3,3}\}$ and setting these derivatives to zero to find $\hat{\theta}$. □

Example 5.14 Equivalence of SUR and Least Squares Estimates

Consider the class of SUR models where the independent variables are the same in each equation. An example is

$$y_{i,t} = \alpha_i x_t + u_{i,t},$$

in which $u_t = [u_{1,t}, u_{2,t}, \cdots, u_{N,t}]' \sim iid \ N(0, V)$. For this model, $A = [-\alpha_1, -\alpha_2, \cdots, -\alpha_N]'$ and estimation by maximum likelihood yields the same estimates as ordinary least squares applied to each equation individually. □

5.4 Testing

The three tests developed in Chapter 4, namely the likelihood ratio (LR), Wald (W) and Lagrange Multiplier (LM) statistics are now applied to testing the parameters of single and multiple equation linear regression models. Depending

Table 5.2. *Unrestricted and restricted parameter estimates of the single equation regression model*

Parameter	Unrestricted	Restricted
β_0	1.129	1.129
β_1	0.719	0.673
β_2	0.389	0.327
σ^2	3.862	3.868
$\ln L_T(\theta)$	-2.0946	-2.0953

on the choice of covariance matrix, various asymptotically equivalent forms of the test statistics are available (see Chapter 4).

Example 5.15 Testing a Single Equation Model
Consider the regression model

$$y_t = \beta_0 + \beta_1 x_{1,t} + \beta_2 x_{2,t} + u_t, \qquad u_t \sim iid\ N(0, \sigma^2),$$

in which $\theta_0 = \{\beta_0 = 1.0,\ \beta_1 = 0.7,\ \beta_2 = 0.3,\ \sigma^2 = 4\}$ and $(x_{1,t}, x_{2,t})' \sim iid\ N(0, I_2)$. The model is simulated with a sample of size $T = 200$ and maximum likelihood estimates of the parameters are reported in the second column of Table 5.2. Now consider testing the hypotheses

$$H_0 : \beta_1 + \beta_2 = 1, \qquad H_1 : \beta_1 + \beta_2 \neq 1.$$

The restricted maximum likelihood parameter estimates, given in the third column of Table 5.2, are obtained by imposing the restriction $\beta_1 + \beta_2 = 1$ and writing the model as

$$y_t = \beta_0 + \beta_1 x_{1,t} + (1 - \beta_1)x_{2,t} + u_t.$$

The LR statistic is computed as

$$LR = -2T(\ln L_T(\widehat{\theta}_0) - \ln L_T(\widehat{\theta}_1)) = -2 \times 200(-2.0953 + 2.0946)$$
$$= 0.2792,$$

which is distributed asymptotically as χ_1^2 under H_0. The p-value is 0.5972 showing that the restriction is not rejected at the 5% level, a result which is consistent with the population parameters.

Based on the assumption of a normal distribution for the disturbance term, an alternative form for the LR statistic for a single equation model is

$$LR = T(\ln \widehat{\sigma}_0^2 - \ln \widehat{\sigma}_1^2).$$

The alternative form of this statistic yields the same value

$$LR = T(\ln \widehat{\sigma}_0^2 - \ln \widehat{\sigma}_1^2) = 200 \times (\ln 3.868 - \ln 3.862) = 0.2792.$$

To compute the Wald statistic, define

$$R = [0 \quad 1 \quad 1 \quad 0], \qquad Q = [1],$$

and compute the negative Hessian matrix

$$-H_T(\widehat{\theta}_1) = \begin{bmatrix} 0.259 & -0.016 & 0.014 & 0.000 \\ -0.016 & 0.285 & -0.007 & 0.000 \\ 0.014 & -0.007 & 0.214 & 0.000 \\ 0.000 & 0.000 & 0.000 & 0.034 \end{bmatrix}.$$

The Wald statistic is then

$$W = T[R\widehat{\theta}_1 - Q]'[R(-H_T^{-1}(\widehat{\theta}_1))R']^{-1}[R\widehat{\theta}_1 - Q] = 0.2794,$$

which is distributed asymptotically as χ_1^2 under H_0. The p-value is 0.5971 showing that the restriction is not rejected at the 5% level.

The LM statistic requires evaluating the gradients of the unrestricted model at the restricted estimates

$$G_T(\widehat{\theta}_0) = \begin{bmatrix} 0.000 & 0.013 & 0.013 & 0.000 \end{bmatrix}',$$

and computing the inverse of the outer product of gradients matrix evaluated at $\widehat{\theta}_0$

$$J_T^{-1}(\widehat{\theta}_0) = \begin{bmatrix} 3.967 & -0.122 & 0.570 & -0.934 \\ -0.122 & 4.158 & 0.959 & -2.543 \\ 0.570 & 0.959 & 5.963 & -1.260 \\ -0.934 & -2.543 & -1.260 & 28.171 \end{bmatrix}.$$

Using these terms in the LM statistic gives

$$LM = TG_T'(\widehat{\theta}_0)J_T^{-1}(\widehat{\theta}_0)G_T(\widehat{\theta}_0) = 0.3990,$$

which is distributed asymptotically as χ_1^2 under H_0. The p-value is 0.5276 showing that the restriction is still not rejected at the 5% level. □

The form of the LR, Wald and LM test statistics in the case of multiple equation regression models is the same as it is for single equation regression models. Once again an alternative form of the LR statistic is available as a result of the assumption of normality. Recall from equation (5.10) that the log-likelihood function for a multiple equation model is

$$\ln L_T(\theta) = -\frac{N}{2}\ln(2\pi) - \frac{1}{2}\ln|V| + \ln|B|$$

$$-\frac{1}{2T}\sum_{t=1}^{T}(By_t + Ax_t)'V^{-1}(By_t + Ax_t).$$

The unrestricted maximum likelihood estimator of V is

$$\widehat{V}_1 = \frac{1}{T}\sum_{t=1}^{T}\widehat{u}_t\widehat{u}_t', \qquad \widehat{u}_t = \widehat{B}_1 y_t + \widehat{A}_1 x_t.$$

The log-likelihood function evaluated at the unrestricted estimator is

$$\ln L_T(\widehat{\theta}_1) = -\frac{N}{2}\ln(2\pi) - \frac{1}{2}\ln|\widehat{V}_1| + \ln|\widehat{B}_1|$$

$$-\frac{1}{2T}\sum_{t=1}^{T}(\widehat{B}_1 y_t + \widehat{A}_1 x_t)'\widehat{V}_1^{-1}(\widehat{B}_1 y_t + \widehat{A}_1 x_t)$$

$$= -\frac{N}{2}(1 + \ln 2\pi) - \frac{1}{2}\ln|\widehat{V}_1| + \ln|\widehat{B}_1|,$$

which uses the result from Chapter 4 that

$$\frac{1}{T}\sum_{t=1}^{T}\widehat{u}_t'\widehat{V}_1^{-1}\widehat{u}_t = N.$$

Similarly, the log-likelihood function evaluated at the restricted estimator is

$$\ln L_T(\widehat{\theta}_0) = -\frac{N}{2}\ln(2\pi) - \frac{1}{2}\ln|\widehat{V}_0| + \ln|\widehat{B}_0|$$

$$-\frac{1}{2T}\sum_{t=1}^{T}(\widehat{B}_0 y_t + \widehat{A}_0 x_t)'\widehat{V}_0^{-1}(\widehat{B}_0 y_t + \widehat{A}_0 x_t)$$

$$= -\frac{N}{2}(1 + \ln 2\pi) - \frac{1}{2}\ln|\widehat{V}_0| + \ln|\widehat{B}_0|,$$

in which

$$\widehat{V}_0 = \frac{1}{T}\sum_{t=1}^{T}\widehat{u}_t\widehat{u}_t', \qquad \widehat{u}_t = \widehat{B}_0 y_t + \widehat{A}_0 x_t.$$

The LR statistic is

$$LR = -2T(\ln L_T(\widehat{\theta}_0) - \ln L_T(\widehat{\theta}_1))$$
$$= T(\ln|\widehat{V}_0| - \ln|\widehat{V}_1|) - 2T(\ln|\widehat{B}_0| - \ln|\widehat{B}_1|).$$

Table 5.3. *Unrestricted and restricted parameter estimates of the multiple equation regression model*

Parameter	Unrestricted	Restricted
β_1	0.592	0.533
α_1	0.409	0.429
β_2	0.209	0.233
α_2	−0.483	−0.429
$\sigma_{1,1}$	0.952	1.060
$\sigma_{1,2}$	0.444	0.498
$\sigma_{2,2}$	0.967	0.934
$\ln L_T(\theta)$	−2.8079	−2.8217

In the special case of the SUR model ($B = I_N$), the LR statistic is

$$LR = T(\ln|\widehat{V}_0| - \ln|\widehat{V}_1|),$$

which is the alternative form given in Chapter 4.

Example 5.16 Testing a Multiple Equation Model
Consider the model

$$y_{1,t} = \beta_1 y_{2,t} + \alpha_1 x_{1,t} + u_{1,t}$$
$$y_{2,t} = \beta_2 y_{1,t} + \alpha_2 x_{2,t} + u_{2,t},$$
$$u_t \sim iid\, N\left(\begin{bmatrix} 0 \\ 0 \end{bmatrix}, V = \begin{bmatrix} \sigma_{1,1} & \sigma_{1,2} \\ \sigma_{1,2} & \sigma_{2,2} \end{bmatrix}\right),$$

in which the hypotheses

$$H_0 : \alpha_1 + \alpha_2 = 0, \qquad H_1 : \alpha_1 + \alpha_2 \neq 0,$$

are to be tested. The unrestricted and restricted maximum likelihood parameter estimates given in Table 5.3 are based on the simulated data and parameter values given in Example 5.6. The restricted parameter estimates are obtained by imposing the restriction $\alpha_2 = -\alpha_1$, and writing the model as

$$y_{1,t} = \beta_1 y_{2,t} + \alpha_1 x_{1,t} + u_{1,t}$$
$$y_{2,t} = \beta_2 y_{1,t} - \alpha_1 x_{2,t} + u_{2,t}.$$

The LR statistic is computed as

$$LR = -2T(\ln L_T(\widehat{\theta}_0) - \ln L_T(\widehat{\theta}_1)) = -2 \times 500(-2.822 + 2.808)$$
$$= 13.883,$$

which is distributed asymptotically as χ_1^2 under H_0. The p-value is 0.000 showing that the restriction is rejected at the 5% level. The alternative form of this statistic gives

$$LR = T(\ln|\widehat{V}_0| - \ln|\widehat{V}_1|) - 2T(\ln|\widehat{B}_0| - \ln|\widehat{B}_1|)$$

$$= 500\left(\ln\begin{vmatrix}1.060 & 0.498 \\ 0.498 & 0.934\end{vmatrix} - \ln\begin{vmatrix}0.952 & 0.444 \\ 0.444 & 0.967\end{vmatrix}\right)$$

$$-2 \times 500\left(\ln\begin{vmatrix}1.000 & -0.533 \\ -0.233 & 1.000\end{vmatrix} - \ln\begin{vmatrix}1.000 & -0.592 \\ -0.209 & 1.000\end{vmatrix}\right)$$

$$= 13.883,$$

which agrees with the value obtained previously. To compute the Wald statistic, define

$$R = [0 \quad 1 \quad 0 \quad 1], \qquad Q = [0],$$

and compute the negative Hessian matrix

$$-H_T(\widehat{\theta}_1) = \begin{bmatrix} 3.943 & 4.513 & -1.921 & 2.921 \\ 4.513 & 44.620 & -9.613 & 0.133 \\ -1.921 & -9.613 & 10.859 & -3.824 \\ 2.921 & 0.133 & -3.824 & 11.305 \end{bmatrix},$$

where $\widehat{\theta}_1$ corresponds to the parameter vector after concentrating the log-likelihood function. The Wald statistic is

$$W = T[R\widehat{\theta}_1 - Q]'[R(-H_T^{-1}(\widehat{\theta}_1)) R']^{-1}[R\widehat{\theta}_1 - Q] = 13.895,$$

which is distributed asymptotically as χ_1^2 under H_0. The p-value is 0.000 showing that the restriction is rejected at the 5% level.

The LM statistic requires evaluating the gradients of the unrestricted model at the restricted estimates

$$G_T(\widehat{\theta}_0) = [0.000 \quad -0.370 \quad 0.000 \quad -0.370]',$$

and computing the inverse of the outer product of gradients matrix evaluated at $\widehat{\theta}_0$

$$J_T^{-1}(\widehat{\theta}_0) = \begin{bmatrix} 0.493 & -0.071 & -0.007 & -0.133 \\ -0.071 & 0.042 & 0.034 & 0.025 \\ -0.007 & 0.034 & 0.123 & 0.040 \\ -0.133 & 0.025 & 0.040 & 0.131 \end{bmatrix}.$$

Using these terms in the LM statistic gives

$$LM = T G_T'(\widehat{\theta}_0) J_T^{-1}(\widehat{\theta}_0) G_T(\widehat{\theta}_0) = 15.325,$$

which is distributed asymptotically as χ_1^2 under H_0. The p-value is 0.000 showing that the restriction is also rejected at the 5% level.   □

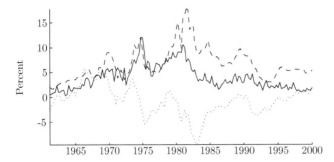

Figure 5.3. United States data on the Federal Funds Rate (dashed line), inflation (solid line) and the output gap (dotted line) as defined by Rudebusch (2002).

5.5 Applications

Two applications of estimation and testing in linear regression models are now presented. The first involves estimating a static version of the Taylor rule for the conduct of monetary policy using macroeconomic data from the United States. The second estimates the well-known Klein macroeconomic model for the United States.

5.5.1 Linear Taylor Rule

Taylor (1993) proposes a simple rule for setting monetary policy where policymakers adjust the Federal funds rate, i_t, in response to inflation, π_t, and the gap between output and its long-run potential level, y_t. To formalise this policy rule, consider the model

$$i_t = \beta_0 + \beta_1 \pi_t + \beta_2 y_t + u_t, \qquad u_t \sim iid\, N(0, \sigma^2),$$

where $\theta = \{\beta_0, \beta_1, \beta_2\}$ are parameters. Taylor suggests values of $\beta_1 = 1.5$ and $\beta_2 = 0.5$. This static linear version of the so-called Taylor rule represents a linear regression model with two exogenous variables of the form discussed in detail in Section 5.3.

The parameters of the model in equation (5.5.1) are estimated using data from the United States for the period March 1987 to December 1999, a total of $T = 52$ observations. Details concerning the construction of the variables are given in Rudebusch (2002, p1164). The data are plotted in Figure 5.3.

The log-likelihood function is

$$\ln L_T(\theta) = -\frac{1}{2}\ln(2\pi) - \frac{1}{2}\ln\sigma^2 - \frac{1}{2\sigma^2 T}\sum_{t=1}^{T}(i_t - \beta_0 - \beta_1\pi_t - \beta_2 y_t)^2,$$

with $\theta = \{\beta_0, \beta_1, \beta_2, \sigma^2\}$. In this particular case, the first-order conditions are solved to yield closed-form solutions for the maximum likelihood estimators that are also the ordinary least squares estimators. The maximum likelihood estimates of $\beta = [\beta_0, \beta_1, \beta_2]'$ are

$$
\begin{bmatrix} \widehat{\beta_0} \\ \widehat{\beta_1} \\ \widehat{\beta_2} \end{bmatrix} = \begin{bmatrix} 53.000 & 132.922 & -40.791 \\ 132.922 & 386.483 & -123.786 \\ -40.791 & -123.786 & 147.772 \end{bmatrix}^{-1} \begin{bmatrix} 305.843 \\ 822.973 \\ -192.157 \end{bmatrix} = \begin{bmatrix} 2.980 \\ 1.300 \\ 0.611 \end{bmatrix}.
$$

Once $\widehat{\beta} = [\ \widehat{\beta_0}\ \widehat{\beta_1}\ \widehat{\beta_2}\ ]'$ is computed, the ordinary least squares estimate of the variance is obtained from the least squares residuals

$$
\widehat{\sigma}^2 = \frac{1}{T} \sum_{t=1}^{T} (i_t - 2.980 - 1.300\pi_t - 0.611y_t)^2 = 1.114.
$$

The covariance matrix of $\widehat{\beta} = \{\widehat{\beta_0}, \widehat{\beta_1}, \widehat{\beta_2}\}$ is

$$
\text{cov}(\widehat{\beta}) = \begin{bmatrix} 0.154 & -0.054 & -0.004 \\ -0.054 & 0.023 & 0.004 \\ -0.003 & 0.004 & 0.010 \end{bmatrix}.
$$

The estimated monetary policy response coefficients, namely, $\widehat{\beta_1} = 1.300$ for inflation and $\widehat{\beta_2} = 0.611$ for the response to the output gap, are not dissimilar to the suggested values of 1.5 and 0.5, respectively. A Wald test of the restrictions $\beta_1 = 1.50$ and $\beta_2 = 0.5$ yields a test statistic of 4.062. From the χ_2^2 distribution, the p-value of this statistic is 0.131 showing that the restrictions cannot be rejected at conventional significance levels.

5.5.2   The Klein Model of the United States Economy

One of the first macroeconomic models constructed for the United States is the Klein (1950) model, which consists of three structural equations and three identities

$$
\begin{aligned}
C_t &= \alpha_0 + \alpha_1 P_t + \alpha_2 P_{t-1} + \alpha_3(PW_t + GW_t) + u_{1,t} \\
I_t &= \beta_0 + \beta_1 P_t + \beta_2 P_{t-1} + \beta_3 K_{t-1} + u_{2,t} \\
PW_t &= \gamma_0 + \gamma_1 D_t + \gamma_2 D_{t-1} + \gamma_3 TREND_t + u_{3,t} \\
D_t &= C_t + I_t + G_t \\
P_t &= D_t - TAX_t - PW_t \\
K_t &= K_{t-1} + I_t\ ,
\end{aligned}
$$

in which $u_t = [u_{1,t}, u_{2,t}, u_{3,t}]'$ is the disturbance vector with distribution

$$
u_t \sim iid\ N \left(\begin{bmatrix} 0 \\ 0 \\ 0 \end{bmatrix}, \begin{bmatrix} \sigma_{1,1} & \sigma_{1,2} & \sigma_{1,3} \\ \sigma_{1,2} & \sigma_{2,2} & \sigma_{2,3} \\ \sigma_{1,3} & \sigma_{2,3} & \sigma_{3,3} \end{bmatrix} \right),
$$

and the key variables are defined as

$$
\begin{aligned}
C_t &= \text{Consumption} \\
P_t &= \text{Profits} \\
PW_t &= \text{Private wages} \\
GW_t &= \text{Government wages} \\
I_t &= \text{Investment} \\
K_t &= \text{Capital stock} \\
D_t &= \text{Aggregate demand} \\
G_t &= \text{Government spending} \\
TAX_t &= \text{Indirect taxes plus nex exports} \\
TREND_t &= \text{Time trend, base in 1931.}
\end{aligned}
$$

The first equation is a consumption function, the second equation is an investment function and the third equation is a labor demand equation. The last three expressions are identities for aggregate demand, private profits and the capital stock, respectively. The variables are classified as

$$
\begin{aligned}
\text{Endogenous} \quad &: \quad C_t, I_t, PW_t, D_t, P_t, K_t \\
\text{Exogenous} \quad &: \quad CONST, G_t, TAX_t, GW_t, TREND, \\
\text{Predetermined} \quad &: \quad P_{t-1}, D_{t-1}, K_{t-1}.
\end{aligned}
$$

To estimate the Klein model by FIML, it is necessary to use the three identities to write the model as a three-equation system just containing the three endogenous variables. Formally, this requires combing the identities for P_t and D_t to derive an expression for P_t as

$$
P_t = D_t - TAX_t - PW_t = C_t + I_t + G_t - TAX_t - PW_t.
$$

This equation together with the identity for D_t are used to substitute D_t and P_t out of the three structural equations as follows

$$
\begin{aligned}
C_t &= \alpha_0 + \alpha_1(C_t + I_t + G_t - TAX_t - PW_t) \\
&\quad + \alpha_2 P_{t-1} + \alpha_3(PW_t + GW_t) + u_{1,t} \\[6pt]
I_t &= \beta_0 + \beta_1(C_t + I_t + G_t - TAX_t - PW_t) \\
&\quad + \beta_2 P_{t-1} + \beta_3 K_{t-1} + u_{2,t} \\[6pt]
PW_t &= \gamma_0 + \gamma_1(C_t + I_t + G_t) + \gamma_2 D_{t-1} + \gamma_3 TREND_t + u_{3,t}.
\end{aligned}
$$

This is now a system of three equations and three endogenous variables (C_t, I_t, PW_t), which can be estimated by FIML. In deriving this form of the Klein model the third identity corresponding to the capital stock accumulation equation is not used as K_t does not appear in any of the three structural

Table 5.4. *Parameter estimates based on ordinary least squares (OLS), instrumental variables (IV) and FIML of the Klein macroeconomic model for the United States, 1921 to 1941*

Parameter	OLS	IV	FIML
α_0	16.237	16.555	16.461
α_1	0.193	0.017	0.177
α_2	0.090	0.216	0.210
α_3	0.796	0.810	0.728
β_0	10.126	20.278	24.130
β_1	0.480	0.150	0.007
β_2	0.333	0.616	0.670
β_3	−0.112	−0.158	−0.172
γ_0	1.497	1.500	1.028
γ_1	0.439	0.439	0.317
γ_2	0.146	0.147	0.253
γ_3	0.130	0.130	0.096

equations. Defining

$$y_t = \begin{bmatrix} C_t & I_t & PW_t \end{bmatrix}'$$

$$x_t = \begin{bmatrix} CONST & G_t & TAX_t & GW_t & TREND_t & P_{t-1} & D_{t-1} & K_{t-1} \end{bmatrix}'$$

$$u_t = \begin{bmatrix} u_{1,t} & u_{2,t} & u_{3,t} \end{bmatrix}'$$

$$B = \begin{bmatrix} (1-\alpha_1) & -\alpha_1 & (\alpha_1 - \alpha_3) \\ -\beta_1 & (1-\beta_1) & \beta_1 \\ -\gamma_1 & -\gamma_1 & 1 \end{bmatrix}$$

$$A = \begin{bmatrix} -\alpha_0 & -\alpha_1 & \alpha_1 & -\alpha_3 & 0 & -\alpha_2 & 0 & 0 \\ -\beta_0 & -\beta_1 & \beta_1 & 0 & 0 & -\beta_2 & 0 & -\beta_3 \\ -\gamma_0 & -\gamma_1 & 0 & 0 & -\gamma_3 & 0 & -\gamma_2 & 0 \end{bmatrix}$$

from (5.1), the system of equations is written as

$$By_t + Ax_t = u_t .$$

The Klein macroeconomic model is estimated over the period 1920 to 1941 using United States annual data. As the system contains one lag the effective sample begins in 1921, resulting in a sample of size $T = 21$. The FIML parameter estimates are contained in the last column of Table 5.4. The value of the log-likelihood function is $\ln L_T(\widehat{\theta}) = -4.065$. For comparison the ordinary least squares and instrumental variables estimates are also given. The instrumental variables estimates are computed using the eight variables given in x_t as the instrument set for each equation. Noticeable differences in the magnitudes

of the parameter estimates are evident in some cases, particularly in the investment equation where the parameters are $\{\beta_0, \beta_1, \beta_2, \beta_3\}$. In this instance, the IV
estimates appear to be closer to the FIML estimates than do the ordinary least
squares estimates, indicating potential simultaneity problems with the ordinary
least squares approach for this equation in particular.

5.6   Exercises

(1) Simulating a Simultaneous System

Program files linear_simulation.*	

Consider the bivariate model

$$y_{1,t} = \beta_1 y_{2,t} + \alpha_1 x_{1,t} + u_{1,t}$$
$$y_{2,t} = \beta_2 y_{1,t} + \alpha_2 x_{2,t} + u_{2,t},$$

in which $y_{1,t}$ and $y_{2,t}$ are the dependent variables, the exogenous variables
are $x_{1,t} \sim iid\ U[0, 10]$ and $x_{2,t} \sim iid\ N(0, 9)$ with $x_{1,t}$ and $x_{2,t}$ independent of each other, and $u_{1,t}$ and $u_{2,t}$ are iid normally distributed disturbances
with zero means and covariance matrix

$$V = \begin{bmatrix} \sigma_{1,1} & \sigma_{1,2} \\ \sigma_{1,2} & \sigma_{2,2} \end{bmatrix} = \begin{bmatrix} 1 & 0.5 \\ 0.5 & 1 \end{bmatrix},$$

while $\beta_1 = 0.6$, $\alpha_1 = 0.4$, $\beta_2 = 0.2$ and $\alpha_2 = -0.5$.
(a) Construct A, B and hence compute $\Pi = -B^{-1}A$.
(b) Simulate the model for $T = 500$ observations and plot the simulated
series of $y_{1,t}$ and $y_{2,t}$.

(2) ML Estimation of a Regression Model

Program files linear_estimate.*	

Simulate the model for a sample of size $T = 200$

$$y_t = \beta_0 + \beta_1 x_{1,t} + \beta_2 x_{2,t} + u_t$$
$$u_t \sim iid\ N(0, 4),$$

in which $\beta_0 = 1.0$, $\beta_1 = 0.7$, $\beta_2 = 0.3$, $\sigma^2 = 4$ and $(x_{1,t}, x_{2,t})' \sim$
$iid\ N(0, I_2)$.
(a) Compute the maximum likelihood parameter estimates using the
Newton-Raphson algorithm, with and without concentrating the log-
likelihood function. Compare the two sets of parameter estimates.
(b) Compute the parameter estimates by ordinary least squares and compare them with those obtained in part (a).

(c) Compute the covariance matrix of the parameter estimates in parts (a) and (b) and compare the results.

(d) Using LR, Wald and LM statistics, test the hypotheses

$$H_0 : \beta_1 + \beta_2 = 1 \qquad H_1 : \beta_1 + \beta_2 \neq 1.$$

(3) FIML Estimation of a Structural Model

Program files   linear_fiml.*

This exercise uses the model and simulated data from Exercise 1.

(a) Estimate the parameters of the structural model

$$y_{1,t} = \beta_1 y_{2,t} + \alpha_1 x_{1,t} + u_{1,t}$$
$$y_{2,t} = \beta_2 y_{1,t} + \alpha_2 x_{2,t} + u_{2,t},$$

by FIML using an iterative algorithm with the starting estimates taken as draws from a uniform distribution.

(b) Repeat part (a) by choosing the starting estimates as draws from a normal distribution. Compare the final estimates with the estimates obtained in part (a).

(c) Test the hypotheses

$$H_0 : \alpha_1 + \alpha_2 = 0 \qquad H_1 : \alpha_1 + \alpha_2 \neq 0,$$

using LR, Wald and LM tests.

(d) Re-estimate the model's parameters using an IV estimator and compare these estimates with the FIML estimates obtained in parts (a) and (b).

(4) Weak Instruments

Program files   linear_weak.*

This exercise extends the results on weak instruments in Example 5.11. Consider the model

$$y_{1,t} = \beta y_{2,t} + u_{1,t}$$
$$y_{2,t} = \alpha x_t + u_{2,t}, \qquad u_t \sim iid\, N \left(\begin{bmatrix} 0 \\ 0 \end{bmatrix}, \begin{bmatrix} 1.00 & 0.99 \\ 0.99 & 1.00 \end{bmatrix} \right),$$

in which $y_{1,t}$ and $y_{2,t}$ are dependent variables, $x_t \sim iid\, U(0, 1)$ is the exogenous variable (held fixed in repeated samples) and the parameters are β and α. The sample size is $T = 5$ and 10000 replications are used to generate the sampling distribution of the estimator.

(a) Generate the sampling distribution of the IV estimator for the parameter values $\beta = 0$ and $\alpha = \{0.5, 1.0, 10\}$. Discuss the sampling properties of the IV estimator in each case.

(b) Generate the sampling distribution of the IV estimator for the parameter values $\beta = 0$ and $\alpha = 0$. Compare this sampling distribution to the three sampling distributions obtained in part (a). Also compute the sampling distribution of the ordinary least squares estimator for this case. Note that for this model the ordinary least squares estimator has the property (see Stock, Wright and Yogo, 2002)

$$\text{plim}(\widehat{\beta}^{LS}) = \frac{\sigma_{1,2}}{\sigma_{2,2}} = 0.99 \, .$$

(c) Repeat parts (a) and (b) for samples of size $T = \{50, 500\}$. Discuss whether the results in parts (a) and (b) are affected by asymptotic arguments.

(5) Regression Model with Gamma Disturbances

Program files   linear_gamma.*

Consider the linear regression model

$$y_t = \beta_0 + \beta_1 x_t + (u_t - \rho\alpha),$$

in which y_t is the dependent variable, x_t is the exogenous variable and the disturbance term u_t is an *iid* drawing from the gamma distribution

$$f(u; \rho, \alpha) = \frac{1}{\Gamma(\rho)} \left(\frac{1}{\alpha}\right)^\rho u^{\rho-1} \exp\left[-\frac{u}{\alpha}\right],$$

with $\Gamma(\rho)$ representing the gamma function. The term $-\rho\alpha$ in the regression model is included to ensure that the disturbance term $u_t - \rho\alpha$ has mean $E[u_t - \rho\alpha] = 0$. For samples of size $T = \{10, 100, 1000, 10000\}$, compute the standardised sampling distributions of the least squares estimators

$$z_{\widehat{\beta}_0} = \frac{\widehat{\beta}_0 - \beta_0}{\text{se}(\widehat{\beta}_0)}, \qquad z_{\widehat{\beta}_1} = \frac{\widehat{\beta}_1 - \beta_1}{\text{se}(\widehat{\beta}_1)},$$

based on 5000 draws, parameter values $\beta_0 = 1, \beta_1 = 2, \rho = 0.25, \alpha = 0.1$ and x_t is drawn from a standard normal distribution. Discuss the limiting properties of the sampling distributions as T changes.

(6) Relationship Between FIML and IV Estimators

Program files   linear_iv.*

Simulate the following structural model for $T = 500$ observations

$$y_{1,t} = \beta_1 y_{2,t} + u_{1,t}$$
$$y_{2,t} = \beta_2 y_{1,t} + \alpha x_t + u_{2,t},$$

in which $y_{1,t}$ and $y_{2,t}$ are the dependent variables, $x_t \sim iid\ N(0, 100)$ is the exogenous variable, $u_{1,t}$ and $u_{2,t}$ are iid normally distributed disturbance terms with zero means and diagonal covariance matrix

$$V = \begin{bmatrix} \sigma_{1,1} & \sigma_{1,2} \\ \sigma_{1,2} & \sigma_{2,2} \end{bmatrix} = \begin{bmatrix} 2.0 & 0.0 \\ 0.0 & 1.0 \end{bmatrix},$$

and the parameters are set at $\beta_1 = 0.6$, $\beta_2 = 0.4$ and $\alpha = -0.5$.

(a) Compute the FIML estimates of the model's parameters using an iterative algorithm with the starting estimates taken as draws from a uniform distribution.

(b) Re-compute the FIML estimates using the analytical expressions given in Example 5.8. Compare these estimates with the estimates obtained in part (a).

(c) Re-estimate the model's parameters using an IV estimator and compare these estimates with the FIML estimates in parts (a) and (b).

(7) Recursive Structural Models

Program files   `linear_recursive.*`

Simulate the trivariate structural model for $T = 200$ observations

$$
\begin{aligned}
y_{1,t} &= & & & & \alpha_1 x_{1,t} & + & u_{1,t} \\
y_{2,t} &= & \beta_1 y_{1,t} & & + & \alpha_2 x_{2,t} & + & u_{2,t} \\
y_{3,t} &= & \beta_2 y_{1,t} & + & \beta_3 y_{2,t} & + & \alpha_3 x_{3,t} & + & u_{3,t},
\end{aligned}
$$

in which the exogenous variables $\{x_{1,t}, x_{2,t}, x_{3,t}\}$ are iid and mutually independent normal random variables with zero means and respective standard deviations of $\{1, 2, 3\}$. The parameters are $\beta_1 = 0.6$, $\beta_2 = 0.2$, $\beta_3 = 1.0$, $\alpha_1 = 0.4$, $\alpha_2 = -0.5$ and $\alpha_3 = 0.2$. The disturbance vector $u_t = [u_{1,t}, u_{2,t}, u_{3,t}]'$ is normally distributed with zero mean and diagonal covariance matrix

$$V = \begin{bmatrix} 2 & 0 & 0 \\ 0 & 1 & 0 \\ 0 & 0 & 5 \end{bmatrix}.$$

(a) Estimate the model by maximum likelihood and compare the parameter estimates with the population parameter values.

(b) Estimate each equation by ordinary least squares and compare the parameter estimates to the maximum likelihood estimates.

(c) Briefly discuss why the two sets of estimates in parts (a) and (b) are the same.

(8) Seemingly Unrelated Regression

Program files	`linear_sur.*`

Simulate the following trivariate SUR model for $T = 500$ observations

$$y_{i,t} = \alpha_i x_{i,t} + u_{i,t}, \qquad i = 1, 2, 3,$$

in which the exogenous variables $\{x_{1,t}, x_{2,t}, x_{3,t}\}$ are iid and mutually independent normal random variables with zero means and respective standard deviations of $\{1, 2, 3\}$. The parameters are $\alpha_1 = 0.4$, $\alpha_2 = -0.5$ and $\alpha_3 = 1.0$. The disturbance vector $u_t = [u_{1,t}, u_{2,t}, u_{3,t}]'$ is iid normally distributed with zero means and covariance matrix

$$V = \begin{bmatrix} 1.0 & 0.5 & -0.1 \\ 0.5 & 1.0 & 0.2 \\ -0.1 & 0.2 & 1.0 \end{bmatrix}.$$

(a) Estimate the model by maximum likelihood and compare the parameter estimates with the population parameter values.

(b) Estimate each equation by ordinary least squares and compare the parameter estimates to the maximum likelihood estimates.

(c) Now simulate the model using the following covariance matrix

$$V = \begin{bmatrix} 2 & 0 & 0 \\ 0 & 1 & 0 \\ 0 & 0 & 5 \end{bmatrix}.$$

Repeat parts (a) and (b) and comment on the results.

(d) Simulate the model

$$y_{i,t} = \alpha_i x_{1,t} + u_{i,t}, \qquad i = 1, 2, 3,$$

for $T = 500$ observations and using the initial covariance matrix of V. Repeat parts (a) and (b) and comment on the results.

(9) Linear Taylor Rule

Program files	`linear_taylor.*`
Data files	`taylor.*`.

The data are $T = 52$ quarterly observations for the United States on the Federal funds rate, i_t, inflation, π_t, and the output gap, y_t.

(a) Consider the static linear Taylor rule equation

$$i_t = \beta_0 + \beta_1 \pi_t + \beta_2 y_t + u_t, \qquad u_t \sim iid\ N(0, \sigma^2),$$

in which π_t and y_t are exogenous. Estimate the parameters by maximum likelihood and compute the covariance matrix of $\widehat{\beta} = \{\beta_0, \beta_1, \beta_2\}$.

(b) Taylor (1993) proposed values of the slope parameters equal to $\beta_1 = 1.5$ and $\beta_2 = 0.5$. Show that the model under these choices can be written as

$$i_t - \pi_t = \beta_0 + \beta_2(y_t - \pi_t) + u_t .$$

Interpret the structure of this equation. To determine whether the parameter values proposed by Taylor are consistent with the data, consider the following hypotheses

$$H_0 : \beta_1 = 1.5, \ \beta_2 = 0.5$$
$$H_1 : \text{at least one restriction does not hold} .$$

Use a Wald test to determine the validity of the parameter values proposed by Taylor.

(10) **Klein's Macroeconomic Model of the United States**

Program files	linear_klein.*
Data files	klein.*

The data file contains 22 annual observations from 1920 to 1941 on the following United States macroeconomic variables:

C_t	$=$	Consumption
P_t	$=$	Profits
PW_t	$=$	Private wages
GW_t	$=$	Government wages
I_t	$=$	Investment
K_t	$=$	Capital stock
D_t	$=$	Aggregate demand
G_t	$=$	Government spending
TAX_t	$=$	Indirect taxes plus nex exports
$TREND_t$	$=$	Time trend, base in 1931.

The Klein (1950) macroeconometric model of the United States is

$$C_t = \alpha_0 + \alpha_1 P_t + \alpha_2 P_{t-1} + \alpha_3(PW_t + GW_t) + u_{1,t}$$
$$I_t = \beta_0 + \beta_1 P_t + \beta_2 P_{t-1} + \beta_3 K_{t-1} + u_{2,t}$$
$$PW_t = \gamma_0 + \gamma_1 D_t + \gamma_2 D_{t-1} + \gamma_3 TREND_t + u_{3,t}$$
$$D_t = C_t + I_t + G_t$$
$$P_t = D_t - TAX_t - PW_t$$
$$K_t = K_{t-1} + I_t ,$$

where the disturbance vector $u_t = [u_{1,t}, u_{2,t}, u_{3,t}]'$ is distributed as

$$
u_t \sim iid \ N \left(\begin{bmatrix} 0 \\ 0 \\ 0 \end{bmatrix}, \begin{bmatrix} \sigma_{1,1} & \sigma_{1,2} & \sigma_{1,3} \\ \sigma_{1,2} & \sigma_{2,2} & \sigma_{2,3} \\ \sigma_{1,3} & \sigma_{2,3} & \sigma_{3,3} \end{bmatrix} \right) .
$$

(a) Estimate each of the three structural equations by ordinary least squares. What is the problem with using this estimator to compute the parameter estimates of this model?

(b) Estimate the model by IV using the following instruments for each equation

$$
x_t = [CONST, \ G_t, \ TAX_t, \ GW_t, \ TREND_t, \ P_{t-1}, \ D_{t-1}, \ K_{t-1}]' .
$$

What are the advantages over ordinary least squares with using IV to compute the parameter estimates of this model?

(c) Use the three identities to re-express the three structural equations as a system containing the three endogenous variables, C_t, I_t and PW_t, and estimate this model by FIML. What are the advantages over IV with using FIML to compute the parameter estimates of this model?

(d) Compare the parameter estimates obtained in parts (a) to (c), with the estimates presented in Table 5.4.

(e) Test the joint restrictions $\alpha_1 = \alpha_2 = \alpha_3 = 1$, using a Wald test and interpret the result.

(f) Test the joint restrictions $\beta_1 = \beta_2 = 1$, using a Wald test and interpret the result.

6   Nonlinear Regression Models

6.1   Introduction

The class of linear regression models with normal disturbances discussed in Chapter 5 is now extended to allow for nonlinearities. Three types of extensions are investigated. The first is where the exogenous variable x_t is specified as a nonlinear function. The second is where the dependent variable y_t is specified as a nonlinear function. The third is where the disturbance term u_t is specified to have a non-normal distribution. Nonlinear specifications of time series models are discussed in Part SIX where nonlinearities in the conditional mean are investigated in Chapter 19, nonlinearities in the conditional variance are discussed in Chapter 20 and nonlinearities arising from models where the dependent variable is a discrete random variable are discussed in Chapter 21.

As with the treatment of linear regression models in the previous chapter, nonlinear regression models are examined within the maximum likelihood framework. Establishing this link ensures that methods typically used to estimate nonlinear regression models, including Gauss-Newton, nonlinear least squares and robust estimators, immediately inherit the same asymptotic properties as the maximum likelihood estimator. Moreover, it is also shown that many of the statistics used to test nonlinear regression models are special cases of the LR, Wald or LM tests discussed in Chapter 4. An important example of this property is a non-nested test used to discriminate between models that is based on a variation of a LR test.

6.2   Specification

A typical form for the nonlinear regression model is

$$g(y_t; \alpha) = \mu(x_t; \beta) + u_t, \qquad u_t \sim iid\ N(0, \sigma^2), \tag{6.1}$$

in which y_t is the dependent variable and x_t is the exogenous variable. Extending this framework to allow for non-normal disturbances is investigated in

194

Section 6.6. The nonlinear functions $g(\cdot)$ and $\mu(\cdot)$ of y_t and x_t have parameter vectors $\alpha = \{\alpha_1, \alpha_2, \cdots, \alpha_m\}$ and $\beta = \{\beta_0, \beta_1, \cdots, \beta_k\}$, respectively. The unknown parameters to be estimated are given by the $(m + k + 2)$ vector $\theta = \{\alpha, \beta, \sigma^2\}$.

Example 6.1 Zellner-Revankar Production Function

Consider the nonlinear production function relating output, y_t, to capital, k_t, and labour, l_t, given by

$$\ln y_t + \alpha y_t = \beta_0 + \beta_1 \ln k_t + \beta_2 \ln l_t + u_t .$$

The nonlinear specifications in equation (6.1) are

$$g(y_t; \alpha) = \ln y_t + \alpha y_t , \qquad \mu(x_t; \beta) = \beta_0 + \beta_1 \ln k_t + \beta_2 \ln l_t .$$

□

Example 6.2 Exponential Regression Model

An example of a nonlinear exponential regression model is given by

$$y_t = \beta_0 \exp [\beta_1 x_t] + u_t ,$$

with

$$g(y_t; \alpha) = y_t , \qquad \mu(x_t; \beta) = \beta_0 \exp [\beta_1 x_t] .$$

□

The models in Examples 6.1 and 6.2 are intrinsically nonlinear, in the sense that they cannot be transformed into linear representations of the form of models discussed in Chapter 5. A model that is not intrinsically nonlinear is given by

$$y_t = \beta_0 \exp [\beta_1 x_t + u_t] . \tag{6.2}$$

By contrast with the model in Example 6.2, this model can be transformed into a linear representation using the logarithmic transformation

$$\ln y_t = \ln \beta_0 + \beta_1 x_t + u_t . \tag{6.3}$$

This model also coincides with the Zellner-Revankar production function in Example 6.1 for the special case where $\alpha = 0$. The properties of the two exponential models in Equations (6.2) and (6.3) are compared in the following example.

Example 6.3 Alternative Exponential Regression Models

Figure 6.1 plots simulated series based on the exponential models

$$y_{1,t} = \beta_0 \exp [\beta_1 x_t + u_{1,t}]$$
$$y_{2,t} = \beta_0 \exp [\beta_1 x_t] + u_{2,t} ,$$

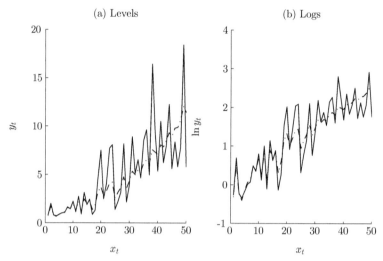

Figure 6.1. Simulated realisations from two exponential regression models, $y_{1,t}$ (solid line) and $y_{2,t}$ (dot-dashed line), in levels and in logarithms with $T = 50$.

in which the sample size is $T = 50$, the exogenous variable x_t is a linear trend, $u_{1,t}, u_{2,t} \sim iid\ N(0, \sigma^2)$ and the parameter values are $\beta_0 = 1.0$, $\beta_1 = 0.05$ and $\sigma = 0.5$. Panel (a) of Figure 6.1 shows that both series are increasing exponentially as x_t increases, with $y_{1,t}$ exhibiting increasing volatility over time whereas the volatility remains constant for $y_{2,t}$. Panel (b) of Figure 6.1 shows that a natural logarithmic transformation captures the exponential property of the trends in the two series. This transformation also renders the volatility of $y_{1,t}$ constant, but appears inappropriate for $y_{2,t}$ where the transformed series now exhibits decreasing volatility over time.   □

6.3   Maximum Likelihood Estimation

The iterative algorithms discussed in Chapter 3 can be used to find the maximum likelihood estimates of the parameters of the nonlinear regression model in equation (6.1), together with their standard errors. The disturbance term, u_t, is assumed to be normally distributed with density given by

$$f(u_t) = \frac{1}{\sqrt{2\pi\sigma^2}} \exp\left[-\frac{u_t^2}{2\sigma^2}\right].$$

(6.4)

The transformation of variable technique (see Appendix A) is used to derive the corresponding density of y_t as

$$f(y_t) = f(u_t)\left|\frac{du_t}{dy_t}\right|.$$

(6.5)

Taking the derivative with respect to y_t on both sides of equation (6.1) gives

$$\frac{du_t}{dy_t} = \frac{dg(y_t; \alpha)}{dy_t},$$

so the conditional probability distribution of y_t is

$$f(y_t \mid x_t; \theta) = \frac{1}{\sqrt{2\pi\sigma^2}} \exp\left[-\frac{(g(y_t; \alpha) - \mu(x_t; \beta))^2}{2\sigma^2} \right] \left| \frac{dg(y_t; \alpha)}{dy_t} \right|,$$

where the unknown parameters are $\theta = \{\alpha, \beta, \sigma^2\}$. The log-likelihood function for $t = 1, 2, \cdots, T$ observations is

$$\ln L_T(\theta) = \frac{1}{T} \sum_{t=1}^{T} \ln f(y_t \mid x_t; \theta) = \frac{1}{T} \sum_{t=1}^{T} \ln l_t(\theta)$$

$$= -\frac{1}{2}\ln(2\pi) - \frac{1}{2}\ln(\sigma^2) - \frac{1}{2\sigma^2 T} \sum_{t=1}^{T} (g(y_t; \alpha) - \mu(x_t; \beta))^2$$

$$+ \frac{1}{T} \sum_{t=1}^{T} \ln \left| \frac{dg(y_t; \alpha)}{dy_t} \right|,$$

which is maximised with respect to θ.

The gradient vector is

$$G_T(\theta) = \begin{bmatrix} \dfrac{1}{T} \displaystyle\sum_{t=1}^{T} \dfrac{\partial \ln l_t}{\partial \alpha} \\[2mm] \dfrac{1}{T} \displaystyle\sum_{t=1}^{T} \dfrac{\partial \ln l_t}{\partial \beta} \\[2mm] \dfrac{1}{T} \displaystyle\sum_{t=1}^{T} \dfrac{\partial \ln l_t}{\partial \sigma^2} \end{bmatrix},$$

where

$$\frac{\partial \ln l_t(\theta)}{\partial \alpha} = -\frac{1}{\sigma^2}(g(y_t; \alpha) - \mu(x_t; \beta))\frac{\partial g(y_t; \alpha)}{\partial \alpha} + \frac{\partial}{\partial \alpha} \ln \left| \frac{dg(y_t; \alpha)}{dy_t} \right|$$

$$\frac{\partial \ln l_t(\theta)}{\partial \beta} = \frac{1}{\sigma^2}(g(y_t; \alpha) - \mu(x_t; \beta))\frac{\partial \mu(x_t; \beta)}{\partial \beta}$$

$$\frac{\partial \ln l_t(\theta)}{\partial \sigma^2} = -\frac{1}{2\sigma^2} + \frac{1}{2\sigma^4}(g(y_t; \alpha) - \mu(x_t; \beta))^2.$$

The Hessian is

$$
H_T(\theta) =
\begin{bmatrix}
\dfrac{1}{T}\displaystyle\sum_{t=1}^{T}\dfrac{\partial^2 \ln l_t}{\partial\alpha^2} & \dfrac{1}{T}\displaystyle\sum_{t=1}^{T}\dfrac{\partial^2 \ln l_t}{\partial\alpha\partial\beta} & \dfrac{1}{T}\displaystyle\sum_{t=1}^{T}\dfrac{\partial^2 \ln l_t}{\partial\alpha\partial\sigma^2} \\[3mm]
\dfrac{1}{T}\displaystyle\sum_{t=1}^{T}\dfrac{\partial^2 \ln l_t}{\partial\beta\partial\alpha} & \dfrac{1}{T}\displaystyle\sum_{t=1}^{T}\dfrac{\partial^2 \ln l_t}{\partial\beta^2} & \dfrac{1}{T}\displaystyle\sum_{t=1}^{T}\dfrac{\partial^2 \ln l_t}{\partial\beta\partial\sigma^2} \\[3mm]
\dfrac{1}{T}\displaystyle\sum_{t=1}^{T}\dfrac{\partial^2 \ln l_t}{\partial\sigma^2\partial\alpha} & \dfrac{1}{T}\displaystyle\sum_{t=1}^{T}\dfrac{\partial^2 \ln l_t}{\partial\sigma^2\partial\beta} & \dfrac{1}{T}\displaystyle\sum_{t=1}^{T}\dfrac{\partial^2 \ln l_t}{\partial(\sigma^2)^2}
\end{bmatrix},
$$

where

$$
\frac{\partial^2 \ln l_t(\theta)}{\partial\alpha\partial\alpha'} = -\frac{1}{\sigma^2}(g(y_t;\alpha)-\mu(x_t;\beta))\frac{\partial g(y_t;\alpha)}{\partial\alpha\partial\alpha'} - \frac{1}{\sigma^2}\frac{\partial g(y_t;\alpha)}{\partial\alpha}\frac{\partial g(y_t;\alpha)}{\partial\alpha'}
$$
$$
+ \frac{\partial^2}{\partial\alpha\partial\alpha'}\ln\left|\frac{dg(y_t;\alpha)}{dy_t}\right|
$$

$$
\frac{\partial^2 \ln l_t(\theta)}{\partial\alpha\partial\beta'} = \frac{1}{\sigma^2}(g(y_t;\alpha)-\mu(x_t;\beta))\frac{\partial g(y_t;\alpha)}{\partial\alpha}\frac{\partial\mu(x_t;\beta)}{\partial\beta'}
$$

$$
\frac{\partial^2 \ln l_t(\theta)}{\partial\beta\partial\beta'} = \frac{1}{\sigma^2}(g(y_t;\alpha)-\mu(x_t;\beta))\frac{\partial^2\mu(x_t;\beta)}{\partial\beta\partial\beta'} - \frac{1}{\sigma^2}\frac{\partial^2\mu(x_t;\beta)}{\partial\beta\partial\beta'}
$$

$$
\frac{\partial^2 \ln l_t}{\partial(\sigma^2)^2} = \frac{1}{2\sigma^4} - \frac{1}{\sigma^6}(g(y_t;\alpha)-\mu(x_t;\beta))^2
$$

$$
\frac{\partial^2 \ln l_t(\theta)}{\partial\alpha\partial\sigma^2} = \frac{1}{\sigma^4}(g(y_t;\alpha)-\mu(x_t;\beta))\frac{\partial g(y_t;\alpha)}{\partial\alpha}
$$

$$
\frac{\partial^2 \ln l_t(\theta)}{\partial\beta\partial\sigma^2} = -\frac{1}{\sigma^4}(g(y_t;\alpha)-\mu(x_t;\beta))\frac{\partial\mu(x_t;\beta)}{\partial\beta}.
$$

The parameter updating scheme of the Newton-Raphson algorithm is

$$
\theta_{(k)} = \theta_{(k-1)} - H_{(k-1)}^{-1}G_{(k-1)}. \tag{6.6}
$$

In the context of the nonlinear regression model the Newton-Raphson algorithm is simplified by concentrating σ^2 from the log-likelihood function by expressing $\widehat{\sigma}^2$ as a function of $\widehat{\beta}$ and $\widehat{\alpha}$. This is achieved by solving the first-order condition for $\widehat{\sigma}^2$ which has the solution

$$
\widehat{\sigma}^2 = \frac{1}{T}\sum_{t=1}^{T}(g(y_t;\widehat{\alpha})-\mu(x_t;\widehat{\beta}))^2. \tag{6.7}
$$

Maximisation of the log-likelihood function is performed by redefining the unknown parameter vector as $\theta = \{\alpha, \beta\}$, with the iterations computed as

$$
\theta_{(k)} = \theta_{(k-1)} - H_{1,1}^{-1}\left(\theta_{(k-1)}\right)G_1(\theta_{(k-1)}), \tag{6.8}
$$

where the gradient vector is now

$$
G_1 = \begin{bmatrix} \dfrac{1}{T} \displaystyle\sum_{t=1}^{T} \dfrac{\partial \ln l_t(\theta)}{\partial \alpha} \\[3ex] \dfrac{1}{T} \displaystyle\sum_{t=1}^{T} \dfrac{\partial \ln l_t(\theta)}{\partial \beta} \end{bmatrix},
\tag{6.9}
$$

the Hessian is now

$$
H_{1,1} = \begin{bmatrix} \dfrac{1}{T} \displaystyle\sum_{t=1}^{T} \dfrac{\partial^2 \ln l_t(\theta)}{\partial \alpha \partial \alpha'} & \dfrac{1}{T} \displaystyle\sum_{t=1}^{T} \dfrac{\partial^2 \ln l_t(\theta)}{\partial \alpha \partial \beta'} \\[3ex] \dfrac{1}{T} \displaystyle\sum_{t=1}^{T} \dfrac{\partial^2 \ln l_t(\theta)}{\partial \beta \partial \alpha'} & \dfrac{1}{T} \displaystyle\sum_{t=1}^{T} \dfrac{\partial^2 \ln l_t(\theta)}{\partial \beta \partial \beta'} \end{bmatrix},
\tag{6.10}
$$

and $\widehat{\sigma}^2$ is replaced by equation (6.7).

The method of scoring replaces $-H_{(k-1)}$ in (6.6), by the information matrix $I(\theta)$ where the unknown parameters are $\theta = \{\alpha, \beta, \sigma^2\}$. The updated parameter vector is calculated as

$$
\theta_{(k)} = \theta_{(k-1)} + I_{(k-1)}^{-1} G_{(k-1)},
\tag{6.11}
$$

where the information matrix, $I(\theta)$, is given by

$$
I(\theta) = -\mathrm{E} \begin{bmatrix} \dfrac{1}{T} \displaystyle\sum_{t=1}^{T} \dfrac{\partial^2 \ln l_t(\theta)}{\partial \alpha \partial \alpha'} & \dfrac{1}{T} \displaystyle\sum_{t=1}^{T} \dfrac{\partial^2 \ln l_t(\theta)}{\partial \alpha \partial \beta'} & \dfrac{1}{T} \displaystyle\sum_{t=1}^{T} \dfrac{\partial^2 \ln l_T(\theta)}{\partial \alpha \partial \sigma^2} \\[3ex] \dfrac{1}{T} \displaystyle\sum_{t=1}^{T} \dfrac{\partial^2 \ln l_t(\theta)}{\partial \beta \partial \alpha'} & \dfrac{1}{T} \displaystyle\sum_{t=1}^{T} \dfrac{\partial^2 \ln l_t(\theta)}{\partial \beta \partial \beta'} & \dfrac{1}{T} \displaystyle\sum_{t=1}^{T} \dfrac{\partial^2 \ln l_t(\theta)}{\partial \beta \partial \sigma^2} \\[3ex] \dfrac{1}{T} \displaystyle\sum_{t=1}^{T} \dfrac{\partial^2 \ln l_t(\theta)}{\partial \sigma^2 \partial \alpha'} & \dfrac{1}{T} \displaystyle\sum_{t=1}^{T} \dfrac{\partial^2 \ln l_t(\theta)}{\partial \sigma^2 \partial \beta'} & \dfrac{1}{T} \displaystyle\sum_{t=1}^{T} \dfrac{\partial^2 \ln l_t(\theta)}{\partial (\sigma^2)^2} \end{bmatrix}.
$$

Example 6.4 Estimation of a Nonlinear Production Function

Consider the Zellner-Revankar production function in Example 6.1. The probability density function of u_t is

$$
f(u_t) = \frac{1}{\sqrt{2\pi\sigma^2}} \exp\left[-\frac{u_t^2}{2\sigma^2} \right].
$$

Using equation (6.5) with

$$
\frac{du_t}{dy_t} = \frac{1}{y_t} + \alpha,
$$

the conditional density for y_t is

$$f(y_t|k_t, l_t; \theta) = \frac{1}{\sqrt{2\pi\sigma^2}} \exp\left[-\frac{(\ln y_t + \alpha y_t - \beta_0 - \beta_1 \ln k_t - \beta_2 \ln l_t)^2}{2\sigma^2}\right]$$
$$\times \left|\frac{1}{y_t} + \alpha\right|.$$

The log-likelihood function for a sample of $t = 1, \cdots, T$ observations is

$$\ln L_T(\theta) = -\frac{1}{2}\ln(2\pi) - \frac{1}{2}\ln(\sigma^2) + \frac{1}{T}\sum_{t=1}^{T}\ln\left|\frac{1}{y_t} + \alpha\right|$$
$$-\frac{1}{2\sigma^2 T}\sum_{t=1}^{T}(\ln y_t + \alpha y_t - \beta_0 - \beta_1 \ln k_t - \beta_2 \ln l_t)^2.$$

This function is maximised with respect to the unknown parameters $\theta = \{\alpha, \beta_0, \beta_1, \beta_2, \sigma^2\}$. The problem is simplified by concentrating the log-likelihood function with respect to $\hat{\sigma}^2$ which is given by the variance of the residuals

$$\hat{\sigma}^2 = \frac{1}{T}\sum_{t=1}^{T}(\ln y_t + \hat{\alpha}y_t - \hat{\beta}_0 - \hat{\beta}_1 \ln k_t - \hat{\beta}_2 \ln l_t)^2. \qquad \square$$

Example 6.5 Estimation of a Nonlinear Exponential Model

Consider the nonlinear model in Example 6.2. The disturbance term u_t is assumed to have a normal distribution

$$f(u_t) = \frac{1}{\sqrt{2\pi\sigma^2}} \exp\left[-\frac{u_t^2}{2\sigma^2}\right],$$

so the conditional density of y_t is

$$f(y_t|x_t; \theta) = \frac{1}{\sqrt{2\pi\sigma^2}} \exp\left[-\frac{(y_t - \beta_0 \exp[\beta_1 x_t])^2}{2\sigma^2}\right].$$

The log-likelihood function for a sample of $t = 1, \cdots, T$ observations is

$$\ln L_T(\theta) = -\frac{1}{2}\ln(2\pi) - \frac{1}{2}\ln(\sigma^2) - \frac{1}{2\sigma^2 T}\sum_{t=1}^{T}(y_t - \beta_0 \exp[\beta_1 x_t])^2.$$

This function is to be maximised with respect to $\theta = \{\beta_0, \beta_1, \sigma^2\}$.

The derivatives of the log-likelihood function with respect to θ are

$$\frac{\partial \ln L_T(\theta)}{\partial \beta_0} = \frac{1}{\sigma^2 T} \sum_{t=1}^{T} (y_t - \beta_0 \exp[\beta_1 x_t]) \exp[\beta_1 x_t]$$

$$\frac{\partial \ln L_T(\theta)}{\partial \beta_1} = \frac{1}{\sigma^2 T} \sum_{t=1}^{T} (y_t - \beta_0 \exp[\beta_1 x_t]) \beta_0 \exp[\beta_1 x_t] x_t$$

$$\frac{\partial \ln L_T(\theta)}{\partial \sigma^2} = -\frac{1}{2\sigma^2} + \frac{1}{2\sigma^4 T} \sum_{t=1}^{T} (y_t - \beta_0 \exp[\beta_1 x_t])^2.$$

The maximum likelihood estimators of the parameters are obtained by setting these derivatives to zero and solving the system of equations

$$\frac{1}{\widehat{\sigma}^2 T} \sum_{t=1}^{T} (y_t - \widehat{\beta}_0 \exp[\widehat{\beta}_1 x_t]) \exp[\widehat{\beta}_1 x_t] = 0$$

$$\frac{1}{\widehat{\sigma}^2 T} \sum_{t=1}^{T} (y_t - \widehat{\beta}_0 \exp[\widehat{\beta}_1 x_t]) \widehat{\beta}_0 \exp[\widehat{\beta}_1 x_t] x_t = 0$$

$$-\frac{1}{2\widehat{\sigma}^2} + \frac{1}{2\widehat{\sigma}^4 T} \sum_{t=1}^{T} (y_t - \widehat{\beta}_0 \exp[\widehat{\beta}_1 x_t])^2 = 0.$$

Estimation of the parameters is simplified as in the previous example, by concentrating the log-likelihood and expressing $\widehat{\sigma}^2$ as a function of the other estimated parameters according to

$$\widehat{\sigma}^2 = \frac{1}{T} \sum_{t=1}^{T} (y_t - \widehat{\beta}_0 \exp[\widehat{\beta}_1 x_t])^2. \tag{6.12}$$

Using the simulated $y_{2,t}$ data in Panel (a) of Figure 6.1, the maximum likelihood estimates based on the concentrated log-likelihood are $\widehat{\beta} = \{\widehat{\beta}_0 = 1.027, \widehat{\beta}_1 = 0.049\}$. The estimated negative Hessian matrix is

$$-H_T(\widehat{\beta}) = \begin{bmatrix} 117.521 & 4913.334 \\ 4913.334 & 215992.398 \end{bmatrix},$$

and the covariance matrix of $\widehat{\beta}$ is

$$\mathrm{cov}(\widehat{\beta}) = -\frac{1}{T} H_T^{-1}(\widehat{\beta}) = \begin{bmatrix} 0.003476 & -0.000079 \\ -0.000079 & 0.000002 \end{bmatrix}.$$

The standard errors of the maximum likelihood estimates of β_0 and β_1 are found by taking the square roots of the diagonal terms of this matrix

$$se(\widehat{\beta}_0) = \sqrt{0.003476} = 0.059$$
$$se(\widehat{\beta}_1) = \sqrt{0.000002} = 0.001 .$$

The residual at time t is computed as

$$\widehat{u}_t = y_t - \widehat{\beta}_0 \exp[\widehat{\beta}_1 x_t] = y_t - 1.027 \exp[0.049 \, x_t],$$

and the residual sum of squares is given by $\sum_{t=1}^{T} \widehat{u}_t^2 = 12.374$. Finally, the residual variance is computed as

$$\widehat{\sigma}^2 = \frac{1}{T} \sum_{t=1}^{T} (y_t - \widehat{\beta}_0 \exp[\widehat{\beta}_1 x_t])^2 = \frac{12.374}{50} = 0.247 ,$$

with standard error

$$se(\widehat{\sigma}^2) = \sqrt{\frac{2\widehat{\sigma}^4}{T}} = \sqrt{\frac{2 \times 0.247^2}{50}} = 0.049 . \qquad \square$$

6.4   Gauss-Newton

For the special case of the nonlinear regression model in which $g(y_t; \alpha) = y_t$ in (6.1), the scoring algorithm can be simplified further so that parameter updating can be achieved by means of a least squares regression. This form of the scoring algorithm is known as the Gauss-Newton algorithm.

Consider the nonlinear regression model

$$y_t = \mu(x_t; \beta) + u_t , \qquad u_t \sim iid \, N(0, \sigma^2), \qquad (6.13)$$

with unknown parameters $\theta = \{\beta, \sigma^2\}$. The conditional distribution of y_t is

$$f(y_t \mid x_t; \theta) = \frac{1}{\sqrt{2\pi\sigma^2}} \exp \left[-\frac{1}{2\sigma^2} \sum_{t=1}^{T} (y_t - \mu(x_t; \beta))^2 \right] , \qquad (6.14)$$

and the corresponding log-likelihood function at time t is

$$\ln l_t(\theta) = -\frac{1}{2} \ln(2\pi) - \frac{1}{2} \ln(\sigma^2) - \frac{1}{2\sigma^2} (y_t - \mu(x_t; \beta))^2 , \qquad (6.15)$$

with first derivative

$$g_t(\beta) = \frac{1}{\sigma^2} \frac{\partial(\mu(x_t; \beta))}{\partial \beta} (y_t - \mu(x_t; \beta)) = \frac{1}{\sigma^2} z_t u_t , \qquad (6.16)$$

in which

$$u_t = y_t - \mu(x_t; \beta), \qquad z_t = \frac{\partial(\mu(x_t; \beta))}{\partial \beta} .$$

The gradient vector with respect to β is

$$G_T(\beta) = \frac{1}{T} \sum_{t=1}^{T} g_t(\beta) = \frac{1}{\sigma^2 T} \sum_{t=1}^{T} z_t u_t \,, \tag{6.17}$$

and the information matrix is, therefore,

$$I(\beta) = \mathrm{E}\left[\frac{1}{T} \sum_{t=1}^{T} g_t(\beta) g_t(\beta)'\right] = \frac{1}{T} \sum_{t=1}^{T} \mathrm{E}\left[\left(\frac{1}{\sigma^2} z_t u_t\right)\left(\frac{1}{\sigma^2} z_t u_t\right)'\right]$$

$$= \frac{1}{\sigma^4 T} \mathrm{E}\left[\sum_{t=1}^{T} u_t^2 z_t z_t'\right] = \frac{1}{\sigma^2 T} \sum_{t=1}^{T} \mathrm{E}\left[z_t z_t'\right] \,, \tag{6.18}$$

where use has been made of the assumption that u_t is *iid* with $\mathrm{E}[u_t^2] = \sigma^2$.

The Gauss-Newton algorithm is implemented by approximating the expression for $I(\beta)$ in (6.18) by excluding the expectations operator $\mathrm{E}[.]$, and evaluating this expression and the gradient $G_T(\beta)$ in (6.17) at $\beta_{(k-1)}$. The iterations proceed according to

$$\beta_{(k)} = \beta_{(k-1)} + I_{(k-1)}^{-1} G_{(k-1)} = \beta_{(k-1)} + \left[\sum_{t=1}^{T} z_t z_t'\right]^{-1} \sum_{t=1}^{T} z_t u_t \,.$$

Let the change in the parameters at iteration k be defined as

$$\widehat{\Delta} = \beta_{(k)} - \beta_{(k-1)} = \left[\sum_{t=1}^{T} z_t z_t'\right]^{-1} \sum_{t=1}^{T} z_t u_t \,. \tag{6.19}$$

The Gauss-Newton algorithm, therefore, requires the evaluation of u_t and z_t at $\beta_{(k-1)}$ followed by a simple linear regression of u_t on z_t to obtain $\widehat{\Delta}$. The updated parameter vector at the next iteration $\beta_{(k)}$, is simply obtained by adding the parameter estimates from this regression on to the estimates from the previous iteration $\beta_{(k-1)}$.

Once the Gauss-Newton scheme has converged, the final estimates of $\widehat{\beta}$ are the maximum likelihood estimates. In turn, the maximum likelihood estimate of σ^2 is computed as

$$\widehat{\sigma}^2 = \frac{1}{T} \sum_{t=1}^{T} (y_t - \mu(x_t; \widehat{\beta}))^2 \,. \tag{6.20}$$

Example 6.6 Nonlinear Exponential Model Revisited

Consider again the nonlinear exponential model in Examples 6.2 and 6.5

$$y_t = \beta_0 \exp\left[\beta_1 x_t\right] + u_t \,.$$

Estimating this model using the Gauss-Newton algorithm requires the following steps.

Step 1: Compute the derivatives of $\mu(x_t; \beta)$ with respect to $\beta = \{\beta_0, \beta_1\}$

$$z_{1,t} = \frac{\partial \mu(x_t; \beta)}{\partial \beta_0} = \exp[\beta_1 x_t]$$

$$z_{2,t} = \frac{\partial \mu(x_t; \beta)}{\partial \beta_1} = \beta_0 \exp[\beta_1 x_t] x_t .$$

Step 2: Evaluate u_t, $z_{1,t}$ and $z_{2,t}$ at the starting values of β.
Step 3: Regress u_t on $z_{1,t}$ and $z_{2,t}$ to obtain $\widehat{\Delta}_{\beta_0}$ and $\widehat{\Delta}_{\beta_1}$.
Step 4: Update the parameter estimates at iteration $k = 1$

$$\begin{bmatrix} \beta_0 \\ \beta_1 \end{bmatrix}_{(k)} = \begin{bmatrix} \beta_0 \\ \beta_1 \end{bmatrix}_{(k-1)} + \begin{bmatrix} \widehat{\Delta}_{\beta_0} \\ \widehat{\Delta}_{\beta_1} \end{bmatrix} .$$

Step 5: The iterations continue until convergence is achieved, $|\widehat{\Delta}_{\beta_0}|, |\widehat{\Delta}_{\beta_1}| < \varepsilon$, where ε is the tolerance level. □

Example 6.7 Estimating a Nonlinear Consumption Function

Consider the following nonlinear consumption function

$$c_t = \beta_0 + \beta_1 y_t^{\beta_2} + u_t , \qquad u_t \sim iid \ N(0, \sigma^2) ,$$

in which c_t is real consumption, y_t is real disposable income, u_t is an $iid \ N(0, \sigma^2)$ disturbance term that is assumed independent of y_t and $\theta = \{\beta_0, \beta_1, \beta_2, \sigma^2\}$ are unknown parameters. Estimating this model using the Gauss-Newton algorithm requires the following steps.

Step 1: Compute the derivatives of $\mu(y_t; \beta) = \beta_0 + \beta_1 y_t^{\beta_2}$ with respect to $\beta = \{\beta_0, \beta_1, \beta_2\}$

$$z_{1,t} = \frac{\partial \mu(y_t; \beta)}{\partial \beta_0} = 1$$

$$z_{2,t} = \frac{\partial \mu(y_t; \beta)}{\partial \beta_1} = y_t^{\beta_2}$$

$$z_{3,t} = \frac{\partial \mu(y_t; \beta)}{\partial \beta_2} = \beta_1 y_t^{\beta_2} \ln(y_t) .$$

Step 2: Evaluate u_t, $z_{1,t}$, $z_{2,t}$ and $z_{3,t}$ at the starting values for β.
Step 3: Regress u_t on $z_{1,t}$, $z_{2,t}$ and $z_{3,t}$, to get $\widehat{\Delta} = \{\widehat{\Delta}_{\beta_0}, \widehat{\Delta}_{\beta_1}, \widehat{\Delta}_{\beta_2}\}$ from this auxiliary regression.

Step 4: Update the parameter estimates at iteration $k = 1$

$$
\begin{bmatrix} \beta_0 \\ \beta_1 \\ \beta_2 \end{bmatrix}_{(k)} = \begin{bmatrix} \beta_0 \\ \beta_1 \\ \beta_2 \end{bmatrix}_{(k-1)} + \begin{bmatrix} \widehat{\Delta}_{\beta_0} \\ \widehat{\Delta}_{\beta_1} \\ \widehat{\Delta}_{\beta_2} \end{bmatrix}.
$$

Step 5: The iterations continue until convergence, $|\widehat{\Delta}_{\beta_0}|, |\widehat{\Delta}_{\beta_1}|, |\widehat{\Delta}_{\beta_2}| < \varepsilon$, where ε is the tolerance level.

United States quarterly data for real consumption expenditure and real disposable personal income for the period March 1960 to December 2009, downloaded from the Federal Reserve Bank of St. Louis, are used to estimate the parameters of this nonlinear consumption function. The starting values for β_0 and β_1, obtained from a linear model with $\beta_2 = 1$, are

$$
\beta_{(0)} = [-228.540, 0.950, 1.000]'.
$$

After constructing u_t and the derivatives $z_t = \{z_{1,t}, z_{2,t}, z_{3,t}\}$, u_t is regressed on z_t to give the parameter values

$$
\widehat{\Delta} = [600.699, -1.145, 0.125].
$$

The updated parameter estimates are

$$
\beta_{(1)} = \begin{bmatrix} -228.5 \\ 0.950 \\ 1.000 \end{bmatrix} + \begin{bmatrix} 600.7 \\ -1.145 \\ 0.125 \end{bmatrix} = \begin{bmatrix} 372.2 \\ -0.195 \\ 1.125 \end{bmatrix}.
$$

The final estimates, achieved after $k = 5$ iterations, are

$$
\beta_{(5)} = [299.019, 0.289, 1.124]'.
$$

The estimated residual for time t, using the parameter estimates at the final iteration, is computed as

$$
\widehat{u}_t = c_t - 299.019 - 0.289 \, y_t^{1.124},
$$

yielding the residual variance

$$
\widehat{\sigma}^2 = \frac{1}{T} \sum_{t=1}^{T} \widehat{u}_t^2 = \frac{1307348.531}{200} = 6536.743.
$$

The estimated information matrix is

$$
I(\widehat{\beta}) = \frac{1}{\widehat{\sigma}^2 T} \sum_{t=1}^{T} z_t z_t' = \begin{bmatrix} 0.000153 & 2.436440 & 6.144954 \\ 2.436440 & 48449.105592 & 124488.159259 \\ 6.144954 & 124488.159259 & 320337.624247 \end{bmatrix},
$$

from which the covariance matrix of $\widehat{\beta}$ is computed as

$$\text{cov}(\widehat{\beta}) = \frac{1}{T} I^{-1}(\widehat{\beta}) = \begin{bmatrix} 2350.782016 & -1.601204 & 0.577158 \\ -1.601204 & 0.001161 & -0.000420 \\ 0.577158 & -0.000420 & 0.000152 \end{bmatrix}.$$

The standard errors of $\widehat{\beta}$ are given as the square roots of the elements on the main diagonal of this matrix

$$\text{se}(\widehat{\beta}_0) = \sqrt{2350.782016} = 48.485$$
$$\text{se}(\widehat{\beta}_1) = \sqrt{0.001161} = 0.034$$
$$\text{se}(\widehat{\beta}_2) = \sqrt{0.000152} = 0.012.$$
□

6.4.1   Relationship to Nonlinear Least Squares

A standard procedure used to estimate nonlinear regression models is known as nonlinear least squares. Consider equation (6.13) where for simplicity β is a scalar. By expanding $\mu(x_t; \beta)$ as a Taylor series expansion around $\beta_{(k-1)}$

$$\mu(x_t; \beta) = \mu\left(x_t; \beta_{(k-1)}\right) + \frac{d\mu}{d\beta'}\left(\beta - \beta_{(k-1)}\right) + \cdots,$$

equation (6.13) is rewritten as

$$y_t - \mu\left(x_t; \beta_{(k-1)}\right) = \frac{d\mu}{d\beta'}\left(\beta - \beta_{(k-1)}\right) + v_t, \qquad (6.21)$$

where v_t is the disturbance which contains u_t and the higher-order terms from the Taylor series expansion. The kth iteration of the nonlinear regression estimation procedure involves regressing $y_t - \mu\left(x_t; \beta_{(k-1)}\right)$ on the derivative $d\mu/d\beta$, to generate the parameter estimate

$$\widehat{\Delta} = \beta_{(k)} - \beta_{(k-1)}.$$

The updated value of the parameter estimate is then computed as

$$\beta_{(k)} = \beta_{k-1} + \widehat{\Delta},$$

which is used to compute $y_t - \mu\left(x_t; \beta_{(k)}\right)$ and $d\mu\left(x_t; \beta_{(k)}\right)/d\beta$. The iterations proceed until convergence.

An alternative way of expressing the linearised regression equation in equation (6.21) is to define

$$u_t = y_t - \mu(x_t; \beta_{(k-1)}), \quad z_t = \frac{d\mu(x_t; \beta_{(k-1)})}{d\beta}, \quad \Delta = \beta - \beta_{(k-1)},$$

and write this equation as

$$u_t = z'_t\left(\beta_{(k)} - \beta_{(k-1)}\right) + v_t. \qquad (6.22)$$

A least squares regression of u_t on z_t yields $\widehat{\Delta} = \beta_{(k)} - \beta_{(k-1)}$, which is equivalent to the updated Gauss-Newton estimator in (6.19).

6.4.2 Relationship to Ordinary Least Squares

For classes of models in equation (6.1) where not only is $g(y_t; \alpha)$ linear in y_t, but also the mean function $\mu(x_t; \beta)$, is linear as well, the Gauss-Newton algorithm converges in one step regardless of the starting value. Consider the linear regression model in which $\mu(x_t; \beta) = x_t'\beta$ and the expressions for u_t and z_t are, respectively,

$$u_t = y_t - x_t'\beta, \qquad z_t = \frac{\partial \mu(x_t; \beta)}{\partial \beta} = x_t.$$

Evaluating these expressions at $\beta_{(k-1)}$ and substituting into the Gauss-Newton algorithm in equation (6.19) gives after rearranging

$$\beta_{(k)} = \beta_{(k-1)} + \left[\sum_{t=1}^{T} x_t x_t' \right]^{-1} \sum_{t=1}^{T} x_t (y_t - x_t'\beta_{(k-1)})$$

$$= \beta_{(k-1)} + \left[\sum_{t=1}^{T} x_t x_t' \right]^{-1} \sum_{t=1}^{T} x_t y_t - \left[\sum_{t=1}^{T} x_t x_t' \right]^{-1} \sum_{t=1}^{T} x_t x_t' \beta_{(k-1)}$$

$$= \beta_{(k-1)} + \left[\sum_{t=1}^{T} x_t x_t' \right]^{-1} \sum_{t=1}^{T} x_t y_t - \beta_{(k-1)}$$

$$= \left[\sum_{t=1}^{T} x_t x_t' \right]^{-1} \sum_{t=1}^{T} x_t y_t, \tag{6.23}$$

which is just the ordinary least squares estimator obtained when regressing y_t on x_t. The scheme converges in just one step for an arbitrary choice of $\beta_{(k-1)}$ because $\beta_{(k-1)}$ does not appear on the right-hand side of equation (6.23).

6.4.3 Asymptotic Distributions

As Chapter 2 shows, maximum likelihood estimators are asymptotically normally distributed. In the context of the nonlinear regression model, this means that

$$\widehat{\theta} \overset{a}{\sim} N(\theta_0, \frac{1}{T} I(\theta_0)^{-1}), \tag{6.24}$$

in which $\theta_0 = \{\beta_0, \sigma_0^2\}$ is the true parameter vector and $I(\theta_0)$ is the information matrix evaluated at θ_0. The fact that $I(\theta)$ is block diagonal in the class of models considered here means that the asymptotic distribution of $\widehat{\beta}$ can be considered separately from that of $\widehat{\sigma}^2$ without any loss of information.

From equation (6.18), the relevant block of the information matrix is

$$I(\beta_0) = \frac{1}{\sigma_0^2 T} \sum_{t=1}^{T} E[z_t z_t'],$$

so that the asymptotic distribution is

$$\widehat{\beta} \overset{a}{\sim} N\left(\beta_0, \sigma_0^2 \left(\sum_{t=1}^{T} E[z_t z_t']\right)^{-1}\right).$$

In practice, σ_0^2 is unknown and is replaced by the maximum likelihood estimator given in equation (6.7). The standard errors of $\widehat{\beta}$ are therefore computed by taking the square root of the diagonal elements of the covariance matrix

$$\text{cov}(\widehat{\beta}) = \widehat{\sigma}^2 \left[\sum_{t=1}^{T} z_t z_t'\right]^{-1}.$$

The asymptotic distribution of $\widehat{\sigma}^2$ is

$$\widehat{\sigma}^2 \overset{a}{\sim} N\left(\sigma_0^2, \frac{1}{T} 2\sigma_0^4\right).$$

As with the standard error of $\widehat{\beta}$, σ_0^2 is replaced by the maximum likelihood estimator of σ^2 given in equation (6.7), so that the standard error of $\widehat{\sigma}^2$ is

$$\text{se}(\widehat{\sigma}^2) = \sqrt{\frac{2\widehat{\sigma}^4}{T}}.$$

6.5   Testing

6.5.1   LR, Wald and LM Tests

The LR, Wald and LM tests discussed in Chapter 4 can all be applied to test the parameters of nonlinear regression models. For those cases where the unrestricted model is relatively easier to estimate than the restricted model, the Wald test is particularly convenient. Alternatively, where the restricted model is relatively easier to estimate than the unrestricted model, the LM test is the natural strategy to adopt.

Example 6.8 Testing a Nonlinear Consumption Function
   A special case of the nonlinear consumption function used in Example 6.7 is the linear model where $\beta_2 = 1$. This suggests that a test of linearity is given by the hypotheses

$$H_0 : \beta_2 = 1 \qquad H_1 : \beta_2 \neq 1.$$

This restriction is tested using the United States quarterly data for the period March 1960 to December 2009, $T = 200$, on real personal consumption expenditure c_t, and real disposable income y_t, from Example 6.7.

To perform a LR test, the values of the restricted ($\beta_2 = 1$) and unrestricted ($\beta_2 \neq 1$) log-likelihood functions are, respectively given by

$$\ln L_T(\theta_0) = -\frac{1}{2}\ln(2\pi) - \frac{1}{2}\ln(\sigma^2) - \frac{1}{T}\sum_{t=1}^{T}\frac{(c_t - \beta_0 - \beta_1 y_t)^2}{2\sigma^2}$$

$$\ln L_T(\theta_1) = -\frac{1}{2}\ln(2\pi) - \frac{1}{2}\ln(\sigma^2) - \frac{1}{T}\sum_{t=1}^{T}\frac{(c_t - \beta_0 - \beta_1 y_t^{\beta_2})^2}{2\sigma^2}\,.$$

The restricted and unrestricted parameter estimates from the concentrated log-likelihood are respectively given by

$$\widehat{\theta}_0 = [\,-228.540 \quad 0.950 \quad 1.000\,]' \text{ and } \widehat{\theta}_1 = [\,298.739 \quad 0.289 \quad 1.124\,]'\,.$$

These estimates produce the respective values of the log-likelihood functions

$$\ln L_T(\widehat{\theta}_0) = -6.023\,, \quad \ln L_T(\widehat{\theta}_1) = -5.812\,.$$

The value of the LR statistic is

$$LR = -2 \times T(\ln L_T(\widehat{\theta}_0) - \ln L_T(\widehat{\theta}_1)) = -2 \times 200 \times (-6.023 + 5.812)$$
$$= 84.676.$$

From the χ_1^2 distribution, the p-value of the LR test statistic is 0.000 showing that the linearity restriction is rejected at conventional significance levels.

To perform a Wald test, define $R = [\,0 \quad 0 \quad 1\,]$ and $Q = [\,1\,]$ and compute the Hessian matrix based on numerical derivatives evaluated at $\widehat{\theta}_1$

$$H_T(\widehat{\theta}_1) = \begin{bmatrix} -0.000153 & -2.434873 & -6.145408 \\ -2.434873 & -48385.661707 & -124422.344597 \\ -6.145408 & -124422.344597 & -320409.721145 \end{bmatrix}\,.$$

The Wald statistic is

$$W = T[R\widehat{\theta}_1 - Q]'[R(-H_T^{-1}(\widehat{\theta}_1))R']^{-1}[R\widehat{\theta}_1 - Q] = 64.268\,.$$

The p-value of the Wald test statistic obtained from the χ_1^2 distribution is 0.000, once again showing that the linearity restriction is strongly rejected at conventional significance levels.

To perform a LM test, the gradient vector of the unrestricted model evaluated at the restricted parameter estimates, $\widehat{\theta}_0$, is

$$G_T(\widehat{\theta}_0) = [\,0.000 \quad 0.000 \quad 2.810\,]'\,,$$

and the outer product of the gradients matrix is

$$
J_T(\widehat{\theta}_0) =
\begin{bmatrix}
0.000 & 0.625 & 5.257 \\
0.625 & 4727.411 & 40412.673 \\
5.257 & 40412.673 & 345921.880
\end{bmatrix} .
$$

The LM statistic is

$$
LM = T G'_T(\widehat{\theta}_0) J_T^{-1}(\widehat{\theta}_0) G_T(\widehat{\theta}_0) = 39.908 ,
$$

which, from the χ_1^2 distribution, has a p-value of 0.000 showing that the restriction is still strongly rejected.   □

Example 6.9 Constant Marginal Propensity to Consume

The nonlinear consumption function used in Examples 6.7 and 6.8 with unknown parameters $\theta = \{\beta_0, \beta_1, \beta_2\}$, has a marginal propensity to consume (MPC) given by

$$
MPC = \frac{dc_t}{dy_t} = \beta_1 \beta_2 y_t^{\beta_2 - 1} ,
$$

the value of which changes over time as it is a function of income, y_t. Testing the restriction that the MPC is constant and hence does not depend on y_t, involves testing the hypotheses

$$
H_0 : \beta_2 = 1 \qquad H_1 : \beta_2 \neq 1.
$$

Define $Q = 0$ and

$$
C(\theta) = \beta_1 \beta_2 y_t^{\beta_2 - 1} - \beta_1
$$

$$
\mathrm{cov}(C(\beta) - Q) = D(\theta)(-H(\theta))^{-1} D^1(\theta)
$$

$$
D(\theta) = \frac{\partial C(\theta)}{\partial \theta'} = [\, 0 \quad \beta_2 y_t^{\beta_2 - 1} - 1 \quad \beta_1 y_t^{\beta_2 - 1}(1 + \beta_2 \ln y_t)\,] ,
$$

then from Chapter 4 the general form of the Wald statistic in the case of nonlinear restrictions is

$$
W = T[C(\widehat{\theta}_1) - Q]'[D(\widehat{\theta}_1)(-H_T^{-1}(\widehat{\theta}_1))D(\widehat{\theta}_1)']^{-1}[C(\widehat{\theta}_1) - Q] .
$$

This statistic is asymptotically distributed as χ_1^2 under the null hypothesis and large values of the test statistic constitute rejection of the null hypothesis.   □

The LM test has a convenient form for nonlinear regression models because of the assumption of normality. To demonstrate this feature, consider the LM statistic from Chapter 4 based on the information matrix which has the form

$$
LM = T G'_T(\widehat{\theta}_0) I^{-1}(\widehat{\theta}_0) G_T(\widehat{\theta}_0) . \tag{6.25}
$$

Under the null hypothesis, this statistic is distributed asymptotically as χ^2_M where M is the number of restrictions. Using the expression for G_T in (6.17) and I in (6.18), the LM statistic is

$$
\begin{aligned}
LM &= \left[\frac{1}{\widehat{\sigma}^2}\sum_{t=1}^T z_t\widehat{u}_t\right]'\left[\frac{1}{\widehat{\sigma}^2}\sum_{t=1}^T z_tz_t'\right]^{-1}\left[\frac{1}{\widehat{\sigma}^2}\sum_{t=1}^T z_t\widehat{u}_t\right] \\
&= \frac{1}{\widehat{\sigma}^2}\left[\sum_{t=1}^T z_t\widehat{u}_t\right]'\left[\sum_{t=1}^T z_tz_t'\right]^{-1}\left[\sum_{t=1}^T z_t\widehat{u}_t\right] \\
&= \frac{T}{\displaystyle\sum_{t=1}^T \widehat{u}_t^2}\left[\sum_{t=1}^T z_t\widehat{u}_t\right]'\left[\sum_{t=1}^T z_tz_t'\right]^{-1}\left[\sum_{t=1}^T z_t\widehat{u}_t\right] \qquad(6.26) \\
&= TR^2, \qquad(6.27)
\end{aligned}
$$

where all quantities are evaluated under H_0,

$$
\begin{aligned}
\widehat{u}_t &= y_t - \mu(x_t;\widehat{\theta}_0) \\
z_t &= -\frac{\partial u_t}{\partial\theta}\Big|_{\theta=\widehat{\theta}_0} \\
\widehat{\sigma}^2 &= \frac{1}{T}\sum_{t=1}^T (y_t - \mu(x_t;\widehat{\theta}_0))^2,
\end{aligned}
$$

and R^2 is the coefficient of determination obtained by regressing $\widehat{u}_t$ on z_t.

The LM test in (6.27) is implemented by means of two linear regressions. The first stage involves estimating the restricted model by a linear regression and extracting the ordinary least squares residuals $\widehat{u}_t$. The second requires a regression of $\widehat{u}_t$ on z_t, where all of the quantities are evaluated at the restricted estimates. The test statistic is $LM = TR^2$, where R^2 is the coefficient of determination from the second stage regression. The implementation of the LM test in terms of two linear regressions is revisited in Chapters 7 and 8.

Example 6.10 Nonlinear Consumption Function

Example 6.9 uses a Wald test to test for a constant marginal propensity to consume in a nonlinear consumption function. To perform an LM test of the same restriction, the following steps are required.

Step 1: Write the model in terms of u_t

$$u_t = c_t - \beta_0 - \beta_1 y_t^{\beta_2}.$$

Step 2: Compute the following derivatives

$$z_{1,t} = -\frac{\partial u_t}{\partial \beta_0} = 1,$$

$$z_{2,t} = -\frac{\partial u_t}{\partial \beta_1} = y_t^{\beta_2},$$

$$z_{3,t} = -\frac{\partial u_t}{\partial \beta_2} = \beta_1 y_t^{\beta_2} \ln(y_t).$$

Step 3: Estimate the restricted model

$$c_t = \beta_0 + \beta_1 y_t + u_t,$$

by regressing c_t on a constant and y_t to generate the restricted estimates $\widehat{\beta}_0$ and $\widehat{\beta}_1$.

Step 4: Evaluate u_t at the restricted estimates

$$\widehat{u}_t = c_t - \widehat{\beta}_0 - \widehat{\beta}_1 y_t.$$

Step 5: Evaluate the derivatives at the restricted estimates

$$z_{1,t} = 1,$$
$$z_{2,t} = y_t,$$
$$z_{3,t} = \widehat{\beta}_0 y_t \ln(y_t).$$

Step 6: Regress $\widehat{u}_t$ on $\{z_{1,t}, z_{2,t}, z_{3,t}\}$ and compute R^2 from this regression.

Step 7: Evaluate the test statistic, $LM = TR^2$. This statistic is asymptotically distributed as χ_1^2 under the null hypothesis. Large values of the test statistic constitute rejection of the null hypothesis. Notice that the strength of the nonlinearity in the consumption function is determined by the third term in the second stage regression in Step 6. If no significant nonlinearity exists, this term should not add to the explanatory power of this regression equation. If the nonlinearity is significant, then it acts as an excluded variable which manifests itself through a non-zero value of R^2.   □

6.5.2 Non-nested Tests

Two models are non-nested if one model cannot be expressed as a subset of the other. While a number of procedures have been developed to test non-nested models, in this application a maximum likelihood approach is discussed following Vuong (1989). The basic idea is to convert the likelihood functions of the two competing models into a common likelihood function using the transformation of variable technique and perform a variation of a LR test.

To highlight the key features of the Vuong non-nested test consider the following two alternative money demand equations

Model 1: $\quad m_t \quad = \quad \beta_0 + \beta_1 r_t + \beta_2 y_t + u_{1,t}, \qquad u_{1,t} \sim iid\ N(0, \sigma_1^2),$
Model 2: $\quad \ln m_t \quad = \quad \alpha_0 + \alpha_1 \ln r_t + \alpha_2 \ln y_t + u_{2,t}, \quad u_{2,t} \sim iid\ N(0, \sigma_2^2),$

in which m_t is real money, y_t is real income, r_t is the nominal interest rate and $\theta_1 = \{\beta_0, \beta_1, \beta_2, \sigma_1^2\}$ and $\theta_2 = \{\alpha_0, \alpha_1, \alpha_2, \sigma_2^2\}$ are the unknown parameters of the two models, respectively. The models are not nested since one model cannot be expressed as a subset of the other. Another way to view this problem is to observe that Model 1 is based on the distribution of m_t whereas Model 2 is based on the distribution of $\ln m_t$,

$$f_1(m_t | r_t, y_t) = \frac{1}{\sqrt{2\pi \sigma_1^2}} \exp\left[-\frac{(m_t - \beta_0 - \beta_1 r_t - \beta_2 y_t)^2}{2\sigma_1^2}\right]$$

$$f_2(\ln m_t | r_t, y_t) = \frac{1}{\sqrt{2\pi \sigma_2^2}} \exp\left[-\frac{(\ln m_t - \alpha_0 - \alpha_1 \ln r_t - \alpha_2 \ln y_t)^2}{2\sigma_2^2}\right].$$

To enable a comparison of the two models, use the transformation of variable technique to convert the distribution f_2 into a distribution of the level of m_t. Formally this link between the two distributions is given by

$$f_1(m_t) = f_2(\ln m_t) \left|\frac{d \ln m_t}{dm_t}\right| = f_2(\ln m_t) \left|\frac{1}{m_t}\right|,$$

which now allows the log-likelihood functions of the two models to be compared. The steps to perform the Vuong test are as follows.

Step 1: Estimate Model 1 by regressing m_t on $\{c, r_t, y_t\}$ and construct the log-likelihood function at each observation

$$\ln l_{1,t}(\widehat{\theta_1}) = -\frac{1}{2}\ln(2\pi) - \frac{1}{2}\ln(\widehat{\sigma}_1^2) - \frac{(m_t - \widehat{\beta}_0 - \widehat{\beta}_1 r_t - \widehat{\beta}_2 y_t)^2}{2\widehat{\sigma}_1^2}.$$

Step 2: Estimate Model 2 by regressing $\ln m_t$ on $\{c, \ln r_t, \ln y_t\}$ and construct the log-likelihood function at each observation for m_t by using

$$\ln l_{2,t}(\widehat{\theta_2}) = -\frac{1}{2}\ln(2\pi) - \frac{1}{2}\ln(\widehat{\sigma}_2^2) - \frac{(\ln m_t - \widehat{\alpha}_0 - \widehat{\alpha}_1 \ln r_t - \widehat{\alpha}_2 \ln y_t)^2}{2\widehat{\sigma}_2^2}$$
$$\qquad\qquad - \ln m_t.$$

Step 3: Compute the difference in the log-likelihood functions of the two models at each observation

$$d_t = \ln l_{1,t}(\widehat{\theta_1}) - \ln l_{2,t}(\widehat{\theta_2}).$$

Step 4: Construct the test statistic

$$V = \sqrt{T} \frac{\overline{d}}{s},$$

in which

$$\overline{d} = \frac{1}{T} \sum_{t=1}^{T} d_t, \qquad s^2 = \frac{1}{T} \sum_{t=1}^{T} (d_t - \overline{d})^2,$$

are the mean and the variance of d_t, respectively.

Step 5: Using the result in Vuong (1989), the statistic V is asymptotically normally distributed

$$V \xrightarrow{d} N(0, 1),$$

under the null hypothesis that the respective fits of the two models to the observed data are not significantly different.

Example 6.11 Vuong's Test and United States Money Demand

The non-nested money demand models discussed earlier are estimated using quarterly data for the United States on real money, m_t, the nominal interest rate, r_t, and real income, y_t, for the period March 1959 to December 2005. The estimates of Model 1 are

$$\widehat{m_t} = 7.131 + 7.660 \, r_t + 0.449 \, y_t.$$

The estimates of Model 2 are

$$\widehat{\ln m_t} = 0.160 + 0.004 \, \ln r_t + 0.829 \, \ln y_t.$$

The mean and variance of d_t are, respectively,

$$\overline{d} = -0.159$$
$$s^2 = 0.054,$$

yielding the value of the test statistic

$$V = \sqrt{T} \frac{\overline{d}}{s} = \sqrt{188} \frac{-0.159}{\sqrt{0.054}} = -9.380.$$

Since the p-value of the statistic obtained from the standard normal distribution is 0.000, the null hypothesis that the models are equivalent representations of money demand is rejected at conventional significance levels. The statistic being negative suggests that Model 2 is to be preferred because it has the higher value of log-likelihood function at the maximum likelihood estimates.   □

6.6 Applications

The previous analysis focusses on including nonlinearities into the linear regression model where the disturbance term is normally distributed. In this section two applications of regression models are discussed where the assumption of normality is relaxed. The first application is based on the capital asset pricing model (CAPM) where a fat-tailed distribution is used to model outliers in the data. The second application investigates the stochastic frontier model where the disturbance term is specified as a mixture of normal and non-normal distributions.

6.6.1 Robust Estimation of the CAPM

One way to ensure that parameter estimates of the nonlinear regression model are robust to the presence of outliers is to use a heavy-tailed distribution such as the Student t distribution. This is a natural approach to modelling outliers since, by definition, an outlier represents an extreme draw from the tails of the distribution. The general idea is that the additional parameters of the heavy-tailed distribution capture the effects of the outliers and thereby help reduce any potential contamination of the parameter estimates that may arise from these outliers.

The approach is demonstrated using the capital asset pricing model

$$r_t = \beta_0 + \beta_1 m_t + u_t, \qquad u_t \sim iid\ N(0, \sigma^2),$$

in which r_t is the return on an asset relative to a risk-free rate and m_t is the return on the market portfolio relative to a risk-free rate. The parameter β_1 is of importance in finance because it provides a measure of the risk of the asset known as the beta risk. Outliers in the data are captured by respecifying the model as

$$r_t = \beta_0 + \beta_1 m_t + \sigma \sqrt{\frac{\nu - 2}{\nu}}\, v_t, \qquad (6.28)$$

where the disturbance term v_t now has a Student t distribution given by

$$f(v_t) = \frac{\Gamma\left(\dfrac{\nu + 1}{2}\right)}{\sqrt{\pi \nu}\, \Gamma\left(\dfrac{\nu}{2}\right)} \left(1 + \frac{v_t^2}{\nu}\right)^{-(\nu+1)/2},$$

where ν is the degrees of freedom parameter and $\Gamma(\cdot)$ is the gamma function. The term $\sigma \sqrt{(\nu - 2)/\nu}$ in equation (6.28) ensures that the variance of r_t is σ^2, because the variance of a Student t distribution is $\nu/(\nu - 2)$.

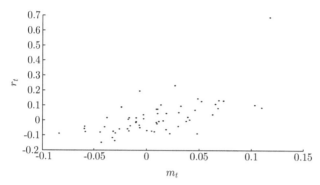

Figure 6.2. Scatterplot of the monthly returns on the company Martin Marietta and return on the market index, both relative to the risk-free rate, over the period January 1982 to December 1986.

Using the transformation of variable technique, the distribution of r_t is

$$f(r_t) = f(v_t) \left| \frac{dv_t}{dr_t} \right| = \frac{\Gamma\left(\frac{v+1}{2}\right)}{\sqrt{\pi v}\, \Gamma\left(\frac{v}{2}\right)} \left(1 + \frac{v_t^2}{v}\right)^{-(v+1)/2} \left| \frac{1}{\sigma} \sqrt{\frac{v}{v-2}} \right|,$$

with

$$v_t = \frac{r_t - \beta_0 - \beta_1 m_t}{\sigma \sqrt{\frac{v-2}{v}}}.$$

The log-likelihood function at observation t is therefore

$$\ln l_t(\theta) = \ln \left(\frac{\Gamma\left(\frac{v+1}{2}\right)}{\sqrt{\pi v}\, \Gamma\left(\frac{v}{2}\right)} \right) - \frac{v+1}{2} \ln\left(1 + \frac{v_t^2}{v}\right) - \ln \sigma + \ln \sqrt{\frac{v}{v-2}}.$$

The parameters $\theta = \{\beta_0, \beta_1, \sigma^2, v\}$ are estimated by maximum likelihood using one of the iterative algorithms discussed in Section 6.3.

As an illustration, consider the monthly returns on the company Martin Marietta, over the period January 1982 to December 1986, taken from Butler, McDonald, Nelson and White (1990, pp321–327). A scatterplot of the data in Figure 6.2 suggests that estimation of the CAPM by least squares may yield an estimate of β_1 that is biased upwards as a result of the outlier in r_t where the monthly excess return of the asset in one month is 0.688.

The results of estimating the CAPM by maximum likelihood assuming normal disturbances, are

$$\widehat{r}_t = 0.001 + 1.803 \, m_t,$$

Table 6.1. *Maximum likelihood estimates of the robust capital asset pricing model. Standard errors based on the inverse of the Hessian*

Parameter	Estimate	se	t stat.
β_0	−0.007	0.008	−0.887
β_1	1.263	0.190	6.665
σ^2	0.008	0.006	1.338
ν	2.837	1.021	2.779

where the estimates are obtained by simply regressing r_t on a constant and m_t. The estimate of 1.803 suggests that this asset is very risky relative to the market portfolio since on average changes in the asset returns amplify the contemporaneous movements in the market excess returns, m_t. A test of the hypothesis that $\beta_1 = 1$, provides a test that movements in the returns on the asset mirror the market one-to-one. The Wald statistic is

$$W = \left(\frac{1.803 - 1}{0.285} \right)^2 = 7.930.$$

The p-value of the statistic obtained from the χ_1^2 distribution is 0.000, showing strong rejection of the null hypothesis.

The maximum likelihood estimates of the robust version of the CAPM model are given in Table 6.1. The estimate of β_1 is now 1.263, which is much lower than the ordinary least squares estimate of 1.803. A Wald test of the hypothesis that $\beta_1 = 1$ now yields

$$W = \left(\frac{1.263 - 1}{0.190} \right)^2 = 1.930.$$

The p-value is 0.164 showing that the null hypothesis that the asset tracks the market one-to-one fails to be rejected.

The use of the Student t distribution to model the outlier has helped to reduce the effect of the outlier on the estimate of β_1. The degrees of freedom parameter estimate of $\hat{\nu} = 2.837$ shows that the tails of the distribution are indeed very fat, with just the first two moments of the distribution existing.

Another approach to estimate regression models that are robust to outliers is to specify the distribution as the Laplace distribution, also known as the double exponential distribution

$$f(y_t; \theta) = \frac{1}{2} \exp\left[-|y_t - \theta| \right].$$

To estimate the unknown parameter θ, for a sample of size T, the log-likelihood function is

$$\ln L_T(\theta) = \frac{1}{T} \sum_{t=1}^{T} f(y_t; \theta) = -\ln(2) - \frac{1}{T} \sum_{t=1}^{T} |y_t - \theta|.$$

In contrast to the log-likelihood functions dealt with thus far, this function is not differentiable everywhere. However, the maximum likelihood estimator can still be derived, which is given as the median of the data (Stuart and Ord, 1999, p59), that is $\hat{\theta} = \text{median}(y_t)$. This result is a reflection of the well-known property that the median is less affected by outliers than is the mean. A generalisation of this feature of the maximum likelihood estimator forms the basis of the class of estimators known as M-estimators and quantile regression.

6.6.2   Stochastic Frontier Models

In stochastic frontier models the disturbance term u_t of a regression model is specified as a mixture of two random disturbances, $u_{1,t}$ and $u_{2,t}$. The most widely used application of this model is in production theory where the production process is assumed to be affected by two types of shocks (Aigner, Lovell and Schmidt, 1977).

(1) Idiosyncratic shocks, $u_{1,t}$, which are either positive or negative.
(2) Technological shocks, $u_{2,t}$, which are either zero or negative, with a zero (negative) shock representing the production function operates efficiently (inefficiently).

Consider the stochastic frontier model

$$y_t = \beta_0 + \beta_1 x_t + u_t$$
$$u_t = u_{1,t} - u_{2,t} ,$$

(6.29)

where y_t is the dependent variable, x_t is the exogenous variable and u_t is a composite disturbance term with mutually independent and iid components, $u_{1,t}$ and $u_{2,t}$, with respective distributions

$$f(u_1) = \frac{1}{\sqrt{2\pi\sigma_1^2}} \exp\left[-\frac{u_1^2}{2\sigma_1^2}\right], \quad -\infty < u_1 < \infty, \quad \text{[Normal]}$$

$$f(u_2) = \frac{1}{\sigma_2} \exp\left[-\frac{u_2}{\sigma_2}\right], \qquad\qquad 0 \le u_2 < \infty. \quad \text{[Exponential]}$$

(6.30)

The distribution of u_t has support on the real line $(-\infty, \infty)$, but the effect of $-u_{2,t}$ is to skew the normal distribution to the left as highlighted in Figure 6.3. The strength of the asymmetry is controlled by the parameter σ_2 in the exponential distribution.

To estimate the parameters $\theta = \{\beta_0, \beta_1, \sigma_1, \sigma_2\}$ in (6.29) and (6.30) by maximum likelihood, it is necessary to derive the distribution of y_t from u_t. Since u_t is a mixture distribution of two components, its distribution is derived from the joint distribution of $u_{1,t}$ and $u_{2,t}$ using the change of variable technique. However, because the model consists of mapping two random variables, $u_{1,t}$ and $u_{2,t}$, into one random variable u_t, it is necessary to choose an additional

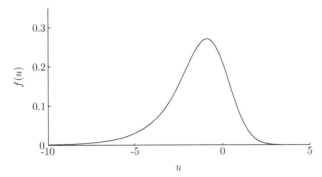

Figure 6.3. Stochastic frontier disturbance distribution based on a mixture of $N(0, \sigma_1^2)$ with standard deviation $\sigma_1 = 1$ and exponential distribution with standard deviation $\sigma_2 = 1.5$.

variable, v_t, to fill out the mapping for the Jacobian to be nonsingular. Once the joint distribution of (u_t, v_t) is derived, the marginal distribution of u_t is obtained by integrating the joint distribution with respect to v_t.

Let $u = u_1 - u_2$ and $v = u_1$ where the t subscript is suppressed to simplify the notation. To derive the Jacobian rearrange these expressions as

$$u_1 = v, \qquad u_2 = v - u, \tag{6.31}$$

so the Jacobian is

$$|J| = \begin{vmatrix} \dfrac{\partial u_1}{\partial u} & \dfrac{\partial u_1}{\partial v} \\[2ex] \dfrac{\partial u_2}{\partial u} & \dfrac{\partial u_2}{\partial v} \end{vmatrix} = \begin{vmatrix} 0 & 1 \\ -1 & 1 \end{vmatrix} = |1| = 1.$$

Using the property that $u_{1,t}$ and $u_{2,t}$ are independent and $|J| = 1$, the joint distribution of (u, v) is

$$
\begin{aligned}
g(u, v) &= |J| \, f(u_1) \, f(u_2) \\[1ex]
&= |1| \frac{1}{\sqrt{2\pi\sigma_1^2}} \exp\left[-\frac{u_1^2}{2\sigma_1^2} \right] \times \frac{1}{\sigma_2} \exp\left[-\frac{u_2}{\sigma_2} \right] \\[1ex]
&= \frac{1}{\sqrt{2\pi\sigma_1^2}} \frac{1}{\sigma_2} \exp\left[-\frac{u_1^2}{2\sigma_1^2} - \frac{u_2}{\sigma_2} \right]. \tag{6.32}
\end{aligned}
$$

Using the substitution $u_1 = v$ and $u_2 = v - u$ the term in the exponent is

$$
-\frac{v^2}{2\sigma_1^2} - \frac{v-u}{\sigma_2} = -\frac{v^2}{2\sigma_1^2} - \frac{v}{\sigma_2} + \frac{u}{\sigma_2} = -\frac{\left(v + \dfrac{\sigma_1^2}{\sigma_2} \right)^2}{2\sigma_1^2} + \frac{\sigma_1^2}{2\sigma_2^2} + \frac{u}{\sigma_2},
$$

where the last step is based on completing the square. Placing this expression into (6.32) and rearranging gives the joint probability density

$$
g(u, v) = \frac{1}{\sigma_2} \exp\left[\frac{\sigma_1^2}{2\sigma_2^2} + \frac{u}{\sigma_2}\right] \frac{1}{\sqrt{2\pi\sigma_1^2}} \exp\left[-\frac{\left(v + \frac{\sigma_1^2}{\sigma_2}\right)^2}{2\sigma_1^2}\right].
$$

(6.33)

To derive the marginal distribution of u as $v = u_1 = u + u_2$ and remembering that u_2 is positive, the range of integration of v is (u, ∞) because

Lower: $u_2 = 0 \Rightarrow v = u$,   Upper: $u_2 > 0 \Rightarrow v > u$.

The marginal distribution of u is now given by integrating out v in (6.33)

$$
g(u) = \int_u^\infty g(u, v)dv
$$

$$
= \frac{1}{\sigma_2} \exp\left[\frac{\sigma_1^2}{2\sigma_2^2} + \frac{u}{\sigma_2}\right] \int_u^\infty \frac{1}{\sqrt{2\pi\sigma_1^2}} \exp\left[-\frac{\left(v + \frac{\sigma_1^2}{\sigma_2}\right)^2}{2\sigma_1^2}\right] dv
$$

$$
= \frac{1}{\sigma_2} \exp\left[\frac{\sigma_1^2}{2\sigma_2^2} + \frac{u}{\sigma_2}\right] \left(1 - \Phi\left(\frac{u + \frac{\sigma_1^2}{\sigma_2}}{\sigma_1}\right)\right)
$$

$$
= \frac{1}{\sigma_2} \exp\left[\frac{\sigma_1^2}{2\sigma_2^2} + \frac{u}{\sigma_2}\right] \Phi\left(-\frac{u + \frac{\sigma_1^2}{\sigma_2}}{\sigma_1}\right),
$$

(6.34)

where $\Phi(\cdot)$ is the cumulative normal distribution function and the last step follows from the symmetry property of the normal distribution. Finally, the distribution in terms of y_t conditional on x_t is given by using (6.29) to substitute out $u_t = u$ in (6.34) to give

$$
g(y_t|x_t) = \frac{1}{\sigma_2} \exp\left[\frac{\sigma_1^2}{2\sigma_2^2} + \frac{(y_t - \beta_0 - \beta_1 x_t)}{\sigma_2}\right] \Phi\left(-\frac{y_t - \beta_0 - \beta_1 x_t - \frac{\sigma_1^2}{\sigma_2}}{\sigma_1}\right).
$$

(6.35)

Table 6.2. *Sampling properties of the maximum likelihood estimator of the stochastic frontier model in equations (6.29) and (6.30). Based on samples of size $T = 1000$ and 5000 replications*

Parameter	True	Mean	Bias	MSE
β_0	1.0000	0.9213	−0.0787	0.0133
β_1	0.5000	0.4991	−0.0009	0.0023
σ_1	1.0000	1.0949	0.0949	0.0153
σ_2	1.5000	1.3994	−0.1006	0.0184

Using expression (6.35) the log-likelihood function for a sample of T observations is

$$\ln L_T(\theta) = \frac{1}{T} \sum_{t=1}^{T} \ln g(y_t|x_t)$$

$$= -\ln \sigma_2 + \frac{\sigma_1^2}{2\sigma_2^2} + \frac{1}{\sigma_2 T} \sum_{t=1}^{T} (y_t - \beta_0 - \beta_1 x_t)$$

$$+ \frac{1}{T} \sum_{t=1}^{T} \ln \Phi \left(-\frac{y_t - \beta_0 - \beta_1 x_t - \frac{\sigma_1^2}{\sigma_2}}{\sigma_1} \right) .$$

This expression is nonlinear in the parameter θ and is maximised using an iterative algorithm.

A Monte Carlo experiment is performed to investigate the sampling properties of the maximum likelihood estimator of the stochastic frontier model in (6.29) and (6.30). The parameters are $\theta_0 = \{\beta_0 = 1, \beta_1 = 0.5, \sigma_1 = 1.0, \sigma_2 = 1.5\}$, the exogenous variable is $x_t \sim iid\ N(0, 1)$, the sample size is $T = 1000$ and the number of replications is 5000. The dependent variable, y_t, is simulated using the inverse cumulative density technique. This involves computing the cumulative density function of u_t from its marginal distribution in (6.35) for a grid of values ranging from -10 to 5. Uniform random variables are then drawn to obtain values of u_t which are added to $\beta_0 + \beta_1 x_t$ to obtain a draw of y_t.

The results of the Monte Carlo experiment are given in Table 6.2 which reports the bias and mean square error (MSE) for each parameter. The estimate of β_0 is biased downwards by about 8% while the slope estimate of β_1 exhibits very little bias. The estimates of the standard deviations exhibit bias in different directions with the estimate of σ_1 biased upwards and the estimate of σ_2 biased downwards.

6.7   Exercises

(1) Simulating Exponential Models

Program files   nls_simulate.*

Consider the exponential models given by

$$y_{1,t} = \beta_0 \exp[\beta_1 x_t + u_t]$$
$$y_{2,t} = \beta_0 \exp[\beta_1 x_t] + u_t,$$

where the exogenous variable is a time trend $x_t = t$ and the disturbance term is $u_t \sim iid\ N(0, \sigma^2)$.

(a) Simulate the exponential models for a sample size of $T = 50$, with parameters $\beta_0 = 1.0$, $\beta_1 = 0.05$, and $\sigma = 0.5$. Plot the level of the series, $y_{1,t}$ and $y_{2,t}$, and the logarithm of the series $\ln y_{1,t}$ and $\ln y_{2,t}$. Discuss the time series properties of the time series.

(b) Repeat part (a) with parameters $\beta_0 = 50.0$, $\beta_1 = -0.05$, and $\sigma = 0.5$.

(c) Reduce the signal to noise ratio in part (a) by choosing the parameters $\beta_0 = 1.0$, $\beta_1 = 0.05$, and $\sigma = 5.0$. Demonstrate that the natural logarithm transformation is no longer an appropriate method of explaining the trend for the series $y_{2,t}$.

(2) Estimating the Exponential Model by Maximum Likelihood

Program files   nls_exponential.*

Simulate the model

$$y_t = \beta_0 \exp[\beta_1 x_t] + u_t, \qquad u_t \sim iid\ N(0, \sigma^2),$$

for a sample size of $T = 50$, where the exogenous variable, the disturbance term and the parameters are as defined in Exercise 1.

(a) Use the Newton-Raphson algorithm to estimate the parameters $\theta = \{\beta_0, \beta_1, \sigma^2\}$, by concentrating out σ^2. Choose as starting values $\beta_0 = 0.1$ and $\beta_1 = 0.1$.

(b) Compute the standard errors of $\widehat{\beta}_0$ and $\widehat{\beta}_1$ based on the Hessian.

(c) Estimate the parameters of the model without concentrating the log-likelihood function with respect to σ^2 and compute the standard errors of $\widehat{\beta}_0$, $\widehat{\beta}_1$ and $\widehat{\sigma}^2$, based on the Hessian.

(3) Estimating the Exponential Model by Gauss-Newton

Program files   nls_exponential_gn.*

Simulate the model

$$y_t = \beta_0 \exp[\beta_1 x_t] + u_t, \qquad u_t \sim iid\ N(0, \sigma^2),$$

for a sample size of $T = 50$, where the exogenous variable and the disturbance term and the parameters are as defined in Exercise 1.
(a) Use the Gauss-Newton algorithm to estimate the parameters $\theta = \{\beta_0, \beta_1, \sigma^2\}$. Choose as starting values $\beta_0 = 0.1$ and $\beta_1 = 0.1$.
(b) Compute the standard errors of $\widehat{\beta}_0$ and $\widehat{\beta}_1$ and compare these estimates with those obtained using the Hessian in Exercise 2.

(4) Nonlinear Consumption Function

Program files	nls_conest.*, nls_contest.*
Data files	usdata.*

This exercise is based on United States quarterly data for real consumption expenditure and real disposable personal income for the period March 1960 to December 2009, downloaded from the Federal Reserve Bank of St. Louis. Consider the nonlinear consumption function

$$c_t = \beta_0 + \beta_1\, y_t^{\beta_2} + u_t, \qquad u_t \sim iid\ N(0, \sigma^2).$$

(a) Estimate a linear consumption function by setting $\beta_2 = 1$.
(b) Estimate the unrestricted nonlinear consumption function using the Gauss-Newton algorithm. Choose the linear parameter estimates computed in part (a) for β_0 and β_1 and $\beta_2 = 1$ as the starting values.
(c) Test the hypotheses

$$H_0 : \beta_2 = 1 \qquad H_1 : \beta_2 \neq 1,$$

using a LR test, a Wald test and a LM test.

(5) Nonlinear Regression 1

Program files	nls_regression1.*

Consider the nonlinear regression model

$$y_t = \frac{1}{x_t - \theta} + u_t, \qquad u_t \sim iid\ N(0, \sigma^2),$$

in which y_t is the dependent variable, x_t is the exogenous variable and u_t is the disturbance term.
(a) Derive the log-likelihood function $L_T(\theta)$, the gradient $G_T(\theta)$, the Hessian $H_T(\theta)$ and the information matrix $I(\theta)$.
(b) Simulate $T = 100$ observations on y_t and x_t, where $\theta = 2$ and $x_t \sim iid\ U[2, 3]$. Perform one step of the scoring algorithm with starting value $\theta_{(0)} = 1.5$.

(c) Compute the maximum likelihood estimates using the BFGS algorithm with starting value $\theta_{(0)} = 1.5$. Compare the performance of the BFGS algorithm with the Newton-Raphson and BHHH algorithms in terms of iterations needed to achieve convergence.

(6) Nonlinear Regression 2

Program files   `nls_regression2.*`

Consider the nonlinear regression model given by

$$y_t^{\beta_2} = \beta_0 + \beta_1 x_t + u_t, \qquad u_t \sim iid\ N(0, \sigma^2),$$

in which y_t is the dependent variable, x_t is the exogenous variable, u_t is the disturbance term and $\theta = \{\beta_0, \beta_1, \beta_2, \sigma^2\}$.

(a) Using the transformation of variable technique, derive the distribution of y_t and hence the log-likelihood function, $L_T(\theta)$.

(b) Show how to estimate the model's parameters by maximum likelihood using the Newton-Raphson, BHHH and Gauss-Newton algorithms.

(c) Simulate $T = 100$ observations on y_t and x_t, where $\beta_0 = 10$, $\beta_1 = 2$, $\beta_2 = 0.5$, $\sigma^2 = 0.1$ and $x_t \sim iid\ \chi_1^2$. Compute the maximum likelihood estimates where σ^2 is concentrated from the log-likelihood function.

(d) Construct LR, Wald and LM tests of the null hypothesis $\beta_2 = 1$. Interpret the results.

(7) Testing for a Liquidity Trap

Program files   `nls_liquiditytrap.*`
Data files   `us_liquiditytrap.*`

The data file contains monthly data on money, real output, CPI and the Federal funds rate for the United States from January 1959 to December 2011. Consider the nonlinear money demand equation used to model a liquidity trap by Konstas and Khouja (1969) given by

$$y_t = \beta_1 x_{1,t} + \frac{\beta_2}{x_{2,t} - \beta_3} + u_t, \qquad u_t \sim iid\ N(0, \sigma^2),$$

in which y_t is the logarithm of real money, $x_{1,t}$ is the logarithm of real income, $x_{2,t}$ is the nominal interest rate, u_t is the disturbance term and $\theta = \{\beta_1, \beta_2, \beta_3, \sigma^2\}$. If $\beta_3 > 0$, then as the interest rate, $x_{2,t}$, falls towards β_3 the semi-elasticity of the interest rate approaches infinity. If $\beta_3 = 0$, there is no liquidity trap and the model is linear in the exogenous variables.

(a) Construct Wald and LM tests of the null hypothesis $\beta_3 = 0$. Discuss the advantage(s) of the LM test over the Wald test in this case.

(b) Estimate the model by maximum likelihood where σ^2 is concentrated from the log-likelihood function. Test for a liquidity trap using the test statistics derived in part (a). Interpret the results.

(8) Vuong's Non-nested Test of Money Demand

Program files	`nls_money.*`
Data files	`moneydemand.*`

This exercise is based on quarterly data for the United States on real money, m_t, the nominal interest rate, r_t, and real income, y_t, for the period March 1959 to December 2005.
Consider the non-nested money demand equations given by

$$
\begin{aligned}
\text{Model 1:} \quad m_t &= \beta_0 + \beta_1 r_t + \beta_2 y_t + u_{1,t} \\
u_{1,t} &\sim iid\ N(0, \sigma_1^2), \\
\text{Model 2:} \quad \ln m_t &= \alpha_0 + \alpha_1 \ln r_t + \alpha_2 \ln y_t + u_{2,t} \\
u_{2,t} &\sim iid\ N(0, \sigma_2^2).
\end{aligned}
$$

(a) Estimate Model 1 by regressing m_t on $\{c, r_t, y_t\}$ and construct the log-likelihood at each observation

$$
\ln l_{1,t} = -\frac{1}{2}\ln(2\pi) - \frac{1}{2}\ln(\widehat{\sigma}_1^2) - \frac{(m_t - \widehat{\beta}_0 - \widehat{\beta}_1 r_t - \widehat{\beta}_2 y_t)^2}{2\widehat{\sigma}_1^2}.
$$

(b) Estimate Model 2 by regressing $\ln m_t$ on $\{c, \ln r_t, \ln y_t\}$ and construct the log-likelihood function of the transformed distribution at each observation

$$
\begin{aligned}
\ln l_{2,t} = {}&-\frac{1}{2}\ln(2\pi) - \frac{1}{2}\ln(\widehat{\sigma}_2^2) - \frac{(\ln m_t - \widehat{\alpha}_0 - \widehat{\alpha}_1 \ln r_t - \widehat{\alpha}_2 \ln y_t)^2}{2\widehat{\sigma}_2^2} \\
&-\ln m_t.
\end{aligned}
$$

(c) Perform Vuong's non-nested test and interpret the result.

(9) Robust Estimation of the CAPM

Program files	`nls_capm.*`

This exercise is based on monthly returns data on the company Martin Marietta from January 1982 to December 1986. The data are taken from Butler et. al. (1990, pp321–327).
(a) Identify any outliers in the data by using a scatterplot of r_t against m_t.
(b) Estimate the CAPM model given by

$$
r_t = \beta_0 + \beta_1 m_t + u_t, \qquad u_t \sim iid\ N(0, \sigma^2),
$$

and interpret the estimate of β_1. Test the hypothesis that $\beta_1 = 1$.

(c) Now estimate the CAPM model given by

$$r_t = \beta_0 + \beta_1 m_t + \sigma \sqrt{\frac{v-2}{v}} v_t, \qquad v_t \sim \text{Student } t(0, v),$$

and interpret the estimate of β_1. Test the hypothesis that $\beta_1 = 1$.

(d) Compare the parameter estimates of $\{\beta_0, \beta_1\}$ in parts (b) and (c) and discuss the robustness properties of these estimates.

(e) An alternative approach to achieving robustness is to exclude any outliers from the data set and re-estimate the model by ordinary least squares using the trimmed data set. A common way to do this is to compute the standardised residual

$$z_t = \frac{\widehat{u}_t}{\sqrt{\widehat{\sigma}^2 \, \text{diag}(I - x_t' \left[\sum_{t=1}^{T} x_t x_t' \right]^{-1} x_t)}},$$

in which $\widehat{u}_t$ is the least squares residual using all of the data and $\widehat{\sigma}^2$ is the residual variance. The standardised residual is approximately distributed as $N(0, 1)$, with absolute values in excess of 3 representing extreme observations. Compare the estimates of $\{\beta_0, \beta_1\}$ using the trimmed data approach with those obtained in parts (b) and (c). Hence discuss the role of the degrees of freedom parameter v in achieving robust parameter estimates to outliers.

(f) Construct a Wald test of normality based on the CAPM equation assuming Student t errors.

(10) Stochastic Frontier Model

Program files   `nls_frontier.*`

The stochastic frontier model is

$$y_t = \beta_0 + \beta_1 x_t + u_t$$
$$u_t = u_{1,t} - u_{2,t},$$

in which $u_{1,t}$ and $u_{2,t}$ are distributed as normal and exponential as defined in (6.30), with standard deviations σ_1 and σ_2, respectively.

(a) Use the change of variable technique to show that the distribution of u_t is

$$g(u_t) = \frac{1}{\sigma_2} \exp\left[\frac{\sigma_1^2}{2\sigma_2^2} + \frac{u_t}{\sigma_2} \right] \Phi\left(-\frac{u_t + \frac{\sigma_1^2}{\sigma_2}}{\sigma_1} \right).$$

Plot the distribution and discuss its shape.

(b) Choose the parameter values $\theta_0 = \{\beta_0 = 1, \beta_1 = 0.5, \sigma_1 = 1.0, \sigma_2 = 1.5\}$. Use the inverse cumulative density technique to simulate u_t, by computing its cumulative density function from its marginal distribution in part (a) for a grid of values of u_t ranging from -10 to 5 and then drawing uniform random numbers to obtain draws of u_t.

(c) Investigate the sampling properties of the maximum likelihood estimator using a Monte Carlo experiment based on the parameters in part (b), $x_t \sim N(0, 1)$, with $T = 1000$ and 5000 replications.

(d) Repeat parts (a) to (c) where now the disturbance is $u_t = u_{1,t} + u_{2,t}$ with density function

$$g(u_t) = \frac{1}{\sigma_2} \exp\left[\frac{\sigma_1^2}{2\sigma_2^2} - \frac{u_t}{\sigma_2}\right] \Phi\left(\frac{u_t - \dfrac{\sigma_1^2}{\sigma_2}}{\sigma_1}\right).$$

(e) Let $u_t = u_{1,t} - u_{2,t}$, where $u_{1,t}$ is normal but now $u_{2,t}$ is half-normal

$$f(u_{2,t}) = \frac{2}{\sqrt{2\pi\sigma_2^2}} \exp\left[-\frac{u_{2,t}^2}{2\sigma_2^2}\right], \qquad 0 \le u_{2,t} < \infty.$$

Repeat parts (a) to (c) by defining $\sigma^2 = \sigma_1^2 + \sigma_2^2$ and $\lambda = \sigma_2/\sigma_1$, hence show that u_t has distribution

$$g(u_t) = \sqrt{\frac{2}{\pi}}\frac{1}{\sigma} \exp\left[-\frac{u_t^2}{2\sigma^2}\right] \Phi\left(-\frac{u_t\lambda}{\sigma}\right).$$

7   Autocorrelated Regression Models

7.1   Introduction

An important feature of the regression models presented in Chapters 5 and 6 is that the disturbance term is assumed to be independent across time. This assumption is now relaxed and the resultant models are referred to as auto-correlated regression models. The aim of this chapter is to use the maximum likelihood framework set up in Part ONE to estimate and test autocorrelated regression models. The structure of the autocorrelation may be autoregressive, moving average or a combination of the two. Both single equation and multiple equation models are analysed.

A property of the maximum likelihood estimator of the autocorrelated regression model is that it nests a number of other estimators, including conditional maximum likelihood, Gauss-Newton, zig-zag algorithms and the Cochrane-Orcutt procedure. Tests of autocorrelation are derived in terms of the LR, Wald and LM tests set out in Chapter 4. In the case of LM tests of auto-correlation, the statistics are shown to be equivalent to a number of diagnostic test statistics widely used in econometrics.

7.2   Specification

In Chapter 5, the focus is on estimating and testing linear regression models of the form

$$y_t = \beta_0 + \beta_1 x_t + u_t, \qquad u_t \sim iid\ N(0, \sigma^2), \tag{7.1}$$

in which y_t is the dependent variable, x_t is the exogenous variable and u_t is the disturbance term. For a sample of $t = 1, 2, \cdots, T$ observations, the joint density function of this model is

$$f(y_1, y_2, \cdots, y_T \,|\, x_1, x_2, \cdots, x_T; \theta) = \prod_{t=1}^{T} f(y_t \,|\, x_t; \theta), \tag{7.2}$$

where $\theta = \{\beta_0, \beta_1, \sigma^2\}$ is the vector of parameters to be estimated.

The assumption that u_t in (7.1) is independent is now relaxed by augmenting the model to include an equation for u_t that is a function of information at time $t - 1$. Common parametric specifications of the disturbance term, u_t, are autoregressive (AR) models, moving average (MA) models, or a combination of the two. Some examples are as follows.

1. AR(1)   : $u_t = \rho_1 u_{t-1} + v_t$
2. AR(p)   : $u_t = \rho_1 u_{t-1} + \rho_2 u_{t-2} + \cdots + \rho_p u_{t-p} + v_t$
3. MA(1)   : $u_t = v_t + \delta_1 v_{t-1}$
4. MA(q)   : $u_t = v_t + \delta_1 v_{t-1} + \delta_2 v_{t-2} + \cdots + \delta_q v_{t-q}$
5. ARMA(p,q)   : $u_t = \sum_{i=1}^{p} \rho_i u_{t-i} + v_t + \sum_{i=1}^{q} \delta_i v_{t-i}$,

where $v_t \sim iid\ N(0, \sigma^2)$. The regression model where u_t has a dynamic structure given by one of these specifications is referred to as the autocorrelated regression model.

A characteristic of autocorrelated regression models is that a shock at time t, as represented by v_t, has an immediate effect on y_t and continues to have an effect at times $t + 1$, $t + 2$, etc. This suggests that the conditional mean in equation (7.1), $\beta_0 + \beta_1 x_t$, underestimates y_t for some periods and overestimates it for other periods.

Example 7.1 A Regression Model with Autocorrelation

Figure 7.1 panel (a) gives a scatterplot of simulated data for a sample of $T = 200$ observations from a regression model with an AR(1) disturbance term given by

$$y_t = \beta_0 + \beta_1 x_t + u_t$$
$$u_t = \rho_1 u_{t-1} + v_t$$
$$v_t \sim iid\ N(0, \sigma^2),$$

with parameter values $\theta_0 = \{\beta_0 = 2, \beta_1 = 1, \rho_1 = 0.95, \sigma^2 = 9\}$ and the exogenous variable is generated as $x_t = 0.5t + e_t$ where $e_t \sim iid\ N(0, 1)$. For comparative purposes, the conditional mean of y_t, $\beta_0 + \beta_1 x_t$, is also plotted.

This figure shows that there are periods when the conditional mean consistently underestimates y_t whilst for other periods consistently overestimates y_t. A similar pattern, although less pronounced than that observed in panel (a), occurs in Figure 7.1 panel (b), where the disturbance is MA(1)

$$y_t = \beta_0 + \beta_1 x_t + u_t$$
$$u_t = v_t + \delta_1 v_{t-1}$$
$$v_t \sim iid\ N(0, \sigma^2),$$

where x_t is as before and $\theta_0 = \{\beta_0 = 2, \beta_1 = 1, \delta_1 = 0.95, \sigma^2 = 9\}$. $\square$

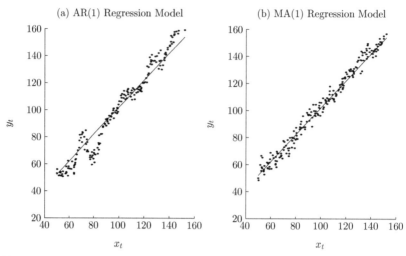

Figure 7.1. Scatterplots of the simulated data from the regression model with an auto-correlated disturbance.

7.3   Maximum Likelihood Estimation

From Chapter 1, the joint pdf of $y_1, y_2, \cdots, y_T$ dependent observations is

$$
\begin{aligned}
f(y_1, y_2, &\cdots, y_T \mid x_1, x_2, \cdots, x_T; \theta) \\
&= f(y_s, y_{s-1}, \cdots, y_1 \mid x_s, x_{s-1}, \cdots, x_1; \theta) \\
&\quad \times \prod_{t=s+1}^{T} f(y_t \mid y_{t-1}, \cdots, x_t, x_{t-1}, \cdots; \theta),
\end{aligned}
\tag{7.3}
$$

where $\theta = \{\beta_0, \beta_1, \rho_1, \rho_2, \cdots, \rho_p, \delta_1, \delta_2, \cdots, \delta_q, \sigma^2\}$ and $s = \max(p, q)$. The first term on the right-hand side in equation (7.3) represents the marginal distribution of $\{y_s, y_{s-1}, \cdots, y_1\}$, while the second term contains the sequence of conditional distributions of y_t. When both terms in the likelihood function in equation (7.3) are used, the estimator is also known as the exact maximum likelihood estimator. By contrast, when only the second term of equation (7.3) is used the estimator is known as the conditional maximum likelihood estimator.

7.3.1   Exact Maximum Likelihood

From equation (7.3), the log-likelihood function for the exact maximum likelihood estimator is

$$
\begin{aligned}
\ln L_T(\theta) = \frac{1}{T} &\ln f(y_s, y_{s-1}, \cdots, y_1 \mid x_s, x_{s-1}, \cdots, x_1; \theta) \\
&+ \frac{1}{T} \sum_{t=s+1}^{T} \ln f(y_t \mid y_{t-1}, \cdots, x_t, x_{t-1}, \cdots; \theta).
\end{aligned}
\tag{7.4}
$$

The log-likelihood function is normally nonlinear in the unknown parameters, θ, and must be maximised using one of the algorithms presented in Chapter 3.

Example 7.2 AR(1) Regression Model

Consider the model

$$y_t = \beta_0 + \beta_1 x_t + u_t$$
$$u_t = \rho_1 u_{t-1} + v_t$$
$$v_t \sim iid\ N(0, \sigma^2),$$

where y_t is the dependent variable, x_t is the exogenous variable and the parameters are $\theta = \{\beta_0, \beta_1, \rho_1, \sigma^2\}$. The distribution of v_t is

$$f(v_t) = \frac{1}{\sqrt{2\pi\sigma^2}} \exp\left[-\frac{v_t^2}{2\sigma^2}\right].$$

The conditional distribution of u_t is

$$f(u_t | u_{t-1}; \theta) = f(v_t) \left|\frac{dv_t}{du_t}\right| = \frac{1}{\sqrt{2\pi\sigma^2}} \exp\left[-\frac{(u_t - \rho_1 u_{t-1})^2}{2\sigma^2}\right],$$

because $|dv_t/du_t| = 1$. Consequently, the conditional distribution of y_t is

$$f(y_t | y_{t-1}, x_t, x_{t-1}; \theta)$$
$$= f(u_t) \left|\frac{du_t}{dy_t}\right|$$
$$= \frac{1}{\sqrt{2\pi\sigma^2}} \exp\left[-\frac{(y_t - \beta_0 - \beta_1 x_t - \rho_1(y_{t-1} - \beta_0 - \beta_1 x_{t-1}))^2}{2\sigma^2}\right],$$

because $|du_t/dy_t| = 1$. To derive the marginal distribution of u_t, use the result that for the AR(1) model with $u_t = \rho_1 u_{t-1} + v_t$, where $v_t \sim N(0, \sigma^2)$, the marginal distribution is $N(0, \sigma^2/(1 - \rho_1^2))$. Hence

$$f(u_t) = \frac{1}{\sqrt{2\pi\sigma^2/(1 - \rho_1^2)}} \exp\left[-\frac{(u_t - 0)^2}{2\sigma^2/(1 - \rho_1^2)}\right],$$

so that the distribution of y_t at $t = 1$ is given by

$$f(y_1 | x_1; \theta) = f(u_1) \left|\frac{du_1}{dy_1}\right| = \frac{1}{\sqrt{2\pi\sigma^2/(1 - \rho_1^2)}} \exp\left[-\frac{(y_1 - \beta_0 - \beta_1 x_1)^2}{2\sigma^2/(1 - \rho_1^2)}\right],$$

because $|du_1/dy_1| = 1$. It follows, therefore, that the joint probability distribution of y_t for the AR(1) regression model is

$$f(y_1, y_2, \cdots, y_T \mid x_1, x_2, \cdots, x_T; \theta)$$
$$= f(y_1 \mid x_1; \theta) \times \prod_{t=2}^{T} f(y_t \mid y_{t-1}, x_t, x_{t-1}; \theta),$$

and the log-likelihood function is

$$\ln L_T(\theta) = \frac{1}{T} \ln f(y_1 \mid x_1; \theta) + \frac{1}{T} \sum_{t=2}^{T} \ln f(y_t \mid y_{t-1}, x_t, x_{t-1}; \theta)$$
$$= -\frac{1}{2} \ln(2\pi) - \frac{1}{2} \ln \sigma^2 + \frac{1}{T} \ln(1 - \rho_1^2) - \frac{1}{2T} \frac{(y_1 - \beta_0 - \beta_1 x_1)^2}{\sigma^2/(1 - \rho_1^2)}$$
$$- \frac{1}{2\sigma^2 T} \sum_{t=2}^{T} (y_t - \rho_1 y_{t-1} - \beta_0(1 - \rho_1) - \beta_1(x_t - \rho_1 x_{t-1}))^2 \,.$$

This expression shows that the log-likelihood function is a nonlinear function of the parameters.   □

7.3.2   Conditional Maximum Likelihood

Example 7.2 deals with a regression model with an AR(1) disturbance term. Estimation of the regression model with an ARMA(p,q) disturbance term is more difficult, however, since it requires deriving the marginal distribution of $f(y_1, y_2, \cdots, y_s)$, where $s = \max(p, q)$. One solution is to ignore this term, in which case the log-likelihood function in (7.4) is taken with respect to an average of the log-likelihoods corresponding to the conditional distributions from $s + 1$ onwards

$$\ln L_T(\theta) = \frac{1}{T - s} \sum_{t=s+1}^{T} \ln f(y_t \mid y_{t-1}, \cdots, x_t, x_{t-1}, \cdots; \theta). \quad (7.5)$$

As the likelihood is now constructed by treating the first s observations as fixed, estimators based on maximising this likelihood are referred to as conditional maximum likelihood estimators. Asymptotically the exact and conditional maximum likelihood estimators are equivalent because the contribution of $\ln f(y_s, y_{s-1}, \cdots, y_1 \mid x_s, x_{s-1}, \cdots, x_1; \theta)$ to the overall log-likelihood function vanishes for $T \to \infty$.

Example 7.3 AR(2) Regression Model
Consider the model

$$y_t = \beta_0 + \beta_1 x_t + u_t$$
$$u_t = \rho_1 u_{t-1} + \rho_2 u_{t-2} + v_t$$
$$v_t \sim N(0, \sigma^2),$$

with parameters $\theta = \{\beta_0, \beta_1, \rho_1, \sigma^2\}$. Given some starting values $\theta_{(0)}$, the conditional log-likelihood function is constructed by computing

$$u_t = y_t - \beta_0 - \beta_1 x_t, \qquad\qquad t = 1, 2, \cdots, T$$
$$v_t = u_t - \rho_1 u_{t-1} - \rho_2 u_{t-2}, \qquad t = 3, 4, \cdots, T,$$

where the parameters are replaced by $\theta_{(0)}$. The conditional log-likelihood function is then computed as

$$\ln L_T(\theta) = -\frac{1}{2} \ln(2\pi) - \frac{1}{2} \ln \sigma^2 - \frac{1}{2\sigma^2(T-2)} \sum_{t=3}^{T} v_t^2. \qquad \square$$

In evaluating the conditional log-likelihood function for ARMA(p,q) models, it is necessary to choose starting values for the first q values of v_t. A common choice is $v_1 = v_2 = \cdots v_q = 0$.

Example 7.4 ARMA(1,1) Regression Model
Consider the model

$$y_t = \beta_0 + \beta_1 x_t + u_t$$
$$u_t = \rho_1 u_{t-1} + v_t + \delta_1 v_{t-1}$$
$$v_t \sim iid \ N(0, \sigma^2),$$

with parameters $\theta = \{\beta_0, \beta_1, \rho_1, \delta_1, \sigma^2\}$. Given some starting values $\theta_{(0)}$, the conditional log-likelihood function is constructed by computing

$$u_t = y_t - \beta_0 - \beta_1 x_t, \qquad\qquad t = 1, 2, \cdots, T$$
$$v_t = u_t - \rho_1 u_{t-1} - \delta_1 v_{t-1}, \qquad t = 2, 3, \cdots, T,$$

with $v_1 = 0$ and where the parameters are replaced by $\theta_{(0)}$. The conditional log-likelihood function is then

$$\ln L_T(\theta) = -\frac{1}{2} \ln(2\pi) - \frac{1}{2} \ln \sigma^2 - \frac{1}{2\sigma^2(T-1)} \sum_{t=2}^{T} v_t^2. \qquad \square$$

Table 7.1. *Maximum likelihood estimates of the investment model using the Newton-Raphson algorithm with derivatives computed numerically. Standard errors and t statistics are based on the Hessian*

Parameter	Exact			Conditional		
	Estimate	se	t stat.	Estimate	se	t stat.
β_0	-0.281	0.157	-1.788	-0.275	0.159	-1.733
β_1	1.570	0.130	12.052	1.567	0.131	11.950
β_2	-0.332	0.165	-2.021	-0.334	0.165	-2.023
ρ_1	0.090	0.081	1.114	0.091	0.081	1.125
σ^2	2.219	0.215	10.344	2.229	0.216	10.320
$\ln L_T(\widehat{\theta})$	-1.817			-1.811		

Example 7.5 A Dynamic Model of United States Investment

This example uses quarterly data for the United States from March 1957 to September 2010 to estimate the following model of investment

$$dri_t = \beta_0 + \beta_1 dry_t + \beta_2 rint_t + u_t$$
$$u_t = \rho_1 u_{t-1} + v_t$$
$$v_t \sim iid\ N(0, \sigma^2),$$

where dri_t is the quarterly percentage change in real investment, dry_t is the quarterly percentage change in real income, $rint_t$ is the real interest rate expressed as a quarterly percentage, and the parameters are $\theta = \{\beta_0, \beta_1, \beta_2, \rho_1, \sigma^2\}$. The sample begins in June 1957 as one observation is lost from constructing the quarterly growth rates, resulting in a sample of size $T = 214$. Given some starting values $\theta_{(0)}$, the conditional log-likelihood function is constructed by computing

$$u_t = dri_t - \beta_0 - \beta_1 dry_t - \beta_2 rint_t, \qquad t = 1, 2, \cdots, T$$
$$v_t = u_t - \rho_1 u_{t-1} \qquad\qquad\qquad t = 2, 3, \cdots, T.$$

The log-likelihood function at $t = 1$ is

$$\ln l_1(\theta) = -\frac{1}{2}\ln(2\pi) - \frac{1}{2}\ln\sigma^2 + \frac{1}{2}\ln(1 - \rho_1^2) - \frac{(u_1 - 0)^2}{2\sigma^2/(1 - \rho_1^2)},$$

while for $t > 1$ it is

$$\ln l_t(\theta) = -\frac{1}{2}\ln(2\pi) - \frac{1}{2}\ln\sigma^2 - \frac{v_t^2}{2\sigma^2}.$$

The exact maximum likelihood estimates of the investment model are given in Table 7.1 under the heading Exact. All parameter estimates are statistically significant at the 5% level with the exception of the autocorrelation parameter estimate, $\widehat{\rho}_1$. For comparison the conditional maximum likelihood estimates are also given in Table 7.1, and give qualitatively similar results to the exact maximum likelihood estimates. □

7.4 Alternative Estimators

In some cases, the maximum likelihood estimator of the autocorrelated regression model nests a number of other estimation methods as special cases. Three algorithms are discussed consisting of the Gauss-Newton algorithm, the zig-zig algorithm and the Cochrane-Orcutt algorithm.

7.4.1 Gauss-Newton

The exact and conditional maximum likelihood estimators of the autocorrelated regression model discussed earlier are presented in terms of the Newton-Raphson algorithm with the derivatives computed numerically. In the case of the conditional likelihood constructing analytical derivatives is straightforward. As the log-likelihood function is based on the normal distribution, the variance of the disturbance, σ^2, can be concentrated out and the nonlinearities arising from the contribution of the marginal distribution of y_1 are no longer present. Once the Newton-Raphson algorithm is re-expressed in terms of analytical derivatives, it reduces to a sequence of least squares regressions known as the Gauss-Newton algorithm, as discussed in Chapter 6.

Consider the first-order derivatives of the conditional log-likelihood function of the AR(1) regression model with respect to the parameters, $\theta = \{\beta_0, \beta_1, \rho_1, \sigma^2\}$, given by

$$
\frac{\partial \ln L_T(\theta)}{\partial \beta_0} = \frac{1}{\sigma^2(T-1)} \sum_{t=2}^{T} v_t(1-\rho_1)
$$

$$
\frac{\partial \ln L_T(\theta)}{\partial \beta_1} = \frac{1}{\sigma^2(T-1)} \sum_{t=2}^{T} v_t(x_t - \rho_1 x_{t-1})
$$

$$
\frac{\partial \ln L_T(\theta)}{\partial \rho_1} = \frac{1}{\sigma^2(T-1)} \sum_{t=2}^{T} v_t u_{t-1} \tag{7.6}
$$

$$
\frac{\partial \ln L_T(\theta)}{\partial \sigma^2} = -\frac{1}{2\sigma^2} + \frac{1}{2\sigma^4(T-1)} \sum_{t=2}^{T} v_t^2 \,,
$$

where

$$
v_t = y_t - \rho_1 y_{t-1} - \beta_0(1-\rho_1) - \beta_1(x_t - \rho_1 x_{t-1}) \,.
$$

The direct second-order derivatives are

$$\frac{\partial^2 \ln L_T(\theta)}{\partial \beta_0^2} = -\frac{1}{\sigma^2(T-1)} \sum_{t=2}^{T}(1-\rho_1)^2$$

$$\frac{\partial^2 \ln L_T(\theta)}{\partial \beta_1^2} = -\frac{1}{\sigma^2(T-1)} \sum_{t=2}^{T}(x_t - \rho_1 x_{t-1})^2$$

$$\frac{\partial^2 \ln L_T(\theta)}{\partial \rho_1^2} = -\frac{1}{\sigma^2(T-1)} \sum_{t=2}^{T} u_{t-1}^2 \qquad (7.7)$$

$$\frac{\partial^2 \ln L_T(\theta)}{\partial (\sigma^2)^2} = \frac{1}{2\sigma^4(T-1)} - \frac{1}{\sigma^6} \sum_{t=2}^{T} v_t^2,$$

and second-order cross derivatives are

$$\frac{\partial^2 \ln L_T(\theta)}{\partial \beta_0 \partial \beta_1} = -\frac{1}{\sigma^2(T-1)} \sum_{t=2}^{T}(x_t - \rho_1 x_{t-1})(1 - \rho_1)$$

$$\frac{\partial^2 \ln L_T(\theta)}{\partial \beta_0 \partial \rho_1} = -\frac{1}{\sigma^2(T-1)} \sum_{t=2}^{T}(u_{t-1}(1 - \rho_1) + v_t)$$

$$\frac{\partial^2 \ln L_T(\theta)}{\partial \beta_0 \partial \sigma^2} = -\frac{1}{\sigma^4(T-1)} \sum_{t=2}^{T} v_t(1 - \rho_1)$$

$$\frac{\partial^2 \ln L_T(\theta)}{\partial \beta_1 \partial \rho_1} = -\frac{1}{\sigma^2(T-1)} \sum_{t=2}^{T}(u_{t-1}(x_t - \rho_1 x_{t-1}) + v_t x_{t-1}) \qquad (7.8)$$

$$\frac{\partial^2 \ln L_T(\theta)}{\partial \beta_1 \partial \sigma^2} = -\frac{1}{\sigma^4(T-1)} \sum_{t=2}^{T} v_t(x_t - \rho_1 x_{t-1})$$

$$\frac{\partial^2 \ln L_T(\theta)}{\partial \rho_1 \partial \sigma^2} = -\frac{1}{\sigma^2(T-1)} \sum_{t=2}^{T} v_t u_{t-1}.$$

Setting $\partial \ln L_T(\theta)/\partial \sigma^2 = 0$ and rearranging gives the solution

$$\widehat{\sigma}^2 = \frac{1}{T-1} \sum_{t=2}^{T} \widehat{v}_t^2, \qquad (7.9)$$

which is used to concentrate σ^2 out of the log-likelihood function. The iterations are now expressed only in terms of the parameters β_0, β_1 and ρ_1

$$\begin{bmatrix} \beta_0 \\ \beta_1 \\ \rho_1 \end{bmatrix}_{(k)} = \begin{bmatrix} \beta_0 \\ \beta_1 \\ \rho_1 \end{bmatrix}_{(k-1)} - H_{(k-1)}^{-1} G_{(k-1)}. \qquad (7.10)$$

The gradient, obtained from (7.6), is

$$G_T(\theta) = \frac{1}{\sigma^2 T} \sum_{t=2}^{T} \begin{bmatrix} 1 - \rho_1 \\ x_t - \rho_1 x_{t-1} \\ u_{t-1} \end{bmatrix} v_t, \qquad (7.11)$$

and the Hessian is based on the terms in equations (7.7) and (7.8). The Hessian is simplified further by using the results $\sum_{t=1}^{T} \widehat{v}_t = 0$ and $\sum_{t=1}^{T} \widehat{v}_t x_t = 0$, which follow from the first-order conditions, so that

$$
H_T(\theta) = -\frac{1}{\sigma^2 T} \sum_{t=2}^{T} \begin{bmatrix} 1 - \rho_1 \\ x_t - \rho_1 x_{t-1} \\ u_{t-1} \end{bmatrix} \begin{bmatrix} 1 - \rho_1 \; x_t - \rho_1 x_{t-1} \; u_{t-1} \end{bmatrix}.
$$

$$(7.12)$$

Substituting expressions (7.11) and (7.12) in equation (7.10) gives

$$
\begin{bmatrix} \beta_0 \\ \beta_1 \\ \rho_1 \end{bmatrix}_{(k)} = \begin{bmatrix} \beta_0 \\ \beta_1 \\ \rho_1 \end{bmatrix}_{(k-1)} + \left[\sum_{t=2}^{T} z_t z_t' \right]^{-1} \left[\sum_{t=2}^{T} z_t v_t \right],
$$

$$(7.13)$$

where

$$
z_t = [1 - \rho_1, \; x_t - \rho_1 x_{t-1}, \; u_{t-1}]'
$$

and

$$
v_t = u_t - \rho_1 u_{t-1} = (y_t - \beta_0 - \beta_1 x_t) - \rho_1 (y_{t-1} - \beta_0 - \beta_1 x_{t-1}),
$$

in which all of the parameters are evaluated at $\theta_{(k-1)}$. This updating algorithm has two important features. First, it does not contain $\widehat{\sigma}^2$ because it is cancelled out in the calculation of $H_T^{-1}(\theta) G_T(\theta)$. Second, the updating part of the algorithm is equivalent to the Gauss-Newton algorithm described in Chapter 6 consisting of regressing $\widehat{v}_t$ on z_t.

A simpler way to motivate the Gauss-Newton algorithm in (7.13) is to express the model in terms of v_t as the dependent variable

$$
v_t = u_t - \rho_1 u_{t-1} = (y_t - \beta_0 - \beta_1 x_t) - \rho_1 (y_{t-1} - \beta_0 - \beta_1 x_{t-1}),
$$

and construct the derivatives

$$
z_{1,t} = -\frac{\partial v_t}{\partial \beta_0} = 1 - \rho_1
$$

$$
z_{2,t} = -\frac{\partial v_t}{\partial \beta_1} = x_t - \rho_1 x_{t-1}
$$

$$
z_{3,t} = -\frac{\partial v_t}{\partial \rho_1} = u_{t-1},
$$

which are the same set of variables as those given in z_t.

Example 7.6 Gauss-Newton Estimator of an ARMA(1,1) Model

Re-express the ARMA(1,1) model in Example 7.4 in terms of v_t as

$$
v_t = u_t - \rho_1 u_{t-1} - \delta_1 v_{t-1}
$$
$$
= (y_t - \beta_0 - \beta_1 x_t) - \rho_1 (y_{t-1} - \beta_0 - \beta_1 x_{t-1}) - \delta_1 v_{t-1}.
$$

Construct the derivatives

$$z_{1,t} = -\frac{\partial v_t}{\partial \beta_0} = 1 - \rho_1 - \delta_1 z_{1,t-1}$$

$$z_{2,t} = -\frac{\partial v_t}{\partial \beta_1} = x_t - \rho_1 x_{t-1} - \delta_1 z_{2,t-1}$$

$$z_{3,t} = -\frac{\partial v_t}{\partial \rho_1} = y_{t-1} - \beta_0 - \beta_1 x_{t-1} - \delta_1 z_{3,t-1}$$

$$z_{4,t} = -\frac{\partial v_t}{\partial \delta_1} = v_{t-1} - \delta_1 z_{4,t-1}.$$

Regress v_t on $z_t = \left[z_{1,t}, z_{2,t}, z_{3,t}, z_{4,t}\right]'$, with all terms evaluated at the starting values $[\beta_0, \beta_1, \rho_1, \delta_1]_{(0)}$. Let the parameter estimates be given by $\Delta_{\beta_0}, \Delta_{\beta_1}, \Delta_{\rho_1}, \Delta_{\delta_1}$. Construct new parameter values as

$$
\begin{bmatrix} \beta_0 \\ \beta_1 \\ \rho_1 \\ \delta_1 \end{bmatrix}_{(1)}
=
\begin{bmatrix} \beta_0 \\ \beta_1 \\ \rho_1 \\ \delta_1 \end{bmatrix}_{(0)}
+
\begin{bmatrix} \Delta_{\beta_0} \\ \Delta_{\beta_1} \\ \Delta_{\rho_1} \\ \Delta_{\delta_1} \end{bmatrix}_{(1)},
$$

and repeat the iterations. The estimate of σ^2 is computed using the final parameter estimates.   □

7.4.2   Zig-Zag Algorithms

The derivation of the Gauss-Newton algorithm is based on using the first-order conditions to simplify the Hessian. Another way to proceed that leads to even further simplification of the Hessian is to use the scoring algorithm of Chapter 3

$$\theta_{(k)} = \theta_{(k-1)} + I_{(k-1)}^{-1} G_{(k-1)}, \tag{7.14}$$

where $G_{(k-1)}$ and $I_{(k-1)}$ are, respectively, the gradient and the information matrix evaluated at $\theta = \theta_{(k-1)}$. This algorithm is slightly more involved to implement than are the Newton-Raphson and Gauss-Newton algorithms because it requires deriving the information matrix. Consider the AR(1) regression model with normal disturbances in Example 7.2. Taking expectations of the second-order derivatives given in (7.7) and (7.8) yields

$$E\left[\frac{\partial^2 \ln L_T(\theta)}{\partial \beta_0^2}\right] = -\frac{1}{\sigma^2(T-1)} \sum_{t=2}^{T} (1 - \rho_1)^2$$

$$E\left[\frac{\partial^2 \ln L_T(\theta)}{\partial \beta_1^2}\right] = -\frac{1}{\sigma^2(T-1)} \sum_{t=2}^{T} E[(x_t - \rho_1 x_{t-1})^2]$$

$$E\left[\frac{\partial^2 \ln L_T(\theta)}{\partial \rho_1^2}\right] = -\frac{1}{\sigma^2(T-1)} \sum_{t=2}^{T} \frac{\sigma^2}{1-\rho_1^2} = -\frac{1}{1-\rho_1^2}$$

$$E\left[\frac{\partial^2 \ln L_T(\theta)}{\partial (\sigma^2)^2}\right] = E\left[\frac{1}{2\sigma^4} - \frac{1}{\sigma^6(T-1)} \sum_{t=2}^{T} v_t^2\right] = -\frac{1}{2\sigma^4},$$

and

$$E\left[\frac{\partial^2 \ln L_T(\theta)}{\partial \beta_0 \partial \beta_1}\right] = -\frac{1}{\sigma^2(T-1)} \sum_{t=2}^{T} E[x_t - \rho_1 x_{t-1}](1 - \rho_1)$$

$$E\left[\frac{\partial^2 \ln L_T(\theta)}{\partial \beta_0 \partial \rho_1}\right] = -\frac{1}{\sigma^2(T-1)} \sum_{t=2}^{T} (E[u_{t-1}](1 - \rho_1) + E[v_t]) = 0$$

$$E\left[\frac{\partial^2 \ln L_T(\theta)}{\partial \beta_0 \partial \sigma^2}\right] = -\frac{1}{\sigma^4(T-1)} \sum_{t=2}^{T} E[v_t](1 - \rho_1) = 0$$

$$E\left[\frac{\partial^2 \ln L_T(\theta)}{\partial \beta_1 \partial \rho_1}\right] = -\frac{1}{\sigma^2(T-1)} \sum_{t=2}^{T} (E[u_{t-1}(x_t - \rho_1 x_{t-1})] + E[v_t x_{t-1}]) = 0$$

$$E\left[\frac{\partial^2 \ln L_T(\theta)}{\partial \beta_1 \partial \sigma^2}\right] = -\frac{1}{\sigma^4(T-1)} \sum_{t=2}^{T} E[v_t(x_t - \rho_1 x_{t-1})] = 0$$

$$E\left[\frac{\partial^2 \ln L_T(\theta)}{\partial \rho_1 \partial \sigma^2}\right] = -\frac{1}{\sigma^2(T-1)} \sum_{t=2}^{T} E[v_t]E[u_{t-1}] = 0.$$

The information matrix is now given by

$$I(\theta) = \begin{bmatrix} I_{1,1} & 0 & 0 \\ 0 & I_{2,2} & 0 \\ 0 & 0 & I_{3,3} \end{bmatrix}, \tag{7.15}$$

in which

$$I_{1,1} = \frac{1}{\sigma^2(T-1)} \sum_{t=2}^{T} \begin{bmatrix} (1-\rho_1)^2 & E[x_t - \rho_1 x_{t-1}](1-\rho_1) \\ E[x_t - \rho_1 x_{t-1}](1-\rho_1) & E[(x_t - \rho_1 x_{t-1})^2] \end{bmatrix}$$

$$I_{2,2} = \frac{1}{1-\rho_1^2} \tag{7.16}$$

$$I_{3,3} = \frac{1}{2\sigma^4}.$$

The key feature of the information matrix in equation (7.15) is that it is block diagonal. This suggests that estimation can proceed in three separate blocks, that is in a zig-zag

$$
\begin{bmatrix} \beta_0 \\ \rho_1 \\ \sigma^2 \end{bmatrix}_{(k)} = \begin{bmatrix} \beta_0 \\ \rho_1 \\ \sigma^2 \end{bmatrix}_{(k-1)} + \begin{bmatrix} I_{1,1}^{-1} & 0 & 0 \\ 0 & I_{2,2}^{-1} & 0 \\ 0 & 0 & I_{3,3}^{-1} \end{bmatrix}_{(k-1)} \begin{bmatrix} G_1 \\ G_2 \\ G_3 \end{bmatrix}_{(k-1)},
$$

(7.17)

in which the gradients from (7.6) are defined as

$$
G_1 = \frac{1}{\sigma^2(T-1)} \sum_{t=2}^{T} \begin{bmatrix} 1 - \rho_1 \\ x_t - \rho_1 x_{t-1} \end{bmatrix} v_t
$$

$$
G_2 = \frac{1}{\sigma^2(T-1)} \sum_{t=2}^{T} \begin{bmatrix} u_{t-1} \end{bmatrix} v_t
$$

(7.18)

$$
G_3 = -\frac{1}{2\sigma^2} + \frac{1}{2\sigma^4(T-1)} \sum_{t=2}^{T} v_t^2,
$$

with all parameters evaluated at $\theta_{(k-1)}$.

Just as in the Gauss-Newton algorithm where the first-order condition for σ^2 is used to derive an explicit solution for $\hat{\sigma}^2$, the iterative scheme is only needed for the first two blocks in (7.17). Compared to the Gauss-Newton algorithm, the zig-zag algorithm has the advantage of simplifying the computations since the regression parameters β_0 and β_1 are computed separately to the autocorrelation parameter ρ_1.

The steps used to update the parameters $\theta = \{\beta_0, \beta_1, \rho_1, \sigma^2\}$ by the zig-zag algorithm are summarised as follows.

Step 1: Choose starting values $\theta_{(0)}$.
Step 2: Update β_0 and β_1 using the first block in (7.17).
Step 3: Update ρ_1 using the second block in (7.17).
Step 4: Repeat steps 2 to 3 until convergence.
Step 5: Estimate σ^2 using (7.9) as the last step.

7.4.3   Cochrane-Orcutt

The zig-zag algorithm is equivalent to the Cochrane-Orcutt algorithm commonly used to estimate regression models with autocorrelated disturbance terms. To see this, consider the updating step of β_0 and β_1 in (7.17) where $I_{1,1}$ and G_1 are given in (7.16) and (7.18), respectively,

$$
\begin{bmatrix} \beta_0 \\ \beta_1 \end{bmatrix}_{(k)} = \begin{bmatrix} \beta_0 \\ \beta_1 \end{bmatrix}_{(k-1)} + \begin{bmatrix} \sum_{t=2}^{T} z_t z_t' \end{bmatrix}^{-1} \begin{bmatrix} \sum_{t=2}^{T} z_t v_t \end{bmatrix},
$$

where now $z_t = [1 - \rho_1, \ x_t - \rho_1 x_{t-1}]'$. Given that

$$v_t = y_t - \rho_1 y_{t-1} - \beta_0(1 - \rho_1) - \beta_1(x_t - \rho_1 x_{t-1})$$

$$= y_t - \rho_1 y_{t-1} - z_t' \begin{bmatrix} \beta_0 \\ \beta_1 \end{bmatrix},$$

the updating equation reduces to

$$\begin{bmatrix} \beta_0 \\ \beta_1 \end{bmatrix}_{(k)} = \left[\sum_{t=2}^{T} z_t z_t' \right]^{-1} \left[\sum_{t=2}^{T} z_t (y_t - \rho_1 y_{t-1}) \right].$$

This equation shows that the updated estimates of β_0 and β_1 are immediately obtained by simply regressing $y_t - \rho_1 y_{t-1}$ on z_t.

The updating step for ρ_1 in (7.17) can also be expressed in terms of a least squares regression by replacing $\sigma^2/(1 - \rho_1^2)$ in the $I_{2,2}$ term in (7.16) by u_{t-1}^2 to give

$$[\rho_1]_{(k)} = [\rho_1]_{(k-1)} + \left[\sum_{t=2}^{T} u_{t-1}^2 \right]^{-1} \left[\sum_{t=2}^{T} u_{t-1} v_t \right]$$

$$= [\rho_1]_{(k-1)} + \left[\sum_{t=2}^{T} u_{t-1}^2 \right]^{-1} \left[\sum_{t=2}^{T} u_{t-1}(u_t - \rho_{1(k-1)} u_{t-1}) \right]$$

$$= \left[\sum_{t=2}^{T} u_{t-1}^2 \right]^{-1} \left[\sum_{t=2}^{T} u_{t-1} u_t \right].$$

This equation shows that the updated estimate of ρ_1 is obtained immediately by simply regressing u_t on u_{t-1}.

The steps used to update the parameters $\theta = \{\beta_0, \beta_1, \rho_1, \sigma^2\}$ by the Cochrane-Orcutt algorithm are summarised as follows.

Step 1: Choose starting values $\theta_{(0)}$.
Step 2: Update β_0 and β_1 by regressing $y_t - \rho_1 y_{t-1}$ on $\{1 - \rho_1, x_t - \rho_1 x_{t-1}\}$.
Step 3: Update ρ_1 by regressing u_t on u_{t-1}.
Step 4: Repeat steps 2 and 3 until convergence.
Step 5: Estimate σ^2 using (7.9) as the last step.

Example 7.7 Cochrane-Orcutt Estimator of an AR(p) Model
Consider the autocorrelated regression model with an AR(p) disturbance

$$y_t = \beta_0 + \beta_1 x_t + u_t$$

$$u_t = \rho_1 u_{t-1} + \rho_2 u_{t-2} + \cdots + \rho_p u_{t-p} + v_t$$

$$v_t \sim iid\ N(0, \sigma^2).$$

The Cochrane-Orcutt algorithm consists of constructing the transformed variables

$$y_t^* = y_t - \rho_1 y_{t-1} - \rho_2 y_{t-2} - \cdots - \rho_p y_{t-p}$$
$$x_t^* = x_t - \rho_1 x_{t-1} - \rho_2 x_{t-2} - \cdots - \rho_p x_{t-p},$$

given starting values for $\rho_1, \rho_2, \cdots \rho_p$ and regressing y_t^* on a constant (scaled by $1 - \rho_1 - \rho_2 - \cdots - \rho_p$) and x_t^* to get updated values of β_0 and β_1. Next, regress u_t on $\{u_{t-1}, u_{t-2}, \cdots, u_{t-p}\}$ to get updated estimates of $\rho_1, \rho_2, \cdots, \rho_p$. Reconstruct the transformed variables y_t^* and x_t^* using the updated values of ρ_i and repeat the steps until convergence, which is assured by the findings in Sargan (1964).   □

The Cochrane-Orcutt algorithm is very similar to the Gauss-Newton algorithm since both procedures involve performing least squares regressions at each iteration. There are two main differences between these algorithms.

(1) All parameters are updated jointly in Gauss-Newton whereas in the Cochrane-Orcutt algorithm the regression parameters are updated separately to the autocorrelation parameters.
(2) Gauss-Newton uses v_t as the dependent variable in the updating of the regression and autocorrelation parameters, whereas Cochrane-Orcutt uses y_t^* as the dependent variable in the updating of the regression parameters and u_t as the dependent variable in the updating of the autocorrelation parameters.

7.5   Distribution Theory

The asymptotic distribution of the maximum likelihood estimator in the case of the autocorrelated regression model is now discussed. Special attention is given to comparing the asymptotic properties of this estimator with the ordinary least squares estimator based on misspecifying the presence of autocorrelation in the disturbance term. Finite sample properties of these estimators are explored in Section 7.9.2.

The asymptotic distributions of the maximum likelihood and ordinary least squares estimators are developed primarily for the AR(1) regression model

$$y_t = \beta x_t + u_t$$
$$u_t = \rho u_{t-1} + v_t \tag{7.19}$$
$$v_t \sim iid \, N(0, \sigma^2),$$

in which y_t is the dependent variable, x_t is a (scalar) exogenous variable assumed to be independent of the disturbance term v_t at all lags and the unknown parameters are $\theta = \{\beta, \rho, \sigma^2\}$ with the stationarity restriction $|\rho| < 1$. Both y_t

and x_t are assumed to have zero mean. As is demonstrated, an important feature of the asymptotic distributions is that they depend upon the data-generating process of x_t in (7.19).

7.5.1 Maximum Likelihood Estimator

The maximum likelihood estimator $\widehat{\theta}$ of the parameter vector $\theta = \{\beta, \rho, \sigma^2\}$ for the autocorrelated regression model (7.19) has all the properties discussed in Chapter 2. It is consistent, asymptotically efficient and has asymptotic distribution

$$\sqrt{T}(\widehat{\theta} - \theta_0) \xrightarrow{d} N(0, I(\theta_0)^{-1}), \tag{7.20}$$

in which $\theta_0 = \{\beta_0, \rho_0, \sigma_0^2\}$ is the true population parameter vector and $I(\theta_0)$ is the information matrix evaluated at the population vector θ_0. Given that the Gauss-Newton, zig-zag and Cochrane-Orcutt algorithms discussed in Section 7.4 are also maximum likelihood estimators, it immediately follows that these estimators also share the same asymptotic properties.

From equation (7.6) it follows that the gradient $g_t(\theta_0)$ at time t of the parameters of the AR(1) regression model in (7.19) consists of

$$g_{1,t} = \frac{1}{\sigma^2} v_t(x_t - \rho x_{t-1})$$

$$g_{2,t} = \frac{1}{\sigma^2} v_t u_{t-1}$$

$$g_{3,t} = -\frac{1}{2\sigma^2} + \frac{1}{2\sigma^4} v_t^2 \,.$$

Taking conditional expectations of $g_{1,t}$ yields

$$\mathrm{E}_{t-1}[g_{1,t}] = \mathrm{E}_{t-1}\left[\frac{1}{\sigma_0^2} v_t(x_t - \rho_0 x_{t-1})\right] = \frac{1}{\sigma_0^2}\mathrm{E}_{t-1}\left[v_t\right]\mathrm{E}_{t-1}\left[(x_t - \rho_0 x_{t-1})\right]$$
$$= 0 \,,$$

where the second last step is based on the assumption of x_t being independent of v_t, while the last step also uses the property $\mathrm{E}_{t-1}[v_t] = 0$. Similarly, for $g_{2,t}$ it follows that

$$\mathrm{E}_{t-1}[g_{2,t}] = \frac{1}{\sigma_0^2}\mathrm{E}_{t-1}[v_t u_{t-1}] = \frac{1}{\sigma_0^2}\mathrm{E}_{t-1}[v_t]u_{t-1} = 0 \,,$$

and finally for $g_{3,t}$

$$\mathrm{E}_{t-1}[g_{3,t}] = \mathrm{E}_{t-1}\left[-\frac{1}{2\sigma_0^2} + \frac{1}{2\sigma_0^4} v_t^2\right] = -\frac{1}{2\sigma_0^2} + \frac{1}{2\sigma_0^4}\sigma_0^2 = 0 \,,$$

since $\mathrm{E}_{t-1}[v_t^2] = \sigma_0^2$. The gradient vector $g_t(\theta_0)$ therefore satisfies the requirements of a mds. The mds central limit theorem from Chapter 2 therefore applies to conclude that

$$\frac{1}{\sqrt{T}} \sum_{t=2}^{T} g_t(\theta_0) \overset{d}{\to} N(0, \lim_{T \to \infty} E[g_t(\theta_0)g_t(\theta_0)']) \tag{7.21}$$

where by definition the information matrix is the limiting variance of the gradient, that is

$$I(\theta_0) = \lim_{T \to \infty} \text{var}(\frac{1}{\sqrt{T}} \sum_{t=2}^{T} g_t(\theta_0)). \tag{7.22}$$

The derivation of the asymptotic normality of the maximum likelihood estimator given in Chapter 2, based on a mean value expansion, then applies to conclude that

$$\sqrt{T}(\widehat{\theta} - \theta_0) \overset{d}{\to} N(0, I(\theta_0)^{-1}), \tag{7.23}$$

as usual.

Because the information matrix in equation (7.15) is block diagonal, the asymptotic distribution of the maximum likelihood estimator separates into three blocks

$$\sqrt{T}(\widehat{\beta} - \beta_0) \overset{d}{\to} N(0, I_{1,1}^{-1})$$

$$\sqrt{T}(\widehat{\rho} - \rho_0) \overset{d}{\to} N(0, I_{2,2}^{-1}) \tag{7.24}$$

$$\sqrt{T}(\widehat{\sigma}^2 - \sigma_0^2) \overset{d}{\to} N(0, I_{3,3}^{-1}).$$

For the conditional maximum likelihood estimator, the relevant information matrices follow from equation (7.16) and are, respectively,

$$I_{1,1} = -\lim_{T \to \infty} E\left[\frac{\partial^2 \ln L_T(\theta)}{\partial \beta^2}\right] = \lim_{T \to \infty} \frac{1}{\sigma_0^2(T-1)} \sum_{t=2}^{T} E[(x_t - \rho_0 x_{t-1})^2]$$

$$I_{2,2} = -\lim_{T \to \infty} E\left[\frac{\partial^2 \ln L_T(\theta)}{\partial \rho^2}\right] = \lim_{T \to \infty} E\left[\frac{1}{\sigma_0^2(T-1)} \sum_{t=2}^{T} \frac{\sigma_0^2}{1 - \rho_0^2}\right] = \frac{1}{1 - \rho_0^2}$$

$$I_{3,3} = -\lim_{T \to \infty} E\left[\frac{\partial^2 \ln L_T(\theta)}{\partial (\sigma^2)^2}\right] = \lim_{T \to \infty} E\left[\frac{1}{\sigma_0^2(T-1)} \sum_{t=2}^{T} \frac{1}{2\sigma_0^2}\right] = \frac{1}{2\sigma_0^4}.$$

It follows immediately that only in the case of the asymptotic distribution of $\widehat{\beta}$ does the form of the information matrix depend upon the assumptions made about the data-generating process of x_t. Two cases are considered next.

Case 1: Deterministic Exogenous Variables

In the case of deterministic x_t, the information matrix of $\widehat{\beta}$ is

$$I_{1,1} = \lim_{T \to \infty} \frac{1}{\sigma_0^2(T-1)} \sum_{t=2}^{T} (x_t - \rho_0 x_{t-1})^2 , \tag{7.25}$$

yielding the approximate variance

$$\text{var}(\widehat{\beta}) = \frac{1}{T-1} I_{1,1}^{-1} = \sigma_0^2 \left[\sum_{t=2}^{T} (x_t - \rho_0 x_{t-1})^2 \right]^{-1} . \tag{7.26}$$

Example 7.8 Simulation Experiment

Consider the AR(1) regression model

$$y_t = \beta_0 + \beta_1 x_t + u_t, \quad u_t = \rho u_{t-1} + v_t ,$$

where $v_t \sim iid\ N(0, \sigma^2)$, $x_t \sim iid\ U(-0.5, 0.5)$ which is fixed in repeated sampling, and the population parameters are $\theta_0 = \{\beta_0 = 1, \beta_1 = 1, \rho = 0.6, \sigma^2 = 10\}$. For a sample of size $T = 500$,

$$\sum_{t=2}^{500} (x_t - \rho x_{t-1})^2 = \sum_{t=2}^{500} (x_t - 0.6 x_{t-1})^2 = 57.4401 ,$$

and the asymptotic variance of $\widehat{\beta}_1$ using (7.26) is

$$\widehat{\beta}_1 = 10 \left[\sum_{t=2}^{T} (x_t - 0.6 x_{t-1})^2 \right]^{-1} = \frac{10}{57.4401} = 0.1741 .$$

The model is simulated 5000 times with the conditional maximum likelihood estimator computed at each replication. As x_t is deterministic it does not vary over the replications. The mean squared error in the case of $\widehat{\beta}_1$ is

$$\text{MSE} = \frac{1}{5000} \sum_{i=1}^{5000} (\widehat{\beta}_{1,i} - 1)^2 = 0.1686 ,$$

which agrees with the theoretical value of 0.1741. A plot of the standardised sampling distribution in Figure 7.2 reveals that it is normally distributed

$$z = \frac{\widehat{\beta}_1 - 1}{\sqrt{0.1686}} \xrightarrow{d} N(0, 1) . \qquad \square$$

Case 2: Stochastic and Independent Exogenous Variables

In the case where the exogenous variable x_t is stochastic and independent of u_t, it is possible to derive analytical expressions for the asymptotic variance of

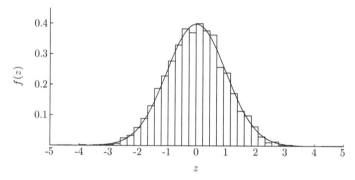

Figure 7.2. Standardised sampling distribution of the maximum likelihood estimator of the slope parameter in the autocorrelated regression model, based on 5000 Monte Carlo replications.

$\widehat{\beta}$ for certain data-generating processes. For example, assume that x_t in (7.19) is the stationary AR(1) process

$$x_t = \phi x_{t-1} + w_t, \qquad w_t \sim iid\ N(0, \eta^2), \tag{7.27}$$

where $|\phi| < 1$ and the corresponding population parameters are ϕ_0 and η_0^2. The information matrix is

$$I_{1,1} = \lim_{T \to \infty} \frac{1}{\sigma_0^2(T-1)} \sum_{t=2}^{T} E\left[x_t^2 - 2\rho_0 x_t x_{t-1} + \rho_0^2 x_{t-1}^2\right]$$

$$= \lim_{T \to \infty} \frac{1}{\sigma_0^2(T-1)} \sum_{t=2}^{T} \left(\frac{\eta_0^2}{1-\phi_0^2} - \frac{2\eta_0^2 \rho_0 \phi_0}{1-\phi_0^2} + \frac{\eta_0^2 \rho_0^2}{1-\phi_0^2} \right)$$

$$= \frac{\eta_0^2}{\sigma_0^2} \left(\frac{1 - 2\rho_0\phi_0 + \rho_0^2}{1-\phi_0^2} \right),$$

where the second line uses a result established in Chapter 13 that for the AR(1) process in (7.27) the autocovariance k periods apart is

$$E\left[x_t x_{t+k}\right] = \eta_0^2 \phi_0^k / \left(1 - \phi_0^2\right), \qquad k \geq 0.$$

The asymptotic variance of $\widehat{\beta}$ in this case is

$$\text{var}(\widehat{\beta}) \approx \frac{1}{T-1} I_{1,1}^{-1} = \frac{1}{(T-1)} \frac{\sigma_0^2}{\eta_0^2} \left(\frac{1-\phi_0^2}{1 - 2\rho_0\phi_0 + \rho_0^2} \right). \tag{7.28}$$

For the case where $\rho_0 = \phi_0$, this expression simplifies to

$$\text{var}(\widehat{\beta}) \approx \frac{1}{T-1} I_{1,1}^{-1} = \frac{1}{(T-1)} \frac{\sigma_0^2}{\eta_0^2}. \tag{7.29}$$

7.5.2 Least Squares Estimator

Consider the least squares estimator obtained by ignoring the autocorrelation in the disturbance term and simply regressing y_t on x_t. Despite misspecifying the dynamics of the model, the ordinary least squares estimator of β is still unbiased and asymptotically normally distributed, provided that x_t is independent of the disturbance term. The cost of ignoring the presence of autocorrelation is that estimation by ordinary least squares is, in general, asymptotically inefficient relative to the maximum likelihood estimator $\widehat{\beta}$ in (7.24).

Case 1: Deterministic Exogenous Variables

The first two derivatives of the log-likelihood function with respect to β in the AR(1) model in (7.19) are

$$\frac{\partial \ln L_T(\theta)}{\partial \beta} = \frac{1}{\sigma^2(T-1)} \sum_{t=2}^{T} v_t (x_t - \rho x_{t-1})$$

$$\frac{\partial^2 \ln L_T(\theta)}{\partial \beta^2} = -\frac{1}{\sigma^2(T-1)} \sum_{t=2}^{T} (x_t - \rho x_{t-1})^2 \ . \tag{7.30}$$

The ordinary least squares estimator is based on imposing the restriction of no autocorrelation, $\rho = 0$, so that these derivatives simplify to

$$\left.\frac{\partial \ln L_T(\theta)}{\partial \beta}\right|_{\rho=0} = \frac{1}{\sigma^2 T} \sum_{t=1}^{T} (y_t - \beta x_t) x_t \ ,$$

$$\left.\frac{\partial^2 \ln L_T(\theta)}{\partial \beta^2}\right|_{\rho=0} = -\frac{1}{\sigma^2 T} \sum_{t=1}^{T} x_t^2 \ , \tag{7.31}$$

since $v_t = u_t = y_t - \beta x_t$ in equation (7.19) when the restriction $\rho = 0$ is imposed and the sample period is now T. The ordinary least squares estimator is obtained by setting the first-order derivative in (7.31) to zero

$$\frac{1}{\sigma^2 T} \sum_{t=1}^{T} (y_t - \widehat{\beta}_{LS} x_t) x_t = 0 \ , \tag{7.32}$$

and solving for $\widehat{\beta}_{LS}$, giving

$$\widehat{\beta}_{LS} = \left[\sum_{t=1}^{T} x_t^2\right]^{-1} \sum_{t=1}^{T} x_t y_t = \beta_0 + \left[\sum_{t=1}^{T} x_t^2\right]^{-1} \sum_{t=1}^{T} x_t u_t \ .$$

With x_t fixed it is simple to show that $\widehat{\beta}_{LS}$ is unbiased, that is

$$E[\widehat{\beta}_{LS}] = \beta_0 + \left[\sum_{t=1}^{T} x_t^2\right]^{-1} \sum_{t=1}^{T} x_t E[u_t] = 0,$$

since $E[u_t] = 0$ for all t.

To show that the ordinary least squares estimator is asymptotically normal, rearranging (7.5.2) and multiplying both sides by $\sqrt{T}$ gives

$$\sqrt{T}(\hat{\beta}_{LS} - \beta_0) = \left[\frac{1}{T}\sum_{t=1}^{T}x_t^2\right]^{-1}\frac{1}{\sqrt{T}}\sum_{t=1}^{T}x_t u_t .$$

It is assumed that the term in square brackets on the right-hand side converges to a finite positive constant

$$\frac{1}{T}\sum_{t=1}^{T}x_t^2 \rightarrow \mathrm{E}[x_t].$$

When $|\rho_0| < 1$ and v_t is normally distributed, the AR(1) process u_t has zero mean, is mixing and all of its moments exist. Since x_t is fixed, the same applies to the product $x_t u_t$, which means the mixing central limit theorem given in equation (2.21) of Chapter 2 can be applied to yield

$$\frac{1}{\sqrt{T}}\sum_{t=1}^{T}x_t u_t \xrightarrow{d} N(0, J),$$

where

$$J = \lim_{T\to\infty}\mathrm{var}\left(\frac{1}{\sqrt{T}}\sum_{t=1}^{T}x_t u_t\right).$$

The variance is

$$\mathrm{var}\left(\frac{1}{\sqrt{T}}\sum_{t=1}^{T}x_t u_t\right) = \frac{1}{T}\mathrm{E}\left[\left(\sum_{t=1}^{T}x_t u_t\right)^2\right]$$

$$= \mathrm{E}\left[\left(\sum_{t=1}^{T}x_t^2 u_t^2 + 2\sum_{i=1}^{T-1}\sum_{t=1}^{T-i}x_t x_{t+i}u_t u_{t+i}\right)^2\right]$$

$$= \left(\sum_{t=1}^{T}x_t^2\mathrm{E}[u_t^2] + 2\sum_{i=1}^{T-1}\sum_{t=1}^{T-i}x_t x_{t+i}\mathrm{E}[u_t u_{t+i}]\right)$$

$$= \left(\sum_{t=1}^{T}x_t^2\frac{\sigma_0^2}{1-\rho_0^2} + 2\sum_{i=1}^{T-1}\sum_{t=1}^{T-i}x_t x_{t+i}\frac{\sigma_0^2\rho_0^i}{1-\rho_0^2}\right)$$

$$= \frac{\sigma_0^2}{(1-\rho_0^2)}\left(\sum_{t=1}^{T}x_t^2 + 2\sum_{i=1}^{T-1}\sum_{t=1}^{T-i}\rho_0^i x_t x_{t+i}\right),$$

$$(7.33)$$

since $\mathrm{E}[u_t u_{t+k}] = \sigma_0^2\rho_0^k/(1-\rho_0^2)$, $k \geqslant 0$, under the true model of first-order autocorrelation. The presence of autocorrelation implies that the gradient vector associated with the ordinary least squares estimator in this case is not a mds.

The efficiency of the least squares estimator is assessed by considering the information and outer product of the gradients matrices of this estimator. Using the second derivative in equation (7.31) gives the information matrix

$$I(\beta_0) = -E\left[\left.\frac{\partial^2 \ln L_T(\theta)}{\partial \beta^2}\right|_{\rho=0}\right] = \frac{1}{\sigma_0^2 T}\sum_{t=1}^T x_t^2 . \tag{7.34}$$

Using the square of the first derivative in (7.31) and taking expectations gives the outer product of gradients matrix

$$J(\beta_0) = E\left[\left(\frac{1}{\sigma^2 T}\sum_{t=1}^T (y_t - \beta_0 x_t)x_t\right)^2\right]$$

$$= \frac{1}{\sigma_0^2(1-\rho_0^2)}\left(\sum_{t=1}^T x_t^2 + 2\sum_{i=1}^{T-1}\sum_{t=1}^{T-i} \rho_0^i x_t x_{t+i}\right), \tag{7.35}$$

which follows immediately from (7.33). Comparing expressions (7.34) and (7.35) shows that $I(\beta_0) \neq J(\beta_0)$ and so the information equality of Chapter 2 does not hold for the ordinary least squares estimator in the case of misspecified autocorrelation. Only for the special case of no autocorrelation, $\rho_0 = 0$, does this equality hold. Chapter 9 shows that the remedy is to combine $I(\beta_0)$ and $J(\beta_0)$ by expressing the ordinary least squares variance as

$$\text{var}(\widehat{\beta}_{LS}) = \frac{1}{T}I^{-1}(\beta_0)\,J(\beta_0)\,I^{-1}(\beta_0) . \tag{7.36}$$

Substituting expressions (7.34) and (7.35) in (7.36) and simplifying yields the variance of the ordinary least squares estimator

$$\text{var}(\widehat{\beta}_{LS}) = \left[\sum_{t=1}^T x_t^2\right]^{-2}\left[\frac{\sigma_0^2}{1-\rho_0^2}\left(\sum_{t=1}^T x_t^2 + 2\sum_{i=1}^{T-1}\sum_{t=1}^{T-i}\rho_0^i x_t x_{t+i}\right)\right]. \tag{7.37}$$

In Chapter 9, the least squares estimator $\widehat{\beta}_{LS}$ with variance given by (7.37) is referred to as a quasi-maximum likelihood estimator.

A measure of relative efficiency is given by the ratio of the ordinary least squares variance in (7.37) and the maximum likelihood variance in (7.26)

$$\frac{\text{var}(\widehat{\beta}_{LS})}{\text{var}(\widehat{\beta})} = \frac{\left[\sum_{t=1}^T x_t^2\right]^{-2}\left[\sum_{t=1}^T x_t^2 + 2\sum_{i=1}^{T-1}\sum_{t=1}^{T-i}\rho_0^i x_t x_{t+i}\right]}{(1-\rho_0^2)\left[\sum_{t=2}^T (x_t - \rho_0 x_{t-1})^2\right]^{-1}}. \tag{7.38}$$

Values of this ratio greater than unity represent a loss of efficiency from using ordinary least squares. The extent of the loss in efficiency depends upon the form of x_t. In the special case of $\rho_0 = 0$, expression (7.38) equals unity and so the asymptotic efficiency of the two estimators is the same.

Example 7.9 Efficiency of $\bar{y}$ in the Presence of Autocorrelation

Let $x_t = 1$ in (7.19) so β represents the intercept. The ordinary least squares estimator of β is the sample mean and the asymptotic variance from (7.37) is

$$
\text{var}(\widehat{\beta}_{LS}) = \frac{T^{-2}\sigma_0^2}{1 - \rho_0^2} \left(T + 2 \sum_{i=1}^{T-1} \sum_{t=1}^{T-i} \rho_0^i \right)
$$

$$
= \frac{T^{-2}\sigma_0^2}{1 - \rho_0^2} \left(\frac{T(1 - \rho_0^2) - 2\rho_0(1 - \rho_0^T)}{(1 - \rho_0)^2} \right).
$$

Setting $x_t = 1$ in (7.26) gives the asymptotic variance of the conditional maximum likelihood estimator

$$
\text{var}(\widehat{\beta}) = \sigma_0^2 \left[\sum_{t=2}^{T} (1 - \rho_0)^2 \right]^{-1} = \frac{\sigma_0^2}{(T - 1)(1 - \rho_0)^2}.
$$

The efficiency ratio in (7.38) is now

$$
\frac{\text{var}(\widehat{\beta}_{LS})}{\text{var}(\widehat{\beta})} = \frac{T^{-2}\sigma_0^2}{1 - \rho_0^2} \left(\frac{T(1 - \rho_0^2) - 2\rho_0(1 - \rho_0^T)}{(1 - \rho_0)^2} \right) \times \frac{(T - 1)(1 - \rho_0)^2}{\sigma_0^2}.
$$

Upon taking limits

$$
\lim_{T \to \infty} \frac{\text{var}(\widehat{\beta}_{LS})}{\text{var}(\widehat{\beta})} = \lim_{T \to \infty} \left(\frac{T(T - 1)}{T^2} - 2\rho_0 \frac{(1 - \rho_0^T)(T - 1)}{1 - \rho_0^2} \frac{}{T^2} \right) = 1,
$$

so that the two estimators are asymptotically efficient. This result is a special case of a more general result established by Anderson (1971, p581). □

Case 2: Stochastic and Independent Exogenous Variables

In the case where the regressor x_t is stochastic, independent of u_t and has the AR(1) structure given in (7.27), it is, like u_t, stationary and mixing and it satisfies the WLLN, that is

$$
\frac{1}{T} \sum_{t=1}^{T} x_t^2 \xrightarrow{P} \text{E}[x_t^2] = \frac{\eta_0^2}{1 - \phi_0^2}.
$$

The product process $x_t u_t$ is therefore also stationary and mixing and satisfies the mixing central limit theorem given in (2.21) of Chapter 2 with variance of the form (2.22), resulting in

$$\lim_{T\to\infty} \text{var}\left(\frac{1}{\sqrt{T}} \sum_{t=1}^{T} x_t u_t\right) = \text{var}(x_t u_t) + 2\sum_{j=1}^{\infty} \text{cov}(x_t u_t, x_{t-j} u_{t-j})$$

$$= \text{var}(x_t)\text{var}(u_t) + 2\sum_{j=1}^{\infty} \text{cov}(x_t, x_{t-j})\text{cov}(u_t, u_{t-j})$$

$$= \frac{\eta_0^2}{1-\phi_0^2}\frac{\sigma_0^2}{1-\rho_0^2} + 2\sum_{j=1}^{\infty} \frac{\eta_0^2 \phi_0^j}{1-\phi_0^2}\frac{\sigma_0^2 \rho_0^j}{1-\rho_0^2}$$

$$= \frac{\eta_0^2}{1-\phi_0^2}\frac{\sigma_0^2}{1-\rho_0^2}\left(1 + 2\frac{\phi_0\rho_0}{1-\phi_0\rho_0}\right)$$

$$= \frac{\eta_0^2}{1-\phi_0^2}\frac{\sigma_0^2}{1-\rho_0^2}\frac{1+\phi_0\rho_0}{1-\phi_0\rho_0}.$$

Combining these limits in (7.5.2) shows that $\widehat{\beta}_{LS}$ is asymptotically normal with asymptotic variance

$$\text{var}(\widehat{\beta}_{LS}) \approx \frac{1}{T}\frac{\sigma_0^2}{\eta_0^2}\frac{1-\phi_0^2}{1-\rho_0^2}\frac{1+\phi_0\rho_0}{1-\phi_0\rho_0}.$$

Using this and (7.28), the asymptotic relative efficiency of the least squares estimator relative to the maximum likelihood estimator is

$$\lim_{T\to\infty} \frac{\text{var}(\widehat{\beta}_{LS})}{\text{var}(\widehat{\beta})} = \frac{(1-2\rho_0\phi_0+\rho_0^2)(1+\rho_0\phi_0)}{(1-\rho_0^2)(1-\rho_0\phi_0)}. \tag{7.39}$$

Example 7.10 Relative Efficiency

If $\rho_0 = \phi_0 = 0.6$, then from (7.39) the efficiency ratio is

$$\frac{\text{var}(\widehat{\beta}_{LS})}{\text{var}(\widehat{\beta})} = \frac{1+\rho_0^2}{1-\rho_0^2} = \frac{1+0.6^2}{1-0.6^2} = 2.125,$$

showing that the asymptotic variance of the ordinary least squares estimator is more than twice that of the maximum likelihood estimator. □

7.6 Lagged Dependent Variables

The set of exogenous variables x_t so far are assumed either to be deterministic, or if stochastic to be independent of the disturbance term u_t. This restriction of independence is now relaxed by augmenting the set of exogenous variables to include lags of the dependent variable. In the case of the AR(1) regression model in equation (7.19), an extension of this model is

$$
\begin{aligned}
y_t &= \beta x_t + \alpha y_{t-1} + u_t \\
u_t &= \rho u_{t-1} + v_t \\
v_t &\sim iid\, N(0, \sigma^2).
\end{aligned}
\tag{7.40}
$$

The parameter α controls the influence of y_{t-1} and is restricted to the range $-1 < \alpha < 1$. To estimate the parameters $\theta = \{\beta, \alpha, \rho, \sigma^2\}$ by maximum likelihood, the conditional log-likelihood function is given by

$$
\begin{aligned}
\ln L_T(\theta) &= \frac{1}{T-1} \sum_{t=2}^{T} \ln f(y_t \,|\, y_{t-1}, x_t, x_{t-1}; \theta) \\
&= -\frac{1}{2}\ln(2\pi) - \frac{1}{2}\ln\sigma^2 - \frac{1}{2\sigma^2(T-1)} \sum_{t=2}^{T} v_t^2,
\end{aligned}
\tag{7.41}
$$

in which

$$
\begin{aligned}
v_t &= u_t - \rho u_{t-1} \\
&= (y_t - \beta x_t - \alpha y_{t-1}) - \rho(y_{t-1} - \beta x_{t-1} - \alpha y_{t-2}).
\end{aligned}
\tag{7.42}
$$

The log-likelihood function is maximised with respect to θ using any of the algorithms discussed previously.

The maximum likelihood estimator remains consistent even where the regressors include lagged dependent variables. In this respect, it contrasts with the ordinary least squares estimator, obtained by regressing y_t on $\{1, x_t, y_{t-1}\}$, which is inconsistent because y_{t-1} is correlated with u_t via u_{t-1}. Asymptotic normality of the maximum likelihood estimator follows by invoking the martingale CLT as the gradient vector g_t, still represents a mds as the inclusion of the exogenous variable y_{t-1} is part of the conditioning set of information resulting in $E_{t-1}[g_t] = 0$.

An alternative efficient estimator for autocorrelated regression models with lagged dependent variables is given by Hatanaka (1974), which is explored further in Exercise 6.

Which is explored further in Exercise 6.

7.7 Testing

Consider the regression model where the disturbance term u_t is ARMA(p,q)

$$
\begin{aligned}
y_t &= \beta_0 + \beta_1 x_t + u_t \\
u_t &= \sum_{i=1}^{p} \rho_i u_{t-i} + v_t + \sum_{i=1}^{q} \delta_i v_{t-i} \\
v_t &\sim iid\, N(0, \sigma^2).
\end{aligned}
$$

A natural test of autocorrelation is a joint test based on the following null and alternative hypotheses:

$$H_0 : \rho_1 = \rho_2 = \cdots = \rho_p = \delta_1 = \delta_2 \cdots = \delta_q = 0 \quad \text{[No Autocorrelation]}$$
$$H_1 : \text{at least one restriction is violated} \quad \text{[Autocorrelation]}.$$

Some examples of other null hypotheses are

1.	Test for AR(1)	:	$H_0 : \rho_1 = 0$
2.	Test for MA(1)	:	$H_0 : \delta_1 = 0$
3.	Test for AR(2)	:	$H_0 : \rho_1 = \rho_2 = 0$
4.	Test for ARMA(1,1)	:	$H_0 : \rho_1 = \delta_1 = 0$
5.	Test for seasonal AR(k)	:	$H_0 : \rho_k = 0$.

The last hypothesis is of interest if autocorrelation is thought to be present in quarterly data ($k = 4$) or monthly data ($k = 12$).

Tests of autocorrelation can be based on the LR, Wald and LM test statistics developed in Chapter 4. The use of the scalar $T - s$, where $s = \max(p, q)$, in the LR and LM tests emphasises that they are constructed by conditioning the log-likelihood function on the first s observations. The LM version of the autocorrelation test has the advantage that it involves estimating the regression model under the null hypothesis only. It is for this reason that regression diagnostics often reported in computer packages are LM tests.

Example 7.11 Autocorrelation in United States Investment
The data used in Example 7.5 are revisited in order to test for first-order autocorrelation in the dynamic model of United States investment. The model is identical to the one presented in Example 7.5 and parameter estimates are based on the conditional log-likelihood function. The hypotheses tested are

$$H_0 : \rho_1 = 0, \qquad H_0 : \rho_1 \neq 0.$$

The LR statistic is computed as

$$LR = -2(T - 1)(\ln L_T(\widehat{\theta}_0) - \ln L_T(\widehat{\theta}_1))$$
$$= -2 \times 213 \times (1.814 + 1.811) = 1.278,$$

in which $\ln L_T(\widehat{\theta}_1) = 1.811$ is obtained from Table 7.1, while $\ln L_T(\widehat{\theta}_0) = -1.814$ is obtained by re-estimating the model subject to the restriction $\rho_1 = 0$. This statistic is distributed asymptotically as χ_1^2 under H_0. The p-value is 0.258 resulting in a failure to reject the null hypothesis at the 5% level of significance. To compute the Wald statistic, the unrestricted parameter estimates are given in Table 7.1

$$\widehat{\theta}_1 = [-0.275 \quad 1.567 \quad -0.334 \quad 0.091 \quad 2.228]',$$

while

$$R = [0 \ 0 \ 0 \ 1 \ 0], \qquad Q = [0],$$

and the covariance matrix of the unconstrained parameter estimates is

$$\text{cov}(\widehat{\theta}_1) = -\frac{1}{T} H_T^{-1}(\widehat{\theta}_1) = \begin{bmatrix} 0.025 & -0.006 & -0.013 & 0.002 & 0.000 \\ -0.006 & 0.017 & -0.009 & -0.006 & 0.000 \\ -0.013 & -0.009 & 0.027 & 0.002 & 0.000 \\ 0.002 & -0.006 & 0.002 & 0.007 & 0.000 \\ 0.000 & 0.000 & 0.000 & 0.000 & 0.047 \end{bmatrix}.$$

The Wald statistic is

$$W = T[R\widehat{\theta}_1 - Q]'[R(-H_T^{-1}(\widehat{\theta}_1))R']^{-1}[R\widehat{\theta}_1 - Q] = 1.266,$$

which is distributed asymptotically as χ_1^2 under H_0. The p-value is 0.261 yielding the same qualitative results as the LR test at the 5% level of significance. As this test is of a single restriction, an alternative form of the Wald statistic in this case is

$$\sqrt{W} = \sqrt{1.266} = 1.125,$$

which agrees with the t statistic reported for ρ_1 in Table 7.1 using the conditional maximum likelihood estimator. The LM statistic requires evaluating the gradients of the unrestricted model at the restricted estimates

$$G_T(\widehat{\theta}_0) = [0.000 \quad 0.000 \quad 0.000 \quad 0.067 \quad 0.000]',$$

while the pertinent covariance matrix based on the outer product of the gradients matrix is

$$J_T(\widehat{\theta}_0) = \begin{bmatrix} 0.446 & 0.235 & 0.309 & -0.079 & -0.103 \\ 0.235 & 0.960 & 0.286 & 0.339 & 0.046 \\ 0.309 & 0.286 & 0.493 & -0.114 & -0.085 \\ -0.079 & 0.339 & -0.114 & 1.216 & 0.144 \\ -0.103 & 0.046 & -0.085 & 0.144 & 0.227 \end{bmatrix}.$$

Using these terms in the LM statistic gives

$$LM = (T-1)G_T'(\widehat{\theta}_0)J_T^{-1}(\widehat{\theta}_0)G_T(\widehat{\theta}_0) = 0.988,$$

which is distributed asymptotically as χ_1^2 under H_0. The p-value is 0.320 thereby having the same qualitative outcome as the LR and W tests at the 5% level of significance. □

7.7.1 Alternative LM Test I

An alternative form of the Lagrange multiplier test of autocorrelation that is commonly used is based on replacing $J_T(\widehat{\theta}_0)$ by the information matrix $I(\theta)$ evaluated under the null hypothesis

$$LM = (T-1)G_T'(\widehat{\theta}_0)I^{-1}(\widehat{\theta}_0)G_T(\widehat{\theta}_0). \tag{7.43}$$

This alternative form of the LM test not only has the advantage of simplifying the implementation of the test, but it highlights how other well-known tests of autocorrelation can be interpreted as an LM test.

Consider once again the model in Example 7.2. The gradient in equation (7.6) evaluated under the null hypothesis $\rho_1 = 0$, becomes

$$G_T(\widehat{\theta}_0) = \frac{1}{\sigma^2(T-1)} \sum_{t=2}^{T} \begin{bmatrix} u_t \\ u_t x_t \\ u_t u_{t-1} \\ -\dfrac{1}{2} + \dfrac{u_t^2}{2\sigma^2} \end{bmatrix}, \tag{7.44}$$

because under the null hypothesis $v_t = u_t = y_t - \beta_0 - \beta_1 x_t$. The information matrix in (7.15) evaluated under the null hypothesis, $\rho_1 = 0$, is

$$I(\widehat{\theta}_0) = \frac{1}{\sigma^2(T-1)} \sum_{t=2}^{T} \begin{bmatrix} 1 & x_t & 0 & 0 \\ x_t & x_t^2 & 0 & 0 \\ 0 & 0 & u_{t-1}^2 & 0 \\ 0 & 0 & 0 & \dfrac{1}{2\sigma^2} \end{bmatrix}, \tag{7.45}$$

where the [3,3] cell is obtained by replacing σ^2 by u_{t-1}^2. This substitution also implies that the last cell of $G(\theta_0)$ is zero and this, together with the block-diagonal structure of the information matrix in (7.45), means that the LM statistic in (7.43) simplifies to

$$LM = \frac{1}{\widehat{\sigma}^2} \begin{bmatrix} \sum_{t=2}^{T} \widehat{u}_t \\ \sum_{t=2}^{T} \widehat{u}_t x_t \\ \sum_{t=2}^{T} \widehat{u}_t \widehat{u}_{t-1} \end{bmatrix}' \begin{bmatrix} T-1 & \sum_{t=2}^{T} x_t & 0 \\ \sum_{t=2}^{T} x_t & \sum_{t=2}^{T} x_t^2 & 0 \\ 0 & 0 & \sum_{t=2}^{T} \widehat{u}_{t-1}^2 \end{bmatrix}^{-1} \begin{bmatrix} \sum_{t=2}^{T} \widehat{u}_t \\ \sum_{t=2}^{T} \widehat{u}_t x_t \\ \sum_{t=2}^{T} \widehat{u}_t \widehat{u}_{t-1} \end{bmatrix}.$$

To understand the structure of this form of the LM test, it is informative to define $z_t = \{1, x_t, \hat{u}_{t-1}\}$, so that the LM statistic is rewritten as

$$
LM = \frac{1}{\hat{\sigma}^2} \left[\sum_{t=2}^{T} z_t \hat{u}_t \right]' \left[\sum_{t=2}^{T} z_t z_t' \right]^{-1} \left[\sum_{t=2}^{T} z_t \hat{u}_t \right]
$$

$$
= \frac{T-1}{\sum_{t=2}^{T} \hat{u}_t^2} \left[\sum_{t=2}^{T} z_t \hat{u}_t \right]' \left[\sum_{t=2}^{T} z_t z_t' \right]^{-1} \left[\sum_{t=2}^{T} z_t \hat{u}_t \right]
$$

$$
= (T-1)R^2, \tag{7.46}
$$

where the second step uses the definition $(T-1)\hat{\sigma}^2 = \sum_{t=2}^{T} \hat{u}_t^2$ and R^2 is the coefficient of determination from regressing $\hat{u}_t$ on z_t. In the case where the dependent variable does not have zero mean, the R^2 in (7.46) is the un-centered coefficient of determination.

This analysis suggests that the LM test can be constructed as follows.

Step 1: Regress y_t on a constant and x_t to get the residuals $\hat{u}_t$.
Step 2: Regress $\hat{u}_t$ on a constant, x_t and the lagged residual $\hat{u}_{t-1}$.
Step 3: Construct the test statistic $LM = (T-1)R^2$ where T is the sample size and R^2 is the coefficient of determination from the second-stage regression. Under the null hypothesis LM is asymptotically distributed as χ_1^2.

This version of the LM test is easily extended to test higher-order autocorrelation. For example, to test for autocorrelation of order p, the steps are as follows.

Step 1: Regress y_t on a constant and x_t, to get the residuals $\hat{u}_t$.
Step 2: Regress $\hat{u}_t$ on a constant, x_t and the lagged residuals $\hat{u}_{t-1}, \cdots, \hat{u}_{t-p}$.
Step 3: Construct the test statistic $LM = (T-p)R^2$, which is asymptotically distributed as χ_p^2 under the null hypothesis.

7.7.2   Alternative LM Test II

An alternative way to motivate the form of the Lagrange multiplier statistic in (7.46) is in terms of the Gauss-Newton algorithm. In the case of the regression model with an AR(1) disturbance, the steps are as follows. First, express the model with v_t as the dependent variable

$$
v_t = u_t - \rho_1 u_{t-1} = (y_t - \beta_0 - \beta_1 x_t) - \rho_1 (y_{t-1} - \beta_0 - \beta_1 x_{t-1}).
$$

Second, construct the derivatives

$$z_{1,t} = -\frac{\partial v_t}{\partial \beta_0} = 1 - \rho_1$$

$$z_{2,t} = -\frac{\partial v_t}{\partial \beta_1} = x_t - \rho_1 x_{t-1}$$

$$z_{3,t} = -\frac{\partial v_t}{\partial \phi_1} = y_{t-1} - \beta_0 - \beta_1 x_{t-1} .$$

Third, evaluate all terms under the null $\rho_1 = 0$

$$v_t = u_t$$

$$z_{1,t} = -\frac{\partial v_t}{\partial \beta_0} = 1$$

$$z_{2,t} = -\frac{\partial v_t}{\partial \beta_1} = x_t$$

$$z_{3,t} = -\frac{\partial v_t}{\partial \rho_1} = y_{t-1} - \beta_0 - \beta_1 x_{t-1} = u_{t-1} .$$

The regression of u_t on $\{z_{1,t}, z_{2,t}, z_{3,t}\}$ is the same regression equation used to construct (7.46).

7.7.3 Alternative LM Test III

An even simpler form of the LM test follows from noting that the gradient vector under the null hypothesis that $\rho_1 = 0$ is

$$G_T(\widehat{\theta}_0) = \frac{1}{\widehat{\sigma}^2(T-1)} \begin{bmatrix} \sum_{t=2}^{T} \widehat{u}_t \\ \sum_{t=2}^{T} \widehat{u}_t x_t \\ \sum_{t=2}^{T} \widehat{u}_t \widehat{u}_{t-1} \end{bmatrix} = \frac{1}{\widehat{\sigma}^2(T-1)} \begin{bmatrix} 0 \\ 0 \\ \sum_{t=2}^{T} \widehat{u}_t \widehat{u}_{t-1} \end{bmatrix} ,$$

and that $I_{2,2}(\widehat{\theta}_0)$ in expression (7.16) under the null hypothesis is

$$I_{2,2}(\widehat{\theta}_0) = 1.$$

Using these terms in expression (7.43) yields the LM statistic

$$LM_I = \frac{T-1}{\hat{\sigma}^4(T-1)^2} \left(\sum_{t=2}^{T} \hat{u}_t \hat{u}_{t-1} \right)^2 = (T-1) \left(\frac{\sum_{t=2}^{T} \hat{u}_t \hat{u}_{t-1}}{\sum_{t=2}^{T} \hat{u}_t^2} \right)^2$$

$$= (T-1)r_1^2,$$

in which r_1 is the first-order autocorrelation coefficient. The asymptotic distribution of this statistic under the null hypothesis is χ_1^2. It follows, therefore, that another form of the test can be based on $\sqrt{T-1}r_1$, whose asymptotic distribution under the null hypothesis is $N(0, 1)$.

7.8   Autocorrelation in Systems of Equations

Estimation and testing of systems of regression equations with autocorrelated disturbances in theory proceeds as in the case of single equations, although estimation is potentially computationally more demanding. An example of a bivariate system of equations with a vector AR(1) disturbance term is

$$y_{1,t} = \beta_1 y_{2,t} + \alpha_1 x_{1,t} + u_{1,t}$$
$$y_{2,t} = \beta_2 y_{1,t} + \alpha_2 x_{2,t} + u_{2,t},$$

where the disturbances follow

$$u_{1,t} = \rho_{1,1} u_{1,t-1} + \rho_{1,2} u_{2,t-1} + v_{1,t}$$
$$u_{2,t} = \rho_{2,1} u_{1,t-1} + \rho_{2,2} u_{2,t-1} + v_{2,t},$$

and

$$\begin{bmatrix} v_{1,t} \\ v_{2,t} \end{bmatrix} \sim iid \, N \left(\begin{bmatrix} 0 \\ 0 \end{bmatrix}, \begin{bmatrix} \sigma_{1,1} & \sigma_{1,2} \\ \sigma_{2,1} & \sigma_{2,2} \end{bmatrix} \right),$$

with $\sigma_{1,2} = \sigma_{2,1}$.

More generally, when the specification of systems of regression equations in Chapter 5 is used, a system of N regression equations with first-order vector autocorrelation is

$$By_t + Ax_t = u_t$$
$$u_t = Pu_{t-1} + v_t \qquad\qquad (7.47)$$
$$v_t \sim iid \, N(0, V),$$

in which y_t is a $(N \times 1)$ vector of dependent variables, x_t is a $(K \times 1)$ vector of exogenous variables, B is a $(N \times N)$ matrix, A is a $(N \times K)$ matrix, P is a

$(N \times N)$ matrix of autocorrelation parameters and V is the $(N \times N)$ covariance matrix of the disturbances. In the bivariate example

$$P = \begin{bmatrix} \rho_{1,1} & \rho_{1,2} \\ \rho_{2,1} & \rho_{2,2} \end{bmatrix} .$$

Higher-order vector autoregressive systems that include lagged dependent variables as exogenous variables, or even vector ARMA(p,q) models, can also be specified.

7.8.1 Estimation

The starting point for estimating the multivariate model with first-order vector autocorrelation by maximum likelihood is the pdf of v_t, assumed to be the multivariate normal distribution

$$f(v_t) = \left(\frac{1}{\sqrt{2\pi}}\right)^N |V|^{-1/2} \exp\left[-\frac{1}{2}v_t' V^{-1} v_t\right] .$$

The transformation of variable technique determines the density of u_t to be

$$
\begin{aligned}
f(u_t &| u_{t-1}, \cdots, u_1) \\
&= f(v_t)\frac{\partial v_t}{\partial u_t'} \\
&= \left(\frac{1}{\sqrt{2\pi}}\right)^N |V|^{-1/2} \exp\left[-\frac{1}{2}(u_t - Pu_{t-1})' V^{-1}(u_t - Pu_{t-1})\right] ,
\end{aligned}
$$

because $|\partial v_t / \partial u_t'| = 1$. Similarly, the transformation of variable technique determines the density of y_t to be

$$
\begin{aligned}
f(y_t &| y_{t-1}, \cdots, y_1, x_t, \cdots, x_1) \\
&= f(u_t)\frac{\partial u_t}{\partial y_t'} \\
&= \left(\frac{1}{\sqrt{2\pi}}\right)^N |V|^{-1/2} \exp\left[-\frac{1}{2}(u_t - Pu_{t-1})' V^{-1}(u_t - Pu_{t-1})\right] |B| ,
\end{aligned}
$$

as $|\partial u_t / \partial y_t'| = B$. Using $u_t = By_t + Ax_t$ the log-likelihood function for the tth observation is

$$\ln l_t(\theta) = -\frac{N}{2}\ln(2\pi) - \frac{1}{2}\ln|V| + \ln|B| - \frac{1}{2}v_t' V^{-1} v_t ,$$

where $v_t = u_t - Pu_{t-1}$. The conditional log-likelihood function is

$$\ln L_T(\theta) = \frac{1}{T-1}\sum_{t=2}^T \ln l_t(\theta) ,$$

which is maximised with respect to $\theta = \{B, A, P, V\}$ in the usual way.

Table 7.2. *Maximum likelihood estimates of the bivariate model with a vector AR(1) disturbance, using the BFGS algorithm with derivatives computed numerically. Standard errors and t statistics are computed based on the Hessian*

Parameter	Population	Estimate	se	t stat.
β_1	0.6	0.589	0.021	27.851
α_1	0.4	0.396	0.010	38.383
β_2	0.2	0.188	0.024	7.915
α_2	−0.5	−0.500	0.017	−29.764
$\rho_{1,1}$	0.8	0.801	0.027	29.499
$\rho_{1,2}$	0.1	0.078	0.034	2.277
$\rho_{2,1}$	−0.2	−0.189	0.028	−6.726
$\rho_{2,2}$	0.6	0.612	0.035	17.344

Example 7.12 Estimation of a Vector AR(1)Model

This example estimates a bivariate system of equations with a vector first-order autocorrelation disturbances using simulated data. The model in equations (7.47) is simulated for $T = 500$ observations with parameter matrices

$$B = \begin{bmatrix} 1 & -\beta_1 \\ -\beta_2 & 1 \end{bmatrix} = \begin{bmatrix} 1.000 & -0.600 \\ -0.200 & 1.000 \end{bmatrix}$$

$$A = \begin{bmatrix} -\alpha_1 & 0 \\ 0 & -\alpha_2 \end{bmatrix} = \begin{bmatrix} -0.400 & 0.000 \\ 0.000 & 0.500 \end{bmatrix}$$

$$P = \begin{bmatrix} \rho_{1,1} & \rho_{1,2} \\ \rho_{2,1} & \rho_{2,2} \end{bmatrix} = \begin{bmatrix} 0.800 & 0.100 \\ -0.200 & 0.600 \end{bmatrix}$$

$$V = \begin{bmatrix} \sigma_{1,1} & \sigma_{1,2} \\ \sigma_{2,1} & \sigma_{2,2} \end{bmatrix} = \begin{bmatrix} 1.0 & 0.5 \\ 0.5 & 1.0 \end{bmatrix}.$$

The exogenous variables are $x_{1,t} \sim U[0, 10]$ and $x_{2,t} \sim N(0, 9)$. The maximum likelihood estimates, given in Table 7.2, are statistically indistinguishable from their population parameter counterparts.   □

7.8.2 Testing

The LR, Wald and LM tests can all be used to test for autocorrelation in systems of equations. An example using the LR test follows.

Example 7.13 Likelihood Ratio Test of a Vector AR(1) Model

To test the null hypothesis of no autocorrelation in the system given by equation (7.47), the restrictions $\rho_{1,1} = \rho_{1,2} = \rho_{2,1} = \rho_{2,2} = 0$ are tested. For the simulated data generated in Example 7.12, the log-likelihood functions of the unrestricted and restricted models are given by

$$\ln L_T(\widehat{\theta}_1) = -2.804 \qquad \ln L_T(\widehat{\theta}_0) = -3.696\,,$$

respectively. The LR statistic is

$$LR = -2(T-1)\big(\ln L_T(\widehat{\theta}_0) - \ln L_T(\widehat{\theta}_1)\big)$$
$$= -2 \times (500-1) \times (-3.696 + 2.804) = 890.212\,,$$

which is distributed asymptotically as χ_4^2 under H_0. The p-value is 0.000 resulting in the null hypothesis being rejected at the 5% level. $\qquad\square$

7.9 Applications

7.9.1 Illiquidity and Hedge Funds

Getmansky, Lo and Makarov (2004) argue that as hedge funds tend to contain assets which are not actively traded, the returns they generate are relatively smoother than the returns generated by highly liquid assets such as the S&P500. In the case of the capital asset pricing model (CAPM), where the excess return on a hedge fund is expressed as a function of the excess return on the S&P500, the discrepancy in the autocorrelation properties of the two series should manifest itself in autocorrelation in the disturbance term.

The results of estimating the CAPM for Equity hedge fund data are (with standard errors in parentheses based on the Hessian)

$$r_{e,t} - f_t = \underset{(0.007)}{0.001} + \underset{(0.005)}{0.226}\,(m_t - f_t) + \widehat{u}_t\,,$$

in which $r_{e,t}$ is the return on the hedge fund, m_t is market return and f_t is the risk-free rate of return. The LM test of first-order autocorrelation yields a value of $LM = 20.490$. The number of restrictions is 1, yielding a p-value of 0.000 thereby suggesting significant evidence of serial correlation. Correcting the model for first-order autocorrelation yields the results

$$r_{e,t} - f_t = \underset{(0.008)}{0.001} + \underset{(0.006)}{0.217}\,(m_t - f_t) + \widehat{u}_t$$
$$\widehat{u}_t = \underset{(0.024)}{0.117}\widehat{u}_{t-1} + \widehat{v}_t\,.$$

Applying the LM test of first-order autocorrelation to these residuals results in a value of $LM = 3.356$. The p-value is now 0.067, showing that at the 5% significance level the adjusted model captures the autocorrelation in the residuals.

When this approach is repeated for the Convertible Arbitrage hedge fund with returns given by $r_{c,t}$, the estimated CAPM without any adjustment for autocorrelation is (with standard errors in parentheses based on the Hessian)

$$r_{c,t} - f_t = \underset{(0.011)}{-0.032} - \underset{(0.008)}{0.030}\,(m_t - f_t) + \widehat{u}_t\,.$$

The LM test of first-order autocorrelation yields a value of $LM = 118.409$. The number of restrictions is 1, yielding a p-value of 0.000 once again providing significant evidence of serial correlation. Correcting the model for first-order autocorrelation yields the results

$$r_{c,t} - f_t = \underset{(0.014)}{-0.032} - \underset{(0.008)}{0.053}\,(m_t - f_t) + \widehat{u}_t$$

$$\widehat{u}_t = \underset{(0.023)}{0.267}\widehat{u}_{t-1} + \widehat{v}_t\,.$$

Applying the LM test of first-order autocorrelation to these residuals results in a value of $LM = 22.836$. Unlike the results of the Equity Hedge fund, this result suggests that it is now necessary to make allowances for even higher autocorrelation because the residuals for the Convertible Arbitrage hedge fund still display significant autocorrelation.

7.9.2   Beach-MacKinnon Simulation Study

Beach and MacKinnon (1978) investigate the finite sampling properties of the exact and conditional maximum likelihood estimators using Monte Carlo experiments based on the AR(1) regression model

$$y_t = \beta_0 + \beta_1 x_t + u_t$$
$$u_t = \rho_1 u_{t-1} + v_t \tag{7.48}$$
$$v_t \sim iid\ N\left(0, \sigma^2\right)\,,$$

in which y_t is the dependent variable, x_t is the exogenous variable and u_t and v_t are disturbance terms. The population parameter values are $\theta_0 = \{\beta_0 = 1, \beta_1 = 1, \rho_1 = 0.6, \sigma^2 = 0.0036\}$. The sample sizes are $T = \{20, 50\}$, and the number of replications is 5000. Finally, the exogenous variable x_t is generated as

$$x_t = \exp\left(0.04t\right) + w_t, \qquad w_t \sim iid\ N(0, 0.0009)\,,$$

where t is a linear trend. The exogenous variable is treated as fixed in repeated samples by drawing random numbers for w_t only once and then holding these values fixed for each of the 5000 replications.

The bias and RMSE of the estimator, computed as

$$\text{Bias} = \frac{1}{5000}\sum_{i=1}^{5000}\widehat{\theta}_i - \theta_0, \qquad \text{RMSE} = \frac{1}{5000}\sum_{i=1}^{5000}(\widehat{\theta}_i - \theta_0)^2\,,$$

are given in Table 7.3. For comparative purposes, the least squares estimates of β_0 and β_1 obtained by regressing y_t on a constant and x_t and based on the

Table 7.3. *Monte Carlo performance of alternative estimators of the autocorrelated regression model parameters in (7.48). The bias and RMSE are expressed as a percentage. The number of replications is 5000*

Parameter	T	Exact Bias ($\times 100$)	Exact RMSE ($\times 100$)	Conditional Bias ($\times 100$)	Conditional RMSE ($\times 100$)	OLS Bias ($\times 100$)	OLS RMSE ($\times 100$)
β_0	20	−0.077	11.939	0.297	44.393	−0.045	12.380
	50	−0.069	3.998	−0.101	4.353	−0.084	4.080
β_1	20	0.026	7.315	−0.141	10.302	0.009	7.607
	50	0.027	1.060	0.034	1.114	0.031	1.091
ρ_1	20	−23.985	32.944	−24.189	33.267	n.a.	n.a.
	50	−8.839	15.455	−8.977	15.583	n.a.	n.a.
σ^2	20	−0.061	0.121	−0.068	0.126	n.a.	n.a.
	50	−0.022	0.073	−0.023	0.074	n.a.	n.a.

assumption of no autocorrelation, are also given. The results show a reduction in bias from using the exact over the conditional maximum likelihood estimators for all four parameter estimates. Both the exact and the conditional maximum likelihood estimators of ρ_1 and σ^2 are biased downwards. The exact maximum likelihood estimator also provides efficiency gains over the conditional maximum likelihood estimator in small samples. In the case of β_0, the ratio of the RMSEs of the conditional maximum likelihood estimator to the exact maximum likelihood estimator for $T = 20$ is $44.393/11.939 = 3.718$, indicating a large efficiency differential. The value of this ratio reduces quickly to $4.353/3.998 = 1.089$ for $T = 50$. In the case of β_1, the ratio for $T = 20$ is $10.302/7.315 = 1.408$ but reduces to $1.114/1.060 = 1.051$ when $T = 50$.

An interesting feature of the finite sample results in Table 7.3 is the performance of the least squares estimator of β_0 and β_1. For $T = 20$, this estimator has smaller bias than both the exact and conditional maximum likelihood estimators while still having lower bias than the conditional maximum likelihood estimator for $T = 50$. Nonetheless, the exact maximum likelihood estimator still exhibits better efficiency over the least squares estimator for $T = 20$.

7.10 Exercises

(1) Simulating a Regression Model with Autocorrelation

Program file(s) `auto_simulate.*`

(a) Simulate the following regression model with an AR(1) disturbance term for a sample of $T = 200$ observations

$$y_t = \beta_0 + \beta_1 x_t + u_t$$
$$u_t = \rho_1 u_{t-1} + v_t$$
$$v_t \sim iid\ N(0, \sigma^2),$$

with $\beta_0 = 2$, $\beta_1 = 1$, $\rho_1 = 0.95$ and $\sigma^2 = 9$ and with the exogenous variable generated as $x_t = 0.5t + w_t \sim iid\ N(0, 1)N(0, 1)$. Compare the simulated data to the conditional mean of y_t given by $\beta_0 + \beta_1 x_t$. Hence reproduce panel (a) of Figure 7.1.

(b) Simulate the following regression model with a MA(1) disturbance term for a sample of $T = 200$ observations

$$y_t = \beta_0 + \beta_1 x_t + u_t$$
$$u_t = v_t + \delta_1 v_{t-1}$$
$$v_t \sim iid\ N(0, \sigma^2),$$

with $\beta_0 = 2$, $\beta_1 = 1$, $\delta_1 = 0.95$ and $\sigma^2 = 9$ and with x_t constructed as before. Compare the simulated data to the conditional mean of y_t. Hence reproduce panel (b) of Figure 7.1.

(c) Simulate the following regression model with an AR(2) disturbance term for a sample of $T = 200$ observations

$$y_t = \beta_0 + \beta_1 x_t + u_t$$
$$u_t = \rho_1 u_{t-1} + \rho_2 u_{t-2} + v_t$$
$$v_t \sim iid\ N(0, \sigma^2),$$

with $\beta_0 = 2$, $\beta_1 = 1$, $\rho_1 = 0.1$, $\rho_2 = -0.9$ and $\sigma^2 = 9$ and with x_t constructed as before. Compare the simulated data to the conditional mean of y_t.

(d) Simulate the following regression model with an ARMA(2,2) disturbance term for a sample of $T = 200$ observations

$$y_t = \beta_0 + \beta_1 x_t + u_t$$
$$u_t = \rho_1 u_{t-1} + \rho_2 u_{t-2} + v_t + \delta_1 v_{t-1} + \delta_2 v_{t-2}$$
$$v_t \sim iid\ N(0, \sigma^2),$$

with $\beta_0 = 2, \beta_1 = 1, \rho_1 = 0.1, \rho_2 = -0.9, \delta_1 = 0.3, \delta_2 = 0.2$ and $\sigma^2 = 9$ and with x_t constructed as before. Compare the simulated data to the conditional mean of y_t.

(2) A Dynamic Model of United States Investment

Program file(s)	`auto_invest.*`, `auto_test.*`
Data file(s)	`usinvest.*`

This exercise uses quarterly United States data from March 1957 to September 2010. Consider the model

$$dri_t = \beta_0 + \beta_1 dry_t + \beta_2 rint_t + u_t$$
$$u_t = \rho_1 u_{t-1} + v_t$$
$$v_t \sim iid \, N(0, \sigma^2),$$

where dri_t is the quarterly percentage change in real investment, dry_t is the quarterly percentage change in real income, $rint_t$ is the real interest rate expressed as a quarterly percentage, and the parameters are $\theta = \{\beta_0, \beta_1, \beta_2, \rho_1, \sigma^2\}$.

(a) Plot the real investment series (dri_t) and interpret its time series properties.

(b) Estimate the model by exact maximum likelihood using the full log-likelihood function and conditional maximum likelihood. Compare the parameter estimates with the estimates reported in Table 7.1.

(c) Compute the standard errors using the Hessian matrix and the outer product of the gradients matrix.

(d) Test the hypotheses

$$H_0 : \rho_1 = 0, \qquad H_0 : \rho_1 \neq 0.$$

using a LR test, a Wald test, a LM test, a LM test based on the Gauss-Newton algorithm version and a LM test based on $\sqrt{T-1} \, r_1$, where r_1 is the first-order autocorrelation coefficient of the residuals obtained by estimating the constrained model.

(3) Asymptotic Distribution

Program file(s)	`auto_distribution.*`

Consider the model

$$y_t = \beta_0 + \beta_1 x_t + u_t$$
$$u_t = \rho u_{t-1} + v_t$$
$$v_t \sim iid \, N(0, \sigma^2),$$

where the exogenous variable x_t is a deterministic variable generated as $x_t \sim U(-0.5, 0.5)$, and the population parameters are $\theta_0 = \{\beta_0 = 1, \beta_1 = 1, \rho = 0.6, \sigma^2 = 10\}$.

(a) Simulate the model for $T = 500$ observations and use the expression in equation (7.26) to compute the asymptotic variance of the conditional maximum likelihood estimator of β_1. Compare this result by computing the MSE of $\widehat{\beta}_1$ using a Monte Carlo experiment with 5000 replications.
(b) Use the 5000 simulated values of $\widehat{\beta}_1$ calculated in part (a) to compute the standardised empirical distribution of $\widehat{\beta}_1$ and compare this distribution with the standard normal distribution.
(c) Repeat part (b) for the maximum likelihood parameter estimator of β_0 in the model

$$y_t = \beta_0 + u_t$$
$$u_t = \rho u_{t-1} + v_t$$
$$v_t \sim iid\ N(0, \sigma^2).$$

(4) Efficiency of the Sample Mean

Program file(s)   auto_mean.*

Consider the model

$$y_t = \beta + u_t$$
$$u_t = \rho u_{t-1} + v_t$$
$$v_t \sim iid\ N(0, \sigma^2).$$

(a) Prove that

$$T + 2\sum_{i=1}^{T-1}\sum_{t=1}^{T-i} \rho_0^i = \frac{T\left(1 - \rho_0^2\right) - 2\rho_0(1 - \rho_0^T)}{(1 - \rho_0)^2}.$$

Verify this result by computing the left-hand side for various values of T and the population parameter ρ_0.
(b) Derive an expression of the asymptotic variance of $\widehat{\beta}$ for the conditional maximum likelihood estimator.
(c) Derive an expression of the asymptotic variance of $\widehat{\beta}$ for the ordinary least squares estimator based on the assumption that $\rho = 0$.
(d) Compare the asymptotic variances of the conditional maximum likelihood estimator and the least squares estimator in parts (b) and (c), respectively, assuming population parameter values of $\rho_0 = 0.6$ and $\sigma_0^2 = 10$ and samples of size $T = \{5, 50, 500\}$.

(5) Relative Efficiency of Maximum Likelihood and Least Squares

---

Program file(s) `auto_efficiency.*`

In Section 7.5 it is shown that the relative efficiency of the maximum likelihood and least squares estimators in large samples depends upon the generating process of the exogenous variable x_t in the model

$$y_t = \beta_0 + \beta_1 x_t + u_t$$
$$u_t = \rho u_{t-1} + v_t$$
$$v_t \sim iid\, N\left(0, \sigma^2\right).$$

The following Monte Carlo experiments are based on the population parameter values $\theta_0 = \{\beta_0 = 1, \beta_1 = 1, \rho = 0.6, \sigma^2 = 0.0036\}$.

(a) Simulate the model for 5000 replications and samples of size $T = \{50, 100, 200, 500, 1000, 2000\}$ where the exogenous variable is a deterministic time trend $x_t = t$. Compute the MSE

$$MSE = \frac{1}{5000} \sum_{i=1}^{5000} (\widehat{\beta}_{j,i} - 1)^2, \quad j = 0, 1$$

of the maximum likelihood and least squares estimators of β_0 and β_1 and discuss the relative efficiency of the two estimators.

(b) Repeat part (a) with $x_t = \sin(2\pi t / T)$, a deterministic sinusoidal trend.

(c) Repeat part (a) where the exogenous variable is the stochastic time series

$$x_t = \phi x_{t-1} + w_t, \qquad w_t \sim N(0, 0.0036),$$

with $\phi = 0.6$. In the simulations, treat x_t as stochastic by redrawing w_t in each replication.

(i) Show that, as the sample size increases, the ratio of the MSE of the least squares and maximum likelihood estimators for the slope parameter β_1 converges to the asymptotic efficiency ratio given by

$$\frac{\left(1 - 2\rho_0\phi_0 + \rho_0^2\right)\left(1 + \rho_0\phi_0\right)}{\left(1 - \rho_0^2\right)\left(1 - \rho_0\phi_0\right)}.$$

(ii) Repeat the exercise for different values of ρ and ϕ.

(iii) Demonstrate that the asymptotic efficiency ratio is independent of the parameters β_0 and β_1 by choosing different values for these parameters in the experiments.

(iv) Demonstrate that the asymptotic efficiency ratio is independent of the parameters σ^2 and $\text{var}(w_t)$ by choosing different values for these parameters in the experiments.

(6) Hatanaka Estimator

Program file(s)   `auto_hatanaka.*`

Consider the model

$$y_t = \beta_0 + \beta_1 x_t + \alpha y_{t-1} + u_t$$
$$u_t = \rho u_{t-1} + v_t$$
$$v_t \sim iid\, N\left(0, \sigma^2\right).$$

(a) Assuming that x_t is deterministic, prove that

$$\text{cov}(y_{t-1}, u_t) = \frac{\rho_0 \sigma_0^2}{(1 - \alpha_0 \rho_0)\left(1 - \rho_0^2\right)},$$

where ρ_0, σ_0^2 and α_0 represent the population equivalents of ρ, α and σ^2, respectively.

(b) Letting the exogenous variable be $x_t \sim U(-0.5, 0.5)$ and choosing population parameter values of $\theta_0 = \{\beta_0 = 1, \beta_1 = 1, \alpha = 0.5, \rho = 0.6, \sigma^2 = 0.1\}$, verify the result in (a) by simulating the model for $T = 1000000$ and computing the sample covariance of y_{t-1} and u_t.

(c) Show how this model can be estimated using the Gauss-Newton algorithm.

(d) Compare the sampling properties of the Hatanaka estimator for various sample sizes with the maximum likelihood estimator, as well as with the ordinary least squares estimator based on a regression of y_t on a constant, x_t and y_{t-1}. Treat x_t as fixed in repeated sampling.

(7) Systems with Autocorrelation

Program file(s)   `auto_system.*`

Simulate the following bivariate system of equations with first-order vector autocorrelation disturbances for $T = 500$ observations

$$By_t + Ax_t = u_t$$
$$u_t = Pu_{t-1} + v_t$$
$$v_t \sim iid\, N(0, V),$$

in which

$$B = \begin{bmatrix} 1 & -\beta_1 \\ -\beta_2 & 1 \end{bmatrix} = \begin{bmatrix} 1.000 & -0.600 \\ -0.100 & 1.000 \end{bmatrix}$$

$$A = \begin{bmatrix} -\alpha_1 & 0 \\ 0 & -\alpha_2 \end{bmatrix} = \begin{bmatrix} -0.400 & 0.000 \\ 0.000 & 0.500 \end{bmatrix}$$

$$P = \begin{bmatrix} \rho_{1,1} & \rho_{1,2} \\ \rho_{2,1} & \rho_{2,2} \end{bmatrix} = \begin{bmatrix} 0.800 & 0.100 \\ -0.200 & 0.600 \end{bmatrix}$$

$$V = \begin{bmatrix} \sigma_{1,1} & \sigma_{1,2} \\ \sigma_{2,1} & \sigma_{2,2} \end{bmatrix} = \begin{bmatrix} 1.0 & 0.5 \\ 0.5 & 1.0 \end{bmatrix}.$$

The exogenous variables are $x_{1,t} \sim iid\ U[0, 10]$ and $x_{2,t} \sim iid\ N(0, 9)$, which are independent of each other.

(a) Estimate the model using the conditional maximum likelihood estimator and compare the results with the parameter estimates reported in Table 7.2.

(b) Perform a LR test of the following restrictions and interpret the results.
   (i) $\rho_{1,1} = \rho_{1,2} = \rho_{2,1} = \rho_{2,2} = 0$.
   (ii) $\rho_{1,2} = \rho_{2,1} = 0$.

(c) Perform a Wald test of the following restrictions and interpret the results.
   (i) $\rho_{1,1} = \rho_{1,2} = \rho_{2,1} = \rho_{2,2} = 0$.
   (ii) $\rho_{1,1} = \rho_{2,2}, \rho_{1,2} = \rho_{2,1}$.

(d) Repeat parts (a) to (c), except simulate the model with no autocorrelation

$$P = \begin{bmatrix} \rho_{1,1} & \rho_{1,2} \\ \rho_{2,1} & \rho_{2,2} \end{bmatrix} = \begin{bmatrix} 0 & 0 \\ 0 & 0 \end{bmatrix}.$$

(8) Illiquidity and Hedge Funds

Program file(s)	auto_hedge.*
Data file(s)	hedge.*

The data consist of $T = 1869$ daily returns for the period 1 April 2003 to the 28 May 2010 on seven hedge funds (Convertible Arbitrage, Distressed Securities, Equity Hedge, Event Driven, Macro, Merger Arbitrage, Equity Market Neutral) and three market indexes (Dow, NASDAQ and S&P500).

(a) For each of the seven hedge funds, estimate the CAPM

$$r_{i,t} - f_t = \beta_0 + \beta_1(m_t - f_t) + u_t,$$

in which $r_{i,t}$ is the return on a hedge fund, m_t is the market return and f_t is the risk-free interest rate. Interpret the parameter estimates. Test for an AR(1) disturbance term.

(b) For each of the seven hedge funds, estimate a dynamic CAPM where

$$u_t = \rho y_{t-1} + v_t \,,$$

and reapply the LM test to the estimated residuals.

(9) Beach-MacKinnon Monte Carlo Study

Program file(s)   `auto_beachmack.g`

Simulate the model

$$y_t = \beta_0 + \beta_1 x_t + u_t$$
$$u_t = \rho_1 u_{t-1} + v_t$$
$$v_t \sim iid\ N(0, \sigma^2) \,,$$

with the population parameters given by

$$\theta_0 = \{\beta_0 = 1, \beta_1 = 1, \rho_1 = 0.6, \sigma^2 = 0.0036\} \,,$$

and the exogenous variable x_t is generated as $x_t \sim \exp(0.04t) + w_t$, where $w_t \sim iid\ N(0, 0.0009)$.

(a) For 200 replications and $T = 20$ observations, compute the following statistics

$$\text{Mean} \quad = \frac{1}{200} \sum_{i=1}^{200} \widehat{\theta}_i$$

$$\text{Bias} \quad = \theta_0 - \frac{1}{200} \sum_{i=1}^{200} \widehat{\theta}_i$$

$$\text{MSE} \quad = \frac{1}{200} \sum_{i=1}^{200} (\widehat{\theta}_i - \theta_0)^2$$

$$\text{RMSE} \quad = \sqrt{MSE}$$

$$\text{Efficiency} = \frac{\text{var}(\widehat{\theta}_{LS})}{\text{var}(\widehat{\theta})} \,,$$

where $\widehat{\theta}$ is the conditional maximum likelihood estimator and $\widehat{\theta}_{LS}$ is the least squares estimator without any adjustment for autocorrelation.

(b) Repeat part (a) using $T = 50$ and comment on the asymptotic properties of the estimators.

(c) Repeat parts (a) and (b) for $\rho_1 = \{0.8, 0.99\}$ and discuss the results.

(d) Repeat parts (a) to (c) where the exogenous variable x_t is the white noise process $x_t \sim iid\ N(0, 0.0625)$, and compare the results with the case of a trending x_t variable.

(e) For the stationary x_t variable case in part (d) compare the MSE of $\widehat{\beta}_1$ to the corresponding asymptotic variances of the maximum likelihood and least squares estimators given in Harvey (1990, pp197–198),

$$\text{MLE:} \quad \text{var}(\widehat{\beta}_1) = \frac{1}{T} \frac{\sigma^2}{\sigma_x^2} \frac{1}{1 + \rho_1^2}$$

$$\text{OLS:} \quad \text{var}(\widehat{\beta}_1) = \frac{1}{T} \frac{\sigma^2}{\sigma_x^2} \frac{1}{1 - \rho_1^2},$$

and compare the simulated efficiency results with the asymptotic efficiency ratio given by

$$\frac{\sqrt{1 + \rho_1^2}}{\sqrt{1 - \rho_1^2}}.$$

(f) Repeat parts (a) to (d) for 10000 and 20000 replications, and discuss the sensitivity of the simulation results to the number of replications.

8   Heteroskedastic Regression Models

8.1   Introduction

The regression models considered in Chapters 5 to 7 allow for the mean of the distribution of the dependent variable to vary over time by specifying the mean as a function of a set of exogenous variables. An important feature of these models is that the mean is specified to be time-varying but the variance is assumed to be constant, or homoskedastic. A natural extension of homoskedastic regression models, therefore, is to specify the variance as a function of a set of exogenous variables thereby allowing the variance to be time-varying as well. This class of model is referred to as the heteroskedastic regression model.

In this chapter, the maximum likelihood framework is applied to estimating and testing the heteroskedastic regression model. More general models, in which both heteroskedasticity and autocorrelation structures are present in systems of equations by combining the variance specifications of this chapter with the autocorrelation specifications of Chapter 7, are also considered. In specifying this class of model, the parametric form of the distribution of the disturbances is usually assumed to be normal but this assumption can also be relaxed.

As with the autocorrelated regression model, estimators and testing procedures commonly applied to the heteroskedastic regression model are shown to be special cases of the maximum likelihood framework developed in Part ONE. The estimators that are discussed include weighted least squares and zig-zag algorithms, while the tests that are covered include the Breusch-Pagan and White tests of heteroskedasticity.

8.2   Specification

The classical linear regression model is

$$y_t = \beta_0 + \beta_1 x_t + u_t \qquad u_t \sim iid\, N(0, \sigma^2), \tag{8.1}$$

Table 8.1. *Descriptive statistics on the daily percentage change in*
bond yields for selected maturities in the United States on FOMC
event dates and non-event days for the period 1 October 1993 to
31 December 2003

Maturity	Mean		Variance	
	Event	Non-event	Event	Non-event
3-month	−0.0290	0.0002	0.0091	0.0023
6-month	−0.0280	0.0001	0.0081	0.0018
1-year	−0.0190	−0.0002	0.0077	0.0024
2-year	−0.0147	−0.0003	0.0084	0.0038
3-year	−0.0155	−0.0002	0.0082	0.0041
5-year	−0.0124	−0.0002	0.0074	0.0043
7-year	−0.0077	−0.0002	0.0059	0.0042
10-year	−0.0051	−0.0002	0.0045	0.0038

where y_t is the dependent variable, x_t is the exogenous variable and u_t is the
disturbance term. To allow for a time-varying variance in equation (8.1), the
model is rewritten as

$$y_t = \beta_0 + \beta_1 x_t + u_t \qquad u_t \sim N(0, \sigma_t^2), \tag{8.2}$$

where u_t remains independently distributed across t. The form of the time-
varying variance in equation (8.2) is usually specified parametrically. To motivate potential specifications of the variance consider the following example of
the effects of monetary policy on asset markets.

Example 8.1 Effects of Monetary Policy on Asset Markets
    The Federal Reserve Open Market Committee (FOMC) meets on selected
days during the year, known as event days, to determine monetary policy
in the United States. To investigate the effects of monetary policy on bond
markets, Table 8.1 gives descriptive statistics of the daily percentage change in
bond yields in the United States for selected maturities from 1 October 1993 to
31 December 2003, a total of $T = 2583$ observations. There is an increase in the
variance of the change in yields for all maturities on event days. Furthermore,
it is the shorter maturities that exhibit the largest increase in variance on event
days with the effect dissipating for the yields on longer maturities of 7 and
10 years.   □

If w_t is an exogenous exogenous variable and d_t is a suitably defined dummy variable, then some common specifications of heteroskedasticity are as follows.

1. Step   : $\sigma_t^2 = \gamma_0 + \gamma_1 d_t$
2. Linear   : $\sigma_t^2 = \gamma_0 + \gamma_1 w_t$
3. Power   : $\sigma_t^2 = \gamma_0 + \gamma_1 w_t^2$
4. Multiplicative : $\sigma_t^2 = \exp(\gamma_0 + \gamma_1 w_t)$.

An important property of σ_t^2 is that it must remain positive for all t. The step function allows for two variances over the sample given by γ_0 and $\gamma_0 + \gamma_1$. An example of this type of specification is presented in the previous example. Provided that the parameters γ_0 and $\gamma_0 + \gamma_1$ are restricted to be positive, the resultant estimate of σ_t^2 is positive. The linear heteroskedasticity model specifies the time variation in the variance as a linear function of the exogenous variable w_t. Even if γ_0, $\gamma_1 > 0$, negative values of the exogenous variable w_t may result in a negative estimate of the variance. The power specification restricts the w_t to be positive so that, if the restrictions γ_0, $\gamma_1 > 0$ are enforced, this specification ensures that the variance is positive for all t. The importance and practical appeal of the multiplicative variance specification is that the estimate of the time-varying variance is guaranteed to be positive without the need to restrict the sign of the parameters or w_t. Examples of these last two specifications are widely used in ARCH models discussed in Chapter 20.

Example 8.2 A Regression Model with Heteroskedasticity
Consider the regression model

$$y_t = \beta_0 + \beta_1 x_t + u_t$$
$$\sigma_t^2 = \gamma_0 + \gamma_1 w_t$$
$$u_t \sim N(0, \sigma_t^2),$$

in which x_t and w_t are exogenous variables and the unknown parameters are $\theta = \{\beta_0, \beta_1, \gamma_0, \gamma_1\}$. The conditional distribution of y_t is

$$f(y|x_t, w_t; \theta) = \frac{1}{\sqrt{2\pi\sigma_t^2}} \exp\left[-\frac{(y - \beta_0 - \beta_1 x_t)^2}{2\sigma_t^2} \right],$$

where the conditional mean of y_t is $\beta_0 + \beta_1 x_t$ and the conditional variance of y_t is $\gamma_0 + \gamma_1 w_t$. In this example, both the mean and the variance of the distribution of y_t are time-varying: the former because of changes in x_t over time and the latter because of changes in w_t over time. Thus, each observation of y_t is drawn from a different distribution for each and every t.

Figure 8.1 illustrates a variety of scatterplots of $T = 500$ observations simulated from this model, where $x_t \sim iid\ N(0, 1)$, $w_t = t$ is a linear time trend and $\theta_0 = \{\beta_0 = 1, \beta_1 = 2, \gamma_0 = 1, \gamma_1 = 0.5\}$ are the population parameters.

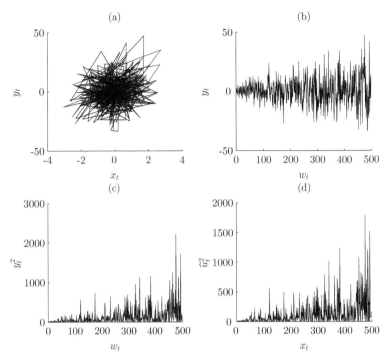

Figure 8.1. Scatterplots of the simulated data from the regression model with heteroskedasticity.

The scatterplot of y_t and x_t in panel (a) of Figure 8.1 does not reveal any evidence of heteroskedasticity. By contrast, the scatterplot between y_t and w_t in panel (b) does provide evidence of a heteroskedastic structure in the variance. The scatterplot in panel (c), between y_t^2 and w_t, provides even stronger evidence of a heteroskedastic structure in the variance, as does panel (d), which replaces y_t^2 with $\widehat{u}_t^2$, where $\widehat{u}_t$ is the ordinary least squares residual of the regression of y_t on a constant and x_t.   □

For the regression model with heteroskedasticity, let $\beta = \{\beta_0, \beta_1, \cdots \beta_K\}$ be the parameters of the mean equation and let $\gamma = \{\gamma_0, \gamma_1, \cdots, \gamma_P\}$ be the parameters of the variance equation. The unknown parameters are, therefore, $\theta = \{\beta_0, \beta_1, \cdots, \beta_K, \gamma_0, \gamma_1, \cdots, \gamma_P\}$, which are to be estimated by maximum likelihood. A general form for the log-likelihood function of the heteroskedastic regression model is

$$\ln L_T(\theta) = \frac{1}{T} \sum_{t=1}^{T} \ln f(y_t \mid x_t, w_t; \theta), \qquad (8.3)$$

where the form of the pdf $f(y_t \mid x_t, w_t; \theta)$ is derived from the assumptions of the regression model using the transformation of variable method.

Example 8.3 Multiplicative Heteroskedasticity

Consider the linear regression model with a multiplicative heteroskedastic disturbance

$$y_t = \beta_0 + \beta_1 x_t + u_t, \qquad u_t \sim N(0, \sigma_t^2),$$
$$\sigma_t^2 = \exp(\gamma_0 + \gamma_1 w_t),$$

in which x_t and w_t are exogenous variables and the unknown parameters are $\theta = \{\beta_0, \beta_1, \gamma_0, \gamma_1\}$. Given the distributional assumptions made for u_t, the distribution of y_t is

$$f(y_t \mid x_t, w_t; \theta) = \frac{1}{\sqrt{2\pi \sigma_t^2}} \exp\left[-\frac{(y_t - \beta_0 - \beta_1 x_t)^2}{2\sigma_t^2}\right].$$

Using the multiplicative specification for σ_t^2, the log-likelihood function for a sample of T observations is

$$\ln L_T(\theta) = -\frac{1}{2}\ln(2\pi) - \frac{1}{2T}\sum_{t=1}^{T}(\gamma_0 + \gamma_1 w_t) - \frac{1}{2T}\sum_{t=1}^{T}\frac{(y_t - \beta_0 - \beta_1 x_t)^2}{\exp(\gamma_0 + \gamma_1 w_t)}.$$

$\square$

8.3   Estimation

8.3.1   Maximum Likelihood

The log-likelihood function of the heteroskedastic regression model may be maximised with respect to the unknown model parameters, θ, using any of the iterative algorithms described in Chapter 3. The algorithms investigated are the Newton-Raphson algorithm and the scoring algorithm where the latter is shown to be related to the weighted least squares estimator.

In the case of the Newton-Raphson algorithm, the parameter vector is updated at iteration k as

$$\theta_{(k)} = \theta_{(k-1)} - H_{(k-1)}^{-1} G_{(k-1)},$$

where the gradient and the Hessian are, respectively,

$$G_{(k-1)} = \left.\frac{\partial \ln L_T(\theta)}{\partial \theta}\right|_{\theta = \theta_{(k-1)}} \qquad H_{(k-1)} = \left.\frac{\partial^2 \ln L_T(\theta)}{\partial \theta \partial \theta'}\right|_{\theta = \theta_{(k-1)}}.$$

Example 8.4 Newton-Raphson Algorithm

The gradient of the multiplicative heteroskedastic model with parameters $\theta = \{\beta_0, \beta_1, \gamma_0, \gamma_1\}$ specified in Example 8.3 is

$$
G_T(\theta) =
\begin{bmatrix}
\dfrac{1}{T} \displaystyle\sum_{t=1}^{T} \dfrac{u_t}{\sigma_t^2} \\[2ex]
\dfrac{1}{T} \displaystyle\sum_{t=1}^{T} \dfrac{x_t u_t}{\sigma_t^2} \\[2ex]
-\dfrac{1}{2} + \dfrac{1}{2T} \displaystyle\sum_{t=1}^{T} \dfrac{u_t^2}{\sigma_t^2} \\[2ex]
-\dfrac{1}{2T} \displaystyle\sum_{t=1}^{T} w_t + \dfrac{1}{2T} \displaystyle\sum_{t=1}^{T} \dfrac{w_t u_t^2}{\sigma_t^2}
\end{bmatrix},
$$

and the Hessian, $H_T(\theta)$, is

$$
\begin{bmatrix}
-\dfrac{1}{T} \displaystyle\sum_{t=1}^{T} \dfrac{1}{\sigma_t^2} & -\dfrac{1}{T} \displaystyle\sum_{t=1}^{T} \dfrac{x_t}{\sigma_t^2} & -\dfrac{1}{T} \displaystyle\sum_{t=1}^{T} \dfrac{u_t}{\sigma_t^2} & -\dfrac{1}{T} \displaystyle\sum_{t=1}^{T} \dfrac{w_t u_t}{\sigma_t^2} \\[2ex]
-\dfrac{1}{T} \displaystyle\sum_{t=1}^{T} \dfrac{x_t}{\sigma_t^2} & -\dfrac{1}{T} \displaystyle\sum_{t=1}^{T} \dfrac{x_t^2}{\sigma_t^2} & -\dfrac{1}{T} \displaystyle\sum_{t=1}^{T} \dfrac{x_t u_t}{\sigma_t^2} & -\dfrac{1}{T} \displaystyle\sum_{t=1}^{T} \dfrac{x_t w_t u_t}{\sigma_t^2} \\[2ex]
-\dfrac{1}{T} \displaystyle\sum_{t=1}^{T} \dfrac{u_t}{\sigma_t^2} & -\dfrac{1}{T} \displaystyle\sum_{t=1}^{T} \dfrac{x_t u_t}{\sigma_t^2} & -\dfrac{1}{2T} \displaystyle\sum_{t=1}^{T} \dfrac{u_t^2}{\sigma_t^2} & -\dfrac{1}{2T} \displaystyle\sum_{t=1}^{T} \dfrac{w_t u_t^2}{\sigma_t^2} \\[2ex]
-\dfrac{1}{T} \displaystyle\sum_{t=1}^{T} \dfrac{w_t u_t}{\sigma_t^2} & -\dfrac{1}{T} \displaystyle\sum_{t=1}^{T} \dfrac{x_t w_t u_t}{\sigma_t^2} & -\dfrac{1}{2T} \displaystyle\sum_{t=1}^{T} \dfrac{w_t u_t^2}{\sigma_t^2} & -\dfrac{1}{2T} \displaystyle\sum_{t=1}^{T} \dfrac{w_t^2 u_t^2}{\sigma_t^2}
\end{bmatrix},
$$

where $u_t = y_t - \beta_0 - \beta_1 x_t$ and $\sigma_t^2 = \exp(\gamma_0 + \gamma_1 w_t)$.

The data are simulated using parameter values $\theta_0 = \{\beta_0 = 1, \beta_1 = 2, \gamma_0 = 0.1, \gamma_1 = 0.1\}$. The exogenous variables are defined as $x_t \sim iid\ N(0, 1)$ and $w_t = t/10$, $t = 0, 1, 2, \cdots$. The results of estimating the heteroskedastic regression model using the Newton-Raphson algorithm are given in Table 8.2. The point estimates agree satisfactorily with the population parameters. For comparison, the estimates of the homoskedastic model, with the restriction $\gamma_1 = 0$, are also reported. □

An alternative algorithm to Newton-Raphson is the method of scoring, which replaces the Hessian in equation (8.31) by the information matrix, $I(\theta)$. The scoring algorithm updating scheme is

$$
\theta_{(k)} = \theta_{(k-1)} + I_{(k-1)}^{-1} G_{(k-1)},
$$

Table 8.2. *Maximum likelihood estimates of the multiplicative heteroskedasticity model. Standard errors based on the inverse of the Hessian matrix are in parentheses*

Parameter	Heteroskedastic Model	Homoskedastic Model
β_0	0.949	0.753
	(0.105)	(0.254)
β_1	1.794	2.136
	(0.103)	(0.240)
γ_0	0.121	3.475
	(0.121)	(0.063)
γ_1	0.098	0.000
	(0.004)	
$\ln L_T(\theta)$	-2.699	-3.157

where the gradient and the information matrix are respectively defined as

$$G_{(k-1)} = \frac{\partial \ln L_T(\theta)}{\partial \theta}\bigg|_{\theta=\theta_{(k-1)}}, \quad I_{(k-1)} = -E\left[\frac{\partial^2 \ln L_T(\theta)}{\partial \theta \partial \theta'}\right]\bigg|_{\theta=\theta_{(k-1)}}.$$

Example 8.5 Scoring Algorithm

In the case of the multiplicative heteroskedastic regression model of Example 8.3, the information matrix is obtained from the Hessian matrix in Example 8.4 by recognising that

$$E[y_t - \beta_0 - \beta_1 x_t] = 0$$

$$E\left[\frac{(y_t - \beta_0 - \beta_1 x_t)^2}{\exp(\gamma_0 + \gamma_1 w_t)}\right] = E\left[\frac{u_t^2}{\sigma_t^2}\right] = 1.$$

The information matrix is, therefore, the block-diagonal matrix

$$I(\theta) = -E\left[\frac{\partial^2 \ln L_T(\theta)}{\partial \theta \partial \theta'}\right]$$

$$= E\begin{bmatrix} \dfrac{1}{T}\displaystyle\sum_{t=1}^{T}\dfrac{1}{\sigma_t^2} & \dfrac{1}{T}\displaystyle\sum_{t=1}^{T}\dfrac{x_t}{\sigma_t^2} & 0 & 0 \\[2ex] \dfrac{1}{T}\displaystyle\sum_{t=1}^{T}\dfrac{x_t}{\sigma_t^2} & \dfrac{1}{T}\displaystyle\sum_{t=1}^{T}\dfrac{x_t^2}{\sigma_t^2} & 0 & 0 \\[2ex] 0 & 0 & \dfrac{1}{2} & \dfrac{1}{2T}\displaystyle\sum_{t=1}^{T}w_t \\[2ex] 0 & 0 & \dfrac{1}{2T}\displaystyle\sum_{t=1}^{T}w_t & \dfrac{1}{2T}\displaystyle\sum_{t=1}^{T}w_t^2 \end{bmatrix}.$$

Letting $\beta = \{\beta_0, \beta_1\}$ and $\gamma = \{\gamma_0, \gamma_1\}$, the block-diagonal property of the information matrix allows estimation to proceed in two separate blocks

$$
\begin{bmatrix} \beta \\ \gamma \end{bmatrix}_{(k)} = \begin{bmatrix} \beta \\ \gamma \end{bmatrix}_{(k-1)} + \begin{bmatrix} I_{1,1} & 0 \\ 0 & I_{2,2} \end{bmatrix}^{-1}_{(k-1)} \begin{bmatrix} G_1 \\ G_2 \end{bmatrix}_{(k-1)}, \tag{8.4}
$$

where the relevant elements of the gradient are

$$
G_1 = \begin{bmatrix} \dfrac{1}{T}\sum_{t=1}^{T}\dfrac{u_t}{\sigma_t^2} \\[2ex] \dfrac{1}{T}\sum_{t=1}^{T}\dfrac{x_t u_t}{\sigma_t^2} \end{bmatrix}, \quad
G_2 = \begin{bmatrix} -\dfrac{1}{2}+\dfrac{1}{2T}\sum_{t=1}^{T}\dfrac{u_t^2}{\sigma_t^2} \\[2ex] -\dfrac{1}{2T}\sum_{t=1}^{T}w_t+\dfrac{1}{2T}\sum_{t=1}^{T}\dfrac{w_t u_t^2}{\sigma_t^2} \end{bmatrix},
$$

and the relevant blocks of the information matrix are

$$
I_{1,1} = \begin{bmatrix} \dfrac{1}{T}\sum_{t=1}^{T}\dfrac{1}{\sigma_t^2} & \dfrac{1}{T}\sum_{t=1}^{T}\dfrac{x_t}{\sigma_t^2} \\[2ex] \dfrac{1}{T}\sum_{t=1}^{T}\dfrac{x_t}{\sigma_t^2} & \dfrac{1}{T}\sum_{t=1}^{T}\dfrac{x_t^2}{\sigma_t^2} \end{bmatrix}, \quad
I_{2,2} = \begin{bmatrix} \dfrac{1}{2} & \dfrac{1}{2T}\sum_{t=1}^{T}w_t \\[2ex] \dfrac{1}{2T}\sum_{t=1}^{T}w_t & \dfrac{1}{2T}\sum_{t=1}^{T}w_t^2 \end{bmatrix},
$$

with $u_t = y_t - \beta_0 - \beta_1 x_t$, $\sigma_t^2 = \exp(\gamma_0 + \gamma_1 w_t)$ and where all parameters are evaluated at $\theta_{(k-1)}$. □

8.3.2 Relationship with Weighted Least Squares

The scoring algorithm in Example 8.5 is an example of a zig-zag algorithm where updated estimates of the mean parameters, $\beta = \{\beta_0, \beta_1\}$, are obtained separately from the updated estimates of the variance parameters, $\gamma = \{\gamma_0, \gamma_1\}$. An important property of the method of scoring for heteroskedastic regression models is that it is equivalent to the weighted least squares estimator.

Example 8.6 Weighted Least Squares Estimation
  A common way to start the weighted least algorithm is to set $\gamma_1 = 0$, and assume that there is no heteroskedasticity. The relevant blocks of the gradient and Hessian of the multiplicative heteroskedastic regression model in Example 8.5 now become, respectively,

$$
G_1 = \begin{bmatrix} \dfrac{1}{T}\sum_{t=1}^{T}\dfrac{u_t}{\exp(\gamma_0)} \\[2ex] \dfrac{1}{T}\sum_{t=1}^{T}\dfrac{x_t u_t}{\exp(\gamma_0)} \end{bmatrix}, \quad
G_2 = \begin{bmatrix} -\dfrac{1}{2}+\dfrac{1}{2T}\sum_{t=1}^{T}\dfrac{u_t^2}{\exp(\gamma_0)} \\[2ex] -\dfrac{1}{2T}\sum_{t=1}^{T}w_t+\dfrac{1}{2T}\sum_{t=1}^{T}\dfrac{w_t u_t^2}{\exp(\gamma_0)} \end{bmatrix},
$$

and

$$
I_{1,1} = \begin{bmatrix} \dfrac{1}{\exp(\gamma_0)} & \dfrac{1}{T}\displaystyle\sum_{t=1}^{T}\dfrac{x_t}{\exp(\gamma_0)} \\[3ex] \dfrac{1}{T}\displaystyle\sum_{t=1}^{T}\dfrac{x_t}{\exp(\gamma_0)} & \dfrac{1}{T}\displaystyle\sum_{t=1}^{T}\dfrac{x_t^2}{\exp(\gamma_0)} \end{bmatrix}, \quad I_{2,2} = \begin{bmatrix} \dfrac{1}{2} & \dfrac{1}{2T}\displaystyle\sum_{t=1}^{T}w_t \\[3ex] \dfrac{1}{2T}\displaystyle\sum_{t=1}^{T}w_t & \dfrac{1}{2T}\displaystyle\sum_{t=1}^{T}w_t^2 \end{bmatrix},
$$

where $u_t = y_t - \beta_0 - \beta_1 x_t$. An important property of the scoring algorithm is that at the first step the update of $\beta = \{\beta_0, \beta_1\}$ does not depend on the choice of the starting value as the first step of the update is

$$
\beta_{(1)} = \beta_{(0)} + I_{1,1}^{-1}(\beta_{(0)})G_1(\beta_{(0)})
$$

$$
= \begin{bmatrix} \beta_0 \\ \beta_1 \end{bmatrix}_{(0)} + \begin{bmatrix} T & \displaystyle\sum_{t=1}^{T}x_t \\[3ex] \displaystyle\sum_{t=1}^{T}x_t & \displaystyle\sum_{t=1}^{T}x_t^2 \end{bmatrix}^{-1} \begin{bmatrix} \displaystyle\sum_{t=1}^{T}(y_t - \beta_0 - \beta_1 x_t) \\[3ex] \displaystyle\sum_{t=1}^{T}x_t(y_t - \beta_0 - \beta_1 x_t) \end{bmatrix}_{(0)}
$$

$$
= \begin{bmatrix} T & \displaystyle\sum_{t=1}^{T}x_t \\[3ex] \displaystyle\sum_{t=1}^{T}x_t & \displaystyle\sum_{t=1}^{T}x_t^2 \end{bmatrix}^{-1} \begin{bmatrix} \displaystyle\sum_{t=1}^{T}y_t \\[3ex] \displaystyle\sum_{t=1}^{T}x_t y_t \end{bmatrix},
$$

which is equivalent to a linear regression of y_t on $\{1, x_t\}$. The starting value for γ_0 is given by

$$
\gamma_{0(0)} = \ln\left(\frac{1}{T}\sum_{t=1}^{T}(y_t - \beta_{0(0)} - \beta_{1(0)}x_t)^2\right).
$$

From the other component of the scoring algorithm in Example 8.5, the variance parameters are updated as

$$
\gamma_{(1)} = \gamma_{(0)} + I_{2,2}^{-1}(\gamma_{(0)})G_2(\gamma_{(0)})
$$

$$
= \begin{bmatrix} \gamma_0 \\ \gamma_1 \end{bmatrix}_{(0)} + \begin{bmatrix} T & \displaystyle\sum_{t=1}^{T}w_t \\[3ex] \displaystyle\sum_{t=1}^{T}w_t & \displaystyle\sum_{t=1}^{T}w_t^2 \end{bmatrix}^{-1} \begin{bmatrix} \displaystyle\sum_{t=1}^{T}v_t \\[3ex] \displaystyle\sum_{t=1}^{T}w_t v_t \end{bmatrix},
$$

where

$$
v_t = \frac{(y_t - \beta_{0(0)} - \beta_{1(0)}x_t)^2}{\exp(\gamma_{0(0)})} - 1.
$$

The update of the variance parameters is therefore obtained from a linear regression of v_t on $\{1, w_t\}$.

These results suggest that estimation by weighted least squares involves the following steps.

Step 1: Estimate $\beta_{(0)}$ by regressing y_t on $\{1, x_t\}$ and compute

$$\gamma_{0(0)} = \ln\left(\frac{1}{T}\sum_{t=1}^{T}(y_t - \beta_{0(0)} - \beta_{1(0)}x_t)^2\right).$$

Step 2: Regress v_t on $\{1, w_t\}$, where

$$v_t = \frac{(y_t - \beta_{0(0)} - \beta_{1(0)}x_t)^2}{\exp(\gamma_{0(0)})} - 1.$$

This regression provides estimates of the updates Δ_{γ_0} and Δ_{γ_1} so that the updated parameter estimates of the variance equation are

$$\begin{bmatrix} \gamma_0 \\ \gamma_1 \end{bmatrix}_{(1)} = \begin{bmatrix} \gamma_0 \\ \gamma_1 \end{bmatrix}_{(0)} + \begin{bmatrix} \Delta_{\gamma_0} \\ \Delta_{\gamma_1} \end{bmatrix}_{(0)}.$$

Step 3: Regress the weighted dependent variable, $y_t/\widehat{\sigma}_t$, on the weighted exogenous variables, $\{1/\widehat{\sigma}_t, x_t/\widehat{\sigma}_t\}$, to obtain $\beta_{(1)} = [\beta_{0(1)}, \beta_{1(1)}]'_1$, where

$$\widehat{\sigma}_t^2 = \exp(\gamma_{0(1)} + \gamma_{1(1)}w_t).$$

Step 4: Regress v_t on $\{1, w_t\}$ where

$$v_t = \frac{(y_t - \beta_{0(1)} - \beta_{1(1)}x_t)^2}{\exp(\gamma_{0(1)} + \gamma_{1(1)})} - 1,$$

and update the parameter estimates of the variance equation again.

Step 5: Repeat steps 3 and 4 until convergence is achieved.

$\square$

8.4 Distribution Theory

The asymptotic distribution of the maximum likelihood estimator of $\theta = \{\beta_0, \beta_1, \gamma_0, \gamma_1\}$ of the heteroskedastic regression model is

$$\widehat{\theta} \overset{a}{\sim} N\left(\theta_0, \frac{1}{T}I(\theta_0)^{-1}\right), \tag{8.5}$$

in which $I(\theta_0)$ is the information matrix evaluated at the population parameter θ_0. Because the information matrix is block-diagonal, the asymptotic distribution of the maximum likelihood estimator of $\beta = \{\beta_0, \beta_1\}$ separates from the asymptotic distribution of σ^2.

From the properties of the maximum likelihood estimator developed in Chapter 2, $\widehat{\beta}$ is a consistent and asymptotically efficient estimator of the population parameter for β. As the weighted least squares estimator is shown to be a maximum likelihood estimator from the discussion in Section 8.3.2, the weighted least squares estimator is also consistent and asymptotically efficient.

The ordinary least squares estimator of $\beta = \{\beta_0, \beta_1\}$ is simply a regression of y_t on $\{1, x_t\}$ without any allowance for heteroskedasticity. That is, this estimator is based on specifying the mean of the model correctly but misspecifying the variance. The implication of this result is that the ordinary least squares estimator is consistent, but inefficient compared to the maximum likelihood estimator $\widehat{\beta}$. The details of this situation are explored further in Chapter 9, Section 9.6.2.

8.5   Testing

Hypothesis tests on the parameters of heteroskedastic regression models can be based on the LR, Wald and LM test statistics developed in Chapter 4. As in Chapters 5 to 7, the Wald and LM test statistics can take various asymptotically equivalent forms.

Consider a linear regression model with multiplicative heteroskedasticity as specified in Examples 8.3 and 8.5 with parameters $\theta = \{\beta_0, \beta_1, \gamma_0, \gamma_1\}$. A test of multiplicative heteroskedasticity is performed by testing the restriction that $\gamma_1 = 0$ because this restriction yields a constant variance, or homoskedasticity. The respective null and alternative hypotheses are

$$H_0 : \quad \gamma_1 = 0 \quad [\text{Homoskedasticity}]$$
$$H_1 : \quad \gamma_1 \neq 0 \quad [\text{Heteroskedasticity}].$$

Let the parameters of the restricted model be $\widehat{\theta}_0$ and the parameters of the unrestricted model be $\widehat{\theta}_1$.

The log-likelihood function evaluated at the maximum likelihood estimator under the alternative hypothesis, $\widehat{\theta}_1$, is

$$\ln L_T(\widehat{\theta}_1) = -\frac{1}{2}\ln(2\pi) - \frac{1}{2T}\sum_{t=1}^{T}(\widehat{\gamma}_0 + \widehat{\gamma}_1 w_t) - \frac{1}{2T}\sum_{t=1}^{T}\frac{(y_t - \widehat{\beta}_0 - \widehat{\beta}_1 x_t)^2}{\exp(\widehat{\gamma}_0 + \widehat{\gamma}_1 w_t)}.$$

The log-likelihood function evaluated at the maximum likelihood estimator under the null hypothesis, $\widehat{\theta}_0$, is

$$\ln L_T(\widehat{\theta}_0) = -\frac{1}{2}\ln(2\pi) - \frac{1}{2}\ln\widehat{\sigma}_0^2 - \frac{1}{2},$$

where $\widehat{\sigma}_0^2$ is the residual variance from regressing y_t on $\{1, x_t\}$. The LR statistic is

$$LR = -2\big(T \ln L_T(\widehat{\theta}_0) - T \ln L_T(\widehat{\theta}_1)\big)$$

$$= T \ln \widehat{\sigma}_0^2 - \sum_{t=1}^{T}(\widehat{\gamma}_0 + \widehat{\gamma}_1 w_t) + T - \sum_{t=1}^{T} \frac{(y_t - \widehat{\beta}_0 - \widehat{\beta}_1 x_t)^2}{\exp(\widehat{\gamma}_0 + \widehat{\gamma}_1 w_t)},$$

which is asymptotically distributed as χ_1^2 under the null hypothesis.

To construct the Wald test statistic define

$$R = [0 \ \ 0 \ \ 0 \ \ 1], \qquad Q = [0].$$

From the properties of partitioned matrices

$$I^{-1}(\widehat{\theta}_1) = \begin{bmatrix} I_{11}^{-1} & 0 \\ 0 & I_{22}^{-1} \end{bmatrix},$$

where

$$I_{11}^{-1} = \begin{bmatrix} \dfrac{1}{T}\displaystyle\sum_{t=1}^{T}\dfrac{1}{\exp(\gamma_0 + \gamma_1 w_t)} & \dfrac{1}{T}\displaystyle\sum_{t=1}^{T}\dfrac{x_t}{\exp(\gamma_0 + \gamma_1 w_t)} \\ \dfrac{1}{T}\displaystyle\sum_{t=1}^{T}\dfrac{x_t}{\exp(\gamma_0 + \gamma_1 w_t)} & \dfrac{1}{T}\displaystyle\sum_{t=1}^{T}\dfrac{x_t^2}{\exp(\gamma_0 + \gamma_1 w_t)} \end{bmatrix}^{-1},$$

and

$$I_{22}^{-1} = \frac{2}{\displaystyle\sum_{t=1}^{T}(w_t - \overline{w})^2} \begin{bmatrix} \displaystyle\sum_{t=1}^{T} w_t^2 & -\sum_{t=1}^{T} w_t \\ -\displaystyle\sum_{t=1}^{T} w_t & T \end{bmatrix},$$

so that the Wald statistic is

$$W = T[R\widehat{\theta}_1 - Q]'[R\,I^{-1}(\widehat{\theta}_1)\,R']^{-1}[R\widehat{\theta}_1 - Q]$$

$$= [\widehat{\gamma}_1 - 0]'\left[\frac{1}{2}\sum_{t=1}^{T}(w_t - \overline{w})^2\right]^{-1}[\widehat{\gamma}_1 - 0]$$

$$= \frac{(\widehat{\gamma}_1 - 0)^2}{\dfrac{1}{2}\displaystyle\sum_{t=1}^{T}(w_t - \overline{w})^2}.$$

An alternative form of the Wald statistic is

$$W_2 = T[R\widehat{\theta}_1 - Q]'[R\,(-H^{-1}(\widehat{\theta}_1))\,R']^{-1}[R\widehat{\theta}_1 - Q].$$

In this case, the statistic simplifies to

$$W_2 = \frac{(\widehat{\gamma}_1 - 0)^2}{\text{var}(\widehat{\gamma}_1)},$$

or, when expressed as a t statistic, is

$$t = \frac{\widehat{\gamma}_1 - 0}{\text{se}(\widehat{\gamma}_1)}.$$

To perform a LM test of heteroskedasticity the gradient vector and information matrix are needed. The elements of the gradient vector evaluated under the null hypothesis are

$$G_T(\widehat{\theta}_0) = \begin{bmatrix} \dfrac{1}{T} \displaystyle\sum_{t=1}^{T} (y_t - \widehat{\beta}_0 - \widehat{\beta}_1 x_t) \exp(-\widehat{\gamma}_0) \\[2ex] \dfrac{1}{T} \displaystyle\sum_{t=1}^{T} x_t (y_t - \widehat{\beta}_0 - \widehat{\beta}_1 x_t) \exp(-\widehat{\gamma}_0) \\[2ex] -\dfrac{1}{2} + \dfrac{1}{2T} \displaystyle\sum_{t=1}^{T} (y_t - \widehat{\beta}_0 - \widehat{\beta}_1 x_t)^2 \exp(-\widehat{\gamma}_0) \\[2ex] -\dfrac{1}{2T} \displaystyle\sum_{t=1}^{T} w_t + \dfrac{1}{2T} \displaystyle\sum_{t=1}^{T} (y_t - \widehat{\beta}_0 - \widehat{\beta}_1 x_t)^2 w_t \exp(-\widehat{\gamma}_0) \end{bmatrix},$$

where the parameters are evaluated at $\widehat{\theta}_0$. The information matrix under the null hypothesis is

$$I(\widehat{\theta}_0) = \begin{bmatrix} \dfrac{1}{T} \displaystyle\sum_{t=1}^{T} \exp(-\widehat{\gamma}_0) & \dfrac{1}{T} \displaystyle\sum_{t=1}^{T} x_t \exp(-\widehat{\gamma}_0) & 0 & 0 \\[2ex] \dfrac{1}{T} \displaystyle\sum_{t=1}^{T} x_t^1 \exp(-\widehat{\gamma}_0) & \dfrac{1}{T} \displaystyle\sum_{t=1}^{T} x_t^2 \exp(-\widehat{\gamma}_0) & 0 & 0 \\[2ex] 0 & 0 & \dfrac{1}{2} & \dfrac{1}{2T} \displaystyle\sum_{t=1}^{T} w_t \\[2ex] 0 & 0 & \dfrac{1}{2T} \displaystyle\sum_{t=1}^{T} w_t & \dfrac{1}{2T} \displaystyle\sum_{t=1}^{T} w_t^2 \end{bmatrix},$$

where the parameters are evaluated at $\widehat{\theta}_0$. As

$$\frac{\partial \ln L_T(\theta)}{\partial \beta} \bigg|_{\theta=\theta_0} = 0,$$

the information matrix under the null hypothesis is block-diagonal, and the LM test statistic simplifies to

$$LM = T G'_T(\widehat{\theta}_0) I^{-1}(\widehat{\theta}_0) G_T(\widehat{\theta}_0)$$

$$= \frac{1}{2} \begin{bmatrix} \sum\limits_{t=1}^{T} \widehat{v}_t \\ \sum\limits_{t=1}^{T} \widehat{v}_t w_t \end{bmatrix}' \begin{bmatrix} T & \sum\limits_{t=1}^{T} w_t \\ \sum\limits_{t=1}^{T} w_t & \sum\limits_{t=1}^{T} w_t^2 \end{bmatrix}^{-1} \begin{bmatrix} \sum\limits_{t=1}^{T} \widehat{v}_t \\ \sum\limits_{t=1}^{T} \widehat{v}_t w_t \end{bmatrix},$$

where

$$\widehat{v}_t = \frac{(y_t - \widehat{\beta}_0 - \widehat{\beta}_1 x_t)^2}{\exp(\widehat{\gamma}_0)} - 1.$$

The parameter $\widehat{\beta} = \{\widehat{\beta}_0, \widehat{\beta}_1\}$ is obtained from a regression of y_t on $\{1, x_t\}$ and

$$\widehat{\gamma}_0 = \ln\left(\frac{1}{T} \sum_{t=1}^{T} (y_t - \widehat{\beta}_0 - \widehat{\beta}_1 x_t)^2\right).$$

Alternatively, consider the standardised random variable

$$z_t = \frac{y_t - \widehat{\beta}_0 - \widehat{\beta}_1 x_t}{\sqrt{\exp(\widehat{\gamma}_0)}},$$

that is distributed asymptotically as $N(0, 1)$. It follows that

$$\text{plim}\left(\frac{1}{T} \sum_{t=1}^{T} \widehat{v}_t^2\right) = \text{plim}\left(\frac{1}{T} \sum_{t=1}^{T} (z_t^2 - 1)^2\right) = \text{plim}\left(\frac{1}{T} \sum_{t=1}^{T} (z_t^4 - 2z_t^2 + 1)\right) = 2,$$

because from the properties of the standard normal distribution $E[z_t^2] = 1$ and $E[z_t^4] = 3$. It follows that the $1/2$ in the LM statistic can be replaced by $T / \sum_{t=1}^{T} \widehat{v}_t^2$, so that another asymptotic form of the LM test is

$$LM_2 = \frac{T}{\sum\limits_{t=1}^{T} \widehat{v}_t^2} \begin{bmatrix} \sum\limits_{t=1}^{T} \widehat{v}_t \\ \sum\limits_{t=1}^{T} \widehat{v}_t w_t \end{bmatrix}' \begin{bmatrix} T & \sum\limits_{t=1}^{T} w_t \\ \sum\limits_{t=1}^{T} w_t & \sum\limits_{t=1}^{T} w_t^2 \end{bmatrix}^{-1} \begin{bmatrix} \sum\limits_{t=1}^{T} \widehat{v}_t \\ \sum\limits_{t=1}^{T} \widehat{v}_t w_t \end{bmatrix} = T R^2,$$

where R^2 is the coefficient of determination from regressing $\widehat{v}_t$ on $\{1, w_t\}$, because under the null hypothesis

$$\bar{v} = \frac{1}{T} \sum_{t=1}^{T} \widehat{v}_t = 0.$$

Alternatively, $\widehat{v}_t$ can be redefined as $\widehat{u}_t^2 = (y_t - \widehat{\beta}_0 - \widehat{\beta}_1 x_t)^2$, because R^2 is invariant to linear transformations. This suggests that a test of multiplicative heteroskedasticity can be implemented as a two-stage regression procedure as follows.

Step 1: Regress y_t on $\{1, x_t\}$ to obtain the restricted residuals $\widehat{u}_t = y_t - \widehat{\beta}_0 - \widehat{\beta}_1 x_t$.

Step 2: Regress $\widehat{u}_t^2$ on $\{1, w_t\}$.

Step 3: Compute TR^2 from this second-stage regression and compare the computed value of the test statistic to the critical value obtained from the χ_1^2 distribution.

Example 8.7 Testing Multiplicative Heteroskedasticity

This example reports LR, Wald and LM tests for heteroskedasticity in the multiplicative heteroskedastic model for alternative forms of the test statistics using the numerical results reported in Table 8.2. The LR statistic is

$$LR = -2T(\ln L_T(\widehat{\theta}_0) - \ln L_T(\widehat{\theta}_1)) = -2 \times 500(-3.157 + 2.699) = 457.800.$$

Also using the results from the same table, the alternative form of the Wald statistic is

$$W_2 = \frac{(\widehat{\gamma}_1 - 0)^2}{\operatorname{var}(\widehat{\gamma}_1)} = \left(\frac{0.097741 - 0}{0.004142}\right)^2 = 556.778.$$

To compute the LM statistic the gradient vector and the Hessian are evaluated at the restricted estimates $\widehat{\theta}_0$ given in Table 8.2

$$G_T(\widehat{\theta}_0) = \begin{bmatrix} 0.000 \\ 0.000 \\ 0.000 \\ 7.978 \end{bmatrix}$$

$$H_T(\widehat{\theta}_0) = \begin{bmatrix} -0.031 & 0.000 & 0.000 & 0.130 \\ 0.000 & -0.035 & 0.000 & -0.143 \\ 0.000 & 0.000 & -0.500 & -20.454 \\ 0.130 & -0.143 & -20.454 & -878.283 \end{bmatrix}.$$

The LM statistic is

$$LM = TG'_T(\widehat{\theta}_0)[-H_T(\widehat{\theta}_0)]^{-1}G_T(\widehat{\theta}_0) = 787.423.$$

To compute the regression form of the LM test, in the first stage use the restricted estimates in Table 8.2 to compute the following ordinary least squares residuals under the null hypothesis

$$\widehat{u}_t = y_t - 0.753 - 2.136 x_t.$$

In the second stage regress $\widehat{u}_t^2$ on $\{1, w_t\}$. The results are

$$\widehat{u}_t^2 = -29.424 + 2.474 w_t + \widehat{e}_t,$$

which yields

$$R^2 = 1 - \frac{\sum \widehat{e}_t^2}{\sum (\widehat{u}_t^2 - \overline{u})^2} = 0.157 .$$

The regression form of the LM statistic is

$$LM_2 = T R^2 = 500 \times 0.157 = 78.447 .$$

The number of restrictions is $M = 1$ and the asymptotic distribution of all the test statistics under the null hypothesis is, therefore, χ_1^2. For the LR, Wald and two LM tests, the p-values are all 0.000, suggesting that the null hypothesis is rejected at the 5% level. The conclusion that significant evidence of heteroskedasticity exists at the 5% level is consistent with the setup of the model.

□

Example 8.8 Breusch-Pagan and White Tests

The regression form of the LM test presented previously is perhaps the most commonly adopted test of heteroskedasticity since it is relatively easy to implement, involving just two least squares regressions. This construction of the LM test is consistent with both the Breusch-Pagan and White tests of heteroskedasticity, with the difference between these two tests being the set of variables (implicitly) specified in the variance equation.

For the Breusch-Pagan test, the variance equation is specified as

$$\sigma_t^2 = \gamma_0 + \sum_{i=1}^{M} \gamma_i w_{i,t} .$$

The test involves regressing y_t on $\{1, x_t\}$ to get the least squares residuals $\widehat{u}_t$, in the first stage. In the second stage, regress $\widehat{u}_t^2$ on $\{1, w_{1,t}, w_{2,t}, \cdots, w_{M,t}\}$ and compute $LM = T R^2$ where R^2 is, as before, the coefficient of determination from the second-stage regression. This statistic is asymptotically distributed as χ_M^2 under the null hypothesis.

For the White test, the variance equation is an extension of the Breusch-Pagan specification involving the inclusion of all the relevant cross-product terms

$$\sigma_t^2 = \gamma_0 + \sum_{i=1}^{M} \gamma_i w_{i,t} + \sum_{i>j}^{M} \gamma_{i,j} w_{i,t} w_{j,t} .$$

The second-stage regression now consists of regressing $\widehat{u}_t^2$ on

$$\{1, w_{1,t}, w_{2,t}, \cdots, w_{M,t}, w_{1,t}^2, w_{2,t}^2, \cdots, w_{M,t}^2, w_{1,t} w_{2,t}, \cdots, w_{M-1,t} w_{M,t}\} .$$

The test statistic is $LM = T R^2$, where R^2 is the coefficient of determination from the second-stage regression, which is asymptotically distributed as χ^2 under the null hypothesis with $(M^2 + 3M)/2$ degrees of freedom.

Implementing the Breusch-Pagan and White tests still requires that the variables in the variance equation, $w_{i,t}$, $i = 1, 2, \cdots, M$, be specified. In practice, it is not uncommon to let the exogenous variables in the mean and the variance be the same by setting $w_t = x_t$.   □

8.6   Heteroskedasticity in Systems of Equations

8.6.1   Specification

Extending the univariate model with heteroskedasticity to a system of equations with heteroskedasticity is relatively straightforward. As in the univariate model where the choice of the specification is needed to ensure that the variance of the disturbance term is positive for all t, the multivariate specification requires that the covariance matrix of the disturbance vector must remain positive-definite for all t.

A system of equations where the disturbance vector is heteroskedastic is specified as

$$By_t + Ax_t = u_t, \qquad u_t \sim N(0, V_t), \tag{8.6}$$

in which y_t is a $(N \times 1)$ vector of dependent variables, x_t is a $(K \times 1)$ vector of exogenous variables, B is a $(N \times N)$ matrix, A is a $(N \times K)$ matrix and V_t is the $(N \times N)$ covariance matrix of the time-varying disturbances driven by the variable w_t assumed here, for simplicity, to be a scalar. This model can easily be extended to allow for additional variables in the variance equation.

To ensure that V_t is positive-definite, the approach is to express the variances and covariances in terms of a lower triangular matrix, S_t, and construct the covariance matrix as

$$V_t = S_t S_t', \qquad S_t = C + Dw_t, \tag{8.7}$$

in which C and D are $(N \times N)$ lower triangular matrices of unknown parameters. For example, consider a bivariate model $N = 2$. The matrix S_t is specified as

$$S_t = \begin{bmatrix} c_{1,1} & 0 \\ c_{2,1} & c_{2,2} \end{bmatrix} + \begin{bmatrix} d_{1,1} & 0 \\ d_{2,1} & d_{2,2} \end{bmatrix} w_t = \begin{bmatrix} c_{1,1} + d_{1,1}w_t & 0 \\ c_{2,1} + d_{2,1}w_t & c_{2,2} + d_{2,2}w_t \end{bmatrix},$$

where

$$C = \begin{bmatrix} c_{1,1} & 0 \\ c_{2,1} & c_{2,2} \end{bmatrix}, \qquad D = \begin{bmatrix} d_{1,1} & 0 \\ d_{2,1} & d_{2,2} \end{bmatrix}.$$

The covariance matrix in (8.7) is then

$$
\begin{aligned}
V_t &= S_t S_t' \\
&= \begin{bmatrix} c_{1,1} + d_{1,1}w_t & 0 \\ c_{2,1} + d_{2,1}w_t & c_{2,2} + d_{2,2}w_t \end{bmatrix} \begin{bmatrix} c_{1,1} + d_{1,1}w_t & c_{2,1} + d_{2,1}w_t \\ 0 & c_{2,2} + d_{2,2}w_t \end{bmatrix} \\
&= \begin{bmatrix} \sigma_{1,1,t} & \sigma_{1,2,t} \\ \sigma_{2,1,t} & \sigma_{2,2,t} \end{bmatrix},
\end{aligned}
$$

where the variances $(\sigma_{1,1,t}, \sigma_{2,2,t})$ and covariance $(\sigma_{1,2,t} = \sigma_{2,1,t})$ are

$$
\begin{aligned}
\sigma_{1,1,t} &= (c_{1,1} + d_{1,1}w_t)^2 \\
&= c_{1,1}^2 + 2c_{1,1}d_{1,1}w_t + d_{1,1}^2 w_t^2
\end{aligned}
$$

$$
\begin{aligned}
\sigma_{1,2,t} &= (c_{1,1} + d_{1,1}w_t)(c_{2,1} + d_{2,1}w_t) \\
&= c_{1,1}c_{2,1} + (c_{1,1}d_{2,1} + c_{2,1}d_{1,1})w_t + d_{1,1}d_{2,1}w_t^2
\end{aligned}
$$

$$
\begin{aligned}
\sigma_{2,2,t} &= (c_{2,1} + d_{2,1}w_t)(c_{2,1} + d_{2,1}w_t) + (c_{2,2} + d_{2,2}w_t)(c_{2,2} + d_{2,2}w_t) \\
&= c_{2,1}^2 + c_{2,2}^2 + (2c_{2,1}d_{2,1} + 2c_{2,2}d_{2,2})w_t + (d_{2,1}^2 + d_{2,2}^2)w_t^2,
\end{aligned}
$$

respectively. This covariance matrix has three features.

(1) V_t is symmetric since $\sigma_{1,2,t} = \sigma_{2,1,t}$.
(2) V_t is positive (semi) definite since $\sigma_{1,1,t}\sigma_{2,2,t} \geq \sigma_{1,2,t}^2$.
(3) The variances, $\sigma_{1,1,t}$ and $\sigma_{2,2,t}$, and the covariance, $\sigma_{1,2,t}$, are all quadratic in w_t.

The matrix S_t in expression (8.7) represents the Choleski decomposition of V_t. In the special case of a univariate model, $N = 1$, when the disturbance is homoskedastic $d_{1,1} = 0$, then $\sigma_{1,1,t} = c_{1,1}^2$ so that $c_{1,1}$ represents the standard deviation. For this reason, the matrix S_t is sometimes referred to as the standard-deviation matrix, or, more generally, as the square-root matrix.

8.6.2 Estimation

The multivariate regression model with vector heteroskedasticity is estimated using the full-information maximum likelihood estimator presented in Chapter 5. From the assumption of multivariate normality in (8.6), the distribution of u_t is

$$
f(u_t) = \left(\frac{1}{\sqrt{2\pi}}\right)^N |V_t|^{-1/2} \exp\left[-\frac{1}{2}u_t' V_t^{-1} u_t\right]. \tag{8.8}
$$

The Jacobian is

$$
\frac{\partial u_t}{\partial y_t'} = B,
$$

so that by the transformation of variable technique, the density of y_t is

$$f(y_t \mid x_t, w_t; \theta) = f(u_t) \left| \frac{\partial u_t}{\partial y_t'} \right|$$

$$= \left(\frac{1}{\sqrt{2\pi}} \right)^N |V_t|^{-1/2} \exp\left[-\frac{1}{2} u_t' V_t^{-1} u_t \right] |B|.$$

The log-likelihood function at observation t is

$$\ln l_t(\theta) = -\frac{N}{2} \ln(2\pi) - \frac{1}{2} \ln |V_t| + \ln |B| - \frac{1}{2} u_t' V_t^{-1} u_t, \tag{8.9}$$

where

$$u_t = By_t + Ax_t,$$

and

$$V_t = S_t S_t' = (C + Dw_t)(C + Dw_t)'.$$

For a sample of T observations, the log-likelihood function

$$\ln L_T(\theta) = \frac{1}{T} \sum_{t=1}^{T} \ln l_t(\theta), \tag{8.10}$$

is maximised with respect to $\theta = \{B, A, C, D\}$ using one of the iterative algorithms discussed in Chapter 3.

Example 8.9 Estimation of a Vector Heteroskedastic Model

This example simulates and estimates a bivariate system of equations where the covariance matrix of the disturbance vector is time-varying. The following model is simulated for $T = 2000$ observations

$$By_t + Ax_t = u_t$$
$$S_t = C + Dw_t$$
$$u_t \sim N(0, V_t = S_t S_t'),$$

in which

$$B = \begin{bmatrix} 1 & -\beta_1 \\ -\beta_2 & 1 \end{bmatrix} = \begin{bmatrix} 1.000 & -0.600 \\ -0.200 & 1.000 \end{bmatrix}$$

$$A = \begin{bmatrix} -\alpha_1 & 0 \\ 0 & -\alpha_2 \end{bmatrix} = \begin{bmatrix} -0.400 & 0.000 \\ 0.000 & 0.500 \end{bmatrix}$$

$$C = \begin{bmatrix} c_{1,1} & 0 \\ c_{2,1} & c_{2,2} \end{bmatrix} = \begin{bmatrix} 1.000 & 0.000 \\ 0.500 & 2.000 \end{bmatrix}$$

$$D = \begin{bmatrix} d_{1,1} & 0 \\ d_{2,1} & d_{2,2} \end{bmatrix} = \begin{bmatrix} 0.500 & 0.000 \\ 0.200 & 0.200 \end{bmatrix},$$

and $x_{1,t} \sim iid\ U(0, 10)$, $x_{2,t} \sim iid\ N(0, 9)$ and $w_t \sim iid\ U(0, 1)$.

Table 8.3. *Maximum likelihood estimates of the vector heteroskedastic model. Standard errors and t statistics are based on the inverse of the Hessian matrix*

Parameter	Population	Estimate	se	t statistic
β_1	0.6	0.591	0.015	38.209
α_1	0.4	0.402	0.005	81.094
β_2	0.2	0.194	0.019	10.349
α_2	−0.5	−0.527	0.018	−29.205
$c_{1,1}$	1.0	1.055	0.037	28.208
$d_{1,1}$	0.5	0.373	0.068	5.491
$c_{2,1}$	0.5	0.502	0.116	4.309
$d_{2,1}$	0.2	0.177	0.170	1.042
$c_{2,2}$	2.0	1.989	0.071	27.960
$d_{2,2}$	0.2	0.304	0.117	2.598

The log-likelihood function is maximised with respect to the parameters

$$\theta = \{\beta_1, \alpha_1, \beta_2, \alpha_2, c_{1,1}, d_{1,1}, c_{2,1}, d_{2,1}, c_{2,2}, d_{2,2}\} \,,$$

using the BFGS algorithm. The maximum likelihood estimates are given in Table 8.3 and demonstrate good agreement with the population values. □

8.6.3 Testing

The LR, Wald and LM tests can all be used to test for heteroskedasticity in systems of equations given by (8.6) and (8.7). The null and alternative hypotheses are

$$\begin{aligned} H_0 &: \quad d_{i,j} = 0, \forall i \geq j \\ H_1 &: \quad \text{at least one restriction is not satisfied}. \end{aligned}$$

Example 8.10 Wald Test of Vector Heteroskedasticity
Consider again the vector heteroskedastic model given in Example 8.9. The null and alternative hypotheses are

$$H_0 : d_{1,1} = d_{2,1} = d_{2,2} = 0,$$

H_1 : at least one restriction is not satisfied,

so that there are three restrictions to be tested. The Wald statistic is

$$W = T[R\widehat{\theta}_1 - Q]'[R\,(-H_T^{-1}(\widehat{\theta}_1))R']^{-1}[R\widehat{\theta}_1 - Q],$$

where $\widehat{\theta}_1$ are the unrestricted parameter estimates given in Table 8.3, $H_T(\widehat{\theta}_1)$ is the Hessian evaluated at $\widehat{\theta}_1$, and

$$R = \begin{bmatrix} 0 & 0 & 0 & 0 & 0 & 1 & 0 & 0 & 0 & 0 \\ 0 & 0 & 0 & 0 & 0 & 0 & 0 & 1 & 0 & 0 \\ 0 & 0 & 0 & 0 & 0 & 0 & 0 & 0 & 0 & 1 \end{bmatrix}, \qquad Q = \begin{bmatrix} 0 \\ 0 \\ 0 \end{bmatrix}.$$

Substituting the terms into W and simplifying gives $W = 36.986$, which is distributed asymptotically as χ_3^2 under H_0. The p-value is 0.000, so the null hypothesis is rejected at the 5% level. ☐

8.6.4   Heteroskedastic and Autocorrelated Disturbances

A system of equations where the disturbance vector is both heteroskedastic and autocorrelated with one lag is specified as

$$\begin{aligned} By_t + Ax_t &= u_t \\ u_t &= Pu_{t-1} + v_t \\ S_t &= C + Dw_t \\ v_t &\sim N(0, V_t = S_t S_t'), \end{aligned} \tag{8.11}$$

in which y_t is a $(N \times 1)$ vector of dependent variables, x_t is a $(K \times 1)$ vector of exogenous variables, B is a $(N \times N)$ matrix, A is a $(N \times K)$ matrix and P is a $(N \times N)$ matrix of autocorrelation parameters. The covariance matrix of the disturbances, V_t, is the $(N \times N)$ matrix with $(N \times N)$ lower triangular parameter matrices C and D and w_t is a positive scalar variable.

The log-likelihood function at observation t is

$$\ln l_t(\theta) = -\frac{N}{2}\ln(2\pi) - \frac{1}{2}\ln|V_t| + \ln|B| - \frac{1}{2}v_t' V_t^{-1} v_t, \tag{8.12}$$

where

$$v_t = u_t - Pu_{t-1}$$
$$u_t = By_t + Ax_t,$$

and

$$V_t = S_t S_t' = (C + Dw_t)(C + Dw_t)'.$$

Conditioning on the first observation, the conditional log-likelihood function is

$$\ln L_T(\theta) = \frac{1}{T-1}\sum_{t=2}^{T}\ln l_t(\theta), \tag{8.13}$$

which is maximised with respect to $\theta = \{B, A, C, D, P\}$.

The system of equations in (8.11) represents a general and flexible linear model in which to analyse time series and draw inferences. This model can also be used to perform a range of hypothesis tests of heteroskedasticity, autocorrelation or both.

Example 8.11 Testing for Heteroskedasticity and Autocorrelation

Consider the bivariate system of equations (8.11), where the disturbance is a vector AR(1) with a time-varying covariance matrix and the population parameters are

$$B = \begin{bmatrix} 1 & -\beta_1 \\ -\beta_2 & 1 \end{bmatrix} = \begin{bmatrix} 1.000 & -0.600 \\ -0.200 & 1.000 \end{bmatrix}$$

$$A = \begin{bmatrix} -\alpha_1 & 0 \\ 0 & -\alpha_2 \end{bmatrix} = \begin{bmatrix} -0.400 & 0.000 \\ 0.000 & 0.500 \end{bmatrix}$$

$$P = \begin{bmatrix} \rho_{1,1} & \rho_{1,2} \\ \rho_{2,1} & \rho_{2,2} \end{bmatrix} = \begin{bmatrix} 0.800 & -0.100 \\ -0.200 & 0.600 \end{bmatrix}$$

$$C = \begin{bmatrix} c_{1,1} & 0 \\ c_{2,1} & c_{2,2} \end{bmatrix} = \begin{bmatrix} 1.000 & 0.000 \\ 0.500 & 2.000 \end{bmatrix}$$

$$D = \begin{bmatrix} d_{1,1} & 0 \\ d_{2,1} & d_{2,2} \end{bmatrix} = \begin{bmatrix} 0.500 & 0.000 \\ 0.200 & 0.200 \end{bmatrix}.$$

The conditional log-likelihood function in (8.13) is maximised with respect to the parameter vector

$$\theta = \left\{ \beta_1, \alpha_1, \beta_2, \alpha_2, \rho_{1,1}, \rho_{1,2}, \rho_{2,1}, \rho_{2,2}, c_{1,1}, d_{1,1}, c_{2,1}, d_{2,1}, c_{2,2}, d_{2,2} \right\},$$

using the BFGS algorithm. As before, standard errors are computed using the negative of the inverse of the Hessian matrix. A joint test of heteroskedasticity and autocorrelation is carried out using a Wald test. The hypotheses are

$$H_0 : d_{1,1} = d_{2,1} = d_{2,2} = \rho_{1,1} = \rho_{1,2} = \rho_{2,1} = \rho_{2,2} = 0$$
$$H_1 : \text{at least one restriction is not satisfied},$$

representing a total of seven restrictions. The Wald statistic is

$$W = T[R\widehat{\theta}_1 - Q]'[R(-H_T^{-1}(\widehat{\theta}_1))R']^{-1}[R\widehat{\theta}_1 - Q],$$

where $\widehat{\theta}_1$ is the vector of unrestricted parameter estimates, $H_T(\widehat{\theta}_1)$ is the Hessian matrix and

$$R = \begin{bmatrix} 0 & 0 & 0 & 0 & 0 & 1 & 0 & 0 & 0 & 0 & 0 & 0 & 0 & 0 \\ 0 & 0 & 0 & 0 & 0 & 0 & 0 & 1 & 0 & 0 & 0 & 0 & 0 & 0 \\ 0 & 0 & 0 & 0 & 0 & 0 & 0 & 0 & 1 & 0 & 0 & 0 & 0 & 0 \\ 0 & 0 & 0 & 0 & 0 & 0 & 0 & 0 & 0 & 1 & 0 & 0 & 0 & 0 \\ 0 & 0 & 0 & 0 & 0 & 0 & 0 & 0 & 0 & 0 & 1 & 0 & 0 & 0 \\ 0 & 0 & 0 & 0 & 0 & 0 & 0 & 0 & 0 & 0 & 0 & 1 & 0 & 0 \\ 0 & 0 & 0 & 0 & 0 & 0 & 0 & 0 & 0 & 0 & 0 & 0 & 0 & 1 \end{bmatrix}, \quad Q = \begin{bmatrix} 0 \\ 0 \\ 0 \\ 0 \\ 0 \\ 0 \\ 0 \end{bmatrix}.$$

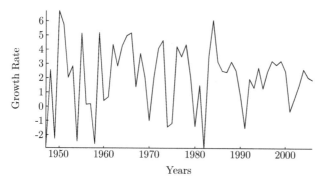

Figure 8.2. Annual percentage growth rate of per capita real GDP in the United States for the period 1947 to 2006.

Substituting these terms into W gives $W = 5590.034$, which is distributed asymptotically as χ^2_7 under H_0. The p-value is 0.000 and the null hypothesis is rejected at the 5% level. □

8.7 Applications

8.7.1 The Great Moderation

The Great Moderation refers to the decrease in the volatility of United States output growth after the early 1980s by comparison with previous volatility levels. This feature of output growth is highlighted in Figure 8.2 which gives the annual percentage growth in per capita real GDP for the United States from 1947 to 2006. The descriptive statistics presented in Table 8.4 show that the variance decreases from 7.489% in the period 1947 to 1983 to 2.049% in the period 1984 to 2006, a reduction of more than 70%.

To model the change in volatility over the period consider the following heteroskedastic regression model

$$y_t = \beta_0 + \beta_1 d_t + u_t, \qquad u_t \sim N(0, \sigma_t^2),$$
$$\sigma_t^2 = \exp(\gamma_0 + \gamma_1 d_t), \tag{8.14}$$

in which y_t is the growth rate in real GDP and

$$d_t = \begin{cases} 1 & : \quad 1947 \text{ to } 1983 \\ 0 & : \quad 1984 \text{ to } 2006, \end{cases} \tag{8.15}$$

is a dummy variable that identifies the structural break in the volatility. This model is an example of the step model of heteroskedasticity where the variances of the two periods are $\sigma^2_{1947-1983} = \exp(\gamma_0)$ and $\sigma^2_{1984-2006} = \exp(\gamma_0 + \gamma_1)$. The model also allows for the mean to change over the two sample periods if $\beta_1 \neq 0$.

Table 8.4. *Descriptive statistics on the annual percentage growth rate of per capita real GDP in the United States for selected sub-periods*

Period	Mean	Variance
1947 to 1983	1.952	7.489
1984 to 2006	2.127	2.049

The results from estimating the parameters of the model in equation (8.14) by maximum likelihood are

$$y_t = \underset{(0.450)}{1.952} + \underset{(0.540)}{0.175}d_t + \widehat{u}_t$$

$$\widehat{\sigma}_t^2 = \exp(\underset{(0.232)}{2.013} - \underset{(0.375)}{1.296}d_t),$$

where standard errors are given in parentheses based on the Hessian. The negative estimate reported for γ_1 shows that there is a fall in the variance in the second sub-period. The estimates of the variances for the two periods are

$$\widehat{\sigma}_{1947-1983}^2 = \exp(\widehat{\gamma}_0) = \exp(2.013) = 7.489$$

$$\widehat{\sigma}_{1984-2006}^2 = \exp(2.013 - 1.296) = 2.049,$$

which equal the variances reported in Table 8.4 for the respective two sub-periods.

A test of the moderation hypothesis is based on the null and alternative hypotheses

$$H_0: \quad \gamma_1 = 0 \quad \text{[No Moderation]}$$
$$H_1: \quad \gamma_1 \neq 0 \quad \text{[Moderation]}.$$

Using the LR, Wald and LM tests the results are

$$LR = 10.226, \qquad W = 11.909, \qquad LM = 9.279.$$

From the χ_1^2 distribution, the respective p-values are 0.001, 0.001 and 0.002, providing strong evidence in favour of the Great Moderation hypothesis.

8.7.2 Finite Sample Properties of the Wald Test

The size and power properties of the Wald test for heteroskedasticity in finite samples are now investigated using a range of Monte Carlo experiments. Consider the model

$$y_t = 1.0 + 2.0x_t + u_t, \qquad u_t \sim N(0, \sigma_t^2),$$
$$\sigma_t^2 = \exp(1.0 + \gamma_1 x_t),$$

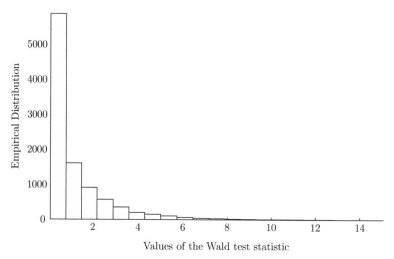

Values of the Wald test statistic

Figure 8.3. Sampling distribution of the Wald statistic for heteroskedasticity under the null hypothesis of constant variance. Based on $T = 50$ observations and 10000 replications.

in which $x_t \sim iid\ U[0, 1]$ and $\gamma_1 = \{0.0, 0.5, 1.0, 1.5, \cdots, 5.0\}$ controls the strength of heteroskedasticity.

To compute the size of the Wald test, the model is simulated under the null hypothesis of homoskedasticity by setting $\gamma_1 = 0$. The finite sample distribution of the Wald statistic under the null hypothesis for $T = 50$ observations and 10000 replications is given in Figure 8.3.

The characteristics of this distribution are similar to the asymptotic distribution given by a chi-square distribution with one degree of freedom. The finite sample critical value corresponding to a size of 5% is computed as that value which 5% of the simulated Wald statistics exceed. The finite sample critical value is in fact 4.435, which is greater than the corresponding asymptotic critical value of 3.841. The size of the test is computed as the average number of times the Wald statistic in the simulations is greater than the asymptotic critical value 3.841

$$\text{SIZE} = \frac{1}{10000} \sum_{i=1}^{10000} D_i(W_i > 3.841) = 0.0653,$$

or 6.530%. This result suggests that the asymptotic distribution is a reasonable approximation to the finite sample distribution for $T = 50$. That the size of the test is slightly greater than the nominal size of 5% suggests that the Wald test rejects the null hypothesis slightly more often that it should when asymptotic critical values are used.

To compute the power of the Wald test the model is simulated under the alternative hypothesis of heteroskedasticity by initially setting $\gamma_1 = 0.5$. Two

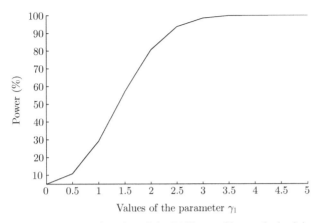

Figure 8.4. Power function of the Wald test of heteroskedasticity, size adjusted. Based on $T = 50$ observations and 10000 replications.

types of power are computed. The first is the average number of times the simulated Wald statistic is greater than the asymptotic critical value

$$\text{POWER}_U = \frac{1}{10000} \sum_{i=1}^{10000} D_i(W_i > 3.841) = 0.1285 \,.$$

This result shows that the probability of rejecting the null hypothesis of homo-skedasticity when it is false, is just 0.1285, or 12.850%. The second method of computing the power is to recognise the result showing that under the null hypothesis with a nominal size of 5% the actual empirical size of this test is 6.530%. For this reason POWER_U is referred to as the unadjusted power of the test. The size-adjusted power of the test is computed as

$$\text{POWER}_A = \frac{1}{10000} \sum_{i=1}^{10000} D_i(W_i > 4.435) = 0.1011 \,,$$

or 10.11%. Figure 8.4 gives the size-adjusted power function for values of $\gamma_1 = \{0.5, 1.0, 1.5, \cdots, 5.0\}$. The power function is monotonically increasing in γ_1, with the power reaching unity for $\gamma_1 \geqslant 4$.

8.8 Exercises

(1) **Properties of Heteroskedastic Regression Models**

Program files	`hetero_simulate.*`

Consider the heteroskedastic regression model

$$y_t = \beta_0 + \beta_1 x_t + u_t, \qquad u_t \sim N(0, \sigma_t^2),$$

in which the exogenous variable is $x_t \sim iid\ N(0, 1)$, and σ_t^2 is the time-varying variance. This exercise uses simulation methods to identify the properties of alternative models of heteroskedasticity.

(a) Simulate the model for $T = 500$ observations where σ_t^2 is the linear heteroskedastic specification

$$\sigma_t^2 = \gamma_0 + \gamma_1 w_t,$$

in which $w_t = t$ is a time trend and the parameter values are $\theta_0 = \{\beta_0 = 1, \beta_1 = 2, \gamma_0 = 1, \gamma_1 = 0.5\}$. Generate and interpret the scatter-plots between y_t and x_t, y_t and w_t, y_t^2 and w_t, and $\hat{u}_t^2$ and w_t, where $\hat{u}_t$ is the residual from regressing y_t on $\{1, x_t\}$.

(b) Repeat part (a) for the power heteroskedastic specification

$$\sigma_t^2 = \gamma_0 + \gamma_1 w_t^2.$$

(c) Repeat part (a) for the step heteroskedastic specification

$$\sigma_t^2 = \gamma_0 + \gamma_1 d_t,$$

in which d_t is a dummy variable defined by

$$d_t = \begin{cases} 0 & : \quad t \le 250 \\ 1 & : \quad t > 250, \end{cases}$$

and the parameter values are $\theta_0 = \{\beta_0 = 1, \beta_1 = 2, \gamma_0 = 1, \gamma_1 = 20\}$.

(2) Estimating and Testing Heteroskedastic Models

Program files   hetero_estimate.*, hetero_test.*

Consider the heteroskedastic regression model

$$y_t = \beta_0 + \beta_1 x_t + u_t, \qquad u_t \sim N(0, \sigma_t^2),$$

in which $x_t \sim iid\ N(0, 1)$, $w_t = t$ is a time trend and the parameter values are $\theta_0 = \{\beta_0 = 1, \beta_1 = 2, \gamma_0 = 0.1, \gamma_1 = 0.1\}$.

(a) Simulate the model for $T = 500$ observations where σ_t^2 is the multiplicative heteroskedastic specification

$$\sigma_t^2 = \exp(\gamma_0 + \gamma_1 w_t).$$

(i) Derive the log-likelihood function.
(ii) Compute the maximum likelihood estimates using the Newton-Raphson algorithm and compare the estimates with the population values.
(iii) Compute LR, Wald and LM tests of heteroskedasticity.

(b) Repeat part (a) for the power heteroskedastic specification

$$\sigma_t^2 = \gamma_0 + \gamma_1 w_t^2 \, ,$$

where the parameters γ_0 and γ_1 are constrained to be positive.

(c) Repeat part (b) where the positivity restriction on the variance parameters are not imposed.

(3) Business Cycles

Computer file(s)	`hetero_g7.*`
Data file(s)	`g7data.*`

The data are percentage quarterly growth rates of output, y_t , and spreads, x_t, for the G7 countries, Canada, France, Germany, Italy, Japan, United Kingdom and the United States. All sample periods end December 1999, but the starting dates vary which are given in the data file.

(a) Consider the following model of the business cycle where output growth in the mean and the variance are functions of lagged output growth and lagged spreads

$$y_t = \beta_0 + \beta_1 y_{t-1} + \beta_2 x_{t-1} + u_t \, , \qquad u_t \sim N\left(0, \sigma_t^2\right) \, ,$$
$$\sigma_t^2 = \exp\left(\gamma_0 + \gamma_1 y_{t-1} + \gamma_2 x_{t-1}\right) \, .$$

Estimate the model for each of the G7 countries and interpret the parameter estimates.

(b) Perform a likelihood ratio test of heteroskedasticity by testing the restrictions

$$\gamma_1 = \gamma_2 = 0 \, .$$

(c) Use the results in parts (a) and (b) to discuss the role of spreads in determining the business cycle.

(4) Testing for Vector Heteroskedasticity

Program files	`hetero_system.*`

Simulate the bivariate heteroskedasticity model for $T = 2000$ observations

$$By_t + Ax_t = u_t$$
$$u_t \sim N(0, V_t = S_t S_t')$$
$$S_t = C + Dw_t,$$

in which

$$B = \begin{bmatrix} 1 & -\beta_1 \\ -\beta_2 & 1 \end{bmatrix} = \begin{bmatrix} 1.000 & -0.600 \\ -0.200 & 1.000 \end{bmatrix}$$

$$A = \begin{bmatrix} -\alpha_1 & 0 \\ 0 & -\alpha_2 \end{bmatrix} = \begin{bmatrix} -0.400 & 0.000 \\ 0.000 & 0.500 \end{bmatrix}$$

$$C = \begin{bmatrix} c_{1,1} & 0 \\ c_{2,1} & c_{2,2} \end{bmatrix} = \begin{bmatrix} 1.000 & 0.000 \\ 0.500 & 2.000 \end{bmatrix}$$

$$D = \begin{bmatrix} d_{1,1} & 0 \\ d_{2,1} & d_{2,2} \end{bmatrix} = \begin{bmatrix} 0.500 & 0.000 \\ 0.200 & 0.200 \end{bmatrix},$$

and $x_{1,t} \sim iid\ U[0, 10]$, $x_{2,t} \sim iid\ N(0, 9)$ and $w_t \sim iid\ U[0, 1]$.
(a) Estimate the model by maximum likelihood using the Newton-Raphson algorithm and comment on the results.
(b) Construct LR and Wald tests for vector heteroskedasticity.

(5) **Monetary Policy and Asset Market Volatility**

Program files	hetero_event.*
Data files	usasset.*

The data consist of $T = 2583$ daily observations from 1 October 1993 to 31 December 2003 for the United States on eight daily bond yields with maturities ranging from 3 months to 10 years, expressed as a percentage. Also contained in the file are equity prices and a dummy variable corresponding to when the Federal Reserve Open Market Committee (FOMC) meets, known as an event day

$$d_t = \begin{cases} 1 & : \quad \text{Event day (meeting of the FOMC)} \\ 0 & : \quad \text{Non-event day.} \end{cases}$$

To investigate the effects of monetary policy on asset market volatility consider the heteroskedastic regression model where the variance is based on a step function

$$y_{i,t} = \beta_0 + \beta_1 d_t + u_t, \qquad u_t \sim N\left(0, \sigma_t^2\right),$$
$$\sigma_t^2 = \exp\left(\gamma_0 + \gamma_1 d_t\right),$$

where $y_{i,t}$, $i = 1, 2, \cdots, 8$, is the change in the yield on the ith bond and d_t is the event dummy variable corresponding to FOMC meeting dates.

(a) Compute the sample means and sample variances of $y_{i,t}$ for each bond yield corresponding to event days and non-event days. Interpret these results.

(b) Estimate the model for each bond yield. Use the estimated model to compute estimates of the mean and the variance on event and non-event days and compare these results to the descriptive statistics computed in part (a).

(c) Perform LR, Wald and LM tests on the restrictions (i) $\gamma_1 = 0$ and (ii) $\beta_1 = \gamma_1 = 0$, respectively. Interpret the results.

(d) Repeat parts (a) to (c) where the change in the bond yield, $y_{i,t}$, is replaced by equity returns

$$r_t = 100(\ln p_t - \ln p_{t-1}),$$

where p_t is the equity price.

(e) Combine the eight bond market yields and the equity return in parts (a) to (d) to form a system of nine variables

$$\{y_{1,t}, y_{2,t}, \cdots, y_{8,t}, r_t\}.$$

Estimate a vector heteroskedastic model by combining the nine heteroskedastic regression models. Perform a LR test of constant volatility. Briefly discuss how money shocks effect asset markets in the United States.

(6) **Testing for Vector Heteroskedasticity and Autocorrelation**

    Program files   hetero_general.*

Simulate the bivariate heteroskedastic model with autocorrelation for $T = 2000$ observations

$$By_t + Ax_t = u_t$$
$$u_t = Pu_{t-1} + v_t$$
$$v_t \sim N(0, V_t = S_t S_t')$$
$$S_t = C + Dw_t,$$

in which

$$B = \begin{bmatrix} 1 & -\beta_1 \\ -\beta_2 & 1 \end{bmatrix} = \begin{bmatrix} 1.000 & -0.600 \\ -0.200 & 1.000 \end{bmatrix}$$

$$A = \begin{bmatrix} -\alpha_1 & 0 \\ 0 & -\alpha_2 \end{bmatrix} = \begin{bmatrix} -0.400 & 0.000 \\ 0.000 & 0.500 \end{bmatrix}$$

$$P = \begin{bmatrix} \rho_{1,1} & \rho_{1,2} \\ \rho_{2,1} & \rho_{2,2} \end{bmatrix} = \begin{bmatrix} 0.800 & 0.100 \\ -0.200 & 0.600 \end{bmatrix}$$

$$C = \begin{bmatrix} c_{1,1} & 0 \\ c_{2,1} & c_{2,2} \end{bmatrix} = \begin{bmatrix} 1.000 & 0.000 \\ 0.500 & 2.000 \end{bmatrix}$$

$$D = \begin{bmatrix} d_{1,1} & 0 \\ d_{2,1} & d_{2,2} \end{bmatrix} = \begin{bmatrix} 0.500 & 0.000 \\ 0.200 & 0.200 \end{bmatrix},$$

and $x_{1,t} \sim iid\ U[0, 10]$, $x_{2,t} \sim iid\ N(0, 9)$ and $w_t \sim iid\ U[0, 1]$.

(a) Estimate the model by maximum likelihood using the Newton-Raphson algorithm and comment on the results.

(b) Construct LR and Wald tests for joint vector heteroskedasticity and autocorrelation.

(c) Construct LR and Wald tests for vector heteroskedasticity.

(7) **The Great Moderation**

Program files   hetero_moderation.*

This exercise is based on annual data on real United States GDP per capita for the period 1946 to 2006. The Great Moderation refers to the decrease in the volatility of United States output growth in the early 1980s. This proposition is tested by specifying the following model

$$y_t = \beta_0 + \beta_1 d_t + u_t, \qquad u_t \sim N(0, \sigma_t^2),$$
$$\sigma_t^2 = \exp(\gamma_0 + \gamma_1 d_t),$$

in which y_t is the growth rate in real GDP and d_t is a dummy variable defined as

$$d_t = \begin{cases} 0 & : & 1947\ \text{to}\ 1983 \\ 1 & : & 1984\ \text{to}\ 2006. \end{cases}$$

(a) Construct the growth rate in real GDP

$$y_t = 100(\ln GDP_t - \ln GDP_{t-1}).$$

and compute the sample means and sample variances of y_t for the sub-periods 1947 to 1983 and 1984 to 2006.

(b) Estimate the parameters of the model, $\theta = \{\beta_0, \beta_1, \gamma_0, \gamma_1\}$, by maximum likelihood. Interpret the parameter estimates by comparing the estimates to the descriptive statistics computed in part (a).

(c) The Great Moderation suggests that the United States GDP growth rate has become less volatile in the post-1983 period. This requires that $\gamma_1 < 0$. Perform LR, Wald and LM tests of this restriction and interpret the results.

(d) The model allows for both the mean and the variance to change. Test the restriction $\beta_1 = 0$. If the null hypothesis is not rejected, then redo part (c) subject to the restriction $\beta_1 = 0$.

(8) Sampling Properties of Heteroskedasticity Estimators

Program files   hetero_sampling.*

Consider the model

$$y_t = \beta_0 + \beta_1 x_t + u_t, \qquad u_t \sim N(0, \sigma_t^2),$$
$$\sigma_t^2 = \exp(\gamma_0 + \gamma_1 x_t),$$

in which the exogenous variable is $x_t \sim iid\, U[0, 1]$, draws from the uniform distribution, and the population parameter values are $\theta_0 = \{\beta_0 = 1.0, \beta_1 = 2.0, \gamma_0 = 1.0, \gamma_1 = 5.0\}$.

(a) Simulate the model for $T = \{20, 50, 100, 200, 500\}$ observations and compute the following statistics on the sampling distribution of the maximum likelihood estimator using 10000 replications,

$$\text{Mean} \quad = \quad \frac{1}{10000} \sum_{i=1}^{10000} \widehat{\theta}_i$$

$$\text{Bias} \quad = \quad \frac{1}{10000} \sum_{i=1}^{10000} \widehat{\theta}_i - \theta_0$$

$$\text{MSE} \quad = \quad \frac{1}{10000} \sum_{i=1}^{10000} (\widehat{\theta}_i - \theta_0)^2$$

$$\text{RMSE} \quad = \quad \sqrt{MSE}.$$

(b) Repeat part (a) for the least squares estimator without adjusting for heteroskedasticity, that is with $\gamma_1 = 0$.

(c) Using the results in parts (a) and (b), discuss the consistency and efficiency properties of the maximum likelihood and the ordinary least squares estimators of β_0 and β_1.

(9) Size and Power Properties of the Wald Heteroskedasticity Test

Program files   hetero_power.*

Consider the multiplicative heteroskedastic regression model

$$y_t = \beta_0 + \beta_1 x_t + u_t, \qquad u_t \sim N(0, \sigma_t^2),$$
$$\sigma_t^2 = \exp(\gamma_0 + \gamma_1 x_t),$$

in which $x_t \sim iid\ U[0, 1]$ is an exogenous variable.

(a) Simulate the model under the null hypothesis of no heteroskedasticity using population parameter values $\theta_0 = \{\beta_0 = 1.0, \beta_1 = 2.0, \gamma_0 = 1.0, \gamma_1 = 0.0\}$. Choose a sample of $T = 50$ observations and 10000 replications.

   (i) For each draw, compute the Wald test of heteroskedasticity

$$W = \frac{(\widehat{\gamma}_1 - 0)^2}{\text{var}(\widehat{\gamma}_1)}.$$

   (ii) Compute the 5% critical value from the sampling distribution.

   (iii) Compute the size of the test based on the 5% critical value from the χ^2 distribution with one degree of freedom.

   (iv) Discuss the size properties of the test.

(b) Simulate the model under the alternative hypothesis with increasing levels of heteroskedasticity by choosing $\gamma_1 = \{0.5, 1.0, 1.5, \cdots, 5.0\}$, with the remaining parameters equal to the values in part (a). Choose a sample of $T = 50$ observations and 10000 replications.

   (i) For each draw compute the Wald test of heteroskedasticity.

   (ii) Compute the power of the test (size unadjusted) based on the 5% critical value from the χ^2 distribution with one degree of freedom.

   (iii) Compute the power of the test (size adjusted) based on the 5% critical value from the sampling distribution of the Wald statistic obtained in part (a).

   (iv) Discuss the power properties of the test.

(c) Repeat parts (a) and (b) for samples of size $T = \{100, 200, 500\}$. Discuss the consistency properties of the Wald test.

PART THREE

Other Estimation Methods

9   Quasi-Maximum Likelihood Estimation

9.1   Introduction

The class of models discussed in Parts ONE and TWO of the book assume that the specification of the likelihood function, in terms of the joint probability distribution of the variables, is correct and that the regularity conditions set out in Chapter 2 are satisfied. Under these conditions, the maximum likelihood estimator has the desirable properties discussed in Chapter 2, namely that it is consistent, asymptotically normally distributed and asymptotically efficient because in the limit it achieves the Cramér-Rao lower bound given by the inverse of the information matrix.

This chapter addresses the problem investigated by White (1982), namely maximum likelihood estimation when the likelihood function is misspecified. In general, the maximum likelihood estimator in the presence of misspecification does not display the usual properties. However, there are a number of important special cases in which the maximum likelihood estimator of a misspecified model still provides a consistent estimator for some of the population parameters in the true model. As the maximum likelihood estimator is based on a misspecified model, this estimator is referred to as the quasi-maximum likelihood estimator. Perhaps the most important case is the estimation of the conditional mean in the linear regression model, discussed in detail in Part TWO, where potential misspecifications arise from assuming either normality, or constant variance, or independence.

One important difference between the maximum likelihood estimator based on the true probability distribution and the quasi-maximum likelihood estimator is that the usual estimator of the variance derived in Chapter 2 and based on the information matrix equality holding, is no longer appropriate for the quasi-maximum likelihood estimator. Nonetheless, an estimator of the variance is still available, being based on a combination of the Hessian and the outer product of gradients matrices.

9.2   Misspecification

Suppose that the true probability distribution of y_t is $f_0(y_t; \theta, \delta)$ with population parameters $\theta = \theta_0$ and $\delta = \delta_0$, but that an incorrect probability distribution given by $f(y_t; \theta, \lambda)$ is used to construct the likelihood function. This situation may be summarised as

True distribution	:	$f_0(y_t; \theta, \delta)$
Misspecified distribution	:	$f(y_t; \theta, \lambda)$.

The parameter vector of interest is θ, which is common to both models. The additional parameter vector δ is part of the true distribution but not the misspecified model, while the reverse holds for the parameter vector λ, which is just part of the misspecified model.

Example 9.1 Duration Analysis

Ensuring positive durations motivates the use of an exponential distribution with mean μ for the true model of duration times between events, while the misspecified model is a normal distribution with mean μ and unit variance, given by

$$f_0(y_t; \mu) = \frac{1}{\mu} \exp\left[-\frac{y_t}{\mu}\right], \qquad f(y_t; \mu) = \frac{1}{\sqrt{2\pi}} \exp\left[-\frac{(y_t - \mu)^2}{2}\right].$$

The common parameter is $\theta = \{\mu\}$ and there are no additional parameters in either the true or misspecified model. While the distribution $f(y_t; \mu)$ is misspecified, the mean is correctly specified to be μ. Panel (a) of Figure 9.1 provides a plot of the true and misspecified log-likelihood functions for a sample of $T = 10$ observations drawn from the (true) exponential distribution with parameter $\theta_0 = \mu_0 = 1$. □

Example 9.2 Durations with Dependence

The true model of y_t is an exponential distribution with an AR(1) structure for the mean conditional on y_{t-1},

$$f_0(y_t | y_{t-1}, \cdots, y_1; \mu, \beta) = \frac{1}{\mu + \beta(y_{t-1} - \mu)} \exp\left[-\frac{y_t}{\mu + \beta(y_{t-1} - \mu)}\right].$$

This specification implies that the unconditional mean of y_t is μ. The misspecified model is an *iid* exponential distribution with mean μ,

$$f(y_t | y_{t-1}, \cdots, y_1; \mu) = \frac{1}{\mu} \exp\left[-\frac{y_t}{\mu}\right],$$

which is misspecified because it omits the dependence induced by the AR(1) structure in the true model. The common parameter is $\theta = \{\mu\}$ while $\delta = \{\beta\}$ is an extra parameter in the true model. □

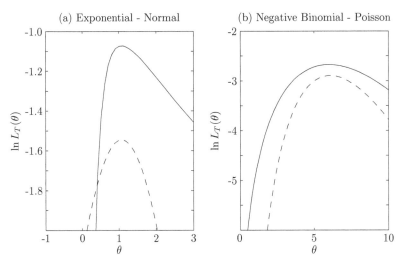

Figure 9.1. Comparison of the true and misspecified log-likelihood functions. Panel (a) compares the true exponential log-likelihood function (solid line) and the misspecified normal log-likelihood function (dashed line) for $T = 10$ observations drawn from an exponential distribution with $\mu_0 = 1$. Panel (b) compares the true negative binomial distribution (solid line) and the misspecified Poisson distribution for $T = 10$ observations drawn from a negative binomial distribution with $\mu_0 = 5$ and $p_0 = 0.5$.

Example 9.3 Modelling Counts

The true distribution of counts is negative binomial with parameters $\mu > 0$ and $0 < p < 1$ and the misspecified distribution is a Poisson distribution with parameter $\mu > 0$ given by

$$f_0(y_t; \mu, p) = \frac{\Gamma(y_t + \mu)}{\Gamma(y_t + 1)\,\Gamma(\mu)}\,(1-p)^\mu\, p^{y_t}, \qquad f(y_t; \mu) = \frac{\mu^{y_t}\exp[-\mu]}{y_t!}.$$

The parameter $\theta = \{\mu\}$ is common to both models, while $\delta = \{p\}$ is an additional parameter in the true model. The mean and the variance of the negative binomial distribution are, respectively, given by

$$\mathrm{E}[y_t] = \mu\frac{p}{1-p}, \qquad \mathrm{var}(y_t) = \mu\frac{p}{(1-p)^2}, \qquad \frac{\mathrm{var}(y_t)}{\mathrm{E}[y_t]} = \frac{1}{1-p} > 1,$$

where the last expression measures the over dispersion of the negative binomial distribution relative to the Poisson distribution. The misspecification is that the Poisson distribution does not exhibit over dispersion because its mean and variance are equal. Panel (b) of Figure 9.1 illustrates the true and misspecified log-likelihood functions for a sample of $T = 10$ observations drawn from the (true) negative binomial distribution with parameters $\theta_0 = \{\mu_0 = 5$ and $p_0 = 0.5\}$. $\qquad\square$

Example 9.4 AR Model with Non-normal Disturbance

The true model is an AR(1)

$$y_t = \phi y_{t-1} + \sigma z_t,$$

in which $|\phi| < 1$ and z_t is an iid $(0, 1)$ disturbance term distributed as standardised Student t with ν degrees of freedom

$$f_0(y_t|y_{t-1}, \cdots, y_1; \phi, \sigma^2, \nu)$$

$$= \frac{\Gamma\left(\dfrac{\nu+1}{2}\right)}{\sqrt{\pi\sigma^2\left(\nu-2\right)}\Gamma\left(\dfrac{\nu}{2}\right)}\left(1 + \frac{(y_t - \phi y_{t-1})^2}{\sigma^2(\nu-2)}\right)^{-\frac{\nu+1}{2}}.$$

The misspecified model assumes that z_t has a standard normal distribution

$$f\left(y_t|y_{t-1}, \cdots, y_1; \phi, \sigma^2\right) = \frac{1}{\sqrt{2\pi\sigma^2}} \exp\left[-\frac{(y_t - \phi y_{t-1})^2}{2\sigma^2}\right].$$

The common parameters are $\theta = \{\phi, \sigma^2\}$ while the degrees of freedom parameter represents an additional parameter in the true model, $\delta = \{\nu\}$. The conditional mean and variance are correctly specified, but the distribution is misspecified as the fatness in the tails of the true distribution is not being modelled. The degree of this misspecification is controlled by the parameter ν, with misspecification disappearing as $\nu \to \infty$. □

Example 9.5 Time Series Dynamics

The time series y_t follows a MA(1) model, but the misspecified model is based on a model having AR(1) dynamics

$$MA(1): y_t = u_t - \psi u_{t-1}, \qquad u_t \sim iid\, N(0, \sigma^2)$$
$$AR(1): y_t = \psi y_{t-1} + v_t, \qquad v_t \sim iid\, N(0, \eta^2).$$

The true and misspecified distributions are, respectively, given by

$$f_0(y_t|y_{t-1}, \cdots, y_1; \psi, \sigma^2) = \frac{1}{\sqrt{2\pi\sigma^2}} \exp\left[-\frac{(y_t - (-\sum_{j=1}^{t-1}\psi^j y_{t-j}))^2}{2\sigma^2}\right]$$

$$f(y_t|y_{t-1}, \cdots, y_1; \psi, \eta^2) = \frac{1}{\sqrt{2\pi\eta^2}} \exp\left[-\frac{(y_t - \psi y_{t-1})^2}{2\eta^2}\right],$$

The common parameter is $\theta = \{\psi\}$, while the additional parameter in the true model is $\delta = \{\sigma^2\}$ and in the misspecified model $\lambda = \{\eta^2\}$. The misspecification corresponds to excluding lags greater than the first lag from the model. □

Example 9.6 Heteroskedasticity
   The true model is a heteroskedastic regression model with conditional mean βx_t and a normal disturbance with conditional variance αx_t, while the misspecified model has the same conditional mean but a conditional variance equal to σ^2 which is constant

$$f_0(y_t | x_t; \beta, \alpha) = \frac{1}{\sqrt{2\pi(\alpha x_t)}} \exp\left[-\frac{(y_t - \beta x_t)^2}{2(\alpha x_t)}\right]$$

$$f(y_t | x_t; \beta, \sigma^2) = \frac{1}{\sqrt{2\pi\sigma^2}} \exp\left[-\frac{(y_t - \beta x_t)^2}{2\sigma^2}\right].$$

The common parameter is $\theta = \{\beta\}$, whereas the additional parameters in the true and misspecified models are, respectively, $\delta = \{\alpha\}$ and $\lambda = \{\sigma^2\}$. □

   In Chapter 2, the maximum likelihood estimator based on a correctly specified likelihood is shown to be consistent and asymptotically normal. It is also shown that the information matrix equality holds which implies that the asymptotic variance of the maximum likelihood estimator is given by the inverse of the information matrix. If the likelihood function is misspecified, however, there are several possible cases to consider. Suppose a conditional mean is being estimated using the misspecified likelihood function, then the following possible cases arise.

(1) The misspecification is mostly harmless because the estimator based on the misspecified log-likelihood function remains consistent, asymptotically normal and has the same asymptotic variance as if it were correctly specified. In general, however, the estimator based on the misspecified model is no longer asymptotically efficient. Examples 9.1 and 9.4 fall into this category.
(2) The estimator is consistent and asymptotically normal, but the information equality no longer holds so that the asymptotic variance of the estimator has a different form. Examples 9.2, 9.3 and 9.6 fall into this category.
(3) The estimator is inconsistent so that any subsequent inference is likely to be misleading. Example 9.5 is an example of this worst-case scenario.

The details of the model and the type of potential misspecification need to be evaluated on a case-by-case basis to determine which of these three situations may be relevant. While this classification does not, therefore, provide a general rule to analyse misspecification in every case, it does provide some guiding intuition that is often useful when estimating (conditional) means. If the misspecified likelihood function correctly specifies the form of both the mean and the variance, even if other aspects are misspecified, then case (1) applies. If, on the other hand, the mean is correctly specified but the variance is misspecified then case (2) applies. Finally, the worst-case scenario arises if the mean is misspecified. The same logic can be applied to estimating a (conditional) variance of y_t, since that is determined by the means of y_t and y_t^2.

9.3   The Quasi-Maximum Likelihood Estimator

The previous examples provide a number of cases where the parameter θ is common to the true likelihood based on $f_0(y_t; \theta, \lambda)$ and the misspecified likelihood based on $f(y_t; \theta, \delta)$. If $\widehat{\theta}$ represents the maximum likelihood estimator of θ_0 using the misspecified model, this estimator is known as the quasi-maximum likelihood estimator since estimation is based on a misspecified distribution and not the true distribution. The true and quasi log-likelihood functions are given by

$$\text{True log-likelihood function} \quad : \quad \frac{1}{T} \sum_{t=1}^{T} \ln f_0(y_t; \theta, \delta)$$

$$\text{Quasi log-likelihood function} \quad : \quad \frac{1}{T} \sum_{t=1}^{T} \ln f(y_t; \theta, \lambda).$$

What is of interest is whether or not the maximum likelihood estimator of the misspecified model, $\widehat{\theta}$, is a consistent estimator of θ_0, even though the specified distribution used to construct the likelihood may not match the true distribution. The conditions that need to be satisfied for this result to occur are now presented.

In Chapter 2, the maximum likelihood estimator is shown to be a consistent estimator of θ_0, provided that

$$(\theta_0, \delta_0) = \arg\max_{\theta, \delta} E[\ln f_0(y_t; \theta, \delta)], \tag{9.1}$$

and the correctly specified maximum likelihood estimator is the sample equivalent of this, given by

$$(\widehat{\theta}_{ML}, \widehat{\delta}_{ML}) = \arg\max_{\theta, \delta} \frac{1}{T} \sum_{t=1}^{T} \ln f_0(y_t; \theta, \delta). \tag{9.2}$$

Now consider replacing the true distribution $f_0(y_t; \theta, \delta)$ in (9.1) by the misspecified distribution $f(y_t; \theta, \lambda)$. If the condition

$$(\theta_0, \lambda_0) = \arg\max_{\theta, \lambda} E[\ln f(y_t; \theta, \lambda)] \tag{9.3}$$

is satisfied, then θ_0 also maximises the expectation of the quasi log-likelihood function. The quasi-maximum likelihood estimator is the solution of

$$(\widehat{\theta}, \widehat{\lambda}) = \arg\max_{\theta, \lambda} \frac{1}{T} \sum_{t=1}^{T} \ln f(y_t; \theta, \lambda). \tag{9.4}$$

Provided that (9.3) is shown to hold and that there is a suitable uniform WLLN such that

$$\frac{1}{T} \sum_{t=1}^{T} \ln f(y_t; \theta, \lambda) \xrightarrow{p} E\left[\ln f(y_t; \theta, \lambda)\right],$$

it follows by the same reasoning outlined in Chapter 2 that the quasi-maximum likelihood estimator is a consistent estimator of θ_0, that is $\widehat{\theta} \xrightarrow{p} \theta_0$.

Example 9.7 Duration Analysis

Consider Example 9.1 where the true model is the exponential distribution and the misspecified model is the normal distribution. Taking expectations of $\ln f(y_t; \theta)$ where $\theta = \mu$ gives

$$
\begin{aligned}
E[\ln f(y_t; \mu)] &= -\frac{1}{2} \ln 2\pi - \frac{1}{2} E[(y_t - \mu)^2] \\
&= -\frac{1}{2} \ln 2\pi - \frac{1}{2} E[(y_t - \mu_0 + \mu_0 - \mu)^2] \\
&= -\frac{1}{2} \ln 2\pi - \frac{1}{2} E[(y_t - \mu_0)^2] - \frac{1}{2}(\mu_0 - \mu)^2 - (\mu_0 - \mu)E[y_t - \mu_0] \\
&= -\frac{1}{2} \ln 2\pi - \frac{1}{2}\mu_0^2 - \frac{1}{2}(\mu_0 - \mu)^2 .
\end{aligned}
$$

As $E[\ln f(y_t; \mu)]$ is maximised at $\mu = \mu_0$, the normal model satisfies (9.3) for the consistent estimation of μ_0, the mean of an exponential distribution. □

Example 9.8 Durations with Dependence

From Example 9.2 the quasi log-likelihood function at time t is given by

$$\ln f(y_t; \mu) = -\ln \mu - y_t/\mu.$$

Now

$$E[\ln f(y_t; \mu)] = -\ln \mu - \frac{E[y_t]}{\mu} = -\ln \mu - \frac{\mu_0}{\mu}.$$

The first and second derivatives of $E[\ln f(y_t; \mu)]$ are

$$\frac{dE[\ln f(y_t; \mu)]}{d\mu} = -\frac{1}{\mu} + \frac{\mu_0}{\mu^2}, \qquad \frac{d^2 E[\ln f(y_t; \mu)]}{d\mu^2} = \frac{1}{\mu^2} - \frac{2\mu_0}{\mu^3}.$$

Setting the first derivative to zero shows that $E[\ln f(y_t; \mu)]$ is maximised at $\mu = \mu_0$. The quasi-maximum likelihood estimator provides a consistent estimator of μ_0, even though it omits the dynamics of the true model. □

Example 9.9 Time Series Dynamics

In Example 9.5 the true model is a MA(1) model and the misspecified model is an AR(1) model. The expectation of the misspecified log-likelihood

function is

$$E[\ln f(y_t|y_{t-1}, \cdots, y_1; \psi, \eta^2)]$$
$$= -\frac{1}{2}\ln 2\pi - \frac{1}{2}\ln \eta^2 - \frac{1}{2\eta^2}E[(y_t - \psi y_{t-1})^2].$$

Given that the true MA(1) model is $y_t = u_t - \psi_0 u_{t-1}$, then

$$E[(y_t - \psi y_{t-1})^2] = E[((u_t - \psi_0 u_{t-1}) - \psi(u_{t-1} - \psi_0 u_{t-2}))^2]$$
$$= \sigma_0^2(1 + (\psi + \psi_0)^2 + \psi^2\psi_0^2),$$

as $u_t \sim iid\,(0, \sigma_0^2)$, resulting in

$$E[\ln f(y_t|y_{t-1}, \cdots, y_1; \psi, \eta^2)]$$
$$= -\frac{1}{2}\ln 2\pi - \frac{1}{2}\ln \eta^2 - \frac{1}{2\eta^2}\sigma_0^2(1 + (\psi + \psi_0)^2 + \psi^2\psi_0^2).$$

Differentiating with respect to ψ and setting the derivative to zero shows that

$$\psi = -\frac{\psi_0}{1 + \psi_0^2} \neq \psi_0,$$

so the condition in (9.3) is not satisfied. Therefore, the estimator of the coefficient of an AR(1) model is not consistent for the coefficient of a MA(1) model as a result of the conditional mean being misspecified. □

9.4   Asymptotic Distribution

Suppose the quasi-maximum likelihood condition (9.3) holds, so that the quasi-maximum likelihood estimator $\widehat{\theta}$ is consistent for θ_0. The derivation of the asymptotic distribution of $\widehat{\theta}$ follows the same steps as those in Chapter 2 except the true likelihood based on $f_0(y_t; \theta, \delta)$ is replaced by the quasi-likelihood based on $f(y_t; \theta, \lambda)$. Let $\{\theta_0, \lambda_0\}$ represent the true parameters, where θ_0 is the population parameter of interest and λ_0 effectively represents a true parameter insofar as it satisfies (9.3) even though it is not actually part of the true model.

The first-order condition of the quasi log-likelihood function corresponding to (9.4) is

$$G_T(\widehat{\theta}, \widehat{\lambda}) = \frac{1}{T}\sum_{t=1}^{T} g_t(\widehat{\theta}, \widehat{\lambda}) = 0, \tag{9.5}$$

where

$$g_t(\theta, \lambda) = \begin{bmatrix} \dfrac{\partial \ln f(y_t; \theta, \lambda)}{\partial \theta} \\ \dfrac{\partial \ln f(y_t; \theta, \lambda)}{\partial \lambda} \end{bmatrix}, \tag{9.6}$$

is the gradient. Provided (9.3) holds and under standard regularity conditions, an important property of $g_t(\theta, \lambda)$ is that

$$E[g_t(\theta_0, \lambda_0)] = 0. \tag{9.7}$$

This expression can be interpreted as the first-order condition of (9.3) and it demonstrates that if the quasi log-likelihood function is well specified for the estimation of θ_0, the gradient evaluated at the true parameter value has mean zero, just as in the case of correctly specified maximum likelihood estimation.

The second-order condition for maximisation is that

$$H_T(\widehat{\theta}, \widehat{\lambda}) = \frac{1}{T} \sum_{t=1}^{T} h_t(\widehat{\theta}, \widehat{\lambda}),$$

be negative definite, where

$$h_t(\theta, \lambda) = \begin{bmatrix} \dfrac{\partial^2 \ln f(y_t; \theta, \lambda)}{\partial\theta\partial\theta'} & \dfrac{\partial^2 \ln f(y_t; \theta, \lambda)}{\partial\theta\partial\lambda'} \\ \dfrac{\partial^2 \ln f(y_t; \theta, \lambda)}{\partial\lambda\partial\theta'} & \dfrac{\partial^2 \ln f(y_t; \theta, \lambda)}{\partial\lambda\partial\lambda'} \end{bmatrix}.$$

A mean value expansion of the first-order condition around the true value, (θ_0, λ_0), gives

$$0 = \frac{1}{T} \sum_{t=1}^{T} g_t(\widehat{\theta}, \widehat{\lambda}) = \frac{1}{T} \sum_{t=1}^{T} g_t(\theta_0, \lambda_0) + \left[\frac{1}{T} \sum_{t=1}^{T} h_t(\theta^*, \lambda^*)\right] \begin{bmatrix} \widehat{\theta} - \theta_0 \\ \widehat{\lambda} - \lambda_0 \end{bmatrix}, \tag{9.8}$$

in which (θ^*, λ^*) lies between $(\widehat{\theta}, \widehat{\lambda})$ and (θ_0, λ_0) and hence $(\theta^*, \lambda^*) \xrightarrow{p} (\theta_0, \lambda_0)$ if $(\widehat{\theta}, \widehat{\lambda}) \xrightarrow{p} (\theta_0, \lambda_0)$. Rearranging and multiplying both sides by $\sqrt{T}$ yields

$$\begin{bmatrix} \sqrt{T}(\widehat{\theta} - \theta_0) \\ \sqrt{T}(\widehat{\lambda} - \lambda_0) \end{bmatrix} = \left[-\frac{1}{T} \sum_{t=1}^{T} h_t(\theta^*, \lambda^*)\right]^{-1} \left[\frac{1}{\sqrt{T}} \sum_{t=1}^{T} g_t(\theta_0, \lambda_0)\right]. \tag{9.9}$$

Now the following conditions are used

$$\frac{1}{T} \sum_{t=1}^{T} h_t(\theta^*, \lambda^*) \xrightarrow{p} H(\theta_0, \lambda_0)$$

$$\frac{1}{\sqrt{T}} \sum_{t=1}^{T} g_t(\theta_0, \lambda_0) \xrightarrow{d} N(0, J(\theta_0, \lambda_0)), \tag{9.10}$$

where

$$H(\theta_0, \lambda_0) = \lim_{T\to\infty} \frac{1}{T} \sum_{t=1}^{T} E[h_t(\theta_0, \lambda_0)], \tag{9.11}$$

and

$$
\begin{aligned}
J(\theta_0, \lambda_0) &= \lim_{T \to \infty} E\left[\left(\frac{1}{\sqrt{T}} \sum_{t=1}^{T} g_t(\theta_0, \lambda_0)\right)\left(\frac{1}{\sqrt{T}} \sum_{t=1}^{T} g_t(\theta_0, \lambda_0)\right)'\right] \\
&= \lim_{T \to \infty} \frac{1}{T} \sum_{t=1}^{T} E[g_t(\theta_0, \lambda_0) g_t'(\theta_0, \lambda_0)] \\
&\quad + \lim_{T \to \infty} \sum_{s=1}^{T-1}\left(\frac{1}{T} \sum_{t=s+1}^{T} E[g_t(\theta_0, \lambda_0) g_{t-s}'(\theta_0, \lambda_0)]\right) \\
&\quad + \lim_{T \to \infty} \sum_{s=1}^{T-1}\left(\frac{1}{T} \sum_{t=s+1}^{T} E[g_{t-s}(\theta_0, \lambda_0) g_t'(\theta_0, \lambda_0)]\right).
\end{aligned} \tag{9.12}
$$

The first condition in (9.10) follows from a uniform WLLN. The second condition relies on (9.7) to apply a suitable central limit theorem to $g_t(\theta_0, \lambda_0)$. The choice of central limit theorem, as outlined in Chapter 2, depends on the time series properties of $g_t(\theta, \lambda)$. Combining (9.9) and (9.10) yields the asymptotic distribution

$$
\begin{bmatrix} \sqrt{T}(\hat{\theta} - \theta_0) \\ \sqrt{T}(\hat{\lambda} - \lambda_0) \end{bmatrix} \xrightarrow{d} N\left(\begin{bmatrix} 0 \\ 0 \end{bmatrix}, \begin{bmatrix} \Omega_{1,1} & \Omega_{1,2} \\ \Omega_{2,1} & \Omega_{2,2} \end{bmatrix}\right), \tag{9.13}
$$

where the asymptotic quasi-maximum likelihood covariance matrix is partitioned conformably in terms of (θ, λ) and given by

$$
\Omega = \begin{bmatrix} \Omega_{1,1} & \Omega_{1,2} \\ \Omega_{2,1} & \Omega_{2,2} \end{bmatrix} = H^{-1}(\theta_0, \lambda_0) J(\theta_0, \lambda_0) H^{-1}(\theta_0, \lambda_0). \tag{9.14}
$$

Partitioning $H(\theta_0, \lambda_0)$ and $J(\theta_0, \lambda_0)$ in (9.14) conformably in terms of $\{\theta, \lambda\}$ as

$$
H(\theta_0, \lambda_0) = \begin{bmatrix} H_{1,1} & H_{1,2} \\ H_{2,1} & H_{2,2} \end{bmatrix}, \qquad J(\theta_0, \lambda_0) = \begin{bmatrix} J_{1,1} & J_{1,2} \\ J_{2,1} & J_{2,2} \end{bmatrix},
$$

the asymptotic distribution of the quasi-maximum likelihood estimator of θ_0 is

$$
\sqrt{T}(\hat{\theta} - \theta_0) \xrightarrow{d} N(0, \Omega_{1,1}), \tag{9.15}
$$

where $\Omega_{1,1}$ is as defined in equation (9.14). Although, in general, the construction of $\Omega_{1,1}$ will require computing the partitioned inverse of $H(\theta_0, \lambda_0)$, the situation is often simplified by the fact that $H(\theta_0, \lambda_0)$ is block-diagonal, in which case $\Omega_{1,1}$ reduces to $H_{1,1}^{-1} J_{1,1} H_{1,1}^{-1}$.

9.4.1 Misspecification and the Information Equality

Misspecification will generally imply that

$$J(\theta_0, \lambda_0) \neq -H(\theta_0, \lambda_0). \tag{9.16}$$

To show this, suppose that y_t is *iid* so that the expressions in (9.11) and (9.12) simplify to

$$J(\theta_0, \lambda_0) = E[g_t(\theta_0, \lambda_0) g_t'(\theta_0, \lambda_0)], \qquad H(\theta_0, \lambda_0) = E[h_t(\theta_0, \lambda_0)].$$

Focussing on the parameter of interest θ, and partitioning $g_t(\theta, \lambda)$ and $h_t(\theta, \lambda)$ conformably, the first element of the gradient in (9.6) of the misspecified model is

$$g_{1,t}(\theta, \lambda) = \frac{\partial \ln f(y_t; \theta, \lambda)}{\partial \theta} = \frac{1}{f(y_t; \theta, \lambda)} \frac{\partial f(y_t; \theta, \lambda)}{\partial \theta}.$$

and the Hessian is

$$h_{1,1,t}(\theta, \lambda) = -\frac{1}{f(y_t; \theta, \lambda)^2} \frac{\partial f(y_t; \theta, \lambda)}{\partial \theta} \frac{\partial f(y_t; \theta, \lambda)}{\partial \theta'} + \frac{1}{f(y_t; \theta, \lambda)} \frac{\partial^2 f(y_t; \theta, \lambda)}{\partial \theta \partial \theta'}$$

$$= -g_{1,t}(\theta, \lambda) g_{1,t}'(\theta, \lambda) + \frac{1}{f(y_t; \theta, \lambda)} \frac{\partial^2 f(y_t; \theta, \lambda)}{\partial \theta \partial \theta'},$$

Taking expectations of this expression under the true model and rearranging gives

$$E[g_{1,t}(\theta_0, \lambda_0) g_{1,t}'(\theta_0, \lambda_0)] = -E[h_{1,1,t}(\theta_0, \lambda_0)]$$

$$+ E\left[\frac{1}{f(y_t; \theta_0, \lambda_0)} \frac{\partial^2 f(y_t; \theta, \lambda)}{\partial \theta \partial \theta'} \bigg|_{\substack{\theta = \theta_0 \\ \lambda = \lambda_0}} \right],$$

which shows that the information equality holds for θ provided that the second term on the right-hand side is zero. This occurs if the model is correctly specified as $f(y_t; \theta, \lambda) = f_0(y_t; \theta, \lambda)$, resulting in this term reducing to

$$\int \frac{1}{f(y_t; \theta_0, \lambda_0)} \frac{\partial^2 f(y_t; \theta, \lambda)}{\partial \theta \partial \theta'} \bigg|_{\substack{\theta = \theta_0 \\ \lambda = \lambda_0}} f_0(y_t; \theta_0, \lambda_0) dy_t$$

$$= \int \frac{\partial^2 f(y_t; \theta, \lambda)}{\partial \theta \partial \theta'} \bigg|_{\substack{\theta = \theta_0 \\ \lambda = \lambda_0}} dy_t = \frac{\partial^2}{\partial \theta \partial \theta'} \int f(y_t; \theta, \lambda) dy_t \bigg|_{\substack{\theta = \theta_0 \\ \lambda = \lambda_0}} = 0,$$

since $\int f(y_t; \theta, \lambda) dy_t = 1$. In general, if the model is misspecified this reasoning does not necessarily apply and the information equality is not necessarily satisfied. An implication of the information matrix equality failing to hold is that neither $J^{-1}(\theta_0, \lambda_0)$ nor $-H^{-1}(\theta_0, \lambda_0)$ are appropriate covariance matrices on which to base standard error calculations, with the consequence that t tests will have sizes that differ from the nominal (5%) level.

Example 9.10 Duration Analysis

In Example 9.1, the misspecified model is $N(\theta, 1)$, with log-likelihood function at t given by

$$\ln f (y_t; \theta) = -\frac{1}{2} \ln 2\pi - \frac{(y_t - \theta)^2}{2}.$$

The respective gradient and Hessian are

$$g_t(\theta) = \frac{d \ln f(y_t; \theta)}{d\theta} = y_t - \theta, \qquad h_t(\theta) = \frac{d^2 \ln f(y_t; \theta)}{d\theta^2} = -1.$$

As the true model is an exponential distribution with mean $E[y_t] = \theta_0$ and variance $\text{var}(y_t) = \theta_0^2$, and given that y_t is iid, $H(\theta_0)$ and $J(\theta_0)$ of the misspecified model are, respectively,

$$H(\theta_0) = E[h_t(\theta_0)] = -1, \qquad J(\theta_0) = E\left[g_t(\theta_0)^2\right] = E\left[(y_t - \theta_0)^2\right] = \theta_0^2,$$

verifying that $J(\theta_0) \neq -H(\theta_0)$. By comparison from Chapter 2, the respective gradient and Hessian based on the true model are

$$g_t(\theta) = \frac{d \ln f(y_t; \theta)}{d\theta} = -\frac{1}{\theta} + \frac{y_t}{\theta^2}, \qquad h_t(\theta) = \frac{d^2 \ln f(y_t; \theta)}{d\theta^2} = \frac{1}{\theta^2} - \frac{2y_t}{\theta^3}.$$

As

$$H(\theta_0) = E[h_t(\theta_0)] = E\left[\frac{1}{\theta_0^2} - \frac{2y_t}{\theta_0^3}\right] = \frac{1}{\theta_0^2} - \frac{2E[y_t]}{\theta_0^3} = \frac{1}{\theta_0^2} - \frac{2\theta_0}{\theta_0^3} = -\frac{1}{\theta_0^2},$$

$$J(\theta_0) = E\left[g_t(\theta_0)^2\right] = E\left[\left(-\frac{1}{\theta_0} + \frac{y_t}{\theta_0^2}\right)^2\right] = E\left[\frac{(y_t - \theta_0)^2}{\theta_0^4}\right] = \frac{\theta_0^2}{\theta_0^4} = \frac{1}{\theta_0^2},$$

the information equality holds for the true model.   □

Example 9.11 AR Model with Non-normal Disturbance

In Example 9.4, the misspecified model is an AR(1) with normal disturbance yielding a log-likelihood function at t given by

$$\ln f (y_t | y_{t-1}; \phi, \sigma^2) = -\frac{1}{2} \ln 2\pi - \frac{1}{2} \ln \sigma^2 - \frac{(y_t - \phi y_{t-1})^2}{2\sigma^2},$$

with common parameters $\theta = \{\phi, \sigma^2\}$. The respective gradient vector and Hessian are

$$
g_t(\theta) = \begin{bmatrix} \dfrac{1}{\sigma^2} y_{t-1}(y_t - \phi y_{t-1}) \\[2mm] -\dfrac{1}{2\sigma^2} + \dfrac{(y_t - \phi y_{t-1})^2}{2\sigma^4} \end{bmatrix},
$$

$$
h_t(\theta) = \begin{bmatrix} -\dfrac{y_{t-1}^2}{\sigma^2} & -\dfrac{y_{t-1}(y_t - \phi y_{t-1})}{\sigma^4} \\[2mm] -\dfrac{y_{t-1}(y_t - \phi y_{t-1})}{\sigma^4} & \dfrac{1}{2\sigma^4} - \dfrac{(y_t - \phi y_{t-1})^2}{\sigma^6} \end{bmatrix}.
$$

Evaluating at $\theta = \theta_0$ and defining $v_t = y_t - \phi_0 y_{t-1} = \sigma_0 z_t$, gives

$$
g_t(\theta_0) = \begin{bmatrix} \dfrac{1}{\sigma_0^2} y_{t-1} v_t \\[2mm] \dfrac{(v_t^2 - \sigma_0^2)}{2\sigma_0^4} \end{bmatrix}, \quad
h_t(\theta_0) = \begin{bmatrix} -\dfrac{y_{t-1}^2}{\sigma_0^2} & -\dfrac{y_{t-1} v_t}{\sigma_0^4} \\[2mm] -\dfrac{y_{t-1} v_t}{\sigma_0^4} & \dfrac{1}{2\sigma_0^4} - \dfrac{v_t^2}{\sigma_0^6} \end{bmatrix}.
$$

The gradient, $g_t(\theta_0)$, is a mds because

$$
E_{t-1}\left[\dfrac{1}{\sigma_0^2} y_{t-1} v_t\right] = \dfrac{1}{\sigma_0^2} y_{t-1} E_{t-1}[v_t] = 0
$$

$$
E_{t-1}\left[\dfrac{v_t^2 - \sigma_0^2}{2\sigma_0^4}\right] = \dfrac{E_{t-1}[v_t^2] - \sigma_0^2}{2\sigma_0^4} = \dfrac{\sigma_0^2 - \sigma_0^2}{2\sigma_0^4} = 0.
$$

For the AR(1) model, y_t is also stationary so that $J(\theta_0)$ is

$$
J(\theta_0) = E[g_t(\theta_0) g_t'(\theta_0)]
$$

$$
= \begin{bmatrix} \dfrac{E[y_{t-1}^2 v_t^2]}{\sigma_0^4} & \dfrac{E[y_{t-1} v_t (v_t^2 - \sigma_0^2)]}{2\sigma_0^6} \\[2mm] \dfrac{E[y_{t-1} v_t (v_t^2 - \sigma_0^2)]}{2\sigma_0^6} & \dfrac{E[(v_t^2 - \sigma_0^2)^2]}{4\sigma_0^8} \end{bmatrix}
$$

$$
= \begin{bmatrix} \dfrac{1}{1 - \phi_0^2} & 0 \\[2mm] 0 & \dfrac{1}{2\sigma_0^4}\left(1 + \dfrac{3}{\nu - 4}\right) \end{bmatrix}.
$$

This expression uses the following results

$$E[y_{t-1}^2 v_t^2] = E[E_{t-1}[y_{t-1}^2 v_t^2]] = E[y_{t-1}^2 E_{t-1}[v_t^2]]$$

$$= E[y_{t-1}^2]\sigma_0^2 = \frac{\sigma_0^4}{1 - \phi_0^2}$$

$$E[y_{t-1} v_t (v_t^2 - \sigma_0^2)] = E[y_{t-1} E_{t-1}[v_t (v_t^2 - \sigma_0^2)]] = E[y_{t-1}]E[v_t^3] = 0$$

$$E[(v_t^2 - \sigma_0^2)^2] = E[v_t^4] - \sigma_0^4 = \sigma_0^4(E[z_t^4] - 1) = \sigma_0^4\left(2 + \frac{6}{v - 4}\right),$$

where the first two terms are based on the law of iterated expectations and the property that the first two unconditional moments of the AR(1) model (see also Chapter 13) are $E[y_t] = E[y_{t-1}] = 0$ and $\text{var}(y_t) = \sigma_0^2/(1 - \phi_0^2)$ respectively, while the third term uses the fourth moment of the t distribution $E[z_t^4] = 3 + 6/(v - 4)$. Finally, $H(\theta_0)$ is given by

$$H(\theta_0) = E[h_t(\theta_0)] = \begin{bmatrix} -\dfrac{E[y_{t-1}^2]}{\sigma_0^2} & -\dfrac{E[y_{t-1}v_t]}{\sigma_0^4} \\ -\dfrac{E[y_{t-1}v_t]}{\sigma_0^4} & \dfrac{1}{2\sigma_0^4} - \dfrac{E[v_t^2]}{\sigma_0^6} \end{bmatrix} = -\begin{bmatrix} \dfrac{1}{1-\phi_0^2} & 0 \\ 0 & \dfrac{1}{2\sigma_0^4} \end{bmatrix},$$

which is based on the same results used to derive $J(\theta_0)$. A comparison of $J(\theta_0)$ and $H(\theta_0)$ shows that the information equality holds for the autoregressive parameter ϕ, but not for the variance parameter σ^2. In the special case of no misspecification where the true model is also normal so that $v \to \infty$ and hence $E[v_t^4] = 3\sigma_0^4$, from $J(\theta_0)$ the pertinent term is $1/2\sigma_0^4$ which now equals the corresponding term in $H(\theta_0)$. □

9.4.2 Independent and Identically Distributed Data

If y_t is *iid*, then $g_t(\theta_0, \lambda_0)$ is also *iid* and the expressions for $H(\theta_0, \lambda_0)$ and $J(\theta_0, \lambda_0)$ in (9.11) and (9.12), respectively, reduce to

$$H(\theta_0, \lambda_0) = E[h_t(\theta_0, \lambda_0)] \tag{9.17}$$

$$J(\theta_0, \lambda_0) = E[g_t(\theta_0, \lambda_0) g_t'(\theta_0, \lambda_0)], \tag{9.18}$$

since the expectations $E[h_t(\theta_0, \lambda_0)]$ and $E[g_t(\theta_0, \lambda_0) g_t'(\theta_0, \lambda_0)]$ are constant over t because of the identical distribution assumption, and the autocovariance terms in $J(\theta_0, \lambda_0)$ disappear because of independence. As $g_t(\theta_0, \lambda_0)$ is *iid*, the asymptotic normality condition in (9.13) follows from the Lindeberg-Levy central limit theorem in Chapter 2.

Example 9.12 Duration Analysis
From Example 9.10 in which there is just one common parameter, θ, the terms

$$H(\theta_0) = -1, \qquad J(\theta_0) = \theta_0^2,$$

when substituted in (9.14) give the quasi-maximum likelihood variance

$$\Omega = H^{-1}(\theta_0)J(\theta_0)H^{-1}(\theta_0) = \theta_0^2 \,.$$

The asymptotic distribution of the quasi-maximum likelihood estimator $\widehat{\theta}$, from (9.13) is

$$\sqrt{T}(\widehat{\theta} - \theta_0) \xrightarrow{d} N\left(0, \theta_0^2\right) .$$

By comparison, the maximum likelihood estimator of θ_0, based on the true distribution, has the same variance and hence the same asymptotic distribution. For this example, the erroneous assumption of normality does not result in an inefficient estimator because the variance of the quasi-maximum likelihood and maximum likelihood estimators is identical. □

Example 9.13 Duration Analysis Extended
Extending Example 9.10, by choosing a quasi log-likelihood function based on $N(\theta, \sigma^2)$, now yields the respective gradient and Hessian

$$g_t(\theta) = \frac{d \ln f(y_t; \theta)}{d\theta} = \frac{y_t - \theta}{\sigma^2}, \qquad h_t(\theta) = \frac{d^2 \ln f(y_t; \theta)}{d\theta^2} = -\frac{1}{\sigma^2}.$$

As the true model is an exponential distribution with mean $E[y_t] = \theta_0$ and variance $\mathrm{var}(y_t) = \theta_0^2 = \sigma_0^2$, the Hessian and the outer product of gradient matrices of the misspecified model are, respectively, given by

$$H(\theta_0) = E[h_t(\theta_0)] = -\frac{1}{\sigma_0^2} = -\frac{1}{\theta_0^2},$$

$$J(\theta_0) = E\left[g_t(\theta_0)^2\right] = E\left[\frac{(y_t - \theta_0)^2}{\sigma_0^4}\right] = \frac{E[(y_t - \theta_0)^2]}{\theta_0^4} = \frac{\theta_0^2}{\theta_0^4} = \frac{1}{\theta_0^2}.$$

The information equality $J(\theta_0) = -H(\theta_0)$ holds even for this misspecified model, as now both the mean and the variance are specified correctly even if the distribution is not. □

9.4.3 Dependent Data and Martingale Difference Score

If the gradient (or score) $g_t(\theta_0, \lambda_0)$ is a mds, the expression for $J(\theta_0, \lambda_0)$ in (9.12) reduces to

$$J(\theta_0, \lambda_0) = \lim_{T \to \infty} \frac{1}{T} \sum_{t=1}^{T} E[g_t(\theta_0, \lambda_0) g_t'(\theta_0, \lambda_0)], \qquad (9.19)$$

since martingale differences are not autocorrelated. If y_t is also stationary, then (9.19) reduces to (9.18) since the covariances are the same at each t and $H(\theta_0, \lambda_0)$, in expression (9.11), reduces to (9.17). As $g_t(\theta_0, \lambda_0)$ is a mds, the asymptotic normality condition in (9.13) follows from the martingale difference central limit theorem in Chapter 2.

Example 9.14 AR Model with Non-normal Disturbance

From Example 9.11 in which the common parameters are $\theta = \{\phi, \sigma^2\}$, it follows that

$$H(\theta_0) = - \begin{bmatrix} \dfrac{1}{1 - \phi_0^2} & 0 \\ 0 & \dfrac{1}{2\sigma_0^4} \end{bmatrix}, \quad J(\theta_0) = \begin{bmatrix} \dfrac{1}{1 - \phi_0^2} & 0 \\ 0 & \dfrac{1}{2\sigma_0^4}\left(1 + \dfrac{3}{\nu - 4}\right) \end{bmatrix}.$$

The asymptotic covariance matrix of the quasi-maximum likelihood estimator is

$$\Omega = H^{-1}(\theta_0) J(\theta_0) H^{-1}(\theta_0) = \begin{bmatrix} 1 - \phi_0^2 & 0 \\ 0 & E[v_t^4] - \sigma_0^4 \end{bmatrix}.$$

This matrix is block-diagonal and the asymptotic distributions therefore decompose into

$$\sqrt{T}\left(\hat{\phi} - \phi_0\right) \overset{d}{\to} N\left(0, 1 - \phi_0^2\right)$$
$$\sqrt{T}\left(\hat{\sigma}^2 - \sigma_0^2\right) \overset{d}{\to} N\left(0, 2\sigma_0^4\left(1 + \frac{3}{\nu - 4}\right)\right).$$

In the special case where the distribution is not misspecified, v_t is normal with fourth moment $E[v_t^4] = 3\sigma_0^4$. Letting $\nu \to \infty$ the asymptotic variance of $\hat{\sigma}^2$ is $2\sigma_0^4$, as derived in Chapter 2 using the information matrix.   □

9.4.4 Dependent Data and Score

If the gradient $g_t(\theta_0, \lambda_0)$ exhibits autocorrelation and is not, therefore, a mds, it is necessary to use the more general expression of $J(\theta_0, \lambda_0)$ in (9.12) to derive the asymptotic covariance matrix. If y_t is also stationary, then the outer product of the gradients matrix reduces to

$$J(\theta_0, \lambda_0) = E[g_t(\theta_0, \lambda_0) g_t'(\theta_0, \lambda_0)]$$

$$+ \sum_{s=1}^{\infty} \Big(E[g_t(\theta_0, \lambda_0) g_{t-s}'(\theta_0, \lambda_0)] + E[g_{t-s}(\theta_0, \lambda_0) g_t'(\theta_0, \lambda_0)] \Big).$$

$$(9.20)$$

Provided that $g_t(\theta_0, \lambda_0)$ is also mixing at a sufficiently fast rate so that it exhibits independence at least asymptotically, the asymptotic normality result in (9.10) follows from the mixing central limit theorem of Chapter 2. Finally, as y_t is also stationary, the Hessian is given by (9.17).

Example 9.15 Durations with Dependence

From Example 9.8, where there is only the common parameter $\theta = \{\mu\}$, the expected Hessian is

$$H(\theta_0) = E[h_t(\theta_0)] = \frac{1}{\mu_0^2} - \frac{2\mu_0}{\mu_0^3} = -\frac{1}{\mu_0^2}.$$

As the gradient is $g_t(\theta) = (y_t - \mu)/\mu^2$ and since the variance is given by $\mathrm{var}(y_t) = \mu_0^2/(1 - 2\beta_0^2)$,[1] the first term of (9.20) is

$$E[g_t(\theta_0) g_t'(\theta_0)] = \frac{1}{\mu_0^4} E\left[(y_t - \mu_0)^2\right] = \frac{1}{\mu_0^4}\frac{\mu_0^2}{1 - 2\beta_0^2}.$$

For the second term of (9.20), the AR(1) structure of the conditional mean implies

$$E[g_t(\theta_0) g_{t-s}'(\theta_0)] = \beta_0^s \frac{1}{\mu_0^4}\frac{\mu_0^2}{1 - 2\beta_0^2}.$$

Thus (9.20) is

$$J(\theta_0) = \frac{1}{\mu_0^4}\frac{\mu_0^2}{1 - 2\beta_0^2}\left(1 + 2\sum_{s=1}^{\infty}\beta_0^s\right) = \frac{1}{\mu_0^4}\frac{\mu_0^2}{1 - 2\beta_0^2}\frac{1 + \beta_0}{1 - \beta_0}.$$

The quasi-maximum likelihood estimator, $\widehat{\mu}$, has variance

$$\Omega = H^{-1}(\theta_0)J(\theta_0)H^{-1}(\theta_0) = \frac{\mu_0^2}{1 - 2\beta_0^2}\frac{1 + \beta_0}{1 - \beta_0},$$

---

[1] To see this, use $\mathrm{var}(y_t) = E[\mathrm{var}(y_t|y_{t-1})] + \mathrm{var}(E[y_t|y_{t-1}])$, and then $E[\mathrm{var}(y_t|y_{t-1})] = \mu_0^2 + \beta_0^2\mathrm{var}(y_{t-1})$, which follows from the exponential property that the variance is the square of the mean, and also $\mathrm{var}(E[y_t|y_{t-1}]) = \beta_0^2\mathrm{var}(y_{t-1})$.

and, from (9.13), has asymptotic distribution

$$\sqrt{T}\left(\widehat{\mu} - \mu_0\right) \overset{d}{\to} N\left(0, \frac{\mu_0^2}{1 - 2\beta_0^2}\frac{1 + \beta_0}{1 - \beta_0}\right).$$

In the special case of $\beta_0 = 0$, the asymptotic distribution simplifies to $\sqrt{T}\left(\widehat{\mu} - \mu_0\right) \overset{d}{\to} N\left(0, \mu_0^2\right)$, which is the *iid* case given in Example 9.12. $\square$

9.5   Variance Estimation

If a quasi-maximum likelihood estimator is consistent and has asymptotic distribution given by (9.13), in practice it is necessary to estimate the asymptotic covariance matrix

$$\Omega = H^{-1}(\theta_0, \lambda_0)J(\theta_0, \lambda_0)H^{-1}(\theta_0, \lambda_0), \tag{9.21}$$

with a consistent estimator. A covariance estimator of this form is also known as a sandwich estimator.

In the case where y_t is stationary, a consistent estimator of $H(\theta_0, \lambda_0)$ in (9.11) is obtained by using a uniform WLLN to replace the expectations operator by the sample average and evaluating $\{\theta_0, \lambda_0\}$ at the quasi-maximum likelihood estimator $\{\widehat{\theta}, \widehat{\lambda}\}$

$$H_T(\widehat{\theta}, \widehat{\lambda}) = \frac{1}{T}\sum_{t=1}^{T} h_t(\widehat{\theta}, \widehat{\lambda}). \tag{9.22}$$

The appropriate form of estimator for $J(\theta_0, \lambda_0)$ depends on the autocorrelation properties of $g_t(\theta_0, \lambda_0)$. If the gradient is not autocorrelated the autocovariance terms in (9.12) are ignored. In this case, an estimator of $J(\theta_0, \lambda_0)$ is obtained by using a uniform WLLN to replace the expectations operator by the sample average. Evaluating $\{\theta_0, \lambda_0\}$ at the quasi-maximum likelihood estimator, $\{\widehat{\theta}, \widehat{\lambda}\}$, yields

$$J_T(\widehat{\theta}, \widehat{\lambda}) = \frac{1}{T}\sum_{t=1}^{T} g_t\left(\widehat{\theta}, \widehat{\lambda}\right) g_t'\left(\widehat{\theta}, \widehat{\lambda}\right), \tag{9.23}$$

which is the outer product of gradients estimator of $J(\theta_0, \lambda_0)$ discussed in Chapter 3. Using (9.22) and (9.23) in (9.21) yields the heteroskedasticity consistent covariance matrix

$$\widehat{\Omega} = \left[\frac{1}{T}\sum_{t=1}^{T} h_t\left(\widehat{\theta}, \widehat{\lambda}\right)\right]^{-1}\left[\frac{1}{T}\sum_{t=1}^{T} g_t\left(\widehat{\theta}, \widehat{\lambda}\right) g_t'\left(\widehat{\theta}, \widehat{\lambda}\right)\right]\left[\frac{1}{T}\sum_{t=1}^{T} h_t\left(\widehat{\theta}, \widehat{\lambda}\right)\right]^{-1}.$$
$$\tag{9.24}$$

If there is autocorrelation in $g_t(\theta_0, \lambda_0)$, it is necessary to allow for the autocovariance terms in (9.12) by defining

$$J_T(\widehat{\theta}, \widehat{\lambda}) = \widehat{\Gamma}_0 + \sum_{i=1}^{P} w_i \left(\widehat{\Gamma}_i + \widehat{\Gamma}'_i \right), \tag{9.25}$$

in which P represents the maximum lag length, w_i are weights that ensure $\widehat{\Omega}$ is positive definite and consistent, and

$$\widehat{\Gamma}_i = \frac{1}{T} \sum_{t=i+1}^{T} g_t(\widehat{\theta}, \widehat{\lambda}) g'_{t-i}(\widehat{\theta}, \widehat{\lambda}), \qquad i = 0, 1, 2, \cdots.$$

Substituting (9.22) and (9.25) in (9.21) yields the heteroskedasticity and autocorrelation consistent asymptotic covariance matrix

$$\widehat{\Omega} = \left[\frac{1}{T} \sum_{t=1}^{T} h_t\left(\widehat{\theta}, \widehat{\lambda}\right) \right]^{-1} \left[\widehat{\Gamma}_0 + \sum_{i=1}^{P} w_i \left(\widehat{\Gamma}_i + \widehat{\Gamma}'_i \right) \right] \left[\frac{1}{T} \sum_{t=1}^{T} h_t\left(\widehat{\theta}, \widehat{\lambda}\right) \right]^{-1}. \tag{9.26}$$

The choices of P and w_i are summarised in Table 9.1 for three weighting schemes, namely Bartlett, Parzen and quadratic spectral. Following Newey and West (1994), the determination of the maximum lag length P is based on minimising the asymptotic mean squared error of $J_T(\theta_0, \lambda_0)$. The steps are as follows.

Step 1: Choose a weighting scheme, and hence a preliminary value of the maximum lag length P, given by the first column of Table 9.1.
Step 2: Compute

$$\widehat{J}_0 = \widehat{\Gamma}_0 + \sum_{i=1}^{P} \left(\widehat{\Gamma}_i + \widehat{\Gamma}'_i \right), \quad \widehat{J}_1 = 2 \sum_{i=1}^{P} i \widehat{\Gamma}_i, \quad \widehat{J}_2 = 2 \sum_{i=1}^{P} i^2 \widehat{\Gamma}_i, \tag{9.27}$$

and update the maximum lag length according to the second column of Table 9.1. For Bartlett weights, the updated value of P is

$$\widehat{P} = \text{int} \left[1.1447 \left(\frac{\widehat{v}_1^2}{\widehat{v}_0^2} T \right)^{1/3} \right], \tag{9.28}$$

in which $\widehat{v}_i = \iota' \widehat{J}_i \iota$ for $i = 0, 1, 2$ and ι is a conformable column vector of ones.
Step 3: Compute the weights using the third column of Table 9.1 and the updated maximum lag length P from Step 2.

Table 9.1. *Alternative choices of lag length, P, and weights, w_i, $i \geq 1$, to compute the quasi-maximum likelihood covariance matrix in equation (9.26). Updated lag lengths computed using equations (9.27) and (9.28)*

Preliminary P	Updated P	Weighting Scheme, w_i

Bartlett:

$$\text{int}\left[4\left(\frac{T}{100}\right)^{\frac{2}{9}}\right] \qquad \text{int}\left[1.1447\left(\frac{\widehat{v}_1^2}{\widetilde{v}_0^2}T\right)^{1/3}\right] \qquad w_i = 1 - \frac{i}{P+1}$$

Parzen:

$$\text{int}\left[4\left(\frac{T}{100}\right)^{\frac{4}{25}}\right] \qquad \text{int}\left[2.6614\left(\frac{\widehat{v}_2^2}{\widetilde{v}_0^2}T\right)^{1/5}\right] \qquad w_i = \begin{cases} 1 - 6\left(\dfrac{i}{P+1}\right)^2 - 6\left(\dfrac{i}{P+1}\right)^3 \\ \qquad\qquad 0 \leq i \leq \dfrac{P+1}{2} \\ 2(1 - \dfrac{i}{P+1})^3 \\ \qquad\qquad \text{otherwise} \end{cases}$$

Quadratic Spectral:

$$\text{int}\left[4\left(\frac{T}{100}\right)^{\frac{2}{25}}\right] \qquad \text{int}\left[1.3221\left(\frac{\widehat{v}_2^2}{\widetilde{v}_0^2}T\right)^{1/5}\right] \qquad w_i = \frac{25}{12\pi^2(\frac{i}{P})^2}\left(\frac{5P}{6\pi i}\sin\frac{6\pi i}{5P} - \cos\frac{6\pi i}{5P}\right)$$

The asymptotic results for the quasi-maximum likelihood estimator, developed in the previous section, have an important implication for choosing among the alternative variance estimators that are available. The implication is that for models which yield gradients that are martingale difference sequences, the appropriate variance is computed using (9.24) and not the autocorrelation version in equation (9.26). A case where this condition applies is the AR(1) model. If an estimated model within this class exhibits autocorrelated residuals, then this is evidence of a misspecified conditional mean caused, for example, by an incorrect choice of lag length or functional form. The remedy is not to use an autocorrelation-consistent variance estimator to correct the standard errors, but rather to re-specify the conditional mean. Correcting the variance to solve a problem in the mean is not a fruitful strategy.

9.6   Quasi-Maximum Likelihood and Linear Regression

Let the true relationship between y_t and x_t be represented by the linear equation

$$y_t = x_t'\beta + u_t, \tag{9.29}$$

with population parameter $\beta = \beta_0$ and where u_t is a disturbance term. The aim of this section is to investigate the properties of the quasi-maximum likelihood estimator of β_0 of a linear regression model that is based on the assumptions of normality, homoskedasticity and independence of the disturbances, u_t. These properties are formalised as $u_t \sim iid\ N\left(0, \sigma^2\right)$, which is independent of the exogenous variable x_t. This assumption may not be true in a variety of ways, resulting in a misspecification of the quasi log-likelihood function. In terms of the notation adopted so far, the common parameter vector θ and additional parameter in the quasi log-likelihood function are, respectively, $\theta = \{\beta\}$ and $\lambda = \{\sigma^2\}$. An important result yet to be derived is that under certain conditions the quasi-maximum likelihood estimator of β_0 is consistent with an asymptotic normal distribution. As these properties still hold in the presence of various types of misspecification, the quasi-maximum likelihood estimator is referred to as a robust estimator.

The quasi log-likelihood function is

$$\ln f\left(y_t|x_t; \beta, \sigma^2\right) = -\frac{1}{2}\ln 2\pi - \frac{1}{2}\ln \sigma^2 - \frac{1}{2\sigma^2}\left(y_t - x_t'\beta\right)^2, \qquad (9.30)$$

which has respective gradient and Hessian

$$g_t\left(\beta, \sigma^2\right) = \begin{bmatrix} \dfrac{1}{\sigma^2}x_t(y_t - \beta x_t) \\[2mm] -\dfrac{1}{2\sigma^2} + \dfrac{1}{2\sigma^4}(y_t - x_t'\beta)^2 \end{bmatrix}, \qquad (9.31)$$

$$h_t\left(\beta, \sigma^2\right) = \begin{bmatrix} -\dfrac{1}{\sigma^2}x_t x_t' & -\dfrac{1}{\sigma^4}x_t(y_t - x_t'\beta) \\[2mm] -\dfrac{1}{\sigma^4}(y_t - x_t'\beta)x_t' & \dfrac{1}{2\sigma^4} - \dfrac{1}{\sigma^6}(y_t - x_t'\beta)^2 \end{bmatrix}. \qquad (9.32)$$

The quasi-maximum likelihood estimator of β_0 is the least squares estimator

$$\widehat{\beta} = \left[\sum_{t=1}^{T} x_t x_t'\right]^{-1} \sum_{t=1}^{T} x_t y_t, \qquad (9.33)$$

in which $\widehat{\sigma}^2 = T^{-1}\sum_{t=1}^{T}(y_t - x_t'\widehat{\beta})^2$ is the residual variance.

Using (9.30) in the quasi-maximum likelihood condition in (9.3) verifies that

$$\beta_0 = \arg\max_{\beta} E\left[\ln f\left(y_t|x_t; \beta, \sigma^2\right)\right],$$

so that $\widehat{\beta}$ in (9.33) is a consistent estimator of β_0, that is $\widehat{\beta} \xrightarrow{p} \beta_0$. This result, which is a general one, is not surprising given the well-known properties of the least squares estimator. An important assumption underlying the result is that the conditional mean of the quasi log-likelihood function is specified correctly as

$$E[y_t|x_t] = x_t'\beta_0.$$

To derive the asymptotic distribution of $\widehat{\beta}$, partition $H(\beta_0, \sigma_0^2)$ and $J(\beta_0, \sigma_0^2)$ in (9.14) conformably as

$$H(\beta_0, \sigma_0^2) = \begin{bmatrix} H_{1,1} & H_{1,2} \\ H_{2,1} & H_{2,2} \end{bmatrix}, \qquad J(\beta_0, \sigma_0^2) = \begin{bmatrix} J_{1,1} & J_{1,2} \\ J_{2,1} & J_{2,2} \end{bmatrix}.$$

The Hessian is block diagonal since

$$H_{1,2} = -\frac{1}{\sigma_0^4} E[x_t(y_t - x_t'\beta_0)] = -\frac{1}{\sigma_0^4} E[x_t(E[y_t|x_t] - x_t'\beta_0)] = 0.$$

Define

$$H(\beta_0) = H_{1,1}, \qquad J(\beta_0) = J_{1,1},$$

so that from (9.13) the asymptotic distribution of $\widehat{\beta}$ is

$$\sqrt{T}(\widehat{\beta} - \beta_0) \xrightarrow{d} N(0, \Omega), \tag{9.34}$$

with asymptotic covariance matrix

$$\Omega = H_{1,1}^{-1} J_{1,1} H_{1,1}^{-1} = H^{-1}(\beta_0) J(\beta_0) H^{-1}(\beta_0). \tag{9.35}$$

For the quasi log-likelihood function based on the linear regression model in (9.29), $H(\beta_0)$ and $J(\beta_0)$ have well-known forms. In the case of $H(\beta_0)$, substituting $h_t(\beta, \sigma^2)$ from (9.32) into (9.11) gives

$$H(\beta_0) = \lim_{T \to \infty} \frac{1}{T} \sum_{t=1}^{T} \left[-\frac{1}{\sigma_0^2} E\left[x_t x_t'\right] \right]. \tag{9.36}$$

For $J(\beta_0)$, the gradient in (9.31) is substituted into (9.12) to give

$$J(\beta_0) = \lim_{T \to \infty} \frac{1}{T} E\left[\left(\sum_{t=1}^{T} g_t(\beta_0) \right) \left(\sum_{t=1}^{T} g_t(\beta_0) \right)' \right]$$

$$= \lim_{T \to \infty} \frac{1}{T} E\left[\left(\sum_{t=1}^{T} \frac{1}{\sigma_0^2} x_t u_t \right) \left(\sum_{t=1}^{T} \frac{1}{\sigma_0^2} x_t u_t \right)' \right],$$

or

$$J(\beta_0) = \lim_{T \to \infty} \frac{1}{T} \sum_{t=1}^{T} \frac{1}{\sigma_0^4} E\left[u_t^2 x_t x_t'\right] + \lim_{T \to \infty} \sum_{s=1}^{T-1} \left(\frac{1}{T} \sum_{t=s+1}^{T} \frac{1}{\sigma_0^4} E\left[u_t u_{t-s} x_t x_{t-s}'\right] \right)$$

$$+ \lim_{T \to \infty} \sum_{s=1}^{T-1} \left(\frac{1}{T} \sum_{t=s+1}^{T} \frac{1}{\sigma_0^4} E[u_t u_{t-s} x_{t-s} x_t'] \right). \tag{9.37}$$

As in the general discussion of the quasi-maximum likelihood estimator in Section 9.4, the form of the asymptotic distribution of $\widehat{\beta}$ in (9.34) varies depending upon the assumptions underlying the data. Three special cases, namely non-normality, heteroskedasticity and autocorrelation, are now discussed in detail.

9.6.1 Misspecification: Non-normality

Suppose that $\{y_t, x_t\}$ is *iid* in the true model. Suppose also that the assumption $\mathrm{var}\,(u_t | x_t) = \sigma_0^2$ is correct but that the assumption of normality is incorrect. The *iid* assumption means that $H(\beta_0)$ and $J(\beta_0)$ in (9.36) and (9.37) are, respectively,

$$H(\beta_0) = -\frac{1}{\sigma_0^2} \mathrm{E}[x_t x_t']$$

$$J(\beta_0) = \frac{1}{\sigma_0^4} \mathrm{E}[u_t^2 x_t x_t'] = \frac{1}{\sigma_0^4} \mathrm{E}[\mathrm{E}[u_t^2 | x_t] x_t x_t'] = \frac{1}{\sigma_0^4} \mathrm{E}[\sigma_0^2 x_t x_t'] = \frac{1}{\sigma_0^2} \mathrm{E}[x_t x_t'].$$

Using these expressions in (9.35) shows that the quasi-maximum likelihood estimator has an asymptotic covariance matrix given by

$$\Omega = H^{-1}(\beta_0) J(\beta_0) H^{-1}(\beta_0) = \sigma_0^2 (\mathrm{E}[x_t x_t'])^{-1}.$$

Other than the conditional variance σ_0^2, the asymptotic distribution of $\widehat{\beta}$ does not depend on the form of the conditional distribution of y_t. The asymptotic variance of $\widehat{\beta}$ can be calculated as if y_t were truly conditionally normal, even if this is not the case. So far as estimating β_0 is concerned, the misspecification of the conditional distribution has no effect on the consistency or the asymptotic distribution of the estimator, although now $\widehat{\beta}$ is asymptotically inefficient relative to the maximum likelihood estimator based on the true conditional distribution.

9.6.2 Misspecification: Heteroskedasticity

Suppose that $\{y_t, x_t\}$ is assumed *iid* but that the assumption of homoskedasticity is incorrect, so that $\sigma_t^2 = \mathrm{var}\,(y_t | x_t) = \mathrm{E}[u_t^2 | x_t]$ depends on x_t. The *iid* assumption means that $H(\beta_0)$ and $J(\beta_0)$ in (9.36) and (9.37) simplify to

$$H(\beta_0) = -\frac{1}{\sigma_0^2} \mathrm{E}[x_t x_t']$$

$$J(\beta_0) = \frac{1}{\sigma_0^4} \mathrm{E}[u_t^2 x_t x_t'] = \frac{1}{\sigma_0^4} \mathrm{E}[\mathrm{E}[u_t^2 | x_t] x_t x_t'] = \frac{1}{\sigma_0^4} \mathrm{E}[\sigma_t^2 x_t x_t'].$$

$$(9.38)$$

The quasi-maximum likelihood estimator has an asymptotic covariance matrix given by

$$\Omega = H^{-1}(\beta_0)J(\beta_0)H^{-1}(\beta_0) = (E[x_t x_t'])^{-1}E[\sigma_t^2 x_t x_t'](E[x_t x_t'])^{-1}.$$

(9.39)

Example 9.16 Exponential Regression Model

The true model is that $\{y_t, x_t\}$ are *iid* with conditional exponential distribution with conditional mean $\mu_t = x_t'\beta_0$. From the properties of the exponential distribution, the conditional variance is $\sigma_t^2 = (x_t'\beta_0)^2$. For this model, the quasi log-likelihood function based on the normal distribution is misspecified in both its distribution and its assumption of homoskedasticity. From (9.38) it follows that

$$H(\beta_0) = -\frac{1}{\sigma_0^2}E[x_t x_t'], \qquad J(\beta_0) = \frac{1}{\sigma_0^4}E[(x_t'\beta_0)^2 x_t x_t'],$$

so that the asymptotic covariance matrix of $\widehat{\beta}$ in (9.39) is

$$\Omega = (E[x_t x_t'])^{-1}E[(x_t'\beta_0)^2 x_t x_t'](E[x_t x_t'])^{-1}.$$

The asymptotic covariance matrix of $\widehat{\beta}$ for this model is a function of the second and fourth moments of x_t. For example, if x_t is a single regressor, the asymptotic variance is $\beta_0^2 E[x_t^4]/E[x_t^2]^2$. □

Even where the quasi-maximum likelihood estimator is consistent, the cost of misspecifying the true model is that the resultant parameter estimates are inefficient relative to the true maximum likelihood estimator.

Example 9.17 Relative Efficiency

From Example 9.16, the log-likelihood function of the true model is

$$\sum_{t=1}^{T} \ln f_0(y_t|x_t; \beta) = \sum_{t=1}^{T}\left(-\ln\mu_t - \frac{y_t}{\mu_t}\right),$$

with $\mu_t = \beta x_t$ and x_t is a single regressor for simplicity. The respective gradient and Hessian are

$$\frac{\partial \ln f_0(y_t|x_t; \beta)}{\partial\beta} = -\frac{1}{\mu_t}x_t + \frac{y_t}{\mu_t^2}x_t, \qquad \frac{\partial^2 \ln f_0(y_t|x_t; \beta)}{\partial\beta\partial\beta'} = \frac{1}{\mu_t^2}x_t^2 - 2\frac{y_t}{\mu_t^3}x_t^2.$$

Taking expectations of the Hessian

$$H(\beta_0) = E\left[\frac{1}{\mu_t^2}x_t^2 - 2\frac{E[y_t|x_t]}{\mu_t^3}x_t^2\right] = E\left[\frac{1}{\mu_t^2}x_t^2 - 2\frac{\mu_t}{\mu_t^3}x_t^2\right]$$

$$= -E\left[\frac{x_t^2}{\mu_t^2}\right] = -\frac{1}{\beta_0^2},$$

the asymptotic variance of the correctly specified maximum likelihood estimator is

$$\Omega_{ML} = -H^{-1}(\beta_0) = \beta_0^2.$$

By comparison from Example 9.16, the asymptotic variance of the quasi-maximum likelihood estimator is

$$\Omega = \beta_0^2 \frac{E\left(x_t^4\right)}{E\left(x_t^2\right)^2} \geq \beta_0^2,$$

from the Cauchy-Schwarz inequality. □

9.6.3 Misspecification: Autocorrelation

Now suppose the *iid* assumption is relaxed to allow dependence among $\{y_t, x_t\}$ in the true model, subject to the mixing condition of Section 9.4.4, while retaining the identical distribution assumption so that (y_t, x_t) is a stationary process. Assuming that the conditional mean is specified correctly, then from (9.36) and (9.37)

$$H(\beta_0) = -\frac{1}{\sigma_0^2} E[x_t x_t']$$

$$J(\beta_0) = \frac{1}{\sigma_0^4}\left(E[u_t^2 x_t x_t'] + \sum_{j=1}^{\infty}\left(E[u_t u_{t-j} x_t x_{t-j}'] + E[u_{t-j} u_t x_{t-j} x_t']\right)\right),$$

in which the stationarity of (y_t, x_t) implies that the expectations in this expression are constant over t. The quasi-maximum likelihood estimator has an asymptotic covariance matrix given by

$$\Omega = H^{-1}(\beta_0)J(\beta_0)H^{-1}(\beta_0)$$

$$= E[x_t x_t']^{-1}\left(E[u_t^2 x_t x_t'] + \sum_{j=1}^{\infty}\left(E[u_t u_{t-j} x_t x_{t-j}'] + E[u_{t-j} u_t x_{t-j} x_t']\right)\right)$$

$$\times E[x_t x_t']^{-1}, \tag{9.40}$$

in which the autocorrelation in $u_t x_t$ is used to adjust the variance.

Example 9.18 Forward Market Efficiency
    Consider a model of the forward exchange rate market consisting of the spot exchange rate s_t and the three-month forward exchange rate $f_{t,3}$, which are observed monthly. Under forward market efficiency, the 3-month forward rate at t is an unbiased predictor of the spot rate at time $t + 3$

$$E_t[s_{t+3}] = f_{t,3}.$$

The unbiasedness property implies that the spread at time t, $y_t = s_t - f_{t-3,3}$, satisfies

$$E_{t-3}[y_t] = E_{t-3}[s_t - f_{t-3,3}] = E_{t-3}[s_t] - f_{t-3,3} = 0.$$

Also, applying the law of iterated expectations, the unconditional expectation is

$$E[y_t] = E[E_{t-3}[y_t]] = 0,$$

from the previous step. These two theoretical implications of market efficiency can be tested empirically by specifying a regression of the form

$$y_t = \beta_1 + \beta_2 y_{t-3} + u_t,$$

in which $\beta_1 = \beta_2 = 0$ if the unbiasedness property holds, while $\beta_1 \neq 0$ or $\beta_2 \neq 0$ implies that it does not hold. Under unbiasedness the disturbance u_t satisfies $u_t = y_t$ and hence $E_{t-3}[u_t] = 0$. This property of u_t implies a MA(2) structure since, for any $h \geq 3$, applying the law of iterated expectations gives

$$E[u_t u_{t-3}] = E[E_{t-3}[u_t]u_{t-3}] = 0,$$

while $E[u_t u_{t-1}]$ and $E[u_t u_{t-2}]$ are not restricted to be zero by $E_{t-3}[u_t] = 0$. The product $y_{t-3} u_t$ also satisfies $E_{t-3}[y_{t-3}u_t] = y_{t-3}E_{t-3}[u_t] = 0$, so it also has a MA(2) structure. The gradient vector for the regression $[u_t, y_{t-3}u_t]'$ therefore has a bivariate MA(2) structure, which implies that the quasi-maximum likelihood covariance in equation (9.40) now has a finite lag structure given by

$$H(\beta_0) = \begin{bmatrix} 1 & 0 \\ 0 & E[y_{t-3}^2] \end{bmatrix}$$

$$J(\beta_0) = E\left[u_t^2 \begin{pmatrix} 1 & y_{t-3} \\ y_{t-3} & y_{t-3}^2 \end{pmatrix}\right]$$

$$+ E\left[u_t u_{t-1} \begin{pmatrix} 1 & y_{t-4} \\ y_{t-3} & y_{t-3}y_{t-4} \end{pmatrix}\right] + E\left[u_t u_{t-1} \begin{pmatrix} 1 & y_{t-3} \\ y_{t-4} & y_{t-3}y_{t-4} \end{pmatrix}\right]$$

$$+ E\left[u_t u_{t-2} \begin{pmatrix} 1 & y_{t-5} \\ y_{t-3} & y_{t-3}y_{t-5} \end{pmatrix}\right] + E\left[u_t u_{t-2} \begin{pmatrix} 1 & y_{t-3} \\ y_{t-5} & y_{t-3}y_{t-5} \end{pmatrix}\right].$$

□

9.6.4   The White Variance Estimator

In the case of neglected heteroskedasticity, a consistent estimator of the asymptotic covariance matrix, Ω, in (9.39) is given by

$$\widehat{\Omega} = H_T^{-1}(\widehat{\beta})J_T(\widehat{\beta})H_T^{-1}(\widehat{\beta}), \tag{9.41}$$

in which $H_T(\widehat{\beta})$ and $J_T(\widehat{\beta})$ are consistent estimators of $H(\beta_0)$ and $J(\beta_0)$. They are computed by replacing the expectations operator by the sample average and evaluating the parameters at the quasi-maximum likelihood estimator $\widehat{\beta}$, to give

$$H_T(\widehat{\beta}) = -\frac{1}{\widehat{\sigma}^2}\frac{1}{T}\sum_{t=1}^{T} x_t x_t', \qquad J_T(\widehat{\beta}) = \frac{1}{\widehat{\sigma}^2}\frac{1}{T}\sum_{t=1}^{T} \widehat{u}_t^2 x_t x_t', \qquad (9.42)$$

in which $\widehat{\sigma}^2 = T^{-1}\sum_{t=1}^{T} \widehat{u}_t^2$ and $\widehat{u}_t = y_t - x_t'\widehat{\beta}$. Substituting (9.42) in (9.41) and simplifying gives

$$\widehat{\Omega} = \left[\frac{1}{T}\sum_{t=1}^{T} x_t x_t'\right]^{-1}\left[\frac{1}{T}\sum_{t=1}^{T} \widehat{u}_t^2 x_t x_t'\right]\left[\frac{1}{T}\sum_{t=1}^{T} x_t x_t'\right]^{-1}. \qquad (9.43)$$

This covariance matrix estimator is also known as the White estimator (White, 1980).

Standard errors are computed as the square roots of the diagonal elements of the normalised covariance matrix

$$\frac{1}{T}\widehat{\Omega} = \left[\sum_{t=1}^{T} x_t x_t'\right]^{-1}\left[\sum_{t=1}^{T} \widehat{u}_t^2 x_t x_t'\right]\left[\sum_{t=1}^{T} x_t x_t'\right]^{-1}. \qquad (9.44)$$

These standard errors are different from the usual ordinary least squares standard errors given by the square roots of the diagonal elements of the matrix

$$\frac{1}{T}\widehat{\Omega}_{LS} = \widehat{\sigma}^2 \left[\sum_{t=1}^{T} x_t x_t'\right]^{-1}, \qquad (9.45)$$

which are inconsistent in the presence of neglected heteroskedasticity.

For computational purposes, it is useful to define the matrices

$$X = \begin{bmatrix} x_1' \\ \vdots \\ x_T' \end{bmatrix}, \quad Z = \begin{bmatrix} \widehat{u}_1 x_1' \\ \vdots \\ \widehat{u}_T x_T' \end{bmatrix}, \qquad (9.46)$$

so that (9.44) is computed as

$$\frac{1}{T}\widehat{\Omega} = [X'X]^{-1}[Z'Z][X'X]^{-1}.$$

Note that to compute $\sum_{t=1}^{T} \widehat{u}_t^2 x_t x_t'$ using the form $Z'Z$ is much faster than using the more commonly cited $X'WX$, where $W = \text{diag}\left(\widehat{u}_1^2, \widehat{u}_2^2, \cdots, \widehat{u}_T^2\right)$ is a $T \times T$ matrix. The $Z'Z$ computations make substantial differences in execution times in Monte Carlo simulations for example.

Table 9.2. *Finite sample properties of the quasi-maximum likelihood estimator where the true model is a heteroskedastic autoregression with population parameter $\beta_0 = 0.5$. Results are based on 100000 Monte Carlo replications*

	Statistics		Pr$(|t| > 1.96)$	
T	Mean $\widehat{\beta}$	Var $\widehat{\beta}$	OLS	White
25	0.406	0.053	0.145	0.100
50	0.431	0.032	0.183	0.082
100	0.450	0.020	0.231	0.069
200	0.464	0.013	0.283	0.061
400	0.474	0.008	0.342	0.059
800	0.482	0.006	0.398	0.053
1600	0.487	0.004	0.454	0.050

Example 9.19 Sampling Properties of the White Estimator
The true model is the heteroskedastic AR(1) model

$$y_t = \beta_0 y_{t-1} + \left(\omega_0 + \alpha_0 y_{t-1}^2\right)^{1/2} z_t, \qquad z_t \sim iid\, N(0, 1),$$

with conditional mean and conditional variance given by $E[y_t|y_{t-1}] = \beta_0 y_{t-1}$ and $var(y_t|y_{t-1}) = \omega_0 + \alpha_0 y_{t-1}^2$, respectively, and population parameters $\{\beta_0 = 0.5, \omega_0 = 1, \alpha_0 = 0.5\}$. Table 9.2 gives statistics from simulating the sampling distribution of the quasi-maximum likelihood estimator $\widehat{\beta}$ based on a homoskedastic AR(1) model, computed by regressing y_t on y_{t-1}. The results demonstrate the consistency of the quasi-maximum likelihood estimator because its mean converges towards the true value of 0.5 and its variance decreases towards zero as the sample size increases. The t statistic, computed as $t = (\widehat{\beta} - 0.5)/se(\widehat{\beta})$, exhibits substantial over-rejections based on ordinary least squares standard errors, with the problem worsening as the sample size increases. The White standard errors largely correct this problem, especially for the larger sample sizes. $\qquad\qquad\square$

9.6.5   The Newey-West Variance Estimator

Provided that the conditional mean is specified correctly, a consistent estimator of the asymptotic covariance matrix, Ω, in (9.40) in the presence of neglected autocorrelation is given by

$$\widehat{\Omega} = H_T^{-1}(\widehat{\beta}) J_T(\widehat{\beta}) H_T^{-1}(\widehat{\beta}). \tag{9.47}$$

Once again, $H_T(\widehat{\beta})$ and $J_T(\widehat{\beta})$ are consistent estimators of $H(\beta_0)$ and $J(\beta_0)$, respectively, and are obtained by replacing the expectations operator by the sample average and evaluating the parameters at the quasi-maximum likelihood estimators $\widehat{\beta}$ and $\widehat{\sigma}^2$ to give

$$
H_T(\widehat{\beta}) = -\frac{1}{\widehat{\sigma}^2}\frac{1}{T}\sum_{t=1}^{T} x_t x_t', \qquad J_T(\widehat{\beta}) = \frac{1}{\widehat{\sigma}^4}\left(\widehat{\Gamma}_0 + \sum_{i=1}^{P} w_i\left(\widehat{\Gamma}_i + \widehat{\Gamma}_i'\right)\right),
$$

$$\tag{9.48}$$

where

$$
\widehat{\Gamma}_i = \frac{1}{T}\sum_{t=i+1}^{T} \widehat{u}_t \widehat{u}_{t-i} x_t x_{t-i}', \quad i = 0, 1, 2, \cdots,
$$

are sample autocovariance matrices and $\widehat{u}_t = y_t - x_t'\widehat{\beta}$ are the least squares residuals with variance $\widehat{\sigma}^2 = T^{-1}\sum_{t=1}^{T}\widehat{u}_t^2$. Substituting (9.48) in (9.47) gives the estimator of the asymptotic covariance matrix

$$
\widehat{\Omega} = \left[\frac{1}{T}\sum_{t=1}^{T} x_t x_t'\right]^{-1}\left[\widehat{\Gamma}_0 + \sum_{i=1}^{P} w_i\left(\widehat{\Gamma}_i + \widehat{\Gamma}_i'\right)\right]\left[\frac{1}{T}\sum_{t=1}^{T} x_t x_t'\right]^{-1},
$$

$$\tag{9.49}$$

commonly known as the Newey-West estimator (Newey and West, 1987). The value of the truncation parameter, P, and the choice of weights, w_t, in (9.49) are determined using Table 9.1.

Standard errors for individual ordinary least squares coefficients are computed as the square roots of the diagonal elements of the normalised covariance matrix

$$
\frac{1}{T}\widehat{\Omega} = \frac{1}{T}H_T^{-1}(\widehat{\beta})J_T(\widehat{\beta})H_T^{-1}(\widehat{\beta}).
$$

$$\tag{9.50}$$

Example 9.20 Forward Market Efficiency Revisited

From the discussion of Example 9.18, a model of forward market efficiency is based on the linear regression equation

$$
y_t = \beta_1 + \beta_2 y_{t-h} + u_t,
$$

in which $y_{t+h} = s_{t+h} - f_{t,h}$ is the spread between the spot rate at $t + h$, s_{t+h}, and the h-period forward contract at t, $f_{t,h}$. The quasi-maximum likelihood estimates of the regression are computed using monthly data on the spot and three-month forward exchange rates ($h = 3$) between the United States dollar

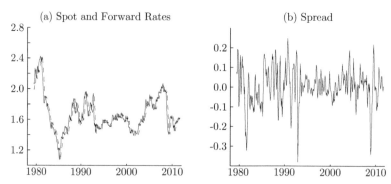

Figure 9.2. Monthly data on the spot (solid line) and three-month forward (dashed line) exchange rates between the United States dollar and the British pound, April 1979 to August 2011.

and the British pound from April 1979 to August 2011. The data are plotted in Figure 9.2 where three observations are lost from computing the spread, resulting in a sample of size $T = 386$.

The least squares estimates are $\widehat{\beta}_1 = 0.0026$ and $\widehat{\beta}_2 = 0.1850$. The first six autocorrelations of the residuals $\widehat{u}_t = y_t - \widehat{\beta}_1 - \widehat{\beta}_2 y_{t-3}$ and the product $\widehat{u}_t y_{t-3}$ are given in the following table.

Lag	1	2	3	4	5	6
$\widehat{u}_t$	0.747	0.337	0.006	−0.061	−0.070	−0.077
$\widehat{u}_t y_{t-3}$	0.600	0.138	−0.074	−0.087	−0.089	−0.061

There is evidence of autocorrelation at lags one and two, which is consistent with the market efficiency theory in Example 9.18. Using the critical value $2/\sqrt{T} = 0.102$, these autocorrelations are also statistically significant while autocorrelations at higher lags are not.

To calculate the Newey-West standard errors for $\widehat{\beta}_1$ and $\widehat{\beta}_2$ using Bartlett weights, from Table 9.1 the preliminary value of the maximum lag in (9.49) is $P = \text{int}\left[4\left(T/100\right)^{2/9}\right] = 5$. Now

$$\widehat{J}_0 = \widehat{\Gamma}_0 + \sum_{i=1}^{5} \left(\widehat{\Gamma}_i + \widehat{\Gamma}'_i\right) = \begin{bmatrix} 9.377 & -0.339 \\ -0.339 & 0.080 \end{bmatrix},$$

$$\widehat{J}_1 = 2\sum_{i=1}^{5} i\widehat{\Gamma}_i = \begin{bmatrix} 5.436 & 0.400 \\ -1.542 & -0.011 \end{bmatrix},$$

and

$$\widehat{v}_0 = \iota' \widehat{J}_0 \iota = \begin{bmatrix} 1 \\ 1 \end{bmatrix}' \begin{bmatrix} 9.377 & -0.339 \\ -0.339 & 0.080 \end{bmatrix} \begin{bmatrix} 1 \\ 1 \end{bmatrix} = 8.78$$

$$\widehat{v}_1 = \iota' \widehat{J}_1 \iota = \begin{bmatrix} 1 \\ 1 \end{bmatrix}' \begin{bmatrix} 5.436 & 0.400 \\ -1.542 & -0.011 \end{bmatrix} \begin{bmatrix} 1 \\ 1 \end{bmatrix} = 4.28,$$

result in an optimal lag length of

$$P = \text{int}\left[1.1447 \left(\frac{\widehat{v}_1^2}{\widehat{v}_0^2} T \right)^{1/3} \right] = \text{int}\left[1.1447 \left(\frac{4.28^2}{8.78^2} \times 386 \right)^{1/3} \right] = 5.$$

The Newey-West standard errors based on $P = 5$ are $\text{se}(\widehat{\beta}_1) = 0.008$ and $\text{se}(\widehat{\beta}_2) = 0.087$. Given the least squares point estimates, it is concluded that $\widehat{\beta}_2$ is significant at the 5% level but $\widehat{\beta}_1$ is not. $\square$

The forward market efficiency example provides an example of a regression equation in which autocorrelation is present in the disturbances even though the conditional mean is specified correctly. This contrasts sharply with the AR(1) model where the presence of autocorrelation in the residuals is symptomatic of a misspecified conditional mean. In the former case, an autocorrelation-consistent Newey-West covariance estimator in equation (9.49) is used to correct for the autocorrelation. In the latter case, the approach is to correct the misspecification of the conditional mean rather than to correct the covariance estimator.

The crucial difference between these two situations is to be found in the conditioning used to form expectations in each model. If the conditioning in a regression model includes the full history of the dependent and exogenous variables so that the conditioning set is $\{x_t, y_{t-1}, x_{t-1}, \cdots\}$, the disturbance is a mds and the relevant covariance estimator is the White estimator in (9.43). Moreover, as in the case of the AR(1) model, the presence of autocorrelation in the residuals of the model with full conditioning would be evidence of a misspecified conditional mean. In the forward exchange rate model, however, expectations are taken with respect to the restricted information set available at time $t - 3$, $\{y_{t-3}, y_{t-4}, \cdots\}$, so that the disturbances are not restricted to be a mds. In general, regressions conditioned on a subset of the full history of variables in the model, including static regressions for y_t conditioned only on an exogenous variable x_t, do not imply mds disturbances. In such cases the Newey-West variance estimator is appropriate.

9.7   Testing

If the quasi-maximum likelihood estimator is consistent, then the Wald and LM test statistics discussed in Chapter 4 are made robust to model misspecification by using the quasi-maximum likelihood covariance matrix $\widehat{\Omega}$ in (9.21). In regression models, the choice of (9.24) will correct the test for heteroskedasticity, while using (9.26) will correct the test for both heteroskedasticity and autocorrelation.

Consider testing the hypotheses

$$H_0 : \theta = \theta_0 , \qquad H_1 : \theta \neq \theta_0 ,$$

in which θ_0 represents the population parameter under the null hypothesis. A robust version of the Wald test is

$$W = T[\widehat{\theta} - \theta_0]' \, \widehat{\Omega}_{1,1}^{-1} [\widehat{\theta} - \theta_0], \tag{9.51}$$

in which $\widehat{\theta}$ is the quasi-maximum likelihood estimator without imposing the constraints and $\widehat{\Omega}_{1,1}$ is the sub-matrix of $\widehat{\Omega}$ corresponding to θ, which is evaluated at $\widehat{\theta}$.

A robust LM test is found by first defining the restricted version of the quasi-maximum likelihood estimator in (9.4) to be $\{\theta_0, \widehat{\lambda}_0\}$, where

$$\widehat{\lambda}_0 = \arg\max_{\lambda} \frac{1}{T} \sum_{t=1}^{T} \ln f(y_t; \theta_0, \lambda)$$

represents the restricted estimator of λ under the null hypothesis. The LM statistic is computed as

$$LM = T G'_T \left(\theta_0, \widehat{\lambda}_0 \right) \widehat{\Omega}_0 G_T \left(\theta_0, \widehat{\lambda}_0 \right), \tag{9.52}$$

where

$$G_T(\theta_0, \widehat{\lambda}_0) = \frac{1}{T} \sum_{t=1}^{T} g_t(\theta_0, \widehat{\lambda}_0),$$

and $\widehat{\Omega}_0$ is computed as in (9.24) or (9.26) but with $g_t(\widehat{\theta}, \widehat{\lambda})$ and $h_t(\widehat{\theta}, \widehat{\lambda})$ replaced by $g_t(\theta_0, \widehat{\lambda}_0)$ and $h_t(\theta_0, \widehat{\lambda}_0)$. The asymptotic distribution of both statistics under the null hypothesis is the same as for their likelihood versions, that is $W, LM \overset{d}{\to} \chi_p^2$ where p is the dimension of θ, and both tests reject for large values of the statistic.

In contrast to the robust versions of the Wald and Lagrange multiplier statistics, no similar robust LR statistic is available. This means that the robust analogues of the Wald and LM tests have correct size under misspecification, whereas the LR test does not.

Example 9.21 Test of Foreign Exchange Market Efficiency

From Example 9.20, a joint test of market efficiency is based on the null hypothesis

$$H_0 : \beta_1 = \beta_2 = 0.$$

Using the calculated value of $\widehat{\Omega}$ in Example 9.20, which is based on the Newey-West covariance matrix with $P = 5$ lags, the Wald test statistic is

$$
W = T \begin{bmatrix} \widehat{\beta}_1 \\ \widehat{\beta}_2 \end{bmatrix}' \begin{bmatrix} \widehat{\Omega}_{1,1} & \widehat{\Omega}_{1,2} \\ \widehat{\Omega}_{2,1} & \widehat{\Omega}_{2,2} \end{bmatrix}^{-1} \begin{bmatrix} \widehat{\beta}_1 \\ \widehat{\beta}_2 \end{bmatrix}
$$

$$
= 386 \begin{bmatrix} 0.0026 \\ 0.1850 \end{bmatrix}' \begin{bmatrix} 0.0226 & -0.0944 \\ -0.0944 & 2.9086 \end{bmatrix}^{-1} \begin{bmatrix} 0.0026 \\ 0.1850 \end{bmatrix}
$$

$$
= 6.013.
$$

The p-value of 0.049 is computed from a χ_2^2 distribution, showing that the null hypothesis of foreign exchange market efficiency is rejected at the 5% level of significance but not at the 1% level. As the test is based on the Newey-West covariance matrix, this joint test is robust to both autocorrelation and heteroskedasticity.

9.8 Applications

The first application is a simulation study that evaluates the properties of two quasi-maximum likelihood estimators when estimating a dynamic model for count data. Count data are also discussed in Chapter 21. The second application continues the theme of exploring estimation issues in time series models of the interest rate, previously discussed in Chapters 1 and 3.

9.8.1 Autoregressive Models for Count Data

Let $y_1, y_2, \cdots , y_T$ represent a time series of count data where the true conditional distribution is negative binomial

$$
f_0 \left(y_t | y_{t-1}; \alpha, \beta \right) = \frac{\Gamma \left(y_t + \mu_t \right)}{\Gamma \left(y_t + 1 \right) \Gamma \left(\mu_t \right)} \left(1 - p \right)^{\mu_t} p^{y_t}, \tag{9.53}
$$

with μ_t and p specified as

$$
\mu_t = \alpha + \beta y_{t-1}, \qquad p = 0.5. \tag{9.54}
$$

From the properties of the negative binomial distribution, the conditional mean and variance are, respectively,

$$E[y_t|y_{t-1}] = \mu_t \frac{p}{1-p} = \mu_t = \alpha + \beta y_{t-1} \tag{9.55}$$

$$\text{var}(y_t|y_{t-1}) = \mu_t \frac{p}{(1-p)^2} = 2\mu_t = 2(\alpha + \beta y_{t-1}). \tag{9.56}$$

This model is characterised by over dispersion since the conditional variance is twice the size of the conditional mean.

Suppose that the model specified is the Poisson distribution

$$f(y_t|y_{t-1}; \alpha, \beta) = \frac{\mu_t^{y_t} \exp[-\mu_t]}{y_t!},$$

where μ_t is defined in (9.54). The parameters of the true and misspecified models that are common are $\theta = \{\alpha, \beta\}$ and the quasi-maximum likelihood estimator of θ is the solution of

$$\widehat{\theta} = \arg\max_{\theta} \frac{1}{T} \sum_{t=1}^{T} \ln f(y_t|y_{t-1}; \theta).$$

The first and second derivatives at observation t are

$$g_t = \frac{y_t - \mu_t}{\mu_t} \frac{\partial \mu_t}{\partial \theta} = \frac{y_t - \mu_t}{\mu_t} \begin{bmatrix} 1 \\ y_{t-1} \end{bmatrix} \tag{9.57}$$

$$h_t = -\frac{y_t}{\mu_t^2} \frac{\partial \mu_t}{\partial \theta} \frac{\partial \mu_t}{\partial \theta'} = -\frac{y_t}{\mu_t^2} \begin{bmatrix} 1 & y_{t-1} \\ y_{t-1} & y_{t-1}^2 \end{bmatrix}. \tag{9.58}$$

Recognising that $E_{t-1}[y_t] = \mu_t$ in (9.55), it follows that the gradient in (9.57) is a mds since

$$E_{t-1}[g_t] = E_{t-1}\left[\frac{y_t - \mu_t}{\mu_t} \frac{\partial \mu_t}{\partial \theta}\right] = \frac{E_{t-1}[y_t] - \mu_t}{\mu_t} \frac{\partial \mu_t}{\partial \theta} = 0.$$

When the law of iterated expectations is used the unconditional expectation under the true model is given by

$$E[g_t] = E[E_{t-1}[g_t]] = 0,$$

which is required for the quasi-maximum likelihood estimator to be consistent.
Taking conditional expectations of the Hessian in (9.58) gives

$$E_{t-1}[h_t] = E_{t-1}\left[-\frac{y_t}{\mu_t^2} \frac{\partial \mu_t}{\partial \theta} \frac{\partial \mu_t}{\partial \theta'}\right] = -\frac{E_{t-1}[y_t]}{\mu_t^2} \frac{\partial \mu_t}{\partial \theta} \frac{\partial \mu_t}{\partial \theta'} = -\frac{1}{\mu_t} \frac{\partial \mu_t}{\partial \theta} \frac{\partial \mu_t}{\partial \theta'} \tag{9.59}$$

since $E_{t-1}[y_t] = \mu_t$. Similarly, taking conditional expectations of the outer product of gradients matrix yields

$$E_{t-1}[g_t g_t'] = E_{t-1}\left[\left(\frac{y_t - \mu_t}{\mu_t}\right)^2 \frac{\partial \mu_t}{\partial \theta} \frac{\partial \mu_t}{\partial \theta'}\right] = \left[\frac{2}{\mu_t} \frac{\partial \mu_t}{\partial \theta} \frac{\partial \mu_t}{\partial \theta'}\right] \quad (9.60)$$

since $E_{t-1}[(y_t - \mu_t)^2] = \text{var}(y_t | y_{t-1}) = 2\mu_t$ from (9.56). Using the law of iterated expectations also shows that the unconditional expectations under the true model of (9.59) and (9.60) are, respectively,

$$H(\theta_0) = E\left[E_{t-1}[h_t]\right] = E\left[-\frac{1}{\mu_t} \frac{\partial \mu_t}{\partial \theta} \frac{\partial \mu_t}{\partial \theta'}\right] = E\left[-\frac{1}{\mu_t}\begin{bmatrix} 1 & y_{t-1} \\ y_{t-1} & y_{t-1}^2 \end{bmatrix}\right]$$

$$J(\theta_0) = E\left[E_{t-1}[g_t g_t']\right] = E\left[\frac{2}{\mu_t} \frac{\partial \mu_t}{\partial \theta} \frac{\partial \mu_t}{\partial \theta'}\right] = E\left[\frac{2}{\mu_t}\begin{bmatrix} 1 & y_{t-1} \\ y_{t-1} & y_{t-1}^2 \end{bmatrix}\right].$$

These results verify that the information equality does not hold since $J(\theta_0) \neq -H(\theta_0)$. The asymptotic distribution of $\widehat{\theta}$ is, therefore,

$$\sqrt{T}\left(\widehat{\theta} - \theta_0\right) \xrightarrow{d} N(0, \Omega), \quad (9.61)$$

in which

$$\Omega = H^{-1}(\theta_0)J(\theta_0)H^{-1}(\theta_0) = 2\left[E\left[\frac{1}{\mu_t} \frac{\partial \mu_t}{\partial \theta} \frac{\partial \mu_t}{\partial \theta'}\right]\right]^{-1}.$$

Consistent estimators of $H(\theta_0)$ and $J(\theta_0)$ are given by

$$H_T(\widehat{\theta}) = -\frac{1}{T}\sum_{t=1}^{T} \frac{1}{(\widehat{\alpha} + \widehat{\beta} y_{t-1})}\begin{bmatrix} 1 & y_{t-1} \\ y_{t-1} & y_{t-1}^2 \end{bmatrix},$$

$$\quad (9.62)$$

$$J_T(\widehat{\theta}) = \frac{2}{T}\sum_{t=1}^{T} \frac{1}{(\widehat{\alpha} + \widehat{\beta} y_{t-1})}\begin{bmatrix} 1 & y_{t-1} \\ y_{t-1} & y_{t-1}^2 \end{bmatrix},$$

in which $\widehat{\theta} = (\widehat{\alpha}, \widehat{\beta})$ is the quasi-maximum likelihood estimator. The form of the outer product of gradients matrix in (9.23) is applicable for $J_T(\widehat{\theta})$ because g_t is a mds and adjusting for autocorrelation is unnecessary. The quasi-maximum likelihood covariance matrix is, therefore, consistently estimated by

$$\widehat{\Omega} = H_T^{-1}(\widehat{\theta})J_T(\widehat{\theta})H_T^{-1}(\widehat{\theta}). \quad (9.63)$$

The square roots of the diagonal elements of $\widehat{\Omega}_T / T$ provide standard errors for the individual coefficients.

The sampling properties of the quasi-maximum likelihood estimator in the case where the true model is a negative binomial distribution and the misspecified model is a Poisson distribution are reported in Table 9.3. Summary statistics on the sampling distribution of the quasi-maximum likelihood

Table 9.3. *Sampling properties of the quasi-maximum likelihood estimator of β, where the true distribution is negative binomial and the misspecified distribution is Poisson. Based on* 10000 *Monte Carlo replications where the true parameters in (9.54) are $\alpha_0 = 1$ and $\beta_0 = 0.5$. The estimate of the standard error is based on the covariance matrix in (9.63) for the Poisson quasi log-likelihood function and (9.44) for the normal quasi log-likelihood function*

T	mean $\widehat{\beta}$		var $\widehat{\beta}$		$\Pr\left(\left|(\widehat{\beta} - \beta_0)/\text{se}(\widehat{\beta})\right| > 1.96\right)$	
	Poisson	Normal	Poisson	Normal	Poisson	Normal
25	0.389	0.357	0.046	0.046	0.159	0.197
50	0.441	0.421	0.024	0.024	0.105	0.142
100	0.471	0.459	0.012	0.013	0.078	0.113
200	0.486	0.478	0.006	0.007	0.069	0.090
400	0.493	0.489	0.003	0.004	0.061	0.075
800	0.496	0.494	0.002	0.002	0.055	0.065
1600	0.498	0.497	0.001	0.001	0.051	0.056

estimator of the autoregressive parameter β from a Monte Carlo experiment using 10000 replications are reported. The true parameter values are $\theta_0 = \{\alpha_0 = 1, \beta_0 = 0.5\}$. For comparative purposes, the results of using a quasi log-likelihood function based on the assumption of a normal distribution are also presented. Both quasi-maximum likelihood estimators behave like consistent estimators. The means of the two sampling distributions approach the true value of $\beta_0 = 0.5$ and the variances both approach zero, roughly halving as the sample size doubles.

Also reported in Table 9.3 is the tail probability from the simulations of the t statistic $(\widehat{\beta} - \beta_0)/\text{se}(\widehat{\beta})$. The standard error $\text{se}(\widehat{\beta})$ for the quasi log-likelihood function based on the Poisson distribution is the square root of the second diagonal element of (9.63). For the quasi log-likelihood function based on the assumption of a normal distribution, the standard error is computed using the White variance estimator in (9.44). The results demonstrate that the quasi-maximum likelihood variance estimators work well for both quasi-maximum likelihood estimators, with the asymptotic normal approximation resulting in tail probabilities approaching 0.05 as the sample size increases.

9.8.2 The CKLS Model of Interest Rates

The CKLS model of Chan, Karolyi, Longstaff and Sanders (1992) specify the interest rate r_t, to evolve as

$$r_t - r_{t-1} = \alpha(\mu - r_{t-1})\Delta + \Delta^{1/2}\sigma r_{t-1}^{\gamma} z_t, \qquad z_t \sim iid\, N(0, 1).$$
$$(9.64)$$

The unknown parameters are $\theta = \{\alpha, \mu, \sigma, \gamma\}$, where α is the adjustment parameter, μ is the mean interest rate, σ is a volatility parameter and γ represents the levels-effect parameter. The scale factor Δ corresponds to the frequency of the data, which is used to annualise the parameters of the model. Imposing the constraint $\gamma = 0.5$ corresponds to the square-root diffusion or CIR model (Cox, Ingersoll and Ross, 1985) in the case of the continuous time version of (9.64) discussed in Section 3.8 of Chapter 3. An important feature of the CIR model is that the conditional distribution of the interest rate is non-normal, having a non-central chi-square distribution. This observation suggests that even for the discrete version of the model in (9.64), the normality assumption of z_t represents a misspecification of the log-likelihood function.

The quasi log-likelihood function is

$$\ln L_T(\theta) = \frac{1}{T-1} \sum_{t=2}^{T} \ln f(r_t | r_{t-1}; \theta), \tag{9.65}$$

where the conditional distribution is given by

$$f(r_t | r_{t-1}; \theta) = \frac{1}{\Delta^{1/2} \sigma r_{t-1}^{\gamma} \sqrt{2\pi}} \exp\left[-\frac{(r_t - r_{t-1} - \alpha(\mu - r_{t-1})\Delta)^2}{2\Delta\sigma^2 r_{t-1}^{2\gamma}} \right]. \tag{9.66}$$

The gradients at time t are

$$
\begin{aligned}
g_{1,t} &= \frac{\partial \ln f(r_t | r_{t-1}; \theta)}{\partial \alpha} = \frac{u_t(\mu - r_{t-1})}{\sigma^2 r_{t-1}^{2\gamma}} \\
g_{2,t} &= \frac{\partial \ln f(r_t | r_{t-1}; \theta)}{\partial \mu} = \frac{u_t \alpha}{\sigma^2 r_{t-1}^{2\gamma}} \\
g_{3,t} &= \frac{\partial \ln f(r_t | r_{t-1}; \theta)}{\partial \sigma^2} = \left(\frac{u_t^2}{\Delta\sigma^2 r_{t-1}^{2\gamma}} - 1 \right) \frac{1}{2\sigma^2} \\
g_{4,t} &= \frac{\partial \ln f(r_t | r_{t-1}; \theta)}{\partial \gamma} = \left(\frac{u_t^2}{\Delta\sigma^2 r_{t-1}^{2\gamma}} - 1 \right) \ln r_{t-1},
\end{aligned}
\tag{9.67}
$$

where the disturbance term, u_t, is

$$u_t = r_t - r_{t-1} - \alpha(\mu - r_{t-1})\Delta.$$

The quasi-maximum likelihood estimator is obtained by maximising (9.65). As the gradients in (9.67) are nonlinear in the parameters, the BFGS algorithm is adopted.

As in Sections 1.5 and 3.8, the data for this application are the daily annualised seven-day Eurodollar interest rate used by Aït-Sahalia (1996) for the period 1 June 1973 to 25 February 1995, $T = 5505$ observations. The scale parameter in (9.64) is set at $\Delta = 1/250$ since the frequency of the data is daily

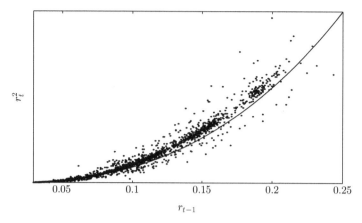

Figure 9.3. Scatterplot of r_t^2 on r_{t-1} together with the model predicted value, $\widehat{\sigma}^2 r_t^{\widehat{2\gamma}}$ (solid line).

and the interest rates are annualised. The method described in Section 3.8.2 is used to obtain starting values for α, μ and σ, and the starting value of γ is set equal to one. The quasi-maximum likelihood estimates are

$$\widehat{\alpha} = \frac{0.300}{(0.303)}, \quad \widehat{\mu} = \frac{0.115}{(0.069)}, \quad \widehat{\sigma} = \frac{1.344}{(0.194)}, \quad \widehat{\gamma} = \frac{1.311}{(0.059)},$$

with quasi-maximum likelihood standard errors based on White's estimator given in parentheses. In this model, the gradients are martingale difference sequences, so the White estimator rather than the Newey-West estimator is the appropriate one.

Interestingly, the estimate of α, the speed of adjustment parameter, is now broadly as expected, unlike the estimate returned by the CIR model in Section 3.8.2. The reason for this is that the diffusion function of the CKLS model is more dynamic than that of the CIR model and thus more capable of capturing the volatility of the short-term interest rate. The estimates of the drift parameters are, therefore, not contaminated by trying to compensate for a specification of the diffusion that is far too restrictive. Note that the estimate of γ is 1.311, which is much larger than the value of 0.5 imposed by the CIR model. The estimated standard error of $\widehat{\gamma}$ suggests that its value is significantly different from 0.5, thereby providing support for the contention that this parameter should be estimated rather than imposed.

Figure 9.3 shows a scatterplot of r_t^2 on r_{t-1} and superimposes on it the predicted value in terms of the model $\widehat{\sigma}^2 r_{t-1}^{\widehat{2\gamma}}$. Comparison of this figure with Figure 3.2 in Chapter 3 demonstrates that the CKLS model is much better able to capture the behaviour of the actual scatter of interest rates as the level of the interest rate increases. This added flexibility is largely due to the influence of γ.

9.9 Exercises

(1) Graphical Analysis

Program files   qmle_graph.*

(a) Simulate $T = 10$ observations from an exponential distribution with parameter $\theta_0 = \mu_0 = 1$. Plot the following log-likelihood functions

$$\text{Exponential:} \quad \ln L_T(\theta) = -\ln \theta - \frac{1}{\theta T} \sum_{t=1}^{T} y_t$$

$$\text{Normal:} \quad \ln L_T(\theta) = -\frac{1}{2} \ln 2\pi - \frac{1}{2T} \sum_{t=1}^{T} (y_t - \theta)^2,$$

for $\theta = \{0.1, 0.2, \cdots, 3\}$. Comment on the results.

(b) Simulate $T = 10$ observations from a negative binomial distribution with parameters $\theta_0 = \mu_0 = 5$ and $p_0 = 0.5$. Plot the following log-likelihood functions

$$\text{Neg. bin.:} \quad \ln L_T(\theta) = \frac{1}{T} \sum_{t=1}^{T} \frac{\ln \Gamma(y_t + \theta)}{\Gamma(y_t + 1)\Gamma(\theta)} + \theta \ln(1 - p)$$
$$+ \frac{1}{T} \sum_{t=1}^{T} y_t \ln p$$

$$\text{Poisson:} \quad \ln L_T(\theta) = \frac{1}{T} \sum_{t=1}^{T} y_t \ln \theta - \theta - \frac{1}{T} \sum_{t=1}^{T} \ln y_t!,$$

for $\theta = \{0.1, 0.2, \cdots, 10\}$. Comment on the results.

(c) Simulate $T = 10$ observations from a standardised Student t distribution with parameters $\theta_0 = \mu_0 = 5$, $\sigma^2 = 1$ and degrees of freedom $\nu = 10$. Plot the following log-likelihood functions

$$\text{Stud. t:} \quad \ln L_T(\theta) = \ln \frac{\Gamma((\nu + 1)/2)}{\sqrt{\pi(\nu - 2)}\Gamma(\nu/2)} - \frac{1}{2} \ln \sigma^2$$
$$- \frac{\nu + 1}{2T} \sum_{t=1}^{T} \ln \left(1 + \frac{(y_t - \theta)^2}{\sigma^2(\nu - 2)}\right)$$

$$\text{Normal:} \quad \ln L_T(\theta) = -\frac{1}{2} \ln 2\pi - \frac{1}{2} \ln \sigma^2 - \frac{1}{2T} \sum_{t=1}^{T} \frac{(y_t - \theta)^2}{\sigma^2},$$

for $\theta = \{-5, -4, \cdots, 15\}$. Comment on the results.

(d) Simulate $T = 10$ observations from a Poisson distribution with parameter $\theta_0 = \mu_0 = 5$. Plot the following log-likelihood functions

Poisson: $\ln L_T(\theta) = \dfrac{1}{T} \sum\limits_{t=1}^{T} y_t \ln \theta - \theta - \dfrac{1}{T} \sum\limits_{t=1}^{T} \ln y_t!$

Normal: $\ln L_T(\theta) = -\dfrac{1}{2} \ln 2\pi - \dfrac{1}{2} \ln \theta - \dfrac{1}{2T} \sum\limits_{t=1}^{T} \dfrac{(y_t - \theta)^2}{\theta},$

for $\theta = \{0.1, 0.2, \cdots, 10\}$. Comment on the results.

(2) Bernoulli Distribution

Program files   qmle_bernoulli.*

The true and misspecified models are respectively, given by

$$f_0(y_t; \theta) = \theta^{y_t} (1 - \theta)^{1-y_t}$$

$$f(y_t; \theta) = \frac{1}{\sqrt{2\pi}} \exp\left[-\frac{(y_t - \theta)^2}{2} \right].$$

(a) Use the true model to derive the following.
  (i) The maximum likelihood estimator of θ_0.
  (ii) The variance based on the information matrix.
  (iii) The variance based on the outer product of the gradients matrix.
(b) Use the misspecified model to derive the following.
  (i) The quasi-maximum likelihood estimator of θ_0.
  (ii) The variance based on the information matrix.
  (iii) The variance based on the outer product of gradients matrix.
  (iv) The quasi-maximum likelihood variance based on the assumption of independence.
(c) Compare the variance expressions based on the true model in part (a) and the misspecified model in part (b).
(d) Generate a sample of size $T = 100$ from the Bernoulli distribution with parameter $\theta_0 = 0.6$. Repeat parts (a) to (c) using the simulated data.

(3) Poisson Distribution

Program files   qmle_poisson.*

The true and misspecified models are respectively, given by

$$f_0(y_t; \theta) = \frac{\theta^{y_t} \exp[-\theta]}{y_t!}$$

$$f(y_t; \theta) = \frac{1}{\sqrt{2\pi}} \exp\left[-\frac{(y_t - \theta)^2}{2} \right].$$

(a) Use the true model to derive the following.

    (i) The maximum likelihood estimator of θ_0.

    (ii) The variance based on the information matrix.

    (iii) The variance based on the outer product of the gradients matrix.

(b) Use the misspecified model to derive the following.

    (i) The quasi-maximum likelihood estimator of θ_0.

    (ii) The variance based on the information matrix.

    (iii) The variance based on the outer product of gradients matrix.

    (iv) The quasi-maximum likelihood variance based on the assumption of independence.

(c) Compare the variance expressions based on the true model in part (a) and the misspecified model in part (b).

(d) Generate a sample of size $T = 100$ from the Poisson distribution with parameter $\theta_0 = 2$. Repeat parts (a) to (c) using the simulated data.

(4) Duration Analysis

    Program files   qmle_exponential.*

The true model of duration times between significant events follows an exponential distribution with parameter θ_0. The misspecified model posits that the durations are normally distributed with mean θ and unit variance

$$f_0(y_t; \theta) = \frac{1}{\theta} \exp\left[-\frac{y_t}{\theta}\right]$$

$$f(y_t; \theta) = \frac{1}{\sqrt{2\pi}} \exp\left[-\frac{(y_t - \theta)^2}{2}\right].$$

(a) Simulate $T = 50000$ observations on y_t from the exponential distribution with parameter $\theta_0 = 1.0$.

(b) Compute the quasi-maximum likelihood estimate $\widehat{\theta}$ based on the misspecified model.

(c) Derive an expression for the Hessian of the misspecified model, $H(\theta)$, and use the data on y_t to compute $H(\widehat{\theta})$.

(d) Derive an expression for the outer product of gradients matrix of the misspecified model, $J(\theta)$, assuming independence and use the data on y_t to compute $J(\widehat{\theta})$.

(e) Compare $-H(\widehat{\theta})$ and $J(\widehat{\theta})$.

(5) Effect of Misspecifying the Log-likelihood Function

    Program files   qmle_student1.*

Suppose the true and misspecified models are

$$f_0(y_t; \theta, v) = \frac{\Gamma\left(\dfrac{v+1}{2}\right)}{\sqrt{\pi \sigma^2 (v-2)} \Gamma\left(\dfrac{v}{2}\right)} \left(1 + \frac{(y_t - \mu)^2}{\sigma^2 (v-2)}\right)^{-(v+1)/2}$$

$$f(y_t; \theta) = \frac{1}{\sqrt{2\pi\sigma^2}} \exp\left[-\frac{(y_t - \mu)^2}{2\sigma^2}\right],$$

with parameters of interest $\theta = \{\mu, \sigma^2\}$.

(a) Simulate $T = 50000$ observations of y_t drawn from the Student t distribution with parameters $\{\mu_0 = 1, \sigma_0^2 = 1\}$ and degrees of freedom values of $v_0 = \{5, 10, 20, 30, 100, 500\}$.

(b) For each choice of v_0, compute the quasi-maximum likelihood estimates of $\theta = \{\mu, \sigma^2\}$.

(c) For each choice of v_0 and associated estimators $\widehat{\theta} = \{\widehat{\mu}, \widehat{\sigma}^2\}$, tabulate the elements of the information matrix, the elements of the outer product of the gradients matrix and the differences between them. Comment on your results.

(6) Student t and Normal Distributions

Program files   qmle_student2.*

Let the true distribution be the standardised Student t distribution defined in the previous exercise with parameters $\mu_0 = 10$, $\sigma_0^2 = 1$ and $v_0 = 5$. The misspecified distribution is a normal distribution with parameters $\theta = \{\mu, \sigma^2\}$.

(a) Simulate a sample of size $T = 50000$ and compute the covariance matrix of the parameter estimates of the true model based on the Hessian, outer product of gradients matrix. Comment on your results.

(b) Compute the covariance matrix of the parameter estimates of the misspecified model based on the Hessian, outer product of gradients and the quasi-maximum likelihood estimate. Comment on your results.

(7) Linear Regression Model

Program files   qmle_ols.*

Consider the linear regression model

$$y_t = \beta_1 + \beta_2 x_t + u_t, \qquad u_t \sim iid\ N(0, \sigma^2),$$

with parameters $\theta = \{\beta_1, \beta_2, \sigma^2\}$. Data on y_t and x_t are $y_t = \{3, 2, 4, 6, 10\}$ and $x_t = \{1, 2, 3, 4, 5\}$.

(a) Compute the maximum likelihood parameter estimates, $\widehat{\theta}$.

(b) Compute the covariance matrix of $\widehat{\beta}_1$ and $\widehat{\beta}_2$ using the Hessian, the outer product of gradients matrix assuming independence and the outer product of gradients matrix assuming dependence. Where appropriate choose the optimal lag length based on the preliminary estimate, $P = \text{int}\left[4\left(\frac{T}{100}\right)^{\frac{2}{9}}\right]$. Compare the estimates of the covariance matrix.

(c) Now suppose the data on y_t and x_t are $y_t = \{3, 2, 4, 6, 5\}$ and $x_t = \{2, 4, 4, 2, 4\}$. Repeat parts (a) and (b).

(8) Simulation Experiment

Program files   qmle_ols_simul.*

Simulate $T = 200$ observations from the heteroskedastic and autocorrelated linear regression model

$$y_t = \beta_1 + \beta_2 x_t + u_t$$
$$u_t = \rho_1 u_{t-1} + v_t$$
$$\sigma_t^2 = \exp(\gamma_1 + \gamma_2 x_t)$$
$$v_t \sim N\left(0, \sigma_t^2\right),$$

using the parameter values $\beta_1 = 1$, $\beta_2 = 0.2$, $\rho_1 = 0.2$, $\gamma_1 = 1$ and $\gamma_2 = 0.2$ and the exogenous variable x_t is computed as $0.1t + 10 \cos(2\pi t/40) + e_t$ where e_t is a uniform random variable.

(a) Compute the quasi-maximum likelihood parameter estimates $\widehat{\theta} = \{\widehat{\beta}_1, \widehat{\beta}_2, \widehat{\sigma}^2\}$ where the misspecified model is

$$y_t = \beta_1 + \beta_2 x_t + u_t, \qquad u_t \sim iid\ N(0, \sigma^2).$$

(b) Compute the covariance matrix of $\widehat{\beta}_1$ and $\widehat{\beta}_2$ using the Hessian, the outer product of gradients matrix assuming independence and the White estimator. Compare these estimates of the covariance matrix.

(c) Estimate the true model and compute the covariance matrix of the maximum likelihood estimates based on the Hessian and the outer product of gradients. Comment on your results.

(9) United States Investment

Program files   qmle_invest.*
Data files   investment.*

This exercise uses quarterly United States data from March 1957 to September 2010. Consider the model

$$dri_t = \beta_1 + \beta_2 dry_t + \beta_3 rint_t + u_t$$
$$u_t \sim iid\ N(0, \sigma^2),$$

in which dri_t is the quarterly percentage change in real investment, and the exogenous variables are dry_t, quarterly percentage change in real income and $rint_t$, the real interest rate expressed as a quarterly percentage. The parameters are $\theta = \{\beta_1, \beta_2, \beta_3, \sigma^2\}$.

(a) Compute the quasi-maximum likelihood parameter estimates $\widehat{\theta} = \{\widehat{\beta}_1, \widehat{\beta}_2, \widehat{\beta}_3, \widehat{\sigma}^2\}$.

(b) Compute the covariance matrix of $\widehat{\theta}$ using the Hessian, the outer product of gradients matrix assuming independence, and the White variance estimator. Compare these estimates of the covariance matrix and interpret the results.

(10) Autoregressive Models for Count Data

Program files	`qmle_nbar1reg.*`

Let $y_1, y_2, \cdots, y_T$ represent a time series of count data where the true conditional distribution is negative binomial

$$f_0(y_t | y_{t-1}; \alpha, \beta) = \frac{\Gamma(y_t + \mu_t)}{\Gamma(y_t + 1)\Gamma(\mu_t)} (1 - p)^{\mu_t} p^{y_t},$$

with μ_t and p specified as

$$\mu_t = \alpha + \beta y_{t-1}, \qquad p = 0.5.$$

(a) For true parameter values of $\theta_0 = \{\alpha_0 = 1, \beta_0 = 0.5\}$, using 10000 replications and with $T = \{25, 50, 100, 200, 400, 800, 1600\}$ conduct a Monte Carlo experiment to explore the consistency of the quasi-maximum likelihood estimator of β using a quasi log-likelihood function based on the Poisson distribution.

(b) Repeat part (a) using a quasi log-likelihood function based on the normal distribution and hence reproduce the results reported in Table 9.3. Comment on the results.

(11) Forward Market Efficiency

Program files	`qmle_sf.*`
Data files	`sf.*`

The data are monthly spot (s_t) and three-month forward $(f_{t,3})$ exchange rates between the United States dollar and the British pound, April 1979 to August 2011.

(a) Construct the spread variable $y_t = s_t - f_{t-3,3}$ and estimate the regression

$$y_t = \beta_1 + \beta_2 y_{t-3} + u_t.$$

(b) Compute an appropriate covariance matrix to find standard errors for the coefficient estimates from the regression.

(c) Carry out hypothesis tests for
   (i) $H_0 : \beta_1 = 0$ against $H_1 : \beta_1 \neq 0$.
   (ii) $H_0 : \beta_2 = 0$ against $H_1 : \beta_2 \neq 0$.
   (iii) $H_0 : \beta_1 = 0$ and $\beta_2 = 0$ against $H_1 : \beta_1 \neq 0$ and/or $\beta_2 \neq 0$.
   Discuss the implications of these results for the forward market efficiency hypothesis.

(d) Repeat this analysis for the expanded regression

$$y_t = \beta_1 + \beta_2 y_{t-3} + \beta_3 y_{t-4} + u_t,$$

to provide a further test of the forward market efficiency hypothesis.

(12) **The CKLS Model of Interest Rates**

Program files	qmle_ckls.*
Data files	eurod.*

The data are the daily seven-day Eurodollar interest rates used by Aït-Sahalia (1996) for the period 1 June 1973 to 25 February 1995, $T = 5505$ observations, expressed in raw units.

(a) The CKLS model of the short-term interest rate, r_t, is given by

$$dr = \alpha(\mu - r)dt + \sigma r^\gamma \, dB,$$

in which $dB \sim N(0, dt)$. Estimate the parameters $\theta = \{\alpha, \mu, \sigma, \gamma\}$ of the model by quasi-maximum likelihood based on the assumption that the unknown transitional pdf required to construct the log-likelihood function is approximated in discrete time by the normal distribution

$$f(r_t | r_{t-1}; \theta) = \frac{1}{\sigma r_{t-1}^\gamma \sqrt{2\pi \Delta}} \exp\left[-\frac{(r_t - r_{t-1} - \alpha(\mu - r_{t-1})\Delta)^2}{\sigma^2 r_{t-1}^{2\gamma}} \right].$$

(b) Compute the quasi-maximum likelihood standard errors and perform a test of the CIR model of interest rates where the levels effect parameter is $\gamma = 0.5$.

(c) Discuss the performance of the estimated model to explain volatility by plotting r_t^2 and $\widehat{\sigma}^2 r_{t-1}^{2\gamma}$ on r_{t-1}. Interpret the results.

10 Generalised Method of Moments

10.1 Introduction

The maximum likelihood method of estimation is based on specifying a likelihood function that, in turn, requires specifying a particular form for the joint distribution of the underlying random variables. This requirement is now relaxed so that the model rests only on the specification of moments of certain functions of the random variables, in an approach known as the generalised method of moments (GMM). In the case where the moments used in the GMM procedure correspond to the distribution specified in the maximum likelihood procedure, the two estimators are equivalent. In essence, the choice between maximum likelihood and GMM then boils down to a trade-off between the statistical efficiency of a maximum likelihood estimator based on the full distribution against the ease of specification and the robustness of a GMM estimator based only on certain moments.

GMM is often a natural estimation framework in economics and finance because the moments of a model often correspond to the first-order conditions of a dynamic optimisation problem. Moreover, as theory tends to provide little or even no guidance on the specification of the distribution, computing maximum likelihood estimators requires making potentially ad hoc assumptions about the underlying stochastic processes. This is not the case with using GMM. On the other hand, GMM estimation requires the construction of a sufficient number of moment conditions by choosing instruments that may not be directly related to the theoretical model.

Under general regularity conditions, GMM estimators are consistent and asymptotically normal. They also have the additional advantage of circumventing the misspecification of the likelihood function. This problem is inherent to the maximum likelihood estimator and is discussed in the context of quasi-maximum likelihood estimation in Chapter 9. It turns out that the covariance matrix of the GMM and quasi-maximum likelihood estimators are in fact identical under certain conditions. The GMM family of estimators also nests a number of well-known estimators, including the maximum likelihood estimator dealt with in Part ONE and the ordinary least squares and instrumental variable estimators discussed in Part TWO. A further property of GMM is that it forms the basis of many recently developed simulation estimation procedures, the subject matter of Chapter 12.

10.2 Motivating Examples

In this section various statistical and economic examples are used to motivate the GMM methodology. The GMM approach is based on specifying certain moments of the random variables, not necessarily their full distribution as the maximum likelihood estimator requires.

10.2.1 Population Moments

Given some random variables $y_1, y_2, \cdots, y_T$ and a $(K \times 1)$ parameter vector θ, a GMM model is specified in terms of an $(N \times 1)$ vector of functions $m(y_t; \theta)$ such that the true value θ_0 satisfies

$$E[m(y_t; \theta_0)] = 0. \tag{10.1}$$

These N equations are called the population moment conditions, or population moments. These population moments define the GMM model.

The usual moments of a random variable can be written in the form of (10.1). Some examples are as follows.

(1) If $E[y_t] = \theta_0$ for all t, then

$$m(y_t; \theta) = y_t - \theta, \tag{10.2}$$

so that (10.1) is satisfied. In this case $K = N = 1$.
(2) If $E[y_t] = \mu_0$ and $\text{var}(y_t) = \sigma_0^2$ for all t, then $\theta = \{\mu, \sigma^2\}$ and

$$m(y_t; \theta) = \begin{bmatrix} y_t - \mu \\ (y_t - \mu)^2 - \sigma^2 \end{bmatrix}, \tag{10.3}$$

so that (10.1) with $\theta_0 = \{\mu_0, \sigma_0^2\}$ implies $E[y_t] = \mu_0$ and $E[(y_t - \mu_0)^2] = \sigma_0^2$, as required. In this case $K = N = 2$.
(3) A GMM model may specify any number of uncentered moments, say $E[y_t^i] = \theta_{i,0}$ for $i = 1, 2, \cdots, K$. Then $\theta = \{\theta_1, \theta_2, \cdots, \theta_K\}$ and

$$m(y_t; \theta) = \begin{bmatrix} y_t - \theta_1 \\ y_t^2 - \theta_2 \\ \vdots \\ y_t^K - \theta_K \end{bmatrix}. \tag{10.4}$$

(4) Centered moments may be specified in a similar manner. In this case, $E[y_t] = \theta_{1,0}$ as before, and then $E[(y_t - \theta_{1,0})^i] = \theta_{i,0}$ so that $\theta = \{\theta_1, \theta_2, \cdots, \theta_K\}$ and

$$m(y_t; \theta) = \begin{bmatrix} y_t - \theta_1 \\ (y_t - \theta_1)^2 - \theta_2 \\ \vdots \\ (y_t - \theta_1)^K - \theta_K \end{bmatrix}. \tag{10.5}$$

(5) Other functions besides polynomials can also be used. For example, if $E[\ln y_t] = \theta_0$ then,

$$m(y_t; \theta) = \ln y_t - \theta, \tag{10.6}$$

or, if $E[1/y_t] = \theta_0$, then

$$m(y_t; \theta) = \frac{1}{y_t} - \theta. \tag{10.7}$$

10.2.2 Empirical Moments

The idea of GMM is to replace the population moments in equation (10.1) with their sample counterparts, the empirical moments. For any θ, the empirical moments have the general form

$$M_T(\theta) = \frac{1}{T} \sum_{t=1}^{T} m(y_t; \theta). \tag{10.8}$$

If $K = N$, as in all of the earlier examples, then the model is exactly identified and the GMM estimator, $\widehat{\theta}$, is defined as the sample counterpart of (10.1)

$$M_T(\widehat{\theta}) = 0. \tag{10.9}$$

If $N > K$, then the model is over-identified and an exact solution to (10.9) is not available because there are more equations than unknowns. GMM estimation for this case is discussed in Section 10.3.

GMM estimators for models that are just-identified are referred to as method of moments estimators. Some examples of GMM estimators in the just-identified case are as follows.

(1) The GMM model to estimate the mean $\theta_0 = E[y_t]$ is specified by (10.2), so that

$$M_T(\theta) = \frac{1}{T} \sum_{t=1}^{T} (y_t - \theta) = \frac{1}{T} \sum_{t=1}^{T} y_t - \theta.$$

Solving (10.9) for $\widehat{\theta}$ gives the sample mean as the estimator of θ

$$\widehat{\theta} = \frac{1}{T} \sum_{t=1}^{T} y_t.$$

(2) The GMM model to estimate both mean and variance is specified by (10.3), so that

$$M_T(\theta) = \begin{bmatrix} \dfrac{1}{T} \sum_{t=1}^{T} y_t - \mu \\[2mm] \dfrac{1}{T} \sum_{t=1}^{T} (y_t - \mu)^2 - \sigma^2 \end{bmatrix},$$

and solving (10.9) gives the sample mean and sample variance, respectively,

$$\widehat{\mu} = \frac{1}{T} \sum_{t=1}^{T} y_t, \qquad \widehat{\sigma}^2 = \frac{1}{T} \sum_{t=1}^{T} (y_t - \widehat{\mu})^2. \tag{10.10}$$

(3) The GMM model to estimate the first K uncentered moments is specified by (10.4), giving

$$M_T(\theta) = \frac{1}{T} \left[\sum_{t=1}^{T} y_t - \theta_1 \quad \sum_{t=1}^{T} y_t^2 - \theta_2 \quad \cdots \quad \sum_{t=1}^{T} y_t^K - \theta_K \right]',$$

so that solving (10.9) gives the usual sample uncentered moments of y_t

$$\widehat{\theta}_i = \frac{1}{T} \sum_{t=1}^{T} y_t^i, \qquad i = 1, 2, \cdots, K.$$

(4) The GMM model to estimate the first K centered moments is specified by (10.5), giving

$$M_T(\theta) = \frac{1}{T} \left[\sum_{t=1}^{T} y_t - \theta_1 \quad \sum_{t=1}^{T} (y_t - \theta_1)^2 - \theta_2 \quad \cdots \quad \sum_{t=1}^{T} (y_t - \theta_1)^K - \theta_K \right]',$$

and solving (10.9) gives

$$\widehat{\theta}_1 = \frac{1}{T} \sum_{t=1}^{T} y_t, \qquad \widehat{\theta}_i = \frac{1}{T} \sum_{t=1}^{T} \left(y_t - \widehat{\theta}_1 \right)^i, \quad i = 2, 3, \cdots, K.$$

(5) If $E[\ln y_t] = \theta_0$, then (10.6) and (10.9) give

$$\widehat{\theta} = \frac{1}{T} \sum_{t=1}^{T} \ln y_t.$$

Table 10.1. *Calculation of various empirical moments for the* $T = 10$ *observations on the variable* y_t

t	y_t	y_t^2	y_t^3	y_t^4	$y_t - m_1$	$(y_t - m_1)^2$	$\ln(y_t)$	$1/y_t$
1	2.0	4.0	8.0	16.0	−2.90	8.410	0.693	0.500
2	7.0	49.0	343.0	2401.0	2.10	4.410	1.946	0.143
3	5.0	25.0	125.0	625.0	0.10	0.010	1.609	0.200
4	6.0	36.0	216.0	1296.0	1.10	1.210	1.792	0.167
5	4.0	16.0	64.0	256.0	−0.90	0.810	1.386	0.250
6	8.0	64.0	512.0	4096.0	3.10	9.610	2.079	0.125
7	5.0	25.0	125.0	625.0	0.10	0.010	1.609	0.200
8	5.0	25.0	125.0	625.0	0.10	0.010	1.609	0.200
9	4.0	16.0	64.0	256.0	−0.90	0.810	1.386	0.250
10	3.0	9.0	27.0	81.0	−1.90	3.610	1.099	0.333
Moment:	4.9	26.9	160.9	1027.70	0.000	2.890	1.521	0.237

If $E[1/y_t] = \theta_0$, then (10.7) and (10.9) give

$$\widehat{\theta} = \frac{1}{T}\sum_{t=1}^{T}\frac{1}{y_t}.$$

Table 10.1 gives some examples of empirical moments for a data set consisting of $T = 10$ observations. It shows the computation of the first four sample uncentered moments of y_t, the first two centered moments and the means of $\ln y_t$ and $1/y_t$.

The approach to GMM model specification is different from that of maximum likelihood. A GMM model specifies only those aspects of the distribution of the random variables that are of interest. A maximum likelihood model specifies the entire joint distribution of the random variables, even if interest is confined only to a small selection of moments. Nevertheless, as shown in the following examples, the GMM approach can be used to estimate the parameters of distributions.

Example 10.1 Normal Distribution

Suppose that the distribution of y_t is normal

$$f(y_t;\theta) = \frac{1}{\sqrt{2\pi\sigma^2}}\exp\left[-\frac{1}{2}\left(\frac{y_t - \mu}{\sigma}\right)^2\right],$$

where μ and σ^2 are the mean and variance, respectively. By definition the mean and variance are

$$E[y_t] = \mu_0, \qquad \text{var}(y_t^2) = \sigma_0^2,$$

and so the GMM model in (10.3) applies. The GMM estimators are, therefore, the sample mean and variance given in (10.10). Using the data reported in

Table 10.1 yields the GMM estimates

$$\widehat{\mu} = 4.900, \qquad \widehat{\sigma}^2 = 2.890.$$

☐

Example 10.2 Student t distribution

Suppose that the distribution of y_t is the Student t distribution given by

$$f(y_t; \theta) = \frac{\Gamma\left((v+1)/2\right)}{\sqrt{\pi v}\,\Gamma\left(v/2\right)} \left[1 + \frac{(y_t - \mu)^2}{v}\right]^{-(v+1)/2},$$

where μ is the mean and v is the degrees of freedom parameter. Consider the population moments

$$E[y_t] = \mu_0, \quad E[(y_t - \mu_0)^2] = \frac{v_0}{v_0 - 2}.$$

The GMM model for $\theta = \{\mu, v\}$ is

$$m(y_t; \theta) = \begin{bmatrix} y_t - \mu \\ (y_t - \mu)^2 - \dfrac{v}{v - 2} \end{bmatrix}.$$

Solving (10.9) in this case gives

$$\widehat{\mu} = \frac{1}{T} \sum_{t=1}^{T} y_t,$$

and

$$\frac{\widehat{v}}{\widehat{v} - 2} = \frac{1}{T} \sum_{t=1}^{T} (y_t - \widehat{\mu})^2,$$

which rearranges to give

$$\widehat{v} = \frac{2T^{-1} \sum_{t=1}^{T} (y_t - \widehat{\mu})^2}{T^{-1} \sum_{t=1}^{T} (y_t - \widehat{\mu})^2 - 1}.$$

Using the data reported in Table 10.1 yields the GMM estimates

$$\widehat{\mu} = 4.900, \quad \widehat{v} = \frac{2 \times 2.890}{2.890 - 1} = 3.058.$$

These estimators are different from the maximum likelihood estimators, but having such estimators in closed form may provide starting values for numerical computation of the maximum likelihood estimators.   ☐

Example 10.3 Gamma Distribution

Suppose that the distribution of y_t is the gamma distribution given by

$$f(y_t; \theta) = \frac{\beta^\alpha}{\Gamma(\alpha)} \exp[-\beta y_t] y_t^{\alpha - 1}, \qquad y_t \geqslant 0, \alpha > 0, \beta > 0,$$

with $\theta = \{\alpha, \beta\}$. Consider the population moments

$$E[y_t] = \frac{\alpha_0}{\beta_0}, \qquad E[y_t^2] = \frac{\alpha_0(\alpha_0 + 1)}{\beta_0^2}, \qquad E\left[\frac{1}{y_t}\right] = \frac{\beta_0}{\alpha_0 - 1},$$

which result in the model

$$m(y_t; \theta) = \left[y_t - \frac{\alpha}{\beta} \quad y_t^2 - \frac{\alpha(\alpha + 1)}{\beta^2} \quad \frac{1}{y_t} - \frac{\beta}{\alpha - 1} \right]'.$$

This model is over-identified, since it has more moments than parameters. An exactly identified model is specified by selecting two of the three moments. In the case of the first and third moments, the model is

$$m(y_t; \theta) = \begin{bmatrix} y_t - \dfrac{\alpha}{\beta} \\ \dfrac{1}{y_t} - \dfrac{\beta}{\alpha - 1} \end{bmatrix}.$$

From (10.9) the equations to solve are

$$\frac{1}{T} \sum_{t=1}^{T} y_t = \frac{\widehat{\alpha}}{\widehat{\beta}}, \qquad \frac{1}{T} \sum_{t=1}^{T} \frac{1}{y_t} = \frac{\widehat{\beta}}{\widehat{\alpha} - 1},$$

which have solutions

$$\widehat{\alpha} = \frac{T^{-1} \sum_{t=1}^{T} y_t}{T^{-1} \sum_{t=1}^{T} y_t - T^{-1} \sum_{t=1}^{T} 1/y_t}, \qquad \widehat{\beta} = \frac{\widehat{\alpha}}{T^{-1} \sum_{t=1}^{T} y_t}.$$

Using the data in Table 10.1 yields the GMM estimates

$$\widehat{\alpha} = \frac{4.900}{4.900 - 0.237} = 1.051, \qquad \widehat{\beta} = \frac{1.051}{4.900} = 0.214.$$

Using another combination of moments yields a different model and hence a different set of estimates. This illustrates that in GMM the specification of the model is often not unique. $\qquad \square$

10.2.3   GMM Models from Conditional Expectations

Many models are expressed in terms of conditional expectations, whether derived from statistical or economic principles. For example, a regression is a model of a conditional mean. In general terms, suppose the model is expressed as

$$E[u(y_t; \theta_0)|w_t] = 0, \tag{10.11}$$

in which $u(y_t; \theta)$ is a function of the random variables and parameters that define the functional form of the model and w_t are conditioning variables. The law of iterated expectations gives

$$E[w_t u(y_t; \theta_0)] = E[w_t E[u(y_t; \theta_0)|w_t]] = 0, \tag{10.12}$$

implying a GMM model of the form

$$m(y_t; \theta) = w_t u(y_t; \theta). \tag{10.13}$$

This logic applies for any subset of the variables contained in w_t; so there is a different GMM model for each subset. This construction is now illustrated in some common modelling situations.

Example 10.4 Linear Regression

Consider the regression equation

$$E[y_t|x_t] = x_t'\beta_0.$$

This equation can be written as

$$E[y_t - x_t'\beta_0|x_t] = 0,$$

implying that $u(y_t, x_t; \beta) = y_t - x_t'\beta$ and $w_t = x_t$ in (10.11). The law of iterated expectations immediately gives

$$E[x_t(y_t - x_t'\beta_0)] = E[x_t E[y_t - x_t'\beta_0|x_t]] = 0,$$

so that the GMM model is

$$m(y_t, x_t; \beta) = x_t \left(y_t - x_t'\beta \right).$$

Applying (10.9) gives

$$M_T(\widehat{\beta}) = \frac{1}{T} \sum_{t=1}^{T} x_t(y_t - x_t'\widehat{\beta}) = 0,$$

which is solved to give the ordinary least squares estimator

$$\widehat{\beta} = \left[\sum_{t=1}^{T} x_t x_t' \right]^{-1} \sum_{t=1}^{T} x_t y_t.$$

$\square$

Example 10.5 Instrumental Variables

Consider a model of the form

$$y_t = x_t'\beta_0 + u_t, \tag{10.14}$$

in which u_t does not satisfy $E[u_t|x_t] = 0$, so that u_t and x_t are correlated. It follows that the regression model $E[y_t|x_t] = x_t'\beta_0$ is misspecified for the estimation of β_0 since $E[y_t|x_t] = x_t'\beta_0 + E[u_t|x_t] \neq x_t'\beta_0$. For example, if $E[u_t|x_t] = x_t'\gamma_0$, then $E[y_t|x_t] = x_t'(\beta_0 + \gamma_0)$, which shows the well-known endogeneity bias in this regression. Instead, suppose there is a vector of instrumental variables w_t that satisfy $E[u_t|w_t] = 0$ and $E[x_t|w_t] \neq E[x_t]$. Taking expectations of (10.14) conditional on w_t gives

$$E[y_t|w_t] = E[x_t|w_t]'\beta_0,$$

or

$$E[y_t - x_t'\beta_0|w_t] = 0,$$

so this conditional expectation is correctly specified for the estimation of β_0. It has the form (10.11) with $u(y_t, x_t; \beta) = y_t - x_t'\beta$. It follows from (10.12) that

$$E[w_t(y_t - x_t'\beta_0)] = 0,$$

and the GMM model is

$$m(y_t, x_t, w_t; \beta) = w_t\left(y_t - x_t'\beta\right).$$

If w_t and x_t have the same dimension, the model is exactly identified, and (10.9) becomes

$$M_T(\widehat{\beta}) = \frac{1}{T}\sum_{t=1}^{T} w_t\left(y_t - x_t'\widehat{\beta}\right) = 0,$$

with solution

$$\widehat{\beta} = \left[\sum_{t=1}^{T} w_t x_t'\right]^{-1} \sum_{t=1}^{T} w_t y_t,$$

which is the IV estimator given in Chapter 5. If there are more instruments than regressors, then the model is over-identified.   □

Example 10.6 C-CAPM

The consumption capital asset pricing model (C-CAPM) is based on the assumption that a representative agent maximises the intertemporal utility function

$$\sum_{i=0}^{\infty} \beta_0^i E_t \left[\frac{c_{t+i}^{1-\gamma_0} - 1}{1 - \gamma_0} \right],$$

subject to a budget constraint, where c_t is real consumption and E_t represents expectations conditional on all relevant variables available at time t. The parameters are the discount rate, β, and the relative risk aversion parameter, γ. The first-order condition is

$$E_t \left[\beta_0 \left(\frac{c_{t+1}}{c_t} \right)^{-\gamma_0} (1 + r_{t+1}) - 1 \right] = 0,$$

where r_t is the interest rate. This has the form (10.11) where

$$u \left(\frac{c_{t+1}}{c_t}, r_{t+1}; \beta, \gamma \right) = \beta \left(\frac{c_{t+1}}{c_t} \right)^{-\gamma} (1 + r_{t+1}) - 1.$$

Letting $w_t = \{1, e_t\}$ represent the relevant conditioning variables, where e_t represents real returns on equities, yields an exactly-identified model of the form (10.13). The GMM estimator, $\widehat{\theta} = \{\widehat{\beta}, \widehat{\gamma}\}$, defined by (10.9) satisfies

$$\frac{1}{T} \sum_{t=1}^{T} \left(\widehat{\beta} \left(\frac{c_{t+1}}{c_t} \right)^{-\widehat{\gamma}} (1 + r_{t+1}) - 1 \right) = 0$$

$$\frac{1}{T} \sum_{t=1}^{T} \left(\widehat{\beta} \left(\frac{c_{t+1}}{c_t} \right)^{-\widehat{\gamma}} (1 + r_{t+1}) - 1 \right) e_t = 0.$$

This nonlinear system of two equations is solved using one of the iterative methods discussed in Chapter 3. Expanding the information set to $w_t = \{1, c_t/c_{t-1}, r_t, e_t\}$ results in an over-identified model with two over-identifying restrictions. □

10.2.4 GMM and Maximum Likelihood

Consider a maximum likelihood model based on a density function $f(y_t; \theta)$ for *iid* random variables $y_1, y_2, \cdots, y_T$. From Chapter 2, the expected gradient at the true value $\theta = \theta_0$ is zero

$$E \left[\frac{\partial \ln f(y_t; \theta)}{\partial \theta} \bigg|_{\theta=\theta_0} \right] = 0. \tag{10.15}$$

This property of the gradient suggests that a GMM model is defined as

$$m(y_t; \theta) = \frac{\partial \ln f(y_t; \theta)}{\partial \theta}. \tag{10.16}$$

This model is exactly identified because an element of the gradient exists for each parameter in θ so the GMM estimator from (10.9) satisfies

$$\frac{1}{T} \sum_{t=1}^{T} \frac{\partial \ln f(y_t; \theta)}{\partial \theta} \bigg|_{\theta=\widehat{\theta}} = 0, \tag{10.17}$$

which also defines the first-order conditions for the maximum likelihood estimator.

Note that the GMM model (10.16) does not fully encapsulate the maximum likelihood model, because it only represents the first-order conditions. The expectations in (10.15) are the first-order conditions of the likelihood equality

$$\theta_0 = \arg\max_{\theta} E\left[\ln f(y_t; \theta)\right], \tag{10.18}$$

and this maximisation aspect of the maximum likelihood model is not captured by the GMM formulation. For example, if there are multiple solutions to the equations

$$E\left[\frac{\partial \ln f(y_t; \theta)}{\partial \theta}\right] = 0,$$

only one of which is $\theta = \theta_0$, the GMM model considered in isolation provides no guidance on which solution is the desired one. In a practical situation solving (10.17), the GMM principle alone is not informative about how to proceed when there are multiple solutions to (10.17). The additional structure provided by the maximum likelihood model suggests that the desired solution of (10.17) is the one that also maximises $T^{-1}\sum_{t=1}^{T} \ln f(y_t; \theta)$.

10.3   Estimation

In the analysis that follows, a GMM estimator is defined that covers over-identified models, and it is shown to include the exactly identified estimator (10.9) as a special case.

10.3.1   The GMM Objective Function

To define the GMM criterion function, it is convenient to adopt the simplified notation

$$m_t(\theta) = m(y_t; \theta),$$

for the GMM model, where $\theta = \{\theta_1, \theta_2, \cdots, \theta_K\}$ is the parameter vector and $m_t(\theta)$ is the $N \times 1$ vector of moments

$$m_t(\theta) = \begin{bmatrix} m_{1,t}(\theta) \\ m_{2,t}(\theta) \\ \vdots \\ m_{N,t}(\theta) \end{bmatrix}.$$

From (10.1), the true value θ_0 satisfies

$$E[m_t(\theta_0)] = 0. \tag{10.19}$$

The sample mean of these moment conditions is

$$M_T(\theta) = \frac{1}{T} \sum_{t=1}^{T} m_t(\theta),$$

but in the over-identified case the GMM estimator cannot be defined to satisfy (10.9), which only works for exactly identified models. Instead the GMM estimator is defined as

$$\widehat{\theta} = \arg\min_{\theta} Q_T(\theta), \tag{10.20}$$

where

$$Q_T(\theta) = \frac{1}{2} M_T'(\theta) W_T^{-1} M_T(\theta), \tag{10.21}$$

and W_T is an $N \times N$ positive definite weighting matrix that determines how each moment condition is weighted in the estimation. The first-order condition for a minimum of this function is

$$\left. \frac{\partial Q_T(\theta)}{\partial \theta} \right|_{\theta=\widehat{\theta}} = D_T'(\widehat{\theta}) W_T^{-1} M_T(\widehat{\theta}) = 0, \tag{10.22}$$

in which

$$D_T(\theta) = \frac{\partial M_T(\theta)}{\partial \theta'}.$$

Solving this first-order condition yields the GMM estimator, $\widehat{\theta}$.

The definition (10.20) is also valid in the just-identified case. The just-identified GMM estimator was initially defined as (10.9) but the two definitions do not conflict. In a just-identified model it is possible to choose $\widehat{\theta}$ to solve $M_T(\widehat{\theta}) = 0$ exactly, so that $Q_T(\widehat{\theta}) = 0$ and the solutions to (10.9) and (10.20) coincide. This result also implies there is no role for the weighting matrix, W_T, in just-identified estimation since, in this case, $D_T(\widehat{\theta})$ is a square matrix and can be inverted. Consequently, expression (10.22) simplifies to $M_T(\widehat{\theta}) = 0$, which is just equation (10.9) again. For all other $\theta \neq \hat{\theta}$, the positive definiteness of W_T^{-1} implies that $Q_T(\theta) > 0$.

10.3.2   *Asymptotic Properties*

Under some general assumptions the GMM estimator defined in (10.20) is consistent and asymptotically normal.

Consistency

Define the population moments

$$M(\theta) = E[m_t(\theta)],$$

for any θ, so that the population moment conditions (10.19) are

$$M(\theta_0) = 0. \tag{10.23}$$

The true value θ_0 is identified by the model

$$M(\theta) = 0, \text{ if, and only if, } \theta = \theta_0. \tag{10.24}$$

The 'if' part of this identification condition is (10.23). The 'only if' part is an extra assumption required to ensure that there is only one candidate value for θ_0 identified by the model. In some particular models, the 'only if' part of the identification assumption might be replaced with some other identification rule, such as (10.18) in a quasi-maximum likelihood model, which would allow for multiple solutions to the first-order conditions.

Example 10.7 Consistency and the Gamma Distribution

From Example 10.3, the gamma distribution of y_t with $\beta = 1$ is given by

$$f(y_t; \alpha) = \frac{1}{\Gamma(\alpha)} \exp[-y_t] y_t^{\alpha-1}, \qquad y_t \geqslant 0, \alpha > 0,$$

where $\theta = \{\alpha\}$ and the first two uncentered population moments are $E[y_t] = \alpha_0$ and $E[y_t^2] = \alpha_0(\alpha_0 + 1)$. The GMM model based on these moments is

$$m_t(\alpha) = \begin{bmatrix} y_t - \alpha \\ y_t^2 - \alpha(\alpha + 1) \end{bmatrix},$$

so that

$$M(\alpha) = \begin{bmatrix} \alpha_0 - \alpha \\ \alpha_0(\alpha_0 + 1) - \alpha(\alpha + 1) \end{bmatrix} = \begin{bmatrix} \alpha_0 - \alpha \\ (\alpha_0 - \alpha)(\alpha + \alpha_0 + 1) \end{bmatrix},$$

which shows that $M(\alpha) = 0$ if, and only if, $\alpha = \alpha_0$.   □

The WLLN provides the convergence in probability of the sample moments to the population moments for any θ, that is

$$M_T(\theta) \overset{p}{\to} M(\theta), \tag{10.25}$$

and it is assumed that the model is sufficiently regular for this convergence to be uniform in θ (see, for example, Theorem 2.6 of Newey and McFadden, 1994). It is also assumed that

$$W_T \overset{p}{\to} W, \tag{10.26}$$

for some positive definite matrix W. Combining (10.25) and (10.26) in the definition of $Q_T(\theta)$ in (10.21) gives

$$Q_T(\theta) \overset{p}{\to} Q(\theta), \tag{10.27}$$

uniformly in θ, where

$$Q(\theta) = \frac{1}{2} M'(\theta) W^{-1} M(\theta). \tag{10.28}$$

The population moment conditions (10.23) imply that $Q(\theta_0) = 0$, while the identification condition (10.24) and the positive definiteness of W together imply that $Q(\theta) > 0$ for all $\theta \neq \theta_0$. Thus

$$\theta_0 = \arg\min_{\theta} Q(\theta), \tag{10.29}$$

which shows that minimising $Q(\theta)$ identifies θ_0. The combination of the definition of the GMM estimator in (10.20), the convergence requirement in (10.27) and the identification property in (10.29) implies the consistency of the GMM estimator, $\widehat{\theta} \overset{p}{\to} \theta_0$. This result does not depend on the choice of W_T provided that it is positive definite in the limit.

Example 10.8 Demonstration of Consistency

Consider a gamma distribution with $\beta = 1$ and moments

$$\mathrm{E}[y_t] = \alpha_0, \qquad \mathrm{E}[y_t^2] = \alpha_0(\alpha_0 + 1), \qquad \mathrm{E}[y_t^{-1}] = (\alpha_0 - 1)^{-1}.$$

The population objective function $Q(\alpha)$ is simulated by using $T = 100000$ draws of y_t from a gamma distribution with $\alpha_0 = 10$ with

$$Q_T(\alpha) = \frac{1}{2} M_T(\alpha)' W_T^{-1}(\alpha) M_T(\alpha),$$

and

$$M_T(\alpha) = \frac{1}{T} \sum_{t=1}^{T} \begin{bmatrix} y_t - \alpha \\ y_t^2 - \alpha(\alpha + 1) \\ y_t^{-1} - \dfrac{1}{\alpha - 1} \end{bmatrix},$$

$$W_T(\alpha) = \frac{1}{T} \sum_{t=1}^{T} \begin{bmatrix} y_t - \alpha \\ y_t^2 - \alpha(\alpha + 1) \\ y_t^{-1} - \dfrac{1}{\alpha - 1} \end{bmatrix} \begin{bmatrix} y_t - \alpha \\ y_t^2 - \alpha(\alpha + 1) \\ y_t^{-1} - \dfrac{1}{\alpha - 1} \end{bmatrix}'.$$

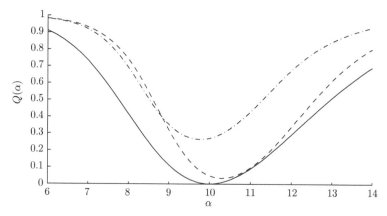

Figure 10.1. Demonstrating the consistency property of the GMM estimator for the gamma distribution with parameter $\alpha_0 = 10$ (solid line). $Q(\widehat{\alpha})$ is computed for samples of size 50 (dot-dashed line) and 100 (dashed line).

Values of $Q_T(\alpha)$ are given in Figure 10.1 for α ranging from 6 to 14. Also given are the finite sample objective functions $Q_T(\alpha)$ for sample sizes $T = \{50, 100\}$. The consistency property of the GMM estimator is clear with $Q_T(\alpha)$ approaching $Q(\alpha)$ as T increases, as well as $\widehat{\alpha}$ approaching $\alpha_0 = 10$. □

Normality

The mean value theorem for $M_T(\theta)$ gives

$$M_T(\widehat{\theta}) = M_T(\theta_0) + D_T(\theta^*)(\widehat{\theta} - \theta_0),$$

for some intermediate value θ^* between $\widehat{\theta}$ and θ_0. Pre-multiplying this expression by $D_T(\widehat{\theta})'W_T^{-1}$ gives

$$D_T'(\widehat{\theta})W_T^{-1}M_T(\widehat{\theta}) = D_T'(\widehat{\theta})W_T^{-1}M_T(\theta_0) + D_T'(\widehat{\theta})W_T^{-1}D_T(\theta^*)(\widehat{\theta} - \theta_0).$$

The left-hand side of this expression is zero by the first-order conditions (10.22) and can be re-arranged to give

$$\sqrt{T}(\widehat{\theta} - \theta_0) = -\left(D_T'(\widehat{\theta})W_T^{-1}D_T(\theta^*)\right)^{-1} D_T'(\widehat{\theta})W_T^{-1}\sqrt{T}M_T(\theta_0).$$

$$(10.30)$$

It is now assumed that there is a uniform WLLN such that

$$D_T(\theta) = \frac{1}{T}\sum_{t=1}^{T}\frac{\partial m_t(\theta)}{\partial \theta'} \xrightarrow{p} E\left[\frac{\partial m_t(\theta)}{\partial \theta'}\right],$$

uniformly in θ and that the expected derivative is continuous so that

$$D_T(\widehat{\theta}), D_T(\theta^*) \xrightarrow{p} D,$$

$$(10.31)$$

where

$$D = E \left[\left. \frac{\partial m_t (\theta)}{\partial \theta'} \right|_{\theta=\theta_0} \right].$$

It is also assumed that there is a central limit theorem such that

$$\sqrt{T} M_T (\theta_0) = \frac{1}{\sqrt{T}} \sum_{t=1}^{T} m_t (\theta_0) \overset{d}{\to} N (0, J), \tag{10.32}$$

for some variance matrix J. The result stated in (10.32) requires that some conditions be imposed on the model, in particular that $m_t (\theta_0)$ have more than two finite moments and that it has at most weak dependence (as in Chapter 9). The form of the variance matrix, J, is governed by the dependence properties of $m_t(\theta_0)$. For example, if $m_t (\theta_0)$ is a stationary mds, including *iid* as a special case, then from Chapter 9 it immediately follows that

$$J = E[m_t (\theta_0) m_t' (\theta_0)], \tag{10.33}$$

while if $m_t (\theta_0)$ is stationary and autocorrelated then

$$J = E[m_t (\theta_0) m_t' (\theta_0)] + \sum_{s=1}^{\infty} \left(E[m_t (\theta_0) m_{t-s}' (\theta_0)] + E[m_{t-s} (\theta_0) m_t' (\theta_0)] \right). \tag{10.34}$$

The covariance matrix J corresponds to the outer product of gradients matrix discussed in Chapter 9 where $m_t (\theta_0)$ corresponds to the gradient vector.

Combining (10.26), (10.31) and (10.32) in (10.30) gives

$$\sqrt{T} \left(\hat{\theta} - \theta_0 \right) \overset{d}{\to} N (0, \Omega_W), \tag{10.35}$$

where

$$\Omega_W = \left(D' W^{-1} D \right)^{-1} D' W^{-1} J W^{-1} D \left(D' W^{-1} D \right)^{-1}.$$

This is the general form of the asymptotic distribution of the GMM estimator in the over-identified case.

The result in (10.35) also applies to the just-identified GMM model, by noting that in this case the matrix D is square, so that $\left(D' W^{-1} D \right)^{-1}$ becomes $D^{-1} W D^{-1'}$ and hence Ω_W simplifies to

$$\Omega_W = D^{-1} J D^{-1'},$$

for any W. The invariance of Ω_W to W under exact identification is consistent with the fact that the GMM estimator itself does not depend on W_T in this case.

Efficiency

The weighting matrix W_T in (10.21) can be any positive definite matrix that satisfies (10.26). The dependence of the asymptotic variance Ω_W on W in (10.35) raises the question of how best to choose W_T. It turns out that if $W = J$, then the expression for Ω_W simplifies to

$$\Omega_J = \left[D'J^{-1}D \right]^{-1}, \tag{10.36}$$

and, most importantly, it can be shown that $\Omega_W - \Omega_J$ is positive semi-definite for any W (Hansen, 1982), so that Ω_J represents a lower bound on the asymptotic variance of a GMM estimator for θ_0 based on the model $m_t(\theta)$. It is, therefore, desirable to implement the GMM estimator defined in terms of (10.21) using a weighting matrix W_T such that $W_T \xrightarrow{p} J$. This will produce a GMM estimator with asymptotic variance Ω_J.

It is important to distinguish between this concept of asymptotic efficiency for GMM and that associated with the maximum likelihood estimator. The GMM estimator computed with weighting matrix satisfying $W_T \xrightarrow{p} J$ is asymptotically efficient among those estimators based on the particular model, $m_t(\theta)$. A different form for the moments will result in a different efficient GMM estimator. This is a more restricted concept of asymptotic efficiency than maximum likelihood, which is asymptotically efficient among all regular consistent estimators. A GMM estimator can match the asymptotic variance of the maximum likelihood estimator if $m_t(\theta)$ happens to be the gradient of the true likelihood function, but otherwise in general a GMM estimator, even with efficient choice of W_T, is less efficient than the maximum likelihood estimator based on a correctly specified model. The trade-off with GMM is that it is not necessary to be able to specify correctly the joint distribution of the random variables, but the price paid for this flexibility is a loss of asymptotic efficiency relative to the maximum likelihood estimator.

Example 10.9 Gamma Distribution

From Example 10.7, the derivative of the model is

$$\frac{\partial m_t(\alpha)}{\partial \alpha} = - \begin{bmatrix} 1 \\ 2\alpha + 1 \end{bmatrix},$$

so

$$D = - \begin{bmatrix} 1 \\ 2\alpha_0 + 1 \end{bmatrix}.$$

To derive J requires making some assumptions about the dynamics of $m_t(\alpha_0)$. If y_t is *iid*, $m_t(\alpha_0)$ is also *iid* and then $J = \text{var}(m_t(\alpha_0))$. From the properties of the gamma distribution with $\beta = 1$, the first four moments are

$$E[y_t] = \alpha_0 , \ E[(y_t - \alpha_0)^2] = \alpha_0 , \ E\left[(y_t - \alpha_0)^3\right] = 2\alpha_0 ,$$
$$E[(y_t - \alpha_0)^4] = 3\alpha_0^2 + 6\alpha_0 ,$$

with

$$J = \mathrm{var}(m_t(\alpha_0))$$
$$= \begin{bmatrix} \mathrm{var}(y_t - \alpha_0) & \mathrm{cov}\left((y_t - \alpha_0), (y_t^2 - \alpha_0(\alpha_0 + 1))\right) \\ \mathrm{cov}\left((y_t - \alpha_0), (y_t^2 - \alpha_0(\alpha_0 + 1))\right) & \mathrm{var}\left(y_t^2 - \alpha_0(\alpha_0 + 1)\right) \end{bmatrix}$$
$$= \begin{bmatrix} \alpha_0 & 2\alpha_0 (\alpha_0 + 1) \\ 2\alpha_0 (\alpha_0 + 1) & \alpha_0 (\alpha_0 + 2)(4\alpha_0 + 3) \end{bmatrix} .$$

The asymptotic variance of the efficient GMM estimator in (10.36) is

$$\Omega_J = \begin{bmatrix} 1 \\ 2\alpha_0 + 1 \end{bmatrix}' \begin{bmatrix} \alpha_0 & 2\alpha_0 (\alpha_0 + 1) \\ 2\alpha_0 (\alpha_0 + 1) & \alpha_0 (\alpha_0 + 2)(4\alpha_0 + 3) \end{bmatrix}^{-1} \begin{bmatrix} 1 \\ 2\alpha_0 + 1 \end{bmatrix}$$
$$= \frac{\alpha_0 (3\alpha_0 + 2)}{3 (\alpha_0 + 1)} ,$$

resulting in the asymptotic distribution

$$\sqrt{T} (\widehat{\alpha} - \alpha_0) \overset{d}{\to} N \left(0, \frac{\alpha_0 (3\alpha_0 + 2)}{3 (\alpha_0 + 1)} \right) .$$

$\square$

10.3.3 Estimation Strategies

Variance Estimation
In order to implement a GMM estimator with a weighting matrix that satisfies $W_T \overset{p}{\to} J$, it is necessary to consider the consistent estimation of J. From Chapter 9, if $m_t (\theta_0)$ is not autocorrelated, then J has the form given in (10.33) and an estimator of $W_T (\theta)$ is

$$W_T (\theta) = \frac{1}{T} \sum_{t=1}^{T} m_t (\theta) m_t' (\theta) , \tag{10.37}$$

which is defined for any θ. If autocorrelation in $m_t (\theta_0)$ is suspected, then J has the general form (10.34) and an estimator of the form

$$W_T (\theta) = \widehat{\Gamma}_0 (\theta) + \sum_{i=1}^{P} w_i \left(\widehat{\Gamma}_i (\theta) + \widehat{\Gamma}_i' (\theta) \right) , \tag{10.38}$$

is used, where

$$\widehat{\Gamma}_i(\theta) = \frac{1}{T} \sum_{t=i+1}^{T} m_t(\theta) m'_{t-i}(\theta), \quad i = 0, 1, 2, \cdots.$$

Efficient GMM Estimators

The estimators $W_T(\theta)$ in (10.37) and (10.38) are consistent for J if evaluated at some consistent estimator of θ_0. One approach is to compute an initial GMM estimator $\widehat{\theta}_{(1)}$, based on a known weighting matrix W_T in (10.21), with $W_T = I_N$ being one possibility. This initial estimator is generally not asymptotically efficient, but it is consistent, since consistency does not depend on the choice of W_T. Thus $W_T(\widehat{\theta}_{(1)})$ provides a consistent estimator for J and

$$\widehat{\theta}_{(2)} = \arg\min_{\theta} \frac{1}{2} M'_T(\theta) W_T^{-1}(\widehat{\theta}_{(1)}) M_T(\theta), \tag{10.39}$$

is then an asymptotically efficient GMM estimator for θ_0. This is referred to as the two-step estimator since two estimators of θ_0 are computed.

The two-step approach can be extended by re-estimating J using the second asymptotically efficient estimator $\widehat{\theta}_{(2)}$ in $W_T(\theta)$, on the grounds that $W_T(\widehat{\theta}_{(2)})$ might give a better estimator of J. This updated estimator of J, in turn, is used to update the estimator of θ_0. This process is repeated, giving a sequence of estimators of the form

$$\widehat{\theta}_{(j+1)} = \arg\min_{\theta} \frac{1}{2} M'_T(\theta) W_T(\widehat{\theta}_{(j)}^{-1}) M_T(\theta), \tag{10.40}$$

for $j = 1, 2, \cdots$ until the estimators and the weighting matrix converge to within some tolerance. The iterations for $j > 2$ provide no further improvement in the asymptotic properties, but it is hoped they provide some improvement in the finite sample properties of the estimator. This is referred to as the iterative estimator.

Rather than switching between the separate estimation of θ_0 and J, an alternative strategy is to estimate them jointly using

$$\widehat{\theta} = \arg\min_{\theta} \frac{1}{2} M'_T(\theta) W_T^{-1}(\theta) M_T(\theta). \tag{10.41}$$

This is referred to as the continuous updating estimator. The dependence of $W_T(\theta)$ on θ makes the first-order conditions more complicated because there is an extra term arising from the derivative of $W_T^{-1}(\theta)$ with respect to θ. Also, the derivations of the asymptotic properties outlined earlier do not allow for the dependence of $W_T(\theta)$ on θ. Nevertheless, as described in Hansen, Heaton and Yaron (1996) and references therein, the asymptotic properties of this continuous updating estimator are the same as those for the other two estimators. They also point out that the continuous updating estimator has some nice invariance properties not shared by the other two estimators and present simulation evidence on the three estimators.

Computations

For models where $m_t(\theta)$ is nonlinear in the unknown parameters θ, implementation of the estimation strategies in (10.39) to (10.41) requires the minimisation to be performed using an iterative algorithm such as the Newton-Raphson method discussed in Chapter 3. In the case of the continuous updating estimator in (10.41), implementation of a gradient algorithm requiring first and second derivatives is even more involved as a result of the effect of θ on the weighting matrix. To see this, given (10.41), consider the criterion function

$$Q_T(\theta) = \frac{1}{2} M_T'(\theta) \, W_T(\theta)^{-1} \, M_T(\theta). \tag{10.42}$$

Letting $M_T(\theta) = (M_{i,T}(\theta))_{i=1}^N$ and $W_T(\theta)^{-1} = \left(w_{i,j}(\theta)\right)_{i,j=1}^N$, the first derivative of $Q_T(\theta)$ is

$$\sum_{i=1}^N \sum_{j=1}^N M_{i,T}(\theta) \, w_{i,j}(\theta) \, \frac{\partial M_{j,T}(\theta)}{\partial \theta} + \frac{1}{2} \sum_{i=1}^N \sum_{j=1}^N M_{i,T}(\theta) \, \frac{\partial w_{i,j}(\theta)}{\partial \theta} M_{j,T}(\theta),$$
$$\tag{10.43}$$

and the second derivative is

$$\sum_{i=1}^N \sum_{j=1}^N \frac{\partial M_{i,T}(\theta)}{\partial \theta} w_{i,j}(\theta) \, \frac{\partial M_{j,T}(\theta)}{\partial \theta'} + \sum_{i=1}^N \sum_{j=1}^N M_{i,T}(\theta) \, w_{i,j}(\theta) \, \frac{\partial^2 M_{j,T}(\theta)}{\partial \theta \partial \theta'}$$

$$+ \sum_{i=1}^N \sum_{j=1}^N M_{i,T}(\theta) \, \frac{\partial w_{i,j}(\theta)}{\partial \theta} \frac{\partial M_{j,T}(\theta)}{\partial \theta'} + \sum_{i=1}^N \sum_{j=1}^N \frac{\partial M_{i,T}(\theta)}{\partial \theta} \frac{\partial w_{i,j}(\theta)}{\partial \theta'} M_{j,T}(\theta)$$

$$+ \frac{1}{2} \sum_{i=1}^N \sum_{j=1}^N M_{i,T}(\theta) \, \frac{\partial^2 w_{i,j}(\theta)}{\partial \theta \partial \theta'} M_{j,T}(\theta). \tag{10.44}$$

The potential complexity of these computations suggests that a more convenient approach is to use a gradient algorithm in which the derivatives are computed numerically (see Chapter 3).

The leading term in the expression for the second derivative of $Q_T(\theta)$ in (10.44) is

$$\left(\frac{\partial M_T(\theta)}{\partial \theta'}\right)' W_T(\theta)^{-1} \left(\frac{\partial M_T(\theta)}{\partial \theta'}\right) = D_T'(\theta) \, W_T^{-1}(\theta) \, D_T(\theta).$$

When evaluated at the estimator $\widehat{\theta}$, the inverse of this expression provides a consistent estimator of the asymptotic variance $\Omega_J = \left(D' J^{-1} D\right)^{-1}$. The remaining terms in the second derivative of $Q_T(\theta)$ in (10.44) all involve $M_{i,T}(\theta)$, and

$M_{i,T}(\widehat{\theta}) \xrightarrow{p} 0$, as $M_T(\widehat{\theta}) \xrightarrow{p} E[m_t(\theta_0)] = 0$. Therefore, the inverse of the second derivative of $Q_T(\theta)$ is a consistent estimator of the asymptotic variance of the efficient GMM estimator. It follows that standard errors can be obtained as the square roots of the diagonal elements of the matrix

$$\text{cov}(\widehat{\theta}) = \frac{1}{T}\widehat{\Omega} = \frac{1}{T}\left[\frac{\partial^2 Q_T(\theta)}{\partial\theta\partial\theta'}\Big|_{\theta=\widehat{\theta}}\right]^{-1},$$

where $Q_T(\theta)$ is as defined in (10.42).

Alternatively, the usual variance estimator suggested in the GMM literature is

$$\widehat{\Omega}_J = \left[D_T'(\widehat{\theta})W_T^{-1}(\widehat{\theta})D_T(\widehat{\theta})\right]^{-1},$$

which is also consistent, and standard errors can be obtained as the square roots of the diagonal elements of $T^{-1}\widehat{\Omega}_J$.

Example 10.10 Estimating the Gamma Distribution

Consider estimating α in the gamma distribution using the $T = 10$ observations on y_t in Table 10.1 based on the over-identified model in Example 10.7. The moments are $m_t(\alpha) = [y_t - \alpha, \; y_t^2 - \alpha(\alpha+1)]'$ and

$$M_T(\alpha) = \frac{1}{T}\sum_{t=1}^{T}\left[\begin{array}{c} y_t - \alpha \\ y_t^2 - \alpha(\alpha+1) \end{array}\right],$$

$$W_T(\alpha) = \frac{1}{T}\sum_{t=1}^{T}\left[\begin{array}{c} y_t - \alpha \\ y_t^2 - \alpha(\alpha+1) \end{array}\right]\left[\begin{array}{c} y_t - \alpha \\ y_t^2 - \alpha(\alpha+1) \end{array}\right]'.$$

Choosing the first moment as the starting value $\alpha_{(0)} = T^{-1}\sum_{t=1}^{T} y_t = 4.9$, then

$$M\left(\alpha_{(0)}\right) = \left[\begin{array}{c} -0.0001 \\ -2.0106 \end{array}\right], \qquad W\left(\alpha_{(0)}\right) = \left[\begin{array}{cc} 2.8900 & 29.0901 \\ 29.0901 & 308.1327 \end{array}\right],$$

resulting in the value of the objective function of

$$Q\left(\alpha_{(0)}\right) = \frac{1}{2}M'\left(\alpha_{(0)}\right)W\left(\alpha_{(0)}\right)^{-1}M\left(\alpha_{(0)}\right)$$

$$= \frac{1}{2}\left[\begin{array}{c} -0.0001 \\ -2.0106 \end{array}\right]'\left[\begin{array}{cc} 2.8900 & 29.0901 \\ 29.0901 & 308.1327 \end{array}\right]^{-1}\left[\begin{array}{c} -0.0001 \\ -2.0106 \end{array}\right] = 0.1319.$$

The first and second numerical derivatives of (10.42) evaluated at $\alpha_{(0)}$ are

$$G_{(0)} = \frac{dQ_T(\alpha)}{d\alpha}\Big|_{\alpha=4.9} = 0.0709, \quad H_{(0)} = \frac{d^2Q_T(\alpha)}{d\alpha^2}\Big|_{\alpha=4.9} = 0.3794,$$

which yield the first Newton-Raphson iteration of

$$\alpha_{(1)} = \alpha_{(0)} - H_{(0)}^{-1}G_{(0)} = 4.9 - \frac{0.0709}{0.3794} = 4.7130.$$

Iterating a second time gives

$$\alpha_{(2)} = \alpha_{(1)} - H_{(1)}^{-1} G_{(1)} = 4.7130 - \frac{-0.0021}{0.3905} = 4.7184,$$

which produces a first derivative of $Q_T(\alpha)$ at $\alpha_{(2)}$ of 1.6×10^{-6}, suggesting that the algorithm has converged. As $H_{(2)} = 0.3912$, $\text{var}(\widehat{\alpha}) = 1/(10 \times 0.3912) = 0.2556$ and the standard error is $\text{se}(\widehat{\alpha}) = \sqrt{0.2556} = 0.5056$. □

Example 10.11 Estimating the C-CAPM

The C-CAPM introduced in Example 10.6 with moments

$$m_t(\theta) = \left(\beta \left(\frac{c_{t+1}}{c_t} \right)^{-\gamma} (1 + r_{t+1}) - 1 \right) w_t = u_t w_t,$$

is now estimated by GMM using a data set consisting of $T = 238$ observations on the ratio of intertemporal real United States consumption, c_{t+1}/c_t, the real return on Treasury bills, r_{t+1}, and the real return on the value weighted index e_{t+1}. The data are a revised version of the original data used by Hansen and Singleton (1982). The full set of instruments is $w_t = \{1, c_t/c_{t-1}, r_t, e_t\}$ resulting in the GMM model

$$m_t'(\theta) = [u_t, u_t c_t/c_{t-1}, u_t r_t, u_t e_t],$$

which represents a set of four nonlinear moments and two unknown parameters, $\theta = \{\beta, \gamma\}$. The GMM parameter estimates are reported in Table 10.2 for various instrument sets based on the continuous updating estimator with all derivatives computed numerically. The estimate of β for all instrument sets is 0.998. This implies a discount rate of

$$d = \frac{1}{\widehat{\beta}} - 1 = \frac{1}{0.998} - 1 = 0.002,$$

or 0.2%, which appears to be quite low. The estimates of the relative risk aversion parameter, γ, range from 0.554 to 0.955. These estimates suggest that relative risk aversion is also low over the sample period considered. □

10.4 Over-identification Testing

An over-identified GMM model for K parameters has $N > K$ population moment conditions of the form

$$M(\theta_0) = 0, \tag{10.45}$$

where $M(\theta) = \text{E}[m_t(\theta)]$ for any θ. However, if some of the moments are misspecified, then some or all of the elements of $M(\theta_0)$ will be non-zero. In the presence of such misspecification, a uniform WLLN can still apply to the

Table 10.2. *GMM estimates of the consumption capital asset pricing model for alternative instrument sets. Estimation is based on continuous updating with standard errors computed using the heteroskedasticity-consistent weighting matrix in (10.37)*

	Instrument Set		
Parameter	$w_t = \{1, c_t/c_{t-1}\}$	$w_t = \{1, c_t/c_{t-1}, r_t\}$	$w_t = \{1, c_t/c_{t-1}, r_t, e_t\}$
β	0.998	0.998	0.998
	(0.004)	(0.004)	(0.004)
γ	0.554	0.955	0.660
	(1.939)	(1.535)	(1.615)
J_{HS}	0.000	1.067	1.278
p-value	(n.a.)	(0.302)	(0.528)

sample moments so that the GMM estimator (10.20) converges in probability to

$$\theta^* = \arg\min_{\theta} \frac{1}{2} M'(\theta) W^{-1} M(\theta). \tag{10.46}$$

The effect of the misspecification is that $\theta^* \neq \theta_0$, so that the GMM estimator is no longer consistent for θ_0. In general, this implies that

$$M(\theta^*) \neq 0. \tag{10.47}$$

An implication of this result is that the probability limit of the GMM estimator now depends on the choice of weighting matrix W. This is in contrast to the GMM estimator of a correctly specified model in which (10.45) holds.

Example 10.12 Misspecifying the Gamma Distribution

In Example 10.7, the estimation of the shape parameter of a gamma distribution with $\beta = 1$ is based on the moments $E[y_t] = \alpha_0$ and $E[y_t^2] = \alpha_0(\alpha_0 + 1)$. Now suppose that the true distribution of y_t is exponential with parameter α_0, for which the moments are $E[y_t] = \alpha_0$ and $E[y_t^2] = 2\alpha_0^2$. This means that the first moment based on the gamma distribution is correctly specified, but the second moment is not, except in the special case of $\alpha_0 = 1$. The moment conditions of the misspecified model are

$$M(\alpha) = E[m_t(\alpha)] = \begin{bmatrix} E[y_t] - \alpha \\ E[y_t^2] - \alpha(\alpha + 1) \end{bmatrix} = \begin{bmatrix} \alpha_0 - \alpha \\ 2\alpha_0^2 - \alpha(\alpha + 1) \end{bmatrix},$$

showing that there is no value of α where $M(\alpha) = 0$, since the first population moment is zero for $\alpha = \alpha_0$, while the second population moment is zero for $\alpha = \sqrt{2\alpha_0^2 + \frac{1}{4}} - \frac{1}{2}$. Following (10.46), the probability limit of the GMM estimator in this model is the value of α that minimises $\frac{1}{2} M(\alpha)' W^{-1} M(\alpha)$, denoted α^*.

The value of α^* will depend on W; for example, if $W = I_2$, then α^* minimises $\left((\alpha_0 - \alpha)^2 + \left(2\alpha_0^2 - \alpha(\alpha + 1)\right)^2\right)/2$. So, if the GMM model based on the gamma distribution is used to estimate α_0, when the truth is an exponential distribution with parameter α_0, the GMM estimator will converge to this implied value of α^*, not the correct value α_0. Also α^* will generally be neither α_0 nor $\sqrt{2\alpha_0^2 + \frac{1}{4}} - \frac{1}{2}$, so neither of the population moment conditions will be equal to zero when evaluated at α^*. The practical implication of this is that, even though only one of the two moment conditions is misspecified, both of them turn out to be non-zero when evaluated at the probability limit of the GMM estimator. Therefore knowing that both elements of $M(\alpha^*)$ are non-zero is not informative about which moments are misspecified. $\qquad\qquad\square$

A general misspecification test is based on the property that (10.45) holds under correct specification, but (10.47) holds under misspecification. In particular, under correct specification it follows that $\widehat{\theta} \overset{p}{\to} \theta_0$ and

$$Q_T(\widehat{\theta}) \overset{p}{\to} \frac{1}{2} M'(\theta_0) W^{-1} M(\theta_0) = 0,$$

by (10.45). Under misspecification, however, it is true that

$$Q_T(\widehat{\theta}) \overset{p}{\to} \frac{1}{2} M'(\theta^*) W^{-1} M(\theta^*) > 0,$$

by (10.47) and the positive-definiteness of W. This result suggests that the value of the minimised criterion function $Q_T(\widehat{\theta})$ provides a test of misspecification.

In general terms the hypotheses are

H_0 : model correctly specified

H_1 : model not correctly specified.

The Hansen-Sargan J test statistic is defined as

$$J_{HS} = 2T\, Q_T(\widehat{\theta}). \tag{10.48}$$

This statistic must be computed from a criterion function in which the weighting matrix is chosen optimally so $W_T \overset{p}{\to} J$. Under the null J_{HS} is distributed asymptotically as χ^2_{N-K}, where the number of over-identifying restrictions, represented by $N - K$, is the number of degrees of freedom. Under the alternative, J_{HS} diverges to $+\infty$ as $T \to \infty$, since $Q_T(\widehat{\theta})$ itself converges to a strictly positive limit. The null hypothesis H_0 is therefore rejected for values of J_{HS} larger than the critical value from the χ^2_{N-K} distribution. As J_{HS} represents a general test of misspecification, it is not informative about which moments are misspecified, as illustrated in Example 10.12.

The J test exploits the presence of over-identification to detect any misspecification. This approach to specification testing therefore does not apply for exactly identified models. In that case misspecification will still generally result in inconsistent estimation, since $\widehat{\theta} \xrightarrow{p} \theta^* \neq \theta_0$, where $M(\theta^*) = 0$. In the sample, the exactly identified estimator is obtained to solve $M_T(\widehat{\theta}) = 0$ so that by construction $Q_T(\widehat{\theta}) = 0$, regardless of any misspecification.

Example 10.13 Gamma Distribution

From Example 10.12, suppose that only the second moment of the gamma distribution is used to define the GMM model

$$m_t(\alpha) = y_t^2 - \alpha(\alpha + 1),$$

while the true distribution of y_t is exponential with parameter α_0. This is an exactly identified model with

$$M(\alpha) = 2\alpha_0^2 - \alpha(\alpha + 1).$$

As $M(\alpha^*) = 0$ yields as the solution $\alpha^* = \sqrt{2\alpha_0^2 + \frac{1}{4}} - \frac{1}{2} \neq \alpha_0$, the GMM estimator is inconsistent for α_0 and the J_{HS} test cannot be used to detect the misspecification. $\qquad\square$

The majority of applications of GMM in econometrics arise from models specified in terms of conditional expectations, such as (10.11). When a sufficient number of instruments is chosen in (10.12) to over-identify the model, the J_{HS} test has the potential to detect whether any of the instruments are invalid or if the functional form of $u(y_t; \theta)$ is misspecified. This is illustrated in the following example.

Example 10.14 Regression with an Invalid Instrument

Consider the model in Example 10.5 where

$$y_t = x_t \beta_0 + u_t,$$

and x_t is a single regressor for which $E[u_t | x_t] \neq 0$. Suppose there are two potential instruments, $z_{1,t}$ and $z_{2,t}$, that are used to specify the GMM model

$$m(y_t, x_t, z_{1,t}, z_{2,t}; \beta) = \begin{bmatrix} z_{1,t}(y_t - x_t \beta) \\ z_{2,t}(y_t - x_t \beta) \end{bmatrix}.$$

This model is correctly specified if $E[z_{i,t}u_t] = 0$ and $E[z_{i,t}x_t] \neq 0$ for $i = 1, 2$. Suppose, however, that the condition $E[z_{2,t}u_t] = 0$ does not hold, so that $z_{2,t}$ is not a valid instrument. The model is then misspecified for the estimation of β_0. This is shown by using $y_t - x_t \beta = u_t - x_t(\beta - \beta_0)$ to rewrite the moment conditions as

$$M(\beta) = E[m(y_t, x_t, z_{1,t}, z_{2,t}; \beta)] = \begin{bmatrix} -E[z_{1,t}x_t](\beta - \beta_0) \\ E[z_{2,t}u_t] - E[z_{2,t}x_t](\beta - \beta_0) \end{bmatrix}.$$

The first of these population moments is zero if $\beta = \beta_0$ (using $E[z_{1,t} x_t] \neq 0$), but the second population moment is zero for

$$\beta = \beta_0 + \frac{E[z_{2,t} u_t]}{E[z_{2,t} x_t]},$$

showing that there is no value of β such that $M(\beta) = 0$. Hence the J test will have power against this misspecification. Note that the J test cannot distinguish which instrument is not valid. ☐

Example 10.15 Regression with Incorrect Functional Form

Suppose the true functional relationship between y_t and x_t is

$$y_t = x_t^2 \beta_0 + u_t,$$

but the GMM model (10.14) is specified assuming linearity. Also assume that both instruments, $z_{1,t}$ and $z_{2,t}$, are valid. The population moments are

$$E[z_{i,t}(y_t - x_t \beta)] = E[z_{i,t}(u_t + x_t^2 \beta_0 - x_t \beta)] = E[z_{i,t} x_t^2]\beta_0 - E[z_{i,t} x_t]\beta,$$

for $i = 1, 2$. The first population moment condition is zero at

$$\beta = \frac{E[z_{1,t} x_t^2]}{E[z_{1,t} x_t]}\beta_0,$$

and the second is zero at a different value

$$\beta = \frac{E[z_{2,t} x_t^2]}{E[z_{2,t} x_t]}\beta_0.$$

Therefore, there is no single value of β such that $M(\beta) = 0$ and the Hansen-Sargan J test will have power against this misspecification. ☐

Example 10.16 Testing the C-CAPM

Tests of the C-CAPM in Example 10.11 are based on the J_{HS} tests reported in Table 10.2. For the first instrument set $w_t = \{1, c_t/c_{t-1}\}$, the model is exactly identified, so $J_{HS} = 0$ and there is nothing to test. For the instrument set $w_t = \{1, c_t/c_{t-1}, r_t\}$, there is one over-identifying restriction resulting in a value of the test statistic of $J_{HS} = 1.067$. The statistic is distributed asymptotically as χ_1^2 under the null yielding a p-value of 0.302. For the instrument set $w_t = \{1, c_t/c_{t-1}, r_t, e_t\}$, there are two over-identifying restrictions resulting in a value of the test statistic of $J_{HS} = 1.278$. This statistic is distributed asymptotically as χ_2^2 under the null yielding a p-value 0.528. For the last two instrument sets, the model specification cannot be rejected at conventional significance levels. ☐

10.5   Applications

Two applications of the GMM estimation framework are presented. The first application focusses on the finite sample properties of the GMM estimator and its associated test statistics using a range of Monte Carlo experiments. The second application is empirical and uses GMM to estimate an interest rate model with level effects.

10.5.1   Monte Carlo Evidence

Estimation

The data-generating process for y_t is *iid* with gamma distribution for $t = 1, 2, \cdots, T$ with shape parameter α_0 and known scale parameter $\beta_0 = 1$, resulting in the moments $E[y_t] = \alpha_0$ and $E[y_t^2] = \alpha_0 (1 + \alpha_0)$. Two GMM estimators of α are computed. The first is based on the first moment with solution

$$\widehat{\alpha}_1 = \frac{1}{T} \sum_{t=1}^{T} y_t.$$

The second GMM estimator is based on both moments and computed as

$$\widehat{\alpha}_2 = \arg \min_{\alpha} \frac{1}{2} M_T' (\alpha) W_T^{-1} (\alpha) M_T (\alpha) ,$$

where

$$m_t(\alpha) = [y_t - \alpha, \ y_t^2 - \alpha(\alpha + 1)]' , \quad M_T(\alpha) = \frac{1}{T} \sum_{t=1}^{T} m_t(\alpha) ,$$

$$W_T (\alpha) = \frac{1}{T} \sum_{t=1}^{T} m_t(\alpha) m_t'(\alpha) .$$

For comparative purposes the maximum likelihood estimator is

$$\widehat{\alpha}_{ML} = \arg \max_{\alpha} \frac{1}{T} \sum_{t=1}^{T} \ln f (y_t; \alpha) ,$$

where

$$\ln f(y_t; \alpha) = (\alpha - 1) \ln y_t - y_t - \ln \Gamma(\alpha) .$$

Results for the bias and standard deviation of the sampling distributions of these three estimators are shown in Table 10.3 for $\alpha_0 = \{1, 2, 3, 4, 5\}$ and $T = \{50, 100, 200\}$. The sample mean $\widehat{\alpha}_1$ is exactly unbiased; so any nonzero bias only reflects simulation error. The GMM estimator $\widehat{\alpha}_2$ shows a small negative bias that tends to increase in magnitude as α_0 increases and decrease in magnitude as T increases, the latter being a reflection of the consistency of

Table 10.3. *Simulation results for maximum likelihood* $\left(\widehat{\alpha}_{ML}\right)$ *and GMM* $\left(\widehat{\alpha}_1, \widehat{\alpha}_2\right)$ *estimators. Based on a gamma distribution with unknown parameter* α_0 *and* $\beta_0 = 1$

	$\widehat{\alpha}_{ML}$		$\widehat{\alpha}_1$		$\widehat{\alpha}_2$	
α_0	Bias	S.D.	Bias	S.D.	Bias	S.D
			$T = 50$			
1	0.0105	0.1125	0.0016	0.1413	−0.0292	0.1374
2	0.0099	0.1748	−0.0020	0.1974	−0.0352	0.1925
3	0.0151	0.2283	0.0050	0.2474	−0.0338	0.2427
4	0.0074	0.2706	−0.0020	0.2863	−0.0431	0.2843
5	0.0100	0.3001	0.0013	0.3156	−0.0426	0.3136
			$T = 100$			
1	0.0050	0.0790	0.0006	0.0997	−0.0110	0.0925
2	0.0066	0.1251	0.0018	0.1406	−0.0136	0.1338
3	0.0044	0.1590	−0.0008	0.1734	−0.0189	0.1663
4	0.0056	0.1877	0.0008	0.1996	−0.0193	0.1940
5	0.0066	0.2117	0.0010	0.2228	−0.0203	0.2180
			$T = 200$			
1	0.0030	0.0557	0.0006	0.0709	−0.0031	0.0637
2	0.0029	0.0876	0.0010	0.0996	−0.0054	0.0932
3	0.0015	0.1116	−0.0005	0.1227	−0.0091	0.1159
4	0.0015	0.1347	−0.0008	0.1438	−0.0102	0.1382
5	0.0021	0.1492	0.0004	0.1575	−0.0106	0.1521

the estimator. The MLE $\widehat{\alpha}_{ML}$ shows a very small positive bias that decreases as T increases.

The variances of all three estimators increase as α_0 increases. For example, the variances of $\widehat{\alpha}_2$ are $0.1374^2 = 0.0189$ (for $T = 50$), 0.0086 ($T = 100$) and 0.0041 ($T = 200$); so the variances approximately halve as the sample size doubles, as is expected from an estimator whose approximate variance has the form $T^{-1}\Omega_J$.

The simulation results show that

$$\text{var}(\widehat{\alpha}_{ML}) < \text{var}(\widehat{\alpha}_2) < \text{var}(\widehat{\alpha}_1).$$

The efficiency of the maximum likelihood estimator with respect to the GMM estimators is a reflection of the fact that maximum likelihood is based on the full distribution of y_t and hence all of the moments of y_t. With respect to the GMM estimators, the efficiency of $\widehat{\alpha}_2$ relative to $\widehat{\alpha}_1$ reflects the fact that the former is based on two moments as opposed to the one moment for the latter.

Table 10.4. *Finite sample properties of t tests of* $\alpha_0 = 1$ *based on the maximum likelihood estimator* (t_{ML}) *and the GMM estimator* (t_1, t_2). *The true model is a gamma distribution with shape parameter* α_0 *and known scale parameter* $\beta_0 = 1$. *The sample size is* $T = 200$. *The size of the test is given for* $\alpha_0 = 1$ *and the power of test is given for values of* $\alpha_0 > 1$

α_0	t_{ML}	t_1	t_2
1.00	0.0539	0.0537	0.0600
1.05	0.1343	0.0847	0.1016
1.10	0.3993	0.2496	0.2995
1.15	0.7173	0.5052	0.5857
1.20	0.9176	0.7626	0.8271
1.25	0.9859	0.9163	0.9506
1.30	0.9981	0.9806	0.9905

Hypothesis Testing

The finite sample properties of hypothesis tests based on the three estimators are now investigated. The hypotheses tested are

$$H_0 : \alpha_0 = 1 \qquad H_1 : \alpha_0 \neq 1,$$

using the t statistic. Under the null hypothesis, $\alpha_0 = 1$, the distribution of y_t is exponential with mean equal to unity, whereas under the alternative, y_t follows gamma distribution with mean $\alpha_0 \neq 1$. The decision rule is to reject H_0 if $|t| > 1.96$, giving a test with an asymptotic significance level of 5%.

The respective standard errors for each of the three estimators are computed as

$$\text{se}\left(\widehat{\alpha}_{ML}\right) = \left[\sum_{t=1}^{T} \frac{\partial^2 \ln f\left(y_t; \alpha\right)}{\partial \alpha \, \partial \alpha} \right]^{-1/2}$$

$$\text{se}\left(\widehat{\alpha}_1\right) = \left[\frac{1}{T} \sum_{t=1}^{T} \left(y_t - \widehat{\alpha}_1\right)^2 \right]^{1/2}$$

$$\text{se}\left(\widehat{\alpha}_2\right) = \left[T \frac{\partial^2 Q_T\left(\alpha\right)}{\partial \alpha \, \partial \alpha'} \right]^{-1/2} .$$

The t statistics using these standard errors are denoted as t_{ML}, t_1 and t_2, respectively.

The simulated finite sample properties of the three t tests are shown in Table 10.4 for $T = 200$. The size of the test is given for $\alpha_0 = 1$ and the power of the test for $\alpha_0 > 1$. The tests based on t_{ML} and t_1 have finite sample sizes closest to the nominal size of 0.05, while the test based on t_2 is marginally over sized. A comparison of the powers of the three tests show that the t_{ML} test has the highest power, by a substantial margin in most cases. This is a direct result of the greater efficiency of the maximum likelihood estimator revealed in Table 10.3. Of the tests based on the GMM estimator the t_2 test has higher power than the t_1 test. Some of this power advantage is due to the t_2 test having slightly higher size, and the rest of the power difference is attributed to the greater efficiency of the estimator based on two moments instead of one. The power results illustrate that more efficient estimators translate to more powerful hypothesis tests.

Misspecification

The finite sample properties of the GMM estimator are based on the assumption that the distribution of y_t is chosen correctly. To explore the effects of misspecifying this distribution on the properties of the maximum likelihood and GMM estimators, the distribution of y_t is now specified as *iid* exponential with parameter α_0, while the maximum likelihood and GMM estimators are still based on the gamma distribution. The GMM estimator based on the first moment is correctly specified for all values of α because the moments of the exponential distribution are $E[y_t] = \alpha_0$ and $E[y_t^2] = 2\alpha_0^2$. On the other hand, the maximum likelihood estimator and the GMM estimator based on both moments are only specified correctly for the special case of $\alpha_0 = 1$ since the exponential and gamma distributions then coincide.

The finite sample properties of the three estimators are shown in Table 10.5 for samples of size $T = 200$ and $T = 400$. As expected, all three estimators have small bias for $\alpha_0 = 1$ when the gamma distribution is correctly specified. As α_0 increases away from one, both $\widehat{\alpha}_{ML}$ and $\widehat{\alpha}_2$ become increasingly negatively biased. For $\alpha_0 = 2$ the ML estimator appears to be converging to a value of about 1.6, while $\widehat{\alpha}_2$ appears to be converging to a value of about 1.7. These biases do not disappear in large samples, as illustrated by doubling the sample size from $T = 200$ to $T = 400$. Regardless of the value of α_0, the sample mean $\widehat{\alpha}_1$ remains unbiased and is a consistent estimator of α_0 in this experiment. These results suggest that if the distributional assumption is incorrect then the maximum likelihood estimator may no longer be consistent and hypothesis tests can be very misleading. These results also suggest that provided that the moments of the distribution are specified correctly, the GMM estimator can be more robust in this situation. Implications of misspecification for hypothesis testing are investigated in Exercise 8.

10.5.2   Levels Effect in Interest Rates

Consider again the discretised version of the CKLS model of the short-term interest rate that was estimated by quasi-maximum likelihood in Section 9.8

$$r_{t+1} - r_t = \alpha + \beta r_t + \sigma r_t^\gamma z_{t+1}, \tag{10.49}$$

Table 10.5. *Finite sample properties of the maximum likelihood and GMM estimators under misspecification. True model is exponential with parameter α_0 whereas the maximum likelihood estimator $(\widehat{\alpha}_{ML})$ and the GMM estimators $(\widehat{\alpha}_1, \widehat{\alpha}_2)$ are based on a gamma distribution with an unknown shape parameter but known scale parameter $\beta = 1$*

	$\widehat{\alpha}_{ML}$		$\widehat{\alpha}_1$		$\widehat{\alpha}_2$	
α_0	Bias	S.D.	Bias	S.D.	Bias	S.D
			$T = 200$			
1.0	0.0030	0.0557	0.0006	0.0709	−0.0031	0.0637
1.2	−0.0763	0.0646	0.0019	0.0842	−0.0485	0.0730
1.4	−0.1578	0.0745	0.0011	0.0987	−0.1071	0.0833
1.6	−0.2407	0.0848	−0.0001	0.1127	−0.1704	0.0947
1.8	−0.3236	0.0947	−0.0008	0.1286	−0.2347	0.1070
2.0	−0.4095	0.1054	−0.0018	0.1410	−0.3012	0.1192
			$T = 400$			
1.0	0.0018	0.0389	0.0011	0.0500	−0.0001	0.0444
1.2	−0.0784	0.0460	0.0004	0.0598	−0.0480	0.0517
1.4	−0.1604	0.0530	−0.0010	0.0700	−0.1052	0.0598
1.6	−0.2426	0.0595	−0.0007	0.0799	−0.1648	0.0679
1.8	−0.3248	0.0664	0.0003	0.0896	−0.2240	0.0777
2.0	−0.4082	0.0743	0.0019	0.0994	−0.2838	0.0879

in which r_t is the interest rate, $z_t \sim iid\ N(0, 1)$, and $\theta = \{\alpha, \beta, \sigma, \gamma\}$ are parameters. This model in (10.49) implies that the conditional first moment is

$$E_t[r_{t+1} - r_t] = \alpha_0 + \beta_0 r_t, \tag{10.50}$$

since $E_t[\sigma_0 r_t^{\gamma_0} z_{t+1}] = \sigma_0 r_t^{\gamma_0} E_t[z_{t+1}] = 0$. It also exhibits heteroskedasticity because

$$\begin{aligned}
\text{var}_t[r_{t+1} - r_t] &= E_t[(r_{t+1} - r_t - E_t[r_{t+1} - r_t])^2] \\
&= E_t[(\sigma_0 r_t^{\gamma_0} z_{t+1})^2] \\
&= \sigma_0^2 r_t^{2\gamma_0} E_t[z_{t+1}^2] \\
&= \sigma_0^2 r_t^{2\gamma_0}. \tag{10.51}
\end{aligned}$$

That is, the variance of the change in the interest rate varies with the level of the interest rate. The strength of this relationship is determined by the parameter γ_0, commonly referred to as the levels effect.

Defining

$$u(r_{t+1}, r_t; \theta) = \begin{bmatrix} r_{t+1} - r_t - \alpha - \beta r_t \\ (r_{t+1} - r_t - \alpha - \beta r_t)^2 - \sigma^2 r_t^{2\gamma} \end{bmatrix},$$

Table 10.6. *GMM estimates computed using the heteroskedastic-consistent weighting matrix in equation (10.37) of interest rate models with levels effect. Standard errors are in parentheses*

Maturity	α	β	σ	γ
0 months	0.183	−0.038	0.198	0.864
	(0.063)	(0.018)	(0.039)	(0.107)
1 month	0.106	−0.020	0.049	1.352
	(0.059)	(0.016)	(0.018)	(0.188)
3 months	0.090	−0.015	0.035	1.425
	(0.054)	(0.014)	(0.017)	(0.231)
6 months	0.089	−0.015	0.026	1.533
	(0.057)	(0.014)	(0.015)	(0.284)
9 months	0.091	−0.015	0.027	1.517
	(0.056)	(0.013)	(0.015)	(0.278)
10 years	0.046	−0.006	0.029	1.178
	(0.027)	(0.006)	(0.007)	(0.114)

allows (10.50) and (10.51) to be expressed as

$$E_t[u(r_{t+1}, r_t; \theta_0)] = E[u(r_{t+1}, r_t; \theta_0)|w_t] = 0, \qquad (10.52)$$

with w_t representing the information set of all relevant variables available up to and including time t. This conditional expectation has the general form (10.11). Using the law of iterated expectations implies a GMM model of the form

$$m(r_{t+1}, r_t; \theta) = u(r_{t+1}, r_t; \theta)w_t'.$$

Letting the instrument set be $w_t = \{1, r_t\}$, the moments are

$$m(r_{t+1}, r_t; \theta) = \begin{bmatrix} r_{t+1} - r_t - \alpha - \beta r_t \\ (r_{t+1} - r_t - \alpha - \beta r_t)r_t \\ (r_{t+1} - r_t - \alpha - \beta r_t)^2 - \sigma^2 r_t^{2\gamma} \\ ((r_{t+1} - r_t - \alpha - \beta r_t)^2 - \sigma^2 r_t^{2\gamma})r_t \end{bmatrix}.$$

As the number of moment conditions equals the number of parameters, the parameters in θ are just-identified.

The results of estimating the interest rate model by GMM are given in Table 10.6. The interest rates are monthly United States zero coupon yields beginning December 1946 and ending February 1991. Equation (10.52) shows that $u(r_{t+1}, r_t; \theta_0)$ is a mds and hence not autocorrelated; consequently the heteroskedastic-consistent weighting matrix estimator is used. The results also show a strong levels effect in United States interest rates that changes over the maturity of the asset. The parameter estimates of γ increase in magnitude as maturity increases from 0 to 6 months, reach a peak at 6 months, and taper off thereafter.

10.6   Exercises

(1) Method of Moments Estimation

Program files   gmm_mom.*

This exercise is based on the data in Table 10.1. The method of moments estimator of θ for a just-identified model is based on the solution of

$$M_T(\widehat{\theta}) = \frac{1}{T} \sum_{t=1}^{T} m_t(y_t; \widehat{\theta}) = 0,$$

where $m_t(\theta) = m_t(y_t; \theta)$ is the moment at time t.

(a) The normal distribution

$$f(y_t; \theta) = \frac{1}{\sqrt{2\pi\sigma^2}} \exp\left[-\frac{1}{2}\left(\frac{y_t - \mu}{\sigma}\right)^2\right],$$

has moments $E[y_t] = \mu_0$, $E[y_t^2] = \sigma_0^2 + \mu_0^2$ and $E[(y_t - \mu_0)^4] = 3\sigma_0^4$.

(i) Estimate μ and σ^2 using the moment conditions

$$m_t(\theta) = \begin{bmatrix} y_t - \mu \\ y_t^2 - \sigma^2 - \mu^2 \end{bmatrix}.$$

(ii) Estimate μ and σ^2 using the moment conditions

$$m_t(\theta) = \begin{bmatrix} y_t - \mu \\ (y_t - \mu)^4 - 3\sigma^4 \end{bmatrix}.$$

Compare the two sets of point estimates of μ and σ^2.

(b) The Student t distribution

$$f(y_t; \theta) = \frac{\Gamma[(v + 1)/2]}{\sqrt{\pi v}\Gamma[v/2]} \left[1 + \frac{(y_t - \mu)^2}{v}\right]^{-(v+1)/2},$$

has moments $E[y_t] = \mu_0$, $E[(y_t - \mu_0)^2] = v_0/(v_0 - 2)$, and $E[(y_t - \mu_0)^4] = 3v_0^2/(v_0 - 2)(v_0 - 4)$.

(i) Estimate μ and v using the moment conditions

$$m_t(\theta) = \begin{bmatrix} y_t - \mu \\ (y_t - \mu)^2 - \dfrac{v}{v - 2} \end{bmatrix}.$$

(ii) Estimate μ and ν using the moment conditions

$$m_t(\theta) = \left[\begin{array}{c} y_t - \mu \\ (y_t - \mu)^4 - \dfrac{3\nu^2}{(\nu - 2)(\nu - 4)} \end{array} \right].$$

Compare the two sets of point estimates of μ and ν.

(c) The gamma distribution

$$f(y_t; \theta) = \frac{\beta^\alpha}{\Gamma(\alpha)} \exp[-\beta y_t] y_t^{\alpha-1}, \qquad y_t \geqslant 0, \alpha > 0, \beta > 0,$$

has moments $E[y_t] = \alpha_0/\beta_0$, $E[y_t^2] = \alpha_0(\alpha_0 + 1)/\beta_0^2$, and $E[1/y_t] = \beta_0/(\alpha_0 - 1)$.

(i) Estimate α and β using the moment conditions

$$m_t(\theta) = \left[\begin{array}{c} y_t - \dfrac{\alpha}{\beta} \\ \dfrac{1}{y_t} - \dfrac{\beta}{\alpha - 1} \end{array} \right].$$

(ii) Estimate α and β using the moment conditions

$$m_t(\theta) = \left[\begin{array}{c} y_t - \dfrac{\alpha}{\beta} \\ y_t^2 - \dfrac{\alpha(\alpha + 1)}{\beta^2} \end{array} \right].$$

Compare the two sets of point estimates for α and β. Briefly discuss the potential problems associated with the estimates based on the moment conditions in part (ii).

(d) The Pareto distribution

$$f(y_t; \alpha) = \frac{\alpha y_{\min}}{y_t^{\alpha+1}}, \qquad y_t > y_{\min},$$

has $E[y_t] = \alpha_0 y_{\min}/(\alpha_0 - 1)$ and $E[y_t^2] = \alpha_0 y_{\min}^2/((\alpha_0 - 1)^2(\alpha_0 - 2))$, where $y_{\min}$ represents the minimum value.

(i) Choosing $y_{\min} = 2$, estimate $\theta = \alpha$ using the moment condition

$$m_t(\theta) = \left[y_t - \frac{\alpha y_{\min}}{\alpha - 1} \right].$$

(ii) Choosing $y_{\min} = 2$, estimate α using the moment condition

$$m_t(\theta) = \left[y_t^2 - \frac{\alpha y_{\min}^2}{(\alpha - 1)^2(\alpha - 2)} \right].$$

(2) Estimating a Gamma Distribution

Program files	gmm_gamma.*

This exercise is based on the data in Table 10.1. The generalised method of moments estimator is based on the solution of

$$\hat{\theta} = \arg\min_{\theta} Q_T(\theta), \tag{10.53}$$

where

$$Q_T(\theta) = \frac{1}{2} M_T'(\theta) W_T^{-1} M_T(\theta), \quad M_T(\theta) = \frac{1}{T} \sum_{t=1}^{T} m_t(\theta),$$

$$W_T(\hat{\theta}) = \frac{1}{T} \sum_{t=1}^{T} m_t(\theta) m_t'(\theta),$$

and where $m_t(\theta) = m_t(y_t; \theta)$ is the moment at time t.

(a) The first two uncentered moments of the gamma distribution with $\beta_0 = 1$ are $E[y_t] = \alpha_0$, $E[y_t^2] = \alpha_0(\alpha_0 + 1)$.

   (i) Using the starting value $\theta_{(0)} = \{\alpha_{(0)} = \bar{y}\}$ compute the following

$$M_T(\theta_{(0)}), \ W_T(\theta_{(0)}), \ Q_T(\theta_{(0)}), \ G_{(0)} = \frac{\partial Q_T(\theta_{(0)})}{\partial \theta}, \ H_{(0)} = \frac{\partial^2 Q_T(\theta_{(0)})}{\partial \theta \partial \theta'},$$

   where the derivatives are computed numerically.

   (ii) Use the results in part (i) to compute the Newton-Raphson update

$$\theta_{(1)} = \theta_{(0)} - H_{(0)}^{-1} G_{(0)},$$

   and compare $Q_T(\theta_{(0)})$ and $Q_T(\theta_{(1)})$. Iterate until convergence to find the GMM parameter estimate of α and its standard error using

$$\text{se}(\hat{\alpha}) = \sqrt{\frac{1}{T} H^{-1}(\hat{\alpha})}.$$

(b) Repeat part (a) using $E[y_t] = \alpha_0$, $E[y_t^2] = \alpha_0(\alpha_0 + 1)$, $E[1/y_t] = 1/(\alpha_0 - 1)$.

(c) Repeat part (a) with α and β unknown using $E[y_t] = \alpha_0/\beta_0$, $E[y_t^2] = \alpha_0(\alpha_0 + 1)/\beta_0^2$, and $E[1/y_t] = \beta_0/(\alpha_0 - 1)$.

(3) Estimating a Student t Distribution

Program files	gmm_student.*

This exercise is based on the data in Table 10.1. The generalised method of moments estimator is based on the solution of

$$\widehat{\theta} = \arg\min_{\theta} Q_T(\theta), \tag{10.54}$$

where

$$Q_T(\theta) = \frac{1}{2} M_T'(\theta) W_T^{-1} M_T(\theta), \quad M_T(\theta) = \frac{1}{T} \sum_{t=1}^{T} m_t(\theta),$$

$$W_T(\widehat{\theta}) = \frac{1}{T} \sum_{t=1}^{T} m_t(\theta) m_t'(\theta),$$

and where $m_t(\theta) = m_t(y_t; \theta)$ is the moment at time t.

(a) Consider the following moments of the Student t distribution $E[y_t] = \mu_0$, $E[(y_t - \mu_0)^2] = \nu_0/(\nu_0 - 2)$.

(i) Using the starting value $\theta_{(0)} = \{\mu_{(0)} = \bar{y}, \nu_{(0)} = 5\}$ compute the following

$$M_T(\theta_{(0)}), \ W_T(\theta_{(0)}), \ Q_T(\theta_{(0)}), \ G_{(0)} = \frac{\partial Q_T(\theta_{(0)})}{\partial \theta}, \ H_{(0)} = \frac{\partial^2 Q_T(\theta_{(0)})}{\partial \theta \partial \theta'},$$

where the derivatives are computed numerically.

(ii) Use the results in part (i) to compute the Newton-Raphson update

$$\theta_{(1)} = \theta_{(0)} - H_{(0)}^{-1} G_{(0)},$$

and compare $Q_T(\theta_{(0)})$ and $Q_T(\theta_{(1)})$. Iterate until convergence to find the GMM parameter estimate of θ and its standard error using

$$se(\widehat{\theta}) = \sqrt{\frac{1}{T} H^{-1}(\widehat{\theta})}.$$

(b) Repeat part (a) using the moments $E[y_t] = \mu_0$, $E[(y_t - \mu_0)^2] = \nu_0/(\nu_0 - 2)$, $E[(y_t - \mu_0)^4] = 3\nu_0^2/(\nu_0 - 2)(\nu_0 - 4)$.

(4) The Consumption Capital Asset Pricing Model

Program files	gmm_ccapm.*
Data files	ccapm.*

The data are 238 observations on the real United States consumption ratio c_{t+1}/c_t (*CRATIO*), the real Treasury bill rate r_{t+1} (*R*), and the real value weighted returns e_{t+1} (*E*). This is the adjusted Hansen and Singleton (1982) data set used in their original paper. Consider the first-order condition of the C-CAPM

$$E_t[\beta_0(c_{t+1}/c_t)^{-\gamma_0}(1 + r_{t+1}) - 1] = 0,$$

where c_t is real consumption and r_t is the real interest rate. The parameters are the discount factor, β, and the relative risk aversion coefficient γ.

(a) Estimate the parameters $\theta = \{\beta, \gamma\}$ by GMM using $w_t = \{1, c_t/c_{t-1}\}$ as instruments and starting values $\theta_{(0)} = \{\beta = 1.0, \gamma = 1.0\}$. Interpret the parameter estimates and test the number of over-identifying restrictions.

(b) Repeat part (a) using $w_t = \{1, c_t/c_{t-1}, r_t\}$ as instruments.

(c) Repeat part (a) using $w_t = \{1, c_t/c_{t-1}, r_t, e_t\}$, as instruments.

(d) Repeat part (a) using $w_t = \{1, c_t/c_{t-1}, r_t, e_t, e_{t-1}\}$, as instruments.

(e) Compare the parameter estimates across the four sets of instruments in parts (a) to (d).

(5) Decomposing International Equity returns

Program files	gmm_equity.*
Data files	equity_decomposition.*

The data file contains daily equity prices (P) on the S&P500, FTSE100 and the EURO50, from 29 July 2004 to 3 March 2009. Let $e_{i,t} = r_{i,t} - \bar{r}_i$ represent the centered daily percentage equity returns where $r_{i,t} = 100(\ln P_{i,t} - \ln P_{i,t-1})$.

(a) Compute the covariance matrix of $e_{i,t}$ and interpret the empirical moments.

(b) Consider the latent factor model

$$e_{i,t} = \lambda_i s_t + \phi_i z_{i,t}, \qquad i = 1, 2, 3,$$

where $\{s_t, z_{1,t}, z_{2,t}, z_{3,t}\}$ are $iid\,(0, 1)$. Show that the theoretical moments of $e_{i,t}$ are

$$\begin{aligned}
E[e_{i,t}^2] &= \lambda_i^2 + \phi_i^2, & i = 1, 2, 3, \\
E[e_{i,t} e_{j,t}] &= \lambda_i \lambda_j, & i \neq j.
\end{aligned}$$

(c) Using the moment structure in part (b) estimate the parameters $\theta = \{\lambda_1, \lambda_2, \lambda_3, \phi_1, \phi_2, \phi_3\}$ by GMM. Interpret the parameter estimates by computing the relative contributions of the common factor (s_t) and the idiosyncratic factors ($z_{1,t}, z_{2,t}, z_{3,t}$) given by

$$\frac{\lambda_i^2}{\lambda_i^2 + \phi_i^2}, \qquad \frac{\phi_i^2}{\lambda_i^2 + \phi_i^2}, \qquad i = 1, 2, 3.$$

(d) Show that the factor decomposition in part (b) gives an exact decomposition of the empirical covariance matrix of $e_{i,t}$ computed in (a).

(6) Modelling Contagion in the Asian Crisis

Program files	gmm_contagion.*
Data files	contagion.*

The data file contains daily data on the exchange rate $(s_{i,t})$ of the following seven countries: South Korea, Indonesia, Malaysia, Japan, Australia, New Zealand and Thailand. The sample period is 2 June 1997 to 31 August 1998, a total of 319 observations. Let $e_{i,t} = r_{i,t} - \bar{r}_i$, represent the zero-mean daily percentage currency returns where $r_{i,t} = 100(\ln s_{i,t} - \ln s_{i,t-1})$.

(a) Estimate the latent factor model of the exchange rate

$$e_{i,t} = \lambda_i s_t + \phi_i z_{i,t} + \gamma_i z_{7,t}, \qquad i = 1, 2, \cdots, 7,$$

by GMM with $\gamma_7 = 0$ and where the factors $\{s_t, z_{1,t}, \cdots, z_{7,t}\}$ are all $iid\,(0, 1)$.

(b) For each country, estimate the proportion of volatility arising from contagion by evaluating

$$\frac{\gamma_i^2}{\lambda_i^2 + \phi_i^2 + \gamma_i^2}, \qquad i = 1, 2, ..., 6.$$

(c) Perform a test of contagion $\gamma_1 = \gamma_2 = \cdots = \gamma_6 = 0$.

(7) Consistency of GMM

Program files gmm_consistency.*

(a) Simulate $T = 100000$ observations from the gamma distribution with parameters $\theta_0 = \{\alpha_0 = 10, \beta_0 = 1\}$. Compute the GMM population objective function

$$Q_T(\alpha) = \frac{1}{2} M_T'(\alpha) W_T^{-1}(\alpha) M_T(\alpha),$$

for values of $\alpha = \{6, \cdots, 14\}$ and $\beta = 1$, where

$$M_T(\alpha) = \frac{1}{T} \sum_{t=1}^{T} m_t(\alpha),$$

$$W_T(\alpha) = \frac{1}{T} \sum_{t=1}^{T} m_t(\alpha) m_t'(\alpha), \quad m_t(\alpha) = \begin{bmatrix} y_t - \alpha \\ y_t^2 - \alpha(\alpha+1) \\ y_t^{-1} - (\alpha-1)^{-1} \end{bmatrix}.$$

(b) Repeat part (a) for the finite samples of size $T = 10, 100, 200, 400$ and discuss the consistency property of the GMM estimator of α.

(c) Repeat parts (a) and (b) with $m_t(\alpha) = \begin{bmatrix} y_t - \alpha & y_t^2 - \alpha(\alpha+1) \end{bmatrix}'$.

(d) Repeat parts (a) and (b) with $m_t(\alpha) = \begin{bmatrix} y_t - \alpha \end{bmatrix}$.

(8) Monte Carlo Evidence for the Gamma Model

Program files gmm_gammasim.*

Let y_t have an *iid* gamma distribution for $t = 1, \cdots, T$ with shape parameter $\alpha_0 = \{1, 2, 3, 4, 5\}$ and scale parameter $\beta_0 = 1$.

(a) Investigate the finite sample bias and variance of the following estimators of α_0 assuming that $\beta_0 = 1$ is known, for sample sizes of $T = \{50, 100, 200, 400\}$ with 10000 replications.

(i) The maximum likelihood estimator.

(ii) The GMM estimator based on the first moment of the gamma distribution $m_t(\alpha) = [y_t - \alpha]'$.

(iii) The GMM estimator based on the first two moments of the gamma distribution $m_t(\alpha) = [y_t - \alpha, \ y_t^2 - \alpha(\alpha + 1)]'$.

(b) Compute the finite sample size of the t statistic $(\widehat{\alpha} - \alpha_0)/se(\widehat{\alpha})$ based on the three estimators in part (a) as well as the J_{HS} statistic of misspecification.

(c) Compute the finite sample power of the t statistic $(\widehat{\alpha} - 1)/se(\widehat{\alpha})$ based on the three estimators in part (a) for parameter values of $\alpha_0 = \{1.05, 1.10, \cdots, 1.30\}$.

(d) Suppose that the data-generating process is now an exponential distribution with parameter values of $\alpha_0 = \{1.0, 1.2, \cdots, 2.0\}$ whereas the estimators in part (a) are still based on the gamma distribution. Redo parts (a) to (c) and discuss the effects of misspecification on the sampling properties of the three estimators, their associated test statistics and the J_{HS} statistic of misspecification.

(9) Levels Effect in United States Interest Rates

Program files	gmm_level.*
Data files	level.*

The data are monthly and cover the period December 1946 to February 1991. The zero coupon bonds have maturities of 0, 1, 3, 6, 9 months and 10 years.

(a) For each yield, estimate the following interest rate equation by GMM

$$r_{t+1} - r_t = \alpha + \beta r_t + \sigma r_t^\gamma z_{t+1},$$

where z_t is *iid* $(0, 1)$ and the instrument set is $w_t = \{1, r_t\}$.

(b) For each yield test the following restrictions: $\gamma = 0.0$, $\gamma = 0.5$ and $\gamma = 1.0$.

(c) If the level effect model of the interest rate captures time-varying volatility and $\alpha, \beta \simeq 0$, then

$$E\left[\left(\frac{r_{t+1} - r_t}{r_t^\gamma}\right)^2\right] \simeq \sigma^2.$$

Plot the series

$$\frac{r_{t+1} - r_t}{r_t^{\gamma}},$$

for $\gamma = \{0.0, 0.5, 1.0, 1.5\}$ and discuss the properties of this series.

(10) **Risk Aversion and the Equity Premium Puzzle**

Program files	gmm_risk_aversion.*
Data files	equity_mp.*

In this exercise, the risk aversion parameter is estimated by GMM using the data originally used by Mehra and Prescott (1985) in their work on the equity premium puzzle. The data are annual for the period 1889 to 1978, a total of 91 observations on the following United States variables: the real stock price, S_t; real dividends, D_t; real per capita consumption, C_t; the nominal risk-free rate on bonds, expressed as a per annum percentage, R_t; and the price of consumption goods, P_t.

(a) Compute the following returns series for equities, bonds and consumption, respectively,

$$R_{s,t+1} = \frac{S_{t+1} + D_t - S_t}{S_t}$$

$$R_{b,t+1} = (1 + R_t)(\frac{P_t}{P_{t+1}}) - 1$$

$$R_{c,t+1} = \frac{C_{t+1} - C_t}{C_t}.$$

(b) Consider the first-order conditions of the C-CAPM model

$$E_t[\beta(1 + R_{c,t+1})^{-\gamma}(1 + R_{b,t+1}) - 1] = 0$$
$$E_t[\beta(1 + R_{c,t+1})^{-\gamma}(1 + R_{s,t+1}) - 1] = 0,$$

where the parameters are the discount factor, β, and the relative risk aversion coefficient, γ. Estimate the parameters $\theta = \{\beta, \gamma\}$ by GMM with instruments $w_t = \{1, R_{c,t}\}$. Interpret the parameter estimates and test the number of over-identifying restrictions.

(c) Repeat part (b) with instruments $w_t = \{1, R_{c,t}, R_{b,t}\}$.

(d) Repeat part (b) with instruments $w_t = \{1, R_{c,t}, R_{b,t}, R_{s,t}\}$.

(e) Discuss the robustness properties of the parameter estimates of θ in parts (b) to (d).

11 Nonparametric Estimation

11.1 Introduction

Earlier chapters in Part THREE of the book explore circumstances in which the likelihood function is misspecified. The case of incorrectly specifying the entire distribution is considered in Chapter 9, while Chapter 10 deals with the situation in which the form of the distribution is unknown but the functional form of the moments of the distribution are known. The assumptions underlying the model are relaxed even further in this chapter to the extent that neither the distribution of the dependent variable nor the functional form of the moments of the distribution are specified. Estimation is nonparametric in the sense that the moments of the dependent variable, y_t, at each point in time, are estimated conditional on a set of exogenous variables, x_t, without specifying the functional form of this relationship. Instead smoothness conditions linking the dependent variable, y_t, and the explanatory variables, x_t, are imposed. This estimator is known as the Nadaraya-Watson kernel estimator of the relevant conditional moment.

The cost of using a nonparametric estimator is that the rate of convergence of the estimator to the true model is slower (less than $\sqrt{T}$) than the case in which a parametric model is correctly specified ($\sqrt{T}$). Intuitively, this slower rate of convergence is the cost of providing less information about the model's structure than would be the case when using parametric estimation methods. The gain however, is that if the parametric form of the model is misspecified then the maximum likelihood estimator is likely to be biased and inconsistent while the nonparametric estimator remains consistent.

Prior to dealing with the nonparametric estimation of regression models, however, it is necessary to establish a number of preliminary results by discussing briefly the problem of estimating an unknown probability density function of a random variable using only sample information. The formal results given in this chapter concerning both density estimation and nonparametric regression are developed initially in the context of independently and identically distributed observations and then extended to the more general case of dependent observations.

11.2 The Kernel Density Estimator

The problem is to estimate the unknown probability density function, $f(y)$, using only the information available in a sample of T observations $y_t = \{y_1, y_2, \cdots, y_T\}$. A simple but useful first approximation to $f(y)$ is the histogram. One possible simple algorithm for constructing a histogram is as follows.

Step 1: Construct a grid of values of y starting at the lowest value of y_t and ending at the highest value of y_t. Let the distance between the y values be h, where h is known as the bandwidth. This interval is also commonly referred to as the bin.

Step 2: Choose the first value of y and count the number of sample values, y_t, falling in the interval $(y - h/2, y + h/2)$.

Step 3: Repeat the exercise for the next value of y in the grid and continue until the last value in the grid.

Formally, the histogram estimator of $f(y)$ for a sample of size T is

$$\widehat{f}(y) = \frac{1}{Th} \sum_{t=1}^{T} [\text{number of observations in } (y - h/2, y + h/2)]$$

$$= \frac{1}{Th} \sum_{t=1}^{T} \mathcal{I}\left(y - \frac{h}{2} \le y_t \le y + \frac{h}{2}\right) = \frac{1}{Th} \sum_{t=1}^{T} \mathcal{I}\left(\left|\frac{y - y_t}{h}\right| \le \frac{1}{2}\right),$$

where

$$\mathcal{I}(\cdot) = \begin{cases} 1 : & \left|\dfrac{y - y_t}{h}\right| \le \dfrac{1}{2} \\[2mm] 0 : & \left|\dfrac{y - y_t}{h}\right| > \dfrac{1}{2}, \end{cases} \tag{11.1}$$

is the indicator function. This estimator can be written as

$$\widehat{f}(y) = \frac{1}{T} \sum_{t=1}^{T} w_t(y), \qquad w_t(y) = \frac{1}{h} \mathcal{I}\left(\left|\frac{y - y_t}{h}\right| \le \frac{1}{2}\right),$$

which emphasises that the histogram is the sample mean of the weights $w_t(y)$, evaluated at y. This estimate of the density is in essence a local histogram where the width of the bin, h, controls the amount of smoothing.

The main disadvantage with the approach based on the histogram is that the weights, $w_t(y)$, are discontinuous, switching from one to zero immediately wherever $|(y_t - y)/h| > 1/2$. This in turn, leads to an estimator of $f(y)$ that is jagged. A natural solution is to replace the indicator function with a smooth function known as the kernel function. In selecting this function, the approach

Table 11.1. *Commonly used kernel functions,*
$z = (y - y_t)/h$

Kernel	$K(z)$	Range
Uniform	1	$I(|z| \leq 1/2)$
Triangle	$(1 - z)$	$I(|z| \leq 1)$
Epanechnikov	$\frac{3}{4}(1 - z^2)$	$I(|z| \leq 1)$
Biweight	$\frac{15}{16}(1 - z^2)^2$	$I(|z| \leq 1)$
Triweight	$(1 - z^2)^3$	$I(|z| \leq 1)$
Gaussian	$\dfrac{1}{\sqrt{2\pi}} \exp(-\dfrac{1}{2}z^2)$	$-\infty < z < \infty$

is to choose kernels that are non-negative functions and which enclose unit probability mass and therefore satisfy automatically the basic prerequisites of a probability distribution. The kernel estimate of a density has the generic form

$$\widehat{f}(y) = \frac{1}{Th} \sum_{t=1}^{T} K\left(\frac{y - y_t}{h}\right) = \frac{1}{T} \sum_{t=1}^{T} w_t(y), \quad w_t(y) = \frac{1}{h} K\left(\frac{y - y_t}{h}\right),$$

$$(11.2)$$

in which h is a window length controlling the averaging, known as the kernel bandwidth, and $K(\cdot)$ is a suitable non-negative function defined over the required interval and enclosing unit mass. As emphasised by expression (11.2), the density estimator is interpreted as a kernel with bandwidth h placed on all the data points with the resultant density mass at y being averaged to obtain $\widehat{f}(y)$. It follows that the greater is the number of observations near y the greater is the probability mass computed at this point.

Table 11.1 presents some well known kernel functions, of which the Gaussian kernel is the most commonly used. All of the tabulated kernel functions have the following properties

$$\int_{-\infty}^{\infty} K(z)dz = 1 \qquad \int_{-\infty}^{\infty} zK(z)dz = 0$$

$$\int_{-\infty}^{\infty} z^2 K(z)dz = \mu_2 \qquad \int_{-\infty}^{\infty} z^3 K(z)dz = 0,$$

$$(11.3)$$

in which the variance of the kernel, μ_2, is a positive constant with a value dependent on the choice of the kernel function. Further, all odd-order moments are zero by virtue of the fact that the kernel is a symmetric function. As will become clear, the choice of kernel function is not particularly crucial to the

Table 11.2. *Kernel density estimation example based on a Gaussian kernel with bandwidths h = {1, 2}, and a sample of size T = 20. The grid points selected are y = {5, 10, 15}*

y_t (ordered)	$w_t(y)\,(h = 1)$			$w_t(y)\,(h = 2)$		
	$y = 5$	$y = 10$	$y = 15$	$y = 5$	$y = 10$	$y = 15$
2.000	0.004	0.000	0.000	0.065	0.000	0.000
3.000	0.054	0.000	0.000	0.121	0.000	0.000
5.000	0.399	0.000	0.000	0.199	0.009	0.000
7.000	0.054	0.004	0.000	0.121	0.065	0.000
8.000	0.004	0.054	0.000	0.065	0.121	0.000
8.000	0.000	0.054	0.000	0.065	0.121	0.000
9.000	0.000	0.242	0.000	0.027	0.176	0.002
9.000	0.000	0.242	0.000	0.027	0.176	0.002
10.000	0.000	0.399	0.000	0.009	0.199	0.009
10.000	0.000	0.399	0.000	0.009	0.199	0.009
11.000	0.000	0.242	0.000	0.002	0.176	0.027
11.000	0.000	0.242	0.000	0.002	0.176	0.027
11.000	0.000	0.242	0.000	0.002	0.176	0.027
12.000	0.000	0.054	0.004	0.000	0.121	0.065
12.000	0.000	0.054	0.004	0.000	0.121	0.065
14.000	0.000	0.000	0.242	0.000	0.027	0.176
15.000	0.000	0.000	0.399	0.000	0.009	0.199
17.000	0.000	0.000	0.054	0.000	0.000	0.121
18.000	0.000	0.000	0.004	0.000	0.000	0.065
20.000	0.000	0.000	0.000	0.000	0.000	0.009
$\widehat{f}(y) = \frac{1}{T}\sum_{t=1}^{T} w_t(y):$	0.026	0.111	0.035	0.036	0.094	0.040

quality of the density estimate; the most important factor is the choice of the bandwidth, h.

A simple algorithm for computing a kernel estimate of the density, $f(y)$, is as follows:

Step 1: Construct a grid of values of y starting at the lowest value of y_t and ending at the highest value of y_t.
Step 2: Choose the first value of y and compute $f(y)$ as in equation (11.2).
Step 3: Repeat for the next value of y in the grid and continue until the last value in the grid.

Example 11.1 Numerical Illustration

Consider the following $T = 20$ ordered observations, given in the first column of Table 11.2, that are drawn from an unknown distribution $f(y)$. The density is estimated at three points $y = \{5, 10, 15\}$ using a Gaussian kernel and two bandwidths $h = \{1, 2\}$. The weights $w_t(y)$ associated with each observation for $y = 5$ and $h = 1$, are given in the second column. The first ordered observation is $y_1 = 2$ and the weight is computed as

$$w_1(y) = \frac{1}{h} K\left(\frac{y - y_1}{h}\right) = \frac{1}{h} \frac{1}{\sqrt{2\pi}} \exp\left(-\frac{1}{2}\left(\frac{y - y_1}{h}\right)^2\right)$$

$$= \frac{1}{1} \frac{1}{\sqrt{2\pi}} \exp\left(-\frac{1}{2}\left(\frac{5 - 2}{1}\right)^2\right) = 0.004 \,.$$

For the second ordered observation

$$w_2(y) = \frac{1}{h} K\left(\frac{y - y_2}{h}\right) = \frac{1}{h} \frac{1}{\sqrt{2\pi}} \exp\left(-\frac{1}{2}\left(\frac{y - y_2}{h}\right)^2\right)$$

$$= \frac{1}{1} \frac{1}{\sqrt{2\pi}} \exp\left(-\frac{1}{2}\left(\frac{5 - 3}{1}\right)^2\right) = 0.054 \,.$$

This procedure is repeated for all $T = 20$ observations, with the kernel estimate at $y = 5$, given by the sample average of the weights

$$\widehat{f}(5) = \frac{1}{20} \sum_{t=1}^{20} w_t(y) = \frac{0.004 + 0.054 + 0.399 + 0.054 \cdots 0.000}{20} = 0.026 \,,$$

which is given in the last row of the second column in Table 11.2. Columns 3 and 4 repeat the calculations for $y = 10$ and $y = 15$ with $h = 1$, yielding the respective estimates of 0.111 and 0.035. Of course, the kernel density estimator can be evaluated at a finer number of grid points.

The last three columns of Table 11.2 repeat the calculations for a wider bandwidth $h = 2$, but using the same values of y. Comparing the two sets of estimates shows that the distribution based on $h = 1$ yields a more peaked distribution than is the case when $h = 2$ is used. Intuitively this is due to the fact that larger bandwidths assign relatively greater weight to observations further away from the grid points $y = \{5, 10, 15\}$, thus creating smoother estimates of $f(y)$ than those obtained using smaller bandwidths. □

The kernel estimator generalises naturally to deal with the multivariate case. The problem in multiple dimensions is to approximate the N-dimensional probability density function evaluated at $f(y_1, \cdots y_N)$ given the matrix of observations $y_{t,n}$ for $t = 1, \cdots, T$ and $n = 1, \cdots, N$. The multivariate kernel density estimator in the N-dimensional case is defined as

$$\widehat{f}(y_1, \cdots, y_N) = \frac{1}{T} \sum_{t=1}^{T} \frac{1}{h_1 \times \cdots \times h_N} K\left(\frac{y_1 - y_{t,1}}{h_1}, \cdots, \frac{y_N - y_{t,N}}{h_N}\right),$$

in which K denotes a multivariate kernel and where it is assumed that the bandwidth h is in fact a vector of bandwidths $\{h_1, \cdots, h_N\}$. In practice the form of this multivariate kernel function is simplified to the so-called product kernel estimator of the multivariate density

$$\widehat{f}(y_1, \cdots, y_N) = \frac{1}{Th_1 \times \cdots \times h_N} \sum_{t=1}^{T} \left\{ \prod_{n=1}^{N} K\left(\frac{y_n - y_{t,n}}{h_n}\right) \right\},$$

which amounts to using the same univariate kernel in each dimension but with a different smoothing parameter for each dimension. A major difficulty with multidimensional estimation, however, is that very large sample sizes are needed to obtain accurate estimates of the density. Yatchew (2003) provides a good discussion of the curse of dimensionality.

11.3 Properties of the Kernel Density Estimator

The properties of the kernel estimator, $\widehat{f}(y)$, outlined in this section are based on the assumption of *iid* sample data. Generalisations to dependent data are discussed at the end of the section. The derivations of some of the properties are presented in Appendix D along with some other useful results.

11.3.1 Finite Sample Properties

Bias
The bias of the kernel estimator, $\widehat{f}(y)$, is given by

$$\text{bias}(\widehat{f}(y)) = \text{E}[\widehat{f}(y)] - f(y) = \frac{h^2}{2} f^{(2)}(y)\mu_2 + O(h^4), \qquad (11.4)$$

in which

$$f^{(k)}(y) = \frac{d^k f(y)}{dy^k}.$$

This expression shows that the bias is an increasing function of the bandwidth h and disappears as $h \rightarrow 0^+$.

Variance
The variance of the kernel estimator, $\widehat{f}(y)$, is given by

$$\text{var}(\widehat{f}(y)) = \frac{1}{Th} f(y) \int_{-\infty}^{\infty} K^2(z)dz + o\left(\frac{1}{Th}\right). \qquad (11.5)$$

By contrast with the expression for the bias, the variance is a decreasing function of the bandwidth h with the variance disappearing as $Th \rightarrow \infty$.

Equations (11.4) and (11.5) show that there is an inverse relationship between bias and variance for different values of h, as illustrated in the following example.

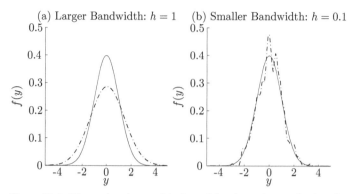

Figure 11.1. Bias and variance of the kernel density estimator (broken line) for different choices of bandwidth. Data are *iid* from the standard normal distribution (continuous line) and the sample size is $T = 500$.

Example 11.2 Bias, Variance and Bandwidth

Consider the problem of estimating the density of $T = 500$ *iid* drawings from a $N(0, 1)$ distribution. The effect on bias of a 'large' bandwidth, $h = 1$, is demonstrated in panel (a) of Figure 11.1 in which the kernel estimator underestimates the peak (biased downwards) and overestimates the tails (biased upwards) because of over-smoothing. Panel (b) of Figure 11.1 shows that for a 'smaller' bandwidth, $h = 0.1$, the bias is considerably smaller in the peak and the tails of the distribution. The cost of the smaller bandwidth is to generate greater variance, as represented by the jagged behaviour of the kernel estimate. This contrasts with panel (a) where the variance of the kernel estimator is lower. □

11.3.2 Optimal Bandwidth Selection

The aim of data-driven bandwidth selection is to choose h to resolve the trade-off between bias and variance in an optimal way. The approach is to choose h to minimise the asymptotic mean integrated squared error of the density estimator, hereafter $AMISE$, obtained by combining expressions (11.4) and (11.5) as

$$AMISE = \int_{-\infty}^{\infty} (\text{bias}^2 \widehat{f}(y) + \text{var}(\widehat{f}(y)))dy = \frac{h^4}{4} \mu_2^2 R(f^{(2)}(y)) + \frac{1}{Th} R(K),$$

in which terms up to order h are retained and $R(\cdot)$ represents the roughness operator (see Appendix D).

The optimal bandwidth is obtained by minimising the AMISE by differentiating this expression with respect to h

$$\frac{d}{dh} AMISE = h^3 \mu_2^2 R(f^{(2)}(y)) - \frac{1}{Th^2} R(K).$$

Setting this derivative to zero

$$0 = h_{opt}^3 \mu_2^2 R(f^{(2)}(y)) - \frac{1}{Th_{opt}^2} R(K),$$

and rearranging gives the optimal bandwidth

$$h_{opt} = \left[\frac{R(K)}{T \mu_2^2 R(f^{(2)}(y))} \right]^{1/5}. \tag{11.6}$$

The bandwidth depends positively on the roughness of the kernel function, $R(K)$, and inversely on the sample size, T, the variance of the kernel function, μ_2, and the roughness of the true distribution, $R(f^{(2)}(y))$. The optimal bandwidth can also be written as

$$h_{opt} = cT^{-1/5}, \qquad c = \left[\frac{R(K)}{\mu_2^2 R(f^{(2)}(y))} \right]^{1/5}, \tag{11.7}$$

which is a useful form for examining the asymptotic properties of the kernel.

The expression for c in (11.7) involves the unknown function $R(f^{(2)}(y))$, the roughness of the second derivative of the true population distribution. The simplest solution is to assume that the population distribution, $f(y)$, is normal with unknown mean μ and variance σ^2. From the properties of the Gaussian kernel,

$$R(f^{(2)}) = \frac{3}{8\sigma^5 \sqrt{\pi}}, \qquad \mu_2 = 1, \qquad R(K) = \frac{1}{2\sqrt{\pi}},$$

and substituting these expressions into equation (11.7) gives

$$c = \left(\frac{1}{2\sqrt{\pi}} \frac{8\sigma^5 \sqrt{\pi}}{3} \right)^{1/5} \simeq 1.06\sigma.$$

From equation (11.6), the optimal bandwidth, in the case where the population distribution is Gaussian, is

$$h_{opt} = 1.06\,\sigma\,T^{-1/5}. \tag{11.8}$$

Replacing σ by an unbiased estimator, s, the sample standard deviation, gives the normal-reference rule or rule-of-thumb bandwidth

$$\widehat{h} = 1.06\,s\,T^{-1/5}. \tag{11.9}$$

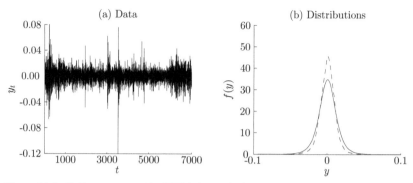

Figure 11.2. Daily returns on the FTSE from 1973 to 2001 and a comparison of the normal distribution (continuous line) and the kernel estimate of the density of returns (broken line).

Example 11.3 FTSE All Ordinaries Index

A plot of the continuously compounded returns of the FTSE All Ordinaries share index is given in panel (a) of Figure 11.2. The returns are daily beginning on 20 November 1973 and ending 23 July 2001, a total of $T = 7000$ observations. The sample mean and standard deviation are, respectively, $\bar{y} = 0.000$ and $s = 0.011$, with a minimum daily return of -0.130 and a maximum daily return of 0.089. The kernel estimate of the distribution is presented in panel (b) of Figure 11.2 using a Gaussian kernel with bandwidth

$$\widehat{h} = 1.06\, s\, T^{-1/5} = 1.06 \times 0.011 \times 7000^{-1/5} = 0.002.$$

As all of the observations, apart from one, fall in the range -0.1 to 0.1, this is chosen as the range of the grid points which increase in steps of 0.001. For comparative purposes, a normal distribution with mean $\mu = 0$ and variance $\sigma^2 = 0.011^2$ is also plotted. The empirical distribution of y_t based on the kernel estimator exhibits a much sharper peak than the normal distribution. In most applications the tails of the distribution are also found to be fatter than the normal distribution. This is a standard empirical result for the distribution of financial returns and the distribution is said to exhibit leptokurtosis.   ◻

The choice of bandwidths for the N-dimensional multivariate product kernels is based on the same principles as in the univariate case. If a normal kernel is used, the bandwidth in each dimension that minimises the multivariate AMISE is given by

$$h_n = \left(\frac{4}{N+2}\right)^{1/(N+4)} \sigma_n\, T^{-1/(N+4)}, \qquad n = 1, 2, \cdots, N, \quad (11.10)$$

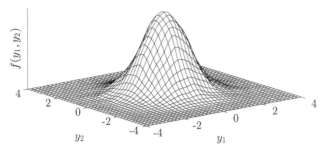

Figure 11.3. Product kernel estimate of the bivariate normal distribution.

in which σ_n is the standard deviation of the nth series $\{y_{1,n}, y_{2,n}, \cdots, y_{T,n}\}$. The univariate bandwidth in (11.8) is recovered by setting $N = 1$ since

$$\left(\frac{4}{1+2}\right)^{1/5} = 1.0592 \approx 1.06\,.$$

Furthermore, when $N = 2$ the constant in equation (11.10) is exactly equal to one. As a consequence, Scott (1992, p152) suggests that an easy-to-remember rule for bandwidth computation in a multivariate setting is

$$\widehat{h}_n = s_n T^{-1/(N+4)}\,. \tag{11.11}$$

Example 11.4 Bivariate Normal Distribution
Figure 11.3 contains a bivariate Gaussian kernel density estimated using a product kernel with bandwidth given by equation (11.11). The sample data are drawn from $N = 2$ independent standardised normal distributions and the sample size is $T = 20000$ observations.

□

11.3.3 Asymptotic Properties

To develop the properties of consistency and asymptotic normality of the kernel estimator, it is useful to write equation (11.7) in the form

$$h = c\,T^{-k}, \qquad \text{where} \quad \begin{cases} k > 1/5 \to \text{ under smoothing} \\ k = 1/5 \to \text{ optimal smoothing} \\ k < 1/5 \to \text{ over smoothing}\,. \end{cases} \tag{11.12}$$

Consistency
Consistency requires that both the bias and the variance approach zero as T increases so that

$$\text{plim}(\widehat{f}(y)) = f(y)\,.$$

Recall from equations (11.4) and (11.5), that the bias decreases as $h \to 0$ and the variance decreases as $Th \to \infty$. Both of these conditions must be satisfied simultaneously for consistency to hold. This is clearly the case for the optimal bandwidth $h = cT^{-1/5}$ given in equation (11.7), but it is also true for other values of k in equation (11.12). If $k = 1$ in equation (11.12), then $h = cT^{-1}$ and $Th = TcT^{-1} = c \nrightarrow \infty$ as T grows so that the variance does not disappear. On the other hand, if $k = 0$ in equation (11.12), then h is the constant cT^0 and $h \nrightarrow 0$ as T grows so that the bias will not disappear. In other words, consistency requires that k satisfies $0 < k < 1$.

Asymptotic normality

The asymptotic distribution of the kernel estimator is

$$\sqrt{Th}\left(\widehat{f}(y) - E[\widehat{f}(y)]\right) \xrightarrow{d} N\left(0, f(y) \int_{-\infty}^{\infty} K^2(z)\,dz\right). \qquad (11.13)$$

For this expression to be of practical use for undertaking inference, it is necessary for $E[\widehat{f}(y)]$ to converge in the limit to the true distribution $f(y)$. It turns out that this convergence is only assured if the bandwidth h satisfies an even tighter constraint than that required for the consistency property. To see why, write the left-hand side of equation (11.13) as

$$\sqrt{Th}\left(\widehat{f}(y) - E[\widehat{f}(y)]\right)$$
$$= \sqrt{Th}\left(\widehat{f}(y) - f(y) + f(y) - E[\widehat{f}(y)]\right) + O(h^2)$$
$$= \sqrt{Th}\left(\widehat{f}(y) - f(y) - \text{bias}(\widehat{f}(y))\right) + O(h^2)$$
$$= \sqrt{Th}\left(\widehat{f}(y) - f(y) - \frac{h^2}{2}f^{(2)}(y)\mu_2\right) + O(h^2)$$
$$= \sqrt{Th}\left(\widehat{f}(y) - f(y)\right) - \sqrt{Th^5}\left(\frac{1}{2}f^{(2)}(y)\mu_2\right) + O(h^2).$$

The expectation $E[\widehat{f}(y)]$ can be replaced by $f(y)$ only if the second term on the right-hand side of this expression disappears as $T \to \infty$. Interestingly enough, this condition is not satisfied by the optimal bandwidth $h = cT^{-1/5}$ because

$$\sqrt{Th^5} = \sqrt{Tc^5(T^{-1/5})^5} = \sqrt{c^5 T^0},$$

is constant as $T \to \infty$. It turns out that by under smoothing, that is, setting $k > 1/5$, the bias term disappears faster than the variance and $E[\widehat{f}(y)]$ converges to $f(y)$. To ensure the asymptotic normality of the kernel estimator, therefore, the relevant condition on k is $1/5 < k < 1$.

Provided that this bandwidth condition is satisfied, the nonparametric estimator of $f(y)$ has an asymptotic normal distribution

$$\sqrt{Th}\left(\widehat{f}(y) - f(y)\right) \overset{d}{\to} N\left(0, f(y)\int_{-\infty}^{\infty} K^2(z)\,dz\right),\qquad(11.14)$$

which is similar to the expression in (11.13), but with $E[\widehat{f}(y)]$ replaced by $f(y)$. Equation (11.14) can be used to construct the 95% confidence interval

$$\widehat{f}(y) \pm 1.96(Th)^{-1/2}\left[f(y)\int_{-\infty}^{\infty} K^2(z)dz\right]^{1/2}.$$

In the case of the Gaussian kernel

$$\int_{-\infty}^{\infty} K^2(z)dz = \frac{3}{8\sqrt{\pi}} = 0.2821,$$

so that the 95% confidence interval simplifies to

$$\widehat{f}(y) \pm 1.96(Th)^{-1/2}[f(y) \times 0.2821]^{1/2},$$

or

$$\widehat{f}(y) \pm 1.041(Th)^{-1/2} f(y)^{1/2}.$$

Finally, to be able to implement this interval in practice it is necessary to replace $f(y)$ by a consistent estimator, $\widehat{f}(y)$, in which case the 95% confidence interval that is used in practice is

$$\widehat{f}(y) \pm 1.041(Th)^{-1/2}\widehat{f}(y)^{1/2}.$$

11.3.4 Dependent Data

The key theoretical results of the nonparametric density estimator presented earlier are based on the assumption that y_t is independent of y_{t-k}, $k \geq 1$. As is generally the case in time series data, these theoretical results still hold under weak conditions (see, Wand and Jones, 1995; Pagan and Ullah, 1999). Intuitively, this result arises because the kernel density estimator is based on the spatial dependence structure of the data in the sense that $\widehat{f}(y)$ is constructed as a weighted average of the observations around y, the support of the density. This weighting procedure effectively reduces the role of the time dependence structure of y_t in estimating $f(y)$, while emphasising instead the spatial dependence structure of y_t. A more formal justification is to assume that y_t is strongly mixing, as defined in Chapter 2.

11.4   Semi-parametric Density Estimation

Density estimators which also use parametric information are referred to as semiparametric estimators. An example is given by Stachurski and Martin (2008) in which parametric information on the transitional density of an autoregressive time series model, $f(y|y_{t-1})$ is used to estimate the marginal density $f(y)$. In this context $f(y)$ represents the stationary density of the time series model as discussed in Chapters 1 and 3. An important advantage of the approach is that the convergence rate is now $\sqrt{T}$ compared to the slower rate of convergence arising from the nonparametric kernel estimator.

Let $f(y|y_{t-1})$ represent the transitional density of a parametric model. Under certain conditions, the stationary density is given by

$$f(y) = E[f(y|y_{t-1})], \qquad (11.15)$$

where the support of the density is taken to be over the real line. This suggests that a suitable estimator of $f(y)$ for a sample of size T is given by the sample average of the heights of the T transitional densities evaluated at each y

$$\widehat{f}(y) = \frac{1}{T} \sum_{t=1}^{T} f(y|y_{t-1}). \qquad (11.16)$$

This estimator is also known as the look-ahead estimator (LAE). As the transitional density approaches regions of higher probability more frequently than regions of lower probability, by averaging across the transitional densities over the sample an estimator of the stationary density is constructed.

The LAE and the nonparametric kernel density estimator can be compared in the case of an AR(1) model with normal disturbances

$$y_t = \phi_0 + \phi_1 y_{t-1} + \sigma z_t, \qquad z_t \sim iid\ N(0, 1). \qquad (11.17)$$

The LAE is

$$\widehat{f}(y) = \frac{1}{T} \sum_{t=1}^{T} f(y|y_{t-1}) = \frac{1}{T} \sum_{t=1}^{T} \frac{1}{\sqrt{2\pi\sigma^2}} \exp\left[-\frac{1}{2} \left(\frac{y - \phi_0 - \phi_1\theta y_{t-1}}{\sigma} \right)^2 \right],$$

By re-defining y_{t-1} as y_t this expression is rewritten as

$$\widehat{f}(y) = \frac{1}{T} \sum_{t=1}^{T} \frac{1}{\sqrt{2\pi\sigma^2}} \exp\left[-\frac{1}{2} \left(\frac{y - \phi_0 - \phi_1\theta y_t}{\sigma} \right)^2 \right]. \qquad (11.18)$$

Comparing the LAE in (11.18) and the nonparametric kernel density estimator using a Gaussian kernel with bandwidth h, shows that the two density estimators are equivalent when $\phi_0 = 0$, $\phi_1 = 1$ and $\sigma = h$. The last condition is appealing as it suggests that if the AR(1) model is derived from economic theory, the

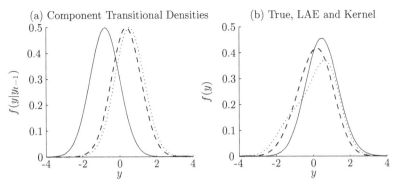

Figure 11.4. Comparison of the LAE and the nonparametric density estimator of the stationary density of a threshold AR(1) model with $\theta = 0.5$. Panel (a) illustrates the component transitional densities of the LAE for the observations $y_t = 0.6$ (dashed line), $y_t = -1.334$ (solid line) and $y_t = 0.894$ (dotted line). Panel (b) compares the true density (solid line), the LAE (dashed line) and the nonparametric kernel estimator (dotted line).

bandwidth has an economic interpretation. Moreover, this relationship also suggests that the choice of the kernel can be motivated from the assumptions underlying the economic model.

Example 11.5 LAE of a Threshold AR(1) Model

Consider the threshold AR(1) model (Zhao, 2010)

$$y_t = \theta \, |y_{t-1}| + \sqrt{1 - \theta^2} z_t, \qquad z_t \sim iid \, N(0, 1),$$

with respective stationary and transitional densities

$$f(y_t) = 2\phi(y_t)\Phi(\delta y_t), \qquad \delta = \theta/\sqrt{1 - \theta^2}$$

$$f(y_t | y_{t-1}) = \frac{1}{\sqrt{2\pi(1 - \theta^2)}} \exp\left[-\frac{1}{2} \left(\frac{y_t - \theta \, |y_{t-1}|}{\sqrt{1 - \theta^2}} \right)^2 \right].$$

For a grid of values of y, the LAE is computed as

$$\widehat{f}(y) = \frac{1}{T} \sum_{t=1}^{T} f(y | y_t) = \frac{1}{T} \sum_{t=1}^{T} \frac{1}{\sqrt{2\pi(1 - \theta^2)}} \exp\left[-\frac{1}{2} \left(\frac{y - \theta \, |y_t|}{\sqrt{1 - \theta^2}} \right)^2 \right].$$

Figure 11.4 gives the LAE estimate of $f(y)$ using the $T = 3$ observations, $y_t = \{-1.334, 0.600, 0.894\}$, simulated from the threshold AR(1) model with parameter $\theta = 0.5$. Panel (a) provides three of the conditional distributions used to compute the LAE. Panel (b) shows that the LAE provides a better approximation of the true density than the fully nonparametric kernel estimate based on a Gaussian kernel using a rule-of-thumb bandwidth. □

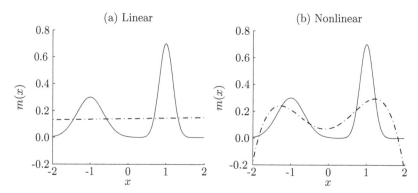

Figure 11.5. Comparison of the true conditional mean (continuous line) with estimated parametric models based on (a) linear, and (b) nonlinear parametric specifications (broken lines).

11.5   The Nadaraya-Watson Kernel Regression Estimator

Consider the simple regression problem of estimating the conditional mean

$$y_t = m(x_t) + u_t , \tag{11.19}$$

in which $m(x_t)$ is the conditional mean and u_t is an *iid* disturbance term. The problem with adopting a parametric specification for $m(x_t)$ is that if the functional form is incorrect, then the estimator of the conditional mean is unlikely to be consistent.

Example 11.6 Parametric Estimates of the Conditional Mean
A sample of $T = 500$ observations are simulated from (11.19) with conditional mean

$$m(x_t) = 0.3 \exp(-4(x_t + 1)^2) + 0.7 \exp(-16(x_t - 1)^2) ,$$

in which $x_t \sim iid\ U[-2, 2]$ and disturbance term $u_t \sim iid\ N(0, 0.01)$. Least squares estimates of a linear and a nonlinear parametric model of $m(x)$ are, respectively,

$$\widehat{m}(x_t)_{\text{linear}} = 0.155 + 0.008\ x_t$$
$$\widehat{m}(x_t)_{\text{nonlinear}} = 0.058 + 0.244\ x_t - 0.035\ x_t^2 - 0.021\ x_t^3 - 0.080\ x_t^4.$$

Figure 11.5 provides a comparison of the linear and nonlinear estimated parametric conditional means and the true conditional mean. The linear model predicts a slight upward drift in y_t, but fails to capture any of the turning points. The nonlinear model identifies some of the nonlinear features of the data, but misses the amplitudes of the peaks and troughs, and performs poorly in the tails. □

To avoid misspecifying the conditional moments of a model, an alternative approach known as nonparametric regression is adopted. The aim of nonparametric regression is to recover (estimate) the conditional mean of the dependent variable, y_t, at each point in time given a set of conditioning variables, x_t, but without specifying the functional form of the relationship between y_t and x_t. The most widely used nonparametric estimator adopted in practice is the Nadaraya-Watson estimator, in which the conditional mean is estimated by smoothing over y_t using an appropriate weighting function that is a function of x_t. In other words, it is essentially the nonparametric kernel regression analogue to nonparametric density estimation.

The Nadaraya-Watson nonparametric regression estimator, for the case where y_t depends only on one exogenous variable x_t, is constructed as follows. From the definition of conditional expectations, the conditional mean, $m(x)$, is defined as

$$m(x) = E[y|x_t = x] = \int y f_{y|x}(y|x)dy = \frac{\int y f_{yx}(y, x)dy}{f_x(x)},$$

(11.20)

in which $f_{y|x}$ is the conditional density of y given x, $f_{yx}(y, x)$ is the joint density of y and x and

$$f_x(x) = \int f_{y,x}(y, x)\,dy,$$

is the marginal density of x. It is understood that all integrals are taken over the relevant support of y. By replacing $f_{yx}(y, x)$ and $f_x(x)$ by nonparametric density estimators, a nonparametric estimator of $m(x)$ is

$$\widehat{m}(x) = \frac{\int y \widehat{f}_{yx}(y, x)dy}{\widehat{f}_x(x)},$$

(11.21)

in which

$$\widehat{f}_{yx}(y, x) = \frac{1}{Th^2} \sum_{t=1}^{T} K\left(\frac{y - y_t}{h}\right) K\left(\frac{x - x_t}{h}\right)$$

(11.22)

$$\widehat{f}_x(x) = \frac{1}{Th} \sum_{t=1}^{T} K\left(\frac{x - x_t}{h}\right),$$

(11.23)

and all bandwidths are assumed to be equal to h. The choice of a product kernel in (11.22) for the bivariate distribution enables the numerator of (11.21) to be written as

$$\int y \hat{f}_{yx}(x)dy = \int y \left[\frac{1}{Th^2} \sum_{t=1}^{T} K\left(\frac{y-y_t}{h}\right) K\left(\frac{x-x_t}{h}\right) \right] dy$$

$$= \frac{1}{Th^2} \sum_{t=1}^{T} K\left(\frac{x-x_t}{h}\right) \int y K\left(\frac{y-y_t}{h}\right) dy$$

$$= \frac{1}{Th} \sum_{t=1}^{T} y_t K\left(\frac{x-x_t}{h}\right). \tag{11.24}$$

The last step follows by using the change of variable $s = (y - y_t)/h$ and writing

$$\int y K\left(\frac{y-y_t}{h}\right) dy = h \int (sh + y_t) K(s) ds = h \left(h \int s K(s) ds + y_t \int K(s) ds \right)$$

$$= h(h \times 0 + y_t) = hy_t,$$

which recognises that $\int K(s)ds = 1$ and $\int s K(s)ds = 0$ for a symmetric kernel. Substituting (11.24) and (11.23) into (11.21) gives

$$\hat{m}(x) = \frac{\dfrac{1}{Th} \sum_{t=1}^{T} y_t K\left(\dfrac{x-x_t}{h}\right)}{\dfrac{1}{Th} \sum_{t=1}^{T} K\left(\dfrac{x-x_t}{h}\right)} = \sum_{t=1}^{T} y_t w_t(x), \tag{11.25}$$

in which $w_t(x)$ represents the weight given by

$$w_t(x) = \frac{\dfrac{1}{Th} K\left(\dfrac{x-x_t}{h}\right)}{\dfrac{1}{Th} \sum_{t=1}^{T} K\left(\dfrac{x-x_t}{h}\right)}. \tag{11.26}$$

The kernel regression estimator therefore has the intuitive interpretation of a weighted average of the dependent variable where the weights are a function of the explanatory variable x_t.

The steps to compute the kernel regression estimator are as follows.

Step 1: Choose a grid of values of x starting at the lowest value of x_t and ending at the highest value of x_t.

Step 2: Choose the first value of x in the grid and weight the observations according to (11.26) with the largest weight given to the x_t values closest to x. This involves choosing a kernel function K and a bandwidth h.

Step 3: Compute (11.25), the estimate of the conditional mean, $E[y|x_t = x]$.

Step 4: Repeat the computation for all of the values of x in the grid. Notice that changing x changes the weights and hence the estimate of the conditional mean.

Table 11.3. *Nadaraya-Watson kernel regression estimates of the conditional mean, $m(x)$, for selected values of x. The bandwidth is $h = 0.5$ and $K(\cdot)$ is the Gaussian kernel*

t	y_t	x_t	$x = -2.0$		$x = -1.75$	
			$K\left(\dfrac{x - x_t}{h}\right)$	$y_t K\left(\dfrac{x - x_t}{h}\right)$	$K\left(\dfrac{x - x_t}{h}\right)$	$y_t K\left(\dfrac{x - x_t}{h}\right)$
1	0.433	0.886	0.000	0.000	0.000	0.000
2	0.236	−1.495	0.239	0.057	0.350	0.083
3	0.299	−1.149	0.094	0.028	0.194	0.058
4	0.030	1.921	0.000	0.000	0.000	0.000
5	−0.041	−1.970	0.398	−0.016	0.362	−0.015
6	0.185	−1.697	0.332	0.062	0.397	0.074
7	0.053	−0.324	0.001	0.000	0.007	0.000
8	0.459	0.844	0.000	0.000	0.000	0.000
9	−0.038	−1.968	0.398	−0.015	0.363	−0.014
10	−0.061	−1.829	0.376	−0.023	0.394	−0.024
11	0.147	0.510	0.000	0.000	0.000	0.000
12	−0.041	−0.380	0.002	0.000	0.009	0.000
13	0.042	0.230	0.000	0.000	0.000	0.000
14	0.224	−0.678	0.012	0.003	0.040	0.009
15	−0.043	1.954	0.000	0.000	0.000	0.000
16	0.046	1.477	0.000	0.000	0.000	0.000
17	−0.055	1.925	0.000	0.000	0.000	0.000
18	−0.054	0.099	0.000	0.000	0.000	0.000
19	0.205	−1.641	0.308	0.063	0.390	0.080
20	−0.084	−0.339	0.002	0.000	0.007	−0.001
		$\displaystyle\sum_{t=1}^{T}$	2.164	0.157	2.514	0.250

Example 11.7 Computing the Nadaraya-Watson Estimator

Table 11.3 provides a breakdown of the computation of the nonparametric kernel regression estimates for $T = 20$ observations on y_t and x_t given in columns 2 and 3 of the table. A Gaussian kernel with a bandwidth of $h = 0.5$ is chosen with seventeen grid points, $x = \{-2.0, -1.75, -0.5, \cdots, 1.75, 2.0\}$.

The calculations are presented for the first two grid points in the table. For $x = -2.0$

$$\frac{1}{Th} \sum_{t=1}^{T} K\left(\frac{-2 - x_t}{h}\right) = \frac{2.164}{20 \times 0.5} = 0.216$$

$$\frac{1}{Th} \sum_{t=1}^{T} y_t K\left(\frac{-2 - x_t}{h}\right) = \frac{0.157}{20 \times 0.5} = 0.016,$$

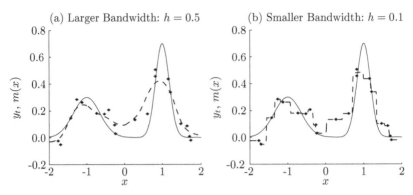

Figure 11.6. Actual values (diamonds), true conditional mean (solid line) and the non-parametric kernel conditional mean estimates (dashed) for different bandwidths.

and (allowing for rounding error)

$$\widehat{m}(-2.0) = \frac{0.016}{0.216} = 0.073 \,.$$

Figure 11.6 illustrates the Nadaraya-Watson conditional mean estimates evaluated at the seventeen grid points of x together with the realised values of y_t. Panel (a) gives the results for $h = 0.5$, and panel (b) gives the results for the smaller bandwidth of $h = 0.1$.

□

11.6   Properties of Kernel Regression Estimators

This section provides a discussion of some of the finite sample and asymptotic properties of the kernel regression estimator. The results are presented for the iid case, with generalisations allowing for data exhibiting limited temporal dependence discussed at the end of the section.

Bias and Variance
Just as in the case of the kernel density estimator, the bias of the kernel regression is positively related to the size of the bandwidth, h, and the variance is negatively related to h.

Example 11.8 Bias and Variance in a Kernel Regression
  A sample of $T = 500$ observations are simulated from the model

$$y_t = 0.3 \exp(-4(x_t + 1)^2) + 0.7 \exp(-16(x_t - 1)^2) + u_t \,,$$

in which $u_t \sim iid\, N(0, 0.01)$ and $x_t \sim iid\, U[-2, 2]$. The kernel regression estimates of the conditional mean for different choices of the bandwidth are illustrated in Figure 11.7.

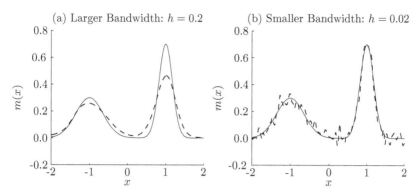

Figure 11.7. True conditional mean (solid line) and nonparametric estimates (dashed lines) demonstrate the effect of the bandwidth h on the kernel regression estimator.

The nonparametric regression estimator exhibits some bias for $h = 0.2$ in panel (a) of Figure 11.7. In particular, the estimator underestimates the two peaks and overestimates the troughs, suggesting that the estimate is over smoothed. Panel (b) of Figure 11.7 shows that reducing the bandwidth to $h = 0.02$ decreases this bias, but at the expense of introducing greater variance. The jagged nature of the estimator in panel (b) is indicative of under smoothing. □

Consistency
Consistency requires that both the respective bias and variance expressions for $\widehat{f}_{yx}(x)$ and $\widehat{f}_{x}(x)$ approach zero as T increases so that

$$\text{plim}(\widehat{f}_{yx}(x)) = f_{yx}(x) \quad \text{and} \quad \text{plim}(\widehat{f}_{x}(x)) = f_{x}(x).$$

Using Slutsky's theorem

$$\text{plim}(\widehat{m}(x)) = \text{plim}\left(\frac{\int y \widehat{f}_{yx}(y, x) dy}{\widehat{f}_{x}(x)}\right) = \frac{\text{plim}(\int y \widehat{f}_{yx}(y, x) dy)}{\text{plim}(\widehat{f}_{x}(x))}$$

$$= \frac{\int y f_{yx}(y, x) dy}{f_{x}(x)} = m(x),$$

which establishes the consistency of the nonparametric kernel regression estimator of the conditional mean. Pagan and Ullah (1999) establish the formal conditions underlying this result. Just as in the case of the kernel density estimator, the required condition on the bandwidth used in the kernel regression is

$$h = cT^{-k}, \qquad 0 < k < 1,$$

where, as before, c is a constant whose value depends upon the kernel function chosen to compute the estimator.

Asymptotic Normality

The asymptotic distribution of $\widehat{m}(x)$ is

$$\sqrt{Th}\left(\widehat{m}(x) - E\left[\widehat{m}(x)\right]\right) \xrightarrow{d} N\left(0, \frac{\sigma^2_{y|x}}{f_x(x)}\int K^2(z)\,dz\right),$$

where

$$\sigma^2_{y|x} = \int (y_t - m(x))^2\, f_{y|x}(y|x)dy\,,$$

is the conditional variance of y given x. Following the argument in Section 11.3.3, to make this result useful for statistical inference it is necessary for $E[\widehat{m}(x)]$ to converge to $m(x)$ sufficiently quickly in which case $\widehat{m}(x)$ has an asymptotic normal distribution

$$\sqrt{Th}\left(\widehat{m}(x) - m(x)\right) \xrightarrow{d} N\left(0, \frac{\sigma^2_{y|x}}{f_x(x)}\int K^2(z)\,dz\right), \qquad (11.27)$$

which is the same as the previous expression, but with $E[\widehat{m}(x)]$ replaced by $m(x)$. The bandwidth condition needed for the convergence of $E[\widehat{m}(x)]$ to $m(x)$ is

$$h_T = cT^{-k}, \qquad 1/5 < k < 1\,,$$

in which c is a constant. This is the same condition used to establish the asymptotic normality property of the kernel density estimator.

The 95% confidence interval for the kernel regression estimator is

$$\widehat{m}(x) \pm 1.96\,(Th)^{-1/2}\left[\frac{\sigma^2_{y|x}}{f_x(x)}\int K^2(z_t)\,dz_t\right]^{1/2}.$$

In the case of a Gaussian kernel

$$\int_{-\infty}^{\infty} K^2(z_t)\,dz_t = \frac{3}{8\sqrt{\pi}} = 0.2821\,,$$

the 95% confidence interval simplifies to

$$\widehat{m}(x) \pm 1.96\,(Th)^{-1/2}\left[\frac{\sigma^2_{y|x}}{f_x(x)} \times 0.2821\right]^{1/2},$$

or

$$\widehat{m}(x) \pm 1.041\,(Th)^{-1/2}\frac{\sigma_{y|x}}{f_x(x)^{1/2}}.$$

Finally, to be able to implement this interval in practice $\sigma_{y|x}$ and $f_x(x)$ are replaced by consistent estimators, giving the 95% confidence interval used in practice as

$$\widehat{m}(x) \pm 1.041 \, (Th)^{-1/2} \, \frac{\widehat{\sigma}_{y|x}}{\widehat{f}_x(x)^{1/2}} \, ,$$

where

$$\widehat{u}_t = y_t - \widehat{m}(x_t), \qquad \widehat{\sigma}^2_{y|x} = \sum_{t=1}^{T} w_t(x)\widehat{u}_t^2 \, ,$$

and the weights $w_t(x)$ are given in equation (11.26).

Dependent Data

As in the case of the nonparametric density estimator where the theoretical results based on *iid* also hold at least asymptotically for dependent data, the theoretical results of the kernel regression estimator derived earlier are still satisfied when y_t and y_{t-k}, $k \geq 1$, are correlated (Robinson, 1983; Pagan and Ullah, 1999). This rule of 'effective dependence' has also been shown to hold in nonparametric cointegrating regressions by Wang and Phillips (2009).

11.7 Bandwidth Selection for Kernel Regression

The problem of bandwidth selection is now one of ensuring the best possible estimator of the mean of y_t conditional on x_t. A natural approach is to treat the bandwidth, h, as a parameter and choose the value that minimises the distance between y_t and its conditional mean, $m(x_t)$, using the criterion

$$\underset{h}{\arg \min} \; \mathcal{S} = \sum_{t=1}^{T} (y_t - \widehat{m}(x_t))^2 \, , \tag{11.28}$$

in which $\widehat{m}(x_t)$ is an estimator of $m(x_t)$. The problem with this approach is that it leads to the degenerate solution of $h = 0$ for which $\widehat{m}(x_t) = y_t$ resulting in a perfect fit with zero error. To see why this is the case, consider the nonparametric estimator of $m(x_t)$ in equation (11.25), evaluated at x_1, the first observation of x_t. The conditional mean is

$$\widehat{m}(x_1) = \frac{\dfrac{1}{Th} \displaystyle\sum_{t=1}^{T} y_t K \left(\dfrac{x_1 - x_t}{h} \right)}{\dfrac{1}{Th} \displaystyle\sum_{t=1}^{T} K \left(\dfrac{x_1 - x_t}{h} \right)} \, ,$$

which for a Gaussian kernel becomes

$$\hat{m}(x_1) = \frac{\dfrac{1}{Th}\left[\dfrac{y_1}{\sqrt{2\pi}} + \displaystyle\sum_{t=2}^{T}\dfrac{y_t}{\sqrt{2\pi}}\exp\left(-\dfrac{1}{2}\left(\dfrac{x_1-x_t}{h}\right)^2\right)\right]}{\dfrac{1}{Th}\left[\dfrac{1}{\sqrt{2\pi}} + \displaystyle\sum_{t=2}^{T}\dfrac{1}{\sqrt{2\pi}}\exp\left(-\dfrac{1}{2}\left(\dfrac{x_1-x_t}{h}\right)^2\right)\right]}$$

$$= \frac{y_1 + \displaystyle\sum_{t=2}^{T}y_t\exp\left(-\dfrac{1}{2}\left(\dfrac{x_1-x_t}{h}\right)^2\right)}{1 + \displaystyle\sum_{t=2}^{T}\exp\left(-\dfrac{1}{2}\left(\dfrac{x_1-x_t}{h}\right)^2\right)}.$$

Allowing $h \to 0^+$ the exponential terms at $t = 2, 3, \cdots$, all approach zero, leaving

$$\lim_{h\to 0^+}\hat{m}(x_1) = y_1 .$$

Repeating these calculations for $t \geqslant 2$, the sum of squares function in equation (11.28) is minimised where

$$\lim_{h\to 0^+}S = 0,$$

as the estimates of the mean equal the data, y_t.

This degenerate solution for the bandwidth is circumvented by removing the jth observation when estimating $m(x_j)$. This results in the so-called leave-one-out kernel estimator of $m(x_t)$ given by

$$\tilde{m}(x_j) = \frac{\dfrac{1}{Th}\displaystyle\sum_{\substack{t=1\\t\neq j}}^{T}y_j K\left(\dfrac{x_j-x_t}{h}\right)}{\dfrac{1}{Th}\displaystyle\sum_{\substack{t=1\\t\neq j}}^{T}K\left(\dfrac{x_j-x_t}{h}\right)}, \qquad (11.29)$$

and the associated criterion for the choice of bandwidth is now

$$\arg\min_{h}\tilde{S} = \sum_{t=1}^{T}(y_t - \tilde{m}(x_t))^2 . \qquad (11.30)$$

This method of bandwidth selection is also known as cross-validation.

The leave-one-out approach to choosing the bandwidth is particularly sensitive to outliers. There are two common ways to address this problem.

(1) Eliminate the values of x_t that fall in the upper and lower 5th percentiles, $P_{0.95}$ and $P_{0.05}$, respectively, of the data by using a non-negative weight

function

$$\omega(x_t) = \mathcal{I}(x \in [P_{0.05}, P_{0.95}]),\tag{11.31}$$

where $\mathcal{I}$ is an indicator function. The objective function is then

$$\underset{h}{\arg\min}\ \widetilde{S} = \sum_{t=1}^{T}(y_t - \widetilde{m}(x_t))^2 \omega(x_t).\tag{11.32}$$

(2) An alternative to cross validation is to penalise the sum of squares function in (11.28) for 'small' choices of h. Here the bandwidth is the solution of the constrained problem

$$\underset{h}{\arg\min}\ \widehat{S} = \sum_{t=1}^{T}(y_t - \widehat{m}(x_t))^2 \omega(x_t)\Xi(h),\tag{11.33}$$

in which $\widehat{m}(x_t)$ is constructed using all the available observations, $\omega(x_t)$ is as defined in (11.31) and $\Xi(h)$ is a suitable penalty function that penalises small bandwidths. Rice (1984) suggests using one of the following penalty functions

$$\Xi(h) = 1 + 2u\,,\qquad \Xi(h) = \exp(2u)\,,\qquad \Xi(h) = (1 - 2u)^{-1}\,,$$

where $u = K(0)/Th$.

Example 11.9 Cross-Validation
A sample of $T = 500$ observations are simulated from the model

$$y_t = 0.3\exp(-4(x_t + 1)^2) + 0.7\exp(-16(x_t - 1)^2) + u_t\,,$$

in which $u_t \sim iid\ N(0, 0.01)$ and $x_t \sim iid\ U[-2, 2]$. Figure 11.8 illustrates the importance of the leave-one-out principle in kernel regression bandwidth selection. The sum of squares function in (11.33) based on the leave-one-out kernel estimator of $m(x_t)$ in (11.29) is plotted using the grid of bandwidths $h = \{0.001, 0.002, \cdots, 0.5\}$. The optimal bandwidth based on cross-validation is $h = 0.07$ and the objective function is $\widehat{S} = 5.378$. For comparative purposes Figure 11.8 also shows that the value of (11.33) without cross-validation based on (11.25) has the degenerate solution $h = 0$. □

Ultimately, however, there are no convenient rules-of-thumb for bandwidth selection in nonparametric regression. Yatchew (2003, p46) argues that trying different bandwidths and examining the resultant estimate of the regression function is often a useful way of obtaining a general indication of possible over- or under-smoothing.

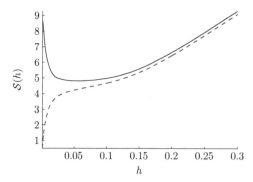

Figure 11.8. The sum of squares function for the cross-validation procedure (solid line) shows a well-defined minimum at $h > 0$, whereas the sum of squares function for the bandwidth with all observations included (dashed line) reaches its minimum at $h = 0$.

11.8   Multivariate Kernel Regression

The analysis of kernel regression so far has concentrated on a single exogenous variable, x_t. In theory the kernel regression estimator can be expanded to allow for N regressors. Consider

$$y_t = m(x_t) + u_t,$$

in which $x_t = \{x_{1,t}, x_{2,t}, \cdots, x_{N,t}\}$ and u_t is a disturbance term. Using the results of multivariate kernel density estimation discussed in Section 11.2, the multivariate analogue of the Nadaraya-Watson kernel regression estimator, based on product kernels, is

$$\widehat{m}(x) = \frac{\displaystyle\int y \widehat{f}_{yx}(y, x)dy}{\widehat{f}_x(x)} \tag{11.34}$$

where

$$\int y \widehat{f}_{yx}(y, x)dy = \frac{1}{T \times h_1 \times \cdots \times h_N} \sum_{t=1}^{T} y_t \prod_{n=1}^{N} K\left(\frac{x_n - x_{n,t}}{h_n}\right)$$

$$\widehat{f}_x(x) = \frac{1}{T \times h_1 \times \cdots \times h_N} \sum_{t=1}^{T} \prod_{n=1}^{N} K\left(\frac{x_n - x_{n,t}}{h_n}\right).$$

Note that in implementing the multivariate kernel regression, a different bandwidth is needed for each $x_{i,t}$ to accommodate differences in scaling. The difficulty of selecting $h_1, \cdots, h_N$ bandwidths means that a commonly-adopted approach is simply to use the Scott (1992) rule-of thumb approach in equation (11.11), for bandwidth selection in a multivariate kernel density setting.

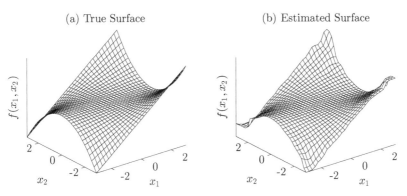

Figure 11.9. True and two-dimensional product kernel estimates of the conditional mean where the regression equation is $y_t = x_{1,t} x_{2,t}^2 + u_t$.

Example 11.10 Two-dimensional Product Kernel Regression

Consider the following nonlinear model

$$y_t = x_{1,t} x_{2,t}^2 + u_t,$$

in which y_t is the dependent variable, $x_{1,t}$ and $x_{2,t}$ are the exogenous variables and $u_t \sim iid\ N(0, 0.01)$ is the disturbance term. The $N = 2$ exogenous variables are taken as realisations from independent $N(0, 1)$ distributions. The model is simulated for $T = 20000$ observations. To perform a multivariate nonparametric kernel regression the bandwidths for each exogenous variable are chosen as

$$\widehat{h}_1 = s_1 T^{-1/(N+4)}, \qquad \widehat{h}_2 = s_2 T^{-1/(N+4)},$$

where s_i is the sample standard deviation of $x_{i,t}$. The Nadaraya-Watson multivariate kernel regression estimator in equation (11.34) requires computation of

$$\widehat{f}_x(x) = \frac{1}{T\widehat{h}_1\widehat{h}_2} \sum_{t=1}^{T} K\left(\frac{x_1 - x_{1,t}}{\widehat{h}_1}\right) K\left(\frac{x_2 - x_{2,t}}{\widehat{h}_2}\right)$$

$$\int y\widehat{f}_{yx}(y, x) dy = \frac{1}{T\widehat{h}_1\widehat{h}_2} \sum_{t=1}^{T} y_t K\left(\frac{x_1 - x_{1,t}}{\widehat{h}_1}\right) K\left(\frac{x_2 - x_{2,t}}{\widehat{h}_2}\right).$$

The true surface in panel (a) of Figure 11.9 is compared with the bivariate kernel estimates in panel (b) based on a Gaussian kernel. The kernel estimates are very accurate at the center of the surface, but become less accurate near the edges where data are sparse. ☐

The previous example highlights a common problem in multi-dimensional nonparametric estimation, already mentioned in Section 11.2, namely the 'curse of dimensionality'. This feature arises because the accuracy of the estimates of a one-dimensional problem with sample size of T can only be reproduced in two-dimensions with T^2 observations. As a result applications of multivariate kernel regressions are less common and alternative approaches that impose more structure on the problem, such as semiparametric regression estimators, are developed.

11.9   Semi-parametric Regression of the Partial Linear Model

Consider the partial linear model where the dependent variable y_t is a function of the exogenous variables $\{x_{1,t}, x_{2,t}, x_{3,t}\}$

$$y_t = \beta_1 x_{1,t} + \beta_2 x_{2,t} + g(x_{3,t}) + u_t, \tag{11.35}$$

in which $g(x_{3,t})$ is an unknown function of $x_{3,t}$ and u_t is an iid disturbance term. Part of the model has a well-defined parametric structure, but the functional form of the remaining part is unknown. Using a multivariate nonparametric kernel to estimate the conditional mean of y in this instance ignores the parametric information $\beta_1 x_{1,t} + \beta_2 x_{2,t}$. One approach to estimating the parameters of this partial linear model is the difference procedure described in detail by Yatchew (2003).The approach presented here is the semiparametric method developed by Robinson (1988).

Take expectations of equation (11.35) conditioning on $x_{3,t}$

$$\mathrm{E}\left[y_t | x_{3,t}\right] = \beta_1 \mathrm{E}\left[x_{1,t} | x_{3,t}\right] + \beta_2 \mathrm{E}\left[x_{2,t} | x_{3,t}\right] + g(x_{3,t}), \tag{11.36}$$

where the results $\mathrm{E}\left[g(x_{3,t}) | x_{3,t}\right] = g(x_{3,t})$ and $\mathrm{E}\left[u_t | x_{3,t}\right] = 0$ are used. Subtracting equation (11.36) from equation (11.35) yields

$$y_t - \mathrm{E}\left[y_t | x_{3,t}\right] = \beta_1(x_{1,t} - \mathrm{E}\left[x_{1,t} | x_{3,t}\right]) + \beta_2(x_{2,t} - \mathrm{E}\left[x_{2,t} | x_{3,t}\right]) + u_t. \tag{11.37}$$

The estimation proceeds as follows.

Step 1: Estimate $\mathrm{E}\left[y_t | x_{3,t}\right]$, $\mathrm{E}\left[x_{1,t} | x_{3,t}\right]$ and $\mathrm{E}\left[x_{2,t} | x_{3,t}\right]$ by three separate bivariate nonparametric regressions.
Step 2: Substitute the nonparametric estimates from Step 1 into equation (11.37), and estimate β_1 and β_2 by an ordinary least squares regression of $y_t - \mathrm{E}\left[y_t | x_{3,t}\right]$ on $x_{1,t} - \mathrm{E}\left[x_{1,t} | x_{3,t}\right]$ and $x_{2,t} - \mathrm{E}\left[x_{2,t} | x_{3,t}\right]$.
Step 3: An estimate of $g(x_{3,t})$ is now obtained as

$$\widehat{g}(x_{3,t}) = \mathrm{E}\left[y_t | x_{3,t}\right] - \widehat{\beta}_1 \mathrm{E}\left[x_{1,t} | x_{3,t}\right] - \widehat{\beta}_2 \mathrm{E}\left[x_{2,t} | x_{3,t}\right],$$

where all quantities are replaced by their sample estimates.

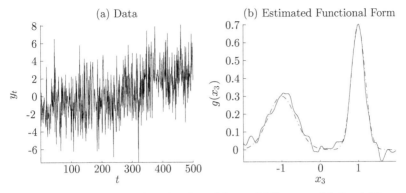

Figure 11.10. Semi-parametric estimation of the partial linear model. Panel (b) compares the true model (dashed line) with the semiparametric estimate (solid line) for x_3.

Example 11.11 The Partial Linear Model

DiNardo and Tobias (2001) consider the model

$$y_t = 2x_{1,t} + x_{2,t} + g(x_{3,t}) + u_t ,$$

in which $x_{1,t}|x_{3,t} \sim N(0.5x_{3,t}, 1)$, $x_{2,t}$ is iid distributed as a Student t distribution with four degrees of freedom, $x_{3,t}$ is iid distributed as $U[-2, 2]$ and $u_t \sim iid\ N(0, 0.1)$. In this example, the true functional form of $g(x_{3,t})$ is

$$g(x_{3,t}) = 0.3 \exp(-4(x_{3,t} + 1)^2) + 0.7 \exp(-16(x_{3,t} - 1)^2) ,$$

which is treated as unknown when using the semiparametric estimator. The simulated data of sample size $T = 500$ are shown in panel (a) of Figure 11.10.

Three kernel regressions are computed with bandwidth $h = 0.05$, to estimate $E[y_t|x_{3,t}]$, $E[x_{1,t}|x_{3,t}]$ and $E[x_{2,t}|x_{3,t}]$. An ordinary least squares regression is then estimated yielding parameter estimates $\widehat{\beta}_1 = 1.999$ and $\widehat{\beta}_2 = 1.001$, which are in good agreement with their true values. The nonparametric estimate of $g(x_{3,t})$ is plotted in panel (b) of Figure 11.10 and compares favourably with the true function.   □

11.10 Applications

The first application requires estimating the derivatives of a nonlinear production function that relates output to two inputs and is adapted from Pagan and Ullah (1999). The second application is based on Chapman and Pearson (2000) which uses a nonparametric regression to estimate the drift and diffusion functions of a stochastic differential equation.

11.10.1   Derivatives of a Nonlinear Production Function

Consider the problem of estimating the derivatives of a nonlinear production function that relates y_t (the natural logarithm of output) and $x_{1,t}$ and $x_{2,t}$ (the natural logarithms of the inputs). As the variables are in logarithms, the derivatives represent elasticities. The true model is given by

$$y_t = m(x_{1,t}, x_{2,t}) + u_t$$
$$= -0.2 \ln(\exp(-5x_{1,t}) + 2\exp(-5x_{2,t})) + u_t,$$

in which $u_t \sim iid\ N(0, 0.01)$ is the disturbance and the logarithms of the inputs are $x_{1,t}, x_{2,t} \sim iid\ U(0, 1)$. The nonlinear production function is simulated for a sample of size $T = 200$.

In computing the first-order derivatives, it is necessary to use a finite-difference approximation with step length h_i. The finite difference approximations are

$$D_1 \approx \frac{m(x_1 + h_1, x_2) - m(x_1 - h_1, x_2)}{2h_1}$$

$$D_2 \approx \frac{m(x_1, x_2 + h_2) - m(x_1, x_2 - h_2)}{2h_2}.$$

These expressions suggest that the nonparametric estimates of the derivatives are obtained by replacing $m(x)$ by $\widehat{m}(x)$. In which case

$$\widehat{D}_1 = \frac{\widehat{m}(x_1 + h_1, x_2) - \widehat{m}(x_1 - h_1, x_2)}{2h_1} \tag{11.38}$$

$$\widehat{D}_2 = \frac{\widehat{m}(x_1, x_2 + h_2) - \widehat{m}(x_1, x_2 - h_2)}{2h_2}. \tag{11.39}$$

In computing these estimates, the optimal bandwidth used is adjusted by the order of the derivative being approximated. Pagan and Ullah (1999, p189) give an estimate of the optimal bandwidth for the Sth derivative for the case of N exogenous variables as

$$\widehat{h}_i = s_i T^{-1/(4+N+2S)}. \tag{11.40}$$

This choice of bandwidth demonstrates that to estimate the derivatives, the nonparametric estimator needs to be based on a larger bandwidth than would be used in the computation of the conditional mean.

Figure 11.11 plots the nonparametric kernel regression estimator of the production function using a Gaussian product kernel, with the bandwidths based on (11.40) with $S = 0$ and $N = 2$

$$\widehat{h}_1 = s_1 T^{-1/(4+N+2S)} = 0.306 \times 200^{-1/(4+2+0)} = 0.126$$
$$\widehat{h}_2 = s_2 T^{-1/(4+N+2S)} = 0.288 \times 200^{-1/(4+2+0)} = 0.119,$$

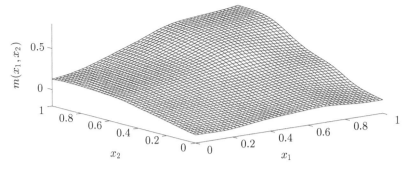

Figure 11.11. Bivariate nonparametric kernel regression estimator of a production function.

where s_i is the sample standard deviation of $x_{i,t}$. The grid points are chosen as

$$x_1, x_2 = \{0.00, 0.02, 0.04, \cdots, 0.98, 1.00\} \ .$$

The nonparametric estimates of the elasticities evaluated at $x_1 = x_2 = 0.5$ and the pertinent conditional mean estimates, $\widehat{m}(x_1, x_2)$, are given in Table 11.4. To compute the first derivatives, the bandwidths with $S = 1$ are

$$\widehat{h}_1 = s_1 T^{-1/(4+N+2S)} = 0.306 \times 200^{-1/(4+2+2)} = 0.158$$
$$\widehat{h}_2 = s_2 T^{-1/(4+N+2S)} = 0.288 \times 200^{-1/(4+2+2)} = 0.149 \ .$$

Using equations (11.38) and (11.39) the elasticities are

$$\widehat{D}_1 = \frac{\widehat{m}(0.5 + 0.158, 0.5) - \widehat{m}(0.5 - 0.158, 0.5)}{2 \times 0.158} = \frac{0.306 - 0.187}{2 \times 0.158} = 0.378$$
$$\widehat{D}_2 = \frac{\widehat{m}(0.5, 0.5 + 0.149) - \widehat{m}(0.5, 0.5 - 0.149)}{2 \times 0.149} = \frac{0.336 - 0.155}{2 \times 0.149} = 0.609.$$

Table 11.4. *Nonparametric estimates of the elasticities of the nonlinear production function example. Derivatives are evaluated at $x_1 = x_2 = 0.5$*

	$\widehat{m}(x_{1,x_2})$			Nonparametric		True	
				$\dfrac{\partial m(x)}{\partial x_1}$	$\dfrac{\partial m(x)}{\partial x_2}$	$\dfrac{\partial m(x)}{\partial x_1}$	$\dfrac{\partial m(x)}{\partial x_2}$
	$x_2 =$						
	0.351	0.500	0.649				
	0.343	0.106	0.187	0.257			
$x_1 =$ 0.500		0.155	0.248	0.336	0.378	0.609	0.333	0.667
	0.658	0.187	0.306	0.409			

The population elasticities, evaluated at $x_1 = x_2 = 0.5$, are

$$D_1 = \frac{\partial m(x_1, x_2)}{\partial x_1} = \frac{\exp(-5x_1)}{\exp(-5x_1) + 2\exp(-5x_2)} = 0.333,$$

$$D_2 = \frac{\partial m(x_1, x_2)}{\partial x_2} = \frac{2\exp(-5x_2)}{\exp(-5x_1) + 2\exp(-5x_2)} = 0.667,$$

showing that the nonparametric estimates of the derivatives are accurate to at least one decimal place.

11.10.2   Drift and Diffusion Functions of SDEs

Consider once again a stochastic differential equation describing the evolution of the instantaneous interest rate

$$dr = a(r)dt + b(r)dB,$$

in which $dB \sim N(0, dt)$, $a(r)dt$ is the expected drift and $b^2(r)dt$ is the conditional variance generated in an interval of duration dt. There exist in the literature a number of parametric representations for $a(r)$ and $b^2(r)$, most of which are linear, although related work by Aït-Sahalia (1996) and Conley, Hansen, Luttmer and Scheinkman (1997) suggest that nonlinear representations may be appropriate for interest rate data. An alternative approach, which circumvents the need to provide parametric representations for the conditional mean and the variance, is to use a nonparametric regression estimator.

To demonstrate the use of the kernel regression estimator, the following simulation experiment is performed. Consider the stochastic differential equation

$$dr = \alpha(\mu - r)dt + \sigma r^{1/2}dB,$$

in which the drift and diffusion functions are linear functions of r. This model is simulated using a discrete time interval, Δ, as

$$r_t - r_{t-1} = \alpha(\mu - r_{t-1})\Delta + \sigma r_{t-1}^{1/2}\Delta^{1/2}z_t,$$

in which $z_t \sim iid \, N(0, 1)$. The parameters chosen are based on the work of Chapman and Pearson (2000, pp361–362). The annualised values are

$$\alpha = 0.21459, \quad \mu = 0.08571, \quad \sigma = 0.07830,$$

and $\Delta = 1/250$ represents an approximate daily frequency. In simulating the model the total length of the sample is chosen as $T = 7500$ with the initial value of the interest rate set at μ.

Defining $E_{t-1}[r_t - r_{t-1}]$ as the conditional expectations operator using information up to time $t - 1$, the conditional mean is then

$$E_{t-1}[r_t - r_{t-1}] = E_{t-1}[\alpha(\mu - r_{t-1})\Delta + \sigma r_{t-1}^{1/2}\Delta^{1/2}z_t] = \alpha(\mu - r_{t-1})\Delta,$$

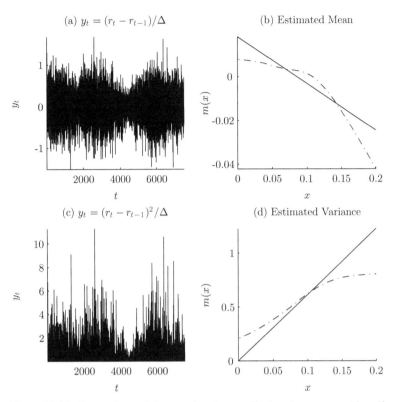

Figure 11.12. Comparison of the true (continuous line) and nonparametric estimates (dashed line) of the mean and variance functions in the stochastic differential equation of the interest rate.

as $E_{t-1}[z_t] = 0$. Alternatively

$$\frac{E_{t-1}[r_t - r_{t-1}]}{\Delta} = \alpha(\mu - r_{t-1}),$$

which is linear in the interest rate. A plot of $(r_t - r_{t-1})/\Delta$ is given in panel (a) of Figure 11.12.

Further, the conditional variance is given by

$$
\begin{aligned}
E_{t-1}[(r_t - r_{t-1})^2] &= E_{t-1}\left[\left(\alpha(\mu - r_{t-1})\Delta + \sigma r_{t-1}^{1/2}\Delta^{1/2}z_t\right)^2\right] \\
&= E_{t-1}[(\sigma r_{t-1}^{1/2}\Delta^{1/2}z_t)^2 + 2\alpha(\mu - r_{t-1})\sigma r_{t-1}^{1/2}\Delta^{3/2}z_t] \\
&\quad + O(\Delta^2) \\
&= \sigma^2 r_{t-1}\Delta E_{t-1}[z_t^2] + 2\alpha(\mu - r_{t-1})\sigma r_{t-1}^{1/2}\Delta^{3/2}E_{t-1}[z_t] \\
&\quad + O(\Delta^2) \\
&= \sigma^2 r_{t-1}\Delta + O(\Delta^2).
\end{aligned}
$$

Ignoring terms of Δ^2, which are of a smaller magnitude than Δ, an alternative expression is

$$\frac{E_{t-1}[(r_t - r_{t-1})^2]}{\Delta} = \sigma^2 r_{t-1},$$

which shows that the conditional variance is also linear in r_t. A plot of $(r_t - r_{t-1})^2/\Delta$ is given in panel (c) of Figure 11.12.

To estimate the conditional mean using the nonparametric regression estimator

$$m(x) = \frac{\displaystyle\sum_{t=1}^{T} y_t K\left(\frac{x - x_t}{h}\right)}{\displaystyle\sum_{t=1}^{T} K\left(\frac{x - x_t}{h}\right)},$$

define the variables

$$y_t = \frac{r_t - r_{t-1}}{\Delta}, \qquad x_t = r_{t-1}.$$

Using a Gaussian kernel with a bandwidth of $h = 0.023$, the nonparametric conditional mean estimates are given in panel (b) of Figure 11.12 based on the grid $x = r = \{0.000, 0.002, 0.004, \cdots, 0.200\}$. For comparison, the true conditional mean, $\alpha(\mu - r)$, is also shown. The nonparametric estimates of the conditional mean suggest a nonlinear structure when in fact the true conditional mean is linear. This finding of the simulation experiment is symptomatic of a more general problem in using nonparametric kernel regression procedures; namely, the estimates can become imprecise in the tails of the data.

To repeat the exercise for the conditional variance, define the variables

$$y_t = \frac{(r_t - r_{t-1})^2}{\Delta} \qquad x_t = r_{t-1}.$$

The nonparametric estimates of the conditional variance are given in panel (d) of Figure 11.12, using a Gaussian kernel with a bandwidth of $h = 0.023$ over the same grid of values for $x = r$ as used in computing the conditional mean. For comparison, the true conditional variance, $\sigma^2 r$, is also given. As with the conditional mean, the nonparametric estimates of the conditional variance exhibit a spurious nonlinearity when compared with the true linear conditional variance.

11.11   Exercises

(1) Parametric Approximations

Program files   npd_parametric.*

Simulate $T = 200$ random numbers from a normal distribution

$$f(y; \theta) = \frac{1}{\sqrt{2\pi\sigma^2}} \exp\left(-\frac{(y - \mu)^2}{2\sigma^2}\right),$$

with parameters $\mu = 0$ and $\sigma^2 = 9$.

(a) Estimate the population distribution using a normal distribution parametric density estimator where the mean and the variance are estimated as

$$\bar{y} = \frac{1}{T} \sum_{t=1}^{200} y_t \qquad s^2 = \frac{1}{T-1} \sum_{t=1}^{200} (y_t - \bar{y})^2.$$

(b) Estimate the population distribution using a Student t parametric density estimator where the mean and variance are computed as in (a) and the degrees of freedom parameter is computed as

$$\nu = \frac{2s^2}{s^2 - 1}.$$

(c) Plot the parametric density estimates and compare the results with the normal distribution, $N(0, 9)$.

(2) Numerical Illustration of the Kernel Density Estimator

Program files   npd_kernel.*

This exercise uses the $T = 20$ observations on y_t that are tabulated in Table 11.2 and which are drawn from an unknown distribution, $f(y; \theta)$.

(a) Using the Gaussian kernel with a bandwidth of $h = 1$, estimate the nonparametric density at the points $y = \{5, 10, 15\}$. Repeat for $h = 2$.

(b) Plot the nonparametric density estimates for the two bandwidths and comment on the differences between the two estimates. Compare your results with the estimates reported in Table 11.2.

(3) Normal Distribution

Program files   npd_normal.*

Simulate $T = 200$ random numbers from a normal distribution

$$f(y; \theta) = \frac{1}{\sqrt{2\pi\sigma^2}} \exp\left(-\frac{(y - \mu)^2}{2\sigma^2}\right),$$

with parameters $\mu = 0$ and $\sigma^2 = 9$. Define a grid of points $y = \{-10, -0.99, \cdots, 10\}$.

(a) Use a nonparametric kernel estimator to estimate the density with the Gaussian kernel and bandwidths of $h = \{1.0, 2.0\}$.

(b) Use a nonparametric kernel estimator to estimate the density with the Gaussian kernel and a bandwidth of $\hat{h} = 1.06 \, s \, T^{-1/5}$, where s is the sample standard deviation.

(c) Estimate the density using the normal distribution where the mean and the variance are the corresponding sample statistics.

(d) Compare the parametric and nonparametric results.

(4) Sampling Properties of Kernel Density Estimators

Program files   npd_property.*

Generate a sample of size $T = 500$ from a standardised normal distribution.

(a) Compute Gaussian kernel density estimators with $h = \{0.1, 1.0\}$ and compare your estimate with the population distribution. Compare the results with Figure 11.1.

(b) Discuss the relationship between bias and bandwidth, and between variance and bandwidth.

(5) Distribution of Equity Returns

Program files   npd_ftse.*, npd_sp500.*
Data files   ftse.*, s&p500.*

(a) Estimate a kernel density using a Gaussian kernel for the $T = 7000$ daily returns on the FTSE index over the period 20 November 1973 to 23 July 2001, with bandwidths $h = \{0.0001, 0.01, 0.05\}$ and for $\hat{h} = 1.06s \, T^{-1/5}$ where s is the sample standard deviation. Compare the kernel estimates associated with each bandwidth and comment on the size of the bias and variance of each of the estimates. Also compare the kernel estimates with the normal distribution where the mean and the variance are the corresponding sample statistics.

(b) Repeat part (a) for the $T = 12000$ daily returns on the S&P500 index over the period 9 February 1954 to 23 July 2001.

(6) Sampling Distribution of the t statistic

Program files   npd_cauchy.*

An important application of kernel density estimation is in the calculation of the sampling distribution of statistics obtained from simulation. Simulate 10000 samples of size $T = 100$ observations from the Cauchy distribution

$$f(y) = \frac{1}{\pi} \frac{1}{1 + y^2}.$$

(a) For each replication compute the t statistic

$$t = \frac{\sqrt{T}\bar{y}}{s_y},$$

where

$$\bar{y} = \frac{1}{T} \sum_{t=1}^{T} y_t, \qquad s_y^2 = \frac{1}{T-1} \sum_{t=1}^{T} (y_t - \bar{y})^2,$$

are, respectively, the sample mean and the sample variance.
(b) Compute the histogram of the t statistics with 21 bins. Discuss the shape of the sampling distribution.
(c) Compute kernel density estimates of the t statistics using the following bandwidths $h = \{0.1, 0.2, 0.5, 1.0, \}$ and for $\hat{h} = 1.06\, s\, T^{-1/5}$.
(d) Compare the estimated sampling distributions with the asymptotic (normal) distribution. Why are the two distributions different in this case? *Hint: Redo the experiment with the degrees of freedom equal to two.*

(7) **Multivariate Kernel Density Estimation**

Program files   npd_bivariate.*

Estimate a bivariate Gaussian product kernel based on $T = 20000$ observations drawn from two independent standardised normal distributions and using the multivariate variant of the rule-of-thumb bandwidth. Compare your answer with the results in Figure 11.3.

(8) **Semi-parametric Density Estimation**

Program files   npd_semilin.*, npd_seminonlin.*

(a) Consider the AR(1) linear model

$$y_t = \phi_0 + \phi_1 y_{t-1} + \sigma z_t, \qquad z_t \sim iid\, N(0, 1).$$

Using the observations $y_t = \{1.000, 0.701, -0.527, 0.794, 1.880\}$ and the parameter values $\theta = \{\phi_0 = 1.0, \phi_1 = 0.5, \sigma^2 = 1.0\}$ estimate the stationary density using the LAE and the nonparametric kernel density estimator based on a Gaussian kernel with a rule-of-thumb bandwidth. Compare these estimates with the true stationary density.

(b) Repeat part (a) for the nonlinear model

$$y_t = \theta |y_{t-1}| + \sqrt{1 - \theta^2} z_t, \qquad z_t \sim iid\ N(0, 1),$$

in which the observations are $y_t = \{0.600, -0.279, -1.334, 0.847, 0.894\}$ and the parameter is $\theta = 0.5$.

(9) Parametric Conditional Mean Estimator

Program files npr_parametric.*

Simulate the following model for $T = 500$ observations

$$y_t = 0.3 \exp(-4(x_t + 1)^2) + 0.7 \exp(-16(x_t - 1)^2) + u_t,$$

in which $u_t \sim iid\ N(0, 0.1)$ and $x_t \sim iid\ U[-2, 2]$.

(a) Estimate the conditional mean of the linear model

$$y_t = \beta_0 + \beta_1 x_t + v_t.$$

(b) Estimate the conditional mean of the cubic model

$$y_t = \beta_0 + \beta_1 x_t + \beta_2 x_t^2 + \beta_3 x_t^3 + v_t.$$

(c) Estimate the conditional mean of the quartic polynomial model

$$y_t = \beta_0 + \beta_1 x_t + \beta_2 x_t^2 + \beta_3 x_t^3 + \beta_4 x_t^4 + v_t.$$

(d) Compare the conditional mean estimates in parts (a) to (c) with the true conditional mean

$$m(x) = 0.3 \exp(-4(x + 1)^2) + 0.7 \exp(-16(x - 1)^2).$$

Also compare your results with Figure 11.5.

(10) Nadaraya-Watson Conditional Mean Estimator

Program files npr_nadwatson.*

Simulate $T = 20$ observations from the model used in Exercise 9.

(a) Using a Gaussian kernel with a bandwidth of $h = 0.5$ for $x = -2.0$, compute

$$\widehat{f}_{xx}(-2.0), \quad \widehat{f}_{yx}(-2.0), \quad \widehat{m}(-2.0).$$

Compare these results with Table 11.3.

(b) Using a Gaussian kernel with a bandwidth of $h = 0.5$ for $x = -1.75$, compute

$$\widehat{f}_{xx}(-1.75), \quad \widehat{f}_{yx}(-1.75), \quad \widehat{m}(-1.75).$$

Compare these results with Table 11.3.

(c) Compute the Nadaraya-Watson estimator using a Gaussian kernel with a bandwidth of $h = 0.5$ for the $N = 17$ grid points

$$x = \{-2.0, -1.75, -0.5, \cdots, 1.75, 2.0\} .$$

Compare the conditional mean estimates with the actual values y_t, and the true conditional mean

$$m(x) = 0.3 \exp(-4(x + 1)^2) + 0.7 \exp(-16(x - 1)^2) .$$

Also compare your results with Figure 11.6 panel (a).

(d) Repeat part (c) with $h = 0.1$. Compare your results with Figure 11.6 panel (b). Discuss the effects on the nonparametric estimates of $m(x)$ by changing the bandwidth from $h = 0.5$ to $h = 0.1$.

(11) **Properties of the Nadaraya-Watson Estimator**

Program files   `npr_property.*`

Simulate $T = 500$ observations from the model used in Exercises 9 and 10.

(a) Estimate the conditional mean using the Nadaraya-Watson estimator with a Gaussian kernel and bandwidths $h = \{0.02, 0.2\}$.

(b) Compare the nonparametric estimates with the true conditional mean and comment on the bias and the variance of the estimator as a function of the bandwidth h.

(12) **Cross-Validation Bandwidth Selection**

Program files   `npr_crossvalid.*`

Simulate $T = 100$ observations from the model used in Exercises 9, 10 and 11.

(a) Find the optimal bandwidth by cross-validation using a grid of bandwidths, $h = \{0.001, 0.002, \cdots, 0.5\}$.

(b) Repeat the exercise for samples of size $T = \{200, 500, 1000\}$ and comment on the relationship between the optimal bandwidth based on cross-validation and the sample size.

(c) Show that by not using cross-validation, in which the conditional mean is computed using (11.25), leads to the degenerate solution of $h = 0$.

(13) **Bivariate Nonparametric Regression**

Program files   `npr_bivariate.*`

(a) Simulate the model

$$y_t = x_{1,t} x_{2,t}^2 + u_t ,$$

in which $u_t \sim iid\ N(0, 0.01)$ and $x_{i,t} \sim iid\ N(0, 1), i = 1, 2,$ for $T = 20000$ observations. Compute the Nadaraya-Watson estimator and compare the result with Figure 11.9.

(b) Repeat part (a) for the model

$$y_t = x_{1,t}x_{2,t}^3 + u_t.$$

(c) Repeat part (a) for the model

$$y_t = x_{1,t}^2 x_{2,t}^2 + u_t.$$

(14) Estimating the Elasticity of a Production Function

Program files npr_production.*

Consider $T = 200$ observations from the nonlinear production function relating output y_t and the inputs $x_{1,t}$ and $x_{2,t}$

$$y_t = -0.2\ln(\exp(-5x_{1,t}) + 2\exp(-5x_{2,t})) + u_t,$$

in which $u_t \sim iid\ N(0, 0.01)$ and $x_{1,t}, x_{2,t} \sim iid\ U(0, 1)$.

(a) Compute the nonparametric estimates of the first derivatives

$$D_1 = \frac{\partial m(x_1, x_2)}{\partial x_1}, \qquad D_2 = \frac{\partial m(x_1, x_2)}{\partial x_2},$$

with the derivatives evaluated at $x_1 = x_2 = 0.5$. Compare these estimates with the true values of the derivatives.

(b) Repeat part (a) for the second derivatives

$$\frac{\partial^2 m(x_1, x_2)}{\partial x_1^2}, \frac{\partial^2 m(x_1, x_2)}{\partial x_2^2}, \frac{\partial^2 m(x_1, x_2)}{\partial x_1 \partial x_2}.$$

(15) Estimating Drift and Diffusion Functions

Program files npr_chapman.*

The true data generating process of the interest rate is given by the stochastic differential equation

$$dr = \alpha(\mu - r)dt + \sigma r^{1/2}dB,$$

in which $dB \sim N(0, dt)$ and $\{\alpha, \mu, \sigma\}$ are parameters.

(a) Generate a sample of daily observations of size $T = 7500$ by simulating the following model of the interest rate r_t

$$r_t - r_{t-1} = \alpha(\mu - r_{t-1})\Delta + \sigma r_{t-1}^{1/2}\Delta^{1/2}z_t,$$

in which $\Delta = 1/250$, $z_t \sim iid \; N(0, 1)$ and the parameters are

$$\alpha = 0.21459 \quad \mu = 0.08571 \quad \sigma = 0.07830 \,.$$

(b) Plot the series

$$y_{1,t} = \frac{r_t - r_{t-1}}{\Delta} \,, \qquad y_{2,t} = \frac{(r_t - r_{t-1})^2}{\Delta} \,,$$

and discuss their time series properties.

(c) Define

$$y_t = \frac{r_t - r_{t-1}}{\Delta} \qquad x_t = r_{t-1} \,,$$

and estimate the drift (conditional mean) using the nonparametric estimator with a Gaussian kernel and a bandwidth of $h = 0.023$ over the grid of values $x = r = \{0.000, 0.002, 0.004, \cdots, 0.200\}$. Compare the estimated values with the true value, $\alpha(\mu - r)$.

(d) Define

$$y_t = \frac{(r_t - r_{t-1})^2}{\Delta} \qquad x_t = r_{t-1} \,,$$

and estimate the diffusion (conditional variance) using the nonparametric estimator with a Gaussian kernel and a bandwidth of $h = 0.023$ over the same grid of values as in part (c). Compare the estimated values with the true value, $\sigma^2 r$.

12 Estimation by Simulation

12.1 Introduction

An important feature of the maximum likelihood estimator emphasised in Chapter 1 is that the likelihood function, defined in terms of the probability distribution of the observed data, y_t, is tractable. Some important examples in economics and finance where the likelihood cannot be evaluated easily are continuous-time models where data are observed discretely, factor GARCH models and ARMA models where the random variable is discrete.

A popular solution to the problem of an intractable likelihood function is to use an estimation procedure based on simulation. There are two important requirements for the successful implementation of this approach.

(1) The actual model with the intractable likelihood function whose parameters, θ, are to be estimated, can be simulated.
(2) There exists an alternative (auxiliary) model with parameters β that provides a good approximation to the true model and can be estimated by conventional methods.

The underlying idea behind the simulation estimator is that the estimates $\widehat{\theta}$ are chosen in such a way as to ensure that the data simulated using the true model yield the same estimates of the auxiliary model, $\widehat{\beta}_s(\theta)$, as does the observed data, $\widehat{\beta}$.

Under certain conditions the simulation estimator is consistent, asymptotically normally distributed and achieves the same asymptotic efficiency as the maximum likelihood estimator. The algorithm for computing the simulation estimator is based on the GMM estimator discussed in Chapter 10 as it involves choosing the unknown parameters of the true model so that the empirical moments (based on the data) are equated to the theoretical moments (based on the simulated data), with the form of the moments determined by the auxiliary

model. Three simulation estimators are discussed here, namely, Indirect Inference (Gouriéroux, Monfort and Renault, 1993); Efficient Method of Moments
(Gallant and Tauchen, 1996); and Simulated Method of Moments (Duffie and
Singleton, 1993; Smith, 1993). Although not discussed in this chapter, Bayesian
numerical methods are frequently used in estimation by simulation. For a general introduction to these methods, see Chib and Greenberg (1996), Geweke
(1999) and Chib (2001, 2008).

12.2 Motivating Example

To motivate the simulation procedures and to establish notation, consider the
problem of estimating the parameters of the MA(1)

$$y_t = u_t - \theta u_{t-1}, \qquad u_t \sim iid\ N(0, 1), \tag{12.1}$$

in which $|\theta| < 1$ to ensure that the process is invertible (see Chapter 13). The
aim is to estimate the unknown parameter θ. An appropriate estimation strategy
is to use maximum likelihood. The conditional log-likelihood function is

$$\ln L_T(\theta) = \frac{1}{T-1} \sum_{t=2}^{T} \ln f_0(y_t | y_{t-1}, y_{t-2}, \cdots ; \theta)$$

$$= -\frac{1}{2} \ln(2\pi) - \frac{1}{2(T-1)} \sum_{t=2}^{T} (y_t + \theta u_{t-1})^2,$$

which is maximised using a nonlinear iterative algorithm. Of course this is not
a difficult numerical problem, but it does highlight the key estimation issues
that underlie more difficult problems which motivate the need for a simulation
based estimation procedure.

Suppose that instead of specifying the MA(1) model, an AR(1) model is
incorrectly specified instead

$$y_t = \rho y_{t-1} + v_t, \qquad v_t \sim iid\ N(0, 1), \tag{12.2}$$

and $\beta = \{\rho\}$ is an unknown parameter. Estimation of the AR(1) model is
certainly more simple as ρ can be estimated by maximum likelihood in one
iteration. The conditional log-likelihood function for this model is

$$\ln L_T(\theta) = \frac{1}{T-1} \sum_{t=2}^{T} \ln f(y_t | y_{t-1}; \rho)$$

$$= -\frac{1}{2} \ln(2\pi) - \frac{1}{2(T-1)} \sum_{t=2}^{T} (y_t - \rho y_{t-1})^2,$$

where conditioning is on the first observation y_1. Solving the first-order condition

$$\frac{1}{T-1} \sum_{t=2}^{T} y_{t-1}(y_t - \hat{\rho} y_{t-1}) = 0, \tag{12.3}$$

yields the maximum likelihood estimator

$$\hat{\rho} = \frac{\sum_{t=2}^{T} y_{t-1} y_t}{\sum_{t=2}^{T} y_{t-1}^2}, \tag{12.4}$$

which is simply the ordinary least squares estimator obtained by regressing y_t on y_{t-1}.

To show the relationship between the true model in equation (12.1) and the misspecified model in equation (12.2), take expectations of the first-order condition in (12.3) with respect to the true MA(1) model

$$E\left[\frac{1}{T-1} \sum_{t=2}^{T} y_{t-1}(y_t - \hat{\rho} y_{t-1})\right] = 0.$$

Using the properties of the MA(1) model, the expectations are

$$E[y_t^2] = (1 + \theta_0^2), \qquad E[y_{t-1} y_t] = -\theta_0,$$

and the first-order condition becomes

$$-\theta_0 - \rho_0(1 + \theta_0^2) = 0,$$

which uses the result $\operatorname{plim} \hat{\rho} = \rho_0$. If follows that

$$\rho_0 = -\frac{\theta_0}{(1 + \theta_0^2)},$$

which provides an analytical expression relating the parameter of the auxiliary model, ρ_0, to the parameter of the true model, θ_0. A natural way to estimate θ_0 is to replace ρ_0 with its estimate, $\hat{\rho}$, obtained from the auxiliary model

$$\hat{\rho} = -\frac{\hat{\theta}}{(1 + \hat{\theta}^2)},$$

and solve for $\hat{\theta}$. The solution is a quadratic equation in $\hat{\theta}$

$$\hat{\rho}\hat{\theta}^2 + \hat{\theta} + \hat{\rho} = 0.$$

This equation has two roots, with the root falling within the unit circle (see Chapter 13) taken as the estimator of θ

$$\hat{\theta} = \frac{-1 + \sqrt{1 - 4\hat{\rho}^2}}{2\hat{\rho}}.$$

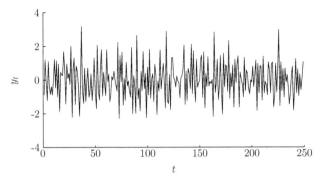

Figure 12.1. Simulated data from a MA(1) model.

Example 12.1 Method of Moments Estimation of a MA(1) Model

The MA(1) model in equation (12.1) is simulated with $\theta_0 = 0.5$ and $u_t \sim$ $iid\ N(0, 1)$ to obtain $T = 250$ observations. The simulated data are presented in Figure 12.1.

The first-order autocorrelation coefficient, estimated on the zero mean data, is $\widehat{\rho} = -0.411$. The estimate of θ is therefore

$$\widehat{\theta} = \frac{-1 + \sqrt{1 - 4\widehat{\rho}^2}}{2\widehat{\rho}} = \frac{-1 + \sqrt{1 - 4(-0.411)^2}}{-20.411} = 0.525\,,$$

which is in good agreement with the population parameter $\theta_0 = 0.5$.   □

In the analysis of the MA(1) model the empirical AR(1) coefficient estimated from the sample data, $\widehat{\rho}$, is equated with the theoretical AR(1) coefficient, $-\theta/(1 + \theta^2)$ and used to obtain an estimate of the MA(1) parameter. Simulation estimation methods use this approach more generally, but with the theoretical parameter replaced by coefficient estimates obtained from data simulated using the true model.

12.3   Indirect Inference

This estimator was first proposed by Gouriéroux, Monfort and Renault (1993). In this approach, parameters of the true model are not estimated directly by maximising the log-likelihood function, but indirectly through another model, known as the auxiliary model. There is also a developing literature on approximate Bayesian computation which is linked to indirect inference (Beaumont, Cornuet, Marin and Robert, 2009; Drovandi, Pettitt and Faddy, 2011).

12.3.1 Estimation

As usual, let θ denote the parameter vector of the true model to be estimated and let β represent the parameters of an auxiliary model, which is easily estimated. Indirect estimation extracts information about θ indirectly through the estimates of β, by ensuring that the estimates of the parameters of the auxiliary model are linked to the parameters of the true model by a binding function $\beta = g(\theta)$. If the dimension of β is identical to that of θ, then the binding function is invertible and θ is estimated indirectly using $\theta = g^{-1}(\beta)$. In practice, the binding function between the β and θ is recovered by simulation. Observations are simulated from the true model for given θ and then used to find the corresponding estimate for β thus creating a realisation of the binding function.

A central feature of estimation is the simulation of the true model for given values of θ. The length of the simulated series is $S = T \times K$ where K is a constant. When simulating the model it is common practice to simulate more observations than strictly required and then to discard the supernumerary initial observations. This practice, known as burn in, has the effect of reducing dependence of the simulated series on the choice of initial conditions. Another advantage of using this practice is that if p lagged values of y_t are present in the auxiliary model the last p discarded observations from the burn-in sample may be treated as the initial conditions for these lags. This means that none of the S observations are lost when estimating the auxiliary model using the simulated data.

The estimation procedure is now as follows. Estimate the parameters of the auxiliary model using the observed sample data, $\widehat{\beta}$. Simulate the model for given θ and use the S simulated observations to estimate the parameters of the auxiliary model from the simulated data, $\widehat{\beta}_s$. The indirect estimator is the solution of

$$\widehat{\theta} = \arg\min_{\theta} \frac{1}{2} (\widehat{\beta} - \widehat{\beta}_s(\theta))' W_T^{-1} (\widehat{\beta} - \widehat{\beta}_s(\theta)). \tag{12.5}$$

The matrix W_T is the optimal weighting matrix discussed in Chapters 9 and 10, which is given by $W_T = H_T J_T^{-1} H_T$ where H_T is the Hessian of the auxiliary model and J_T is the outer product of gradients matrix of the auxiliary model. The need for a weighting matrix stems from the fact that the auxiliary model with parameters β represents a misspecification of the true model with parameters θ. The solution of the indirect estimator requires a gradient algorithm as the objective function is in general a nonlinear function of the parameters θ. The model is just-identified if the dimension of β equals the dimension of θ. The model is over-identified if the dimension of β exceeds the dimension of θ. If the dimension of β is less than the dimension of θ, then the model is under-identified in which case it is not possible to compute the indirect estimator. For the over-identified models where the weighting matrix is chosen to be the identity matrix, the indirect estimator is still consistent but not asymptotically efficient.

Example 12.2 Indirect Estimation of a MA(1) Model

Consider the MA(1) model in equation (12.1) which is simulated in Example 12.1. The MA(1) parameter θ is estimated by indirect inference using an AR(1) model as the auxiliary model by implementing the following steps.

Step 1: Estimate the parameter of the auxiliary model, $\beta = \{\rho\}$, using the observed data y_t to give

$$\widehat{\rho} = \frac{\sum_{t=2}^{T} y_t y_{t-1}}{\sum_{t=2}^{T} y_{t-1}^2}.$$

Step 2: Choose a value of θ initially, say $\theta_{(0)}$.

Step 3: Let $y_{s,t}$ represent a time series of simulated data of length $S = T \times K$ from the true model, in this case a MA(1) model, given $\theta = \theta_{(0)}$.

Step 4: Compute the first-order autocorrelation coefficient using the simulated data

$$\widehat{\rho}_s = \frac{\sum_{t=1}^{S} y_{s,t-1} y_{s,t}}{\sum_{t=1}^{S} y_{s,t-1}^2},$$

where the limits of the summation reflect the fact that the starting value $y_{s,0}$ is available from the discarded burn-in observations.

Step 5: The indirect estimator is to choose θ, so that

$$\widehat{\rho} = \widehat{\rho}_s,$$

which means that $-\widehat{\theta}/(1 + \widehat{\theta}^2)$ is replaced by $\widehat{\rho}_s$.   □

Setting $K = 1$ in Example 12.2, results in the simulated series having the same length as the actual series. As K increases, the simulated AR(1) coefficient, $\widehat{\rho}_s$, approaches the theoretical AR(1) coefficient, ρ_0. In the limit as $K \to \infty$, the simulated and theoretical AR(1) coefficients are equal, as the following example demonstrates.

Example 12.3 Accuracy of Simulated Moments

The true model is a MA(1)

$$y_t = u_t - \theta u_{t-1}, \qquad u_t \sim iid\ N(0, 1),$$

with $\theta_0 = 0.5$. The sample size is $T = 250$. Table 12.1 gives the AR(1) coefficient estimates for various values of K. The true AR(1) parameter is

$$\rho_0 = -\frac{\theta_0}{(1 + \theta_0^2)} = -\frac{0.5}{(1 + 0.5^2)} = -0.4.$$

Table 12.1. *Estimated AR(1) coefficient
estimates obtained from simulating a MA(1)
model with $\theta_0 = 0.5$, for various simulation
sample sizes, S. The sample size of the
observed data is $T = 250$*

K	$S = T \times K$	AR(1)
1	250	−0.411
2	500	−0.375
3	750	−0.360
4	1000	−0.385
5	1250	−0.399
10	2500	−0.403
100	5000	−0.399
True:		−0.400

The results reported in Table 12.1 demonstrate that as K increases, the simulated AR(1) coefficient estimates approach the true population autocorrelation parameter value of −0.4. Note that the sequence of AR(1) estimates do not monotonically approach $\rho = -0.4$. This is simply a reflection of simulation error, where for different simulation runs, different seeds for the random number generator will yield different numerical results. The overall qualitative behaviour of the results, however, remains the same. □

The choice of an AR(1) log-likelihood to approximate the MA(1) log-likelihood can be improved by choosing AR models with longer lags. To motivate this point, rewrite the MA(1) model from Examples 12.1 to 12.3 as an infinite AR model as follows:

$$y_t = u_t - \theta u_{t-1}$$
$$y_t = (1 - \theta L)u_t$$
$$(1 - \theta L)^{-1}y_t = u_t$$
$$(1 + \theta L + \theta^2 L^2 + \cdots)y_t = u_t$$
$$y_t = -\theta y_{t-1} - \theta^2 y_{t-2} - \cdots + u_t, \qquad (12.6)$$

in which L is the lag operator (see Appendix B). The AR(1) model represents a first-order approximation of the more correct auxiliary model, given by an infinite AR model. This suggests that a better approximation to the true model is obtained by choosing as the auxiliary model an AR model with P lags. In the limit the auxiliary model approaches the true model as $P \to \infty$. In this case the efficiency of the indirect estimator approaches the maximum likelihood estimator as given by the Cramér-Rao lower bound. In practice, the indirect estimator achieves a comparable efficiency level as that of the maximum likelihood estimator for a finite lag structure.

Table 12.2. *Finite sample properties of the indirect estimator of θ for the MA(1) example. Based on a Monte Carlo experiment with* 1000 *replications. The sample size is* $T = 250$

Statistics	Auxiliary model		
	AR(1)	AR(2)	AR(3)
True	0.5000	0.5000	0.5000
Mean	0.5335	0.5109	0.5066
St. dev.	0.1835	0.1125	0.0906
RMSE	0.1866	0.1130	0.0909

Example 12.4 Finite Sample Properties

Table 12.2 gives statistics on the sampling properties of the indirect estimator for a sample of size $T = 250$ using a Monte Carlo experiment based on 1000 replications. The indirect estimator is computed by setting the length of the simulated series to be $S = T = 250$ observations, that is $K = 1$. Three auxiliary models are used, beginning with an AR(1) model, then an AR(2) model and finally an AR(3) model. For convenience, the weighting matrix is taken to be the identity matrix in this example.

The mean of the simulations shows that the bias of the indirect estimator decreases as the dimension of the auxiliary model increases. There is also a decrease in the RMSE showing that the indirect estimator based on the AR(3) model is statistically more efficient than the indirect estimators based on lower AR lags. □

12.3.2 Relationship with Indirect Least Squares

The goal of indirect inference is to obtain a consistent estimator of the true model even when the estimated auxiliary model is misspecified. This objective is not new to econometrics and has been around for a long time as a method for obtaining consistent estimates of the parameters of simultaneous equation models (see Chapter 5).

Consider the simple Keynesian two-sector model consisting of a consumption function and the income identity

$$c_t = \alpha + \phi y_t + u_t$$
$$y_t = c_t + i_t \tag{12.7}$$
$$u_t \sim iid\ N\left(0, \sigma^2\right),$$

in which c_t is consumption, y_t is income, i_t is investment which is assumed to be exogenous so that $E[i_t u_t]$ and $\theta = \{\alpha, \phi\}$ are the parameters to be estimated.

Estimation of the first equation by least squares is inappropriate as a result of simultaneity bias. The equation for y_t can be written as

$$y_t = \frac{\alpha}{1-\phi} + \frac{1}{1-\phi} i_t + \frac{1}{1-\phi} u_t ,$$

so that

$$E[y_t u_t] = E\left[\left(\frac{\alpha}{1-\phi} + \frac{1}{1-\phi} i_t + \frac{1}{1-\phi} u_t\right) u_t\right] = \frac{\sigma^2}{1-\phi} \neq 0 .$$

The earliest method to obtain a consistent parameter estimator of θ is known as indirect least squares. This is obtained by first solving (12.7) for the reduced form. In the case of the consumption equation the pertinent equation is

$$c_t = \frac{\alpha}{1-\phi} + \frac{\phi}{1-\phi} i_t + \frac{1}{1-\phi} u_t = \delta + \gamma i_t + v_t , \qquad (12.8)$$

where $v_t = (1-\phi)^{-1} u_t$ and

$$\delta = \frac{\alpha}{1-\phi}, \qquad \gamma = \frac{\phi}{1-\phi}, \qquad (12.9)$$

are the reduced form parameters. Estimation of (12.8) by least squares yields consistent estimators of $\widehat{\delta}$ and $\widehat{\gamma}$. Consistent estimators of the consumption function parameters in (12.7) are obtained by rearranging (12.9) and evaluating at $\widehat{\delta}$ and $\widehat{\gamma}$ to give the indirect least squares estimators

$$\widehat{\alpha} = \frac{\widehat{\delta}}{1+\widehat{\gamma}}, \qquad \widehat{\phi} = \frac{\widehat{\gamma}}{1+\widehat{\gamma}} . \qquad (12.10)$$

The indirect least squares solution in (12.10) is equivalent to the indirect inference solution where the simulation length is $K \to \infty$. The reduced form equation in (12.8) is nothing other than the auxiliary model and (12.9) corresponds to the binding function that links the true parameters $\theta = \{\alpha, \phi\}$ to the auxiliary parameters $\beta = \{\delta, \gamma\}$. Thus to estimate the consumption function parameters in (12.7) by indirect inference, the strategy is to estimate the auxiliary model (reduced form) in (12.8) by least squares using the actual data to yield $\widehat{\beta} = \{\widehat{\delta}, \widehat{\gamma}\}$. The consumption function in (12.7) is then simulated using some starting values of $\{\alpha_{(0)}, \phi_{(0)}\}$ to generate simulated consumption data $c_{s,t}$. The auxiliary model (reduced form) in (12.8) is then re-estimated using the simulated consumption data, $c_{s,t}$, and the actual investment data, i_t, to generate $\widehat{\beta}_s = \{\widehat{\delta}_s, \widehat{\gamma}_s\}$. As the model is just-identified, the indirect inference estimators are obtained when $\theta = \{\alpha, \phi\}$ is iterated until $\widehat{\beta} = \widehat{\beta}_s$.

12.4   Efficient Method of Moments (EMM)

The indirect estimator is based on matching the parameter estimates of the auxiliary model using actual and simulated data. The efficient method of moments
estimator (EMM) proposed by Gallant and Tauchen (1996) focusses on the
gradient of the auxiliary model instead.

12.4.1   Estimation

Let β represent the $M \times 1$ vector of parameters of the auxiliary model and $\widehat{\beta}$ the
corresponding parameter estimates using the actual data. The EMM estimator
is the solution of

$$\widehat{\theta} = \arg\min_{\theta} \frac{1}{2} G'_S(\theta, \widehat{\beta}) W_T^{-1} G_S(\theta, \widehat{\beta}), \tag{12.11}$$

in which $G_S(\theta, \widehat{\beta})$ is a $M \times 1$ vector of gradients of the auxiliary model evaluated at the maximum likelihood estimates of the auxiliary model, $\widehat{\beta}$, but using
the simulated data, $y_{s,t}$. The use of the simulated data in computing the gradients establishes the required binding function between θ and β. Gallant and
Tauchen (1996) choose the optimal weighting matrix as $W_T = J_T$, where J_T
is the outer product of gradients matrix of the auxiliary model as defined in
Chapters 9 and 10. The solution of the EMM estimator requires a gradient
algorithm as the objective function is in general a nonlinear function of the
parameters θ.

The intuition behind the EMM estimator is as follows. The gradient of the
auxiliary model, $G_T(\beta)$, computed using the actual data and evaluated at the
maximum likelihood estimator, $\beta = \widehat{\beta}$, is zero by definition, that is $G_T(\widehat{\beta}) = 0$.
EMM chooses that θ which generates simulated data such that the gradients
of the auxiliary model, $G_S(\widehat{\theta})$ match the gradients obtained using the actual
data, namely $G_T(\widehat{\beta}) = 0$. An important computational advantage of the EMM
estimator is that it is necessary to estimate the auxiliary model only once when
solving (12.11). This is in contrast to the indirect estimator in (12.5) where it is
necessary to re-estimate the auxiliary model at each iteration of the algorithm.

Example 12.5 EMM Estimation of a MA(1) Model

Consider again the MA(1) model in equation (12.1) with $\theta_0 = 0.5$. Three
auxiliary models are used to estimate the parameter θ, an AR(1) model, an
AR(2) model and an AR(3) model. If the model is simulated $S = T \times K$
times, in the case of the AR(1) model, the gradient in equation (12.11) is given
by

$$G_S(\theta, \widehat{\beta}) = \frac{1}{S} \sum_{t=1}^{S} y_{s,t-1}(y_{s,t} - \widehat{\rho}_1 y_{s,t-1}),$$

Table 12.3. *Finite sample properties of the EMM estimator of* θ *for the MA(1) model. Based on a Monte Carlo experiment with 1000 replications. The sample size is* $T = 250$

	Auxiliary model		
Statistics	AR(1)	AR(2)	AR(3)
True	0.5000	0.5000	0.5000
Mean	0.5308	0.4843	0.4745
St. dev.	0.1773	0.1096	0.0956
RMSE	0.1799	0.1107	0.0990

in which the starting value y_0 is available from the burn-in sample. The approach is to choose θ so that (12.11) is satisfied.

Table 12.3 gives statistics on the sampling properties of the EMM estimator for a sample of size $T = 250$ using a Monte Carlo experiment. The number of replications is 1000. The EMM estimator is based on $S = T = 250$ observations, that is $K = 1$.

The sampling distribution of the EMM estimator in Table 12.3 is similar to the sampling distribution of the indirect estimator given in Table 12.2. In particular, the fall in the RMSE as the lag length of the auxiliary model increases shows the improvement in the efficiency of this estimator as the approximation of the auxiliary model improves. □

12.4.2   Relationship with Instrumental Variables

The relationship between simulation estimation and simultaneous equations estimators can be generalised by showing that the instrumental variables estimator is equivalent to the EMM estimator. Consider the model

$$y_t = \theta x_t + u_t, \qquad u_t \sim iid\, N(0, 1), \tag{12.12}$$

in which $E[x_t u_t] \neq 0$, in which case least squares is inappropriate. The EMM estimator is based on estimating an auxiliary model specified as

$$x_t = \phi z_t + v_t, \qquad v_t \sim iid\, N(0, 1), \tag{12.13}$$

where the variable z_t has the property that $E[z_t v_t] = 0$. In the simultaneous equations literature, (12.12) is the structural equation and (12.13) is the reduced form. The restriction $E[z_t u_t] = 0$, means that z_t represents a valid instrument.

The reduced form in the case of y_t is obtained by substituting x_t from (12.13) into (12.12)

$$y_t = \beta z_t + w_t,$$ (12.14)

in which $\beta = \phi\theta$ and $w_t = u_t + \theta v_t$. The population moment condition is

$$E[(y_t - \beta_0 z_t)z_t] = 0.$$ (12.15)

Evaluating the expectation by the sample average yields the first-order condition

$$\frac{1}{T}\sum_{t=1}^{T}(y_t - \widehat{\beta}z_t)z_t = 0,$$ (12.16)

where $\widehat{\beta}$ is obtained as a least squares regression of y_t on z_t. The EMM estimator, $\widehat{\theta}$, is computed by simulating (12.12) according to $y_{s,t} = \theta x_t + u_{s,t}$, with x_t treated as given, and evaluating y_t in equation (12.16) at $y_{s,t}$ according to

$$\frac{1}{S}\sum_{t=1}^{S}(y_{s,t} - \widehat{\beta}z_t)z_t = \frac{1}{S}\sum_{t=1}^{S}(\widehat{\theta}x_t + u_{s,t} - \widehat{\beta}z_t)z_t = 0.$$

Letting $S \to \infty$ amounts to replacing the summation by the expectations operator

$$\lim_{S\to\infty}\frac{1}{S}\sum_{t=1}^{S}(\widehat{\theta}x_t + u_{t,s} - \widehat{\beta}z_t)z_t = E[(\theta_0 x_t - \beta_0 z_t)z_t]$$

$$= \theta_0 E[x_t z_t] - E[y_t z_t] = 0,$$

where the first equality uses $E[u_{t,s}z_t] = 0$, and the second equality uses $\beta_0 E[z_t^2] = E[y_t z_t]$ from (12.15). Solving for θ_0 gives

$$\theta_0 = \frac{E[y_t z_t]}{E[x_t z_t]}.$$

Replacing the expectations by the sample moments gives the instrumental variables estimator discussed in Chapter 5

$$\widehat{\theta} = \frac{T^{-1}\sum_{t=1}^{T}y_t z_t}{T^{-1}\sum_{t=1}^{T}x_t z_t},$$

which corresponds to the EMM estimator as $S \to \infty$.

The establishment of the link between the EMM estimator and the instrumental variables estimator means that statements concerning the quality of the instrument are equivalent to statements about the quality of the auxiliary model to approximate the true model. If the auxiliary model represents a good approximation of the true model, the sampling distribution of the EMM estimator under the regularity conditions in Chapter 2 is asymptotically normal. However, if the approximation is poor, the sampling distribution will not be asymptotically normal, but will inherit the sampling distribution of the instrumental variables estimator when the instruments are weak, as investigated in Chapter 5.

12.5   Simulated Generalised Method of Moments (SMM)

An important feature of the indirect estimator defined by (12.5) is that it involves estimating the parameter vector of the true model, θ, by equating the parameter estimates of the auxiliary model using the observed data, $\widehat{\beta}$, with the parameter vector of the auxiliary model computed using the simulated data, $\widehat{\beta}_s$. In the case of the MA(1) example where the auxiliary model is chosen to be an AR(1), $\widehat{\beta}$ is the first-order autocorrelation coefficient based on the actual data and $\widehat{\beta}_s$ is the first-order autocorrelation coefficient based on the simulated data. More succinctly, the indirect estimator amounts to equating the empirical moment, $\widehat{\beta}$, with the theoretical moments, $\widehat{\beta}_s$,

$$\underset{\text{(Empirical)}}{\widehat{\beta}} = \underset{\text{(Theoretical)}}{\widehat{\beta}_s} .$$

This interpretation of the indirect estimator is also equivalent to the simulated generalised method of moments estimator proposed by Duffie and Singleton (1993). Perhaps the relationship between SMM and EMM estimators is even more transparent since the EMM estimator is based on the scores, which is equivalent to the moments used in SMM.

In general, the auxiliary model can represent a (misspecified) likelihood function that yields first-order conditions corresponding to a range of moments. These moments and hence the auxiliary model, should be chosen to capture the empirical characteristics of the data. In turn, these empirical moments are used to identify the parameters of the true model being estimated by a simulation estimation procedure. In fact, Gallant and Tauchen (1996) suggest a semi-nonparametric model that provides sufficient flexibility to approximate many models. This class of models captures empirical characteristics such as autocorrelation in the mean, autocorrelation in the variance and non-normality.

A further relationship between the three simulation procedures discussed are the diagnostic tests of the models proposed. For example, the Hansen-Sargan J test of the number of over-identifying restrictions, discussed in Chapter 10, can also be applied in the indirect and EMM estimation frameworks. To implement

Table 12.4. *Over-identification test of the AR(1) model
based on the EMM estimator. The sample size is
$T = 250$ and the optimal weighting matrix is based on
$P = 0$ lags*

	Auxiliary model		
Statistics	AR(1)	AR(2)	AR(3)
Q_T	0.0000	0.0001	0.0039
$J_{HS} = 2TQ_T$	0.0000	0.0388	1.9596
$N - M$	0.0000	1.0000	2.0000
p-value	n.a.	0.8437	0.3754

the test, the value of the objective function is

$$Q_T(\widehat{\theta}) = \frac{1}{2} G_S'(\widehat{\theta}, \widehat{\beta}) W_T^{-1} G_S(\widehat{\theta}, \widehat{\beta}), \tag{12.17}$$

where all quantities are evaluated at the EMM estimator, $\widehat{\theta}$. Under the null
hypothesis that the model is correctly specified, the test statistic is

$$J_{HS} = 2TQ_T \overset{d}{\to} \chi^2_{N-M},$$

in which N is the number of moment conditions and M is the number of
parameters.

Example 12.6 Over-Identification Test of a MA(1)
The true model is a MA(1)

$$y_t = u_t - \theta u_{t-1}, \qquad u_t \sim iid\, N(0, 1),$$

with $\theta_0 = 0.5$. Table 12.4 gives the results of the over-identification test using
the EMM estimator for a sample of size $T = 250$. The EMM estimator is based
on $S = T = 250$ observations, that is $K = 1$. For the AR(1) auxiliary model,
the system is just-identified in which case there is nothing to test. For the AR(2)
and AR(3) auxiliary models the computed values of the J_{HS} test statistic are
0.0388 and 1.9596, respectively, with associated p-values of 0.8437 and 0.3754.
In both cases the null hypothesis that the true model is specified correctly is
not rejected at conventional significance levels.

12.6 Estimating Continuous-Time Models

An important area of the use of simulation estimation in economics and finance
is the estimation of continuous-time models as in the application presented in
Section 3.8 of Chapter 3. This class of models is summarised by the following

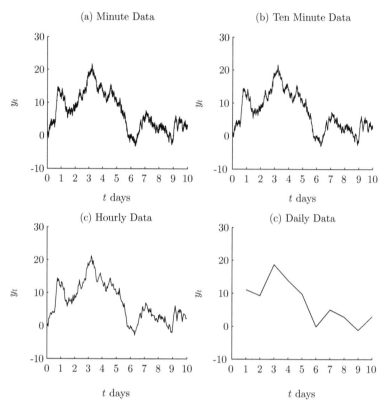

Figure 12.2. Continuous, ten minute, hourly and daily, sampled by simulating equation (12.18) with $\mu(y_t; \alpha) = 0$, $\sigma^2(y_t; \phi) = 1$ (Brownian motion) and $\Delta t = 1/60$.

stochastic differential equation

$$dy_t = \mu(y_t; \alpha)dt + \sigma(y_t; \phi)dB , \qquad (12.18)$$

in which $dB \sim N(0, dt)$. The function $\mu(y_t; \alpha)$ is the mean of dy_t, with parameter vector α, and the function $\sigma^2(y_t; \phi)$ is the variance of dy_t, with parameter vector ϕ.

Panel (a) of Figure 12.2 gives an example of a continuous time series with $\mu(y_t; \alpha) = 0$ and $\sigma^2(y_t; \phi) = 1$, by simulating (12.18) using a time interval of $\Delta t = 1/60$. This choice of Δt is chosen to correspond to minute data. In practice continuous data are not available, but are measured at discrete points in time, $y_1, y_2, \cdots, y_T$. For example, in panel (b) of Figure 12.2 the data correspond to measuring y every 10 minutes, in panel (c) the data are hourly as y is observed every 60 minutes and in panel (d) the data are daily as y is observed every $60 \times 24 = 1440$ minutes.

In general, maximum likelihood estimation for continuous-time processes is intractable as the following simple illustration demonstrates. Consider two discrete observations y_{t+1} and y_t. The records of continuous data between these two observations may be regarded as missing observations. Based on the assumption that there are $n - 1$ missing observations between y_{t+1} and y_t the joint pdf may be represented schematically as

$$f(\underbrace{y_{t+1}}_{\text{known}}, \underbrace{y_{t+(n-1)/n}, \cdots, y_{t+1/n}}_{\text{missing}}, \underbrace{y_t}_{\text{known}}). \tag{12.19}$$

To derive the conditional distribution $f(y_{t+1}|y_t)$ all the missing observations in equation (12.19) must be integrated out an operation that requires the computation of an $(n - 1)$-dimensional integral

$$f(y_{t+1}|y_t) = \int_{-\infty}^{\infty} \cdots \int_{-\infty}^{\infty} f(y_{t+1}, \cdots |y_t) \, dy_{t+1/n} \, dy_{t+2/n} \cdots dy_{t+(n-1)/n} .$$

The construction of the likelihood function requires that this integration be computed for each transition in the data, effectively involving the evaluation of a $T \times (n - 1)$-dimensional integral.

To estimate the parameters α and ϕ of (12.18), using standard estimation methods including maximum likelihood, it is necessary to have continuous data. The earliest approach adopted to resolve the difference in frequency between the model and the data, was to discretise the model thereby matching the frequency of the model to the data. The problem with this strategy is that discretising a continuous-time model results in a misspecification of the functional form of the model so that the parameters of the discrete model are, in general, not the parameters of the continuous-time model, resulting in biased estimators of α and ϕ.

To introduce the form of the misspecification from converting a continuous-time model into discrete time, consider the simplest of all models containing no parameters

$$dy_t = y \, dB , \qquad dB \sim N(0, dt) . \tag{12.20}$$

An exact discretisation of this model is given by

$$y_t = y_{t-1} \exp[u_t - 0.5] , \tag{12.21}$$

in which $u_t \sim iid \, N(0, 1)$. An inexact discretisation is given by choosing the time interval as $\Delta t = 1$ in (12.20)

$$y_t - y_{t-1} = y_{t-1} v_t \iff \frac{y_t - y_{t-1}}{y_{t-1}} = v_t , \tag{12.22}$$

in which $v_t \sim iid \, N(0, 1)$. In both (12.21) and (12.22) y_t is growing at a certain rate, but in (12.21) the growth is continuous whereas in (12.22) the growth is discrete. The functional forms of the two models differ because the discrete time model imposes a linear growth rate while the growth in the continuous-time model is exponential.

Simulation estimation procedures circumvent this misspecification problem by simulating the continuous model, and constructing a discrete time series of simulated data which are calibrated with the observed discrete data through a set of moment conditions based on a chosen auxiliary model. Even though the misspecified discretised model is estimated, these parameter estimates are not of interest, but rather it is the parameter estimates obtained from simulating the continuous-time model that are of interest. To highlight the approach, a simulation estimation framework is developed to estimate models of Brownian motion, geometric Brownian motion and a continuous time model of stochastic volatility.

12.6.1   Brownian Motion

Consider estimating the parameters $\theta = \{\mu, \sigma\}$ of the stochastic differential equation

$$dy_t = \mu \, dt + \sigma \, dB, \tag{12.23}$$

in which $dB \sim N(0, dt)$. The auxiliary model is chosen as a discretisation of this model, obtained by setting $\Delta t = 1$

$$y_t - y_{t-1} = \mu_\Delta + \sigma_\Delta u_t, \qquad u_t \sim iid \; N(0, 1), \tag{12.24}$$

in which $\beta = \{\mu_\Delta, \sigma_\Delta\}$ are the parameters of the auxiliary model. The log-likelihood function of this model is

$$\ln L_T(\beta) = -\frac{1}{2} \ln 2\pi - \frac{1}{2} \ln \sigma_\Delta^2 - \frac{1}{2\sigma_\Delta^2(T-1)} \sum_{t=2}^{T} (y_t - y_{t-1} - \mu_\Delta)^2,$$

$$\tag{12.25}$$

with gradient vector

$$G_T(\beta) = \begin{bmatrix} \dfrac{1}{\sigma_\Delta^2(T-1)} \displaystyle\sum_{t=2}^{T} (y_t - y_{t-1} - \mu_\Delta) \\[3mm] -\dfrac{1}{2\sigma_\Delta^2} + \dfrac{1}{2\sigma_\Delta^4(T-1)} \displaystyle\sum_{t=2}^{T} (y_t - y_{t-1} - \mu_\Delta)^2 \end{bmatrix}. \tag{12.26}$$

Setting $G_T(\widehat{\beta}) = 0$, yields the maximum likelihood estimators

$$
\begin{aligned}
\widehat{\mu}_\Delta &= \frac{1}{T-1} \sum_{t=2}^{T} (y_t - y_{t-1}) \\
\widehat{\sigma}_\Delta^2 &= \frac{1}{T-1} \sum_{t=2}^{T} (y_t - y_{t-1} - \widehat{\mu}_\Delta)^2.
\end{aligned}
\tag{12.27}
$$

Indirect Inference

The indirect estimator of the parameters of the model in (12.23) uses (12.27) to form the moment conditions. To estimate (12.23) by indirect inference requires the following steps.

Step 1: Compute $\widehat{\beta} = \{\widehat{\mu}_\Delta, \widehat{\sigma}_\Delta\}$ from the auxiliary model using (12.27) based on the observed data and compute the optimal weighting matrix $W_T = H_T J_T^{-1} H_T$.

Step 2: Choose starting values for $\theta_{(0)} = \{\mu_{(0)}, \sigma_{(0)}\}$, and generate continuous time data using a small time step, say $\Delta t = 0.1$

$$
y_{s,t+\Delta t} - y_{s,t} = \mu_{(0)} \Delta t + \sigma_{(0)} u_{t+\Delta t}, \qquad u_t \sim iid\ N(0, \Delta t).
$$

Let the length of the simulated series be $S = T \times K$.

Step 3: Generate discrete time data $y_{s,1}, y_{s,2}, \cdots, y_{s,S}$, by choosing every $1/\Delta t$ observations from the simulated continuous time series.

Step 4: Compute the parameter estimates of the auxiliary model, $\widehat{\beta}_s = \{\widehat{\mu}_{\Delta,s}, \widehat{\sigma}_{\Delta,s}\}$, based on the simulated data

$$
\widehat{\mu}_{\Delta,s} = \frac{1}{S} \sum_{t=1}^{S} (y_{s,t} - y_{s,t-1})
$$

$$
\widehat{\sigma}_{\Delta,s}^2 = \frac{1}{S} \sum_{t=1}^{S} (y_{s,t} - y_{s,t-1} - \widehat{\mu}_{\Delta,s})^2.
$$

Step 5: Define the moment conditions

$$
G_S(\theta_{(0)}, \widehat{\beta}) = \begin{bmatrix} \widehat{\mu}_\Delta - \widehat{\mu}_{\Delta,s} \\ \widehat{\sigma}_\Delta^2 - \widehat{\sigma}_{\Delta,s}^2 \end{bmatrix}.
$$

Step 6: Choose $\theta = \{\mu, \sigma\}$ to satisfy

$$
\widehat{\theta} = \arg\min_\theta \frac{1}{2} G_S'(\theta, \widehat{\beta}) W_T^{-1} G_S(\theta, \widehat{\beta}).
$$

EMM Estimation

The EMM estimator of (12.23) uses (12.26) to form the moment conditions. To estimate the parameters of the model in equation (12.23) by EMM, the steps are as follows:

Step 1: Compute $\widehat{\beta} = \{\widehat{\mu}_{\Delta}, \widehat{\sigma}_{\Delta}\}$ from the auxiliary model using (12.27) based on the observed data.

Step 2: Using equation (12.26) evaluate $G_T(\widehat{\beta})$ in equation (12.26) at the maximum likelihood estimators of the auxiliary model, $\widehat{\mu}_{\Delta}$ and $\widehat{\sigma}_{\Delta}$, obtained in Step 1 and compute the weighting matrix $W_T = J_T$.

Step 3: Choose starting values $\theta_{(0)} = \{\mu_{(0)}, \sigma_{(0)}\}$, and generate continuous time data using a small time step, say $\Delta t = 0.1$

$$y_{s,t+\Delta t} - y_{s,t} = \mu_{(0)}\Delta t + \sigma_{(0)}u_{t+\Delta t}, \qquad v_t \sim iid \ N(0, \Delta t).$$

Step 4: Generate discrete time data $y_{s,1}, y_{s,2}, \dots, y_{s,S}$, by choosing every $1/\Delta t$ observations from the simulated continuous time series.

Step 5: Evaluate the gradients in (12.26) using the simulated data and the maximum likelihood parameter estimates in (12.27)

$$G_S(\theta_{(0)}, \widehat{\beta}) = \begin{bmatrix} \dfrac{1}{\widehat{\sigma}_{\Delta}^2 S} \displaystyle\sum_{t=1}^{S}(y_{s,t} - y_{s,t-1} - \widehat{\mu}_{\Delta}) \\[2ex] -\dfrac{1}{2\widehat{\sigma}_{\Delta}^2} + \dfrac{1}{2\widehat{\sigma}_{\Delta}^4 S}\displaystyle\sum_{t=1}^{S}(y_{s,t} - y_{s,t-1} - \widehat{\mu}_{\Delta})^2 \end{bmatrix}.$$

Step 6: Choose $\theta = \{\mu, \sigma\}$ to satisfy

$$\widehat{\theta} = \arg\min_{\theta} \frac{1}{2} G'_S(\theta, \widehat{\beta}) W_T^{-1} G_S(\theta, , \widehat{\beta}).$$

Example 12.7 Simulation Estimation of Brownian Motion

Table 12.5 gives the sampling properties of the indirect and EMM estimators from estimating the parameters of the model in (12.23) with true parameter values $\mu_0 = 0.5$ and $\sigma_0 = 0.5$. The sample size is $T = 500$, the time interval is set at $\Delta t = 0.1$, $K = 1/\Delta t = 10$ and the length of the simulated data is $S = TK = 500 \times 10 = 5000$. The optimal weighting matrix used to compute the EMM estimates allows for heteroskedasticity. The sampling distributions are based on 1000 Monte Carlo replications.

The results in Table 12.5 show that the sampling distributions of the two estimators are nearly equivalent. Apart from asymptotic reasons why the two estimators should be similar for large samples at least, this is to be expected in this particular example as the moment conditions used in both estimation procedures are equivalent. As this model is just-identified, the EMM solution is where the first moment condition of the EMM estimator is satisfied, namely,

$$\frac{1}{\widehat{\sigma}_{\Delta}^2 S} \sum_{t=1}^{S}(y_{s,t} - y_{s,t-1} - \widehat{\mu}_{\Delta}) = 0.$$

Table 12.5. *Sampling properties of the indirect and EMM estimators of the Brownian motion parameters μ_0 and σ_0. The sample size is $T = 500$, $\Delta t = 0.1$, $K = 1/\Delta t$, and the number of Monte Carlo replications is 1000*

Estimator	Parameter	Mean	Std dev.	RMSE
Indirect	μ	0.5015	0.0314	0.0314
	σ	0.5018	0.0231	0.0232
EMM	μ	0.5015	0.0314	0.0314
	σ	0.5018	0.0231	0.0232
True	μ	0.500	n.a.	n.a.
	σ	0.500	n.a.	n.a.

This is equivalent to

$$\frac{1}{S} \sum_{t=12}^{S} (y_{s,t} - y_{s,t-1}) - \widehat{\mu}_\Delta = \widehat{\mu}_{\Delta,s} - \widehat{\mu}_\Delta ,$$

which is the first moment used in the indirect inference procedure. The same result applies for the second moment condition. $\square$

12.6.2 Geometric Brownian Motion

Consider estimating the parameters $\theta = \{\mu, \sigma\}$, of the geometric Brownian motion given by the stochastic differential equation

$$dy_t = \mu y_t \, dt + \sigma y_t \, dB , \qquad dB \sim N(0, dt). \qquad (12.28)$$

An exact discretisation of this model is

$$\ln y_t - \ln y_{t-1} = (\mu - 0.5\sigma^2)\Delta t + \sigma u_t , \qquad u_t \sim iid \, N(0, 1). \qquad (12.29)$$

An Euler discretisation of this model is obtained by setting $\Delta t = 1$ in equation (12.28)

$$y_t - y_{t-1} = \mu_\Delta y_{t-1} + \sigma_\Delta y_{t-1} v_t , \qquad v_t \sim iid \, N(0, 1). \qquad (12.30)$$

Alternatively, the auxiliary model is expressed as

$$z_t = \mu_\Delta + \sigma_\Delta v_t, \qquad (12.31)$$

where

$$z_t = \frac{y_t - y_{t-1}}{y_{t-1}},$$

is the (discrete) growth rate. The log-likelihood function of the auxiliary model is

$$\ln L_T(\beta) = -\frac{1}{2}\ln 2\pi - \frac{1}{2}\ln \sigma_\Delta^2 - \frac{1}{2\sigma_\Delta^2(T-1)}\sum_{t=2}^{T}(z_t - \mu_\Delta)^2 .$$

$$(12.32)$$

The gradient is given by

$$G_T(\beta) = \begin{bmatrix} \dfrac{1}{\sigma_\Delta^2(T-1)}\displaystyle\sum_{t=2}^{T}(z_t - \mu_\Delta) \\[2ex] -\dfrac{1}{2\sigma_\Delta^2} + \dfrac{1}{2\sigma_\Delta^4(T-1)}\displaystyle\sum_{t=2}^{T}(z_t - \mu_\Delta)^2 \end{bmatrix},$$

$$(12.33)$$

and setting $G_T(\widehat{\beta}) = 0$ yields the maximum likelihood estimators

$$\begin{aligned} \widehat{\mu}_\Delta &= \frac{1}{T-1}\sum_{t=2}^{T} z_t \\ \widehat{\sigma}_\Delta^2 &= \frac{1}{T-1}\sum_{t=2}^{T}(z_t - \widehat{\mu}_\Delta)^2 . \end{aligned}$$

$$(12.34)$$

Indirect Inference

The indirect estimator of (12.28) uses (12.34) to form the moment conditions. To estimate (12.28) by indirect inference, the steps are as follows.

Step 1: Compute $\widehat{\beta} = \{\widehat{\mu}_\Delta, \widehat{\sigma}_\Delta\}$ from the auxiliary model using (12.34) based on the observed data and W_T.

Step 2: Choose starting values $\theta_{(0)} = \{\mu_{(0)}, \sigma_{(0)}\}$, and generate continuous time data using a small time step, say $\Delta t = 0.1$

$$y_{s,t+\Delta t} - y_{s,t} = \mu_{(0)} y_{s,t}\Delta t + \sigma_{(0)} y_{s,t} u_{t+\Delta t}, \qquad u_t \sim iid\, N(0, \Delta t).$$

Let the length of the simulated series be $S = T \times K$. Alternatively, simulate

$$z_{s,t+\Delta t} = \mu\Delta t + \sigma u_{t+\Delta t},$$

and construct $y_{s,t+\Delta t}$ using the recursive product

$$y_{s,t+\Delta t} = y_{s,t}(1 + z_{s,t+\Delta t}).$$

Step 3: Generate discrete time data $y_{s,1}, y_{s,2}, \cdots, y_{s,S}$, by choosing every $1/\Delta t$ observations from the simulated continuous time series.

Step 4: Compute the parameter estimates of the auxiliary model, $\widehat{\beta}_s = \{\widehat{\mu}_{\Delta,s}, \widehat{\sigma}_{\Delta,s}\}$ based on the simulated data

$$\widehat{\mu}_{\Delta,s} = \frac{1}{S} \sum_{t=1}^{S} z_{s,t}$$

$$\widehat{\sigma}_{\Delta,s}^2 = \frac{1}{S} \sum_{t=1}^{S} (z_{s,t} - \widehat{\mu}_{\Delta,s})^2.$$

Step 5: Define the moment conditions

$$G_S(\theta_{(0)}, \widehat{\beta}) = \begin{bmatrix} \widehat{\mu} - \widehat{\mu}_{\Delta,s} \\ \widehat{\sigma}^2 - \widehat{\sigma}_{\Delta,s}^2 \end{bmatrix}.$$

Step 6: Choose $\theta = \{\mu, \sigma\}$ to satisfy

$$\widehat{\theta} = \arg\min_{\theta} \frac{1}{2} G_S'(\theta, \widehat{\beta}) W_T^{-1} G_S(\theta, \widehat{\beta}).$$

EMM Estimation

The EMM estimator is computed as follows.

Step 1: Compute $\widehat{\beta} = \{\widehat{\mu}_\Delta, \widehat{\sigma}_\Delta\}$ from the auxiliary model using (12.34) based on the observed data.

Step 2: Compute the gradient vector in equation (12.33) using the maximum likelihood estimators $\widehat{\mu}_\Delta$ and $\widehat{\sigma}_\Delta$ and compute the weighting matrix W_T.

Step 3: Choose starting values for $\theta_{(0)} = \{\mu_{(0)}, \sigma_{(0)}\}$, and generate continuous time data using a small time step, say $\Delta t = 0.1$

$$y_{s,t+\Delta t} - y_{s,t} = \mu_{(0)}\Delta t + \sigma_{(0)}u_{t+\Delta t}, \qquad u_t \sim iid\ N(0, \Delta t).$$

Step 4: Generate discrete time data $y_{s,1}, y_{s,2}, ..., y_{s,S}$, by choosing every $1/\Delta t$ observations from the simulated continuous time series.

Step 5: Evaluate the gradients in (12.33) using the simulated data and the maximum likelihood parameter estimates in (12.34)

$$G_S(\theta_{(0)}, \widehat{\beta}) = \begin{bmatrix} \dfrac{1}{\widehat{\sigma}_\Delta^2 S} \sum_{t=1}^{S}(z_t - \widehat{\mu}_\Delta) \\ -\dfrac{1}{2\widehat{\sigma}_\Delta^2} + \dfrac{1}{2\widehat{\sigma}_\Delta^4 S} \sum_{t=1}^{S}(z_t - \widehat{\mu}_\Delta)^2 \end{bmatrix}.$$

Step 6: Choose $\theta = \{\mu, \sigma\}$ to satisfy

$$\widehat{\theta} = \arg\min_{\theta} \frac{1}{2} G_S'(\theta, \widehat{\beta}) W_T^{-1} G_S(\theta, \widehat{\beta}).$$

12.6.3   Stochastic Volatility

Consider estimating the parameters $\theta = \{\mu, \alpha, \kappa, \gamma\}$, of the continuous-time stochastic volatility model

$$
\begin{aligned}
dy_t &= \mu y_t \, dt + \sigma_t y_t \, dB_1 \\
d \ln \sigma_t^2 &= \alpha(\kappa - \ln \sigma_t^2) \, dt + \gamma \, dB_2,
\end{aligned}
\tag{12.35}
$$

in which $dB_1, dB_2 \sim N(0, dt)$ are assumed to be independent for simplicity, although this assumption can be easily relaxed. In the first equation y_t follows geometric Brownian motion whilst in the second equation $\ln \sigma_t$ follows an Ornstein-Uhlenbeck process. Estimation of this model is more involved than the previous continuous time models because not only are the data observed discretely but the volatility series σ_t is latent.

To estimate the parameters of (12.35), it is necessary to have at least four moments, the dimension of the parameter space. Consider the auxiliary model obtained by discretising (12.35) with the time interval $\Delta t = 1$

$$
\begin{aligned}
\ln y_t - \ln y_{t-1} &= \mu_\Delta + \sigma_t v_{1,t} \\
\ln \sigma_t^2 - \ln \sigma_{t-1}^2 &= \alpha_\Delta(\kappa_\Delta - \ln \sigma_{t-1}^2) + \gamma_\Delta v_{2,t},
\end{aligned}
\tag{12.36}
$$

in which $v_{i,t} \sim N(0, 1)$. The parameter μ_Δ is estimated as

$$
\widehat{\mu}_\Delta = \frac{1}{T-1} \sum_{t=2}^{T} (\ln y_t - \ln y_{t-1}).
\tag{12.37}
$$

To estimate the volatility parameters, consider transforming the first equation in (12.36) as

$$
r_t^2 = \ln(\ln y_t - \ln y_{t-1} - \mu_\Delta)^2 = \ln \sigma_t^2 + \ln v_{1,t}^2,
$$

which represents the logarithm of the mean-adjusted squared return. Use this expression to substitute out $\ln \sigma_t^2$ and $\ln \sigma_{t-1}^2$ in the second equation in (12.36)

$$
r_t^2 - \ln v_{1,t}^2 - r_{t-1}^2 + \ln v_{1,t-1}^2 = \alpha_\Delta(\kappa_\Delta - r_{t-1}^2 + \ln v_{1,t-1}^2) + \gamma_\Delta v_{2,t},
$$

which is simplified as

$$
r_t^2 = \delta_0 + \delta_1 r_{t-1}^2 + \delta_2 \eta_t.
\tag{12.38}
$$

The parameters $\{\delta_0, \delta_1, \delta_2\}$ are functions of the parameters $\{\alpha_\Delta, \kappa_\Delta, \gamma_\Delta\}$, and η_t is a disturbance term which has a moving average structure since it combines $v_{2,t}$, $\ln v_{i,t}^2$ and $\ln v_{i,t-1}^2$. Estimates of $\{\delta_0, \delta_1, \delta_2\}$ can be obtained by regressing r_t^2 on a constant and r_{t-1}^2, with the estimate of δ_2 obtained from the standard deviation of the ordinary least squares residuals corresponding to η_t.

Indirect Inference

The indirect estimator of (12.35) is based on the following steps:

Step 1: Compute $\widehat{\beta}$, the parameters of the auxiliary model using the observed data. The parameter $\widehat{\mu}_\Delta$ is estimated using equation (12.37) and $\widehat{\delta}_0$, $\widehat{\delta}_1$ and $\widehat{\delta}_2$ are estimated using equation (12.38). Also compute the optimal weighting matrix W_T.

Step 2: Choose starting values for $\theta = \{\mu, \alpha, \kappa, \gamma\}$ and a small time step, say $\Delta t = 0.1$ to generate continuous time data using

$$\ln y_{s,t+\Delta t} - \ln y_{s,t} = \mu_{(0)}\Delta t + \sigma_{s,t+\Delta t}u_{1,t+\Delta t}$$
$$\ln \sigma^2_{s,t+\Delta t} - \ln \sigma^2_{s,t} = \alpha_{(0)}(\kappa_{(0)} - \ln \sigma^2_{s,t})\Delta t + \gamma_{(0)}u_{2,t+\Delta t},$$

in which $u_{i,t} \sim N(0, \Delta t)$. Let the length of the simulated series be $S = T \times K$.

Step 3: Generate discrete time data $y_{s,1}, y_{s,2}, \cdots, y_{s,N}$, by choosing every $1/\Delta t$ observations from the simulated continuous time series.

Step 4: Compute the parameter estimates of the auxiliary model based on the simulated data $\widehat{\beta}_s = \{\widehat{\mu}_{\Delta,s}, \widehat{\delta}_{0,s}, \widehat{\delta}_{1,s}, \widehat{\delta}_{2,s}\}$, where

$$\widehat{\mu}_{\Delta,s} = \frac{1}{S}\sum_{t=1}^{S}(\ln y_{s,t} - \ln y_{s,t-1}),$$

and $\widehat{\delta}_{0,s}, \widehat{\delta}_{1,s}, \widehat{\delta}_{2,s}$ are the ordinary least squares estimates obtained by estimating the regression equation

$$r^2_{s,t} = \delta_0 + \delta_1 r^2_{s,t-1} + \delta_2 \eta_{s,t},$$

where $r_{s,t} = \ln y_{s,t} - \ln y_{s,t-1} - \widehat{\mu}_{\Delta,s}$.

Step 5: Define the moment conditions

$$G'_S(\theta, \widehat{\beta}) = \begin{bmatrix} \widehat{\mu}_s - \widehat{\mu} & \widehat{\delta}_{0,s} - \widehat{\delta}_0 & \widehat{\delta}_{1,s} - \widehat{\delta}_1 & \widehat{\delta}^2_{2,s} - \widehat{\delta}^2_2 \end{bmatrix}.$$

Step 6: Choose $\theta = \{\mu, \alpha, \kappa, \gamma\}$ to satisfy

$$\widehat{\theta} = \arg\min_{\theta} \frac{1}{2} G'_S(\theta, \widehat{\beta})W_T^{-1}G_S(\theta, \widehat{\beta}).$$

The quality of the approximation of the auxiliary model can also be improved by estimating (12.38) with a first-order moving average disturbance for η_t. This modification to computing the empirical moments does not change the consistency properties of the indirect estimator, but it can improve its efficiency in small samples.

An alternative auxiliary model is not to transform the auxiliary model into the regression equation (12.38), but treat

$$\ln(\ln y_t - \ln y_{t-1} - \mu_\Delta)^2 = \ln \sigma^2_t + \ln v^2_{1,t},$$
$$\ln \sigma^2_t - \ln \sigma^2_{t-1} = \alpha_\Delta(\kappa_\Delta - \ln \sigma^2_{t-1}) + \gamma_\Delta v_{2,t},$$

as a state-space model where the first equation is the measurement equation and the second equation is the state equation. This model can be estimated by maximum likelihood using a Kalman filter (see Chapter 15), first with the actual data $(\widehat{\beta})$ and second with the simulated data $(\widehat{\beta}_s)$, with the indirect estimates of the stochastic volatility model (θ) obtained by equating the two sets of parameter estimates of the auxiliary (state-space) model. However, this involves a nonlinear estimation problem at each iteration of the indirect algorithm to compute $(\widehat{\beta}_s)$, which is circumvented by using the EMM estimator. This alternative approach requires estimating the state-space model using the actual data $(\widehat{\beta})$. The gradients of the likelihood of the Kalman filter then act as the moments in the EMM algorithm which are simply evaluated at the parameter estimates of the Kalman filter $(\widehat{\beta})$ but using the simulated data. Bayesian methods have also featured prominently in the estimation of stochastic volatility models (Jacquier, Polson and Rossi, 2002, 2004; Chib, Nardari and Shephard, 2002).

12.7   Applications

Consider the following one-factor model of the business cycle proposed by Stock and Watson (2005)

$$
\begin{aligned}
y_{i,t} &= \lambda_i s_t + \sigma_i z_{i,t}, \qquad i = 1, 2, \cdots, N, \\
s_t &= \phi s_{t-1} + \eta_t, \\
z_{i,t}, \eta_t &\sim iid\, N(0, 1),
\end{aligned}
\tag{12.39}
$$

in which $y_{i,t}$ is an indicator, s_t is the business cycle factor and the unknown parameters are

$$
\theta = \{\lambda_1, \lambda_{2,}, \cdots, \lambda_N, \sigma_1, \sigma_2, \cdots, \sigma_N, \phi\}.
$$

The distinguishing feature of the model is that data are available on the indicators, $y_{i,t}$, but not on the business cycle so s_t is treated as a latent process.

In this application an EMM estimator is devised to estimate the parameters in (12.39). To investigate the properties of the estimator, a Monte Carlo experiment is presented initially, followed by an empirical application where the model is applied to Australian business cycle data. For the class of latent factor models in (12.39) it is shown in Chapter 15 that the parameters can be estimated directly by maximum likelihood methods using a Kalman filter. However, this is not the case for generalisations of the latent process in (12.39) that allow for either conditional volatility (Diebold and Nerlove, 1989), or Markov switching (Kim, 1994), or both (Diebold and Rudebusch, 1996). For these extensions it is necessary to use simulation methods such as EMM.

12.7.1 Finite Sample Properties

To motivate the choice of the auxiliary model to estimate the latent-factor business cycle model in (12.39) by EMM, write the first equation of (12.39) as

$$(1 - \phi L) y_{i,t} = \lambda_i (1 - \phi L) s_t + \sigma_i (1 - \phi L) z_{i,t}$$
$$(1 - \phi L) y_{i,t} = \lambda_i \eta_t + \sigma_i (1 - \phi L) z_{i,t}, \qquad i = 1, 2, \cdots, N, \qquad (12.40)$$

where the second step uses the second equation of (12.39). The latent factor model is now expressed as a system of N univariate ARMA(1,1) equations.

Following the earlier discussion concerning the choice of the auxiliary model to estimate a MA(1) model, an AR(2) model represents a suitable specification for the auxiliary model

$$y_{i,t} = \rho_{i,0} + \rho_{i,1} y_{i,t-1} + \rho_{i,2} y_{i,t-2} + \sigma_{v,i} v_{i,t}, \qquad i = 1, 2, \cdots, N, \qquad (12.41)$$

in which the parameters of the auxiliary model are $\beta = \{\rho_{i,0}, \rho_{i,1}, \rho_{i,2}, \sigma_{v,i}\}$ and $v_{i,t} \sim iid\ N(0, 1)$. The auxiliary log-likelihood function at time t for the ith indicator is

$$\ln l_{t,i}(\beta) = -\frac{1}{2} \ln 2\pi - \frac{1}{2} \ln \sigma_{v,i}^2 - \frac{1}{2} \frac{1}{\sigma_{v,i}^2} (y_{i,t} - \rho_{i,0} - \rho_{i,1} y_{i,t-1} - \rho_{i,2} y_{i,t-2})^2.$$

Differentiating with respect to the auxiliary parameters gives the gradients for $i = 1, 2, \cdots, N$

$$\frac{\partial \ln l_{t,i}(\beta)}{\partial \rho_{i,1}} = \frac{1}{\sigma_{v,i}^2} (y_{i,t} - \rho_{i,0} - \rho_{i,1} y_{i,t-1} - \rho_{i,2} y_{i,t-2})$$
$$\frac{\partial \ln l_{t,i}(\beta)}{\partial \rho_{i,1}} = \frac{1}{\sigma_{v,i}^2} (y_{i,t} - \rho_{i,0} - \rho_{i,1} y_{i,t-1} - \rho_{i,2} y_{i,t-2}) y_{i,t-1}$$
$$\frac{\partial \ln l_{t,i}(\beta)}{\partial \rho_{i,2}} = \frac{1}{\sigma_{v,i}^2} (y_{i,t} - \rho_{i,0} - \rho_{i,1} y_{i,t-1} - \rho_{i,2} y_{i,t-2}) y_{i,t-2}$$
$$\frac{\partial \ln l_{t,i}(\beta)}{\partial \sigma_{v,i}^2} = -\frac{1}{2\sigma_{v,i}^2} + \frac{1}{2\sigma_{v,i}^4} (y_{i,t} - \rho_{i,0} - \rho_{i,1} y_{i,t-1} - \rho_{i,2} y_{i,t-2})^2 .$$

$$(12.42)$$

The log-likelihood function for a sample of size T and the N auxiliary models, is given by

$$\ln L_T(\beta) = \frac{1}{T-2} \sum_{t=3}^{T} \sum_{i=1}^{N} \ln l_{t,i}.$$

The log-likelihood function separates into N components because the information matrix is block-diagonal and therefore each of the N AR(2) models are estimated by ordinary least squares separately.

To investigate the ability of the EMM estimator to recover the population parameters, the following Monte Carlo experiment is performed. The DGP has $N = 6$ indicators with parameter values θ given by $\lambda_{(0)} = \{1, 0.8, 0.7, 0.5, -0.5, -1\}$, $\sigma_{(0)} = \{0.2, 0.4, 0.6, 0.8, 1.0, 1.2\}$ and $\phi_{(0)} = 0.8$, a total of 13 parameters. The model in (12.39) is simulated for a sample of size $T = 600$, which corresponds to the length of data used in the empirical application.

The first step of the EMM algorithm is to estimate the auxiliary model based on the $N = 6$ univariate AR(2) models in (12.41). The estimated auxiliary models are

$$
\begin{aligned}
y_{1,t} &= 0.019 + 0.801 y_{1,t-1} + 0.012 y_{1,t-2} + 0.988 \widehat{v}_{1,t} \\
y_{2,t} &= 0.023 + 0.660 y_{2,t-1} + 0.101 y_{2,t-2} + 0.838 \widehat{v}_{2,t} \\
y_{3,t} &= 0.021 + 0.533 y_{3,t-1} + 0.180 y_{3,t-2} + 1.009 \widehat{v}_{3,t} \\
y_{4,t} &= 0.036 + 0.345 y_{4,t-1} + 0.209 y_{4,t-2} + 1.117 \widehat{v}_{4,t} \\
y_{5,t} &= -0.017 + 0.256 y_{5,t-1} + 0.208 y_{5,t-2} + 1.457 \widehat{v}_{5,t} \\
y_{6,t} &= -0.029 + 0.423 y_{6,t-1} + 0.210 y_{6,t-2} + 2.787 \widehat{v}_{6,t} ,
\end{aligned}
\tag{12.43}
$$

where the total number of estimated parameters is 24. Also computed is the (24×24) weighting matrix W_T which is the average of the outer product of the gradients in (12.42) evaluated using the auxiliary parameter estimates in (12.43).

The first iteration of the EMM estimator involves choosing starting values of the parameters in (12.39) and simulating the model to generate a simulated sample of $K \times T = 10 \times 600 = 6000$ observations. The iterations continue by solving

$$
\widehat{\theta} = \arg\min_{\theta} \frac{1}{2} G_S'(\theta, \widehat{\beta}) W_T^{-1} G_S(\theta, \widehat{\beta}) ,
\tag{12.44}
$$

where $G_S(\theta, \widehat{\beta})$ is evaluated using the estimates of the parameters of the auxiliary models given in (12.43) by replacing $y_{i,t}$ in (12.42) with the simulated data and averaging the gradients in (12.42) over the $S = 6000$ simulated observations. The algorithm converges in 16 iterations. The estimated model with standard errors in parentheses is

$$
y_{1,t} = \underset{(0.051)}{0.958} \widehat{s}_t + \underset{(0.127)}{0.224} \widehat{z}_{1,t} \qquad\qquad y_{2,t} = \underset{(0.049)}{0.741} \widehat{s}_t + \underset{(0.056)}{0.418} \widehat{z}_{2,t} ,
$$

$$
y_{3,t} = \underset{(0.052)}{0.689} \widehat{s}_t + \underset{(0.050)}{0.620} \widehat{z}_{3,t} \qquad\qquad y_{4,t} = \underset{(0.047)}{0.503} \widehat{s}_t + \underset{(0.038)}{0.822} \widehat{z}_{4,t} ,
$$

$$
y_{5,t} = \underset{(0.046)}{-0.478} \widehat{s}_t + \underset{(0.038)}{0.973} \widehat{z}_{5,t} , \qquad y_{6,t} = \underset{(0.075)}{-0.937} \widehat{s}_t + \underset{(0.063)}{1.205} \widehat{z}_{6,t} ,
$$

$$
\widehat{s}_t = \underset{(0.025)}{0.828} \widehat{s}_{t-1} + \widehat{\eta}_t .
\tag{12.45}
$$

The EMM parameter estimates in (12.45) compare favourably with the true population parameter values. The value of the objective function at the minimum is $Q(\widehat{\theta}) = 0.0023$, which produces a Hansen-Sargan J test statistic of the over-identifying restrictions given by

$$J_{HS} = 2T Q_T(\widehat{\theta}) = 2 \times 600 \times 0.0023 = 2.8180 .$$

As the number of over-identifying restrictions is $24 - 13 = 11$, the p-value of the test statistic using the χ^2_{11} distribution is 0.9929, a result that provides strong support for the estimated model.

12.7.2 Empirical Properties

The EMM estimator of the latent factor business cycle model in (12.39) is applied to Australian business cycle data using the AR(2) auxiliary model developed in the previous section. The data are monthly beginning September 1959 and ending September 2009. Six indicators are chosen corresponding to the indicators used to construct the coincident index: employment, $y_{1,t}$, GDP, $y_{2,t}$, household income, $y_{3,t}$, industrial production, $y_{4,t}$, retail sales, $y_{5,t}$, and the unemployment rate, $y_{6,t}$. When necessary, quarterly data are converted to monthly data by linear interpolation over the quarter. All indicators are expressed as quarterly percentage growth rates by computing the quarterly span of the natural logarithm of the raw series. In the case of the unemployment rate, this series is inverted to make it move pro-cyclically over the business cycle. Finally, each growth rate is standardised by subtracting the sample mean and dividing by the sample standard deviation. The total sample after computing quarterly growth rates is $T = 598$.

A measure of the business cycle commonly used in practice is the coincident index, which is a weighted average of the 6 indicators. The correlations between the six indicators and the quarterly percentage growth rate of the coincident index are

Coincident index	Employ.	GDP	Income	Prod.	Sales	Unemp.
	0.833	0.830	0.081	0.611	0.199	0.795

All series move positively with the coincident index, although the correlation with household income is relatively low at 0.081.

As the data are standardised, the auxiliary model is an AR(2) without a constant, resulting in a total of 18 parameters. The starting values of θ to solve (12.44) are chosen from a uniform distribution with the exception of ϕ, which is constrained using the hyperbolic tangent function to ensure that it is within the unit circle. Once the algorithm has converged, this restriction is relaxed and the estimation repeated in order to compute the standard error on $\widehat{\phi}$. The length of the simulated series in the EMM algorithm is chosen as

$K \times T = 30 \times 598 = 17940$ observations. The estimated latent factor model, with standard errors in parentheses, is

Employment : $y_{1,t} = \underset{(0.048)}{0.470}\widehat{s}_t + \underset{(0.053)}{0.353}\widehat{z}_{1,t}$

GDP : $y_{2,t} = \underset{(0.015)}{0.338}\widehat{s}_t + \underset{(0.049)}{0.010}\widehat{z}_{2,t}$

Household Income : $y_{3,t} = \underset{(0.015)}{0.376}\widehat{s}_t + \underset{(0.002)}{0.009}\widehat{z}_{3,t}$

Industrial Production : $y_{4,t} = \underset{(0.150)}{0.281}\widehat{s}_t + \underset{(0.012)}{0.147}\widehat{z}_{4,t}$

Retail Sales : $y_{5,t} = \underset{(0.076)}{0.548}\widehat{s}_t + \underset{(0.093)}{0.503}\widehat{z}_{5,t}$

Unemployment Rate : $y_{6,t} = \underset{(0.031)}{0.586}\widehat{s}_t + \underset{(0.091)}{0.002}\widehat{z}_{6,t}$

Factor : $\widehat{s}_t = \underset{(0.028)}{0.775}\widehat{s}_{t-1} + \widehat{\eta}_t$.

The loadings on each indicator are similar with values ranging from 0.281 for industrial production to 0.586 for the unemployment rate. The business cycle exhibits a strong positive correlation structure with $\widehat{\phi} = 0.775$.

The value of the objective function at the minimum is $Q(\widehat{\theta}) = 0.0803$, resulting in the Hansen-Sargan J test of the $18 - 13 = 5$ over-identifying restrictions given by

$$J_{HS} = 2T Q(\widehat{\theta}) = 2 \times 598 \times 0.0803 = 96.085.$$

This value of J_{HS} produces a p-value of 0.000 using the χ_5^2 distribution, suggesting some evidence of misspecification. Four possible sources of misspecification are: (i) the number of latent factors is greater than one; (ii) the dynamics of the latent factor is of a higher order; (iii) the disturbance terms $z_{i,t}$ are not white noise but also exhibit some autocorrelation; (iv) additional dynamic structures including conditional volatility and Markov Switching which may affect the latent factor. The first three types of misspecification are investigated in Chapter 15. Markov switching is discussed in Chapter 19 and conditional volatility is discussed in Chapter 20.

12.8   Exercises

(1) Method of Moments Estimation of a MA(1)

Program files   sim_mom.*

Simulate a MA(1) model

$$y_t = u_t - \theta u_{t-1}, \qquad u_t \sim iid\ N(0, 1),$$

for a sample size of $T = 250$ observations with $\theta_0 = 0.5$.

(a) Estimate the model using the method of moments estimator in equation (12.2) and compare the parameter estimate with θ_0.
(b) Repeat part (a) for samples of size $T = \{500, 1000, 2000\}$. Compare the parameter estimate with θ_0 in each case and discuss the statistical properties of the method of moments estimator.

(2) Computing Autocorrelation Coefficients by Simulation

Program files   sim_accuracy.*

Simulate the MA(1) model

$$y_t = u_t - \theta u_{t-1}, \qquad u_t \sim iid\ N(0, 1),$$

for a sample size of $T = 250$ observations with $\theta_0 = 0.5$.
(a) Compute the true AR(1) parameter ρ_0 from θ_0.
(b) Simulate the MA(1) model and compute the first-order autocorrelation coefficient using the simulated data based on θ_0 for simulated series of length $S = T \times K$, with $T = 250$ and $K = \{1, 2, 3, 4, 5, 10, 100\}$. Compare the results with the theoretical autocorrelation parameter in part (a) and hence reproduce Table 12.1.
(c) Repeat part (b) for $\theta_{(0)} = 0.8$ and $\theta_{(0)} = -0.5$.

(3) Simulation Estimation of a MA(1)

Program files   sim_malindirect.*, sim_malemm.*

This exercise is concerned with reproducing the Monte Carlo results presented in Gouriéroux, Monfort and Renault (1993, Table I, p.S98).
(a) Simulate a MA(1) model

$$y_t = u_t - \theta u_{t-1}, \qquad u_t \sim iid\ N(0, 1),$$

for a sample size of $T = 250$ observations with $\theta_0 = 0.5$.
(b) Estimate the model using the indirect estimator and the EMM estimator. Choose as the auxiliary models an AR(1) model, an AR(2) model and an AR(3) model.
(c) Repeat parts (a) and (b) 1000 times and compare the sampling properties of the indirect and EMM estimators for each auxiliary model. Compare the results with Tables 12.2 and 12.3.

(4) Over-identification Test of a MA(1)

Program files   sim_maloverid.*

(a) Simulate a MA(1) model

$$y_t = u_t - \theta u_{t-1}, \qquad u_t \sim iid\, N(0, 1),$$

for a sample size of $T = 250$ observations with $\theta_0 = 0.5$.
(b) Perform the over-identification test of the true model based on the EMM estimator using the AR(1), AR(2) and AR(3) auxiliary models.
(c) Compare the results with Table 12.4.

(5) Simulating a Stochastic Differential Equation

Program files   sim_brown.*

Consider the stochastic differential equation

$$dy = \mu\, dt + \sigma\, dB, \qquad dB \sim N(0, dt),$$

in which $\theta_{(0)} = \{\mu = 0, \sigma = 1\}$ are parameters.
(a) Generate a minute time series of length $T = 14400$ (10 days), by simulating the model for $\Delta t = 1/60$. Compare the results with panel (a) of Figure 12.2.
(b) Generate a 10 minute series by extracting every 10th observation, an 'hourly' series by extracting every 60th observation and a 'daily' time series by extracting every 1440th observation. Compare the results with panels (b), (c) and (d) of Figure 12.2.
(c) Repeat parts (a) and (b) using as parameters $\mu_{(0)} = 0.05$ and $\sigma = 1$.
(d) Repeat parts (a) and (b) using as parameters $\mu_{(0)} = 0.00$ and $\sigma = 2$.

(6) Brownian Motion

Program files   sim_brownind.*, sim_brownemm.*

Consider estimating the parameters $\theta = \{\mu, \sigma\}$ of the stochastic differential equation

$$dy = \mu\, dt + \sigma\, dB, \qquad dB \sim N(0, dt).$$

Let the sample size be $T = 500$ and the true parameter values be $\theta_0 = \{\mu_0 = 0.5, \sigma_0 = 0.5\}$.
(a) Compute the indirect estimates of the parameters using simulated samples of size $S = TK$ where $K = \{1/\Delta t, 2/\Delta t\}$ and $\Delta t = 0.1$. Compare the finite sample properties of the indirect estimator using 1000 replications.
(b) Repeat part (a) using the EMM estimator.

(7) Geometric Brownian Motion

Program files `sim_geobrind.*`

This exercise reproduces the Monte Carlo results presented in Gouriéroux, Monfort and Renault (1993, Table II, p.S101). Consider estimating the parameters $\theta = \{\mu, \sigma\}$ of

$$dy = \mu y\, dt + \sigma y\, dB\,, \qquad dB \sim N(0, dt)\,.$$

Let the sample size be $T = 150$ and the true parameter values be $\theta_0 = \{\mu_0 = 0.2, \sigma_0 = 0.5\}$.

(a) Compute the indirect estimates of the parameters using simulated samples of size $S = TK$ where $K = \{1/\Delta t, 2/\Delta t\}$ and $\Delta t = 0.1$.

(b) Compare the finite sample properties of the resultant estimators in part (a) using 1000 replications.

(8) Ornstein-Uhlenbeck Process

Program files `sim_ouind.*`

This exercise reproduces the Monte Carlo results presented in Gouriéroux, Monfort and Renault (1993, Table III, p.S103). The Ornstein-Uhlenbeck process is given by

$$dy = \alpha(\kappa - y)\, dt + \sigma\, dB\,, \qquad dB \sim N(0, dt)\,.$$

Let the sample size be $T = 250$ and the true parameters values be $\theta_0 = \{\alpha_0 = 0.1, \kappa_0 = 0.8, \sigma_0 = 0.06\}$. An exact discretisation is

$$y_t = \alpha(1 - \exp[-\kappa]) + \exp[-\kappa]y_{t-1} + \sigma \left[\frac{1 - \exp[-2\kappa]}{2\kappa} \right] u_t,$$

in which $u_t \sim N(0, \Delta t)$. Choose as the auxiliary model

$$y_t = \alpha\kappa + (1 - \kappa)y_{t-1} + \sigma v_t\,, \qquad v_t \sim N(0, 1)\,.$$

(a) Compute the indirect estimates of the parameters using simulated samples of size $S = TK$ where $K = \{10/\Delta t, 20/\Delta t\}$ and $\Delta t = 0.1$.

(b) Compare the finite sample properties of the resultant estimators using 1000 replications.

(9) Business Cycles

Program files `sim_bcycle.*,sim_stockwatson.*,`
Data files `bcycle.*`

(a) Simulate the latent factor business cycle model

$$y_{i,t} = \lambda_i s_t + \sigma_i z_{i,t}, \qquad i = 1, 2, \cdots, 6$$
$$s_t = \phi s_{t-1} + \eta_t$$
$$z_{i,t}, \eta_t \sim iid\ N(0, 1),$$

for a sample of size $T = 600$ and parameter values

$$\lambda_0 = \{1, 0.8, 0.7, 0.5, -0.5, -1\}$$
$$\sigma_0 = \{0.2, 0.4, 0.6, 0.8, 1.0, 1.2\},$$

and $\phi_0 = 0.8$. Choosing the auxiliary model as a set of $N = 6$ AR(2) equations, estimate the model by EMM and compare the parameter estimates with the true values. Discuss other choices of auxiliary models.

(b) Estimate the latent factor business cycle model in part (a) using data on employment, GDP, household income, industrial production, retail sales and the unemployment rate from September 1959 to September 2009 for Australia. Comment on the estimated model and perform an overall test of the specification of the estimated model.

PART FOUR

Stationary Time Series

13 Linear Time Series Models

13.1 Introduction

The maximum likelihood framework presented in Part ONE is now applied to estimating and testing a general class of dynamic models known as stationary time series models. Both univariate and multivariate models are discussed. The dynamics enter the model in one of two ways. The first is through lags of the variables, referred to as the autoregressive part, and the second is through lags of the disturbance term, referred to as the moving average part. In the case where the dynamics of a single variable are being modelled, these models are referred to as autoregressive moving average (ARMA) models. In the multivariate case, where the dynamics of multiple variables are modelled, these models are referred to as vector autoregressive moving average (VARMA) models. Jointly, these models are called stationary time series models where stationarity refers to the types of dynamics allowed for. The case of nonstationary dynamics is discussed in Part FIVE.

The specification of dynamics through the inclusion of lagged variables and lagged disturbances is not new. It was discussed in Part TWO in the context of the linear regression model in Chapter 5 and more directly in Chapter 7 where autoregressive and moving-average dynamics were specified in the context of the autocorrelated regression model. In fact, a one-to-one relationship exists between the VARMA class of models investigated in this chapter and the structural class of regression models of Part TWO, where the VARMA model is interpreted as the reduced form of a structural model. However, as the VARMA class of models is widely used in applied econometric modelling, it is appropriate to discuss the properties of these models separately.

The VARMA model includes an important special case distinguished by dynamics that are just driven by the lags of the variables themselves. This special case is known as a vector autoregression, or VAR model, which was first investigated by Sims (1980) using United States data on the nominal interest rate, money, prices and output. Given the widespread use of VARs in empirical work, a large part of this chapter is devoted to understanding their properties.

Despite their apparent generality, VARs rely on implicit identification assumptions that impose very strict relationships among the variables. These restrictions are identified here and then generalised in Chapter 14 where the VAR class of models is extended to another class of models known as structural vector autoregressive, or SVAR, models. Another potential problem of VARs is the dimension of the specified system. In practice, VARs are specified for relatively small systems as estimation involves many unknown parameters. One solution to this problem is to use economic theory to impose restrictions on the dynamics of a VAR. Some examples of this strategy are given at the end of the chapter. Another approach is discussed in Chapter 15 where the dimensionality problem is reduced by specifying the model in terms of latent factors and model parameters are estimated using a Kalman filter. An alternative approach, not treated here, is to adopt a Bayesian strategy by specifying priors on the VAR parameters (Banbura, Giannone and Reichlin, 2010; Koop, 2012).

13.2   Time Series Properties of Data

Figure 13.1 gives plots from January 1960 to December 1998 of key United States macroeconomic variables in which r_t is the interest rate, lm_t is the logarithm of money, lp_t is the logarithm of prices and lo_t is the logarithm of output, so that $y_t = [r_t, lm_t, lp_t, lo_t]'$. Money, price and output all display smooth upward trends, whereas the interest rate tends to display relatively greater volatility over the sample with a positive trend in the first part of the period followed by a negative trend in the second part. Taking first differences of the variables (column 2), $\Delta y_t = y_t - y_{t-1}$, expresses the variables in monthly changes or monthly growth rates. The times series of the differenced variables do not have trends and exhibit noisy behaviour relative to their levels. Money in particular displays very strong seasonal behaviour. By taking 12th differences (column 3), $\Delta_{12} y_t = y_t - y_{t-12}$, the variables are expressed in annual changes or annual growth rates. These transformed variables still do not exhibit trends but now reveal stronger cyclical behaviour over the sample period.

To understand the dynamic properties of the variables in Figure 13.1, Table 13.1 gives the autocorrelation functions (ACF) and partial autocorrelation functions (PACF) of each variable. The ACF and PACF at lag k are the parameter estimates on the explanatory variable y_{t-k} in each of the following regressions

ACF: Regress y_t on $\{const, y_{t-k}\}$
PACF: Regress y_t on $\{const, y_{t-1}, y_{t-2}, \cdots, y_{t-k}\}$.

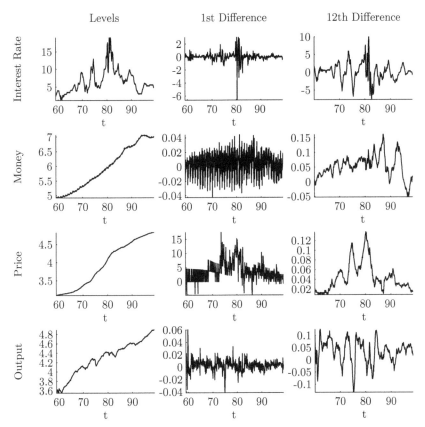

Figure 13.1. Plots of United States monthly macroeconomic data, January 1960 to December 1998. The interest rate is the nominal interest rate expressed as an annual percentage, money is the logarithm of nominal money, price is the logarithm of the CPI, and output is the logarithm of industrial production.

The ACF at lag k is the estimated coefficient on y_{t-k} in the linear regression of y_t on a constant and y_{t-k}, while the PACF is the estimated coefficient on y_{t-k} in the linear regression of y_t on a constant and $y_{t-1}, y_{t-2}, \cdots, y_{t-k}$.

The ACFs of the levels of the variables in Table 13.1 show very slow decay, which is representative of the strong trends exhibited by these variables. The PACFs reveal that it is the first lag that is the most important in explaining y_t. The ACF and PACF of the first-differenced variables reveal quite different dynamics, with output dynamics dominated by the first lag, whereas for the other variables higher-order lags are important. The ACF of the 12th-differenced variables decay slowly, which is consistent with the relatively smooth time series properties of these variables given in Figure 13.1. The corresponding PACFs show the importance of higher-order lags in all of the variables.

Table 13.1. *Estimated ACF and PACF of United States macroeconomic data, January 1959 to December 1998: interest rate, r_t, the logarithm of money, lm_t, the logarithm of price, lp_t and logarithm of real output, lo_t*

	ACF				PACF			
Lag	r_t	lm_t	lp_t	lo_t	r_t	lm_t	lp_t	lo_t
				Level (y_t)				
1	0.98	1.00	1.00	1.00	0.98	1.00	1.00	1.00
2	0.95	1.00	1.00	1.00	−0.39	0.08	−0.56	−0.37
3	0.92	1.00	1.00	0.99	0.16	0.37	−0.28	−0.07
4	0.89	1.00	1.00	0.99	0.02	−0.20	−0.18	−0.05
5	0.87	1.00	1.00	0.99	0.09	0.15	−0.11	0.06
6	0.85	1.00	1.00	0.99	0.00	−0.06	−0.14	0.08
				1st Difference ($\Delta y_t = y_t - y_{t-1}$)				
1	0.37	−0.08	0.56	0.37	0.37	−0.08	0.56	0.37
2	−0.01	−0.36	0.51	0.20	−0.18	−0.37	0.28	0.07
3	−0.10	0.25	0.48	0.13	−0.04	0.20	0.18	0.05
4	−0.14	−0.02	0.45	0.03	−0.10	−0.15	0.11	−0.05
5	−0.09	−0.11	0.46	−0.06	−0.01	0.06	0.14	−0.08
6	−0.06	0.22	0.44	−0.02	−0.05	0.13	0.09	0.02
				12th Difference ($\Delta_{12} y_t = y_t - y_{t-12}$)				
1	0.92	0.98	0.99	0.96	0.92	0.98	0.99	0.96
2	0.79	0.96	0.98	0.90	−0.41	−0.32	−0.25	−0.37
3	0.67	0.93	0.97	0.83	0.17	0.01	−0.16	−0.17
4	0.58	0.90	0.96	0.74	0.08	−0.13	−0.02	−0.10
5	0.53	0.87	0.94	0.66	0.07	0.10	−0.01	−0.02
6	0.49	0.83	0.93	0.58	−0.07	−0.17	−0.08	0.03

13.3 Specification

From Chapter 7, the class of single equation linear regression models with an ARMA(p,q) disturbance is specified as

$$
\begin{aligned}
y_t &= \beta_0 + \beta_1 x_t + u_t \\
u_t &= \sum_{i=1}^{p} \rho_i u_{t-i} + v_t + \sum_{i=1}^{q} \delta_i v_{t-i} \\
v_t &\sim iid\ N(0, \sigma_v^2),
\end{aligned}
\tag{13.1}
$$

in which y_t is the dependent variable, x_t is the explanatory variable and v_t is the disturbance term. Consider a special case of this model by setting $\beta_1 = 0$ so that y_t is fully determined by its own dynamics

$$
y_t = \beta_0 + u_t = \mu + \sum_{i=1}^{p} \phi_i y_{t-i} + v_t + \sum_{i=1}^{q} \psi_i v_{t-i},
\tag{13.2}
$$

where $\mu = \beta_0 - \beta_0 \sum_{i=1}^{p} \rho_i$, $\phi_i = \rho_i$ and $\psi_i = \delta_i$. This model represents the univariate class of linear autoregressive moving average models with p autoregressive lags and q moving average lags, ARMA(p,q). The multivariate analogue of this model is known as the VARMA(p,q) model.

13.3.1   Univariate Model Classification

Some common specifications of the ARMA(p,q) model in (13.2) are

1. ARMA(0, 0) = White noise : $y_t = \mu + v_t$
2. ARMA(1, 0) = AR(1)   : $y_t = \mu + \phi_1 y_{t-1} + v_t$
3. ARMA(2, 0) = AR(2)   : $y_t = \mu + \phi_1 y_{t-1} + \phi_2 y_{t-2} + v_t$
4. ARMA(0, 1) = MA(1)   : $y_t = \mu + v_t + \psi_1 v_{t-1}$
5. ARMA(0, 2) = MA(2)   : $y_t = \mu + v_t + \psi_1 v_{t-1} + \psi_2 v_{t-2}$
6. ARMA(1, 1)   : $y_t = \mu + \phi_1 y_{t-1} + v_t + \psi_1 v_{t-1}$.

The ARMA(p,q) model in (13.2) is rewritten more conveniently in terms of lag polynomials

$$\phi_p(L) y_t = \mu + \psi_q(L) v_t, \qquad v_t \sim iid\ N(0, \sigma_v^2), \qquad (13.3)$$

in which

$$\begin{aligned} \phi_p(L) &= (1 - \phi_1 L - \phi_2 L^2 - \cdots - \phi_p L^p) \\ \psi_q(L) &= (1 + \psi_1 L + \psi_2 L^2 + \cdots + \psi_q L^q), \end{aligned} \qquad (13.4)$$

are polynomials in the lag operator L and $\{\mu, \phi_1, \cdots, \phi_p, \psi_1, \cdots, \psi_q, \sigma_v^2\}$ are unknown parameters. Appendix B contains further details on lag operators. This model provides a general framework to capture the dynamics of a univariate time series y_t. Some of the properties of these models are explored in the following example.

Example 13.1 Simulation Properties of an ARMA(2,2) Model
  Consider the ARMA(2,2) model

$$\begin{aligned} y_t &= \mu + \phi_1 y_{t-1} + \phi_2 y_{t-2} + v_t + \psi_1 v_{t-1} + \psi_2 v_{t-2} \\ v_t &\sim iid\ N(0, \sigma_v^2). \end{aligned}$$

The first column of Figure 13.2 gives plots of y_t obtained by simulating the model for alternative parameterisations. The relevant starting values for y_t are taken to be 0 and $\sigma_v^2 = 0.1$. The first 100 simulated values are discarded to reduce the dependence on the choice of starting values and the remaining $T = 200$ observations are used.
  Inspection of the time series tends not to reveal any clear patterns in the data, whereas inspection of the ACF and the PACF in the second and third columns, respectively, identify strong dynamical behaviour. The ACF for the AR(2)

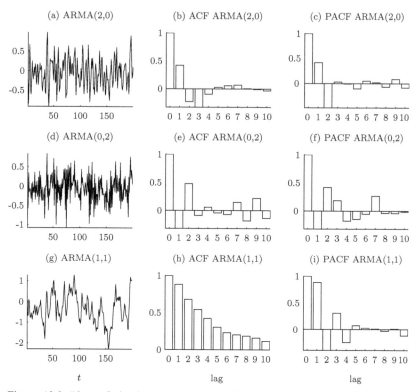

Figure 13.2. Plots of simulated series for AR(2), MA(2) and ARMA(1,1) models together with their autocorrelation (ACF) and partial autocorrelation (PACF) functions.

model exhibits damped oscillatory behaviour, while the PACF is characterised by spikes equal to the number of significant lags of y_t. The MA(2) model displays qualitatively the opposite pattern to the AR model, with the ACF now exhibiting spikes equal to the number of moving average lags and the PACF characterised by damped oscillatory behaviour. The ARMA(1,1) model is a combination of AR and MA models and exhibits both a damped ACF and PACF.   ☐

To understand the properties of the estimated ACF and PACF in Figure 13.2, the population moments of y_t are now derived. The population autocovariance function is defined as

$$\gamma_k = E[(y_t - E[y_t])(y_{t-k} - E[y_{t-k}])].$$ (13.5)

Setting $k = 0$ gives the variance. The related autocorrelation function is

$$\rho_k = \frac{\gamma_k}{\gamma_0}.$$ (13.6)

Example 13.2 Moments of ARMA Models

Consider the ARMA(p,q) model in equation (13.2). The first two moments for alternative parameterisations are as follows

MA(1)   Mean: $E[y_t] = E[\mu + v_t + \psi_1 v_{t-1}] = \mu$

         Variance: $\gamma_0 = \sigma_v^2(1 + \psi_1^2)$

         Covariance: $\gamma_k = \begin{cases} \sigma_v^2 \psi_1 & \text{if } k = \pm 1 \\ 0 & \text{otherwise.} \end{cases}$

MA(q)   Mean: $E[y_t] = \mu$

         Variance: $\gamma_0 = \sigma_v^2(1 + \psi_1^2 + \psi_2^2 + \cdots + \psi_q^2)$

         Covariance: $\gamma_k = \begin{cases} \sigma_v^2 \sum_{i=0}^{q-k} \psi_i \psi_{i+k} & \text{if } k = 1, 2, \cdots, q \\ 0 & k > q. \end{cases}$

AR(1)   Mean: $E[y_t] = E[\mu + \phi_1 y_{t-1}] = \dfrac{\mu}{1 - \phi_1}, \qquad |\phi_1| < 1$

         Variance: $\gamma_0 = \dfrac{\sigma_v^2}{1 - \phi_1^2}$

         Covariance: $\gamma_k = \dfrac{\sigma_v^2 \phi_1^k}{1 - \phi_1^2}, \quad k \geqslant 1,$

where use is made of the fact that $\psi_0 = 1$. The patterns of the empirical ACF and PACF illustrated in Figure 13.2 are consistent with these theoretical results. The condition $|\phi_1| < 1$ in the AR(1) model is needed to ensure that its moments exist.   □

The following example is of an AR(1) model where the condition $|\phi_1| < 1$ is not satisfied.

Example 13.3 Random Walk with Drift

Consider the model

$$y_t = \mu + y_{t-1} + v_t,$$

which is a special case of the AR(1) model with $\phi_1 = 1$. If it is assumed that $y_0 = 0$, then the first two moments are

     Mean: $E[y_t] = t\mu$
     Variance: $\gamma_0 = t\sigma_v^2$
     Covariance: $\gamma_k = (t - k)\sigma_v^2.$

In contrast to the moments of the models in Example 13.2, the first two moments of the random walk with drift are now a function of t. The time series properties of y_t are characterised by an increasing trend ($\mu > 0$) and increasing volatility. In the special case of a random walk without drift ($\mu = 0$), the second moment of y_t is still a function of t even though its mean is zero.   □

13.3.2   *Multivariate Model Classification*

A natural extension of the univariate ARMA class of models is one in which y_t represents a vector of N time series. Let Φ_i and Ψ_i be $(N \times N)$ matrices

$$
\Phi_i = \begin{bmatrix} \phi_{i,1,1} & \cdots & \phi_{i,1,N} \\ \vdots & \ddots & \vdots \\ \phi_{i,N,1} & \cdots & \phi_{i,N,N} \end{bmatrix}, \quad \Psi_i = \begin{bmatrix} \psi_{i,1,1} & \cdots & \psi_{i,1,N} \\ \vdots & \ddots & \vdots \\ \psi_{i,N,1} & \cdots & \psi_{i,N,N} \end{bmatrix}, \quad (13.7)
$$

in which $\phi_{i,j,k}$ is the autoregressive parameter at lag i in equation j on variable k and $\psi_{i,j,k}$ is the corresponding moving-average parameter. The multivariate analogue of the ARMA(p,q) model in (13.2) is the vector autoregressive model VARMA(p,q)

$$
y_t = \mu + \sum_{i=1}^{p} \Phi_i y_{t-i} + v_t + \sum_{i=1}^{q} \Psi_i v_{t-i}, \qquad v_t \sim iid\ N(0, V),
$$

$$(13.8)$$

in which v_t is an N dimensional disturbance vector with zero mean vector and $(N \times N)$ covariance matrix V and $\{\mu, \Phi_1, \Phi_2, \cdots, \Phi_p, \Psi_1, \Psi_2, \cdots, \Psi_q, V\}$ are unknown parameters. Using lag operators, the VARMA(p,q) class of model is represented as

$$
\Phi_p(L)y_t = \mu + \Psi_q(L)v_t, \qquad v_t \sim iid\ N(0, V), \qquad (13.9)
$$

in which

$$
\begin{aligned}
\Phi_p(L) &= I - \Phi_1 L - \Phi_2 L^2 - \cdots - \Phi_p L^p \\
\Psi_q(L) &= I + \Psi_1 L + \Psi_2 L^2 + \cdots + \Psi_q L^q,
\end{aligned} \qquad (13.10)
$$

are matrix polynomials in the lag operator L.

An important special case of the VARMA model is one in which there are p autoregressive lags and no moving-average lags, $q = 0$. This special case is known as a VAR(p) model

$$
y_t = \mu + \Phi_1 y_{t-1} + \cdots + \Phi_p y_{t-p} + v_t. \qquad (13.11)
$$

A VAR has the property that each variable is expressed as a function of its own lags and the lags of all of the other variables in the system, with the result that the lag structure on all variables in all equations is the same. Thus, the right-hand side variables in each equation in a VAR are identical.

Example 13.4 VAR(1) Model
A trivariate ($N = 3$) VAR with one lag is

$$
\begin{aligned}
y_{1,t} &= \mu_1 + \phi_{1,1,1} y_{1,t-1} + \phi_{1,1,2} y_{2,t-1} + \phi_{1,1,3} y_{3,t-1} + v_{1,t} \\
y_{2,t} &= \mu_2 + \phi_{1,2,1} y_{1,t-1} + \phi_{1,2,2} y_{2,t-1} + \phi_{1,2,3} y_{3,t-1} + v_{2,t} \\
y_{3,t} &= \mu_3 + \phi_{1,3,1} y_{1,t-1} + \phi_{1,3,2} y_{2,t-1} + \phi_{1,3,3} y_{3,t-1} + v_{3,t}.
\end{aligned}
$$

In matrix notation, the model becomes

$$\begin{bmatrix} y_{1,t} \\ y_{2,t} \\ y_{3,t} \end{bmatrix} = \begin{bmatrix} \mu_1 \\ \mu_2 \\ \mu_3 \end{bmatrix} + \begin{bmatrix} \phi_{1,1,1} & \phi_{1,1,2} & \phi_{1,1,3} \\ \phi_{1,2,1} & \phi_{1,2,2} & \phi_{1,2,3} \\ \phi_{1,3,1} & \phi_{1,3,2} & \phi_{1,3,3} \end{bmatrix} \begin{bmatrix} y_{1,t-1} \\ y_{2,t-1} \\ y_{3,t-1} \end{bmatrix} + \begin{bmatrix} v_{1,t} \\ v_{2,t} \\ v_{3,t} \end{bmatrix},$$

or, more compactly,

$$y_t = \mu + \Phi_1 y_{t-1} + v_t.$$

This model contains three intercepts, nine autoregressive parameters and six parameters in the covariance matrix, V, for a total of 18 parameters. ☐

A second special case involves a VARMA model with q moving-average lags and no autoregressive lags, $p = 0$, known as a VMA(q) model

$$y_t = \mu + v_t + \Psi_1 v_{t-1} + \Psi_2 v_{t-2} + \cdots + \Psi_q v_{t-q}. \tag{13.12}$$

A VMA(q) has the property that each variable is expressed as a function of its own disturbance and the lags of all of the other disturbances in the system, with the lag structure on all disturbances in all equations being the same.

Example 13.5 VMA(2) Model
A trivariate ($N = 3$) VMA with two lags is

$$\begin{bmatrix} y_{1,t} \\ y_{2,t} \\ y_{3,t} \end{bmatrix} = \begin{bmatrix} \mu_1 \\ \mu_2 \\ \mu_3 \end{bmatrix} + \begin{bmatrix} v_{1,t} \\ v_{2,t} \\ v_{3,t} \end{bmatrix} + \begin{bmatrix} \psi_{1,1,1} & \psi_{1,1,2} & \psi_{1,1,3} \\ \psi_{1,2,1} & \psi_{1,2,2} & \psi_{1,2,3} \\ \psi_{1,3,1} & \psi_{1,3,2} & \psi_{1,3,3} \end{bmatrix} \begin{bmatrix} v_{1,t-1} \\ v_{2,t-1} \\ v_{3,t-1} \end{bmatrix}$$

$$+ \begin{bmatrix} \psi_{2,1,1} & \psi_{2,1,2} & \psi_{2,1,3} \\ \psi_{2,2,1} & \psi_{2,2,2} & \psi_{2,2,3} \\ \psi_{2,3,1} & \psi_{2,3,2} & \psi_{2,3,3} \end{bmatrix} \begin{bmatrix} v_{1,t-2} \\ v_{2,t-2} \\ v_{3,t-2} \end{bmatrix}$$

$$y_t = \mu + v_t + \Psi_1 v_{t-1} + \Psi_2 v_{t-2}.$$ ☐

The multivariate analogue of the autocovariance function in (13.5) is

$$\Gamma_k = \mathrm{E}\left[(y_t - \mathrm{E}[y_t])(y_{t-k} - \mathrm{E}[y_{t-k}])' \right], \tag{13.13}$$

in which y_t is now a ($N \times 1$) vector. Setting $k = 0$ gives the ($N \times N$) covariance matrix of y_t. A property of the autocovariance matrix is

$$\Gamma_k = \Gamma'_{-k}. \tag{13.14}$$

The autocorrelation matrix is

$$P_k = D^{-1/2} \Gamma_k D^{-1/2}, \tag{13.15}$$

where D is a diagonal matrix with the variances down the main diagonal.

Example 13.6 Moments of VARMA Models

Consider the n-dimensional VARMA(p,q) model in equation (13.8). The first two moments for alternative parameterisations are as follows.

VMA(1)   Mean: $E[y_t] = E[\mu + v_t + \Psi_1 v_{t-1}] = \mu$

Variance: $\Gamma_0 = V + \Psi_1 V \Psi_1'$

Covariance: $\gamma_k = \begin{cases} \Psi_1 V & \text{if } k = 1 \\ V \Psi_1' & \text{if } k = -1 \\ 0 & \text{otherwise.} \end{cases}$

VAR(1)   Mean: $E[y_t] = E[\mu + \Phi_1 y_{t-1}] = [I - \Phi_1]^{-1} \mu$

Variance: $\text{vec}(\Gamma_0) = [I_N - \Phi_1 \otimes \Phi_1]^{-1} \text{vec}(V)$

Covariance: $\Gamma_k = \Phi_1 \Gamma_{k-1}, \quad k \geqslant 1$.

The symbol $\otimes$ is the Kronecker product operator. The condition for the moments of the VAR(1) model to exist is the multivariate analogue of the univariate AR(1) condition, that all eigenvalues of Φ_1 are less than one in magnitude.   □

13.4   Stationarity

An important feature of the changes and the growth rates of the macroeconomic variables in Figure 13.1 is that they do not exhibit trends. This characteristic in time series is formally referred to as stationarity, which is defined in Chapter 2.

13.4.1   The Stationarity Condition

The approach to identify the weak stationarity properties of y_t is to look at the first two moments of the distribution and determine if the moments are a function of t. In both the univariate and multivariate cases presented in Example 13.2 and 13.6 the population moments are independent of time and y_t is therefore weakly stationary. Furthermore, if the disturbance term, v_t, in these models is *iid* then y_t is also strictly stationary. Moreover, the fact that the moving average models have moments that are finite sums of the moving-average parameters, implies that all (finite) moving-average models are stationary.

A formal statement of the stationarity condition is as follows. The N dimensional variable y_t is stationary provided that the roots of the polynomial $|\Phi_p(z)| = 0$ lie outside the unit circle. The notation $|\cdot|$ represents the determinant of the matrix argument.

Example 13.7 Stationarity of an AR(1) Model

The relevant polynomial $\phi_p(L) = 1 - \phi_1 L$ is

$$|1 - \phi_1 z| = 1 - \phi_1 z = 0.$$

This equation has only one root, which is given by $z_1 = \phi_1^{-1}$. For stationarity $|z_1| > 1$, which is satisfied if $|\phi_1^{-1}| > 1$, or $|\phi_1| < 1$, a result which corresponds to the moment existence condition stated in Example 13.2 which is also the condition required for the moments not to be a function of time. □

Example 13.8 Stationarity of the Interest Rate
Consider the following AR(4) model of the interest rate, $y_t = r_t$,

$$r_t = 0.141 + 1.418\, r_{t-1} - 0.588\, r_{t-2} + 0.125\, r_{t-3} + 0.024\, r_{t-4} + v_t.$$

The polynomial $1 - 1.418\, z + 0.588\, z^2 - 0.125\, z^3 - 0.024\, z^4 = 0$ has two real roots and two complex roots given by

$$z_1 = -8.772, \quad z_2 = 1.285 - 1.713i, \quad z_3 = 1.285 + 1.713i, \quad z_4 = 1.030.$$

Because $|z_1| = 8.772 > 1$, $|z_2| = |z_3| = 2.141 > 1$ and $|z_4| = 1.030 > 1$, the nominal interest rate is stationary. □

Example 13.9 Stationarity of Money Growth and Inflation
Consider a VAR(2) model with $N = 2$ variables containing annual percentage money growth and inflation, $y_t = [100\Delta_{12}lm_t, 100\Delta_{12}lp_t]'$, with autoregressive parameter matrices

$$\Phi_1 = \begin{bmatrix} 1.279 & -0.355 \\ 0.002 & 1.234 \end{bmatrix}, \quad \Phi_2 = \begin{bmatrix} -0.296 & 0.353 \\ 0.007 & -0.244 \end{bmatrix}.$$

The polynomial $|I - \Phi_1 z - \Phi_2 z^2| = 0$, has four real roots

$$z_1 = 4.757, \quad z_2 = 2.874, \quad z_3 = 1.036, \quad z_4 = 1.011.$$

Because $|z_i| > 1$, $\forall i$ both variables are jointly stationary. □

13.4.2 Wold's Representation Theorem

Suppose that y_t is purely stochastic so that it contains no mean, trends, structural breaks or other deterministic terms. This assumption implies that $E[y_t] = 0$. If y_t is also weakly stationary, then Wold's theorem gives a useful representation for understanding its second moment properties.

Wold Representation Theorem
If y_t is weakly stationary, then it can be represented as

$$y_t = \sum_{j=0}^{\infty} \psi_j v_{t-j}, \tag{13.16}$$

in which $\sum_{j=0}^{\infty} \psi_j^2 < \infty$ and v_t is white noise. The infinite sum is understood as the mean square limit of $\sum_{j=0}^{n} \psi_j v_{t-j}$ as $n \to \infty$. ■

The intuition behind this representation is that the left- and right-hand sides of (13.16) have the same first and second moments. Note that Wold's theorem does not state that all weakly stationary time series must be generated according to (13.16), only that they can be represented as (13.16).

Example 13.10 Bilinearity Model

Consider the random sequence, y_t, generated by

$$y_t = u_t u_{t-1}, \qquad u_t \sim iid\,(0, \sigma^2).$$

The variable y_t is white noise and has a Wold representation of the form

$$y_t = v_t,$$

where $v_t = u_t u_{t-1}$ has variance

$$E[v_t^2] = E[u_t^2 u_{t-1}^2] = E[u_t^2]E[u_{t-1}^2] = \sigma^2\sigma^2 = \sigma^4.$$

This Wold representation captures the second-order properties of y_t but overlooks higher-order dependence such as

$$\mathrm{cov}(y_t^2, y_{t-1}^2) = \sigma^4\left(E[v_t^4] - \sigma^4\right). \qquad\qquad\square$$

It is common and convenient to assume that a weakly stationary process is generated by (13.16). In this case, y_t is referred to as a linear process. In view of the preceding comments, Wold's theorem can not be invoked to state that every zero mean weakly stationary process is generated by a linear process, only that for every weakly stationary process there exists a linear process with the same first and second moments. Moreover, for the development of asymptotic distribution theory, it is necessary to strengthen the condition on v_t in the linear process so that it is *iid* or at least a martingale difference sequence, since first- and second-moment conditions alone are not sufficient for asymptotics. This is just a cautionary note that all results for linear processes need not extend automatically to all weakly stationary processes by appeal to Wold's theorem.

13.4.3 Transforming a VAR to a VMA

An important feature of the AR and MA examples given in Figure 13.2 is that they mirror each other, with the AR model generating a decaying ACF and a PACF that cuts-off at the lag length of the AR model, whereas the MA model gives the opposite result with the PACF exhibiting a decaying pattern and the ACF cutting-off at the lag length of the MA model. The relationship between autoregressive and moving-average models is now formalised. Consider initially the simplest example of converting an AR(1) model to an infinite MA model.

Example 13.11 Transforming an AR(1) to a MA(∞)

The AR(1) model expressed in terms of lag operators is

$$(1 - \phi_1 L)y_t = v_t.$$

The polynomial $(1 - \phi_1 L)$ is inverted as (see Appendix B)

$$y_t = (1 - \phi_1 L)^{-1} v_t = (1 + \phi_1 L + \phi_1^2 L^2 + \cdots) v_t$$

$$= v_t + \phi_1 v_{t-1} + \phi_1^2 v_{t-2} + \cdots = \sum_{i=0}^{\infty} \psi_i v_{t-i},$$

which is now an infinite moving average model with $\psi_i = \phi_1^i$. Provided that $|\phi_1| < 1$, the observed time path of y_t is determined by the complete history of shocks $\{v_t, v_{t-1}, \cdots\}$, with the weights ϕ_1^i in the summation decaying at an exponential rate. $\qquad\square$

The conversion of an autoregressive model into a moving-average model where there are several autoregressive lags and the dimension is $N > 1$ requires a recursive algorithm. To express a VAR(p) model as an infinite VMA model, consider

$$(I - \Phi_1 L - \Phi_2 L^2 - \cdots - \Phi_p L^p)y_t = v_t, \qquad (13.17)$$

where, for simplicity, the vector of intercepts is set to zero. Invert the polynomial $\Phi_p(L)$ to generate an infinite moving-average process

$$y_t = (I - \Phi_1 L - \Phi_2 L^2 - \cdots - \Phi_p L^p)^{-1} v_t = (I + \Psi_1 L + \Psi_2 L^2 + \cdots) v_t, \qquad (13.18)$$

where by definition

$$(I - \Phi_1 L - \Phi_2 L^2 - \cdots - \Phi_p L^p)^{-1} = (I + \Psi_1 L + \Psi_2 L^2 + \cdots). \qquad (13.19)$$

It follows from expression (13.19) that

$$(I - \Phi_1 L - \Phi_2 L^2 - \cdots - \Phi_p L^p)(I + \Psi_1 L + \Psi_2 L^2 + \cdots) = I \quad (13.20)$$

$$I + (\Psi_1 - \Phi_1)L + (\Psi_2 - \Phi_1 \Psi_1 - \Phi_2)L^2 + \cdots = I. \quad (13.21)$$

Equating the parameters on the powers on L using expressions (13.20) and (13.21) gives a recursion for deriving the moving-average parameter matrices from the autoregressive parameter matrices

$$\begin{aligned}
\Psi_1 &= \Phi_1 \\
\Psi_2 &= \Phi_1 \Psi_1 + \Phi_2 \\
\Psi_3 &= \Phi_1 \Psi_2 + \Phi_2 \Psi_1 + \Phi_3 \\
&\vdots \\
\Psi_i &= \sum_{j=1}^{i} \Phi_j \Psi_{i-j} \qquad \text{where } \Phi_j = 0, j > p.
\end{aligned} \tag{13.22}$$

Example 13.12 Transforming a VAR(1) to a VMA(∞)

As $\Phi_i = 0$ for $i > 1$, the VMA parameter matrices associated with the first three lags using the recursion in (13.22) are

$$\begin{aligned}
\Psi_1 &= \Phi_1 \\
\Psi_2 &= \Phi_1 \Psi_1 + \Phi_2 = \Phi_1 \Psi_1 = \Phi_1 \Phi_1 \\
\Psi_3 &= \Phi_1 \Psi_2 + \Phi_2 \Psi_1 + \Phi_3 = \Phi_1 \Psi_2 = \Phi_1 \Phi_1 \Phi_1.
\end{aligned}$$

This result is a multivariate version of the univariate AR(1) example shown previously in which $\psi_i = \phi_1^i$. $\qquad \square$

Example 13.13 Transforming a VAR(2) to a VMA(∞)

Recall the VAR(2) model of money growth and inflation from Example 13.9, where the VAR parameter matrices are

$$\Phi_1 = \begin{bmatrix} 1.28 & -0.36 \\ 0.00 & 1.23 \end{bmatrix}, \qquad \Phi_2 = \begin{bmatrix} -0.30 & 0.35 \\ 0.01 & -0.24 \end{bmatrix}.$$

As $\Phi_i = 0$ for $i > 2$, the first three lagged VMA parameter matrices are

$$\Psi_1 = \Phi_1 = \begin{bmatrix} 1.28 & -0.36 \\ 0.00 & 1.23 \end{bmatrix}$$

$$\begin{aligned}
\Psi_2 &= \Phi_1 \Psi_1 + \Phi_2 \\
&= \begin{bmatrix} 1.28 & -0.36 \\ 0.00 & 1.23 \end{bmatrix} \begin{bmatrix} 1.28 & -0.36 \\ 0.00 & 1.23 \end{bmatrix} + \begin{bmatrix} -0.30 & 0.35 \\ 0.01 & -0.24 \end{bmatrix} \\
&= \begin{bmatrix} 1.34 & -0.54 \\ 0.01 & 1.28 \end{bmatrix}
\end{aligned}$$

$$\begin{aligned}
\Psi_3 &= \Phi_1 \Psi_2 + \Phi_2 \Psi_1 \\
&= \begin{bmatrix} 1.28 & -0.36 \\ 0.00 & 1.23 \end{bmatrix} \begin{bmatrix} 1.34 & -0.54 \\ 0.01 & 1.28 \end{bmatrix} \\
&\quad + \begin{bmatrix} -0.30 & 0.35 \\ 0.01 & -0.24 \end{bmatrix} \begin{bmatrix} 1.28 & -0.36 \\ 0.00 & 1.23 \end{bmatrix} \\
&= \begin{bmatrix} 1.33 & -0.60 \\ 0.03 & 1.27 \end{bmatrix}.
\end{aligned}$$

$\qquad \square$

13.5 Invertibility

The results of the previous section on stationarity relate to the conditions needed for transforming a VAR to a VMA. Reversing this transformation and working from a VMA to a VAR requires the same type of condition, known as the invertibility property. As will be seen in the section on estimation, invertibility is required for estimation of the parameters.

13.5.1 The Invertibility Condition

The N dimensional variable y_t is invertible provided that the roots of the polynomial $\left| \Psi_q(z) \right| = 0$ lie outside the unit circle, where as before $| \cdot |$ represents the determinant of a matrix and $\Psi_q(z)$ is defined in equation (13.10).

Example 13.14 MA(1)
The polynomial is $\psi_p(L) = 1 + \psi_1 L$ so the equation to be solved is $1 + \psi_1 z = 0$. There is only one root, which is given by $z_1 = -\psi_1^{-1}$. For invertibility $|z_1| > 1$, which is satisfied if $\left| -\psi_1^{-1} \right| > 1$, or $|\psi_1| < 1$. $\qquad\square$

13.5.2 Transforming a VMA to a VAR

Now consider the problem of transforming a moving average model into an autoregressive model.

Example 13.15 Transforming a MA(1) to an AR(∞)
Consider the MA(1) model

$$y_t = (1 + \psi_1 L) v_t,$$

where $|\psi_1| < 1$. Inverting the lag polynomial $(1 + \psi_1 L)$ gives

$$(1 + \psi_1 L)^{-1} y_t = v_t$$
$$(1 - \psi_1 L + \psi_1^2 L^2 - \cdots) y_t = v_t$$
$$y_t - \phi_1 y_{t-1} - \phi_2 y_{t-2} - \cdots = v_t$$
$$y_t = \sum_{i=1}^{\infty} \phi_i y_{t-i} + v_t,$$

which is now an infinite autoregressive model with $\phi_i = \psi_1^i (-1)^{i+1}$. Provided that $|\psi_1| < 1$, the weights ϕ_i in the summation decay at an exponential rate for longer lags. $\qquad\square$

An important result is that all finite autoregressive processes are invertible, which is the mirror of the stationarity result found for moving average processes. The invertibility results for the univariate MA model generalise to an N dimensional process. Once again a recursion as in expression (13.23) is required, with the roles of the parameters being reversed.

13.6   Estimation

Specifying the likelihood function for a VARMA(p,q) model requires deriving the joint probability density function of y_t. As the process y_t is dependent, it follows from Chapter 1 that the joint pdf factorises as

$$f(y_1, y_2, ..., y_T; \theta) = f(y_s, y_{s-1}, \cdots, y_1; \theta) \times \prod_{t=s+1}^{T} f(y_t | y_{t-1}, \cdots, y_1; \theta),$$

in which $s = \max(p, q)$ represents the maximum lag in the model and θ contains the unknown parameters $\theta = \{\Phi_1, \Phi_2, ..., \Phi_p, \Psi_1, \Psi_2, ...\Psi_q, V\}$. The log-likelihood function is

$$\ln L_T(\theta) = \frac{1}{T} \left(\ln f(y_s, y_{s-1}, \cdots, y_1; \theta) + \sum_{t=s+1}^{T} \ln f(y_t | y_{t-1}, ..., y_1; \theta) \right).$$

The specification of the log-likelihood function is complicated by the presence of $f(y_s, y_{s-1}, \cdots, y_1; \theta)$, the joint distribution of the initial observations to allow for the s lags. The solution adopted in Chapter 7, in which these s observations are treated as fixed, is also adopted here. In this case the conditional log-likelihood function is

$$\ln L_T(\theta) = \frac{1}{T-s} \sum_{t=s+1}^{T} \ln f(y_t | y_{t-1}, ..., y_1; \theta). \qquad (13.23)$$

The parameters of the ARMA and VARMA models are estimated by maximum likelihood methods by choosing the parameter vector θ to maximise the conditional log-likelihood function in (13.23). One of the iterative algorithms presented in Chapter 3 is needed because the inclusion of moving average terms in the model results in the likelihood being nonlinear in the parameters. As the assumption of normality is commonly adopted in specifying linear time series models, the Gauss-Newton algorithm, as discussed in Chapter 6, can also be used. For the important special case where there are no moving average terms, it is shown that the maximum likelihood estimates are obtained by ordinary least squares and so convergence is achieved in one iteration.

Example 13.16 Estimating an ARMA($1, 1$) Model
Consider the ARMA($1,1$) model

$$y_t = \mu + \phi_1 y_{t-1} + v_t + \psi_1 v_{t-1}, \qquad v_t \sim iid\ N(0, \sigma_v^2),$$

with unknown parameters $\theta = \{\mu, \phi_1, \psi_1, \sigma_v^2\}$. The conditional log-likelihood function with $s = \max(p, q) = 1$ in (13.23) is

$$\ln L_T(\theta)$$

$$= \frac{1}{T-1} \sum_{t=2}^{T} \ln f(y_t | y_{t-1}, ..., y_1; \theta)$$

$$= \frac{1}{T-1} \sum_{t=2}^{T} \left(-\frac{1}{2} \ln 2\pi - \frac{1}{2} \ln \sigma_v^2 - \frac{1}{2\sigma_v^2} (y_t - \mu - \phi_1 y_{t-1} - \psi_1 v_{t-1})^2 \right)$$

$$= -\frac{1}{2} \ln 2\pi - \frac{1}{2} \ln \sigma_v^2 - \frac{1}{2\sigma_v^2(T-1)} \sum_{t=2}^{T} (y_t - \mu - \phi_1 y_{t-1} - \psi_1 v_{t-1})^2,$$

with gradients

$$\frac{\partial \ln L_T(\theta)}{\partial \mu} = \frac{1}{\sigma_v^2(T-1)} \sum_{t=2}^{T} v_t \left(1 + \psi_1 \frac{\partial v_{t-1}}{\partial \mu} \right)$$

$$\frac{\partial \ln L_T(\theta)}{\partial \phi_1} = \frac{1}{\sigma_v^2(T-1)} \sum_{t=2}^{T} v_t \left(y_{t-1} + \psi_1 \frac{\partial v_{t-1}}{\partial \phi_1} \right)$$

$$\frac{\partial \ln L_T(\theta)}{\partial \psi_1} = \frac{1}{\sigma_v^2(T-1)} \sum_{t=2}^{T} v_t \left(v_{t-1} + \psi_1 \frac{\partial v_{t-1}}{\partial \psi_1} \right)$$

$$\frac{\partial \ln L_T(\theta)}{\partial \sigma_v^2} = -\frac{1}{2\sigma_v^2} + \frac{1}{2\sigma_v^4(T-1)} \sum_{t=2}^{T} v_t^2.$$

An iterative algorithm is needed to maximise the likelihood since the gradients are nonlinear functions of the parameters because of the presence of $\partial v_{t-1}/\partial \theta$. To circumvent the need to derive $\partial v_{t-1}/\partial \theta$, it is convenient to use numerical derivatives in the optimisation algorithm. This algorithm is simplified by concentrating out σ_v^2 using the maximum likelihood estimator

$$\widehat{\sigma}_v^2 = (T-1)^{-1} \sum_{t=2}^{T} \widehat{v}_t^2, \qquad \widehat{v}_t = y_t - \widehat{\mu} - \widehat{\phi}_1 y_{t-1} - \widehat{\psi}_1 \widehat{v}_{t-1},$$

computed at each iteration of the algorithm. □

This example highlights the importance of the invertibility property of ARMA and VARMA models in estimation. Consider the gradient expression in the previous example corresponding to ϕ_1 that contains the term

$$\frac{\partial v_t}{\partial \phi_1} = y_{t-1} + \psi_1 \frac{\partial v_{t-1}}{\partial \phi_1}.$$

This is a first-order difference equation in $\partial v_{t-1}/\partial \phi_1$ with parameter ψ_1. If the MA term is not invertible, $|\psi_1| > 1$, then this equation may eventually explode resulting in the algorithm failing.

Example 13.17 Estimating a VARMA(1,1) Model

Consider the VARMA(1,1) model

$$y_t = \mu + \Phi_1 y_{t-1} + v_t + \Psi_1 v_{t-1}, \qquad v_t \sim iid\ N(0, V),$$

where y_t is of dimension N. The conditional log-likelihood function with $s = 1$ in (13.23) is

$$\ln L_T(\theta) = \frac{1}{T-1} \sum_{t=2}^{T} \ln f(y_t|y_{t-1}, ..., y_1; \theta)$$

$$= -\frac{N}{2} \ln 2\pi - \frac{1}{2} \ln |V| - \frac{1}{2(T-1)} \sum_{t=2}^{T} v_t' V^{-1} v_t,$$

where the $(N \times 1)$ disturbance vector at time t is $v_t = y_t - \mu - \Phi_1 y_{t-1} - \Psi_1 v_{t-1}$. Table 13.2 gives the maximum likelihood estimates from estimating the VARMA(1,1)

$$y_{1,t} = \mu_1 + \phi_{1,1,1} y_{1,t-1} + v_{1,t} + \psi_{1,1,1} v_{1,t-1} + \psi_{1,1,2} v_{2,t-1}$$

$$y_{2,t} = \mu_2 + \phi_{1,2,2} y_{2,t-1} + v_{2,t} + \psi_{1,2,1} v_{1,t-1} + \psi_{1,2,2} v_{2,t-1}.$$

The $T = 500$ observations are generated by simulating the model with the true parameters given in Table 13.2. The disturbance term, v_t, has zero mean and covariance matrix given by the identity matrix. There is good agreement between the parameter estimates and the true population parameters. Also reported are the quasi-maximum likelihood standard errors and t statistics that allow for heteroskedasticity. The residual covariance matrix is

$$\widehat{V} = \frac{1}{499} \sum_{t=2}^{500} \widehat{v}_t \widehat{v}_t' = \begin{bmatrix} 0.956 & 0.040 \\ 0.040 & 0.966 \end{bmatrix},$$

which is obtained at the final iteration. $\square$

Example 13.18 Estimating a VAR(p) Model

The conditional log-likelihood function of the N dimensional VAR(p) model in (13.23) is

$$\ln L_T(\theta) = \frac{1}{T-p} \sum_{t=p+1}^{T} \ln f(y_t|y_{t-1}, ..., y_{t-p}; \theta)$$

$$= -\frac{N}{2} \ln 2\pi - \frac{1}{2} \ln |V| - \frac{1}{2(T-p)} \sum_{t=p+1}^{T} v_t' V^{-1} v_t,$$

Table 13.2. *Maximum likelihood estimates of the VARMA(1,1)*
model: standard errors and t statistics are based on
quasi-maximum likelihood estimates of the covariance matrix
allowing for heteroskedasticity

Parameter	Population	Estimate	se	t statistic
μ_1	0.0	0.028	0.059	0.471
$\phi_{1,1,1}$	0.6	0.600	0.045	13.354
$\psi_{1,1,1}$	0.2	0.244	0.063	3.871
$\psi_{1,1,2}$	−0.5	−0.485	0.046	−10.619
μ_2	0.0	0.083	0.072	1.164
$\phi_{2,2,2}$	0.4	0.415	0.053	7.756
$\psi_{1,2,1}$	0.2	0.255	0.029	8.717
$\psi_{1,2,2}$	0.6	0.576	0.051	11.400
$\ln L_T(\theta) = -2.789$				

where the $(N \times 1)$ disturbance vector at time t is

$$v_t = y_t - \mu - \Phi_1 y_{t-1} - \Phi_2 y_{t-2} - \cdots - \Phi_p y_{t-p},$$

and $\theta = \{\mu, \Phi_1, \Phi_2, \cdots, \Phi_p, V\}$, is the set of unknown parameters. As all of the explanatory variables in each of the equations are identical, it follows from the results in Chapter 5 that the maximum likelihood estimates are obtained by ordinary least squares applied to each equation separately. There are no efficiency gains from estimating the system jointly. Once these estimates are obtained, V is estimated as

$$\widehat{V} = \frac{1}{T-p} \sum_{t=p+1}^{T} \widehat{v}_t \widehat{v}_t'.$$

In the special case where $N = 1$, the maximum likelihood estimates of the AR(p) model are obtained by regressing y_t on a constant and its lags. □

Example 13.19 A VAR Model of the United States

Consider the following VAR(2) model of the United States consisting of an interest rate, money growth, inflation and output growth so that $N = 4$. Define $y_t = [r_t, 100\Delta_{12}lm_t, 100\Delta_{12}lp_t, 100\Delta_{12}lo_t]'$ so that the VAR is

$$y_t = \mu + \Phi_1 y_{t-1} + \Phi_2 y_{t-2} + v_t.$$

The maximum likelihood estimates are

$$\widehat{\Phi}_1 = \begin{bmatrix} 1.31 & 0.29 & 0.12 & 0.04 \\ -0.21 & 1.25 & -0.24 & 0.04 \\ 0.07 & 0.03 & 1.16 & 0.01 \\ 0.08 & 0.27 & -0.07 & 1.25 \end{bmatrix},$$

$$
\widehat{\Phi}_2 = \begin{bmatrix} -0.35 & -0.28 & -0.07 & -0.02 \\ 0.19 & -0.26 & 0.24 & -0.05 \\ -0.07 & -0.02 & -0.16 & 0.01 \\ -0.13 & -0.23 & 0.03 & -0.31 \end{bmatrix},
$$

$$
\widehat{\mu} = \begin{bmatrix} -0.04 \\ 0.22 \\ -0.11 \\ 0.49 \end{bmatrix}, \quad \widehat{V} = \begin{bmatrix} 0.29 & -0.02 & 0.01 & 0.11 \\ -0.02 & 0.38 & -0.01 & -0.05 \\ 0.01 & -0.01 & 0.10 & 0.00 \\ 0.11 & -0.05 & 0.00 & 1.27 \end{bmatrix}.
$$

The log-likelihood function evaluated at $\widehat{\theta}$ is $\ln L_T(\widehat{\theta}) = -3.471$.   □

13.7 Optimal Choice of Lag Order

An important practical consideration in estimating the parameters of the general VARMA(p, q) class of stationary time series model is the optimal choice of lag order. A common data-driven way of selecting the lag order is to use information criteria. An information criterion is a scalar that is a simple but effective way of balancing the improvement in the value of the log-likelihood function with the loss of degrees of freedom which results from increasing the lag order of a time series model.

The three most commonly used information criteria for selecting a parsimonious time series model are the Akaike information criterion (AIC) (Akaike, 1974, 1976), the Hannan information criterion (HIC) (Hannan and Quinn, 1979; Hannan, 1980) and the Schwarz information criterion (SIC) (Schwarz, 1978). If k is the number of parameters estimated in the model, these information criteria are given by

$$
\begin{aligned}
AIC &= -2\ln L_T(\widehat{\theta}) + \frac{2k}{T-s} \\
HIC &= -2\ln L_T(\widehat{\theta}) + \frac{2k\ln(\ln(T-s))}{T-s} \\
SIC &= -2\ln L_T(\widehat{\theta}) + \frac{k\ln(T-s)}{T-s},
\end{aligned} \tag{13.24}
$$

in which $s = \max(p_{max}, q_{max})$ and p_{max} and q_{max} are, respectively, the maximum number of lags considered for the AR and MA components of the VARMA(p, q) model.

For the VARMA(p, q) model given in equation (13.8) in which the disturbances, v_t, are assumed to be normally distributed, the information criteria in equation (13.24) take on a simple form. Using the results established in Chapter 4, the log-likelihood function evaluated at the maximum likelihood estimates is

$$\ln L_T(\widehat{\theta}) = -\frac{N}{2}(1 + \ln 2\pi) - \frac{1}{2}\ln|\widehat{V}|. \qquad (13.25)$$

Recognising that the first term on the right-hand side of (13.25) is a constant and does not depend on the choice of lag order, the three information criteria in equation (13.24) are redefined as

$$AIC = \ln|\widehat{V}| + \frac{2k}{T - s}$$

$$HIC = \ln|\widehat{V}| + \frac{2k\ln(\ln(T - s))}{T - s} \qquad (13.26)$$

$$SIC = \ln|\widehat{V}| + \frac{k\ln(T - s)}{T - s}.$$

In the scalar case, the determinant of the estimated covariance matrix, $|\widehat{V}|$, is replaced by the residual variance, $\widehat{\sigma}_v^2$.

Choosing an optimal lag order using information criteria requires the following steps.

Step 1: Choose a maximum number of lags for the AR and MA components of the time series model, respectively, $p_{max} > p_0$ and $q_{max} > q_0$, where p_0 and q_0 are the true but unknown lag lengths. The choice of p_{max} and q_{max} is informed by the ACFs and PACFs of the data, the frequency with which the data are observed and also the sample size.

Step 2: Systematically estimate the model for all combinations of lag orders where the sample size, T, is fixed across all model specifications. For VAR(p) models this involves estimating the model sequentially for $p = 1, 2, \cdots p_{max}$. For a VMA(q) specification, the model is estimated sequentially for $q = 1, 2, \cdots q_{max}$. For VARMA(p, q) specifications, the model is systematically estimated for all combinations of $p = 1, 2, \cdots p_{max}$ and $q = 1, 2, \cdots q_{max}$. For each regression the relevant information criteria are computed.

Step 3: Choose the specification of the model corresponding to the minimum values of the information criteria. In some cases there will be disagreement between different information criteria and the final choice is then an issue of judgement.

Example 13.20 Lag Length Selection in an AR(3) Model
Consider the AR(3) model

$$y_t = 0.0 + 0.2y_{t-1} - 0.15y_{t-2} + 0.05y_{t-3} + v_t, \qquad v_t \sim iid\, N(0, 0.5).$$

The model is simulated to generate 300 realisations of y_t using starting values of 0.0 for y_{t-i}, $i = 1, 2, 3$. The first 100 simulated values are discarded to reduce the dependence on initial conditions and the $T = 200$ remaining observations

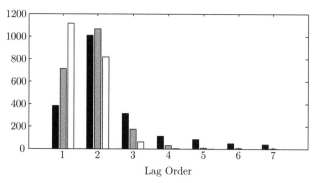

Figure 13.3. Bar graph of the optimal choice of lag order returned by the AIC (black bar), HIC (gray bar) and SIC (white bar). The true lag order is $p_0 = 3$.

are used in the estimation. The AIC, HIC and SIC are used to select the optimal lag order in 2000 replications and the results are summarised in Figure 13.3.

In this example, the AIC and HIC select 2 lags as the optimal lag length most often, while the SIC favours the choice of only 1 lag. The SIC penalises additional variables more harshly than the AIC because $k \ln(T)/T > 2k/T$ for $T \geq 8$, so this result is not surprising. It is also apparent from Figure 13.3 that only the AIC chooses a lag length greater than 3 a significant number of times.

□

13.8   Distribution Theory

Let θ_0 be the true population parameter. Assuming that y_t is stationary and the conditions of the mds central limit theorem from Chapter 2 are satisfied, the asymptotic distribution of the maximum likelihood estimator, $\widehat{\theta}$, is

$$\sqrt{T}(\widehat{\theta} - \theta_0) \xrightarrow{d} N\left(0, H^{-1}(\theta_0)J(\theta_0)H^{-1}(\theta_0)\right),$$ (13.27)

in which

$$H(\theta_0) = \mathrm{E}[h_t(\theta_0)]$$
$$J(\theta_0) = \mathrm{E}[g_t(\theta_0)g_t'(\theta_0)],$$

where $g_t(\theta_0)$ and $h_t(\theta_0)$ are respectively the gradient and the Hessian of the log-likelihood function at observation t evaluated at the population parameter θ_0.

Example 13.21 Distribution of the AR(1) Model
Consider the AR(1) model

$$y_t = \phi y_{t-1} + v_t, \qquad v_t \sim iid\ N(0, \sigma_v^2).$$

The gradient and Hessian of the log-likelihood function at t in the case of ϕ are respectively

$$g_t = \frac{1}{\sigma_v^2} v_t y_{t-1} = \frac{1}{\sigma_v^2} (y_t - \phi y_{t-1}) y_{t-1}, \qquad h_t = -\frac{1}{\sigma_v^2} y_{t-1}^2.$$

The maximum likelihood estimator is the sample correlation coefficient

$$\widehat{\phi} = r_1 = \frac{\sum_{t=2}^{T} y_t y_{t-1}}{\sum_{t=2}^{T} y_{t-1}^2}.$$

Letting $\theta_0 = \phi_0$ represent the population parameter, from the definition of the variance of an AR(1) model

$$H(\theta_0) = \mathrm{E}[h_t(\theta_0)] = -\frac{1}{\sigma_v^2} \mathrm{E}[y_{t-1}^2] = -\frac{1}{\sigma_v^2} \frac{\sigma_v^2}{1 - \phi_0^2} = -\frac{1}{1 - \phi_0^2}.$$

As $-H(\theta_0) = J(\theta_0)$, the asymptotic distribution of r_1 is

$$\sqrt{T}(r_1 - \phi_0) \overset{d}{\to} N(0, 1 - \phi_0^2).$$

In the special case where the population parameter is $\phi = 0$, the asymptotic distribution simplifies further to $\sqrt{T} r_1 \overset{d}{\to} N(0, 1)$. See also Example 2.14 in Chapter 2. □

13.9 Testing

The LR, Wald and LM test statistics, presented in Chapter 4, can be used to test hypotheses on the parameters of ARMA and VARMA models. Many of the statistics used to test hypotheses in stationary time series models are LM tests. This is because the models are relatively easy to estimate under the null hypothesis.

Example 13.22 Testing the Autocorrelation Coefficient
Consider testing for the independence of y_t using the AR(1) model

$$y_t = \phi y_{t-1} + v_t, \qquad v_t \sim iid\, N(0, \sigma^2),$$

which amounts to testing the restriction $\phi = 0$. As demonstrated previously, the asymptotic distribution of $\widehat{\phi}$ corresponds to the asymptotic distribution of the sample autocorrelation coefficient r_1. Evaluating this distribution under the null hypothesis gives $r_1 \overset{a}{\sim} N(0, T^{-1})$, suggesting that a LM test of independence is based on $\sqrt{T} r_1 \overset{d}{\to} N(0, 1)$. □

The general form of the LM test statistic is

$$LM = T G_T'(\widehat{\theta}_0) J_T^{-1}(\widehat{\theta}_0) G_T(\widehat{\theta}_0), \tag{13.28}$$

in which $G_T(\widehat{\theta}_0)$ is the gradient and $J_T(\widehat{\theta}_0)$ is the sample outer product of the gradients, both evaluated at the restricted estimator $\widehat{\theta}_0$. From Chapter 4, the Lagrange multiplier statistic in the case of normality becomes

$$
\begin{aligned}
LM &= T\left[\frac{1}{\widehat{\sigma}_v^2 T}\sum_{t=1}^{T} z_t\widehat{v}_t\right]'\left[\frac{1}{\widehat{\sigma}_v^2 T}\sum_{t=1}^{T} z_t z_t'\right]^{-1}\left[\frac{1}{\widehat{\sigma}_v^2 T}\sum_{t=1}^{T} z_t\widehat{v}_t\right] \\
&= \frac{T}{\sum_{t=1}^{T}\widehat{v}_t^2}\left[\sum_{t=1}^{T} z_t\widehat{v}_t\right]'\left[\sum_{t=1}^{T} z_t z_t'\right]^{-1}\left[\sum_{t=1}^{T} z_t\widehat{v}_t\right] \\
&= T R^2,
\end{aligned}
\tag{13.29}
$$

where R^2 is the coefficient of determination from a regression of $\widehat{v}_t$ on $z_t = -\partial v_t/\partial\theta$, evaluated under the null hypothesis. The LM statistic is distributed asymptotically under the null hypothesis as χ_K^2 where K is the number of restrictions.

Example 13.23 LM Test of a MA(1) Model

Consider testing the ARMA(1, 1) model

$$ y_t = \phi_1 y_{t-1} + v_t + \psi_1 v_{t-1}, $$

for no moving average term, $\psi_1 = 0$. Write the model as

$$ v_t = y_t - \phi_1 y_{t-1} - \psi_1 v_{t-1}, $$

and construct the derivatives

$$ z_{1,t} = -\frac{\partial v_t}{\partial\phi_1} = y_{t-1} - \psi_1 z_{1,t-1} $$

$$ z_{2,t} = -\frac{\partial v_t}{\partial\psi_1} = -\psi_1 z_{2,t-1} + v_{t-1}. $$

Evaluating these expressions under the null hypothesis at $\psi_1 = 0$ gives

$$ v_t = y_t - \phi_1 y_{t-1} $$
$$ z_{1,t} = y_{t-1} $$
$$ z_{2,t} = v_{t-1}. $$

To perform the LM test the following steps are required.

Step 1: Estimate the restricted model by regressing y_t on y_{t-1} and get the restricted residuals $\widehat{v}_t$.

Step 2: Estimate the second-stage regression by regressing $\widehat{v}_t$ on $\{y_{t-1}, \widehat{v}_{t-1}\}$.

Step 3: Compute the test statistic $LM = TR^2$, where T is the sample size and R^2 is the coefficient of determination from the second-stage regression. Under the null hypothesis, LM is asymptotically distributed as χ_1^2.

□

13.10 Analysing Vector Autoregressions

This section focusses on some of the tools used to analyse the dynamic inter-relationships between the variables of VARs. As outlined previously, a VAR(p) model is specified as

$$y_t = \mu + \Phi_1 y_{t-1} + \cdots + \Phi_p y_{t-p} + v_t, \qquad v_t \sim iid\ N(0, V), \tag{13.30}$$

with all of the dynamics captured by the lagged variables and no additional dynamics arising from any moving average terms. In specifying a VAR, the key determinants are the number of variables, N, and the number of lags, p. It is this simplicity of the specification of a VAR that is an important reason for its popularity in modelling economic systems.

The VAR represents the reduced form of a dynamic structural model of the type discussed in Chapter 5. For example, consider the following structural model

$$B_0 y_t = B_1 y_{t-1} + u_t, \tag{13.31}$$

where B_0 and B_1 are matrices of parameters. The ($N \times 1$) structural disturbance vector u_t has the properties

$$E[u_t] = 0, \quad E[u_t u_t'] = D, \tag{13.32}$$

where D is a diagonal matrix containing the variances on the main diagonal. The fact that D is a diagonal matrix means that the disturbances are uncorrelated, a restriction implied by the structural model. Expressing this system in terms of its reduced form gives

$$y_t = B_0^{-1} B_1 y_{t-1} + B_0^{-1} u_t = \Phi_1 y_{t-1} + v_t, \tag{13.33}$$

which is a VAR(1) where the parameters of the VAR and the structural model are related by

$$\Phi_1 = B_0^{-1} B_1, \tag{13.34}$$

while the disturbance vector of the VAR is related to the structural disturbance vector by

$$v_t = B_0^{-1} u_t. \tag{13.35}$$

One of the costs of a VAR is that it generates a large number of parameters, even for relatively small models. For example, a VAR with $N = 4$ variables and $p = 2$ lags, yields $N^2 \times p = 32$ autoregressive parameters and $N = 4$ constants. The fact that VARs produce large numbers of parameters creates difficulties in understanding the dynamic interrelationships amongst the variables in the system. There are three common methods used in empirical work to circumvent this problem, namely, Granger causality, impulse response analysis and variance decomposition.

13.10.1   Granger Causality Testing

A natural approach to understanding the dynamic structure of a VAR is to determine if a particular variable is explained by the lags of any other variable in the VAR other than its own lags. This suggests testing whether the parameters on blocks of lags are jointly zero, commonly referred to as the Granger causality test. To implement the Granger causality test, it is convenient to use the Wald statistic from Chapter 4, given by

$$W = T[R\widehat{\theta}_1 - Q]'[R\,\widehat{\Omega}R']^{-1}[R\widehat{\theta}_1 - Q], \qquad (13.36)$$

where $\widehat{\theta}_1$ is the vector of unrestricted parameter estimates and R and Q are matrices based on the restrictions. Under the null hypothesis, the Wald statistic is distributed asymptotically as χ^2 where the degrees of freedom equals the number of zero restrictions being tested.

Example 13.24 Causality Tests of the United States VAR
   In the VAR(2) macroeconometric model of the United States in Example 13.19, θ is (36×1) with the parameters ordered as

$$\theta = \left[\mu_1, \phi_{1,1,1}, \phi_{1,1,2}, \phi_{1,1,3}, \phi_{1,1,4}, \phi_{2,1,1}, \phi_{2,1,2}, \phi_{2,1,3}, \phi_{2,1,4}, \mu_2, \cdots\right]'.$$

To test whether money fails to Granger cause the interest rate, denoted as $money \nrightarrow interest$, the hypotheses are

$$\begin{array}{lll} H_0: & \phi_{1,1,2} = \phi_{2,1,2} = 0 & (money \nrightarrow interest) \\ H_1: & \text{at least one restriction fails} & (money \rightarrow interest). \end{array}$$

To implement the Wald statistic in (13.36), $\widehat{\theta}_1$ is obtained from Example 13.19, while R is (2×36) and Q is (2×1) defined as

$$R = \begin{bmatrix} 0 & 0 & 1 & 0 & 0 & 0 & 0 & 0 & 0 & 0 & \cdots & 0 \\ 0 & 0 & 0 & 0 & 0 & 0 & 1 & 0 & 0 & 0 & \cdots & 0 \end{bmatrix}, \quad Q = \begin{bmatrix} 0 \\ 0 \end{bmatrix}.$$

To implement other combinations of Granger causality tests defined in terms of the $N = 4$ variables in the model it is merely necessary to change R.
   The Granger causality tests of the interest rate equation are given in the first block of Table 13.3. All restrictions are statistically significant showing that

Table 13.3. *Granger causality tests of the VAR(2) model of the United States economy containing the interest rate, r_t, and annual percentage changes in the money stock, $100\Delta_{12}lm_t$, prices, $100\Delta_{12}lp_t$, and output, $100\Delta_{12}lo_t$. Results are presented for the interest rate and output equations*

Null hypothesis			Wald statistic	DOF	p-value
money	$\nrightarrow$	interest rate	57.366	2	0.000
price	$\nrightarrow$	interest rate	15.839	2	0.000
output	$\nrightarrow$	interest rate	12.602	2	0.002
interest rate	$\nrightarrow$	output	5.036	2	0.081
money	$\nrightarrow$	output	16.958	2	0.000
price	$\nrightarrow$	output	1.927	2	0.382

money growth, inflation and output growth all Granger cause the interest rate. The second block gives Granger causality tests for output. There is Granger causality from money to output, while the causal link from the interest rate to output is significant, but only at the 10% level. The results show that price fails to Granger cause output with a p-value of 0.382. □

13.10.2   Impulse Response Functions

The Granger causality test of the previous section focusses on the lags of the VAR. An alternative approach is to transform the VAR into a vector moving average and identify the dynamic properties of the VAR from the parameters of the VMA. Consider the VAR(p) in (13.30) where, without loss of generality, $\mu = 0$. Assuming stationarity, the VMA is infinite dimensional

$$y_t = v_t + \Psi_1 v_{t-1} + \Psi_2 v_{t-2} + \Psi_3 v_{t-3} + \cdots . \tag{13.37}$$

Taking conditional expectations of (13.37) based on information at time $t - 1$ and subtracting from (13.37) gives the one-step-ahead forecast error

$$y_t - E_{t-1}[y_t] = y_t - (\Psi_1 v_{t-1} + \Psi_2 v_{t-2} + \Psi_3 v_{t-3} + \cdots) = v_t.$$

Writing the model at $t + 1$

$$y_{t+1} = v_{t+1} + \Psi_1 v_t + \Psi_2 v_{t-1} + \Psi_3 v_{t-2} + \cdots \tag{13.38}$$

reveals that v_t also affects y_{t+1} through Ψ_1. By deduction, v_t affects y_{t+h} by Ψ_h, which suggests that a natural way to understand the dynamics of a VAR is to analyse the VMA parameters Ψ_h.

Interpreting the dynamics of the VAR in terms of v_t in (13.38) is problematic because V is, in general, a non-diagonal matrix and therefore the disturbances are correlated with each other. To circumvent this problem, v_t in (13.38) is replaced by the structural shocks, u_t, in (13.35)

$$y_t = B_0^{-1} u_t + \Psi_1 B_0^{-1} u_{t-1} + \Psi_2 B_0^{-1} u_{t-2} + \Psi_3 B_0^{-1} u_{t-3} + \cdots .$$

(13.39)

But this is just shifting the problem, since the structural parameters in B_0 now need to be identified. The most common way to solve this problem dates back to Sims (1980) where B_0 is specified as a triangular matrix, so the contemporaneous relationships among the variables in y_t is recursive. This is the implicit assumption in performing VAR analysis and reporting the results in terms of equation (13.39). A more general identification approach, that does not rely on a strict recursive structure, is given in Chapter 14.

In the case of a VAR(2) model estimated in Example 13.19, for example, the structural model (not the VAR) is specified as

$$
\begin{aligned}
y_{1t} &= & + \{lags\} &+ u_{1,t} \\
y_{2,t} &= \beta_{2,1} y_{1,t} & + \{lags\} &+ u_{2,t} \\
y_{3,t} &= \beta_{3,1} y_{1,t} + \beta_{3,2} y_{2,t} & + \{lags\} &+ u_{3,t} \\
y_{4,t} &= \beta_{4,1} y_{1,t} + \beta_{4,2} y_{2,t} + \beta_{4,3} y_{3,t} & + \{lags\} &+ u_{4,t} ,
\end{aligned}
$$

(13.40)

where B_0 in (13.31) and D in (13.32) are, respectively,

$$
B_0 = \begin{bmatrix} 1 & 0 & 0 & 0 \\ -\beta_{2,1} & 1 & 0 & 0 \\ -\beta_{3,1} & -\beta_{3,2} & 1 & 0 \\ -\beta_{4,1} & -\beta_{4,2} & -\beta_{4,3} & 1 \end{bmatrix}, \quad D = \mathrm{diag} \begin{pmatrix} d_{1,1} \\ d_{2,2} \\ d_{3,3} \\ d_{4,4} \end{pmatrix} .
$$

(13.41)

A natural way to compute B_0 and D is to estimate the full structural model in (13.40) by maximum likelihood. In fact, given the recursive structure of the specified model, there are four possible ways to estimate the structural model which are numerically equivalent.

Structural Equation Approach

Each structural equation in (13.40) is estimated by ordinary least squares

$$y_{1,t} = -0.036$$
$$+1.309 y_{1,t-1} + 0.287 y_{2,t-1} + 0.043 y_{3,t-1} + 0.044 y_{4,t-1}$$
$$-0.353 y_{1,t-2} - 0.280 y_{2,t-2} - 0.071 y_{3,t-2} - 0.023 y_{4,t-2} + \widehat{u}_{1,t},$$
$$y_{2,t} = 0.219 - 0.053 y_{1,t}$$
$$-0.137 y_{1,t-1} + 1.263 y_{2,t-1} - 0.235 y_{3,t-1} + 0.040 y_{4,t-1}$$
$$+0.172 y_{1,t-2} - 0.278 y_{2,t-2} + 0.241 y_{3,t-2} - 0.053 y_{4,t-2} + \widehat{u}_{2,t},$$

$$y_{3,t} = -0.109 + 0.027y_{1,t} - 0.013y_{2,t}$$
$$+0.032y_{1,t-1} + 0.035y_{2,t-1} + 1.149y_{3,t-1} + 0.007y_{4,t-1}$$
$$-0.054y_{1,t-2} - 0.016y_{2,t-2} - 0.153y_{3,t-2} + 0.010y_{4,t-2} + \widehat{u}_{3,t},$$
$$y_{4,t} = 0.519 + 0.387y_{1,t} - 0.112y_{2,t} - 0.042y_{3,t}$$
$$-0.444y_{1,t-1} + 0.296y_{2,t-1} - 0.091y_{3,t-1} + 1.239y_{4,t-1}$$
$$+0.026y_{1,t-2} - 0.152y_{2,t-2} + 0.076y_{3,t-2} - 0.308y_{4,t-2} + \widehat{u}_{4,t},$$

yielding the matrices

$$\widehat{B}_0 = \begin{bmatrix} 1.000 & 0.000 & 0.000 & 0.000 \\ 0.053 & 1.000 & 0.000 & 0.000 \\ -0.027 & 0.013 & 1.000 & 0.000 \\ -0.387 & 0.112 & 0.042 & 1.000 \end{bmatrix}, \quad \widehat{D} = \text{diag} \begin{pmatrix} 0.285 \\ 0.370 \\ 0.097 \\ 1.192 \end{pmatrix},$$

where the ith diagonal element of $\widehat{D}$ is computed as $T^{-1} \sum_{t=1}^{T} \widehat{u}_{i,t}^2$.

Reduced Form Approach

Each equation of the VAR (reduced form) is estimated by ordinary least squares to yield estimates of $\widehat{v}_t$. Now rewrite (13.35) as $B_0 v_t = u_t$, which corresponds to a recursive structure in the VAR residuals. This system of equations can also be estimated by ordinary least squares with $v_t = [v_{1,t}, v_{2,t}, v_{3,t}, v_{4,t}]'$ replaced by $\widehat{v}_t$, the VAR residuals. The results from estimating this system by least squares are

$$\widehat{v}_{1,t} = \widehat{u}_{1,t}$$
$$\widehat{v}_{2,t} = -0.053\,\widehat{v}_{1,t} + \widehat{u}_{2,t}$$
$$\widehat{v}_{3,t} = 0.027\,\widehat{v}_{1,t} - 0.013\,\widehat{v}_{2,t} + \widehat{u}_{3,t}$$
$$\widehat{v}_{4,t} = 0.387\,\widehat{v}_{1,t} - 0.112\,\widehat{v}_{2,t} - 0.042\widehat{v}_{3,t} + \widehat{u}_{4,t},$$

where the $\widehat{u}_{i,t}$s are the residuals from the estimated equations, which also correspond to the structural residuals. Notice that the parameter estimates of this system, apart from a change in sign, do indeed correspond to the $\widehat{B}_0$ matrix using the structural equation approach. The estimates of the structural variances computed from these residuals are used to calculate $\widehat{D}$.

Choleski Decomposition Approach

The first stage is as in the reduced form approach where each equation of the VAR is estimated by least squares and the VAR residuals are used to compute $\widehat{V}$. At the second stage, a Choleski decomposition of $\widehat{V}$ is performed by defining

$$\widehat{V} = \widehat{S}\widehat{S}',$$

where

$$
\widehat{S} = \begin{bmatrix}
0.534 & 0.000 & 0.000 & 0.000 \\
-0.028 & 0.608 & 0.000 & 0.000 \\
0.015 & -0.008 & 0.311 & 0.000 \\
0.209 & -0.068 & -0.013 & 1.092
\end{bmatrix}.
$$

To recover B_0 from S define the structural variances as the square of the diagonal elements of S

$$
\widehat{D} = \mathrm{diag} \begin{pmatrix}
0.534^2 \\
0.608^2 \\
0.311^2 \\
1.092^2
\end{pmatrix} = \mathrm{diag} \begin{pmatrix}
0.285 \\
0.370 \\
0.097 \\
1.192
\end{pmatrix},
$$

which agrees with $\widehat{D}$ given by the structural equation approach. Now from (13.35)

$$
V = \mathrm{E}\left[v_t v_t'\right] = \mathrm{E}\left[B_0^{-1} u_t u_t' B_0^{-1\prime}\right] = B_0^{-1} \mathrm{E}\left[u_t u_t'\right] B_0^{-1\prime} = B_0^{-1} D B_0^{-1\prime},
$$

which implies that $S = B_0^{-1} D^{1/2}$ and hence

$$
B_0 = (SD^{-1/2})^{-1}.
$$

Performing this calculation gives

$$
\widehat{B}_0 = \begin{bmatrix}
0.534/0.534 & 0.000/0.608 & 0.000/0.311 & 0.000/1.092 \\
-0.028/0.534 & 0.608/0.608 & 0.000/0.311 & 0.000/1.092 \\
0.015/0.534 & -0.008/0.608 & 0.311/0.311 & 0.000/1.092 \\
0.209/0.534 & -0.068/0.608 & -0.013/0.311 & 1.092/1.092
\end{bmatrix}^{-1}
$$

$$
= \begin{bmatrix}
1.000 & 0.000 & 0.000 & 0.000 \\
0.053 & 1.000 & 0.000 & 0.000 \\
-0.027 & 0.013 & 1.000 & 0.000 \\
-0.386 & 0.112 & 0.042 & 1.000
\end{bmatrix},
$$

which is the same $\widehat{B}_0$ matrix as obtained using the structural equation method.

Maximum Likelihood Approach

As before, the VAR is estimated by least squares to yield the VAR residuals $\widehat{v}_t$. The log-likelihood function given by

$$
\ln L_T(\theta) = -\frac{N}{2} \ln 2\pi - \frac{1}{2} \ln |V| - \frac{1}{2(T-2)} \sum_{t=3}^{T} \widehat{v}_t' V^{-1} \widehat{v}_t,
$$

which is maximised with respect to $\theta = \{B_0, D\}$ subject to the restriction $V = B_0^{-1} D B_0^{-1}$, with

$$
B_0 = \begin{bmatrix} 1 & 0 & 0 & 0 \\ -b_{2,1} & 1 & 0 & 0 \\ -b_{3,1} & -b_{3,2} & 1 & 0 \\ -b_{4,1} & -b_{4,2} & -b_{4,3} & 1 \end{bmatrix}, \quad D = \begin{bmatrix} d_{1,1} & 0 & 0 & 0 \\ 0 & d_{2,2} & 0 & 0 \\ 0 & 0 & d_{3,3} & 0 \\ 0 & 0 & 0 & d_{4,4} \end{bmatrix}.
$$

The maximum likelihood estimates, with standard errors based on the Hessian in parentheses, are given by

$$
\widehat{B}_0 = \begin{bmatrix} 1.000 & 0.000 & 0.000 & 0.000 \\ {\scriptstyle(-)} & {\scriptstyle(-)} & {\scriptstyle(-)} & {\scriptstyle(-)} \\ 0.053 & 1.000 & 0.000 & 0.000 \\ {\scriptstyle(0.053)} & {\scriptstyle(-)} & {\scriptstyle(-)} & {\scriptstyle(-)} \\ -0.027 & 0.013 & 1.000 & 0.000 \\ {\scriptstyle(0.027)} & {\scriptstyle(0.024)} & {\scriptstyle(-)} & {\scriptstyle(-)} \\ -0.386 & 0.112 & 0.042 & 1.000 \\ {\scriptstyle(0.095)} & {\scriptstyle(0.083)} & {\scriptstyle(0.165)} & {\scriptstyle(-)} \end{bmatrix}, \quad \widehat{D} = \mathrm{diag} \begin{pmatrix} 0.285 \\ {\scriptstyle(0.019)} \\ 0.370 \\ {\scriptstyle(0.024)} \\ 0.097 \\ {\scriptstyle(0.006)} \\ 1.192 \\ {\scriptstyle(0.078)} \end{pmatrix},
$$

where the value of the log-likelihood function is $\ln L_T(\widehat{\theta}) = -3.471$. These estimates are the same as the estimates obtained using the other three approaches. An important advantage of the maximum likelihood approach, however, is that it yields standard errors thereby facilitating hypothesis testing. By contrast, the Choleski method only delivers point estimates.

The structural shocks, u_t, in equation (13.39) can also be expressed in terms of standardised structural shocks by defining

$$
z_t = D^{-1/2} u_t, \tag{13.42}
$$

in which $D^{1/2}$ represents a diagonal matrix with the structural standard deviations down the main diagonal. Using (13.42) to substitute out u_t in (13.39) gives

$$
\begin{aligned}
y_t &= B_0^{-1} D^{1/2} z_t + \Psi_1 B_0^{-1} D^{1/2} z_{t-1} + \Psi_2 B_0^{-1} D^{1/2} z_{t-2} + \cdots \\
&= S z_t + \Psi_1 S z_{t-1} + \Psi_2 S z_{t-2} + \Psi_3 S z_{t-3} + \cdots ,
\end{aligned} \tag{13.43}
$$

in which, as before, $S = B_0^{-1} D^{1/2}$. The parameters on current and lagged z_t represent one standard deviation orthogonalised impulse response functions which are formally defined as

$$
IRF_h = \frac{\partial y_{t+h-1}}{\partial z_t'} = \Psi_{h-1} S, \quad h = 1, 2, \cdots . \tag{13.44}
$$

Example 13.25 Impulse Responses of the United States VAR

Consider again the VAR(2) estimated using the United States macroeconomic data in Example 13.19 with $N = 4$. At $h = 1$, the one standard deviation orthogonalised impulse responses are estimated as

$$IRF_1(\widehat{\theta}) = \widehat{\Psi}_0 \widehat{S} = I_4 \widehat{S} = \widehat{S} = \begin{bmatrix} 0.53 & 0.00 & 0.00 & 0.00 \\ -0.03 & 0.61 & 0.00 & 0.00 \\ 0.02 & -0.01 & 0.31 & 0.00 \\ 0.21 & -0.07 & -0.01 & 1.09 \end{bmatrix}.$$

At $h = 2$ the impulse responses are

$$IRF_2(\widehat{\theta}) = \widehat{\Psi}_1 \widehat{S}$$

$$= \begin{bmatrix} 1.31 & 0.29 & 0.12 & 0.04 \\ -0.21 & 1.25 & -0.24 & 0.04 \\ 0.07 & 0.03 & 1.16 & 0.01 \\ 0.08 & 0.27 & -0.07 & 1.25 \end{bmatrix} \begin{bmatrix} 0.53 & 0.00 & 0.00 & 0.00 \\ -0.03 & 0.61 & 0.00 & 0.00 \\ 0.02 & -0.01 & 0.31 & 0.00 \\ 0.21 & -0.07 & -0.01 & 1.09 \end{bmatrix}$$

$$= \begin{bmatrix} 0.70 & 0.17 & 0.04 & 0.05 \\ -0.14 & 0.76 & -0.08 & 0.04 \\ 0.06 & 0.01 & 0.36 & 0.01 \\ 0.30 & 0.08 & -0.04 & 1.37 \end{bmatrix}.$$

The impulse responses for longer lags are computed as $IRF_h(\widehat{\theta}) = \widehat{\Psi}_{h-1}(\widehat{\theta})\widehat{S}$. For this example, there are $N^2 = 4^2 = 16$ impulse response functions for each h, with the effects of an interest rate shock of the $N = 4$ variables given in the first column, the effects of a money shock in the second column, etc.   □

Impulse responses are nonlinear functions of the estimated parameters of the VAR. To compute standard errors, three approaches are commonly used, namely, the delta method, Monte Carlo techniques and bootstrapping. An example of the Monte Carlo approach is given in Exercise 12.

13.10.3   Variance Decompositions

The one standard deviation impulse response function in (13.43) gives the conditional mean of the distribution of y_t. The variance decomposition is concerned with the conditional variance of the impulse responses. Write the VAR in equation (13.43) at time $t + h$ as

$$y_{t+h} = Sz_{t+h} + \Psi_1 Sz_{t+h-1} + \Psi_2 Sz_{t+h-2} + \Psi_3 Sz_{t+h-3} + \cdots.$$

From the properties of z_t, the conditional mean is

$$E_t[y_{t+h}] = E_t[Sz_{t+h} + \Psi_1 Sz_{t+h-1} + \Psi_2 Sz_{t+h-2} + \Psi_3 Sz_{t+h-3} + \cdots]$$
$$= \Psi_h Sz_t + \Psi_{h+1} Sz_{t-1} + \cdots.$$

The conditional variance is decomposed as

$$
\begin{aligned}
VD_h &= E_t \left[(y_{t+h} - E_t[y_{t+h}])(y_{t+h} - E_t[y_{t+h}])' \right] \\
&= E_t \left[(Sz_{t+h} + \cdots + \Psi_{h-1} Sz_{t+1})(Sz_{t+h} + \cdots + \Psi_{h-1} Sz_{t+1})' \right] \\
&= SE_t \left[z_{t+h} z'_{t+h} \right] S' + \Psi_1 SE_t \left[z_{t+h-1} z'_{t+h-1} \right] S' \Psi'_1 + \cdots \\
&\quad + \Psi_{h-1} SE_t \left[z_{t+1} z'_{t+1} \right] S' \Psi'_{h-1} \\
&= \sum_{i=0}^{h-1} \Psi_i SS' \Psi'_i, \quad h = 1, 2, \cdots,
\end{aligned}
\tag{13.45}
$$

with $\Psi_0 = I_N$. The last step follows since $E[z_t z'_t] = I_N$ by definition.

Alternatively, (13.45) is written in terms of the separate contributions of each of the N shocks in the system to the h-step ahead variances

$$
VD_h = \sum_{i=0}^{h-1} \Psi_i S_1 S'_1 \Psi'_i + \sum_{i=0}^{h-1} \Psi_i S_2 S'_2 \Psi'_i + \cdots + \sum_{i=0}^{h-1} \Psi_i S_N S'_N \Psi'_i, \, h = 1, 2, \cdots,
$$

where S_i is the ith column of S. An even simpler expression of the variance decomposition is just

$$
VD_h = \sum_{i=0}^{h-1} \left[\Psi_i S \right] \odot \left[\Psi_i S \right] = \sum_{i=1}^{h} IRF_i \odot IRF_i,
$$

where $\odot$ is the Hadamard product, which in this case is simply computed by squaring each element of the matrix IRF_i defined in (13.44).

Example 13.26 Variance Decomposition of the United States VAR

Consider again the VAR(2) model estimated in Example 13.19 and used for the illustration of impulse response analysis in Example 13.25. The computation of the first two variance decompositions requires

$$
\begin{aligned}
IRF_1(\widehat{\theta}) \odot IRF_1(\widehat{\theta}) &=
\begin{bmatrix}
0.53^2 & 0.00^2 & 0.00^2 & 0.00^2 \\
-0.03^2 & 0.61^2 & 0.00^2 & 0.00^2 \\
0.02^2 & -0.01^2 & 0.31^2 & 0.00^2 \\
0.21^2 & -0.07^2 & -0.01^2 & 1.09^2
\end{bmatrix} \\
&=
\begin{bmatrix}
0.29 & 0.00 & 0.00 & 0.00 \\
0.00 & 0.37 & 0.00 & 0.00 \\
0.00 & 0.00 & 0.10 & 0.00 \\
0.04 & 0.01 & 0.00 & 1.19
\end{bmatrix},
\end{aligned}
$$

and

$$IRF_2(\widehat{\theta}) \odot IRF_2(\widehat{\theta}) = \begin{bmatrix} 0.70^2 & 0.17^2 & 0.04^2 & 0.05^2 \\ -0.14^2 & 0.76^2 & -0.08^2 & 0.04^2 \\ 0.06^2 & 0.01^2 & 0.36^2 & 0.01^2 \\ 0.30^2 & 0.08^2 & -0.04^2 & 1.37^2 \end{bmatrix}$$

$$= \begin{bmatrix} 0.49 & 0.03 & 0.00 & 0.00 \\ 0.02 & 0.58 & 0.01 & 0.00 \\ 0.00 & 0.00 & 0.13 & 0.00 \\ 0.09 & 0.01 & 0.00 & 1.87 \end{bmatrix},$$

The variance decompositions at $h = 1$ are

$$VD_1 = IRF_1(\widehat{\theta}) \odot IRF_1(\widehat{\theta}) = \begin{bmatrix} 0.29 & 0.00 & 0.00 & 0.00 \\ 0.00 & 0.37 & 0.00 & 0.00 \\ 0.00 & 0.00 & 0.10 & 0.00 \\ 0.04 & 0.01 & 0.00 & 1.19 \end{bmatrix},$$

and the variance decompositions at $h = 2$ are

$$VD_2 = IRF_1(\widehat{\theta}) \odot IRF_1(\widehat{\theta}) + IRF_2(\widehat{\theta}) \odot IRF_2(\widehat{\theta})$$

$$= \begin{bmatrix} 0.78 & 0.03 & 0.00 & 0.00 \\ 0.02 & 0.95 & 0.01 & 0.00 \\ 0.00 & 0.00 & 0.23 & 0.00 \\ 0.13 & 0.01 & 0.00 & 3.06 \end{bmatrix}.$$

The total variance of each variable is given by the row sums of each VD, with the elements representing the contribution of each of the $N = 4$ variables to the total variance. For example, the total variance of the $h = 2$ step ahead forecast error in the output equation of the VAR is given by the last row of VD_2

$$\text{var}(output) = 0.13 + 0.01 + 0.00 + 3.06 = 3.20,$$

where 0.13 is the contribution of the interest rate, 0.01 is the contribution of money, 0.00 is the contribution of price and 3.06 is the contribution of output.

□

13.11 Applications

This section provides two examples to show how theoretical economic models can be represented as a VAR. An important implication of the analysis is that economic theory imposes cross-equation restrictions on the parameters of a VAR reducing the number of unknown parameters that need to be estimated.

13.11.1 Barro's Rational Expectations Model

Consider a rational expectations model of nominal money, m_t, and real output, o_t,

$$\Delta \ln m_t = \alpha_0 + \alpha_1 \Delta \ln m_{t-1} + \alpha_2 \Delta \ln m_{t-2} + v_{1,t} \tag{13.46}$$

$$\Delta \ln o_t = \beta_0 + \beta_1(\Delta \ln m_{t-1} - E_{t-2}[\Delta \ln m_{t-1}])$$
$$+ \beta_2(\Delta \ln m_{t-2} - E_{t-3}[\Delta \ln m_{t-2}]) + v_{2,t}. \tag{13.47}$$

This is an abbreviated version of the model originally specified by Barro (1978). The first equation is an AR(2) model of the growth rate of nominal money, while the second equation shows that the growth rate of real output responds to lags in the unanticipated growth rate in nominal money, m_t.

Using (13.46) to form the conditional expectations of m_t, the unanticipated money shock is

$$v_{1,t} = \Delta \ln m_t - E_{t-1}[\Delta \ln m_t]$$
$$= \Delta \ln m_t - \alpha_0 - \alpha_1 \Delta \ln m_{t-1} - \alpha_2 \Delta \ln m_{t-2}.$$

Using this expression in equation (13.47) gives

$$\Delta \ln o_t = \delta_0 + \delta_1 \Delta \ln m_{t-1} + \delta_2 \Delta \ln m_{t-2} + \delta_3 \Delta \ln m_{t-3}$$
$$+ \delta_4 \Delta \ln m_{t-4} + v_{2,t}, \tag{13.48}$$

where

$$\delta_0 = \beta_0 - \beta_1 \alpha_0 - \beta_2 \alpha_0$$
$$\delta_1 = \beta_1$$
$$\delta_2 = \beta_2 - \beta_1 \alpha_1$$
$$\delta_3 = -\beta_1 \alpha_2 - \beta_2 \alpha_1$$
$$\delta_4 = -\beta_2 \alpha_2.$$

Equations (13.46) and (13.48) form a restricted bivariate VAR in the sense that lags in $\Delta \ln o_t$ are excluded from the model, the lags of $\Delta \ln m_t$ in the two equations differ and, most important from a rational expectations perspective, there are two cross-equation restrictions given by

$$\delta_3 = -\delta_1 \alpha_2 - (\delta_2 + \delta_1 \alpha_1)\alpha_1, \qquad \delta_4 = -(\delta_2 + \delta_1 \alpha_1)\alpha_2.$$

The restricted VAR can be estimated by maximum likelihood methods using an iterative algorithm to yield consistent and asymptotically efficient parameters estimates.

This contrasts with the earlier approaches used to estimate (13.46) and (13.47), in which equation (13.46) would be estimated by ordinary least squares to get estimates of the α_is and, in particular, the residuals $\widehat{v}_{i,t}$. The output equation would then be estimated by regressing $\Delta \ln o_t$ on a constant and the lagged residuals $\widehat{v}_{1,t-1}$ and $\widehat{v}_{1,t-2}$. The problem with this method is that the standard errors are incorrect because the regressors based on lags of $\widehat{v}_{1,t}$ do not recognise that these variables contain the estimated parameters $\widehat{a}_i$s, which are estimated subject to error, the so-called generated regressors problem. The maximum likelihood method avoids this problem as the system is estimated jointly with the restrictions imposed.

A test of rational expectations is a test of the cross-equation restrictions. One approach is to estimate equations (13.46) and (13.48) jointly by maximum likelihood methods and use the nonlinear form of the Wald test to determine if the restrictions are consistent with the data. From Chapter 4, the nonlinear version of the Wald statistic is

$$W = T[C(\widehat{\theta}_1) - Q]'[D(\theta)\widehat{\Omega}D(\theta)']^{-1}[C(\widehat{\theta}_1) - Q)],$$

in which $\theta = \{\alpha_0, \alpha_1, \alpha_2, \delta_0, \delta_1, \delta_2, \delta_3, \delta_4\}$, and

$$C(\theta) = \begin{bmatrix} \delta_3 + \delta_1\alpha_2 + (\delta_2 + \delta_1\alpha_1)\alpha_1 \\ \delta_4 + (\delta_2 + \delta_1\alpha_1)\alpha_2 \end{bmatrix}, \quad Q = \begin{bmatrix} 0 \\ 0 \end{bmatrix},$$

$$D(\theta) = \frac{\partial C}{\partial \theta'} = \begin{bmatrix} 0 & 2\delta_1\alpha_1 & \delta_1 & 0 & \alpha_2 & \alpha_1 & 1 & 0 \\ 0 & \delta_1\alpha_2 & \delta_1\alpha_1 & 0 & \alpha_1\alpha_2 & \alpha_2 & 0 & 1 \end{bmatrix}.$$

Under the null hypothesis that the restrictions are valid, W is distributed asymptotically as χ^2 with two degrees of freedom. A failure to reject the null hypothesis is evidence in favour of rational expectations.

13.11.2   The Campbell-Shiller Present Value Model

The present value model relates the stock price, s_t, to the discounted stream of dividends, d_t. Campbell and Shiller (1987) show that the present value of the stock price is given by

$$s_t = \alpha(1 - \delta)E_t \sum_{i=0}^{\infty} \delta^i d_{t+i}, \tag{13.49}$$

in which δ is the discount factor and $\alpha = 27.342$ is a coefficient of proportionality which is estimated from the least squares equation

$$s_t = \beta + \alpha d_t + \eta_t, \tag{13.50}$$

where β is an intercept and η_t is a disturbance term. Although α is estimated, which again raises the potential problem of a generated regressor, Part FIVE shows that this estimator is superconsistent under certain conditions because (13.50) represents what is known as a cointegrating equation.

Table 13.4. *Maximum likelihood estimates of the unrestricted and restricted present value models for the United States, January 1933 to December 1990. Standard errors and t statistics are based on quasi-maximum likelihood estimates allowing for heteroskedasticity*

Unrestricted				Restricted			
Param.	Est.	se	t stat.	Param.	Est.	se	t stat.
μ_1	0.105	0.042	2.491	μ_1	1.630	0.094	17.323
$\phi_{1,1,1}$	0.945	0.021	44.411	$\phi_{1,1,1}$	0.026	0.009	2.850
$\phi_{1,1,2}$	0.002	0.002	1.428	$\phi_{1,1,2}$	0.009	0.006	1.460
μ_2	0.190	0.124	1.529	μ_2	1.177	0.395	2.982
$\phi_{1,2,1}$	−0.110	0.097	−1.134	δ	0.806	0.116	6.960
$\phi_{1,2,2}$	0.982	0.016	61.827				
$\ln L_T(\widehat{\theta}_1) = -4.100$				$\ln L_T(\widehat{\theta}_0) = -5.172$			

Campbell and Shiller argue that the superconsistency of α circumvents the generated-regressors problem, a result that is formalised in Section 18.6.2 of Chapter 18. Let the dynamics of $y_t = [\Delta d_t, \eta_t]'$ be represented by a VAR(1)

$$\begin{bmatrix} \Delta d_t \\ \eta_t \end{bmatrix} = \begin{bmatrix} \mu_1 \\ \mu_2 \end{bmatrix} + \begin{bmatrix} \phi_{1,1,1} & \phi_{1,1,2} \\ \phi_{1,2,1} & \phi_{1,2,2} \end{bmatrix} \begin{bmatrix} \Delta d_{t-1} \\ \eta_{t-1} \end{bmatrix} + \begin{bmatrix} v_{1,t} \\ v_{2,t} \end{bmatrix}. \quad (13.51)$$

Campbell and Shiller show that

$$\phi_{1,2,1} = -\alpha\phi_{1,1,1}, \quad \phi_{1,2,2} = \delta^{-1} - \alpha\phi_{1,1,2}. \quad (13.52)$$

Substituting these parameters into (13.51) gives the restricted VAR

$$\begin{bmatrix} \Delta d_t \\ \eta_t \end{bmatrix} = \begin{bmatrix} \mu_1 \\ \mu_2 \end{bmatrix} + \begin{bmatrix} \phi_{1,1,1} & \phi_{1,1,2} \\ -\alpha\phi_{1,1,1} & \delta^{-1} - \alpha\phi_{1,1,2} \end{bmatrix} \begin{bmatrix} \Delta d_{t-1} \\ \eta_{t-1} \end{bmatrix} + \begin{bmatrix} v_{1,t} \\ v_{2,t} \end{bmatrix}. \quad (13.53)$$

There are five parameters to be estimated $\theta = \{\mu_1, \mu_2, \phi_{1,1,1}, \phi_{1,1,2}, \delta\}$, compared to the unrestricted VAR in equation (13.51) in which there are six parameters. There is, thus, one cross-equation restriction imposed by theory.

Table 13.4 gives the maximum likelihood estimates of the unrestricted model in equation (13.52) and the restricted model in equation (13.53) using data on monthly real equity prices, s_t, and real dividends, d_t, from January 1933 to December 1990 for the United States in a sample size of 696 observations. Allowing for one lag and the calculation of Δd_t, the sample size used in the estimation is $T = 694$. The estimate of the discount parameter is $\widehat{\delta} = 0.806$, which implies a discount rate of 24.07% as

$$\widehat{r} = \widehat{\delta}^{-1} - 1 = \frac{1}{0.806} - 1 = 0.2407.$$

To test the cross-equation restriction, a LR statistic is used. Using the unrestricted and restricted log-likelihood values reported in Table 13.4 gives

$$LR = -2T(\ln L_T(\widehat{\theta}_0) - \ln L_T(\widehat{\theta}_1)) = -2 \times 694 \times (-5.172 + 4.100)$$
$$= 1489.171.$$

The p-value is 0.000, resulting in a clear rejection of the restriction at the 5% level.

13.12   Exercises

(1) Time Series Properties of Macroeconomic Variables

Program files	stsm_properties.*
Data files	sims_data.*

The data file contains monthly macroeconomic data for the United States for $y_t = [r_t, lm_t, lp_t, lo_t]'$, in which r_t is the interest rate, lm_t is the logarithm of money, lp_t is the logarithm of prices and lo_t is the logarithm of output.

(a) Plot the variables and interpret their time series properties.
(b) Repeat part (a) for the 1st differenced variables, Δy_t.
(c) Repeat part (a) for the 12th differenced variables, $\Delta_{12} y_t$.
(d) Repeat part (a) using the filter proposed by Sims (1972), namely $(1 - 0.75L^2)y_t$.
(e) Compute the ACF and PACF for y_t, Δy_t and $\Delta_{12} y_t$ and interpret the results.

(2) Simulating ARMA Models

Program files	stsm_simulate.*

Consider the ARMA(2, 2) model

$$y_t = \mu + \phi_1 y_{t-1} + \phi_2 y_{t-2} + v_t + \psi_1 v_{t-1} + \psi_2 v_{t-2},$$

in which $v_t \sim iid\ N(0, \sigma_v^2)$.

(a) Simulate the following models for $T = 200$ observations using the parameter values given in the table.

Model	μ	ϕ_1	ϕ_2	ψ_1	ψ_2	σ_v^2
ARMA(0, 0) :	0.0	0.0	0.0	0.0	0.0	0.1
ARMA(1, 0) :	0.0	0.7	0.0	0.0	0.0	0.1
ARMA(2, 0) :	0.0	0.7	−0.5	0.0	0.0	0.1
ARMA(0, 1) :	0.0	0.0	0.0	0.9	0.0	0.1
ARMA(0, 2) :	0.0	0.0	0.0	−0.2	0.7	0.1
ARMA(1, 1) :	0.0	0.8	0.0	0.7	0.0	0.1

(*Hint: You should simulate $T + 100$ observations and then exclude the first 100 observations to avoid the initialisation problem*).
(b) Estimate the ACF for each model and interpret the results. Compare the estimated ACF with the theoretical ACF in (13.6).
(c) Estimate the PACF for each model and interpret the results.

(3) Stationarity Properties of Macroeconomic Variables

Program files	stsm_roots.*
Data files	sims_data.*

The data file contains monthly macroeconomic data for the United States from January 1959 to December 1998.
(a) Estimate an AR(4) model for the interest rate and determine if the process is stationary by computing the roots of the polynomial $1 - \phi_1 z - \phi_2 z^2 - \phi_3 z^3 - \phi_4 z^4 = 0$.
(b) Estimate an AR(2) model for the annual percentage growth rate in output, $100\Delta_{12} \ln o_t$, and determine if the process is stationary by computing the roots of the polynomial $1 - \phi_1 z - \phi_2 z^2 = 0$.
(c) Repeat part (b) but now for the level of the logarithm of output, $\ln o_t$.
(d) Estimate a VAR(2) containing a constant, the annual percentage growth rate of money $100\Delta_{12} \ln m_t$, and the annual percentage inflation rate, $100\Delta_{12} \ln p_t$, and determine if the processes are stationary by computing the roots of the polynomial $|1 - \Phi_1 z - \Phi_2 z^2| = 0$.
(e) Estimate a VAR(2) containing a constant, the interest rate, r_t, the annual percentage growth rate of money, $100\Delta_{12} \ln m_t$, the annual percentage inflation rate, $100\Delta_{12} \ln p_t$, and the annual percentage growth rate of output, $100\Delta_{12} \ln o_t$, and determine if the processes are stationary by computing the roots of the polynomial $|1 - \Phi_1 z - \Phi_2 z^2| = 0$.
(f) Repeat part (e) for a VAR(4).

(4) ARMA Models for Macroeconomic Variables

Program files	stsm_arma.*
Data files	sims_data.*

The data file contains monthly macroeconomic data for the United States from January 1959 to December 1998.

(a) Use the BFGS algorithm to estimate an ARMA(1,1) model for the interest rate, r_t,

$$y_t = \mu + \phi_1 y_{t-1} + v_t + \psi_1 v_{t-1}, \qquad v_t \sim iid \; N(0, \sigma_v^2),$$

and perform LR and Wald tests of the restrictions (i) $\phi_1 = 0$; and (ii) $\psi_1 = 0$.

(b) Repeat part (a) for the annual percentage inflation rate, $100\Delta_{12} l p_t$.

(c) Repeat part (a) for the annual percentage growth rate of output, $100\Delta_{12} l o_t$.

(5) The Gauss-Newton Algorithm

Program files	stsm_gaussn.*

Consider the ARMA(1,1) model

$$y_t = \mu + \phi_1 y_{t-1} + v_t + \psi_1 v_{t-1}, \qquad v_t \sim iid \; N(0, \sigma_v^2).$$

(a) Show how the parameters of the model can be estimated using the Gauss-Newton algorithm. Show all of the steps.

(b) Simulate the ARMA(1,1) model for $T = 200$ observations using the population parameters $\theta_0 = \{\mu = 0.0, \phi_1 = 0.8, \psi_1 = 0.3, \sigma_v^2 = 1\}$.

(c) Using the simulated data in part (b), estimate the model using the Gauss-Newton algorithm where the starting values are chosen as $\theta_{(0)} = \{\mu = 0.2, \phi_1 = 0.2, \psi_1 = 0.2\}$ and where σ_v^2 is concentrated from the log-likelihood function. In addition, estimate the asymptotic covariance matrix as well as the t statistics. Compare the maximum likelihood estimates $\widehat{\theta}$ with θ_0.

(d) Perform Wald and LM tests of the hypothesis $\psi_1 = 0$. What relative advantage does the LM test have over the Wald test in this example?

(e) Repeat part (c) with the starting values $\theta_{(0)} = \{\mu = 0.0, \phi_1 = 0.0, \psi_1 = 0.0\}$. Why does the algorithm fail in this case?

(f) Repeat part (c) with the starting values $\theta_{(0)} = \{\mu = 0.0, \phi_1 = 0.3, \psi_1 = 1.1\}$. Estimate the model for a larger sample size of $T = 500$. Why does the algorithm fail for the larger sample of $T = 500$, but not for the smaller sample size of $T = 200$? Should not more data provide greater precision?

(g) Repeat part (c) with the starting values $\theta_{(0)} = \{\mu = 0.0, \phi_1 = 1.1, \psi_1 = 0.3\}$. Comparing the results to part (f), why does the algorithm not fail for this model? In addition, suggest an alternative and perhaps better way of estimating this model still using the same algorithm.

(6) Properties of LM Tests of ARMA Models

Program files   stsm_lm.*

Simulate $T = 200$ observations using the ARMA(1, 1) model of Exercise 5.

(a) *(Equivalence Result)* Derive the following LM regression-based tests.
  (i) A test of $\phi_1 = 0$ in the AR(1) $y_t = \mu + \phi_1 y_{t-1} + v_t$.
  (ii) A test of $\psi_1 = 0$ in the MA(1) model $y_t = \mu + v_t + \psi_1 v_{t-1}$. Hence show the equivalence of the two LM tests analytically and numerically using simulated data (Poskitt and Tremayne, 1980).

(b) *(Singularity Result)* Use the simulated data to perform a LM regression-based test of $\phi_1 = \psi_1 = 0$ in the ARMA(1, 1) model $y_t = \mu + \phi_1 y_{t-1} + v_t + \psi_1 v_{t-1}$. Hence show both analytically and numerically using simulated data that the test breaks down because of a singularity in the second-stage regression equation.

(7) Estimating and Testing VARMA Models

Program files   stsm_varma.*

Simulate $T = 500$ observations from the VARMA(1, 1) model

$$y_{1,t} = \mu_1 + \phi_{1,1,1} y_{1,t-1} + v_{1,t} + \psi_{1,1,1} v_{1,t-1} + \psi_{1,1,2} v_{2,t-1}$$
$$y_{2,t} = \mu_2 + \phi_{1,2,2} y_{2,t-1} + v_{2,t} + \psi_{1,2,1} v_{1,t-1} + \psi_{1,2,2} v_{2,t-1},$$

in which v_t is bivariate normal with zero mean and covariance matrix given by the identity matrix, and the population parameters are given in Table 13.2.

(a) Compute the maximum likelihood estimates using the Newton-Raphson algorithm.

(b) Repeat part (a) using $T = 1000$ observations. Discuss the asymptotic properties of the maximum likelihood estimator.

(c) Perform LR and Wald tests of the hypothesis

$$H_0 : \psi_{1,1,1} = \psi_{1,1,2} = \psi_{1,2,1} = \psi_{1,2,2} = 0.$$

Choose $T = \{500, 1000\}$ and discuss the consistency properties of the tests.

(8) Testing VARMA Models for Nonlinearities

Program files   stsm_varmab.*

Simulate $T = 500$ observations of the VARMA(1, 1) model set out in Exercise 7, using the population parameters given in Table 13.2.

(a) Use the simulated data to estimate the following nonlinear time series model

$$y_{1,t} = \mu_1 + \phi_{1,1,1} y_{1,t-1} + v_{1,t} + \psi_{1,1,1} v_{1,t-1} + \psi_{1,1,2} v_{2,t-1}$$
$$+ \delta_1 y_{1,t-1} v_{1,t-1}$$
$$y_{2,t} = \mu_2 + \phi_{1,2,2} y_{2,t-1} + v_{2,t} + \psi_{1,2,1} v_{1,t-1} + \psi_{1,2,2} v_{2,t-1}$$
$$+ \delta_2 y_{2,t-1} v_{2,t-1}.$$

The inclusion of the nonlinearities yields a multivariate bilinear model that is studied in greater detail in Chapter 19. Perform LR and Wald tests of multivariate bilinearity

$$H_0 : \delta_1 = \delta_2 = 0 .$$

(b) Briefly discuss how you could make the multivariate test of bilinearity robust to non-normality.

(9) Finite Sample Distribution

Program files   stsm_finite.*

Simulate the AR(1) model $y_t = \phi_1 y_{t-1} + v_t$ in which $v_t \sim iid \, N(0, 1)$ and $\phi_1 = \{0.5, 0.6, 0.7, 0.8, 0.9, 0.95, 0.99\}$. Choose 20000 replications and a sample size of $T = 50$.

(a) Compute the finite sample distribution of the maximum likelihood estimator of ϕ_1 and show that this estimator is biased downwards with the size of the bias approximately equal to $2\phi_1 T^{-1}$ (Shenton and Johnson, 1975).

(b) Show that the bias decreases as the sample size increases, by repeating part (a) for $T = \{100, 500\}$.

(10) Lag Length Determination

Program files   stsm_laglength.*

Simulate the AR(3) model

$$y_t = 0.0 + 0.2 y_{t-1} - 0.15 y_{t-2} + 0.05 y_{t-3} + v_t, \qquad v_t \sim iid \, N(0, 1),$$

2000 times for a sample of size $T = 200$.

(a) For each replication estimate AR(1) to AR(7) models and choose the optimal lag structure based on minimising the AIC, HIC and SIC. Interpret the properties of the statistics to identify the true lag structure of 3.

(b) Redo part (a) for samples of size $T = \{500, 1000, 2000, 5000\}$.

(11) Granger Causality

Program files	stsm_granger.*
Data files	sims_data.*

The data file contains monthly macroeconomic data for the United States from January 1959 to December 1998.

(a) Estimate a VAR(2) containing a constant, the interest rate, the annual percentage growth rate of money, the annual percentage inflation rate and the annual percentage growth of output.

(b) Use a Wald test to construct Granger causality tests between the 4 variables and interpret the results.

(c) Use a Wald test to construct a joint test that a variable fails to be Granger caused by the other 3 variables. That is, test the exogeneity of each of the 4 variables. Interpret the results.

(12) Impulse Responses and Variance Decompositions

Program files	stsm_recursive.*
Data files	sims_data.*

The data file contains monthly macroeconomic data for the United States from January 1959 to December 1998.

(a) Estimate a VAR(2) containing a constant, the interest rate, the annual percentage growth rate of money, the annual percentage inflation rate and the annual percentage growth rate of output.

(b) Compute the moving average parameter matrices, Ψ_0, Ψ_1, Ψ_2, Ψ_3, Ψ_4 and Ψ_5.

(c) Estimate the orthogonalised one standard deviation impulse responses

$$IRF_h = \Psi_{h-1}S, \quad h = 1, 2, \cdots, 5,$$

where $V = SS'$ and $V = \mathrm{E}[v_t v_t']$. Interpret the results.

(d) Estimate the variance decompositions based on the orthogonalised one standard deviation impulse responses

$$VD_h = \sum_{i=1}^{h} IRF_i \odot IRF_i, \quad h = 1, 2, \cdots, 5,$$

and interpret the results.

(e) Generate 95% confidence intervals for the orthogonalised impulses in part (c) and variance decompositions in part (d) using Monte Carlo methods based on the asymptotic distribution of the parameter estimators of the VAR given by $N(\theta_0, \text{cov}(\theta_0))$ in which $\theta_0 = \{\Phi_1, \Phi_2, B_0, D\}$. To implement the approach in practice θ_0 is replaced by $\widehat{\theta}$ so the draws are taken from $N(\widehat{\theta}, \text{cov}(\widehat{\theta}))$. Letting the ith draw from the asymptotic distribution be $\theta^{(i)} = \{\Phi_1^{(i)}, \Phi_2^{(i)}, B_0^{(i)}, D^{(i)}\}$, compute $IRF_h(\theta^{(i)})$ and $VD_h(\theta^{(i)})$. Repeat the process for 10000 draws and extract the 2.5% and 97.5% quantiles to be the 95% confidence intervals for $IRF_h(\widehat{\theta})$ and $VD_h(\widehat{\theta})$.

(13) Diebold-Yilmaz Spillover Index

Program file(s)	stsm_spillover.*
Data file(s)	diebold_yilmaz.*

Diebold and Yilmaz (2009) construct spillover indexes of international real asset returns and volatility based on the variance decomposition of a VAR. The data file contains weekly data on real asset returns, $rets$, and volatility, vol, of 7 developed countries and 12 emerging countries from the first week of January 1992 to the fourth week of November 2007.

(a) Compute descriptive statistics of the 19 real asset market returns given in $rets$. Compare the estimates with the results reported in Table 1 of Diebold and Yilmaz.

(b) Estimate a VAR(2) containing a constant and the 19 real asset market returns.

(c) Estimate VD_{10}, the variance decomposition for horizon $h = 10$, and compare the estimates with the results reported in Table 3 of Diebold and Yilmaz.

(d) Using the results in part (c) compute the 'Contribution from Others' by summing each row of VD_{10} excluding the diagonal elements, and the 'Contribution to Others' by summing each column of VD_{10} excluding the diagonal elements. Interpret the results.

(e) Repeat parts (a) to (d) with the 19 series in $rets$ replaced by vol, and the comparisons now based on Tables 2 and 4 in Diebold and Yilmaz.

(14) Campbell-Shiller Present Value Model

Program file(s)	stsm_camshiller.*
Data file(s)	campbell_shiller.*

The data file contains monthly data on real equity prices, s_t, and real dividends, d_t, for the United States from January 1933 to December 1990.

Consider the present value model of Campbell and Shiller (1987)

$$
\begin{bmatrix} \Delta d_t \\ \eta_t \end{bmatrix} = \begin{bmatrix} \mu_1 \\ \mu_2 \end{bmatrix} + \begin{bmatrix} \phi_{1,1,1} & \phi_{1,1,2} \\ -\alpha\phi_{1,1,1} & \delta^{-1} - \alpha\phi_{1,1,2} \end{bmatrix} \begin{bmatrix} \Delta d_{t-1} \\ \eta_{t-1} \end{bmatrix} + \begin{bmatrix} v_{1,t} \\ v_{2,t} \end{bmatrix}.
$$

in which η_t is the disturbance of the regression equation

$$
s_t = \beta + \alpha d_t + \eta_t .
$$

(a) Estimate the parameter α by regressing s_t on a constant and d.
(b) Given an estimate of α in part (a), compute the maximum likelihood estimates of $\theta = \{\mu_1, \mu_2, \phi_{1,1,1}, \phi_{1,1,2}, \delta\}$.
(c) Perform a LR test of the restriction of the model and interpret the result.
(d) Repeat parts (b) and (c) by increasing the number of lags to two.

14 Structural Vector Autoregressions

14.1 Introduction

The vector autoregression model (VAR) discussed in Chapter 13 provides a convenient framework for modelling dynamic systems of equations. Maximum likelihood estimation of the model is performed one equation at a time using ordinary least squares, while the dynamics of the system are analysed using Granger causality, impulse response analysis and variance decompositions. Although the VAR framework is widely applied in econometrics, it requires the imposition of additional structure on the model in order to give the impulse responses and variance decompositions structural interpretations. For example, in macroeconometric applications, the key focus is often on understanding the effects of a monetary shock on the economy, but this requires the ability to identify precisely what the monetary shock is. In Chapter 13, a recursive structure known as a triangular ordering is adopted to identify shocks. This is a purely statistical approach to identification that imposes a very strict and rigid structure on the dynamics of the model that may not necessarily be consistent with the true structure of the underlying processes. This approach becomes even more problematic when alternative orderings of variables are tried, since the number of combinations of orderings increases dramatically as the number of variables in the model increases.

Structural vector autoregressive (SVAR) models alleviate the problems of imposing a strict recursive structure on the model by specifying restrictions that, in general, are motivated by economic theory. Four common sets of restrictions are used to identify SVARs, namely, short-run restrictions, long-run restrictions, a combination of the two and sign restrictions. Despite the additional acronyms associated with the SVAR literature and the fact that the nature of the applications may seem different at first glance, SVARs simply represent a subset of the class of dynamic linear simultaneous equations models discussed in Part TWO.

14.2 Specification

The most general representation of a SVAR is where all variables in the system are endogenous, as in the following model

$$B_0 y_t = \sum_{i=1}^{p} B_i y_{t-i} + u_t, \qquad u_t \sim iid\ N(0, D), \qquad (14.1)$$

in which y_t is a $(N \times 1)$ vector of the endogenous variables and B_i is a $(N \times N)$ matrix containing the parameters on the ith lag, with B_0 representing the contemporaneous interactions between the variables. The $(N \times 1)$ vector of disturbances, u_t, represents the structural shocks and has covariance matrix D, which is a diagonal matrix containing the variances. It is the fact that the covariances of u_t are all zero that gives u_t its structural interpretation, since each shock is, by definition, independent. As will be seen, the matrices B_0 and D are fundamental to the specification and estimation of SVAR models.

In macroeconomic applications of SVARs, the structural shocks, u_t, may consist of policy shocks, monetary or fiscal, goods market shocks arising from either aggregate demand or supply, nominal shocks and asset market shocks. The following example helps to clarify the relationship between y_t and u_t.

Example 14.1 A Prototype Macroeconomic Model

Consider the four-variable macroeconomic model consisting of the logarithm of output, the interest rate, the logarithm of prices and the logarithm of money: $y_t = [\ln o_t\ r_t\ \ln p_t\ \ln m_t]'$. The model is

$$
\begin{aligned}
\ln\left(\frac{p_t}{p_{t-1}}\right) &= b_1(\ln o_t - u_{as,t}) && \text{Aggregate supply} \\
\ln o_t &= -b_2\left(r_t - \ln\left(\frac{p_t}{p_{t-1}}\right)\right) - u_{is,t} && \text{IS equation} \\
\ln\left(\frac{m_t}{p_t}\right) &= b_3 \ln o_t - b_4 r_t - u_{md,t} && \text{Money demand} \\
\ln m_t &= u_{ms,t}, && \text{Money supply}
\end{aligned}
$$

in which all parameters b_i are positive. The aggregate supply equation expresses inflation as a positive function of real output. The IS equation represents a negative relationship between real output and the real interest rate. The money demand equation shows that real money is a function of real output and the nominal interest rate and the money supply is exogenous as specified by the last equation. The structural shocks are $u_t = [u_{as,t}\ u_{is,t}\ u_{md,t}\ u_{ms,t}]'$, which correspond to shocks in aggregate supply, the IS schedule, money demand and money supply. The parameter matrices for the specification in equation (14.1) with $p = 1$ are

$$
B_0 = \begin{bmatrix} 1 & 0 & -b_1^{-1} & 0 \\ b_2^{-1} & 1 & -1 & 0 \\ b_3 & -b_4 & 1 & -1 \\ 0 & 0 & 0 & 1 \end{bmatrix}, \qquad B_1 = \begin{bmatrix} 0 & 0 & -b_1^{-1} & 0 \\ 0 & 0 & -1 & 0 \\ 0 & 0 & 0 & 0 \\ 0 & 0 & 0 & 0 \end{bmatrix},
$$

in which B_0 represents the contemporaneous effects of shocks of y_t, and B_1 captures the dynamics of the model.   □

An alternative representation of equation (14.1), discussed in Chapter 13, commonly adopted in modelling SVARs, is to define the standardised random variable

$$
z_t = D^{-1/2} u_t, \tag{14.2}
$$

in which $D^{1/2}$ contains the standard deviations on the diagonal and

$$
\begin{aligned}
E[z_t] &= D^{-1/2} E[u_t] = 0 \\
E[z_t z_t'] &= D^{-1/2} E[u_t u_t'](D^{-1/2})' = D^{-1/2} DD^{-1/2} = I_N.
\end{aligned} \tag{14.3}
$$

It follows from equations (14.1) and (14.3) that $z_t \sim iid\, N(0, I_N)$, in which case equation (14.1) is rewritten in terms of standard deviation shocks z_t

$$
B_0 y_t = \sum_{i=1}^{p} B_i y_{t-i} + D^{1/2} z_t. \tag{14.4}
$$

Shocks presented in this form are referred to as one-standard deviation shocks since an increase in $z_{i,t}$ is multiplied by $D_{i,i}^{1/2}$, which is by definition the standard deviation of the structural shock $u_{i,t}$.

The dynamics of the structural model in equation (14.4) are summarised by its VAR representation (see Chapter 13) and also by its reduced-form representation (see Chapter 5)

$$
y_t = \sum_{i=1}^{p} B_0^{-1} B_i y_{t-i} + B_0^{-1} D^{1/2} z_t = \sum_{i=1}^{p} \Phi_i y_{t-i} + v_t, \tag{14.5}
$$

where

$$
\Phi_i = B_0^{-1} B_i, \tag{14.6}
$$

is the matrix of autoregressive parameters at lag i and

$$
v_t = B_0^{-1} D^{1/2} z_t = S z_t, \tag{14.7}
$$

is the reduced-form disturbance vector with

$$
S = B_0^{-1} D^{1/2}. \tag{14.8}
$$

From the properties of z_t in equation (14.3), v_t satisfies

$$
\begin{aligned}
\mathrm{E}\,[v_t] &= S\,\mathrm{E}[z_t] = 0 \\
\mathrm{E}\,[v_t v_t'] &= S\,\mathrm{E}[z_t z_t']S' = S\,I_N\,S' = SS' = V\,,
\end{aligned}
\tag{14.9}
$$

and it follows from the distribution of z_t that $v_t \sim iid\ N(0, V)$. Unlike the structural shocks z_t, which are orthogonal, v_t in (14.5) is not orthogonal since V is not necessarily a diagonal matrix.

The dynamics of the reduced form in equation (14.5) are explored by writing this equation in terms of the lag operator (see Appendix B)

$$
y_t - \sum_{i=1}^{p} \Phi_i y_{t-i} = v_t
$$

$$
(I - \Phi_1 L - \Phi_2 L^2 - \cdots - \Phi_p L^p)y_t = v_t
$$

$$
\Phi(L)y_t = v_t\,,
\tag{14.10}
$$

in which $L^k y_t = y_{t-k}$ defines the lag operator and

$$
\Phi(L) = I_N - \Phi_1 L - \Phi_2 L^2 - \cdots - \Phi_p L^p\,.
\tag{14.11}
$$

From Chapter 13, inverting equation (14.11) gives the vector moving average representation

$$
y_t = \Phi(L)^{-1}v_t = \Psi(L)v_t\,,
\tag{14.12}
$$

where

$$
\Psi(L) = \Psi_0 + \Psi_1 L + \Psi_2 L^2 + \cdots + \Psi_q L^q + \cdots\,,
\tag{14.13}
$$

and $\Psi_0 = I_N$. The effect of a shock in v_t on the future time path of the dependent variables, $y_t, y_{t+1}, y_{t+2}, \cdots$, are, respectively, the $(N \times N)$ parameter matrices $\Psi_0, \Psi_1, \Psi_2, \cdots$.

Example 14.2 A Bivariate VAR of Output and Prices

Consider a VAR(2) model consisting of the logarithm of output and the logarithm of prices, so that $y_t = \begin{bmatrix} \Delta \ln o_t & \Delta \ln p_t \end{bmatrix}'$ in which the variables are scaled by 400 and the parameter matrices are defined as

$$
\mu = \begin{bmatrix} 2.606 \\ 0.250 \end{bmatrix}, \quad
\Phi_1 = \begin{bmatrix} 0.352 & -0.773 \\ 0.059 & 0.577 \end{bmatrix}, \quad
\Phi_2 = \begin{bmatrix} 0.069 & 0.487 \\ -0.032 & 0.300 \end{bmatrix},
$$

and the covariance matrix of v_t is

$$
V = \begin{bmatrix} 7.066 & 0.357 \\ 0.357 & 1.092 \end{bmatrix}.
$$

The first VMA matrix in equation (14.13) is $\Psi_0 = I_2$ and the next three are

$$
\Psi_1 = \begin{bmatrix} 0.352 & -0.773 \\ 0.059 & 0.577 \end{bmatrix}, \quad
\Psi_2 = \begin{bmatrix} 0.147 & -0.232 \\ 0.023 & 0.587 \end{bmatrix}, \quad
\Psi_3 = \begin{bmatrix} 0.087 & -0.308 \\ 0.028 & 0.523 \end{bmatrix}.
$$

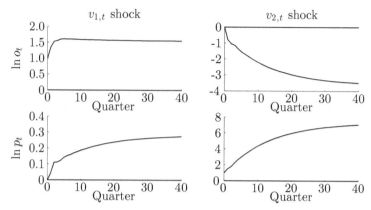

Figure 14.1. The effects of non-orthogonalised shocks, v_t on $\ln o_t$ and $\ln p_t$ in a bivariate VAR model of output and prices.

Cumulating these VMA matrices expresses the effects of v_t on the level of the variables $\ln o_t$ and $\ln p_t$, which are given in Figure 14.1 for an horizon of $h = 40$ quarters. The contemporaneous short-run effects at $h = 0$ of the shocks are given by $\Psi_0 = I_2$, while the long-run effects at $h = 40$ are computed as

$$\sum_{i=0}^{40} \Psi_i = \begin{bmatrix} 1.560 & -3.585 \\ 0.338 & 7.245 \end{bmatrix},$$

corresponding to the last elements in Figure 14.1.   □

The link between a VAR in equation (14.5) and the structural model in equation (14.4) is important in practice, because it is a VAR that is commonly estimated at the first stage of SVAR modelling. But this initial estimation causes a problem since the VAR generates non-orthogonalised shocks, v_t, that are not the structural shocks, z_t. This problem is addressed at the second stage of SVAR modelling where identification of the structural shocks from the VAR shocks is achieved through the imposition of restrictions on the model. What this means in practice is that estimates of the structural parameters $B_0, B_1, \cdots, B_p$ and D in equation (14.4) need to be identified from the estimates of the VAR in equation (14.5), because it is these structural parameters that represent the effects of z_t on y_t. Four sets of restrictions are used to achieve identification.

14.2.1   Short-Run Restrictions

The earliest method of identifying the shocks in SVAR models is based on short-run restrictions. This is formally obtained by imposing zero restrictions on the matrix B_0 in (14.4) since it represents the contemporaneous relationships between the variables y_t.

Example 14.3 The Sims Recursive Model

The Sims (1980) model of the United States economy, discussed in Chapter 13, can be interpreted as representing the first SVAR model that imposes a recursive structure on the short-run parameters. The model contains $N = 4$ variables: the interest rate, the logarithm of money, the logarithm of prices and the logarithm of output, $y_t = [r_t \ \ln m_t \ \ln p_t \ \ln o_t]'$. The model has a recursive structure with the contemporaneous matrix B_0 restricted to be lower triangular

$$
B_0 = \begin{bmatrix}
1 & 0 & 0 & 0 \\
-b_{2,1} & 1 & 0 & 0 \\
-b_{3,1} & -b_{3,2} & 1 & 0 \\
-b_{4,1} & -b_{4,2} & -b_{4,3} & 1
\end{bmatrix} .
$$

This means that the model imposes the following short-run ordering

$$
r_t \ \longrightarrow \ \ln m_t \ \longrightarrow \ \ln p_t \ \longrightarrow \ \ln o_t .
$$

$\square$

Example 14.4 The Kim and Roubini Nonrecursive Model

Kim and Roubini (2000) specify a seven-variable macroeconomic model with nonrecursive restrictions imposed on the short-run parameters. The model includes the variables used in the Sims model but also adds three other variables: the logarithm of the oil price, the Federal funds rate and the logarithm of the exchange rate, $y_t = [r_t \ \ln m_t \ \ln p_t \ \ln o_t \ \ln oil_t \ fed_t \ \ln e_t]'$. The standardised structural shocks comprise shocks to the money supply, money demand, prices, output, the oil price, monetary policy and the exchange rate, $z_t = [z_{ms,t} \ z_{md,t} \ z_{p,t} \ z_{o,t} \ z_{oil,t} \ z_{fed,t} \ z_{e,t}]'$. The contemporaneous matrix, B_0, is specified as

$$
B_0 = \begin{bmatrix}
1 & -b_{1,2} & 0 & 0 & -b_{1,5} & 0 & -b_{1,7} \\
-b_{2,1} & 1 & -b_{2,2} & -b_{2,3} & 0 & 0 & 0 \\
0 & 0 & 1 & -b_{3,4} & -b_{3,5} & 0 & 0 \\
0 & 0 & 0 & 1 & -b_{4,5} & 0 & 0 \\
0 & 0 & 0 & 0 & 1 & 0 & 0 \\
0 & 0 & 0 & 0 & -b_{6,5} & 1 & 0 \\
-b_{7,1} & -b_{7,2} & -b_{7,3} & -b_{7,4} & -b_{7,5} & -b_{7,6} & 1
\end{bmatrix} .
$$

As B_0 is non-triangular, the model has a nonrecursive structure. The absence of zero cells in the last row of B_0 shows that the exchange rate is jointly affected by all $N = 7$ shocks in the model. $\square$

To translate the short-run restrictions given in B_0 to the orthogonalised structural shocks, z_t, rewrite the moving average representation in equation (14.12) in terms of the orthogonalised shocks z_t by using v_t in (14.7) to substitute v_t as follows

$$
\begin{aligned}
y_t &= v_t + \Psi_1 v_{t-1} + \Psi_2 v_{t-2} + \cdots \\
&= B_0^{-1} D^{1/2} z_t + \Psi_1 B_0^{-1} D^{1/2} z_{t-1} + \Psi_2 B_0^{-1} D^{1/2} z_{t-2} + \cdots \\
&= S z_t + \Psi_1 S z_{t-1} + \Psi_2 S z_{t-2} + \Psi_3 S z_{t-3} + \cdots .
\end{aligned}
\tag{14.14}
$$

From Chapter 13, the $(N \times N)$ matrices S, $\Psi_1 S$, $\Psi_2 S$, $\cdots$ represent the orthogonalised one-standard deviation impulses.

Once B_0 and D are specified, S is determined from $S = B_0^{-1} D^{1/2}$. This also suggests that short-run restrictions can be imposed either on B_0 or on S directly, or even D. Restrictions on B_0 control contemporaneous relationships between the y_t variables, whereas restrictions on S control the contemporaneous relationships between the y_t variables and the structural shocks. Both methods are commonly adopted in SVAR models. Finally, if B_0 is triangular, then B_0^{-1} and S are both triangular, resulting in the equivalence of the two methods for imposing short-run restrictions. This is not the case for non-recursive models.

Example 14.5 A SVAR Model with Short-run Restrictions

Consider a bivariate SVAR model of the logarithm of output and the logarithm of prices, $y_t = \begin{bmatrix} \Delta \ln o_t & \Delta \ln p_t \end{bmatrix}'$ where the variables are scaled by 400. The structural shocks, $(z_{1,t})$ and $(z_{2,t})$, represent real and nominal shocks, respectively, and the restriction is that nominal shocks do not affect changes in output in the short run. Suppose that the matrix S in (14.14) is defined as

$$
S = \begin{bmatrix} 3 & 0 \\ -1 & 2 \end{bmatrix},
$$

where the zero element corresponds to the short-run restriction. This matrix also shows that real shocks have a short-run negative impact on changes in prices $\Delta y_{2,t}$ equal to -1. Using the VMA parameter matrices from Example 14.2, the cumulated impulse responses of the orthogonalised shocks are given in Figure 14.2 for an horizon of $h = 40$ quarters. By construction the short-run effects at $h = 0$ are represented by S, with $z_{2,t}$ having no contemporaneous effect on $y_{1,t}$ and $z_{1,t}$ having a negative impact on $y_{2,t}$. In the long-run at $h = 40$, both shocks have non-zero effects on the variables where the long-run is computed as

$$
\sum_{i=0}^{40} \Psi_i S = \begin{bmatrix} 1.560 & -3.585 \\ 0.338 & 7.245 \end{bmatrix} \begin{bmatrix} 3 & 0 \\ -1 & 2 \end{bmatrix} = \begin{bmatrix} 8.263 & -7.170 \\ -6.231 & 14.490 \end{bmatrix},
$$

corresponding to the last elements in Figure 14.2.	□

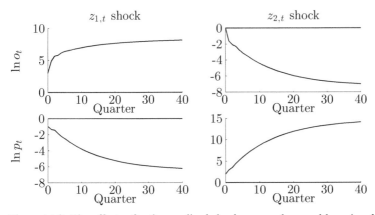

Figure 14.2. The effects of orthogonalised shocks, z_t, on $\ln o_t$ and $\ln p_t$ in a bivariate SVAR model of output and prices with short-run restrictions.

14.2.2 Long-Run Restrictions

The next way to impose restrictions is to constrain the impulse responses in the long run to have values that are motivated by economic theory. The following example exploits the long-run solution of the prototype theoretical model presented earlier.

Example 14.6 A Prototype Macroeconomic Model Revisited

Consider the prototype macroeconomic model of Example 14.1 where long-run equilibrium requires $\ln p_t - \ln p_{t-1} = 0$ and the model reduces to

$$
\begin{aligned}
\ln o_t &= u_{as,t} \\
r_t &= u_{is,t} - b_2^{-1} u_{as,t} \\
\ln p_t &= u_{ms,t} + b_4 u_{is,t} - (b_3 + b_4 b_2^{-1}) u_{as,t} + u_{md,t} \\
m_t &= u_{ms,t}.
\end{aligned}
$$

These equations impose a number of restrictions on the long-run relationship between the model variables $y_t = [\ln o_t \ r_t \ \ln p_t \ \ln m_t]'$ and the structural shocks $u_t = [u_{as,t} \ u_{is,t} \ u_{md,t} \ u_{ms,t}]'$. □

To impose long-run restrictions on the orthogonalised impulse responses, assume that all variables in y_t are expressed in first differences. The long-run effects of a one-standard deviation shock in z_t on the levels of these variables are computed as previously by summing the impulse responses $\Psi_i S$. Letting F represent the long-run matrix, from equation (14.14) the long-run impulse responses are obtained as

$$
F = S + \Psi_1 S + \Psi_2 S + \Psi_3 S + \cdots = \Psi(1)S, \tag{14.15}
$$

with

$$\Psi(1) = I_N + \Psi_1 + \Psi_2 + \Psi_3 + \cdots.$$

It follows from equation (14.15) that the way to restrict impulse responses in the long-run is to impose restrictions on F. Re-arranging equation (14.15) as

$$S = \Psi(1)^{-1} F = \Phi(1) F, \qquad (14.16)$$

shows that S is now expressed in terms of the long-run matrix F weighted by the sum of the VAR parameters in equation (14.10)

$$\Phi(1) = I - \Phi_1 - \Phi_2 - \cdots - \Phi_p. \qquad (14.17)$$

Not surprisingly, in the special case of no dynamics, there is no distinction between the short-run and long-run because $\Phi(1) = I_N$ since $\Phi_i = 0 \; \forall i$.

Example 14.7 A SVAR Model with Long-run Restrictions

Consider the bivariate SVAR model of the logarithm of output and logarithm of prices in Example 14.5 except now nominal shocks do not affect output in the long-run. The long-run matrix F in (14.16) is defined as

$$F = \begin{bmatrix} 3 & 0 \\ -1 & 2 \end{bmatrix},$$

Using the VAR parameter matrices from Example 14.2, $\Phi(1)$ is

$$
\begin{aligned}
\Phi(1) &= I_2 - \Phi_1 - \Phi_2 \\
&= \begin{bmatrix} 1 & 0 \\ 0 & 1 \end{bmatrix} - \begin{bmatrix} 0.352 & -0.773 \\ 0.059 & 0.577 \end{bmatrix} - \begin{bmatrix} 0.069 & 0.487 \\ -0.032 & 0.300 \end{bmatrix} \\
&= \begin{bmatrix} 0.579 & 0.287 \\ -0.027 & 0.123 \end{bmatrix},
\end{aligned}
$$

and from equation (14.16) the S matrix is computed as

$$S = \Phi(1) F = \begin{bmatrix} 0.579 & 0.287 \\ -0.027 & 0.123 \end{bmatrix} \begin{bmatrix} 3 & 0 \\ -1 & 2 \end{bmatrix} = \begin{bmatrix} 1.451 & 0.573 \\ -0.204 & 0.246 \end{bmatrix}.$$

The cumulated impulse responses in Figure 14.3 show that both shocks have short-run effects at $h = 0$ given by S, while the long-run effects are given by F, with the effect of $z_{2,t}$ on $y_{1,t}$ approaching its long-run value of zero. □

Example 14.8 The Blanchard and Quah Model

Blanchard and Quah (1989) specify a bivariate macroeconomic model consisting of the growth rate in output and the unemployment rate, $y_t = [400\Delta \ln o_t \; ue_t]'$. The one-standard deviation structural shocks correspond to aggregate supply and aggregate demand, $z_t = [z_{as,t} \; z_{ad,t}]'$. The model has a

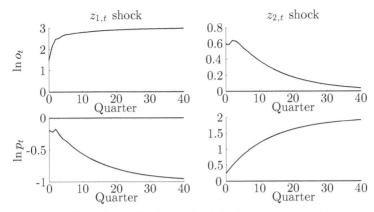

Figure 14.3. The effects of orthogonalised shocks z_t on $\ln o_t$ and $\ln p_t$ in a bivariate SVAR model of output and prices with long-run restrictions.

recursive long-run structure with the long-run parameter matrix F specified as

$$F = \begin{bmatrix} f_{1,1} & 0 \\ f_{2,1} & f_{2,2} \end{bmatrix},$$

where the zero shows that aggregate demand shocks have no long-run effect on output ($f_{1,2} = 0$). □

The Blanchard and Quah model in Example 14.8 emphasises the role of zero restrictions in the long run. The next example uses zero long-run restrictions in conjunction with cross-equation restrictions.

Example 14.9 The Rapach Model

Rapach (2001) specifies a four-variable model consisting of the first differences of the logarithm of prices, the logarithm of real stock prices, the interest rate and the logarithm of output, $y_t = [\Delta \ln p_t \; \Delta \ln s_t \; \Delta r_t \; \Delta \ln o_t]'$. The one-standard deviation structural shocks comprise nominal shocks, portfolio shocks, aggregate demand shocks and aggregate supply shocks, $z_t = [z_{n,t} \; z_{s,t} \; z_{ad,t} \; z_{as,t}]'$. The model has a non-recursive long-run structure with long-run parameter matrix, F, given by

$$F = \begin{bmatrix} f_{1,1} & f_{1,2} & f_{1,3} & f_{1,4} \\ 0 & f_{2,2} & f_{2,3} & f_{2,4} \\ 0 & 0.025 f_{2,2} & f_{3,3} & f_{3,4} \\ 0 & 0 & 0 & f_{4,4} \end{bmatrix}.$$

The first row of the F matrix shows that all shocks affect nominal prices in the long run. The zeros in the second and third rows show that nominal shocks have no long-run effect on the real stock price and the interest rate. The last row represents the natural rate hypothesis whereby only supply shocks affect output in the long run. The restriction $0.025 f_{2,2}$ imposes a long-run relationship between real stock prices and the interest rate, so that a $f_{22} = 10\%$ permanent increase in stock prices requires a $0.025 \times 10 = 2.5\%$ permanent increase in the interest rate to maintain long-run portfolio equilibrium. An alternative identification mechanism is proposed by Fry, Hocking and Martin (2008) discussed later in Section 14.6.   □

14.2.3 Short-Run and Long-Run Restrictions

Another way to impose structure on the model is to use a combination of short-run and long-run restrictions. This requires that constraints are imposed on the contemporaneous impulse responses and on their long-run behaviour. In so doing, the aim is still to specify the structure of the matrix S in terms of these restrictions.

Example 14.10 Combining Short-run and Long-run Restrictions

Consider the bivariate SVAR model of output and prices in Example 14.5, but with the restriction that real structural shocks $z_{1,t}$ do not affect prices $y_{2,t}$ in the short-run and nominal structural shocks $z_{2,t}$ do not affect output $y_{1,t}$ in the long-run. The short-run restriction is $s_{2,1} = 0$. To derive the long-run restriction, as $F = \Phi(1)^{-1} S$ from rearranging (14.16) and where from the VAR in Example 14.2

$$\Phi(1)^{-1} = \begin{bmatrix} 0.579 & 0.287 \\ -0.027 & 0.123 \end{bmatrix}^{-1} = \begin{bmatrix} 1.557 & -3.630 \\ 0.342 & 7.336 \end{bmatrix},$$

the long-run restriction is

$$0 = f_{1,2} = \phi^{1,1} s_{1,2} + \phi^{1,2} s_{2,2} = 1.557 s_{1,2} - 3.630 s_{2,2},$$

in which $\phi^{i,j}$ is the pertinent element of $\Phi(1)^{-1}$. Solving this equation for $s_{2,2}$ yields an expression for S in terms of $s_{1,1}$ and $s_{1,2}$ given by

$$S = \begin{bmatrix} s_{1,1} & s_{1,2} \\ 0 & -\dfrac{\phi^{1,1}}{\phi^{1,2}} s_{1,2} \end{bmatrix} = \begin{bmatrix} s_{1,1} & s_{1,2} \\ 0 & \dfrac{1.557}{3.630} s_{1,2} \end{bmatrix}.$$

The cumulated impulse responses are given in Figure 14.4 for $s_{1,1} = 2$ and $s_{1,2} = 1$. The short-run effects at $h = 0$ are given by S and the long-run effects at $h = 40$ are

$$\sum_{i=0}^{40} \Psi_i S = \begin{bmatrix} 1.560 & -3.585 \\ 0.338 & 7.245 \end{bmatrix} \begin{bmatrix} 2 & 1 \\ 0 & \dfrac{1.557}{3.630} \end{bmatrix} = \begin{bmatrix} 3.119 & 0.022 \\ 0.676 & 3.446 \end{bmatrix}.$$

Increasing the number of moving average terms in this sum from 40 to 100 reduces the long-run value of $f_{1,2}$ from 0.022 to 0.000.   □

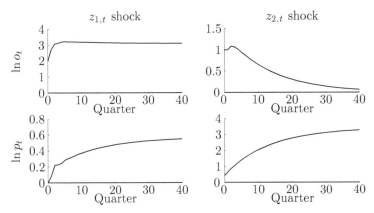

Figure 14.4. The effects of orthogonalised shocks z_t on $\ln o_t$ and $\ln p_t$ in a bivariate SVAR model of output and prices with short- and long-restrictions.

Example 14.11 The Gali Model

The Gali (1992) model consists of the growth rate of output, the change in the nominal interest rate, the real interest rate and the growth rate of real money, so that $y_t = [\Delta \ln o_t \ \ \Delta r_t \ \ (r_t - \Delta \ln p_t) \ \ (\Delta \ln m_t - \Delta \ln p_t)]'$. The one-standard deviation structural shocks, $z_t = [z_{as,t} \ z_{ms,t} \ z_{md,t} \ z_{ad,t}]'$, consist of shocks to aggregate supply, the money supply, money demand and aggregate demand. The restrictions are as follows.

(1) **Short-run (money):** The money market shocks, $z_{ms,t}$ and $z_{md,t}$, do not have a contemporaneous effect on output (Bernanke and Blinder, 1992), $s_{1,2} = s_{1,3} = 0$, where $s_{i,j}$ is the relevant entry of S in equation (14.16).

(2) **Short-run (output):** Output does not enter the monetary policy rule contemporaneously, $b_{2,1} = 0$, where $b_{i,j}$ is a representative element of B_0. To derive the effect of this restriction on S, rewrite (14.8) as $B_0 = D^{1/2} S^{-1}$ so that the restriction becomes

$$0 = d_{1,1}^{1/2} s^{2,1},$$

where $s^{2,1}$ is now the pertinent element of S^{-1}. For $d_{1,1} \neq 0$ it follows that $s^{2,1} = 0$. This equation represents a nonlinear restriction on all of the N elements of S which in theory can be solved for any $s_{i,j}$. However, because $s^{2,1} = 0$ it is also true that $s_{2,1} = 0$, resulting in S now having the structure

$$S = \begin{bmatrix} s_{1,1} & 0 & 0 & s_{1,4} \\ 0 & s_{2,2} & s_{2,3} & s_{2,4} \\ s_{3,1} & s_{3,2} & s_{3,3} & s_{3,4} \\ s_{4,1} & s_{4,2} & s_{4,3} & s_{4,4} \end{bmatrix},$$

after all three short-run restrictions have been imposed.

(3) **Long-run: (output)** Output is assumed to operate at its natural rate so that nominal shocks, $z_{ms,t}$, $z_{md,t}$ and $z_{ad,t}$, have no long-run effect. These long-run restrictions imply that $f_{1,2} = f_{1,3} = f_{1,4} = 0$ in the long-run matrix, F. To derive the effect of these restriction on S, rewrite equation (14.16) as $F = \Phi(1)^{-1}S$, which implies that

$$0 = f_{1,2} = \phi^{1,1}s_{1,2} + \phi^{1,2}s_{2,2} + \phi^{1,3}s_{3,2} + \phi^{1,4}s_{4,2}$$
$$0 = f_{1,3} = \phi^{1,1}s_{1,3} + \phi^{1,2}s_{2,3} + \phi^{1,3}s_{3,3} + \phi^{1,4}s_{4,3}$$
$$0 = f_{1,4} = \phi^{1,1}s_{1,4} + \phi^{1,2}s_{2,4} + \phi^{1,3}s_{3,4} + \phi^{1,4}s_{4,4},$$

in which, as before, $\phi^{i,j}$ is an element of $\Phi(1)^{-1}$. Recalling that $s_{1,2} = s_{1,3} = 0$ from the short-run restrictions, it follows that

$$s_{2,2} = -\frac{\phi^{1,3}}{\phi^{1,2}}s_{3,2} - \frac{\phi^{1,4}}{\phi^{1,2}}s_{4,2}$$

$$s_{2,3} = -\frac{\phi^{1,3}}{\phi^{1,2}}s_{3,3} - \frac{\phi^{1,4}}{\phi^{1,2}}s_{4,3}$$

$$s_{1,4} = -\frac{\phi^{1,2}}{\phi^{1,1}}s_{2,4} - \frac{\phi^{1,3}}{\phi^{1,1}}s_{3,4} - \frac{\phi^{1,4}}{\phi^{1,1}}s_{4,4}.$$

Substituting these expressions into S reduces the number of unknowns to ten, namely $\{s_{1,1}, s_{2,4}, s_{3,1}, s_{3,2}, s_{3,3}, s_{3,4}, s_{4,1}, s_{4,2}, s_{4,3}, s_{4,4}\}$.   □

14.2.4   Sign Restrictions

The earliest method of imposing restrictions is to specify recursive SVAR models for different variable orderings as discussed in Chapter 13. In a recursive bivariate model consisting of $y_{1,t}$ and $y_{2,t}$, the two orderings are identified by the respective S matrices

$$S_{y_1 \to y_2} = \begin{bmatrix} s_{1,1} & 0 \\ s_{2,1} & s_{2,2} \end{bmatrix} \qquad S_{y_2 \to y_1} = \begin{bmatrix} s_{1,1} & s_{1,2} \\ 0 & s_{2,2} \end{bmatrix}. \qquad (14.18)$$

In the first case, a shock in $y_{2,t}$ does not contemporaneously affect $y_{1,t}$, whereas, in the second case, a shock in $y_{1,t}$ does not contemporaneously affect $y_{2,t}$. The choice of variable ordering, and hence SVAR model, is based on the model that yields impulse responses with signs consistent with economic theory. The sign restriction methodology to specifying SVAR models represents a generalisation of this approach.

The strategy for choosing different variable orderings can be understood by defining the matrix

$$Q = \begin{bmatrix} \cos\vartheta & -\sin\vartheta \\ \sin\vartheta & \cos\vartheta \end{bmatrix}, \qquad 0 \le \vartheta \le \pi, \qquad (14.19)$$

which is orthogonal as $QQ' = Q'Q = I_N$. Now rewrite (14.7) as

$$v_t = Sz_t = SQ'Qz_t = SQ'w_t, \tag{14.20}$$

in which $w_t = Qz_t$ represents a new set of standardised structural shocks that are also orthogonal because

$$\mathrm{E}\left[w_t\right] = Q\,\mathrm{E}\left[z_t\right] = 0, \qquad \mathrm{E}\left[w_t w_t'\right] = Q\,\mathrm{E}\left[z_t z_t'\right]Q' = QQ' = I_N.$$

These new structural shocks are simply a weighted average of the original structural shocks, z_t, since

$$w_t = Qz_t = \begin{bmatrix} \cos\vartheta & -\sin\vartheta \\ \sin\vartheta & \cos\vartheta \end{bmatrix} \begin{bmatrix} z_{1,t} \\ z_{2,t} \end{bmatrix} = \begin{bmatrix} z_{1,t}\cos\vartheta - z_{2,t}\sin\vartheta \\ z_{1,t}\sin\vartheta + z_{2,t}\cos\vartheta \end{bmatrix}.$$

The two variable orderings given for the bivariate model in (14.18) are special cases of (14.20). For a lower triangular matrix S, as in the first ordering in equation (14.18), and for Q, as defined in equation (14.19),

$$\begin{aligned} SQ' &= \begin{bmatrix} s_{1,1} & 0 \\ s_{2,1} & s_{2,2} \end{bmatrix} \begin{bmatrix} \cos\vartheta & -\sin\vartheta \\ \sin\vartheta & \cos\vartheta \end{bmatrix}' \\ &= \begin{bmatrix} s_{1,1}\cos\vartheta & s_{1,1}\sin\vartheta \\ s_{2,1}\cos\vartheta - s_{2,2}\sin\vartheta & s_{2,1}\sin\vartheta + s_{2,2}\cos\vartheta \end{bmatrix}. \end{aligned}$$

Setting $\vartheta = 0$ yields the first ordering in equation (14.18). Setting $\vartheta = \vartheta^*$ where ϑ^* is chosen so that $s_{2,1}\cos\vartheta^* - s_{2,2}\sin\vartheta^* = 0$ gives the second ordering. More generally, other structural shocks are identified by choosing alternative values of ϑ within the range $0 \le \vartheta \le \pi$.

The approach of generating alternative models using the orthonormal rotation SQ' and selecting those models that generate impulse responses consistent with economic theory is known as the sign restrictions approach. Canova and de Nicolo (2002) and Peersman (2005) provide examples of this method. For models with dimensions greater than two, Q in (14.20) is based on either the Givens transformation (Uhlig, 2005) or the Householder transformation (Fry and Pagan, 2011). In practice the sign restrictions approach to specifying a SVAR consists of the following steps.

Step 1: Estimate a VAR and construct the VMA parameters, Ψ_i. Compute S, where $SS' = V$.

Step 2: Draw a value of ϑ from $[0, \pi]$ and compute Q from equation (14.19).

Step 3: Compute a finite number of impulse responses. For quarterly data, it is common to choose SQ', $\Psi_1 SQ'$, $\Psi_2 SQ'$, $\Psi_3 SQ'$, where the Ψ_i matrices are obtained in Step 1.

Step 4: If all impulses have the correct sign, select the model, otherwise discard it.

Step 5: Repeat steps 2 to 4 and generate other models that satisfy the restrictions.

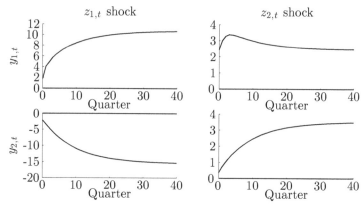

Figure 14.5. The effects of orthogonalised shocks, z_t, on $\ln o_t$ and $\ln p_t$ in a bivariate SVAR model with sign restrictions.

Step 6: Select a final model from the set of candidate models according to some rule. See Fry and Pagan (2011) for a discussion of alternative rules.

Example 14.12 A SVAR Model with Sign Restrictions

Consider again the bivariate SVAR model introduced in Example 14.5, but imposing the sign restrictions that $z_{1,t}$ has a positive effect on $y_{1,t}$ and a negative effect on $y_{2,t}$, whereas $z_{2,t}$ has positive effects on both $y_{1,t}$ and $y_{2,t}$. For comparative purposes, let the matrix S be

$$S = \begin{bmatrix} 3 & 0 \\ -1 & 2 \end{bmatrix},$$

which was used earlier to generate the impulse responses of the short-run restricted version of the model. If $\vartheta = 0.3\pi$, the orthonormal matrix Q is

$$Q = \begin{bmatrix} \cos 0.3\pi & -\sin 0.3\pi \\ \sin 0.3\pi & \cos 0.3\pi \end{bmatrix} = \begin{bmatrix} 0.588 & -0.809 \\ 0.809 & 0.588 \end{bmatrix},$$

and the matrix used to generate the orthogonal impulse responses is

$$SQ' = \begin{bmatrix} 3 & 0 \\ -1 & 2 \end{bmatrix} \begin{bmatrix} 0.588 & -0.809 \\ 0.809 & 0.588 \end{bmatrix} = \begin{bmatrix} 1.763 & 2.427 \\ -2.206 & 0.367 \end{bmatrix}.$$

The cumulated impulse responses given in Figure 14.5 reveal a different pattern to the impulses given in Figure 14.2 where the latter are equivalent to setting $\vartheta = 0.0$ despite both sets of impulses being based on orthogonalised shocks. Imposing the sign restrictions results in choosing impulses based on $\vartheta = 0.3\pi$ but not those based on $\vartheta = 0$. ☐

14.3 Estimation

Let the parameters of the SVAR model be given by $\theta = \{S, B_1, \cdots, B_p\}$, in which

$$S = \begin{cases} B_0^{-1} D^{1/2} & : \quad \text{Short-run restrictions} \\ \Phi(1)F & : \quad \text{Long-run restrictions}, \end{cases} \qquad (14.21)$$

and $\Phi(1)$ is obtained from the VAR in equation (14.5). The parameters can be estimated by maximum likelihood using the iterative algorithms discussed in Chapter 3. Conditioning on the first p observations, the log-likelihood function is

$$\ln L_T(\theta) = \frac{1}{T-p} \sum_{t=p+1}^{T} \ln l_t(\theta).$$

There are two strategies in performing maximum likelihood estimation, depending on whether the log-likelihood function is expressed in terms of the structural model or the reduced form.

Structural Form The log-likelihood function is

$$\ln L_T(\theta) = -\frac{N}{2} \ln 2\pi - \frac{1}{2} \ln |D| - \frac{1}{2(T-p)} \sum_{t=p+1}^{T} u_t' D^{-1} u_t,$$

$$(14.22)$$

where u_t is defined in equation (14.1).

Reduced Form The log-likelihood function is

$$\ln L_T(\theta) = -\frac{N}{2} \ln 2\pi - \frac{1}{2} \ln |V| - \frac{1}{2(T-p)} \sum_{t=p+1}^{T} v_t' V^{-1} v_t,$$

$$(14.23)$$

where v_t is defined in equation (14.5) and $V = SS'$.

Maximising either log-likelihood function produces the same parameter estimates since both procedures are full information maximum likelihood (FIML) procedures, as discussed in Chapter 5. In practice, however, estimation of SVARs tends to be based on the reduced form log-likelihood function because historically a VAR is usually estimated first. As the log-likelihood function is based on the assumption of normality, estimation of the mean and the variance parameters can be performed separately as the information matrix is block diagonal. Thus estimation can proceed in two stages.

Stage 1: Mean Parameters

The maximum likelihood estimates of the VAR are obtained by maximising the log-likelihood function with respect to

$$\Phi_1, \Phi_2, \cdots, \Phi_p,$$

with V concentrated out of the log-likelihood function. This means that each equation of the VAR (reduced form) is estimated individually by ordinary least squares to yield

$$\widehat{\Phi}_1, \widehat{\Phi}_2, \cdots, \widehat{\Phi}_p.$$

The VAR residuals are given by

$$\widehat{v}_t = y_t - \sum_{i=1}^{p} \widehat{\Phi}_i y_{t-i},$$

which are used to compute the $(N \times N)$ covariance matrix

$$\widehat{V} = \frac{1}{T-p} \sum_{t=p+1}^{T} \widehat{v}_t \widehat{v}_t'.$$

Stage 2: Variance Parameters

The maximum likelihood estimates of B_0 and D, in the case of the short-run parameters, and F, in the case of the long-run parameters, are obtained by maximising

$$\ln L_T(\theta) = -\frac{N}{2} \ln 2\pi - \frac{1}{2} \ln |V| - \frac{1}{2(T-p)} \sum_{t=p+1}^{T} \widehat{v}_t' V^{-1} \widehat{v}_t',$$

with $V = SS'$ and S defined in equation (14.21). This maximisation problem is equivalent to solving the nonlinear system of equations

$$\widehat{V} = \widehat{S}\widehat{S}',$$

with $\widehat{V}$ determined from the first stage of the estimation. This expression defines the first-order conditions of the maximum likelihood estimator with respect to these parameters. From equation (14.8) $S = B_0^{-1} D^{1/2}$, in which case estimates of B_0 and D are obtained from $\widehat{S}$ and hence $\widehat{V}$. One B_0 is obtained the $\widehat{B}_i s$ are then obtained from $\widehat{B}_i = \widehat{B}_0 \widehat{\Phi}_i$, where the $\widehat{\Phi}_i s$ are computed from the VAR in the first stage.

Example 14.13 Estimating a SVAR with Short-Run Restrictions

As an example of estimating a SVAR with short-run restrictions, consider a dynamic system of interest rates $y_t = [r_{1,t} \ r_{2,t} \ r_{3,t}]'$, where $r_{1,t}$ is the instantaneous yield, $r_{2,t}$ is the 1-month yield and $r_{3,t}$ is the 3-month yield. The structural model is given by

$$B_0 y_t = B_1 y_{t-1} + u_t,$$

with unknown parameters

$$B_0 = \begin{bmatrix} 1 & 0 & 0 \\ -b_{2,1} & 1 & 0 \\ -b_{3,1} & 0 & 1 \end{bmatrix}, \qquad D = \begin{bmatrix} d_{1,1} & 0 & 0 \\ 0 & d_{2,2} & 0 \\ 0 & 0 & d_{3,3} \end{bmatrix},$$

plus the nine unknown parameters in B_1. The short-run restrictions show that the only contemporaneous relationships are $r_{1,t}$ to $r_{2,t}$ and $r_{1,t}$ to $r_{3,t}$. The parameters to be estimated are $\theta = \{b_{2,1}, b_{3,1}, d_{1,1}, d_{2,2}, d_{3,3}, B_1\}$. The data are monthly United States zero coupon yields from December 1946 to February 1991. Estimation is performed in two stages. In the first stage, a VAR(1) is estimated with the results given by

$$r_{1,t} = -0.124 + 0.060 r_{1,t-1} + 0.321 r_{2,t-1} + 0.559 r_{3,t-1} + \widehat{v}_{1,t}$$
$$r_{2,t} = -0.032 - 0.146 r_{1,t-1} + 0.472 r_{2,t-1} + 0.635 r_{3,t-1} + \widehat{v}_{2,t}$$
$$r_{3,t} = 0.068 + 0.074 r_{1,t-1} - 0.279 r_{2,t-1} + 1.185 r_{3,t-1} + \widehat{v}_{3,t}.$$

In the second stage, the estimates of $\{b_{2,1}, b_{3,1}, d_{1,1}, d_{2,2}, d_{3,3}\}$ are computed by maximising the log-likelihood function in equation (14.23) with $T = 530$, $p = 1$ and, from equation (14.21),

$$S = \begin{bmatrix} 1 & 0 & 0 \\ -b_{2,1} & 1 & 0 \\ -b_{3,1} & 0 & 1 \end{bmatrix}^{-1} \begin{bmatrix} d_{1,1}^{1/2} & 0 & 0 \\ 0 & d_{2,2}^{1/2} & 0 \\ 0 & 0 & d_{3,3}^{1/2} \end{bmatrix},$$

with $V = SS'$. The value of the log-likelihood function evaluated at the maximum likelihood estimates is $\ln L_T(\widehat{\theta}) = -1.744$. The parameter estimates, with standard errors based on the Hessian matrix given in parentheses, are

$$\widehat{B}_0 = \begin{bmatrix} 1.000 & 0.000 & 0.000 \\ \underline{} & \underline{} & \underline{} \\ -0.703 & 1.000 & 0.000 \\ {\scriptstyle(0.017)} & \underline{} & \underline{} \\ -0.457 & 0.000 & 1.000 \\ {\scriptstyle(0.027)} & \underline{} & \underline{} \end{bmatrix} \qquad \widehat{D} = \begin{bmatrix} 0.491 & 0.000 & 0.000 \\ {\scriptstyle(0.030)} & \underline{} & \underline{} \\ 0.000 & 0.072 & 0.000 \\ \underline{} & {\scriptstyle(0.004)} & \underline{} \\ 0.000 & 0.000 & 0.187 \\ \underline{} & \underline{} & {\scriptstyle(0.012)} \end{bmatrix},$$

and hence the estimates of the short-run impact at $h = 0$ of the three structural shocks on the three interest rates are

$$\widehat{S} = \widehat{B}_0^{-1} \widehat{D}^{1/2} = \begin{bmatrix} 0.700 & 0.000 & 0.000 \\ 0.492 & 0.268 & 0.000 \\ 0.320 & 0.000 & 0.432 \end{bmatrix}.$$

□

Example 14.14 Estimating a SVAR with Long-Run Restrictions

Consider again the SVAR in Example 14.13, except that the interest rates are expressed in first differences and identification is now based on imposing the long-run restrictions that only shocks in $r_{1,t}$ have a long-run effect on all three interest rates. This implies that the long-run parameter matrix is

$$
F = \begin{bmatrix} f_{1,1} & 0 & 0 \\ f_{2,1} & f_{2,2} & 0 \\ f_{3,1} & 0 & f_{3,3} \end{bmatrix}.
$$

The parameters to be estimated are $\theta = \{f_{1,1}, f_{2,1}, f_{3,1}, f_{2,2}, f_{3,3}, B_1\}$. The results are based on the same data as given in Example 14.13, namely monthly United States zero coupon yields from December 1946 to February 1991. Estimation is performed in two stages with the first stage the same as the first stage in the previous example. In the second stage, estimates of $\{f_{1,1}, f_{2,1}, f_{3,1}, f_{2,2}, f_{3,3}\}$ are computed by maximising the log-likelihood function in equation (14.23) with $T = 530$, $p = 1$ and

$$
\widehat{\Phi}(1) = I_3 - \begin{bmatrix} -0.373 & -0.057 & -0.017 \\ -0.168 & -0.391 & -0.034 \\ 0.852 & 0.639 & 0.156 \end{bmatrix} = \begin{bmatrix} 1.373 & 0.168 & -0.852 \\ 0.057 & 1.391 & -0.639 \\ 0.017 & 0.034 & 0.844 \end{bmatrix}.
$$

From equation (14.21), in the second stage of the estimation

$$
S = \widehat{\Phi}(1)F = \begin{bmatrix} 1.373 & 0.168 & -0.852 \\ 0.057 & 1.391 & -0.639 \\ 0.017 & 0.034 & 0.844 \end{bmatrix} \begin{bmatrix} f_{1,1} & 0 & 0 \\ f_{2,1} & f_{2,2} & 0 \\ f_{3,1} & 0 & f_{3,3} \end{bmatrix},
$$

where $V = SS'$. The value of the log-likelihood function evaluated at the maximum likelihood estimates is $\ln L_T(\widehat{\theta}) = -1.988$. The long-run parameter estimates, with standard errors based on the Hessian matrix given in parentheses, are

$$
\widehat{F} = \begin{bmatrix} 0.735 & 0.000 & 0.000 \\ {\scriptstyle(0.023)} & - & - \\ 0.590 & 0.233 & 0.000 \\ {\scriptstyle(0.021)} & {\scriptstyle(0.007)} & - \\ 0.477 & 0.000 & 0.366 \\ {\scriptstyle(0.022)} & - & {\scriptstyle(0.011)} \end{bmatrix}.
$$

The estimates of the short-run impact at $h = 0$ of the three structural shocks on the three interest rates are

$$
\widehat{S} = (I - \widehat{\Phi}_1)\widehat{F} = \begin{bmatrix} 0.702 & 0.039 & -0.312 \\ 0.558 & 0.324 & -0.234 \\ 0.435 & 0.008 & 0.309 \end{bmatrix}.
$$

□

An important special case of SVAR models occurs when B_0 is recursive. Under these conditions, all of the parameters θ can be estimated without any need for an iterative algorithm. In fact, Chapter 13 shows four ways of estimating θ that are all numerically equivalent. Here the focus is on the maximum likelihood method.

Example 14.15 Estimating a Recursive SVAR
Consider again the SVAR in Example 14.13 and the monthly United States zero coupon yields from December 1946 to February 1991. The maximum likelihood approach consists of estimating the VAR by ordinary least squares to obtain the VAR residuals $\hat{v}_t$. The log-likelihood function in equation (14.23) is then maximised with respect to $\{b_{2,1}, b_{3,1}, b_{3,2}, d_{1,1}, d_{2,2}, d_{3,3}\}$, with $T = 530$, $p = 1$ and from equation (14.21)

$$
S = \begin{bmatrix} 1 & 0 & 0 \\ -b_{2,1} & 1 & 0 \\ -b_{3,1} & -b_{3,2} & 1 \end{bmatrix}^{-1} \begin{bmatrix} d_{1,1}^{1/2} & 0 & 0 \\ 0 & d_{2,2}^{1/2} & 0 \\ 0 & 0 & d_{3,3}^{1/2} \end{bmatrix},
$$

where $V = SS'$. The value of the log-likelihood function evaluated at the maximum likelihood estimates is $\ln L_T(\hat{\theta}) = -0.535$. The parameter estimates, with standard errors based on the Hessian matrix, are

$$
\hat{B}_0 = \begin{bmatrix} 1.000 & 0.000 & 0.000 \\ - & - & - \\ -0.703 & 1.000 & 0.000 \\ {\scriptstyle(0.017)} & - & - \\ 0.627 & -1.542 & 1.000 \\ {\scriptstyle(0.017)} & {\scriptstyle(0.021)} & - \end{bmatrix} \quad \hat{D} = \begin{bmatrix} 0.491 & 0.000 & 0.000 \\ {\scriptstyle(0.030)} & - & - \\ 0.000 & 0.072 & 0.000 \\ - & {\scriptstyle(0.004)} & - \\ 0.000 & 0.000 & 0.017 \\ - & - & {\scriptstyle(0.001)} \end{bmatrix}.
$$

□

In the case where the model is partially recursive in the sense that the lower triangular part of B_0 contains some zero elements, ordinary least squares estimates of each equation are still consistent but not asymptotically efficient. To achieve asymptotic efficiency in this case it would be necessary to use maximum likelihood methods. If the SVAR is non-recursive, ordinary least squares will not be consistent because there will be simultaneity bias arising from the presence of endogenous variables in each equation. In this situation maximum likelihood methods are needed. Alternatively, instrumental variable methods can be used to achieve consistent estimates following the approach of Pagan and Robertson (1989).

14.4 Identification

The discussion of the estimation of the SVAR parameters is based on the assumption that the unknown parameters in θ are identified, where identification is based on the imposition of either short-run or long-run or sign restrictions. The issue of identification is now formalised.

As pointed out in Section 14.3, in the second estimation stage the maximum likelihood estimator is found as the solution of the expression $V = SS'$. As V contains N variances and $N(N - 1)/2$ covariances, the maximum number of parameters that can be identified from this set of equations is $N(N + 1)/2$. This restriction on the number of identifiable parameters is the order condition, which is a necessary condition for identification. If $\theta = \{B_0, D\}$ is the vector of parameters to be estimated at the second stage, there are three cases to consider:

$$
\begin{array}{llrcl}
\text{Just identified} & : & \dim(\theta) & = & N(N + 1)/2 \\
\text{Over identified} & : & \dim(\theta) & < & N(N + 1)/2 \\
\text{Under identified} & : & \dim(\theta) & > & N(N + 1)/2.
\end{array}
$$

In the just-identified case, V is exactly equal to SS'. In the over-identified case, this does not necessarily hold, but, if the model is correctly specified, then the difference between V and SS' should not be statistically significant. These over-identifying restrictions can be verified by testing, which is the subject matter of Section 14.5. In the under-identified case, insufficient information exists to be able to identify all of the parameters, implying the need for further restrictions on the model.

Example 14.16 Order Conditions of Empirical SVAR Models
The order conditions for some of the SVAR models used in the previous examples, with $\theta = \{B_0, D\}$ in each case, are as follows.

Model	N	$\dfrac{N(N + 1)}{2}$	$\dim(\theta)$	Order condition
Sims	4	10	10	Just-identified model
Kim and Roubini	7	28	23	Over-identified model
Blanchard and Quah	3	3	3	Just-identified model
Rapach	4	10	10	Just-identified model
Gali	4	10	10	Just-identified model

□

Example 14.16 is based on the order condition, which is a necessary condition for identification. As discussed in Chapter 5, a necessary and sufficient condition for identification is the rank condition, which requires that the Hessian of the log-likelihood function in equation (14.23) is negative definite. As $V = SS'$ is the first-order condition satisfied by the maximum likelihood estimator, the rank condition is based on the matrix

$$
\frac{\partial \operatorname{vech}(V)}{\partial \theta'} = \frac{\partial \operatorname{vech}(B_0^{-1} D(B_0^{-1})')}{\partial \theta'},
$$

which has $N(N+1)/2$ rows and $\dim(\theta)$ columns and $\text{vech}\,(V)$ represents the $N(N+1)/2$ dimensional column vector of the unique elements of V. The rank condition requires that this matrix has full column rank, while the order condition is that the $N(N+1)/2$ rows are at least as great as the number of columns.

14.5 Testing

Hypothesis tests on SVAR models can be performed using the LR, Wald and LM test statistics discussed in Chapter 4. Of particular interest in the context of SVARs is a test of the number of over-identifying restrictions. In the second stage of the estimation, an important question is whether or not the covariance matrix of the VAR disturbances from the first stage, V, is equal to the covariance matrix from the second stage, SS'. As stated previously, this condition does not hold for over-identified models, but, if the restrictions are valid, the difference should not be statistically significant. Consequently, a test of the over-identifying restrictions is based on comparing each (unique) element of V with each element of SS'. The hypotheses are

$$H_0 : \text{vech}(V - SS') = 0\,, \qquad H_1 : \text{vech}(V - SS') \neq 0\,.$$

A straightforward way to perform the test is to use the LR statistic

$$LR = -2T(\ln L_T(\widehat{\theta}_0) - \ln L_T(\widehat{\theta}_1)), \tag{14.24}$$

where $\ln L_T(\widehat{\theta}_0)$ is the value of the log-likelihood function subject to the over-identifying restrictions (restricted), and $\ln L_T(\widehat{\theta}_1)$ is the value of the log-likelihood function corresponding to the just-identified model (unrestricted). Under the null hypothesis that the over-identifying restrictions are valid, LR is asymptotically distributed as χ^2 with degrees of freedom equal to the number of over-identifying restrictions

$$\frac{N(N+1)}{2} - \dim(\theta)\,.$$

Example 14.17 Over-identifying Test of the Interest Rate Model
    Consider again the estimation of the SVAR model for the system of United States interest rates with $N=3$ introduced in Example 14.13. The interest rate model based on a recursive structure corresponds to the just-identified case where the value of the (unrestricted) log-likelihood function is $\ln L_T(\widehat{\theta}_1) = -0.535$. Using the results of the over-identified interest rate model based on short-run restrictions, yields the value of the (restricted) log-likelihood function $\ln L_T(\widehat{\theta}_0) = -1.744$. The value of the LR statistic is

$$LR = -2T(\ln L_T(\widehat{\theta}_0) - \ln L_T(\widehat{\theta}_1)) = -2 \times 530(-1.744 + 0.535)$$
$$= 1281.872\,,$$

where the number of over-identifying restrictions is

$$\frac{N(N+1)}{2} - \dim(\theta_0) = 6 - 5 = 1.$$

From the chi-square distribution with one degree of freedom, the p-value is 0.000 giving a clear rejection of the over-identifying restriction.   □

The LR form of the over-identifying test requires estimating the model under the null and alternative hypotheses. A more convenient form of this test is to recognise that the covariance matrix of the VAR residuals $\widehat{V}$ represents the unrestricted covariance matrix and $\widehat{S}\widehat{S}'$ represents the restricted covariance matrix obtained from maximising the log-likelihood function. As the disturbance term is assumed to be normal, from Chapter 4 an alternative form of the LR statistic in equation (14.24) is

$$LR = T(\ln|\widehat{S}\widehat{S}'| - \ln|\widehat{V}|).$$

Example 14.18 Over-identifying Test Revisited

Using the parameter estimates from Example 14.17, the unconstrained VAR residual covariance matrix is

$$\widehat{V} = \begin{bmatrix} 0.491 & 0.345 & 0.224 \\ 0.345 & 0.314 & 0.268 \\ 0.224 & 0.268 & 0.289 \end{bmatrix}.$$

The residual covariance matrix of the SVAR with the over-identifying restrictions is

$$\widehat{S}\widehat{S}' = \begin{bmatrix} 0.700 & 0.000 & 0.000 \\ 0.492 & 0.268 & 0.000 \\ 0.320 & 0.000 & 0.432 \end{bmatrix} \begin{bmatrix} 0.700 & 0.492 & 0.320 \\ 0.000 & 0.268 & 0.000 \\ 0.000 & 0.000 & 0.432 \end{bmatrix}$$

$$= \begin{bmatrix} 0.491 & 0.345 & 0.224 \\ 0.345 & 0.314 & 0.158 \\ 0.224 & 0.158 & 0.289 \end{bmatrix}.$$

Computing the determinants

$$|\widehat{V}| = 0.000585, \qquad |\widehat{S}\widehat{S}'| = 0.006571,$$

yields the value of the LR statistic

$$LR = T(\ln|\widehat{S}\widehat{S}'| - \ln|\widehat{V}|)$$
$$= 530 \times (\ln(0.006571) - \ln(0.000585)) = 1281.969,$$

which is the same as the value reported in Example 14.17.   □

14.6 Applications

14.6.1 Peersman's Model of Oil Price Shocks

Peersman (2005) specifies and estimates a four-variable SVAR model using United States data from June 1979 to June 2002 to identify the effects of oil price shocks on the United States economy. The variables in the model are the growth rate in oil prices, the growth rate of output, the inflation rate and the interest rate, $y_t = \begin{bmatrix} \Delta \ln oil_t & \Delta \ln o_t & \Delta \ln p_t & r_t \end{bmatrix}'$.

The VAR is estimated with $p = 3$ lags, a constant and a time trend. From the first stage of estimation, the VAR residual covariance matrix is

$$\widehat{V} = \begin{bmatrix} 168.123 & 0.173 & 1.190 & 1.935 \\ 0.173 & 0.281 & 0.013 & 0.173 \\ 1.190 & 0.013 & 0.047 & 0.026 \\ 1.935 & 0.173 & 0.026 & 0.763 \end{bmatrix}, \tag{14.25}$$

and

$$\widehat{\Phi}(1) = I_4 - \widehat{\Phi}_1 - \widehat{\Phi}_2 - \widehat{\Phi}_3 = \begin{bmatrix} 1.053 & -4.035 & -5.155 & -0.414 \\ -0.007 & 0.342 & -0.039 & 0.099 \\ -0.004 & 0.066 & 0.256 & 0.012 \\ -0.003 & -1.158 & -2.040 & 0.233 \end{bmatrix}, \tag{14.26}$$

so that

$$\widehat{\Phi}(1)^{-1} = \begin{bmatrix} 1.028 & 5.736 & 11.902 & -1.211 \\ -0.006 & 1.802 & -4.258 & -0.555 \\ 0.013 & -0.566 & 4.377 & 0.038 \\ 0.097 & 4.075 & 17.286 & 1.851 \end{bmatrix}. \tag{14.27}$$

The one-standard deviation structural shocks comprise shocks to oil prices, aggregate supply, aggregate demand and money, $z_t = \begin{bmatrix} z_{oil,t} & z_{as,t} & z_{ad,t} & z_{m,t} \end{bmatrix}'$. Identification of these shocks is based on a combination of four short-run and two long-run restrictions on the SVAR, which results in a just-identified system.

(1) **Short-run (oil):** The non-oil price shocks have no contemporaneous effects on oil prices, $s_{1,2} = s_{1,3} = s_{1,4} = 0$.
(2) **Short-run (output):** Money shocks have no contemporaneous effect on output, $s_{2,4} = 0$.
(3) **Long-run (output):** Aggregate demand shocks and money shocks have no long-run effects on output, $f_{2,3} = f_{2,4} = 0$.

The effect of the two long-run restrictions on S are derived from the second and third rows of $F = \Phi(1)^{-1}S$, which are

$$f_{2,3} = \phi^{2,1}s_{1,3} + \phi^{2,2}s_{2,3} + \phi^{2,3}s_{3,3} + \phi^{2,4}s_{4,3}$$
$$f_{2,4} = \phi^{2,1}s_{1,4} + \phi^{2,2}s_{2,4} + \phi^{2,3}s_{3,4} + \phi^{2,4}s_{4,4},$$

in which $\phi^{i,j}$ is an element of $\Phi(1)^{-1}$ given in (14.27). As $f_{2,3} = f_{2,4} = 0$ and $s_{1,3} = s_{1,4} = s_{2,4} = 0$, these equations are rearranged to give

$$s_{4,3} = -\frac{\phi^{2,2}}{\phi^{2,4}}s_{2,3} - \frac{\phi^{2,3}}{\phi^{2,4}}s_{3,3} = \frac{1.802}{0.555}s_{2,3} - \frac{4.258}{0.555}s_{3,3}$$

$$s_{3,4} = -\frac{\phi^{2,4}}{\phi^{2,3}}s_{4,4} = -\frac{0.555}{4.258}s_{4,4}.$$

Once all short-run and long-run restrictions are imposed, the matrix S is

$$S = \begin{bmatrix} s_{1,1} & 0 & 0 & 0 \\ s_{2,1} & s_{2,2} & s_{2,3} & 0 \\ s_{3,1} & s_{3,2} & s_{3,3} & -\dfrac{0.555}{4.258}s_{4,4} \\ s_{4,1} & s_{4,2} & \dfrac{1.802}{0.555}s_{2,3} - \dfrac{4.258}{0.555}s_{3,3} & s_{4,4} \end{bmatrix}. \quad (14.28)$$

The parameters of the SVAR

$$\theta = \{s_{1,1}, s_{2,1}, s_{2,2}, s_{2,3}, s_{3,1}, s_{3,2}, s_{3,3}, s_{4,1}, s_{4,2}, s_{4,4}\},$$

are estimated by maximising the reduced form log-likelihood function in (14.23) subject to the restriction $V = SS'$, in which v_t is replaced by $\hat{v}_t$, V is replaced by $\hat{V}$ in (14.25) and S is given by (14.28). The short-run and long-run estimates are, respectively,

$$\hat{S} = \begin{bmatrix} 12.966 & 0.000 & 0.000 & 0.000 \\ 0.013 & 0.309 & 0.431 & 0.000 \\ 0.092 & -0.128 & 0.118 & -0.090 \\ 0.149 & -0.131 & 0.491 & 0.695 \end{bmatrix} \quad (14.29)$$

$$\hat{F} = \hat{\Phi}(1)^{-1}\hat{S} = \begin{bmatrix} 14.317 & 0.412 & 3.284 & -1.918 \\ -0.525 & 1.174 & 0.000 & 0.000 \\ 0.566 & -0.739 & 0.293 & -0.369 \\ 3.171 & -1.191 & 4.709 & -0.278 \end{bmatrix}. \quad (14.30)$$

The full set of impulse responses are presented in Figure 14.6 with the initial values given by $\hat{S}$ in equation (14.29). The impulse responses on the logarithms of oil, output and prices are cumulated, because these variables are expressed in first differences in the model. This means that the final impulse values of these variables correspond to the first three rows of $\hat{F}$ in equation (14.30). The impulses on the interest rate are not cumulated because this variable is already

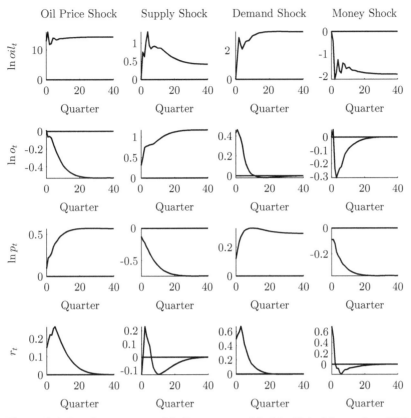

Figure 14.6. Impulse responses of the Peersman model of the United States, June 1979 to June 2002. All impulses are expressed in terms of the levels of the variables.

expressed in levels in the model. However, cumulating these impulses would indeed result in estimates given, by construction, in the last row of $\widehat{F}$.

The oil price shock in Figure 14.6 represents a negative supply shock with output falling and prices increasing. There is a positive effect on the interest rate, which dissipates in the long run.

14.6.2 A Portfolio SVAR Model of Australia

Fry, Hocking and Martin (2008) specify a five-variable SVAR model of the Australian economy that focusses on the transmission of wealth effects arising from portfolio shocks, with identification based on the imposition of long-run restrictions. The variables are the growth rate in output, the change in the logarithm of the interest rate, real stock returns on Australian equities, goods

Table 14.1. *Maximum likelihood estimates of the long-run parameters of the Australian SVAR model. Quasi-maximum likelihood standard errors (allowing for heteroskedasticity) and p-values are also reported*

Equation	Shock	Parameter	Estimate	se	pv
Output	Aggregate supply	$f_{1,1}$	1.039	0.075	0.000
Interest	Aggregate supply	$f_{2,1}$	4.301	1.158	0.000
	Aggregate demand	$f_{2,2}$	5.181	0.376	0.000
	Australian portfolio	$f_{2,3}$	10.109	0.927	0.000
Aust. equity	Aggregate supply	$f_{3,1}$	2.708	0.535	0.000
	Aggregate demand	$-f_{2,2}$	−5.181	0.376	0.000
	Australian portfolio	$f_{3,3}$	1.429	0.751	0.057
	U.S. portfolio	$f_{3,5}$	3.513	0.525	0.000
Price	Aggregate supply	$f_{4,1}$	−0.712	0.274	0.009
	Aggregate demand	$f_{4,2}$	0.777	0.153	0.000
	Australian portfolio	$f_{4,3}$	1.621	0.223	0.000
	Nominal	$f_{4,4}$	1.349	0.099	0.000
U.S. equity	U.S. portfolio	$f_{5,5}$	10.752	0.809	0.000

$\ln L_T(\widehat{\theta}) = -11.440$

market inflation and real stock returns on United States equities, $y_t = [\Delta \ln o_t \; \Delta \ln r_t \; \Delta \ln s_t \; \Delta \ln p_t \; \Delta \ln f_t]'$. The one-standard deviation structural shocks comprise aggregate supply shocks, aggregate demand shocks, Australian portfolio shocks, nominal shocks and United States portfolio shocks, $z_t = [z_{as,t} \; z_{ad,t} \; z_{au,t} \; z_{p,t} \; z_{us,t}]'$.

Identification is based on imposing the following long-run restrictions

$$
F = \begin{bmatrix}
f_{1,1} & 0 & 0 & 0 & 0 \\
f_{2,1} & f_{2,2} & f_{2,3} & 0 & 0 \\
f_{3,1} & -f_{2,2} & f_{3,3} & 0 & f_{3,5} \\
f_{4,1} & f_{4,2} & f_{4,3} & f_{4,4} & 0 \\
0 & 0 & 0 & 0 & f_{5,5}
\end{bmatrix}.
\tag{14.31}
$$

The long-run restriction

$$
\frac{\partial \ln r_t}{\partial z_{ad,t}} = -\frac{\partial \ln s_t}{\partial z_{ad,t}} = f_{2,2},
$$

is obtained from assuming that financial assets are priced in the long run at present value levels. This specification contrasts with the long-run restrictions imposed by Rapach (2001) given in Example 14.9.

The SVAR is estimated using quarterly Australian data from March 1980 to June 2005, with the lag length set at $p = 2$ lags. The results of estimating the long-run parameters by maximum likelihood are given in Table 14.1.

14.7 Exercises

(1) Different Ways to Impose Restrictions

Program files	svar_bivariate.*
Data files	peersman_data.*

Consider a SVAR model consisting of the logarithm of output and the logarithm of prices $y_t = [\,\Delta \ln o_t \quad \Delta \ln p_t\,]'$ in which the variables are scaled by 400 and with structural shocks $u_t = [\,u_{1,t} \quad u_{2,t}\,]'$. Compute impulse responses for $\ln o_t$ and $\ln p_t$ where the VAR is estimated with two lags and a constant.

(a) $S = [3\ 0, -1\ 2]$.

(b) $S = [3\ 1, 0\ 2]$.

(c) $s_{1,1} = 3, s_{2,2} = 2, s_{1,2} = s_{2,1} = 1$.

(d) $S = \Phi(1)F$, where $F = [3\ 0, -1\ 2]$.

(e) $S = \Phi(1)F$, where $F = [3 - 1, 0\ 2]$.

(f) $S = \Phi(1)F$, where $F = [3\ 0, 0\ 2]$.

(g) $s_{1,1} = 3, s_{2,2} = 2, u_{1,t}$ does not affect $y_{2,t}$ in the short run and $u_{2,t}$ does not affect $y_{1,t}$ in the long run.

(h) $s_{1,1} = 3, s_{2,2} = 2, u_{1,t}$ does not affect $y_{2,t}$ in the long run and $u_{2,t}$ does not affect $y_{1,t}$ in the short run.

(i) SQ' where $S = [3\ 0, -1\ 2]$ and Q is given by (14.19) with $\vartheta = 0.1\pi$.

(j) SQ' where $S = [3\ 0, -1\ 2]$ and Q is given by (14.19) with $\vartheta = 0.2\pi$.

(k) SQ' where $S = [3\ 0, -1\ 2]$ and Q is given by (14.19) with $\vartheta = 0.3\pi$.

(2) A Model of Interest Rates with Short-Run Restrictions

Program files	svar_shortrun.*
Data files	mcnew.dat

Consider a system of three interest rates, $y_t = [\,r_{1,t} \quad r_{2,t} \quad r_{3,t}\,]'$, where $r_{1,t}$ is the instantaneous yield, $r_{2,t}$ is the 1-month yield and $r_{3,t}$ is the 3-month yield. The structural model is

$$B_0 y_t = B_1 y_{t-1} + D^{1/2} z_t,$$

where the short-run restrictions are

$$B_0 = \begin{bmatrix} 1 & 0 & 0 \\ -b_{2,1} & 1 & 0 \\ 0 & -b_{3,2} & 1 \end{bmatrix}, \qquad D = \begin{bmatrix} d_{1,1} & 0 & 0 \\ 0 & d_{2,2} & 0 \\ 0 & 0 & d_{3,3} \end{bmatrix}.$$

Using monthly data on United States zero coupon yields from December 1946 to February 1991, estimate the parameters of the model by maximum likelihood and test the number of over-identifying restrictions.

(3) A Model of Interest Rates with Long-Run Restrictions

Program files	svar_longrun.*
Data files	mcnew.*

Consider a system of three interest rates $y_t = \begin{bmatrix} \Delta r_{1,t} & \Delta r_{2,t} & \Delta r_{3,t} \end{bmatrix}'$, where $r_{1,t}$ is the instantaneous yield, $r_{2,t}$ is the 1-month yield and $r_{3,t}$ is the 3-month yield. Using monthly data on United States zero coupon yields from December 1946 to February 1991, estimate the parameters of the SVAR model by maximum likelihood using the long-run restrictions

$$F = \begin{bmatrix} f_{1,1} & 0 & 0 \\ f_{1,1} & f_{2,2} & 0 \\ f_{1,1} & 0 & f_{3,3} \end{bmatrix}.$$

Test the over-identifying restrictions.

(4) The Extended Sims Model

Program files	svar_sims.*
Data files	simsdata.*

Consider the 6-variable Sims model with

$$y_t = [r_t, \ln e_t, \ln cp_t, \ln m_t, \ln p_t, \ln o_t]',$$

where r_t is the interest rate, $\ln e_t$ is the logarithm of the exchange rate, $\ln cp_t$ is the logarithm of commodity prices, $\ln m_t$ is the logarithm of money, $\ln p_t$ is the logarithm of prices, and $\ln o_t$ is the logarithm of output. The data are monthly beginning January 1959 and ending December 1998.

(a) Estimate a recursive SVAR where the VAR has 14 lags, a constant and 11 seasonal dummy variables.

(b) Choosing the ordering of variables as

$$r_t \rightarrow \ln e_t \rightarrow \ln cp_t \rightarrow \ln m_t \rightarrow \ln p_t \rightarrow \ln o_t,$$

compute B_0, D and hence $S = B_0^{-1} D$ using the reduced from method and the Choleski decomposition method.

(5) The Peersman SVAR Model of Oil Price Shocks

Program files	svar_peersman.*
Data files	peersman_data.*

Consider a four-variable model of the United States containing the growth rate in the oil price, the growth rate in output, the inflation rate and the interest rate, $y_t = [\, 100\Delta \ln oil_t \quad 100\Delta \ln o_t \quad 100\Delta \ln p_t \quad r_t\,]'$. The structural shocks comprise oil price, aggregate supply, aggregate demand and money shocks, $z_t = [\, z_{oil,t} \quad z_{as,t} \quad z_{ad,t} \quad z_{m,t}\,]'$.

(a) Estimate the VAR with $p = 3$ lags, a constant and a time trend using data from June 1979 to June 2002.

(b) Estimate the SVAR subject to the restrictions:

   (i) the three non-oil price shocks, $z_{as,t}$, $z_{ad,t}$ and $z_{m,t}$ do not have a short-run effect on oil prices;

   (ii) the money shock, $z_{m,t}$ has no short-run effect on output;

   (iii) the aggregate demand shock, $z_{ad,t}$, and the money shock, $z_{m,t}$, have no long-run effect on output.

(c) Compute the impulse responses for $\ln oil_t$, $\ln o_t$, $\ln p_t$ and r_t and interpret the results. Verify that the impulse responses are given by S at $h = 0$ and by $F = \Phi(1)^{-1}S$ at $h = 100$.

(6) A Portfolio SVAR Model

Program files	svar_port.*
Data files	portfolio_data.*

Consider a five-variable portfolio SVAR model of Australia containing output, the interest rate, real Australian equity prices, the goods market price and real equity prices in the United States converted into Australian dollars,

$$y_t = [\Delta \ln o_t, \Delta \ln r_t, \Delta \ln s_t, \Delta \ln p_t, \Delta \ln f_t]',$$

with all the variables scaled by 100.

(a) Using quarterly data from January 1980 to June 2002, estimate a VAR containing a constant, 2 lags, a dummy variable corresponding to the stock market crash in September 1987 and a dummy variable to capture the introduction of the GST in September 2000.

(b) Estimate a portfolio SVAR model of the Australian economy where identification is based on the long-run restrictions in (14.31). Compute and interpret the impulse response functions and the variance decompositions.

(c) The portfolio model in part (b) is based on the restriction that an aggregate demand shock simultaneously raises interest rates and lowers real equity values in Australia, $f_{3,2} = -f_{2,2}$. Use a LR statistic to test this restriction.

(7) The Blanchard-Quah Model and Okun's Law

Gauss file(s)	svar_bq.*
Matlab file(s)	bq_us.*, bq_uk.*, bq_jp.*

The Blanchard and Quah (1989) model is a bivariate SVAR consisting of the annualised quarterly growth rate in output and the unemployment rate, $y_t = [400\Delta \ln o_t, \ ue_t]'$. The one-standard deviation structural shocks correspond to aggregate supply and aggregate demand, $z_t = [z_{as,t}, z_{ad,t}]'$, which are identified by the long-run restriction that aggregate demand shocks have no long-run effect on output

$$F = \begin{bmatrix} f_{1,1} & 0 \\ f_{2,1} & f_{2,2} \end{bmatrix}.$$

(a) Estimate a SVAR for the United States using quarterly data over the period March 1950 to September 2009, where the VAR is specified to have $p = 8$ lags and a constant. Interpret the parameter estimates of F.

(b) Compute impulse responses for positive shocks to aggregate supply and demand. Interpret the patterns of the impulse responses and compare the results to the impulses reported by Blanchard and Quah in Figures 1 to 6, which are based on the smaller sample of 1950 to 1987. *Hint: In computing the impulses for positive shocks, it may be necessary to change the sign on some of the diagonal elements of the long-run restriction matrix, F, since a positive demand shock, for example, should result in a decrease in unemployment and an increase in output.*

(c) Okun's Law predicts that a 1% decrease in the unemployment rate corresponds to a 3% increase in output (see also Blanchard and Quah (1989, p663), who choose 2.5%). Interpreting this as a long-run relationship, use the estimates of the long-run matrix, F, to construct a Wald test of Okun's Law based first on supply shocks and then also on aggregate demand shocks. Re-estimate the SVAR with the additional restriction that Okun's Law holds.

(d) Repeat parts (a) to (c) for the United Kingdom (June 1971 to September 2009) and Japan (March 1980 to September 2009).

(8) **Identifying a Goods Market Shock using Sign Restrictions**

Program files	svar_sign.*
Data files	sign.*

Consider a bivariate SVAR consisting of the annualised quarterly growth rates in output and prices, $y_t = [400\Delta \ln o_t \; 400\Delta \ln p_t]'$. Sign restrictions are used to identify aggregate supply and aggregate demand shocks, $z_t = [z_{as,t} \; z_{ad,t}]'$, where an aggregate supply shock has a positive effect on output and a negative effect on prices, whereas an aggregate demand shock has a positive effect on both output and prices.

(a) Estimate a VAR for the United States using quarterly data over the period March 1950 to December 2009, where the VAR is specified to have $p = 2$ lags and a constant and a time trend. Show that the residual covariance matrix is

$$\widehat{V} = \begin{bmatrix} 12.172 & -0.309 \\ -0.309 & 5.923 \end{bmatrix}.$$

(b) Use $\widehat{V}$ in part (a) to compute S based on a Choleski decomposition. Hence, show that the impulse responses do not conform with shocks corresponding to aggregate supply and aggregate demand.

(c) Re-do the impulse responses by re-defining S as SQ', where Q is defined in (14.19) with $\vartheta = 0.2\pi$. Show that the impulse responses now correspond to aggregate supply and aggregate demand shocks.

(d) Generate 10000 simulated values of ϑ from the interval $[0, \pi]$ and select the set of impulse responses for each draw that satisfy the sign restrictions. Compute the median impulse responses from this set. In computing the median it is important to ensure that the four impulses chosen come from the same model, otherwise the shocks are not ortho-gonalised. *Hint: The approach adopted is to extract the contemporan-eous impulse values from the selected impulses and group these values into the four impulse sets. These are each standardised by subtracting the respective median and dividing by the respective standard deviation. The median set of impulses is taken as the model that has the smallest absolute deviation from summing across the four impulses.*

15 Latent Factor Models

15.1 Introduction

The simplest representation of the models specified and estimated so far is that of an observed dependent variable, y_t, expressed as a function of an observable explanatory variable, x_t, and an unobservable disturbance term, u_t. For a linear specification this relationship is

$$y_t = \beta x_t + u_t .\tag{15.1}$$

In this chapter, the assumption that the explanatory variable, x_t, is observed is relaxed. So that the notation reflects this change in the status of the explanatory variable, the model is rewritten as

$$y_t = \lambda s_t + u_t ,\tag{15.2}$$

in which s_t represents an unobserved or latent factor. This model is easily extended to include N dependent variables, $y_t = \{y_{1,t}, \cdots y_{N,t}\}$, and K latent factors, $s_t = \{s_{1,t}, \cdots s_{K,t}\}$, where $K < N$.

Models with latent factors are encountered frequently in economics and finance and prominent examples include multi-factor models of the term structure of interest rates, dating of business cycles, the identification of *ex ante* real interest rates, real business cycle models with technology shocks, the capital asset pricing model and models of stochastic volatility. A number of advantages stem from being able to identify the existence of a latent factor structure underlying the behaviour of economic and financial time series. First, it provides a parsimonious way of modelling dynamic multivariate systems. As seen in Chapter 13, the curse of dimensionality arises even in relatively small systems of unrestricted VARs. Second, it avoids the need to use ad hoc proxy variables for the unobservable variables which can result in biased and inconsistent parameter estimates. Examples of this include the capital asset pricing model and the identification of *ex ante* real interest rates.

Despite the fact that it is latent, the factor s_t in equation (15.2) can nonetheless be characterised via the time series properties of the observed dependent variables, y_t. The system of equations capturing this structure is commonly referred to as a state-space model and the technique that enables the identification and extraction of latent factors is known as the Kalman filter. An important assumption underlying the Kalman filter is that the disturbance term, u_t, in equation (15.2) is normally distributed. This assumption makes it possible to summarise the entire distribution of the latent factors using conditional means and variances alone. Consequently, these moments feature prominently in the derivations of the recursions that define the Kalman filter. For the case in which the assumption of normality of the disturbance terms is inappropriate, a quasi-maximum likelihood estimator, based on the methods of Chapter 9, may be available. An alternative approach, which does not require making any distributional assumptions about u_t in (15.2) is the generalised method of moments discussed in Chapter 10. Bayesian approaches to estimating state-space models are dealt with by Carter and Kohn (1994) and Stroud, Muller and Polson (2003).

15.2 Motivating Examples

To motivate the Kalman filter, two sets of examples are explored.

15.2.1 Empirical

The first set of examples is essentially empirical and emphasises the usefulness of the filter in overcoming the curse of dimensionality.

Example 15.1 Term Structure of Interest Rates

Figure 15.1 plots United States daily zero coupon bond yields from 4 October 1988 to 28 December 2001. The maturities are, respectively, 3 months, $r_{1,t}$, 1 year, $r_{2,t}$, 3 years, $r_{3,t}$, 5 years, $r_{4,t}$, 7 years, $r_{5,t}$, and 10 years, $r_{6,t}$. Visual inspection shows that all the yields exhibit very similar dynamics, suggesting that they are all driven by one or two unobservable factors.

$\square$

In the case of a single latent factor, $K = 1$, the previous example suggests that a model of the term structure of interest rates is

$$r_{i,t} = \lambda_i s_t + u_{i,t}, \qquad i = 1, \cdots, 6, \tag{15.3}$$

in which s_t is a latent factor and $u_{i,t} \sim iid\, N(0, \sigma_i^2)$. The parameter λ_i controls the strength of the relationship between the ith yield and the latent factor, s_t. These parameters are commonly referred to as the factor loadings and this equation is commonly referred to as the measurement equation. The disturbance term, $u_{i,t}$, allows for idiosyncratic movements in the ith yield which are not explained by movements in the factor. The strength of these idiosyncratic

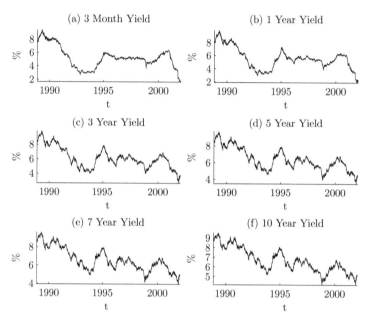

Figure 15.1. Daily United States zero coupon rates from 4 October 1988 to 28 December 2001.

movements are controlled by the parameters σ_i. This set of equations can be written as a single equation in matrix form as

$$r_t = \Lambda s_t + u_t, \qquad (15.4)$$

in which r_t is a (6×1) column vector of yields, u_t is a (6×1) column vector of idiosyncratic terms and

$$\Lambda = \begin{bmatrix} \lambda_1 & \lambda_2 & \lambda_3 & \lambda_4 & \lambda_5 & \lambda_6 \end{bmatrix}'. \qquad (15.5)$$

To complete the specification of the model in equation (15.3), it remains only to specify the dynamics of the latent factor, s_t. As the disturbance terms are independent, any dynamics displayed by the yields must be captured by the dynamics of the factor. The simplest representation is to let the factor follow a first-order autoregressive process

$$s_t = \phi s_{t-1} + v_t, \qquad v_t \sim iid\, N(0, \sigma_v^2), \qquad (15.6)$$

in which ϕ is the autoregressive parameter and v_t is a disturbance term. This equation is commonly known as the state equation and together with the measurement equation (15.3) the system is known as a state-space model.

Example 15.2 Business Cycle Dating

A common approach to identifying the peaks and troughs of a business cycle is to look at the turning points of a range of indicators of economic activity. Typical examples of indicators include GDP growth rates, $y_{1,t}$, changes in unemployment, $y_{2,t}$, movements in employment, $y_{3,t}$, and retail sales, $y_{4,t}$. The business cycle is unobservable and is to be inferred from these observable indicators. □

The business cycle example suggests the following model for the indicators, $y_{i,t}$,

$$y_{i,t} = \lambda_i s_t + u_{i,t}, \qquad i = 1, \cdots, 4, \tag{15.7}$$

in which s_t is the latent business cycle and $u_{i,t} \sim iid\ N(0, \sigma_i^2)$ is a disturbance term. To capture potential cycles in s_t, the dynamics of the business cycle are represented by a second-order autoregressive model

$$s_t = \phi_1 s_{t-1} + \phi_2 s_{t-2} + v_t, \qquad v_t \sim iid\ N(0, \sigma_v^2). \tag{15.8}$$

The assumption that the $u_{i,t}$'s are independent can be relaxed to allow additional dynamics over and above the dynamics induced by the business cycle s_t, by specifying

$$u_{i,t} = \delta_i u_{i,t-1} + w_{i,t}, \qquad w_{i,t} \sim iid\ N(0, \sigma_{w,i}^2). \tag{15.9}$$

15.2.2 Theoretical

The second set of examples is more theoretical in nature and illustrates the importance of being able to deal effectively with latent factors in econometrics.

Example 15.3 Capital Asset Pricing Model

The capital asset pricing model (CAPM) regression equation is

$$y_{i,t} = \alpha_i + \beta_i m_t + u_{i,t},$$

in which $y_{i,t}$ is the observed excess return on an asset, m_t is the observed excess return on the market portfolio, β_i is known as the beta of the ith asset and $u_{i,t} \sim iid\ N(0, \sigma_i^2)$. In theory, the CAPM equation should be specified in terms of the excess return on all invested wealth. As this is an unobservable variable, the excess return on the market portfolio, m_t, is essentially serving as a proxy. □

The alternative approach that avoids the use of a proxy variable, m_t, is to treat the excess return on wealth as a latent factor, s_t, and re-specify the CAPM as

$$y_{i,t} = \alpha_i + \beta_i s_t + u_{i,t}, \qquad i = 1, \cdots, N. \tag{15.10}$$

An important feature of this model is that aggregate wealth is identified by the dynamics of the excess returns on all of the assets in the system. The model is completed by specifying the dynamics of the excess return on wealth, s_t.

Example 15.4 *Ex Ante* Real Interest Rates
   In economic models, decisions are made on *ex ante* real interest rates that are unobserved because they are based on the expected inflation rate. The relationship between the *ex post* and *ex ante* real interest rates is as follows. The *ex post* real interest rate is

$$r_t = i_t - \pi_t,$$

in which i_t is the nominal interest rate and π_t is the observed inflation rate. Expanding this expression to allow for a constant α and expected inflation, π_t^e, gives

$$r_t = \alpha + i_t - \pi_t^e - \alpha + \pi_t^e - \pi_t$$
$$y_t = \alpha + s_t + u_t,$$

where $y_t = r_t$, $s_t + \alpha = i_t - \pi_t^e$ represents the *ex ante* real interest rate and $u_t = \pi_t^e - \pi_t$ is the inflation expectations error.   □

15.3   The Recursions of the Kalman Filter

The Kalman filter is an algorithm to form predictions of the K latent factors, s_t, based on their conditional means and then to update these predictions in a systematic fashion as more measurements of the N observed variables, y_t, become available. Presenting both univariate ($N = K = 1$) and multivariate ($N > K \geq 1$) versions of the Kalman filter highlights the recursive structure and other properties of this algorithm. In deriving the algorithm, it is assumed that the parameters of the model are known. This assumption is relaxed in Section 15.6 and the parameters of the model are estimated by maximum likelihood.

15.3.1   *Univariate*

Consider the univariate model relating a single ($N = 1$) observed dependent variable, y_t, to a single ($K = 1$) latent factor, s_t, given by

$$y_t = \lambda s_t + u_t \tag{15.11}$$
$$s_t = \phi s_{t-1} + v_t, \tag{15.12}$$

in which the disturbances are distributed as

$$u_t \sim iid\ N(0, \sigma^2) \tag{15.13}$$
$$v_t \sim iid\ N(0, \sigma_v^2), \tag{15.14}$$

where $E[u_t v_t] = 0$ and λ, ϕ, σ^2 and σ_v^2 are known parameters.

Prediction

Consider forming a prediction of s_t using information at time $t - 1$, defined as $s_{t|t-1} = E_{t-1}[s_t]$. This can be achieved by taking conditional expectations of equation (15.12)

$$s_{t|t-1} = E_{t-1}[s_t] = E_{t-1}[\phi s_{t-1} + v_t] = \phi E_{t-1}[s_{t-1}] = \phi s_{t-1|t-1}, \tag{15.15}$$

where $E_{t-1}[v_t] = 0$ by assumption and by definition

$$s_{t-1|t-1} = E_{t-1}[s_{t-1}]. \tag{15.16}$$

The variance of s_t given information at time $t - 1$ is by definition

$$P_{t|t-1} = E_{t-1}\left[(s_t - s_{t|t-1})^2\right]. \tag{15.17}$$

An expression for $P_{t|t-1}$ can be obtained by subtracting $s_{t|t-1}$, given in equation (15.15), from both sides of (15.12) to give

$$s_t - s_{t|t-1} = \phi(s_{t-1} - s_{t-1|t-1}) + v_t. \tag{15.18}$$

Squaring and taking expectations gives

$$\begin{aligned}
P_{t|t-1} &= E_{t-1}\left[(s_t - s_{t|t-1})^2\right] \\
&= \phi^2 E_{t-1}\left[(s_{t-1} - s_{t-1|t-1})^2\right] + E_{t-1}\left[v_t^2\right] \\
&\quad + 2\phi E_{t-1}\left[(s_{t-1} - s_{t-1|t-1})v_t\right] \\
&= \phi^2 P_{t-1|t-1} + \sigma_v^2,
\end{aligned}$$

where the following definitions are used

$$P_{t-1|t-1} = E_{t-1}\left[(s_{t-1} - s_{t-1|t-1})^2\right]$$
$$E_{t-1}\left[(s_{t-1} - s_{t-1|t-1})v_t\right] = (E_{t-1}[s_{t-1}] - s_{t-1|t-1})E_{t-1}[v_t] = 0$$
$$E_{t-1}\left[v_t^2\right] = \sigma_v^2.$$

The expressions for the conditional mean and variance of s_t given information at $t - 1$ require values for $s_{t-1|t-1}$ and $P_{t-1|t-1}$, respectively. This highlights the iterative nature of the Kalman filter algorithm as $s_{t-1|t-1}$ and $P_{t-1|t-1}$ will be available from the updating phase of the previous iteration of the filter.

Observation

From (15.11), the conditional expectation of y_t based on information at time $t - 1$ is

$$\mu_{t|t-1} = E_{t-1}[y_t] = E_{t-1}[\lambda s_t + u_t] = \lambda E_{t-1}[s_t] = \lambda s_{t|t-1}, \quad (15.19)$$

where $E_{t-1}[u_t] = 0$, by assumption, and $s_{t|t-1}$ is available from the prediction phase.

The conditional variance of y_t is derived by defining the one-step ahead conditional prediction error by subtracting (15.19) from (15.11)

$$y_t - \mu_{t|t-1} = \lambda s_t + u_t - \lambda s_{t|t-1} = \lambda(s_t - s_{t|t-1}) + u_t. \quad (15.20)$$

The variance of y_t is then

$$
\begin{aligned}
V_{t|t-1} &= E_{t-1}\left[(y_t - \mu_{t|t-1})^2\right] \\
&= \lambda^2 E_{t-1}\left[(s_t - s_{t|t-1})^2\right] + E_{t-1}\left[u_t^2\right] + 2\lambda E_{t-1}\left[(s_t - s_{t|t-1})u_t\right] \\
&= \lambda^2 P_{t|t-1} + \sigma^2, \quad (15.21)
\end{aligned}
$$

where $E_{t-1}\left[u_t^2\right] = \sigma^2$ by assumption, $P_{t|t-1}$ is available from the prediction phase, and the simplification in the last step uses

$$
\begin{aligned}
E_{t-1}\left[(s_t - s_{t|t-1})u_t\right] &= E_{t-1}[(\phi(s_{t-1} - s_{t-1|t-1}) + v_t)u_t] \\
&= \phi(E_{t-1}[s_{t-1}] - s_{t-1|t-1})E_{t-1}[u_t] + E_{t-1}[v_t u_t] = 0. \\
& \quad\quad\quad\quad\quad\quad\quad\quad\quad\quad\quad\quad\quad\quad\quad\quad\quad (15.22)
\end{aligned}
$$

Updating

The conditional forecast of the factor s_t in (15.15) is based on information at time $t - 1$. However, y_t is available at time t so an improved forecast of s_t can be derived using this information. To achieve this objective, the joint conditional normality of y_t and s_t implied by the normality assumptions on u_t and v_t implies that the conditional mean of s_t given y_t has a linear functional form, which can be expressed as the regression equation

$$s_t - s_{t|t-1} = \kappa_t(y_t - \mu_{t|t-1}) + \zeta_t, \quad (15.23)$$

in which ζ_t is a disturbance term and κ_t is a parameter to be derived. This equation can be rewritten as

$$s_t = s_{t|t} + \zeta_t,$$

where

$$s_{t|t} = s_{t|t-1} + \kappa_t(y_t - \mu_{t|t-1}), \quad (15.24)$$

represents the conditional expectation of s_t at time t using all of the information up to and including time t.

Equation (15.23) represents a least squares regression where $s_t - s_{t|t-1}$ is the dependent variable, $y_t - \mu_{t|t-1}$ is the explanatory variable and κ_t is the unknown parameter. It follows immediately that κ is given by

$$\kappa_t = \frac{E_t \left[(s_t - s_{t|t-1})(y_t - \mu_{t|t-1}) \right]}{E_t \left[(y_t - \mu_{t|t-1})^2 \right]}. \tag{15.25}$$

The numerator of equation (15.25) is simplified by substituting for $y_t - \mu_{t|t-1}$ using equation (15.20) to give

$$\begin{aligned} E_t \left[(s_t - s_{t|t-1})(y_t - \mu_{t|t-1}) \right] &= E_t \left[(s_t - s_{t|t-1})(\lambda(s_t - s_{t|t-1}) + u_t) \right] \\ &= \lambda E_t \left[(s_t - s_{t|t-1})^2 \right] \\ &\quad + E_t \left[(s_t - s_{t|t-1})u_t \right] \\ &= \lambda P_{t|t-1} . \end{aligned} \tag{15.26}$$

The simplification in equation (15.26) uses the definition of $P_{t|t-1}$ given in equation (15.17) and also equation (15.22). This result also uses the fact that in this instance conditioning at t is equivalent to conditioning at $t - 1$. Now using equation (15.26) as the numerator in equation (15.25) and equation (15.21) as the denominator gives

$$\kappa_t = \frac{\lambda P_{t|t-1}}{V_{t|t-1}} . \tag{15.27}$$

This term is commonly referred to as the Kalman gain. Using equation (15.27) in (15.24) gives

$$\begin{aligned} s_{t|t} &= s_{t|t-1} + \frac{\lambda P_{t|t-1}}{V_{t|t-1}}(y_t - \mu_{t|t-1}) \\ &= s_{t|t-1} + \frac{\lambda P_{t|t-1}}{V_{t|t-1}}(y_t - \lambda s_{t|t-1}), \end{aligned} \tag{15.28}$$

where the last step is based on using $\mu_{t|t-1} = \lambda s_{t|t-1}$ in (15.19).

The variance of s_t based on information at time t is

$$P_{t|t} = E_t \left[(s_t - s_{t|t})^2 \right] .$$

Using equation (15.28) for $s_{t|t}$ and expanding gives

$$
\begin{aligned}
P_{t|t} &= E_t\left[\left(s_t - s_{t|t-1} - \frac{\lambda P_{t|t-1}}{V_{t|t-1}}\left(y_t - \lambda s_{t|t-1}\right)\right)^2\right] \\
&= E_t\left[\left(s_t - s_{t|t-1}\right)^2 + \left(\frac{\lambda P_{t|t-1}}{V_{t|t-1}}\left(y_t - \lambda s_{t|t-1}\right)\right)^2\right. \\
&\qquad \left. -2\frac{\lambda P_{t|t-1}}{V_{t|t-1}}\left(s_t - s_{t|t-1}\right)\left(y_t - \lambda s_{t|t-1}\right)\right] \\
&= E_t\left[\left(s_t - s_{t|t-1}\right)^2\right] + \left(\frac{\lambda P_{t|t-1}}{V_{t|t-1}}\right)^2 E_t\left[\left(y_t - \lambda s_{t|t-1}\right)^2\right] \\
&\qquad -2\frac{\lambda P_{t|t-1}}{V_{t|t-1}} E_t\left[\left(s_t - s_{t|t-1}\right)\left(y_t - \lambda s_{t|t-1}\right)\right].
\end{aligned}
$$

Defining

$$
E_t\left[\left(s_t - s_{t|t-1}\right)^2\right] = P_{t|t-1}
$$
$$
E_t\left[\left(y_t - \lambda s_{t|t-1}\right)^2\right] = V_{t|t-1}
$$
$$
E_t\left[\left(s_t - s_{t|t-1}\right)\left(y_t - \lambda s_{t|t-1}\right)\right] = \lambda P_{t|t-1},
$$

where the last result uses equation (15.26) with $\mu_{t|t-1} = \lambda s_{t|t-1}$, the updated variance of the factor is simply

$$
P_{t|t} = P_{t|t-1} - \frac{\lambda^2 P_{t|t-1}^2}{V_{t|t-1}}.
$$

Iterating

Now consider predicting y_{t+1} using information at time t. From (15.19) this prediction requires $s_{t+1|t}$ which from (15.15) is based on $s_{t|t}$ where the latter is computed from the previous step given in (15.28). This means that the entire sequence of one-step-ahead predictions can be constructed for both the observable variable, y_t, and the unobservable factor, s_t.

Initialisation

For the first observation, $t = 1$, the algorithm requires some starting values for $s_{1|0}$ and $P_{1|0}$ (see Hamilton, 1994; Harvey, 1989). The simplest approach is to assume stationarity and set the starting values equal to the unconditional moments of s_t obtained from equation (15.12). Using the properties of a stationary AR(1) model from Chapter 13, these are, respectively,

$$
s_{1|0} = 0, \qquad P_{1|0} = \frac{\sigma_v^2}{1 - \phi^2}.
$$

Table 15.1. *Numerical illustration of the recursions of the Kalman filter.*
Parameters are $\lambda = 1.0$, $\phi = 0.8$, $\sigma = 0.5$ and $\sigma_v = 1$

	Data	Prediction		Observation		Updating		Like.
t	y_t	$s_{t\|t-1}$	$P_{t\|t-1}$	$\mu_{t\|t-1}$	$V_{t\|t-1}$	$s_{t\|t}$	$P_{t\|t}$	$\ln l_t$
(1)	(2)	(3)	(4)	(5)	(6)	(7)	(8)	(9)
1	−0.680	0.000	2.778	0.000	3.028	−0.624	0.229	−1.549
2	0.670	−0.499	1.147	−0.499	1.397	0.461	0.205	−1.576
3	0.012	0.369	1.131	0.369	1.381	0.077	0.205	−1.126
4	−0.390	0.062	1.131	0.062	1.381	−0.308	0.205	−1.154
5	−1.477	−0.246	1.131	−0.246	1.381	−1.255	0.205	−1.629

Example 15.5 Recursions of the Univariate Kalman Filter

The recursive features of the Kalman filter algorithm for the model in equations (15.11) to (15.14) are demonstrated with a simple numerical example in Table 15.1. The parameters are specified as $\lambda = 1.0$, $\phi = 0.8$, $\sigma = 0.5$ and $\sigma_v = 1$. The sample size is $T = 5$, with the actual values of y_t given in column (2) of Table 15.1.

The numerical calculations of the recursions of the Kalman filter proceed as follows.

(1) **Prediction:** $t = 1$ **(Initialisation)**

The starting values for the conditional mean and variance of the factor at $t = 1$ are given in columns (3) and (4),

$$s_{1|0} = 0.0, \qquad P_{1|0} = \frac{1}{1 - \phi^2} = \frac{1}{1 - 0.8^2} = 2.778.$$

(2) **Observation:** $t = 1$

The conditional mean and variance of y_1 are given in columns (5) and (6), respectively,

$$\mu_{1|0} = \lambda s_{1|0} = 1.0 \times 0.0 = 0.0,$$
$$V_{1|0} = \lambda^2 P_{1|0} + \sigma^2 = 1.0^2 \times 2.778 + 0.5^2 = 3.028,$$

while the forecast error of y_1 is

$$y_1 - \mu_{1|0} = -0.680 - 0.0 = -0.680.$$

(3) **Updating:** $t = 1$

The update of the mean and the variance of the factor are given in columns (7) and (8). These are

$$s_{1|1} = s_{1|0} + \frac{\lambda P_{1|0}}{V_{1|0}}(y_1 - \mu_{1|0}) = 0 + \frac{1.0 \times 2.778}{3.028}(-0.680 - 0)$$
$$= -0.624$$

$$P_{1|1} = P_{1|0} - \frac{\lambda^2 P_{1|0}^2}{V_{1|0}} = 2.778 - \frac{1.0^2 \times 2.778^2}{3.028} = 0.229.$$

(4) **Prediction:** $t = 2$

From columns (3) and (4),

$$s_{2|1} = \phi s_{1|1} = 0.8 \times (-0.624) = -0.499,$$
$$P_{2|1} = \phi^2 P_{1|1} + 1 = 0.8^2 \times 0.229 + 1.0 = 1.147.$$

See Exercise 1 for the repeat calculations for $t = 2, 3, 4, 5$.

□

15.3.2   Multivariate

Consider the case of N variables $\{y_{1,t}, \cdots, y_{N,t}\}$ and K factors $\{s_{1,t}, \cdots, s_{K,t}\}$. The multivariate version of the state-space system is

$$y_t = \Lambda s_t + u_t \tag{15.29}$$
$$s_t = \Phi s_{t-1} + v_t, \tag{15.30}$$

in which the disturbances are distributed as

$$u_t \sim iid\ N(0, R) \qquad v_t \sim iid\ N(0, Q), \tag{15.31}$$

where

$$E\left[u_t u_t'\right] = R, \qquad E\left[v_t v_t'\right] = Q, \qquad E\left[u_t v_t'\right] = 0_{N \times K}. \tag{15.32}$$

The dimensions of the parameter matrices are as follows: Λ is $(N \times K)$, Φ is $(K \times K)$, R is $(N \times N)$ and Q is $(K \times K)$.

The recursions of the multivariate Kalman filter are as follows.

(1) **Prediction:**

$$s_{t|t-1} = \Phi s_{t-1|t-1}$$
$$P_{t|t-1} = \Phi P_{t-1|t-1} \Phi' + Q.$$

(2) **Observation:**

$$\mu_{t|t-1} = \Lambda s_{t|t-1}$$
$$V_{t|t-1} = \Lambda P_{t|t-1} \Lambda' + R .$$

(3) **Updating:**

$$s_{t|t} = s_{t|t-1} + P_{t|t-1} \Lambda' V_{t|t-1}^{-1} (y_t - \mu_{t|t-1})$$
$$P_{t|t} = P_{t|t-1} - P_{t|t-1} \Lambda' V_{t|t-1}^{-1} \Lambda P_{t|t-1} ,$$

where the Kalman gain is given by

$$\mathcal{K}_t = P_{t|t-1} \Lambda' V_{t|t-1}^{-1}.$$

To start the recursion, the initial values $s_{1|0}$ and $P_{1|0}$ for the multivariate K factor model, assuming stationarity, are

$$s_{1|0} = 0, \tag{15.33}$$
$$\text{vec}(P_{1|0}) = (I_K - (\Phi \otimes \Phi))^{-1} \text{vec}(Q). \tag{15.34}$$

Example 15.6 Recursions of the Multivariate Kalman Filter
Consider a factor model as in equations (15.29) to (15.32), with three observable variables ($N = 3$), two factors ($K = 2$) and parameter matrices

$$\Lambda = \begin{bmatrix} 1.00 & 0.50 \\ 1.00 & 0.00 \\ 1.00 & -0.50 \end{bmatrix}, \quad \Phi = \begin{bmatrix} 0.80 & 0.00 \\ 0.00 & 0.50 \end{bmatrix}, \quad R = \begin{bmatrix} 0.25 & 0.00 & 0.00 \\ 0.00 & 0.16 & 0.00 \\ 0.00 & 0.00 & 0.09 \end{bmatrix},$$

and $Q = I_2$. For $T = 5$ observations, the variables are

$$y_1 = \{1.140, 2.315, -0.054, -1.545, -0.576\}$$
$$y_2 = \{3.235, 0.552, -0.689, 1.382, 0.718\}$$
$$y_3 = \{1.748, 1.472, -1.413, -0.199, 1.481\}.$$

The Kalman filter iterations proceed as follows.

(1) **Prediction:** $t = 1$ **(Initialisation)**

$$s_{1|0} = \begin{bmatrix} 0 \\ 0 \end{bmatrix}$$

$$\text{vec}(P_{1|0}) = \left(I_4 - \left(\begin{bmatrix} 0.80 & 0.00 \\ 0.00 & 0.50 \end{bmatrix} \otimes \begin{bmatrix} 0.80 & 0.00 \\ 0.00 & 0.50 \end{bmatrix} \right) \right)^{-1} \text{vec}(I_2),$$

so that

$$P_{1|0} = \begin{bmatrix} 2.778 & 0.000 \\ 0.000 & 1.333 \end{bmatrix}.$$

(2) Observation: $t = 1$

$$\mu_{t|t-1} = \Lambda s_{t|t-1} = \begin{bmatrix} 1.00 & 0.50 \\ 1.00 & 0.00 \\ 1.00 & -0.50 \end{bmatrix} \begin{bmatrix} 0 \\ 0 \end{bmatrix} = \begin{bmatrix} 0.0 \\ 0.0 \\ 0.0 \end{bmatrix}$$

$$V_{t|t-1} = \Lambda P_{t|t-1} \Lambda' + R$$

$$= \begin{bmatrix} 1.00 & 0.50 \\ 1.00 & 0.00 \\ 1.00 & -0.50 \end{bmatrix} \begin{bmatrix} 2.778 & 0.000 \\ 0.000 & 1.333 \end{bmatrix} \begin{bmatrix} 1.00 & 0.50 \\ 1.00 & 0.00 \\ 1.00 & -0.50 \end{bmatrix}' + \mathrm{diag} \begin{pmatrix} 0.25 \\ 0.16 \\ 0.09 \end{pmatrix}$$

$$= \begin{bmatrix} 3.361 & 2.778 & 2.444 \\ 2.778 & 2.938 & 2.778 \\ 2.444 & 2.778 & 3.201 \end{bmatrix}$$

$$y_t - \mu_{t|t-1} = \begin{bmatrix} 2.5 \\ 2.0 \\ 1.5 \end{bmatrix} - \begin{bmatrix} 0.0 \\ 0.0 \\ 0.0 \end{bmatrix} = \begin{bmatrix} 2.5 \\ 2.0 \\ 1.5 \end{bmatrix}.$$

(3) Updating: $t = 1$

$$s_{t|t} = s_{t|t-1} + P_{t|t-1} \Lambda' V_{t|t-1}^{-1} \left(y_t - \mu_{t|t-1} \right)$$

$$= \begin{bmatrix} 0 \\ 0 \end{bmatrix} + \begin{bmatrix} 2.778 & 0.000 \\ 0.000 & 1.333 \end{bmatrix} \begin{bmatrix} 1.00 & 0.50 \\ 1.00 & 0.00 \\ 1.00 & -0.50 \end{bmatrix}'$$

$$\times \begin{bmatrix} 3.361 & 2.778 & 2.444 \\ 2.778 & 2.938 & 2.778 \\ 2.444 & 2.778 & 3.201 \end{bmatrix}^{-1} \begin{bmatrix} 1.140 \\ 3.235 \\ 1.748 \end{bmatrix}$$

$$= \begin{bmatrix} 2.027 \\ -0.049 \end{bmatrix}.$$

$$P_{t|t} = P_{t|t-1} - P_{t|t-1} \Lambda' V_{t|t-1}^{-1} \Lambda P_{t|t-1}$$

$$= \begin{bmatrix} 2.778 & 0.000 \\ 0.000 & 1.333 \end{bmatrix} - \begin{bmatrix} 2.778 & 0.000 \\ 0.000 & 1.333 \end{bmatrix} \begin{bmatrix} 1.00 & 0.50 \\ 1.00 & 0.00 \\ 1.00 & -0.50 \end{bmatrix}'$$

$$\times \begin{bmatrix} 3.361 & 2.778 & 2.444 \\ 2.778 & 2.938 & 2.778 \\ 2.444 & 2.778 & 3.201 \end{bmatrix}^{-1} \begin{bmatrix} 1.00 & 0.50 \\ 1.00 & 0.00 \\ 1.00 & -0.50 \end{bmatrix} \begin{bmatrix} 2.778 & 0.000 \\ 0.000 & 1.333 \end{bmatrix}$$

$$= \begin{bmatrix} 0.053 & 0.041 \\ 0.041 & 0.253 \end{bmatrix}.$$

□

15.4   Extensions

The derivation of the Kalman filter in Section 15.3 is based on a state-space model in which the latent factors have zero mean, AR(1) dynamics which are stationary and no exogenous or predetermined variables. These assumptions are now relaxed.

15.4.1   Intercepts

The state-space representation can be extended to allow for intercepts as in the case of the expected real interest rate example discussed in Section 15.2. In the case of the univariate model, the model is now re-written as

$$y_t = \lambda_0 + \lambda s_t + u_t$$
$$s_t = \phi_0 + \phi s_{t-1} + v_t.$$

If the factor, s_t, is specified to have a zero mean, $\phi_0 = 0$, then λ_0 is the sample mean of y_t.

15.4.2   Dynamics

To allow for greater generality in the dynamics of the state-space model, consider the following two extensions.

(1) Suppose that the latent factor model has p lags given by

$$s_t = \phi_1 s_{t-1} + \phi_2 s_{t-2} + \cdots + \phi_p s_{t-p} + v_t,$$

in which v_t is the disturbance term. This equation is rewritten as a vector AR(1) model as follows

$$\begin{bmatrix} s_t \\ s_{t-1} \\ s_{t-2} \\ \vdots \\ s_{t-p+1} \end{bmatrix} = \begin{bmatrix} \phi_1 & \phi_2 & \cdots & \phi_{p-1} & \phi_p \\ 1 & 0 & \cdots & 0 & 0 \\ 0 & 1 & \cdots & 0 & 0 \\ \vdots & \vdots & \ddots & \vdots & \vdots \\ 0 & 0 & \cdots & 1 & 0 \end{bmatrix} \begin{bmatrix} s_{t-1} \\ s_{t-2} \\ s_{t-3} \\ \vdots \\ s_{t-p} \end{bmatrix} + \begin{bmatrix} v_t \\ 0 \\ 0 \\ \vdots \\ 0 \end{bmatrix}.$$

The model can be viewed as having p factors $\{s_t, s_{t-1}, \cdots, s_{t-p+1}\}$, although it is really just the first element of this set of factors that is of interest. The measurement equation now becomes

$$y_t = \begin{bmatrix} \lambda & 0 & 0 & \cdots & 0 \end{bmatrix} \begin{bmatrix} s_t \\ s_{t-1} \\ \vdots \\ s_{t-p+1} \end{bmatrix} + \begin{bmatrix} u_t \\ 0 \\ \vdots \\ 0 \end{bmatrix}.$$

(2) Idiosyncratic Dynamics

Consider rewriting the business cycle model in equations (15.7) to (15.9) as

$$y_{i,t} = \lambda_i s_t + \sigma_i z_{i,t}, \qquad i = 1, \cdots, 4$$
$$s_t = \phi_1 s_{t-1} + \phi_2 s_{t-2} + v_t,$$
$$z_{i,t} = \gamma_i z_{i,t-1} + w_{i,t},$$

in which $z_{i,t}, w_{i,t} \sim iid\ N(0, 1)$ and $\gamma_i = \delta_i \sigma_i$. The state equation is now augmented to accommodate the dynamics in the idiosyncratic terms as follows

$$
\begin{bmatrix} s_t \\ s_{t-1} \\ z_{1,t} \\ z_{2,t} \\ z_{3,t} \\ z_{4,t} \end{bmatrix}
=
\begin{bmatrix}
\phi_1 & \phi_2 & 0 & 0 & 0 & 0 \\
1 & 0 & 0 & 0 & 0 & 0 \\
0 & 0 & \gamma_1 & 0 & 0 & 0 \\
0 & 0 & 0 & \gamma_2 & 0 & 0 \\
0 & 0 & 0 & 0 & \gamma_3 & 0 \\
0 & 0 & 0 & 0 & 0 & \gamma_4
\end{bmatrix}
\begin{bmatrix} s_{t-1} \\ s_{t-2} \\ z_{1,t-1} \\ z_{2,t-1} \\ z_{3,t-1} \\ z_{4,t-1} \end{bmatrix}
+
\begin{bmatrix} v_t \\ 0 \\ w_{1,t} \\ w_{2,t} \\ w_{3,t} \\ w_{4,t} \end{bmatrix} .
$$

The model has six factors, $\{s_t, s_{t-1}, z_{1,t}, z_{2,t}, z_{3,t}, z_{4,t}\}$, which now include the idiosyncratic terms. The measurement equation becomes

$$
y_t =
\begin{bmatrix}
\lambda_1 & 0 & \sigma_1 & 0 & 0 & 0 \\
\lambda_2 & 0 & 0 & \sigma_2 & 0 & 0 \\
\lambda_3 & 0 & 0 & 0 & \sigma_3 & 0 \\
\lambda_4 & 0 & 0 & 0 & 0 & \sigma_4
\end{bmatrix}
\begin{bmatrix} s_t \\ s_{t-1} \\ z_{1,t} \\ z_{2,t} \\ z_{3,t} \\ z_{4,t} \end{bmatrix} ,
$$

and, since it now contains no disturbance term, the covariance matrix R in (15.32) is now $R = 0_N$.

15.4.3 Nonstationary Factors

The assumption that s_t is stationary may be relaxed. In the case of nonstationarity, some of the eigenvalues of Φ in equation (15.30) lie on the unit circle resulting in the variance in equation (15.34) being undefined. To circumvent this problem, starting values in equations (15.33) and (15.34) are now specified as

$$s_{1|0} = \psi \tag{15.35}$$
$$P_{1|0} = \omega\ \text{vec}(Q), \tag{15.36}$$

in which ψ represents the best guess of starting value for the conditional mean and ω is a positive constant (also, see Harvey, 1989, pp 120–121). For big values of ω, the distribution has large variance and is thus diffuse. This can be viewed as

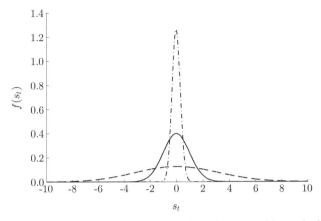

Figure 15.2. The initial distribution of the factor s_t with standard normal prior (solid line), diffuse prior (dashed line) and tight prior (dot-dashed line).

a device for controlling numerical precision when the factors are nonstationary. Alternatively, setting $\omega = 0$ yields a degenerate initial distribution for s_t where the mass of the distribution falls on ψ. Figure 15.2 plots the distribution of the factor s_t for various choices of ω.

Example 15.7 The Bai-Ng PANIC Model

Bai and Ng (2004) propose the following factor model to capture nonstationarity in panel data

$$y_{i,t} = \lambda_{0,i} + \lambda_i s_t + u_{i,t}, \qquad i = 1, 2, \cdots, N,$$
$$s_t = s_{t-1} + v_t,$$
$$u_{i,t} = \delta_i u_{i,t-1} + w_{i,t}$$
$$v_t \sim iid\, N(0, 1), \quad w_{i,t} \sim iid\, N\left(0, \sigma_i^2\right),$$

known as Panel Analysis of Nonstationarity in Idiosyncratic and Common components (PANIC). The intercept $\lambda_{0,i}$ represents a fixed effect, while the dynamics in the dependent variables, $y_{i,t}$, are captured by the nonstationary factor, s_t. $\qquad\square$

15.4.4 *Exogenous and Predetermined Variables*

A set of M exogenous or lagged dependent variables, x_t, can be included in the state-space model in one of two different ways. The first is in the measurement equation

$$y_t = \Lambda f_t + \Gamma x_t + u_t,$$

in which Γ is $(N \times M)$ and x_t is $(M \times 1)$. A special case of this model is the factor VAR model (F-VAR), where $x_t = y_{t-1}$ and Γ is a $(N \times N)$ diagonal matrix. The second approach is to include the exogenous or predetermined variables in the state equation

$$s_t = \Phi s_{t-1} + \Gamma x_t + u_t,$$

in which Γ is now a $(K \times M)$ matrix of parameters.

15.5   Factor Extraction

In many applications, an important objective is to extract estimates of the latent factors, s_t, and interpret their time series properties. By assumption at each t, s_t is normally distributed with a conditional mean and conditional variance. From the discussion in Section 15.3, estimates of these conditional moments are automatically obtained as a by-product of the recursions of the Kalman filter. In fact, three possible estimates of the factor are available depending on the form of the conditioning information set. These are as follows.

$$
\begin{aligned}
s_{t|t-1} &= E_{t-1}[s_t] & \text{[Predicted]} \\
s_{t|t} &= E_t[s_t] & \text{[Updated]} \\
s_{t|T} &= E_T[s_t] & \text{[Smoothed]}
\end{aligned}
$$

The predicted and updated estimates are as defined in Section 15.3. Formally, the equations for the smoothed conditional mean and variance are, respectively,

$$s_{t|T} = s_{t|t} + J_t(s_{t+1|T} - s_{t+1|t}) \tag{15.37}$$
$$P_{t|T} = P_{t|t} + J_t(P_{t+1|T} - P_{t+1|t})J_t', \tag{15.38}$$

where

$$J_t = P_{t|t} \Phi' P_{t+1|t}^{-1}. \tag{15.39}$$

The practical process of computing $s_{t|T}$ and $P_{t|T}$ essentially requires that the Kalman filter algorithm be run backwards starting at T. This approach, also known as fixed interval smoothing, has the effect of generating smoother estimates than either $s_{t|t-1}$ or $s_{t|t}$ as it represents a two-sided moving average with variable weights that uses all of the sample data.

In practice, which of these three methods is adopted depends on the problem context. In the business cycle example, $s_{t|T}$, is an appropriate measure since it is used to date business cycles historically. It provides more precise information of the timing of peaks and troughs than the other measures because it uses all the information in the sample data. In the *ex ante* interest rate model, $s_{t|t-1}$ is the appropriate choice as it provides an expectation of the interest rate at time t conditional on previous information.

Example 15.8 Computing Smooth-Factor Estimates

Using the results in Table 15.1 where the sample size is $T = 5$, at $t = 5$ the smoothed estimates equal the updated factor estimates

$$s_{5|5} = -1.255$$
$$P_{5|5} = 0.205.$$

Using equation (15.39) at $t = 4$

$$J_4 = P_{4|4}\Phi'P_{5|4}^{-1} = 0.205 \times 0.8 \times 1.131^{-1} = 0.145,$$

and from (15.37) and (15.38) yields the respective smoothed estimates

$$\begin{aligned} s_{4|5} &= s_{4|4} + J_4\left(s_{5|5} - s_{5|4}\right) \\ &= -0.308 + 0.145 \times (-1.255 + 0.246) = -0.454, \end{aligned}$$

and

$$\begin{aligned} P_{4|5} &= P_{4|4} + J_4\left(P_{5|5} - P_{5|4}\right)J_4' \\ &= 0.205 + 0.145 \times (0.205 - 1.131) \times 0.145 = 0.185. \end{aligned}$$

Similarly, the remaining smooth-factor estimates conditional on information at time $T = 5$ are

$$s_{3|5} = 0.002, s_{2|5} = 0.408, s_{1|5} = -0.479$$
$$P_{3|5} = 0.185, P_{2|5} = 0.185, P_{1|5} = 0.205.$$

□

15.6 Estimation

The discussion so far has assumed given values for the population parameters Λ, Φ, R and Q in equations (15.29) to (15.32). In general, however, it is necessary to estimate these parameters. If the factors are observable, then the parameters are estimated by simply regressing y_t on s_t and regressing s_t on s_{t-1}. But as s_t is unobservable, an alternative estimation strategy is needed. Two estimators are discussed. The first is the maximum likelihood estimator that constructs the log-likelihood function from the prediction errors of the Kalman filter. The second approach is a sequence of least squares regressions proposed by Stock and Watson (2005) that circumvents potential numerical problems associated with maximum likelihood estimation in high-dimensional systems. Before dealing with the mechanics of estimation, the issue of identification is addressed.

15.6.1 Identification

The multivariate state-space model in (15.29) to (15.32) is under-identified and therefore all of the parameters cannot be estimated unless some further restrictions are imposed. The difficulty is seen by noting that the volatility in the factor, s_t, is controlled by Q, but the impact of this factor on y_t is given by Λ. This suggests that an infinite number of combinations of Q and Λ are consistent with the volatility of y_t, making it necessary that one of these quantities be fixed in order to achieve identification. A common approach is to set

$$Q = I_K. \tag{15.40}$$

This is the case in the term structure example in Section 15.2 in which $Q = \sigma_v^2 = 1$. Another approach is to place restrictions on Λ and allow Q to be estimated as is the case in the *ex ante* real interest rate example in the same section where $\Lambda = \lambda = 1$.

15.6.2 Maximum Likelihood

The maximum likelihood approach is to choose values of the parameters that generate latent factors that maximise the likelihood of the observed variables. Given the assumption of normality in equation (15.31), the conditional distribution of the $(N \times 1)$ vector y_t is multivariate normal

$$y_t \sim N(\mu_{t|t-1}, V_{t|t-1}),$$

where the conditional mean and variance of the observation equation are, respectively,

$$\mu_{t|t-1} = \Lambda s_{t|t-1}$$
$$V_{t|t-1} = \Lambda P_{t|t-1} \Lambda' + R.$$

The log-likelihood function for the tth observation is given by

$$\ln l_t = -\frac{N}{2} \ln(2\pi) - \frac{1}{2} \ln |V_{t|t-1}| - \frac{1}{2}(y_t - \mu_{t|t-1})' V_{t|t-1}^{-1}(y_t - \mu_{t|t-1}).$$

Example 15.9 Log-Likelihood Function of the Kalman Filter
Consider the univariate Kalman filter example in Table 15.1 for $N = 1$. As $y_1 = -0.680$ and the conditional moments of the observation equation are $\mu_{1|0} = 0.0$ and $V_{1|0} = 3.028$, the log-likelihood function at $t = 1$, reported in column (9), is computed as

$$\ln l_1 = -\frac{1}{2} \ln(2\pi) - \frac{1}{2} \ln |V_{1|0}| - \frac{1}{2}(y_1 - \mu_{1|0})' V_{1|0}^{-1}(y_1 - \mu_{1|0})$$
$$= -\frac{1}{2} \ln(2\pi) - \frac{1}{2} \ln |3.028| - \frac{1}{2}(-0.680)' 3.028^{-1}(-0.680)$$
$$= -1.549.$$

The values for $\ln l_2, \ln l_3, \cdots, \ln l_5$ are also given in Table 15.1. □

Table 15.2. *Maximum likelihood estimates of the one-factor term structure model, yields expressed in basis points. Standard errors are based on the Hessian matrix*

Variable	Parameter	Estimate	se	pv
3 month	λ_1	7.354	0.157	0.000
1 year	λ_2	7.636	0.157	0.000
3 year	λ_3	7.004	0.139	0.000
5 year	λ_4	6.293	0.127	0.000
7 year	λ_5	5.848	0.120	0.000
10 year	λ_6	5.536	0.118	0.000
3 month	σ_1	65.743	0.818	0.000
1 year	σ_2	43.667	0.554	0.000
3 year	σ_3	6.287	0.130	0.000
5 year	σ_4	26.591	0.345	0.000
7 year	σ_5	36.680	0.463	0.000
10 year	σ_6	50.466	0.629	0.000
Factor	ϕ	0.999	0.001	0.000

$\ln L_T(\widehat{\theta}) = -29.675$

For a sample of $t = 1, 2, \cdots, T$ observations, the log-likelihood function is

$$\ln L_T(\theta) = \frac{1}{T} \sum_{t=1}^{T} \ln l_t(\theta), \qquad (15.41)$$

in which $\theta = \{\Lambda, \Phi, R, Q\}$. As the parameters enter $\mu_{t|t-1}$ and $V_{t|t-1}$ nonlinearly, the log-likelihood function in equation (15.41) is maximised using an iterative algorithm from Chapter 3.

Example 15.10 A One-Factor Model of the Term Structure
Consider the yields $r_{i,t}$, $i = 1, 2, ..., 6$ on United States zero coupon bonds given in Figure 15.1. From equations (15.4) to (15.6), a one-factor model is given by the state-space representation

$$r_t = \Lambda s_t + u_t \qquad u_t \sim iid\ N(0, R)$$
$$s_t = \phi s_{t-1} + v_t \qquad v_t \sim iid\ N(0, Q),$$

in which s_t is the factor, $R = \text{diag}(\sigma_i^2)$ and $Q = \sigma_v^2 = 1$. The maximum likelihood estimates obtained by maximising (15.41) with respect to $\theta = \{\Lambda, \phi, R\}$ are given in Table 15.2, with standard errors based on the Hessian matrix. A diffuse prior is used to allow for a possible nonstationary factor by specifying the starting values to be $\psi = 0$ and $\omega = 0.1$ as in equations (15.35) and (15.36). The estimates of λ_i are similar in magnitude suggesting that s_t captures the level of the yield curve. The estimates of the idiosyncratic parameter, σ_i, exhibit a U-shape with the shortest and longest maturities having the greatest volatility and with the 3-year yield having the smallest. The adoption of a diffuse prior to initialise the filter is supported by the estimate of ϕ, which is close to unity.

□

15.6.3 *Principal Components Estimator*

When the number of measurement and state equations is large, estimation by maximum likelihood can be problematic. To circumvent this situation Stock and Watson (2005) suggest an iterative least squares approach. To outline the steps involved in this algorithm, consider the F-VAR model

$$y_t = \Lambda s_t + \Gamma y_{t-1} + u_t \qquad u_t \sim iid \, N(0, R)$$
$$s_t = \Phi s_{t-1} + v_t \qquad v_t \sim iid \, N(0, Q),$$
(15.42)

in which y_t is $(N \times 1)$, s_t is $(K \times 1)$, Λ is $(N \times K)$, Γ is $(N \times N)$, Φ is $(K \times K)$, R is $(N \times N)$ and Q is $(K \times K)$. The algorithm proceeds as follows.

Step 1: Standardise the y_t variables to have zero mean and unit variance.
Step 2: Perform a principal components decomposition on the standardised y_t variables to obtain an initial estimate of the K factors, $\widehat{s}_t$, where K is based on the magnitude of the eigenvalues. Bai and Ng (2002) provide a more formal testing procedure to choose the number of factors.
Step 3: Regress $y_{i,t}$ on $\{\widehat{s}_t, y_{i,t-1}\}$, $i = 1, 2, \cdots, N$ and compute $\widehat{\Lambda}$ and $\widehat{\Gamma}$.
Step 4: Redefine y_t as $y_t - \widehat{\Gamma} y_{t-1}$.
Step 5: Repeat steps 2 to 4 until there is no change in the parameter estimates across iterations to some desired tolerance level.
Step 6: At the final iteration, regress $\widehat{s}_t$ on $\widehat{s}_{t-1}$ and compute $\widehat{\Phi}$.

Example 15.11 A F-VAR Model of the Term Structure
The F-VAR model in (15.42) is estimated using the Stock and Watson estimator for $N = 30$ United States yields, with maturities ranging from 1 year to 30 years, inclusive, and $K = 3$ factors. The data are daily, beginning on 2nd of January 1990 and ending on 21st of August 2006. The estimates of the factor loadings on the three factors are given in Figure 15.3 and demonstrate that the factors represent the level, slope and curvature of the yield curve. The estimates of the factor dynamics are

$$\widehat{\Phi} = \begin{bmatrix} 0.853 & 0.451 & -0.039 \\ 0.034 & 0.835 & 0.056 \\ -0.020 & 0.131 & 0.316 \end{bmatrix}.$$

These estimates reveal an interesting causal relationship between the three factors, with the estimates of 0.451 and 0.131 showing unidirectional Granger

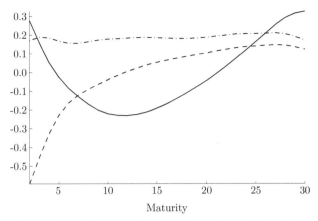

Figure 15.3. Stock-Watson factor loading estimates of standardised United States yields for yearly maturities from 1 year to 30 years. The three factors are the level (dot-dashed line), slope (dashed line) and curvature (solid line).

causality, as defined in Chapter 13, from the slope factor to both the level and curvature factors, respectively.   □

Assuming stationary s_t and u_t, the principal components estimator based on y_t yields consistent estimators of s_t (Stock and Watson, 2002), and Λ (Bai and Ng, 2004) for $N, T \to \infty$. Consistency of this estimator also holds for nonstationary s_t and stationary u_t, but not for nonstationary s_t and u_t (Bai and Ng, 2004). In the latter case, a consistent estimator proposed by Bai and Ng is to perform the principal components decomposition on Δy_t to generate $\Delta \widehat{s}_t$ and estimate Λ by regressing Δy_t on a constant and $\Delta \widehat{s}_t$ and estimate the level of the factor as $\widehat{s}_t = \sum_{i=1}^{t} \Delta \widehat{s}_t$.

Example 15.12 Properties of Principal Component Estimators

The finite sample properties of the Stock-Watson and Bai-Ng estimators are demonstrated in Table 15.3 using some Monte Carlo experiments conducted on the PANIC model

$$y_{i,t} = \lambda_i s_t + u_{i,t}, \qquad i = 1, 2, \cdots, N,$$
$$u_{i,t} = \delta u_{i,t-1} + w_{i,t},$$
$$s_t = s_{t-1} + v_t,$$
$$w_{i,t} \sim iid\ N(0, \sigma_i^2), \qquad v_t \sim iid\ N(0, 1).$$

The efficiency of the Stock-Watson estimator over the Bai-Ng estimator for the stationary case, $\delta < 1$, is evident by the lower MSEs. For the nonstationary case, $\delta = 1$, this is no longer true with the Bai-Ng estimator now giving smaller MSEs. The inconsistency property of the Stock-Watson estimator is highlighted

Table 15.3. *Finite sample properties of principal component estimators of*
$\lambda_i, i = 1, 2, \cdots, N$ *in the PANIC 1-factor model given in Example 15.7. The Bias*
and MSE are averages across the N estimates of λ_i based on 5000 replications

Estimator		$N = 10$		$N = 30$		$N = 50$	
		Bias	MSE	Bias	MSE	Bias	MSE
				$T = 100$			
Stock-Watson	$\delta = 0.0$	−0.031	0.215	0.008	0.010	0.005	0.010
	$\delta = 0.5$	−0.290	1.160	0.009	0.039	0.006	0.037
	$\delta = 1.0$	−0.672	13.260	−0.681	12.605	−0.787	12.628
Bai-Ng	$\delta = 0.0$	−0.894	1.850	−0.633	1.210	−0.731	1.157
	$\delta = 0.5$	−0.872	1.636	−0.594	1.001	−0.716	1.061
	$\delta = 1.0$	−0.847	1.488	−0.581	0.923	−0.714	1.041
				$T = 200$			
Stock-Watson	$\delta = 0.0$	0.019	0.040	0.008	0.005	0.005	0.005
	$\delta = 0.5$	−0.123	0.570	0.010	0.020	0.006	0.019
	$\delta = 1.0$	−0.594	24.223	−0.665	22.989	−0.848	23.050
Bai-Ng	$\delta = 0.0$	−0.929	1.864	−0.689	1.338	−0.817	1.384
	$\delta = 0.5$	−0.910	1.671	−0.658	1.168	−0.801	1.292
	$\delta = 1.0$	−0.889	1.542	−0.643	1.083	−0.800	1.277

by the large increase in MSE as the sample is increased from $T = 100$ to
$T = 200$. $\qquad\square$

15.7   Relationship to VARMA Models

Consider the N variable state-space model

$$y_{i,t} = \lambda_i s_t + u_{i,t}, \qquad i = 1, 2, \cdots, N$$
$$s_t = \phi s_{t-1} + v_t,$$

in which $u_{i,t} \sim iid\, N(0, \sigma_i^2)$ and $v_{i,t} \sim iid\, N(0, 1)$. Rewrite the state equation
using the lag operator

$$(1 - \phi L) s_t = v_t.$$

Multiplying the measurement equation on both sides by $1 - \phi L$ gives

$$(1 - \phi L) y_{i,t} = \lambda_i (1 - \phi L) s_t + (1 - \phi L) u_{i,t}$$
$$= \lambda_i v_t + (1 - \phi L) u_{i,t},$$

or

$$y_{i,t} = \phi y_{i,t-1} + v_{i,t}, \qquad i = 1, 2, \cdots, N, \qquad (15.43)$$

with

$$v_{i,t} = \lambda_i v_t + u_{i,t} - \phi u_{i,t-1} . \tag{15.44}$$

This is a restricted VARMA(1, 1) model, of a similar form to the factor models of contagion proposed by Dungey and Martin (2007) where a VAR is estimated to extract the dynamics and a factor structure of the form $\lambda_i v_t + u_{i,t}$ is used to model the contemporaneous linkages.

Estimation of equation (15.43) by maximum likelihood is complicated by the composite disturbance term containing v_t and $u_{i,t}$ in (15.44). One way to proceed is to use a GMM estimator as discussed in Chapter 10. The theoretical moments all have zero means by assumption. The pertinent moments of v_t are

$$
\begin{aligned}
\mathrm{E}[v_{i,t}^2] &= \lambda_i^2 + \sigma_i^2 \left(1 + \phi^2\right) , \\
\mathrm{E}[v_{i,t} v_{j,t}] &= \lambda_i \lambda_j , \\
\mathrm{E}[v_{i,t} v_{i,t-1}] &= -\phi \sigma_i^2 , \\
\mathrm{E}[v_{i,t} v_{j,t-1}] &= 0.
\end{aligned}
\tag{15.45}
$$

A GMM estimator uses (15.43) to estimate the scalar ϕ from a stacked (pooled) regression of $\mathrm{vec}(y_t)$ on $\mathrm{vec}(y_{t-1})$. Having estimated ϕ, the residuals $\widehat{v}_t$ from this regression are used to estimate the σ_i^2 from the second-last moment condition in (15.45). Estimates of λ_i are then obtained from the first moment condition in (15.45). The second moment condition can also be used in the estimation so that a cross-equation restriction is imposed, which causes the system of equations to become over-identified.

15.8   Applications

15.8.1   The Hodrick-Prescott Filter

Separating out trends and cycles is fundamental to much of macroeconomic analysis and represents an important example of factor extraction. A commonly used technique for estimating the trend in economic and financial time series is the Hodrick-Prescott filter (Hodrick and Prescott, 1997). In this application, this filter is recast in a state-space representation following Harvey and Jaeger (1993). This alternative formulation allows the estimation of an important parameter that the conventional Hodrick-Prescott filter simply imposes. Consequently, this parameter may be tested against the value commonly adopted in the conventional approach.

Let the series, y_t, be decomposed in terms of a trend, τ_t, and a cycle or transitory component, c_t

$$y_t = \tau_t + c_t , \qquad t = 1, 2, \cdots, T . \tag{15.46}$$

The Hodrick-Prescott filter defines the trend, τ_t, in terms of the following minimisation problem

$$\arg\min_{\{\tau_t\}} Q = \left[\sum_{t=1}^{T} (y_t - \tau_t)^2 + \gamma \sum_{t=1}^{T} [(\tau_{t+1} - \tau_t) - (\tau_t - \tau_{t-1})]^2 \right],$$

$$(15.47)$$

for some appropriate choice of the smoothing parameter γ. The first term in equation (15.47) penalises the lack of fit of the trend component while the second term penalises the lack of smoothness in τ_t.

A convenient analytical solution to the minimisation problem in equation (15.47) is to rewrite this equation using lag operators (see Appendix B for details) resulting in

$$\arg\min_{\{\tau_t\}} Q = \sum_{t=1}^{T} (y_t - \tau_t)^2 + \gamma \sum_{t=1}^{T} ((L^{-1} - 1)\tau_t - (1 - L)\tau_t)^2$$

$$= \sum_{t=1}^{T} (y_t - \tau_t)^2 + \gamma \sum_{t=1}^{T} (L^{-1} - 2 + L)^2 \tau_t^2$$

$$= \sum_{t=1}^{T} (y_t - \tau_t)^2 + \gamma \sum_{t=1}^{T} (L^{-2} - 4L^{-1} + 6 - 4L + L^2)\tau_t^2,$$

where the last term represents a fifth-order weighted moving average in the squared trend. Differentiating this expression with respect to τ_t and setting the derivative to zero yields the first-order condition

$$-2(y_t - \widehat{\tau}_t) + 2\gamma(L^{-2} - 4L^{-1} + 6 - 4L + L^2)\widehat{\tau}_t = 0,$$

and rearranging gives

$$\gamma(L^{-2} - 4L^{-1} + 6 - 4L + L^2)\widehat{\tau}_t + \widehat{\tau}_t = y_t, \qquad (15.48)$$

where $\widehat{\tau}_t$ is the estimator of the trend. To derive the solution for all t, define $\widehat{\tau}$ as a $(T \times 1)$ vector containing the trend estimator and y as a $(T \times 1)$ vector of the observed data so that equation (15.48) becomes

$$(\gamma F + I_T)\widehat{\tau} = y.$$

The matrix F is a $(T \times T)$ matrix given by

$$
\begin{bmatrix}
1 & -2 & 1 & 0 & \cdots & & & & & & & & \cdots & 0 \\
-2 & 5 & -4 & 1 & 0 & \cdots & & & & & & & & 0 \\
1 & -4 & 6 & -4 & 1 & 0 & \cdots & & & & & & & 0 \\
0 & 1 & -4 & 6 & -4 & 1 & 0 & \cdots & & & & & & \vdots \\
\vdots & \ddots & & & & & & \ddots & & & & & & \\
& & & & & & \ddots & & & & & \ddots & & \vdots \\
\vdots & & & & & & & 0 & 1 & -4 & 6 & -4 & 1 & 0 \\
0 & & & & & & \cdots & & 0 & 1 & -4 & 6 & -4 & 1 \\
0 & & & & & & \cdots & & & 0 & 1 & -4 & 5 & -2 \\
0 & & & & & & \cdots & & & & 0 & 1 & -2 & 1
\end{bmatrix},
$$

where suitable adjustments are made at the beginning and at the end of the sample. Upon solving this expression for $\widehat{\tau}$, the Hodrick-Prescott estimator becomes

$$\widehat{\tau} = (\gamma F + I_T)^{-1} y. \tag{15.49}$$

The estimator of the trend $\widehat{\tau}$ at each time t is a weighted average of all of the sample observations y.

The smoothness parameter, γ in equation (15.49), is central to estimating the trend: as $\gamma \to 0$, the trend component approaches the actual series and, as $\gamma \to \infty$, τ_t becomes the linear trend. Conventional choices for γ are

$$
\begin{aligned}
\gamma &= 100 &&\text{[Annual data]} \\
\gamma &= 1600 &&\text{[Quarterly data]} \\
\gamma &= 14400 &&\text{[Monthly data]}.
\end{aligned}
$$

An alternative approach is to estimate the smoothing parameter from the data by recasting the Hodrick-Prescott filter as a state-space model

$$
\begin{aligned}
y_t &= \tau_t + c_t && c_t \sim iid\, N(0, \sigma_c^2) \\
\tau_t &= \tau_{t-1} + \beta_{t-1} \\
\beta_t &= \beta_{t-1} + \zeta_t, && \zeta_t \sim iid\, N(0, \sigma_\zeta^2),
\end{aligned}
$$

where, as before, τ_t is the stochastic trend component and c_t is the cyclical component of y_t. The transitory component, c_t, and ζ_t are mutually independent normally distributed variables. This model is commonly known as an unobserved-component model.

Define

$$c_t = u_t, \qquad s_t = \begin{bmatrix} \tau_t \\ \beta_t \end{bmatrix},$$

Table 15.4. *Maximum likelihood estimates of the Hodrick-Prescott factor model. Standard errors based on the Hessian matrix in brackets*

Parameter	Unrestricted	Partially Restricted	Fully Constrained
σ_c	0.363	1.000	1.000
	(0.051)		
σ_ζ	0.716	0.465	1/40
	(0.073)	(0.056)	
$\ln L_T(\widehat{\theta})$	-1.508	-1.741	-2.856

and parameter matrices

$$\Lambda = [1 \quad 0], \quad \Phi = \begin{bmatrix} 1 & 1 \\ 0 & 1 \end{bmatrix} \quad R = \sigma_c^2, \quad Q = \begin{bmatrix} 0 & 0 \\ 0 & \sigma_\zeta^2 \end{bmatrix}.$$

The model now has exactly the representation of the multivariate Kalman filter as in equations (15.29) to (15.32). This system contains two unknown parameters, namely the variances σ_c^2 and σ_ζ^2, which together define the signal-to-noise ratio $q = \sigma_c^2/\sigma_\zeta^2$.

The results of estimating this model using quarterly real United States GDP for the period March 1940 to December 2000, T $=244$ observations, by maximum likelihood for different restrictions on the parameters σ_c and σ_ζ are reported in Table 15.4. The variable y_t is defined as $\ln GDP_t$, centred to have zero mean and scaled by 100.

The maximum likelihood estimates of the parameters for the unrestricted model yield a value of $\ln L_T(\widehat{\theta}_2) = -1.508$. Imposing the normalisation $\sigma_c = 1$ yields a value for the partially restricted model of $\ln L_T(\widehat{\theta}_1) = -1.741$. Harvey and Jaeger (1993) show that when the further restriction

$$\sigma_\zeta^2 = \frac{1}{\gamma} = \frac{1}{1600},$$

is imposed on the partially restricted model, the trend component obtained by the Kalman filter with this restricted signal-to-noise ratio is identical to that obtained from a conventional Hodrick-Prescott filter based on equation (15.49). In this case, there are no parameters to estimate, resulting in a value of the log-likelihood function of $\ln L_T(\widehat{\theta}_0) = -2.856$. Performing a LR test of this restriction yields a value of

$$LR = -2 \times 244 \times (-2.856 + 1.741) = 543.958.$$

The p-value from the chi-square distribution with one degree of freedom is 0.000, which indicates that the Hodrick-Prescott choice of γ is strongly rejected by the data.

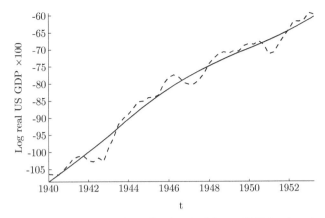

Figure 15.4. The logarithm of real United States GDP for the sub-period 1940 to 1952 (dashed line) with the smoothed trend component extracted using the Kalman filter (solid line). The data are centred to have zero mean and scaled by a factor of 100.

Figure 15.4 shows a plot of real United States GDP together with the smoothed trend component extracted the Kalman filter implementation of the Hodrick-Prescott filter for the sub-period 1940 to 1952. The smoothed estimator, $s_{t|T}$, is also numerically identical to the conventional Hodrick-Prescott filter in equation (15.49).

15.8.2 A Factor Model of Spreads with Money Shocks

The earlier empirical work on the term structure of interest rates focussed on identifying statistical factors from sets of interest rates of differing maturities. These factors are commonly classified in terms of level, slope and curvature encountered previously in Figure 15.3 in Section 15.5. More recently, understanding the economic processes underlying these statistical factors has generated interest (Gurkaynak, Sack, and Swanson, 2005; Cochrane and Piazzesi, 2009; Craine and Martin 2008, 2009). In this application, the focus is on identifying the role of money shocks in determining the factors and hence the movements in the term structure over time.

The spread at time t between a one-year forward rate maturing at time $t + n$, $f_{n,t}$, and the one-year interest rate at time t, $r_{1,t}$ is given by

$$sp_{t,n} = \ln\left(1 + \frac{f_{n,t}}{100}\right) - \ln\left(1 + \frac{r_{1,t}}{100}\right), \qquad (15.50)$$

where both rates are expressed as a percentage. Let y_t be a (5×1) vector containing the $n = 2, 4, 6, 8, 10$ year spreads, which are expressed in basis points and whose mean has been removed. To identify the role of money

Table 15.5. *Estimates of the factor model for spreads expressed in basis points. Standard errors based on the Hessian matrix are in brackets*

Spread	Slope ($s_{1,t}$)		Curvature ($s_{2,t}$)		Idiosyncratic (u_t)	
2 year	$\lambda_{1,1}$	1.377 (0.244)	$\lambda_{1,2}$	2.168 (0.163)	σ_1	11.285 (0.125)
4 year	$\lambda_{2,1}$	6.245 (0.289)	$\lambda_{2,2}$	2.454 (0.711)	σ_2	0.766 (0.126)
6 year	$\lambda_{3,1}$	8.397 (0.135)	$\lambda_{3,3}$	0.487 (0.954)	σ_3	5.055 (0.058)
8 year	$\lambda_{4,1}$	9.278 (0.200)	$\lambda_{4,4}$	−1.272 (1.055)	σ_4	1.182 (0.098)
10 year	$\lambda_{5,1}$	9.567 (0.319)	$\lambda_{5,4}$	−2.512 (1.089)	σ_5	8.399 (0.096)
Factor	ϕ_1	1.000 (0.001)	ϕ_2	0.993 (0.002)		
Money	γ_1	−3.863 (0.780)	γ_2	0.612 (0.960)		

$\ln L_T(\widehat{\theta}) = -16.823$

shocks, x_t, in determining the statistical factors, consider the following $K = 2$ factor model of the $N = 5$ spreads:

$$
\begin{bmatrix} y_{1,t} \\ y_{2,t} \\ y_{3,t} \\ y_{4,t} \\ y_{5,t} \end{bmatrix} = \begin{bmatrix} \lambda_{1,1} & \lambda_{1,2} \\ \lambda_{2,1} & \lambda_{2,2} \\ \lambda_{3,1} & \lambda_{3,2} \\ \lambda_{4,1} & \lambda_{4,2} \\ \lambda_{5,1} & \lambda_{5,2} \end{bmatrix} \begin{bmatrix} s_{1,t} \\ s_{2,t} \end{bmatrix} + \begin{bmatrix} u_{1,t} \\ u_{2,t} \\ u_{3,t} \\ u_{4,t} \\ u_{5,t} \end{bmatrix}
$$

$$
\begin{bmatrix} s_{1,t} \\ s_{2,t} \end{bmatrix} = \begin{bmatrix} \phi_1 & 0 \\ 0 & \phi_2 \end{bmatrix} \begin{bmatrix} s_{1,t-1} \\ s_{2,t-1} \end{bmatrix} + \begin{bmatrix} \gamma_1 \\ \gamma_2 \end{bmatrix} \begin{bmatrix} x_t \end{bmatrix} + \begin{bmatrix} v_{1,t} \\ v_{2,t} \end{bmatrix} ,
$$

in which $R = E[u_t u_t'] = \text{diag}(\sigma_i^2)$ and $Q = E[v_t v_t'] = I_2$. The parameter vector $\Gamma = [\gamma_1 \ \gamma_2]'$ controls the effect of money shocks on the factors. An alternative model specification is to include x_t directly in the measurement equation. This would result in five parameters associated with x_t compared to the two parameters, γ_1 and γ_2, in the existing model. It is these three restrictions that enable the model to decompose the effects of money shocks on the spreads in terms of the two factors, $s_{1,t}$ and $s_{2,t}$.

The maximum likelihood estimates from estimating the factor model are given in Table 15.5 based on daily United States spreads from 2 January 1990 to 21 August 2006. Money shocks are defined as the change in the Eurodollar 1-month rate on Federal Reserve Board meeting dates. The estimates of the loadings on the first factor, $\lambda_{i,1}$, suggest a slope factor with a positive shock to the factor widening all spreads, with longer maturities being most affected. The loading estimates on the second factor, $\lambda_{i,2}$, suggest a curvature factor with a shock to the factor increasing (decreasing) spreads on shorter (longer) maturities, although only the parameter estimates on the 2- and 4-year spreads are statistically significant.

The parameter estimates on the money shock show that money has a significant effect on the slope factor, but not the curvature factor, a result which suggests that the slope factor could be re-labelled as a money factor. The negative sign on γ_1 also suggests that positive money shocks have the effect of narrowing spreads, with the longer-term spreads being the most affected.

15.9 Exercises

(1) Recursions of the Univariate Kalman Filter

Program files	`1fac_uni.*, 1fac_smooth.*`

Consider the univariate latent factor model with $N = 1$ variable and $K = 1$ factor

$$y_t = \lambda s_t + u_t, \qquad u_t \sim iid\ N(0, \sigma^2)$$
$$s_t = \phi s_{t-1} + v_t, \qquad v_t \sim iid\ N(0, \sigma_v^2),$$

with parameters $\lambda = 1.0$, $\phi = 0.8$, $\sigma = 0.5$ and $\sigma_v = 1$. The sample size is $T = 5$ with realised values $y_t = \{-0.608, 0.670, 0.012, -0.390, -1.477\}$.

(a) At time $t = 1$ compute the following equations.

Pred.: $s_{1|0} = 0.0$, $P_{1|0} = \dfrac{1}{1 - \phi^2}$

Obs.: $\mu_{1|0} = \lambda s_{1|0}$, $V_{1|0} = \lambda^2 P_{1|0} + \sigma^2$

Update: $s_{1|1} = s_{1|0} + \dfrac{\lambda P_{1|0}}{V_{1|0}}(y_1 - \mu_{1|0})$, $P_{1|1} = P_{1|0} - \dfrac{\lambda^2 P_{1|0}^2}{V_{1|0}}$.

(b) At time $t = 2$ compute the following equations.

Pred.: $s_{2|1} = \phi s_{1|1}$, $P_{2|1} = \phi^2 P_{1|1} + \sigma_v^2$

Obs.: $\mu_{2|1} = \lambda s_{2|1}$, $V_{2|1} = \lambda^2 P_{2|1} + \sigma^2$

Update: $s_{2|2} = s_{2|1} + \dfrac{\lambda P_{2|1}}{V_{2|1}}(y_2 - \mu_{2|1})$, $P_{2|2} = P_{2|1} - \dfrac{\lambda^2 P_{2|1}^2}{V_{2|1}}$.

(c) Continue for $t = 3, 4, 5$ and compare the results with those reported in Table 15.1.

(d) Using the estimates of the conditional factor means and variances obtained previously, compute the smoothed factor estimates $s_{t|T}$ and $P_{t|T}$ for $t = 5, 4, 3, 2, 1$.

(e) Repeat parts (a) to (d) for $y_t = \{-0.403, 1.424, 0.807, 2.299, 1.750\}$.

(2) Recursions of the Multivariate Kalman Filter

Program files   `1fac_multi.*`

Consider the multivariate latent factor model with $N = 3$ variables and $K = 2$ factors

$$y_t = \Lambda s_t + u_t, \qquad u_t \sim iid\ N(0, R),$$
$$s_t = \Phi s_{t-1} + v_t, \qquad v_t \sim iid\ N(0, Q).$$

(a) Compute the prediction, observation and updating equations for $t = 1, 2, 3, 4, 5$, where the parameter matrices are

$$\Lambda = \begin{bmatrix} 1.00 & 0.50 \\ 1.00 & 0.00 \\ 1.00 & -0.50 \end{bmatrix}, \qquad \Phi = \begin{bmatrix} 0.80 & 0.00 \\ 0.00 & 0.50 \end{bmatrix},$$

$$R = \begin{bmatrix} 0.25 & 0.00 & 0.00 \\ 0.00 & 0.16 & 0.00 \\ 0.00 & 0.00 & 0.09 \end{bmatrix}, \qquad Q = I_2,$$

and the $T = 5$ observations on $y_t = \{y_{1,t}, y_{2,t}, y_{3,t}\}$ are

$$y_1 = \{2.500, 2.017, -0.107, -0.739, -0.992\}$$
$$y_2 = \{2.000, 1.032, -0.535, 0.061, 0.459\}$$
$$y_3 = \{1.500, 0.047, -0.964, 0.862, 1.910\}.$$

(b) Repeat part (a) where the observations are

$$y_1 = \{1.695, 4.741, 4.607, 2.324, 1.645\}$$
$$y_2 = \{2.610, 1.998, 3.403, 0.126, 2.043\}$$
$$y_3 = \{0.230, 1.077, 2.890, 0.155, 2.054\}.$$

(3) Term Structure of Interest Rates

Program files   `1fac_term.*, 1fac_termfig.m`
Data files   `usdata.*`

The data are daily United States zero coupon bond yields beginning 4 October 1988 and ending 28 December 2001, $T = 3306$. The maturities are 3 months, 1 year, 3 years, 5 years, 7 years and 10 years.

(a) Plot the yields and discuss the time series properties of the series.
(b) Let $y_{i,t}$, $i = 1, 2, ..., 6$, be the 6 yields scaled by 100 and centered. Estimate the following one-factor model

$$y_{i,t} = \lambda_i s_t + u_{i,t}, \qquad u_t \sim iid\ N(0, R),$$
$$s_t = \phi s_{t-1} + v_t, \qquad v_t \sim iid\ N(0, Q),$$

in which $R = diag(\sigma_i^2)$ and $Q = 1$. Interpret the parameter estimates.
(c) Compute $s_{t|T}$ and compare this estimate with y_t.
(d) Test the restrictions $\lambda_1 = \lambda_2 = \cdots = \lambda_6$ and interpret the result.

(4) Alternative Formulation of the Kalman Filter

Program files	1fac_term_adj.*
Data files	usdata.*

An alternative way to express the state-space model of the term structure is to treat the disturbance term $u_{i,t}$ in the measurement equation as a latent (idiosyncratic) factor with loading σ_i. The factor model is now expressed as with measurement equation

$$
\begin{bmatrix} r_{1,t} \\ r_{2,t} \\ r_{3,t} \\ r_{4,t} \\ r_{5,t} \\ r_{6,t} \end{bmatrix}
=
\begin{bmatrix}
\lambda_1 & \sigma_1 & 0 & 0 & 0 & 0 & 0 \\
\lambda_2 & 0 & \sigma_2 & 0 & 0 & 0 & 0 \\
\lambda_3 & 0 & 0 & \sigma_3 & 0 & 0 & 0 \\
\lambda_2 & 0 & 0 & 0 & \sigma_4 & 0 & 0 \\
\lambda_1 & 0 & 0 & 0 & 0 & \sigma_5 & 0 \\
\lambda_2 & 0 & 0 & 0 & 0 & 0 & \sigma_6
\end{bmatrix}
\begin{bmatrix} s_{1,t} \\ s_{2,t} \\ s_{3,t} \\ s_{4,t} \\ s_{5,t} \\ s_{6,t} \\ s_{7,t} \end{bmatrix},
$$

and state equation

$$
\begin{bmatrix} s_{1,t} \\ s_{2,t} \\ s_{3,t} \\ s_{4,t} \\ s_{5,t} \\ s_{6,t} \\ s_{7,t} \end{bmatrix}
= diag
\begin{pmatrix} \phi \\ 0 \\ 0 \\ 0 \\ 0 \\ 0 \\ 0 \end{pmatrix}
\begin{bmatrix} s_{1,t-1} \\ s_{2,t-1} \\ s_{3,t-1} \\ s_{4,t-1} \\ s_{5,t-1} \\ s_{6,t-1} \\ s_{7,t-1} \end{bmatrix}
+
\begin{bmatrix} v_{1,t} \\ v_{2,t} \\ v_{3,t} \\ v_{4,t} \\ v_{5,t} \\ v_{6,t} \\ v_{7,t} \end{bmatrix},
$$

in which $R = E\left[u_t u_t'\right] = 0$ and $Q = E\left[v_t v_t'\right] = I_7$. Re-estimate the term structure model in the previous exercise by maximum likelihood using the adjusted state-space representation and show that the parameter estimates are the same as the estimates obtained in the previous exercise. *Hint: The previous exercise uses a prior on $s_{1|0}$ and $P_{1|0}$ associated with the first factor, s_1, whereas for the other factors, s_2 to s_7, the initial values are $s_{1|0} = 0$ and $P_{1|0} = 1.0$.*

(5) An F-VAR Model of the Term Structure

Program files	`lfac_fvar.*`
Data files	`daily_finance.*`

The data are daily United States yields, beginning 2 January 1990, and ending 21 August 2006 ($T = 4142$) with maturities ranging from 1 year to 30 years, inclusive ($N = 30$). Consider the F-VAR model with $N = 30$ variables and $K = 3$ factors

$$y_t = \Lambda s_t + \Gamma y_{t-1} + u_t, \qquad u_t \sim iid \ N(0, R),$$
$$s_t = \Phi s_{t-1} + v_t, \qquad v_t \sim iid \ N(0, Q),$$

in which Λ is a (30×3) matrix, Γ is a (30×30) diagonal matrix, Φ is a (3×3) matrix, R is a (30×30) matrix and Q is a (3×3) matrix.

(a) Letting y_t represent a (30×1) vector of yields that are standardised to have zero mean and unit variance, estimate the parameters of the model using the Stock and Watson estimator.

(b) Plot the estimated factor loadings of Λ, and show that the $K = 3$ factors represent level, slope and curvature factors consistent with the analysis of the term structure by Knez, Litterman and Scheinkman (1994).

(c) Interpret the dynamical interrelationships amongst the factors using the estimator of Φ.

(d) Repeat parts (a) to (c) for $K = 4$ factors. Discuss the interpretation of the fourth factor.

(6) Sampling Properties of the Principal Components Estimator

Program files	`lfac_panic.*`

Consider the $K = 1$ factor PANIC model

$$y_{it} = \lambda_i s_t + u_{i,t}, \qquad i = 1, 2, \cdots, N$$
$$s_t = s_{t-1} + v_t$$
$$u_{i,t} = \delta u_{i,t-1} + w_{i,t},$$

in which $w_{i,t} \sim iid \ N(0, 1)$, $v_t \sim iid \ N(0, 1)$ and the loading parameters are chosen as $\lambda_i \sim N(1, 1)$.

(a) The Stock-Watson estimator of λ is based on estimating the factor s_t, from a principal components decomposition of y_t and regressing y_t on a constant and $\hat{s}_t$. Compute the mean, bias and MSE of the sampling distribution of λ for cross-sections of $N = 10, 30, 50$ idiosyncratic dynamics for $\delta = \{0, 0.5, 1.0\}$ and a sample size of $T = \{100, 200\}$. Choose 5000 replications.

(b) Repeat part (a) for the Bai-Ng estimator of λ which is based on estimating the factor from a principal components decomposition of Δy_t and regressing Δy_t on a constant and $\Delta \hat{s}_t$.

(c) Compare the results in parts (a) and (b) and demonstrate that (i) for $\delta < 1$ both estimators are consistent with the Stock-Watson estimator being more efficient; (ii) for $\delta = 1$ the Bai-Ng estimator is consistent whereas the Stock-Watson estimator is inconsistent.

(7) Hodrick-Prescott Filter

Program files	lfac_hp.*
Data files	usgdp.*

The data are quarterly real United States GDP for the period March 1940 to December 2000. Letting y_t be the logarithm of GDP, centered to have zero mean and scaled by 100, consider the following $K = 2$ factor model

$$y_t = \tau_t + c_t, \qquad c_t \sim iid \ N(0, \sigma_c^2),$$
$$\tau_t = \tau_{t-1} + \beta_{t-1}$$
$$\beta_t = \beta_{t-1} + \zeta_t, \qquad \zeta_t \sim iid \ N(0, \sigma_\zeta^2),$$

where

$$\Lambda = [1 \quad 0], \quad s_t = \begin{bmatrix} \tau_t \\ \beta_t \end{bmatrix}, \quad \Phi = \begin{bmatrix} 1 & 1 \\ 0 & 1 \end{bmatrix},$$
$$R = \sigma_c^2, \quad Q = \begin{bmatrix} 0 & 0 \\ 0 & \sigma_\zeta^2 \end{bmatrix}.$$

(a) Estimate the parameters $\theta = \{\sigma_c^2, \sigma_\zeta^2\}$ by maximum likelihood. Interpret the parameters in terms of the signal-to-noise ratio $q = \sigma_c^2/\sigma_\zeta^2$.

(b) Estimate the parameter $\theta = \{\sigma_\zeta^2\}$ by maximum likelihood subject to the normalisation restriction $\sigma_c^2 = 1$.

(c) Evaluate the log-likelihood function subject to the restrictions $\sigma_c^2 = 1$ and $\sigma_\zeta^2 = 1/1600$. Letting the estimated log-likelihood in part (b) be the unrestricted log-likelihood value, perform a likelihood ratio test of the restriction $\sigma_\zeta^2 = 1/1600$. Hence test the validity of using the commonly adopted choice for the Hodrick-Prescott filter of the smoothing parameter for quarterly data of $\gamma = 1600$.

(d) Compute the smoothed factor estimate of τ_t for the models in parts (a) to (c) and compare these estimates with the estimate obtained using the Hodrick-Prescott filter.

(8) A Multi-Factor Model of Spreads with Money Shocks

Program files	lfac_spreads.*
Data files	daily_finance.*

Let y_t be a (5×1) vector containing the spreads, adjusted to have zero mean and expressed in basis points, between the one year forward rate maturing at $n = 2, 4, 6, 8, 10$ years and the 1-year interest rate.

(a) Estimate the two-factor model by maximum likelihood methods

$$
\begin{bmatrix} y_{1,t} \\ y_{2,t} \\ y_{3,t} \\ y_{4,t} \\ y_{5,t} \end{bmatrix} = \begin{bmatrix} \lambda_{1,1} & \lambda_{1,2} \\ \lambda_{2,1} & \lambda_{2,2} \\ \lambda_{3,1} & \lambda_{3,2} \\ \lambda_{4,1} & \lambda_{4,2} \\ \lambda_{5,1} & \lambda_{5,2} \end{bmatrix} \begin{bmatrix} s_{1,t} \\ s_{2,t} \end{bmatrix} + \begin{bmatrix} u_{1,t} \\ u_{2,t} \\ u_{3,t} \\ u_{4,t} \\ u_{5,t} \end{bmatrix}
$$

$$
\begin{bmatrix} s_{1,t} \\ s_{2,t} \end{bmatrix} = \begin{bmatrix} \phi_1 & 0 \\ 0 & \phi_2 \end{bmatrix} \begin{bmatrix} s_{1,t-1} \\ s_{2,t-1} \end{bmatrix} + \begin{bmatrix} \gamma_1 \\ \gamma_2 \end{bmatrix} \begin{bmatrix} x_t \end{bmatrix} + \begin{bmatrix} v_{1,t} \\ v_{2,t} \end{bmatrix},
$$

in which x_t is the money factor, $R = \mathrm{E}\left[u_t u_t'\right] = \mathrm{diag}\left(\sigma_i^2\right)$ and $Q = \mathrm{E}\left[v_t v_t'\right] = I_2$. Interpret the parameter vector $\Gamma = [\gamma_1 \; \gamma_2]'$, which controls the effect of money shocks on the factors.

(b) Test the restriction $\gamma_1 = \gamma_2 = 0$, and interpret the result.

(c) Extend the analysis to include a set of macroeconomic shocks given by capacity utilisation, consumer confidence, the CPI, advance GDP, the index of business activity, non-farm payroll, new home sales and retail sales.

(d) Extend the analysis by assigning the money shock to the first factor and the macroeconomic shocks to the second factor, so the two factors represent money and macro factors respectively.

(9) *Ex Ante* **Real Interest Rates**

Program files	1fac_exante.*
Data files	exante.*

The data are monthly consisting of the United States Consumer Price Index, p_t, and the 1-month (% p.a.) Eurodollar rate, r_t, from January 1971 to December 2009, a total of $T = 468$ observations. A state-space model of the *ex ante* real interest rate is

$$
\begin{aligned}
y_t &= \alpha + s_t + u_t, & u_t &\sim iid \; N(0, \sigma^2), \\
s_t &= \phi s_{t-1} + v_t, & v_t &\sim iid \; N(0, \sigma_v^2),
\end{aligned}
$$

in which y_t is the *ex post* real interest rate, $s_t + \alpha$ is the *ex ante* real interest rate and u_t is the expectations error in measuring inflation.

(a) Letting the 1-month *ex post* real interest rate (% p.a.) be defined as

$$
y_t = r_t - 1200 \times (\ln p_t - \ln p_{t-12}),
$$

estimate the parameters $\theta = \{\alpha, \phi, \sigma^2, \sigma_v^2\}$ by maximum likelihood.

(b) Use the parameter estimates to compute the unconditional mean and variance of the *ex ante* real interest rate and compare these estimates with the corresponding sample moments of the *ex post* real interest rate y_t.

(c) Compute a time series on the *ex ante* real interest rate using $s_{t|t-1} + \alpha$ and compare the result with the ex post real interest rate y_t.

(d) Compute a time series on the expectations error in measuring inflation and interpret its time series properties.

(10) **Capital Asset Pricing Model**

Program files	lfac_capm.*
Data files	capm.*

The data are quarterly from March 1990 to March 2010, a total of $T = 81$ observations, on the United States stock prices for Microsoft, Intel, Pfizer, Exxon, Procter & Gamble, Boeing, AT&T, General Electric, Chevron and Bank of America, the S&P500 index and the United States 3-month Treasury rate (p.a.). The state-space representation of the CAPM is

$$
\begin{aligned}
y_{i,t} &= \lambda_{0,i} + \lambda_i s_t + u_{i,t}, & u_{i,t} &\sim iid\ N(0, \sigma_i^2), & i = 1, \cdots, 10, \\
s_t &= \phi s_{t-1} + \eta_t, & \eta_t &\sim iid\ N(0, 1),
\end{aligned}
$$

in which $y_{i,t}$ is the excess return on asset i and the unknown parameters are

$$
\theta = \{\lambda_{0,1}, \cdots, \lambda_{0,10}, \lambda_1, \cdots, \lambda_{10}, \phi, \sigma_1^2, \cdots, \sigma_{10}^2\}.
$$

(a) Letting the annual excess return of each asset be defined as

$$
y_{i,t} = 4 \times (\ln p_{i,t} - \ln p_{i,t-1}) - r_t/100, \qquad i = 1, \cdots, 10,
$$

in which $p_{i,t}$ is the price of asset i and r_t is the risk-free rate of interest, estimate θ by maximum likelihood.

(b) Compute the excess return on all invested wealth using the updated conditional mean $s_{t|t}$ and compare this estimate with the proxy variable

$$
m_t = 4 \times (\ln sp500_t - \ln sp500_{t-4}) - r_t/100,
$$

the annual excess market return based on the S&P500 index.

(c) Compare the estimate of λ_i with the estimate of β_i for each of the 10 assets, where the latter is obtained as the least squares estimate from the proxy CAPM regression equation

$$
y_{i,t} = \alpha_i + \beta_i m_t + e_{i,t}.
$$

In comparing the estimators λ_i and β_i, it may be helpful to rescale λ_i by the ratio of the standard deviation of $s_{t|t}$ to the standard deviation of m_t.

(11) Business Cycles

Program files	1fac_bcycle.*
Data files	bcycle.*

The data are monthly consisting of 6 Australian indicators on the business cycle (GDP, unemployment rate, employment, retail sales, household income and industrial production) and the coincident index, beginning in January 1980 and ending in September 2009, a total of $T = 357$ observations. Consider the $K = 1$ factor model of the business cycle

$$y_{i,t} = \lambda_i s_t + u_{i,t}, \qquad u_{i,t} \sim iid\ N(0, \sigma_i^2), \quad i = 1, \cdots, 6,$$
$$s_t = \phi_1 s_{t-1} + \phi_2 s_{t-2} + v_t, \qquad v_t \sim iid\ N(0, 1),$$

in which $y_t = \{y_{1,t}, \cdots, y_{6,t}\}$ are defined in terms of the indicators $I_{i,t}$ as

$$y_{i,t} = 100 \times (\ln I_{i,t} - \ln I_{i,t-12}), \quad i = 1, \cdots, 6.$$

and then centered to have zero mean.

(a) Estimate the parameters $\theta = \{\lambda_1, \cdots, \lambda_6, \phi_1, \phi_2, \sigma_1^2, \cdots, \sigma_6^2\}$ by maximum likelihood and interpret the parameter estimates.

(b) Estimate the business cycle using the smoothed conditional mean $s_{t|T}$ and the usual estimate based on the coincident index

$$bc_t = 100 \times (\ln CI_t - \ln CI_{t-12}),$$

and compare the turning points of the two estimators. In comparing the two estimators it may be helpful to rescale $s_{t|T}$ to have the same sample variance as bc_t by multiplying $s_{t|T}$ by the ratio of the standard deviation of bc_t to the standard deviation of $s_{t|T}$.

PART FIVE

Nonstationary Time Series

16 Nonstationary Distribution Theory

16.1 Introduction

A common feature of many economic and financial time series is that they exhibit trending behaviour. Typical examples in economics are output and consumption, while, in finance, examples consist of asset prices and dividends. The earliest approach to capture trends involves augmenting the specification of the model with a deterministic time trend. Nelson and Plosser (1982), however, show that this strategy can represent a misspecification of the dynamics of the model and argue that a stochastic trend modelled by a random walk is the more appropriate specification to capture trends in the data. Not only does this observation have important implications for the interpretation of the model's parameters, it also has implications for the distribution theory of the maximum likelihood estimator and associated test statistics used to perform inference.

The aim of this chapter is to develop the distribution theory of nonstationary processes with stochastic trends. Formally, the move from a stationary world to a nonstationary world based on stochastic trends involves increasing the absolute value of the parameter ϕ of the AR(1) model investigated in Chapter 13

$$y_t = \phi y_{t-1} + v_t, \qquad v_t \sim iid\,(0, \sigma^2),$$

from the stationary region, $|\phi| < 1$, to the nonstationary region, $|\phi| \geq 1$. This seemingly innocuous change in ϕ, however, leads to fundamental changes to the distribution theory in three significant ways.

(1) Sample moments no longer have fixed limits, as they do for stationary processes, but converge (weakly) to random variables.
(2) The least squares estimator of ϕ is superconsistent with convergence rate greater that the usual rate of $\sqrt{T}$ for stationary processes.
(3) The asymptotic distribution of the least squares estimator is non-standard in contrast to the asymptotic normality result for stationary processes.

The non-standard behaviour of the asymptotic distribution of nonstationary processes with stochastic trends carries over into hypothesis testing for unit roots (Chapter 17) and to estimation and testing using maximum likelihood methods in multivariate nonstationary models (Chapter 18), where the focus is on identifying linear combinations of random walk processes that are stationary, known as cointegration.

16.2   Specification

In this section, two competing models of trends are proposed to model non-stationary time series. The first is a deterministic trend and the second is a stochastic trend modelled using a random walk as discussed in Chapter 13. The following example re-visits the original data set used by Nelson and Plosser (1982) to illustrate the empirical relevance of trends in economic and financial time series.

Example 16.1 Nelson and Plosser Study
Figure 16.1 provides plots of 14 United States annual macroeconomic variables from 1860 to 1970. The variables are expressed in natural logarithms with the exception of the bond yield. All variables exhibit an upward trend with the exception of velocity, which shows a strong downward trend, and the unemployment rate, which tends to fluctuate around a constant level.   □

16.2.1   Models of Trends

Two possible specifications to model trends in the data are

$$\begin{aligned} y_t &= \beta_0 + \beta_1 t + e_t \quad \text{[Deterministic trend]} \\ y_t &= \delta + y_{t-1} + v_t , \quad \text{[Stochastic trend]} \end{aligned} \tag{16.1}$$

in which e_t and v_t are *iid* disturbance terms. Either specification represents a nonstationary model. The deterministic trend specification assumes transitory (stationary) deviations (e_t) around a deterministic trend (t). The stochastic trend model is a random walk with drift ($\delta \neq 0$) in which y_t drifts upwards (if $\delta > 0$) without following a deterministic path. For this model, it is the changes in the variable ($y_t - y_{t-1}$) that are transitory (v_t).

Example 16.2 Simulating Trends
Figure 16.1 also gives plots of simulated data from the two nonstationary models in (16.1) for a sample size of $T = 111$. The simulated time paths of the two series are very different. The deterministic trend has a clear positive linear trajectory while the stochastic trend displays a more circuitous positive path. A comparison of the two simulated trends with the actual data in Figure 16.1 suggests that the stochastic trend model is the more appropriate specification for characterising the trends observed in the data.   □

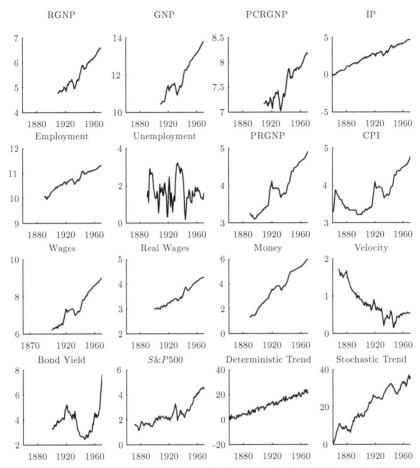

Figure 16.1. US annual macroeconomic variables from 1860 to 1970. All variables are expressed in natural logarithms with the exception of the bond yield. Also given are simulated series based on a deterministic trend and a stochastic trend, as given in (16.1). The parameter values of these two models are $\beta_0 = 0.1$, $\beta_1 = 0.2$ and $\delta_0 = 0.3$, with $e_t, v_t \sim iid\ N(0, 1)$.

Differences in the two trend models in (16.1) are formally derived by solving the stochastic trend model backwards recursively to give

$$y_t = y_0 + \delta t + v_t + v_{t-1} + v_{t-2} + \cdots + v_1 , \tag{16.2}$$

in which y_0 represents the initial value of y_t which for exposition is assumed to be fixed. This equation is of a form similar to the deterministic trend model in (16.1) with y_0 representing the intercept and δ now representing the slope parameter on the time trend, t. However, the fundamental difference between the deterministic trend model in (16.1) and (16.2) is that the disturbance term in the latter is the cumulative sum of all shocks to the system

$$e_t = \sum_{i=1}^{t} v_i . \tag{16.3}$$

As the weight on each shock is the same, the effect of a shock on y_t does not decay over time. This means that if the data generating process is based on a stochastic trend, the specification of a deterministic trend model corresponds to a disturbance term having permanent (nonstationary) shocks rather than transitory (stationary) shocks.

Example 16.3 Nelson and Plosser Data Revisited

Table 16.1 provides estimates of the two trend models in (16.1) applied to the Nelson-Plosser data, and also of a combined model given by

$$y_t = \delta + \gamma t + \phi y_{t-1} + w_t ,$$

in which w_t is an *iid* disturbance term. Estimates of ϕ in the stochastic trend model are near unity, with the exception of the unemployment rate where the estimate is 0.754. Including a deterministic time trend and estimating the combined model results in slightly smaller estimates of ϕ but does not qualitatively change the conclusion that the trends in the data appear to be best characterised as random walks and not as deterministic trends.   □

16.2.2   Integration

Another way to write the stochastic trend model in (16.1) is

$$\Delta y_t = y_t - y_{t-1} = \delta + v_t . \tag{16.4}$$

This expression shows that the first difference of y_t is stationary provided that v_t is stationary. In this case, y_t is commonly referred to as being difference stationary, since by differencing the series once it is rendered stationary. Similarly, in the case of the deterministic trend model, y_t is interpreted as being trend stationary because the subtraction of a deterministic trend from y_t renders the variable stationary. If differencing a series once achieves stationarity, the series is identified as integrated of order one, or $I(1)$. This definition follows from the fact that y_t is a partial sum as in (16.3), the integral, of lagged disturbances.

In some cases, it is necessary to difference a series twice before rendering it stationary

$$\Delta^2 y_t = (1 - L)^2 y_t = (1 - 2L + L^2) y_t = y_t - 2y_{t-1} + y_{t-2} = \delta + v_t ,$$

in which L is the lag operator (see Appendix B). Now y_t is integrated of order two, or $I(2)$. Variables that are $I(2)$ tend to be relatively more smoothly evolving

Table 16.1. *Ordinary least squares estimates of the deterministic and stochastic trend models in (16.1) and a combined trend model applied to the Nelson-Plosser data with standard errors in parentheses. The point estimates and standard errors of the deterministic time trend are scaled up by 100 by defining the time trend as $t/100$ in the regression equations*

Variable	Deterministic		Stochastic		Combined		
	β_0	β_1	δ	ϕ	δ	γ	ϕ
Real GNP	4.614	3.099	0.007	1.004	0.591	0.418	0.876
	(0.033)	(0.093)	(0.082)	(0.015)	(0.276)	(0.189)	(0.060)
Nominal GNP	10.341	5.343	0.021	1.003	0.710	0.386	0.935
	(0.066)	(0.186)	(0.154)	(0.013)	(0.483)	(0.257)	(0.047)
Real GNP	7.002	1.810	0.034	0.998	0.928	0.273	0.868
(per capita)	(0.033)	(0.093)	(0.182)	(0.024)	(0.424)	(0.118)	(0.060)
Industrial Prod.	0.050	4.212	0.055	0.995	0.056	0.662	0.841
	(0.034)	(0.053)	(0.019)	(0.007)	(0.018)	(0.217)	(0.051)
Employment	10.095	1.532	0.127	0.990	1.136	0.162	0.889
	(0.018)	(0.039)	(0.125)	(0.012)	(0.504)	(0.079)	(0.050)
Unemployment	1.871	−0.391	0.424	0.754	0.491	−0.142	0.748
	(0.151)	(0.325)	(0.136)	(0.073)	(0.171)	(0.222)	(0.074)
GNP deflator	3.003	2.188	−0.015	1.009	0.208	0.182	0.933
	(0.034)	(0.072)	(0.042)	(0.011)	(0.109)	(0.082)	(0.036)
CPI	3.161	1.090	−0.026	1.010	0.041	0.041	0.987
	(0.050)	(0.079)	(0.048)	(0.013)	(0.065)	(0.028)	(0.020)
Wages	6.083	4.011	0.016	1.003	0.410	0.276	0.938
	(0.044)	(0.110)	(0.073)	(0.010)	(0.254)	(0.171)	(0.042)
Real wages	2.848	1.996	0.008	1.003	0.380	0.272	0.871
	(0.018)	(0.045)	(0.038)	(0.011)	(0.154)	(0.110)	(0.054)
Money stock	1.344	5.796	0.068	0.997	0.131	0.287	0.949
	(0.042)	(0.089)	(0.019)	(0.005)	(0.049)	(0.205)	(0.035)
Velocity	1.408	−1.209	0.019	0.962	0.052	−0.032	0.941
	(0.038)	(0.064)	(0.015)	(0.016)	(0.051)	(0.049)	(0.035)
Bond yield	3.685	0.486	−0.227	1.076	−0.359	0.393	1.075
	(0.223)	(0.550)	(0.160)	(0.041)	(0.164)	(0.166)	(0.040)
Stock price	1.064	2.819	0.021	1.003	0.082	0.285	0.921
	(0.078)	(0.137)	(0.047)	(0.018)	(0.053)	(0.124)	(0.040)
Det. trend	0.017	20.122	0.480	0.975	0.216	20.426	−0.015
	(0.180)	(0.283)	(0.293)	(0.023)	(0.182)	(1.949)	(0.096)
Random walk	−1.524	30.696	0.500	0.980	0.242	0.935	0.969
	(0.723)	(1.136)	(0.211)	(0.013)	(0.187)	(0.794)	(0.024)

over time, in contrast to $I(1)$ variables, which are also nonstationary but tend to show more jagged movements. This characteristic of an $I(2)$ process is not too surprising since y_t is a function of both y_{t-1} and y_{t-2}, which means that movements in y_t are averaged across two periods. This is not the case for an $I(1)$ process where no such averaging takes place since y_t is simply a function of y_{t-1}.

Extending the definition of integration to the case where y_t is $I(d)$, then

$$\Delta^d y_t = (1 - L)^d y_t = \delta + v_t ,$$

is stationary. In the special case where y_t is $I(0)$, the series does not need to be differenced ($d = 0$) to achieve stationarity because it already is stationary.

16.3   Estimation

The parameter estimates of the deterministic and stochastic trend models in (16.1) for the Nelson and Plosser data are reported in Table 16.1. These estimates are based on the least squares estimator, which also corresponds to the maximum likelihood estimator in the case where the disturbance term is normally distributed. For this estimator to have the same asymptotic properties as the maximum likelihood estimator discussed in Chapters 2 and 13, it is necessary that certain sample moments have fixed and finite limits for the weak law of large numbers (WLLN) to be satisfied.

Given that the deterministic and stochastic trend models discussed in Section 16.2 yield nonstationary processes, it is not immediately obvious that a WLLN holds for the sample moments of these models. This section shows that, provided different scale factors are adopted to those used for stationary processes, the moments of both the deterministic and the stochastic trend models converge. For the deterministic trend model the sample moments converge to fixed limits, but, in the case of the stochastic trend model, the sample moments converge to random variables.

In order to provide a benchmark in terms of the properties of the least squares estimator with which the asymptotic properties of these nonstationary models may be compared, the stationary AR(1) model of Chapter 13 is discussed initially.

16.3.1   Stationary Case

Consider the stationary AR(1) model

$$y_t = \delta + \phi y_{t-1} + v_t , \qquad v_t \sim iid\,(0, \sigma^2), \tag{16.5}$$

in which $|\phi| < 1$ is required for the process to be stationary. The ordinary least squares estimator of this equation is

$$
\begin{bmatrix} \widehat{\delta} \\ \widehat{\phi} \end{bmatrix} = \begin{bmatrix} \sum_{t=2}^{T} 1 & \sum_{t=2}^{T} y_{t-1} \\ \sum_{t=2}^{T} y_{t-1} & \sum_{t=2}^{T} y_{t-1}^2 \end{bmatrix}^{-1} \begin{bmatrix} \sum_{t=2}^{T} y_t \\ \sum_{t=2}^{T} y_{t-1} y_t \end{bmatrix} .
\tag{16.6}
$$

Using (16.5) to substitute out y_t and rearranging gives

$$
\begin{bmatrix} \widehat{\delta} \\ \widehat{\phi} \end{bmatrix} - \begin{bmatrix} \delta \\ \phi \end{bmatrix} = \begin{bmatrix} \sum_{t=2}^{T} 1 & \sum_{t=2}^{T} y_{t-1} \\ \sum_{t=2}^{T} y_{t-1} & \sum_{t=2}^{T} y_{t-1}^2 \end{bmatrix}^{-1} \begin{bmatrix} \sum_{t=2}^{T} v_t \\ \sum_{t=2}^{T} y_{t-1} v_t \end{bmatrix} .
\tag{16.7}
$$

Now scale both sides by $\sqrt{T}$

$$
\sqrt{T} \begin{bmatrix} \widehat{\delta} - \delta \\ \widehat{\phi} - \phi \end{bmatrix} = \sqrt{T} \begin{bmatrix} \sum_{t=2}^{T} 1 & \sum_{t=2}^{T} y_{t-1} \\ \sum_{t=2}^{T} y_{t-1} & \sum_{t=2}^{T} y_{t-1}^2 \end{bmatrix}^{-1} \begin{bmatrix} \sum_{t=2}^{T} v_t \\ \sum_{t=2}^{T} y_{t-1} v_t \end{bmatrix}
$$

$$
= \begin{bmatrix} \frac{1}{T} \sum_{t=2}^{T} 1 & \frac{1}{T} \sum_{t=2}^{T} y_{t-1} \\ \frac{1}{T} \sum_{t=2}^{T} y_{t-1} & \frac{1}{T} \sum_{t=2}^{T} y_{t-1}^2 \end{bmatrix}^{-1} \begin{bmatrix} \frac{1}{\sqrt{T}} \sum_{t=2}^{T} v_t \\ \frac{1}{\sqrt{T}} \sum_{t=2}^{T} y_{t-1} v_t \end{bmatrix} .
\tag{16.8}
$$

To understand the asymptotic distribution of the least squares estimator in expression (16.8), it is necessary to understand the convergence properties of the moments on the right-hand side of this equation. From Chapter 13, the AR(1) model in (16.5) is re-written as

$$
y_t = \delta \sum_{j=0}^{t-1} \phi^j + \sum_{j=0}^{t-1} \phi^j v_{t-j} + \phi^t y_0 ,
\tag{16.9}
$$

in which the initial observation, y_0, is assumed to be fixed. Formally, a fixed initial value means that y_t is not stationary, but it is nonetheless asymptotically stationary in the sense that the first two moments have fixed and finite limits as $t \to \infty$. In the analysis that follows the initial condition in general is set at $y_0 = 0$. Implications where this assumption is relaxed are investigated in Section 17.9 of Chapter 17. The mean is

$$
E[y_t] = \delta \sum_{j=0}^{t-1} \phi^j + \sum_{j=0}^{t-1} \phi^j E[v_{t-j}] + \phi^t y_0 = \phi^t y_0 + \delta \sum_{j=0}^{t-1} \phi^j ,
\tag{16.10}
$$

and the variance is

$$\text{var}(y_t) = E[(y_t - E[y_t])^2] = E\left[\left(\sum_{j=0}^{t-1} \phi^j v_{t-j}\right)^2\right] = \sigma^2 \sum_{j=0}^{t-1} \phi^{2j},$$

(16.11)

where the last step follows from the *iid* assumption about v_t and $E[v_t^2] = \sigma^2$. Taking the limits of (16.10) and (16.11) gives, respectively,

$$\lim_{t\to\infty} E[y_t] = \lim_{t\to\infty} \phi^t y_0 + \lim_{t\to\infty} \sum_{j=0}^{t-1} \phi^j \delta = \frac{\delta}{1 - \phi}$$

(16.12)

$$\lim_{t\to\infty} \text{var}(y_t) = \lim_{t\to\infty} \sigma^2 \sum_{j=0}^{t-1} \phi^{2j} = \sigma^2(1 + \phi^2 + \cdots) = \frac{\sigma^2}{1 - \phi^2},$$

(16.13)

and hence

$$\lim_{t\to\infty} E[y_t^2] = \frac{\sigma^2}{1 - \phi^2} + \frac{\delta^2}{(1 - \phi)^2}.$$

See also the analysis of the moments of stationary processes in Chapter 13.

The first two moments have fixed and finite limits and the WLLN can be shown to apply, so that

$$\frac{1}{T} \sum_{t=2}^{T} y_{t-1} \xrightarrow{p} \lim_{t\to\infty} E[y_t], \qquad \frac{1}{T} \sum_{t=2}^{T} y_{t-1}^2 \xrightarrow{p} \lim_{t\to\infty} E[y_t^2].$$

Example 16.4 Simulating a Stationary AR(1) Model

The AR(1) model in (16.5) is simulated for $T = \{50, 100, 200, 400, 800, 1600\}$, using 50000 draws, with parameters $\theta = \{\delta = 0.0, \phi = 0.8, \sigma^2 = 1.0\}$ and starting value of $y_0 = 0.0$. For each draw, the sample moments

$$m_1 = \frac{1}{T} \sum_{t=2}^{T} y_{t-1}, \qquad m_2 = \frac{1}{T} \sum_{t=2}^{T} y_{t-1}^2,$$

are computed, with the means and variances of these quantities reported in Table 16.2. The two means converge to their respective theoretical values given by (16.12) and (16.13),

$$\lim_{t\to\infty} E[y_t] = \frac{\delta}{1 - \phi} = \frac{0.0}{1 - 0.8} = 0.0$$

$$\lim_{t\to\infty} \text{var}(y_t) = \frac{\sigma^2}{1 - \phi^2} = \frac{1.0}{1 - 0.8^2} = 2.778,$$

as T increases. The limits of these moments are finite with both variances approaching zero with the variances roughly halving as T is doubled.   □

Table 16.2. *Simulation properties of the stationary AR(1)
model in (16.5) for various samples of size T. The parameters
are $\theta = \{\delta = 0.0, \phi = 0.8, \sigma^2 = 1.0\}$ with a starting value
of $y_0 = 0.0$. The number of replications is* 50000

T	$m_1 = \dfrac{1}{T} \sum_{t=2}^{T} y_{t-1}$		$m_2 = \dfrac{1}{T} \sum_{t=2}^{T} y_{t-1}^2$	
	Mean	Variance	Mean	Variance
50	−0.001	0.428	2.620	1.240
100	−0.003	0.231	2.701	0.661
200	−0.002	0.120	2.738	0.340
400	−0.002	0.061	2.756	0.173
800	0.000	0.031	2.767	0.087
1600	0.000	0.016	2.772	0.044

From Chapter 2, the least squares estimator in (16.6) has an asymptotic
normal distribution because $y_{t-1} v_t$ in (16.8) is a martingale difference sequence.
This property is illustrated in panel (a) of Figure 16.2 which gives simulated
sampling distributions of the standardised least squares estimator of ϕ where
the true parameter is 0.8. The normal approximation for the smaller sample
sizes is reasonable except in the tails, but the quality of the approximation
quickly improves as the sample size increases.

16.3.2 Nonstationary Case: Stochastic Trends

Consider the stochastic trend model in (16.1), which is obtained by setting
$\phi = 1$ in equation (16.5). Now using $\phi = 1$ in (16.10) and (16.11) to find the

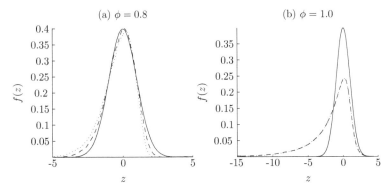

Figure 16.2. Finite sample distributions, based on 50000 replications, of the standardised
least squares estimator of the AR(1) model for sample size $T = 50$ (dotted line) and
$T = 200$ (dashed line) compared to the standard normal distribution (solid line). Choices
of standardisation are $z = \sqrt{T}(\hat{\phi} - \phi)/\sqrt{1 - \phi^2}$ in panel (a) and $z = T(\hat{\phi} - \phi)$ in
panel (b).

moments of y_t reveals a very different result than the one obtained for the stationary model. The mean is

$$E[y_t] = \phi^t y_0 + \sum_{j=0}^{t-1} \phi^j \delta = y_0 + \delta t \,,$$

whereas the variance is

$$\text{var}(y_t) = \sigma^2 \sum_{j=0}^{t-1} \phi^{2j} = \sigma^2(1 + \phi^2 + \phi^4 + \cdots) = \sigma^2 t \,.$$

Both moments are nonstationary because they are functions of t. This suggests that the scaling of the moments $\sum_{t=2}^{T} y_{t-1}$ and $\sum_{t=2}^{T} y_{t-1}^2$ by T^{-1} in (16.8), as adopted in the stationary case, does not result in a convergent sequence in the nonstationary case. In fact, the appropriate scaling factors for these moments differ as the following example demonstrates.

Example 16.5 Sample Moments of a Stochastic Trend Model
The stochastic trend model

$$y_t = \delta + \phi y_{t-1} + v_t \,, \qquad v_t \sim iid\, N(0, \sigma^2) \,,$$

is simulated for samples of size $T = \{50, 100, 200, 400, 800, 1600\}$, using 50000 replications, with parameters $\theta = \{\delta = 0.0, \phi = 1.0, \sigma^2 = 1.0\}$ and starting value $y_0 = 0.0$. For each replication the moments

$$m_1 = \frac{1}{T^{3/2}} \sum_{t=2}^{T} y_{t-1}, \quad m_2 = \frac{1}{T^2} \sum_{t=2}^{T} y_{t-1}^2 \,,$$

are computed with the means and variances of these quantities reported in Table 16.3. The means of the two quantities converge, respectively, to 0.0 and 0.5. In contrast to the stationary case, the variances of both quantities do not approach zero, but tend to converge to $1/3$. This property is a reflection that m_1 and m_2 now converge to random variables and not to fixed limits as is the case for stationary processes. $\qquad\square$

Example 16.5 demonstrates a fundamental difference between the moments of a stationary process and the moments of an integrated process. Whilst the moments of a stationary process converge to a fixed limit using a suitable scaling, the moments of the integrated process converge, after suitable scaling, to a random variable, not a fixed limit. Moreover, the scaling factors needed for the moments of integrated processes are not only higher than for the moments of stationary processes, but also vary across moments of different orders. In the case of the sample moment m_1 in Example 16.5 the scale factor is $T^{-3/2}$ and for the sample moment m_2 it is T^{-2}.

Table 16.3. *Simulation properties of the first two moments of the nonstationary AR(1) model in Example 16.5. The number of replications is 50000*

T	$m_1 = \dfrac{1}{T^{3/2}} \displaystyle\sum_{t=2}^{T} y_{t-1}$		$m_2 = \dfrac{1}{T^2} \displaystyle\sum_{t=2}^{T} y_{t-1}^2$	
	Mean	Variance	Mean	Variance
50	−0.001	0.323	0.490	0.317
100	−0.002	0.329	0.496	0.330
200	−0.003	0.331	0.497	0.334
400	−0.002	0.328	0.494	0.324
800	−0.001	0.335	0.501	0.339
1600	0.003	0.336	0.503	0.339

The fact that sample moments of stochastic trends converge to random variables and not fixed limits, suggests that the distribution of the least squares estimator in (16.6) is affected by this result. This is indeed the case as the following extension of Example 16.5 demonstrates.

Example 16.6 Distribution of the Least Squares Estimator

Consider the AR(1) model

$$y_t = \phi y_{t-1} + v_t, \qquad v_t \sim iid\, N(0, \sigma^2).$$

It follows from equation (16.7) that the least squares estimator is

$$\widehat{\phi} - \phi = \frac{\displaystyle\sum_{t=2}^{T} y_{t-1} v_{t-1}}{\displaystyle\sum_{t=2}^{T} y_{t-1}^2}.$$

Now using the appropriate scale factors from Example 16.5 and rearranging gives

$$z = T(\widehat{\phi} - \phi) = \frac{\dfrac{1}{T} \displaystyle\sum_{t=2}^{T} y_{t-1} v_{t-1}}{\dfrac{1}{T^2} \displaystyle\sum_{t=2}^{T} y_{t-1}^2}.$$

The sampling distribution of z for $\phi = 1$ is given in panel (b) of Figure 16.2 for samples of size 50 and 200. The distribution of $\widehat{\phi}$ is non-normal exhibiting negative skewness with a relatively long left tail. Increasing the sample size from $T = 50$ to $T = 200$ reveals no sign of convergence to normality. The non-normality feature of the distribution is also shown in Table 16.4 which provides third (skewness) and fourth (kurtosis) order sample moments from simulating

Table 16.4. *Distributional properties of the sampling distribution of the least squares estimator of the AR(1) model in equation (16.5). The parameters are $\delta = 0.0$, $\phi = \{0.0, 0.8, 1.0\}$ and $\sigma^2 = 1.0$, with a starting value of $y_0 = 0.0$. The sample sizes are $T = \{50, 100, 200, 400, 800\}$ and the number of replications is 50000. Statistics given are skewness (Skew), kurtosis (Kurt) and the proportion of simulated values of $\widehat{\phi}$ less than ϕ (Prop)*

	$\phi = 0.0$			$\phi = 0.8$			$\phi = 1.0$		
T	Skew.	Kurt.	Prop.	Skew.	Kurt.	Prop.	Skew.	Kurt.	Prop.
50	−0.005	2.871	0.496	−1.947	6.286	0.568	−3.882	16.134	0.677
100	−0.007	2.946	0.498	−1.461	4.854	0.550	−3.991	17.121	0.682
200	0.007	2.927	0.503	−1.094	4.028	0.538	−4.129	18.345	0.684
400	0.013	2.960	0.500	−0.757	3.496	0.527	−4.151	18.896	0.680
800	−0.023	2.984	0.502	−0.576	3.270	0.516	−4.097	18.022	0.681

the AR(1) model for alternative values of ϕ. The results show that for the stochastic trend case where $\phi = 1$, there is very little difference in the sampling distributions of $\widehat{\phi}$ for the various sample sizes, suggesting that convergence to the asymptotic distribution is indeed super fast. This contrasts with the stationary case in panel (a) of Figure 16.2 where $\phi = 0.8$ as convergence to the asymptotic distribution of normality is relatively slower. These properties are formally derived in Section 16.6. □

16.3.3   Nonstationary Case: Deterministic Trends

Consider the nonstationary deterministic trend model in (16.1). The ordinary least squares estimator of the parameters of the model is

$$
\begin{bmatrix} \widehat{\beta_0} \\ \widehat{\beta_1} \end{bmatrix} = \begin{bmatrix} \sum\limits_{t=1}^{T} 1 & \sum\limits_{t=1}^{T} t \\ \sum\limits_{t=1}^{T} t & \sum\limits_{t=1}^{T} t^2 \end{bmatrix}^{-1} \begin{bmatrix} \sum\limits_{t=1}^{T} y_t \\ \sum\limits_{t=1}^{T} t y_t \end{bmatrix}.
\tag{16.14}
$$

Substituting for y_t and rearranging gives

$$
\begin{bmatrix} \widehat{\beta_0} \\ \widehat{\beta_1} \end{bmatrix} - \begin{bmatrix} \beta_0 \\ \beta_1 \end{bmatrix} = \begin{bmatrix} \sum\limits_{t=1}^{T} 1 & \sum\limits_{t=1}^{T} t \\ \sum\limits_{t=1}^{T} t & \sum\limits_{t=1}^{T} t^2 \end{bmatrix}^{-1} \begin{bmatrix} \sum\limits_{t=1}^{T} e_t \\ \sum\limits_{t=1}^{T} t e_t \end{bmatrix}.
\tag{16.15}
$$

In the stationary case both sides are multiplied by $\sqrt{T}$ since all elements in the matrix on the right-hand side of the equation converge to a stationary value in the limit. As with the nonstationary stochastic trend model, this result does not hold here because the rates of convergence of the estimators $\widehat{\beta}_0$ and $\widehat{\beta}_1$, differ.

From the properties of time trends, the following results hold

$$\sum_{t=1}^{T} 1 = T = O(T)$$

$$\sum_{t=1}^{T} t = \frac{1}{2}T(T+1) = O(T^2)$$

$$\sum_{t=1}^{T} t^2 = \frac{1}{6}T(T+1)(2T+1) = O(T^3),$$

and consequently

$$\lim_{T\to\infty} \frac{1}{T} \sum_{t=1}^{T} 1 = \lim_{T\to\infty} \frac{T}{T} = 1$$

$$\lim_{T\to\infty} \frac{1}{T^2} \sum_{t=1}^{T} t = \frac{1}{2} \lim_{T\to\infty} \frac{T(T+1)}{T^2} = \frac{1}{2} \lim_{T\to\infty} (1 + \frac{1}{T}) = \frac{1}{2} \qquad (16.16)$$

$$\lim_{T\to\infty} \frac{1}{T^3} \sum_{t=1}^{T} t^2 = \frac{1}{6} \lim_{T\to\infty} \frac{T(T+1)(2T+1)}{T^3} = \frac{1}{6} \lim_{T\to\infty} (2 + \frac{3}{T} + \frac{1}{T^2}) = \frac{1}{3}.$$

The results in (16.16) suggest that (16.15) be scaled as follows

$$\begin{bmatrix} T^{1/2} & 0 \\ 0 & T^{3/2} \end{bmatrix} \begin{bmatrix} \hat{\beta}_0 - \beta_0 \\ \hat{\beta}_1 - \beta_1 \end{bmatrix} = \begin{bmatrix} T^{1/2} & 0 \\ 0 & T^{3/2} \end{bmatrix} \begin{bmatrix} \sum_{t=1}^{T} 1 & \sum_{t=1}^{T} t \\ \sum_{t=1}^{T} t & \sum_{t=1}^{T} t^2 \end{bmatrix}^{-1} \begin{bmatrix} \sum_{t=1}^{T} e_t \\ \sum_{t=1}^{T} te_t \end{bmatrix}$$

$$= \left[\begin{bmatrix} T^{1/2} & 0 \\ 0 & T^{3/2} \end{bmatrix}^{-1} \begin{bmatrix} \sum_{t=1}^{T} 1 & \sum_{t=1}^{T} t \\ \sum_{t=1}^{T} t & \sum_{t=1}^{T} t^2 \end{bmatrix} \begin{bmatrix} T^{1/2} & 0 \\ 0 & T^{3/2} \end{bmatrix}^{-1} \right]^{-1}$$

$$\times \begin{bmatrix} T^{1/2} & 0 \\ 0 & T^{3/2} \end{bmatrix}^{-1} \begin{bmatrix} \sum_{t=1}^{T} e_t \\ \sum_{t=1}^{T} te_t \end{bmatrix},$$

or

$$\begin{bmatrix} T^{1/2}(\hat{\beta}_0 - \beta_0) \\ T^{3/2}(\hat{\beta}_1 - \beta_1) \end{bmatrix} = \begin{bmatrix} \frac{1}{T}\sum_{t=1}^{T} 1 & \frac{1}{T^2}\sum_{t=1}^{T} t \\ \frac{1}{T^2}\sum_{t=1}^{T} t & \frac{1}{T^3}\sum_{t=1}^{T} t^2 \end{bmatrix}^{-1} \begin{bmatrix} \frac{1}{T^{1/2}}\sum_{t=1}^{T} e_t \\ \frac{1}{T^{1/2}}\sum_{t=1}^{T} te_t \end{bmatrix}. \qquad (16.17)$$

From (16.16), the first term on the right-hand side has the limit

$$
\lim_{T \to \infty}
\begin{bmatrix}
\dfrac{1}{T}\sum_{t=1}^{T} 1 & \dfrac{1}{T^2}\sum_{t=1}^{T} t \\[2ex]
\dfrac{1}{T^2}\sum_{t=1}^{T} t & \dfrac{1}{T^3}\sum_{t=1}^{T} t^2
\end{bmatrix}
=
\begin{bmatrix}
1 & \tfrac{1}{2} \\[1ex]
\tfrac{1}{2} & \tfrac{1}{3}
\end{bmatrix}.
\tag{16.18}
$$

As with the stationary AR(1) model, this is a fixed limit, in contrast to the nonstationary stochastic trend model where the limit is a random variable.

Finally, since the second term on the right-hand side of equation (16.17) satisfies the Lindeberg-Feller central limit theorem of Chapter 2, the asymptotic distribution of the least squares estimator is

$$
\begin{bmatrix}
T^{1/2}(\widehat{\beta}_0 - \beta_0) \\[1ex]
T^{3/2}(\widehat{\beta}_1 - \beta_1)
\end{bmatrix}
\xrightarrow{d}
N\left(
\begin{bmatrix} 0 \\ 0 \end{bmatrix}, \sigma^2
\begin{bmatrix}
1 & \tfrac{1}{2} \\[1ex]
\tfrac{1}{2} & \tfrac{1}{3}
\end{bmatrix}^{-1}
\right).
\tag{16.19}
$$

This result shows that the least squares estimator of the nonstationary deterministic trend model is consistent, although the rates of convergence differ: the intercept rate of convergence is $\sqrt{T}$ for the stationary model, whereas $\widehat{\beta}_1$ converges at the much faster rate $T^{3/2}$. This higher rate of convergence is referred to as super-consistency. Furthermore, unlike the nonstationary stochastic trend model but similar to the stationary model, the asymptotic distribution of the estimator of the deterministic trend model is normal.

16.4   Asymptotics for Integrated Processes

The discussion in the previous section comparing the properties of the deterministic and stochastic trend models, suggests that the distinction between these two specifications is fundamental to time series analysis of nonstationary processes. The distribution theory associated with estimation and hypothesis testing in the case of the deterministic trend model is standard since from equation (16.19), it is based on asymptotic normality. However, in the case of the stochastic trend model, the distribution theory is non-standard. Given the importance of the stochastic trend model in characterising economic and financial variables, the tools for understanding the non-standard nature of this distribution theory are now investigated.

This section aims to outline the asymptotic distribution theory for integrated processes. Three fundamental tools are developed following the approach of Phillips (1987). The first is to express the discrete time random walk as a continuous-time stochastic process. The second is to introduce a new central limit theorem known as the functional central limit theorem (FCLT), which shows that this continuous-time process converges to a normally distributed stochastic process called Brownian motion. The third is to use a result known as the continuous mapping theorem which provides a generalisation of the

Slutsky theorem discussed in Chapter 2. The main theoretical result is that statistics based on $I(1)$ processes converge (weakly) to random variables that are functionals of Brownian motion.

16.4.1 Brownian Motion

As outlined in Chapter 12, Brownian motion is the continuous-time analogue of the discrete time random walk model

$$y_t = y_{t-1} + v_t, \qquad v_t \sim iid \, N(0, \sigma^2), \qquad (16.20)$$

or the equivalent representation

$$y_t = y_{t-1} + \sigma z_t, \qquad z_t \sim iid \, N(0, 1). \qquad (16.21)$$

The movement from $t - 1$ to t, $\Delta y_t = y_t - y_{t-1}$, involves a discrete step of size σz_t.

To motivate the continuous-time feature of Brownian motion, consider breaking the step in (16.21) into smaller intervals. For example, suppose that the full step z_t represents a working week, broken down into $n = 5$ independent steps

$$z_t = z_{1,t} + z_{2,t} + z_{3,t} + z_{4,t} + z_{5,t},$$

corresponding to each day of the working week, with each daily step distributed as

$$z_{i,t} \sim N\left(0, \frac{1}{5}\right).$$

As the $z_{i,t}$ are independent, the moments of the full step, z_t, still have zero mean

$$\begin{aligned} E[z_t] &= E[z_{1,t} + z_{2,t} + z_{3,t} + z_{4,t} + z_{5,t}] \\ &= E[z_{1,t}] + E[z_{2,t}] + E[z_{3,t}] + E[z_{4,t}] + E[z_{5,t}] \\ &= 0, \end{aligned}$$

and unit variance

$$\begin{aligned} E[z_t^2] &= E[(z_{1,t} + z_{2,t} + z_{3,t} + z_{4,t} + z_{5,t})^2] \\ &= E[z_{1,t}^2] + E[z_{2,t}^2] + E[z_{3,t}^2] + E[z_{4,t}^2] + E[z_{5,t}^2] \\ &= \frac{1}{5} + \frac{1}{5} + \frac{1}{5} + \frac{1}{5} + \frac{1}{5} \\ &= 1. \end{aligned}$$

For n steps, the random walk in (16.21) becomes

$$y_t = y_{t-1} + \sigma \sum_{i=1}^{n} z_{i,t},$$

where now each step is

$$z_{i,t} \sim N\left(0, \frac{1}{n}\right).$$

Allowing for infinitely smaller time intervals, $n \to \infty$, the limit is a continuous-time process y_t where the t subscript is now placed in parentheses to emphasise that the function is continuous in time. This suggests the following continuous-time representation of a discrete random walk where the continuous movement in $y(t)$ over a small time interval, dt, is given by

$$dy(t) = \sigma \, dB(t),$$

in which $B(t)$ represents standard Brownian motion which has independent increments and distributed as

$$dB(t) \sim N(0, dt).$$

The properties of Brownian motion are summarised as follows. A stochastic process given by $B(s)$ represents standard Brownian motion over the time interval $s \in [0, 1]$ if it satisfies the properties

(i) $B(0) = 0$
(ii) $B(s) \sim N(0, s)$
(iii) $B(s) - B(r)$, is independent of $B(r)$ for all $0 \le r < s \le 1$.

Brownian motion is, thus, a normally distributed stochastic process whose increments are independent. The intuition behind the independence property is that future changes in a Brownian motion cannot be predicted by past Brownian motion. This result follows from the fact that $B(s)$ is the sum of independent random variables that also contains the independent random variables in $B(r)$. It follows, therefore, that as $B(s) - B(r)$ contains just random variables that are in $B(s)$ but not in $B(r)$, it is independent of $B(r)$. The sample paths of Brownian motion are continuous but nowhere differentiable, see Figure 12.2 of Chapter 12.

16.4.2   Functional Central Limit Theorem

To derive asymptotic theory for a random walk, consider again the partial summation representation of (16.20)

$$y_t = y_0 + \sum_{j=1}^{t} v_j, \qquad v_j \sim iid\,(0, \sigma^2). \tag{16.22}$$

It is assumed that $T^{-1/2}y_0 \overset{p}{\to} 0$ so y_0 can be treated as either fixed or random. It is useful to re-express (16.22) using alternative notation as

$$y_{[Ts]} = y_0 + \sum_{j=1}^{[Ts]} v_j, \quad 0 < s \le 1, \tag{16.23}$$

in which $[x]$ represents the largest integer less than or equal to x. The function $y_{[Ts]}$ is a right-continuous step function on $[0, 1]$. In this representation, a particular value of s measures the sth proportion of the sample used in the summation. For example, if $T = 200$ and $s = 1/4$, $y_{[Ts]} = y_{50}$ is the first quartile and the first 25% of observations are used in the summation. Setting $s = 1$, $y_{[Ts]} = y_{200}$ is the last observation in the sample so summation is over the full sample. As $T \to \infty$, $y_{[Ts]}$ in (16.23) becomes continuously observed on the unit interval $0 \le s \le 1$, in contrast to y_t, which is still defined discretely on the integers $t = 1, 2, \cdots, T$, as in (16.22).

Example 16.7 Constructing a Continuous-Time Process

Panel (a) of Figure 16.3 gives a plot of $T = 5$ observations simulated from a random walk, $y_t = \{2.3, 3.3, 2.7, 4.7, 5.3\}$, with the construction of the right-continuous step function $y_{[Ts]}$ over $s \in [0, 1]$ given in panel (c). Increasing the sample size to $T = 40$, as in panel (b) of Figure 16.3, shows that the picture becomes more dense with the horizontal axis increasing in t, while for the continuous representation in panel (d) of Figure 16.3 the horizontal axis still remains in the interval $[0, 1]$. □

The relationship between the discretely observed time series y_t in (16.22) and the continuous function $y_{[Ts]}$ in (16.23) is conveniently represented as

$$y_{[Ts]} = \begin{cases} 0 & : \quad 0/T \le s < 1/T \\ y_1 = v_1 & : \quad 1/T \le s < 2/T \\ y_2 = v_1 + v_2 & : \quad 2/T \le s < 3/T \\ \quad \vdots & \qquad \vdots \\ y_T = v_1 + v_2 + \cdots + v_T & : \quad s = 1. \end{cases} \tag{16.24}$$

Figure 16.3 shows that y_t is a constant within the tth interval, so the height and the width of the tth bar of the histogram are, respectively, given by

$$\text{HEIGHT}_t = y_t, \qquad \text{WIDTH}_t = \frac{t+1}{T} - \frac{t}{T} = \frac{1}{T},$$

and the associated area for observation $s = t/T$ is

$$\text{AREA}_t = \int_{t/T}^{(t+1)/T} y_{[Ts]} ds = \int_{t/T}^{(t+1)/T} y_{[T \times \frac{t}{T}]} ds = \text{HEIGHT}_t \times \text{WIDTH}_t = \frac{y_t}{T}.$$

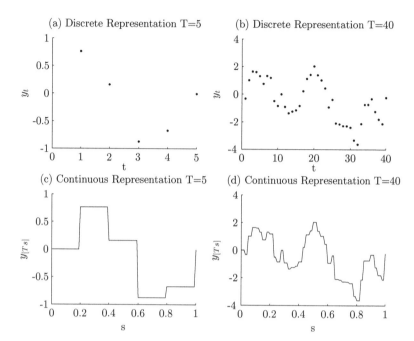

Figure 16.3. Construction of $y_{[Ts]}$ for sample sizes of $T = 5$ and $T = 40$.

The total area corresponding to the $y_{[Ts]}$ function is

$$\text{AREA} = \int_0^1 y_{[Ts]} ds \tag{16.25}$$

$$= \sum_{t=1}^{T} \int_{t/T}^{(t+1)/T} y_{[T \times \frac{t}{T}]} ds$$

$$= \int_{1/T}^{2/T} y_{[T \times \frac{1}{T}]} ds + \int_{2/T}^{3/T} y_{[T \times \frac{2}{T}]} ds + \cdots$$

$$= \frac{y_1}{T} + \frac{y_2}{T} + \cdots + \frac{y_T}{T}$$

$$= \frac{1}{T} \sum_{t=1}^{T} y_t , \tag{16.26}$$

which is the sample mean, so that each bar of the histogram in panels (c) and (d) of Figure 16.3 represents the contribution of each respective observation to the sample mean of y_t.

To construct asymptotic theory for $y_{[Ts]}$ defined in (16.24) for a given $s \in [0, 1]$, note that $[Ts] \to \infty$ as $T \to \infty$. Equation (16.23) is then rescaled to yield

$$[Ts]^{-1/2} y_{[Ts]} = [Ts]^{-1/2} y_0 + [Ts]^{-1/2} \sum_{j=1}^{[Ts]} v_j \overset{d}{\to} N(0, \sigma^2),$$

or, by using the result $[Ts]/T \to s$, this expression is re-expressed as

$$T^{-1/2} y_{[Ts]} = \left(\frac{[Ts]}{T}\right)^{1/2} [Ts]^{-1/2} y_{[Ts]} \overset{d}{\to} s^{1/2} N(0, \sigma^2) = N(0, \sigma^2 s).$$

Alternatively, the standardised function

$$Y_T(s) = \sigma^{-1} T^{-1/2} y_{[Ts]}, \qquad 0 \le s \le 1, \tag{16.27}$$

satisfies

$$Y_T(s) \overset{d}{\to} N(0, s), \tag{16.28}$$

for a given s. As an important special case, the standard central limit theorem arises from (16.28) where $s = 1$.

Now consider the entire random function $Y_T(\cdot)$ on $[0, 1]$, not just for a single s. The convergence properties of $Y_T(\cdot)$ are based on the following theorem.

Functional Central Limit Theorem
If y_t is the random walk $y_t = y_{t-1} + v_t$, where $T^{-1/2} y_0 \overset{p}{\to} 0$ and v_t is iid $(0, \sigma^2)$, the standardised function Y_T in (16.27) satisfies

$$Y_T(\cdot) \overset{d}{\to} B(\cdot), \tag{16.29}$$

where $B(s)$ is standard Brownian motion on $[0, 1]$. ∎

Despite their apparent similarity, the FCLT result (16.29) and the asymptotic normality result (16.28) show important mathematical differences. The simple manipulations leading to (16.28) do not constitute a proof of the FCLT because convergence in distribution of $Y_T(s)$ to $N(0, s)$ for each s is not sufficient to conclude that $Y_T(\cdot)$ converges as a function to Brownian motion $B(\cdot)$ (Billingsley, 1968; Davidson, 1994). Technically, the convergence of $Y_T(\cdot)$ to $B(\cdot)$ in (16.29) involves a generalisation of convergence in distribution, which applies to random variables and vectors, to the concept of weak convergence, which applies to more general objects such as functions. Details of weak convergence can be found in Section 26.3 of Davidson (1994).

Example 16.8 Order Statistics of a Random Walk
The random walk

$$y_t = y_{t-1} + v_t, \qquad v_t \sim iid\ N(0, \sigma^2),$$

is simulated 10000 times with a starting value of $y_0 = 0$, $\sigma^2 = 1$ and a sample size of $T = 500$. The distributions of the standardised functions

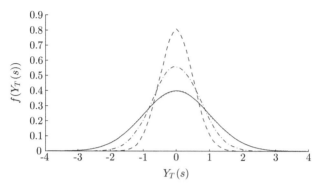

Figure 16.4. Sampling distributions of $Y_T(s)$ for the standardised first quartile (dashed line) with $s = 1/4$, the median (dot-dashed line) with $s = 1/2$ and the last observation (dotted line) with $s = 1$, compared to the standard normal distribution (solid line). The sampling distributions are based on a sample size of $T = 500$ and 10000 replications.

$Y_T(s) = \sigma^{-1} T^{-1/2} y_{[Ts]}$, for $s = 1/4$ (first quartile), $s = 1/2$ (median) and $s = 1$ (last observation) are given in Figure 16.4. All three sampling distributions are normally distributed with zero means but with differing variances. The variances of the simulated standardised functions are computed, respectively, as 0.2478, 0.4976 and 1.0004, which agree with the theoretical values of $s = \{1/4, 1/2, 1.0\}$.   □

16.4.3   Continuous Mapping Theorem

An important additional tool to derive the distribution of statistics based on stochastic trends is the continuous mapping theorem. This theorem represents an extension of Slutsky's theorem encountered in Chapter 2, which is used in standard asymptotic distribution theory to derive the properties of continuous functions of random variables. Now the approach is to derive the properties of continuous functions of random functions. For example Brownian motion $B(s)$ is a random function of s, so that $f(B(s))$ represents a function of a function, commonly referred to as a functional (Davidson, Section 5.4, 1994).

Continuous Mapping Theorem
Let $f(\cdot)$ be a continuous function. If $Y_T(s)$ is a sequence of functions such that $Y_T(s) \overset{d}{\to} B(s)$ then $f(Y_T(s)) \overset{d}{\to} f(B(s))$.   ■

The continuous mapping theorem allows further results to be derived from the FCLT such as

$$Y_T(s)^2 \overset{d}{\to} B(s)^2,$$

$$\int_0^1 Y_T(s)ds \overset{d}{\to} \int_0^1 B(s)ds, \qquad (16.30)$$

$$\left[\int_0^1 Y_T(s)ds\right]^{-1} \overset{d}{\to} \left[\int_0^1 B(s)ds\right]^{-1}.$$

Example 16.9 Sample Mean of a Random Walk
From equation (16.26) the sample mean is

$$\frac{1}{T}\sum_{t=1}^T y_t = \int_0^1 y_{[Ts]}ds.$$

Multiplying both sides by $\sigma^{-1}T^{-1/2}$ and using the definition of $Y_T(s)$ in (16.27) shows that

$$\frac{1}{\sigma T^{3/2}}\sum_{t=1}^T y_t = \int_0^1 \sigma^{-1}T^{-1/2}y_{[Ts]}ds = \int_0^1 Y_T(s)ds \overset{d}{\to} \int_0^1 B(s)ds,$$

where the last step uses the second result in the continuous mapping theorem in (16.30). This is a fundamental result as it shows that a suitably standardised sample mean of a random walk converges weakly to an integral of a Brownian motion. □

From property (ii) of the definition of Brownian motion, $\int_0^1 B(s)ds$ is a continuous sum of normal random variables over s and is therefore also normally distributed. From the properties of the normal distribution, the mean of this term is zero since it is the continuous sum of normal random variables each having zero mean. In the case of the random walk, the variance of the standardised mean is $1/3$ (Banerjee, Dolado, Galbraith and Hendry, 1993), in which case

$$\frac{1}{\sigma T^{1/2}}\bar{y} = \frac{1}{\sigma T^{3/2}}\sum_{t=1}^T y_t \overset{d}{\to} N(0, 1/3), \qquad (16.31)$$

so the variance of $\int_0^1 B(s)ds$ is $\frac{1}{3}$. This result is developed in Exercise 6.

16.4.4 Stochastic Integrals

The discussion of the asymptotic properties of the least squares estimator in (16.8) in the presence of a random walk has focussed on the moments just

Table 16.5. *Simulation properties of the stochastic moment of the nonstationary stochastic trend model in Example 16.10 for alternative scale factors. The number of draws is 50000*

T	$\dfrac{1}{T^{1/2}}\sum_{t=1}^{T} y_{t-1}v_t$		$\dfrac{1}{T}\sum_{t=1}^{T} y_{t-1}v_t$		$\dfrac{1}{T^{3/2}}\sum_{t=1}^{T} y_{t-1}v_t$	
	Mean	Var.	Mean	Var.	Mean	Var.
50	-0.061	23.501	-0.009	0.470	-0.001	0.009
100	-0.092	47.193	-0.009	0.472	-0.001	0.005
200	-0.055	98.383	-0.004	0.492	0.000	0.002
400	-0.123	196.140	-0.006	0.490	0.000	0.001
800	0.058	396.763	0.002	0.496	0.000	0.001
1600	0.001	798.034	0.000	0.499	0.000	0.000

involving y_t such as $\sum_{t=2}^{T} y_{t-1}$. Now the focus is on the sample moment

$$\sum_{t=2}^{T} y_{t-1}v_t \, ,$$

which is important in establishing the asymptotic distribution of the least squares estimator given in Section 16.3. The asymptotic properties of this expression are given by the following theorem.

Example 16.10 Stochastic Moment of a Random Walk
The random walk

$$y_t = y_{t-1} + v_t \, , \qquad v_t \sim iid\ N(0, 1) \, ,$$

is simulated 50000 times with initial condition $y_0 = 0$, for samples of size $T = \{50, 100, 200, 400, 800, 1600\}$. For each replication the stochastic moment

$$m = \frac{1}{T^k}\sum_{t=2}^{T} y_{t-1}v_t \, ,$$

with scale factors $k = \{1/2, 1.0, 3/2\}$ is computed with the mean and the variance reported in Table 16.5. The only scale factor that stabilises the variance of m is $k = 1$. The scale factor $k = 1/2$ used in the stationary case for this moment does not dampen down the variance, whereas the scale factor $k = 3/2$ results in a degenerate stochastic moment with its variance approaching zero as T increases.   □

Stochastic Integral Theorem
If y_t is a random walk $y_t = y_{t-1} + v_t$ and v_t is iid $(0, \sigma^2)$, then

$$\frac{1}{\sigma^2 T} \sum_{t=2}^{T} y_{t-1} v_t \overset{d}{\to} \int_0^1 B(s) dB(s),$$ (16.32)

where $B(s)$ is standard Brownian motion. ■

An integral taken with respect to a Brownian motion is called a stochastic integral. This differs from an integral such as $\int_0^1 B(s) ds$, which is a random variable, but is not termed a stochastic integral since it is taken with respect to s. This functional can be expressed in terms of a centered chi-squared distribution as the following example demonstrates.

Example 16.11 Distribution of a Stochastic Integral
Consider the random walk

$$y_t = y_{t-1} + v_t, \qquad v_t \sim iid(0, \sigma^2).$$

Squaring both sides, summing from $t = 2, 3, \cdots, T$ and rearranging gives

$$\sum_{t=2}^{T} y_{t-1} v_t = \frac{1}{2}(y_T^2 - y_1^2 - \sum_{t=2}^{T} v_t^2).$$

Scaling this expression by $(\sigma^2 T)^{-1}$ results in the sample moment

$$\frac{1}{\sigma^2 T} \sum_{t=2}^{T} y_{t-1} v_t = \frac{1}{2}\left(\frac{1}{\sigma^2 T} y_T^2 - \frac{1}{\sigma^2 T} y_1^2 - \frac{1}{\sigma^2 T} \sum_{t=2}^{T} v_t^2\right) \overset{d}{\to} \frac{1}{2}(B(1)^2 - 1),$$

by using (16.28) with $s = 1$, plim $T^{-1} y_1^2 = 0$ and plim $T^{-1} \sum_{t=2}^{T} v_t^2 = \sigma^2$. As $B(1)$ is $N(0,1)$ then $B(1)^2$ by definition is χ^2 with one degree of freedom with mean 1 and variance 2. Therefore, $(B(1)^2 - 1)/2$ is a centred chi-square distribution with mean 0 and variance of $1/2$. This result is verified in Figure 16.5, which compares the analytical distribution with the sampling distribution obtained by 50000 simulations of a random walk and computing the standardised statistic

$$m = \frac{1}{\sigma^2 T} \sum_{t=2}^{T} y_{t-1} v_t,$$

for each draw. The mean is 0.0002 and the variance is 0.4914, which agree with the theoretical moments of 0.0 and 0.5 respectively. □

The stochastic integral theorem can be generalised, so that if

$$f\left(\frac{1}{\sigma\sqrt{T}} y_{[Ts]}\right) = f(Y_T(s)) \overset{d}{\to} f(B(s)),$$

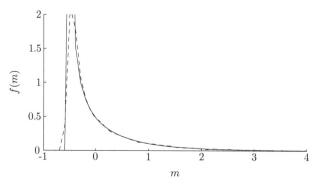

Figure 16.5. Sampling distribution of the standardised statistic $m = \sigma^{-2}T^{-1}\sum_{t=2}^{T} y_{t-1}v_t$ of a random walk. The distribution is based on a sample size of $T = 500$ (dashed line) and 50000 replications, compared to the centered χ_1^2 distribution (solid line).

for some continuous functional $f(\cdot)$, then

$$\frac{1}{T}\sum_{t=2}^{T} f(y_{t-1})v_t \overset{d}{\to} \int_0^1 f(B(s))dB(s).$$

This result is developed in Exercise 7.

16.5 Multivariate Analysis

The derivation of the asymptotic distribution of the previous section is based on a single integrated process. Extending the scalar case to N integrated processes is relatively straightforward and provides a natural generalisation of the results from the previous section. Consider an N dimensional random walk

$$y_{i,t} = y_{i,t-1} + v_{i,t}, \qquad i = 1, 2, \cdots, N, \tag{16.33}$$

and $v_t = \begin{bmatrix} v_{1,t}, v_{2,t}, \cdots, v_{N,t} \end{bmatrix}'$ is a $(N \times 1)$ *iid* vector of disturbances with zero mean and covariance matrix

$$V = \mathrm{E}\begin{bmatrix} v_t v_t' \end{bmatrix} = \begin{bmatrix} \sigma_{1,1} & \sigma_{1,2} & \cdots & \sigma_{1,N} \\ \sigma_{2,1} & \sigma_{2,2} & \cdots & \sigma_{2,N} \\ \vdots & \vdots & \ddots & \vdots \\ \sigma_{N,1} & \sigma_{N,2} & \cdots & \sigma_{N,N} \end{bmatrix}.$$

The key multivariate results are summarised as follows.

Multivariate Functional Central Limit Theorem

Let $B(s)$ be an N dimensional Brownian motion with covariance matrix V with properties

> (i) $B(0) = 0$
> (ii) $B(s) \sim N(0, sV)$
> (iii) $B(s) - B(r)$, is independent of $B(r)$ for all $0 \leq r < s \leq 1$.

It follows that

$$\frac{1}{\sqrt{T}} \sum_{t=1}^{[Ts]} v_t \overset{d}{\to} B(s) \text{ on } s \in [0, 1] . \qquad \blacksquare$$

Stochastic Integral Convergence

Defining the N dimensional cumulative sum as $y_t = \sum_{j=1}^{t} v_j$ yields the $(N \times N)$ matrix

$$\frac{1}{T} \sum_{t=2}^{T} y_{t-1} v_t' \overset{d}{\to} \int_0^1 B(s) dB(s)' . \qquad \blacksquare$$

Example 16.12 Estimation of a Nonstationary VAR

Let $N = 2$ and consider the VAR(1) model

$$y_t = \Phi y_{t-1} + v_t,$$

in which $v_t \sim iid\, N(0, I_2)$ and the true parameter matrix is $\Phi = I_2$ so that both $y_{1,t}$ and $y_{2,t}$ are random walks. The ordinary least squares estimator of Φ is

$$\widehat{\Phi} = \left(\sum_{t=2}^{T} y_{t-1} y_{t-1}' \right)^{-1} \sum_{t=2}^{T} y_{t-1} y_t' ,$$

and simple substitution for y_t gives the representation

$$T(\widehat{\Phi} - \Phi) = \left(\frac{1}{T^2} \sum_{t=2}^{T} y_{t-1} y_{t-1}' \right)^{-1} \frac{1}{T} \sum_{t=2}^{T} y_{t-1} v_t' .$$

Applying the multivariate FCLT to y_t gives

$$\frac{1}{\sqrt{T}} y_{[Ts]} = \begin{bmatrix} \frac{1}{\sqrt{T}} y_{1,[Ts]} \\ \frac{1}{\sqrt{T}} y_{2,[Ts]} \end{bmatrix} \overset{d}{\to} \begin{bmatrix} B_1(s) \\ B_2(s) \end{bmatrix} = B(s),$$

and the multivariate stochastic integral convergence gives

$$\frac{1}{T}\sum_{t=2}^{T} y_{t-1} v_t' = \begin{bmatrix} \frac{1}{T}\sum_{t=2}^{T} y_{1,t-1} v_{1,t} & \frac{1}{T}\sum_{t=2}^{T} y_{1,t-1} v_{2,t} \\ \frac{1}{T}\sum_{t=2}^{T} y_{2,t-1} v_{1,t} & \frac{1}{T}\sum_{t=2}^{T} y_{2,t-1} v_{2,t} \end{bmatrix}$$

$$\xrightarrow{d} \begin{bmatrix} \int_0^1 B_1(s)d B_1(s) & \int_0^1 B_1(s)d B_2(s) \\ \int_0^1 B_2(s)d B_1(s) & \int_0^1 B_2(s)d B_2(s) \end{bmatrix} = \int_0^1 B(s)d B(s)'.$$

It therefore follows that

$$T(\widehat{\Phi} - \Phi) \xrightarrow{d} \left[\int_0^1 B(s)B(s)'ds \right]^{-1} \int_0^1 B(s)d B(s)'. \qquad \square$$

Example 16.13 Mixed Normality
   Consider the bivariate functional given by

$$\int_0^1 B(s)d B(s)' = \begin{bmatrix} \int_0^1 B_1(s)d B_1(s) & \int_0^1 B_1(s)d B_2(s) \\ \int_0^1 B_2(s)d B_1(s) & \int_0^1 B_2(s)d B_2(s) \end{bmatrix}.$$

The diagonal elements are centered chi-squared distributions from Example 16.11. For the off-diagonal elements, suppose B_1 and B_2 are independent, $\sigma_{1,2} = 0$. The distribution of $\int_0^1 B_2(s)d B_1(s)$ conditional on B_2 is

$$\int_0^1 B_2(s)d B_1(s) \Big| B_2 \sim N\left(0, \sigma_{1,1} \int_0^1 B_2(s)^2 ds \right).$$

Thus, $\int_0^1 B_2(s)d B_1(s)$ is conditionally normal given B_2. That is, conditional on a given realisation of B_2, the stochastic integral has a normal distribution whose variance depends on B_2. Unconditionally, however, the distribution of the stochastic integral is mixed normal, since it involves averaging over the conditional normal distributions weighted by the density of the random variance $\int_0^1 B_2(s)^2 ds$. Figure 16.6 compares a mixed normal to a standard normal distribution. If B_1 and B_2 are dependent, $\sigma_{1,2} \neq 0$, then $\int_0^1 B_2(s)d B_1(s)$ is no longer unconditionally mixed normal, but a combination of mixed normal and χ_1^2 components. To see this, express B_1 as $B_1 = (\sigma_{1,2}/\sigma_{2,2})B_2 + B_{1|2}$, which is essentially a population regression of B_1 on B_2 with residual $B_{1|2}$, which is

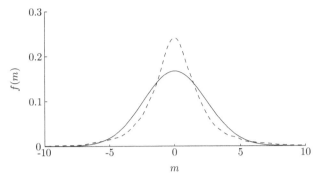

Figure 16.6. Comparison of a mixed normal (dashed line) and a normal distribution (solid line). The mixed normal distribution is obtained by simulating $v_{1,t}, v_{2,t} \sim iid\, N(0, 1)$ with $T = 4000$ and regressing $v_{2,t}$ on $y_{1,t}$ where $y_{1,t} = y_{1,t-1} + v_{1,t}$ to obtain an estimate of the regression parameter $\widehat{\beta}$. The statistic is $m = T\widehat{\beta}$. The number of replications is 20000.

independent of B_2 by construction. It follows that

$$\int_0^1 B_2(s)\,d B_1(s) = \int_0^1 B_2(s)\,d B_{1|2}(s) + \frac{\sigma_{1,2}}{\sigma_{2,2}} \int_0^1 B_2(s)\,d B_2(s),$$

which is the sum of mixed normal and χ_1^2 components. $\qquad\square$

16.6 Applications

The following two applications use the FCLT, stochastic integral convergence and the continuous mapping theorem to derive the asymptotic distribution of the least squares estimator in the presence of integrated processes for two types of models. The first application focusses on estimating an AR(1) model where the true model is $I(1)$. The shape of the derived asymptotic distribution is nonstandard, which has important implications for understanding the properties of unit root tests discussed in Chapter 17. The second application looks at the problem of estimating a deterministic trend in the presence of a random walk.

16.6.1 Least Squares Estimator of the AR(1) Model

Consider an AR(1) model

$$y_t = \phi y_{t-1} + v_t, \qquad v_t \sim iid\,(0, \sigma^2). \tag{16.34}$$

Suppose the true value is $\phi = 1$, so that y_t is a random walk without drift. The least squares estimator is

$$\widehat{\phi} = \frac{\sum_{t=2}^T y_{t-1} y_t}{\sum_{t=2}^T y_{t-1}^2}. \tag{16.35}$$

As y_t is generated by the random walk in (16.34), this expression is used to rewrite (16.35) as

$$\widehat{\phi} = \frac{\sum_{t=2}^{T} y_{t-1}(y_{t-1} + v_t)}{\sum_{t=2}^{T} y_{t-1}^2} = 1 + \frac{\sum_{t=2}^{T} y_{t-1} v_t}{\sum_{t=2}^{T} y_{t-1}^2}.$$

Rearranging and scaling both sides by T gives

$$T(\widehat{\phi} - 1) = \frac{T^{-1} \sum_{t=2}^{T} y_{t-1} v_t}{T^{-2} \sum_{t=2}^{T} y_{t-1}^2}, \tag{16.36}$$

where the choice of scaling is motivated by Example (16.5) and equation (16.32). Thus,

$$\frac{1}{T^2} \sum_{t=2}^{T} y_{t-1}^2 \xrightarrow{d} \sigma^2 \int_0^1 B(s)^2 ds$$

$$\frac{1}{T} \sum_{t=2}^{T} y_{t-1} v_t \xrightarrow{d} \sigma^2 \int_0^1 B(s) dB(s) = \frac{\sigma^2}{2}(B(1)^2 - 1).$$

Using these expressions in (16.36) shows that the least squares estimator, $\widehat{\phi}$, converges weakly to the random variable

$$T(\widehat{\phi} - 1) \xrightarrow{d} \frac{\frac{\sigma^2}{2}(B(1)^2 - 1)}{\sigma^2 \int_0^1 B(s)^2 ds} = \frac{(B(1)^2 - 1)}{2 \int_0^1 B(s)^2 ds}. \tag{16.37}$$

There are two main implications of (16.37).

(1) **Super Consistency**

Since the right-hand side of (16.37) is a random variable independent of T, it follows that

$$T(\widehat{\phi} - 1) = O_p(1),$$

where the subscript p denotes probability. Dividing both sides by T yields

$$\widehat{\phi} - 1 = O_p(T^{-1}),$$

and taking the limit as $T \to \infty$, the right-hand side goes to zero as the random variable is eventually dominated by T^{-1}. That is,

$$\widehat{\phi} - 1 \xrightarrow{p} 0,$$

and $\widehat{\phi}$ is a consistent estimator of $\phi = 1$. As the rate of convergence is T, which is faster than the usual convergence rate of $\sqrt{T}$, the least squares estimator in (16.35) is super consistent.

(2) Non-standard Distribution

The distribution of the random variable in (16.37) is non-standard because it is the ratio of a centered chi-square random variable with one degree of freedom, $0.5(B(1)^2 - 1)$, and a non-normal random variable, $\int_0^1 B(s)^2 ds$. The distribution of the least squares estimator in (16.35) was given in panel (b) of Figure 16.2 based on Monte Carlo simulation, where it was shown to be strongly negatively skewed.

16.6.2   Trend Estimation in the Presence of a Random Walk

Consider the case where the true form of nonstationarity is stochastic given by a random walk with drift but the data are modelled using a deterministic linear trend

$$
\begin{aligned}
\text{True:} \quad & y_t = \delta + y_{t-1} + v_t \\
\text{Specified:} \quad & y_t = \beta_0 + \beta_1 t + e_t,
\end{aligned}
\tag{16.38}
$$

in which v_t and e_t are disturbances, with v_t assumed to be iid $(0, \sigma^2)$. Rewrite the true model as

$$
y_t = \delta t + u_t,
\tag{16.39}
$$

in which, for simplicity, $y_0 = 0$ and u_t is also a disturbance term given by the accumulation of the true disturbance, v_t in (16.38),

$$
u_t = \sum_{i=1}^{t} v_i.
\tag{16.40}
$$

Equation (16.39) shows that if y_t is a random walk with drift δ then it has a linear trend with slope $\beta_1 = \delta$ and a stochastic trend u_t.

The least squares slope estimator of the specified deterministic trend model in (16.38) is

$$
\widehat{\beta}_1 = \frac{\sum_{t=1}^{T}(t - \bar{t})(y_t - \bar{y})}{\sum_{t=1}^{T}(t - \bar{t})^2} = \frac{T\sum_{t=1}^{T} t y_t - \left(\sum_{t=1}^{T} t\right)\left(\sum_{t=1}^{T} y_t\right)}{T\sum_{t=1}^{T} t^2 - \left(\sum_{t=1}^{T} t\right)^2}.
\tag{16.41}
$$

As y_t is generated by (16.39), equation (16.41) is rewritten as

$$
\widehat{\beta}_1 - \delta = \frac{T\sum_{t=1}^{T} t u_t - \sum_{t=1}^{T} t \sum_{t=1}^{T} u_t}{T\sum_{t=1}^{T} t^2 - \left(\sum_{t=1}^{T} t\right)^2},
$$

or

$$
\sqrt{T}(\widehat{\beta}_1 - \delta) = \frac{T^{-5/2}\sum_{t=1}^{T} t u_t - (T^{-2}\sum_{t=1}^{T} t)(T^{-3/2}\sum_{t=1}^{T} u_t)}{T^{-3}\sum_{t=1}^{T} t^2 - (T^{-2}\sum_{t=1}^{T} t)^2}.
\tag{16.42}
$$

Now consider

$$\frac{1}{T^{5/2}} \sum_{t=1}^{T} t u_t \xrightarrow{d} \sigma \int_0^1 s B(s) ds, \qquad \frac{1}{T^{3/2}} \sum_{t=1}^{T} u_t \xrightarrow{d} \sigma \int_0^1 B(s) ds,$$

and from (16.16)

$$\lim_{T \to \infty} \frac{1}{T^2} \sum_{t=1}^{T} t = \frac{1}{2}, \qquad \lim_{T \to \infty} \frac{1}{T^3} \sum_{t=1}^{T} t^2 = \frac{1}{3}.$$

Using these expressions in (16.42) shows that

$$\sqrt{T}(\widehat{\beta}_1 - \delta) \xrightarrow{d} \frac{\sigma \int_0^1 s B(s) ds - \left(\frac{1}{2}\right)\left(\sigma \int_0^1 B(s) ds\right)}{\frac{1}{3} - \left(\frac{1}{2}\right)^2}$$

$$= 12\sigma \left(\int_0^1 s B(s) ds - \frac{1}{2} \int_0^1 B(s) ds \right)$$

$$= 12\sigma \left(\int_0^1 (s - \frac{1}{2}) B(s) ds \right).$$

The distribution of this random variable is known and given by Durlauf and Phillips (1988)

$$\sqrt{T}(\widehat{\beta}_1 - \delta) \xrightarrow{d} N\left(0, \frac{6\sigma^2}{5}\right). \qquad (16.43)$$

Equation (16.43) shows that the least squares estimator $\widehat{\beta}_1$ in (16.41) is consistent and converges to δ at the rate $\sqrt{T}$. To illustrate, the following random walk with drift of $\delta = 0.5$ is simulated for a sample of size $T = 100$

$$y_t = 0.5 + y_{t-1} + v_t,$$

in which $v_t \sim iid\ N(0, 1)$ and $y_0 = 0.0$. The least squares estimates of the deterministic trend model, with t statistics in parentheses, are

$$y_t = \underset{(-1.739)}{-0.683} + \underset{(81.189)}{0.557t} + \widehat{v}_t.$$

The estimate of the slope on the time trend provides a good estimate of the drift parameter $\delta = 0.5$. The t statistic shows that this parameter estimate is highly significant, which is the correct finding in this case since the true value of δ is non-zero. However, Durlauf and Phillips (1988) show that the pertinent t statistic diverges even when $\delta = 0$, so that this t test has an asymptotic size of one and hence cannot be used to test for the presence of a linear trend in the presence of a unit root. Tests of stochastic trends are investigated in Chapter 17.

16.7 Exercises

(1) Nelson-Plosser Data

Program files	nts_nelplos.*
Data files	nelson_plosser.*

The data consist of 14 annual United States macroeconomic time series with varying starting dates spanning the period 1860 to 1970. All of the variables are expressed in natural logarithms with the exception of the bond yield.

(a) Plot the 14 times series and discuss their time series properties.

(b) Compute and interpret the ACF of each series. Compare the results with those reported in Nelson and Plosser (1982, Table 2, p147) as well as in Table 16.1.

(c) Consider the regression equation

$$y_t = \delta + \gamma t + \phi y_{t-1} + v_t, \qquad v_t \sim iid\,(0, \sigma^2).$$

For each series, estimate the following models and interpret the results
(i) Deterministic trend model ($\phi = 0$).
(ii) AR(1) model with drift ($\gamma = 0$).
(iii) AR(1) model with drift and a deterministic trend ($\gamma \neq 0, \sigma \neq 0$).

(d) Simulate the deterministic trend model

$$y_t = 0.1 + 0.2t + e_t, \qquad e_t \sim iid\,N(0, \sigma^2),$$

with $\sigma^2 = 1$ and $T = 111$. Repeat parts (a) to (c).

(e) Simulate the stochastic trend model (random walk with drift)

$$y_t = 0.3 + y_{t-1} + v_t, \qquad v_t \sim iid\,N(0, \sigma^2),$$

with $\sigma^2 = 1$ and $T = 111$. Repeat parts (a) to (c).

(2) Integration

Program files	nts_integration.*

Consider the following four models:

(i) $y_t = \delta + v_t$ [I(0), White noise]
(ii) $y_t = \delta + 0.5y_{t-1} + v_t$ [I(0), Stationary]
(iii) $y_t = \delta + y_{t-1} + v_t$ [I(1), Nonstationary]
(iv) $y_t = \delta + 2y_{t-1} - y_{t-2} + v_t,$ [I(2), Nonstationary]

in which $v_t \sim iid\,N(0, \sigma^2)$ with $\sigma^2 = 1$.

(a) For each model, simulate $T = 200$ observations with the initial condition $y_0 = 0.0$ and with drift parameter $\delta = 0$. Plot the series and compare their time series properties.

(b) Repeat part (a) with drift parameters $\delta = \{0.1, 0.5\}$.

(3) Properties of Moments for Alternative Models

Program files   nts_moment.*

(a) Simulate the AR(1) model

$$y_t = 0.0 + 0.8y_{t-1} + v_t, \qquad v_t \sim iid\ N(0, \sigma^2),$$

with $\sigma^2 = 1$ for $T = \{50, 100, 200, 400, 800, 1600\}$ using 50000 draws and a starting value of $y_0 = 0.0$. For each draw, compute the moments

$$m_i = \frac{1}{T} \sum_{t=1}^{T} y_t^i, \qquad i = 1, 2, 3, 4,$$

and hence the means and variances of these quantities.

(b) Simulate the stochastic trend model (random walk without drift)

$$y_t = y_{t-1} + v_t, \qquad v_t \sim iid\ N(0, \sigma^2),$$

with $\sigma^2 = 1$ for $T = \{50, 100, 200, 400, 800, 1600\}$ using 50000 draws and a starting value of $y_0 = 0.0$. For each draw, compute the moments

$$m_i = \frac{1}{T^{(1+i/2)}} \sum_{t=1}^{T} y_t^i, \qquad i = 1, 2, 3, 4,$$

and the means and variances of these quantities.

(c) Simulate the deterministic trend model

$$y_t = 0.1 + 0.2t + v_t, \qquad v_t \sim iid\ N(0, \sigma^2),$$

with $\sigma^2 = 1$ for $T = \{50, 100, 200, 400, 800, 1600\}$ using 50000 draws and a starting value of $y_0 = 0.0$. For each draw, compute the moments

$$m_i = \frac{1}{T^{(1+i)}} \sum_{t=1}^{T} y_t^i, \qquad i = 1, 2, 3, 4,$$

and the means and variances of these quantities.

(d) Discuss the properties of the moments computed in (a) to (c).

(4) Sampling Distribution of the AR(1) Least Squares Estimator

---

Program files   nts_distribution.*

Consider the AR(1) model

$$y_t = \phi y_{t-1} + v_t, \qquad v_t \sim iid\, N(0, \sigma^2).$$

(a) Simulate the model with $\phi = 0$ and $\sigma^2 = 1$ for samples of size $T = \{50, 100, 200, 400, 800, 1600\}$ using 50000 draws. For each draw, compute the standardised statistic

$$z = \frac{\sqrt{T}(\widehat{\phi} - \phi)}{\sqrt{1 - \phi^2}},$$

where $\widehat{\phi}$ is the least squares estimator from regressing y_t on y_{t-1}. Use a nonparametric kernel to compute the sampling distributions and compare these distributions with the standardised normal distribution. Compute the skewness and kurtosis of the sampling distributions as well as the proportion of $\widehat{\phi}$ draws less than ϕ.

(b) Repeat part (a) with $\phi = 0.8$.

(c) Repeat part (a) with $\phi = 1.0$, except compute the statistic

$$z = T(\widehat{\phi} - \phi).$$

(5) Demonstrating the Functional Central Limit Theorem

Program files   nts_yts.*, nts_fclt.*

(a) Simulate the random walk

$$y_t = y_{t-1} + v_t, \qquad v_t \sim iid\, N(0, \sigma^2),$$

with $\sigma^2 = 1$ and $y_0 = 0$ for a sample size of $T = 5$. Construct the variable

$$y_{[Ts]} = \sum_{j=1}^{[Ts]} v_j,$$

for $s = \{0.2, 0.4, 0.6, 0, 8, 1.0\}$.

(b) Repeat part (a) for $T = 10$ and $s = \{0.1, 0.2, 0.3, \cdots, 1.0\}$.

(c) Repeat part (a) for $T = 40$ and $s = \{1/40, 2/40, 3/40, \cdots, 1.0\}$.

(d) Now simulate the random walk in part (a) 50000 times with a sample of size $T = 500$. For each draw, compute the standardised statistic

$$Y_T(s) = \sigma^{-1} T^{-1/2} y_{[Ts]}, \qquad s = 1/40 \le s \le 1,$$

with $s = \{0.25, 0.5, 1.0\}$ and show that the simulated distributions are $Y_T(s) \xrightarrow{d} N(0, s)$.

(6) Demonstrating the Continuous Mapping Theorem

Program files   nts_cmt.*

Simulate the random walk

$$y_t = y_{t-1} + v_t, \qquad v_t \sim iid\ N(0, \sigma^2),$$

with $\sigma^2 = 1$ and $y_0 = 0$ for a sample size of $T = 500$. The number of draws is 10000.

(a) Given that the moment $m = \sigma^{-1} T^{-1/2} \bar{y} \xrightarrow{d} \int_0^1 B(s) ds$, simulate the sampling distribution of m and verify that its asymptotic distribution is $N(0, 1/3)$.

(b) Given that the moment $m = \sigma^{-1} T^{-5/2} \sum_{t=1}^{T} t y_t \xrightarrow{d} \int_0^1 s B(s) ds$, simulate the sampling distribution of m and verify that its asymptotic distribution is $N(0, 2/15)$.

(7) Simulating the Distribution of Stochastic Integrals

Program files   nts_stochint.*

Consider the random walk

$$y_t = y_{t-1} + v_t, \qquad v_t \sim iid\ N(0, \sigma^2),$$

with $\sigma^2 = 1$ and $y_0 = 0$.

(a) For samples of size $T = \{50, 100, 200, 400, 800, 1600\}$. Simulate the model 50000 times For each draw compute $\frac{1}{T^k} \sum_{t=2}^{T} y_{t-1} v_t$, with scale factors $k = \{1/2, 1.0, 3/2\}$. Compute the mean and variance of the simulated statistics and discuss the properties of these moments for the three different scale factors.

(b) Given that $m = \sigma^{-2} T^{-1} \sum_{t=2}^{T} y_{t-1} v_t \xrightarrow{d} \int_0^1 B(s) d B(s)$, simulate the sampling distribution of m by simulating the model 50000 times for a sample of size $T = 500$. Verify that the asymptotic distribution of m is a centered chi-squared distribution with zero mean and variance $1/2$.

(c) Given that $m = \sigma^{-3} T^{-3/2} \sum_{t=2}^{T} y_{t-1}^2 v_t \xrightarrow{d} \int_0^1 B(s)^2 d B(s)$ from applying the continuous mapping theorem to a stochastic integral, simulate the distribution of the functional by simulating the model 50000 times for a sample of size $T = 500$. Compare the shape of the simulated distribution with the standard normal distribution, $N(0, 1)$.

(8) Simulating a Mixed Normal Distribution

Program files   nts_mixednormal.*

For a sample of size $T = 4000$, simulate two iid normal random variables $v_{1,t}, v_{2,t} \sim N(0, 1)$ and compute the slope coefficient, $\widehat{\beta}$, from a regression of $v_{2,t}$ on $y_{1,t}$, where

$$y_{1,t} = y_{1,t-1} + v_{1,t}.$$

Compute the scaled statistic $T\widehat{\beta}$ and repeat 20000 times. Plot the distribution of $T\widehat{\beta}$ and compare the shape of this distribution with the standard normal distribution based on the mean and the variance of $\widehat{\beta}$.

(9) **Spurious Regression Problem**

Program files   nts_spurious1.*, nts_spurious2.*

A spurious relationship occurs when two independent variables are incorrectly identified as being related. A simple test of independence is based on the estimated correlation coefficient, $\widehat{\rho}$.

(a) Consider the following bivariate models

(i)	$y_{1,t} = v_{1,t}$,		$y_{2,t} = v_{2,t}$
(ii)	$y_{1,t} = y_{1,t-1} + v_{1,t}$,		$y_{2,t} = y_{2,t-1} + v_{2,t}$
(iii)	$y_{1,t} = y_{1,t-1} + v_{1,t}$,		$y_{2,t} = 2y_{2,t-1} - y_{2,t-2} + v_{2,t}$
(iv)	$y_{1,t} = 2y_{1,t-1} - y_{1,t-2} + v_{1,t}$,		$y_{2,t} = 2y_{2,t-1} - y_{2,t-2} + v_{2,t}$

in which $v_{1,t}, v_{2,t}$ are iid $N(0, \sigma^2)$ with $\sigma^2 = 1$. Simulate each bivariate model 10000 times for a sample of size $T = 100$ and compute the correlation coefficient, $\widehat{\rho}$, of each draw. Compute the sampling distributions of $\widehat{\rho}$ for the four sets of bivariate models and discuss the properties of these distributions in the context of the spurious regression problem.

(b) Repeat part (a) with $T = 500$. What do you conclude?

(c) Repeat part (a), except for each draw estimate the regression model

$$y_{2,t} = \beta_0 + \beta_1 y_{1,t} + u_t, \qquad u_t \sim iid\,(0, \sigma^2).$$

Compute the sampling distributions of the least squares estimator $\widehat{\beta}_1$ and its t statistic for the four sets of bivariate models. Discuss the properties of these distributions in the context of the spurious regression problem.

(10) **Trend Estimation in the Presence of a Random Walk**

Program files   nts_trend.*

(a) Simulate the random walk with drift

$$y_t = \delta + y_{t-1} + v_t, \qquad v_t \sim iid\, N(0, \sigma^2),$$

in which the drift parameter is $\delta = 0.5$, $\sigma^2 = 1$ and $y_0 = 0$ for a sample size of $T = 100$. Using the simulated data, estimate the deterministic trend model

$$y_t = \beta_0 + \beta_1 t + e_t,$$

and comment on the parameter estimates $\widehat{\beta}_0$ and $\widehat{\beta}_1$ and the associated t statistics.

(b) Repeat part (a) with drift parameter $\delta = 0.0$.
(c) Repeat parts (a) and (b) for $T = 1000$. Discuss whether increasing the sample size changes the results in parts (a) and (b).
(d) Simulate the random walk with drift model in part (a) 50000 times for a sample of size $T = 5000$. Compute the mean and the variance of the sampling distribution of $\widehat{\beta}_1$ in the deterministic trend model of part (a) and compare these statistics with the moments of the asymptotic distribution $N(0, 6\sigma^2/5)$ given in (16.43).

17 Unit Root Testing

17.1 Introduction

An important conclusion to emerge from Chapter 16 is that many economic and financial time series may exhibit stochastic trends as described by a random walk. This observation suggests that a natural test of a random walk is to estimate the AR(1) model

$$y_t = \phi y_{t-1} + v_t, \qquad v_t \sim iid\,(0, \sigma^2), \tag{17.1}$$

and test whether the slope parameter ϕ is equal to unity using a t test. As the test on the slope is equivalent to testing that the root of the polynomial $(1 - \phi L)$ is unity, these tests are commonly referred to as unit root tests.

When a unit root test is performed, the distribution of the t statistic is non-standard because the process is nonstationary under the null hypothesis of $\phi = 1$. This situation is different from hypothesis tests performed on stationary processes under the null conducted in Chapter 13, where a standard asymptotic distribution arises, based on $\sqrt{T}$ consistency and normality. The results of Chapter 16 show that the least squares estimator $\widehat{\phi}$ in (17.1) has a non-standard distribution expressed in terms of functionals of Brownian motion. It is not too surprising, therefore, that this non-standard distribution of $\widehat{\phi}$ also manifests itself in the distribution of the t statistic.

17.2 Specification

Since the original unit root test proposed by Dickey and Fuller (1979, 1981), there has been an explosion of proposed testing procedures, a survey of which is to be found in Stock (1994) and Maddala and Kim (1998). The major themes of unit root testing may be summarised as follows:

(1) choice of detrending method;
(2) procedures to test $\phi = 1$;
(3) size and power properties of the test statistics;

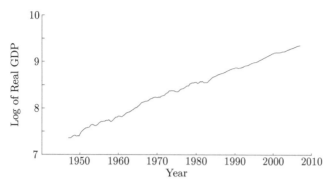

Figure 17.1. The logarithm of real United States GDP for the period March 1947 to March 2007, $T = 241$.

(4) autocorrelation dynamics;
(5) structural breaks; and
(6) the role of initial conditions.

To motivate some of these themes, consider Figure 17.1, which shows a plot of the log of real quarterly United States GDP from March 1947 to March 2007, a sample size of $T = 241$. The series exhibits fluctuations around a strong positive trend, beginning with an initial value of 7.359 in March 1947. The durations and magnitudes of the fluctuations around the trend vary over time reflecting the presence of the business cycle. There also appears to be a break in the trend in the early 1970s corresponding to the slowdown in economic growth following the OPEC oil crisis of 1973.

The time series characteristics of United States GDP in Figure 17.1 suggest the following specification to model its dynamics

$$y_t = \delta + \gamma t + u_t \tag{17.2}$$

$$u_t = \phi u_{t-1} + v_t, \qquad v_t \sim iid\,(0, \sigma^2). \tag{17.3}$$

The first equation captures the deterministic trend features of y_t through the linear trend $\delta + \gamma t$. The second equation captures the stochastic trend features of y_t where a unit root corresponds to $\phi = 1$. Further extensions allowing for richer dynamics are investigated where v_t in (17.3) is permitted to have stationary autocorrelation of a general form (Section 17.7), the inclusion of structural breaks (Section 17.8) and issues related to initial conditions (Section 17.9).

The aim is to test for a unit root in y_t, which, from (17.3), is achieved by testing for a unit root in u_t. The null and alternative hypotheses are

$$\begin{aligned} H_0 &: \phi = 1 \quad \text{[Nonstationary]}\\ H_1 &: \phi < 1. \quad \text{[Stationary]} \end{aligned} \tag{17.4}$$

To implement the test, a two-step approach is adopted.

Step 1: Detrending
Equation (17.2) is estimated to yield the least squares residuals $\widehat{u}_t$, which represent the (deterministic) detrended data

$$\widehat{u}_t = y_t - \widehat{\delta} - \widehat{\gamma} t. \tag{17.5}$$

Step 2: Testing
Using the residuals $\widehat{u}_t$ from the first step, the second step tests for a unit root in (17.3) with u_t replaced by $\widehat{u}_t$.

An advantage of this two-step approach is that within each step a range of options occur, each designed to improve the performance of the unit root test. A further advantage of the two-step approach is that it provides a broad conceptual framework in which to compare alternative strategies to test for unit roots.

17.3   Detrending

Equations (17.2) and (17.3) represent an autocorrelated regression model as discussed in Chapter 7. As the disturbance term has an AR(1) structure, the log-likelihood function for a sample of $t = 1, 2, \cdots, T$, is

$$\ln L_T(\theta) = \frac{1}{T} \ln f(y_1; \theta) + \frac{1}{T} \sum_{t=2}^{T} \ln f(y_t | y_{t-1}; \theta), \tag{17.6}$$

with unknown parameters $\theta = \{\delta, \gamma, \phi\}$. The conditional distribution, $f(y_t | y_{t-1}; \theta)$, in (17.6) is obtained by combining equations (17.2) and (17.3) to derive an expression for y_t, applying the lag operator $(1 - \phi L)$ to both sides of (17.2) and using (17.3) to substitute out u_t. The expression for y_t is

$$(1 - \phi L) y_t = \delta (1 - \phi) + \gamma (1 - \phi L) t + v_t,$$

or

$$y_t - \phi y_{t-1} = \delta (1 - \phi) + \gamma (t - \phi (t - 1)) + v_t. \tag{17.7}$$

Assuming that $v_t \sim iid\ N(0, \sigma^2)$, the logarithm of the conditional distribution in equation (17.6) is

$$\ln f(y_t | y_{t-1}; \theta) = -\frac{1}{2} \ln(2\pi) - \frac{1}{2} \ln \sigma^2$$
$$- \frac{1}{2\sigma^2} (y_t - \phi y_{t-1} - \delta(1 - \phi) - \gamma(t - \phi(t - 1)))^2. \tag{17.8}$$

The marginal distribution, $f(y_1; \theta)$, in equation (17.6) is obtained by writing equations (17.2) and (17.3) at $t = 1$ as

$$y_1 = \delta + \gamma \times 1 + u_1$$
$$u_1 = \phi u_0 + v_1 .$$

By assuming the initial condition $u_0 = 0$, it follows that $u_1 = v_1$. An alternative approach is to specify $u_0 \sim iid(0, \sigma^2/(1 - \phi^2))$ following Elliot (1999). If the assumption of normality for v_t is invoked, the logarithm of the marginal distribution with $u_0 = 0$ is

$$\ln f(y_1; \theta) = -\frac{1}{2} \ln(2\pi) - \frac{1}{2} \ln \sigma^2 - \frac{1}{2\sigma^2} (y_1 - \delta - \gamma)^2 . \qquad (17.9)$$

Substituting (17.8) and (17.9) into (17.6) gives the full log-likelihood function

$$\ln L_T(\theta) = -\frac{1}{2} \ln(2\pi) - \frac{1}{2} \ln \sigma^2 - \frac{1}{2T} \frac{(y_1 - \delta - \gamma)^2}{\sigma^2}$$
$$- \frac{1}{2T\sigma^2} \sum_{t=2}^{T} (y_t - \phi y_{t-1} - \delta(1 - \phi) - \gamma(t - \phi(t - 1)))^2 .$$
$$(17.10)$$

The approach adopted in Chapter 7 to estimate θ is to use an iterative algorithm to compute $\widehat{\theta}$ because of the nonlinear parameter structure of the log-likelihood function. An alternative approach that is commonly followed to test for unit roots is to set $\phi = \phi^*$ in equation (17.7), where ϕ^* is a constant, and estimate the remaining parameters using the full sample of $t = 1, 2, \cdots, T$. Formally the approach consists of using the filter $(1 - \phi^* L)$ to rewrite equation (17.2) as

$$y_t - \phi^* y_{t-1} = \delta(1 - \phi^*) + \gamma(t - \phi^*(t - 1)) + u_t - \phi^* u_{t-1} .$$
$$(17.11)$$

It is convenient to re-express this equation in terms of matrices as

$$y^* = x^* \beta^* + u^* , \qquad (17.12)$$

in which $\beta^* = [\delta \ \gamma]'$ is a (2×1) vector, u^* is the disturbance term of this equation and y^* and x^* are defined, respectively, as

$$y^* = \begin{bmatrix} y_1 \\ y_2 - \phi^* y_1 \\ y_3 - \phi^* y_2 \\ \vdots \\ y_T - \phi^* y_{T-1} \end{bmatrix}, \qquad x^* = \begin{bmatrix} 1 & 1 \\ 1 - \phi^* & 2 - \phi^* \\ 1 - \phi^* & 3 - 2\phi^* \\ \vdots & \vdots \\ 1 - \phi^* & T - (T-1)\phi^* \end{bmatrix} .$$
$$(17.13)$$

Least squares estimation of (17.12) for a particular choice of ϕ^* gives the least squares estimates $\widehat{\beta}^* = \{\widehat{\delta}, \widehat{\gamma}\}$ which are used in (17.5) to compute $\widehat{u}_t$.

Three choices of ϕ^* are as follows:

    1. *Ordinary Least Squares* (Dickey and Fuller, 1979, 1981)
$$\phi^* = 0$$

    2. *Differencing* (Schmidt and Phillips, 1992)
$$\phi^* = 1$$

    3. *Generalised Least Squares* (Elliott, Rothenberg and Stock, 1996)
$$\phi^* = 1 + \frac{\overline{c}}{T}, \text{ where } \begin{cases} \overline{c} = -7 & [\text{Constant } (\delta \neq 0, \gamma = 0)] \\ \overline{c} = -13.5 & [\text{Trend } (\delta \neq 0, \gamma \neq 0)]. \end{cases}$$

17.3.1 Ordinary Least Squares (OLS)

The ordinary least squares detrending approach of setting $\phi^* = 0$ in (17.13) means that the transformed variables y^* and x^* are the original variables

$$y^* = \begin{bmatrix} y_1 \\ y_2 \\ y_3 \\ \vdots \\ y_T \end{bmatrix}, \qquad x^* = \begin{bmatrix} 1 & 1 \\ 1 & 2 \\ 1 & 3 \\ \vdots & \vdots \\ 1 & T \end{bmatrix}. \tag{17.14}$$

In this case estimation of (17.12) by ordinary least squares is equivalent to estimating (17.2) directly by ordinary least squares and the residuals from this regression are then the detrended data as in (17.5).

This suggestion is very closely related to the original Dickey-Fuller regressions. Suppose that (17.2) just includes a constant ($\gamma = 0$), in which case (17.7) is

$$y_t = \delta (1 - \phi) + \phi y_{t-1} + v_t, \quad t = 2, \cdots, T. \tag{17.15}$$

The ordinary least squares estimator of ϕ in (17.15) is

$$\widehat{\phi}_{DF} = \frac{\sum_{t=2}^{T} (y_t - \overline{y}_{(0)}) (y_{t-1} - \overline{y}_{(1)})}{\sum_{t=2}^{T} (y_{t-1} - \overline{y}_{(1)})^2}, \tag{17.16}$$

in which $\overline{y}_{(0)} = (T-1)^{-1} \sum_{t=2}^{T} y_t$ and $\overline{y}_{(1)} = (T-1)^{-1} \sum_{t=2}^{T} y_{t-1}$. By comparison, (17.5) in this case is $\widehat{u}_t = y_t - \overline{y}$, where $\overline{y} = T^{-1} \sum_{t=1}^{T} y_t$, and so the ordinary least squares estimator of ϕ obtained by substituting $\widehat{u}_t$ into (17.3) is

$$\widehat{\phi} = \frac{\sum_{t=2}^{T} (y_t - \overline{y}) (y_{t-1} - \overline{y})}{\sum_{t=2}^{T} (y_{t-1} - \overline{y})^2}. \tag{17.17}$$

The terms $\bar{y}$, $\bar{y}_{(0)}$ and $\bar{y}_{(1)}$ only differ in whether or not they include the observations y_1 and y_T. Comparing (17.16) and (17.17) shows that the estimation of (17.15) by ordinary least squares is very closely related to the two-step estimation of (17.2) and (17.3). Indeed, $\widehat{\phi}_{DF}$ and $\widehat{\phi}$ are asymptotically equivalent.

17.3.2   First Differences

This approach involves evaluating the model under the null hypothesis of a unit root by imposing the restrictions $\phi^* = 1$ and $u_0 = 0$ on (17.3) so that the transformed variables y^* and x^* in (17.13) become

$$
y^* = \begin{bmatrix} y_1 \\ y_2 - y_1 \\ y_3 - y_2 \\ \vdots \\ y_T - y_{T-1} \end{bmatrix}, \qquad x^* = \begin{bmatrix} 1 & 1 \\ 0 & 1 \\ 0 & 1 \\ \vdots & \vdots \\ 0 & 1 \end{bmatrix}. \tag{17.18}
$$

Once the parameter estimates $\widehat{\delta}$ and $\widehat{\gamma}$ are computed by least squares applied to equation (17.12) with y^* and x^* defined as in (17.18), the detrended data are computed using (17.5).

The first differencing detrending method is equivalent to estimating (17.2) in first differences to obtain the parameter estimates, but using the levels equation in (17.2) to compute the detrended data given by $\widehat{u}_t$. The ability of the first-differenced form of (17.2) to estimate all parameters, including the intercept δ, stems from the treatment of the initial condition in (17.18). In the case where (17.2) just includes a constant ($\gamma = 0$), the least squares estimator of δ is

$$
\widehat{\delta} = \frac{\sum_{t=1}^{T} x_t^* y_t^*}{\sum_{t=1}^{T} (x_t^*)^2} = y_1.
$$

The mean of y_t is now estimated by the single observation y_1, which is an unbiased but inconsistent estimator of δ. If (17.2) includes a constant and a time trend, the least squares estimators of δ and γ are

$$
\begin{bmatrix} \widehat{\delta} \\ \widehat{\gamma} \end{bmatrix} = \begin{bmatrix} 1 & 1 \\ 1 & T \end{bmatrix}^{-1} \begin{bmatrix} y_1 \\ y_1 + \sum_{t=2}^{T} \Delta y_t \end{bmatrix} = \frac{1}{T-1} \begin{bmatrix} T y_1 - y_T \\ y_T - y_1 \end{bmatrix},
$$

which have the property

$$
\widehat{\delta} + \widehat{\gamma} = \frac{T y_1 - y_T}{T-1} + \frac{y_T - y_1}{T-1} = \frac{(T-1) y_1}{T-1} = y_1.
$$

17.3.3 Generalised Least Squares (GLS)

Instead of evaluating ϕ at the null as in the first differencing detrending method, the GLS approach is to choose a value that is in the stationary region, but nonetheless near $\phi = 1$, that is local to the null. The approach is to define some fixed value $\phi^* < 1$ as

$$\phi^* = 1 + \frac{\bar{c}}{T},$$

in which $\bar{c} < 0$ is itself a fixed value that depends on which deterministic variables are included in (17.2). The choices of $\bar{c} = -7$ (constant) and $\bar{c} = -13.5$ (constant and linear trend) are justified in Section 17.6. The transformed variables y^* and x^* in (17.13) for the case of a constant and a time trend become

$$y^* = \begin{bmatrix} y_1 \\ y_2 - (1 + \frac{\bar{c}}{T})y_1 \\ y_3 - (1 + \frac{\bar{c}}{T})y_2 \\ \vdots \\ y_T - (1 + \frac{\bar{c}}{T})y_{T-1} \end{bmatrix}, \quad x^* = \begin{bmatrix} 1 & 1 \\ 1 - (1 + \frac{\bar{c}}{T}) & 2 - (1 + \frac{\bar{c}}{T}) \\ 1 - (1 + \frac{\bar{c}}{T}) & 3 - 2(1 + \frac{\bar{c}}{T}) \\ \vdots & \vdots \\ 1 - (1 + \frac{\bar{c}}{T}) & T - (T - 1)(1 + \frac{\bar{c}}{T}) \end{bmatrix},$$

$$(17.19)$$

which depend on the sample size, T. Least squares estimation of equation (17.12), with y^* and x^* defined as in (17.19), yields the parameter estimates $\widehat{\delta}$ and $\widehat{\gamma}$ and the detrended data are again computed using (17.5).

The previous two detrending methods are special cases of the generalised least squares approach based on fixed values of the AR(1) coefficient. This method is also referred to as quasi-differencing and partial generalised least squares, see Phillips and Lee (1995). The ordinary least squares detrending approach is given by setting $\bar{c} = -T$, and the first-difference detrending approach is given by setting $\bar{c} = 0$.

Example 17.1 Effects of Different Detrending Methods on GDP
The effects of the three detrending methods on United States GDP are given in Figure 17.2, which contains plots of the residuals $\widehat{u}_t$ from estimating (17.5). A time trend is included in the detrending so $\bar{c} = -13.5$ and the generalised least squares filter is based on setting

$$\phi^* = 1 - \frac{13.5}{241} = 0.9440.$$

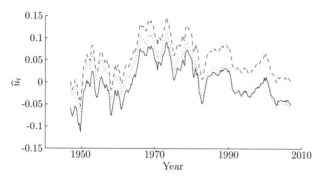

Figure 17.2. Different detrending methods applied to the logarithm of real United States GDP for the period March 1947 to March 2007. The detrending methods used are ordinary least squares detrending (solid line), first-difference detrending (dashed line) and generalised least squares detrending (dotted line).

The estimated trend equations are

OLS	$(\phi^* = 0)$	:	$y_t = 7.410223 + 0.008281\ t + \widehat{u}_t$
Differencing	$(\phi^* = 1)$	:	$y_t = 7.350836 + 0.008313\ t + \widehat{u}_t$
GLS	$(\phi^* = 0.9440)$	:	$y_t = 7.362268 + 0.008521\ t + \widehat{u}_t$.

All three methods yield very similar patterns. The generalised least squares detrended GDP initially tracks the first-differenced detrended GDP, eventually drifting towards the ordinary least squares detrended series. □

17.4 Testing

Tests of the null hypothesis set out in expression (17.4) that $\phi = 1$ in equation (17.3) are now considered. These tests are based on the detrended data $\widehat{u}_t$ from equation (17.5), with the estimates $\widehat{\beta}^*$ obtained from estimating (17.12) using one of the detrending methods described in Section 17.3. Two broad classes of tests are discussed: the Dickey-Fuller test proposed by Dickey and Fuller (1979, 1981) and the class of M tests proposed by Stock (1999) and Perron and Ng (1996). For an alternative Bayesian perspective on testing for unit roots, see Phillips (1991c).

17.4.1 Dickey-Fuller Tests

As v_t is *iid*, the ordinary least squares estimator of ϕ in (17.3) is obtained by regressing $\widehat{u}_t$ on $\widehat{u}_{t-1}$ to obtain

$$\widehat{\phi} = \frac{\sum_{t=2}^{T} \widehat{u}_t \widehat{u}_{t-1}}{\sum_{t=2}^{T} \widehat{u}_{t-1}^2}.$$

(17.20)

Two versions of the Dickey-Fuller test are given based on (17.20). The first is

$$DF_\alpha = T(\widehat{\phi} - 1),$$ (17.21)

while the second is the t statistic evaluated under the null of a unit root, $\phi = 1$, given by

$$DF_t = \frac{\widehat{\phi} - 1}{\text{se}(\widehat{\phi})}.$$ (17.22)

An equivalent approach is to rearrange (17.3) by subtracting u_{t-1} from both sides to obtain

$$\Delta u_t = (\phi - 1)u_{t-1} + v_t$$
$$= \alpha u_{t-1} + v_t,$$ (17.23)

in which $\alpha = \phi - 1$. A test of $\phi = 1$ is now a test of $\alpha = 0$ so that the hypotheses in terms of α are

$$\begin{aligned} H_0 &: \alpha = 0 \quad \text{[Nonstationary]} \\ H_1 &: \alpha < 0. \quad \text{[Stationary]} \end{aligned}$$ (17.24)

The Dickey-Fuller test now requires regressing $\Delta \widehat{u}_t$ on $\widehat{u}_{t-1}$ to obtain

$$\widehat{\alpha} = \frac{\sum_{t=2}^{T} \Delta \widehat{u}_t \widehat{u}_{t-1}}{\sum_{t=2}^{T} \widehat{u}_{t-1}^2},$$ (17.25)

and computing the usual regression t statistic

$$DF_t = \frac{\widehat{\alpha}}{\text{se}(\widehat{\alpha})}.$$ (17.26)

The test statistics (17.22) and (17.26) give identical results since $\widehat{\alpha} = \widehat{\phi} - 1$ and $\text{se}(\widehat{\alpha}) = \text{se}(\widehat{\phi})$, although (17.26) is often computed for convenience as all computer packages automatically report t tests of parameters being zero.

17.4.2 M Tests

The M tests are given by

$$MZ_\alpha = \frac{\dfrac{1}{2}\left(T^{-1}\widehat{u}_T^2 - \widehat{\sigma}^2\right)}{\left(T^{-2}\sum_{t=2}^{T}\widehat{u}_{t-1}^2\right)}$$ (17.27)

$$MSB = \left(\frac{T^{-2}\sum_{t=2}^{T}\widehat{u}_{t-1}^2}{\widehat{\sigma}^2}\right)^{1/2}$$ (17.28)

$$MZ_t = MZ_\alpha \times MSB = \frac{\frac{1}{2}\left(T^{-1}\widehat{u}_T^2 - \widehat{\sigma}^2\right)}{\widehat{\sigma}\left(T^{-2}\sum_{t=2}^{T}\widehat{u}_{t-1}^2\right)^{1/2}},$$ (17.29)

where

$$\widehat{\sigma}^2 = \frac{1}{T-1}\sum_{t=2}^{T}\widehat{v}_t^2,$$ (17.30)

and $\widehat{v}_t$ are the residuals from the regression of $\Delta\widehat{u}_t$ on $\widehat{u}_{t-1}$ used to compute the Dickey-Fuller test.

The two Dickey-Fuller statistics in (17.21) and (17.26) and the three M tests in (17.27) to (17.29) are quite closely related. To understand this relationship, consider the identity $\widehat{u}_t = \widehat{u}_{t-1} + \Delta\widehat{u}_t$. Squaring both sides of this identity and summing over t gives

$$\sum_{t=2}^{T}\widehat{u}_t^2 = \sum_{t=2}^{T}\widehat{u}_{t-1}^2 + 2\sum_{t=2}^{T}\Delta\widehat{u}_t\widehat{u}_{t-1} + \sum_{t=2}^{T}(\Delta\widehat{u}_t)^2,$$

which, upon rearranging, yields

$$\sum_{t=2}^{T}\Delta\widehat{u}_t\widehat{u}_{t-1} = \frac{1}{2}\left(\sum_{t=2}^{T}\widehat{u}_t^2 - \sum_{t=2}^{T}\widehat{u}_{t-1}^2 - \sum_{t=2}^{T}(\Delta\widehat{u}_t)^2\right)$$

$$= \frac{1}{2}\left(\widehat{u}_T^2 - \widehat{u}_1^2 - \sum_{t=2}^{T}\Delta\widehat{u}_t^2\right).$$

From the Dickey-Fuller statistic in (17.21) with $\widehat{\alpha}$ defined as (17.25), it follows that

$$DF_\alpha = T\widehat{\alpha} = \frac{T\sum_{t=2}^{T}\Delta\widehat{u}_t\widehat{u}_{t-1}}{\sum_{t=2}^{T}\widehat{u}_{t-1}^2}$$

$$= \frac{\frac{1}{2}\left(T^{-1}\widehat{u}_T^2 - T^{-1}\widehat{u}_1^2 - T^{-1}\sum_{t=2}^{T}\Delta\widehat{u}_t^2\right)}{T^{-2}\sum_{t=2}^{T}\widehat{u}_{t-1}^2}.$$ (17.31)

Using (17.31), the Dickey-Fuller version of the t test in (17.26) is

$$DF_t = \frac{\frac{1}{2}\left(T^{-1}\widehat{u}_T^2 - T^{-1}\widehat{u}_1^2 - T^{-1}\sum_{t=2}^{T}\Delta\widehat{u}_t^2\right)}{\widehat{\sigma}\left(T^{-2}\sum_{t=2}^{T}\widehat{u}_{t-1}^2\right)^{1/2}}.$$ (17.32)

A comparison of MZ_α in (17.27) and DF_α in (17.31) shows that the two tests are closely related, with two differences. The first is that the initial residual term $T^{-1}\widehat{u}_1^2$ appears in DF_α but not in MZ_α. This initial term disappears asymptotically in some cases. The second difference is that MZ_α has the residual variance $\widehat{\sigma}^2$ while DF_α uses the dependent variable variance $T^{-1}\sum_{t=2}^{T}\Delta\widehat{u}_t^2$. These variances are asymptotically equivalent under the null hypothesis. Similarly, the MZ_t test is closely related to the Dickey-Fuller t test.

17.5   Distribution Theory

This section presents the asymptotic null distributions of five possible test statistics, namely DF_α, DF_t, MZ_α, MSB and MZ_t statistics. A feature of these unit root tests is that they depend only on the residual process $\widehat{u}_t$. With an appropriate FCLT from Chapter 16 for $\widehat{u}_t$, the asymptotic distributions of all of the statistics follow reasonably straightforwardly and are all functionals of Brownian motion. The specific form of the Brownian motion appearing in these distributions depends on the type of detrending used and on the choice of deterministic variables in the detrending regression. For ease of exposition, the basic distributional results are given first in terms of a generic Brownian motion functional $B_X(s)$, the various forms of which are then derived in Sections 17.5.1 and 17.5.2.

Distribution of the DF_α test
The asymptotic distribution of the DF_α test in equation (17.31) is

$$DF_\alpha = \frac{\frac{1}{2}\left(\frac{1}{T}\widehat{u}_T^2 - \frac{1}{T}\widehat{u}_1^2 - \frac{1}{T}\sum_{t=2}^{T}\Delta\widehat{u}_t^2\right)}{\frac{1}{T^2}\sum_{t=2}^{T}\widehat{u}_{t-1}^2} \xrightarrow{d} \frac{\frac{1}{2}\left(B_X(1)^2 - B_X(0)^2 - 1\right)}{\int_0^1 B_X(s)^2 ds},$$

(17.33)

which uses the results

$$\frac{1}{T}\widehat{u}_T^2 \xrightarrow{d} \sigma^2 B_X(1)^2, \quad \frac{1}{T}\widehat{u}_0^2 \xrightarrow{d} \sigma^2 B_X(0)^2, \quad \frac{1}{T^2}\sum_{t=2}^{T}\widehat{u}_{t-1}^2 \xrightarrow{d} \sigma^2\int_0^1 B_X(s)^2 ds.$$

Distribution of the DF_t test
The asymptotic distribution of the DF_t test in equation (17.32) is

$$DF_t = \frac{\frac{1}{2}\left(\frac{1}{T}\widehat{u}_T^2 - \frac{1}{T}\widehat{u}_1^2 - \frac{1}{T}\sum_{t=2}^{T}\Delta\widehat{u}_t^2\right)}{\widehat{\sigma}\left(\frac{1}{T^2}\sum_{t=2}^{T}\widehat{u}_{t-1}^2\right)^{1/2}} \xrightarrow{d} \frac{\frac{1}{2}\left(B_X(1)^2 - B_X(0)^2 - 1\right)}{\left(\int_0^1 B_X(s)^2 ds\right)^{1/2}},$$

(17.34)

which uses the additional result

$$
\begin{aligned}
\frac{1}{T} \sum_{t=2}^{T} \widehat{v}_t^2 &= \frac{1}{T} \sum_{t=2}^{T} (\Delta \widehat{u}_t - \widehat{\alpha} \widehat{u}_{t-1})^2 \\
&= \frac{1}{T} \sum_{t=2}^{T} \Delta \widehat{u}_t^2 - \frac{1}{T} \times (T\widehat{\alpha})^2 \times \frac{1}{T^2} \sum_{t=2}^{T} \widehat{u}_{t-1}^2 \\
&= \frac{1}{T} \sum_{t=2}^{T} \Delta \widehat{u}_t^2 + o_p(1),
\end{aligned}
$$

so that $\widehat{\sigma}^2 \overset{p}{\to} \sigma^2$.

Distribution of the MZ_α test
The asymptotic distribution of the MZ_α test in equation (17.27) is

$$
MZ_\alpha = \frac{\frac{1}{2} \left(\frac{1}{T} \widehat{u}_T^2 - \widehat{\sigma}^2 \right)}{\left(\frac{1}{T^2} \sum_{t=2}^{T} \widehat{u}_{t-1}^2 \right)} \overset{d}{\to} \frac{\frac{1}{2} \left(B_X(1)^2 - 1 \right)}{\int_0^1 B_X(s)^2 ds}. \tag{17.35}
$$

Distribution of the MSB test
The asymptotic distribution of the MSB test (17.28) is

$$
MSB = \left(\frac{\frac{1}{T^2} \sum_{t=2}^{T} \widehat{u}_{t-1}^2}{\widehat{\sigma}^2} \right)^{1/2} \overset{d}{\to} \left(\int_0^1 B_X(s)^2 ds \right)^{1/2}. \tag{17.36}
$$

Distribution of the MZ_t test
The asymptotic distribution of the MZ_t test (17.29) is

$$
MZ_t = \frac{\frac{1}{2} \left(\frac{1}{T} \widehat{u}_T^2 - \widehat{\sigma}^2 \right)}{\widehat{\sigma} \left(\frac{1}{T^2} \sum_{t=2}^{T} \widehat{u}_{t-1}^2 \right)^{1/2}} \overset{d}{\to} \frac{\frac{1}{2} \left(B_X(1)^2 - 1 \right)}{\left(\int_0^1 B_X(s)^2 ds \right)^{1/2}}. \tag{17.37}
$$

The relevant forms of the Brownian motions in the asymptotic distributions in equations (17.33) to (17.37) are now derived for ordinary least squares and generalised least squares detrending. To derive these results it is useful to express the detrended residuals from (17.5) in the form

$$
\widehat{u}_t = u_t - x_t' \left[\sum_{t=1}^{T} x_t^* x_t^{*'} \right]^{-1} \sum_{t=1}^{T} x_t^* u_t^*, \tag{17.38}
$$

where u^* is defined in (17.12). Under the null hypothesis of a unit root in $\widehat{u}_t$, the basic FCLT states

$$\frac{1}{\sqrt{T}} u_{[Ts]} = \frac{1}{\sqrt{T}} \sum_{t=1}^{[Ts]} u_t \xrightarrow{d} \sigma B(s),$$

which is used in the derivations that follow.

17.5.1 Ordinary Least Squares Detrending

The detrended ordinary least squares residuals are given by equation (17.38) where y^* and x^* are defined in equation (17.14).

Constant

In the case of detrending based on a constant, $x_t^* = 1$ and

$$\widehat{u}_t = u_t - \frac{1}{T} \sum_{t=1}^{T} u_t .$$

since now $u_t^* = u_t$. It follows, therefore, that

$$\frac{1}{\sqrt{T}} \widehat{u}_{[Ts]} = \frac{1}{\sqrt{T}} u_{[Ts]} - \frac{1}{T^{3/2}} \sum_{t=1}^{T} u_{[Ts]} \xrightarrow{d} \sigma \left(B(s) - \int_0^1 B(s)ds \right)$$

$$= \sigma B_X(s) . \tag{17.39}$$

which is demeaned Brownian motion.

Constant and Time Trend

In the case of detrending based on a constant and a time trend, $x_t^* = [\,1\ t\,]'$ and

$$\widehat{u}_t = u_t - \begin{bmatrix} 1 \\ t \end{bmatrix}' \left[\sum_{t=1}^{T} \begin{bmatrix} 1 & t \\ t & t^2 \end{bmatrix} \right]^{-1} \sum_{t=1}^{T} \begin{bmatrix} 1 \\ t \end{bmatrix} u_t.$$

Let $D_T = \text{diag}(1, T^{-1})$ so that

$$D_T x_{[Ts]}^* = \begin{bmatrix} 1 & 0 \\ 0 & T^{-1} \end{bmatrix} \begin{bmatrix} 1 \\ [Ts] \end{bmatrix} \xrightarrow{d} \begin{bmatrix} 1 \\ s \end{bmatrix} .$$

Now

$$\frac{1}{\sqrt{T}}\widehat{u}_{[Ts]} = \frac{1}{\sqrt{T}}u_{[Ts]}$$

$$-\begin{bmatrix}1\\t\end{bmatrix}' D_T \left[D_T \sum_{t=1}^{T} \begin{bmatrix}1 & t\\t & t^2\end{bmatrix} D_T \right]^{-1} \frac{1}{\sqrt{T}} \sum_{t=1}^{T} D_T \begin{bmatrix}1\\t\end{bmatrix} u_t$$

$$\xrightarrow{d} \sigma \left(B(s) - \begin{bmatrix}1\\s\end{bmatrix}' \left[\int_0^1 \begin{bmatrix}1 & t\\t & t^2\end{bmatrix} ds \right]^{-1} \int_0^1 \begin{bmatrix}1\\s\end{bmatrix} B(s) ds \right)$$

$$= \sigma \left(B(s) - \begin{bmatrix}1\\s\end{bmatrix}' \begin{bmatrix}1 & 1/2\\1/2 & 1/3\end{bmatrix}^{-1} \int_0^1 \begin{bmatrix}1\\s\end{bmatrix} B(s) ds \right)$$

$$= \sigma \left(B(s) - (4 - 6s) \int_0^1 B(s) ds + (6 - 12s) \int_0^1 s B(s) ds \right)$$

$$= \sigma B_X(s),\tag{17.40}$$

which represents detrended Brownian motion.

It follows, therefore, that for detrending by ordinary least squares, the appropriate Brownian motions for the purposes of deriving the asymptotic distributions of the unit root tests in expressions (17.33) to (17.37) are the expressions for $B_X(s)$ in equations (17.39) and (17.40), respectively.

17.5.2 Generalised Least Squares Detrending

The detrended generalised least squares residuals are given by equation (17.38) where y^* and x^* are defined in equation (17.19) with $\phi^* = 1 + \bar{c}/T$.

Constant

In the case of detrending based on a constant, $x_1^* = 1$ and $x_t^* = -\bar{c}/T$ for $t = 2, \cdots, T$ so that

$$\sum_{t=1}^{T} x_t^* x_t^{*\prime} = x_1^* x_1^{*\prime} + \sum_{t=2}^{T} x_t^* x_t^{*\prime} = 1^2 + \sum_{t=2}^{T} \left(\frac{\bar{c}}{T}\right)^2 = 1 + \bar{c}^2 \frac{T-1}{T^2}$$

$$= 1 + o(1).\tag{17.41}$$

Since $\phi^* = 1 + \bar{c}T^{-1}$ it follows that

$$u_t^* = u_t - (1 + \bar{c}T^{-1})u_{t-1} = \Delta u_t - \bar{c}T^{-1}u_{t-1},$$

and

$$\sum_{t=1}^{T} x_t^* u_t^* = x_1^* u_1^* + \sum_{t=2}^{T} x_t^* u_t^*$$

$$= u_1 - \frac{\bar{c}}{T} \sum_{t=2}^{T} u_t^*$$

$$= u_1 - \frac{\bar{c}}{T} \sum_{t=2}^{T} (\Delta u_t - \frac{\bar{c}}{T} u_{t-1})$$

$$= u_1 - \frac{\bar{c}}{T} \sum_{t=2}^{T} \Delta u_t + \left(\frac{\bar{c}}{T}\right)^2 \sum_{t=2}^{T} u_{t-1}$$

$$= u_1 - \frac{\bar{c}}{T} (u_T - u_1) + \left(\frac{\bar{c}}{T}\right)^2 \sum_{t=2}^{T} u_{t-1}$$

$$= \left(1 + \frac{\bar{c}}{T}\right) u_1 - \frac{\bar{c}}{T} u_T + \left(\frac{\bar{c}}{T}\right)^2 \sum_{t=2}^{T} u_{t-1}$$

$$= u_1 + o_p(1). \tag{17.42}$$

The results in (17.41) and (17.42) may now be substituted in equation (17.38) to give

$$\frac{1}{\sqrt{T}} \widehat{u}_{[Ts]} = \frac{1}{\sqrt{T}} u_{[Ts]} - \frac{1}{\sqrt{T}} (1 + o(1))^{-1} (u_1 + o_p(1)) \xrightarrow{d} \sigma B(s). \tag{17.43}$$

The unit root tests have asymptotic distributions as given in equations (17.33) to (17.37), where $B_X(s) = B(s)$. That is, unlike ordinary least squares detrending on a constant, generalised least squares has no asymptotic effect on the asymptotic distribution of the residual process $\widehat{u}_{[Ts]}$. Furthermore, since $B(0) = 0$, it follows that DF_α^{GLS} and DF_t^{GLS} are asymptotically equivalent to MZ_α^{GLS} and MZ_t^{GLS}, respectively, under the null hypothesis.

Constant and Time Trend
In the case of detrending based on a constant and linear trend, $x_1^* = [1 \ 1]'$ and $x_t^* = [-\bar{c}T^{-1}, 1 - (t-1)\bar{c}T^{-1}]'$ for $t > 1$, which uses the result that the quasi-differenced trend variable is given by

$$t - (t-1)\phi^* = t - (t-1)\left(1 + \bar{c}T^{-1}\right) = 1 - (t-1)\bar{c}T^{-1}.$$

The procedure is now similar to that adopted for generalised least squares detrending with only a constant term present. Expressions are sought for the appropriately scaled sums $\sum_{t=1}^{T} D_T x_t^* x_t^{*'} D_T$ and $D_T \sum_{t=1}^{T} x_t^* u_t^*$, where the scaling is given by the diagonal matrix $D_T = \text{diag}(1, T^{-1/2})$. In this case it can be shown that

$$T^{-1/2}\widehat{u}_{[Ts]} = T^{-1/2}u_{[Ts]} - T^{-1/2}x'_{[Ts]}D_T\left[D_T\sum_{t=1}^{T}x_t^*x_t^{*\prime}D_T\right]^{-1}\left[D_T\sum_{t=1}^{T}x_t^*u_t^*\right]$$

$$= T^{-1/2}u_{[Ts]} - \left[\begin{array}{c}T^{-1/2}\\ [Ts]/T\end{array}\right]'\left[\begin{array}{cc}1 & 0\\ 0 & 1-\bar{c}+\bar{c}^2/3\end{array}\right]^{-1}$$

$$\times\left[\begin{array}{c}(1+\dfrac{\bar{c}}{T})u_1 - \bar{c}T^{-1}u_T + \bar{c}^2 T^{-2}\displaystyle\sum_{t=2}^{T}u_{t-1}\\[2mm] (1-\bar{c}\dfrac{T-1}{T})T^{-1/2}u_T + \dfrac{\bar{c}^2}{T^{5/2}}\displaystyle\sum_{t=2}^{T-1}tu_t - (1-\dfrac{\bar{c}^2}{T^2})T^{-1/2}u_1\end{array}\right]$$

$$+\; o_p(1)$$

$$\xrightarrow{d}\;\sigma(B(s) - s\left(\frac{1-\bar{c}}{1-\bar{c}+\bar{c}^2/3}B(1) + \frac{\bar{c}^2}{1-\bar{c}+\bar{c}^2/3}\int_0^1 sB(s)ds\right))$$

$$= \sigma B_{\bar{c}}(s)\,, \tag{17.44}$$

in which $B_{\bar{c}}(s)$ represents generalised least squares detrended Brownian motion.

For generalised least squares detrending with both a constant and linear trend, therefore, the asymptotic distributions given in equations (17.33) to (17.37) require that $B_X(s)$ is replaced by $B_{\bar{c}}(s)$ from (17.44). Since $B_{\bar{c}}(0) = 0$, it again follows that DF_α^{GLS} and DF_t^{GLS} are asymptotically equivalent to MZ_α^{GLS} and MZ_t^{GLS}, respectively, under the null hypothesis.

17.5.3   Simulating Critical Values

The simplest method of obtaining critical values from the non-standard distributions involving Brownian motion is to simulate the distributions of the relevant test statistics. To obtain the critical values for unit root tests by simulation requires the following steps.

Step 1: Generate a sample of size T from $y_t = y_{t-1} + v_t$, $v_t \sim iid\ N(0, \sigma^2)$ with $\sigma^2 = 1$ and $y_0 = 0$.

Step 2: Compute each of the unit root statistics using (a) ordinary and generalised least squares demeaning and (b) ordinary and generalised least squares linear detrending.

Step 3: Repeat Steps 1 and 2 a large number of times, say 1000000 replications to generate a distribution of each statistic.

Step 4: Compute the quantiles of the various statistics.

The simulated 5% critical values are reported in Table 17.1 for the DF_t and the MZ_t tests for sample sizes $T = \{25, 50, 100, 250, 500, 1000\}$. Computed

Table 17.1. *Simulated 5% critical values for the Dickey-Fuller and M tests for alternative sample sizes. Based on 1000000 replications*

	Sample Size					
	25	50	100	250	500	1000
	Constant					
DF_t^{OLS}	−3.089	−2.972	−2.913	−2.885	−2.872	−2.866
MZ_t^{OLS}	−2.036	−2.250	−2.357	−2.432	−2.455	−2.467
DF_t/MZ_t^{GLS}	−2.559	−2.297	−2.138	−2.031	−1.988	−1.966
	Constant and linear trend					
DF_t^{OLS}	−3.812	−3.601	−3.500	−3.446	−3.428	−3.420
MZ_t^{OLS}	−2.327	−2.710	−2.921	−3.059	−3.107	−3.130
DF_t/MZ_t^{GLS}	−3.580	−3.219	−3.035	−2.925	−2.886	−2.867

values of the test statistic less than the critical value lead to a rejection of the null hypothesis of a unit root at the 5% level.

These simulated critical values should not be considered as exact finite sample critical values but rather as asymptotic approximations. They would only be exact if the disturbances in the observed data are actually normally distributed. Whether or not asymptotic critical values are superior to finite sample critical values is a question for Monte Carlo experimentation in each different case.

Example 17.2 Unit Root Test of GDP

The ordinary least squares detrended residuals from detrending GDP in Example 17.1 have the following summary statistics

$$\sum_{t=2}^{T} \widehat{u}_{t-1}^2 = 0.4103, \quad \sum_{t=2}^{T} (\widehat{u}_t - \widehat{u}_{t-1}) \widehat{u}_{t-1} = -0.0120, \quad \widehat{u}_T = -0.0515,$$

where $T = 241$. The estimated regression equation to perform the unit root tests is

$$\widehat{u}_t - \widehat{u}_{t-1} = -0.0291 \widehat{u}_{t-1} + \widehat{v}_t,$$

where the sum of squared residuals from this regression is $\sum_{t=2}^{T} \widehat{v}_t^2 = 0.0227$. The slope is computed using the summary statistics as $\widehat{\alpha} = -0.0120/0.4103 = -0.0291$ and the residual variance is

$$\widehat{\sigma}^2 = \frac{1}{T-1} \sum_{t=2}^{T} \widehat{v}_t^2 = \frac{0.0227}{241-1} = 0.9457 \times 10^{-4}.$$

The Dickey-Fuller statistics based on ordinary least squares detrending are

$$DF_\alpha^{OLS} = T\widehat{\alpha} = -241 \times 0.0291 = -7.0238$$

$$DF_t^{OLS} = \frac{\widehat{\alpha}}{se\,(\widehat{\alpha})} = \frac{-0.0291}{\sqrt{\dfrac{0.9457 \times 10^{-4}}{0.4103}}} = -1.9197\,.$$

The M statistics based on ordinary least squares detrending are calculated as

$$MZ_\alpha^{OLS} = \frac{\dfrac{1}{2}\left(T^{-1}\widehat{u}_T^2 - \widehat{\sigma}^2\right)}{T^{-2}\sum_{t=2}^{T}\widehat{u}_{t-1}^2} = \frac{\dfrac{1}{2}\left(241^{-1}(-0.0515)^2 - 0.9457 \times 10^{-4}\right)}{241^{-2} \times 0.4103}$$

$$= -5.9146$$

$$MSB^{OLS} = \left(\frac{T^{-2}\sum_{t=2}^{T}\widehat{u}_{t-1}^2}{\widehat{\sigma}^2}\right)^{1/2} = \left(\frac{241^{-2} \times 0.4103}{0.9457 \times 10^{-4}}\right)^{1/2} = 0.2733$$

$$MZ_t^{OLS} = MZ_\alpha^{OLS} \times MSB^{OLS} = -5.9146 \times 0.2733 = -1.6166\,.$$

Replacing the ordinary least squares detrended residuals with the generalised least squares detrended residuals from Example 17.1 yields the alternative test statistics

$$DF_\alpha^{GLS} = -4.1587, \quad DF_t^{GLS} = -1.3249$$

$$MZ_\alpha^{GLS} = -4.1142, \quad MSB^{GLS} = 0.3186, \quad MZ_t^{GLS} = -1.3108\,.$$

As the sample size is $T = 241$ and detrending is based on a linear time trend, the 5% critical values from Table 17.1 in the case of the DF_t and the MZ_t tests are taken as -3.446 for DF_t^{OLS}, -3.059 for MZ_t^{OLS}, and -2.925 for DF_t^{GLS} and MZ_t^{GLS}. In all cases the null hypothesis of a unit root is not rejected at the 5% level.   □

17.6 Power

The critical values of the unit root tests presented in Table 17.1 are constructed to generate a test with asymptotic size of 5% under the null hypothesis of a unit root. In this section the focus is on examining the power of unit root tests to reject the null hypothesis of $\phi = 1$ when in fact the process is stationary $-1 < \phi < 1$. For values of ϕ just less than unity, say 0.99, even though the process is stationary, the behaviour of the process in finite samples is nearer to a unit root process than a stationary process as illustrated in Figure 17.3. This behaviour makes the detection of stationarity difficult and consequently the test statistics may have low power against nearly nonstationary alternatives. As ϕ moves further into the stationary region the process will exhibit more of the characteristics of a stationary process resulting in an increase in power.

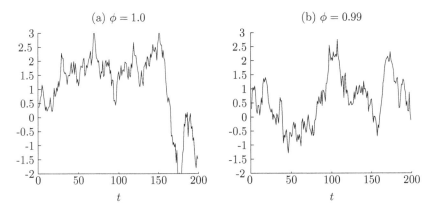

Figure 17.3. Illustrating the similarity of a unit root process ($\phi = 1$) and a near unit root process ($\phi = 0.99$) with $\sigma^2 = 0.1$ and sample size $T = 200$.

To model the sequence of stationary alternatives near the null hypothesis of a unit root, ϕ in (17.3) is given by

$$\phi = \phi_c = 1 + \frac{c}{T}, \quad c < 0. \tag{17.45}$$

A process y_t having this specification for ϕ is referred to as a near unit root process. The choice of the sign of the constant c ensures that values of ϕ occur in the stationary region. As T increases, ϕ approaches one and the alternative hypothesis approaches the null hypothesis. The asymptotic power of a test against such a sequence is called the asymptotic local power and is given as a function of c. In standard hypothesis tests, as opposed to unit root tests, the appropriate sequence of local alternatives uses an exponent of $-\frac{1}{2}$ for T. In this instance, the exponent of T in (17.45), namely -1, is chosen so that the asymptotic local power function is not degenerate. If this exponent were -2 ($-\frac{1}{2}$), then the asymptotic local power function would be one (zero) for all c. Phillips (1988) uses $\phi = \exp[c/T]$, which is asymptotically equivalent to (17.45).

17.6.1 Near Integration

The asymptotic theory for near integrated processes is more like that for integrated processes than it is for stationary processes, which is unsurprising given the observation made concerning the time series patterns of the near unit processes given in Figure 17.3. The asymptotic distribution theory for near integrated processes is an extension of the FCLT. If u_t is generated by (17.3) with ϕ given by (17.45), then

$$\frac{1}{\sigma\sqrt{T}} u_{[Ts]} \overset{d}{\to} B_c(s), \quad 0 \le s \le 1, \tag{17.46}$$

in which $B_c(s)$ is an Ornstein–Uhlenbeck (OU) process given by

$$B_c(s) = \int_0^s \exp[c(s-r)]d\,B(r), \tag{17.47}$$

and $B(s)$ is standard Brownian motion. The process $B_c(s)$ is similar to Brownian motion in that it is a normally distributed continuous stochastic process, but its variance for a fixed s and $c \ne 0$ is

$$\int_0^s \exp[2c(s-r)]dr = \frac{e^{2cs} - 1}{2c}.$$

In the special case of the null hypothesis of a unit root, $c = 0$ and (17.47) reduces to $B_0(s) = \int_0^s d\,B(r) = B(s)$, which is the basic FCLT result for a unit root process.

The asymptotic distributions of the unit root statistics under (17.45) have the same form as the distributions under the null hypothesis given earlier, except with the standard Brownian $B(s)$ replaced by the OU process $B_c(s)$ in (17.47). For example, in the case of ordinary least squares detrending, the asymptotic distribution of DF_t^{OLS} when ϕ is given by (17.45) is

$$DF_t^{OLS} \overset{d}{\to} \frac{\frac{1}{2}(B_{X,c}(1)^2 - B_{X,c}(0)^2 - 1)}{\left(\int_0^1 B_{X,c}(s)^2 ds\right)^{1/2}}. \tag{17.48}$$

where $B_X(s)$ in (17.34) is replaced by

$$B_{X,c}(s) = B_c(s) - (4 - 6s)\int_0^1 B_c(s)ds + (6 - 12s)\int_0^1 s B_c(s)ds.$$

For generalised least squares detrending, the asymptotic distribution is

$$DF_t^{GLS} \overset{d}{\to} \frac{\frac{1}{2}(B_{\bar{c},c}(1)^2 - 1)}{\left(\int_0^1 B_{\bar{c},c}(s)^2 ds\right)^{1/2}} \tag{17.49}$$

in which

$$B_{\bar{c},c}(s) = B_c(s) - s\left(\frac{1 - \bar{c}}{1 - \bar{c} + \bar{c}^2/3}B_c(1) + \frac{\bar{c}^2}{1 - \bar{c} + \bar{c}^2/3}\int_0^1 s B_c(s)ds\right),$$

noting that $B_{\bar{c},c}(0) = 0$.

17.6.2 Asymptotic Local Power

The asymptotic local power of a unit root test is its asymptotic power against local alternatives of the form (17.45). To illustrate the ideas, consider a comparison of the asymptotic local power of the DF_t test under ordinary and generalised least squares detrending. The asymptotic local power function for the DF_t test is

$$POWER(c) = \lim_{T \to \infty} \Pr\left(DF_t < cv_\infty\right),$$

where cv_∞ is the asymptotic critical value from Table 17.1 corresponding to a size of 5% and the limit is taken to reflect the fact it is the asymptotic power function that is required. For ordinary least squares detrending based on a linear time trend cv_∞ is -3.420 and for generalised least squares detrending it is -2.867 which corresponds to $\bar{c} = -13.5$.

Example 17.3 Asymptotic Local Power Curves
  Consider the near unit root model

$$y_t = \left(1 + \frac{c}{T}\right) y_{t-1} + v_t, \qquad v_t \sim iid\, N(0, \sigma^2),$$

with $\sigma^2 = 1$, $y_0 = 0$, $T = 1000$ and $c = -30, -29, \cdots, -1, 0$ controlling the size of the departure from a unit root. The powers of the DF_t^{OLS} and DF_t^{GLS} tests where detrending is based on a linear time trend are computed for each c by simulating the test statistics 100000 times and computing the proportion of values less than their respective critical values, -3.420 and -2.867, respectively. The results in Figure 17.4 show a clear power advantage for using generalised least squares over ordinary least squares detrending. However, it is important to note that this power advantage relies on the assumption that $y_0 = 0$, a point developed in Section 17.9.1. □

  The asymptotic local power can be used to approximate the power of a test in finite samples. In Figure 17.4 associated with Example 17.3, when $c = -20$ the asymptotic local powers of the ordinary least squares and generalised least squares DF_t tests are, respectively, 0.61 and 0.85. In a finite sample of size $T = 100$ these powers would approximate the finite sample power corresponding to $\phi = 1 - 20/100 = 0.8$. If $T = 200$ then those powers would apply to $\phi = 1 - 20/200 = 0.9$.

17.6.3 Point Optimal Tests

It is possible to place an upper bound on the asymptotic local power that can be obtained by unit root tests, assuming normality. Consider the log-likelihood

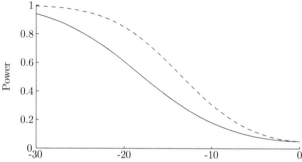

Figure 17.4. Approximate size-adjusted asymptotic power curves of the DF_t^{OLS} test (solid line) and the DF_t^{GLS} test (dashed line) using alternative detrending methods. Computed using Monte Carlo methods with 100000 replications and a sample size of 1000.

in (17.10) with ϕ defined as (17.45)

$$
\ln L_T(c, \delta, \gamma) = -\frac{1}{2}\ln(2\pi) - \frac{1}{2}\ln\sigma^2
$$
$$
- \frac{1}{2\sigma^2}(y_t - \phi y_{t-1} - \delta(1 - \phi) - \gamma(t - \phi(t-1)))^2,
$$

so c is a parameter in the likelihood together with δ and γ. A test of a unit root under the null hypothesis and a near unit root under the alternative can be based on the parameter c according to

$$H_0 : c = 0 \qquad \text{[Unit root]}$$
$$H_1 : c = \overline{c} \qquad \text{[Near unit root]}$$

for some fixed $\overline{c} < 0$. Elliott, Rothenberg and Stock (1996) show that the most powerful invariant test has the form of the LR test (see Chapter 4) given by

$$
LR = -2(T \ln L_T(0, \widehat{\delta}_0, \widehat{\gamma}_0) - T \ln L_T(\overline{c}, \widehat{\delta}_{\overline{c}}, \widehat{\gamma}_{\overline{c}})),
$$

in which $\widehat{\delta}_c$ and $\widehat{\gamma}_c$ are the generalised least squares detrending estimators using either $c = \overline{c}$ or $c = 0$. The null hypothesis of a unit root is rejected for large values of this statistic. An alternative form of the LR statistic is

$$
\frac{\sum_{t=1}^{T}\widehat{v}_{\overline{c},t}^2 - \sum_{t=1}^{T}\widehat{v}_{0,t}^2}{\sigma^2},
$$

where the null hypothesis is rejected for small values. This statistic is infeasible in practice since it depends on the unknown parameter σ^2. An asymptotically equivalent version of this LR test is

$$
P_{\overline{c}} = \frac{\sum_{t=1}^{T}\widehat{v}_{\overline{c},t}^2 - (1 + \overline{c}/T)\sum_{t=1}^{T}\widehat{v}_{0,t}^2}{\widehat{\sigma}^2}, \tag{17.50}
$$

in which $\widehat{\sigma}^2$ is an estimator such as $T^{-1}\sum_{t=1}^{T}v_{\widehat{c},t}^2$. The inclusion of the additional $(1 + \overline{c}/T)$ term in the numerator only changes the statistic by a constant asymptotically but allows the statistic to be easily modified to allow for autocorrelation in v_t by replacing $\widehat{\sigma}^2$ with a different estimator, a point taken up in Section 17.7.

For a particular value of $\overline{c}$, the $P_{\overline{c}}$ test can be used as a benchmark against which to compare the power of the other unit root tests. Since $P_{\overline{c}}$ is constructed to be optimal against a particular point of the alternative hypothesis, it is referred to as a point optimal test. The asymptotic distribution of $P_{\overline{c}}$ is derived using the FCLT result used previously and is given by

$$P_{\overline{c}} \xrightarrow{d} \overline{c}^2 \int_0^1 B_c(s)^2 ds - \overline{c}B_c(1)^2 \qquad \text{[Constant]}$$

$$P_{\overline{c}} \xrightarrow{d} \overline{c}^2 \int_0^1 B_{\overline{c},c}(s)^2 + (1 - \overline{c})B_{\overline{c},c}(1)^2 \quad \text{[Constant and Trend]}.$$

17.6.4 Asymptotic Power Envelope

The $P_{\overline{c}}$ test in (17.50) can be used as a practical unit root test. Although asymptotically optimal only at the fixed value $\overline{c}$, it does have good asymptotic local power properties against other values of c. However, it is also used in the construction of the asymptotic local power envelope, which defines the maximum local power attainable by any unit root test, under the joint assumptions of normality, of asymptotically negligible initial value and of invariance to the deterministic regressors.

The asymptotic local power function for the point optimal test $P_{\overline{c}}$ in (17.6.3) is

$$POWER(c) = \lim_{T \to \infty} \Pr\left(P_{\overline{c}} < cv_\infty\right), \tag{17.51}$$

where the critical value cv_∞ corresponds to a size of 0.05 ($c = 0$). By construction, this is the maximum attainable power for a unit root test when $c = \overline{c}$. The asymptotic local power envelope is defined by evaluating the point optimal test in (17.50) at all values of c and not just $\overline{c}$

$$POWER^{\text{env}}(c) = \lim_{T \to \infty} \Pr\left(P_c < cv_\infty\right).$$

Elliott, Rothenberg and Stock (1996) show there is no uniformly most powerful unit root test, implying that no single unit root test can attain this envelope. As a result, there is no single optimal choice for $\overline{c}$ in the point optimal test. However, choosing $\overline{c}$ to be the value at which the asymptotic local power envelope has power of 0.5 produces tests with good power properties across a wide range of values of c. Values of $\overline{c} = -7$ (for a constant) and $\overline{c} = -13.5$ (for a constant and linear trend) are appropriate practical choices for these constants, which

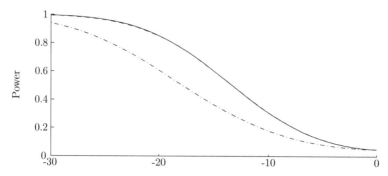

Figure 17.5. The approximate size-adjusted asymptotic power curves of the point optimal test and the DF_t^{GLS} which are indistinguishable from the asymptotic power envelope (solid line). The DF_t^{OLS} test (dot-dashed line) clearly has inferior asymptotic local power. Power is computed using 100000 replications and a sample size of $T = 1000$.

correspond to the choices adopted for generalised least squares detrending in Section 17.3.3.

Example 17.4 Asymptotic Local Power Envelope
   The simulation design in Example 17.3 is extended to produce the asymptotic power envelope and the asymptotic local power of the DF_t^{OLS} and DF_t^{GLS} tests as well as the point optimal test $P_{\bar{c}}$. Detrending is based on a linear time trend so $\bar{c} = -13.5$ for the point optimal test. Figure 17.5 shows that the asymptotic local power of the DF_t^{GLS} test and the point optimal test are barely distinguishable from the power envelope, which shows that there is no point in searching for asymptotic power improvements in this particular model. The DF_t^{OLS} test has inferior asymptotic local power.   □

17.7   Autocorrelation

In practice, an AR(1) model for u_t, as in equation (17.3), is unlikely to be sufficient to ensure that v_t is not autocorrelated. Consequently, this section explores unit root testing in the presence of autocorrelation.

17.7.1   Dickey-Fuller Test with Autocorrelation

The Dickey-Fuller regression (17.23) requires augmenting with lagged differences of u_t to correct for autocorrelation. The test regression is

$$\Delta u_t = \alpha u_{t-1} + \sum_{j=1}^{p} \delta_j \Delta u_{t-j} + v_t ,$$ (17.52)

in which p is a lag length chosen to ensure that v_t is not autocorrelated, at least approximately. A Dickey-Fuller unit root test of $\alpha = 0$ in equation (17.52) is commonly known as the augmented Dickey-Fuller test. It is not necessary that the true data generating process be a finite-order AR model; only that the data generating process can be approximated by an AR model. Chang and Park (2002) formalise the sense of this approximation, showing that a general class of linear processes can be approximated by (17.52) by letting $p \to \infty$ as $T \to \infty$. This allows unit root inference to be carried out semi-parametrically with respect to the form of the autocorrelation in Δu_t. The selection of p affects both the size and power properties of a unit root test. If p is chosen to be too small, then substantial autocorrelation will remain in the error term of equation (17.52) and this will result in size distortions since the asymptotic distribution under the null hypothesis no longer applies in the presence of autocorrelation. However, including an excessive number of lags will have an adverse effect on the power of the test.

A lag-length selection procedure that has good properties in unit root testing is the modified Akaike information criterion (MAIC) method proposed by Ng and Perron (2001). The lag length is chosen to satisfy

$$\widehat{p} = \arg\min_{p} \text{MAIC}(p) = \log(\widehat{\sigma}^2) + \frac{2(\tau_p + p)}{T - p_{\max}}, \tag{17.53}$$

in which

$$\tau_p = \frac{\widehat{\alpha}^2}{\widehat{\sigma}^2} \sum_{t=p_{\max}+1}^{T} \widehat{u}_{t-1}^2,$$

and the maximum lag length is chosen as $p_{\max} = \text{int}[12(T/100)^{1/4}]$. In estimating $\widehat{p}$, it is important that the sample over which the computations are performed is held constant. The stochastic penalty term, τ_p, in the AIC allows for the possible presence of MA terms in the true data generating process for (17.52). The autoregression (17.52) can be used to approximate moving average autocorrelation provided p is allowed to be sufficiently large. This is especially important for MA processes with roots close to -1. The penalty, τ_p, will be small in the presence of such MA processes, hence allowing the selection of longer lags. The MAIC will work much like the standard AIC in other situations.

17.7.2 M Tests with Autocorrelation

Consider the MZ_t statistic

$$MZ_t = \frac{\frac{1}{2}\left(\frac{1}{T}\widehat{u}_T^2 - \widehat{\sigma}^2\right)}{\widehat{\sigma}\left(\frac{1}{T^2}\sum_{t=2}^{T}\widehat{u}_{t-1}^2\right)^{1/2}}$$

with

$$\widehat{\sigma}^2 = \frac{1}{T-1} \sum_{t=2}^{T} \widehat{v}_t^2 \,,$$

but where v_t is now autocorrelated. If the long-run variance of v_t is given by

$$\omega^2 = \sum_{j=-\infty}^{\infty} \mathrm{E}[v_t v_{t-j}] \,,$$

then Phillips (1987) and Phillips and Perron (1988) suggest replacing $\widehat{\sigma}^2$ in the definition of MZ_t with a consistent estimator of ω^2. Perron and Ng (1998) and Stock (1999) propose an estimator of ω^2 given by

$$\widehat{\omega}^2 = \frac{\widehat{\sigma}_p^2}{(1 - \sum_{j=1}^{p} \widehat{\delta}_j)^2} \,,$$

in which $\widehat{\delta}_j$ and $\widehat{\sigma}_p^2$ are the estimators from the Dickey-Fuller equation (17.52). This is a consistent estimator for ω^2 under the null and local alternative hypotheses. The resultant MZ_t test

$$MZ_t = \frac{\frac{1}{2}\left(\frac{1}{T}\widehat{u}_T^2 - \widehat{\omega}^2\right)}{\widehat{\omega}\left(\frac{1}{T^2}\sum_{t=2}^{T}\widehat{u}_{t-1}^2\right)^{1/2}}$$

has the same asymptotic distribution under the null hypothesis given in (17.37). This form of the test, therefore, has the advantage that the asymptotic critical values reported earlier for MZ_t apply in the presence of autocorrelation in v_t. The MZ_α and MSB statistics are similarly modified to allow for autocorrelation in v_t. If p in (17.52) is selected using the MAIC, then the resulting unit root tests are found to have good finite sample properties.

Example 17.5 Unit Root Tests and Autocorrelation

Monte Carlo simulations are used to derive the finite sample properties of the DF_t test and the MZ_t test in the presence of autocorrelation in v_t. The data generating process is given by expressions (17.2), (17.3) and

$$(1 - \rho L)v_t = (1 + \theta L)e_t \,, \qquad e_t \sim iid\ N(0, \sigma_e^2) \,,$$

with $\sigma_e^2 = 1$, $\rho = \{0, 0.3, 0.6\}$ and $\theta = \{-0.8, -0.4, 0.0, 0.4, 0.8\}$. The sample size is $T = 200$ and $\phi = 1.0$ to compute sizes of the tests and $\phi = \{0.90, 0.95\}$ to compute the powers of the test. For the MZ_t test, two methods of choosing p are considered, namely, the MAIC and the AIC, where the latter is obtained by setting $\tau_p = 1$ in (17.53). All three tests are computed using generalised least squares detrending.

Table 17.2. *Finite sample sizes* ($\phi = 1.0$) *of the* DF_t^{GLS} *and* MZ_t^{GLS}
tests with v_t *autocorrelated. Lag length selection based on the AIC*
and MAIC criteria for $T = 200$ *and using* 10000 *replications*

Test	ρ	θ				
		-0.8	-0.4	0.0	0.4	0.8
MZ_t^{GLS}, MAIC	0.0	0.058	0.042	0.030	0.046	0.032
	0.3	0.060	0.042	0.043	0.049	0.084
	0.6	0.068	0.041	0.049	0.014	0.144
MZ_t^{GLS}, AIC	0.0	0.198	0.122	0.085	0.126	0.318
	0.3	0.200	0.128	0.107	0.116	0.426
	0.6	0.220	0.134	0.115	0.098	0.405
DF_t^{GLS}, MAIC	0.0	0.026	0.037	0.040	0.058	0.105
	0.3	0.026	0.033	0.043	0.060	0.130
	0.6	0.024	0.028	0.043	0.013	0.153

The results in Table 17.2 show that the MZ_t test with lag length selected by MAIC generates the best sizes with values close to 0.05. Basing the lag length on the AIC generally results in over sized tests, while the DF_t test tends to be under sized for negative moving average parameters and more over sized than the MZ_t test for positive moving average parameters. The finite sample powers of the tests given in Table 17.3 suggest that the MZ_t test, with the lag length chosen by MAIC, has the highest power, rejecting the null hypothesis 20% of the time for $\phi = 0.95$ and 50% of the time for $\phi = 0.90$. The DF_t test has similar power, except where it is under sized in which case the power is correspondingly reduced. ☐

17.8 Structural Breaks

The analysis is now extended to allow for structural breaks in the linear trend when testing for a unit root in y_t. Both known break points and unknown break points are dealt with. To allow for a structural break in the trend, equation (17.2) is augmented as follows

$$y_t = \delta + \gamma t + \beta DT_t + u_t, \tag{17.54}$$

in which DT_t is the break dummy variable with T_B representing the timing of the break, defined as

$$DT_t = \begin{cases} 0, & t \leq T_B, \\ t - T_B, & t > T_B. \end{cases}$$

The following example highlights the potential structural break in United States real GDP following the oil crisis of 1973 (Perron, 1989).

Table 17.3. *Finite sample powers ($\phi = \{0.90, 0.95\}$) of the DF_t^{GLS} and MZ_t^{GLS} tests with v_t autocorrelated. Lag length selection based on the AIC and MAIC criteria for $T = 200$ and using* 10000 *replications*

Test	ϕ	ρ	θ				
	0.90		−0.8	−0.4	0.0	0.4	0.8
MZ_t, MAIC		0.0	0.478	0.596	0.641	0.498	0.236
		0.3	0.473	0.551	0.528	0.628	0.410
		0.6	0.434	0.477	0.591	0.262	0.644
MZ_t, AIC		0.0	0.499	0.425	0.348	0.446	0.629
		0.3	0.502	0.411	0.384	0.474	0.763
		0.6	0.500	0.408	0.385	0.334	0.828
DF_t, MAIC		0.0	0.373	0.571	0.682	0.561	0.433
		0.3	0.346	0.514	0.541	0.641	0.535
		0.6	0.291	0.435	0.557	0.305	0.677
Test	ϕ	ρ	θ				
	0.95		−0.8	−0.4	0.0	0.4	0.8
MZ_t, MAIC		0.0	0.215	0.225	0.204	0.216	0.102
		0.3	0.220	0.205	0.214	0.274	0.233
		0.6	0.221	0.196	0.236	0.078	0.421
MZ_t, AIC		0.0	0.198	0.122	0.085	0.126	0.318
		0.3	0.200	0.128	0.107	0.116	0.426
		0.6	0.220	0.134	0.115	0.098	0.405
DF_t, MAIC		0.0	0.130	0.206	0.250	0.261	0.257
		0.3	0.126	0.177	0.213	0.307	0.337
		0.6	0.119	0.160	0.217	0.082	0.445

Example 17.6 United States Post-war GDP

Panel (a) of Figure 17.6 gives a plot of the log of quarterly United States real GDP, y_t, from March 1947 to March 2007 with two different trend functions superimposed corresponding to a structural break in March 1973. The trend lines are computed by estimating equation (17.54) with $T_B = 105$, which corresponds to the timing of the structural break in the sample. The dashed trend line shows a break in the trend compared to the dotted line based on a linear trend ($\beta = 0$) estimated on the first 105 observations. Panel (b) shows that the residuals from the structural break appear to be more stationary. This may reflect a general result that an omitted structural break can make a time series appear to be more like a unit root process than it actually is.   □

Example 17.7 The Effect of Omitted Breaks

The data generating process is as specified in Example 17.6, with $\delta = \gamma = 0$ and $\beta = \{0, 0.2, 0.4\}$. The disturbances, u_t, are generated using equation (17.3) with parameter $\phi = \{1, 0.95, 0.90\}$. The sample size is $T = 200$ and the

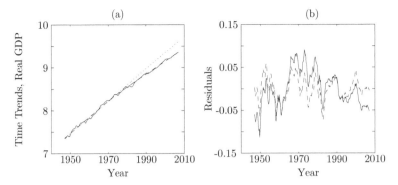

Figure 17.6. Comparison of residuals from excluding and including a structural break in the logarithm of real United States GDP in March 1973. Panel (a) shows the series (solid line) together with the fitted linear trend (dotted line) and the trend allowing for the break (dashed line). Panel (b) compares the residuals from the linear trend (solid line) to the residuals from the trend incorporating the break (dashed line).

time of the break is parameterised as $T_B = [\lambda T]$, where $\lambda = \{0.25, 0.50, 0.75\}$ represents the fraction of the sample at which the break occurs.

Table 17.4 shows that by neglecting a structural break there is a strong tendency not to reject the null hypothesis of a unit root. The extent to which this occurs varies with the type of test and the timing of the break, but the overall finding is very clear. Therefore, it is necessary to be able to allow for structural breaks in the deterministic component to be able to carry out an effective unit root test.   □

17.8.1 Known Break Point

To derive the asymptotic distribution in the presence of a known structural break, the dummy variable DT_t in equation (17.54) is re-defined as

$$DT_t = \begin{cases} 0, & t \leq [\lambda T], \\ t - [\lambda T], & t > [\lambda T], \end{cases}$$

where λ is the known break fraction. The distribution theory for ordinary least squares and generalised least squares detrending is now derived.

Ordinary Least Squares Detrending
Define $D_T = \text{diag}(1, T^{-1}, T^{-1})$, so that

$$D_T^{-1} x_{[Ts]} = \begin{bmatrix} 1 \\ T^{-1}[Ts] \\ T^{-1}(\max(0, [Ts] - [\lambda T])) \end{bmatrix} \rightarrow \begin{bmatrix} 1 \\ s \\ \max(0, s - \lambda) \end{bmatrix} = X(s).$$

Hence

$$\frac{1}{\sqrt{T}} \widehat{u}_{[Ts]} \xrightarrow{d} \sigma B_X(s), \tag{17.55}$$

Table 17.4. *The effects of omitted breaks on the performance of unit root tests. Detrending is based on a linear time trend, with $T = 200$ and 10000 replications*

β	λ	ϕ	DF_t^{OLS}	DF_t^{GLS}	MZ_t^{OLS}	MZ_t^{GLS}
0	n.a.	1.00	0.060	0.065	0.041	0.049
		0.95	0.197	0.345	0.211	0.279
		0.90	0.647	0.880	0.706	0.819
0.2	0.25	1.00	0.052	0.032	0.023	0.025
		0.95	0.125	0.034	0.045	0.025
		0.90	0.259	0.028	0.098	0.018
0.2	0.5	1.00	0.026	0.027	0.015	0.020
		0.95	0.025	0.010	0.009	0.007
		0.90	0.012	0.002	0.004	0.001
0.2	0.75	1.00	0.032	0.036	0.022	0.026
		0.95	0.045	0.069	0.042	0.053
		0.90	0.062	0.115	0.064	0.086
0.4	0.25	1.00	0.050	0.005	0.003	0.003
		0.95	0.053	0.000	0.000	0.000
		0.90	0.046	0.000	0.000	0.000
0.4	0.5	1.00	0.006	0.003	0.002	0.002
		0.95	0.000	0.000	0.000	0.000
		0.90	0.000	0.000	0.000	0.000
0.4	0.75	1.00	0.007	0.006	0.004	0.004
		0.95	0.001	0.001	0.000	0.000
		0.90	0.000	0.000	0.000	0.000

in which

$$B_X(s) = B(s) - X(s)' \left[\int_0^1 X(s)X(s)' \right]^{-1} \int_0^1 X(s)B(s)ds$$

$$= B(s) - \begin{bmatrix} 1 \\ s \\ s - \lambda \end{bmatrix}' \begin{bmatrix} 1 & \dfrac{1}{2} & \dfrac{(1-\lambda)^2}{2} \\ \dfrac{1}{2} & \dfrac{1}{3} & \dfrac{(\lambda+2)(1-\lambda)^2}{6} \\ \dfrac{(1-\lambda)^2}{2} & \dfrac{(\lambda+2)(1-\lambda)^2}{6} & \dfrac{(1-\lambda)^3}{3} \end{bmatrix}^{-1}$$

$$\times \begin{bmatrix} \displaystyle\int_0^1 B(s)\,ds \\ \displaystyle\int_0^1 s\,B(s)\,ds \\ \displaystyle\int_\lambda^1 (s-\lambda)B(s)\,ds \end{bmatrix}$$

$$= B(s) - \frac{3s - \lambda - 2}{1 - \lambda} \int_0^1 B(s)ds + \frac{3(3s - \lambda - 2)}{\lambda(1 - \lambda)} \int_0^1 sB(s)ds$$

$$+ \frac{3(2s\lambda - \lambda - 3s + 2)}{\lambda(1 - \lambda)^3} \int_\lambda^1 (s - \lambda)B(s)ds .$$

The distributions of the unit root tests under ordinary least squares detrending in the presence of a known structural break are given by equations (17.33) to (17.37) with $B_X(s)$ now given by (17.55).

Generalised Least Squares Detrending

For generalised least squares detrending, similar derivations show that

$$\frac{1}{\sqrt{T}}\widehat{u}_{[Ts]} \xrightarrow{d} \sigma B_{\overline{c},\lambda}(s), \tag{17.56}$$

in which

$$B_{\overline{c},\lambda}(s) = B(s) - \left[\frac{s}{\max(0, s - \lambda)} \right]'$$

$$\times \left[\begin{array}{cc} \int_0^1 (1 - \overline{c}s)^2 \, ds & \int_\lambda^1 (1 - \overline{c}s)(1 - \overline{c}(s - \lambda)) \, ds \\ \int_\lambda^1 (1 - \overline{c}s)(1 - \overline{c}(s - \lambda)) \, ds & \int_\lambda^1 (1 - \overline{c}(s - \lambda))^2 \, ds \end{array} \right]^{-1}$$

$$\times \left[\begin{array}{c} (1 - \overline{c})B(1) + \overline{c}^2 \int_0^1 sB(s) \, ds \\ (1 - \overline{c}(1 - \lambda))B(1) + \overline{c}^2 \int_\lambda^1 (s - \lambda)B(s) \, ds - B(\lambda) \end{array} \right] .$$

The asymptotic distributions of the generalised least squares-based tests are all functions of $B_{\overline{c},\lambda}(s)$ (see Theorem 1 of Perron and Rodriguez (2003) for further details). The distributions of the unit root tests under generalised least squares detrending in the presence of a known structural break are given by equations (17.33) to (17.37) with $B_X(s)$ now replaced by $B_{\overline{c},\lambda}(s)$ given by expression (17.56).

The important thing to note from equations (17.55) and (17.56) is that the Brownian motions are functions of the break fraction λ. Consequently, the asymptotic distributions of the unit root tests also depend on the timing of the break, although, by construction, they are invariant to the size of the break. Two important implications follow from this result.

(1) The choice of $\overline{c}$ for generalised least squares detrending depends on λ. Appropriate choices of $\overline{c}$ for different values of the break fraction parameter, λ, are given in Table 17.5.

Table 17.5. *Values of $\bar{c}$ for generalised least squares detrending based on a linear trend in the presence of a known trend break with break fraction λ*

λ	0.15	0.20	0.25	0.30	0.35
$\bar{c}$	−17.6	−18.1	−18.3	−18.4	−18.4
λ	0.40	0.45	0.50	0.55	0.60
$\bar{c}$	−18.4	−18.4	−18.2	−18.1	−17.8
λ	0.65	0.70	0.75	0.80	0.85
$\bar{c}$	−17.8	−17.5	−17.0	−16.6	−16.0

(2) Critical values of unit root tests depend on λ. Approximate asymptotic critical values are given in Table 17.6 for various unit root tests with detrending based on a linear time trend.

Example 17.8 Unit Root Test of GDP with Known Break

Consider testing for a unit root in United States GDP while allowing for a trend break in March 1973. The timing of the break corresponds to $\lambda = 0.44$ so that the MZ_t^{OLS} and MZ_t^{GLS} tests have 5% asymptotic critical values of −3.61 and −3.45, respectively. Computation of the test statistics gives $MZ_t^{OLS} = -4.111$ and $MZ_t^{GLS} = -4.106$, so each individual test rejects the null hypothesis of the unit root. The conclusion from these tests is that real

Table 17.6. *Asymptotic 5% critical values with a trend break with break fraction λ. Detrending is based on a linear time trend*

λ	DF_t^{OLS}	DF_t/MZ_t^{GLS}	MZ_t^{OLS}
0.15	−3.58	−3.38	−3.42
0.20	−3.67	−3.42	−3.48
0.25	−3.73	−3.43	−3.53
0.30	−3.77	−3.44	−3.56
0.35	−3.81	−3.45	−3.58
0.40	−3.84	−3.45	−3.60
0.45	−3.86	−3.45	−3.61
0.50	−3.87	−3.44	−3.62
0.55	−3.87	−3.43	−3.62
0.60	−3.88	−3.42	−3.61
0.65	−3.87	−3.40	−3.60
0.70	−3.85	−3.37	−3.58
0.75	−3.83	−3.33	−3.55
0.80	−3.79	−3.28	−3.51
0.85	−3.74	−3.23	−3.46

GDP is stationary around a broken trend, which is not a surprising finding given the graphical evidence in Figure 17.6.   □

17.8.2   Unknown Break Point

The preceding analysis is based on the assumption that the timing of the break in the trend is known. A straightforward way to proceed in the more likely event of the break point being unknown is to estimate the break point initially, use that break point to estimate the rest of the detrending regression and then perform the unit root test. The critical requirement for this approach is that λ be consistently estimated with a rate of convergence faster than the standard $O_p(T^{-1/2})$ rate. In particular, if an estimator $\widehat{\lambda}$ is obtained such that $\widehat{\lambda} - \lambda = o_p(T^{-1/2})$, then $\widehat{\lambda}$ can be used in the detrending regression and the unit root test as if it were the true value without changing the asymptotic properties of the test.

To make the role of λ explicit, consider

$$y_t = \delta + \gamma t + \beta_2 DT_t(\lambda) + u_t, \tag{17.57}$$

in which

$$DT_t(\lambda) = \begin{cases} 0, & t \le [\lambda T], \\ t - [\lambda T], & t > [\lambda T]. \end{cases} \tag{17.58}$$

A two-step approach suggested by Carrion-i Silverstre, Kim and Perron (2009) satisfies this condition.

Step 1 Choose λ to satisfy

$$\widehat{\lambda} = \arg\min_{\lambda} \sum_{t=1}^{T} \widehat{u}_t(\lambda)^2, \tag{17.59}$$

in which $\widehat{u}_t(\lambda)$ denotes the ordinary least squares residuals in (17.57) for an arbitrary choice of λ. The range of values for λ is typically restricted to some subset of $[0, 1]$, say $[0.15, 0.85]$.

Step 2 Using Table 17.5, look up the appropriate value for $\bar{c}$ corresponding to $\widehat{\lambda}$ and then re-estimate λ from the generalised least squares regression in (17.57).

Setting $\bar{c} = 0$ in Step 2 results in the generalised least squares detrending approach becoming a one step first-differencing procedure. Harris, Harvey, Leybourne and Taylor (2009) show that this simple approach is also asymptotically valid for unit root testing.

Example 17.9 Unit Root Test of GDP with Unknown Break
   The Carrion-i Silvestre, Kim and Perron (2009) procedure of testing for a unit root when the timing of the structural break is unknown is now applied

to the United States GDP data. The break fraction estimator from the levels regression (17.57) is $\widehat{\lambda} = 0.39$, which corresponds to a break date of March 1970, somewhat earlier than the assumed date of March 1973. However, this is only a preliminary estimate used to obtain a value of $\overline{c}$ that is then used to compute the generalised least squares estimate. Since $\widehat{\lambda} = 0.39$ is closest to $\lambda = 0.4$, the appropriate choice is $\overline{c} = -18.5$. This value is used to construct the generalised least squares transformation of (17.57) and then to re-estimate λ, giving $\widehat{\lambda} = 0.44$ or a break date of June 1973. Recall that the convergence properties of these estimates of λ mean that $\overline{c}$ can be obtained from Table 17.5. Based on $\widehat{\lambda} = 0.44$, the appropriate choice is $\overline{c} = -18.4$. The critical values for the ordinary least squares and generalised least squares tests are taken from Table 17.6 and are -3.61 and -3.45, respectively. The test statistics are found to be $MZ_t^{OLS} = -4.095$ and $MZ_t^{GLS} = -4.091$ so each test rejects the null hypothesis of a unit root. It appears, therefore, that irrespective of a break being imposed in March 1973 based on historical knowledge, or estimated to be in June 1973, post-war United States real GDP is stationary around a broken trend. □

17.9   Applications

17.9.1   Power and the Initial Value

The preceding analysis suggests that tests based on generalised least squares rather than ordinary least squares detrending provide a substantial power advantage. This conclusion stems from the seemingly innocuous assumption that the extent to which the time series, y_t, differs from its underlying trend is asymptotically negligible, that is $u_0 = 0$ at least asymptotically. It turns out, however, that the power of unit root tests does depend critically on u_0.

The effects of the initial condition on the power properties of unit root tests are evident in Figure 17.7, which gives the results of simulating the MZ_t test for a sample of $T = 200$ using ordinary least squares and generalised least squares detrending and initial condition values of $u_0 = \{0, 2.5, 5.0\}$. The results demonstrate that the ordering of the power functions of the ordinary least squares and generalised least squares tests changes as u_0 is varied. For $u_0 = 0$ in panel (a), the generalised least squares test is superior to the ordinary least squares test for all values of c. As u_0 increases from $u_0 = 2.5$ (panel (b)) to $u_0 = 5.0$ (panel (c)) the power advantage associated with generalised least squares detrending diminishes while the performance of ordinary least squares is largely unchanged.

Muller and Elliott (2001) construct an asymptotic theory for unit root tests that captures this dependence on the initial value by allowing u_0 to grow with the sample size, specifically $u_0 = O(T^{1/2})$. In that case, u_0 is no longer asymptotically negligible and its role in determining power can be analysed theoretically.

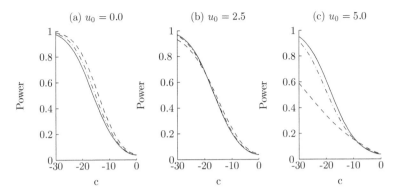

Figure 17.7. The effects of alternative initial conditions on the power of the MZ_t^{OLS} test (solid line) and MZ_t^{GLS} test (dashed line) and union of rejections method (dot-dashed line). Computed using Monte Carlo methods with 50000 replications and a sample size of 200.

A practical approach to this problem, proposed by Harvey, Leybourne and Taylor (2009), is to do both the MZ_t^{OLS} and MZ_t^{GLS} tests and reject the null hypothesis if either or both tests reject it. If u_0 is small, then rejections will tend to come from the more powerful MZ_t^{GLS} test. If u_0 is large, then rejections will tend to come from the MZ_t^{OLS} test. This is known as a union of rejections strategy. To control the overall size of this joint procedure, the decision rule is to reject H_0 if $MZ_t^{OLS} < \tau \cdot cv^{OLS}$ and/or $MZ_t^{GLS} < \tau \cdot cv^{GLS}$, where τ is a constant chosen to ensure a size of 5%.

Figure 17.7 shows the performance of the union of rejections strategy for a linear trend, a sample size of $T = 200$ and $\tau = 1.038$. Doing two tests instead of one means that the critical values have been increased by a factor of τ and hence the union of rejections approach can never achieve the power of the individual MZ_t^{OLS} or MZ_t^{GLS} tests. Nevertheless, it does not fall far short of the best test in each case and avoids the worst of the power losses that can arise.

17.9.2   Nelson-Plosser Data Revisited

Unit root tests are applied to the 14 United States annual macroeconomic variables of the Nelson-Plosser data set analysed in Chapter 16. The results are presented for the MZ_t unit root test with the lag length chosen by MAIC and a union of rejections decision rule used to combine the ordinary least squares and generalised least squares detrending methods assuming a linear trend and no structural break. Three decision rules are adopted, namely,

(1) reject H_0 if $MZ_t^{OLS} < -3.130$, [M test OLS detrending]
(2) reject H_0 if $MZ_t^{GLS} < -2.867$, [M test GLS detrending]

Table 17.7. *Unit root tests for the Nelson-Plosser data using the* MZ_t^{OLS} *and* MZ_t^{GLS} *tests, together with the union of rejections (UR) test*

Variable	Statistics		Classifications		
	MZ_t^{OLS}	MZ_t^{GLS}	MZ_t^{OLS}	MZ_t^{GLS}	UR
Real GNP	−1.813	−1.740	$I(1)$	$I(1)$	$I(1)$
Nominal GNP	−2.455	−2.450	$I(1)$	$I(1)$	$I(1)$
Real per cap. GNP	−1.858	−1.769	$I(1)$	$I(1)$	$I(1)$
Ind. production	−2.830	−2.725	$I(1)$	$I(1)$	$I(1)$
Employment	−2.829	−2.717	$I(1)$	$I(1)$	$I(1)$
Unemployment rate	−3.109	−2.996	$I(1)$	$I(0)$	$I(0)$
GNP deflator	−2.410	−2.169	$I(1)$	$I(1)$	$I(1)$
Consumer prices	−1.427	−1.442	$I(1)$	$I(1)$	$I(1)$
Wages	−2.413	−2.378	$I(1)$	$I(1)$	$I(1)$
Real wages	−1.928	−1.776	$I(1)$	$I(1)$	$I(1)$
Money stock	−3.097	−3.077	$I(1)$	$I(0)$	$I(0)$
Velocity	−1.292	−1.102	$I(1)$	$I(1)$	$I(1)$
Bond Yield	−1.997	−2.326	$I(1)$	$I(1)$	$I(1)$
S&P500	−1.365	−1.193	$I(1)$	$I(1)$	$I(1)$

(3) reject H_0 if $MZ_t^{OLS} < (\tau \times -3.130)$ and/or $MZ_t^{GLS} < (\tau \times -2.867)$, where $\tau = 1.038$ [Union of Rejections test].

The critical values for the first two decision rules are the asymptotic values ($T = 1000$) from Table 17.1.

The results are shown in Table 17.7. All series are found to be $I(1)$ using the MZ_t^{OLS} test. For the MZ_t^{GLS} version of the test, the unemployment rate and the money stock are found to be $I(0)$, a finding supported by the union of rejections rule. This result is reinforced by inspection of Figure 16.1 in Chapter 16, which suggests that the money stock is trend stationary. Moreover, the ability of the generalised least squares version of the test to reject the null hypothesis may reflect the extra power of this test established previously.

In the case of the unemployment rate, inspection of Figure 16.1 in Chapter 16 suggests that a linear trend is not required for this series. Repeating the calculations where detrending includes only a constant term for the unemployment rate yields values of −3.062 (MZ_t^{OLS}) and −2.876 (MZ_t^{GLS}) for the two tests. The asymptotic critical values from Table 17.1 are −2.467 (OLS) and −1.966 (GLS), so the null hypothesis of a unit root is rejected by both tests. This is confirmed by the union of rejections approach with $\tau = 1.084$, which also finds the unemployment rate to be $I(0)$. The change in the classification of the unemployment rate for the MZ_t^{OLS} test suggests that the failure to reject the null hypothesis of a unit when a time trend is included indicates that the time trend is redundant and its inclusion results in a loss of power. The simple remedy is to perform the test based on just a constant.

17.10   Exercises

(1) Critical values for unit root tests

Program files	`unit_critval.*`

(a) Carry out a simulation to compute critical values for unit root tests in the model

$$y_t = \delta + u_t ,$$
$$u_t = \phi u_{t-1} + v_t ,$$
$$v_t \sim iid N(0, \sigma^2).$$

Include the coefficient test DF_α, the t test DF_t and the MZ_t and MSB tests. Each test should be carried out using each of OLS demeaning and GLS demeaning using $\bar{c} = -7$. Use sample sizes $T = \{25, 50, 100, 250, 500, 1000,$ and $100000\}$ replications.

(b) Carry out a simulation to estimate critical values for the same unit root tests in the model that also allows for a linear trend:

$$y_t = \delta + \gamma t + u_t ,$$
$$u_t = \phi u_{t-1} + v_t ,$$
$$v_t \sim iid N(0, \sigma^2).$$

Each test should be carried out using each of OLS detrending and GLS detrending using $\bar{c} = -13.5$.

(2) United States GDP

Program files	`unit_qusgdp.*`
Data files	`usgdp.*`

The data are real quarterly United States GDP from March 1947 to March 2007. Let y_t be the natural logarithm of the data.

(a) Test for a unit root test in y_t without making any allowance for autocorrelation in the residuals of the test regression.

(b) Repeat part (a) allowing for autocorrelation in the residuals of the test regression.

(c) Repeat part (a) based on the assumption of a structural break in the trend in March 1973.

(d) Test for a unit root test in y_t based on the assumption of a structural break whose location is unknown.

(e) Does an answer to the question of whether or not United States GDP has a unit root emerge?

(3) Near Unit Root Processes

Program files   unit_nearunitroot.*

Consider the AR(1) model

$$y_t = \phi y_{t-1} + v_t, \qquad v_t \sim iid\ N(0, \sigma^2).$$

(a) Simulate a unit root process with parameters $\phi = 1$ and $\sigma^2 = 0.1$ for a sample of size of $T = 200$.
(b) Repeat part (a) for a near unit root process with $\phi = 0.99$.
(c) Repeat part (a) for a near unit root process with $\phi = 0.95$.
(d) Plot the simulated series in parts (a) to (c) and compare their time series properties.
(e) For parts (a) to (c) compute the ACF and the PACF and compare their values.

(4) Asymptotic Local Power

Program files   unit_asypower.*

Consider the data generating process

$$y_t = \phi y_{t-1} + v_t, \qquad t = 2, \cdots, T,$$
$$y_1 = v_1,$$

with $v_t \sim iid\ N(0, 1)$, $T = 1000$ and $\phi = 1 + c/T$ with $c \in \{-30, -29, \cdots, 0\}$.

(a) For $c = 0$, carry out a simulation of 100000 replications to obtain the 5% critical values of the DF_t^{OLS} and DF_t^{GLS} tests where the initial regression includes only a constant term. Use $\bar{c} = -7$ for the DF_t^{GLS} test.
(b) For each $c = \{-1, -2, \cdots, -30\}$, simulate the power of the DF_t^{OLS} and DF_t^{GLS} tests and plot the resulting asymptotic local power curves.
(c) Repeat part (a) using an initial regression on a constant and time trend and using $\bar{c} = -13.5$ for the DF_t^{GLS} test.
(d) In the case of a constant and time trend, generate asymptotic local power curves for the DF_t^{GLS} test using $\bar{c} = -5$ and $\bar{c} = -20$ to get some idea of the effect of changing this constant.
(e) Repeat the previous two parts using the Schmidt-Phillips demeaning and detrending procedure.

(5) Asymptotic Power Envelope

Program files   `unit_asypowerenv.*`

Consider the problem of obtaining the asymptotic local power envelope for unit root testing in the model

$$y_t = x_t'\beta + u_t,$$
$$u_t = \phi u_{t-1} + v_t,$$
$$u_0 = \xi,$$
$$v_t \sim iid\,(0, \sigma^2),$$

for $x_t = 1$, $x_t = (1, t)'$ and ξ is a constant.

(a) Simulate the power envelope for $c = \{-1, -2, \cdots, -30\}$, $T = 1000$ and using 100000 repetitions.

(b) Repeat for quadratic detrending. Observe the effect of increasing the degree of the detrending regression on the power available to a unit root test.

(6) Critical Values and $\bar{c}$ in the Presence of a Trend Break

---
Program files   `unit_cbar.*`, `unit_breakcv.*`

(a) The asymptotic distribution of unit root tests in the presence of a trend break depends on the timing of the break. Simulate the asymptotic local power envelope in the presence of a trend break at a given fraction λ, and hence obtain the values of generalised least squares detrending constants for each of $\lambda = \{0.15, 0.20, \cdots, 0.85\}$.

(b) Using these values of $\bar{c}$, carry out a simulation to obtain approximate asymptotic critical values for MZ_t^{GLS} for each λ. Also obtain critical values for MZ_t^{GLS}.

(c) Carry out a simulation to investigate the effect of the initial condition on the power of MZ_t^{GLS} and MZ_t^{OLS} for $\lambda = \{0.25, 0.50, 0.75\}$.

(7) Phillips-Perron Test

Program files   `unit_ppcv.*`, `unit_ppsim.*`

Consider the AR(1) model

$$y_t = \phi y_{t-1} + v_t,$$

in which v_t is a stationary autocorrelated disturbance with mean zero, variance σ^2 and satisfying the FCLT for autocorrelated processes

$$\frac{1}{\sqrt{T}} \sum_{t=1}^{[Ts]} v_t \xrightarrow{d} \omega B(s),$$

in which B is standard Brownian motion and ω^2 is the long-run variance $\omega^2 = \sum_{j=-\infty}^{\infty} E(v_t v_{t-j})$.

(a) Derive the asymptotic distribution of the ordinary least squares estimator of ϕ in the AR(1) model where $\phi = 1$ and show that it depends on the autocorrelation properties of v_t.

(b) Suppose that consistent estimators $\widehat{\omega}^2$ and $\widehat{\sigma}^2$ of ω^2 and σ^2, respectively, are available. Define the transformed estimator

$$\tilde{\phi} = \widehat{\phi} - \frac{1}{2} \frac{\widehat{\omega}^2 - \widehat{\sigma}^2}{T^{-1} \sum_{t=2}^{T} y_{t-1}^2}$$

and derive its asymptotic distribution when $\phi = 1$, hence showing that the asymptotic distribution of $\tilde{\phi}$ does not depend on the autocorrelation properties of v_t.

(c) Define a unit root test based on $\tilde{\phi}$ and simulate approximate asymptotic critical values. This test is the Z_α test suggested in Phillips (1986) and extended to allow for a constant and time trend in Phillips and Perron (1988).

(d) Carry out a Monte Carlo experiment to investigate the finite sample size properties of the test in part (c). Use $T = \{100, 200\}$ with v_t given by

$$(1 - \phi L)v_t = (1 + \theta L)e_t, \qquad e_t \sim iid\ N(0, 1)$$

in which $\phi = \{0, 0.3, 0.6, 0.9\}$ and $\theta = \{-0.8, -0.4, 0, 0.4, 0.8\}$. Use $\widehat{\sigma}^2 = (T - 1)^{-1} \sum_{t=2}^{T} \widehat{v}_t^2$ and let $\widehat{\omega}^2$ be the Newey-West long-run variance estimator with quadratic spectral lag weights (see Chapter 9) and pre-whitening as suggested by Andrews and Monahan (1992).

(8) Unit Root Test Without Lags or Long-Run Variance

Program files `unit_breitung_size.*`, `unit_breitung_power.*`

Consider the AR(1) model $y_t = \phi y_{t-1} + v_t$ where v_t is a disturbance satisfying the same conditions as set out in Exercise 7. Consider the unit root test statistic

$$\rho = \frac{T^{-4} \sum_{t=1}^{T} S_t^2}{T^{-2} \sum_{t=1}^{T} y_t^2},$$

in which $S_t = \sum_{j=1}^{t} y_j$, as proposed by Breitung (2002).

(a) Show that the asymptotic distribution of this statistic under $H_0 : \phi = 1$ is

$$\rho \xrightarrow{d} \frac{\int_0^1 B_S(r)^2 dr}{\int_0^1 B(r)^2 dr},$$

in which $B_S(r) = \int_0^r B(s)ds$, regardless of the autocorrelation properties of v_t (no autoregression or long-run variance is required to make this test operational).

(b) Carry out a Monte Carlo experiment to investigate the finite sample size properties of this test. Use the design from part (d) of the previous exercise.

(c) Use a simulation to compare the asymptotic local power of the test to that of the DF_t test.

(9) **Testing the Null Hypothesis of Stationarity**

Program files   `unit_kpss_cv.*`, `unit_kpssmc.*`

Consider the regression model

$$y_t = x_t'\beta + z_t,$$

in which x_t is a $(k \times 1)$ vector of fixed regressors (constant, time trend), β is $(k \times 1)$ vector of coefficients and z_t has the unobserved components representation

$$z_t = w_t + u_t,$$
$$w_t = w_{t-1} + v_t,$$

in which $w_0 = 0$ and

$$\begin{bmatrix} u_t \\ v_t \end{bmatrix} \sim iid\, N\left(\begin{bmatrix} 0 \\ 0 \end{bmatrix}, \begin{bmatrix} \sigma_u^2 & 0 \\ 0 & \sigma_v^2 \end{bmatrix} \right).$$

Define the standardised test statistic

$$s = \frac{T^{-2} \sum_{t=1}^T S_t^2}{\widehat{\omega}^2},$$

in which $S_t = \sum_{j=1}^t \widehat{z}_j$, $\widehat{z} = (\widehat{z}_1, \cdots, \widehat{z}_T)'$ is the vector of ordinary least squares residuals from a regression of y on x and $\widehat{\omega}^2$ is a consistent Newey-West form of estimator of ω^2 based on $\widehat{z}_t$. This test statistic can be interpreted as a test of over-differencing and/or a moving average unit root and is most commonly known as the KPSS test, after Kwiatkowski, Phillips, Schmidt and Shin (1992).

(a) Show that z_t is $I(1)$ if $\sigma_v^2 > 0$ and z_t is $I(0)$ if $\sigma_v^2 = 0$ and hence that a test of $\sigma_v^2 = 0$ against $\sigma_v^2 > 0$ is a test of $I(0)$ against $I(1)$.

(b) Use the Newey-West form of the long-run variance estimator, but without pre-whitening, carry out a simulation of the size properties of the test when $x_t = 1$. Use $T = \{100, 200\}$ with u_t given by

$$(1 - \phi L)u_t = (1 + \theta L)\varepsilon_t, \qquad \varepsilon_t \sim iid\, N(0, 1)$$

in which $\phi = \{0, 0.3, 0.6, 0.9\}$ and $\theta = \{-0.8, -0.4, 0, 0.4, 0.8\}$.

(10) **Union of Rejections Tests**

Program files   unit_urtau.*, unit_urbreak.*, unit_pow0.*

(a) Carry out a simulation to obtain the value of τ for the MZ_t^{OLS} and MZ_t^{GLS} tests such that the decision rule is to reject H_0 if $MZ_t^{OLS} < \tau \cdot cv^{OLS}$ and/or $MZ_t^{GLS} < \tau \cdot cv^{GLS}$ has asymptotic size of 5%, where cv^{OLS} and cv^{GLS} are the usual 5% asymptotic critical values for the tests taken from Table 17.1. To do this, choose $T = 1000$, generate data under the null hypothesis (y_t will be a random walk) and obtain a large number of replications of both MZ_t^{OLS} and MZ_t^{GLS}. Once these replications are available, search for the appropriate value of τ such that $MZ_t^{OLS} < \tau \cdot cv^{OLS}$ and/or $MZ_t^{GLS} < \tau \cdot cv^{GLS}$ occurs in just 5% of the replications. Carry this out for $x_t = [1]$ and $x_t = [1\ t]'$.
(b) Repeat the simulation for $x_t = [1\ t\ DT_t]'$, where DT_t is the trend break variable for $\lambda = \{0.25, 0.50, 0.75\}$ and observe the insensitivity of τ to λ.
(c) Carry out a simulation to compare the power properties of the union of rejections test based on MZ_t^{OLS} and MZ_t^{GLS} with the individual tests. Obtain results for $x_t = 1$ and $x_t = [1\ t]'$. Obtain results for $u_0 = \{0, 2.5, 5.0\}$ to evaluate the robustness of the union of rejections test to the initial value.

(11) **Role of Initial Conditions and Union of Rejections**

Program files   unit_poweru0.*, unit_powerour.*

To investigate the effect of the initial condition on unit root tests, consider the model

$$y_t = x_t'\beta + u_t,$$
$$u_t = \phi u_{t-1} + v_t,$$
$$u_0 = \xi,$$
$$v_t \sim iid\,(0, \sigma^2),$$

in which ξ is a constant.

(a) Show that any unit root test that includes demeaning (x_t includes 1 so that the test is invariant to adding a constant to y_t) is invariant to ξ under the null hypothesis that $\phi = 1$. Show that this does not apply when $\phi < 1$.

(b) Carry out a simulation to explore the effect of ξ on the finite sample power of the MZ_t^{OLS} and MZ_t^{GLS} tests. Use $T = 200$ and consider the values $\xi = \{0, 2.5, 5\}$.

(c) Repeat the simulation with $\xi = -2.5$ and $\xi = -5$ to see if the effects of ξ on the power of the tests are symmetric.

(d) Using the same simulation design, include the union of rejections test in the comparison. That is, the null hypothesis is rejected if $MZ_t^{OLS} < \tau \cdot cv_{OLS}$ and/or $MZ_t^{GLS} < \tau \cdot cv_{GLS}$ where $cv^{OLS} = -2.467$, $cv^{GLS} = -1.966$, $\tau = 1.084$ when $x_t = 1$, and $cv^{OLS} = -3.130$, $cv^{GLS} = -2.867$, $\tau = 1.038$ when $x_t = (1, t)'$.

(12) **Unit Roots Tests of the Nelson and Plosser Data**

Program files	`unit_nelplos.*`
Data files	`nelson_plosser.*`

(a) Test for a unit root in each of the Nelson and Plosser series using the MZ_t^{OLS} and MZ_t^{GLS} tests and the union of rejections of the two tests. Use a constant and linear trend for each series except unemployment, for which a constant is sufficient. Use the MAIC for lag length selection. The results should replicate those in Table 17.7.

(b) Test whether nominal GNP can be considered to be $I(2)$ (test for a unit root in the first difference of nominal GNP).

18 Cointegration

18.1 Introduction

An important implication of the analysis of stochastic trends presented in Chapter 16 and of the unit root tests discussed in Chapter 17 is that nonstationary time series can be rendered stationary through differencing the series. This use of the differencing operator represents a univariate approach to achieving stationarity since the discussion of nonstationary processes so far has concentrated on a single time series. In the case of $N > 1$ nonstationary time series $y_t = \{y_{1,t}, y_{2,t}, \cdots, y_{N,t}\}$, an alternative method of achieving stationarity is to form linear combinations of the series. The ability to find stationary linear combinations of nonstationary time series is known as cointegration (Engle and Granger, 1987).

The existence of cointegration among sets of nonstationary time series has three important implications.

(1) Cointegration implies a set of dynamic long-run equilibria where the weights used to achieve stationarity represent the parameters of the equilibrium relationship.
(2) The estimates of the weights to achieve stationarity (the long-run parameter estimates) converge to their population values at a super-consistent rate of T compared to the usual $\sqrt{T}$ rate of convergence.
(3) Modelling a system of cointegrated variables allows for specification of both long-run and short-run dynamics. The resultant model is known as a vector error correction model (VECM).

Maximum likelihood methods are used to estimate the parameters of and test restrictions on VECMs. As cointegration yields a set of nonlinear restrictions on the VECM, estimation proceeds using either the iterative gradient algorithms of Chapter 3, or the Johansen algorithm (1988, 1991, 1995b) that decomposes the log-likelihood function in terms of its eigenvalues. Hypothesis tests of the VECM are computed using the statistics discussed in Chapter 4. A widely

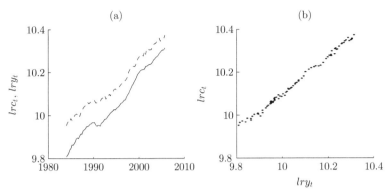

Figure 18.1. United States data on the log real consumption per capita, lrc_t, (solid line) and the log real income per capita, lry_t, (dashed line) for the period March 1984 to December 2005.

adopted test is the LR test of cointegration, commonly known as the trace test, which represents a multivariate generalisation of the Dickey-Fuller unit root test discussed in Chapter 17.

18.2   Long-Run Economic Models

To highlight the dynamic interrelationships between economic processes with stochastic trends and how linear combinations of nonstationary variables can result in stationary series, three examples are presented.

Example 18.1 Permanent Income Hypothesis

The permanent income hypothesis represents a long-run relationship between log real consumption, lrc_t, and log real income, lry_t, given by

$$lrc_t = \beta_c + \beta_y lry_t + u_t,$$

where u_t is a disturbance term and β_c and β_y are parameters. Panel (a) of Figure 18.1 shows that even though lrc_t and lry_t are nonstationary, the two-dimensional scatterplot in panel (b) of Figure 18.1 reveals a one-dimensional relationship between the two variables suggesting that lrc_t does not drift too far from its permanent income level of $\beta_c + \beta_y lry_t$ Transient movements in consumption are captured by u_t, caused by business cycles for example.   □

Example 18.2 Demand for Money

The long-run theory of the demand for money specifies that log real money, lrm_t, is jointly determined by log real income, lry_t, and the spread between the yields on bonds and money, $spread_t$,

$$lrm_t = \beta_c + \beta_y lry_t + \beta_s spread_t + u_t,$$

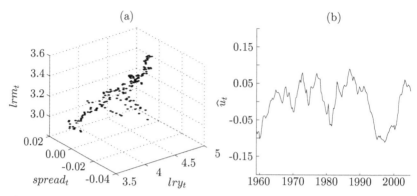

Figure 18.2. United States data on log real M2, lrm_t, log real GDP, lry_t, and the spread between the Treasury bill rate and Federal funds rate, $spread_t$, for the period March 1959 to December 2005. The residuals are computed from the least squares estimated equation $lrm_t = 0.149 + 0.828 \ lry_t - 0.785 \ spread_t + \widehat{u}_t$.

where u_t is a disturbance term and β_c, β_y and β_s are parameters. A three-dimensional scatterplot of the data in panel (a) of Figure 18.2 reveals a two-dimensional surface suggesting that lrm_t does not persistently deviate from its long-run level of $\beta_c + \beta_y lry_t + \beta_s spread_t$. This finding is illustrated further in panel (b) of Figure 18.2, which shows that short-run movements given by the residuals from estimating the long-run money demand equation by ordinary least squares, do not exhibit a trend even though the individual variables in the long-run equation do exhibit a trend.   □

Example 18.3 Term Structure of Interest Rates

The term structure is the relationship between the yields on bonds of differing maturities. Panel (a) of Figure 18.3 shows that the 1-year ($r_{1,t}$), 5-year ($r_{2,t}$) and 10-year ($r_{3,t}$) yields are nonstationary, while a three-dimensional scatterplot in panel (b) of Figure 18.3 shows that all three yields fall on a one-dimensional line. This suggests two long-run relationships between the three yields

$$r_{3,t} = \beta_{c,1} + \beta_{r,1}r_{1,t} + u_{1,t}$$
$$r_{2,t} = \beta_{c,2} + \beta_{r,2}r_{1,t} + u_{2,t},$$

where $u_{1,t}$ and $u_{2,t}$ are stationary disturbances. By extension, N yields would result in $N-1$ long-run relationships. In the special case where $\beta_{r,1} = \beta_{r,2} = 1$ and $\beta_{c,1} = \beta_{c,2} = 0$, the disturbance terms are equal to the spreads, which are stationary.   □

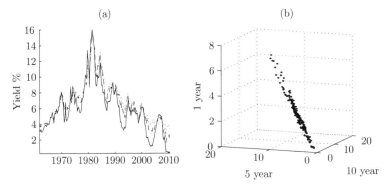

Figure 18.3. Yields (% p.a.) on 1-year, 5-year and 10-year United States bonds, for the period March 1962 to September 2010.

18.3 Specification of a VECM

The examples in Section 18.2 demonstrate the existence of long-run equilibrium relationships between nonstationary variables where short-run deviations from equilibrium are stationary.

18.3.1 Bivariate Models

Consider a bivariate model as given by the permanent income hypothesis in Example 18.1, containing two $I(1)$ variables, $y_{1,t}$ and $y_{2,t}$, with the long-run relationship given by

$$y_{1,t} = \beta_c + \beta_y y_{2,t} + u_t, \qquad (18.1)$$

in which $\beta_c + \beta_y y_{2,t}$ represents the long-run equilibrium, and u_t represents the short-run deviations from equilibrium, which by assumption is stationary. The long run is represented in Figure 18.4 by the straight line assuming $\beta_y > 0$. Suppose that the two variables are in equilibrium at point A. From (18.1), the effect of a positive shock in the previous period ($u_{t-1} > 0$) immediately raises $y_{1,t-1}$ to point B while leaving $y_{2,t-1}$ unaffected. For the process to converge back to its long-run equilibrium, there are three possible trajectories.

(1) *Adjustments are made by $y_{1,t}$*

Equilibrium is restored by $y_{1,t}$ decreasing and returning to point A while $y_{2,t}$ remains unchanged at its initial position. Assuming that the short-run movements in $y_{1,t}$ are a linear function of the size of the shock, u_{t-1}, the adjustment in $y_{1,t}$ is given by

$$y_{1,t} - y_{1,t-1} = \alpha_1 u_{t-1} + v_{1,t} = \alpha_1(y_{1,t-1} - \beta_c - \beta_y y_{2,t-1}) + v_{1,t}, \quad (18.2)$$

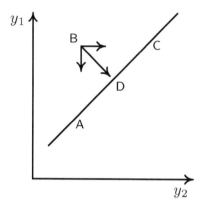

Figure 18.4. Phase diagram demonstrating a vector error correction model.

in which $\alpha_1 < 0$, is a parameter in which the sign reflects the negative adjustment in $y_{1,t}$ needed to restore equilibrium, and $v_{1,t}$ is a disturbance term.

(2) *Adjustments are made by* $y_{2,t}$

Equilibrium is restored by $y_{2,t}$ increasing towards point C, with $y_{1,t}$ remaining unchanged after the initial shock. Assuming that the short-run movements in $y_{2,t}$ are a linear function of the size of the shock, u_{t-1}, the adjustment in $y_{2,t}$ is given by

$$y_{2,t} - y_{2,t-1} = \alpha_2 u_{t-1} + v_{2,t} = \alpha_2 (y_{1,t-1} - \beta_c - \beta_y y_{2,t-1}) + v_{2,t},$$

(18.3)

in which $\alpha_2 > 0$ is a parameter with the sign reflecting the direction of adjustment in $y_{2,t}$ needed to achieve equilibrium and $v_{2,t}$ is a disturbance term.

(3) *Adjustments are made by both* $y_{1,t}$ *and* $y_{2,t}$

Both equations (18.2) and (18.3) are now in operation with $y_{1,t}$ and $y_{2,t}$ converging to a point on the long-run equilibrium such as D. The relative strengths of the two adjustment paths depend upon the relative magnitudes of the adjustment parameters α_1 and α_2.

Equations (18.2) and (18.3) represent a VECM as the two variables correct themselves in the next period according to the error from being out of equilibrium. For this reason, the parameters α_1 and α_2 are known as the error correction parameters. An important characteristic of the VECM is that it is a special case of a vector autoregression (VAR) as studied in Chapter 13 where the parameters are subject to a set of cross-equation restrictions because all the variables are governed by the same long-run equation(s). To demonstrate this, rewrite the VECM in (18.2) and (18.3) as

$$\begin{bmatrix} \Delta y_{1,t} \\ \Delta y_{2,t} \end{bmatrix} = \begin{bmatrix} -\alpha_1 \beta_c \\ -\alpha_2 \beta_c \end{bmatrix} + \begin{bmatrix} \alpha_1 \\ \alpha_2 \end{bmatrix} \begin{bmatrix} 1 & -\beta_y \end{bmatrix} \begin{bmatrix} y_{1,t-1} \\ y_{2,t-1} \end{bmatrix} + \begin{bmatrix} v_{1,t} \\ v_{2,t} \end{bmatrix},$$

or, in terms of a VAR

$$\begin{bmatrix} y_{1,t} \\ y_{2,t} \end{bmatrix} = \begin{bmatrix} -\alpha_1 \beta_c \\ -\alpha_2 \beta_c \end{bmatrix} + \begin{bmatrix} 1+\alpha_1 & -\alpha_1 \beta_y \\ \alpha_2 & 1 - \alpha_2 \beta_y \end{bmatrix} \begin{bmatrix} y_{1,t-1} \\ y_{2,t-1} \end{bmatrix} + \begin{bmatrix} v_{1,t} \\ v_{2,t} \end{bmatrix}$$

$$y_t = \mu + \Phi_1 y_{t-1} + v_t,$$

in which

$$\mu = \begin{bmatrix} -\alpha_1 \beta_c \\ -\alpha_2 \beta_c \end{bmatrix}, \qquad \Phi_1 = \begin{bmatrix} 1+\alpha_1 & -\alpha_1 \beta_y \\ \alpha_2 & 1 - \alpha_2 \beta_y \end{bmatrix}. \tag{18.4}$$

This is a first-order VAR with two restrictions on the parameters in the system. In an unconstrained VAR, the vector of intercepts μ contains 2 parameters, and the matrix of autocorrelation parameters Φ_1, contains 4 parameters, for a total of 6 parameters. However, from (18.4), the model consists of just 4 parameters $\{\beta_c, \beta_y, \alpha_1, \alpha_2\}$, resulting in a total of $6 - 4 = 2$ restrictions.

18.3.2   Multivariate Models

The relationship between a VECM and a VAR generalises to N variables $y_t = [y_{1,t}, \cdots, y_{N,t}]'$ and p lags. First consider the case of an N dimensional model with $p = 1$ lags

$$y_t = \mu + \Phi_1 y_{t-1} + v_t. \tag{18.5}$$

Subtracting y_{t-1} from both sides and rearranging gives

$$\Delta y_t = \mu - (I_N - \Phi_1)y_{t-1} + v_t = \mu - \Phi(1)y_{t-1} + v_t, \tag{18.6}$$

in which $\Phi(1) = I_N - \Phi_1$. This is a VECM, but with $p - 1 = 0$ lags. The operation to transform the VAR in (18.5) to the VECM in (18.6) is exactly the same operation used in Chapter 17 to derive the Dickey-Fuller regression equation from an AR(1) model to test for a unit root.

Expanding the VAR in (18.5) to include p lags gives

$$\Phi(L)y_t = \mu + v_t, \tag{18.7}$$

in which v_t is an N dimensional vector of iid disturbances and $\Phi(L) = I_N - \Phi_1 L - \cdots - \Phi_p L^p$ is a polynomial in the lag operator (see Appendix B). The resulting VECM has $p - 1$ lags given by

$$\Delta y_t = \mu - \Phi(1)y_{t-1} + \sum_{j=1}^{p-1} \Gamma_j \Delta y_{t-j} + v_t, \tag{18.8}$$

in which $\Phi(1) = I_N - \Phi_1 - \cdots - \Phi_p$. In the special case $N = 1$, (18.8) reduces to the augmented Dickey-Fuller equation to test for a unit root discussed in Chapter 17.

The formal operation linking (18.7) and (18.8) is the Beveridge-Nelson decomposition, (Beveridge and Nelson, 1981) which re-expresses the polynomial $\Phi(L)$ in (18.7) as

$$\Phi(L) = \Phi(1)L + \Gamma(L)(1 - L), \tag{18.9}$$

in which

$$\Gamma(L) = I_N - \sum_{j=1}^{p-1} \Gamma_j L^j, \quad \Gamma_j = -\sum_{i=j+1}^{p} \Phi_i. \tag{18.10}$$

Substituting (18.9) into (18.7) gives the VECM in (18.8), as

$$(\Phi(1)L + \Gamma(L)(1 - L))y_t = \Phi(1)y_{t-1} + \Delta y_t - \sum_{j=1}^{p-1} \Gamma_j \Delta y_{t-j} = \mu + v_t.$$

18.3.3   Cointegration

If the vector time series y_t is assumed to be $I(1)$, then y_t is cointegrated if there exists an $(N \times r)$ full column rank matrix, β, with $1 \leq r < N$, such that the r linear combinations

$$\beta' y_t = u_t, \tag{18.11}$$

are $I(0)$. The dimension r is called the cointegrating rank and the columns of β are called the cointegrating vectors. In matrix notation the cointegrating system is given by

$$\begin{bmatrix} \beta_{1,1} & \beta_{1,2} & \cdots & \beta_{1,r} \\ \beta_{2,1} & \beta_{2,2} & \cdots & \beta_{2,r} \\ \beta_{3,1} & \beta_{3,2} & \cdots & \beta_{3,r} \\ \vdots & \vdots & \ddots & \vdots \\ \beta_{N,1} & \beta_{N,2} & \cdots & \beta_{N,r} \end{bmatrix}' \begin{bmatrix} y_{1,t} \\ y_{2,t} \\ y_{3,t} \\ \vdots \\ y_{N,t} \end{bmatrix} = \begin{bmatrix} u_{1,t} \\ u_{2,t} \\ u_{3,t} \\ \vdots \\ u_{N,t} \end{bmatrix}.$$

If an N dimensional system has r $I(0)$ components, this suggests there are $N - r$ $I(1)$ components, commonly referred to as common trends, which are the driving factors behind the $I(1)$ features of y_t.

Example 18.4 Graphical Detection of the Rank
   In panel (b) of Figure 18.1, the $N = 2$ dimensional area of the scatterplot of the permanent income example, a single line suggests a rank of $r = 1$

and $N - r = 2 - 1 = 1$ common trend. In the $N = 3$ dimensional area of the scatterplot of the money demand example, panel (b) of Figure 18.2, a two-dimensional surface suggests a rank of $r = 1$ and $N - r = 3 - 1 = 2$ common trends. Finally, in the $N = 3$ dimensional area of the scatterplot of the term structure example, panel (b) of Figure 18.3, a single line suggests a rank of $r = 2$ and $N - r = 3 - 2 = 1$ common trend.   □

The Granger representation theorem (Engle and Granger, 1987) is the fundamental result showing the formal connection between cointegration in equation (18.11) and the vector error correction model in (18.8). The main result of the theorem is that all of the information needed to analyse cointegration is contained in the $\Phi(1)$ matrix in (18.8).

Granger Representation Theorem
Suppose y_t, generated by (18.8), is either $I(1)$ or $I(0)$.

(a) If $\Phi(1)$ has full rank, $r = N$, then y_t is $I(0)$.
(b) If $\Phi(1)$ has reduced rank, r for $0 < r < N$, $\Phi(1) = -\alpha\beta'$ where α and β are each $(N \times r)$ matrices with full column rank, then y_t is $I(1)$ and $\beta'y_t$ is $I(0)$ with cointegrating vectors(s) given by the columns of β.
(c) If $\Phi(1)$ has zero rank, $r = 0$, $\Phi(1) = 0$ and y_t is $I(1)$ and not cointegrated. ∎

Example 18.5 Cointegrating Rank of Long-Run Economic Models
The form of $\Phi(1)$ for the long-run economic models in Section 18.2 is

Permanent income:
$(N = 2, r = 1)$
$$\Phi(1) = -\alpha\beta' = -\begin{bmatrix} \alpha_{1,1} \\ \alpha_{2,1} \end{bmatrix}\begin{bmatrix} 1 \\ -\beta_y \end{bmatrix}'$$

Money demand:
$(N = 3, r = 1)$
$$\Phi(1) = -\alpha\beta' = -\begin{bmatrix} \alpha_{1,1} \\ \alpha_{2,1} \\ \alpha_{3,1} \end{bmatrix}\begin{bmatrix} 1 \\ -\beta_y \\ -\beta_s \end{bmatrix}'$$

Term structure:
$(N = 3, r = 2)$
$$\Phi(1) = -\alpha\beta' = -\begin{bmatrix} \alpha_{1,1} & \alpha_{1,2} \\ \alpha_{2,1} & \alpha_{2,2} \\ \alpha_{3,1} & \alpha_{3,2} \end{bmatrix}\begin{bmatrix} 1 & 0 \\ 0 & 1 \\ -\beta_{r,1} & -\beta_{r,2} \end{bmatrix}'.$$

□

The Granger representation theorem shows how cointegration arises from the rearranged VAR in (18.7) and suggests the form of the model that should be estimated. If $\Phi(1)$ has full rank N, then all of the time series in y_t are stationary and the original VAR in (18.7) is specified in levels. If $\Phi(1) = 0$, then equation (18.8) shows that the appropriate model is a VAR($p - 1$) in first differences

$$\Delta y_t = \mu + \sum_{j=1}^{p-1} \Gamma_j \Delta y_{t-j} + v_t. \tag{18.12}$$

If $\Phi(1)$ has reduced rank, r with $0 < r < N$, then the VECM in (18.8) is a restricted VAR subject to the cointegrating restrictions $\Phi(1) = -\alpha\beta'$, given by

$$\Delta y_t = \mu + \alpha\beta' y_{t-1} + \sum_{j=1}^{p-1} \Gamma_j \Delta y_{t-j} + v_t \,. \tag{18.13}$$

18.3.4 Deterministic Components

A natural extension of the VECM in (18.13) is to include a deterministic time trend t as follows

$$\Delta y_t = \mu_0 + \mu_1 t + \alpha\beta' y_{t-1} + \sum_{j=1}^{p-1} \Gamma_j \Delta y_{t-j} + v_t \,, \tag{18.14}$$

in which μ_0 and μ_1 are $(N \times 1)$ vectors of parameters associated with the intercept and time trend, respectively. These deterministic components have a dual role by contributing both to the short-run and long-run properties of y_t. To demonstrate this, the deterministic elements in (18.14) are decomposed into their short-run and long-run contributions by defining

$$\underbrace{\mu_j}_{\text{Total}} = \underbrace{\delta_j}_{\text{Short run}} + \underbrace{\alpha\beta'_j}_{\text{Long run}} \,, \qquad j = 0, 1 \,, \tag{18.15}$$

in which δ_j is $(N \times 1)$ and β_j is $(1 \times r)$. Using (18.15) to rewrite (18.14) gives

$$\Delta y_t = \delta_0 + \delta_1 t + \alpha(\beta'_0 + \beta'_1 t + \beta' y_{t-1}) + \sum_{j=1}^{p-1} \Gamma_j \Delta y_{t-j} + v_t \,. \tag{18.16}$$

The term $\beta'_0 + \beta'_1 t + \beta' y_{t-1}$ in (18.16) represents the long-run relationship among the variables. The parameter δ_0 provides a drift component in the equation of Δy_t that contributes a linear trend to y_t. Similarly $\delta_1 t$ allows for a linear time trend in Δy_t that contributes a quadratic trend to y_t. By contrast, β_0 contributes just a constant to y_t and $\beta'_1 t$ contributes a linear trend. Thus the unrestricted term μ_0 in (18.14) has potentially two effects on y_t, contributing both a constant to the long-run economic model and a linear trend to the data. Similarly the unrestricted term μ_1 in (18.14) contributes to both a linear trend in the long-run and a quadratic trend in the data.

The decomposition of μ_j in (18.15) into β_j and δ_j is formally expressed as

$$\delta_j = \alpha_\perp (\alpha'_\perp \alpha_\perp)^{-1} \alpha'_\perp \mu_i \,, \qquad \beta_j = (\alpha'\alpha)^{-1}\alpha'\mu_i \,, \tag{18.17}$$

in which $\alpha_\perp$ is the $(N \times (N-r))$ orthogonal complement matrix of the $(N \times r)$ matrix of error correction parameters α, such that $\alpha'_\perp \alpha = 0_{(N-r) \times r}$. To

Table 18.1. *Summary of alternative VECM specifications with*
$\mu_j = \delta_j + \alpha\beta'_j, \, j = 0, 1$

Model	Specification
1	$\Delta y_t \;=\; \alpha\beta' y_{t-1} + \sum_{j=1}^{p-1} \Gamma_j \Delta y_{t-j} + v_t$
	Restrictions: $\{\delta_0 = 0, \delta_1 = 0, \beta_0 = 0, \beta_1 = 0\}$
2	$\Delta y_t \;=\; \alpha(\beta'_0 + \beta' y_{t-1}) + \sum_{j=1}^{p-1} \Gamma_j \Delta y_{t-j} + v_t$
	Restrictions: $\{\delta_0 = 0, \delta_1 = 0, \beta_1 = 0\}$
3	$\Delta y_t \;=\; \delta_0 + \alpha(\beta'_0 + \beta' y_{t-1}) + \sum_{j=1}^{p-1} \Gamma_j \Delta y_{t-j} + v_t$
	$\;=\; \mu_0 + \alpha\beta' y_{t-1} + \sum_{j=1}^{p-1} \Gamma_j \Delta y_{t-j} + v_t$
	Restrictions: $\{\delta_1 = 0, \beta_1 = 0\}$
4	$\Delta y_t \;=\; \delta_0 + \alpha(\beta'_0 + \beta'_1 t + \beta' y_{t-1}) + \sum_{j=1}^{p-1} \Gamma_j \Delta y_{t-j} + v_t$
	$\;=\; \mu_0 + \alpha(\beta'_1 t + \beta' y_{t-1}) + \sum_{j=1}^{p-1} \Gamma_j \Delta y_{t-j} + v_t$
	Restrictions: $\{\delta_1 = 0\}$
5	$\Delta y_t \;=\; \delta_0 + \delta_1 t + \alpha(\beta'_0 + \beta'_1 t + \beta' y_{t-1}) + \sum_{j=1}^{p-1} \Gamma_j \Delta y_{t-j} + v_t$
	$\;=\; \mu_0 + \mu_1 t + \alpha\beta' y_{t-1} + \sum_{j=1}^{p-1} \Gamma_j \Delta y_{t-j} + v_t$
	Restrictions: None

derive these expressions, multiply both sides of the identity $I_N = \alpha(\alpha'\alpha)^{-1}\alpha' + \alpha_\perp(\alpha'_\perp\alpha_\perp)^{-1}\alpha'_\perp$, by μ_j to give

$$\mu_j = \alpha_\perp(\alpha'_\perp\alpha_\perp)^{-1}\alpha'_\perp\mu_j + \alpha(\alpha'\alpha)^{-1}\alpha'\mu_j = \delta_j + \alpha\beta_j \,.$$

An important implication of this decomposition is that even though δ_j has N elements in (18.16), there are at most only $N - r$ linear independent elements, which is the difference between the dimension of the total system μ_j and the dimension of the number of cointegrating vectors β_j. Alternatively, the VECM in (18.16) contains $N + r$ intercepts with r cross-equation restrictions on the parameters given by (18.17), thereby giving a total of N unique intercepts.

Equation (18.16) is a general specification to model nonstationary time series containing five important special cases summarised in Table 18.1. Model 1 is the simplest and most restricted version of the VECM as it contains no deterministic components. Model 2 allows for just r intercepts corresponding to the r long-run equations, whereas Model 3 allows for contributions of the intercepts in the short run and the long run for a total of N intercepts. Model 4 extends Model 3 by including r time trends just in the long-run equation, whereas Model 5 allows for N time trends that contribute to y_t in both the short run and the long run. The time series properties of these alternative models are investigated in Exercise 2.

Additional types of deterministic components allowing for dummy variables as a result of seasonality or structural breaks can also be included. Seasonal dummy variables are included in the model by appending them to the constant term. Provided that the dummy variables are standardised to sum to zero, they do not have any effect on the asymptotic properties of the estimated parameters of the model (Johansen, 1995b, p166). Structural breaks can arise from:

(1) a change in the number of cointegrating equations; and/or
(2) a change in the parameters of the VECM.

As with unit roots tests in the presence of structural breaks, the statistical properties of the estimators depend upon whether the timing of the break is known as well as on when the break occurs in the sample (Johansen, Mosconi and Nielsen, 2000; Trenkler, Saikkonen and Lütkephol, 2007).

18.4   Estimation

Assuming a parametric specification for the distribution of the disturbance vector v_t in (18.14), the parameters of a VECM are estimated by maximum likelihood by estimating a VAR subject to the cross-equation restrictions arising from cointegration. Two maximum likelihood estimators are presented. The first is an iterative estimator based on the algorithms of Chapter 3 as a result of the cross-equation restrictions on the parameters of the VAR. The second is the estimator proposed by Johansen (1988, 1991) based on an eigenvalue decomposition of the log-likelihood function. Both estimators yield identical point estimates. The second estimator has a computational advantage since it does not require an iterative solution but the former estimator has the advantage of being appropriate for more general classes of cointegrating models where long-run restrictions arising from economic theory are imposed on the individual parameters contained in the cointegrating vectors.

If v_t is assumed to be distributed as $v_t \sim iid\ N(0, V)$, the conditional log-likelihood function of the VECM based on p lags is

$$\ln L_T(\theta) = \frac{1}{T-p} \sum_{t=p+1}^{T} \ln f(y_t | y_{t-1}, y_{t-2}, \cdots y_{t-p}; \theta)$$

$$= -\frac{N}{2} \ln 2\pi - \frac{1}{2} \ln |V| - \frac{1}{2(T-p)} \sum_{t=p+1}^{T} v_t' V^{-1} v_t , \qquad (18.18)$$

with unknown parameters θ. The maximum likelihood estimator is obtained by choosing θ to maximise $\ln L_T(\theta)$, by solving the first-order conditions

$$G_T(\widehat{\theta}) = \frac{\partial \ln L_T(\theta)}{\partial \theta}\bigg|_{\theta=\widehat{\theta}} = 0, \tag{18.19}$$

for $\widehat{\theta}$. The solution of (18.19) depends upon the rank of the matrix $\Phi(1)$ in (18.8). From the Granger representation theorem, three cases need to be considered: full rank $(r = N)$, reduced rank $(0 < r < N)$ and zero rank $(r = 0)$.

18.4.1   Full-Rank Case

In the case where $\Phi(1)$ in (18.8) has full rank, the VECM is equivalent to the unconstrained VAR in (18.7) with unknown parameters

$$\theta = \{\mu_0, \mu_1, \Phi_1, \Phi_2, \cdots, \Phi_p, V\} = \{\mu_0, \mu_1, \Phi(1), \Gamma_1, \Gamma_2, \cdots, \Gamma_{p-1}, V\},$$

where a time trend is included. When the results of Chapter 13 are used, the maximum likelihood estimator of θ is simply obtained by applying ordinary least squares to each equation separately to obtain $\{\widehat{\mu}_0, \widehat{\mu}_1, \widehat{\Phi}_1, \widehat{\Phi}_2, \cdots, \widehat{\Phi}_p\}$, with V estimated from the least squares residuals $\{\widehat{v}_{1,t}, \widehat{v}_{2,t}, \cdots, \widehat{v}_{N,t}\}$ at the last step as

$$\widehat{V} = \frac{1}{T-p} \sum_{t=p+1}^{T} \widehat{v}_t \widehat{v}_t'. \tag{18.20}$$

Evaluating (18.18) at $\widehat{\theta}$, by using $\widehat{V}$ in (18.20), from Chapter 4, the maximised log-likelihood function reduces to

$$\ln L_T(\widehat{\theta}) = -\frac{N}{2}(\ln 2\pi + 1) - \frac{1}{2}\ln|\widehat{V}|. \tag{18.21}$$

Example 18.6 Full-Rank Estimates of the Term Structure Model
Consider a bivariate model of the term structure of interest rates where $y_{1,t}$ and $y_{2,t}$ are the 10-year and 1-year interest rates, respectively, given in Figure 18.3 and the sample size is $T = 195$ observations. Using $p = 1$ lags in (18.7) with a constant and no time trend, the estimated model with standard errors in parentheses, is

$$y_{1,t} = \underset{(0.120)}{0.257} + \underset{(0.039)}{0.888}y_{1,t-1} + \underset{(0.034)}{0.085}y_{2,t-1} + \widehat{v}_{1,t}$$

$$y_{2,t} = \underset{(0.189)}{0.221} - \underset{(0.062)}{0.026}y_{1,t-1} + \underset{(0.053)}{0.990}y_{2,t-1} + \widehat{v}_{2,t}.$$

The residual covariance matrix is estimated as

$$\widehat{V} = \frac{1}{194} \sum_{t=2}^{195} \widehat{v}_t \widehat{v}_t' = \begin{bmatrix} 0.2743 & 0.3408 \\ 0.3408 & 0.6748 \end{bmatrix},$$

and $|\widehat{V}| = 0.0689$. From (18.21), the value of the log-likelihood function evaluated at $\widehat{\theta}$ is

$$\ln L_T(\widehat{\theta}) = -\frac{2}{2}(\ln 2\pi + 1) - \frac{1}{2}\ln(0.0689) = -1.5009.$$

$\square$

18.4.2   Reduced-Rank Case: Iterative Estimator

If $\Phi(1)$ in (18.8) has reduced rank, then the cross-equation restrictions in (18.11) are imposed on the model and it is the constrained VECM in (18.16) that is estimated. The unknown parameters

$$\theta = \{\delta_0, \delta_1, \alpha, \beta_0, \beta_1, \beta, \Gamma_1, \Gamma_2, \cdots, \Gamma_{p-1}, V\},$$

are estimated by means of an iterative algorithm from Chapter 3.

Consider the bivariate VECM,

$$\Delta y_t = \alpha u_{t-1} + v_t, \qquad u_{t-1} = y_{1,t-1} - \beta y_{2,t-1}, \qquad (18.22)$$

in which $\Delta y_t = \left[\Delta y_{1,t}, \Delta y_{2,t}\right]'$, $\alpha = [\alpha_1, \alpha_2]'$, $v_t = [v_{1,t}, v_{2,t}]'$ and the parameters are $\theta = \{\alpha_1, \alpha_2, \beta\}$. The gradient and Hessian of (18.18) are, respectively,

$$G_T(\theta) = \frac{1}{T-1}\sum_{t=2}^{T}\begin{bmatrix} V^{-1}v_t u_{t-1} \\ -\alpha'V^{-1}v_t y_{2,t-1} \end{bmatrix},$$

$$H_T(\theta) = \frac{1}{T-1}\sum_{t=2}^{T}\begin{bmatrix} -V^{-1}u_{t-1}^2 & -V^{-1}(v_t - \alpha u_{t-1})y_{2,t-1} \\ -V^{-1}(v_t - \alpha u_{t-1})y_{2,t-1} & -\alpha'V^{-1}\alpha y_{2,t-1}^2 \end{bmatrix}.$$

$$(18.23)$$

The Newton-Raphson algorithm requires evaluating $G_T(\theta)$ and $H_T(\theta)$ at the starting values $\theta_{(0)}$ and updating according to $\theta_{(1)} = \theta_{(0)} - H_{(0)}^{-1}G_{(0)}$, until convergence.

A convenient way of providing starting estimates for the gradient algorithm is to use the Engle-Granger two-step estimator. In the case of two variables, $y_{1,t}$ and $y_{2,t}$, the first step involves estimating the cointegrating equation by ordinary least squares by regressing $y_{1,t}$ on a constant and $y_{2,t}$ to get $\widehat{u}_t$ and an estimate of the cointegrating vector $\widehat{\beta}$. The second step involves regressing $\Delta y_{1,t}$ on $\widehat{u}_{t-1}$ to get $\widehat{\alpha}_1$, and $\Delta y_{2,t}$ on $\widehat{u}_{t-1}$ to get $\widehat{\alpha}_2$. Any lags of $\Delta y_{1,t}$ and $\Delta y_{2,t}$ in the VECM are included in the second-stage regressions.

Example 18.7 Iterative Estimates of the Term Structure Model

A bivariate VECM containing the 10-year, $y_{1,t}$, and 1-year yields, $y_{2,t}$, using Model 2 in Table 18.1, with $p = 1$ lags and rank of $r = 1$, is specified as

$$y_{1,t} - y_{1,t-1} = \alpha_1(y_{1,t-1} - \beta_c - \beta_r y_{2,t-1}) + v_{1,t}$$
$$y_{2,t} - y_{2,t-1} = \alpha_2(y_{1,t-1} - \beta_c - \beta_r y_{2,t-1}) + v_{2,t},$$

in which $v_t = [v_{1,t}, v_{t,2}]$ is distributed as iid $N(0, V)$ and the unknown parameters are $\theta = \{\beta_c, \beta_r, \alpha_1, \alpha_2\}$. The conditional log-likelihood in (18.18) is maximised in five iterations using the Newton-Raphson algorithm with starting estimates obtained from the Engle-Granger two-step estimator. The parameter estimates are

$$\widehat{\theta} = [\widehat{\beta}_c, \widehat{\beta}_r, \widehat{\alpha}_1, \widehat{\alpha}_2]' = [1.434, 0.921, -0.092, 0.012]',$$

with the estimated covariance matrix based on the Hessian given by

$$\text{cov}(\widehat{\theta}) = \begin{bmatrix} 0.3324 & -0.0475 & -0.0104 & -0.0101 \\ -0.0475 & 0.0081 & 0.0019 & 0.0018 \\ -0.0104 & 0.0019 & 0.0017 & 0.0020 \\ -0.0101 & 0.0018 & 0.0020 & 0.0036 \end{bmatrix}.$$

The estimated VECM, with standard errors in parentheses based on the square roots of the diagonal elements in $\text{cov}(\widehat{\theta})$, is

$$\Delta y_{1,t} = \underset{(0.042)}{-0.092}(y_{1,t-1} - \underset{(0.576)}{1.434} - \underset{(0.090)}{0.921}y_{2,t-1}) + \widehat{v}_{1,t}$$

$$\Delta y_{2,t} = \underset{(0.060)}{0.012}(y_{1,t-1} - \underset{(0.576)}{1.434} - \underset{(0.090)}{0.921}y_{2,t-1}) + \widehat{v}_{2,t},$$

and the residual covariance matrix is estimated as

$$\widehat{V} = \frac{1}{194}\sum_{t=2}^{195} \widehat{v}_t\widehat{v}_t' = \begin{bmatrix} 0.684 & 0.346 \\ 0.346 & 0.277 \end{bmatrix}.$$

From (18.21), the value of the log-likelihood function evaluated at $\widehat{\theta}$ is

$$\ln L_T(\widehat{\theta}) = -\frac{2}{2}(\ln 2\pi + 1) - \frac{1}{2}\ln(0.069914) = -1.5076.$$

$\square$

18.4.3 Reduced-Rank Case: Johansen Estimator

An alternative maximum likelihood estimator proposed by Johansen (1988, 1991) has the advantage that the restricted VECM in (18.16) is estimated without the need for an iterative algorithm. The fundamental difference between the iterative and Johansen estimators is that the iterative approach imposes identifying restrictions on the parameters of the cointegrating vector and then estimates the remaining parameters. The Johansen approach, on the other hand, estimates a basis for the vector space spanned by the cointegrating vectors, and then imposes identification on the coefficients afterwards.

Each of the VECM specifications in Table 18.1 can be written in the general form

$$\Delta y_t = \alpha\gamma'z_{1,t} + \Psi z_{2,t} + v_t, \tag{18.24}$$

where for model 1:

$$z_{1,t} = y_{t-1}, \qquad\qquad\qquad \gamma = \beta,$$
$$z_{2,t} = (\Delta y'_{t-1}, \cdots, \Delta y'_{t-p+1})', \qquad \Psi = (\Gamma_1, \cdots, \Gamma_{p-1}),$$

for model 2:

$$z_{1,t} = (1, y_{t-1})', \qquad\qquad \gamma = (\beta'_0, \beta')',$$
$$z_{2,t} = (\Delta y'_{t-1}, \cdots, \Delta y'_{t-p+1})', \qquad \Psi = (\Gamma_1, \cdots, \Gamma_{p-1}),$$

for model 3:

$$z_{1,t} = y_{t-1}, \qquad\qquad\qquad \gamma = \beta,$$
$$z_{2,t} = (1, \Delta y'_{t-1}, \cdots, \Delta y'_{t-p+1})', \qquad \Psi = (\mu_0, \Gamma_1, \cdots, \Gamma_{p-1}),$$

for model 4:

$$z_{1,t} = (1, t, y_{t-1})', \qquad\qquad \gamma = (\beta'_0, \beta'_1, \beta')',$$
$$z_{2,t} = (1, \Delta y'_{t-1}, \cdots, \Delta y'_{t-p+1})', \qquad \Psi = (\delta_0, \Gamma_1, \cdots, \Gamma_{p-1}),$$

and for model 5:

$$z_{1,t} = y_{t-1}, \qquad\qquad\qquad \gamma = \beta,$$
$$z_{2,t} = (1, t, \Delta y'_{t-1}, \cdots, \Delta y'_{t-p+1})', \qquad \Psi = (\mu_0, \mu_1, \Gamma_1, \cdots, \Gamma_{p-1}).$$

Estimation is achieved by concentrating the log-likelihood function (see Chapter 3) on γ to yield

$$\ln L_T(\gamma) = \ln L_T(\widehat{\alpha}, \gamma, \widehat{\Psi}, \widehat{V}).$$

The idea behind this strategy is based on the recognition that if γ is known, estimation of the remaining parameters of the VECM in (18.24) no longer involves a nonlinear algorithm and simply requires an N dimensional multivariate regression of Δy_t on $\gamma' z_{1,t}$ and $z_{2,t}$. This second step also constitutes the second step of the Engle-Granger estimator used to generate starting estimates for the iterative estimator in Section 18.4.2. As each equation contains the same set of variables, the maximum likelihood estimator is ordinary least squares applied to each equation separately.

Concentrating the log-likelihood function involves three stages. The first stage uses (18.20) to estimate V to yield the log-likelihood function in (18.21), concentrated on α, γ and Ψ. The second stage involves estimating Ψ for fixed α and γ using two multivariate regressions of Δy_t on $z_{2,t}$ and $z_{1,t}$ on $z_{2,t}$ to obtain residuals $R_{0,t}$ and $R_{1,t}$, respectively. The details of these regressions are summarised in Table 18.2. For example, in the case of Model 2, first regress Δy_t on $\{\Delta y_{t-1}, \Delta y_{t-2}, \cdots, \Delta y_{t-p+1}\}$ to obtain the ($N \times 1$) vector of residuals $R_{0,t}$ and then regress $\{1, y_{t-1}\}$ on $\{\Delta y_{t-1}, \Delta y_{t-2}, \cdots, \Delta y_{t-p+1}\}$ to obtain the

Table 18.2. *Summary of intermediate ordinary least squares regressions to concentrate out the deterministic and lagged variable parameters from the log-likelihood function for alternative model specifications of the VECM*

Model	Dep. Variables	Independent Variables	Residuals
1	$\{\Delta y_t\}$	$\{\Delta y_{t-1}, \Delta y_{t-2}, \cdots, \Delta y_{t-p+1}\}$	$R_{0,t}$
	$\{y_{t-1}\}$	$\{\Delta y_{t-1}, \Delta y_{t-2}, \cdots, \Delta y_{t-p+1}\}$	$R_{1,t}$
2	$\{\Delta y_t\}$	$\{\Delta y_{t-1}, \Delta y_{t-2}, \cdots, \Delta y_{t-p+1}\}$	$R_{0,t}$
	$\{1, y_{t-1}\}$	$\{\Delta y_{t-1}, \Delta y_{t-2}, \cdots, \Delta y_{t-p+1}\}$	$R_{1,t}$
3	$\{\Delta y_t\}$	$\{1, \Delta y_{t-1}, \Delta y_{t-2}, \cdots, \Delta y_{t-p+1}\}$	$R_{0,t}$
	$\{y_{t-1}\}$	$\{1, \Delta y_{t-1}, \Delta y_{t-2}, \cdots, \Delta y_{t-p+1}\}$	$R_{1,t}$
4	$\{\Delta y_t\}$	$\{1, \Delta y_{t-1}, \Delta y_{t-2}, \cdots, \Delta y_{t-p+1}\}$	$R_{0,t}$
	$\{t, y_{t-1}\}$	$\{1, \Delta y_{t-1}, \Delta y_{t-2}, \cdots, \Delta y_{t-p+1}\}$	$R_{1,t}$
5	$\{\Delta y_t\}$	$\{1, t, \Delta y_{t-1}, \Delta y_{t-2}, \cdots, \Delta y_{t-p+1}\}$	$R_{0,t}$
	$\{y_{t-1}\}$	$\{1, t, \Delta y_{t-1}, \Delta y_{t-2}, \cdots, \Delta y_{t-p+1}\}$	$R_{1,t}$

$((N+1) \times 1)$ vector of residuals $R_{1,t}$. The estimated covariance matrix $\widehat{V}$ in (18.20) is now defined as

$$\widehat{V} = \frac{1}{T-p} \sum_{t=p+1}^{T} (R_{0,t} - \alpha\gamma' R_{1,t})(R_{0,t} - \alpha\gamma' R_{1,t})'$$
$$= S_{00} - \alpha\gamma' S_{10} - S_{01}\gamma\alpha' + \alpha\gamma' S_{11}\gamma\alpha',$$

in which

$$S_{ij} = \frac{1}{T-p} \sum_{t=p+1}^{T} R_{i,t} R'_{j,t}, \tag{18.25}$$

and the concentrated log-likelihood function is

$$\ln L_T(\alpha, \gamma) = -\frac{N}{2}(\ln 2\pi + 1)$$
$$- \frac{1}{2} \ln \left| S_{00} - \alpha\gamma' S_{10} - S_{01}\gamma\alpha' + \alpha\gamma' S_{11}\gamma\alpha' \right|. \tag{18.26}$$

The third stage is to maximise (18.26) with respect to α. The first-order condition is

$$S_{01}\gamma - \widehat{\alpha}\gamma' S_{11}\gamma = 0,$$

and solving for $\widehat{\alpha}$ gives

$$\widehat{\alpha} = S_{01}\gamma(\gamma' S_{11}\gamma)^{-1}.$$

This is the ordinary least squares estimator of α for a known γ. That is, $\hat{\alpha}$ is found from a regression of $R_{0,t}$ on $\gamma' R_{1,t}$. Substituting this expression for $\hat{\alpha}$ into (18.26) gives the concentrated log-likelihood function

$$\ln L_T(\gamma) = -\frac{N}{2}(\ln 2\pi + 1) - \frac{1}{2}\ln|S_{00} - S_{01}\gamma(\gamma' S_{11}\gamma)^{-1}\gamma' S_{10}|$$

$$= -\frac{N}{2}(\ln 2\pi + 1) - \frac{1}{2}\ln|S_{00}|$$

$$- \frac{1}{2}\ln|\gamma'(S_{11} - S_{10}S_{00}^{-1}S_{01})\gamma|,$$

which uses the property of determinants that

$$|S_{00} - S_{01}\gamma(\gamma' S_{11}\gamma)^{-1}\gamma' S_{10}| = |\gamma' S_{11}\gamma|^{-1}|S_{00}||\gamma' S_{11}\gamma - \gamma' S_{10}S_{00}^{-1}S_{01}\gamma|$$

$$= |S_{00}||\gamma'(S_{11} - S_{10}S_{00}^{-1}S_{01})\gamma|,$$

where the normalisation $\gamma' S_{11}\gamma = I_r$ is imposed. The maximum likelihood estimator, $\hat{\gamma}$, is the value of γ that maximises $\ln L_T(\gamma)$, which is equivalent to solving the following eigenvalue problem (Anderson, 1984)

$$|\hat{\lambda} S_{11} - S_{10}S_{00}^{-1}S_{01}| = 0, \tag{18.27}$$

where $\hat{\lambda}_1 \geqslant \hat{\lambda}_2 \cdots \geqslant \hat{\lambda}_r \cdots \geqslant \hat{\lambda}_N \geqslant 0$ and choosing $\hat{\gamma}$ to be the eigenvectors corresponding to the largest r eigenvalues.

To solve (18.27), use the Choleski decomposition $S_{11} = LL'$ to rewrite equation (18.27) as

$$|\hat{\lambda} I - L^{-1}S_{10}S_{00}^{-1}S_{01}L'^{-1}| = 0, \tag{18.28}$$

which is based on the result $LS_{11}L' = I_N$. Solving this eigenvalue problem yields $\hat{\lambda}_1, \hat{\lambda}_2, \cdots, \hat{\lambda}_N$ and the corresponding matrix of eigenvectors E. The estimates of the eigenvalues have the property $0 < \hat{\lambda}_i < 1$. The estimated eigenvectors of (18.27) are normalised as $L'^{-1}E$ in order to satisfy $\hat{\gamma}' S_{11}\hat{\gamma} = I_r$. Finally, the maximised log-likelihood function is

$$\ln L_T(\hat{\gamma}) = -\frac{N}{2}(1 + \ln 2\pi) - \frac{1}{2}\ln|S_{00}| - \frac{1}{2}\sum_{i=1}^{r}\ln(1 - \hat{\lambda}_i), \tag{18.29}$$

which represents a decomposition of the log-likelihood function in terms of the r largest eigenvalues.

A summary of the steps to implement the Johansen estimator are as follows.

Step 1: Compute the residual vectors $R_{0,t}$ and $R_{1,t}$ as given in Table 18.2.
Step 2: Compute the sums of squares matrices S_{ij} in (18.25).
Step 3: Compute the Choleski decomposition $S_{11} = LL'$.

Step 4: Perform an eigen decomposition on $L^{-1} S_{10} S_{00}^{-1} S_{01} L'^{-1}$, which yields the estimated eigenvalues $\widehat{\lambda}$ and the matrix of eigenvectors E.

Step 5: Normalise the eigenvector matrix as $L'^{-1} E$ and obtain $\widehat{\gamma}$ as the r columns of $L'^{-1} E$ corresponding to the largest r eigenvalues. From $\widehat{\gamma}$, obtain $\widehat{\beta}$ and, if necessary, $\widehat{\beta}_0$ and $\widehat{\beta}_1$.

Example 18.8 Johansen Estimates of the Term Structure Model

To re-estimate the bivariate term structure model in Example 18.7 by the Johansen estimator, the sums of squares matrices are

$$S_{00} = \frac{1}{T-1} \sum_{t=2}^{T} R_{0,t} R_{0,t}' = \begin{bmatrix} 0.286 & 0.344 \\ 0.344 & 0.684 \end{bmatrix}$$

$$S_{11} = \frac{1}{T-1} \sum_{t=2}^{T} R_{1,t} R_{1,t}' = \begin{bmatrix} 53.971 & 48.103 & 6.882 \\ 48.103 & 44.444 & 5.942 \\ 6.882 & 5.942 & 1.000 \end{bmatrix}$$

$$S_{01} = \frac{1}{T-1} \sum_{t=2}^{T} R_{0,t} R_{1,t}' = \begin{bmatrix} -0.163 & -0.060 & -0.006 \\ -0.349 & -0.369 & -0.015 \end{bmatrix},$$

in which $R_{0,t} = \begin{bmatrix} \Delta y_{1,t}, \Delta y_{2,t} \end{bmatrix}'$ and $R_{1,t} = \begin{bmatrix} y_{1,t-1}, y_{2,t-1}, 1 \end{bmatrix}'$. The Choleski decomposition of S_{11} is

$$L = \begin{bmatrix} 7.346 & 0.000 & 0.000 \\ 6.548 & 1.253 & 0.000 \\ 0.937 & -0.153 & 0.315 \end{bmatrix}.$$

Also compute

$$L^{-1} S_{10} S_{00}^{-1} S_{01} L^{-1'} = \begin{bmatrix} 0.003327 & 0.004630 & -0.004132 \\ 0.004630 & 0.076978 & 0.032473 \\ -0.004132 & 0.032473 & 0.025845 \end{bmatrix}.$$

The estimated eigenvalues and eigenvectors of this matrix are, respectively,

$$\widehat{\lambda} = \begin{bmatrix} 0.092804 \\ 0.013346 \\ 0.000000 \end{bmatrix}, \quad E = \begin{bmatrix} 0.026 & -0.494 & 0.869 \\ 0.900 & -0.366 & -0.236 \\ 0.435 & 0.788 & 0.435 \end{bmatrix},$$

and the rescaled eigenvectors are

$$L^{-1'} E = \begin{bmatrix} 7.346 & 0.000 & 0.000 \\ 6.548 & 1.253 & 0.000 \\ 0.937 & -0.153 & 0.315 \end{bmatrix}^{-1'} \begin{bmatrix} 0.026 & -0.494 & 0.869 \\ 0.900 & -0.366 & -0.236 \\ 0.435 & 0.788 & 0.435 \end{bmatrix}$$

$$= \begin{bmatrix} -0.962494 & -0.397778 & -0.040307 \\ 0.886447 & 0.012790 & -0.019751 \\ 1.380589 & 2.502564 & 1.381752 \end{bmatrix}.$$

In this application there is a single cointegrating vector, so just the first vector is taken from $L^{-1\prime}E$ to give

$$\widehat{\gamma} = [-0.962494, 0.886447, 1.380589]'.$$

These coefficients correspond to $y_{1,t}$, $y_{2,t}$ and a constant, respectively. Identification is achieved by normalising on $y_{1,t}$ to give

$$\widehat{\gamma} = \left[1, \frac{0.886447}{-0.962494}, \frac{1.380589}{-0.962494}\right]'$$
$$= [1, -0.921, -1.434]',$$

or, in terms of the parameters of the long-run model

$$\widehat{\beta}_c = 1.434, \quad \widehat{\beta}_r = 0.921,$$

which agree with the estimates obtained using the iterative estimator in Example 18.7. From (18.29) with $p = 1$ and $r = 1$,

$$\ln L_T(\widehat{\theta}) = -\frac{N}{2}(\ln 2\pi + 1) - \frac{1}{2}\ln|S_{00}| - \frac{1}{2}\sum_{i=1}^{r}\ln(1 - \widehat{\lambda}_i)$$
$$= -\frac{2}{2}(\ln 2\pi + 1) - \frac{1}{2}\ln 0.077066 - \frac{1}{2}\ln(1 - 0.092804)$$
$$= -1.5076,$$

which also matches the value of the log-likelihood reported in Example 18.7.

□

Example 18.9 Permanent Income Hypothesis
A bivariate VECM consisting of log real consumption per capita, $y_{1,t}$, and the logarithm real income per capita, $y_{2,t}$, is specified using Model 3 in Table 18.1 with $r = 1$ long-run equation and $p = 4$ lags. Based on the data in Figure 18.1, the eigenvalues and rescaled eigenvectors are, respectively,

$$\widehat{\lambda} = \begin{bmatrix} 0.200582 \\ 0.000010 \end{bmatrix}, \quad L^{-1\prime}E = \begin{bmatrix} -134.915366 & -18.086849 \\ 155.253208 & 29.423442 \end{bmatrix},$$

so that

$$\widehat{\gamma} = [-134.915366, 155.253208]'.$$

Normalising $\widehat{\gamma}$ in terms of real consumption ($y_{1,t}$) gives

$$\widehat{\beta} = \left[\frac{134.915}{134.915}, -\frac{155.253}{134.915}\right]' = [1, -1.151]'.$$

The estimates of μ_0 and α from the Johansen estimator are

$$\widehat{\mu}_0 = [-0.208390, 0.504582]', \quad \widehat{\alpha} = [-0.130, 0.309]' .$$

The estimates of β_0 and δ_0 are recovered using (18.17) by first computing the orthogonal complement matrix $\widehat{\alpha}_\perp = \begin{bmatrix} 0.922 & 0.387 \end{bmatrix}'$. The estimates are

$$\widehat{\beta}_0 = (\widehat{\alpha}'\widehat{\alpha})^{-1}\widehat{\alpha}'\widehat{\mu}$$

$$= \begin{bmatrix} 0.130^2 + 0.309^2 \end{bmatrix}^{-1} [-0.130, 0.309] \begin{bmatrix} -0.208390 \\ 0.504582 \end{bmatrix} = 1.628$$

$$\widehat{\delta}_0 = \widehat{\alpha}_\perp(\widehat{\alpha}'_\perp\widehat{\alpha}_\perp)^{-1}\widehat{\alpha}'_\perp\widehat{\mu}$$

$$= \begin{bmatrix} 0.922 \\ 0.387 \end{bmatrix} \begin{bmatrix} 0.922^2 + 0.387^2 \end{bmatrix}^{-1} \begin{bmatrix} 0.922 \\ 0.387 \end{bmatrix}' \begin{bmatrix} -0.208390 \\ 0.504582 \end{bmatrix} = \begin{bmatrix} 0.003 \\ 0.001 \end{bmatrix} .$$

The estimated long-run permanent income equation is

$$y_{1,t} = -1.628 + 1.151 \, y_{2,t} + \widehat{u}_t \, .$$

The estimated long-run marginal propensity to consume is 1.151, which is similar to the least squares estimate given by

$$y_{1,t} = -1.771 + 1.165 \, y_{2,t} + \widehat{u}_t \, . \qquad \qquad \square$$

18.4.4   Zero-Rank Case

The final case is where $\Phi(1)$ in (18.8) has zero rank, resulting in the VECM reducing to a VAR in first differences, as in (18.12), with unknown parameters $\theta = \{\mu_0, \mu_1, \Gamma_1, \Gamma_2, \cdots, \Gamma_{p-1}, V\}$. As with the full-rank model, the maximum likelihood estimator of (18.12) is the ordinary least squares estimator applied to each equation separately to estimate $\mu_0, \mu_1, \Gamma_1, \Gamma_2, \cdots, \Gamma_{p-1}$, with V estimated at the last step using (18.20).

Example 18.10 Bivariate Term Structure Model with Zero Rank
In the case of $r = 0$ rank, the VECM in Example 18.8 reduces to

$$y_{1,t} - y_{1,t-1} = v_{1,t}, \qquad y_{2,t} - y_{2,t-1} = v_{2,t} \, .$$

The residual covariance matrix is computed immediately using $\widehat{v}_t = v_t$ as

$$\widehat{V} = \frac{1}{194} \sum_{t=2}^{195} \widehat{v}_t\widehat{v}'_t = \begin{bmatrix} 0.286 & 0.344 \\ 0.344 & 0.684 \end{bmatrix} .$$

From (18.21), the value of the log-likelihood function evaluated at $\widehat{\theta}$ is

$$\ln L_T(\widehat{\theta}) = -\frac{2}{2}(\ln 2\pi + 1) - \frac{1}{2}\ln(0.077066) = -1.5563 \, . \qquad \square$$

18.5   Identification

An important feature of the Johansen estimator is the need to normalise the rescaled matrix of eigenvectors to estimate the cointegrating vectors $\widehat{\beta}$. In the bivariate term structure and permanent income examples, the normalisation takes the form of designating one of the variables in the system as the dependent variable. When this normalisation is adopted, the estimates from the Johansen and iterative estimators match, as is demonstrated in the bivariate term structure example. Two general approaches to normalisation are now discussed.

18.5.1   Triangular Restrictions

Triangular restrictions on a model with r long-run relationships, involve transforming the top ($r \times r$) block of $\widehat{\beta}$ to be the identity matrix (Ahn and Reinsel, 1990; Phillips, 1991a). Formally this is achieved by deriving the row echelon form of $\widehat{\beta}$. If $r = 1$ then this corresponds to normalising one of the coefficients to one as in the previous two examples. If there are $N = 3$ variables and $r = 2$ cointegrating equations, $\widehat{\beta}$ is normalised as

$$\widehat{\beta} = \begin{bmatrix} 1 & 0 \\ 0 & 1 \\ \widehat{\beta}_{3,1} & \widehat{\beta}_{3,2} \end{bmatrix}.$$

This structure is appropriate for the trivariate term structure model in Example 18.3 where the cointegrating vectors are related to the spreads in the interest rates, with two of the interest rates being expressed as a function of the third rate.

Example 18.11 Normalising a Trivariate Term Structure Model
A trivariate VECM consisting of the 10-year, $y_{1,t}$, 5-year, $y_{2,t}$ and 1-year, $y_{3,t}$, yields is specified using Model 2 with $p = 1$ lags. The estimates of the eigenvalues and the matrix of rescaled eigenvectors using the Johansen reduced-rank estimator are, respectively, given by

$$\widehat{\lambda} = \begin{bmatrix} 0.159 \\ 0.087 \\ 0.015 \\ 0.000 \end{bmatrix} \qquad L^{-1\prime}E = \begin{bmatrix} 4.358 & 2.513 & -0.370 & -0.339 \\ -6.306 & -2.152 & -0.013 & 0.441 \\ 2.064 & -0.231 & -0.004 & -0.081 \\ -0.542 & -1.733 & 2.561 & -1.098 \end{bmatrix},$$

where the variables are ordered as $\{y_{1,t}, y_{2,t}, y_{3,t}, 1\}$. Choosing a rank of $r = 2$, inspection of the first two columns of $L^{-1\prime}E$ does not reveal a standard term structure relationship among the yields. However, adopting a triangular normalisation by expressing this matrix in its row echelon form, gives

$$\widehat{\beta} = \begin{bmatrix} 1.000 & 0.000 & -0.912 & -1.510 \\ 0.000 & 1.000 & -0.958 & -0.957 \end{bmatrix}',$$

resulting in the following two estimtaed long-run equations

$$y_{1,t} = 1.510 + 0.912 y_{3,t} + \hat{u}_{1,t}$$
$$y_{2,t} = 0.957 + 0.958 y_{3,t} + \hat{u}_{2,t} \,.$$

These equations now have a term structure interpretation with the 10-year, $y_{1,t}$, and 5-year, $y_{2,t}$, yields expressed as a function of the 1-year yield, $y_{3,t}$, with slope estimates numerically close to unity. □

18.5.2 Structural Restrictions

Along the lines of the discussion of identification in Chapter 5, alternative restrictions can be imposed for identification, including exclusion restrictions, cross-equation restrictions, and restrictions on the disturbance covariance matrix (also see the discussion of identification of SVARs in Chapter 14). In the context of cointegration and VECMs, this topic is discussed from different perspectives by Johansen (1995a), Boswijk (1995), Hsiao (1997), Davidson (1998) and Pesaran and Shin (2002).

Example 18.12 Open Economy Model
  Johansen and Juselius (1992) propose an open economy model in which $y_t = \{s_t, p_t, p_t^*, i_t, i_t^*\}$ represent, respectively, the spot exchange rate, the domestic price, the foreign price, the domestic interest rate and the foreign interest rate. Assuming $r = 2$ long-run equations, applying normalisation, exclusion and linear restrictions on the long-run parameters, yields the normalised long-run parameter matrix

$$\beta' = \begin{bmatrix} 1 & -\beta_{2,1} & \beta_{2,1} & 0 & 0 \\ 0 & 0 & 0 & 1 & -\beta_{5,1} \end{bmatrix}.$$

The long-run equations now represent PPP and UIP

$$
\begin{aligned}
s_t &= \beta_{2,1}(p_t - p_t^*) + u_{1,t} && \text{[Purchasing power parity]} \\
i_t &= \beta_{5,1} i_t^* + u_{2,t} && \text{[Uncovered interest parity]}.
\end{aligned}
$$

Stricter forms of PPP and UIP are given where $\beta_{2,1} = \beta_{5,1} = 1$. □

  Alternative identification strategies are investigated in Exercise 11. One implication of this analysis is that the Johansen estimator is inappropriate when imposing over-identifying restrictions on the cointegrating vector. In these cases, the iterative estimator is implemented by imposing the restrictions on the long-run parameters and estimating the remaining parameters by maximum likelihood.

18.6   Distribution Theory

This section provides a summary of the key results regarding the asymptotic properties of the estimated VECM parameters. Understandably, the asymptotics are a function of the type of identifying restrictions discussed in Section 18.5 that are imposed on the model. For full derivations of the results, see Johansen (1995b) for statistical restrictions, Ahn and Reinsel (1990) and Phillips (1991a) for systems based on triangular identification and Pesaran and Shin (2002) for systems with general nonlinear identifying restrictions.

18.6.1   *Asymptotic Distribution of the Eigenvalues*

The Johansen approach leads to the maximised log-likelihood function given in equation (18.29) in which $\widehat{\lambda}_1 > \widehat{\lambda}_2 > \cdots > \widehat{\lambda}_N$ are the ordered estimated eigenvalues. For a model with reduced rank r, the first r estimated eigenvalues converge in probability to constants, with the remaining $N - r$ estimated eigenvalues converging to zero. These properties are summarised as follows.

Let $\lambda_j(M)$ denote the jth largest eigenvalue of the matrix M. Under the conditions of the Granger representation theorem, the estimated eigenvalues $\widehat{\lambda}_1 > \cdots > \widehat{\lambda}_N$ satisfy

Largest eigenvalues   : $\widehat{\lambda}_j \overset{p}{\to} \lambda_j(\Omega_{uu}^{-1}\Omega_{u0}\Omega_{00}^{-1}\Omega_{0u})$, $j = 1, 2, \cdots, r$

Smallest eigenvalues : $T(\widehat{\lambda}_j - 0) \overset{d}{\to} \lambda_{j-r}(M)$, $j = r + 1, \cdots, N$,

in which

$$\Omega_{00} = E[\Delta y_t \Delta y_t'], \qquad \Omega_{u0} = E[u_{t-1}\Delta y_t'] = \Omega_{0u}', \qquad \Omega_{uu} = E[u_{t-1}u_{t-1}'],$$

and $u_t = \beta' y_t$ is the error correction term. The stochastic matrix, M, is given by

$$M = \int_0^1 dB_{N-r}(s)F(s)' \left[\int_0^1 F(s)F(s)'ds\right]^{-1} \int_0^1 F(s)dB_{N-r}(s)',$$

$$(18.30)$$

in which $B_{N-r}(s)$ is an $N - r$ dimensional Brownian motion and $F(s)$ is a function of $B(s)$ and s that depends upon the model type in Table 18.1. The derivation is presented in Theorem 11.1 of Johansen (1995b). In the univariate case ($N = 1$), the distribution of M is the same as that of the asymptotic distribution of the square of the DF_t statistic given in Chapter 17.

The r largest eigenvalues are $O_p(1)$ and converge to constants. The $N - r$ smallest eigenvalues are $O_p(T^{-1})$. As this rate of convergence is T compared to the usual $\sqrt{T}$ rate, $\widehat{\lambda}_{r+1} > \cdots > \widehat{\lambda}_N$ are super-consistent estimators of $\lambda_{r+1} = \cdots = \lambda_N = 0$. This contrasting order of the eigenvalues provides the basis for

Table 18.3. *Summary statistics of the sampling distribution of* $\widehat{\lambda}_1$ *and* $\widehat{\lambda}_2$ *from a bivariate VECM with rank r* $= 1$. *Based on* 10000 *replications*

			$\widehat{\lambda}_1$				$\widehat{\lambda}_2$		
Statistic	$T =$	100	200	300	400	100	200	300	400
Mean		0.510	0.505	0.502	0.501	0.050	0.035	0.025	0.018
Std. Dev.		0.011	0.006	0.003	0.001	0.015	0.007	0.004	0.002

the asymptotic properties of the various methods for selecting r. The properties of the asymptotic distribution of $\widehat{\lambda}$ are illustrated in the following example.

Example 18.13 Asymptotic Properties of Estimated Eigenvalues
The data generating process is a triangular bivariate VECM based on Model 1 in Table 18.1 with rank $r = 1$, given by

$$ y_{1,t} = y_{2,t} + u_t, \qquad y_{2,t} = y_{2,t-1} + v_t, \qquad \begin{bmatrix} u_t \\ v_t \end{bmatrix} \sim iid\ N(0, I_2). $$

The model is simulated 10000 times with samples of size $T = \{100, 200, 400, 800\}$. As

$$ \Delta y_{1,t} = \Delta y_{2,t} + \Delta u_t = \Delta u_t + v_t, $$

the population quantities are

$$ \Omega_{00} = E \begin{bmatrix} \Delta y_{1,t}^2 & \Delta y_{1,t} \Delta y_{2,t} \\ \Delta y_{1,t} \Delta y_{2,t} & \Delta y_{2,t}^2 \end{bmatrix} $$

$$ = E \begin{bmatrix} (\Delta u_t + v_t)^2 & (\Delta u_t + v_t) v_t \\ (\Delta u_t + v_t) v_t & u_t^2 \end{bmatrix} = \begin{bmatrix} 3 & 1 \\ 1 & 1 \end{bmatrix} $$

$$ \Omega_{0u} = E \begin{bmatrix} \Delta y_{1,t} u_{t-1} \\ \Delta y_{2,t} u_{t-1} \end{bmatrix} = E \begin{bmatrix} (\Delta u_t + v_t) u_t \\ v_t u_t \end{bmatrix} = \begin{bmatrix} -1 \\ 0 \end{bmatrix} $$

$$ \Omega_{uu} = E \begin{bmatrix} u_{t-1}^2 \end{bmatrix} = E \begin{bmatrix} v_{1,t-1}^2 \end{bmatrix} = 1, $$

in which case the population eigenvalue is simply

$$ \Omega_{uu}^{-1} \Omega_{u0} \Omega_{00}^{-1} \Omega_{0u} = 1^{-1} \begin{bmatrix} 0 & -1 \end{bmatrix} \begin{bmatrix} 1 & 1 \\ 1 & 3 \end{bmatrix}^{-1} \begin{bmatrix} 0 \\ -1 \end{bmatrix} = 0.5. $$

For each simulation, the eigenvalues are computed using $L^{-1} S_{10} S_{00}^{-1} S_{01} L^{-1'}$, where S_{ij} are the sums of squares matrices in (18.25) with $R_{0,t} = \Delta y_t$ and $R_{1,t} = y_{t-1}$ and $LL' = S_{11}$. Summary descriptive statistics of the sampling distribution of $\widehat{\lambda}_1$ and $\widehat{\lambda}_2$ are given in Table 18.3. The results demonstrate that as T increases $\widehat{\lambda}_1$ converges to a constant equal to the population eigenvalue of

$\lambda_1 = 0.5$, while $\widehat{\lambda}_2$ approaches $\lambda_2 = 0$. The rate of convergence of $\widehat{\lambda}_2$ to λ_2 is the super-consistent rate of T because the sample standard deviation approximately halves as T doubles.   □

18.6.2   Asymptotic Distribution of the Parameters

The asymptotic distribution of the maximum likelihood estimator $\widehat{\theta}$ is derived using the approach of Chapter 2 by expanding the gradient $G_T(\widehat{\theta})$ in (18.19) around the true population parameter θ_0. Upon rearranging,

$$\widehat{\theta} - \theta_0 = -H_T^{-1}(\theta_0)G_T(\theta_0) + o_p(\widehat{\theta} - \theta_0),\tag{18.31}$$

where $H_T(\theta_0)$ is the Hessian and the remainder term contains the higher-order derivatives of the Taylor series, which is small provided that $\widehat{\theta}$ is a consistent estimator of θ_0. In Chapters 2 and 13, the scale factor used to derive the asymptotic distribution is $T^{1/2}$ as the processes there are assumed to be stationary. This is not the case for nonstationary processes as demonstrated in Chapter 16, where the scale factor in general not only has to vary across parameters but also has to be of an order higher than $T^{1/2}$ when sums of nonstationary variables are involved.

To find the scale parameters needed to derive the asymptotic distribution of $\widehat{\theta}$, reconsider the bivariate VECM in (18.22), which involves the error correction parameters $\alpha = [\alpha_1, \alpha_2]'$ and the cointegrating parameter β. As α is associated with the error correction term $u_{t-1} = \beta' y_{t-1}$, which is stationary, and β is associated with the variable $y_{2,t-1}$, which is nonstationary, a suitable choice of the scale factors corresponding to the elements of $\theta = \{\alpha, \beta\}$ is

$$D_T = \begin{bmatrix} \sqrt{T} & 0 \\ 0 & T \end{bmatrix}.\tag{18.32}$$

Applying this expression to (18.31) gives

$$D_T \begin{bmatrix} \widehat{\alpha} - \alpha_0 \\ \widehat{\beta} - \beta_0 \end{bmatrix} = \left[(T-1)D_T^{-1}H_T(\theta_0)D_T^{-1}\right]^{-1}(T-1)D_T^{-1}G_T(\theta_0) + o_p(1).\tag{18.33}$$

When the expressions of the gradient and the Hessian in (18.23) are used, then

$$(T-1)D_T^{-1}G_T(\theta_0) = \sum_{t=2}^{T}\begin{bmatrix} \dfrac{1}{\sqrt{T}}V_0^{-1}v_t u_{t-1} \\[2mm] -\dfrac{1}{T}\alpha_0' V_0^{-1}v_t y_{2,t-1} \end{bmatrix},\tag{18.34}$$

and $(T-1)D_T^{-1}H_T(\theta_0)D_T^{-1}$ is given by the expression

$$
\sum_{t=2}^{T}
\begin{bmatrix}
-\dfrac{1}{T}V_0^{-1}u_{t-1}^2 & -\dfrac{1}{T^{3/2}}V_0^{-1}(v_t-\alpha_0 u_{t-1})y_{2,t-1} \\
-\dfrac{1}{T^{3/2}}V_0^{-1}(v_t-\alpha_0 u_{t-1})'y_{2,t-1} & -\dfrac{1}{T^2}\alpha_0'V_0^{-1}\alpha_0 y_{2,t-1}^2
\end{bmatrix},
$$

(18.35)

where V_0 is the true value of the disturbance covariance matrix because $G_T(\theta)$ and $H_T(\theta)$ are evaluated at the population parameter.

From Chapter 16, the diagonal terms of the Hessian in (18.35) are

$$
\frac{1}{T}\sum_{t=2}^{T}u_{t-1}^2=O_p(1),\qquad \frac{1}{T^2}\sum_{t=2}^{T}y_{2,t-1}^2=O_p(1),
$$

where the first term converges to a fixed limit and the second term converges to a random variable that is a functional of Brownian motion. In the case of the off-diagonal term in (18.35), from the stochastic integral theorem of Chapter 16

$$
\frac{1}{T}\sum_{t=2}^{T}(v_t-\alpha_0 u_{t-1})y_{2,t-1}=O_p(1),
$$

(18.36)

which also converges to a functional of Brownian motion. But, as the scale factor in the off-diagonal term in (18.35) is $T^{-3/2}$, then multiplying both sides of (18.36) by $T^{-1/2}$ shows that

$$
\frac{1}{T^{3/2}}\sum_{t=2}^{T}\Delta(v_t-\alpha_0 u_{t-1})y_{2,t-1}=O_p(T^{-1/2}),
$$

(18.37)

which disappears in the limit. The implication of (18.37) is that the scaled Hessian in (18.35) becomes block diagonal asymptotically, allowing the expressions in (18.33) to separate as

$$
\sqrt{T}(\hat{\alpha}-\alpha_0)=\left[\frac{1}{T}\sum_{t=2}^{T}u_{t-1}^2\right]^{-1}\left[\frac{1}{T^{1/2}}\sum_{t=2}^{T}v_t u_{t-1}\right]+o_p(1),
$$

(18.38)

and

$$
T(\hat{\beta}-\beta_0)=\left[\frac{1}{T^2}\sum_{t=2}^{T}y_{2,t-1}^2\right]^{-1}\left[\frac{1}{T}\sum_{t=2}^{T}z_t y_{2,t-1}\right]+o_p(1),\quad(18.39)
$$

where

$$z_t = -[\alpha_0' V_0^{-1} \alpha_0]^{-1} \alpha_0' V_0^{-1} v_t. \tag{18.40}$$

Asymptotic Theory for $\widehat{\alpha}$

The asymptotic theory for $\widehat{\alpha}$ is standard being based on the results of Chapter 2. When the WLLN is used for the first term on the right-hand side of (18.38) and the martingale difference central limit theorem is used for the second term

$$\text{plim} \frac{1}{T} \sum_{t=2}^{T} u_{t-1}^2 = \sigma_u^2, \qquad \frac{1}{\sqrt{T}} \sum_{t=2}^{T} v_t u_{t-1} \overset{d}{\to} N(0, \sigma_u^2 V_0),$$

it immediately follows that

$$\sqrt{T}(\widehat{\alpha} - \alpha_0) \overset{d}{\to} N(0, \sigma_u^{-2} V_0). \tag{18.41}$$

This result shows that the error correction parameter estimator $\widehat{\alpha}$ is consistent at the standard rate of $T^{1/2}$ and is asymptotically normally distributed. The asymptotic properties of $\widehat{\alpha}$ are the same as if β is known, a result due to the super-consistency of $\widehat{\beta}$. This means that α_0 is estimated by regressing Δy_t on u_{t-1} and that the distribution theory for $\widehat{\alpha}$ is standard. This result is used by Campbell and Shiller (1987), see Section 13.11.2 of Chapter 13.

Asymptotic Theory for $\widehat{\beta}$

The asymptotic theory for $\widehat{\beta}$ requires the functional central limit theorem of Chapter 16. The basic FCLT using the iid disturbances of the VECM is

$$\frac{1}{\sqrt{T}} \sum_{t=1}^{[Ts]} v_t \overset{d}{\to} V(s),$$

where $V(s) = \text{BM}(V_0)$, which is used to derive the asymptotic theory for the terms involving $y_{2,t}$ and z_t as defined in (18.40). From the Granger representation theorem (see Theorem 4.2 of Johansen, 1995b, omitting deterministic terms and initial values) y_t in (18.22) is rewritten as

$$y_t = \beta_\perp (\alpha_\perp' \beta_\perp)^{-1} \alpha_\perp' \sum_{j=1}^{t} v_j + \eta_t,$$

where $\eta_t \sim I(0)$. By defining $e_2 = \begin{bmatrix} 0 & 1 \end{bmatrix}$ then

$$\frac{1}{\sqrt{T}} y_{2,[Ts]-1} = e_2' \beta_\perp (\alpha_\perp' \beta_\perp)^{-1} \alpha_\perp' \frac{1}{\sqrt{T}} \sum_{t=1}^{[Ts]-1} v_t + O_p(T^{-1/2})$$

$$\overset{d}{\to} e_2' \beta_\perp (\alpha_\perp' \beta_\perp)^{-1} \alpha_\perp' V(s) = Y_2(s). \tag{18.42}$$

In addition, from (18.40)

$$\frac{1}{\sqrt{T}}\sum_{t=1}^{[Ts]} z_t = -(\alpha_0' V_0^{-1}\alpha_0)^{-1}\alpha_0' V_0^{-1}\frac{1}{\sqrt{T}}\sum_{t=1}^{[Ts]} v_t$$

$$\xrightarrow{d} -(\alpha_0' V_0^{-1}\alpha_0)^{-1}\alpha_0' V_0^{-1} V(s) = Z(s). \tag{18.43}$$

These two Brownian motions are independent because

$$E\left[Y_2(s)Z(s)\right] = -(\alpha_0' V_0^{-1}\alpha_0)^{-1}\alpha_0' V_0^{-1} E\left[V(s)V(s)'\right]\alpha_\perp(\beta_\perp'\alpha_\perp)^{-1}\beta_\perp' e_2$$

$$= -s(\alpha_0' V_0^{-1}\alpha_0)^{-1}\alpha_0' V_0^{-1}\Omega_0\alpha_\perp(\beta_\perp'\alpha_\perp)^{-1}\beta_\perp' e_2$$

$$= -s(\alpha_0' V_0^{-1}\alpha_0)^{-1}\alpha_0'\alpha_\perp(\beta_\perp'\alpha_\perp)^{-1}\beta_\perp' e_2$$

$$= 0,$$

using $E(V(s)V(s)') = sV_0$ and $\alpha_0'\alpha_\perp = 0$. Combining (18.42) and (18.43) in (18.39) gives

$$T(\widehat{\beta} - \beta_0) \xrightarrow{d} \left[\int_0^1 Y_2(s)^2 ds\right]^{-1}\int_0^1 Y_2(s)dZ(s). \tag{18.44}$$

Since Y_2 and Z are independent, it follows from Chapter 16 that the second term in (18.44) is mixed normal, in which case $T(\widehat{\beta} - \beta_0)$ is asymptotically mixed normal. By contrast to the error correction parameter estimator, $\widehat{\alpha}$, the estimator of the cointegrating parameter $\widehat{\beta}$ is super-consistent, converging at the rate T, whilst the asymptotic distribution of $T(\widehat{\beta} - \beta_0)$ has fatter tails than a normal distribution. Nevertheless, the results of Phillips (1991a) and Saikkonen (1991) show that $\widehat{\beta}$ is asymptotically efficient.

Remaining Parameters
The asymptotic distribution of the remaining parameters, including the lagged dependent variables in the VECM, Γ_i, the intercepts, μ, and the disturbance covariance matrix, V, all have standard asymptotic distributions following the line of reasoning given for (18.41). In particular, when it is assumed that β is known, the VECM is characterised by all of its variables being stationary: (i) since y_t is $I(1)$ the dependent variable Δy_t is $I(0)$ as are the lags of Δy_t; (ii) since there is cointegration, the error correction term, $u_{t-1} = \beta' y_{t-1}$, is also $I(0)$.

18.7 Testing

This section uses the distribution theory results of the previous section to undertake a range of tests on the parameters of the VECM.

18.7.1   Cointegrating Rank

In estimating models of the term structure of interest rates, three models have been estimated without making any judgement as to whether the model has full $(r = N)$, reduced $(0 < r < N)$ or zero rank $(r = 0)$. A test of these alternative models amounts to testing the cointegrating rank r, with the aim of identifying the true cointegrating rank r_0 by determining the number of estimated eigenvalues $\widehat{\lambda} = \{\widehat{\lambda}_1, \widehat{\lambda}_2, \cdots, \widehat{\lambda}_N\}$ that are significantly greater than zero. The null and alternative hypotheses are

$$H_0 : r = r_0 \qquad \text{[Reduced Rank]}$$
$$H_1 : r = N \qquad \text{[Full Rank]}.$$

Since the three models are nested within each other, with the full rank model being the most unrestricted and the zero rank model being the most restricted, the LR test discussed in Chapter 4 can be used to choose among the models and hence r. The LR statistic, where the effective sample size is $T - p$ after adjusting for p lags in the VAR, is

$$LR = -2(T - p)\big(\ln L_T(\widehat{\theta}_0) - \ln L_T(\widehat{\theta}_1)\big), \qquad (18.45)$$

in which $\widehat{\theta}_0$ and $\widehat{\theta}_1$ are, respectively, the restricted and unrestricted parameter estimates corresponding to models with different ranks. Another way of constructing this statistic is to use the eigen decomposition form of the log-likelihood function in (18.29). The full-rank $(r = N)$ and reduced-rank $(r < N)$ log-likelihood functions are, respectively, given by

$$\ln L_T(\widehat{\theta}_1) = -\frac{N}{2}(1 + \ln 2\pi) - \frac{1}{2}\ln|S_{00}| - \frac{1}{2}\sum_{i=1}^{N}\ln(1 - \widehat{\lambda}_i)$$

$$\ln L_T(\widehat{\theta}_0) = -\frac{N}{2}(1 + \ln 2\pi) - \frac{1}{2}\ln|S_{00}| - \frac{1}{2}\sum_{i=1}^{r}\ln(1 - \widehat{\lambda}_i).$$

Using these expressions in (18.45) gives an alternative but numerically equivalent form for the LR statistic, known as the trace statistic

$$LR = -(T - p)\sum_{i=r+1}^{N}\ln(1 - \widehat{\lambda}_i). \qquad (18.46)$$

The asymptotic distribution of LR in (18.46) is non-standard, being based on the trace of the stochastic matrix M

$$LR \xrightarrow{d} \operatorname{tr} M, \qquad (18.47)$$

where M is defined in expression (18.30). This result contrasts with the standard asymptotic distribution given by the chi-square distribution. The quantiles of LR are given in Table 18.4 and vary for each model type in Table 18.1.

Table 18.4. *Quantiles of* tr*M where M is defined in expression (18.30). Based on a sample of size* $T = 1000$ *and* 100000 *replications*

		\multicolumn{6}{c}{Number of common trends $(N - r)$}					
		1	2	3	4	5	6
Model 1	0.90	2.983	10.460	21.677	36.877	56.041	78.991
	0.95	4.173	12.285	24.102	39.921	59.829	83.428
	0.99	6.967	16.380	29.406	46.267	67.174	92.221
Model 2	0.90	7.540	17.869	32.058	50.206	72.448	98.338
	0.95	9.142	20.205	34.938	53.734	76.559	103.022
	0.99	12.733	25.256	41.023	60.943	84.780	112.655
Model 3	0.90	2.691	13.347	26.948	44.181	65.419	90.412
	0.95	3.822	15.430	29.616	47.502	69.293	95.105
	0.99	6.695	19.810	35.130	54.307	77.291	103.980
Model 4	0.90	10.624	23.224	39.482	59.532	83.681	111.651
	0.95	12.501	25.726	42.585	63.336	88.089	116.781
	0.99	16.500	30.855	49.047	70.842	96.726	126.510
Model 5	0.90	2.706	16.090	31.874	51.136	74.462	101.484
	0.95	3.839	18.293	34.788	54.680	78.588	106.265
	0.99	6.648	22.978	40.776	61.744	86.952	115.570

Example 18.14 Bivariate Term Structure Model

To test the hypothesis $H_0 : r = 0$ against $H_1 : r = 2$ in a model of the term structure given by Model 2 in Table 18.1, the LR statistic in (18.45) using the log-likelihood function values from Examples 18.10 and 18.6, is

$$LR = -2 \times (195 - 1) \times (-1.5563 + 1.5009) = 21.502 \,.$$

Alternatively, using the eigenvalues in Example 18.8 produces the same value of LR as using (18.46) since

$$LR = -(T - p) \sum_{i=1}^{2} \ln(1 - \widehat{\lambda}_i)$$
$$= -(195 - 1)(\ln(1 - 0.092804) + \ln(1 - 0.013346)) = 21.502 \,.$$

There are $N - r = 2 - 0 = 2$ common trends under the null hypothesis, so, from Table 18.4, the 5% critical value is 20.205. As $21.502 > 20.205$, the null of zero rank is rejected at the 5% level. To test the hypothesis $H_0 : r = 1$ against $H_1 : r = 2$, the value of the LR statistic, based on the log-likelihood function values from Examples 18.7 and 18.6, is

$$LR = -2 \times (195 - 1) \times (-1.5076 + 1.5009) = 2.607 \,,$$

Table 18.5. *Cointegration tests of a trivariate VECM consisting of quarterly observations on the 10-year, 5-year and 1-year yields on United States bonds for the period March 1962 to September 2010. Critical values are from Table 18.4*

H_0	H_1	$\widehat{\lambda}$	LR	$CV(5\%)$
$r = 0$	$r = 3$	0.159	54.120	34.938
$r = 1$	$r = 3$	0.087	20.557	20.205
$r = 2$	$r = 3$	0.015	2.900	9.142

which also agrees with the LR statistic based on (18.46) as

$$LR = -(T - p) \sum_{i=2}^{2} \ln(1 - \widehat{\lambda}_i) = -(195 - 1)\ln(1 - 0.013346) = 2.607 .$$

The number of common trends under the null hypothesis is now $N - 1 = 2 - 1 = 1$, which corresponds to a critical value of 9.142 for a test with size 5%. As $2.607 > 9.142$, the null cannot be rejected at the 5% level, leading to the conclusion that there is only one cointegrating vector. This result is consistent with the bivariate term structure of interest rates model.   □

Example 18.15 Trivariate Term Structure Model
   The results of the cointegration test for a trivariate VECM consisting of the 10-year, $y_{1,t}$, 5-year, $y_{2,t}$, and 1-year, $y_{3,t}$, yields estimated in Example 18.11, are summarised in Table 18.5.
   The critical values are based on Table 18.4 for Model 2. The first null hypothesis is rejected at the 5% level ($54.120 > 34.938$) as is the second null hypothesis ($20.557 > 20.205$). In contrast, the third null is not rejected ($2.900 < 9.142$), thereby providing evidence of $r = 2$ cointegrating equations at the 5% level, a result which is consistent with the term structure model in Example 18.3.   □

   As $\widehat{\lambda}$ is a random variable, the estimated cointegrating rank, $\widehat{r}$, is also a random variable, albeit a discrete random variable. A property of the trace test (see Johansen, 1995b, Theorem 12.3) with asymptotic size of δ at each stage as $T \to \infty$, is

$$\Pr(\widehat{r} = r) \to \begin{cases} 0, & r < r_0 \\ 1 - \delta, & r = r_0 \\ \leq \delta, & r > r_0 . \end{cases} \qquad (18.48)$$

This result shows that if the test is computed using an asymptotic size of $\delta = 0.05$, the probability of selecting the true cointegrating rank of r_0 converges to $1 - \delta = 0.95$. Even though this result suggests that $\widehat{r}$ is not consistent as

$\Pr(\widehat{r} = r_0) \nrightarrow 1$, the degree of inconsistency of $\widehat{r}$ arises only from a small probability (δ) of overspecifying $(r > r_0)$ the cointegrating rank. The finite sample properties of this test are investigated and compared with another cointegration test based on the information criteria in Section 18.9.

18.7.2 Cointegrating Vector

Hypothesis tests on the cointegrating vector using the procedures of Chapter 4, constitute tests of long-run economic theories. In the term structure example, a test that the cointegrating vector is $(1, -1)$ is a test that yields move one to one in the long run, so the spreads between yields are stationary. In contrast to the cointegration test discussed in Section 18.7.1, where the distribution is non-standard, the Wald, LR and LM statistics are distributed asymptotically as χ^2 under the null hypothesis that the restrictions are valid. The Wald test has the advantage that only the unrestricted model needs to be estimated. If there are M linear restrictions of the form $R\theta_1 - Q$, where R is $(M \times K)$ and Q is $(M \times 1)$, the Wald statistic is

$$W = (T - p)[R\widehat{\theta}_1 - Q]'[R\widehat{\Omega}R']^{-1}[R\widehat{\theta}_1 - Q],$$

in which $\widehat{\Omega}/(T - p)$ is the estimated covariance matrix of $\widehat{\theta}_1$. Alternatively, a LR test can be adopted that involves estimating both the restricted and unrestricted models. As with the cointegration test, the LR statistic can be computed using the log-likelihood values evaluated at the null and alternative hypotheses or expressed in terms of its estimated eigenvalues.

Example 18.16 Testing for the Spread in the Term Structure
From Example 18.7, the null and alternative hypotheses are

$$H_0 : \beta_r = 1, \qquad H_1 : \beta_r \neq 1,$$

so the VECM under the null becomes

$$y_{1,t} - y_{1,t-1} = \alpha_1(y_{2,t-1} - \beta_c - y_{1,t-1}) + v_{1,t}$$
$$y_{2,t} - y_{2,t-1} = \alpha_2(y_{2,t-1} - \beta_c - y_{1,t-1}) + v_{2,t}.$$

Given that $\theta = \{\beta_c, \beta_r, \alpha_1, \alpha_2\}$, define $R = [0\ 1\ 0\ 0]$ and $Q = [1]$, with $\widehat{\theta}_1$ and the relevant covariance matrix given in Example 18.7, the Wald statistic is

$$W = \frac{(0.921 - 1.000)^2}{0.008104} = 0.766,$$

which is distributed under the null hypothesis as chi-square with one degree of freedom. The p-value is 0.382 resulting in a failure to reject the null hypothesis that $\beta_r = 1$ at the 5% level. $\square$

The practical usefulness of the asymptotic mixed normality of $\widehat{\beta}$ can be demonstrated by considering a t test of $H_0 : \beta = \beta_0$ with statistic

$$t = \frac{\widehat{\beta} - \beta_0}{se(\widehat{\beta})}.$$

The standard error is

$$se(\widehat{\beta}) = \frac{1}{T^{1/2}}\left[-\left(H_{\beta\beta}(\widehat{\theta}) - H_{\beta\alpha}(\widehat{\theta})H_{\alpha\alpha}^{-1}(\widehat{\theta})H_{\alpha\beta}(\widehat{\theta})\right)\right]^{-1/2},$$

where the Hessian is partitioned as

$$H_T(\theta) = \begin{bmatrix} H_{\alpha\alpha}(\theta) & H_{\alpha\beta}(\theta) \\ H_{\beta\alpha}(\theta) & H_{\beta\beta}(\theta) \end{bmatrix}.$$

Following the same steps used to deal with (18.35) shows that

$$T se(\widehat{\beta}) = \left[-\left(T^{-1}H_{\beta\beta}(\widehat{\theta}) - T^{-1/2}H_{\beta\alpha}(\widehat{\theta})H_{\alpha\alpha}(\widehat{\theta})T^{-1/2}H_{\alpha\beta}(\widehat{\theta})\right)\right]^{-1/2}$$

$$= \left[\widehat{\alpha}'\widehat{V}^{-1}\widehat{\alpha} \cdot T^{-2}\sum_{t=2}^{T}y_{2,t-1}^2\right]^{-1/2} + o_p(1)$$

$$= \left[\alpha_0'V_0^{-1}\alpha_0 \cdot T^{-2}\sum_{t=2}^{T}y_{2,t-1}^2\right]^{-1/2} + o_p(1).$$

This suggests that $H_{\beta\beta}(\widehat{\theta})^{-1/2}$ can be used as an alternative formula for $se(\widehat{\beta})$. Combining this expression with (18.39) gives

$$t = \frac{T(\widehat{\beta} - \beta_0)}{T se(\widehat{\beta})}$$

$$= \left[\alpha_0'V_0^{-1}\alpha_0\right]^{1/2}\left[\frac{1}{T^2}\sum_{t=2}^{T}y_{2,t-1}^2\right]^{-1/2}\frac{1}{T}\sum_{t=2}^{T}z_t y_{2,t-1} + o_p(1)$$

$$\xrightarrow{d} \left[\int_0^1 Y_2(s)^2 ds\right]^{-1/2}\int_0^1 Y_2(s)dZ^*(s),$$

in which $Z^* = (\alpha_0'V_0^{-1}\alpha_0)^{1/2}Z$. Note that $var(Z) = (\alpha_0'V_0^{-1}\alpha_0)^{-1}$ implies that $var(Z^*) = 1$. Thus, following Example 16.13 of Chapter 16, the conditional distribution of

$$\left[\int_0^1 Y_2(s)^2 ds\right]^{-1/2}\int_0^1 Y_2(s)dZ^*(s),$$

is

$$\left[\int_0^1 Y_2(s)^2 ds\right]^{-1/2}\int_0^1 Y_2(s)dZ^*(s)\bigg| Y_2 \sim N(0, 1).$$

As this conditional distribution does not depend on Y_2, it is also the unconditional distribution. In this case, the asymptotic distribution of the t statistic under the null hypothesis is

$$t \overset{a}{\sim} N(0, 1).$$

The same reasoning can be generalised to show that the usual tests based on the LR, Wald and LM statistics for β have asymptotic χ^2 distributions, even though $\widehat{\beta}$ (and its gradient) are asymptotically mixed normal rather than asymptotically normal.

18.7.3 Exogeneity

An important feature of a VECM is that all of the variables in the system are endogenous. When the system is out of long-run equilibrium, all of the variables interact with each other to move the system back into equilibrium, as is demonstrated in Figure 18.4 for the bivariate case. In a VECM, this interaction formally occurs through the impact of lagged variables so that variable $y_{i,t}$ is affected by the lags of the other variables either through the error correction term, $u_{t-1} = \beta' y_{t-1}$, with parameter α_i, or through the lags of $\Delta y_{j,t}$, $j \neq i$, with parameters given by the rows of $\Gamma_1, \Gamma_2, \cdots \Gamma_{p-1}$.

If the first channel does not exist so that the error correction parameter satisfies the restriction $\alpha_i = 0$, the variable $y_{i,t}$ is weakly exogenous. If both channels do not exist, $y_{i,t}$ is strongly exogenous as only lagged values of $y_{i,t}$ are important in explaining movements in itself. This definition of strong exogeneity is also equivalent to the other variables failing to Granger cause $y_{i,t}$, as discussed in Chapter 13.

Tests of weak and strong exogeneity are conveniently based on the Wald test if the unrestricted model is estimated. From Section 18.6, this statistic has a standard distribution asymptotically. If there is a single cointegrating equation ($r = 1$), weak exogeneity tests reduce to a t test since only one error correction parameter associated with each variable in the system exists. An alternative approach based on the LR test is explored in Exercise 12.

Example 18.17 Exogeneity Tests of the Term Structure Model
   The t test of the restriction that the error correction parameter in the 10-year yield VECM equation in Example 18.7 is zero is $(-0.092 - 0.000)/0.042 = -2.161$. The p-value is 0.031 showing that the 10-year yield is not weakly exogenous. In contrast, performing the same test on the error correction parameter in the 1-year yield VECM equation produces a t statistic of $(0.012 - 0.000)/0.060 = 0.198$, which is now statistically insignificant with a p-value of 0.843, providing evidence that this yield is weakly exogenous. As $p = 1$ in this example, there are no lags of Δy_t in the VECM, in which case the

1-year yield is also strongly exogenous, a result consistent with longer yields adjusting to movements in shorter yields.   □

An implication of weak exogeneity is that, as the cointegrating vector β does not appear in the equations corresponding to the weakly exogenous variables, inference on β can be performed without loss of generality using a partial model of dimension r, which excludes the weakly exogenous variables. For example, consider the bivariate VECM

$$
\begin{bmatrix} \Delta y_{1,t} \\ \Delta y_{2,t} \end{bmatrix} = \begin{bmatrix} \alpha_1 \\ \alpha_2 \end{bmatrix} \begin{bmatrix} 1 \\ -\beta \end{bmatrix}' \begin{bmatrix} y_{1,t-1} \\ y_{2,t-1} \end{bmatrix} + \begin{bmatrix} \Gamma_{1,1} & \Gamma_{1,2} \\ \Gamma_{2,1} & \Gamma_{2,2} \end{bmatrix} \begin{bmatrix} \Delta y_{1,t-1} \\ \Delta y_{2,t-1} \end{bmatrix} + \begin{bmatrix} v_{1,t} \\ v_{2,t} \end{bmatrix} ,
$$

in which

$$
\begin{bmatrix} v_{1,t} \\ v_{2,t} \end{bmatrix} \sim N \left(\begin{bmatrix} 0 \\ 0 \end{bmatrix} , \begin{bmatrix} 1 & \rho \\ \rho & 1 \end{bmatrix} \right) ,
$$

and $\alpha_2 = 0$ so $y_{2,t}$ is weakly exogenous. Now define the regression equation

$$
v_{1,t} = \rho v_{2,t} + w_t ,
$$

in which the disturbance term w_t has the property $E\left[v_{2,t} w_t\right] = 0$, and use the VECM to substitute out $v_{1,t}$ and $v_{2,t}$ to derive the partial model for $y_{1,t}$ as

$$
\Delta y_{1,t} = \alpha_1 (y_{1,t-1} - \beta y_{2,t-1}) + \rho \Delta y_{2,t} + (\Gamma_{1,1} - \rho \Gamma_{2,1}) \Delta y_{1,t-1}
$$
$$
+ (\Gamma_{1,2} - \rho \Gamma_{2,2}) \Delta y_{2,t-1} + w_t .
$$

This equation can be used to estimate β without the need for the equation of $y_{2,t}$ by simply regressing $\Delta y_{1,t}$ on $\{c, y_{1,t-1}, y_{2,t-1}, \Delta y_{2,t}, \Delta y_{1,t-1}, \Delta y_{2,t-1}\}$. This estimator is also equivalent to the maximum likelihood estimator of β from estimating the bivariate VECM subject to the weak exogeneity restriction $\alpha_2 = 0$. This result immediately generalises to the case where $y_{1,t}$ and $y_{2,t}$ consist of r and $N - r$ variables, respectively, with the partial VECM of $y_{1,t}$ now representing a system of r equations.

18.8   Dynamics

18.8.1   Impulse Responses

The dynamics of a VECM can be investigated using impulse response functions as discussed in Chapter 13. As the impulse response functions of Chapter 13 are derived within the context of a VAR, the approach is to re-express a VECM as a VAR by using the property that a VECM is a VAR subject to cross-equation restrictions. For example, the VECM

$$
\Delta y_t = \mu + \alpha \beta' y_{t-1} + \sum_{j=1}^{p-1} \Gamma_j \Delta y_{t-j} + v_t , \tag{18.49}
$$

is a VAR in levels

$$y_t = \mu + \sum_{j=1}^{p} \Phi_j y_{t-j} + v_t \,, \tag{18.50}$$

subject to the restrictions $\Phi_1 = \alpha\beta' + \Gamma_1 + I_N$, and $\Phi_j = \Gamma_j - \Gamma_{j-1}$, $j = 2, 3, \cdots, p$.

The impulses are computed as

$$I R_i = \Psi_i S \,, \tag{18.51}$$

where Ψ_i are obtained from the VMA and S is obtained as $V = SS'$, the Choleski decomposition of V, if a triangular ordering is adopted (see Chapter 14). Shocks are characterised as having restricted contemporaneous channels determined by the triangular ordering, but unrestricted channels thereafter. For an alternative way of identifying structural shocks in VECMs, see Pagan and Pesaran (2008).

Phillips (1998) shows that restricted and unrestricted estimation of (18.50) gives consistent estimators of the short-run impulse responses, but only the VECM gives consistent estimators of the long-run impulse responses.

18.8.2   Cointegrating Vector Interpretation

Interpretation of the cointegrating vector itself can be clarified using impulse responses. Suppose there is a cointegrating equation of the form

$$y_{1,t} = \beta_2 y_{2,t} + \beta_3 y_{3,t} + u_t \,, \tag{18.52}$$

in which u_t is $I(0)$. The coefficient β_2 is interpreted as the expected long-run change in $y_{1,t}$ given a one unit long-run change in $y_{2,t}$, while holding $y_{3,t}$ constant in the long run. This is very similar to the standard interpretation of a regression coefficient, but the emphasis on long-run changes is important. For example, this cointegrating equation does not necessarily imply that a single period one unit shock to $y_{2,t}$, holding $y_{3,t}$ constant, is expected to change $y_{1,t}$ by β_2 in either the short or long run.

In terms of impulse responses, Johansen (2005) shows that an impulse of the form $S = \Gamma(1)F$, where $\Gamma(1)$ is defined in (18.10) and $F = [\beta_2, 1, 0]'$, produces the desired long-run changes of a one unit change in $y_{2,t}$, a zero unit change in $y_{3,t}$ and the resulting β_2 change in $y_{1,t}$. That is, there exists some shock that can be applied to (18.49) to produce the long-run changes implied by (18.52).

The shock $S = \Gamma(1)F$ is different from those implied by other identifications, such as the Choleski decomposition of V. These latter shocks will, therefore, have different effects in both the short run and the long run. In some cases the long-run effects of the Choleski shocks can even differ in sign from what might be expected from (18.52). This is because the long-run dynamics of the model are determined by $\Gamma(1)$ as well as α and β.

18.9   Applications

Two applications are presented that focus on extensions of the trace LR test of cointegration. The first investigates the performance of information criteria to select the rank, while the second focusses on the size properties of the trace test when the *iid* assumption is relaxed.

18.9.1   *Rank Selection Based on Information Criteria*

Identifying the cointegrating rank by means of information criteria (see also Chapter 13 for an application to the selection of lags in a VAR) requires that the log-likelihood in (18.29) be augmented by a penalty factor, c_T,

$$IC(r) = -2(T - p)\ln L_T(r) + c_T m_r \,,$$

where $c_T = \ln T$ for the Schwarz information criterion (SIC) and $m_r = \dim(\alpha, \beta, V) = Nr + (N - r)r + N(N + 1)/2$, is the number of free parameters corresponding to rank r, having normalised r of the N variables in the system. The estimated rank is chosen to satisfy

$$\widehat{r} = \underset{0 \leq r \leq N}{\arg\min} \, IC(r). \tag{18.53}$$

Asymptotic Properties

  If r_0 represents the true cointegrating rank, then from Section 18.6.1, $\{\widehat{\lambda}_1, \cdots, \widehat{\lambda}_{r_0}\}$ are $O_p(1)$ and $\{\widehat{\lambda}_{r_0+1}, \cdots, \widehat{\lambda}_N\}$ are $O_p(T^{-1})$. If the model is underspecified, $(r < r_0)$, the asymptotic difference between the information criteria based on r and the true rank r_0, is

$$\lim_{T \to \infty} (IC(r) - IC(r_0)) = \lim_{T \to \infty} (T - p) \sum_{j=r+1}^{r_0} \ln(1 - \widehat{\lambda}_j) + \lim_{T \to \infty} c_T(m_r - m_{r_0}).$$

The first term diverges to $+\infty$ at the rate T,

$$\lim_{T \to \infty} (T - p) \sum_{j=r+1}^{r_0} \ln(1 - \widehat{\lambda}_j) = O(T)O_p(1) = O_p(T).$$

The second term

$$\lim_{T \to \infty} c_T(m_r - m_{r_0}),$$

Table 18.6. *Estimates of* $\Pr(\widehat{r} = r)$ *for alternative tests of cointegration where the true rank is* r_0, *with the value of* r_0 *in each case indicated with an asterisk. The simulations are based on (18.54) with a sample of size* $T = 100$ *and 10000 replications*

	Experiment I ($\phi_1 = 1, \phi_2 = 1$)			Experiment II ($\phi_1 = 1, \phi_2 = 0.8$)			Experiment III ($\phi_1 = \phi_2 = 0.8$)		
Stat.	$r = 0^*$	$r = 1$	$r = 2$	$r = 0$	$r = 1^*$	$r = 2$	$r = 0$	$r = 1$	$r = 2^*$
SIC	0.984	0.016	0.000	0.590	0.391	0.019	0.136	0.010	0.854
LR	0.949	0.046	0.005	0.329	0.626	0.045	0.003	0.013	0.984

diverges to $-\infty$ since $m_r - m_{r_0} < 0$ and $\lim_{T \to \infty} c_T = \ln T \to \infty$. However, because this is a lower rate of convergence than T, the first term dominates, resulting in $\Pr(IC(r) > IC(r_0)) = 1$ as $T \to \infty$, and hence $\Pr(\widehat{r} < r_0) \to 0$.

If the model is overspecified ($r > r_0$), the asymptotic difference between the information criteria based on r and the true rank r_0 is now

$$\lim_{T \to \infty} (IC(r) - IC(r_0)) = \lim_{T \to \infty} (T - p) \sum_{j=r_0+1}^{r} \ln(1 - \widehat{\lambda}_j)$$
$$+ \lim_{T \to \infty} c_T (m_r - m_{r_0}).$$

The first term satisfies

$$\lim_{T \to \infty} (T - 1) \sum_{j=r_0+1}^{r} \ln(1 - \widehat{\lambda}_j) = O(T)O_p(T^{-1}) = O_p(1).$$

The second term converges to $+\infty$ as $m_r - m_{r_0} > 0$ and $\lim_{T \to \infty} c_T = \ln T \to \infty$. In this case, $IC(r) - IC(r_0) \to \infty$ for $r > r_0$ and hence $\Pr(\widehat{r} > r_0) \to 0$. The combination of $\Pr(\widehat{r} < r_0) \to 0$ and $\Pr(\widehat{r} > r_0) \to 0$ for the SIC imply that $\Pr(\widehat{r} = r_0) \to 1$, so $\widehat{r}$ is a consistent estimator of r_0.

Finite Sample Properties

To identify the finite sample properties of the SIC in determining the true cointegrating rank, r_0, the following Monte Carlo experiments are conducted using the data generating process ($N = 2$)

$$\begin{bmatrix} y_{1,t} \\ y_{2,t} \end{bmatrix} = \begin{bmatrix} \phi_1 & 0 \\ 0 & \phi_2 \end{bmatrix} \begin{bmatrix} y_{1,t-1} \\ y_{2,t-1} \end{bmatrix} + \begin{bmatrix} v_{1,t} \\ v_{2,t} \end{bmatrix}, \qquad (18.54)$$

in which $v_t = [v_{1,t}, v_{2,t}]'$ and $v_t \sim iid\ N(0, I_2)$. Three experiments are conducted with the true cointegrating rank of $r_0 = \{0, 1, 2\}$, respectively, with the results for a sample of size $T = 100$ and 10000 replications reported in Table 18.6. For comparative purposes, the results are also presented for the trace LR test based on Model 1 with the selection of the rank determined using the asymptotic 5% critical value.

The SIC tends to be a conservative test in finite samples with a tendency to under-select the cointegrating rank. In Experiment II ($r_0 = 1$), the probability of choosing $r = 0$ is 0.590, whereas for Experiment III ($r_0 = 2$), the probability of choosing a lower rank is $0.136 + 0.010$. The trace LR test yields empirical sizes close to the nominal size of 5% in Experiment I ($0.046 + 0.005$) and Experiment III ($0.003 + 0.013$). In Experiment II where the true rank is $r_0 = 1$, the probability of choosing this rank is just 0.626. For this experiment the estimated probability of 0.329 shows that the power of the trace test of testing $H_0: r = 0$ against $H_1: r > 0$, is $1 - 0.329 = 0.671$.

Alternative cointegrating rank selection procedures that do not require knowledge of the lag length of the VECM include Poskitt (2000), Harris and Poskitt (2004) and Cheng and Phillips (2009).

18.9.2   Effects of Heteroskedasticity on the Trace Test

An important assumption underlying the computation of the critical values of the trace test in Table 18.4 is that the disturbance term v_t is *iid*. This assumption is now relaxed by using a range of Monte Carlo experiments to investigate the effects of heteroskedasticity on the size of the trace test. Two forms of heteroskedasticity are considered with the first based on a generalised autoregressive conditional heteroskedastic (or GARCH) variance (see Chapter 20 for a discussion of GARCH models) and the second based on a one-off structural break in the variance. A sufficient condition for the asymptotic null distribution theory of the trace test to remain valid in the first case is for the GARCH process to have at least finite fourth moments (Cavaliere, Rahbek and Taylor, 2010). In the case of structural breaks in the variance, the asymptotic distribution is affected by the timing of the structural break.

The data generating process under the null of no cointegration ($r = 0$) is an $N = 2$ dimensional VECM based on Model 1 with $p = 1$ lags

$$\Delta y_t = v_t \, ,$$

in which $v_t = [v_{1,t}, v_{2,t}]'$ is now a heteroskedastic martingale difference disturbance term, with zero mean and variance $\text{var}(v_{j,t}) = \sigma_{j,t}^2$, given by

GARCH	:	$\sigma_{j,t}^2 = (1 - \phi_1 - \phi_2) + \phi_1 v_{i,t-1}^2 + \phi_2 \sigma_{j,t-1}^2 , \quad \forall j \, ,$
Structural Breaks	:	$\sigma_{j,t}^2 = \begin{cases} 1 & : \ t \leq \lfloor \tau T \rfloor \\ 2 & : \ t > \lfloor \tau T \rfloor \, , \end{cases} \quad \forall j.$

The results of the Monte Carlo experiments are given in Table 18.7 for samples ranging from $T = 100$ to $T = 3200$. The size of the trace test is computed by simulating the DGP 10000 times and computing the proportion of calculated values of the trace statistic in excess of the pertinent critical values given in Table 18.4. As a benchmark, the results of the *iid* case are also

Table 18.7. *Size of the trace test in the presence of heteroskedasticity from GARCH and structural breaks. Results are based on $N = 2$ with 10000 replications and the critical values of Model 1 in Table 18.4*

T	iid	GARCH ($\phi_1 = 0.3$)		Structural Break		
		$\phi_2 = 0.6$	$\phi_2 = 0.69$	($\tau = 0.1$)	($\tau = 0.5$)	($\tau = 0.9$)
100	0.0538	0.0704	0.0912	0.0645	0.1081	0.0915
200	0.0506	0.0698	0.0901	0.0671	0.1027	0.0888
400	0.0501	0.0676	0.0932	0.0632	0.1051	0.0964
800	0.0528	0.0638	0.1009	0.0690	0.1054	0.0943
1600	0.0511	0.0571	0.0971	0.0679	0.1057	0.0923
3200	0.0513	0.0560	0.0994	0.0658	0.1057	0.0926

presented. Two sets of parameters are used for the GARCH model. In the first set, $\{\phi_1 = 0.3, \phi_2 = 0.6\}$ yields a finite fourth moment for v_t (Lee and Tse, 1996) because

$$3\phi_1^2 + 2\phi_1\phi_2 + \phi_2^2 < 1, \tag{18.55}$$

and the trace test has its usual asymptotic distribution. For the second set of parameters $\{\phi_1 = 0.3, \phi_2 = 0.69\}$, the fourth moment condition in (18.55) is no longer satisfied.

The Monte Carlo results in Table 18.7 show that the size of the trace test approaches the nominal size of 0.05 as T increases for the first parameter set which results in the GARCH model having a finite fourth moment. In contrast, for the GARCH model which does not satisfy the fourth moment condition, the usual asymptotic distribution is affected since there is now no evidence of the size approaching 0.05 as T increases.

A structural break in the variance results in size distortions that are largest when the break is in the middle of the sample ($\tau = 0.5$), although the other choices of τ also result in significant size distortions. Furthermore, there is no sign of amelioration in the size distortion as T increases.

18.10 Exercises

(1) Graphical Analysis of Long-Run Economic Theories

Program files	coint_lrgraphs.*
Data files	permincome.*, moneydemand.*, usmacro.*

The data are quarterly macroeconomic variables for the United States for various sample periods.

(a) In the context of the permanent income hypothesis, discuss the time series properties of and relationships between the logarithms of real consumption per capita and real income per capita from March 1984 to December 2005.

(b) In the context of the long-run demand for money, discuss the time series properties of and relationships between the logarithms of real money and real income, and the relative interest rate from March 1959 to December 2005.

(c) In the context of the term structure of interest rates, discuss the time series properties of and relationships between the yields on 10-year, 5-year and 1-year bonds from March 1962 to September 2010.

(2) **Time Series Properties of a VECM**

Program files   coint_ecmsim.*

The following question explores the time series properties of a VECM by simulating the model under various parameterisations. Consider the bivariate VECM with rank $r = 1$

$$\begin{bmatrix} y_{1,t} \\ y_{2,t} \end{bmatrix} = \begin{bmatrix} \delta_{1,0} \\ \delta_{2,0} \end{bmatrix} + \begin{bmatrix} \alpha_{1,1} \\ \alpha_{2,1} \end{bmatrix} (2 + \beta_1 t + y_{1,t-1} - y_{2,t-1}) + \begin{bmatrix} v_{1,t} \\ v_{2,t} \end{bmatrix},$$

in which $v_t = \begin{bmatrix} v_{1,t}, v_{2,t} \end{bmatrix}'$ is $N(0, V)$ with $V = I_2$. For a sample of size $T = 200$, simulate the model for the parameterisations given in the following table and interpret the time series properties of $y_t = \begin{bmatrix} y_{1,t}, y_{2,t} \end{bmatrix}'$.

Experiment	Model	$\delta_{1,0}$	$\delta_{2,0}$	β_1	$\alpha_{1,1}$	$\alpha_{2,1}$
I	2	0.0	0.0	0.0	−0.1	0.1
II	2	0.0	0.0	0.0	−0.01	0.01
III	3	0.1414	0.1414	0.0	−0.1	0.1
IV	4	0.0	0.0	0.1	−0.1	0.1

(3) **Term Structure of Interest Rates**

Program files   coint_bivterm.*, coint_triterm.*
Data files   usmacro.*

The data are quarterly 1-year, 5-year and 10-year yields for the United States from March 1962 to September 2010.

(a) Estimate a bivariate VAR containing the 10-year and 1-year yields, with a constant and $p = 1$ lags. Interpret the parameter estimates.

(b) Using the results of part (a), estimate a bivariate VECM with a constant in the cointegrating equation only (Model 2). Interpret the parameter estimates. Use both the iterative and Johansen estimators.

(c) Estimate a bivariate VAR containing the first differences of the 10-year and 1-year yields, no constant and the lag length corresponding to the lag length of the VECM in part (b). Interpret the parameter estimates.

(d) Use the log-likelihood values of the estimated models in parts (a) to (c) to test for cointegration.

(e) Test for weak exogeneity and strong exogeneity.

(f) Repeat parts (a) to (e) for the 10-year and 5-year yields.

(g) Repeat parts (a) to (e) for the 5-year and 1-year yields.

(h) Repeat parts (a) to (e) for the 10-year, 5-year and 1-year yields.

(4) Permanent Income Hypothesis

Program files	`coint_permincome.*`
Data files	`permincome.*`

The data are quarterly real consumption per capita, rc_t, and real income per capita, ry_t, for the United States from March 1984 to December 2005.

(a) Test for cointegration between $\ln rc_t$ and $\ln ry_t$ using a VECM based on Model 3 in Table 18.1 with $p = 4$ lags.

(b) Given the results of the cointegration test in part (a), estimate a VECM and interpret the long-run parameter estimates, $\hat{\beta}$, and the error correction parameter estimates, $\hat{\alpha}$.

(c) Using the results of parts (a) and (b), discuss whether the permanent income hypothesis is satisfied.

(5) Simulating the Eigenvalue Distribution

Program files	`coint_simevals.*`

(a) Consider the bivariate VECM based on Model 1 in Table 18.1 with rank $r = 1$

$$y_{1,t} = y_{2,t} + v_{1,t}, \qquad y_{2,t} = y_{2,t-1} + v_{2,t},$$

in which $v_t = \begin{bmatrix} v_{1,t}, v_{2,t} \end{bmatrix}' \sim iid\, N(0, V)$ with $V = I_2$. Simulate the model 10000 times with samples of size $T = \{100, 200, 400, 800\}$ and discuss the asymptotic properties of the sampling distributions of the estimated eigenvalues obtained from

$$L^{-1} S_{10} S_{00}^{-1} S_{01} L^{-1'},$$

in which $S_{i,j}$ are defined in (18.25) with $R_{0,t} = \Delta y_t$ and $R_{1,t} = y_{t-1}$ and $LL' = S_{1,1}$.

(b) Repeat part (a) for the trivariate VECM

$$y_{1,t} = 0.5y_{2,t} + 0.5y_{3,t} + v_{1,t}$$
$$y_{2,t} = y_{2,t-1} + v_{2,t}$$
$$y_{3,t} = y_{3,t-1} + v_{3,t} \,.$$

(c) Repeat part (a) for the trivariate VECM

$$y_{1,t} = y_{3,t} + v_{1,t}$$
$$y_{2,t} = y_{3,t} + v_{1,t}$$
$$y_{3,t} = y_{3,t-1} + v_{3,t} \,.$$

(6) Computing the Quantiles of the Trace Statistic by Simulation

Program files   coint_tracecv.*

The quantiles of the trace statistic reported in Table 18.4 for Models 1 to 5 are computed by simulating the model under the null hypothesis of $N - r$ common trends.

(a) For Model 1, simulate the following K dimensional process under the null hypothesis

$$\Delta y_t = v_t, \quad v_t \sim iid\ N(0, V),$$

in which $V = I_K$ and v_t is $(T \times K)$ matrix which approximates the Brownian increments $dB(s)$ and y_t approximates $B(s)$. In the computation of $B(s)$ and $dB(s)$, the latter is treated as a forward difference relative to $B(s)$. Compute the trace statistic

$$LR = \text{tr}\left([T^{-1}\sum_{t=1}^{T} v_t y'_{t-1}][T^{-2}\sum_{t=1}^{T} y_{t-1}y'_{t-1}]^{-1}[T^{-1}\sum_{t=1}^{T} y_{t-1}v'_t]\right),$$

100000 times and find the 90%, 95% and 99% quantiles of LR for $K = 1, 2, \cdots, 6$ common trends.

(b) For Model 2, repeat part (a), except that $B(s)$ is augmented by including a constant.

(c) For Model 3, repeat part (a), except replace one of the common trends in $B(s)$ by a deterministic time trend and then center $B(s)$.

(d) For Model 4, repeat part (a), except augment $B(s)$ by including a deterministic time trend and then center $B(s)$.

(e) For Model 5, repeat part (a), except replace one of the common trends in $B(s)$ by a squared deterministic time trend and then detrend $B(s)$ by regressing $B(s)$ on a constant and a deterministic time trend.

(7) Demand for Money

Program files	`coint_impulse.*`
Data files	`moneydemand.*`

The data are quarterly nominal M2, m_t, nominal GDP, gdp_t, the consumer price level, cpi_t, the Treasury bill yield, $tbill_t$ and the Federal funds rate, $funds_t$, for the United States from March 1959 to December 2005.

(a) Test for cointegration among $\ln(m_t/p_t)$, $\ln(gdp_t/p_t)$, $tbill_t$ and $funds_t$, where the VECM is based on Model 3 from Table 18.1 with $p = 4$ lags.

(b) Given the results of the cointegration test in part (a), estimate a VECM and interpret the normalised long-run parameter estimates, $\widehat{\beta}$, and the error-correction parameter estimates, $\widehat{\alpha}$.

(c) Test the following restrictions on the long-run parameters and interpret the results.

   (i) The income elasticity is unity.
   (ii) The two interest rate semi-elasticities sum to zero.

(d) Given the results of part (c), compute the impulse responses of the VECM based on short-run restrictions given by a triangular ordering and interpret the results.

(e) Compute the impulse responses for an income shock based on the long-run restrictions between money and income while holding the two yields fixed.

(8) Information Criteria Test of Cointegration

Program files	`coint_ic.*`

The information criteria approach to choosing the cointegrating rank is based on solving

$$\widehat{r} = \arg\min_{0 \leq r \leq N} (-2(T - p)\ln L_T(r) + c_T m_r),$$

where $c_T = 2$ (AIC), $\ln T$ (SIC), $2\ln\ln T$ (HIC) and $m_r = \dim(\alpha, \beta, V) = Nr + (N - r)r + N(N + 1)/2$, the number of free parameters corresponding to rank r having normalised r of the N variables in the system.

(a) Show that the BIC and the HIC yield consistent estimators of the true cointegrating rank r_0, unlike the AIC.

(b) The following data generating process is used to investigate the small sample properties of the information criteria to select the cointegrating rank

$$\begin{bmatrix} y_{1,t} \\ y_{2,t} \end{bmatrix} = \begin{bmatrix} \phi_1 & 0 \\ 0 & \phi_2 \end{bmatrix} \begin{bmatrix} y_{1,t-1} \\ y_{2,t-1} \end{bmatrix} + \begin{bmatrix} v_{1,t} \\ v_{2,t} \end{bmatrix},$$

$$\begin{bmatrix} v_{1,t} \\ v_{2,t} \end{bmatrix} \sim iid\ N\left(\begin{bmatrix} 0 \\ 0 \end{bmatrix}, \begin{bmatrix} 1 & \rho \\ \rho & 1 \end{bmatrix} \right),$$

where the sample size is $T = 100$, the number of replications is 10000 and the parameter values are
(i) $r_0 = 0 : \phi_1 = 1.0, \phi_2 = 1.0, \rho = 0.0$
(ii) $r_0 = 1 : \phi_1 = 1.0, \phi_2 = 0.8, \rho = 0.0$
(iii) $r_0 = 1 : \phi_1 = 1.0, \phi_2 = 0.8, \rho = 0.9$
(iv) $r_0 = 2 : \phi_1 = 0.8, \phi_2 = 0.8, \rho = 0.0$.

(c) Redo the Monte Carlo experiment in part (b) for the trace test using the asymptotic 5% critical value reported in Table 18.4. Compare the finite sample performance of the trace and information criteria approaches to select the cointegrating rank.

(9) Heteroskedasticity and the Distribution of the Trace Statistic

Program files   coint_hetero.*

Consider the following VECM with heteroskedasticity

$$\Delta y_{i,t} = v_{i,t}, \quad v_{i,t} = \sqrt{h_{i,t}} z_{i,t}, \quad z_{i,t} \sim N(0, 1), \quad i = 1, 2, \cdots, N.$$

(a) Assume that the heteroskedasticity is of the form

$$\sigma_{i,t}^2 = (1 - \phi_1 - \phi_2) + \phi_1 v_{i,t-1}^2 + \phi_2 \sigma_{j,t-1}^2.$$

Simulate the size of the trace test for $N = 2$, a sample of $T = 100$ and using 10000 replications. Choose two sets of parameters given by $\{\phi_1 = 0.3, \phi_2 = 0.6\}$ and $\{\phi_1 = 0.3, \phi_2 = 0.69\}$. Discuss the results.
(b) Repeat part (a) for dimensions of $N = 4, 6, 8$. Discuss the results.
(c) Assume that the heteroskedasticity is a structural break

$$\sigma_{j,t}^2 = \begin{cases} 1 & : \ t \leq \lfloor \tau T \rfloor \\ 2 & : \ t > \lfloor \tau T \rfloor \end{cases}.$$

Simulate the size of the trace test for a sample of $T = 100$ using 10000 replications and break points of $\tau = \{0.1, 0.25, 0.5, 0.75, 0.9\}$. Discuss the results.
(d) Repeat part (c) for dimensions of $N = 4, 6, 8$. Discuss the results.

(10) Likelihood Ratio Test of a Deterministic Time Trends

Program files   coint_trend.*

Simulate the following bivariate VECM based on Model 3 for a sample of size $T = 200$

$$\begin{bmatrix} \Delta y_{1,t} \\ \Delta y_{2,t} \end{bmatrix} = \begin{bmatrix} 0.2 \\ 0.2 \end{bmatrix} + \begin{bmatrix} -0.2 \\ 0.2 \end{bmatrix} \begin{bmatrix} 1 \\ -1 \\ 4 \end{bmatrix}' \begin{bmatrix} y_{1,t-1} \\ y_{2,t-1} \\ 1 \end{bmatrix}$$

$$+ \begin{bmatrix} -0.2 & 0 \\ 0 & 0.4 \end{bmatrix} \begin{bmatrix} \Delta y_{1,t-1} \\ \Delta y_{2,t-1} \end{bmatrix} + \begin{bmatrix} v_{1,t} \\ v_{2,t} \end{bmatrix},$$

in which $v_t = [\, v_{1,t} \; v_{2,t} \,]'$ and $v_t \sim iid \; N(0, V)$ with $V = I_2$.

(a) Estimate two VECMs using the Johansen estimator with the first based on Model 5 in Table 18.1 and the second based on Model 4. Perform a LR test and interpret the result given that the true DGP is based on Model 3. Use the property that under the null hypothesis the LR test is distributed asymptotically as χ^2 with $\dim(\mu_1) - \dim(\beta_1) = N - r$ degrees of freedom since the total number of deterministic time trends in the unrestricted model is N, while in the restricted model the number of trends is r.

(b) Estimate two VECMs using the Johansen estimator with the first based on Model 4 in Table 18.1 and the second based on Model 3. Perform a LR test and interpret the result given that the true DGP is based on Model 3. Use the property that under the null hypothesis the LR test is distributed asymptotically as χ^2 with $\dim(\beta_1) = r$ restrictions.

(11) **Identification of VECMs**

Program files `coint_ident.*`

Simulate the following trivariate VECM based on Model 3 for a sample of size $T = 200$

$$\begin{bmatrix} \Delta y_{1,t} \\ \Delta y_{2,t} \\ \Delta y_{3,t} \end{bmatrix} = \begin{bmatrix} 0.04286 \\ 0.02857 \\ 0.08571 \end{bmatrix} + \begin{bmatrix} -0.2 & 0.0 \\ 0.0 & -0.3 \\ 0.1 & 0.1 \end{bmatrix} \begin{bmatrix} 1 & 0 \\ 0 & 1 \\ -0.8 & -0.8 \\ 4 & 1 \end{bmatrix}' \begin{bmatrix} y_{1,t-1} \\ y_{2,t-1} \\ y_{3,t-1} \\ 1 \end{bmatrix}$$

$$+ \begin{bmatrix} -0.2 & 0 & 0 \\ 0 & 0.4 & 0 \\ 0 & 0 & 0.1 \end{bmatrix} \begin{bmatrix} \Delta y_{1,t-1} \\ \Delta y_{2,t-1} \\ \Delta y_{3,t-1} \end{bmatrix} + \begin{bmatrix} v_{1,t} \\ v_{2,t} \\ v_{3,t} \end{bmatrix},$$

where $v_t = [\, v_{1,t} \; v_{2,t} \; v_{3,t} \,]' \sim iid \; N(0, V)$ with $V = I_3$ and $y_0 = y_{-1} = 0$.

(a) Use the Johansen algorithm to estimate the VECM based on model 3 with rank $r = 2$.

(b) Estimate the non-normalised cointegrating vectors using the first two columns of $\widehat{\gamma} = L'^{-1} E$ and compare the estimates with the population parameter values.

(c) Estimate β using the triangular normalisation and compare the estimates with the population parameter values.
(d) Use the iterative algorithm to estimate the VECM based on model 3 with rank $r = 2$, where the triangular normalisation is subject to the cross-equation restriction that the long-run parameter estimates on $y_{3,t}$ in the two cointegrating equations are equal.

(12) Exogeneity Testing

Program files   `coint_exogeneity.*`

Simulate the bivariate VECM based on Model 1 for a sample of size $T = 200$

$$\begin{bmatrix} \Delta y_{1,t} \\ \Delta y_{2,t} \end{bmatrix} = \begin{bmatrix} -0.4 \\ 0.0 \end{bmatrix} \begin{bmatrix} 1 \\ -1 \end{bmatrix}' \begin{bmatrix} y_{1,t-1} \\ y_{2,t-1} \end{bmatrix}$$
$$+ \begin{bmatrix} -0.2 & 0.0 \\ 0.0 & 0.4 \end{bmatrix} \begin{bmatrix} \Delta y_{1,t-1} \\ \Delta y_{2,t-1} \end{bmatrix} + \begin{bmatrix} v_{1,t} \\ v_{2,t} \end{bmatrix}$$
$$\begin{bmatrix} v_{1,t} \\ v_{2,t} \end{bmatrix} \sim iid\ N \left(\begin{bmatrix} 0 \\ 0 \end{bmatrix}, \begin{bmatrix} 1.0 & 0.5 \\ 0.5 & 1.0 \end{bmatrix} \right).$$

In this model $y_{2,t}$ is both weakly and strongly exogenous.
(a) Estimate the following VECM based on Model 1 with $p = 2$ lags

$$\begin{bmatrix} \Delta y_{1,t} \\ \Delta y_{2,t} \end{bmatrix} = \begin{bmatrix} \alpha_{1,1} \\ \alpha_{2,1} \end{bmatrix} \begin{bmatrix} 1.0 \\ \beta_{2,1} \end{bmatrix}' \begin{bmatrix} y_{1,t-1} \\ y_{2,t-1} \end{bmatrix}$$
$$+ \begin{bmatrix} \Gamma_{1,1} & \Gamma_{1,2} \\ \Gamma_{2,1} & \Gamma_{2,2} \end{bmatrix} \begin{bmatrix} \Delta y_{1,t-1} \\ \Delta y_{2,t-1} \end{bmatrix} + \begin{bmatrix} v_{1,t} \\ v_{2,t} \end{bmatrix},$$

using the iterative estimator based on Newton-Raphson. Test the following hypotheses

$$H_0 : \alpha_{2,1} = 0 \qquad\qquad \text{[Weak exogeneity]}$$
$$H_0 : \alpha_{2,1} = 0, \Gamma_{2,1} = 0 \quad \text{[Strong exogeneity]},$$

using a Wald statistic.
(b) Estimate the VECM in part (a) subject to the restriction $\alpha_{2,1} = 0$. Test for weak exogeneity using a LR statistic.
(c) Estimate the VECM in part (a) subject to the restrictions $\alpha_{2,1} = 0$ and $\Gamma_{2,1} = 0$. Test for strong exogeneity using a LR statistic.
(d) Show that, under weak exogeneity, the estimate of the cointegrating parameter $\beta_{2,1}$, obtained in part (b), can also be recovered from estimating the regression equation

$$\Delta y_{1,t} = v_1 y_{1,t-1} + v_2 y_{2,t-1} + v_3 \Delta y_{2,t} + v_4 \Delta y_{1,t-1} + v_5 \Delta y_{2,t-1} + w_t,$$

by ordinary least squares and defining $\beta_{2,1} = -v_2/v_1$. Compare the estimate of $\beta_{2,1}$ obtained using the partial model with the estimate using the full system obtained in part (b) subject to the restriction $\alpha_{2,1} = 0$.

(e) Estimate the VECM in part (a) based on Model 1 with $p = 2$ lags using the Johansen estimator and compare with the results obtained using the Newton-Raphson algorithm.

(13) **Term Structure of Interest Rates with Level Effects**

Program files	coint_level.*
Data files	usmacro.*

The data are quarterly 1-year, 5-year and 10-year yields for the United States from March 1962 to September 2010.

(a) Consider the bivariate VECM of y_t containing the 10-year and 1-year yields, using Model 2 with $p = 1$ lags,

$$\begin{bmatrix} \Delta y_{1,t} \\ \Delta y_{2,t} \end{bmatrix} = \begin{bmatrix} \alpha_{1,1} \\ \alpha_{2,1} \end{bmatrix} (y_{1,t-1} - \beta_0 - \beta_s y_{2,t-1}) + v_t$$

$$L = \begin{bmatrix} L_{1,1} & 0 \\ L_{1,2} & L_{2,2} \end{bmatrix}$$

$$v_t \sim iid\, N(0, V = LL').$$

Estimate the parameters $\theta = \{\alpha_1, \alpha_2, \beta_c, \beta_s, L_{1,1}, L_{1,2}, L_{2,2}\}$ using the iterative estimator based on the Newton-Raphson algorithm. Compare the estimates with those in part (b) of Exercise 3.

(b) Now estimate the VECM with level effects parameters κ_1 and κ_2 by redefining L and V in part (a) as

$$L_t = \begin{bmatrix} L_{1,1} & 0 \\ L_{1,2} & L_{2,2} \end{bmatrix} \begin{bmatrix} y_{1,t-1}^{\kappa_1} \\ y_{2,t-1}^{\kappa_2} \end{bmatrix}, \qquad V_t = L_t L_t'.$$

(c) Compare the estimates obtained in parts (a) and (b). Test for weak and strong exogeneity. Perform a joint test of level effects in the term structure of interest rates by testing the restrictions $\kappa_1 = \kappa_2 = 0$.

(14) **Cointegrating Regression**

Program files	coint_reg.*

In the case of a single cointegrating vector, the coefficients of a cointegrating equation can be estimated by regression methods. This situation can be represented by the model

$$y_t = x_t'\beta + u_t, \tag{18.56}$$
$$\Delta x_t = v_t, \tag{18.57}$$

in which $[u_t \; v_t']'$ is a vector of $I(0)$ disturbances. In general, these disturbances may be allowed to be autocorrelated and correlated with each other. The regressors x_t are clearly $I(1)$ and are assumed to be not cointegrated among themselves. Under these conditions, the vector time series $[y_t \; x_t']'$ is cointegrated with cointegrating vector $[1, \; -\beta']'$.

The ordinary least squares estimator of β in (18.56) was suggested and analysed by, among others, Engle and Granger (1987), Stock (1987), and Park and Phillips (1988). It was shown that ordinary least squares is an $O_p(T^{-1})$ consistent estimator of β, even in situations where u_t and v_t are correlated with each other. However such correlation was shown to induce a second-order bias in the ordinary least squares estimator, as well as nuisance parameters in its asymptotic distribution. As a remedy to this, Phillips and Hansen (1990) introduced the Fully Modified ordinary least squares estimator (FMOLS), which involves the following steps.

(a) Estimate (18.56) by ordinary least squares to obtain $\widehat{\beta}_{OLS}$ and $\widehat{u}_t$.
(b) Form the vector $z_t = (\widehat{u}_t, \Delta x_t')'$ and obtain estimates of the long run variance matrices

$$\Omega_{zz} = \sum_{j=-\infty}^{\infty} E[z_t z_{t-j}'], \quad \Delta_{zz} = \sum_{j=0}^{\infty} E[z_t z_{t-j}'],$$

using the Newey-West approach outlined in Chapter 9. Partition these estimators as

$$\widehat{\Omega}_{zz} = \begin{bmatrix} \widehat{\omega}_u^2 & \widehat{\omega}_{vu}' \\ \widehat{\omega}_{vu} & \widehat{\Omega}_{vv} \end{bmatrix}, \quad \widehat{\Delta}_{zz} = \begin{bmatrix} \widehat{\delta}_u & \widehat{\delta}_{vu}' \\ \widehat{\delta}_{vu} & \widehat{\Delta}_{vv} \end{bmatrix}.$$

(c) The FMOLS estimator is

$$\widehat{\beta}_{FM} = \left[\sum_{t=2}^{T} x_t x_t' \right]^{-1} \left[\sum_{t=2}^{T} x_t y_t^* - T \widehat{\delta}_{vu}^* \right],$$

in which

$$y_t^* = y_t - \Delta x_t' \widehat{\Omega}_{vv}^{-1} \widehat{\omega}_{vu},$$

and

$$\widehat{\delta}_{vu}^* = \widehat{\delta}_{vu} - \widehat{\Delta}_{vv} \widehat{\Omega}_{vv}^{-1} \widehat{\omega}_{vu}.$$

This modified estimator does not have the second-order bias that ordinary least squares does and its asymptotic distribution is mixed normal.

Alternative estimators of (18.56) that achieve the same result include those of Saikkonen (1991), Phillips (1991b), Park (1992), Stock and Watson (1993) and Marinucci and Robinson (2001). Carry out a Monte Carlo experiment to explore the finite sample properties of the ordinary least squares and FMOLS estimators in comparison to the Johansen VECM estimator. The data generating process should have

$$u_t = \alpha u_{t-1} + e_{1,t},$$

$$v_t = e_{2,t},$$

in which

$$\begin{bmatrix} e_{1,t} \\ e_{2,t} \end{bmatrix} \sim iid\ N \left(\begin{bmatrix} 0 \\ 0 \end{bmatrix}, \begin{bmatrix} 1 & \rho \\ \rho & 1 \end{bmatrix} \right),$$

with $\rho = \{0, 0.4, 0.8\}$, $\alpha = \{0, 0.4, 0.8\}$ and $T = \{100, 200, 400\}$. Evaluate the biases and standard deviations of the sampling distributions of the three estimators and use these to observe
(a) the super-consistency of all three estimators,
(b) the effects of regressor endogeneity (controlled by ρ),
(c) the effects of disturbance autocorrelation (controlled by α).

PART SIX

Nonlinear Time Series

19 Nonlinearities in Mean

19.1 Introduction

The stationary time series models developed in Part FOUR and the nonstationary time series models developed in Part FIVE are characterised by the mean being a linear function of the lagged dependent variables (autoregressive) and/or the lagged disturbances (moving average). These models are able to capture many of the characteristics observed in time series data, including randomness, cycles and stochastic trends. Where these models come up short, however, is in capturing more extreme events such as jumps and asymmetric adjustments across cycles that cannot be captured adequately by a linear representation. This chapter deals with models in which the linear mean specification is augmented by the inclusion of nonlinear terms so that the conditional mean becomes nonlinear in the lagged dependent variables and lagged disturbances.

Examples of nonlinear models investigated are thresholds time series models (TAR), artificial neural networks (ANN), bilinear models and Markov switching models. Nonparametric methods are also investigated where a parametric specification of the nonlinearity is not imposed on the structure of the model. Further nonlinear specifications are investigated in Chapters 20 and 21. In Chapter 20, nonlinearities in variance are introduced and developed in the context of GARCH and MGARCH models. In Chapter 21, nonlinearities arise from the specification of time series models of discrete random variables.

19.2 Motivating Examples

The class of stationary linear time series models presented in Chapter 13 yields solutions that are characterised by convergence to a single equilibrium point, with the trajectory path exhibiting either monotonic or oscillatory behaviour.

Example 19.1 AR(2) Model
Consider the linear AR(2) process

$$y_t = 0.9 + 0.7y_{t-1} - 0.6y_{t-2}. \tag{19.1}$$

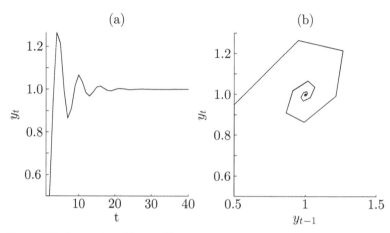

Figure 19.1. Properties of the AR(2) process, $y_t = 0.9 + 0.7y_{t-1} - 0.6y_{t-2}$, with $y_0 = 0.5$.

Panel (a) of Figure 19.1 shows that the dynamics exhibit damped oscillatory behaviour, starting from the initial value $y_0 = 0.5$ and converging to the equilibrium point $y = 0.9/(1 - 0.7 + 0.6) = 1.0$. The phase diagram in Panel (b) of Figure 19.1 shows how the process spirals towards this equilibrium point. □

While this linear class of models can capture a wide range of patterns commonly observed in time series data, there are some empirical characteristics that these models cannot explain. Examples of this nonlinear behaviour include limit cycles, strange attractors, multiple equilibria and asymmetries.

Example 19.2 Limit Cycle
Consider the following model, proposed by Tong (1983, p85), where y_t is governed by separate AR processes depending upon whether it is above or below the threshold value of 3.05

$$y_t = \begin{cases} 0.8023 + 1.0676y_{t-1} - 0.2099y_{t-2} + 0.1712y_{t-3} & : y_{t-2} \leq 3.05 \\ \quad -0.4528y_{t-4} + 0.2237y_{t-5} - 0.0331y_{t-6} & \\ \\ 2.2964 + 1.4246y_{t-1} - 1.0795y_{t-2} - 0.0900y_{t-3} & : y_{t-2} > 3.05. \end{cases}$$

Panel (a) of Figure 19.2 shows that the process converges to a nine-period cycle. The phase diagram in panel (b) of Figure 19.2 illustrates how the process eventually settles down into a cycle, known as a limit cycle. This behaviour contrasts with the pattern observed for the linear time series model in Figure 19.1 where the limit of the process is a single point. □

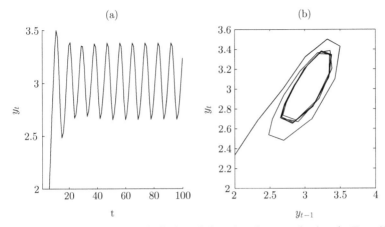

Figure 19.2. Demonstration of a limit cycle based on the example given by Tong (1983).

Example 19.3 Strange Attractors

Strange attractors are regions to which a process converges, but once in the region the process exhibits aperiodic behaviour, commonly known as chaos. This behaviour contrasts with the limit cycle depicted in Figure 19.2 where the process settles upon the outer perimeter of the region. An example of a strange attractor is the nonlinear business cycle model of Kaldor (see Lorenz, 1989, p130; Creedy and Martin, 1994) given by

$$
\begin{aligned}
y_{t+1} - y_t &= 20(i_t - s_t) && \text{[Output]} \\
k_{t+1} - k_t &= i_t - 0.05 k_t && \text{[Capital]} \\
i_t &= 20(2^{-(0.01 y_t + 0.00001)^{-2}}) + 0.05 y_t + 5(280 k_t^{-1})^{4.5} && \text{[Investment]} \\
s_t &= 0.21 y_t, && \text{[Savings]}
\end{aligned}
$$

where y_t is output, k_t is capital, i_t is investment and s_t is savings.

The dynamic properties of the model are given in Figure 19.3. The phase diagrams, in panels (a) to (c) of Figure 19.3, highlight the strange attraction properties of the model with regions of attraction characterised by aperiodic behaviour. Panel (d) of Figure 19.3 demonstrates the sensitive dependence to initial conditions property of chaotic attractors whereby the time paths of two processes with very similar initial conditions eventually diverge and follow completely different time trajectories.   □

Example 19.4 Multiple Equilibria

The stationary linear times series model exhibits a unique equilibrium. However, more than one equilibrium arises in many situations in economics. The nonlinear business cycle model of Kaldor presented in Figure 19.3 provides an example of an equilibrium region, referred to as a strange attractor, where

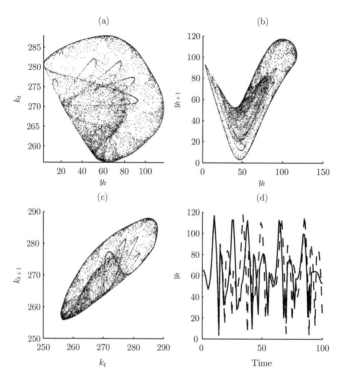

Figure 19.3. Strange attractor properties of the Kaldorian nonlinear business cycle model, where y_t is output and k_t is capital.

the process never remains at any single point because of chaotic behaviour. As another example of multiple equilibria, consider the nonlinear error correction model of the logarithm of real money, m_t, which is a simplification of the model estimated in Ericsson, Hendry and Prestwich (1998, p. 296)

$$\Delta m_t = 0.45\Delta m_{t-1} - 0.10\Delta^2 m_{t-2} - 2.54(m_{t-1} - 0.1)m_{t-1}^2 + v_t ,$$

where $v_t \sim iid\ N(0, 0.005^2)$, $\Delta m_t = m_t - m_{t-1}$, and $\Delta^2 m_{t-2} = m_{t-2} - 2m_{t-3} + m_{t-4}$. The nonlinearity is given by the error correction term $(m_{t-1} - 0.1)m_{t-1}^2$, which is a cubic with three roots: one at 0.1 (stable) and two at 0.0 (point of inflection). Simulating this model for a sample of size $T = 50000$ generates the histogram given in Figure 19.4. The manifestation of a nonlinear stochastic model with multiple equilibria is a multimodal distribution with the majority of the mass around the stable equilibrium value of 0.1, and a smaller mass at around the inflection point of 0.0.   □

Example 19.5 Asymmetries
A property of linearity is that positive and negative shocks have the same effect on the absolute value of y_t, so that a positive shock followed by a negative

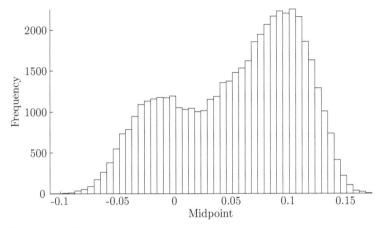

Figure 19.4. Histogram obtained from simulating the nonlinear error correction model of Ericsson, Hendry and Prestwich (1998).

shock of equal magnitude would return the process to its original position. This degree of symmetry is not always evident in the data. An example where adjustment is asymmetric arises in the analysis of business cycles where strong empirical evidence exists that the duration of expansions is longer on average than the duration of contractions (Harding and Pagan, 2002, p372).

Table 19.1 gives the business cycle turning points for United States monthly data from 1945 to 2007. The average duration of contractions is about 10 months, compared to 57 months for expansions. Figure 19.5 shows the monthly unemployment rate from 1947 to 2010, which reveals the asymmetric behaviour of the business cycle. Large, sharp upward movements in unemployment (contraction phase) are followed by slow, downward drifts (expansion phase). This suggests that separate time series models may be needed to capture differences in the expansion and contraction phases of the business cycle. □

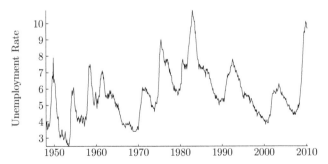

Figure 19.5. United States monthly aggregate unemployment rate measured for the period January 1947 to March 2010.

Table 19.1. *United States business cycle turning points*
(month/year) for the period 1945 to 2007

Peak	Trough	Duration of Contraction (Peak to Trough)	Duration of Expansion (Trough to Peak)
02/1945	10/1945	8	80
11/1948	10/1949	11	37
07/1953	05/1954	10	45
08/1957	04/1958	8	39
04/1960	02/1961	10	24
12/1969	11/1970	11	106
11/1973	03/1975	16	36
01/1980	07/1980	6	58
07/1981	11/1982	16	12
07/1990	03/1991	8	92
03/2001	11/2001	8	120
12/2007	——	–	73
	Mean	10	57

Source: http://www.nber.org/cycles.html

19.3   Threshold Models

19.3.1   *Specification*

Threshold time series models assume that the dependent variable y_t, is governed by more than a single regime at any point in time. In the case of two regimes where each sub-model has an autoregressive process, the model is expressed as

$$y_t = \mathrm{E}_{t-1}[y_t] + v_t , \qquad v_t \sim iid\,(0, \sigma^2), \tag{19.2}$$

in which $\mathrm{E}_{t-1}[y_t]$ is the conditional model given by

$$\mathrm{E}_{t-1}[y_t] = \begin{cases} \phi_0 + \sum_{i=1}^{p} \phi_i y_{t-i} & : \text{ with probability } 1 - w_t \\[2ex] \alpha_0 + \sum_{i=1}^{p} \alpha_i y_{t-i} & : \text{ with probability } w_t . \end{cases} \tag{19.3}$$

The variable w_t represents a time-varying weighting function with the property

$$0 \le w_t \le 1, \tag{19.4}$$

which, in general, is specified to be a function of lagged values of y_t and a set of explanatory variables x_t. For values of w_t close to zero (unity) the conditional mean of y_t is dominated by the first (second) regime. Combining equations (19.2) and (19.3), the model is written more compactly as

$$
\begin{aligned}
y_t &= (\phi_0 + \sum_{i=1}^{p} \phi_i y_{t-i})(1 - w_t) + (\alpha_0 + \sum_{i=1}^{p} \alpha_i y_{t-i})w_t + v_t \\
&= \phi_0 + \sum_{i=1}^{p} \phi_i y_{t-i} + (\beta_0 + \sum_{i=1}^{p} \beta_i y_{t-i})w_t + v_t,
\end{aligned}
\tag{19.5}
$$

with $\beta_0 = \alpha_0 - \phi_0$ and $\beta_i = \alpha_i - \phi_i$. Equation (19.5) forms the basis of the class of threshold time series models, which, in turn, nests a number of well-known nonlinear time series models.

The key distinguishing feature of the nonlinear class of time series models in (19.5) is the way the weighting function, w_t, is specified. Four popular choices of this function are

$$
\text{STAR} \quad : \quad w_t = \frac{1}{\sqrt{2\pi}} \int_{-\infty}^{\gamma(y_{t-d}-c)} e^{-0.5s^2} ds,
$$

$$
\text{LSTAR} \quad : \quad w_t = \frac{1}{1 + \exp(-\gamma(y_{t-d} - c))}, \quad \gamma > 0,
\tag{19.6}
$$

$$
\text{SETAR} \quad : \quad w_t = \begin{bmatrix} 1 & y_{t-d} \geq c \\ 0 & y_{t-d} < c, \end{bmatrix}
$$

$$
\text{ESTAR} \quad : \quad w_t = 1 - \exp(-\gamma(y_{t-d} - c)^2), \quad \gamma > 0,
$$

which represent, respectively, the smooth transition autoregressive model (STAR), the logistic smooth transition autoregressive (LSTAR) model, the self-exciting threshold autoregressive model (SETAR) and the exponential smooth transition autoregressive model (ESTAR).

The properties of w_t in (19.6) are displayed in Figure 19.6 for the four models with $\gamma = 1$, $c = 0$ and $d = 1$. The parameter d controls the delay in moving between regimes, the parameter c represents the threshold where switching occurs and the parameter γ determines the speed of adjustment in switching between regimes. At $\gamma = 0$ there is no switching with the STAR, LSTAR and ESTAR models reducing to the linear model. For $\gamma > 0$, there is smooth adjustment between the two regimes for the STAR, LSTAR and ESTAR models. As $\gamma \to \infty$, there is infinitely fast switching between regimes with the STAR and LSTAR models reducing to the SETAR model, whilst the ESTAR model approaches the linear model again. For the STAR, LSTAR and SETAR models, switching occurs from regime 1 to regime 2 in (19.3) since y_{t-d} increases from values less than c to values greater than c. In the case of the ESTAR model, the dynamics of y_t are governed by regime 1 for values of

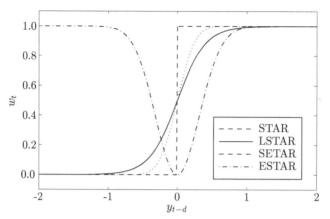

Figure 19.6. Alternative threshold functions used in threshold autoregressive models: $\gamma = 1, c = 0$ and $d = 1$.

y_{t-d} near $c = 0$ and by a weighted average of the two regimes for high and low values of y_{t-d}.

19.3.2   Estimation

Threshold models can be estimated by maximum likelihood using standard iterative algorithms. Assuming a normal disturbance term, $v_t \sim iid\ N(0, \sigma^2)$, the conditional probability distribution of y_t for the threshold model in equation (19.5) with weighting function w_t in (19.6) is

$$f(y_t|y_{t-1}, \ldots, y_{t-s}) = \frac{1}{\sqrt{2\pi\sigma^2}} \exp\left[-\frac{v_t^2}{2\sigma^2}\right], \tag{19.7}$$

where $s = \max(p, d)$. For a sample of $t = 1, 2, \cdots, T$, observations, the conditional log-likelihood function from Chapter 7 for the case of known delay parameter, d, is

$$\ln L_T(\theta) = \frac{1}{T-s} \sum_{t=s+1}^{T} \ln f(y_t|y_{t-1}, \ldots, y_{t-s})$$

$$= -\frac{1}{2}\ln 2\pi - \frac{1}{2}\ln \sigma^2$$

$$- \frac{1}{2\sigma^2(T-s)} \sum_{t=s+1}^{T} \left(y_t - \phi_0 - \sum_{i=1}^{p}\phi_i y_{t-i} - (\beta_0 - \sum_{i=1}^{p}\beta_i y_{t-i})w_t\right)^2,$$

where $\theta = \{\phi_0, \phi_1, \cdots, \phi_p, \beta_0, \beta_1, \cdots, \beta_p, \gamma, c, \sigma^2\}$ are the unknown parameters. The log-likelihood function is maximised with respect to θ using one of the iterative algorithms discussed in Chapter 3. This algorithm is simplified by using the maximum likelihood estimator $\widehat{\sigma}^2 = (T - s)^{-1} \sum_{t=s+1}^{T} \widehat{v}_t^2$ to concentrate out σ^2 from $\ln L_T(\theta)$, where $\widehat{v}_t$ is the residual. For the case of unknown d, a grid search is performed by estimating the model for values of $d = \{1, 2, 3. \cdots\}$ and choosing $\widehat{d}$ that maximises $\ln L_T(\theta)$. An alternative method to compute the maximum likelihood estimator is to perform a grid search on both d and c. The advantage of this method is that for each choice of d and c, w_t is now an observable time series so the maximum likelihood estimator of the remaining parameters is computed by regressing y_t on $\{\text{constant}, y_{t-1}, y_{t-2}, \cdots, y_{t-p}, w_t, y_{t-1}w_t, \cdots, y_{t-p}w_t\}$.

19.3.3 Testing

A natural test of the threshold model in (19.5) is to perform a test of linearity by seeing if the model reduces to the linear autoregressive model

$$y_t = \phi_0 + \sum_{i=1}^{p} \phi_i y_{t-i} + v_t. \tag{19.8}$$

A comparison of (19.5) and (19.8) suggests that a natural test statistic to determine whether or not the parameters in the second regime are zero, $\beta_i = 0, \forall i$, can be based on either the Wald or LM principle. The distribution of any test statistic that tests this hypothesis, however, is non-standard because the parameters γ and c are not defined under the null hypothesis and conventional maximum likelihood theory is, therefore, not directly applicable. An alternative approach is to test $\gamma = 0$ as w_t in (19.6) becomes a constant resulting in the STAR, LSTAR and ESTAR models reducing to a linear AR model. However, in this case it is the parameters c and β_i that are now not identified under the null hypothesis. There are two possible ways to address this problem. Luukkonen, Saikkonen and Teräsvirta (1988) suggest focussing on local asymptotics at $\gamma = 0$. This approach has the advantage of yielding a test statistic with a standard distribution under the null hypothesis. Alternatively, Hansen (1996) proposes a solution based on local asymptotics at $\beta = 0$, which yields a test statistic whose distribution must be approximated by bootstrapping. The discussion that follows focusses on the first approach.

Let $z_t = \gamma(y_{t-d} - c)$ so that under the null hypothesis $\gamma = 0$ and thus $z_t = 0$. For the LSTAR weighting function $w_t = 1/(1 + \exp[-z_t])$. The first three derivatives of the LSTAR weighting function with respect to z_t, evaluated at

$z_t = 0$, are as follows

$$w^{(1)}(0) = \left.\frac{\partial w_t}{\partial z_t}\right|_{z_t=0} = \left.\frac{\exp(-z_t)}{(1 + \exp(-z_t))^2}\right|_{z_t=0} = \frac{1}{4}$$

$$w^{(2)}(0) = \left.\frac{\partial^2 w_t}{\partial z_t^2}\right|_{z_t=0} = \left.-\frac{\exp(-z_t) - \exp(-2z_t)}{(1 + \exp(-z_t))^3}\right|_{z_t=0} = 0$$

$$w^{(3)}(0) = \left.\frac{\partial^3 w_t}{\partial z_t^3}\right|_{z_t=0} = \left.\frac{\exp(3z_t) - 4\exp(2z_t) + \exp(z_t)}{6\exp(2z_t) + 4\exp(3z_t) + \exp(4z_t) + 4\exp(z_t) + 1}\right|_{z_t=0}$$

$$= -\frac{1}{8}.$$

Using these derivatives in a third-order Taylor expansion of $w(z_t)$ around $z_t = 0$ gives

$$w_t \approx w(0) + w^{(1)}(0)(z_t - 0) + \frac{1}{2}w^{(2)}(0)(z_t - 0)^2 + \frac{1}{6}w^{(3)}(0)(z_t - 0)^3$$

$$= \frac{1}{2} + \frac{1}{4}z_t + 0 - \frac{1}{48}z_t^3.$$

The expansion of $z_t^3 = (y_{t-d} - c)^3$ has terms in y_{t-d}^3, y_{t-d}^2 and y_{t-d}, so that the weighting function is approximated by the cubic

$$w_t \approx \delta_0 + \delta_1 y_{t-d} + \delta_2 y_{t-d}^2 + \delta_3 y_{t-d}^3. \tag{19.9}$$

This Taylor series approximation represents the local behaviour of the function in the vicinity of $\gamma = 0$ and therefore provides a basis of a test for linearity.

Substituting (19.9) in (19.5) for w_t gives the regression equation

$$y_t = \pi_0 + \sum_{i=1}^{p} \pi_{0,i} y_{t-i} + \sum_{i=1}^{p} \pi_{1,i} y_{t-i} y_{t-d} + \sum_{i=1}^{p} \pi_{2,i} y_{t-i} y_{t-d}^2$$

$$+ \sum_{i=1}^{p} \pi_{3,i} y_{t-i} y_{t-d}^3 + u_t, \tag{19.10}$$

where the disturbance term u_t is a function of v_t in (19.5) and the approximation error from truncating the Taylor series expansion in (19.9). Where the delay parameter is known, this regression equation forms the basis of the LST linearity test of Luukkonen, Saikkonen and Teräsvirta (1988). Under the null hypothesis, there are no interaction terms, $\pi_{j,i} = 0$ with $j = 1, 2, 3$ and $i = 1, 2, \cdots, p$. The steps to perform the linearity test are as follows.

Step 1: Regress y_t on $\{1, y_{t-1}, \cdots, y_{t-p}\}$ to get the restricted residuals $\widehat{u}_t$.

Table 19.2. *Sampling properties of the linearity test in (19.10), for a sample of size $T = 100$ and 10000 replications. The null hypothesis is $\beta = 0$, which gives the size of the test (%) based on a nominal size of 5%. The alternative hypothesis is $\beta > 0$, which gives the size-adjusted power of the test (%)*

	w_t is STAR			w_t is LSTAR		
	$\beta = 0.0$	$\beta = 0.5$	$\beta = 1.0$	$\beta = 0.0$	$\beta = 0.5$	$\beta = 1.0$
$\gamma = 0.5$	4.360	24.480	67.930	4.360	25.230	70.550
$\gamma = 1.0$	4.360	22.880	63.320	4.360	24.080	66.560
$\gamma = 5.0$	4.360	22.200	61.170	4.360	22.290	61.310

Step 2: Regress $\widehat{u}_t$ on

$$\{1, y_{t-1}, \cdots, y_{t-p}, y_{t-1}y_{t-d}, \cdots, y_{t-p}y_{t-d},$$
$$y_{t-1}y_{t-d}^2, \cdots, y_{t-p}y_{t-d}^2, y_{t-1}y_{t-d}^3, \cdots, y_{t-p}y_{t-d}^3\}.$$

Step 3: Compute the test statistic $LM = TR^2$, where T is the sample size and R^2 is the coefficient of determination from the second-stage regression. Under the null hypothesis, LM is asymptotically distributed as χ^2 with $3p$ degrees of freedom.

Three other variants of a test based on equation (19.10) are obtained by imposing restrictions on the parameters of the higher-order terms: (i) $\pi_{2,i} = \pi_{3,i} = 0, \forall i$; (ii) $\pi_{2,i} = 0, \forall i$; and (iii) $\pi_{3,i} = 0, \forall i$. These alternative versions of the test may improve the power properties of the test if the lower-order terms in the Taylor series expansion in (19.9) are sufficient to capture the nonlinearities in the model. This may occur, for example, if the weighting function in (19.6) is of the ESTAR type, a property which is developed in the exercises.

Example 19.6 Sampling Properties of the LST Linearity Test
Table 19.2 gives the finite sample performance of the linearity test based on (19.10) using a small Monte Carlo experiment. The data generating process is identical to that used by Luukkonen, Saikkonen and Teräsvirta (1988) and is given by

$$y_t = -0.5y_{t-1} + \beta y_{t-1}w_t + v_t$$
$$w_t = \begin{cases} \Phi(\gamma(y_{t-1} - 0)) \\ (1 + \exp(-\gamma(y_{t-1} - 0)))^{-1}, \end{cases}$$

in which $v_t \sim iid\ N(0, 25)$. The size of the test is 4.36%, given in the column headed $\beta = 0$, which is close to the nominal size of 5%. The size-adjusted power function increases monotonically as β becomes more positive. This pattern holds for all values of γ, although the power tends to taper off for larger values of γ. □

In the case where the delay parameter d is unknown, the regression equation in (19.10) includes the intermediate lags of y_{t-d}^2 as well. Assuming $d = p$ for simplicity, the augmented regression equation is

$$y_t = \pi + \sum_{i=1}^{p} \pi_{0,i} y_{t-i} + \sum_{i=1}^{p} \sum_{j=1}^{p} \pi_{1,i,j} y_{t-i} y_{t-j} + \sum_{i=1}^{p} \sum_{j=1}^{p} \pi_{2,i,j} y_{t-i} y_{t-j}^2$$

$$+ \sum_{i=1}^{p} \sum_{j=1}^{p} \pi_{3,i,j} y_{t-i} y_{t-j}^3 + u_t . \qquad (19.11)$$

A potential problem with this auxiliary regression is that the presence of a large number of regressors may result in a loss in power of the test statistic. One solution is to choose one of the variants of the test outlined earlier by excluding some of the higher-order terms. For example, by setting $\pi_{2,i,j} = 0$, under the null hypothesis the test is now based on the restrictions $\pi_{1,i,j} = \pi_{3,i,j} = 0$ with $i, j = 1, 2, \cdots, p$. This version of the test statistic has a χ^2 distribution with $p(p+1)/2 + p$ degrees of freedom.

19.4   Artificial Neural Networks

An artificial neural network (ANN) provides a flexible framework in which to approximate nonlinear processes. In their simplest form, they represent a threshold time series model in which the weighting function in (19.6) is now referred to as a squasher. This colourful choice of terminology stems from engineering where ANNs were initially developed. Following Creedy and Martin (1994), ANNs are presented in an econometric framework in terms of model specification, estimation and testing. Further discussion is given in Kuan and White (1994) and Lee, White and Granger (1993).

19.4.1   Specification

Consider the nonlinear time series model

$$y_t = \phi y_{t-1} + \beta \left[\frac{1}{1 + \exp\left(-\left(\delta_0 + \delta_1 y_{t-1} \right) \right)} \right] + v_t, \qquad (19.12)$$

where v_t is an $iid\,(0, \sigma^2)$ disturbance term. This is a special case of the TAR model in equation (19.5) with lag $p = 1$ and weighting function in (19.6) given by the logistic function. In artificial neural network parlance, the nonlinear time series model in (19.12) is known as a hidden-layer, feed-forward artificial neural network. The hidden layer refers to the term $\delta_0 + \delta_1 y_{t-1}$, because it provides for an additional linkage between y_t and y_{t-1} that is nested/hidden within the logistic function. Feed-forward indicates that the model uses information at time $t - 1$ to make predictions of the process at t. The artificial neural network

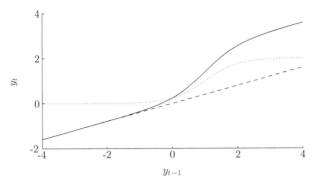

Figure 19.7. Decomposition of the predictions of an ANN (solid line) into linear (dashed line) and nonlinear (dotted line) components, based on equation (19.12). Parameter values are $\phi = 0.4$, $\beta = 2.0$, $\delta_0 = -2$ and $\delta_1 = 2$.

component is given by the parameters δ_0 and δ_1 while the logistic function is commonly referred to as a squasher as this function dampens the impact on large movements in the lagged values of y_t. The logistic function is perhaps the most commonly used squasher, although other alternatives such as the cumulative normal distribution and the hyperbolic tangent are also used.

Example 19.7 Decomposition of an Artificial Neural Network
Figure 19.7 decomposes the conditional mean of the ANN in equation (19.12) into a linear and a nonlinear component

$$
\begin{aligned}
\text{Linear} \quad &: \quad \phi y_{t-1} \\
\text{Nonlinear} \quad &: \quad \frac{\beta}{1 + \exp\left(-\left(\delta_0 + \delta_1 y_{t-1}\right)\right)} \\
\text{Total} \quad &: \quad \phi y_{t-1} + \frac{\beta}{1 + \exp\left(-\left(\delta_0 + \delta_1 y_{t-1}\right)\right)} \ .
\end{aligned}
$$

The nonlinear prediction ranges from 0 to $\beta = 2$ since the parameter β has the effect of stretching the unit-interval domain of the logistic function. The parameter δ_0 causes the nonlinear function to shift to the right, while the parameter δ_1 controls the steepness of the nonlinear function around its point of inflection. □

The specification of the model in (19.12) is commonly referred to as architecture. Other forms of architecture, that is model specifications, consist of including additional lags, additional logistic functions, different types of nonlinear functions and additional variables. For example, the following hidden-layer feed-forward artificial neural network has four lags and three logistic functions,

Table 19.3. *Artificial neural network terminology*

Terminology	Translation
Architecture	Specification
Target	Dependent variable, y_t
Input	Explanatory variable, y_{t-1}
Output	Predictor, $E_{t-1}[y]$
Squasher	Logistic function
Hidden layer	Equation inside the squasher, $\delta_0 + \delta_1 y_{t-1}$
Neurodes	The unknown parameters, $\theta = \{\phi, \beta, \delta_0, \delta_1\}$
Bias	The parameter δ_0 in the logistic function
Connection strengths	The parameter δ_1 in the logistic function
Training, Learning	Estimation
Fitness function	Objective function used in estimation
Tolerance	Convergence criteria
Epochs	Number of iterations used in estimation
Learning rate	Line search parameter used in estimation
Momentum	Back-step parameter used in estimation

with two of the logistic functions feeding into a third logistic function

$$y_t = \sum_{i=1}^{4} \phi_i y_{t-i} + \beta \left[\frac{1}{1 + \exp(-(\delta_{0,0} + \delta_{0,1} w_{1,t} + \delta_{0,2} w_{2,t}))} \right] + v_t,$$

$$(19.13)$$

where

$$w_{j,t} = \left[\frac{1}{1 + \exp(-(\delta_{j,0} + \sum_{i=1}^{4} \delta_{j,i} y_{t-i}))} \right], \qquad j = 1, 2.$$

The econometric equivalents of other commonly adopted engineering terms used in the context of ANNs are given in Table 19.3. The unknown parameters are called nodes (or neurodes). The parameter δ_0 in (19.12) is called the bias as it pushes the point of inflection of the logistic function away from zero. The parameter δ_1 in (19.12) is called the connection strength since it controls the influence of the lag y_{t-1} on the squasher and hence the output (predictor).

19.4.2 Estimation

Maximum Likelihood

For a sample of $t = 1, 2, \cdots, T$ observations, the unknown parameters $\theta = \{\phi, \beta, \delta_0, \delta_1, \sigma^2\}$ of the ANN given in equation (19.12), can be estimated by maximum likelihood methods. Assuming that $v_t \sim iid\ N(0, \sigma^2)$ in (19.12) and the maximum lag length is $p = 1$, the conditional log-likelihood

function is

$$\ln L_T (\theta) = -\frac{1}{2} \ln 2\pi - \frac{1}{2} \ln \sigma^2 - \frac{1}{2\sigma^2(T-1)} \sum_{t=2}^{T} (y_t - \phi y_{t-1} - \beta w_t)^2 ,$$

(19.14)

with

$$w_t = \frac{1}{1 + \exp\left(-(\delta_0 + \delta_1 y_{t-1})\right)}.$$

This function is maximised using one of the iterative algorithms discussed in Chapter 3.

In most applications of ANNs, there is no explicit discussion of estimation issues. Instead the terminology refers to presenting the data to the neural network and the ANN being trained to learn the unknown structure underlying the dynamic processes connecting the target to the inputs. Learning is based on a fitness function as well as additional controls for tolerance, momentum and the number of epochs. Table 19.3 shows that training and leaning are just synonyms for estimation and the fitness function is simply the log-likelihood function. Learning arises because starting with some initial parameter values, $\theta_{(0)}$, does not generally yield good outputs (predictors) of the target (dependent) variable. As the algorithm is an iterative procedure, there is learning at the next step with the updated parameters yielding better predictors of y_t. The number of iterations required to achieve convergence is referred to as the number of epochs and the convergence criteria used is called the tolerance.

Back Propagation

The gradient algorithms discussed in Chapter 3 to estimate the unknown parameters of an econometric model are based on first and second derivatives. Although these algorithms are well-known and widely used in econometrics, they tend not to be widely adopted in ANN applications. Instead the so-called back-propagation algorithm is most commonly used. A representative iteration of this algorithm is given by

$$\theta_{(k)} = \theta_{(k-1)} - \eta \left. \frac{\partial \ln l_t(\theta)}{\partial \theta} \right|_{\theta=\theta_{(k-1)}} + v(\theta_{(k-1)} - \theta_{(k-2)}),$$

(19.15)

where $\theta_{(k)}$ is the parameter vector at iteration k, $\ln l_t(\theta)$ is the log-likelihood function at observation t, η is the learning rate and v is the momentum. The latter two parameters are used to aid convergence and correspond to line searching and back stepping respectively (see Table 19.3). White (1989) and Kuan and

White (1994) show that by choosing the learning parameter as

$$\eta \propto T^{-k} \qquad 0.5 < k \leq 1, \tag{19.16}$$

$\theta_{(k)}$ converges almost surely to θ_0.

The most notable features of the back-propagation algorithm are that it uses first derivatives only and that its iterations correspond to scrolling through the sample evaluating the log-likelihood function at time t only and not averaging over all t as would be the case with standard gradient algorithms. This suggests that the back propagation algorithm is computationally less efficient than gradient algorithms that use all of the information in the data at each iteration as well as additional information in the form of second derivatives.

Neural Methods

For certain ANNs, the number of neurodes (unknown parameters) can be extremely large. In fact, it is not uncommon in some applications for the number of neurodes to exceed the number of observations, T. Apart from the potential problems of imprecision in the parameter estimates in trying to train an ANN with this number of neurodes, a gradient algorithm used to compute the maximum likelihood estimates can be expected to breakdown as a result of multicollinearity causing the information matrix to be singular. Even for the ANN given by equation (19.13), a gradient algorithm can still be expected to have problems in achieving convergence.

One approach that is used in training the ANN, is to choose values of the δ_i neurodes (parameters) from a random number generator. The motivation for doing this is that squashers with many neurodes can begin to mimic the brain which has millions of neurons. One advantage of this approach is that the ANN in equation (19.12), for example, now becomes linear in the remaining parameters

$$y_t = \phi y_{t-1} + \beta w_t^{(0)} + v_t,$$

with

$$w_t^{(0)} = \left[\frac{1}{1 + \exp(-(\delta_0^{(0)} + \delta_1^{(0)} y_{t-1}))} \right],$$

and $\delta_0^{(0)}$ and $\delta_1^{(0)}$ are random draws at the initial step. The parameters ϕ and β are then estimated by regressing y_t on $\{y_{t-1}, w_t^{(0)}\}$. The procedure is repeated for another draw of δ_0 and δ_1, with ϕ and β once again estimated by ordinary least squares. After performing the algorithm N times, the parameter estimates are chosen as the values that maximise the fitness function if it is expressed as a log-likelihood function.

19.4.3 Testing

Under the regularity conditions discussed in Chapter 2, the maximum likelihood estimator $\widehat{\theta}$ has an asymptotic normal distribution

$$\widehat{\theta} \overset{a}{\sim} N\left(\theta_0, \frac{1}{T}I^{-1}(\theta_0)\right).$$

In general, this asymptotic distribution can be used as the basis of undertaking tests on the parameters of the ANN. However, as already observed in the case of the threshold time series class of models, care needs to be exercised when performing hypothesis tests when some of the parameters are not identified under the null hypothesis. This problem arises in testing for a hidden layer based on the hypotheses

$$H_0 : \beta = 0 \qquad H_1 : \beta \neq 0,$$

as δ_0 and δ_1 are not identified under H_0. Restrictions of this form also constitute a natural test of nonlinearity as the ANN in equation (19.12) reduces to a linear model under the null hypothesis.

To circumvent the issue of some parameters not being identified under the null hypothesis, one solution is to condition the model on values of δ_0 and δ_1, which are drawn randomly from a specified distribution following the neural methods approach to estimate ANNs. Given values for these parameters, the first-order conditions for ϕ and β under H_0 are used to construct a LM test similar to the approach adopted to test for linearity in the threshold time series model. This approach is suggested by Lee, Granger and White (1993), who choose a rectangular distribution with range $[-2, 2]$ to draw the random numbers for δ_0 and δ_1. The steps of the LM test are as follows.

Step 1: Estimate the (linear) model under the null by regressing y_t on y_{t-1} and extract the ordinary least squares residuals $\widehat{v}_t$.

Step 2: Choose δ_0, δ_1 randomly from a rectangular distribution in the range $[-2, 2]$, say $\delta_0^{(0)}$, and $\delta_1^{(0)}$.

Step 3: Construct the activation variable(s)

$$w_t^{(0)} = \left[\frac{1}{1 + \exp(-(\delta_0^{(0)} + \delta_1^{(0)} y_{t-1}))}\right].$$

Step 4: Regress $\widehat{v}_t$ on $\{y_{t-1}, w_t^{(0)}\}$ and extract the coefficient of determination R^2, from this regression.

Step 5: Compute $LM = TR^2$, where T is the sample size.

Step 6: Reject the null hypothesis for $LM > \chi_1^2$.

The intuition behind this test is that any important nonlinearity in the data excluded at the first stage (Step 1), will show up in the second-stage regression (Step 4) in the form of a high value for the coefficient of determination R^2.

19.5   Bilinear Time Series Models

Bilinear times series models constitute a class of nonlinear models where the linear ARMA model is augmented by the product of the AR and MA terms (Granger and Anderson, 1978; Subba Rao and Gabr, 1984). These models are able to generate a wide range of time series patterns including bursting behaviour as observed in stock market bubbles.

19.5.1   Specification

Consider the ARMA(1, 1) model

$$y_t = \phi y_{t-1} + v_t + \psi v_{t-1}, \tag{19.17}$$

where v_t is an $iid\,(0, \sigma^2)$ disturbance. From Example 19.1, values of $|\phi| < 1$ result in the model exhibiting uniform variation around its unconditional mean $E[y_t] = 0$ (see also Chapter 13). Now consider the introduction of a nonlinear term $y_{t-1}v_{t-1}$, which is simply the product of the AR(1) and MA(1) components of the model

$$y_t = \phi y_{t-1} + v_t + \psi v_{t-1} + \gamma y_{t-1}v_{t-1}. \tag{19.18}$$

This additional component is known as the bilinear term, which has the effect of generating a range of interesting nonlinear features that cannot be generated from the linear ARMA(1, 1) model in (19.17).

Example 19.8 Properties of the Bilinear Time Series Model
Simulated time series of size $T = 200$ from the bilinear model

$$y_t = 0.4y_{t-1} + v_t + 0.2v_{t-1} + \gamma y_{t-1}v_{t-1}, \qquad v_t \sim iid\,N\,(0, 1)\,,$$

are given in Figure 19.8 for alternative values of the bilinear parameter γ. For values of $\gamma = 0$ and $\gamma = 0.4$, y_t exhibits the typical pattern of a linear ARMA(1,1) model. Increasing γ further causes the model to exhibit bursting ($\gamma = 0.8$) and extreme bursting ($\gamma = 1.2$) behaviour which is characteristic of stock markets self-correcting to shocks.   □

The specification of the bilinear model in (19.18) is easily extended for longer lags, alternative bilinear product terms and higher dimensions. An example of a bivariate bilinear model with two lags is

$$y_{1,t} = \phi_{1,1}y_{1,t-1} + \phi_{1,2}y_{1,t-2} + v_{1,t} + \psi_{1,1}v_{1,t-1} + \gamma_{2,1}y_{1,t-1}v_{2,t-1}$$
$$y_{2,t} = \phi_{2,1}y_{2,t-1} + \phi_{2,2}y_{2,t-2} + v_{2,t} + \psi_{2,1}v_{2,t-1} + \gamma_{2,2}y_{1,t-1}v_{1,t-1}.$$

The terms $y_{1,t-1}v_{2,t-1}$ and $y_{1,t-1}v_{1,t-1}$ capture alternative types of spillovers that may represent a way to model contagion (Dungey and Martin, 2007).

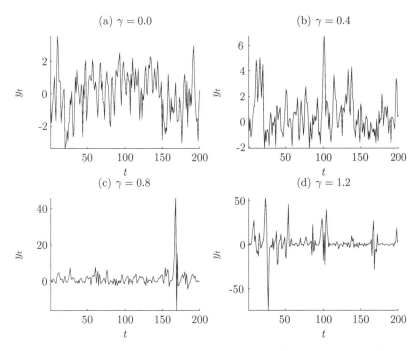

Figure 19.8. Simulated bilinear time series models for different values of γ with $T = 200$, AR parameter 0.4 and MA parameter 0.2.

19.5.2 Estimation

Estimation of a bilinear time series model using maximum likelihood methods requires specifying the conditional log-likelihood function. In the case of the bilinear model in (19.18) where the disturbance term is $N(0, \sigma^2)$, the number of lags is $p = q = 1$ and the unknown parameters are $\theta = \{\phi, \psi, \gamma, \sigma^2\}$, the conditional log-likelihood function for a sample of $t = 1, 2, \cdots, T$ observations is

$$
\ln L_T(\theta) = -\frac{1}{2} \ln 2\pi - \frac{1}{2} \ln \sigma^2
$$
$$
- \frac{1}{2\sigma^2(T-1)} \sum_{t=2}^{T} (y_t - \phi y_{t-1} - \psi v_{t-1} - \gamma y_{t-1} v_{t-1})^2 \ .
$$

This function is maximised with respect to θ using one of the algorithms discussed in Chapter 3. As an alternative iterative procedure, the Gauss-Newton algorithm discussed in Chapter 6 can also be used because the log-likelihood function is expressed in terms of a sum of squared disturbances.

19.5.3 Testing

A special case of the bilinear model is the ARMA(p, q) model. This suggests that the hypothesis testing methods discussed in Chapter 4 can be used to construct general tests of bilinearity. In the case where there is no moving average term, the regression form of the LM given in Chapter 6 is particularly simple to implement. Consider the bilinear model given by

$$y_t = \phi y_{t-1} + v_t + \gamma y_{t-1} v_{t-1}, \qquad v_t \sim iid\, N(0, \sigma^2). \qquad (19.19)$$

A test of bilinearity is based on the following hypotheses

$$H_0 : \gamma = 0, \qquad H_1 : \gamma \neq 0.$$

To implement an LM test of bilinearity, the steps are as follows.

Step 1: Rewrite (19.19) as

$$v_t = y_t - \phi y_{t-1} - \gamma y_{t-1} v_{t-1},$$

and compute the derivatives

$$z_{1,t} = -\frac{\partial v_t}{\partial \phi} = y_{t-1} + \gamma y_{t-1}\frac{\partial v_{t-1}}{\partial \phi}$$

$$z_{2,t} = -\frac{\partial v_t}{\partial \gamma} = y_{t-1} v_{t-1} + \gamma y_{t-1}\frac{\partial v_{t-1}}{\partial \gamma}.$$

Step 2: Evaluate the expressions in Step 1 under the null, $\gamma = 0$

$$v_t = y_t - \phi y_{t-1}$$
$$z_{1,t} = y_{t-1} \qquad\qquad\qquad (19.20)$$
$$z_{2,t} = y_{t-1} v_{t-1}.$$

Step 3: Estimate the model under the null hypothesis by regressing y_t on y_{t-1} and extract the ordinary least squares residuals $\widehat{v}_t$.

Step 4: Regress $\widehat{v}_t$ on $\{y_{t-1}, y_{t-1}\widehat{v}_{t-1}\}$ and compute R^2.

Step 5: Form the LM statistic $LM = TR^2$, where T is the sample size, and compare with a χ_1^2 distribution. The null hypothesis is rejected for large values of the test statistic because this result implies that the bilinear component, $y_{t-1} v_{t-1}$, has been excluded from the first-stage regression.

19.6 Markov Switching Model

The Markov switching model is widely used to model nonlinearities in economic and financial processes. Examples include business cycles (Hamilton, 1989), the term structure of interest rates (Hamilton, 1988), exchange rates (Engel and Hamilton, 1990), stock returns (Hamilton and Susmel, 1994) and business cycle factor models (Kim, 1994). This model has much in common with the threshold time series models discussed previously, except in those models switching is deterministic whereas in the Markov switching model it is stochastic. This model is also similar to the latent factor models analysed in Chapter 15 with the minor difference that the factor is discrete in the present context.

Let w_t, represent a stochastic weighting variable that switches between regimes according to

$$w_t = \begin{cases} 1 & : \quad \text{Regime 1} \\ 0 & : \quad \text{Regime 2}. \end{cases} \tag{19.21}$$

Unlike the threshold time series models where the weighting function is identified by expressing it in terms of lagged observed variables, w_t is not observable. Moreover, w_t is binary for the Markov switching model compared to the weighting function in the threshold models where in general it takes on intermediate values in the unit circle. A Markov switching model for y_t is specified as

$$
\begin{aligned}
y_t &= \alpha + \beta w_t + u_t \\
\sigma_t^2 &= \gamma + \delta w_t \\
u_t &\sim N(0, \sigma_t^2) \\
p &= P\left[w_t = 1 \mid w_{t-1} = 1, y_{t-1}, y_{t-2}, \cdots \right] \\
q &= P\left[w_t = 0 \mid w_{t-1} = 0, y_{t-1}, y_{t-2}, \cdots \right],
\end{aligned}
\tag{19.22}
$$

where $\theta = \{\alpha, \beta, \gamma, \delta, p, q\}$ are unknown parameters and u_t is a heteroskedastic disturbance. In regime 1 the mean is $E[y_t] = \alpha + \beta$ with variance $\gamma + \delta$, whereas in regime 2 the mean is $E[y_t] = \alpha$ with variance γ. The weighting variable w_t is specified in terms of the parameters p and q which represent the conditional probabilities of staying in each regime.

An important extension of the model is to allow for p lags by writing the first equation in (19.22) as

$$y_t = \alpha + \beta w_t + \sum_{i=1}^{p} \phi_i(y_{t-i} - \alpha - \beta w_{t-i}) + u_t.$$

Further extensions consist of specifying y_t as a vector of variables, and allowing for time-varying conditional probabilities p and q by expressing these probabilities as functions of explanatory variables. This extension is investigated in Exercise 6.

Estimation of the model by maximum likelihood requires the joint conditional distribution $f(y_t, w_t | y_{t-1}, y_{t-2}, \cdots ; \theta)$, which is complicated by the fact that w_t is not observed. To circumvent this problem, it is necessary to integrate, or more correctly sum, out w_t, thereby expressing the likelihood just in terms of the observable variable y_t. A similar strategy is adopted for the stochastic frontier model in Chapter 6. As w_t is binary this strategy is relatively straightforward as the summation involves just two terms. To demonstrate the mechanics of the approach, conditioning on $y_{t-1}, y_{t-2}, \cdots$ is initially suppressed to simplify the notation. From the rules of probability, the marginal distribution of y_t is given by

$$f(y_t) = P[w_t = 1, y_t] + P[w_t = 0, y_t]$$
$$= P[w_t = 1] f(y_t | w_t = 1) + P[w_t = 0] f(y_t | w_t = 0),$$

which shows that the marginal is obtained by summing over the joint distribution which, in turn, is expressed in terms of the product of the marginal and conditional distributions. This expression is re-expressed by making conditioning on past values of y_t explicit

$$f(y_t | y_{t-1}, y_{t-2}, \cdots) = w_{1,t|t-1} f_{1,t|t-1} + w_{0,t|t-1} f_{0,t|t-1}, \quad (19.23)$$

where

$$w_{i,t|t-1} = P[w_t = i | y_{t-1}, y_{t-2}, \cdots],$$
$$f_{i,t|t-1} = f(y_t | w_t = i, y_{t-1}, y_{t-2}, \cdots), \quad i = 0, 1.$$

Equation (19.23) represents the likelihood function at time t which excludes w_t by construction with the weights at time t now expressed in terms of conditional probabilities which are implicit functions of all previous lags of y_t. This likelihood function has the form of a mixture distribution with weights $w_{i,t|t-1}$ that vary over the sample.

To evaluate the likelihood function in (19.23), from equation (19.22)

$$
\begin{aligned}
f_{1,t|t-1} &= \frac{1}{\sqrt{2\pi(\gamma + \delta)}} \exp\left[-\frac{(y_t - \alpha - \beta)^2}{2(\gamma + \delta)} \right] \\
f_{0,t|t-1} &= \frac{1}{\sqrt{2\pi\gamma}} \exp\left[-\frac{(y_t - \alpha)^2}{2\gamma} \right].
\end{aligned}
\qquad (19.24)
$$

To derive expressions for $w_{1,t|t-1}$ and $w_{0,t|t-1}$ from equation (19.23) the updated conditional probabilities based on observing the dependent variable at time t, are

$$
\begin{aligned}
w_{1,t|t} &= P[w_t = 1 | y_t, y_{t-1}, \cdots] = \frac{w_{1,t|t-1} f_{1,t|t-1}}{w_{1,t|t-1} f_{1,t|t-1} + w_{0,t|t-1} f_{0,t|t-1}} \\
w_{0,t|t} &= P[w_t = 1 | y_t, y_{t-1}, \cdots] = \frac{w_{0,t|t-1} f_{0,t|t-1}}{w_{1,t|t-1} f_{1,t|t-1} + w_{0,t|t-1} f_{0,t|t-1}}.
\end{aligned}
$$
$$(19.25)$$

Using the definition of p and q in equation (19.22), it follows that

$$
\begin{bmatrix} w_{1,t+1|t} \\ w_{0,t+1|t} \end{bmatrix} = \begin{bmatrix} p & 1-q \\ 1-p & q \end{bmatrix} \begin{bmatrix} w_{1,t|t} \\ w_{0,t|t} \end{bmatrix}.
\qquad (19.26)
$$

For a sample of $t = 1, 2, \cdots, T$ observations, combining equations (19.23) and (19.24) the log-likelihood function is

$$\ln L_T(\theta) = \frac{1}{T} \sum_{t=1}^{T} \ln f(y_t \mid y_{t-1}, y_{t-2}, \cdots; \theta)$$

$$= \frac{1}{T} \sum_{t=1}^{T} \ln(w_{1,t|t-1} f_{1,t|t-1} + w_{0,t|t-1} f_{0,t|t-1}), \qquad (19.27)$$

where $w_{i,t|t-1}$ and $f_{i,t|t-1}$ are defined in equations (19.26) and (19.24), respectively. This function is maximised with respect to θ using the iterative algorithms presented in Chapter 3. At $t = 1$, it is necessary to be able to evaluate $w_{1,1|0}$ and $w_{0,1|0}$, which are set equal to their respective stationary probabilities

$$w_{1,1|0} = \frac{1-q}{1-p+1-q}, \qquad w_{0,1|0} = \frac{1-p}{1-p+1-q}.$$

Example 19.9 Markov Switching Model of the Business Cycle

A Markov switching model of the business cycle is specified where

$$w_t = \begin{cases} 1 & : \text{ Expansionary phase of the business cycle} \\ 0 & : \text{ Contractionary phase of the business cycle.} \end{cases}$$

Using the quarterly percentage growth rate of United States GNP from June 1951 to December 1984, given in Figure 19.9, the log-likelihood function in (19.27) is maximised with respect to θ, with the parameter estimates reported in Table 19.4. To ensure that the conditional probabilities p and q are in the unit interval these parameters are restricted using the logistic transformation

$$p = \frac{1}{1 + \exp(-\kappa)}, \qquad q = \frac{1}{1 + \exp(-\lambda)},$$

with (19.27) now maximised with respect to $\theta = \{\alpha, \beta, \gamma, \delta, \kappa, \lambda\}$. The unrestricted parameter estimates are then obtained by maximising (19.27) with respect to $\theta = \{\alpha, \beta, \gamma, \delta, p, q\}$ using one more iteration.

The average growth rate in the expansionary phase of the business cycle is $\widehat{\alpha} + \widehat{\beta} = -0.224 + 1.401 = 1.177\%$ per quarter, compared to the average growth rate in the contractionary phase of $\widehat{\alpha} = -0.224\%$ per quarter. The expansionary phase exhibits smaller variance $\widehat{\gamma} + \widehat{\delta} = 0.942 - 0.323 = 0.619$, compared to $\widehat{\gamma} = 0.942$ in the contractionary period. Expansions tend to last longer than contractions with $\widehat{p} = 0.892$ greater than $\widehat{q} = 0.753$. An estimate of the average duration of each phase is, respectively,

Table 19.4. *Maximum likelihood parameter estimates of the Markov switching model of the United States business cycle. The quasi-maximum likelihood standard errors are adjusted for heteroskedasticity*

Parameter	Estimate	se	p-value
α	−0.224	0.417	0.591
β	1.401	0.283	0.000
γ	0.942	0.223	0.000
δ	−0.323	0.275	0.241
p	0.892	0.055	0.000
q	0.753	0.130	0.000

(Hamilton, 1989, p. 374)

$$\text{DURATION(Expansion)} = \frac{1}{1 - \widehat{p}} = \frac{1}{1 - 0.892} = 9.270 \text{ quarters}$$

$$\text{DURATION(Contraction)} = \frac{1}{1 - \widehat{q}} = \frac{1}{1 - 0.753} = 4.050 \text{ quarters.}$$

$\square$

19.7 Nonparametric Autoregression

The nonlinear time series models discussed in this chapter are based on parametric specifications which are primarily designed to capture specific types of

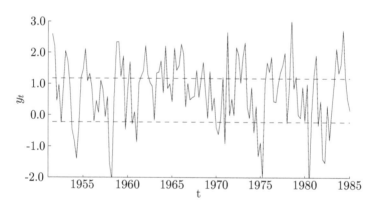

Figure 19.9. Quarterly percentage growth rate of United States GNP, June 1951 to December 1984. Also given are maximum likelihood estimates of expansionary and contractionary average growth rates. Source: Hamilton (1989).

nonlinearities. A nonparametric approach allows for general nonlinear structures by specifying the model

$$y_t = m\left(y_{t-k}\right) + v_t, \tag{19.28}$$

where $m(y_{t-k})$ is the conditional mean with $k > 0$ and v_t is an iid disturbance
term.

From Chapter 11 the Nadaraya-Watson kernel regression estimator of the
conditional mean is given by

$$\widehat{m}\left(y_{t-k}\right) = \frac{1}{T} \sum_{t=1}^{T} y_t w_t, \tag{19.29}$$

where w_t is the weight at time t, which, in the case of a Gaussian kernel with
bandwidth h, is

$$w_t = \frac{\dfrac{1}{\sqrt{2\pi h^2}} \exp\left[-\left(\dfrac{y - y_{t-k}}{h}\right)^2\right]}{\displaystyle\sum_{t=1}^{T} \dfrac{1}{\sqrt{2\pi h^2}} \exp\left[-\left(\dfrac{y - y_{t-k}}{h}\right)^2\right]}, \qquad k \geq 1. \tag{19.30}$$

By computing equation (19.29) for each k, a nonparametric autocorrelation
function of a nonlinear time series model is constructed. Parametric information
can also be included by specifying a parametric form for the distribution of
v_t in (19.28), or for the conditional mean, $m(y_{t-k})$. Chapter 11 provides an
example by Robinson (1988) of a semiparametric estimator of a nonlinear time
series model. This approach is extended by Chen and Fan (1999) who develop
a general class of tests in nonparametric models. An alternative approach based
on the time-varying parameter model proposed by Granger (2008) is developed
in Exercise 12.

Example 19.10 Estimating a Nonlinear AR(1) Model
The nonlinear autoregressive model

$$y_t = \theta\,|y_{t-1}| + \sqrt{1 - \theta^2}z_t, \qquad z_t \sim iid\ N(0, 1),$$

is simulated for $T = 5000$ observations with $\theta = 0.8$. Figure 19.10 shows
the nonparametric estimate of the conditional mean based on a Gaussian kernel using a rule-of-thumb bandwidth. The true conditional mean given by
$m(y_{t-1}) = \theta\,|y_{t-1}|$ is also shown together with the conditional mean of a linear AR(1) model, θy_{t-1}. The nonparametric estimator tracks the linear conditional mean for $y_{t-1} > 0$, but also captures the nonlinearity of the model
for $y_{t-1} < 0$. $\qquad\qquad\square$

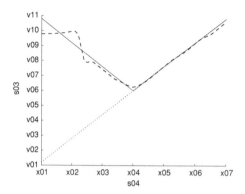

Figure 19.10. Nonparametric estimate of a nonlinear AR(1) model. The nonparametric estimate (dashed line) is compared to a linear AR(1) model (dotted line) and the true conditional mean (solid line).

19.8 Nonlinear Impulse Responses

The impulse response functions discussed in Chapter 13 show how a shock in a variable, y_t, is propagated through all of the variables in the model. Because the impulse response functions are discussed in the context of linear time series models, the impact of a shock on y_t has two key properties.

(i) Symmetry: The effects on y_t of positive and negative shocks of the same magnitude differ only in sign.
(ii) Independence: The effects of shocks on y_t are independent of the history of the process.

To explore the properties of impulse responses of linear time series models, consider a linear univariate AR(1) model

$$y_t = \phi_1 y_{t-1} + v_t, \tag{19.31}$$

where v_t is an *iid* disturbance term. Writing the model out at time $t+1$ gives

$$y_{t+1} = \phi_1 (\phi_1 y_{t-1} + v_t) + v_{t+1} = \phi_1^2 y_{t-1} + \phi_1 v_t + v_{t+1}. \tag{19.32}$$

Choosing a shock at time t of size $v_t = \delta$, setting $v_{t+1} = 0$ and conditioning on information at time $t-1$, yields the conditional expectations with and without the shock as

$$\begin{aligned} E_{t-1}\left[y_{t+1} \mid v_{t+1} = 0, v_t = \delta\right] &= \phi_1^2 y_{t-1} + \phi_1 \times \delta + 0 \\ E_{t-1}\left[y_{t+1} \mid v_{t+1} = 0, v_t = 0\right] &= \phi_1^2 y_{t-1} + \phi_1 \times 0 + 0, \end{aligned} \tag{19.33}$$

respectively. The difference of the two conditional expectations gives the impulse response at $t + 1$, namely,

$$IRF_1 = E_{t-1}[y_{t+1}|v_{t+1} = 0, v_t = \delta] - E_{t-1}[y_{t+1}|v_{t+1} = 0, v_t = 0]$$
$$= \phi_1 \delta. \tag{19.34}$$

Inspection of (19.34) shows that the impulse response function is both symmetric, because the impulse response is a linear function of the shock, δ, and independent of the history of y_t.

The properties of symmetry and independence that characterise impulse response functions of linear time series models do not, in general, arise in nonlinear time series models. For example, Figure 19.10 of Example 19.10 illustrates a relationship between y_t and y_{t-1} characterised by the absolute function $|y_{t-1}|$. A positive shock results in an increase in y_t the next period if $y_{t-1} > 0$ whereas the effect of the same shock yields a decrease in y_t if $y_{t-1} < 0$. By contrast, for the linear model in Figure 19.10 a positive shock results in an increase in y_t regardless of the value of y_{t-1}.

To demonstrate the features of impulse responses of nonlinear time series models more formally, consider the nonlinear model

$$y_t = \phi_1 y_{t-1} + \phi_2 y_{t-1}^2 + v_t, \tag{19.35}$$

which reduces to the linear time series model in (19.31) for $\phi_2 = 0$. Proceeding as before, express the model at time $t + 1$ and substitute for y_t to give

$$y_{t+1} = \phi_1 \left(\phi_1 y_{t-1} + \phi_2 y_{t-1}^2 + v_t \right) + \phi_2 \left(\phi_1 y_{t-1} + \phi_2 y_{t-1}^2 + v_t \right)^2 + v_{t+1}.$$

Choosing a shock of size $v_t = \delta$, setting $v_{t+1} = 0$ and conditioning on information at time $t - 1$ yields the conditional expectations with and without the shock, respectively, as

$$E_{t-1}[y_{t+1}|v_{t+1} = 0, v_t = \delta] = \phi_1 \left(\phi_1 y_{t-1} + \phi_2 y_{t-1}^2 + \delta \right)$$
$$+ \phi_2 \left(\phi_1 y_{t-1} + \phi_2 y_{t-1}^2 + \delta \right)^2 + 0$$

$$E_{t-1}[y_{t+1}|v_{t+1} = 0, v_t = 0] = \phi_1 \left(\phi_1 y_{t-1} + \phi_2 y_{t-1}^2 + 0 \right)$$
$$+ \phi_2 \left(\phi_1 y_{t-1} + \phi_2 y_{t-1}^2 + 0 \right)^2 + 0.$$

The impulse response function is therefore

$$\begin{aligned} IRF_1 &= E_{t-1}[y_{t+1}|v_{t+1} = 0, v_t = \delta] - E_{t-1}[y_{t+1}|v_{t+1} = 0, v_t = 0] \\ &= \phi_1 \delta + \phi_2 \left(\left(\phi_1 y_{t-1} + \phi_2 y_{t-1}^2 + \delta \right)^2 - \left(\phi_1 y_{t-1} + \phi_2 y_{t-1}^2 + 0 \right)^2 \right) \\ &= \underbrace{\phi_1 \delta}_{\text{linear}} + \underbrace{\delta^2 \phi_2 + 2\delta \phi_1 \phi_2 y_{t-1} + 2\delta \phi_2^2 y_{t-1}^2}_{\text{nonlinear}}. \end{aligned}$$

$$\tag{19.36}$$

This expression encapsulates all of the key issues in generating impulse responses of nonlinear time series models. The first term in equation (19.36) is identical to the impulse response for the linear model in equation (19.34). The second term in equation (19.36) reflects the nonlinear features of the model. It is clear from inspection of this term that the impulse response is now no longer symmetrical in the size or the sign of the shock δ. Positive and negative shocks of the same magnitude yield impulses that are not opposite in sign as they are in the case of the linear model. The impulse response in equation (19.36) is also dependent on the history of the process, as it contains y_{t-1}. A shock occurring when $y_{t-1} < 0$, now does not necessarily have the same effect on y_t as a shock occurring when $y_{t-1} > 0$. An example of this phenomenon is in nonlinear models of the business cycle where a shock during a recession results in a different response in output to the same shock in an expansion period.

To compute impulse responses over $n + 1$ horizons for nonlinear time series models, it is necessary to compute the conditional expectations in (19.36) over all possible histories of y_t. One way to proceed is to use simulation methods where the conditional expectations are calculated as sample averages across a range of histories obtained from the data. The steps involved are as follows.

Step 1: Estimate the model and obtain the residuals $\widehat{v}_t$, $t = 1, 2 \cdots , T$.

Step 2: Simulate the estimated model for $n + 1$ periods where the $n + 1$ residuals are randomly drawn from $\{\widehat{v}_1, \widehat{v}_2, \cdots , \widehat{v}_T\}$. Repeat the simulations R times and take the sample average of the R impulse responses for each of the $n + 1$ horizons to compute the base conditional expectation.

Step 3: Repeat Step 2 with the same randomly drawn residuals except replace the initial condition by $\widehat{v}_1 + \delta$ where $\widehat{v}_1$ is the first residual and δ is the shock. Again repeat the simulations R times and take the sample average of the R impulse responses for each of the $n + 1$ horizons to compute the conditional expectation corresponding to the shock δ.

Step 4: Repeat Steps 2 and 3 for a new set of random draws and where the initial condition in Step 3 is now $\widehat{v}_2 + \delta$, where $\widehat{v}_2$ is the second residual.

Step 5: Repeating Step 4 results in T impulse responses of length $n + 1$ for the base and the shock conditional expectations. Averaging across these T impulses for each horizon and taking the difference in the two sample averages, yields the nonlinear impulse response functions.

The process of random sampling from $\{\widehat{v}_1, \widehat{v}_2, \cdots , \widehat{v}_T\}$ to construct the impulse responses is known as bootstrapping. There are two averaging processes going on here. The first is averaging across sample paths for alternative forecast horizons. The second is averaging across the initial conditions. Koop, Pesaran and Potter (1996) call impulses computed this way generalised impulse response functions (GIRF). Having obtained the conditional mean of the impulse response function from the bootstraps, standard errors can also be computed from this information as well.

Table 19.5. *Impulse responses for shocks of size δ*
computed for a TAR model and for an AR(1) model

Horizon	TAR(1)		AR(1)	
	$\delta = 1$	$\delta = -1$	$\delta = 1$	$\delta = -1$
0	1.001	−0.999	1.000	−1.000
1	0.593	−0.406	0.750	−0.750
2	0.357	−0.214	0.563	−0.563
3	0.220	−0.125	0.422	−0.422
4	0.137	−0.076	0.316	−0.316
5	0.086	−0.047	0.237	−0.237
6	0.054	−0.030	0.178	−0.178
7	0.034	−0.019	0.133	−0.133
8	0.022	−0.012	0.100	−0.100
9	0.014	−0.007	0.075	−0.075
10	0.009	−0.005	0.056	−0.056

Example 19.11 Impulse Responses of a Threshold Autoregression

Consider the threshold autoregressive model

$$y_t = \phi_1 y_{t-1} + \phi_2 y_{t-1} w_t + v_t, \qquad v_t \sim iid\, N(0, 1)$$
$$w_t = \begin{cases} 1 & y_{t-1} \geq 0 \\ 0 & y_{t-1} < 0. \end{cases}$$

The model is simulated for $T = 1000$ observations for parameter values $\phi_1 = 0.25$ and $\phi_2 = 0.50$, which for simplicity are directly used to compute the impulse responses without estimating the model. The number of bootstrapped samples is set at T. The simulated impulse responses are given in Table 19.5 for horizons of $n = 10$ and for shocks of size $\delta = \{1, -1\}$. For comparison the analytical impulse response of an AR(1) model are also given by setting $\phi_2 = 0$. Reversing the shock from $\delta = 1$ to $\delta = -1$ results in asymmetrical impulse responses for the TAR model, with the impulse responses decaying at a relatively faster rate for the negative shock. In contrast, the linear AR model impulse responses exhibit symmetry with the rate of decay being the same for $\delta = 1$ and $\delta = -1$. □

The construction of the impulse responses presented in the previous example is obtained by averaging across all of the shocks in the data. An alternative refinement is to average across histories where the initial condition is a particular sign. Finally, whilst the approach is presented for single equation nonlinear time series models, it generalises to multivariate nonlinear time series models. For example, Koop, Pesaran and Potter (1996) provides an example based on a bivariate TAR model of output and unemployment.

19.9 Applications

19.9.1 A Multiple Equilibrium Model of Unemployment

In this application, an LSTAR model of the United States monthly unemployment rate given in Figure 19.5, is specified and estimated. Following Skalin and Teräsvirta (2002), a two-regime error correction model of the change in the unemployment rate Δy_t, is specified as

$$\Delta y_t = \mu_1 + \alpha_1 y_{t-1} + (\mu_2 + \alpha_2 y_{t-1}) w_t + v_t, \qquad \mu_i > 0, \quad (19.37)$$

where v_t is an *iid* disturbance term. The weighting function w_t is

$$w_t = \frac{1}{1 + \exp[-\gamma(\Delta_{12} y_{t-1} - c)/s)]}, \qquad \gamma > 0,$$

where $\Delta_{12} y_{t-1} = y_{t-1} - y_{t-13}$ is the lagged annual change in the unemployment rate, c is the threshold and s is a scaling factor equal to the sample standard deviation of $\Delta_{12} y_{t-1}$ (Teräsvirta, 1994). Rewriting equation (19.37) as

$$\Delta y_t = \alpha_1 \left(\frac{\mu_1}{\alpha_1} + y_{t-1} \right) + \alpha_2 \left(\frac{\mu_2}{\alpha_2} + y_{t-1} \right) w_t + v_t, \qquad (19.38)$$

expresses the model in an error correction form, as discussed in Chapter 18, where the parameters α_1 and α_2 represent the error correction parameters. As a result of the nonlinear specification, two unemployment rates satisfy the equilibrium condition $\Delta y_t = 0$, namely,

$$y_{\text{low}} = -\frac{\mu_1}{\alpha_1}, \qquad y_{\text{high}} = -\frac{\mu_1 + \mu_2}{\alpha_1 + \alpha_2}, \qquad (19.39)$$

which correspond, respectively, to the low state where $w_t = 0$ and to the high state where $w_t = 1$. The error correction parameters associated with these two equilibrium states are respectively, α_1 and $\alpha_1 + \alpha_2$, which need to be negative to ensure that the low and high multiple equilibria exist and satisfy the stability restriction $-1 < \alpha_1 + \alpha_2 < 0$.

The results from estimating the LSTAR model in (19.37) by maximum likelihood are given in Table 19.6 for a sample of size $T = 734$. The value of the log-likelihood function at the maximum likelihood estimates is $\ln L_T(\widehat{\theta}) = 0.160$. The parameter estimates of the error-correction parameters are negative, which is consistent with the presence of multiple equilibria. The second error correction parameter estimate, $\widehat{\alpha}_2$, is statistically insignificant suggesting that the speed of adjustment to both low and high equilibria are the same and equal to $\widehat{\alpha}_1$. The point estimates also satisfy the stability restriction as $-1 < \widehat{\alpha}_1 + \widehat{\alpha}_2 < 0$. Finally, the estimates of the low and high equilibrium unemployment rates

Table 19.6. *Maximum likelihood parameter estimates of the LSTAR multiple equilibrium model of the United States monthly unemployment rate in (19.38), with standard errors based on the Hessian matrix in parentheses*

Parameter	Estimate	s.e.
μ_1	0.077	0.040
α_1	−0.021	0.007
μ_2	0.282	0.083
α_2	−0.017	0.012
γ	6.886	3.272
c	0.420	0.115

are, respectively,

$$\widehat{y}_{\text{low}} = -\frac{\widehat{\mu}_1}{\widehat{\alpha}_1} = -\frac{0.077}{-0.021} = 3.691$$

$$\widehat{y}_{\text{high}} = -\frac{\widehat{\mu}_1 + \widehat{\mu}_2}{\widehat{\alpha}_1 + \widehat{\alpha}_2} = -\frac{0.077 + 0.282}{-0.021 - 0.017} = 9.431 \ .$$

Inspection of Figure 19.5 shows that these estimates represent sensible estimates for the means of the different states of the United States unemployment rate.

19.9.2 Bivariate Threshold Models of G7 Countries

Anderson, Anthansopoulos and Vahid (2007) investigate the relationship between the real output growth rate and the interest rate spread of G7 countries using a range of nonlinear time series models. The variables are

$$y_{1,t} = 100 \times (\ln RGDP_t - \ln RGDP_{t-1}), \qquad y_{2,t} = R_{10yr,t} - R_{3mth,t} \ ,$$

where $RGDP_t$ is real GDP, and $R_{10yr,t}$ and $R_{3mth,t}$ are, respectively, the 10-year and 3-month interest rates, both expressed in percentages. The sample periods vary for each country and are as follows:

Canada	:	June 1961 to December 1999
France	:	March 1970 to September 1998
Germany	:	June 1960 to December 1999
Italy	:	June 1971 to December 1999
Japan	:	March 1970 to June 1999
United Kingdom	:	June 1960 to December 1999
United States	:	June 1960 to December 1999.

Table 19.7. *Log-likelihood function values and residual covariance matrices of G7 threshold models given in equations (19.40) to (19.42)*

Country	$(T-2)\ln L$	$\widehat{V}$	
Canada	-322.274	$\begin{bmatrix} 0.587 & -0.003 \\ -0.003 & 0.417 \end{bmatrix}$	
France	-233.199	$\begin{bmatrix} 0.318 & -0.042 \\ -0.042 & 0.725 \end{bmatrix}$	
Germany	-440.403	$\begin{bmatrix} 1.326 & -0.035 \\ -0.035 & 0.760 \end{bmatrix}$	
Italy	-295.208	$\begin{bmatrix} 0.489 & 0.070 \\ 0.070 & 1.439 \end{bmatrix}$	
Japan	-275.014	$\begin{bmatrix} 0.801 & 0.044 \\ 0.044 & 0.535 \end{bmatrix}$	
United Kingdom	-373.531	$\begin{bmatrix} 0.942 & -0.038 \\ -0.038 & 0.452 \end{bmatrix}$	
United States	-298.734	$\begin{bmatrix} 0.613 & -0.054 \\ -0.054 & 0.269 \end{bmatrix}$	

For each G7 country a generic bivariate threshold time series model is specified

$$
\begin{aligned}
y_{1,t} &= \phi_{1,0} + \sum_{i=1}^{2} \phi_{i,1,1} y_{1,t-i} + \sum_{i=1}^{2} \phi_{i,1,2} y_{2,t-1} \\
&\quad + \left(\beta_{1,0} + \sum_{i=1}^{2} \beta_{i,1,1} y_{1,t-i} + \sum_{i=1}^{2} \beta_{i,1,2} y_{2,t-i} \right) w_{1,t} + v_{1,t} \\
y_{2,t} &= \phi_{2,0} + \sum_{i=1}^{2} \phi_{i,2,1} y_{1,t-i} + \sum_{i=1}^{2} \phi_{i,2,2} y_{2,t-2} \\
&\quad + \left(\beta_{2,0} + \sum_{i=1}^{2} \beta_{i,2,1} y_{1,t-i} + \sum_{i=1}^{2} \beta_{i,2,2} y_{2,t-i} \right) w_{2,t} + v_{2,t},
\end{aligned}
$$

$$(19.40)$$

where the disturbance vector $v_t = \left[v_{1,t}, v_{2,t} \right]'$ is distributed as $v_t \sim iid N(0, V)$ with

$$
V = \begin{bmatrix} \sigma_{1,1} & \sigma_{1,2} \\ \sigma_{2,1} & \sigma_{2,2} \end{bmatrix},
$$

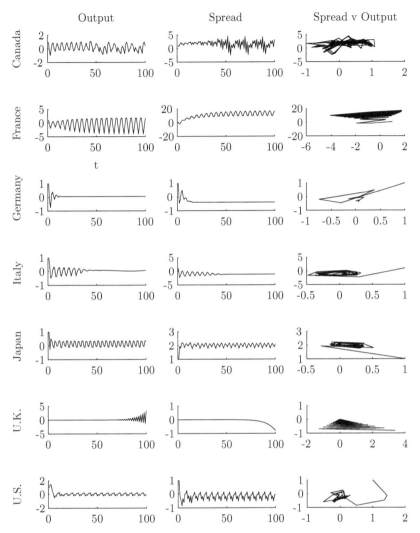

Figure 19.11. Simulated TAR models of G7 countries based on the maximum likelihood estimates in Table 19.7.

and the weighting functions are given by the LSTAR specifications

$$w_{1,t} = \frac{1}{1 + \exp(-\gamma_1(y_{1,t-2} - c_1))} \tag{19.41}$$

$$w_{2,t} = \frac{1}{1 + \exp(-\gamma_2(y_{1,t-1} - c_2))} \, . \tag{19.42}$$

The specifications of the weighting functions show that adjustments between regimes in the rate of growth in output and the interest rate spread are governed by lagged output growth. Other specifications of the model can be entertained including longer lag structures in each regime and alternative threshold specifications. For example, Anderson, Anthansopoulos and Vahid (2007) choose longer lag structures and threshold specifications that vary for each country. They also delete parameter estimates that are statistically insignificant.

The log-likelihood function at observation t is

$$
\ln l_T(\theta) = -\frac{N}{2} \ln (2\pi) - \frac{1}{2} \ln |V| - \frac{1}{2} v_t' V^{-1} v_t, \tag{19.43}
$$

with $N = 2$. The full log-likelihood function for a sample of size T is maximised using the BFGS algorithm discussed in Chapter 3. When estimating the model, the adjustment parameters in equations (19.41) and (19.42) are fixed at $\gamma_1 = \gamma_2 = 100$, which has the effect of forcing the LSTAR model to become a SETAR model. The log-likelihood values and residual variance-covariance matrices are reported in Table 19.7.

To explore the dynamical properties of the estimated models the results of simulating the bivariate threshold models for each G7 country with parameter values replaced by their maximum likelihood estimates are given in Figure 19.11. The dynamics of the simulated models vary across the countries. Canada tends to exhibit chaotic behaviour with the dynamics of output and the spread characterised by a strange attractor. Germany and Italy converge to a fixed point. France, Japan and the United States converge to stable limit cycles, whereas the United Kingdom exhibits an unstable cycle.

19.10   Exercises

(1) Features of Nonlinear Models

Program files	nlm_features.*
Data files	usunemp.*

Consider the AR(2) process

$$
y_t = 0.9 + 0.7 y_{t-1} - 0.6 y_{t-2} .
$$

(a) Simulate the model for $T = 40$ observations where the initial value is $y_0 = 0.5$. Show that the model converges to the equilibrium point $y = 1.0$. Derive this result analytically.

(b) Show that the following process converges to a nine-period cycle.

$$
y_t = \begin{cases} 0.8023 + 1.0676 y_{t-1} - 0.2099 y_{t-2} + 0.1712 y_{t-3} & : y_{t-2} \le 3.05 \\ -0.4528 y_{t-4} + 0.2237 y_{t-5} - 0.0331 y_{t-6} & \\ 2.2964 + 1.4246 y_{t-1} - 1.0795 y_{t-2} - 0.0900 y_{t-3} & : y_{t-2} > 3.05 . \end{cases}
$$

(c) Consider the nonlinear business cycle model of Kaldor

$$y_{t+1} - y_t = 20(i_t - s_t)$$
$$k_{t+1} - k_t = i_t - 0.05k_t$$
$$i_t = 20(2^{-(0.01y_t + 0.00001)^{-2}}) + 0.05y_t + 5(280k_t^{-1})^{4.5}$$
$$s_t = 0.21y_t,$$

in which y_t is output, k_t is capital, i_t is investment and s_t is savings. Simulate the model for $T = 15000$ observations and discard the first 5000 observations. Show that the dynamics represent a strange attractor.

(d) Consider the nonlinear error correction model of the logarithm of real money, m_t, which is a simplification of the model estimated in Ericsson, Hendry and Prestwich (1998, p. 296)

$$\Delta m_t = 0.45\Delta m_{t-1} - 0.10\Delta^2 m_{t-2} - 2.54(m_{t-1} - 0.1)m_{t-1}^2 + v_t$$
$$v_t \sim iid\ N(0, 0.005^2),$$

where $\Delta m_t = m_t - m_{t-1}$ and $\Delta^2 m_{t-2} = m_{t-2} - 2m_{t-3} + m_{t-4}$. Simulate the model for $T = 50000$ observations and show that the majority of the mass is around the stable equilibrium value of 0.1 with smaller mass at the inflection point of 0.0.

(e) Plot the United States monthly unemployment rate from January 1948 to March 2010. Describe its statistical properties including potential differences in the duration of expansion and contraction periods.

(2) Sampling Properties of the LST Linearity Test

Program files   nlm_tarsim.*

This exercise is based on the Monte Carlo experiments of Luukkonen, Saikkonen and Teräsvirta (1988) where the data generating process is

$$y_t = -0.5y_{t-1} + \beta y_{t-1}w_t + v_t$$
$$w_t = (1 + \exp(-\gamma(y_{t-1} - 0)))^{-1}$$
$$v_t \sim iid\ N(0, 25),$$

where the parameters are $\beta = \{0.0, 0.5, 1.0\}$ and $\gamma = \{0.5, 1.0, 5.0\}$. The number of replications is set at 10000.

(a) For $T = 100$, compute the size of the LST linearity test in (19.10) assuming a nominal size of 5%, and the size-adjusted power function. Compare the results with Table 19.2.

(b) Repeat part (a) for $T = 200$ and discuss the consistency property of the test.

(c) Show that improvements in the power of the test are obtained by imposing the restrictions $\pi_{3,i} = 0, \forall i$ in the auxiliary equation in (19.10).
Interpret this result.

(d) Replace the LSTAR model with a STAR model in the data generating
process and redo parts (a) and (b). Compare the two power functions.

(e) Let the weighting function w_t be given by the ESTAR model and redo
parts (a) and (b). Show that for this model

$$\frac{\partial w_t}{\partial z_t}\bigg|_{z_t=0} = 0, \qquad \frac{\partial^2 w_t}{\partial z_t^2}\bigg|_{z_t=0} = 2, \qquad \frac{\partial^3 w_t}{\partial z_t^3}\bigg|_{z_t=0} = 0,$$

and that improvements in the power of the test are obtained by imposing
the restrictions $\pi_{3,i} = 0, \forall i$, in the auxiliary equation (19.10).

(f) Now choose as the data generating process

$$y_t = 1 - 0.5y_{t-1} + \beta w_t + v_t$$
$$w_t = (1 + \exp(-\gamma(y_{t-1} - 0)))^{-1}$$
$$v_t \sim iid\, N(0, 1),$$

where the parameters are $\beta = \{0.0, -1, -2, -3, -4\}$ and $\gamma = \{2\}$.
Show that the linearity test based on (19.10) has power in the direction
of β, but that the version of the test with the restrictions $\pi_{2,i} = \pi_{3,i} = 0, \forall i$, in (19.10) has lower power.

(3) Artificial Neural Networks

Program files   nlm_ann.*, nlm_neural.*

(a) Simulate the ANN model

$$y_t = \phi y_{t-1} + \gamma \left[\frac{1}{1 + \exp(-(\delta_0 + \delta_1 y_{t-1}))}\right] + v_t, \qquad v_t \sim iid\, N(0, \sigma^2),$$

where the parameter values are $\phi = 0.2, \gamma = 2.0, \delta_0 = -2, \delta_1 = 2$,
$\sigma^2 = 0.1$ and the initial condition is $y_0 = 0.0$. Choose a sample size
of $T = 2100$ observations and discard the first 100 observations.

(b) Estimate the unknown parameters $\theta = \{\phi, \gamma, \delta_0, \delta_1, \sigma^2\}$ by maximum
likelihood using the Newton-Raphson algorithm.

(c) Estimate the unknown parameters $\theta = \{\phi, \gamma, \delta_0, \delta_1, \sigma^2\}$ using the
neural algorithm where the parameters δ_0 and δ_1 are chosen at each
iteration by drawing from the rectangular distribution $[-5, 5]$. Let the
total number of iterations be 10000.

(4) Neural Network Test

Program files   nlm_lgwtest.*

(a) Simulate the linear model

$$y_t = 0.6y_{t-1} + v_t, \qquad v_t \sim iid\ N(0, 1),$$

2000 times with samples of size $T = 250$. Determine the size properties of the neural network test for the case of $q = 1, 2$ activation functions.

(b) Simulate the nonlinear model

$$y_t = \gamma y_{t-1} v_{t-2} + v_t, \qquad v_t \sim iid\ N(0, 1),$$

2000 times for samples of size $T = 250$ with $\gamma = 0.7$. Determine the size-adjusted power properties of the neural network test for the case of $q = 1, 2$ activation functions.

(c) Extend part (b) by computing the power of the test for $\gamma = 0.8, 0.9$.

(5) **Bilinearity**

Program files   nlm_blinear.*, nlm_blinest.*

(a) Simulate the bilinear model

$$y_t = 0.4y_{t-1} + v_t + 0.2v_{t-1} + \gamma y_{t-1} v_{t-1}, \qquad v_t \sim iid\ N(0, 1),$$

for $\gamma = \{0.0, 0.4, 0.8, 1.2\}$, with starting values $y_0 = 0.0$ and $v_0 = 0.0$. Choose the sample size to be $T = 300$ and then discard the first 100 observations. Describe the properties of the four time series corresponding to each value of γ.

(b) Simulate the bilinear model

$$y_t = 0.1 + 0.4y_{t-1} + v_t + \gamma y_{t-1} v_{t-1}, \qquad v_t \sim iid\ N(0, 0.1),$$

for $\gamma = 0.4$ with starting values $y_0 = 0.0$ and $v_0 = 0.0$. Choose the sample size to be $T = 1100$ observations and discard the first 100 observations. Estimate the parameters by maximum likelihood.

(c) Using the results in part (b), test for bilinearity using a LR test, a Wald test and a LM test.

(d) Repeat parts (b) and (c) where the bilinearity parameter is $\gamma = 0.0$.

(6) **A Markov Switching Model of the Business Cycle**

Program files   nlm_bcycle.*
Data files   gnp.*, urate.*

The data file contains $T = 136$ quarterly observations on United States GNP from March 1951 to December 1984. Consider the following model of the business cycle

$$
\begin{aligned}
y_t &= \alpha + \beta w_t + u_t \\
\sigma_t^2 &= \gamma + \delta w_t \\
u_t &\sim N(0, \sigma_t^2) \\
p &= P\left[w_t = 1 \mid w_{t-1} = 1, y_{t-1}, y_{t-2}, \cdots\right] \\
q &= P\left[w_t = 0 \mid w_{t-1} = 0, y_{t-1}, y_{t-2}, \cdots\right],
\end{aligned}
$$

where y_t is the quarterly percentage growth rate in output, w_t is a stochastic binary variable representing the business cycle, u_t is a disturbance and $\theta = \{\alpha, \beta, \gamma, \delta, p, q\}$ are unknown parameters.

(a) Estimate the unknown parameters θ by maximum likelihood and interpret the parameter estimates. Compare these estimates to the values reported in Table 19.4 and in Hamilton (1989, Table 1, p.372).

(b) A measure of duration of an expansion is given by $(1 - p)^{-1}$ and of a contraction by $(1 - q)^{-1}$. Estimate the duration of the two phases of the business cycle together with their standard errors.

(c) Test the restriction $\delta = 0$ and interpret the result.

(d) A potential test of Markov switching is based on the joint restriction $\beta = \delta = 0$. Briefly discuss the statistical issues associated in performing this test.

(e) Re-estimate the model by allowing the conditional probabilities to be time-varying functions of the unemployment rate, x_t,

$$
p_t = \frac{1}{1 + \exp\left(-\kappa_0 - \kappa_1 x_t\right)}, \qquad q_t = \frac{1}{1 + \exp\left(-\lambda_0 - \lambda_1 x_t\right)}.
$$

Perform a LR test of time-invariant transitional probabilities by testing the joint restriction $\kappa_1 = \lambda_1 = 0$.

(7) Nonparametric Autoregression

Program files   nlm_linear.*, nlm_tar.*

(a) Simulate $T = 5000$ observations from the linear AR(k) model

$$
y_t = \mu + \phi y_{t-k} + \sigma z_t, \qquad z_t \sim iid\ N(0, 1),
$$

with $k = 1, 2, 3, 4, 5$ lags and parameter values $\mu = 0.0$, $\phi = 0.8$, $\sigma^2 = 1$. For each k estimate the conditional mean, $m(y_{t-k})$, using the Nadaraya-Watson kernel regression estimator with a Gaussian kernel and the rule-of-thumb bandwidth. Compare the estimated conditional mean and the true conditional mean given by $m(y) = \phi^k y$.

(b) Repeat part (a) for the nonlinear autoregressive model

$$
y_t = \theta |y_{t-k}| + \sqrt{1 - \theta^2} z_t, \qquad z_t \sim iid\ N(0, 1),
$$

with $k = 1, 2, 3, 4, 5$ lags and parameter $\theta = 0.8$. For each k, compare the nonparametric estimate of the conditional mean with the linear conditional mean in part (a). Interpret the results.

(8) Impulse Response Function of Nonlinear Time Series Models

---

Program files   nlm_girf.*

Simulate $T = 1000$ observations from the nonlinear model

$$y_t = \phi_1 y_{t-1} + \phi_2 y_{t-1} w_t + v_t,$$

$$w_t = \begin{cases} 1 & y_{t-1} \geq 0 \\ 0 & y_{t-1} < 0. \end{cases}$$

$$v_t \sim iid\ N(0, 1),$$

with parameter values $\phi_1 = 0.25$ and $\phi_2 = 0.50$.

(a) Compute the generalised impulse responses for horizons of $n = 10$ and shocks of $\delta = \{2, 1, -1, -2\}$. Interpret the results.

(b) Compare the results in part (a) to the impulse responses of a linear model by setting $\phi_2 = 0.0$.

(c) Repeat parts (a) and (b) for alternative values of ϕ_1 and ϕ_2.

(9) LSTAR Model of Unemployment

Program files   nlm_usurate.*,nlm_ozurate.*
Data files   usunemp.*, ausu.*

(a) Consider the case of the United States in which the data are observations on the monthly percentage unemployment rate from January 1948 to March 2010. Estimate an AR(1) model with a constant for the unemployment rate, y_t. Use the results to estimate the long-run equilibrium level of unemployment.

(b) Perform the LST linearity test on the unemployment rate.

(c) Estimate the LSTAR model

$$\Delta y_t = \mu_1 + \alpha_1 u_{t-1} + (\mu_2 + \alpha_2 u_{t-1}) w_t + v_t$$

$$w_t = \frac{1}{1 + \exp(-\gamma(\Delta_{12} y_{t-1} - c)/s)},$$

in which $v_t \sim iid\ N(0, \sigma^2)$ and s is a scale factor equal to the standard deviation of $\Delta_{12} y_{t-1}$. Interpret the parameter estimates.

(d) Estimate the long-run equilibrium level of unemployment in the 'low' state and the 'high' state and compare these estimates with the estimate obtained in part (a) based on the linear model. Discuss these results in the light of the linearity test conducted in part (b).

(e) Repeat parts (a) to (d) where now y_t are observations on the quarterly percentage unemployment rate in Australia beginning March 1971 and ending December 2008.

(10) Bivariate LSTAR Model of G7 Countries

Program files	nlm_g7.*
Data files	G7Data.*

The data are percentage quarterly growth rates of output, $y_{1,t}$, and spreads, $y_{2,t}$, for the G7 countries, Canada, France, Germany, Italy, Japan, the United Kingdom and the United States. All sample periods end December 1999, but the starting dates vary which are given in the data file.

(a) Estimate a bivariate VAR of $y_{1,t}$ and $y_{2,t}$ with a constant and two lags. Describe the dynamic properties of this model.

(b) A bivariate analogue of the LST test is based on the regression equation

$$
v_{j,t} = \pi_0 + \sum_{i=1}^{p} \pi_{0,i,1} y_{1,t-i} + \sum_{i=1}^{p} \pi_{0,i,2} y_{2,t-i}
$$

$$
+ \sum_{i=1}^{p} \pi_{1,i,1} y_{1,t-i} y_{k,t-d} + \sum_{i=1}^{p} \pi_{1,i,2} y_{2,t-i} y_{k,t-d}
$$

$$
+ \sum_{i=1}^{p} \pi_{2,i,1} y_{1,t-i} y_{k,t-d}^2 + \sum_{i=1}^{p} \pi_{2,i,2} y_{2,t-i} y_{k,t-d}^2
$$

$$
+ \sum_{i=1}^{p} \pi_{3,i,1} y_{1,t-i} y_{k,t-d}^3 + \sum_{i=1}^{p} \pi_{3,i,2} y_{2,t-i} y_{k,t-d}^3 + e_t \, ,
$$

where $v_{j,t}$ is the residual of variable j from estimating the linear VAR in part (a). Apply this test for $j, d = 1, 2$.

(c) Estimate the following bivariate LSTAR model by maximum likelihood for each of the G7 countries

$$
y_{1,t} = \phi_{1,0} + \sum_{i=1}^{2} \phi_{i,1,1} y_{1,t-i} + \sum_{i=1}^{2} \phi_{i,1,2} y_{2,t-1}
$$

$$
+ \ (\beta_{1,0} + \sum_{i=1}^{2} \beta_{i,1,1} y_{1,t-i} + \sum_{i=1}^{2} \beta_{i,1,2} y_{2,t-i}) w_{1,t} + v_{1,t}
$$

$$
y_{2,t} = \phi_{2,0} + \sum_{i=1}^{2} \phi_{i,2,1} y_{1,t-i} + \sum_{i=1}^{2} \phi_{i,2,2} y_{2,t-2}
$$

$$
+ \ (\beta_{2,0} + \sum_{i=1}^{2} \beta_{i,2,1} y_{1,t-i} + \sum_{i=1}^{2} \beta_{i,2,2} y_{2,t-i}) w_{2,t} + v_{2,t} \, ,
$$

and

$$w_{1,t} = \frac{1}{1 + \exp(-\gamma_1(y_{1,t-2} - c_1))},$$

$$w_{2,t} = \frac{1}{1 + \exp(-\gamma_2(y_{1,t-1} - c_2))},$$

where $v_t = \begin{bmatrix} v_{1,t}, v_{2,t} \end{bmatrix}'$ is distributed as $v_t \sim iid\ N(0, V)$ and the threshold parameters are restricted to be $\gamma_1 = \gamma_2 = 100$.

(d) Simulate each of the estimated models and discuss the dynamic properties of these models. Compare the results with Figure 19.11.

(11) **Sunspots**

Program files	nlm_sunspots.*
Data files	sunspots.*

The data, y_t, are the monthly averages of daily sunspot numbers from January 1749 to June 2009, compiled by the Solar Influences Data Analysis Centre in Belgium. Sunspots are magnetic regions on the sun with magnetic field strengths thousands of times stronger than the earth's magnetic field. They appear as dark spots on the surface of the sun and typically last for several days. They were first observed in the early 1600s following the invention of the telescope.

(a) Plot the sunspots data and discuss the time series properties of this series.

(b) Perform the LST linearity test on the sunspots data and interpret.

(c) Estimate the following LSTAR model of sunspots by maximum likelihood methods

$$y_t = \phi_0 + \sum_{i=1}^{6} \phi_i y_{t-i} + (\beta_0 + \sum_{i=1}^{3} \beta_i y_{t-i})w_t + v_t,$$

$$w_t = \frac{1}{1 + \exp(-\gamma(y_{t-d} - c))},$$

where the disturbance is distributed as $v_t \sim iid\ N(0, \sigma^2)$, the delay parameter is fixed at $d = 2$, and the threshold parameter is fixed at the following values $\gamma = \{1, 5, 10, 50, 100\}$. Use these results to estimate γ conditional on $d = 2$.

(d) Repeat part (c) for alternative values of the delay parameter d and use these results to derive maximum likelihood estimates d and γ.

(12) **Relationship with Time-varying Parameter Models**

Program files	nlm_tvarying.*

Granger (2008) uses White's theorem to argue that nonlinear models can be approximated using time-varying parameter models. To understand the theorem consider the regression equation

$$y_t = E[y_t|y_{t-1}, y_{t-2}, \cdots] + v_t,$$

where v_t is a disturbance term. Assuming that $y_{t-1} > 0$, this equation is rewritten as

$$y_t = (E[y_t|y_{t-1}, y_{t-2}, \cdots]/y_{t-1})y_{t-1} + v_t = s_t y_{t-1} + v_t,$$

where $s_t = (E[y_t|y_{t-1}, y_{t-2}, \cdots]/y_{t-1})$. This is an AR(1) model with a time-varying parameter given by s_t, which can be used to approximate $E[y_t|y_{t-1}, y_{t-2}, \cdots]$ by either a Kalman filter (Chapter 15) or a nonparametric regression estimator (Chapter 11).

(a) To examine the approximation properties of the time-varying model for the simplest case of a linear model, simulate the following AR(2) model with $\gamma = 0.0$ for $T = 200$ observations

$$y_t = 10 + 0.6y_{t-1} + 0.3y_{t-2} + \gamma y_{t-1}v_{t-1} + v_t, \qquad v_t \sim iid\ N(0, 3).$$

(b) Using the simulated data in part (a) estimate the time-varying Kalman filter model

$$
\begin{aligned}
y_t &= \lambda_t s_t + v_t, & v_t &\sim iid\ N(0, \sigma^2) \\
s_t &= \phi s_{t-1} + \eta_t, & \eta_t &\sim iid\ N(0, 1),
\end{aligned}
$$

for the unknown parameters $\theta = \{\sigma^2, \phi\}$, with $\lambda_t = y_{t-1}$. Approximate the conditional mean of y_t by $y_{t-1}s_{t|T}$, where $s_{t|T}$ is the smoothed estimate of the latent factor s_t.

(c) Now estimate the conditional mean of y_t using a nonparametric estimator.

(d) Compare the approximating conditional means obtained in parts (b) and (c) with the true conditional mean which is given by

$$E[y_t|y_{t-1}] = 10 + 0.6y_{t-1} + 0.3y_{t-2}.$$

(e) Repeat parts (a) to (d) where the true model is nonlinear based on the bilinear specification with $\gamma = 0.8$.

(13) **GENTS**

Program files	nlm_gents.*
Data files	ftse.*

The data are the daily percentage returns on the FTSE, y_t, beginning 20 November 1973 and ending 23 July 2001, $T = 7000$ observations. The generalised exponential nonlinear time series (GENTS) model of Lye and

Martin (1994) consists of specifying a generalised Student t distribution with time-varying parameters

$$f(y_t | y_{t-1})$$
$$= \exp\left[\theta_{1,t} \tan^{-1}\left(\frac{y_t}{\gamma}\right) + \theta_{2,t} \ln\left(\gamma^2 + y_t^2\right) + \theta_{3,t} y_t - \frac{1}{2} y_t^2 - \eta_t\right],$$

where

$$\theta_{1,t} = \alpha y_{t-1}, \quad \theta_{2,t} = -\frac{(1-\gamma^2)}{2}, \quad \theta_{3,t} = \beta y_{t-1},$$

and η_t is the normalising constant given by

$$\eta_t = \ln \int_{-\infty}^{\infty} \exp\left[\theta_{1,t} \tan^{-1}\left(\frac{y}{\gamma}\right)\right.$$
$$\left. + \theta_{2,t} \ln(\gamma^2 + y^2) + \theta_{3,t} y - \frac{1}{2} y^2 - \eta_t\right] dy.$$

This model not only allows for a time-varying conditional mean, but also time-varying higher-order moments, as well as endogenous jumping during periods where the distribution exhibits multimodality.

(a) Estimate the parameters $\theta = \{\gamma, \alpha, \beta\}$ by maximum likelihood. In computing the log-likelihood function all integrals are evaluated numerically.

(b) Estimate the conditional mean

$$E[y_t | y_{t-1}] = \int_{-\infty}^{\infty} y_t \, f(y_t | y_{t-1}) dy,$$

and discuss its time series properties.

(c) Use the estimated model to perform a test of skewness on exchange rate returns based on the Wald test.

20 Nonlinearities in Variance

20.1 Introduction

This chapter addresses time series models that are nonlinear in the variance. It transpires that the variance of the returns of financial assets, commonly referred to as the volatility, is a crucial aspect of much of modern finance theory, because it is a key input to areas such as portfolio construction, risk management and option pricing. In this chapter, the particular nonlinear variance specification investigated is the autoregressive conditional heteroskedasticity (ARCH) class of models introduced by Engle (1982). This model also represents a special case of heteroskedastic regression models discussed in Chapter 8 where lags of the dependent variable are now included as explanatory variables of the variance.

As in the case with nonlinear models in the mean, however, a wide range of potential nonlinearities can be entertained when modelling the variance. There are two other important approaches to modelling the variance of financial asset returns which are only briefly touched on. The first is the stochastic volatility model, introduced by Taylor (1982) and discussed in Chapters 9 and 12. The second is realised volatility proposed by Andersen, Bollerslev, Diebold and Labys (2001, 2003) which is only explored in the context of the MIDAS model of Ghysels, Santa-Clara and Valkanov (2005) in Exercise 10 of this chapter.

20.2 Statistical Properties of Asset Returns

Panel (a) of Figure 20.1 provides a plot of the returns of the daily percentage returns, y_t, on the FTSE from 5 January 1989 to 31 December 2007, $T = 4952$. At first sight, the returns appear to be random, a point highlighted in panel (c), which shows that the autocorrelation function of returns is flat. Closer inspection of the returns reveals periods when returns hardly change (market tranquility) and others where large movements in returns are followed by further large changes (market turbulence). This property is demonstrated in panel (b)

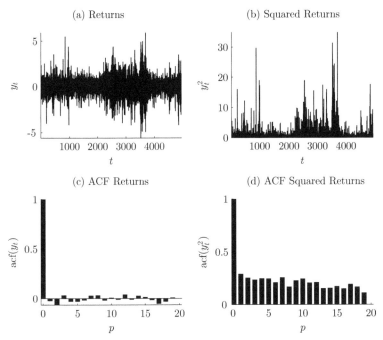

Figure 20.1. Statistical properties of daily percentage returns, y_t, on the FTSE from 5 January 1989 to 31 December 2007.

of Figure 20.1, which gives a time series plot of the squares of returns, y_t^2. This clustering of volatility is a commonly-observed empirical characteristic of financial returns and it gives rise to autocorrelation in the squared returns, as is demonstrated in panel (d) of Figure 20.1.

The properties observed in Figure 20.1 for the returns to the FTSE are commonly observed in the returns of other equity markets and more generally, in other financial markets including currency, futures, options and bond markets. The properties of returns are summarised as follows.

Property 1: No Autocorrelation in Returns

The autocorrelation in the levels of returns demonstrated in Figure 20.1 shows that predicting the direction of asset returns is not possible. This suggests the following model of y_t

$$y_t = \rho y_{t-1} + v_t, \qquad v_t \sim N(0, \sigma^2),$$

in which restriction of no autocorrelation requires that $\rho = 0$. In this case the unconditional mean and variance of y_t are, respectively,

$$
\begin{aligned}
\text{Mean} &: \quad \mathrm{E}[y_t] = \mathrm{E}[v_t] = 0 \\
\text{Variance} &: \quad \mathrm{E}[y_t^2] - \mathrm{E}[y_t]^2 = \mathrm{E}[y_t^2] = \mathrm{E}[v_t^2] = \sigma^2 .
\end{aligned}
\tag{20.1}
$$

Also, the conditional mean at time t, based on information at time $t - 1$, is

$$E_{t-1}[y_t] = E_{t-1}[\rho y_{t-1} + v_t] = \rho E_{t-1}[y_{t-1}] + E_{t-1}[v_t] = \rho y_{t-1} = 0,$$
(20.2)

since $\rho = 0$.

Property 2: Autocorrelation in Squared Returns

The autocorrelation in the squares of returns demonstrated in Figure 20.1 shows that while predicting the direction of returns is not possible, predicting their volatility is. This suggests a model of squared returns, y_t^2, of the following form

$$y_t^2 = \alpha_0 + \alpha_1 y_{t-1}^2 + e_t,$$
(20.3)

where e_t is an *iid* disturbance term and α_0 and α_1 are parameters.

An alternative expression of the unconditional variance of y_t given in (20.1) is obtained by using the law of iterated expectations and taking unconditional expectations of (20.3)

$$E[y_t^2] = E[\alpha_0 + \alpha_1 y_{t-1}^2 + e_t] = \alpha_0 + \alpha_1 E[y_{t-1}^2] + E[e_t].$$
(20.4)

Using the fact that $E[y_t^2] = E[y_{t-1}^2] = \sigma^2$ and given that $E_{t-1}[y_t] = 0$ from (20.2), expression (20.4) is rewritten as

$$\sigma^2 = \alpha_0 + \alpha_1 \sigma^2 + 0,$$

or

$$\sigma^2 = \frac{\alpha_0}{1 - \alpha_1}.$$
(20.5)

It follows that, for the unconditional variance to be positive, the restrictions $\alpha_0 > 0$ and $|\alpha_1| < 1$ are needed. Another important implication of this expression is that if $\alpha_1 = 1$ the unconditional variance is undefined.

Now consider the conditional variance of y_t based on information at $t - 1$

$$\sigma_t^2 = E_{t-1}[y_t^2] - E_{t-1}[y_t]^2.$$

Using (20.2) reduces this expression to

$$\sigma_t^2 = E_{t-1}[y_t^2].$$

It follows from (20.3) that the conditional variance is

$$\sigma_t^2 = \text{E}_{t-1}[\alpha_0 + \alpha_1 y_{t-1}^2 + e_t] = \alpha_0 + \alpha_1 y_{t-1}^2 + \text{E}_{t-1}[e_t] = \alpha_0 + \alpha_1 y_{t-1}^2.$$
(20.6)

Unlike the conditional mean in (20.2), which is time invariant, the conditional variance does change over time as a result of y_{t-1}^2.

Property 3: Volatility Clustering

The volatility clustering property demonstrated in panel (d) of Figure 20.1 shows that small movements in returns tend to be followed by small returns in the next period, whereas large movements in returns tend to be followed by large returns. These movements imply that the autocorrelation of squared returns is positive and suggests that in the expression of the conditional variance in (20.6), volatility clustering requires the tighter restriction $0 < \alpha_1 < 1$.

Property 4: Conditional Normality

The conditional distribution of returns is normal with conditional mean given by (20.2) and conditional variance given by (20.6)

$$f(y_t | y_{t-1}) \sim N(0, \alpha_0 + \alpha_1 y_{t-1}^2).$$
(20.7)

for small values of y_{t-1}, the conditional variance is drawn from a relatively compact distribution with mean of zero and approximate variance α_0. This indicates a high probability of drawing another small value of y_t in the next period. By contrast, for larger values of y_{t-1} the conditional variance is drawn from a more dispersed distribution with mean zero and variance $\alpha_0 + \alpha_1 y_{t-1}^2$. There is, therefore, a high probability of drawing another large value of y_t in the next period.

Property 5: Unconditional Leptokurtosis

The unconditional distribution is derived by averaging over all T conditional distributions. Even though the conditional distribution is normal, the unconditional distribution is not. For conditional distributions with relatively low-volatility, the normal distributions are relatively compact with high peaks, whereas, for the relatively high-volatility conditional distributions, the normal distributions are relatively more dispersed with low peaks. Averaging across the conditional distributions yields a non-normal unconditional distribution, $f(y_t)$, that has fat-tails and a sharp peak compared to the normal distribution. A distribution with these two properties is said to exhibit leptokurtosis.

The unconditional distribution of the FTSE returns estimated using a non-parametric kernel estimator with a rule-of-thumb bandwidth is given in Figure 20.2 and is compared to the conditional distribution given by the standard normal distribution. The unconditional distribution exhibits leptokurtosis since it

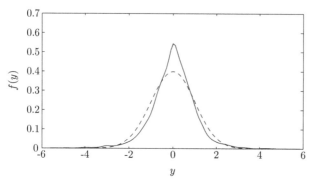

Figure 20.2. Unconditional (empirical) distribution of FTSE percentage returns (solid line) compared to the conditional (standardised normal) distribution (dashed line).

has a sharper peak and fatter tails than the standard normal distribution. The peak of the empirical distribution is 0.522 and the estimated kurtosis is 6.077. These values are to be compared to their standard normal counterparts of 0.399 and 3 respectively.

20.3   The ARCH Model

The analysis of the empirical characteristics of asset returns in the previous section suggests that modelling the autocorrelation structure of the variance is relatively more important than modelling the autocorrelation structure in the mean. This section discusses the ARCH class of model, which captures the autocorrelation properties in the variance.

20.3.1   Specification

The specification of the ARCH model is motivated by the discussion in the previous section and, in particular, equation (20.6) in which the conditional variance is expressed as a function of lagged squared returns. The model is

$$
\begin{aligned}
y_t &= v_t \\
v_t &\sim N(0, \sigma_t^2) \\
\sigma_t^2 &= \alpha_0 + \sum_{i=1}^{q} \alpha_j v_{t-i}^2 \, .
\end{aligned}
\tag{20.8}
$$

This model is referred to as ARCH(q), where q refers to the order of the lagged squared returns included in the model. The conditional variance is given by

$$
\sigma_t^2 = \alpha_0 + \alpha_1 v_{t-1}^2 + \cdots + \alpha_q v_{t-q}^2 = \alpha_0 + \alpha_1 y_{t-1}^2 + \cdots + \alpha_q y_{t-q}^2 \, ,
$$

where $\theta = \{\alpha_0, \alpha_1, \cdots, \alpha_q\}$ is a vector of parameters to be estimated.

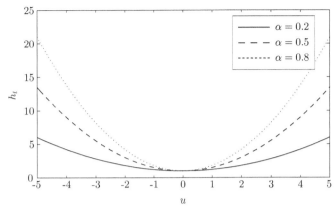

Figure 20.3. The news impact curve (NIC) for alternative parameterisations of the ARCH(1) model given in equation (20.9).

A special case of (20.8) is the ARCH(1) model given by

$$y_t = v_t$$
$$v_t \sim N(0, \sigma_t^2) \tag{20.9}$$
$$\sigma_t^2 = \alpha_0 + \alpha_1 v_{t-1}^2 = \alpha_0 + \alpha_1 y_{t-1}^2,$$

with the conditional distribution of y_t given by

$$f(y_t | y_{t-1}; \theta) = \frac{1}{\sqrt{2\pi\sigma_t^2}} \exp\left[-\frac{y_t^2}{2\sigma_t^2}\right]$$

$$= \frac{1}{\sqrt{2\pi(\alpha_0 + \alpha_1 y_{t-1}^2)}} \exp\left[-\frac{y_t^2}{2(\alpha_0 + \alpha_1 y_{t-1}^2)}\right]. \tag{20.10}$$

Clearly the shape of this distribution changes over time as y_{t-1} changes.

Example 20.1 The News Impact Curve (NIC)

A property of the ARCH(1) model in (20.9) is that the conditional variance, σ_t^2, changes as the disturbance in the previous period changes. This relationship is presented in Figure 20.3, which shows that σ_t^2 increases as the absolute value of v_{t-1} increases. This figure also shows that the relationship between σ_t^2 and v_{t-1} is symmetric since a positive disturbance has the same effect on σ_t^2 as does a negative disturbance of the same magnitude. $\qquad\square$

20.3.2 Estimation

For ease of exposition, the details of the estimation of ARCH models are presented for the ARCH(1) specification in equation (20.9). The model can be estimated by maximum likelihood using a standard iterative algorithm discussed in Chapter 3. For a sample of $t = 1, 2, \cdots, T$ observations, the conditional log-likelihood function is

$$\ln L_T(\theta) = \frac{1}{T} \sum_{t=1}^{T} \ln f(y_t | y_{t-1}; \theta), \qquad (20.11)$$

where $f(y_t | y_{t-1}; \theta)$ is the conditional distribution in (20.10). For the ARCH model in equation (20.10), the conditional log-likelihood function becomes

$$
\begin{aligned}
\ln L_T(\theta) &= \frac{1}{T} \sum_{t=1}^{T} \ln f(y_t | y_{t-1}; \theta) \\
&= -\frac{1}{2} \ln(2\pi) - \frac{1}{2T} \sum_{t=1}^{T} \ln(\sigma_t^2) - \frac{1}{2T} \sum_{t=1}^{T} \frac{y_t^2}{\sigma_t^2} \qquad (20.12) \\
&= -\frac{1}{2} \ln(2\pi) - \frac{1}{2T} \sum_{t=1}^{T} \ln(\alpha_0 + \alpha_1 y_{t-1}^2) - \frac{1}{2T} \sum_{t=1}^{T} \frac{y_t^2}{\alpha_0 + \alpha_1 y_{t-1}^2}.
\end{aligned}
$$

The first and second derivative of the log-likelihood function in equation (20.12) are required if the parameters $\theta = \{\alpha_0, \alpha_1\}$ are to be estimated by means of a gradient algorithm. Analytical derivatives are easily computed. The first derivatives are

$$
\begin{aligned}
\frac{\partial \ln L_T(\theta)}{\partial \alpha_0} &= \frac{\partial \ln L_T(\theta)}{\partial \sigma_t^2} \frac{\partial \sigma_t^2}{\partial \alpha_0} \\
&= \frac{1}{T} \sum_{t=1}^{T} \left[-\frac{1}{2\sigma_t^2} + \frac{y_t^2}{2\sigma_t^4} \right] \frac{\partial \sigma_t^2}{\partial \alpha_0} = \frac{1}{T} \sum_{t=1}^{T} \frac{1}{2\sigma_t^2} \left[\frac{y_t^2}{\sigma_t^2} - 1 \right],
\end{aligned}
$$

$$
\begin{aligned}
\frac{\partial \ln L_T(\theta)}{\partial \alpha_1} &= \frac{\partial \ln L_T(\theta)}{\partial \sigma_t^2} \frac{\partial \sigma_t^2}{\partial \alpha_1} \\
&= \frac{1}{T} \sum_{t=1}^{T} \left[-\frac{1}{2\sigma_t^2} + \frac{y_t^2}{2\sigma_t^4} \right] \frac{\partial \sigma_t^2}{\partial \alpha_1} = \frac{1}{T} \sum_{t=1}^{T} \frac{1}{2\sigma_t^2} \left[\frac{y_t^2}{\sigma_t^2} - 1 \right] y_{t-1}^2,
\end{aligned}
$$

so that the gradient vector is

$$
G_T(\theta) = \frac{\partial \ln L_T(\theta)}{\partial \theta} = \frac{1}{T} \sum_{t=1}^{T} \frac{1}{2\sigma_t^2} \left[\frac{y_t^2}{\sigma_t^2} - 1 \right] \begin{bmatrix} 1 \\ y_{t-1}^2 \end{bmatrix}. \qquad (20.13)
$$

The second derivatives are

$$\frac{\partial^2 \ln L_T(\theta)}{\partial \alpha_0^2} = \frac{1}{T} \sum_{t=1}^{T} \left(\frac{1}{2\sigma_t^4} - \frac{y_t^2}{\sigma_t^6} \right)$$

$$\frac{\partial^2 \ln L_T(\theta)}{\partial \alpha_0 \partial \alpha_1} = \frac{1}{T} \sum_{t=1}^{T} \left(\frac{1}{2\sigma_t^4} - \frac{y_t^2}{\sigma_t^6} \right) y_{t-1}^2$$

$$\frac{\partial^2 \ln L_T(\theta)}{\partial \alpha_1^2} = \frac{1}{T} \sum_{t=1}^{T} \left(\frac{1}{2\sigma_t^4} - \frac{y_t^2}{\sigma_t^6} \right) y_{t-1}^4 ,$$

which yields the Hessian matrix

$$H_T(\theta) = \frac{\partial^2 \ln L_T(\theta)}{\partial \theta \, \partial \theta'} = \frac{1}{T} \sum_{t=1}^{T} \left(\frac{1}{2\sigma_t^4} - \frac{y_t^2}{\sigma_t^6} \right) \begin{bmatrix} 1 & y_{t-1}^2 \\ y_{t-1}^2 & y_{t-1}^4 \end{bmatrix}.$$

$$(20.14)$$

Beginning with some starting values of the parameters, say $\theta_{(0)}$, the Newton-Raphson algorithm can be used to update the parameter values using the iterative scheme

$$\theta_{(k)} = \theta_{(k-1)} - H_{(k-1)}^{-1} G_{(k-1)} , \qquad (20.15)$$

where $G_{(k-1)} = G_T(\theta_{(k-1)})$ using equation (20.13), $H_{(k-1)} = H_T(\theta_{(k-1)})$ using equation (20.14), and σ_t^2 is evaluated at $\theta_{(k-1)}$.

The scoring algorithm can also be used. In deriving the information matrix, however, it is convenient to modify the algorithm by using the conditional expectation instead of the usual unconditional expectation. By definition as $\sigma_t^2 = \mathrm{E}_{t-1}[y_t^2]$, from equation (20.14) the information matrix is

$$I(\theta) = -\mathrm{E}_{t-1}[H_T(\theta)]$$

$$= \frac{1}{T} \sum_{t=1}^{T} \left(\frac{1}{2\sigma_t^4} - \frac{\mathrm{E}_{t-1}[y_t^2]}{\sigma_t^6} \right) \begin{bmatrix} 1 & y_{t-1}^2 \\ y_{t-1}^2 & y_{t-1}^4 \end{bmatrix}$$

$$= -\frac{1}{T} \sum_{t=1}^{T} \left(\frac{1}{2\sigma_t^4} - \frac{\sigma_t^2}{\sigma_t^6} \right) \begin{bmatrix} 1 & y_{t-1}^2 \\ y_{t-1}^2 & y_{t-1}^4 \end{bmatrix}$$

$$= \frac{1}{T} \sum_{t=1}^{T} \frac{1}{2\sigma_t^4} \begin{bmatrix} 1 & y_{t-1}^2 \\ y_{t-1}^2 & y_{t-1}^4 \end{bmatrix}. \qquad (20.16)$$

The modified scoring algorithm proceeds as follows

$$\theta_{(k)} = \theta_{(k-1)} + I_{(k-1)}^{-1} G_{(k-1)} , \qquad (20.17)$$

where as before $G_{(k-1)} = G_T(\theta_{(k-1)})$, using equation (20.13), and $I_{(k-1)} = I(\theta_{(k-1)})$, using equation (20.16).

The maximisation of the log-likelihood function in equation (20.12) requires a starting value for σ_1^2

$$\sigma_1^2 = \alpha_0 + \alpha_1 y_0^2\,,$$

which, in turn, requires a starting value for y_0. The simplest solution is to choose σ_1^2 as the sample variance of y_t, which represents an estimate of the unconditional variance of y_t. Another approach is to compute σ_1^2 by setting $y_0 = 0$, which is the unconditional mean of y_t for the model in equation (20.9).

A potential problem in estimating the parameters of the ARCH model is that the specification of the variance in equation (20.9) does not necessarily ensure that σ_t^2 is always non-negative. For example, a negative estimate of the conditional variance may arise if α_0 and/or α_1 become negative during the iterations. If this happens, even for just one observation, the optimisation algorithm will break down because $\ln \sigma_t^2$ in (20.12) cannot be computed. One possible solution is to follow the suggestion made in Chapter 3 and transform α_0 and α_1 using an appropriate mapping that ensures positive estimates. A popular choice is exponential tilting in which the algorithm estimates the transformed parameters δ_i where $\alpha_i = \exp \delta_i$. Standard errors of $\widehat{\alpha}_i$ can be computed by the delta method or the model can be iterated one more time with $\exp(\widehat{\delta}_i)$ replaced by $\widehat{\alpha}_i$. From the invariance property of maximum likelihood estimators, the estimates of α_i obtained using this strategy are also the maximum likelihood estimates.

It is also usual to confine attention to cases in which the process generating the disturbances is variance stationary, that is, the unconditional variance of u_t is unchanging over time. This requires that $\alpha_1 < 1$ in equation (20.9), which can also be imposed by using an appropriate transformation of the parameter as discussed in Chapter 3.

Example 20.2 Estimating an ARCH Model

Consider the daily percentage returns, y_t, on the FTSE from 5 January 1989 to 31 December 2007, $T = 4952$. The maximum likelihood estimates of the parameters of the ARCH(1) model in equation (20.9) applied to this data are

$$y_t = \widehat{v}_t$$
$$\widehat{\sigma}_t^2 = \widehat{\alpha}_0 + \widehat{\alpha}_1 \widehat{v}_{t-1}^2 = 0.739 + 0.255\ y_{t-1}^2\,.$$

The value of the log-likelihood function is $\ln L_T(\theta) = -1.378$. An estimate of the theoretical unconditional variance using (20.5) is

$$\widehat{\sigma}^2 = \frac{0.739}{1 - 0.255} = 0.993\,,$$

which is consistent with the sample variance of 0.984 obtained for y_t.   □

20.3.3   Testing

A test of ARCH is given by testing that $\alpha_1 = 0$ in (20.9) so that the model under the null hypothesis reduces to a normal distribution with zero mean and constant variance $\sigma_t^2 = \alpha_0$, given by

$$f(y; \alpha_0) \sim iid\, N(0, \alpha_0).$$

The null and alternative hypotheses are

$$H_0 : \alpha_1 = 0 \quad \text{[No ARCH]}, \qquad H_1 : \alpha_1 \neq 0 \quad \text{[ARCH]}.$$

Let the parameters of the restricted model under the null hypothesis be given by $\widehat{\theta}_0 = \{\widehat{\alpha}_0, 0\}$, where $\widehat{\alpha}_0$ is the maximum likelihood estimator of α_0 under the null hypothesis. For the model in equation (20.9) the maximum likelihood estimator of α_0 is simply

$$\widehat{\alpha}_0 = \frac{1}{T} \sum_{t=1}^{T} y_t^2. \tag{20.18}$$

The test of ARCH can be performed by using either the LR, Wald or LM tests. In practice the LM test is commonly used since it simply involves estimating an ordinary least squares regression equation and performing a goodness-of-fit test.

The information matrix version of the LM test is based on the test statistic

$$LM = T G_T(\widehat{\theta}_0)' I(\widehat{\theta}_0)^{-1} G_T(\widehat{\theta}_0), \tag{20.19}$$

where $G_T(\widehat{\theta}_0)$ and $I(\widehat{\theta}_0)$ are the gradient vector and information matrix, respectively, evaluated at the parameter estimates under the null hypothesis. From equations (20.13) and (20.16) these terms are

$$G_T(\widehat{\theta}_0) = \frac{1}{T} \sum_{t=1}^{T} \frac{1}{2\widehat{\alpha}_0} \left[\frac{y_t^2}{\widehat{\alpha}_0} - 1 \right] \begin{bmatrix} 1 \\ y_{t-1}^2 \end{bmatrix}$$

$$I_t(\widehat{\theta}_0) = \frac{1}{T} \sum_{t=1}^{T} \frac{1}{2\widehat{\alpha}_0^2} \begin{bmatrix} 1 & y_{t-1}^2 \\ y_{t-1}^2 & y_{t-1}^4 \end{bmatrix}.$$

Using these expressions in (20.19) and simplifying gives

$$LM = \frac{1}{2} \begin{bmatrix} \sum_{t=1}^{T} \widehat{e}_t \\ \sum_{t=1}^{T} \widehat{e}_t y_{t-1}^2 \end{bmatrix}' \begin{bmatrix} T & \sum_{t=1}^{T} y_{t-1}^2 \\ \sum_{t=1}^{T} y_{t-1}^2 & \sum_{t=1}^{T} y_{t-1}^4 \end{bmatrix}^{-1} \begin{bmatrix} \sum_{t=1}^{T} \widehat{e}_t \\ \sum_{t=1}^{T} \widehat{e}_t y_{t-1}^2 \end{bmatrix},$$

$$\tag{20.20}$$

where

$$\widehat{e}_t = \frac{y_t^2}{\widehat{\alpha}_0} - 1.$$

(20.21)

Alternatively, since under the null hypothesis

$$z_t = \frac{y_t}{\sqrt{\widehat{\alpha}_0}} \sim N(0, 1),$$

it follows that $\widehat{e}_t$ in equation (20.21) has the property

$$\text{plim}\left(\frac{1}{T}\sum_{t=1}^{T}\widehat{e}_t^2\right) = \text{plim}\left(\frac{1}{T}\sum_{t=1}^{T}(z_t^2 - 1)^2\right)$$

$$= \text{plim}\left(\frac{1}{T}\sum_{t=1}^{T}(z_t^4 - 2z_t^2 + 1)\right) = 2,$$

because $\text{plim}(T^{-1}\sum_{t=1}^{T} z_t^2) = 1$ and $\text{plim}(T^{-1}\sum_{t=1}^{T} z_t^4) = 3$ from the properties of the normal distribution. Consequently, another asymptotic form for the LM test in equation (20.20) is to the replace the $1/2$ in equation (20.20) by $T/\sum_{t=1}^{T}\widehat{e}_t^2$ which is the inverse of the variance of $\widehat{e}_t$. This yields the test statistic

$$LM = \frac{T}{\sum_{t=1}^{T}\widehat{e}_t^2}\begin{bmatrix}\sum_{t=1}^{T}\widehat{e}_t \\ \sum_{t=1}^{T}\widehat{e}_t y_{t-1}^2\end{bmatrix}'\begin{bmatrix}T & \sum_{t=1}^{T}y_{t-1}^2 \\ \sum_{t=1}^{T}y_{t-1}^2 & \sum_{t=1}^{T}y_{t-1}^4\end{bmatrix}^{-1}\begin{bmatrix}\sum_{t=1}^{T}\widehat{e}_t \\ \sum_{t=1}^{T}\widehat{e}_t y_{t-1}^2\end{bmatrix}.$$

(20.22)

This form of the LM test may be computed as $T R^2$, where R^2 is the coefficient of determination from regressing $\widehat{e}_t$ on $\{1, y_{t-1}^2\}$ because under the null hypothesis $\bar{e} = T^{-1}\sum_{t=1}^{T}\widehat{e}_t = 0$. An even simpler form is to replace $\widehat{e}_t$ in equation (20.21) by y_t^2, since R^2 is invariant to linear transformations. The ARCH test now involves regressing y_t^2 on $\{1, y_{t-1}^2\}$ and computing the R^2 from this regression. This form of the ARCH test corresponds to the regression equation initially proposed in equation (20.3) as a model of squared returns. Under the null hypothesis, the LM statistic is distributed as χ_1^2.

Generalising the LM test to the ARCH(q) model in (20.8) is straightforward. The null and alternative hypotheses are now

$$H_0 : \quad \alpha_1 = \alpha_2 = \cdots \alpha_q = 0 \qquad \text{[No ARCH]}$$
$$H_1 : \quad \text{at least one of the restrictions is violated} \quad \text{[ARCH]}.$$

The ARCH(q) test is implemented using the following steps.

Table 20.1. *LM test for ARCH(1) and ARCH(2) in equity returns for the period 5 January 1989 to 31 December 2007, T = 4952. The parameter estimates, $\widehat{\alpha}_i$, are the least squares estimates for the specification in equation (20.23) and R^2 is the coefficient of determination from this regression*

Index	$\widehat{\alpha}_0$	$\widehat{\alpha}_1$	$\widehat{\alpha}_2$	T	R^2	$LM = TR^2$	pv
			ARCH(1)				
FTSE	0.765	0.223		4951	0.050	245.306	0.000
DOW	0.774	0.158		4951	0.025	123.382	0.000
NIKKEI	1.716	0.108		4951	0.012	57.840	0.000
			ARCH(2)				
FTSE	0.573	0.167	0.251	4950	0.109	541.888	0.000
DOW	0.674	0.137	0.130	4950	0.041	204.805	0.000
NIKKEI	1.503	0.095	0.124	4950	0.027	133.006	0.000

Step 1: Estimate the regression equation

$$y_t^2 = \alpha_0 + \sum_{i=1}^{q} \alpha_i y_{t-i}^2 + e_t , \tag{20.23}$$

by least squares, where e_t is an *iid* disturbance term.

Step 2: Compute TR^2 from this regression and the corresponding p-value using the χ_q^2 distribution. A p-value less than 0.05 is evidence of ARCH in y_t at the 5% level.

Example 20.3 Testing for ARCH

Daily percentage returns of the FTSE, Dow Jones Industrial Average (DOW) and the NIKKEI indices for the period 5 January 1989 to 31 December 2007 are used to test for ARCH(1) and ARCH(2) with the results summarised in Table 20.1. As the LM test is based on the model in equation (20.8) has zero mean, the returns are first transformed to have zero mean by subtracting the sample mean, $\overline{y}$. All p-values given in the last column are clearly less than 0.05, showing strong evidence of first-order and second-order ARCH in all three equity returns. □

20.4   Univariate Extensions

A vast number of extensions to the ARCH model have been proposed in the literature and applied to modelling financial data. In this section, some of the more popular extensions are discussed briefly.

20.4.1   GARCH

The ARCH(q) model in (20.8) has the property that the memory in the variance stops at lag q. This suggests that, for processes exhibiting long memory in the variance, it would be necessary to specify and estimate a high dimensional model. A natural way to circumvent this problem is to specify the conditional variance as a function of its own lags. The equation for the conditional variance then becomes

$$\sigma_t^2 = \alpha_0 + \sum_{i=1}^{q} \alpha_i v_{t-i}^2 + \sum_{i=1}^{p} \beta_i \sigma_{t-i}^2 , \qquad (20.24)$$

which is known as GARCH(p,q) where the p and the q identify the lags of the model and the 'G' stands for generalised ARCH. Once again, without loss of generality, it is convenient to work with the GARCH(1, 1) model

$$y_t = v_t , \qquad v_t \sim N(0, \sigma_t^2) \qquad (20.25)$$
$$\sigma_t^2 = \alpha_0 + \alpha_1 y_{t-1}^2 + \beta_1 \sigma_{t-1}^2 . \qquad (20.26)$$

To highlight the memory properties of this model, using the lag operator $L^k y_t = y_{t-k}$ (see Appendix B) rewrite the expression for the conditional variance, σ_t^2, as

$$(1 - \beta_1 L)\sigma_t^2 = \alpha_0 + \alpha_1 y_{t-1}^2 .$$

Assuming that $|\beta_1| < 1$ and using the properties of the lag operator, the conditional variance is expressed as

$$\sigma_t^2 = (1 - \beta_1 L)^{-1}\alpha_0 + \alpha_1(1 - \beta_1 L)^{-1}y_{t-1}^2$$

$$= \frac{\alpha_0}{1 - \beta_1} + \alpha_1 y_{t-1}^2 + \alpha_1 \sum_{i=1}^{\infty} \beta_1^i y_{t-1-i}^2 , \qquad (20.27)$$

which is instantly recognisable as an ARCH(∞) model. The third term in equation (20.27) captures the effects of higher-order lags $\{y_{t-2}^2, y_{t-3}^2, y_{t-4}^2, \cdots\}$ on the conditional variance, which are now controlled by the parameter, β_1. The GARCH model is therefore an attractive specification to use in modelling financial data because it provides a parsimonious representation of the memory characteristics commonly observed in the variance of financial returns.

Another way to highlight the memory characteristics of the GARCH conditional variance is to define the (forecast) error

$$e_t = y_t^2 - \sigma_t^2 , \qquad (20.28)$$

which has the property $E_{t-1}[e_t] = 0$. Rearranging this expression and using (20.26) gives

$$y_t^2 = \sigma_t^2 + e_t$$
$$y_t^2 = \alpha_0 + \alpha_1 y_{t-1}^2 + \beta_1 \sigma_{t-1}^2 + e_t$$
$$y_t^2 = \alpha_0 + \alpha_1 y_{t-1}^2 + \beta_1(y_{t-1}^2 - e_{t-1}) + e_t$$
$$y_t^2 = \alpha_0 + (\alpha_1 + \beta_1)y_{t-1}^2 - \beta_1 e_{t-1} + e_t , \qquad (20.29)$$

which is an ARMA(1, 1) model in terms of y_t^2. The memory of this process is determined by the autoregressive parameter $\alpha_1 + \beta_1$. The closer $\alpha_1 + \beta_1$ is to unity the longer the effect of a shock on volatility.

The effect of a shock on volatility in the long-run is obtained from the unconditional variance of y_t, defined as $\sigma^2 = E[y_t^2]$. Taking unconditional expectations of (20.29) and using $E[e_t] = E[e_{t-1}] = 0$, it follows that

$$E[y_t^2] = E[\alpha_0 + (\alpha_1 + \beta_1)y_{t-1}^2 - \beta_1 e_{t-1} + e_t],$$
$$\sigma^2 = \alpha_0 + (\alpha_1 + \beta_1)\sigma^2,$$

which gives, upon rearranging, an expression of the unconditional, or long-run, variance

$$\sigma^2 = \frac{\alpha_0}{1 - \alpha_1 - \beta_1}. \tag{20.30}$$

Example 20.4 ACF of a GARCH(1,1) Model
The autocorrelation function (ACF) of the GARCH(1,1) model in (20.26) is simulated for $T = 1000$ observations. Two sets of parameter values are used:

Model 1 (short memory) : $\alpha_0 = 0.10, \alpha_1 = 0.70, \beta_1 = 0.20$
Model 2 (long memory) : $\alpha_0 = 0.05, \alpha_1 = 0.15, \beta_1 = 0.80,$

where the memory classification of the model is determined by the relative size of β_1. The ACFs of the two models are given in Figure 20.4. The short memory feature of model 1 is highlighted by the ACF approaching zero at lag 10, compared to the longer memory model where the decay is slower. □

As with the ARCH model, the GARCH model can be estimated by maximising the log-likelihood function in (20.11) using a gradient algorithm. For the GARCH(1,1) model the unknown parameters are $\theta = \{\alpha_0, \alpha_1, \beta_1\}$ and the log-likelihood function at observation t is

$$\ln l_t(\theta) = \ln f(y_t | y_{t-1})$$
$$= -\frac{1}{2}\ln(2\pi) - \frac{1}{2}\ln(\sigma_t^2) - \frac{1}{2}\frac{y_t^2}{\sigma_t^2}$$
$$= -\frac{1}{2}\ln(2\pi) - \frac{1}{2}\ln(\alpha_0 + \alpha_1 y_{t-1}^2 + \beta_1 \sigma_{t-1}^2)$$
$$- \frac{1}{2}\frac{y_t^2}{\alpha_0 + \alpha_1 y_{t-1}^2 + \beta_1 \sigma_{t-1}^2}. \tag{20.31}$$

In estimating this model, as with the ARCH model, it may be necessary to restrict the parameters α_0, α_1 and β_1 to be positive in order to ensure that the conditional variance is positive for all t.

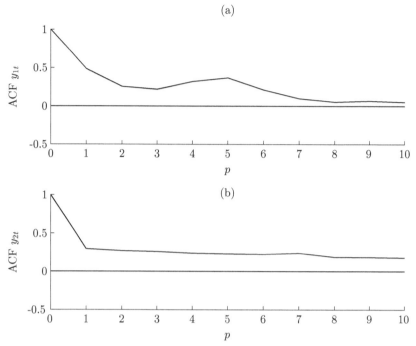

Figure 20.4. Autocorrelation function of two GARCH(1,1) models. The first model has parameter values $\alpha_0 = 0.10$, $\alpha_1 = 0.70$ and $\beta_1 = 0.20$. The second model has parameter values $\alpha_0 = 0.05$, $\alpha_1 = 0.15$, and $\beta_1 = 0.8$.

The LR, Wald and LM testing methods can also be used to test the GARCH model. The LM test derived previously in the context of the ARCH model is still relevant for the GARCH model. It should be noted that finding ARCH at relatively longer lags is evidence of a GARCH(1,1) or, possibly, a GARCH(2,2) specification. Another natural test is given by the hypotheses

$$H_0 : \beta_1 = 0 \quad \text{[No GARCH]}, \qquad H_1 : \beta_1 \neq 0 \quad \text{[GARCH]},$$

which may be implemented using either the Wald or LR test.

Example 20.5 A GARCH Model of Equity Returns

Table 20.2 contains the maximum likelihood parameter estimates of the GARCH(1,1) model in equation (20.26) for the daily percentage returns of the FTSE, DOW and NIKKEI used in Example 20.3. For comparative purposes, the results for the GARCH(0,1) or ARCH(1) model are also given.

An important feature of the empirical results is the consistency of the parameter estimates across all three equity returns, with the estimates of β_1 being around 0.9 and the estimates of α_1 being between 0.05 and 0.10. Also given in Table 20.2 are the theoretical variances computed using equation (20.30) and

Table 20.2. *Maximum likelihood estimates of GARCH(1,1) and GARCH(0,1) = ARCH(1) models of equity returns. Standard errors in parentheses are based on the Hessian. The sample size is T = 4952*

					Unconditional Variance	
Index	α_0	α_1	β_1	$T \ln L$	(Theoretical)	(Empirical)
FTSE	0.013	0.079	0.907	−6348.796	0.964	0.984
	(0.003)	(0.008)	(0.012)			
	0.740	0.255		−6824.029	0.993	0.984
	(0.020)	(0.023)				
DOW	0.009	0.051	0.940	−6316.263	0.975	0.919
	(0.002)	(0.006)	(0.008)			
	0.748	0.195		−6712.500	0.929	0.919
	(0.019)	(0.022)				
NIKKEI	0.026	0.088	0.903	−8187.337	2.728	1.924
	(0.005)	(0.008)	(0.008)			
	1.587	0.182		−8561.058	1.940	1.924
	(0.040)	(0.020)				

the empirical variances. There is good agreement between these two statistics for all indexes and all models with the exception of the NIKKEI in the case of the GARCH(1,1) model.

Figure 20.5 provides a plot of the estimated conditional variance of the FTSE. The first three observations of $\widehat{h}_t$ are computed recursively as

$$\widehat{\sigma}_1^2 = \frac{1}{T} \sum_{t=1}^{T} y_t^2 = 0.984,$$

$$\widehat{\sigma}_2^2 = \widehat{\alpha}_0 + \widehat{\alpha}_1 y_1^2 + \widehat{\beta}_1 \widehat{\sigma}_1^2 = 0.013 + 0.079 \times 0.628^2 + 0.907 \times 0.984 = 0.937,$$

$$\widehat{\sigma}_3^2 = \widehat{\alpha}_0 + \widehat{\alpha}_1 y_2^2 + \widehat{\beta}_1 \widehat{\sigma}_2^2 = 0.013 + 0.079 \times 1.083^2 + 0.907 \times 0.937 = 0.956,$$

where $y_1 = 0.628$ and $y_2 = 0.083$ are the first two observations of the zero-mean returns.

From Table 20.2, in the case of the FTSE, $T \ln L_T(\widehat{\theta}_1) = -6348.796$ for the GARCH(1,1) model and $T \ln L_T(\widehat{\theta}_0) = -6824.029$ for the ARCH(1) model. The LR statistic is

$$LR = -2(T \ln L(\widehat{\theta}_0) - T \ln L(\widehat{\theta}_1))$$
$$= -2 \times (-6824.029 + 6348.796) = 950.467,$$

which is distributed as χ_1^2 under the null hypothesis. The p-value is 0.000 indicating a strong rejection of the ARCH(1) model at the 5% level in favour of the GARCH(1,1) model. □

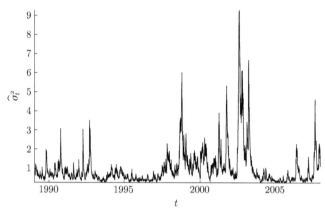

Figure 20.5. Conditional variance estimate of the zero-mean percentage daily returns to FTSE from 5 January 1989 to 31 December 2007.

20.4.2   Integrated GARCH

A feature of the volatility estimates of the GARCH(1,1) model of equity returns in Table 20.2 is that $\widehat{\alpha}_1 + \widehat{\beta}_1 \simeq 1$. For the FTSE it is

$$\widehat{\alpha}_1 + \widehat{\beta}_1 = 0.079 + 0.907 = 0.986\,.$$

From (20.29) this suggests that the volatility series has a (near) unit root. GARCH models with a unit root are referred to as IGARCH, where the 'I' stands for integrated following the discussion of nonstationary models in Part FIVE.

One way to proceed in estimating IGARCH models is to impose the unit root restriction. In the case of the GARCH(1,1) model, the restriction is $\alpha_1 + \beta_1 = 1$, in which case β_1 is replaced by $1 - \alpha_1$ so the conditional variance in equation (20.26) becomes

$$\sigma_t^2 = \alpha_0 + \alpha_1 y_{t-1}^2 + (1 - \alpha_1)\sigma_{t-1}^2\,. \tag{20.32}$$

The log-likelihood function is now maximised with respect to the variance parameters $\{\alpha_0, \alpha_1\}$, with the estimate of β_1 is obtained after the algorithm has converged. From Slutsky's theorem, this estimator is also a maximum likelihood estimator. Moreover, from the invariance property of maximum likelihood estimators the alternative strategy of substituting out α_1 and maximising the log-likelihood with respect to the parameters $\{\alpha_0, \beta_1\}$ produces identical parameter estimates.

A generalisation of the IGARCH model is the fractional integrated GARCH model (FIGARCH) proposed by Baillie, Bollerslev and Mikkelsen (1996). The

FIGARCH $(1, d, 1)$ model is

$$\sigma_t^2 = \alpha_0 + \left[1 - \beta_1 L - \frac{(1 - \alpha_1 L - \beta_1 L)(1 - L)^d}{1 - L} \right] v_t^2 + \beta_1 \sigma_{t-1}^2 , \tag{20.33}$$

where

$$(1 - L)^d = \sum_{j=0}^{\infty} \frac{\Gamma(j - d)}{\Gamma(-d) \Gamma(j + 1)} L^j ,$$

and $\Gamma(\cdot)$ is the gamma function. This model is equivalent to a GARCH $(1, \infty)$ where the infinite lag on the ARCH component is fully parameterised in terms of α_1, β_1 and the fractional differencing parameter d. The IGARCH model in (20.32) is a special case occurring when $\alpha_1 + \beta_1 = 1$ and $d = 1$. Estimation of the FIGARCH model requires starting values of v_t^2 to begin the recursion. To allow for long memory in the conditional variance a common choice is $v_0^2 = v_{-1}^2 = \cdots = v_{-1000}^2 = s^2$, the sample variance of y_t.

20.4.3 Additional Variables

A further extension of the ARCH class of model is to include additional variables in both the mean and the variance. An example, using the GARCH(1,1) conditional variance specification, is given by

$$y_t = \gamma_0 + \gamma_1 x_t + v_t , \qquad v_t \sim N(0, \sigma_t^2) \tag{20.34}$$
$$\sigma_t^2 = \alpha_0 + \alpha_1 v_{t-1}^2 + \beta_1 \sigma_{t-1}^2 + \lambda w_t , \tag{20.35}$$

where x_t and w_t are additional explanatory variables which are important in explaining the mean and the variance, respectively. Examples of w_t include trade volume, policy announcements and day-of-the-week and holiday effects. Han and Park (2008) allow for nonstationary variables in the variance to model the IGARCH properties discussed earlier (see Exercise 5).

Example 20.6 LR Test of Day-of-the-Week Effects
Consider the GARCH(1,1) model of financial returns

$$y_t = v_t , \qquad v_t \sim N(0, \sigma_t^2)$$
$$\sigma_t^2 = \alpha_0 + \alpha_1 v_{t-1}^2 + \beta_1 \sigma_{t-1}^2 + \lambda_1 d_{1,t} + \lambda_2 d_{2,t} + \lambda_3 d_{3,t} + \lambda_4 d_{4,t} ,$$

where $d_{1,t}$, $d_{2,t}$, $d_{3,t}$ and $d_{4,t}$ are dummy variables corresponding to Tuesday, Wednesday, Thursday and Friday respectively, taking the value 1 on the appropriate day and 0 otherwise. A test of day-of-the-week effects is given by the hypotheses

$$H_0 \ : \ \lambda_1 = \lambda_2 = \lambda_3 = \lambda_4 = 0 \quad \text{[No Day-of-the-Week Effects]}$$
$$H_1 \ : \ \lambda_i \neq 0 \text{ for at least one } i \quad \text{[Day-of-the-Week Effects]}.$$

When the FTSE data from Example 20.5 are used, the unrestricted model yields a value of $T \ln L_T(\widehat{\theta}_1) = -6347.691$, whereas the restricted value is $T \ln L_T(\widehat{\theta}_0) = -6348.796$, which is obtained from Table 20.2. The LR statistic is

$$LR = -2(T \ln L_T(\widehat{\theta}_0) - T \ln L_T(\widehat{\theta}_1))$$
$$= -2 \times (-6348.796 + 6347.691) = 2.210,$$

which is distributed under the null as χ_4^2. The p-value is 0.697 resulting in a failure to reject the null of no day-of-the-week effects at the 5% level.   □

To construct a LM test of ARCH where explanatory variables are included in the model, the assumption of normality enables the test to be implemented using two least squares regressions because the information matrix separates into two blocks. The first block contains the mean parameters $\{\gamma_0, \gamma_1\}$ and the second block contains the variance parameters $\{\alpha_0, \alpha_1, \beta_1, \lambda\}$. The steps to test for ARCH of order q in the model

$$y_t = \gamma_0 + \gamma_1 x_t + v_t, \qquad v_t \sim N(0, \sigma_t^2) \tag{20.36}$$

$$\sigma_t^2 = \alpha_0 + \sum_{i=1}^{q} \alpha_i v_{t-i}^2, \tag{20.37}$$

are as follows.

Step 1 Regress y_t on $\{1, x_t\}$ and compute the least squares residuals $\widehat{v}_t$.
Step 2 Regress $\widehat{v}_t^2$ on $\{1, \widehat{v}_{t-1}^2, \widehat{v}_{t-2}^2, \cdots, \widehat{v}_{t-q}^2\}$.
Step 3 Compute $T R^2$ from Step 2 and the corresponding p-value using the χ_q^2 distribution. A p-value of less than 0.05 is evidence of ARCH in y_t at the 5% level.

20.4.4 Asymmetries

The GARCH model assumes that negative and positive shocks have the same impact on volatility, an assumption which ensures that the NIC of the GARCH model, like that of the ARCH model in Figure 20.3, is symmetric. A natural extension of the GARCH model is to allow the effects of negative and positive shocks on the conditional variance to differ. This is especially important in modelling equity markets where negative shocks are expected to have a relatively bigger impact on volatility than positive shocks as a result of leverage effects.

One way to model asymmetries in volatility is the threshold GARCH model (TARCH). The variance is now specified as

$$\sigma_t^2 = \alpha_0 + \sum_{i=1}^{q} \alpha_i v_{t-i}^2 + \sum_{i=1}^{p} \beta_i \sigma_{t-i}^2 + \phi v_{t-1}^2 d_{t-1} , \qquad (20.38)$$

where d_{t-1} is a dummy variable given by

$$d_{t-1} = \begin{cases} 1 : & v_{t-1} < 0 \\ 0 : & v_{t-1} \geq 0 . \end{cases}$$

If $\phi > 0$, the effect of positive shocks $v_{t-1} \geq 0$, on volatility equals to α_1, whereas the effect of negative shocks, $v_{t-1} < 0$, on volatility equals $\alpha_1 + \phi$. If falls in the equity market are followed by relatively higher volatility, then $\phi > 0$. For the case of $p = q = 1$ lags, these features of the model are conveniently summarised as

$$\begin{aligned} \sigma_t^2(\text{positive}) &= \alpha_0 + \alpha_1 v_{t-1}^2 + \beta_1 \sigma_{t-1}^2 \\ \sigma_t^2(\text{negative}) &= \alpha_0 + (\alpha_1 + \phi) v_{t-1}^2 + \beta_1 \sigma_{t-1}^2 . \end{aligned}$$

The effect of $\phi \neq 0$ is to make the NIC asymmetric. The TARCH model can be estimated using maximum likelihood methods and a test of the model can be conducted using a Wald test of the hypothesis $\phi = 0$.

An alternative asymmetric model of the variance is the exponential GARCH (EGARCH) model of Nelson (1991). An example of an EGARCH(1, 1) model is

$$\ln \sigma_t^2 = \alpha_0 + \alpha_1 \frac{v_{t-1}}{\sigma_{t-1}} + \phi \left| \frac{v_{t-1}}{\sigma_{t-1}} \right| + \beta_1 \ln \sigma_{t-1}^2 . \qquad (20.39)$$

The asymmetry in the conditional variance is governed by the parameter ϕ. As it is the logarithm of the conditional variance that is being modelled, the EGARCH conditional variance is constrained to be non-negative for all observations, regardless of the sign of the parameter estimates. This feature of the EGARCH model simplifies estimation as there is now no need to constrain the parameter estimates to be positive to ensure that the conditional variance is non-negative at each t.

20.4.5   Garch-in-Mean

An important application of the ARCH class of volatility models is in modelling the trade-off between the expected return, μ, and risk, σ, of an asset

$$\mu = \gamma_0 + \varphi \sigma^\rho , \qquad (20.40)$$

where γ_0, φ, ρ are parameters. The relationship between the risk and the expected return of an asset depends upon the attitudes toward risk of asset holders.

Three categories of risk behaviour are identified assuming that $\rho > 0$

$$
\begin{array}{lll}
\text{Risk aversion} & : & \varphi > 0 \\
\text{Risk neutral} & : & \varphi = 0 \\
\text{Risk lover} & : & \varphi < 0 .
\end{array}
\tag{20.41}
$$

The ARCH model provides a natural and convenient way to model the dynamic trade-off between expected return and risk by simply including the conditional standard deviation σ_t, into the conditional mean, μ_t. This model is known as the GARCH-M model and is given by

$$
\begin{aligned}
y_t &= \mu_t + v_t, & v_t &\sim N(0, \sigma_t^2) \\
\mu_t &= \gamma_0 + \varphi \sigma_t^\rho \\
\sigma_t^2 &= \alpha_0 + \alpha_1 v_{t-1}^2 + \beta_1 \sigma_{t-1}^2 .
\end{aligned}
\tag{20.42}
$$

The second equation gives the relationship between the expected return (μ_t) and the risk (σ_t) of an asset, while the third equation gives the dynamics of the conditional variance (σ_t^2) assuming a GARCH(1,1) process.

The parameters $\theta = \{\gamma_0, \varphi, \rho, \alpha_0, \alpha_1 \beta_1\}$ can be estimated by maximum likelihood methods as usual and hypothesis tests can be performed to test the hypotheses embodied, for example, in equation (20.41).

Example 20.7 Risk in the Term Structure of Interest Rates

A GARCH-M model is estimated using daily interest rates on United States zero coupon bonds from 10 October 1988 to 28 December 2001 ($T = 3307$) for the 10-year yield, $r_{10y,t}$, and the 3-month yield, $r_{3m,t}$. The estimated model is

$$
\begin{aligned}
r_{10,t} &= \underset{(0.018)}{2.259} + \underset{(0.003)}{0.776 r_{3m,t}} + \underset{(0.020)}{0.117 \widehat{\sigma}_t^{\,2.071\,(0.211)}} + \widehat{v}_t \\
\widehat{\sigma}_t^2 &= \underset{(0.004)}{0.049} + \underset{(0.019)}{0.962 \widehat{v}_{t-1}^2} + \underset{(0.050)}{0.275 \widehat{\sigma}_{t-1}^2} .
\end{aligned}
$$

Standard errors based on the Hessian are shown in parentheses. The point estimate of $\widehat{\varphi} = 0.117$ is positive, providing evidence of risk aversion. A test of the hypotheses

$$
\begin{array}{lll}
H_0 : & \varphi = 0 & [\text{Risk neutral}] \\
H_1 : & \varphi > 0 & [\text{Risk aversion}],
\end{array}
$$

is based on a Wald test given by the t statistic

$$
t = \frac{0.117 - 0.0}{0.020} = 9.816.
$$

The p-value is 0.000 providing strong evidence against the null of risk neutrality.

□

20.4.6 Diagnostics

A summary of diagnostic tests commonly employed to test the adequacy of (G)ARCH models will complete this section. These tests, which are designed to ascertain whether or not the estimated model captures the nonlinearity in the conditional variance, are usually implemented using the standardised disturbance

$$z_t = \frac{v_t}{\sigma_t},$$

where σ_t is the conditional standard deviation of the model. The role of σ_t in the denominator of z_t is to eliminate the ARCH structure embedded in the disturbance term, v_t. The null and alternative hypotheses are respectively

$$
\begin{aligned}
H_0 &: \quad \text{variance specified correctly} &\quad [\text{No ARCH}] \\
H_1 &: \quad \text{variance not specified correctly} &\quad [\text{ARCH}].
\end{aligned}
$$

Under the null hypothesis, there is no evidence of ARCH in z_t, suggesting that the model is specified correctly. If the statistical evidence favours the alternative hypothesis, the model needs to be re-estimated with a different specification for the conditional variance and the testing procedure repeated. To implement a test of these hypotheses in terms of z_t, v_t is replaced by $\widehat{v}_t$ and σ_t by $\widehat{\sigma}_t$. Four types of diagnostics are presented.

(1) *ARCH test on standardised residuals*

Apply a test for ARCH(q) to the standardised residuals. Evidence of ARCH suggests that the initial specification of σ_t^2 is insufficient to be able to capture all of the dynamics in the conditional variance.

(2) *Overfitting*

Estimate GARCH(p, q) models by increasing the lag order for both p and q and compute the following information criteria (see Chapter 13)

$$
\begin{aligned}
AIC &= -2 \ln L_T + \frac{2k}{T} \\
HIC &= -2 \ln L_T + \frac{2k \ln(\ln T)}{T} \\
SIC &= -2 \ln L_T + \frac{k \ln T}{T},
\end{aligned}
$$

where k is the number of parameters in the model and it is understood that the number of observations, T, is suitably adjusted for the maximum lag order. The best lag order corresponds to where these statistics are minimised.

(3) *Conditional distribution test*

Use a Kolmogorov-Smirnov test to compare the empirical distribution of z_t with the theoretical conditional distribution used to specify the log-likelihood function. Under the null hypothesis of no specification error, the two distributions should not be significantly different from each other.

(4) *Unconditional distribution test*

Use a Kolmogorov-Smirnov test to compare the empirical distribution of y_t with the theoretical unconditional distribution of the model. Under the null hypothesis of no specification error, any differences in two distributions should not be statistically significant. As no analytical solution exists for the unconditional distribution of the ARCH model, one way to make this comparison is to simulate the model several (say 1000) steps ahead and repeat this many times (say 10000). Choosing the last simulated value from each of the replications will yield 10000 draws from the unconditional distribution of the estimated ARCH model and a nonparametric estimate of this distribution can then be obtained using a kernel density estimator.

20.5   Conditional Non-normality

An important feature of the volatility models discussed so far is the role of conditional normality. The combination of conditional normality and GARCH variance yields an unconditional distribution of financial returns that is lepto-kurtotic. In practice, a simple GARCH model specified with normal disturbances is not able to model all of the leptokurtosis in the data. Consequently, there are three common approaches to generalise the GARCH model to account for leptokurtosis.

20.5.1   *Parametric*

The parametric solution to leptokurtosis is to replace the conditional normality specification by a parametric distribution that also exhibits kurtosis. Consider the GARCH(1,1) model

$$y_t = v_t, \qquad v_t = \sigma_t z_t,$$
$$\sigma_t^2 = \alpha_0 + \alpha_1 v_{t-1}^2 + \beta_1 \sigma_{t-1}^2, \qquad (20.43)$$

where the conditional distribution of z_t is chosen as the standardised Student t distribution, $St(0, 1, \nu)$, with ν degrees of freedom and with the property that $E[z_t] = 0$ and $E[z_t^2] = 1$. To derive this distribution, consider the (non-standardised) Student t distribution

$$f(e_t) = \frac{\Gamma\left(\dfrac{\nu + 1}{2}\right)}{\sqrt{\pi \nu}\, \Gamma\left(\dfrac{\nu}{2}\right)} \left(1 + \frac{e_t^2}{\nu}\right)^{-\left(\frac{\nu + 1}{2}\right)},$$

where $E[e_t] = 0$ and $E[e_t^2] = \nu/(\nu - 2)$. Defining the standardised random variable $z_t = e_t/\sqrt{\nu/(\nu - 2)}$, it follows from the transformation of variable technique that

$$
f(z_t) = f(e_t) \left| \frac{de_t}{dz_t} \right| = f\left(z_t \sqrt{\frac{v}{v-2}} \right) \left| \sqrt{\frac{v}{v-2}} \right|.
$$

which yields the standardised Student t distribution

$$
f(z_t) = \frac{\Gamma\left(\frac{v+1}{2} \right)}{\sqrt{\pi(v-2)}\, \Gamma\left(\frac{v}{2} \right)} \left(1 + \frac{z_t^2}{v-2} \right)^{-\left(\frac{v+1}{2} \right)}. \tag{20.44}
$$

The parameter v in (20.44) provides additional flexibility required to model the non-normality in the data. Using equations (20.43) and (20.44), the log-likelihood function is

$$
\ln L_T(\theta) = \frac{1}{T} \sum_{t=1}^{T} \ln l_t(\theta), \tag{20.45}
$$

where

$$
\ln l_t(\theta) = -\frac{1}{2} \ln \sigma_t^2 + \ln f(z_t)
$$

$$
= -\frac{1}{2} \ln \sigma_t^2 + \ln \left(\frac{\Gamma\left(\frac{v+1}{2} \right)}{\sqrt{\pi(v-2)}\, \Gamma\left(\frac{v}{2} \right)} \right) - \frac{(v+1)}{2} \ln \left(1 + \frac{z_t^2}{v-2} \right), \tag{20.46}
$$

and $\theta = \{\alpha_0, \alpha_1, \beta_1, v\}$. Maximising (20.45) may require enforcing the restriction $v > 2$ to circumvent the algorithm breaking down.

To derive the covariance matrix of the maximum likelihood estimator corresponding to (20.46) consider focussing on the GARCH parameters by conditioning on the degrees of freedom parameter, so now $\theta = \{\alpha_0, \alpha_1, \beta_1\}$. The first derivative at observation t is

$$
g_t = \frac{\partial \ln l_t}{\partial \theta} = -\frac{1}{2} \frac{1}{\sigma_t^2} \frac{\partial \sigma_t^2}{\partial \theta} \left(1 - \frac{(v+1)y_t^2}{(\sigma_t^2(v-2) + y_t^2)} \right), \tag{20.47}
$$

where

$$
\frac{\partial \sigma_t^2}{\partial \theta} = \begin{bmatrix} \dfrac{\partial \sigma_t^2}{\partial \alpha_0} \\[2mm] \dfrac{\partial \sigma_t^2}{\partial \alpha_1} \\[2mm] \dfrac{\partial \sigma_t^2}{\partial \beta_1} \end{bmatrix} = \begin{bmatrix} 1 + \beta_1 \dfrac{\partial \sigma_{t-1}^2}{\partial \alpha_0} \\[2mm] y_{t-1}^2 + \beta_1 \dfrac{\partial \sigma_{t-1}^2}{\partial \alpha_1} \\[2mm] \sigma_{t-1}^2 + \beta_1 \dfrac{\partial \sigma_{t-1}^2}{\partial \beta_1} \end{bmatrix}. \tag{20.48}
$$

The covariance matrix is based on $J(\theta) = E[g_t g_t']$, which is consistently estimated by

$$J_T(\widehat{\theta}) = \frac{1}{T}\sum_{t=1}^{T} g_t g_t' = \frac{1}{4}\frac{1}{T}\sum_{t=1}^{T}\left[\left(\frac{1}{\sigma_t^4}\left(1 - \frac{(\nu+1)y_t^2}{(\sigma_t^2(\nu-2)+y_t^2)}\right)^2\right)\frac{\partial\sigma_t^2}{\partial\theta}\frac{\partial\sigma_t^2}{\partial\theta'}\right],$$

$$(20.49)$$

where σ_t^2 in (20.43) and $\partial\sigma_t^2/\partial\theta$ in (20.48) are evaluated at $\theta = \widehat{\theta}$. The estimated covariance matrix is

$$\widehat{\Omega} = J_T^{-1}(\widehat{\theta}),$$

$$(20.50)$$

with $J_T(\widehat{\theta})$ given by (20.49).

20.5.2   Semi-parametric

A semi-parametric approach to dealing with leptokurtosis is to specify the conditional mean and conditional variance equations parametrically but to use a nonparametric density estimator, as discussed in Chapter 11, for the distribution of the disturbance term. Consider extending the GARCH(1, 1) model in (20.43) to allow for a regressor in the mean

$$y_t = \gamma_0 + \gamma_1 x_t + v_t, \qquad v_t = \sigma_t z_t$$
$$\sigma_t^2 = \alpha_0 + \alpha_1 v_{t-1}^2 + \beta_1 \sigma_{t-1}^2,$$

where $f(z_t)$ is to be estimated using nonparametric methods. Estimation would proceed as follows.

Step 1: Choose starting values for the parameters $\theta_{(0)} = \{\gamma_0, \gamma_1, \alpha_0, \alpha_1, \beta_1\}$.
Step 2: For each t construct the conditional mean $\gamma_0 + \gamma_1 x_t$, the residual $v_t = y_t - \gamma_0 - \gamma_1 x_t$ and the conditional variance $\sigma_t^2 = \alpha_0 + \alpha_1 v_{t-1}^2 + \beta_1 \sigma_{t-1}^2$, where all parameters are evaluated at $\theta_{(0)}$.
Step 3: For each t construct the standardised residual

$$z_t = \frac{y_t - \gamma_0 - \gamma_1 x_t}{\sigma_t},$$

with the parameters evaluated at $\theta_{(0)}$.
Step 4: Use a kernel estimator to obtain a nonparametric estimate of the density of the standardised residuals, $f_{np}(z)$. Evaluate $f_{np}(z)$ at each observation and hence compute $f_{np}(z_t)$.
Step 5: For each t compute

$$\ln l_t(\theta) = -0.5 \ln \sigma_t^2 + \ln f_{np}(z_t),$$

and maximise the log-likelihood function for the entire sample using an iterative algorithm.

20.5.3 *Nonparametric*

A simpler approach to dealing with the problem of leptokurtosis is to recognise that the assumption of normally distributed disturbances results in the misspecification of the log-likelihood function. Despite the shape of the distribution being incorrect, the mean and variance of this distribution are, however, correctly specified. From the analysis of Chapter 9, maximum likelihood estimation in terms of the misspecified log-likelihood function yields quasi-maximum likelihood estimators of θ that are consistent. The standard errors of θ, known as Bollerslev-Wooldridge standard errors in this context (Bollerslev and Wooldridge, 1992), are given by the square root of the diagonal elements of

$$\text{cov}(\widehat{\theta}) = \frac{1}{T}\widehat{\Omega} = \frac{1}{T}H_T^{-1}(\widehat{\theta})J_T(\widehat{\theta})H_T^{-1}(\widehat{\theta}), \tag{20.51}$$

where

$$H_T(\widehat{\theta}) = \frac{1}{T}\sum_{t=1}^{T}h_t, \qquad J_T(\widehat{\theta}) = \frac{1}{T}\sum_{t=1}^{T}g_t g_t', \tag{20.52}$$

with g_t and h_t respectively representing the gradient and the Hessian at time t of the misspecified model corresponding to the normal distribution. It is understood that all derivatives are evaluated at $\widehat{\theta}$. The vector $\widehat{\theta}$ represents the quasi-maximum likelihood parameter estimates at the final iteration.

In the case where the true distribution is the Standardised Student t distribution in (20.44), an analytical expression of the quasi-maximum likelihood estimator covariance matrix in (20.51) is available. As the misspecified model is normal, the log-likelihood function at observation t is

$$\ln l_t(\theta) = -\frac{1}{2}\ln 2\pi - \frac{1}{2}\ln \sigma_t^2 - \frac{1}{2}\frac{y_t^2}{\sigma_t^2}. \tag{20.53}$$

For the model in (20.43) where conditioning is again on the degrees of freedom parameter so the parameter vector is $\theta = \{\alpha_0, \alpha_1, \beta_1\}$, the first derivatives and second derivatives in (20.52) are respectively

$$g_t = -\frac{1}{2}\frac{1}{\sigma_t^2}\frac{\partial \sigma_t^2}{\partial \theta}\left(1 - \frac{y_t^2}{\sigma_t^2}\right),$$

$$h_t = -\frac{1}{2}\left(-\frac{1}{\sigma_t^4}\frac{\partial \sigma_t^2}{\partial \theta}\frac{\partial \sigma_t^2}{\partial \theta'}\left(1 - \frac{y_t^2}{\sigma_t^2}\right) + \frac{1}{\sigma_t^2}\frac{\partial^2 \sigma_t^2}{\partial \theta \partial \theta'}\left(1 - \frac{y_t^2}{\sigma_t^2}\right)\right.$$

$$\left. + \frac{1}{\sigma_t^4}\frac{\partial \sigma_t^2}{\partial \theta}\frac{\partial \sigma_t^2}{\partial \theta'}\frac{y_t^2}{\sigma_t^2}\right).$$

To derive the quasi-maximum likelihood estimator covariance matrix of $\widehat{\theta}$, expectations of the derivatives are taken initially with respect to the conditional expectations operator. In the case of the first derivative, it follows that

$$E_{t-1}[g_t] = E_{t-1}\left[-\frac{1}{2}\frac{1}{\sigma_t^2}\frac{\partial \sigma_t^2}{\partial \theta}\left(1 - \frac{y_t^2}{\sigma_t^2}\right)\right] = -\frac{1}{2}\frac{1}{\sigma_t^2}\frac{\partial \sigma_t^2}{\partial \theta}\left(1 - \frac{E_{t-1}[y_t^2]}{\sigma_t^2}\right) = 0\,,$$

because $E_{t-1}[y_t^2]/\sigma_t^2 = E_{t-1}[z_t^2] = 1$ by definition. Using the law of iterated expectations, it immediately follows that $E[E_{t-1}[g_t]] = 0$, which from Chapter 9 establishes that the quasi-maximum likelihood estimator, $\widehat{\theta}$, is a consistent estimator of the true population parameter, θ_0.

For the second derivative

$$E_{t-1}[h_t] = E_{t-1}\left[-\frac{1}{2}\left(-\frac{1}{\sigma_t^4}\frac{\partial \sigma_t^2}{\partial \theta}\frac{\partial \sigma_t^2}{\partial \theta'}\left(1 - \frac{y_t^2}{\sigma_t^2}\right) + \frac{1}{\sigma_t^2}\frac{\partial^2 h_t}{\partial \theta \partial \theta'}\left(1 - \frac{y_t^2}{\sigma_t^2}\right)\right.\right.$$

$$\left.\left.\left(\frac{1}{\sigma_t^4}\frac{\partial \sigma_t^2}{\partial \theta}\frac{\partial \sigma_t^2}{\partial \theta'}\frac{y_t^2}{\sigma_t^2}\right)\right)\right]$$

$$= E_{t-1}\left[-\frac{1}{2}\left(\frac{1}{\sigma_t^4}\frac{\partial \sigma_t^2}{\partial \theta}\frac{\partial \sigma_t^2}{\partial \theta'}\right)\right]\,, \tag{20.54}$$

which again uses the property $E_{t-1}[z_t^2] = E_{t-1}[y_t^2]/\sigma_t^2 = 1$, so the first two terms are zero. Finally, for the outer product of gradients matrix

$$E_{t-1}[g_t g_t'] = E_{t-1}\left[\left(-\frac{1}{2}\frac{1}{\sigma_t^2}\frac{\partial \sigma_t^2}{\partial \theta}\left(1 - \frac{y_t^2}{\sigma_t^2}\right)\right)\left(-\frac{1}{2}\frac{1}{\sigma_t^2}\frac{\partial \sigma_t^2}{\partial \theta'}\left(1 - \frac{y_t^2}{\sigma_t^2}\right)\right)\right]$$

$$= \frac{1}{4}\frac{1}{\sigma_t^4}E_{t-1}\left[\left(1 - \frac{y_t^2}{\sigma_t^2}\right)^2\right]\frac{\partial \sigma_t^2}{\partial \theta}\frac{\partial \sigma_t^2}{\partial \theta'}$$

$$= \frac{1}{4}\frac{1}{\sigma_t^4}\left(2 + \frac{6}{\nu - 4}\right)\frac{\partial \sigma_t^2}{\partial \theta}\frac{\partial \sigma_t^2}{\partial \theta'}\,, \tag{20.55}$$

because

$$E_{t-1}[(1 - y_t^2\sigma_t^{-2})^2] = E_{t-1}[(1 - z_t^2)^2] = E_{t-1}[1 + z_t^4 - 2z_t^2]$$
$$= 1 + E_{t-1}[z_t^4] - 2E_{t-1}[z_t^2] = 2 + 6/(\nu - 4)\,,$$

which uses the properties of the standardised Student t distribution that $E_{t-1}[z_t^2] = 1$ and $E_{t-1}[z_t^4] = 3 + 6/(\nu - 4)$. By using the law of iterated expectations again, the unconditional expectations under the true model of (20.54) and (20.55) are respectively

$$H(\theta_0) = E\left[E_{t-1}[h_t]\right] = E\left[-\frac{1}{2}\left(\frac{1}{\sigma_t^4}\frac{\partial \sigma_t^2}{\partial \theta}\frac{\partial \sigma_t^2}{\partial \theta'}\right)\right]$$

$$J(\theta_0) = E\left[E_{t-1}[g_t g_t']\right] = E\left[\frac{1}{4}\frac{1}{\sigma_t^4}\left(\frac{\partial \sigma_t^2}{\partial \theta}\right)^2\left(2 + \frac{6}{\nu - 4}\right)\right]\,,$$

where $\partial\sigma_t^2/\partial\theta$ is given by (20.48). Consistent estimates of these matrices are obtained as

$$
\begin{aligned}
H_T(\widehat{\theta}) &= -\frac{1}{2}\frac{1}{T}\sum_{t=1}^{T}\frac{1}{\sigma_t^4}\frac{\partial\sigma_t^2}{\partial\theta}\frac{\partial\sigma_t^2}{\partial\theta'} \\
J_T(\widehat{\theta}) &= \frac{1}{4}\left(2+\frac{6}{\nu-4}\right)\frac{1}{T}\sum_{t=1}^{T}\frac{1}{\sigma_t^4}\left(\frac{\partial\sigma_t^2}{\partial\theta}\right)^2 ,
\end{aligned}
\tag{20.56}
$$

where σ_t^2 in (20.43) and $\partial\sigma_t^2/\partial\theta$ in (20.48) are evaluated at $\theta = \widehat{\theta}$. Substituting these expressions into (20.51) yields the estimated quasi-maximum likelihood covariance matrix estimator. In practice, the analytical expressions of H_T and J_T for more general classes of GARCH models with other types of non-normal conditional specifications of the disturbance are derived using numerical derivatives.

Example 20.8 Efficiency Comparisons

Engle and González-Rivera (1991) investigate the relative efficiency properties of the quasi-maximum likelihood estimator in GARCH models where the true conditional distribution is Student t and the misspecified distribution is normal. The results are given in Table 20.3 where the relative efficiency is computed by simulating the GARCH(1,1) model in (20.43) for $T = 10000000$ observations subject to the restriction $\alpha_0 = 1 - \alpha_1 - \beta_1$ and forming the ratio of the diagonal elements of (20.50) and (20.51). The population parameters are $\alpha_1 = 0.1$ and $\beta_1 = 0.8$ and the GARCH intercept is restricted to $a_0 = 1 - \alpha_1 - \beta_1 = 1 - 0.1 - 0.8 = 0.1$. In computing the variances the derivative $\partial\sigma_t^2/\partial\theta$ is computed recursively as

$$
\frac{\partial\sigma_t^2}{\partial\theta} = \begin{bmatrix} \dfrac{\partial\sigma_t^2}{\partial\alpha_1} \\[2mm] \dfrac{\partial\sigma_t^2}{\partial\beta_1} \end{bmatrix} = \begin{bmatrix} -1 + u_{t-1}^2 + \beta_1\dfrac{\partial\sigma_{t-1}^2}{\partial\alpha_1} \\[2mm] -1 + \sigma_{t-1}^2 + \beta_1\dfrac{\partial\sigma_{t-1}^2}{\partial\beta_1} \end{bmatrix} ,
$$

with the startup values of the derivatives set to zero.

For comparative purposes the analytical efficiency ratios taken from Table 1 in González-Rivera and Drost (1999) are also reported. These analytical results are transformed from the original where they are quoted as the percentage change in the quasi-maximum likelihood variance over the maximum likelihood variance. For example, González-Rivera and Drost report a value of 150 for the variance parameters where $\nu = 5$. Transforming this number as $1/(1 + 150/100) = 0.400$ gives the value reported in Table 20.3.

The simulated and analytical relative efficiency results are in strong agreement. For relatively small values of ν there is a large efficiency loss from using the quasi-maximum likelihood estimator in the presence of misspecification.

Table 20.3. *Relative efficiency of the maximum likelihood*
estimator and the quasi-maximum likelihood estimator for
the parameters of a GARCH(1,1) model. Simulated results
are based on T = 10000000 and analytical results are
based on González-Rivera and Drost (1999)

	Simulated		Analytical	
ν	α_1	β_1	α_1	β_1
5	0.400	0.400	0.400	0.400
8	0.787	0.787	0.787	0.787
12	0.911	0.911	0.909	0.909

In the limit as $\nu \to \infty$ the two variances approach each other signifying no
efficiency loss as the extent of the misspecification diminishes.   □

20.6   Multivariate GARCH

The models discussed so far are univariate since they focus on modelling the
variance of the returns on a single financial asset. A natural extension is to
consider a multivariate model and specify both conditional variances as well as
conditional covariances. A simple multivariate specification is

$$ y_t = v_t, \qquad v_t \sim N(0, V_t), $$

where $y_t = [y_{1,t}, y_{2,t}, \cdots, y_{N,t}]'$ is a $(N \times 1)$ vectors of time series, $v_t =$
$[v_{1,t}, v_{2,t}, \cdots, v_{N,t}]'$ is a $(N \times 1)$ vector of disturbance terms and V_t is a
$(N \times N)$ symmetric positive definite matrix containing the variances $(\sigma_{i,i,t})$
on the main diagonal and covariances $(\sigma_{i,j,t})$ on the off diagonals. For $N = 2$,
V_t is

$$ V_t = \begin{bmatrix} \sigma_{1,1,t} & \sigma_{1,2,t} \\ \sigma_{2,1,t} & \sigma_{2,2,t} \end{bmatrix}, $$

where the convention $\sigma_{1,t}^2 = \sigma_{1,1,t}$ and $\sigma_{2,t}^2 = \sigma_{2,2,t}$ is adopted to represent the
conditional variances and $\sigma_{1,2,t} = \sigma_{2,1,t}$ is the conditional covariance.

Assuming conditional normality, the log-likelihood function at time t is

$$ \ln l_t(\theta) = -\frac{N}{2} \ln(2\pi) - \frac{1}{2} \ln |V_t| - \frac{1}{2} v_t' V_t^{-1} v_t . \qquad (20.57) $$

To compute the maximum likelihood estimates two computational problems
arise in the case of MGARCH models. First, the covariance matrix, V_t, must
be positive definite for all t. This is the multivariate analogue of the univariate
GARCH requirement that the conditional variance is positive at each t. The
restrictions needed to satisfy this condition are that the conditional variances

are all positive at each t, $\sigma_{i,i,t}^2 > 0$, and that the determinant of the covariance matrix is positive also at each t, $|V_t| > 0$. These restrictions are necessary from a statistical perspective since V_t represents a covariance matrix and, from a computational perspective, violation of this condition will result in numerical error when computing the term $\ln |V_t|$ in equation (20.57). Second, the number of unknown parameters governing the behaviour of the variances and covariances in MGARCH models increases exponentially as the dimension N increases.

Four multivariate models are discussed each of which, to a greater or lesser degree, deal with these two problems.

(i) The VECH model, which is a direct generalisation of the univariate GARCH model to multiple dimensions.
(ii) The BEKK model of Engle and Kroner (1995), which reduces the parameter dimension of the VECH model and has the advantage that V_t is restricted to be positive definite at each t.
(iii) The DCC model of Engle (2002) and Engle and Sheppard (2001), which reduces the dimension of the unknown parameters of the BEKK model further, thus making estimation of higher dimensional MGARCH models more feasible.
(iv) The DECO model of Engle and Kelly (2009), which further simplifies the DCC model by restricting all correlations to be equal contemporaneously with the result that estimation is simplified dramatically.

20.6.1   VECH

The VECH specification is the simplest and natural multivariate analogue of the univariate GARCH model. For the case of $N = 2$ variables, V_t is specified as

$$
\text{vech}(V_t) = C + A\ \text{vech}(v_{t-1}v_{t-1}') + D\ \text{vech}(V_{t-1}),
$$

$$
\begin{bmatrix} \sigma_{1,1,t} \\ \sigma_{1,2,t} \\ \sigma_{2,2,t} \end{bmatrix} = \begin{bmatrix} c_1 \\ c_2 \\ c_3 \end{bmatrix} + \begin{bmatrix} a_{1,1} & a_{1,2} & a_{1,3} \\ a_{2,1} & a_{2,2} & a_{2,3} \\ a_{3,1} & a_{3,2} & a_{3,3} \end{bmatrix} \begin{bmatrix} v_{1,t-1}^2 \\ v_{1,t-1}v_{2,t-1} \\ v_{2,t-1}^2 \end{bmatrix}
$$
$$
+ \begin{bmatrix} d_{1,1} & d_{1,2} & d_{1,3} \\ d_{2,1} & d_{2,2} & d_{2,3} \\ d_{3,1} & d_{3,2} & d_{3,3} \end{bmatrix} \begin{bmatrix} \sigma_{1,1,t-1} \\ \sigma_{1,2,t-1} \\ \sigma_{2,2,t-1} \end{bmatrix}, \tag{20.58}
$$

where vech($\cdot$) represents the column stacking of the unique elements of a symmetric matrix. The VECH model does not guarantee that V_t will be positive definite at each t and, even in the bivariate case, there are a large number of parameters (21 in total) that need to be estimated.

The total number of parameters for an N dimensional VECH model is made up as follows:

$$C \text{ matrix} \quad : \quad \# \text{ parameters} \quad = \quad \frac{N(N+1)}{2}$$

$$A \text{ matrix} \quad : \quad \# \text{ parameters} \quad = \quad \left(\frac{N(N+1)}{2}\right)^2$$

$$D \text{ matrix} \quad : \quad \# \text{ parameters} \quad = \quad \left(\frac{N(N+1)}{2}\right)^2 ,$$

so that the total number of parameters is

$$\frac{N(N+1)}{2} + \left(\frac{N(N+1)}{2}\right)^2 + \left(\frac{N(N+1)}{2}\right)^2 = \frac{N^4 + 2N^3 + 2N^2 + N}{2} .$$

For the case of $N = 3$ variables, the number of unknown parameters is

$$\frac{N^4 + 2N^3 + 2N^2 + N}{2} = \frac{3^4 + 2 \times 3^3 + 2 \times 3^2 + 3}{2} = 78 ,$$

and for $N = 4$ variables, this number grows to 210.

20.6.2 BEKK

To impose the positive definiteness restriction on V_t while simultaneously reducing the dimension of the parameter vector, the BEKK model is

$$V_t = CC' + A v_{t-1} v'_{t-1} A' + D V_{t-1} D' , \tag{20.59}$$

where C is a $(N \times N)$ lower (Choleski) triangular matrix and A and D are $(N \times N)$ matrices that need not be symmetric.

For illustrative purposes, the matrices of the BEKK model in equation (20.59) are now spelled out for the cases of $N = 1$ and $N = 2$. In the univariate case, the matrices are

$$V_{t-1} = \begin{bmatrix} \sigma_{1,1,t-1} \end{bmatrix}, \quad v_{t-1} = \begin{bmatrix} v_{1,t-1} \end{bmatrix},$$
$$C = \begin{bmatrix} c_{1,1} \end{bmatrix}, \quad A = \begin{bmatrix} a_{1,1} \end{bmatrix}, \quad D = \begin{bmatrix} d_{1,1} \end{bmatrix} ,$$

with V_t having the form

$$V_t = \begin{bmatrix} c_{1,1} \end{bmatrix} \begin{bmatrix} c_{1,1} \end{bmatrix}' + \begin{bmatrix} a_{1,1} \end{bmatrix} \begin{bmatrix} v_{1,t-1} \end{bmatrix} \begin{bmatrix} v_{1,t-1} \end{bmatrix}' \begin{bmatrix} a_{1,1} \end{bmatrix}'$$
$$+ \begin{bmatrix} d_{1,1} \end{bmatrix} \begin{bmatrix} \sigma_{1,1,t-1} \end{bmatrix} \begin{bmatrix} d_{1,1} \end{bmatrix}'$$
$$= c_{1,1}^2 + a_{1,1}^2 v_{1,t-1}^2 + d_{1,1}^2 \sigma_{1,1,t-1} .$$

This is just a univariate GARCH model with three parameters that are all restricted to be positive because they are specified in terms of squares.

With $N = 2$, the matrices of the BEKK model in equation (20.59) are

$$V_{t-1} = \begin{bmatrix} \sigma_{1,1,t-1} & \sigma_{1,2,t-1} \\ \sigma_{1,2,t-1} & \sigma_{2,2,t-1} \end{bmatrix}, \quad v_{t-1} = \begin{bmatrix} v_{1,t-1} \\ v_{2,t-1} \end{bmatrix},$$

$$C = \begin{bmatrix} c_{1,1} & 0 \\ c_{2,1} & c_{2,2} \end{bmatrix}, \quad A = \begin{bmatrix} a_{1,1} & a_{1,2} \\ a_{2,1} & a_{2,2} \end{bmatrix}, \quad D = \begin{bmatrix} d_{1,1} & d_{1,2} \\ d_{2,1} & d_{2,2} \end{bmatrix}.$$

The matrix V_t has the form

$$V_t = \begin{bmatrix} c_{1,1} & 0 \\ c_{2,1} & c_{2,2} \end{bmatrix} \begin{bmatrix} c_{1,1} & 0 \\ c_{2,1} & c_{2,2} \end{bmatrix}'$$
$$+ \begin{bmatrix} a_{1,1} & a_{1,2} \\ a_{2,1} & a_{2,2} \end{bmatrix} \begin{bmatrix} v_{1,t-1} \\ v_{2,t-1} \end{bmatrix} \begin{bmatrix} v_{1,t-1} \\ v_{2,t-1} \end{bmatrix}' \begin{bmatrix} a_{1,1} & a_{1,2} \\ a_{2,1} & a_{2,2} \end{bmatrix}'$$
$$+ \begin{bmatrix} d_{1,1} & d_{1,2} \\ d_{2,1} & d_{2,2} \end{bmatrix} \begin{bmatrix} \sigma_{1,1,t-1} & \sigma_{1,2,t-1} \\ \sigma_{1,2,t-1} & \sigma_{2,2,t-1} \end{bmatrix} \begin{bmatrix} d_{1,1} & d_{1,2} \\ d_{2,1} & d_{2,2} \end{bmatrix}',$$

which is simplified as

$$V_t = \begin{bmatrix} c_{1,1} & 0 \\ c_{2,1} & c_{2,2} \end{bmatrix} \begin{bmatrix} c_{1,1} & c_{2,1} \\ 0 & c_{2,2} \end{bmatrix}$$
$$+ \begin{bmatrix} a_{1,1} & a_{1,2} \\ a_{2,1} & a_{2,2} \end{bmatrix} \begin{bmatrix} v_{1,t-1}^2 & v_{1,t-1}v_{2,t-1} \\ v_{1,t-1}v_{2,t-1} & v_{2,t-1}^2 \end{bmatrix} \begin{bmatrix} a_{1,1} & a_{2,1} \\ a_{1,2} & a_{2,2} \end{bmatrix}$$
$$+ \begin{bmatrix} d_{1,1} & d_{1,2} \\ d_{2,1} & d_{2,2} \end{bmatrix} \begin{bmatrix} \sigma_{1,1,t-1} & \sigma_{1,2,t-1} \\ \sigma_{1,2,t-1} & \sigma_{2,2,t-1} \end{bmatrix} \begin{bmatrix} d_{1,1} & d_{2,1} \\ d_{1,2} & d_{2,2} \end{bmatrix}.$$

The number of unknown parameters is 11 compared to 21 parameters in the VECH specification given in equation (20.58).

The number of unknown parameters may be further reduced by restricting the A and D parameter matrices to be symmetric

$$A = \begin{bmatrix} a_{1,1} & a_{1,2} \\ a_{1,2} & a_{2,2} \end{bmatrix}, \quad D = \begin{bmatrix} d_{1,1} & d_{1,2} \\ d_{1,2} & d_{2,2} \end{bmatrix}. \tag{20.60}$$

These restrictions can be tested by performing a LR test of

$$a_{1,2} = a_{2,1}, \qquad d_{1,2} = d_{2,1}.$$

Another class of models is to assume that the covariance is constant. The restrictions to be tested for the asymmetric BEKK model are

$$a_{1,2} = a_{2,1} = d_{1,2} = d_{2,1} = 0.$$

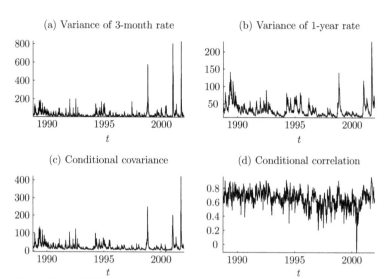

Figure 20.6. BEKK estimates of the conditional variances, the covariance and the correlation of the changes in the yields on 3-month and 1-year United States zero coupon bonds.

Example 20.9 Bivariate BEKK Model of Interest Rates

Consider the bivariate asymmetric BEKK model

$$
\begin{aligned}
y_{1,t} &= \gamma_1 + v_{1,t} \\
y_{2,t} &= \gamma_2 + v_{2,t} \\
V_t &= CC' + A v_{t-1} v'_{t-1} A' + D V_{t-1} D' \\
v_t &\sim N(0, V_t).
\end{aligned}
$$

The model is estimated using the same data as in Example 20.7, where now $y_{1,t}$ and $y_{2,t}$ are, respectively, the daily changes on the yields of 3-month and 1-year United States zero coupon bonds, expressed in basis points ($T = 3306$). The estimated parameter matrices are

$$
\widehat{\gamma} = \begin{bmatrix} \widehat{\gamma}_1 \\ \widehat{\gamma}_2 \end{bmatrix} = \begin{bmatrix} 0.060 \\ 0.059 \end{bmatrix}, \qquad \widehat{C} = \begin{bmatrix} 1.071 & 0.000 \\ 0.285 & 0.567 \end{bmatrix},
$$

$$
\widehat{A} = \begin{bmatrix} 0.385 & 0.049 \\ 0.008 & 0.224 \end{bmatrix}, \qquad \widehat{D} = \begin{bmatrix} 0.881 & 0.027 \\ -0.006 & 0.973 \end{bmatrix},
$$

with a log-likelihood value of $\ln L_T(\widehat{\theta}) = -5.807$. Time series plots of the two conditional variances and the covariance are given in Figures 20.6 as well as the conditional correlation given by

$$
r_{1,2,t} = \frac{\sigma_{1,2,t}}{\sqrt{\sigma_{1,1,t}\sigma_{2,2,t}}}.
$$

A test of a constant covariance between the two interest rates is based on estimating the model subject to the restrictions $a_{1,2} = a_{2,1} = d_{1,2} = d_{2,1} = 0$. The log-likelihood value of the restricted model is $\ln L_T(\widehat{\theta}_0) = -5.814$. The LR test statistic is

$$LR = -2T(\ln L_T(\widehat{\theta}_0) - \ln L_T(\widehat{\theta}_1)) = -2 \times 3306(-5.814 + 5.807) = 44.485,$$

which is distributed as χ_4^2 under the null hypothesis. The p-value is 0.000, leading to a strong rejection of the null hypothesis. □

20.6.3 DCC

The Dynamic Conditional Correlation (DCC) model imposes positive definiteness on V_t and achieves a large reduction in the number of parameters by specifying univariate conditional GARCH variances $\sigma_{i,t}^2$ together with a parsimonious conditional correlation matrix, R_t. The conditional covariance matrix is recovered from

$$V_t = S_t R_t S_t , \qquad (20.61)$$

where R_t is a $(N \times N)$ conditional correlation matrix and S_t is a diagonal matrix containing the conditional standard deviations along the main diagonal

$$S_t = \begin{bmatrix} \sigma_{1,t} & & 0 \\ & \ddots & \\ 0 & & \sigma_{N,t} \end{bmatrix} . \qquad (20.62)$$

The conditional variances have univariate GARCH representations

$$\sigma_{i,t}^2 = \alpha_{0,i} + \alpha_{1,i} v_{i,t-1}^2 + \beta_{1,i} \sigma_{i,t-1}^2 . \qquad (20.63)$$

The specification of the conditional correlation matrix R_t is given by

$$R_t = \mathrm{diag}(Q_t)^{-1/2} Q_t \, \mathrm{diag}(Q_t)^{-1/2} , \qquad (20.64)$$

where Q_t has the GARCH(1,1) specification

$$Q_t = (1 - \alpha - \beta)\overline{Q} + \alpha z_{t-1} z_{t-1}' + \beta Q_{t-1} , \qquad (20.65)$$

which is a function of just two unknown scalar parameters α and β, and the unconditional covariance matrix of the standardised residuals

$$z_{i,t} = \frac{v_{i,t}}{\sigma_{i,t}} ,$$

which is given by

$$
\overline{Q} = \frac{1}{T} \sum_{t=1}^{T}
\begin{bmatrix}
z_{1,t}^2 & z_{1,t}z_{2,t} & \cdots & z_{1,t}z_{N,t} \\
z_{2,t}z_{1,t} & z_{2,t}^2 & \cdots & z_{2,t}z_{N,t} \\
\vdots & \vdots & \ddots & \vdots \\
z_{N,t}z_{1,t} & z_{N,t}z_{2,t} & \cdots & z_{N,t}^2
\end{bmatrix}.
\tag{20.66}
$$

A special case of the DCC model is the constant correlation matrix that arises when $\alpha = \beta = 0$. These restrictions can be tested using a LR test.

Example 20.10 Bivariate DCC Model

For illustrative purposes, it is useful to outline the construction of the conditional covariance matrix of the DCC model for the 2 asset case.

Step 1: Estimate univariate GARCH(1, 1) models for the two assets

$$
\sigma_{1,t}^2 = \alpha_{0,1} + \alpha_{1,1}v_{1,t-1}^2 + \beta_{1,i}\sigma_{1,t-1}^2
$$
$$
\sigma_{2,t}^2 = \alpha_{0,2} + \alpha_{1,2}v_{2,t-1}^2 + \beta_{2,i}\sigma_{2,t-1}^2 ,
$$

and construct the matrix

$$
S_t =
\begin{bmatrix}
\sigma_{1,t} & 0 \\
0 & \sigma_{2,t}
\end{bmatrix}.
$$

Step 2: Compute the standardised residuals

$$
\begin{bmatrix}
z_{1,t} \\
z_{2,t}
\end{bmatrix}
= S_t^{-1}u_t =
\begin{bmatrix}
\dfrac{1}{\sigma_{1,t}} & 0 \\
0 & \dfrac{1}{\sigma_{2,t}}
\end{bmatrix}
\begin{bmatrix}
v_{1,t} \\
v_{2,t}
\end{bmatrix}
=
\begin{bmatrix}
\dfrac{v_{1,t}}{\sigma_{1,t}} \\
\dfrac{v_{2,t}}{\sigma_{2,t}}
\end{bmatrix}.
$$

Step 3: Compute $\overline{Q}$

$$
\overline{Q} =
\begin{bmatrix}
\overline{\rho}_{1,1} & \overline{\rho}_{1,2} \\
\overline{\rho}_{1,2} & \overline{\rho}_{2,2}
\end{bmatrix}
= \frac{1}{T} \sum_{t=1}^{T}
\begin{bmatrix}
z_{1,t}^2 & z_{1,t}z_{2,t} \\
z_{2,t}z_{1,t} & z_{2,t}^2
\end{bmatrix},
$$

and use the result to construct the elements of the matrix Q using a simple GARCH(1, 1) specification for the conditional correlations. The relevant equations are, respectively,

$$
q_{1,1,t} = \overline{\rho}_{1,1}(1 - \alpha - \beta) + \alpha z_{1,t-1}z_{1,t-1} + \beta q_{1,1,t-1}
$$
$$
q_{2,2,t} = \overline{\rho}_{2,2}(1 - \alpha - \beta) + \alpha z_{2,t-1}z_{2,t-1} + \beta q_{2,2,t-1}
$$
$$
q_{1,2,t} = \overline{\rho}_{1,2}(1 - \alpha - \beta) + \alpha z_{1,t-1}z_{2,t-1} + \beta q_{1,2,t-1} .
$$

Step 4: Construct the matrix of conditional correlations

$$
R_t = \begin{bmatrix} \dfrac{1}{\sqrt{q_{1,1,t}}} & 0 \\ 0 & \dfrac{1}{\sqrt{q_{2,2,t}}} \end{bmatrix} \begin{bmatrix} q_{1,1,t} & q_{1,2,t} \\ q_{1,2,t} & q_{2,2,t} \end{bmatrix} \begin{bmatrix} \dfrac{1}{\sqrt{q_{1,1,t}}} & 0 \\ 0 & \dfrac{1}{\sqrt{q_{2,2,t}}} \end{bmatrix}
$$

$$
= \begin{bmatrix} 1 & \dfrac{q_{1,2,t}}{\sqrt{q_{1,1,t} q_{2,2,t}}} \\ \dfrac{q_{1,2,t}}{\sqrt{q_{1,1,t} q_{2,2,t}}} & 1 \end{bmatrix}.
$$

Step 5: The estimate of the conditional covariance matrix is then

$$
V_t = \begin{bmatrix} \sigma_{1,t} & 0 \\ 0 & \sigma_{2,t} \end{bmatrix} \begin{bmatrix} 1 & \rho_{1,2,t} \\ \rho_{1,2,t} & 1 \end{bmatrix} \begin{bmatrix} \sigma_{1,t} & 0 \\ 0 & \sigma_{2,t} \end{bmatrix}
$$

$$
= \begin{bmatrix} \sigma_{1,t}^2 & \rho_{1,2,t}\sigma_{1,t}\sigma_{2,t} \\ \rho_{1,2,t}\sigma_{1,t}\sigma_{2,t} & \sigma_{2,t}^2 \end{bmatrix}.
$$

□

Maximum Likelihood Estimation: Small N

Let the parameter vector be partitioned into $\theta = \{\theta_1, \theta_2\}$, where θ_1 are the volatility parameters and $\theta_2 = \{\alpha, \beta\}$ are the correlation parameters. Using expression (20.61) for V_t in (20.57), the log-likelihood function at observation t is

$$
\ln l_t(\theta) = -\frac{N}{2}\ln(2\pi) - \frac{1}{2}\ln|S_t R_t S_t| - \frac{1}{2}v_t'[S_t R_t S_t]^{-1} v_t. \quad (20.67)
$$

Using the results $|AB| = |A||B|$ and $[AB]^{-1} = B^{-1}A^{-1}$, expression (20.67) is rearranged into two components given by

$$
\ln l_t(\theta) = -\frac{N}{2}\ln(2\pi) - \frac{1}{2}(2\ln|S_t| + \ln|R_t|) - \frac{1}{2}z_t'R_t^{-1}z_t
$$

$$
= -\frac{N}{2}\ln(2\pi) - \frac{1}{2}\ln|S_t|^2 - \frac{1}{2}\ln|R_t| - \frac{1}{2}z_t'R_t^{-1}z_t,
$$

where $z_t = S_t^{-1} v_t$ is the standardised variable. Since $z_t' z_t = v_t' S_t^{-1} S_t^{-1} v_t$, adding and subtracting $z_t' z_t / 2$ gives

$$
\begin{aligned}
\ln l_t(\theta) &= -\frac{N}{2} \ln(2\pi) - \frac{1}{2} \ln |S_t|^2 - \frac{1}{2} \ln |R_t| - \frac{1}{2} z_t' R_t^{-1} z_t \\
&\quad - \frac{1}{2} (v_t' S_t^{-1} S_t^{-1} v_t - z_t' z_t) \\
&= -\frac{N}{2} \ln(2\pi) - \frac{1}{2} \ln |S_t|^2 - \frac{1}{2} v_t' S_t^{-1} S_t^{-1} v_t - \frac{1}{2} \ln |R_t| \\
&\quad - \frac{1}{2} z_t' R_t^{-1} z_t + \frac{1}{2} z_t' z_t \\
&= \ln l_{1,t}(\theta_1) + \ln l_{2,t}(\theta_1, \theta_2),
\end{aligned}
\tag{20.68}
$$

where

$$
\ln l_{1,t}(\theta_1) = -\frac{N}{2} \ln(2\pi) - \frac{1}{2} \ln |S_t|^2 - \frac{1}{2} v_t' S_t^{-2} v_t,
\tag{20.69}
$$

contains just the GARCH parameters and

$$
\ln l_{2,t}(\theta_1, \theta_2) = -\frac{1}{2} \ln |R_t| - \frac{1}{2} z_t' R_t^{-1} z_t + \frac{1}{2} z_t' z_t,
\tag{20.70}
$$

contains the GARCH and correlation parameters.

From (20.68), the full log-likelihood function is

$$
\begin{aligned}
\ln L_T(\theta) &= \frac{1}{T} \sum_{t=1}^{T} \ln l_{1,t}(\theta_1) + \frac{1}{T} \sum_{t=1}^{T} \ln l_{2,t}(\theta_1, \theta_2) \\
&= \ln L_{1,T}(\theta_1) + \ln L_{2,T}(\theta_1, \theta_2).
\end{aligned}
\tag{20.71}
$$

The gradient is

$$
G_T(\theta) = \begin{bmatrix} \dfrac{\partial \ln L_T(\theta)}{\partial \theta_1} \\[2ex] \dfrac{\partial \ln L_T(\theta)}{\partial \theta_2} \end{bmatrix} = \begin{bmatrix} \dfrac{\partial \ln L_1(\theta_1)}{\partial \theta_1} + \dfrac{\partial \ln L_2(\theta_1, \theta_2)}{\partial \theta_1} \\[2ex] \dfrac{\partial \ln L_2(\theta_1, \theta_2)}{\partial \theta_2} \end{bmatrix},
\tag{20.72}
$$

and the Hessian is

$$
H_T(\theta) = \begin{bmatrix} \dfrac{\partial^2 \ln L_T(\theta)}{\partial \theta_1 \partial \theta_1'} & \dfrac{\partial^2 \ln L_T(\theta)}{\partial \theta_1 \partial \theta_2'} \\[2ex] \dfrac{\partial^2 \ln L_T(\theta)}{\partial \theta_2 \partial \theta_1'} & \dfrac{\partial^2 \ln L_T(\theta)}{\partial \theta_2 \partial \theta_2'} \end{bmatrix} = \begin{bmatrix} \dfrac{\partial^2 \ln L_1}{\partial \theta_1 \partial \theta_1'} + \dfrac{\partial^2 \ln L_2}{\partial \theta_1 \partial \theta_1'} & \dfrac{\partial^2 \ln L_2}{\partial \theta_1 \partial \theta_2'} \\[2ex] \dfrac{\partial^2 \ln L_2}{\partial \theta_2 \partial \theta_1'} & \dfrac{\partial^2 \ln L_2}{\partial \theta_2 \partial \theta_2'} \end{bmatrix}.
$$

As with the BEKK model, for relatively small values of N, standard iterative algorithms can be used to maximise (20.71) with respect to θ. The total number of unknown parameters is $3N + 2$, consisting of the $3N$ univariate GARCH parameters in (20.63) and the correlation parameters α and β in (20.65). For larger values of N this approach may not be feasible.

Two-step Estimation: Large N

For large N, a two-step estimator has significant computational advantages. This estimator proceeds as follows.

Step 1: *Volatility parameters (θ_1)*

In the first step the log-likelihood function in (20.69) is maximised with respect to the GARCH parameters by solving

$$\frac{\partial \ln L_1(\theta_1)}{\partial \theta_1}\bigg|_{\theta_1 = \widehat{\theta}_1} = 0 .$$

Since S_t is a diagonal matrix, $|S_t|$ is simply the product of the diagonal elements, the log-likelihood function in equation (20.69) decomposes into N separate components

$$\ln l_{1,t}(\theta_1) = -\frac{1}{2} \sum_{i=1}^{N} \left(\ln(2\pi) + \ln \sigma_{i,t}^2 + \frac{v_{i,t}^2}{\sigma_{i,t}^2} \right) , \tag{20.73}$$

suggesting that the volatility parameters in each GARCH equation can be estimated individually.

Step 2: *Correlation parameters (θ_2)*

The second step involves maximising (20.70) to obtain consistent estimates of the conditional correlation parameters α and β, given the estimates of the GARCH parameters in the first step, by solving

$$\frac{\partial \ln L_2(\widehat{\theta}_1, \theta_2)}{\partial \theta_2}\bigg|_{\theta_2 = \widehat{\theta}_2} = 0 .$$

As z_t does not contain θ_2, the expression to be maximised is simply

$$\ln L_{2,t}(\theta_2) = -\frac{1}{2} \ln |R_t| - \frac{1}{2} z_t' R_t^{-1} z_t . \tag{20.74}$$

The two-step estimator is consistent, but not asymptotically efficient because the full log-likelihood function is not maximised with respect to all parameters. This occurs as the second step ignores the term $\partial \ln L_2 / \partial \theta_1$ in the first element of the gradient vector in (20.72) by treating the volatility parameters as fixed. Moreover, the standard errors of $\widehat{\theta}$ obtained from estimating θ_1 and θ_2 separately are not correct as a result of treating $\widehat{\theta}_1$ as fixed at the second step. It is, in fact, just the standard errors on $\widehat{\theta}_2$ that are not correct, because the standard errors on the volatility parameters, $\widehat{\theta}_1$, from estimating the GARCH equations separately in the first step are correct.

To derive the correct standard errors for the two-step estimator, the gradients of this estimator are written as

$$G_1(\theta_1) = \frac{\partial \ln L_1(\theta_1)}{\partial \theta_1}$$

$$G_2(\theta_1, \theta_2) = \frac{\partial \ln L_2(\theta_1, \theta_2)}{\partial \theta_2},$$

$$(20.75)$$

where $\widehat{\theta}_1$ is replaced by θ_1 in the expression for G_2 so as to derive the correct standard error. The corresponding Hessian is block-triangular

$$H_T(\theta) = \begin{bmatrix} \dfrac{\partial G_1}{\partial \theta_1} & \dfrac{\partial G_1}{\partial \theta_2'} \\[2mm] \dfrac{\partial G_2}{\partial \theta_1} & \dfrac{\partial G_2}{\partial \theta_2'} \end{bmatrix} = \begin{bmatrix} H_{11} & 0 \\ H_{21} & H_{22} \end{bmatrix}.$$

From the properties of partitioned inverses it follows that

$$H_T^{-1}(\theta) = \begin{bmatrix} H_{11} & 0 \\ H_{21} & H_{22} \end{bmatrix}^{-1} = \begin{bmatrix} H_{11}^{-1} & 0 \\ -H_{22}^{-1} H_{21} H_{11}^{-1} & H_{22}^{-1} \end{bmatrix}$$

$$= \begin{bmatrix} H_{11}^{-1} & 0 \\ -H_{22}^{-1} \Psi & H_{22}^{-1} \end{bmatrix},$$

where $\Psi = H_{21} H_{11}^{-1}$. Defining $J_T(\theta)$ as the outer product of gradients matrix associated with (20.75), the quasi-maximum likelihood covariance matrix is

$$\widehat{\Omega} = H_T^{-1}(\widehat{\theta}) J_T(\widehat{\theta}) H_T^{-1}(\widehat{\theta})'$$

$$= \begin{bmatrix} H_{11}^{-1} & 0 \\ -H_{22}^{-1}\Psi & H_{22}^{-1} \end{bmatrix} \begin{bmatrix} J_{11} & J_{12} \\ J_{21} & J_{22} \end{bmatrix} \begin{bmatrix} H_{11}^{-1} & 0 \\ -H_{22}^{-1}\Psi & H_{22}^{-1} \end{bmatrix}'$$

$$= \begin{bmatrix} H_{11}^{-1} J_{11} & H_{11}^{-1} J_{12} \\ -H_{22}^{-1}\Psi J_{11} + H_{22}^{-1} J_{21} & -H_{22}^{-1}\Psi J_{12} + H_{22}^{-1} J_{22} \end{bmatrix} \begin{bmatrix} H_{11}^{-1} & -\Psi' H_{22}^{-1} \\ 0 & H_{22}^{-1} \end{bmatrix}$$

$$= \begin{bmatrix} \widehat{\omega}_{11} & \widehat{\omega}_{12} \\ \widehat{\omega}_{21} & \widehat{\omega}_{22} \end{bmatrix}, \qquad (20.76)$$

where

$$\widehat{\omega}_{11} = H_{11}^{-1} J_{11} H_{11}^{-1}$$

$$\widehat{\omega}_{12} = -H_{11}^{-1} J_{11} \Psi' H_{22}^{-1} + H_{11}^{-1} J_{12} H_{22}^{-1}$$

$$\widehat{\omega}_{21} = -H_{22}^{-1} \Psi J_{11} H_{11}^{-1} + H_{22}^{-1} J_{21} H_{11}^{-1}$$

$$\widehat{\omega}_{22} = H_{22}^{-1} (J_{22} - J_{21} \Psi' - \Psi J_{12} + \Psi J_{11} \Psi') H_{22}^{-1}.$$

From the block-diagonal components of (20.76), the correct covariance matrices of the two-step estimator are

$$\widehat{\Omega}(\widehat{\theta}_1) = H_{11}^{-1} J_{11} H_{11}^{-1} \tag{20.77}$$

$$\widehat{\Omega}(\widehat{\theta}_2) = H_{22}^{-1}(J_{22} - J_{21}\Psi' - \Psi J_{12} + \Psi J_{11}\Psi')H_{22}^{-1}. \tag{20.78}$$

From (20.73), $\widehat{\Omega}(\widehat{\theta}_1)$ is also block diagonal and the quasi-maximum likelihood covariance matrices from estimating each GARCH equation separately in the first step are correct. Also note that only in the special case of

$$\widehat{\omega}_{12} = -H_{11}^{-1} J_{11} \Psi' H_{22}^{-1} + H_{11}^{-1} J_{12} H_{22}^{-1} = 0,$$

is the quasi-maximum likelihood covariance matrix at the second step correct. Finally, standard errors, $\text{se}(\widehat{\theta})$, are computed as the square roots of the diagonal elements of the normalized covariance matrix

$$\text{cov}(\widehat{\theta}) = \frac{1}{T}\widehat{\Omega}.$$

20.6.4 DECO

The key assumption underlying the Dynamic Equicorrelation (DECO) model of Engle and Kelly (2009) is that the unconditional correlation matrix of systems of financial returns has entries of roughly similar magnitude. The correlations of the DCC model in (20.64) are therefore assumed to be equal contemporaneously across all N variables, but not over time. The pertinent restrictions on the correlation matrix are

$$R_t = \begin{bmatrix} 1 & r_{1,2,t} & \cdots & r_{1,N,t} \\ r_{2,1,t} & 1 & \cdots & \vdots \\ \vdots & \vdots & \ddots & r_{N-1,N,t} \\ r_{N,1,t} & \cdots & r_{N,N-1,t} & 1 \end{bmatrix} = \begin{bmatrix} 1 & \bar{r}_t & \cdots & \bar{r}_t \\ \bar{r}_t & 1 & \cdots & \vdots \\ \vdots & \vdots & \ddots & \bar{r}_t \\ \bar{r}_t & \cdots & \bar{r}_t & 1 \end{bmatrix},$$

where $\bar{r}_t$ represents the average of the $N(N-1)/2$ correlations at time t in (20.64)

$$\bar{r}_t = \frac{2}{N(N-1)} \sum_{i>j} r_{i,j,t}.$$

The advantage of the DECO restrictions on the correlation matrix is that, as N increases, it becomes relatively easier to maximise the log-likelihood function corresponding to the correlation component of the DECO model in

(20.71). Rewriting these restrictions shows that

$$
R_t = (1 - \bar{r}_t)
\begin{bmatrix}
1 & 0 & \cdots & 0 \\
0 & 1 & \cdots & \vdots \\
\vdots & \vdots & \ddots & 0 \\
0 & 0 & \cdots & 1
\end{bmatrix}
+ \bar{r}_t
\begin{bmatrix}
1 & 1 & \cdots & 1 \\
1 & 1 & \cdots & \vdots \\
\vdots & \vdots & \ddots & 1 \\
1 & 1 & \cdots & 1
\end{bmatrix}
= (1 - \bar{r}_t) I_N + \bar{r}_t O_N ,
$$

where I_N is the identity matrix and O_N is a $(N \times N)$ matrix of ones. This form of the correlation matrix, R_t, has the following analytical properties

$$
|R_t| = (1 - \bar{r}_t)^{N-1} (1 + (N-1)\bar{r}_t)
$$

$$
R_t^{-1} = \frac{1}{1 - \bar{r}_t} I_N - \frac{\bar{r}_t}{(1 - \bar{r}_t)(1 + (N-1)\bar{r}_t)} O_N .
$$

Substituting these expressions in equation (20.70) simplifies the computation of the log-likelihood function since now no large determinants or inverses need to be computed at each t.

20.7 Applications

In this section, two applications based on multivariate methods for volatility modelling are presented. The first is a simple implementation of the DCC and DECO models using United States data, and the second illustrates how the SVAR models of Chapter 14 can be augmented to allow the shocks to have a time-varying conditional variance.

20.7.1   DCC and DECO Models of United States Yields

Let $y_{1,t}, y_{2,t} \cdots, y_{5,t}$ be daily observations on the changes in United States zero coupon yields with maturities 1, 5, 10, 15 and 20 years, respectively, which are transformed to have zero mean. The data are for the period 3 January 2000 to 21 August 2006.

Table 20.4 gives parameter estimates of the DCC and DECO models.

(i) The parameter estimates for the individual GARCH models for each yield, $\alpha_{0,i}$, $\alpha_{1,i}$ and $\beta_{1,i}$ correspond to the specification given in (20.63). The $\alpha_{1,i}$ and $\beta_{1,i}$ parameters are initially transformed to be constrained in the unit circle and then untransformed at the final iteration to obtain the appropriate standard errors.

(ii) The parameters corresponding to the correlation specification in (20.65) taken to be α and β are given in the second last row of Table 20.4.

The results indicate that the correlation parameter estimates of α and β are statistically significant for the DCC model, whereas just the estimate of β is

Table 20.4. *Maximum likelihood estimates of the DCC and DECO models of daily changes in United States zero coupon yields, expressed in basis points, with maturities 1, 5, 10, 15 and 20 years. The data period is 3 January 2000 to 21 August 2006. Quasi-maximum likelihood standard errors in parentheses assuming heteroskedasticity*

Yield	DCC			DECO		
	$\alpha_{0,i}$	$\alpha_{1,i}$	$\beta_{1,i}$	$\alpha_{0,i}$	$\alpha_{1,i}$	$\beta_{1,i}$
1-year	0.771	0.108	0.873	1.006	0.152	0.843
	(0.209)	(0.021)	(0.022)	(0.329)	(0.047)	(0.036)
5-year	1.514	0.069	0.898	0.792	0.065	0.912
	(0.337)	(0.014)	(0.016)	(0.351)	(0.019)	(0.025)
10-year	1.548	0.059	0.899	0.631	0.054	0.920
	(0.308)	(0.012)	(0.014)	(0.265)	(0.013)	(0.020)
15-year	1.633	0.054	0.895	0.814	0.055	0.913
	(0.324)	(0.010)	(0.013)	(0.359)	(0.014)	(0.024)
20-year	1.446	0.046	0.902	0.796	0.055	0.912
	(0.323)	(0.010)	(0.014)	(0.370)	(0.015)	(0.026)
Correlation		0.074	0.942		0.180	0.953
		(0.024)	(0.014)		(0.253)	(0.031)
	$\ln L = -8.654$			$\ln L = -12.218$		

statistically significant for the DECO model. Setting the correlation parameters of the DCC model to zero yields $\ln L_T(\widehat{\theta}_0) = -9.074$. A joint test of constant correlation is given by the LR statistic

$$LR = -2T(\ln L_T(\widehat{\theta}_0) - \ln L_T(\widehat{\theta}_1))$$
$$= -2 \times 1658(-9.074 + 8.654) = 1395.218,$$

which is distributed as χ_2^2 under the null hypothesis. The p-value is 0.000, leading to a strong rejection of the null hypothesis of a constant correlation matrix. A comparison of the DCC and DECO parameter estimates indicates a large degree of similarity between the two sets of estimates. A plot of the average correlation of the five interest rates for the DECO model given in Figure 20.7 shows that it is relatively stable over the sample, varying between 0.85 and 0.95.

20.7.2 A Time-Varying Volatility SVAR Model

The following application uses an SVAR model with short-run restrictions to estimate a model for the 3-month United Kingdom LIBOR rate. The data are for the period 1 January 2004 to 28 May 2008. An important feature of the

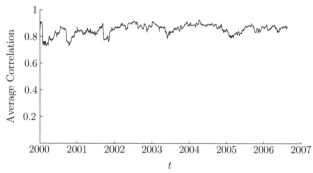

Figure 20.7. DECO estimate of the average correlation of United States zero-coupon yields, 3 January 2000 to 21 August 2006.

model is an allowance for the structural shocks to have time-varying conditional volatilities thereby providing an alternative method for modelling multivariate GARCH models.

Let y_t contain the following six variables: the VIX index which is a measure of volatility constructed from European put and call option prices such that at any given time it reflects the risk-neutral expectation of the integrated variance averaged over the next 30 calendar days (or 22 trading days); the on-off run United States 5-year spread which provides a measure of liquidity in the market; the GBP/USD swap rate; the REPO spread which is a measure of credit spreads; a measure of the default risk for the United Kingdom; and the 3-month United Kingdom LIBOR rate spread.

Consider the following dynamic structural model of y_t

$$B_0 y_t = B_1 y_{t-1} + B_2 y_{t-2} + \cdots + B_k y_{t-k} + u_t \tag{20.79}$$

$$\mathrm{E}[u_t] = 0, \qquad \mathrm{E}[u_t u_t'] = D_t, \qquad \mathrm{E}[u_t u_s'] = 0, t \neq s \tag{20.80}$$

$$\sigma_{i,t}^2 = \delta_i + \alpha_i u_{i,t-1}^2 + \beta_i \sigma_{i,t-1}^2, \tag{20.81}$$

where B_i, $i = 0, 1, \cdots, k$ are matrices of structural parameters with B_0 having coefficients of unity down the main diagonal to represent the usual normalisation, k represents the order of the lags and u_t is a vector of independent structural disturbances with separate GARCH(1,1) conditional variances with the conditional variances in (20.81) given by the diagonal elements of D_t.

The VAR is

$$\begin{aligned} y_t &= B_0^{-1} B_1 y_{t-1} + B_0^{-1} B_2 y_{t-2} + \cdots + B_0^{-1} B_k y_{t-k} + B_0^{-1} u_t \\ &= \Phi_1 y_{t-1} + \Phi_2 y_{t-2} + \cdots + \Phi_k y_{t-k} + v_t, \end{aligned} \tag{20.82}$$

where the VAR parameters are related to the structural parameters by

$$\Phi_i = B_0^{-1} B_i, \forall i, \tag{20.83}$$

and the VAR disturbances are

$$v_t = B_0^{-1} u_t = B_0^{-1} D_t^{1/2} z_t = S_t z_t , \qquad (20.84)$$

with

$$S_t = B_0^{-1} D_t^{1/2} .$$

The VAR disturbances have time-varying covariances as

$$E[v_t v_t'] = E[B_0^{-1} u_t u_t' B_0^{-1'}] = B_0^{-1} E[u_t u_t'] B_0^{-1'} = B_0^{-1} D_t B_0^{-1'} = S_t S_t' = V_t .$$

Unlike the structural disturbances, this matrix is not diagonal, provided that B_0 and hence S are not diagonal, in which case the volatility of all factors has an effect on all the variables in the VAR.

To identify the parameters of the SVAR, the following short-run restrictions are imposed on B_0^{-1}

$$B_0^{-1} = \begin{bmatrix} 1 & 0 & 0 & 0 & 0 & 0 \\ b^{2,1} & 1 & b^{2,3} & 0 & 0 & 0 \\ b^{3,1} & 0 & 1 & 0 & 0 & 0 \\ b^{4,1} & 0 & 0 & 1 & 0 & 0 \\ b^{5,1} & b^{5,2} & b^{5,3} & b^{5,4} & 1 & 0 \\ b^{6,1} & b^{6,2} & b^{6,3} & b^{6,4} & b^{6,5} & 1 \end{bmatrix} . \qquad (20.85)$$

The interpretation of the structural shocks, u_t, is

$$u_t = \begin{bmatrix} \text{Global risk factor} \\ \text{Narrow liquidity factor} \\ \text{Broad liquidity factor} \\ \text{Credit factor} \\ \text{Default factor} \\ \text{Idiosyncratic factor} \end{bmatrix} .$$

Notice that all factors are designed to impact on the LIBOR, as given by the last row in the matrix B_0^{-1} in (20.85).

The variance decompositions are given in Figure 20.8, for 1-period shocks, 5-period shocks and 20-period shocks respectively. These decompositions are time-varying as $B_0^{-1} D_t^{1/2}$ is used to compute the orthogonalised impulse responses which is time-varying through the conditional variance matrix D_t. The results of the 1-period variance decompositions over time for the United Kingdom LIBOR spread given in the first row of Figure 20.8 show that the key factors are the idiosyncratic factor and the broader liquidity factor. Over the next 5 periods (second row of Figure 20.8) and 20 periods (third row of Figure 20.8) the global risk factor progressively increases in importance.

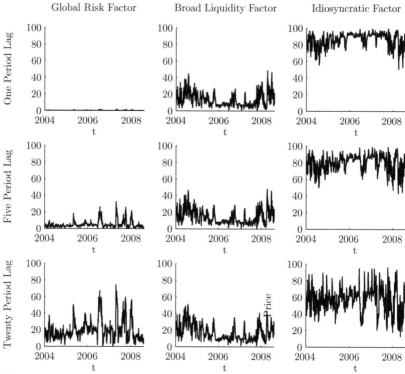

Figure 20.8. Time-varying variance decompositions of the United Kingdom LIBOR spread for selected periods: instantaneous (first row), 5-period (second row) and 20-period (third row).

20.8   Exercises

(1) Statistical Properties of Equity Returns

Program files	garch_statistic.*
Data files	equity.*

The data are daily observations on the FTSE, DOW and NIKKEI stock indexes from 5 January 1989 to 31 December 2007, a total of $T = 4953$ sample observations.

(a) Compute the daily percentage return on the FTSE index, y_t.

(b) Plot y_t and y_t^2 and compare the results with Figures 20.1(a) and 20.1(b). Interpret the plots.

(c) Compute the ACF of y_t and y_t^2, for 20 lags and compare the results with ACFs reported in Figure 20.1, panels (c) and (d). Interpret the plots.

(d) Compute the skewness and kurtosis coefficients of y_t. Compare these values with the corresponding moments of the standardised normal distribution, namely 0 and 3, respectively.

(e) Estimate the unconditional distribution of y_t using a nonparametric kernel density estimator and compare the result with the conditional distribution based on the standardised normal distribution.

(f) Repeat parts (a) to (e) for the DOW and the NIKKEI.

(2) Testing for ARCH in Equity Returns

Program files	garch_test.*
Data files	equity.*

This exercise is based on the same data used in Exercise 1.

(a) Compute the daily percentage return on the FTSE index, y_t.

(b) Test y_t for ARCH(1), ARCH(2) and ARCH(3) using the LM test and compare the results for the first two tests with those presented in Table 20.1.

(c) Repeat parts (a) and (b) for the DOW and the NIKKEI.

(3) GARCH Model Properties

Program files	garch_simulate.*

(a) Simulate the following GARCH(1,1) model

$$y_t = v_t, \qquad v_t \sim N(0, \sigma_t^2)$$
$$\sigma_t^2 = \alpha_0 + \alpha_1 v_{t-1}^2 + \beta_1 \sigma_{t-1}^2,$$

for a sample of size $T = 100000$, using the parameters $\alpha_0 = 0.10$, $\alpha_1 = 0.70$ and $\beta_1 = 0.20$. Let the starting value for v_0 be a draw from its unconditional distribution $N(0, \alpha_0/(1 - \alpha_1 - \beta_1))$ and $\sigma_0^2 = (1 - \alpha_1 - \beta_1)$ which is the variance of the unconditional distribution.

(b) Compute the ACF of y_t^2 and compare the results with the ACF reported in Figure 20.4, panel (a).

(c) Repeat parts (a) and (b) using the parameters $\alpha_0 = 0.05$, $\alpha_1 = 0.15$ and $\beta_1 = 0.80$. Compare the results with the ACF reported in Figure 20.4, panel (b).

(d) Repeat parts (a) and (b) using the parameters $\alpha_0 = 0.05$, $\alpha_1 = 0.05$, $\beta_1 = 0.90$ and compare the memory characteristics of the GARCH models in parts (b) and (c).

(4) Estimating a GARCH Model of Equity Returns

Program files	garch_equity.*
Data files	equity.*

This exercise is based on the same data used in Exercise 1.

(a) Estimate the following GARCH(1,1) model

$$y_t = v_t, \qquad v_t \sim N(0, \sigma_t^2)$$
$$\sigma_t^2 = \alpha_0 + \alpha_1 v_{t-1}^2 + \beta_1 \sigma_{t-1}^2,$$

where y_t is the zero-mean percentage return on the FTSE. Compare the results with those presented in Table 20.2.

(b) Plot the conditional variance and interpret the time series patterns of the series.

(c) Compare the quasi-maximum likelihood standard errors assuming heteroskedasticity with the standard errors based on the Hessian and outer product of the gradients, respectively.

(d) Compute the unconditional variance using (20.30) and compare the value to the empirical estimate.

(e) Test a GARCH(1,1) model against a GARCH(0,1) = ARCH(1) model using a LR test.

(f) Re-estimate the model with an IGARCH conditional variance by imposing the restriction $\beta_1 = 1 - \alpha_1$ given in (20.32). Reverse this operation by imposing the restriction $\alpha_1 = 1 - \beta_1$ and discuss the invariance property of the maximum likelihood estimator.

(g) Repeat parts (a) to (f) for the DOW and the NIKKEI.

(5) ARCH-NNH Model

Program files	garch_nnh.*
Data files	han_park.*

The exercise is based on Han and Park (2008) who model GARCH non-stationary conditional variances using nonstationary variables. The data consist of S&P500 stock returns, y_t, and the interest rate spread between AAA and BBB bonds, w_t, which are recorded monthly, weekly and daily.

(a) Estimate the GARCH(1,1) model

$$y_t = \mu + v_t, \qquad v_t \sim N(0, \sigma_t^2)$$
$$\sigma_t^2 = \alpha_0 + \alpha_1 v_{t-1}^2 + \beta_1 \sigma_{t-1}^2,$$

by maximum likelihood using the monthly, weekly and daily data. Discuss the time series properties of the estimate of σ_t^2.

(b) Consider the nonstationary ARCH model with nonlinear heteroskedasticity (ARCH-NNH)

$$y_t = \mu + v_t, \qquad v_t \sim N(0, \sigma_t^2)$$
$$\sigma_t^2 = \alpha_1 v_{t-1}^2 + \lambda |w_{t-1}|^\phi,$$

where w_{t-1} represents the lagged spread. Estimate the parameters $\theta = \{\mu, \alpha_1, \lambda, \phi\}$ by maximum likelihood for the monthly, weekly and daily data. Test the restriction $\phi = 1$.

(c) Estimate the GARCH-NNH model

$$y_t = \mu + v_t, \qquad v_t \sim N(0, \sigma_t^2)$$
$$\sigma_t^2 = \alpha_0 + \alpha_1 v_{t-1}^2 + \beta_1 \sigma_{t-1}^2 + \lambda |w_{t-1}|^{\phi} .$$

Compare these parameter estimates with those in parts (a) and (b) and discuss the ability of the nonstationary variable w_{t-1} to capture the nonstationarity properties of the conditional variance.

(d) Perform a Wald test of the restriction $\lambda = 0$ in part (c). Briefly discuss the problem(s) in implementing this test.

(6) Testing for Day-of-the-Week Effects in Equity Returns

Program files	garch_seasonality.*
Data files	equity.*

This exercise is based on the same data used in Exercise 1.

(a) Consider the GARCH(1,1) model

$$y_t = v_t, \qquad v_t \sim N(0, \sigma_t^2)$$
$$\sigma_t^2 = \alpha_0 + \alpha_1 v_{t-1}^2 + \beta_1 \sigma_{t-1}^2 + \lambda_1 d_{1,t} + \lambda_2 d_{2,t} + \lambda_3 d_{3,t} + \lambda_4 d_{4,t} ,$$

where y_t is the zero-mean percentage return on the FTSE and $d_{i,t}$ are dummy variables corresponding to Tuesday, Wednesday, Thursday and Friday. Perform a LR test of seasonality.

(b) Extend the variance to include a holiday dummy variable, and perform a joint test of day-of-the-week and holiday effects.

(c) Repeat parts (a) and (b) for the DOW and the NIKKEI.

(7) Modelling Risk in the Term Structure of Interest Rates

Program files	garch_m.*
Data files	yields_us.*

The data consist of daily yields, r_t, on United States zero coupon bonds, expressed as a percentage, over the period 10 October 1988 to 28 December 2001, a total of 3307 observations. The maturities of the bonds are 3 months, 1 year, 3 year, 5 year, 7 year and 10 year.

(a) Estimate the following GARCH-M model

$$r_{10y,t} = \mu_t + v_t, \qquad v_t \sim N(0, \sigma_t^2)$$
$$\mu_t = \gamma_0 + \gamma_1 r_{3m,t} + \varphi \sigma_t^{\rho}$$
$$\sigma_t^2 = \alpha_0 + \alpha_1 v_{t-1}^2 + \beta_1 \sigma_{t-1}^2 ,$$

where $r_{10y,t}$ is the 10-year yield and $r_{3m,t}$ is the 3-month yield on United States zero coupon bonds.

(b) Perform a test of risk neutrality by testing the restriction $\varphi = 0$.

(c) Perform a test of a linear risk-return relationship by testing the restriction $\rho = 1.0$.

(d) Repeat parts (a) to (c) by choosing the 1-year, 3-year, 5-year and 7-year bond yields as the dependent variables, respectively.

(8) GARCH Model with Conditional Student t

Program files	garch_student.*
Data files	equity.*

This exercise is based on the same data used in Exercise 1.

(a) Estimate the following GARCH(1,1) model

$$y_t = \gamma_0 + v_t, \qquad v_t \sim St(0, \sigma_t^2, v)$$
$$\sigma_t^2 = \alpha_0 + \alpha_1 v_{t-1}^2 + \beta_1 \sigma_{t-1}^2,$$

where y_t is the percentage return on the FTSE. Compare the GARCH point estimates with those presented in Table 20.2, which are based on conditional normality.

(b) Interpret the estimate of the degrees of freedom parameter v and discuss its implications for the existence of the moments of the conditional distribution of y_t.

(c) A limiting case of the Student t distribution occurs when the degrees of freedom approaches infinity, $v \to \infty$. Construct a Wald test of normality. *Hint: under the null* $v^{-1} = 0$.

(d) Re-estimate the model assuming a constant conditional variance by imposing the restrictions $\alpha_1 = \beta_1 = 0$. Compare the estimate of the degrees of freedom parameter obtained in part (b) and hence discuss the effects of the GARCH conditional variance on modelling the distribution of y_t.

(e) Repeat parts (a) to (d) for the DOW and the NIKKEI.

(9) Efficiency of the Quasi-Maximum Likelihood Estimator

Program files	garch_studt.*, garch_gam.*

Consider the GARCH(1, 1) model

$$y_t = v_t, \qquad v_t = \sigma_t z_t$$
$$\sigma_t^2 = 1 - \alpha_1 - \beta_1 + a_1 v_{t-1}^2 + \beta_1 \sigma_{t-1}^2.$$

The aim of this exercise is to investigate the efficiency of the quasi-maximum likelihood estimator relative to the maximum likelihood estimator of the parameters $\theta = \{\alpha_1, \beta_1\}$.

(a) Let the true distribution of z_t be Student t with ν_0 degrees of freedom. Write the log-likelihood function for observation t and derive an expression for the covariance matrix of the maximum likelihood estimator, $\widehat{\theta}$, of the true model. Let the variances be given by $\text{cov}_0(\widehat{\alpha}_1)$ and $\text{cov}_0(\widehat{\beta}_1)$.

(b) Let the misspecified distribution of z_t be $N(0, 1)$. Write the log-likelihood function for observation t and derive an expression for the covariance matrix of the quasi-maximum likelihood estimator, $\widehat{\theta}$, of the misspecified model. Let the QMLE variances be given by $\text{cov}(\widehat{\alpha}_1)$ and $\text{cov}(\widehat{\beta}_1)$.

(c) Simulate $T = 1000000$ observations from the true model with the degrees of freedom parameter $\nu_0 = \{5, 8, 12\}$. For each value of ν_0 evaluate

$$\frac{\text{cov}_0(\widehat{\alpha}_1)}{\text{cov}(\widehat{\alpha}_1)}, \qquad \frac{\text{cov}_0(\widehat{\beta}_1)}{\text{cov}(\widehat{\beta}_1)}.$$

Compare the simulation results to the analytical results of González-Rivera and Drost (1999).

(d) Repeat parts (a) to (c) when the true distribution of z_t is the gamma distribution,

$$f(z_t) = \frac{\sqrt{c}}{\Gamma(c)} \left(\sqrt{c}z_t\right)^{c-1} \exp[-\sqrt{c}z_t - c],$$

with shape parameter $c = 50$.

(10) Mixed-Data-Sampling Estimator (MIDAS)

Program files	`garch_midas.*`
Data files	`daily_hedge.*`

The data are $T = 2179$ daily prices on the convertible arbitrage hedge fund index and the S&P500 index from 31 March 2003 to 4 August 2011. As an alternative to the ARCH-M model, Ghysels, Santa-Clara and Valkanov (2005) propose the MIDAS estimator where the monthly conditional variance is computed as a realised volatility being a weighted average of lagged squared daily returns. The model is

$$R_t = \beta_0 + \beta_1 M_t + \beta_2 \sigma_t^2 + \beta_3 D_t + v_t, \qquad v_t \sim iid\ N(0, \sigma_v^2),$$

where R_t is the monthly return on the hedge fund, M_t is the monthly return on the market, σ_t^2 is the MIDAS conditional variance computed from lagged daily returns according to

$$\sigma_t^2 = \sum_{i=0}^{NL-1} 22r_{t-1-i}^2 w_i, \qquad w_i = \frac{\exp(\alpha_1 i + \alpha_2 i^2)}{\sum_{i=0}^{NL-1} \exp(\alpha_1 i + \alpha_2 i^2)},$$

with r_{t-1-i}^2 representing the lagged squared daily return and w_i the weight. The variable D_t is a dummy to capture the effects of the Global Financial crisis which equals unity on the day of the biggest fall in the monthly return R_t and zero otherwise. The number of days in a month is set at $N = 22$ and L is the lag length in months.

(a) Compute monthly returns R_t from the daily returns r_t assuming that there are $N = 22$ days in a month.
(b) Estimate the parameters $\theta = \{\beta_0, \beta_1, \beta_2, \beta_3, \alpha_1, \alpha_2\}$ by maximum likelihood with the MIDAS variance based on a lag length of $L = 18$ months. Plot the weight function w_i and interpret its shape.
(c) Test the restriction $\alpha_1 = \alpha_2 = 0$ and interpret the result.
(d) In the inter-temporal capital asset pricing model the parameter β_2 represents the coefficient of relative risk aversion. Interpret the parameter estimate obtained in part (b).
(e) For a hedge fund to be market neutral the restriction is that $\beta_1 = 0$. Test this restriction using the results in part (b) and compare this result by estimating the standard capital asset pricing model based on the restriction $\beta_2 = 0$. Briefly discuss the potential problem(s) of testing the restriction β_2 using the estimates obtained in part (b).
(f) Repeat part (b) for the lag lengths $L = \{1, 6, 12, 24\}$ and determine the sensitivity of the estimate of β_2 to the choice of L.

(11) Mean Impact Curve (MIC)

Program files	garch_mic.*
Data files	intequity.*

The data are daily equity prices of the AORD in Australia, the Hang Seng and the Straits Times, beginning May 29th, 1992 for the AORD ($T = 5001$ observations), January 2nd, 1990 for the Hang Seng ($T = 5629$ observations) and August 31st, 1999 for the Straits Times ($T = 3109$ observations), with all indexes ending on July 29th, 2011. Sarkar, Kanto and Martin (2012) investigate the relationship between the conditional mean μ_t and the lagged shock, v_{t-1}, called the mean impact curve, which is an extension of the news impact curve.

(a) For each index estimate the nonlinear model

$$
\begin{aligned}
y_t &= \mu_t + v_t, & v_t &\sim N(0, \sigma_t^2) \\
\mu_t &= \gamma_0 + \gamma_1 y_{t-1} + \gamma_2 \sigma_t^2 + \gamma_3 \sigma_t^2 y_{t-1} \\
\sigma_t^2 &= \alpha_0 + \alpha_1 v_{t-1}^2 + \beta_1 \sigma_{t-1}^2 + \phi v_{t-1}^2 d_{t-1},
\end{aligned}
$$

where y_t is the daily percentage equity return and d_{t-1} is the asymmetry dummy variable defined in equation (20.38).

(b) Show that for the model in part (a) the MIC is characterised as a cubic equation in v_{t-1}. For each equity return plot the estimated MIC and interpret its shape.

(c) Use the delta method to derive standard errors of the MIC for each equity return and compute confidence intervals for the MIC.

(12) BEKK Model of United States Yields

Program files	mgarch_bekk.*, mgarch_student.m
Data files	yields_us.*

This exercise is based on the same data used in Exercise 7.

(a) Construct the variables

$$
y_{1,t} = 100(r_{3m,t} - r_{3m,t-1}), \qquad y_{2,t} = 100(r_{1y,t} - r_{1y,t-1}),
$$

where $r_{3m,t}$ is the 3-month yield and r_{1y} is the 1-year yield, expressed as a percentage.

(b) Estimate the following asymmetric BEKK specification

$$
\begin{aligned}
y_{1,t} &= \gamma_1 + v_{1,t} \\
y_{2,t} &= \gamma_2 + v_{2,t} \\
v_t &\sim N(0, V_t) \\
V_t &= CC' + A v_{t-1} v_{t-1}' A' + D V_{t-1} D',
\end{aligned}
$$

where C, A and D are matrices of parameters.

(c) Perform a LR test of the constant covariance BEKK model by testing the restrictions $a_{1,2} = a_{2,1} = d_{1,2} = d_{2,1} = 0$.

(d) Perform a LR test of the symmetric BEKK model by testing the restrictions $a_{1,2} = a_{2,1}$ and $d_{1,2} = d_{2,1}$.

(e) Re-estimate the symmetric BEKK model using the standardised multivariate Student t distribution

$$
f(v_t) = \frac{\Gamma\left(\dfrac{v+N}{2}\right)}{(\pi(v-2))^{N/2}\Gamma\left(\dfrac{v}{2}\right)} |V_t|^{-1/2} \left(1 + \frac{v_t' V_t^{-1} v_t}{v-2}\right)^{-\left(\frac{v+N}{2}\right)},
$$

where $N = 2$ and v is the degrees of freedom parameter. Interpret the estimate of the degrees of freedom parameter.

(13) DCC and DECO Model of United States Yields

Program files	mgarch_dcc.*, mgarch_deco.*
Data files	yields_us.*

The data file contains daily yields, r_t, on United States zero coupon bonds, expressed as a percentage, over the period 3 January 2000 to 21 August 2006 ($T = 1658$). The maturities of the bonds are 1, 5, 10, 15 and 20 years.

(a) Let

$$y_{i,t} = 100(r_{i,t} - r_{i,t-1}), \qquad i = 1, 2, \cdots, 5,$$

which are further transformed to have zero mean. Compute the maximum likelihood estimates of a DCC model for $y_{i,t}$ and interpret the parameter values.

(b) Perform a LR test of the constant correlation model by testing the restrictions $\alpha = \beta = 0$ in equation (20.65).

(c) Compute the maximum likelihood estimates of a DECO model for $y_{i,t}$ and compare the estimated parameters with the estimates obtained using the DCC model. Plot the average correlation of the five interest rates and interpret the result.

(14) International CAPM with Time-Varying Beta

Program files	mgarch_icapm.*
Data files	icapm.*

The data are the excess returns on the NYSE, $y_{1,t}$, and the excess returns on a world equity index based on the MSCI index, $y_{2,t}$. The sample period is 3 February 1988 to 29 December 1995, a total of $T = 2000$ observations.

(a) Estimate the following international CAPM using the symmetric BEKK multivariate conditional variance specification with conditional normality

$$y_{1,t} = \alpha + \beta_t y_{2,t} + v_{1,t}$$

$$y_{2,t} = v_{2,t}$$

$$\beta_t = \frac{\sigma_{1,2,t}}{\sigma_{2,2,t}}.$$

(b) Plot the estimate of β_t over the sample period.

(c) Estimate the constant beta risk model ($\beta_t = \beta$) by regressing $y_{1,t}$ on a constant and $y_{2,t}$, and compare this estimate to the plot of β_t given in part (b).

(15) **Modelling LIBOR Rates with Time-Varying Volatility**

Program files	mgarch_liboruk.*
Data files	libor_data.*

The data, y_t, are daily, beginning 1 January 2004 and ending 28 May 2008, and correspond to the six variables listed in Section 20.7.2, namely, the VIX, the on-off run United States 5-year spread, the GBP/USD swap rate, the REPO spread, the default risk for the United Kingdom and the 3-month United Kingdom LIBOR rate spread. Consider the dynamic structural model of y_t with GARCH conditional variances

$$B_0 y_t = B_1 y_{t-1} + B_2 y_{t-2} + \cdots + B_k y_{t-k} + u_t$$
$$E[u_t] = 0, \qquad E[u_t u_t'] = D_t, \qquad E[u_t u_s'] = 0, t \neq s$$
$$\sigma_{i,t}^2 = \delta_i + \alpha_i u_{i,t-1}^2 + \beta_i \sigma_{i,t-1}^2,$$

where u_t represent structural shocks and identification is based on the restrictions in (20.85).
(a) Estimate the model and interpret the factors.
(b) Compute the variance decompositions at lags 1, 5 and 20 and interpret the results.

21   Discrete Time Series Models

21.1   Introduction

In most of the models previously discussed, the dependent variable, y_t, is assumed to be a continuous random variable. There are a number of situations where the continuity assumption is inappropriate and alternative classes of models must be specified to explain the time series features of discrete random variables. This chapter reviews the important class of discrete time series models commonly used in microeconometrics namely the probit, ordered probit and Poisson regression models. It also discusses some recent advances in the modelling of discrete random variables with particular emphasis on the binomial thinning model of Steutel and Van Harn (1979) and the Autoregressive Conditional Duration (ACD) model of Engle and Russell (1998), together with some of its extensions.

21.2   Motivating Examples

Recent empirical research in financial econometrics has emphasised the importance of discrete random variables. Here, data on the number of trades and the duration between trades are recorded at very high frequencies. The examples which follow all highlight the need for econometric models that deal with discrete random variables by preserving the distributional characteristics of the data.

Example 21.1 Transactions Data on Trades
Table 21.1 provides a snapshot of transactions data recorded every second, on the United States stock AMR, the parent company of American Airlines, on 1 August 2006. Three examples of discrete random variables can be obtained from the data in Table 21.1.

Table 21.1. *Snapshot of transactions data on AMR: 1 August 2006, 9.30am to 4.00pm*

9:42:Seconds	Trade (1 sec. interval)	Trade (3 sec. interval)	Duration (between trades)	Price
5	1		1	21.58
6	0		1	21.58
7	0	1	1	21.58
8	0		1	21.58
9	0		1	21.58
10	0	0	1	21.58
11	1		6	21.59
12	1		1	21.59
13	0	2	1	21.59
14	1		2	21.59
15	1		1	21.59
16	0	2	1	21.59
17	1		2	21.59
18	1		1	21.59
19	0	2	1	21.59

Binary data
Data on whether a trade on AMR stock occurs within a second are given in the second column in Table 21.1, with the binary variable defined as

$$y_t = \begin{cases} 1 & : \quad \text{Trade occurs} \\ 0 & : \quad \text{Trade does not occur.} \end{cases}$$

The data in this column represent a binary random variable which is modelled using a Bernoulli distribution

$$f(y_t; \theta) = \theta^{y_t}(1 - \theta)^{1 - y_t}, \qquad 0 < \theta < 1.$$

Count data
In the third column of Table 21.1, the number of trades in every 3-second interval is recorded. The frequency of trades now ranges from zero to two and represents a discrete counting variable. A potential model of the random variable y_t now is the Poisson distribution

$$f(y_t; \theta) = \frac{\theta^{y_t} \exp(-\theta)}{y_t!}, \qquad \theta > 0.$$

Duration data
The time interval between trades is given in the fourth column of Table 21.1. If the trade counts represents a Poisson random variable, then the duration

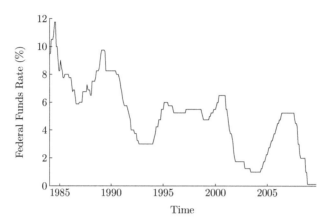

Figure 21.1. United States Federal funds target rate (%) from 1984 to 2009.

between trades is modelled as an exponential random variable

$$f(y_t; \theta) = \frac{1}{\theta} \exp\left[\frac{y_t}{\theta}\right], \qquad \theta > 0,$$

where y_t now represents the duration between trades.   □

Example 21.2 United States Monetary Policy
The key instrument of monetary policy in the United States is the Federal funds target rate. A plot of the monthly target rate over the period 1984 to 2009 given in Figure 21.1 shows that the series, in general, moves in discrete steps of ±0.25%. The change in the target rate ranges from extreme easing of interest rates (changes of −1%), as experienced during the global financial crisis of 2007 to 2009, to extreme tightening (changes of 1%). This variable represents an ordered polychotomous variable.   □

Example 21.3 Interest Rate Floors and Money Demand
The demand for money expresses the interest rate, r_t, as a function of real income, ry_t, and the real stock of money, m_t,

$$r_t = \beta_0 + \beta_1 ry_t + \beta_2 m_t + u_t,$$

where u_t is a disturbance term. If the monetary authorities set an interest rate floor of r_{FLOOR}, then r_t is given by

$$r_t = \begin{cases} r_t & : \quad r_t > r_{\text{FLOOR}} \\ r_{\text{FLOOR}} & : \quad r_t \leq r_{\text{FLOOR}}. \end{cases}$$

Even though the money demand equation without the floor is linear, with the floor it is nonlinear. This is highlighted in Figure 21.2 where the floor interest rate is 4%. Even if u_t in the demand for money equation has a normal

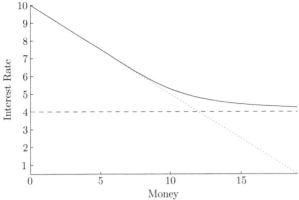

Figure 21.2. Money demand equation with a floor interest rate of 4% (solid line). The demand equation without the floor is linear (dashed line).

distribution, it does not follow that the distribution of r_t is also normal because it is now a censored random variable. □

21.3 Qualitative Data

Before recent developments in dynamic discrete time series models are investigated, traditional methods commonly used in microeconometrics for modelling and estimating qualitative response models are presented.

21.3.1 Specification

Consider the following normal linear regression model

$$y_t^* = \beta_0 + \beta_1 x_t^* + u_t^*, \qquad u_t^* \sim iid \, N(0, \sigma^2), \tag{21.1}$$

where y_t^* and x_t^* are the quantitative dependent and exogenous variables, respectively, and u_t^* is the disturbance term. The $*$ notation is introduced to distinguish between quantitative (not filtered) and qualitative (filtered) variables. The fundamental difference between the different kinds of qualitative response models concerns the way that the data are transformed, or filtered. These models are now demonstrated with reference to the sample of $T = 10$ simulated realisations from the model in equation (21.1) for y_t^* and x_t^*. The simulated observations are tabulated in Table 21.2.

In the first two columns of Table 21.2 headed Full, there is no filtering so that $y_t = y_t^*$ and $x_t = x_t^*$. In each of the other columns, Binary, Censored and Truncated, the data are subject to the application of a filter so that the quantitative and qualitative data are not identical. The qualitative data y_t and x_t are observed and the underlying quantitative data y_t^* and x_t^* are unobserved. Simply ignoring

Table 21.2. *Data used to compare alternative filtering methods; $T = 10$*

Full		Binary		Censored		Truncated	
$x_t = x_t^*$	$y_t = y_t^*$	x_t	y_t	x_t	y_t	x_t	y_t
5	-1	5	0	5	0	n.a.	n.a.
4	3	4	1	4	3	4	3
2	-4	2	0	2	0	n.a.	n.a.
1	-2	1	0	1	0	n.a.	n.a.
5	2	5	1	5	2	5	2
6	0	6	0	6	0	n.a.	n.a.
7	1	7	1	7	1	7	1
3	2	3	1	3	2	3	2
3	-3	3	0	3	0	n.a.	n.a.
9	4	9	1	9	4	9	4

the filter and estimating (21.1) using the observed qualitative variables y_t and x_t

$$y_t = \alpha_0 + \alpha_1 x_t + u_t, \tag{21.2}$$

by ordinary least squares results in biased estimates of the unknown parameters $\theta = \{\beta_0, \beta_1, \sigma^2\}$ as

$$\text{plim}(\widehat{\alpha}_0) \neq \beta_0, \qquad \text{plim}(\widehat{\alpha}_1) \neq \beta_1 .$$

The maximum likelihood estimator, however, offers a means of still obtaining a consistent estimator of θ. It surmounts the potential statistical problems caused from filtering by explicitly building into the likelihood the form of the filter. Each of the cases represented in Table 21.2 is now discussed in more detail.

Full Information: Linear Regression Model
The data are in the columns headed Full in Table 21.2 where $y_t = y_t^*$ and $x_t = x_t^*$. This case corresponds to the simple linear regression model. The distribution of y_t is

$$f(y_t | x_t; \theta) = \frac{1}{\sigma} \phi_t,$$

in which ϕ_t is the standard normal distribution

$$\phi_t = \frac{1}{\sqrt{2\pi}} \exp\left[-\frac{1}{2\sigma^2}(y_t - \beta_0 - \beta_1 x_t)^2 \right] . \tag{21.3}$$

The log-likelihood function for a sample of T observations is

$$\ln L_T(\theta) = \frac{1}{T} \sum_{t=1}^{T} [-\ln \sigma + \ln \phi_t] .$$

Binary Information: Probit Regression Model

The binary data for the probit regression model are created by applying the filter

$$
\begin{aligned}
y_t &= \begin{cases} 1 & : \ y_t^* > 0 \\ 0 & : \ y_t^* \le 0 \end{cases} \\
x_t &= x_t^*,
\end{aligned}
\tag{21.4}
$$

with the results recorded in the columns headed Binary in Table 21.2. Because y_t is a binary random variable, it has a Bernoulli distribution

$$
f(y_t \mid x_t; \theta) = \Phi_t^{y_t}(1 - \Phi_t)^{1-y_t} ,
\tag{21.5}
$$

in which $\Phi_t = \Pr(y = 1)$ and $1 - \Phi_t = \Pr(y = 0)$. As u_t in (21.1) is normally distributed, Φ_t is defined in terms of the cumulative normal distribution

$$
\Phi_t = \int_{-\infty}^{\dfrac{\beta_0 + \beta_1 x_t}{\sigma}} \frac{1}{\sqrt{2\pi}} \exp\left[-\frac{s^2}{2}\right] ds .
\tag{21.6}
$$

This represents the probit regression model. The log-likelihood function for a sample of T observations is

$$
\ln L_T(\theta) = \frac{1}{T} \sum_{t=1}^{T} [y_t \ln \Phi_t + (1 - y_t)\ln(1 - \Phi_t)] .
$$

For the probit regression model as the upper limit of the integration in equation (21.6) is

$$
\frac{\beta_0 + \beta_1 x_t}{\sigma} = \frac{\beta_0}{\sigma} + \frac{\beta_1}{\sigma} x_t ,
$$

it is only possible to identify the ratios β_0/σ and β_1/σ and not the individual terms. It is common practice therefore to adopt the normalisation $\sigma = 1$.

Censored Information: Censored Regression Model

In the case of the censored model, the data are constructed using the filter

$$
\begin{aligned}
y_t &= \begin{cases} y_t^* & : \ y_t^* > 0 \\ 0 & : \ y_t^* \le 0 \end{cases} \\
x_t &= x_t^*,
\end{aligned}
\tag{21.7}
$$

with the results recorded in the columns headed Censored in Table 21.2. This model is a mixture of the full information model where $y_t^* > 0$, and the binary information model where $y_t^* > 0$. The distribution of y_t thus consists of two parts

$$
f(y_t \mid x_t; \theta) = \left(\frac{1}{\sigma}\right)^{d_t} \phi_t^{d_t}(1 - \Phi_t)^{1-d_t},
\tag{21.8}
$$

where ϕ_t and Φ_t are defined in (21.3) and (21.6), respectively, and d_t is a dummy variable

$$d_t = \begin{cases} 1 & : \quad y_t^* > 0 \\ 0 & : \quad y_t^* \leq 0. \end{cases} \qquad (21.9)$$

This is the censored regression model, or the Tobit model. The log-likelihood function for a sample of T observations is

$$\ln L_T(\theta) = \frac{1}{T} \sum_{t=1}^{T} [-d_t \ln \sigma + d_t \ln \phi_t + (1 - d_t) \ln(1 - \Phi_t)] .$$

Truncated Information: Truncated Regression Model

Finally, the data for the truncated model are constructed using the filter

$$y_t = \begin{cases} y_t^* & : \quad y_t^* > 0 \\ n.a & : \quad y_t^* \leq 0, \end{cases} \qquad x_t = \begin{cases} x_t^* & : \quad y_t^* > 0 \\ n.a & : \quad y_t^* \leq 0, \end{cases} \qquad (21.10)$$

with the results recorded in the Truncated columns in Table 21.2. The distribution of the dependent variable is the truncated normal distribution

$$f(y_t | x_t; \theta) = \frac{\phi_t}{\sigma \Phi_t}, \qquad (21.11)$$

where ϕ_t and Φ_t are defined in (21.3) and (21.6), respectively. This is the truncated regression model. The log-likelihood function for a sample of T observations is

$$\ln L_T(\theta) = \frac{1}{T} \sum_{t=1}^{T} [-d_t \ln \sigma + d_t \ln \phi_t - d_t \ln \Phi_t] ,$$

where d_t is as defined in equation (21.9).

The main difference between the models presented is the degree of information lost from filtering the data. To quantify this loss of information a Monte Carlo experiment is now used to demonstrate the finite sample properties of the maximum likelihood estimator of these models.

Example 21.4 Finite Sample Properties of Estimators

The model is specified as in equation (21.1) in which $x_t^* \sim N(0, 1)$, $u_t^* \sim N(0, \sigma^2)$, the parameters are $\theta = \{\beta_0 = 1, \beta_1 = 1, \sigma^2 = 1\}$ and truncation is at zero. The results obtained by simulating the model using 5000 replications with samples of size $T = 100$ are given in Table 21.3. The maximum likelihood estimator shows little bias for the probit, Tobit and truncated regression models, demonstrating that this estimator is able to correct for the different data filters. The root mean square errors satisfy the relationship

RMSE(Censored) < RMSE(Truncated) < RMSE(Probit),

Table 21.3. *Finite sample properties of the maximum likelihood estimator of alternative models, based on equation (21.1). The restricted model is estimated using data on $y_t > 0$ only. The sample size is $T = 100$ and the number of repetitions is 5000*

Statistics	Linear	Probit	Censored	Truncated	Restricted
True (β_0)	1.000	1.000	1.000	1.000	1.000
Mean	0.999	1.039	0.996	0.990	1.372
Bias	−0.001	0.039	−0.004	−0.010	0.372
RMSE	0.103	0.211	0.110	0.170	0.384
True (β_1)	1.000	1.000	1.000	1.000	1.000
Mean	1.000	1.057	1.005	1.006	0.704
Bias	0.000	0.057	0.005	0.006	−0.296
RMSE	0.102	0.254	0.116	0.172	0.317

showing that the greatest loss of efficiency, not surprisingly, occurs for the probit regression model. In comparison, the last column of Table 21.3 shows that least squares estimation using data on values of $y_t > 0$ only, yields biased parameter estimates with the size of the bias being approximately 30%. □

21.3.2 Estimation

With the exception of the linear regression model, the probit, censored and truncated regression models are nonlinear in the parameters. The parameters of these models must, therefore, be estimated using one of the numerical algorithms discussed in Chapter 3. In practice, it is convenient to compute the gradient vector and Hessian numerically, although for all of these models analytical solutions are easily derived.

The probit regression model with just a constant in the regression model is an example of a case in which an analytical expression is available for the maximum likelihood estimator. In this situation, estimation of the model reduces to estimating the parameter of the Bernoulli distribution.

Example 21.5 Bernoulli Distribution
Let $y_t, t = 1, 2, \cdots, T$ be *iid* observations from the Bernoulli distribution

$$f(y_t; \theta) = \theta^{y_t}(1 - \theta)^{1-y_t}, \qquad y_t = 0, 1,$$

where $\theta > 0$, is an unknown parameter (probability). The log-likelihood is

$$\ln L_T(\theta) = \frac{1}{T} \sum_{t=1}^{T} y_t \ln \theta + \frac{1}{T} \sum_{t=1}^{T} (1 - y_t) \ln(1 - \theta).$$

The gradient and Hessian are, respectively,

$$G_T(\theta) = \frac{d \ln L_T(\theta)}{d\theta} = \frac{1}{\theta T} \sum_{t=1}^{T} y_t - \frac{1}{(1-\theta)T} \sum_{t=1}^{T} (1 - y_t)$$

$$H_T(\theta) = \frac{d^2 \ln L_T(\theta)}{d\theta^2} = -\frac{1}{\theta^2 T} \sum_{t=1}^{T} y_t - \frac{1}{(1-\theta)^2 T} \sum_{t=1}^{T} (1 - y_t).$$

The maximum likelihood estimator is given as the solution of $G_T(\widehat{\theta}) = 0$,

$$0 = \frac{1}{\widehat{\theta} T} \sum_{t=1}^{T} y_t - \frac{1}{(1-\widehat{\theta})T} \sum_{t=1}^{T} (1 - y_t) = \frac{1}{\widehat{\theta}(1-\widehat{\theta})T} \sum_{t=1}^{T} (y_t - \widehat{\theta}),$$

which yields the sample mean of y_t as the maximum likelihood estimator

$$\widehat{\theta} = \frac{1}{T} \sum_{t=1}^{T} y_t = \bar{y}.$$

As the data are binary, the sample mean also corresponds to the sample proportion. Evaluating the Hessian at $\widehat{\theta}$ gives

$$H_T(\widehat{\theta}) = -\frac{1}{\widehat{\theta}^2 T} \sum_{t=1}^{T} y_t - \frac{1}{(1-\widehat{\theta})^2 T} \sum_{t=1}^{T} (1 - y_t)$$

$$= -\frac{\widehat{\theta}}{\widehat{\theta}^2} - \frac{(1-\widehat{\theta})}{(1-\widehat{\theta})^2} = -\frac{1}{\widehat{\theta}(1-\widehat{\theta})}.$$

The variance of $\widehat{\theta}$ is

$$\text{var}(\widehat{\theta}) = -\frac{1}{T} H_T^{-1}(\widehat{\theta}) = \frac{\widehat{\theta}(1-\widehat{\theta})}{T},$$

which is the usual variance reported for testing the sample proportion.   □

Example 21.6 BHHH Estimation of the Probit Model

Consider the binary variable, y_t, that has a Bernoulli distribution

$$f(y_t|x_t; \theta) = \Phi_t^{y_t}(1 - \Phi_t)^{1-y_t},$$

where Φ_t is defined by (21.6), x_t is an exogenous variable and $\theta = \{\beta_0, \beta_1\}$. The log-likelihood function of the probit regression model is

$$\ln L_T(\theta) = \frac{1}{T} \sum_{t=1}^{T} y_t \ln \Phi_t + \frac{1}{T} \sum_{t=1}^{T} (1 - y_t) \ln(1 - \Phi_t).$$

The first derivatives are

$$
\frac{\partial \ln L_T(\theta)}{\partial \beta_0} = \frac{1}{T} \sum_{t=1}^{T} y_t \frac{\phi_t}{\Phi_t} - \frac{1}{T} \sum_{t=1}^{T} (1 - y_t) \frac{\phi_t}{1 - \Phi_t}
$$

$$
= \frac{1}{T} \sum_{t=1}^{T} \frac{(y_t - \Phi_t)\phi_t}{\Phi_t(1 - \Phi_t)}
$$

$$
\frac{\partial \ln L_T(\theta)}{\partial \beta_1} = \frac{1}{T} \sum_{t=1}^{T} y_t x_t \frac{\phi_t}{\Phi_t} - \frac{1}{T} \sum_{t=1}^{T} (1 - y_t) x_t \frac{\phi_t}{1 - \Phi_t}
$$

$$
= \frac{1}{T} \sum_{t=1}^{T} \frac{(y_t - \Phi_t)\phi_t}{\Phi_t(1 - \Phi_t)} x_t \,,
$$

where ϕ_t is defined by (21.3). The BHHH algorithm amounts to updating using a weighted least squares regression with weights given by $w_t = \sqrt{\phi_t / \Phi_t(1 - \Phi_t)}$. The approach is to regress the weighted residual $(y_t - \Phi_t)w_t$ on the weighted exogenous variables $\{w_t, x_t w_t\}$, evaluated at the starting value $\theta_{(0)}$, to get Δ_θ. The updated parameter values are computed as

$$
\theta_{(1)} = \theta_{(0)} + \Delta_\theta \,. \qquad \qquad \square
$$

Example 21.7 A Probit Model of Monetary Policy

Consider the Federal funds rate data introduced in Example 21.2. Changes in the target rate, Δr_t, are assumed to be a function of the spread between the 6-month Treasury bill rate and the Federal funds rate, s_t, the 1-month lagged inflation rate, π_{t-4}, and the growth rate in output, gdp_t. If just the direction of monetary policy is known, the model is specified as

$$
y_t = \begin{cases} 1 & : \quad \Delta r_t > 0 \quad \text{[Monetary tightening]} \\ 0 & : \quad \Delta r_t \leq 0 \quad \text{[Monetary easing or no change]}, \end{cases}
$$

and

$$
f(y_t | x_t; \theta) = \Phi_t^{y_t} (1 - \Phi_t)^{1 - y_t},
$$
$$
\Phi_t = \Phi(\beta_0 + \beta_1 s_t + \beta_2 \pi_{t-4} + \beta_3 gdp_t),
$$

where the exogenous variables are $x_t = \{s_t, \pi_{t-4}, gdp_t\}$.

Summary statistics of the movements in the Federal funds target rate, r_t, given in Table 21.4, show that of the $T = 106$ meeting days from 1984 to 1997, 10 resulted in monetary tightening ($\Delta r_t > 0$) and 96 resulted in either monetary easing or no change in policy ($\Delta r_t \leq 0$). The parameter estimates given in Table 21.5 show that s_t is significant at the 5% level of significance, gdp_t is significant at the 10% level of significance and π_{t-4} is not statistically significant. The restricted model given by setting $\beta_1 = \beta_2 = \beta_3 = 0$, yields an

Table 21.4. *Descriptive statistics of movements in the Federal funds target rate on Federal open Market Committee (FOMC) meeting days, February 1984 to June 1997*

Target change (%)	Number	Proportion
−0.50	3	0.028
−0.25	11	0.104
0.00	82	0.774
0.25	6	0.057
0.50	4	0.034
		106

estimate of the intercept of −1.315. Substituting this value into the cumulative normal distribution gives

$$\int_{-\infty}^{-1.315} \frac{1}{\sqrt{2\pi}} \exp\left[-\frac{s^2}{2}\right] ds = 0.094 \,,$$

which equals the observed proportion of FOMC days of monetary tightening, that is 10 out of 106. ☐

21.3.3 Testing

The LR, Wald and LM testing procedures can be used to perform hypothesis tests on the parameters $\theta = \{\beta_0, \beta_1\}$. Consider testing the hypotheses for the model in (21.1) in the case of the probit regression model

$$H_0 : \beta_1 = 0, \qquad H_1 : \beta_1 \neq 0 \,.$$

Table 21.5. *Maximum likelihood estimates of the probit model of monetary policy, with calculations based on the BFGS algorithm with derivatives computed numerically*

| Parameter | Unrestricted | | Restricted | |
	Estimate	p-value	Estimate	p-value
β_0	−3.859	0.024	−1.315	0.000
β_1	2.328	0.001		
β_2	58.545	0.136		
β_3	0.277	0.098		
$T \ln L_T(\widehat{\theta})$	−20.335		−33.121	

Choosing the LM test has the advantage that, under the null hypothesis of $\beta_1 = 0$, the maximum likelihood estimator $\widehat{\theta}_0 = \{\widehat{\beta}_0, 0\}$, has an analytical solution where $\Phi(\widehat{\beta}_0) = \overline{y}$. The LM statistic is

$$LM = T G'_T(\widehat{\theta}_0) I^{-1}(\widehat{\theta}_0) G_T(\widehat{\theta}_0). \tag{21.12}$$

In the case of the probit regression model, the gradient vector and information matrix under the null are, respectively,

$$G_T(\widehat{\theta}_0) = \frac{1}{T} \sum_{t=1}^{T} \widehat{u}_t \frac{\widehat{\phi}}{\widehat{\Phi}(1 - \widehat{\Phi})} \begin{bmatrix} 1 \\ x_t \end{bmatrix} \tag{21.13}$$

$$I(\widehat{\theta}_0) = -E\left[H_T(\widehat{\theta}_0)\right] = \frac{1}{T} \sum_{t=1}^{T} \frac{\widehat{\phi}^2}{\widehat{\Phi}(1 - \widehat{\Phi})} \begin{bmatrix} 1 & x_t \\ x_t & x_t^2 \end{bmatrix}, \tag{21.14}$$

where $\widehat{u}_t = y_t - \widehat{\Phi}$ represents the residual and

$$\widehat{\phi} = \frac{1}{\sqrt{2\pi}} \exp\left[-\frac{1}{2}(y_t - \widehat{\beta}_0)^2\right], \qquad \widehat{\Phi} = \int_{-\infty}^{\widehat{\beta}_0} \frac{1}{\sqrt{2\pi}} \exp\left[-\frac{s^2}{2}\right] ds,$$

and the normalisation $\sigma = 1$ is adopted. Substituting into the LM statistic in (21.12) and rearranging gives

$$LM = \frac{1}{\widehat{\Phi}(1 - \widehat{\Phi})} \begin{bmatrix} \sum_{t=1}^{T} \widehat{u}_t \\ \sum_{t=1}^{T} \widehat{u}_t x_t \end{bmatrix}' \begin{bmatrix} T & \sum_{t=1}^{T} x_t \\ \sum_{t=1}^{T} x_t & \sum_{t=1}^{T} x_t^2 \end{bmatrix}^{-1} \begin{bmatrix} \sum_{t=1}^{T} \widehat{u}_t \\ \sum_{t=1}^{T} \widehat{u}_t x_t \end{bmatrix}$$

$$= \frac{T}{\sum_{t=1}^{T} \widehat{u}_t^2} \begin{bmatrix} \sum_{t=1}^{T} \widehat{u}_t \\ \sum_{t=1}^{T} \widehat{u}_t x_t \end{bmatrix}' \begin{bmatrix} T & \sum_{t=1}^{T} x_t \\ \sum_{t=1}^{T} x_t & \sum_{t=1}^{T} x_t^2 \end{bmatrix}^{-1} \begin{bmatrix} \sum_{t=1}^{T} \widehat{u}_t \\ \sum_{t=1}^{T} \widehat{u}_t x_t \end{bmatrix}$$

$$= T R^2. \tag{21.15}$$

The second step is based on the property of the Bernoulli distribution that $\text{var}(y_t) = \Phi(1 - \Phi)$, which suggests that under the null hypothesis $\widehat{\Phi}(1 - \widehat{\Phi})$ can be replaced by the sample variance

$$s^2 = \frac{1}{T} \sum_{t=1}^{T} (y_t - \overline{y})^2 = \frac{1}{T} \sum_{t=1}^{T} (y_t - \widehat{\Phi})^2 = \frac{1}{T} \sum_{t=1}^{T} \widehat{u}_t^2.$$

The LM statistic in (21.15) shows that small values of R^2 suggest that x_t does not contribute to explaining the difference between y_t and its sample mean, that is its sample proportion. Consequently, a LM test of the overall explanatory power of the model is implemented as a two-stage regression procedure as follows.

Step 1: Regress y_t on a constant to obtain the residual, $\widehat{u}_t = y_t - \overline{y}$.
Step 2: Regress $\widehat{u}_t$ on $\{1 \; x_t\}$.
Step 3: Compute $T R^2$ from this second-stage regression and the corresponding p-value from the χ_K^2 distribution, where K is the number of variables in x_t. A p-value of less than 0.05 represents rejection of the null hypothesis at the 5% level.

Example 21.8 Joint LM Test in a Probit Model

Consider the probit model of monetary policy in Example 21.7. Defining $\widehat{u}_t = y_t - \overline{y}$ from the first stage, the estimated regression equation at the second stage is

$$\widehat{u}_t = -0.013 + 0.278 \, s_t + 4.022 \, \pi_{t-4} + 0.030 \, gdp_t + \widehat{e}_t \,,$$

with coefficient of determination of $R^2 = 0.231322$. The LM statistic of the joint test that $\beta_1 = \beta_2 = \beta_3 = 0$ is

$$LM = T R^2 = 106 \times 0.231322 = 24.520 \,,$$

which is distributed under the null hypothesis as χ_3^2. The p-value is 0.000 showing strong rejection of the null hypothesis at the 5% level.   □

21.3.4 *Binary Autoregressive Models*

In the models discussed in this chapter so far, the distribution of the dependent variable y_t is conditional on a set of explanatory variables x_t. Without loss of generality, this set can also include lagged values of the x_t variables. However, extending the set of explanatory variables to include lagged values of the dependent variable requires more careful modelling. One possible specification is the AR class of models investigated in Chapter 13. In the case of an AR(1) model the dynamics are represented by

$$y_t = \phi_0 + \phi_1 y_{t-1} + v_t \,, \tag{21.16}$$

in which $-1 < \phi_1 < 1$ is the AR parameter and v_t is a continuous *iid* disturbance term. As y_t represents binary integers, the proposed model needs to preserve this property. This is not the case with the model in equation (21.16) as (i) the conditional expectation $E_{t-1}[y_t] = \phi_1 y_{t-1}$ is unlikely to be a binary integer even if y_{t-1} is; (ii) the disturbance term v_t is continuous suggesting that y_t is also continuous. An alternative strategy is needed for the present case of a binary random variable.

Let y_t be a binary random variable corresponding to one of two states

$$y_t = \begin{cases} 1 & : \quad \text{State 1} \\ 0 & : \quad \text{State 0}. \end{cases}$$

In the next period, y_{t+1} is also a binary random variable taking on the values $\{1, 0\}$ depending upon its value in the previous state. The dynamics of y_t are represented by the AR(1) model

$$y_t = (1 - q) + (p + q - 1)y_{t-1} + u_t. \tag{21.17}$$

The parameters p and q represent the conditional probabilities of staying in each respective state

$$\begin{aligned} p &= P[y_t = 1 \mid y_{t-1} = 1] \\ q &= P[y_t = 0 \mid y_{t-1} = 0]. \end{aligned} \tag{21.18}$$

As y_t is binary, the disturbance term u_t also needs to be binary in order to preserve the characteristics of the dependent variable. The disturbance term has the following form depending upon the conditional value of y_{t-1}. If $y_{t-1} = 1$

$$u_t = \begin{cases} 1 - p & : \quad \text{with probability } p \\ -p & : \quad \text{with probability } 1 - p, \end{cases} \tag{21.19}$$

whereas, if $y_{t-1} = 0$

$$u_t = \begin{cases} -(1 - q) & : \quad \text{with probability } q \\ q & : \quad \text{with probability } 1 - q. \end{cases} \tag{21.20}$$

To show that the model given by equations (21.17) to (21.20) preserves the binary characteristics of y_t suppose that $y_{t-1} = 1$. From (21.17)

$$y_t = (1 - q) + (p + q - 1) \times 1 + u_t = p + u_t,$$

and, from (21.18), $u_t = 1 - p$ with probability p, which means that

$$y_t = p + (1 - p) = 1,$$

with probability p, which is the definition of p in (21.18). Alternatively, $u_t = -p$ with probability $1 - p$, which means that

$$y_t = p + (-p) = 0,$$

with probability $1 - p$. A similar result occurs for the case of $y_{t-1} = 0$.

An alternative way of summarising these transition probabilities is to define the transition matrix

$$\begin{bmatrix} p & 1 - q \\ 1 - p & q \end{bmatrix}, \tag{21.21}$$

where the first row is used to compute the probability of ending in state $y_t = 1$, while the second row gives the probability of ending in state $y_t = 0$. Thus,

$$
\begin{bmatrix} P(y_t = 1) \\ P(y_t = 0) \end{bmatrix} = \begin{bmatrix} p & 1-q \\ 1-p & q \end{bmatrix} \begin{bmatrix} P(y_{t-1} = 1) \\ P(y_{t-1} = 0) \end{bmatrix}.
$$

Estimation of the parameters $\theta = \{p, q\}$ in equation (21.17) can be accomplished using the EMM estimator discussed in Chapter 12. A natural choice of the auxiliary model is the continuous time AR(1) model in equation (21.16) which is fully specified as

$$
y_t = \phi_0 + \phi_1 y_{t-1} + v_t, \qquad v_t \sim iid \; N(0, \sigma_v^2). \tag{21.22}
$$

The algorithm proceeds as follows. Estimate the auxiliary model in (21.22) using the actual data by regressing y_t on a constant and y_{t-1} to obtain $\widehat{\beta} = \widehat{\phi}_0, \widehat{\phi}_1$, as well as the residual variance $\widehat{\sigma}_v^2$. Simulate the model in equations (21.17) to (21.20) for starting values of $\theta = \{p, q\}$ and generate simulated data $y_{s,t}$. Evaluate the (2×1) gradient function of the auxiliary model, replacing the actual data by the simulated data

$$
G_S(\theta, \widehat{\beta}) = \begin{bmatrix} \dfrac{1}{S\widehat{\sigma}_v^2} \displaystyle\sum_{t=2}^{S} (y_{s,t} - \widehat{\phi}_0 - \widehat{\phi}_1 y_{s,t-1}) \\ \dfrac{1}{S\widehat{\sigma}_v^2} \displaystyle\sum_{t=2}^{S} (y_{s,t} - \widehat{\phi}_0 - \widehat{\phi}_1 y_{s,t-1}) y_{s,t-1} \end{bmatrix},
$$

in which $S = T \times K$ and K is the number of simulated paths. The EMM estimator is the solution of

$$
\widehat{\theta} = \arg \max_{\theta} \frac{1}{2} G_S'(\theta, \widehat{\beta}) W_T^{-1} G_S(\theta, \widehat{\beta}), \tag{21.23}
$$

where W_T is the optimal weighting matrix encountered in Chapters 9, 10 and 12. An example of this class of model is the Markov switching model of Hamilton (1989), discussed in Chapter 19.

21.4   Ordered Data

In the probit model of monetary policy discussed in Example 21.7, the dependent variable is defined in terms of two regimes that capture the sign of movements in the target rate. Inspection of Table 21.4 reveals that there is also additional information available about the size of the change in terms of monetary tightening and easing. It is possible to characterise monetary policy in terms of five regimes over the period 1984 to 1997, ranging from -0.50% to 0.50% in steps of 0.25%. As the dependent variable is an ordered discrete random variable, a simple probit model is no longer appropriate and an ordered probit model is required.

To specify the ordered probit model, the dependent variable y_t is defined in terms of the dummy variable d_t as

$$
d_t = \begin{cases}
0 & : & y_t = -0.50 & \text{[Extreme easing]} \\
1 & : & y_t = -0.25 & \text{[Easing]} \\
2 & : & y_t = 0.00 & \text{[No change]} \\
3 & : & y_t = 0.25 & \text{[Tightening]} \\
4 & : & y_t = 0.50 & \text{[Extreme tightening]}.
\end{cases}
$$

The probabilities associated with each regime are

$$
\begin{aligned}
\Phi_{0,t} &= \Pr(d_t = 0) = \Phi(c_0 - x_t\beta) \\
\Phi_{1,t} &= \Pr(d_t = 1) = \Phi(c_1 - x_t\beta) - \Phi(c_0 - x_t\beta) \\
\Phi_{2,t} &= \Pr(d_t = 2) = \Phi(c_2 - x_t\beta) - \Phi(c_1 - x_t\beta) \\
\Phi_{3,t} &= \Pr(d_t = 3) = \Phi(c_3 - x_t\beta) - \Phi(c_2 - x_t\beta) \\
\Phi_{4,t} &= \Pr(d_t = 4) = 1 - \Phi(c_3 - x_t\beta),
\end{aligned}
$$

where x_t is the set of explanatory variables with parameter vector β and $c_0 < c_1 < c_2 < c_3$ are parameters corresponding to the intercepts of each regime. The order restriction on the c parameters is needed to ensure that the probabilities of each regime are positive. In the special case of two regimes, $c_0 = -\beta_0$ is the intercept of the probit regression model in which

$$
d_t = \begin{cases}
0 & : & \text{with probability } \Phi_{0,t} & \text{[Easing or no change]} \\
1 & : & \text{with probability } \Phi_{1,t} & \text{[Tightening]},
\end{cases}
$$

where

$$
\begin{aligned}
\Phi_{0,t} &= \Pr(d_t = 0) = \Phi(-\beta_0 - x_t\beta) = 1 - \Phi(\beta_0 + x_t\beta) \\
\Phi_{1,t} &= \Pr(d_t = 1) = 1 - \Phi(-\beta_0 - x_t\beta) = \Phi(\beta_0 + x_t\beta).
\end{aligned}
$$

The log-likelihood function for a sample of size T is

$$
\ln L_T(\theta) = \frac{1}{T} \sum_{t=1}^{T} \sum_{j=0}^{4} d_{j,t} \ln \Phi_{j,t},
$$

where the unknown parameters are $\theta = \{\beta, c_0, c_1, c_2, c_3\}$. This function is maximised with respect to θ using the iterative algorithms discussed in Chapter 3.

Example 21.9 An Ordered Probit Model of Monetary Policy

Table 21.6 gives the results of estimating the ordered probit model of United States monetary policy, with the same explanatory variables as used in the probit version of this model given in Example 21.7, namely, the spread between the Federal funds rate and the 6-month Treasury bill rate, s_t, the 1-month lagged inflation rate, π_{t-4}, and the growth rate in output, gdp_t. Similar to the empirical results reported for the probit model in Table 21.7, s_t is statistically the most important explanatory variable of monetary policy. The restricted model is

Table 21.6. *Maximum likelihood estimates of the ordered probit model of monetary policy: calculations based on the BFGS algorithm with derivatives computed numerically. Reported p-values are based on the Hessian*

Parameter	Unrestricted		Restricted	
	Estimate	p-value	Estimate	p-value
c_0	-2.587	0.003	-1.906	0.000
c_1	-1.668	0.048	-1.117	0.000
c_2	1.542	0.063	1.315	0.000
c_3	2.321	0.008	1.778	0.000
β_1	1.641	0.000		
β_2	4.587	0.823		
β_3	0.125	0.109		
$T \ln L_T$	-68.154		-87.005	

estimated by setting $\beta_1 = \beta_2 = \beta_3 = 0$. Substituting these estimates into the cumulative normal distribution recovers the empirical probabilities of each regime given in Table 21.4. For example

$$\Pr(d_t = 0) = \int_{-\infty}^{-1.906} \frac{1}{\sqrt{2\pi}} \exp\left[-\frac{s^2}{2}\right] ds = 0.028$$

$$\Pr(d_t = 1) = \int_{-1.906}^{-1.117} \frac{1}{\sqrt{2\pi}} \exp\left[-\frac{s^2}{2}\right] ds = 0.132 - 0.028 = 0.104\,,$$

correspond to $3/106$ and $10/106$, respectively.   □

21.5   Count Data

Count data measure the number of times that an event occurs within a given time period. An example was given in Table 21.1 where the number of trades, y, occurring in the 3-second interval was

$$y_t = \begin{cases} 0 \\ 1 \\ 2. \end{cases}$$

The data are positive integer counts and, therefore, represent a discrete random variable.

A natural way to model a dependent variable that measures counts is to assume that y_t has a Poisson distribution

$$f(y_t; \theta) = \frac{\theta^{y_t} \exp(-\theta)}{y_t!}, \qquad y_t = 0, 1, 2, \cdots, \qquad \theta > 0, \quad (21.24)$$

where θ is an unknown parameter, which represents the mean of the distribution $\theta = E[y_t]$.

Example 21.10 Poisson Distribution

For a sample of T observations on y_t assumed to be independent drawings from the Poisson distribution, the log-likelihood function is

$$\ln L_T(\theta) = \frac{1}{T} \sum_{t=1}^{T} \ln f(y_t; \theta)$$

$$= \frac{1}{T} \sum_{t=1}^{T} \ln \left(\frac{\theta^{y_t} \exp(-\theta)}{y_t!} \right) = \ln \theta \frac{1}{T} \sum_{t=1}^{T} y_t - \theta - \frac{1}{T} \sum_{t=1}^{T} \ln y_t!.$$

The gradient and Hessian are, respectively,

$$G_T(\theta) = \frac{d \ln L_T(\theta)}{d\theta} = \frac{1}{\theta T} \sum_{t=1}^{T} y_t - 1,$$

$$H_T(\theta) = \frac{d^2 \ln L_T(\theta)}{d\theta^2} = -\frac{1}{\theta^2 T} \sum_{t=1}^{T} y_t .$$

Setting the gradient to zero yields the sample mean as the maximum likelihood estimator

$$\widehat{\theta} = \frac{1}{T} \sum_{t=1}^{T} y_t .$$

Evaluating the Hessian at $\widehat{\theta}$ shows that the maximum likelihood estimator satisfies the second-order condition

$$H_T(\widehat{\theta}) = -\frac{1}{\widehat{\theta}^2 T} \sum_{t=1}^{T} y_t = -\frac{1}{\widehat{\theta}^2 T} T\widehat{\theta} = -\frac{1}{\widehat{\theta}} < 0 .$$

The variance of $\widehat{\theta}$ is

$$\text{var}(\widehat{\theta}) = -\frac{1}{T} H_T^{-1}(\widehat{\theta}) = \frac{\widehat{\theta}}{T},$$

which is the usual formula given for computing the variance of the sample mean from the Poisson distribution. ☐

21.5.1   *The Poisson Regression Model*

The Poisson regression model is obtained by specifying the mean of the Poisson distribution in equation (21.24) as a function of the exogenous variable x_t,

$$f(y_t \mid x_t; \theta) = \frac{\mu_t^{y_t} \exp(-\mu_t)}{y_t!}, \qquad y_t = 0, 1, 2, \cdots \tag{21.25}$$

$$\mu_t = \exp(\beta_0 + \beta_1 x_t), \qquad \mu_t > 0, \tag{21.26}$$

in which $\theta = \{\beta_0, \beta_1\}$ are the unknown parameters and the nonlinear function $\exp(\beta_0 + \beta_1 x_t)$ ensures that the conditional mean is positive for all t.

For a sample of T observations, the log-likelihood function is

$$\ln L_T(\theta) = \frac{1}{T} \sum_{t=1}^{T} \ln f(y_t \mid x_t; \theta) = \frac{1}{T} \sum_{t=1}^{T} (y_t \ln \mu_t - \mu_t - \ln y_t!)$$

$$= \frac{1}{T} \sum_{t=1}^{T} (y_t(\beta_0 + \beta_1 x_t) - \exp(\beta_0 + \beta_1 x_t) - \ln y_t!).$$

The gradient is

$$G_T(\theta) = \begin{bmatrix} \dfrac{\partial \ln L_T(\theta)}{\partial \beta_0} \\[2mm] \dfrac{\partial \ln L_T(\theta)}{\partial \beta_1} \end{bmatrix} = \frac{1}{T} \sum_{t=1}^{T} (y_t - \mu_t) \begin{bmatrix} 1 \\ x_t \end{bmatrix}.$$

The Hessian is

$$H_T(\theta) = \begin{bmatrix} \dfrac{\partial^2 \ln L_T(\theta)}{\partial \beta_0^2} & \dfrac{\partial^2 \ln L_T(\theta)}{\partial \beta_0 \partial \beta_1} \\[2mm] \dfrac{\partial^2 \ln L_T(\theta)}{\partial \beta_0 \partial \beta_1} & \dfrac{\partial^2 \ln L_T(\theta)}{\partial \beta_1^2} \end{bmatrix} = -\frac{1}{T} \sum_{t=1}^{T} \mu_t \begin{bmatrix} 1 & x_t \\ x_t & x_t^2 \end{bmatrix},$$

yielding the information matrix

$$I(\theta) = -E[H_T(\theta)] = \frac{1}{T} \sum_{t=1}^{T} \mu_t \begin{bmatrix} 1 & x_t \\ x_t & x_t^2 \end{bmatrix}.$$

As there is no analytical solution for $\hat{\theta} = \{\hat{\beta}_0, \hat{\beta}_1\}$, it is necessary to use an iterative algorithm.

Hypothesis tests are performed using the LR, Wald and LM testing frameworks. As with the probit model, the LM statistic

$$LM = T G_T'(\hat{\theta}_0) I^{-1}(\hat{\theta}_0) G_T(\hat{\theta}_0),$$

where $\hat{\theta}_0$ is the maximum likelihood estimator under the null hypothesis, is often a convenient testing strategy. Consider a test of the hypothesis $\beta_1 = 0$ in equation (21.26). The maximum likelihood estimator is $\widehat{\mu} = \exp(\widehat{\beta}_0) = \overline{y}$. The gradient and information matrix under the null hypothesis are, respectively,

$$G_T(\widehat{\theta}_0) = \frac{1}{T}\sum_{t=1}^{T}(y_t - \overline{y})\begin{bmatrix}1\\x_t\end{bmatrix} = \frac{1}{T}\sum_{t=1}^{T}\widehat{u}_t\begin{bmatrix}1\\x_t\end{bmatrix}$$

$$I(\widehat{\theta}_0) = \frac{1}{T}\sum_{t=1}^{T}\overline{y}\begin{bmatrix}1 & x_t\\x_t & x_t^2\end{bmatrix},$$

where $\widehat{u}_t = y_t - \overline{y}$. Substituting the expressions for $G_T(\widehat{\theta}_0)$ and $I(\widehat{\theta}_0)$ into the LM statistic and rearranging gives

$$LM = \frac{1}{\overline{y}}\begin{bmatrix}\sum_{t=1}^{T}\widehat{u}_t\\\sum_{t=1}^{T}\widehat{u}_t x_t\end{bmatrix}'\begin{bmatrix}T & \sum_{t=1}^{T}x_t\\\sum_{t=1}^{T}x_t & \sum_{t=1}^{T}x_t^2\end{bmatrix}^{-1}\begin{bmatrix}\sum_{t=1}^{T}\widehat{u}_t\\\sum_{t=1}^{T}\widehat{u}_t x_t\end{bmatrix}$$

$$= \frac{T}{\sum_{t=1}^{T}\widehat{u}_t^2}\begin{bmatrix}\sum_{t=1}^{T}\widehat{u}_t\\\sum_{t=1}^{T}\widehat{u}_t x_t\end{bmatrix}'\begin{bmatrix}T & \sum_{t=1}^{T}x_t\\\sum_{t=1}^{T}x_t & \sum_{t=1}^{T}x_t^2\end{bmatrix}^{-1}\begin{bmatrix}\sum_{t=1}^{T}\widehat{u}_t\\\sum_{t=1}^{T}\widehat{u}_t x_t\end{bmatrix}$$

$$= T R^2,$$

where the second step is based on the property of the Poisson distribution that $\mu = \text{var}(y_t)$, which suggests that under the null hypothesis $\overline{y}$ can be replaced by the sample variance

$$s^2 = \frac{1}{T}\sum_{t=1}^{T}(y_t - \overline{y})^2 = \frac{1}{T}\sum_{t=1}^{T}\widehat{u}_t^2.$$

The LM test of the overall explanatory power of the model is implemented as a two-stage regression procedure as follows:

Step 1: Regress y_t on a constant to obtain the residual, $\widehat{u}_t = y_t - \overline{y}$.
Step 2: Regress $\widehat{u}_t$ on $\{1, x_t\}$.
Step 3: Compute $T R^2$ from this second-stage regression and the corresponding p-value from the χ_K^2 distribution, where K is the number of variables in x_t. A p-value of less than 0.05 represents rejection of the null hypothesis at the 5% level.

21.5.2 Integer Autoregressive Models

Consider specifying a Poisson autoregressive model where y_t is a Poisson random variable representing count data assumed to be a function of its own lag y_{t-1}. As discussed in Section 21.3.4, the continuous time AR(1) model in equation (21.16) is not appropriate to model autoregressive discrete random variables as (i) the conditional expectation $E_{t-1}[y_t]$ is unlikely to be an integer; (ii) the disturbance term v_t is continuous suggesting that y_t is also continuous. The second problem is easily rectified by replacing the continuous distribution of v_t by a discrete distribution such as the Poisson distribution. The first problem is solved by replacing the multiplication operator ρy_{t-1} in equation (21.16) by the binomial thinning operator introduced by Steutel and Van Harn (1979) and extended by McKenzie (1988) and Al-Osh and Alzaid (1987). See also Jung, Ronning and Tremayne (2005) for a review.

A first-order Poisson autoregressive model is specified as

$$ y_t = \underbrace{\rho \circ y_{t-1}}_{departures\ (Bernoulli)} + \underbrace{u_t}_{arrivals\ (Poisson)} , \tag{21.27}$$

in which

$$ \rho \circ y_{t-1} = \sum_{s=1}^{y_{t-1}} e_{s,t-1} $$
$$ e_{s,t-1} = \begin{cases} 1: & Prob = \rho \\ 0: & Prob = 1 - \rho \end{cases} \tag{21.28}$$
$$ u_t \sim iid\ P(\lambda). $$

The notation $\circ$ is referred to as the binomial thinning operator because it sums y_{t-1} Bernoulli random variables, $e_{s,t-1}$, each with probability of success equal to ρ. The disturbance term u_t is a Poisson random variable with parameter λ, given by $P(\lambda)$. This model has two sources of randomness.

Thinning: Departures at each t are determined by the thinning operator assuming Bernoulli random variables.

Disturbance: Arrivals at each t are determined by a Poisson random variable.

Example 21.11 Simulating a Poisson AR(1) Model

The parameters of the Poisson autoregressive model are $\rho = 0.3$ and $\lambda = 3.5$, with the initial value of y_t given by $y_1 = 5$. To simulate y_t at $t = 2$, $y_1 = 5$ uniform random numbers are drawn with values $\{0.51, 0.24, 0.26, 0.51, 0.59\}$. As two of these random variables are less than $\rho = 0.3$, the value of the thinning operator is

$$ \rho \circ y_1 = \sum_{s=1}^{y_1} e_{s,1} = \sum_{s=1}^{5} e_{s,1} = 0 + 1 + 1 + 0 + 0 = 2. $$

Drawing from the Poisson distribution with parameter $\lambda = 3.5$ yields the disturbance term $u_2 = 2$. The updated value of y_2 is

$$ y_2 = \rho \circ y_1 + u_2 = 2 + 2 = 4. $$

To simulate y_t at $t = 3$, $y_2 = 4$ new uniform random numbers are drawn with values $\{0.297, 0.844, 0.115, 0.600\}$, resulting in the thinning operation

$$\rho \circ y_2 = \sum_{s=1}^{y_2} e_{s,1} = \sum_{s=1}^{4} e_{s,1} = 1 + 0 + 1 + 0 = 2 \,.$$

Drawing from the Poisson distribution with parameter $\lambda = 3.5$ yields the disturbance term $u_3 = 1$, so the updated value of y_3 is

$$y_3 = \rho \circ y_2 + u_3 = 2 + 1 = 3 \,.$$

These calculations are repeated for $t = 4$ with the initial value $y_3 = 3$. $\qquad\square$

The parameters of the first-order Poisson autoregressive model, $\theta = \{\rho, \lambda\}$ in equations (21.27) and (21.28), can be estimated by maximum likelihood methods. The conditional distribution of y_t is shown by Al-Osh and Alzaid (1987) to be

$$f(y_t \mid y_{t-1}; \theta) = \sum_{k=0}^{\min(y_t, y_{t-1})} \frac{y_{t-1}! \rho^k (1 - \rho)^{y_{t-1}-k}}{k!(y_{t-1} - k)!} \frac{\lambda^{y_t - k} \exp(-\lambda)}{(y_t - k)!} \,.$$

$$(21.29)$$

This distribution represents a mixture of a binomial distribution and a Poisson distribution which naturally follows from the two sources of randomness underlying the model in equation (21.27). Conditioning on the first observation, the log-likelihood for a sample of $t = 2, 3, \cdots, T$ observations is

$$\ln L_T(\theta) = \frac{1}{T-1} \sum_{t=2}^{T} \ln f(y_t \mid y_{t-1}; \theta)$$

$$= -\lambda + \frac{1}{T-1} \sum_{t=2}^{T} \ln \left(\sum_{k=0}^{\min(y_t, y_{t-1})} \frac{y_{t-1}! \rho^k (1 - \rho)^{y_{t-1}-k}}{k!(y_{t-1} - k)!} \frac{\lambda^{y_t - k}}{(y_t - k)!} \right) \,.$$

The numerical optimisation algorithms presented in Chapter 3 are used to maximise this function with respect to θ.

Example 21.12 Sampling Properties
This example reproduces the results of Jung, Ronning and Tremayne (2005, Table 1) for the case of maximum likelihood estimation. The sample size is $T = 100$ and the number of draws is 5000. The results are given in Table 21.7 where the population parameter values are $\rho = 0.3$ and $\lambda = 3.5$ and $E[y] = \lambda/(1 - \rho) = 3.5/(1 - 0.3) = 5$. Also reported are the sampling properties of the conditional least squares (CLS) estimator of Klimko and Nelson (1978), where ρ and λ are estimated, respectively, from a least squares regression of y_t on y_{t-1} and a constant. The maximum likelihood estimator has superior

Table 21.7. *Finite sample properties of the maximum likelihood estimator (MLE) and the conditional least squares estimator (CLS) of the parameters of the Poisson first-order autoregressive model. The sample size is $T = 100$ and the number of draws is 5000*

Statistics	MLE		CLS	
	ρ	λ	ρ	λ
True	0.300	3.500	0.300	3.500
Mean	0.295	3.528	0.279	3.609
Bias	−0.005	0.028	−0.021	0.109
St. dev.	0.096	0.504	0.100	0.521
RMSE	0.096	0.505	0.102	0.533
MSE	0.009	0.225	0.010	0.284

sampling properties to the CLS estimator, producing smaller bias and lower variances. A measure of the asymptotic relative efficiency (ARE) is given by the ratio of the MSE of the maximum likelihood estimator to the CLS estimator

$$\text{ARE}(\widehat{\rho}) = \frac{\text{MSE}(\widehat{\rho}_{MLE})}{\text{MSE}(\widehat{\rho}_{CLS})} = \frac{0.009}{0.010} = 0.886$$

$$\text{ARE}(\widehat{\lambda}) = \frac{\text{MSE}(\widehat{\lambda}_{MLE})}{\text{MSE}(\widehat{\lambda}_{CLS})} = \frac{0.225}{0.284} = 0.898,$$

which show efficiency gains of around 10% in the maximum likelihood estimator compared to the CLS estimator. □

The testing procedures discussed in Chapter 4 can be used to conduct hypothesis tests on θ. For example, a test of the hypothesis $\rho = 0$, provides a test of independence. Imposing this restriction on the conditional distribution in (21.29) gives

$$
\begin{aligned}
f(y_t \,|\, y_{t-1}; \rho = 0, \lambda) &= \sum_{k=0}^{\min(y_t, y_{t-1})} \frac{y_{t-1}! 0^k (1-0)^{y_{t-1}-k}}{k!(y_{t-1}-k)!} \frac{\lambda^{y_t-k} \exp(-\lambda)}{(y_t - k)!} \\
&= \left(\frac{y_{t-1}! 0^k (1-0)^{y_{t-1}-0}}{0!(y_{t-1}-0)!} \frac{\lambda^{y_t-0} \exp(-\lambda)}{(y_t - 0)!} \right. \\
&\quad \left. + \frac{y_{t-1}! 0^1 (1-0)^{y_{t-1}-1}}{1!(y_{t-1}-1)!} \frac{\lambda^{y-1} \exp(-\lambda)}{(y - 1)!} + \cdots \right) \\
&= \frac{\lambda^{y_t} \exp(-\lambda)}{y_t!},
\end{aligned}
$$

which is the unconditional Poisson distribution of y_t. Under the null hypothesis, the consequence of $\rho = 0$ is the suppression of the randomness of the thinning operator thus leaving the Poisson component as the only source of error.

Extending the specification of the first-order Poisson autoregressive model to include longer lags and moving average dynamics immediately involves more complicated estimation issues. Maximum likelihood estimation of higher-order integer autoregressive models are discussed by Bu, McCabe and Hadri (2008) where the binomial model is replaced by a multinomial model. In the case of MA dynamics estimation by maximum likelihood methods is infeasible as the likelihood function is no longer tractable. For integer MA models and more generally integer ARMA specifications Martin, Tremayne and Jung (2011) propose an EMM estimator. The sampling properties of this estimator are investigated in Section 21.7. Bayesian methods for dealing with time series counts are discussed in McCabe and Martin (2005) and Frühwirth-Schnatter and Wagner (2006).

21.6 Duration Data

In the previous section, the Poisson distribution with parameter $\theta = \{\mu\}$ is used to model the number of counts within a given time period. From the properties of the Poisson distribution, the durations between counts have an exponential distribution with the same parameter μ. Letting y_t represent the duration between counts, the distribution of y_t is given by

$$f(y_t; \theta) = \frac{1}{\mu} \exp\left(-\frac{y_t}{\mu}\right), \qquad \mu > 0. \tag{21.30}$$

From Chapter 1, the maximum likelihood estimator of μ is the sample mean of y_t.

As with the Poisson regression model exogenous variables can be included in the duration model by expressing the mean μ as a function of x_t. The duration regression model is specified as

$$f(y_t \mid x_t; \theta) = \frac{1}{\mu_t} \exp\left(-\frac{y_t}{\mu_t}\right), \qquad \mu_t > 0, \tag{21.31}$$

where μ_t is the conditional mean of the exponential distribution, which is a function of the exogenous variable x_t. To ensure that μ_t is strictly positive for all t, the following restriction is imposed

$$\mu_t = \exp(\beta_0 + \beta_1 x_t). \tag{21.32}$$

For a sample of T observations, the log-likelihood function for the duration regression model is

$$\ln L_T(\theta) = \frac{1}{T}\sum_{t=1}^{T} \ln f(y|x_t;\theta) = \frac{1}{T}\sum_{t=1}^{T}(-\ln \mu_t - \frac{y_t}{\mu_t})$$

$$= \frac{1}{T}\sum_{t=1}^{T}\left(-(\beta_0 + \beta_1 x_t) - \frac{y_t}{\exp(\beta_0 + \beta_1 x_t)}\right), \qquad (21.33)$$

which is maximised with respect to the parameters $\theta = \{\beta_0, \beta_1\}$ using an iterative algorithm.

Example 21.13 The Engle-Russell ACD Model A class of models used in empirical finance to model the duration between trades, y_t, is the autoregressive conditional duration model (ACD) of Engle and Russell (1998), where y is distributed exponentially as in (21.31) and the conditional mean in (21.32) is specified as

$$\mu_t = \alpha_0 + \sum_{j=1}^{q}\alpha_j y_{t-j} + \sum_{j=1}^{p}\beta_j \mu_{t-j}.$$

To ensure that the conditional mean is stationary, the condition

$$\sum_{j=1}^{q}\alpha_j + \sum_{j=1}^{p}\beta_j < 1,$$

is needed. The parameters β_j control the memory of the process, being a weighted sum of lagged durations. □

An important concept in modelling durations is the hazard rate which represents the probability of an event occurring in the next time interval

$$h_t = \frac{f(y_t)}{S(y_t)} = \frac{f(y_t)}{1 - F(y_t)}, \qquad (21.34)$$

where $f(y_t)$ is the probability density of y_t, $S(y_t)$ is the survival function and $F(y_t)$ is the corresponding cumulative probability distribution. In the case where $f(y_t)$ is the exponential distribution given in (21.31), the survival function is $S(y_t) = \exp(-y_t\mu_t^{-1})$ and the hazard rate reduces to

$$h_t = \frac{f(y_t)}{S(y_t)} = \frac{\mu_t^{-1}\exp(-y_t\mu_t^{-1})}{\exp(-y_t\mu_t^{-1})} = \frac{1}{\mu_t}. \qquad (21.35)$$

The hazard rate represents a probability and must satisfy the restriction $0 \leq h_t \leq 1$.

Example 21.14 The Hamilton-Jorda ACH Model of Trades

Let y_t be a binary variable with $y_t = 1$ if an event occurs and $y_t = 0$ if no event occurs. The autoregressive conditional hazard model (ACH) of Hamilton and Jordà (2002) is given by

$$f(y_t \mid x_t; \theta) = h_t^{y_t}(1 - h_t)^{1-y_t}$$

$$h_t = \frac{1}{1 + \exp(\psi_t)}$$

$$\psi_t = \alpha_0 + \alpha_1 d_{t-1} + \beta_1 \psi_{t-1},$$

where x_t consists of lags of d_t, the observed duration between events, h_t is the hazard rate, and ψ_t represents the conditional duration. The specification of the hazard rate ensures that $0 < h_t < 1$. This is a dynamic probit regression model where the probability represents the hazard rate which is time-varying according to durations in the previous period d_{t-1}, and the lagged hazard rate as $\psi_{t-1} = \ln(h_{t-1}^{-1} - 1)$. If $\alpha_1 > 0$, an increase in d_{t-1} decreases the probability (hazard rate) of an event occurring the next period. The equation for ψ_t corresponds to the conditional mean equation in the ACD model. The difference in the ACD and ACH models is that the dependent variable of the ACD model is the duration time between events at time t, whereas it is the binary variable that an event occurs at time t in the ACH model. An application of the ACH model is given next. □

21.7 Applications

21.7.1 An ACH Model of United States Airline Trades

Nowak (2008) uses an ACH model to investigate the effects of firm-specific and macroeconomic-specific news announcements on transactions of United States airline stocks. Let y_t be a binary variable at time t that identifies whether a trade has occurred

$$y_t = \begin{cases} 1 & : & \text{Trade occurs in a second} \\ 0 & : & \text{No trade occurs.} \end{cases}$$

The model is specified as

$$f(y_t \mid x_t; \theta) = h_t^{y_t}(1 - h_t)^{1-y_t}$$

$$h_t = \frac{1}{1 + \exp(\psi_t + \delta_1 Firm_{t-1} + \delta_2 Macro_{t-1})}$$

$$\psi_t = \alpha_0 + \alpha_1 d_{t-1} + \beta_1 \psi_{t-1},$$

where x_t consists of lags of d_t, the observed duration between events, as well as the dummy variables $Firm_{t-1}$ and $Macro_{t-1}$ which represent respectively, lagged news announcements of the firm and the macroeconomy. The hazard

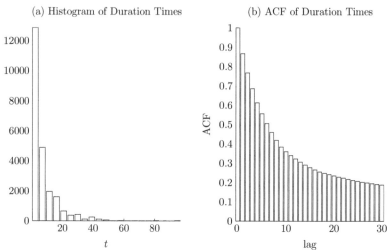

Figure 21.3. Histogram and ACF of the durations between AMR trades.

rate is h_t and ψ_t is the conditional duration. The conditional log-likelihood function for a sample of $t = 1, 2, \cdots, T$ observations is

$$\ln L_T(\theta) = \frac{1}{T-1} \sum_{t=2}^{T} \left(y_t \ln(h_t) + (1 - y_t) \ln(1 - h_t) \right),$$

which is maximised with respect to $\theta = \{\alpha_0, \alpha_1, \beta_1, \delta_1, \delta_2\}$.

The data consist of trades per second on the United States company AMR, which is the parent company of American Airlines. The data are recorded on 1 August 2006, from 9.30am to 4.00pm. The total number of time periods is $23,367$ second intervals, of which $3,641$ intervals correspond to a trade ($y_t = 1$). A snapshot of the data is given in Table 21.1. The average time between trades is $\bar{d} = 7.28$ seconds. This corresponds to an unconditional hazard rate of

$$\bar{h} = \bar{d}^{-1} = 7.28^{-1} = 0.137,$$

showing that the (unconditional) probability of a trade occurring in the next second is 0.137. A histogram of duration times given in panel (a) of Figure 21.3 shows that the distribution has an exponential shape which is consistent with the assumptions of the hazard rate in the ACH model. A plot of the autocorrelation function of d_t in panel (b) of Figure 21.3 shows that the series exhibits long-memory characteristics with the ACF decaying slowly.

The maximum likelihood estimates of the model are given in Table 21.8 for the unrestricted model as well as for the restricted model where the news

Table 21.8. *Maximum likelihood estimates of the ACH model of trades for the AMR data recorded on 1 August 2006. Estimation uses the BFGS algorithm with numerical derivatives. Quasi-maximum likelihood standard errors are given in parentheses*

Variable	Parameter	Unrestricted		Restricted	
		Estimate	se	Estimate	se
$Const$	α_0	0.020	0.004	0.020	0.004
d_{t-1}	α_1	0.001	0.0001	0.001	0.0001
ψ_{t-1}	β_1	0.984	0.002	0.984	0.002
$Firm_{t-1}$	δ_1	0.503	1.123		
$Macro_{t-1}$	δ_2	-1.747	1.294		
	$T \ln L$	-10024.460		-10025.172	

announcement variables are excluded. The estimate of

$$\widehat{\alpha}_1 + \widehat{\beta}_1 = 0.001 + 0.984 = 0.985 \,,$$

is consistent with the long-memory property of the autocorrelation structure of durations identified in panel (b) of Figure 21.3.

To identify the effect of the news variables on trades, the hazard rate is computed with and without the two news dummy variables as follows

$$\overline{h}(Firm = 0, Macro = 0) = \frac{1}{1 + \exp(1.722)} = 0.152$$

$$\overline{h}(Firm = 1, Macro = 1) = \frac{1}{1 + \exp(1.722 + 0.503 - 1.747)} = 0.383 \,,$$

where $\overline{\psi} = 1.722$ is the sample average of the estimated conditional duration function $\widehat{\psi}_t$, obtained from the last iteration of the maximum likelihood algorithm. With the inclusion of the two news variables, the probability of a trade occurring in the next second immediately after a news announcement more than doubles from 0.152 to 0.383. The estimate of the average length of time to the next trade is $1/0.383 = 2.613$ seconds when there is a news announcement and increases in duration to $1/0.152 = 6.594$ seconds when there is no news announcement. Whilst these results suggest that the news variables are economically significant in terms of the overall effect on trades of AMR stock, the individual t statistics reported in Table 21.8 show that these variables are nonetheless statistically insignificant at conventional levels.

21.7.2   *EMM Estimator of Integer Models*

An important feature of the maximum likelihood estimator of the Poisson binomial thinning model presented in Section 21.5.2, is that while the likelihood
function of an AR(1) model is tractible, it becomes increasingly more complicated for higher-order integer autoregressive models. Expanding the class
of models further to allow for integer moving average processes as well as
mixed integer ARMA processes, the log-likelihood function becomes intract-
ible. As demonstrated in Example 21.12, conditional least squares (CLS) offers
a solution in the case of autoregressive models as it is simple to implement and
has relatively good sampling properties relative to the maximum likelihood
estimator.

   Martin, Tremayne and Jung (2011) propose a variant of the efficient method
of moments estimator (EMM) introduced in Chapter 12, to compute the parameters of Poisson binomial thinning models which include AR(p), MA(q) and
mixed ARMA(p, q) models. This choice of the EMM estimator is motivated
by the following considerations.

(1) The binomial thinning model is easily simulated for integer ARMA models
    of arbitrary lag orders.
(2) There exists a natural auxiliary model that provides a suitable approximation
    to the likelihood of the true binomial thinning model.

   To simulate a mixed process, consider the integer ARMA(1,1) specification
proposed by McKenzie (1988)

$$s_t = \rho \circ s_{t-1} + u_t$$
$$y_t = s_{t-1} + \psi \circ u_t , \qquad (21.36)$$

where y_t is observable, s_t is unobservable, u_t is an *iid* Poisson random variable
with parameter λ, and ρ and ψ are the autoregressive and moving average
parameters respectively. Given starting parameters for $\theta = \{\rho, \lambda, \psi\}$ as well
as a starting value for the latent variable s_t, simulated values of y_t are easily
obtained following the approach of Example 21.11.

   The choice of the auxiliary model is based on a linear AR model where the
lag structure is chosen to be of sufficient length to identify the parameters in
(21.36)

$$y_t = \phi_0 + \sum_{i=1}^{p} \phi_i y_{t-i} + v_t , \qquad (21.37)$$

in which $v_t \sim iid \ N(0, \sigma_v^2)$. For the model in (21.36) a minimum choice of the
lag structure is $p = 2$ so that ϕ_1 and ϕ_2 are used to identify the parameters ρ
and ψ. The disturbance variance σ_v^2 and the intercept ϕ_0 are used to identify λ.

Table 21.9. *Mean and Root Mean Square Error (RMSE) of the EMM estimator for the INARMA(1, 1) model in finite samples. Population parameters are* $\rho_0 = 0.3$, $\lambda_0 = 3.5$ *and* $\psi_0 = 0.7$. *The number of draws is 5000*

Auxiliary	Mean $(\widehat{\rho})$			RMSE $(\widehat{\rho})$		
lag (p)	$T = 50$	$T = 100$	$T = 200$	$T = 50$	$T = 100$	$T = 200$
2	0.280	0.287	0.290	0.183	0.162	0.145
3	0.306	0.309	0.306	0.190	0.162	0.140
	Mean $(\widehat{\lambda})$			RMSE $(\widehat{\lambda})$		
	$T = 50$	$T = 100$	$T = 200$	$T = 50$	$T = 100$	$T = 200$
2	3.561	3.537	3.519	0.673	0.508	0.405
3	3.485	3.487	3.483	0.744	0.545	0.417
	Mean $(\widehat{\psi})$			RMSE $(\widehat{\psi})$		
	$T = 50$	$T = 100$	$T = 200$	$T = 50$	$T = 100$	$T = 200$
2	0.642	0.653	0.663	0.276	0.254	0.232
3	0.620	0.629	0.651	0.278	0.260	0.218

The moment conditions of the auxiliary model are

$$G_T(\theta, \beta) = \frac{1}{T - p} \sum_{t=p+1}^{T} \left[\frac{v_t}{\sigma_v^2} \quad \frac{v_t y_{t-1}}{\sigma_v^2} \quad \frac{v_t y_{t-2}}{\sigma_v^2} \quad \cdots \quad \left(\frac{v_t^2}{\sigma_v^2} - 1 \right) \frac{1}{2\sigma_v^2} \right]'.$$

(21.38)

The EMM estimator is based on solving

$$\widehat{\theta} = \arg\min_{\theta} \frac{1}{2} G_S'(\theta, \widehat{\beta}) W_T^{-1} G_S(\theta, \widehat{\beta}),$$

(21.39)

where $G_S(\theta, \widehat{\beta})$ is the gradient vector in (21.38) with y_t replaced by the simulated data and the auxiliary parameters $\widehat{\beta}$ given by the $\phi_i s$ in equation (21.37) which are estimated by least squares. The matrix W_T is the optimal weighting matrix which is based on the outer product of the gradient vector of the auxiliary model evaluated at y_t (see Chapter 12). As a result of the discrete nature of the underlying process, the objective function in expression (21.39) is not continuous in θ. To circumvent this problem a grid search algorithm is used instead of a gradient algorithm to maximise the log-likelihood function. Under certain regularity conditions, the EMM estimator has the same asymptotic properties as the maximum likelihood estimator and, in some instances, can yield better small sample properties, as the following simulation experiment demonstrates.

The finite sample results of the EMM estimator for the INARMA(1, 1) model in (21.36) are given in Table 21.9. Two auxiliary models are chosen with the lag structure of the auxiliary model in (21.37) varying from $p = 2$ (just-identified) to $p = 3$ (over-identified). The true parameter values are set at

$$\theta_0 = \{\rho_0 = 0.3, \lambda_0 = 3.5, \psi_0 = 0.7\}\ .$$

The sample sizes are $T = \{50, 100, 200\}$, the length of a simulation run is fixed at $S = 500T$ and the number of replications is 5000.

Inspection of the results in Table 21.9 shows that the biases are relatively small and that they decrease as the sample size increases. The percentage bias of $\widehat{\rho}$, in the case of the auxiliary model with $p = 2$ and a sample of size $T = 50$, is just $-100 \times 0.020/0.3 = -6.67\%$. Increasing the sample size to $T = 200$ halves the bias to $-100 \times 0.010/0.3 = -3.33\%$. A comparison of the root mean square error for alternative values of p in the auxiliary model suggests that for smaller samples of size $T = 50$ choosing a smaller lag length for the auxiliary model yields marginally more efficient parameter estimates. The opposite appears to be true for larger samples of size $T = 200$.

21.8   Exercises

(1) Finite Sample Properties of Qualitative Response Estimators

---

Program files   discrete_simulation.*

The model is

$$y_t^* = \beta_0 + \beta_1 x_t^* + u_t^*$$
$$u_t^* \sim iid\ N(0, \sigma^2),$$

where $x_t^* \sim N(0, 1)$ and $\theta_0 = \{\beta_0 = 1, \beta_1 = 1, \sigma^2 = 1\}$.

(a) Simulate 5000 replications of the model with sample size $T = 100$, and compute the bias and root mean square error of the following estimators and compare the results with those reported in Table 21.7.

   (i) Estimate the linear regression model where $y_t = y_t^*$ and $x_t = x_t^*$.
   (ii) Estimate the probit regression model where

$$y_t = \begin{cases} 1 & : & y_t^* > 0 \\ 0 & : & y_t^* \le 0 \end{cases}$$
$$x_t = x_t^*\ .$$

(iii) Estimate the censored regression model where

$$y_t = \begin{cases} y_t^* & : & y_t^* > 0 \\ 0 & : & y_t^* \le 0 \end{cases}$$
$$x_t = x_t^*\ .$$

(iv) Estimate the truncated regression model where

$$y_t = \begin{cases} y_t^* & : & y_t^* > 0 \\ n.a & : & y_t^* \le 0 \end{cases}, \qquad x_t = \begin{cases} x_t^* & : & y_t^* > 0 \\ n.a & : & y_t^* \le 0. \end{cases}$$

(v) Estimate the restricted regression model where $y_t > 0$ is regressed on a constant and the corresponding values of x_t.

(b) Repeat part (a) for $T = \{200, 500, 1000\}$ and discuss the asymptotic properties of the various estimation procedures and their ability to correct for alternative filtering procedures.

(2) A Probit Model of Monetary Policy

Program files	discrete_probit.*
Data files	usmoney.*

The data file contains 693 weekly observations for the United States starting in the first week of February 1984 and ending in the first week of June 1997 for the Federal funds rate, r_t, the spread between the Federal funds rate and the 6-month Treasury bill rate, s_t, the 1-month lagged inflation rate, π_{t-4} and the growth rate in output, gdp_t.

(a) Using just Federal Open Market Committee (FOMC) meeting days, estimate a probit model of monetary policy where

$$y_t = \begin{cases} 1 & : & \Delta r_t > 0 \quad \text{[Monetary tightening]} \\ 0 & : & \Delta r_t \le 0 \quad \text{[Monetary easing or no change]}, \end{cases}$$

and $\{const, s_t, \pi_{t-1}, gdp_t\}$ are the explanatory variables. Compare the results with the estimates given in Table 21.5 and interpret the parameter estimates.
(b) Consider the restricted probit model where all of the parameters on the explanatory variables are zero, with the exception of the intercept. Verify that convergence of a gradient algorithm is achieved in one step if the starting value on the intercept is chosen as $\Phi^{-1}(\bar{y})$, the inverse of the cumulative normal distribution evaluated at the sample mean $\bar{y}$.
(c) Test the validity of the restrictions of the restricted probit model in part (b) using the LR, Wald and LM tests.

(3) An Ordered Probit Model of Monetary Policy

Program files	discrete_ordered.*
Data files	usmoney.*

This exercise uses the same data as Exercise 2.

(a) Using just FOMC meeting days, estimate an ordered probit model of monetary policy where

$$
d_t = \begin{cases}
0 & : & \Delta r_t = -0.50 & \text{[Extreme easing]} \\
1 & : & \Delta r_t = -0.25 & \text{[Easing]} \\
2 & : & \Delta r_t = 0.00 & \text{[No change]} \\
3 & : & \Delta r_t = 0.25 & \text{[Tightening]} \\
4 & : & \Delta r_t = 0.50 & \text{[Extreme tightening]},
\end{cases}
$$

and $\{const, s_t, \pi_{t-4}, gdp_t\}$ are the explanatory variables. Compare the results with the estimates given in Table 21.6 and interpret the parameter estimates.

(b) Consider the restricted ordered probit model where the parameters on the three explanatory variables are zero. Verify that convergence of a gradient algorithm is achieved in one step if the starting values on the intercepts in each regime are chosen as $\Phi^{-1}(p_i)$, the inverse of the cumulative normal distribution evaluated at the proportion of observations in regime i.

(c) Test the validity of the restrictions of the restricted ordered probit model in part (b) using the LR and Wald tests.

(4) Hamiton-Jorda Ordered Probit Model of Monetary Policy

Program files	discrete_hamilton_jorda.*
Data files	usmoney.*

This exercise uses weekly United States data from the first week in February 1984 to the last week of April 2001, being an extended version of the data used in Exercises 2 and 3.

(a) Using just event days, estimate the ordered probit model in Exercise 3 using data from the first week in February 1984 to the first week of June 1997, where the explanatory variables are the magnitude of the last target change as of the previous week and the spread between the 6-month Treasury bill rate and the Federal funds rate. Compare the parameter estimates reported in Hamilton and Jordà (2002, Table 6).

(b) Re-estimate the model in part (a), extending the sample period to April 2001. Check the robustness properties of the parameter estimates over the two sample periods.

(5) Simulating the Binomial Thinning Model

Program files	discrete_thinning.*

Consider the binomial thinning model

$$
y_t = \rho \circ y_{t-1} + u_t,
$$

where

$$\rho \circ y_{t-1} = \sum_{s=1}^{y_{t-1}} e_{s,t-1}$$

$$e_{s,t-1} = \begin{cases} 1: & \text{Prob} = \rho \\ 0: & \text{Prob} = 1 - \rho \end{cases}$$

$$u_t \sim P(\lambda),$$

and $P(\lambda)$ represents iid draws from the Poisson distribution with parameter λ.

(a) Simulate the model for $t = 2, 3, 4, 5$, with parameters $\rho = 0.3$ and $\lambda = 3.5$, and initial value $y_1 = 5$.

(b) Repeat part (a) with parameters $\rho = 0.8$ and $\lambda = 3$.

(c) Repeat part (a) with parameters $\rho = 0.3$ and $\lambda = 3$.

(6) Finite Sample Properties of the Binomial Thinning Model

Program files   discrete_poissonauto.*

This exercise uses Monte Carlo experiments to investigate the finite sample properties of the maximum likelihood estimator of the binomial thinning model in Exercise 5, where the parameters are $\rho = 0.3$ and $\lambda = 3.5$. Simulate the model with 5000 replications and a sample of size $T = 100$.

(a) Compute the maximum likelihood estimator and construct summary statistics of the finite sample distribution of the estimators. Compare the results with those reported in Table 21.7 as well as with the results in Jung, Ronning and Tremayne (2005, Table 1).

(b) Repeat part (a) for the conditional least squares (CLS) estimator of Klimko and Nelson (1978) and compare the finite sample properties of the two estimators.

(c) Repeat parts (a) and (b) for the alternative parameterisations given in Jung, Ronning and Tremayne (2005).

(7) A Duration Model of Strikes

Program files   discrete_strike.*
Data files   strike.*

The data file contains 62 observations on the duration of strikes, y_t, expressed in days, in the United States from 1968 to 1976. Also given are annual data on unanticipated output, $output_t$. All data are based on Kennan (1985). Consider the Weibull model of durations

$$\ln y_t = \beta_0 + \beta_1 \, output_t + \sigma z_t$$
$$f(z_t) = \exp(z_t - e^{z_t}).$$

(a) Estimate the parameters $\theta = \{\beta_0, \beta_1, \sigma^2\}$ by maximum likelihood. As starting values for β_0 and β_1, use the least squares parameter estimates from regressing $\ln y_t$ on a constant and *output*$_t$ and for σ^2 choose 1.0.

(b) Re-estimate the model with z_t having an exponential distribution by imposing the restriction $\sigma^2 = 1$. Perform a LR test of this restriction.

(8) Equivalence of ACD and GARCH Models

Program files	discrete_acd.*
Data files	amr_aug1.*

The data file contains trades per second of the United States airline AMR on 1 August 2006, from 9.30am to 4.00pm, a total of $T = 23367$ observations.

(a) Estimate the following ACD model

$$f(y_t | y_{t-1}, y_{t-2}, \cdots; \theta) = \frac{1}{\mu_t} \exp\left(-\frac{y_t}{\mu_t}\right), \qquad \mu_t > 0,$$

$$\mu_t = \alpha_0 + \alpha_1 y_{t-1} + \beta_1 \mu_{t-1},$$

by maximum likelihood where y_t is the duration between trades.

(b) Estimate the GARCH(1,1) model

$$\sqrt{y_t} = v_t, \qquad v_t \sim N(0, \sigma_t^2),$$

$$\sigma_t^2 = \alpha_0 + \alpha_1 v_{t-1}^2 + \beta_1 \sigma_{t-1}^2.$$

Show that the parameter estimates equal the parameter estimates obtained in part (a). Hence show that the ACD model can be estimated using a GARCH model where the dependent variable is $\sqrt{y_t}$, which is normally distributed with zero mean and variance σ_t^2.

(9) An ACH Model of United States Airline Trades

Program files	discrete_trade.*
Data files	amr_aug1.*

The data file contains trades per second of the United States airline AMR on 1 August 2006, from 9.30am to 4.00pm, a total of $T = 23367$ observations.

(a) Estimate the following ACH model

$$f(y_t | x_t; \theta) = h_t^{y_t} (1 - h_t^{1-y_t}),$$

$$h_t = \frac{1}{1 + \exp(\psi_t + \delta_1 Firm_{t-1} + \delta_2 Macro_{t-1})}$$

$$\psi_t = \alpha_0 + \alpha_1 d_{t-1} + \beta_1 \psi_{t-1},$$

where

$$y_t = \begin{cases} 1 & : & \text{Trade occurs in a second} \\ 0 & : & \text{No trade occurs}, \end{cases}$$

and x_t consists of lags of d_t, the observed duration between events, as well as the dummy variables $Firm_{t-1}$ and $Macro_{t-1}$ which represent respectively, lagged news announcements of the firm and the macroeconomy. Compare the estimates with those reported in Table 21.8.

(b) Compute the effect on the hazard rate h_t of the two news announcement variables.

(10) **EMM Estimator of Integer Models**

Program files   `discrete_emm.*`

Consider the integer ARMA(1,1) specification

$$s_t = \rho \circ s_{t-1} + u_t$$
$$y_t = s_{t-1} + \psi \circ u_t,$$

where y_t is observable, s_t is unobservable, and u_t is an iid Poisson random variable with parameter λ.

(a) Derive the finite sample properties of the EMM estimator of θ for the integer ARMA(1,1) model where the parameters of the model are $\theta_0 = \{\rho_0 = 0.3, \lambda_0 = 3.5, \psi_0 = 0.7\}$. Choose sample sizes of $T = \{50, 100, 200\}$ and 5000 replications.

(b) Repeat part (a) for the integer AR(1) model by setting $\psi_0 = 0.0$.

(c) Repeat part (a) for the integer MA(1) model by setting $\rho_0 = 0.0$.

Appendix A. Change of Variable in Density Functions

Let X be a continuous random variable with pdf $f(x)$. Define a new random variable Y by means of the relation $Y = g(X)$ where g is a monotonic mapping, so that its inverse function exists. The pdf of the continuous random variable Y, $h(y)$ is given by

$$h(y) = f(g^{-1}(y)) \left| \frac{dg^{-1}(y)}{dy} \right| = f(x) \left| \frac{dx}{dy} \right|,$$

where dx/dy is a Jacobian of the transformation.

This result generalises to functions of more than one variable. Let $X_1, \cdots, X_n$ be random variables with joint pdf given by $f(x_1, \cdots, x_n)$. Let $Y_i = g_i(X_1, \cdots, X_n)$, $i = 1, \cdots, n$, be a suitably differentiable one-to-one mapping from $X_1, \cdots, X_n$ to $Y_1, \cdots, Y_n$, then the joint pdf of $Y_1, \cdots, Y_n$ is

$$h(y_1, \cdots, y_n) = f(x_1, \cdots, x_n) |J|,$$

in which J is a Jacobian of the transformation, defined as the determinant of

$$J = \begin{vmatrix} \dfrac{\partial x_1}{\partial y_1} & \cdots & \dfrac{\partial x_1}{\partial y_n} \\ \vdots & \ddots & \vdots \\ \dfrac{\partial x_n}{\partial y_1} & \cdots & \dfrac{\partial x_n}{\partial y_n} \end{vmatrix}.$$

In all cases the new sample space is obtained by mapping the boundary or the old sample space using the $Y = g(X)$ in the univariate case and $Y_i = g_i(X_1, \cdots, X_n)$ in the multivariate case.

Appendix B. The Lag Operator

B.1 Basics

The lag operator, L, takes the time series y_t and lags it once, that is

$$Ly_t = y_{t-1}.$$

From this definition, it follows that

$$L^2 y_t = LLy_t = Ly_{t-1} = y_{t-2}$$
$$L^p y_t = y_{t-p}$$
$$L^{-p} y_t = y_{t+p}.$$

It is also possible to define polynomials in the lag operator. Two polynomials in the lag operator that are often encountered are of the form

$$\phi(L) = \phi_0 + \phi_1 L + \phi_2 L^2 + \phi_3 L^3 + \cdots$$
$$\psi(L) = 1 - \psi_1 L - \psi_2 L^2 - \psi_3 L^3 - \cdots$$

or, in the multivariate case,

$$\Phi(L) = \Phi_0 + \Phi_1 L + \Phi_2 L^2 + \Phi_3 L^3 + \cdots$$
$$\Psi(L) = I - \Psi_1 L - \Psi_2 L^2 - \Psi_3 L^3 - \cdots,$$

where Φ_i and Ψ_i are now square matrices of parameters. Without loss of generality, this appendix presents the univariate case, but each result extends naturally to the multivariate case.

B.2 Polynomial Convolution

Consider the two infinite polynomials in the lag operator

$$\phi(L) = \phi_0 + \phi_1 L + \phi_2 L^2 + \phi_3 L^3 + \cdots$$
$$\psi(L) = \psi_0 + \psi_1 L + \psi_2 L^2 + \psi_3 L^3 + \cdots$$

The multiplication or convolution of the two polynomials gives

$$\varphi(L) = \phi(L)\psi(L)$$

where

$$\varphi_0 = \phi_0 \psi_0$$
$$\varphi_1 = \phi_0 \psi_1 + \phi_1 \psi_0$$
$$\varphi_2 = \phi_0 \psi_2 + \phi_1 \psi_1 + \phi_2 \psi_0$$
$$\varphi_3 = \phi_0 \psi_3 + \phi_1 \psi_2 + \phi_2 \psi_1 + \phi_3 \psi_0$$
$$\vdots = \vdots$$
$$\varphi_n = \phi_0 \psi_n + \phi_1 \psi_{n-1} + \phi_2 \psi_{n-2} + \cdots + \phi_n \psi_0$$
$$\vdots = \vdots$$

Therefore, for the convolution of two infinite-order polynomials, the elements of the resultant polynomial $\varphi(L)$ are given by the simple rule

$$\varphi_k = \sum_{j=0}^{k} \phi_j \psi_{k-j} .$$

Any finite-order polynomial may be viewed as an infinite-order polynomial with all its coefficients zero after a certain order. It therefore follows from the previous result that in the case of a convolution of polynomials of finite order that the rule for generating the coefficients of $\varphi_k(L)$ is

$$\varphi_k = \sum_{j=\max(0;k-p)}^{\min(k;q+1)} \phi_j \psi_{k-j} .$$

B.3 Polynomial Inversion

In some cases, it is possible to invert polynomials in the lag operator. Consider the infinite series

$$1 + \lambda + \lambda^2 + \lambda^3 + \cdots = \frac{1}{1-\lambda} \qquad |\lambda| < 1 .$$

This series suggests that if $|\phi L| < 1$ then

$$\frac{1}{1-\phi L} = 1 + \phi L + \phi^2 L^2 + \phi^3 L^3 + \cdots .$$

Simple multiplication verifies this conjecture as

$$(1 - \phi L) \times (1 + \phi L + \phi^2 L^2 + \phi^3 L^3 + \cdots)$$
$$= (1 + \phi L + \phi^2 L^2 + \phi^3 L^3 + \cdots)$$
$$-(\phi L + \phi L^2 + \phi^3 L^3 + \phi^4 L^4 + \cdots)$$
$$= 1.$$

The situation is more complicated when trying to find the inverse of higher-order polynomials in the lag operator. Consider, for example, the second-order polynomial

$$1 - \phi_1 L - \phi_2 L^2.$$

Factorising this expression gives

$$1 - \phi_1 L - \phi_2 L^2 = (1 - \gamma L)(1 - \rho L),$$

with

$$\gamma + \rho = \phi_1 \qquad \gamma\rho = -\phi_2.$$

Note that although ϕ_1 and ϕ_2 take real values, γ and ρ need not be real, but can be complex conjugates. Using the result for a first-order polynomial it follows that

$$(1 - \gamma L)^{-1}(1 - \rho L)^{-1}$$
$$= (1 + \gamma + \gamma^2 L^2 + \gamma^3 L^3 + \cdots)(1 + \rho + \rho^2 L^2 + \rho^3 L^3 + \cdots).$$

The result is, therefore, a convolution of two polynomials in the lag operator of infinite order, and it is straightforward to evaluate this convolution using the results on polynomial convolution presented earlier.

B.4   Polynomial Decomposition

There is an important decomposition of a lag polynomial. Define the operator

$$a(L) = 1 - a_1 L - a_2 L^2 - a_3 L^3 - \cdots - a_n L^n = 1 - \sum_{k=1}^{n} a_k L^k$$

and let $a(1) = 1 - \sum_{k=1}^{n} a_k$ (the sum of the coefficients). In this case,

$$a(L) - a(1) = \left(1 - \sum_{k=1}^{n} a_k L^k\right) - \left(1 - \sum_{k=1}^{n} a_k\right) = \sum_{k=1}^{n} a_k(1 - L^k).$$

It is a fact that $1 - x^k = (1 - x)(1 + x + x^2 + \cdots + x^{k-1})$ (just check it by multiplication), or,

$$1 - x^k = (1 - x) \sum_{r=0}^{k-1} x^r .$$

Therefore,

$$a(L) - a(1) = \sum_{k=1}^{n} a_k(1 - L)\left(\sum_{r=0}^{k-1} L^r \right) = (1 - L) \sum_{k=1}^{n} a_k \left(\sum_{r=0}^{k-1} L^r \right) .$$

The task is now to re-index the summation on the right-hand side of the previous expression. The result is

$$a(L) - a(1) = (1 - L) \sum_{r=0}^{n-1} L^r \left(\sum_{k=r+1}^{n} a_k \right) = (1 - L) \sum_{r=0}^{n-1} b_r L^r ,$$

where

$$b_r = \sum_{k=r+1}^{n} a_k .$$

Appendix C. FIML Estimation of a Structural Model

C.1 Log-Likelihood Function

Consider the bivariate simultaneous equation model discussed in Chapter 5

$$y_{1,t} = \beta_1 y_{2,t} + u_{1,t}$$
$$y_{2,t} = \beta_2 y_{1,t} + \alpha x_t + u_{2,t} \, ,$$

where the disturbance term $u_t = (u_{1,t}, u_{2,t})'$ has a bivariate normal distribution with variance parameters $\sigma_{1,1}$ and $\sigma_{2,2}$, respectively. The log-likelihood function is

$$\ln L_T(\theta) = -\ln(2\pi) - \frac{1}{2}\ln\left|\sigma_{1,1}\sigma_{2,2}\right| + \ln\left|1 - \beta_1\beta_2\right|$$

$$-\frac{1}{2\sigma_{1,1}T}\sum_{t=1}^{T}(y_{1,t} - \beta_1 y_{2,t})^2$$

$$-\frac{1}{2\sigma_{2,2}T}\sum_{t=1}^{T}(y_{2,t} - \beta_2 y_{1,t} - \alpha x_t)^2 \, .$$

The model imposes the restriction that the disturbances are not contemporaneously correlated, that is $\sigma_{1,2} = \sigma_{2,1} = 0$.

C.2 First-Order Conditions

To derive the maximum likelihood estimators of the parameter vector $\theta = \{\beta_1, \beta_2, \alpha, \sigma_{1,1}, \sigma_{2,2}\}$, set the first-order derivatives of the log-likelihood function equal to zero to yield

$$\frac{\partial \ln L_T(\theta)}{\partial \beta_1} = -\frac{\widehat{\beta}_2}{1 - \widehat{\beta}_1\widehat{\beta}_2} + \frac{1}{\widehat{\sigma}_{1,1}T}\sum_{t=1}^{T}(y_{1,t} - \widehat{\beta}_1 y_{2,t})y_{2,t} = 0 \quad \text{(C.1)}$$

$$\frac{\partial \ln L_T}{\partial \beta_2} = -\frac{\widehat{\beta}_1}{1 - \widehat{\beta}_1 \widehat{\beta}_2} + \frac{1}{\widehat{\sigma}_{2,2} T} \sum_{t=1}^{T} (y_{2,t} - \widehat{\beta}_2 y_{1,t} - \widehat{\alpha} x_t) y_{1,t} = 0 \quad \text{(C.2)}$$

$$\frac{\partial \ln L_T}{\partial \alpha} = \frac{1}{\widehat{\sigma}_{2,2} T} \sum_{t=1}^{T} (y_{2,t} - \widehat{\beta}_2 y_{1,t} - \widehat{\alpha} x_t) x_t = 0 \quad \text{(C.3)}$$

$$\frac{\partial \ln L_T}{\partial \sigma_{1,1}} = -\frac{1}{2\widehat{\sigma}_{1,1}} + \frac{1}{2\widehat{\sigma}_{1,1}^2 T} \sum_{t=1}^{T} (y_{1,t} - \widehat{\beta}_1 y_{2,t})^2 = 0 \quad \text{(C.4)}$$

$$\frac{\partial \ln L_T}{\partial \sigma_{2,2}} = -\frac{1}{2\widehat{\sigma}_{2,2}} + \frac{1}{2\widehat{\sigma}_{2,2}^2 T} \sum_{t=1}^{T} (y_{2,t} - \widehat{\beta}_2 y_{1,t} - \widehat{\alpha} x_t)^2 = 0. \quad \text{(C.5)}$$

C.3   Solution

Solving these first-order conditions proceeds as follows. Self-evidently, the equations for $\partial \ln L / \partial \sigma_{1,1}$ and $\partial \ln L / \partial \sigma_{2,2}$ may be simplified directly to yield

$$\widehat{\sigma}_{1,1} = \frac{1}{T} \sum_{t=1}^{T} (y_{1,t} - \widehat{\beta}_1 y_{2,t})^2 = \frac{1}{T} \sum_{t=1}^{T} \widehat{u}_{1,t}^2 \quad \text{(C.6)}$$

$$\widehat{\sigma}_{2,2} = \frac{1}{T} \sum_{t=1}^{T} (y_{2,t} - \widehat{\beta}_2 y_{1,t} - \widehat{\alpha} x_t)^2 = \frac{1}{T} \sum_{t=1}^{T} \widehat{u}_{2,t}^2. \quad \text{(C.7)}$$

Multiply equation (C.1) by $(\widehat{\sigma}_{1,1} T)(1 - \widehat{\beta}_1 \widehat{\beta}_2)$ and then replace $\widehat{\sigma}_{1,1} T$ in the resulting equation by equation (C.6) to get

$$-\widehat{\beta}_2 \sum_{t=1}^{T} (y_{1,t} - \widehat{\beta}_1 y_{2,t})^2 + (1 - \widehat{\beta}_1 \widehat{\beta}_2) \sum_{t=1}^{T} (y_{1,t} - \widehat{\beta}_1 y_{2,t}) y_{2,t} = 0.$$

Because $\widehat{u}_{1,t} = y_{1,t} - \widehat{\beta}_1 y_{2,t}$ is a common factor in both sums, they may be combined to obtain after some cancellation

$$\sum_{t=1}^{T} (y_{1,t} - \widehat{\beta}_1 y_{2,t})(y_{2,t} - \widehat{\beta}_2 y_{1,t}) = 0. \quad \text{(C.8)}$$

A similar procedure applied to equation (C.2), in this case multiplying by $(\widehat{\sigma}_{2,2} T)(1 - \widehat{\beta}_1 \widehat{\beta}_2)$ and then replacing $\widehat{\sigma}_{2,2} T$ by equation (C.7) yields

$$\sum_{t=1}^{T} (y_{2,t} - \widehat{\beta}_2 y_{1,t} - \widehat{\alpha} x_t)(-\widehat{\beta}_1 y_{2,t} + \widehat{\alpha} \widehat{\beta}_1 x_t + y_{1,t}) = 0. \quad \text{(C.9)}$$

In the derivation of equation (C.9) the fact that $\widehat{u}_{2,t} = y_{2,t} - \widehat{\beta}_2 y_{1,t} - \widehat{\alpha} x_t$ is a common factor has been used to make the simplification. Equation (C.9) is now divided into the component sums

$$\sum_{t=1}^{T}(y_{2,t} - \widehat{\beta}_2 y_{1,t} - \widehat{\alpha} x_t)(-\widehat{\beta}_1 y_{2,t} + y_{1,t}) + \widehat{\alpha}\widehat{\beta}\sum_{t=1}^{T}(y_{2,t} - \widehat{\beta}_2 y_{1,t} - \widehat{\alpha} x_t)x_t = 0,$$

and equation (C.3) is used to eliminate the second sum to give the final result

$$\sum_{t=1}^{T}(y_{2,t} - \widehat{\beta}_2 y_{1,t} - \widehat{\alpha} x_t)(y_{1,t} - \widehat{\beta}_1 y_{2,t}) = 0. \tag{C.10}$$

The definition of the residuals reveals that equation (C.10) is equivalent to

$$\sum_{t=1}^{T}\widehat{u}_{2,t}\widehat{u}_{1,t} = 0,$$

which, of course, comes from the restriction of the model that the disturbances are contemporaneously independent, that is $\sigma_{1,2} = 0$.

Now subtract (C.8) from (C.10) to give

$$\widehat{\alpha}\sum_{t=1}^{T}(y_{1,t} - \widehat{\beta}_1 y_{2,t})x_t = 0. \tag{C.11}$$

Since $\widehat{\alpha}$ is not zero, equation (C.11) may be solved to give

$$\widehat{\beta}_1 = \frac{\sum_{t=1}^{T} y_{1,t} x_t}{\sum_{t=1}^{T} y_{2,t} x_t}.$$

The solution for $\widehat{\beta}_2$ is obtained by rearranging (C.8) to give

$$\widehat{\beta}_2 = \frac{\sum_{t=1}^{T} y_{2,t}\widehat{u}_{1,t}}{\sum_{t=1}^{T} y_{1,t}\widehat{u}_{1,t}}.$$

Finally, given the solution for $\widehat{\beta}_2$, equation (C.10) is solved for $\widehat{\alpha}$ to give

$$\widehat{\alpha} = \frac{\sum_{t=1}^{T} y_{2,t}\widehat{u}_{1,t} - \widehat{\beta}_2 \sum_{t=1}^{T} y_{1,t}\widehat{u}_{1,t}}{\sum_{t=1}^{T} x_t\widehat{u}_{1,t}}$$

Appendix D. Additional Nonparametric Results

D.1 Mean

The kernel estimate of a density is given by

$$\widehat{f}(y) = \frac{1}{Th} \sum_{t=1}^{T} K\left(\frac{y - y_t}{h}\right) = \frac{1}{T} \sum_{t=1}^{T} w_t, \qquad w_t = \frac{1}{h} K\left(\frac{y - y_t}{h}\right),$$

where h is the kernel bandwidth and $K(\cdot)$ is the kernel function. The expectation of $\widehat{f}(y)$ is

$$\mathrm{E}\left[\widehat{f}(y)\right] = \mathrm{E}\left[\frac{1}{T} \sum_{t=1}^{T} w_t\right] = \frac{1}{T} \sum_{t=1}^{T} \mathrm{E}[w_t].$$

Because of the identically distributed assumption

$$\mathrm{E}[w_1] = \mathrm{E}[w_2] = \cdots = \mathrm{E}[w_T],$$

the mean value of $\widehat{f}(y)$ reduces to

$$\begin{aligned}
\mathrm{E}\left[\widehat{f}(y)\right] &= \mathrm{E}[w_t] \\
&= \mathrm{E}\left[\frac{1}{h} K(\frac{y - y_t}{h})\right] \\
&= \frac{1}{h} \int_{-\infty}^{\infty} K(\frac{y - y_t}{h}) f(y_t) dy_t,
\end{aligned}$$

where w_t is taken as a 'representative' random variable.

Now define the standardised random variable

$$z_t = \frac{y - y_t}{h},$$

in which $h > 0$. It follows that $E\left[\widehat{f}(y)\right]$ may be rewritten in terms of z_t (by using the change of variable technique) as

$$
\begin{aligned}
E\left[\widehat{f}(y)\right] &= \frac{1}{h}\int_{-\infty}^{\infty} K(\frac{y-y_t}{h})f(y_t)\left|\frac{dy_t}{dz_t}\right|dz_t \\
&= \frac{1}{h}\int_{-\infty}^{\infty} K(z_t)f(y-hz_t)hdz_t \\
&= \int_{-\infty}^{\infty} K(z_t)f(y-hz_t)dz_t.
\end{aligned} \tag{D.1}
$$

This expression shows that the mean of the kernel density estimator at y is related to the unknown distribution, $f(y)$, in a nonlinear way. To highlight this relationship, consider expanding $f(y-hz_t)$ in a Taylor series expansion for small h to get

$$
f(y-hz_t) = f(y) - \frac{hz_t}{1}f^{(1)}(y) + \frac{(hz_t)^2}{2}f^{(2)}(y) - \frac{(hz_t)^3}{6}f^{(3)}(y) + O(h^4),
$$

in which

$$
f^{(k)}(y) = \frac{d^k f(y)}{dy^k},
$$

represents the kth derivative of $f(y)$. Substituting into the expression for $E\left[\widehat{f}(y)\right]$ and rearranging gives

$$
\begin{aligned}
E\left[\widehat{f}(y)\right] &= \int_{-\infty}^{\infty} K(z_t)\left(f(y) - hz_t f^{(1)}(y) + \frac{(hz_t)^2}{2}f^{(2)}(y)\right.\\
&\qquad\left. -\frac{(hz_t)^3}{6}f^{(3)}(y) + O(h^4)\right)dz_t \\
&= f(y)\int_{-\infty}^{\infty} K(z_t)dz_t - hf^{(1)}(y)\int_{-\infty}^{\infty} z_t K(z_t)dz_t \\
&\quad +\frac{h^2}{2}f^{(2)}(y)\int_{-\infty}^{\infty} z_t^2 K(z_t)dz_t - \frac{h^3}{6}f^{(3)}(y)\int_{-\infty}^{\infty} z_t^3 K(z_t)dz_t + O(h^4) \\
&= f(y) - 0 + \frac{h^2}{2}f^{(2)}(y)\mu_2 - 0 + O(h^4) \\
&= f(y) + \frac{h^2}{2}f^{(2)}(y)\mu_2 + O(h^4),
\end{aligned} \tag{D.2}
$$

by using the properties of the kernel functions (see Chapter 11) and, in particularly, the property that higher odd-order moments are zero by virtue of the fact that the kernel is a symmetric function. The term $\frac{h^2}{2}f^{(2)}(y)\mu_2$ is simply a correction of order $O(h^2)$ that controls the bias which is given by

$$\text{bias}(\widehat{f}(y)) = \text{E}\left[\widehat{f}(y)\right] - f(y) = \frac{h^2}{2} f^{(2)}(y)\mu_2 + O(h^4). \qquad (D.3)$$

D.2   Variance

The variance of $\widehat{f}(y)$ is given by

$$
\begin{aligned}
\text{var}(\widehat{f}(y)) &= \text{E}\left[(\widehat{f}(y) - \text{E}[\widehat{f}(y)])^2\right] \\
&= \text{E}\left[\left(\frac{1}{T}\sum_{t=1}^{T}(w_t - \text{E}[w_t])\right)^2\right] \\
&= \frac{1}{T^2}\text{E}\left[\left(\sum_{t=1}^{T}(w_t - \text{E}[w_t])\right)^2\right] \\
&= \frac{1}{T^2}\left[\sum_{t=1}^{T}\text{var}(w_t) + 2\text{cov}(w_1, w_2) + 2\text{cov}(w_1, w_3) + \cdots\right] \\
&= \frac{1}{T^2}\sum_{t=1}^{T}\text{var}(w_t),
\end{aligned}
$$

where the $T(T-1)/2$ covariances are each zero because of the independence assumption. When the identically distributed assumption is invoked, the variance expression reduces to

$$\text{var}\left[\widehat{f}(y)\right] = \frac{1}{T}\text{var}(w_t),$$

where, once again, w_t is taken as the representative random variable. Now, by definition

$$
\begin{aligned}
\text{var}(w_t) &= \text{E}[(w_t - \text{E}[w_t])^2] \\
&= \text{E}[w_t^2] - (\text{E}[w_t])^2.
\end{aligned}
$$

Consider

$$
\begin{aligned}
\text{E}[w_t^2] &= \text{E}\left[\left(\frac{1}{h}K\left(\frac{y - y_t}{h}\right)\right)^2\right] \\
&= \frac{1}{h^2}\text{E}\left[\left(K\left(\frac{y - y_t}{h}\right)\right)^2\right] \\
&= \frac{1}{h^2}\int_{-\infty}^{\infty}\left(K\left(\frac{y - y_t}{h}\right)\right)^2 f(y_t)dy_t.
\end{aligned}
$$

Rewriting in terms of the standardised random variable z_t, gives

$$E[w_t^2] = \frac{1}{h^2} \int_{-\infty}^{\infty} \left(K\left(\frac{y-y_t}{h}\right)\right)^2 f(y_t) \left|\frac{dy_t}{dz_t}\right| dz_t$$

$$= \frac{1}{h^2} \int_{-\infty}^{\infty} K^2(z_t) f(y - hz_t) h \, dz_t$$

$$= \frac{1}{h} \int_{-\infty}^{\infty} K^2(z_t) f(y - hz_t) \, dz_t.$$

Substituting into the variance expression for $\text{var}(w_t)$ gives

$$\text{var}(w_t) = \frac{1}{h} \int_{-\infty}^{\infty} K^2(z_t) f(y - hz_t) \, dz_t - \left(\int_{-\infty}^{\infty} K(z_t) f(y - hz_t) \, dz_t\right)^2,$$

which, in turn, yields an expression for the variance of the kernel estimator given by

$$\text{var}(\widehat{f}(y)) = \frac{1}{T} \left[\frac{1}{h} \int_{-\infty}^{\infty} K^2(z_t) f(y - hz_t) \, dz_t - \left(\int_{-\infty}^{\infty} K(z_t) f(y - hz_t) \, dz_t\right)^2\right].$$

A Taylor series expansion of $f(y - hz_t)$ around a small value of h, gives

$$\text{var}(\widehat{f}(y)) = \frac{1}{Th} \int_{-\infty}^{\infty} K^2(z_t)\left(f(y) - hz_t f^{(1)}(y) + \frac{(hz_t)^2}{2} f^{(2)}(y) - \cdots\right) dz_t$$

$$- \frac{1}{T}\left(\int_{-\infty}^{\infty} K(z_t)\left(f(y) - hz_t f^{(1)}(y)\right.\right.$$

$$\left.\left. + \frac{(hz_t)^2}{2} f^{(2)}(y) - \cdots\right) dz_t.\right)^2$$

$$= \frac{1}{Th} f(y) \int_{-\infty}^{\infty} K^2(z_t) \, dz_t - 0$$

$$+ \frac{1}{Th} \frac{h^2}{2} f^{(2)}(y) \int_{-\infty}^{\infty} z_t^2 K^2(z_t) \, dz_t - \cdots$$

$$- \frac{1}{T}\left(f(y) \int_{-\infty}^{\infty} K(z_t) \, dz_t - 0\right.$$

$$\left. + \frac{h^2}{2} f^{(2)}(y) \int_{-\infty}^{\infty} z_t^2 K(z_t) \, dz_t - \cdots\right)^2.$$

Noting that when h is small, $h^2/Th = h/T$ is of a smaller order of magnitude than $(Th)^{-1}$, the previous expression simplifies to yield

$$\text{var}(\widehat{f}(y)) = \frac{1}{Th} f(y) \int_{-\infty}^{\infty} K^2(z_t) \, dz_t + o\left(\frac{1}{Th}\right). \tag{D.4}$$

This expression shows that the variance of the kernel estimator is inversely related to the bandwidth h.

D.3 Mean Square Error

$$\text{AMISE} = \int_{-\infty}^{\infty} \left(\text{bias}^2 + \text{var}(\widehat{f}(y)) \right) dy. \tag{D.5}$$

From (D.2), the aggregate squared bias is

$$
\begin{aligned}
\int_{-\infty}^{\infty} \text{bias}^2 dy &= \int_{-\infty}^{\infty} \left(\frac{h^2}{2} f^{(2)}(y)\mu_2 + O(h^4) \right)^2 dy \\
&= \int_{-\infty}^{\infty} \left(\frac{h^4}{4} (f^{(2)}(y))^2 \mu_2^2 + O(h^8) + h^2 f^{(2)}(y)\mu_2 O(h^4) \right) dy \\
&= \int_{-\infty}^{\infty} \left(\frac{h^4}{4} (f^{(2)}(y))^2 \mu_2^2 + O(h^6) \right) dy \\
&= \int_{-\infty}^{\infty} \frac{h^4}{4} (f^{(2)}(y))^2 \mu_2^2 dy + O(h^6) \\
&= \frac{h^4}{4} \mu_2^2 \int_{-\infty}^{\infty} (f^{(2)}(y))^2 dy + O(h^6) \\
&= \frac{h^4}{4} \mu_2^2 R(f^{(2)}(y)) + O(h^6), \tag{D.6}
\end{aligned}
$$

in which

$$R(\phi) = \int_{-\infty}^{\infty} \phi^2(y)\, dy \tag{D.7}$$

is the roughness operator of the density function.

Similarly, from (D.4), the aggregate squared variance is

$$
\begin{aligned}
\int_{-\infty}^{\infty} \text{var}(\widehat{f}(y))dy &= \int_{-\infty}^{\infty} \left(\frac{1}{Th} f(y) \int_{-\infty}^{\infty} K^2(z_t)\, dz_t + o\left(\frac{1}{Th}\right) \right) dy \\
&= \frac{1}{Th} \int_{-\infty}^{\infty} f(y) \int_{-\infty}^{\infty} K^2(z_t)\, dz_t\, dy + o\left(\frac{1}{Th}\right) \\
&= \frac{1}{Th} \int_{-\infty}^{\infty} f(y) dy \int_{-\infty}^{\infty} K^2(z_t)\, dz_t + o\left(\frac{1}{Th}\right) \\
&= \frac{1}{Th} \int_{-\infty}^{\infty} K^2(z_t)\, dz_t + o\left(\frac{1}{Th}\right) \\
&= \frac{1}{Th} R(K) + o\left(\frac{1}{Th}\right) \tag{D.8}
\end{aligned}
$$

since $\int_{-\infty}^{\infty} f(y)\,dy = 1$ by virtue of the fact that $f(y)$ it is a density and

$$R(K) = \int_{-\infty}^{\infty} K^2(z_t)\,dz_t,$$

is the roughness of the kernel density $K(z_t)$. Combining (D.6) and (D.8) in (D.5) yields the integrated mean squared error. Retaining terms up to order h^4 yields the asymptotic expression

$$\text{AMISE} = \frac{h^4}{4}\mu_2^2 R(f^{(2)}(y)) + \frac{1}{Th}R(K). \tag{D.9}$$

D.4   Roughness

Many of the properties of the kernel density estimator and the algorithms designed for the optimal selection of the bandwidth rely on results relating to the roughness operator R, defined in equation (D.7).

D.4.1   Roughness Results for the Gaussian Distribution

If $f(y;\mu,\sigma^2)$ is the probability density function of the Gaussian distribution then

$$R(f^{(2)}(y)) = \int_{-\infty}^{\infty} \left[f^{(2)}(y)\right]^2 dy$$

$$= \int_{-\infty}^{\infty} \left[\frac{d^2}{dy^2}\left(\frac{1}{\sqrt{2\pi\sigma^2}}\exp\left(-\frac{(y-\mu)^2}{2\sigma^2}\right)\right)\right]^2 dy$$

$$= \int_{-\infty}^{\infty} \left[\frac{1}{\sqrt{2\pi\sigma^2}}\left(\left(\frac{y-\mu}{\sigma^2}\right)^2 - \frac{1}{\sigma^2}\right)\exp\left(-\frac{(y-\mu)^2}{2\sigma^2}\right)\right]^2 dy$$

$$= \frac{1}{2\pi\sigma^6}\int_{-\infty}^{\infty}\left(\left(\frac{y-\mu}{\sigma}\right)^2 - 1\right)^2 \exp\left(-\frac{(y-\mu)^2}{\sigma^2}\right) dy.$$

This expression is simplified with the transformation $u/\sqrt{2} = (y-\mu)/\sigma$

$$R(f^{(2)}(y)) = \frac{1}{2\pi\sigma^6}\int_{-\infty}^{\infty}\left(\frac{u^2}{2} - 1\right)^2 e^{-u^2/2}\left|\frac{dy}{du}\right|du$$

$$= \frac{1}{2\pi\sigma^6}\int_{-\infty}^{\infty}\left(\frac{u^4}{4} - u^2 + 1\right)e^{-u^2/2}\frac{\sigma}{\sqrt{2}}du$$

$$= \frac{1}{2\sqrt{\pi}\sigma^5}\frac{1}{\sqrt{2\pi}}\int_{-\infty}^{\infty}\left(\frac{u^4}{4} - u^2 + 1\right)e^{-u^2/2}\,du$$

$$= \frac{1}{2\sqrt{\pi}\sigma^5}\left(\frac{1}{4}\text{E}\left[u^4\right] - \text{E}[u^2] + 1\right) = \frac{3}{8\sqrt{\pi}\sigma^5}, \tag{D.10}$$

in which the results $E\left[u^4\right] = 3$ and $E\left[u^2\right] = 1$ for a standardised normal random variable are used. In addition, it may be shown that

$$R(f^{(1)}) = \frac{1}{4\sigma^3\sqrt{\pi}}, \quad R(f^{(2)}) = \frac{3}{8\sigma^5\sqrt{\pi}}, \quad R(f^{(3)}) = \frac{15}{16\sigma^7\sqrt{\pi}},$$

$$R(f^{(4)}) = \frac{105}{32\sigma^9\sqrt{\pi}}.$$

D.4.2 Roughness Results for the Gaussian Kernel

The roughness of a Gaussian kernel is

$$R(K) = \int_{-\infty}^{\infty} K^2(z_t)\,dz_t$$

$$= \int_{-\infty}^{\infty} \left(\frac{1}{\sqrt{2\pi}} \exp\left(\frac{-z_t^2}{2}\right)\right)^2 dz_t$$

$$= \frac{1}{2\pi} \int_{-\infty}^{\infty} \exp\left(-z_t^2\right) dz_t .$$

This expression is simplified by using the change of variable technique with the transformation $z_t = u/\sqrt{2}$ to give

$$R(K) = \frac{1}{2\pi} \int_{-\infty}^{\infty} e^{-u^2/2} \frac{1}{\sqrt{2}}\,du$$

$$= \frac{1}{2\sqrt{\pi}} \left(\frac{1}{\sqrt{2\pi}} \int_{-\infty}^{\infty} e^{-u^2/2}\right) du$$

$$= \frac{1}{2\sqrt{\pi}} .$$

In addition,

$$R(K^{(1)}) = \frac{1}{4\sqrt{\pi}}, \quad R(K^{(2)}) = \frac{3}{8\sqrt{\pi}}, \quad R(K^{(3)}) = \frac{15}{16\sqrt{\pi}}.$$

References

Abramowitz, M., and Stegun, I.A. 1965. *Handbook of Mathematical Functions with Formulas, Graphs, and Mathematical Tables*. New York: Dover.

Ahn, S.K., and Reinsel, G.C. 1990. Estimation for partially nonstationary multivariate autoregressive models. *Journal of the American Statistical Association*, **85**, 813–823.

Aigner, D., Lovell, C.A.K., and Schmidt, P. 1977. Formulation and estimation of stochastic frontier production function models. *Journal of Econometrics*, **6**, 21–37.

Aït-Sahalia, Y. 1996. Testing continuous-time models of the spot interest rate. *Review of Financial Studies*, **9**, 385–426.

Akaike, H. 1974. A new look at the statistical model identification. *I.E.E.E. Transactions on Automatic Control*, **19**, 716–723.

Akaike, H. 1976. Canonical correlation analysis of time series and the use of an information criterion. Pages 52–107 of: Mehra, R., and Lainotis, D.G. (eds), *System Identification: Advances and Case Studies*. New York: Academic Press.

Al-Osh, M.A., and Alzaid, A.A. 1987. First-order integer valued autoregressive (INAR(1)) process. *Journal of Time Series Analysis*, **8**, 261–275.

Andel, J., and Barton, T. 1986. A note on the threshold AR(1) model. *Journal of Time Series Analysis*, **7**, 1–5.

Andersen, T.G., Bollerslev, T., Diebold, F.X., and Labys, P. 2001. The distribution of exchange rate volatility. *Journal of the American Statistical Association*, **96**, 42–55.

Andersen, T.G., Bollerslev, T., Diebold, F.X., and Labys, P. 2003. Modeling and forecasting realized volatility. *Econometrica*, **71**, 579–62.

Anderson, H.M., Anthansopoulos, G., and Vahid, F. 2007. Nonlinear autoregressive leading indicator models of output in G-7 countries. *Journal of Applied Econometrics*, **22**, 63–87.

Anderson, T.W. 1971. *The Statistical Analysis of Time Series*. New York: Wiley.

Anderson, T.W. 1984. *An Introduction to Multivariate Statistical*. John Wiley and Sons, Inc.

Andrews, D.W.K. 1984. Non-strong mixing autoregressive processes. *Journal of Applied Probability*, **21**, 930–934.

Andrews, D.W.K., and Monahan, J.C. 1992. An improved heteroskedasticity and autocorrelation consistent covariance matrix. *Econometrica*, **60**, 953–966.

Bai, J., and Ng, S. 2002. Determining the number of factors in approximate factor models. *Econometrica*, **70**, 191–221.

Bai, J., and Ng, S. 2004. A PANIC attack on unit roots and cointegration. *Econometrica*, **72**, 1127–1177.

Baillie, R.T., Bollerslev, T., and Mikkelsen, H.O. 1996. Fractionally integrated generalized autoregressive conditional heteroskedasticity. *Journal of Econometrics*, **74**, 3–30.

Banbura, M., Giannone, D., and Reichlin, L. 2010. Large Bayesian vector autoregressions. *Journal of Applied Econometrics*, **25**, 71–92.

Banerjee, A., Dolado, J.J., Galbraith, J.W., and Hendry, D.F. 1993. *Co-integration, Error-Correction, and the Econometric Analysis of Non-Stationary*. Advanced Texts in Econometrics. Oxford: Oxford University Press.

Barro, R.J. 1978. Unanticipated money, output, and the price level in the United States. *Journal of Political Economy*, **86**, 549–580.

Beach, C.M., and MacKinnon, J.G. 1978. A maximum likelihood procedure for regression with autocorrelated errors. *Econometrica*, **46**, 51–58.

Beaumont, M.A., Cornuet, J-M., Marin, J-M., and Robert, C.P. 2009. Adaptive approximate Bayesian computation. *Biometrika*, **96**, 983–990.

Bera, A.K., Ghosh, A., and Xiao, Z. 2010. *Smooth test for equality of distributions*. Mimeo.

Bernanke, B.S., and Blinder, A.S. 1992. The Federal funds rate and the channels of monetary transmission. *American Economic Review*, **82**, 901–921.

Berndt, E., Hall, B., Hall, R., and Hausman, J. 1974. Estimation and inference in nonlinear structural models. *Annals of Social Measurement*, **3**, 653–665.

Beveridge, S., and Nelson, C.R. 1981. A new approach to decomposition of economic time series into permanent and transitory components with particular attention to measurement of the 'business cycle'. *Journal of Monetary Economics*, **7**, 151–174.

Billingsley, P. 1968. *Convergence of Probability Measures*. New York: Wiley.

Blanchard, O.J., and Quah, D. 1989. The dynamic effects of aggregate demand and supply disturbances. *The American Economic Review*, **79**, 655–673.

Bollerslev, T., and Wooldridge, J.M. 1992. Quasi-maximum likelihood estimation and inference in dynamic model with time-varying covariances. *Econometric Reviews*, **11**, 143–172.

Boswijk, P. 1995. Efficient inference on cointegration parameters in structural error correction models. *Journal of Econometrics*, **69**, 133–158.

Breitung, J. 2002. Nonparametric tests for unit roots and cointegration. *Journal of Econometrics*, **108**, 343–363.

Broyden, C.G. 1970. The convergence of a class of double-rank minimization algorithms. *Journal of the Institute of Mathematical Applications*, **6**, 76–90.

Bu, R., McCabe, B.P.M., and Hadri, K. 2008. Maximum likelihood estimation of higher-order integer-valued autoregressive processes. *Journal of Time Series Analysis*, **29**, 973–994.

Butler, R.J., McDonald, J.B., Nelson, R.D., and White, S.B. 1990. Robust and partially adaptive estimation of regression models. *Review of Economics and Statistics*, **72**, 321–327.

Campbell, J.Y., and Shiller, R.J. 1987. Cointegration and tests of present value models. *Journal of Political Economy*, **95**, 1062–1088.

Canova, F., and de Nicolo, G. 2002. Monetary disturbances matter for business fluctuations in the G7. *Journal of Monetary Economics*, **49**, 1131–1159.

Carrion-i Silvestre, J.L., Kim, D., and Perron, P. 2009. GLS-based unit root tests with multiple structural breaks under both the null and the alternative hypothesis. *Econometric Theory*, **25**, 1754–1792.

Carter, C.K., and Kohn, R. 1994. On Gibbs sampling for state space models. *Biometrika*, **81**, 541–553.

Cavaliere, G., Rahbek, A., and Taylor, A.M.R. 2010. Cointegration rank testing under conditional heteroskedasticity. *Econometric Theory*, **26**, 1719–1760.

Chan, K.C., Karolyi, G.A., Longstaff, F.A., and Sanders, A.B. 1992. An empirical comparison of alternative models of the short term interest rate. *Journal of Finance*, **52**, 1209–1227.

Chang, Y., and Park, J.Y. 2002. On the asymptotics of ADF tests for unit roots. *Econometric Reviews*, **21**, 431–447.

Chapman, D. A., and Pearson, N.D. 2000. Is the short rate drift actually nonlinear? *Journal of Finance*, **55**, 355–388.

Chen, X., and Fan, Y. 1999. Consistent hypothesis testing in semiparametric and nonparametric models for econometric time series. *Journal of Econometrics*, **91**, 373–401.

Cheng, X., and Phillips, P.C.B. 2009. Semiparametric cointegrating rank selection. *Econometrics Journal*, **12**, S83–S104.

Chib, S. 2001. Markov chain Monte Carlo methods: computation and inference. Pages 3569–3649 of: Heckman, J.J., and Leamer, E. (eds), *Handbook of Econometrics, Volume 5*. Amsterdam: North Holland.

Chib, S. 2008. MCMC methods. In: 2 (ed), *New Palgrave Dictionary of Economics*. New York: Palgrave Macmillan.

Chib, S., and Greenberg, E. 1996. Markov chain Monte Carlo simulation methods in econometrics. *Econometric Theory*, **12**, 409–431.

Chib, S., Nardari, F., and Shephard, N. 2002. Markov chain Monte Carlo methods for stochastic volatility models. *Journal of Econometrics*, **108**, 281–316.

Cochrane, J.H., and Piazzesi, M. 2009. *Decomposing the yield curve*. Unpublished manuscript.

Conley, T.G., Hansen, L.P., Luttmer, E.G.J., and Scheinkman, J.A. 1997. Short-term interest rates as subordinated diffusions. *Review of Financial Studies*, **10**, 525–577.

Cox, J.C., Ingersoll, J.E., and Ross, S.A. 1985. A theory of the term structure of interest rates. *Econometrica*, **53**, 385–407.

Craine, R., and Martin, V.L. 2008. International monetary policy surprise spillovers. *Journal of International Economics*, **75**, 180–196.

Craine, R., and Martin, V.L. 2009. *The interest rate conundrum*. Unpublished manuscript.

Creedy, J., and Martin, V.L. 1994. *Chaos and Non-linear Models in Economics: Theory and Applications*. Cheltenham: Edward Elgar.

Davidson, J. 1994. *Stochastic Limit Theory*. Oxford: Oxford University Press.

Davidson, J. 1998. Structural relations, cointegration and identification: Some simple results and their application. *Journal of Econometrics*, **87**, 87–113.

D.E., Rapach. 2001. Macro shocks and real stock prices. *Journal of Economics and Business*, **53**, 5–26.

Dickey, D.A., and Fuller, W.A. 1979. Distributions of the estimators for autoregressive time series with a unit root. *Journal of the American Statistical Association*, **74**, 427–431.

Dickey, D.A., and Fuller, W.A. 1981. Likelihood ratio statistics for autogressive time series with a unit root. *Econometrica*, **49**, 1057–1072.

Diebold, F.X., and Nerlove, M. 1989. The dynamics of exchange rate volatility: A multivariate latent-factor ARCH model. *Journal of Applied Econometrics*, **4**, 1–22.

Diebold, F.X., and Rudebusch, G.D. 1996. Measuring business cycles: A modern perspective. *Review of Economics and Statistics*, **78**, 67–77.

Diebold, F.X., and Yilmaz, K. 2009. Measuring financial asset return and volatility spillovers, with application to global equity. *Economic Journal*, **119**, 158–171.

DiNardo, J., and Tobias, J.L. 2001. Nonparametric density and regression estimation. *Journal of Economic Perspectives*, **15**, 11–28.

Drovandi, C.C., Pettitt, A.N., and Faddy, M.J. 2011. Approximate Bayesian computation using indirect inference. *Journal of the Royal Statistical Society (Series C)*, **60**, 1–21.

Duffie, D., and Singleton, K.J. 1993. Simulated moments estimation of Markov models of asset prices. *Econometrica*, **61**, 929–952.

Dungey, M., and Martin, V.L. 2007. Unravelling financial market linkages during crises. *Journal of Applied Econometrics*, **22**, 89–119.

Durlauf, S.N., and Phillips, P.C.B. 1988. Trends versus random walks in time series analysis. *Econometrica*, **56**, 1333–1354.

Efron, B., and Tibshirani, R.J. 1993. *An Introduction to the Bootstrap*. New York: Chapman and Hall.

Elliot, G. 1999. Efficient tests for a unit root when the initial observation is drawn from its unconditional distribution. *International Economic Review*, **40**, 767–783.

Elliot, G., Rothenberg, T.J., and Stock, J.H. 1996. Efficient tests for an autoregressive unit root. *Econometrica*, **64**, 813–836.

Engel, C., and Hamilton, J.D. 1990. Long swings in the dollar: Are they in the data and do markets know it? *American Economic Review*, **80**, 689–713.

Engle, R.F. 1982. Autoregressive conditional heteroskedasticity with estimates of the variance of United Kingdom inflation. *Econometrica*, **50**, 987–1008.

Engle, R.F. 2002. Dynamic conditional correlation. A simple class of multivariate generalized autoregressive conditional heteroskedasticity models. *Journal of Business and Economic Statistics*, **20**, 339–350.

Engle, R.F., and González-Rivera, G. 1991. Semiparametric ARCH models. *Journal of Business and Economic Statistics*, **9**, 345–359.

Engle, R.F., and Granger, C.W.J. 1987. Cointegration and error correction: Representation, estimation and testing. *Econometrica*, **55**, 251–276.

Engle, R.F., and Kelly, B. 2009. *Dynamic equicorrelation*. Unpublished manuscript.

Engle, R.F., and Kroner, K.F. 1995. Multivariate simultaneous generalized ARCH. *Econometric Theory*, **11**, 122–150.

Engle, R.F., and Russell, J. R. 1998. Autoregressive conditional duration: A new model for irregularly spaced transaction data. *Econometrica*, **66**, 1127–1162.

Engle, R.F., and Sheppard, K. 2001. *Theoretical and empirical properties of dynamic conditional correlation multivariate GARCH*. Working Paper 8554. NBER.

Ericsson, N.R., Hendry, D.F., and Prestwich, K.M. 1998. The demand for broad money in the United Kingdom. *Scandinavian Journal of Economics*, **100**, 289–324.

Favero, C.A., and Giavazzi, F. 2002. Is the international propagation of financial shocks non-linear? Evidence from the ERM. *Journal of International Economics*, **57**, 231–246.

Fletcher, R. 1970. A new approach to variable metric algorithms. *Computer Journal*, **13**, 317–322.

Forchini, G. 2006. On the bimodality of the exact distribution of the TSLS estimator. *Econometric Theory*, **22**, 932–946.

Frühwirth-Schnatter, S., and Wagner, H. 2006. Auxiliary mixture sampling for parameter-driven models of time series of small counts with applications to state space modelling. *Biometrika*, **93**, 827–841.

Fry, R., Hocking, J., and Martin, V.L. 2008. The role of portfolio shocks in a SVAR model of the Australian economy. *Economic Record*, **84**, 17–33.

Fry, R.A., and Pagan, A.R. 2011. Some issues in using sign restrictions for identifying structural VARs. *Journal of Economic Literature*, **49**, 938–960.

Gali, J. 1992. How well does the IS-LM model fit postwar U.S. data? *Quarterly Journal of Economics*, **107**, 709–738.

Gallant, A.R., and Tauchen, G. 1996. Which moments to match? *Econometric Theory*, **12**, 657–681.

Getmansky, M., Lo, A.W., and Makarov, I. 2004. An econometric model of serial correlation and illiquidity in hedge fund returns. *Journal of Financial Econometrics*, **74**, 529–609.

Geweke, J. 1999. Using simulation methods for Bayesian econometric models: inference, development and communication. *Econometric Reviews*, **18**, 1–74.

Geweke, J. 2005. *Contemporary Bayesian Econometrics and Statistics*. New Jersey: John Wiley and Sons, Inc.

Ghysels, E., Santa-Clara, P., and Valkanov, R. 2005. There is a risk-return trade-off after all. *Journal of Financial Economics*, **76**, 509–548.

Gill, P.E., Murray, W., and Wright, M.H. 1981. *Practical Optimization*. New York: Academic Press.

Goldfarb, D. 1970. A family of variable metric methods derived by variational means. *Mathematics of Computation*, **24**, 23–26.

González-Rivera, G., and Drost, F.C. 1999. Efficiency comparisons of maximum-likelihood-based estimators in GARCH models. *Journal of Econometrics*, **93**, 93–111.

Gouriéroux, C., Monfort, A., and Renault, E. 1993. Indirect inference. *Journal of Applied Econometrics*, **8**, 85–118.

Granger, C.W.J. 2008. Non-linear models: where do we go next - time varying parameter models? *Studies in Nonlinear Dynamics and Econometrics*, **12**, 1–9.

Granger, C.W.J., and Anderson, A.P. 1978. *An Introduction to Bilinear Time Series Models*. Gottingen: Vandenhoeck and Ruprecht.

Greenberg, E. 2008. *An Introduction to Bayesian Econometrics*. New York: Cambridge University Press.

Gurkaynak, R.S., Sack, B., and Swanson, E. 2005. The sensitivity of long-term interest rates to economic news: Evidence and implications for macroeconomic models. *American Economic Review*, **95**, 425–436.

Hall, P., and Heyde, C. C. 1980. *Martingale Limit Theory and its Application*. New York: Academic Press Inc. [Harcourt Brace Jovanovich Publishers].

Hamilton, J.D. 1988. Rational expectations econometric analysis of changes in regime: An investigation of the term structure of interest rates. *Journal of Economic Dynamics and Control*, **12**, 385–423.

Hamilton, J.D. 1989. A new approach to the economic analysis of nonstationary time series and the business cycle. *Econometrica*, **57**, 357–384.

Hamilton, J.D. 1994. *Time Series Analysis*. Princeton, New Jersey: Princeton University Press.

Hamilton, J.D., and Jordà, Ò. 2002. A model of the Federal funds rate target. *Journal of Political Economy*, **110**, 1135–1167.

Hamilton, J.D., and Susmel, R. 1994. Autoregressive conditional heteroskedasticity and changes in regime. *Journal of Econometrics*, **64**, 307–333.

Han, H., and Park, J.Y. 2008. Time series properties of ARCH processes with persistent covariates. *Journal of Econometrics*, **146**, 275–292.

Hannan, E.J. 1980. The estimation of the order of an ARMA process. *Annals of Statistics*, **8**, 1071–1081.

Hannan, E.J., and Quinn, B.G. 1979. The determination of the order of an autoregression. *Journal of the Royal Statistical Society (Series B)*, **41**, 190–195.

Hansen, B.E. 1996. Inference when a nuisance parameter is not identified under the null hypothesis. *Econometrica*, **64**, 413–430.

Hansen, L.P. 1982. Large sample properties of generalised method of moments estimators. *Econometrica*, **50**, 1029–1054.

Hansen, L.P., and Singleton, K.J. 1982. Generalized instrumental variables estimation of nonlinear rational expectations models. *Econometrica*, **50**, 1269–1286.

Hansen, L.P., Heaton, J., and Yaron, A. 1996. Finite-sample properties of some alternative GMM estimators. *Journal of Business and Economic Statistics*, **14**, 262–280.

Harding, D., and Pagan, A.R. 2002. Dissecting the cycle: a methodological investigation. *Journal of Monetary Economics*, **49**, 365–381.

Harris, D., and Poskitt, D.S. 2004. Determination of cointegration rank in partially non-stationary processes via a generalised von-Neumann criterion. *Econometrics Journal*, **7**, 191–217.

Harris, D., Harvey, D.I., Leybourne, S.J., and Taylor, A.M.R. 2009. Testing for a unit root in the presence of a possible break in trend. *Econometric Theory*, **25**, 1545–1588.

Harvey, A.C. 1989. *Forecasting, Structural Time Series Models and the Kalman Filter*. Cambridge: Cambridge University Press.

Harvey, A.C. 1990. *The Econometric Analysis of Time Series, 2nd Edition*. London: Philip Allan.

Harvey, A.C., and Jaeger, A. 1993. Detrending, stylized facts and the business cycle. *Journal of Applied Econometrics*, **8**, 231–247.

Harvey, D.I., Leybourne, S.J., and Taylor, A.M.R. 2009. Unit root testing in practice: Dealing with uncertainty over trend and initial condition. *Econometric Theory*, **25**, 587–636.

Hatanaka, M. 1974. An efficient two-step estimator for the dynamic adjustment model with autoregressive errors. *Journal of Econometrics*, **2**, 199–220.

Hillier, G. 2006. Yet more on the exact properties of IV estimators. *Econometric Theory*, **22**, 913–931.

Hodrick, R.J., and Prescott, E.C. 1997. Postwar U.S. business cycles: An empirical investigation. *Journal of Money, Credit and Banking*, **24**, 1–16.

Horowitz, J.L. 1997. Bootstrap methods in econometrics: theory and numerical performance. In: Kreps, D.M., and Wallis, K.F. (eds), *Advances in Economics and Econometrics: Theory and Applications*. Cambridge: Cambridge University Press.

Hsiao, C. 1997. Cointegration and dynamic simultaneous equations model. *Econometrica*, **65**, 647–670.

Hurn, A.S., Jeisman, J., and Lindsay, K.A. 2007. Seeing the wood for the trees: A critical evaluation of methods to estimate the parameters of stochastic differential equations. *Journal of Financial Econometrics*, **5**, 390–455.

Jacquier, E., Polson, N.G., and Rossi, P.E. 2002. Bayesian analysis of stochastic volatility models. *Journal of Business and Economic Statistics*, **20**, 69–87.

Jacquier, E., Polson, N.G., and Rossi, P.E. 2004. Bayesian analysis of stochastic volatility models with fat-tails and correlated errors. *Journal of Econometrics*, **122**, 185–212.

Johansen, S. 1988. Statistical analysis of cointegration vectors. *Journal of Economic Dynamics and Control*, **12**, 231–254.

Johansen, S. 1991. Estimation and hypothesis testing of cointegration vectors in Gaussian vector autoregressive models. *Econometrica*, **59**, 1551–1580.

Johansen, S. 1995a. Identifying restrictions of linear equations: with applications to simultaneous equations and cointegration. *Journal of Econometrics*, **69**, 111–132.

Johansen, S. 1995b. *Likelihood-based Inference in Cointegrated Vector Autoregressive Models*. Oxford: Oxford University Press.

Johansen, S. 2005. Interpretation of cointegrating coefficients in the cointegrated autoregressive model. *Oxford Bulletin of Economics and Statistics*, **67**, 93–104.

Johansen, S., and Juselius, K. 1992. Testing structural hypotheses in a multivariate cointegration analysis of the PPP and UIP for the U.K. *Journal of Econometrics*, **53**, 211–244.

Johansen, S., Mosconi, R., and Nielsen, B. 2000. Cointegration analysis in the presence of structural breaks in the deterministic trend. *Econometrics Journal*, **3**, 216–249.

Jung, R.C., Ronning, G., and Tremayne, A.R. 2005. Estimation in conditional first order autoregression with discrete support. *Statistical Papers*, **46**, 195–224.

Kendall, M., and Stuart, A. 1973. *The Advanced Theory of Statistics*. London: Griffin.

Kennan, J. 1985. The duration of contract strikes in U.S. manufacturing. *Journal of Econometrics*, **28**, 5–28.

Kim, C-J. 1994. Dynamic linear models with Markov switching. *Journal of Econometrics*, **60**, 1–22.

Kim, S., and Roubini, N. 2000. Exchange rate anomalies in the industrial countries: A solution with a structural VAR approach. *Journal of Monetary Economics*, **45**, 561–586.

Klein, L.R. 1950. *Economic Fluctuations in the United States 1921–1941*. Monograph 11. Cowles Commission.

Klimko, L.A., and Nelson, P.I. 1978. On conditional least squares estimation for stochastic processes. *Annals of Statistics*, **6**, 629–642.

Knez, P., Litterman, R., and Scheinkman, J. 1994. Explorations into factors explaining money market returns. *Journal of Finance*, **49**, 1861–1882.

Konstas, P., and Khouja, M.W. 1969. The Keynesian demand-for-money function. *Journal of Money, Credit and Banking*, **1**, 765–777.

Koop, G. 2003. *Bayesian Econometrics*. Chichester: Wiley.

Koop, G. 2012. Forecasting with medium and large Bayesian VARs. *Journal of Applied Econometrics*, **forthcoming**.

Koop, G., Pesaran, M.H., and Potter, S.M. 1996. Impulse response analysis in nonlinear multivariate models. *Journal of Econometrics*, **74**, 119–147.

Koop, G., Poirier, D.J., and Tobias, J.L. 2007. *Bayesian Econometric Methods*. Cambridge: Cambridge University Press.

Kuan, C.M., and White, H. 1994. Adaptive learning with nonlinear dynamics driven by dependent processes. *Econometrica*, **62**, 1087–1114.

Kwiatkowski, D.P., Phillips, P.C.B., Schmidt, P., and Shin, Y. 1992. Testing the null hypothesis of stationarity against the alternative of a unit root: How sure are we that economic series have a unit root? *Journal of Econometrics*, **54**, 159–178.

Lee, T-H., and Tse, Y. 1996. Cointegration tests with conditional heteroskedasticity. *Journal of Econometrics*, **73**, 401–410.

Lee, T-H., White, H., and Granger, C.W.J. 1993. Testing for neglected nonlinearity in time-series models: A comparison of neural network methods and standard tests. *Journal of Econometrics*, **56**, 269–290.

Li, H., and Maddala, G.S. 1996. Bootstrapping time series models. *Econometric Reviews*, **15**, 115–158.

Lorenz, H-W. 1989. *Nonlinear Dynamical Economics and Chaotic Motion*. Lecture Notes in Economics and Mathematical Systems 334. Springer-Verlag.

Luukkonen, R., Saikkonen, P., and Teräsvirta, T. 1988. Testing linearity against smooth transition autoregressive models. *Biometrika*, **75**, 491–499.

Lye, J.N., and Martin, V.L. 1994. Nonlinear time series modelling and distributional flexibility. *Journal of Time Series Analysis*, **15**, 65–84.

Maddala, G.S., and Kim, I-M. 1998. *Unit Roots, Cointegration and Structural Change*. Cambridge: Cambridge University Press.

Maddala, G.S., and Li, H. 1996. Bootstrap based tests in financial models. Pages 463–488 of: Maddala, G.S., and Rao, C.R. (eds), *Statistical Methods in Finance*. Handbook of Statistics, vol. 14. Elsevier.

Marinucci, D., and Robinson, P.M. 2001. Finite sample improvements in statistical inference with I(1) processes. *Journal of Applied Econometrics*, **16**, 431–444.

Martin, V.L., Tremayne, A.R., and Jung, R.C. 2011. Efficient method of moments estimators for integer time series models. In: *Econometric Society Australasian Meeting*.

McCabe, B.P.M., and Martin, G.M. 2005. Bayesian predictions of low count time series. *International Journal of Forecasting*, **21**, 315–330.

McKenzie, E. 1988. Some ARMA models for dependent sequences of Poisson counts. *Advances in Applied Probability*, **20**, 822–835.

Mehra, R., and Prescott, E.C. 1985. The equity premium: a puzzle. *Journal of Monetary Economics*, **15**, 145–162.

Müller, U.K., and Elliot, G. 2001. *Tests for unit roots and the initial observation.* Discussion Paper 2001-19. University of California, San Diego.

Nelder, J.A., and Mead, R. 1965. A simplex method for function minimization. *Computer Journal*, **7**, 308–313.

Nelsen, R.B. 1999. *An Introduction to Copulas.* New York: Springer-Verlag.

Nelson, C.R., and Plosser, C.I. 1982. Trends and random walks in macroeconmic time series: Some evidence and implications. *Journal of Monetary Economics*, **10**, 139–162.

Nelson, D.B. 1991. Conditional heteroskedasticity in asset returns: A new approach. *Econometrica*, **59**, 347–370.

Newey, W.K., and McFadden, D.L. 1994. Large sample estimation and hypothesis testing. In: Engle, R.F., and McFadden, D.L. (eds), *Handbook of Econometrics, Volume 4*. Elsevier.

Newey, W.K., and West, K.D. 1987. A simple, positive semi-definite, heteroscedasticity and autocorrelation consistent covariance matrix. *Econometrica*, **55**, 703–708.

Newey, W.K., and West, K.D. 1994. Automatic lag selection in covariance matrix estimation. *Review of Economic Studies*, **61**, 631–654.

Neyman, J. 1937. Smooth test for goodness of fit. *Skandinaviske Aktuarietidskrift*, **20**, 150–199.

Ng, S., and Perron, P. 2001. Lag length selection and the construction of unit root tests with good size and power. *Econometrica*, **69**, 1519–1554.

Nowak, S. 2008. *How do public announcements affect the frequency of trading in U.S. airline stocks?* Working Paper 38. CAMA.

Pagan, A.R., and Pesaran, M.H. 2008. Econometric analysis of structural systems with permanent and transitory shocks. *Journal of Economic Dynamics and Control*, **32**, 3376–3395.

Pagan, A.R., and Robertson, J.C. 1989. Structural models of the liquidity effect. *Review of Economics and Statistics*, **80**, 202–217.

Pagan, A.R., and Ullah, A. 1999. *Nonparametric Econometrics.* New York: Cambridge University Press.

Park, J.Y. 1992. Canonical cointegrating regressions. *Econometrica*, **60**, 119–143.

Park, J.Y., and Phillips, P.C.B. 1988. Statistical inference in regressions with integrated processes: Part 1. *Econometric Theory*, **4**, 468–498.

Peersman, G. 2005. What caused the early millenium slowdown? Evidence based on vector autoregressions. *Journal of Applied Econometrics*, **20**, 185–207.

Perron, P. 1989. The Great Crash, the oil price shock, and the unit root hypothesis. *Econometrica*, **57**, 1361–1401.

Perron, P., and Ng, S. 1996. Useful modifications to some unit root tests with dependent errors and their local asymptotic properties. *Review of Economic Studies*, **63**, 435–463.

Perron, P., and Ng, S. 1998. An autoregressive spectral density estimator at frequency zero for nonstationarity tests. *Econometric Theory*, **14**, 560–603.

Perron, P., and Rodriguez, G. 2003. GLS detrending efficient unit root tests and structural change. *Journal of Econometrics*, **115**, 1–27.

Pesaran, M.H., and Shin, Y. 2002. Long run structural modelling. *Econometric Reviews*, **21**, 49–87.

Phillips, P.C.B. 1986. Understanding spurious regressions in econometrics. *Journal of Econometrics*, **33**, 311–340.

Phillips, P.C.B. 1987. Time series regression with a unit root. *Econometrica*, **55**, 277–301.

Phillips, P.C.B. 1991a. Optimal inference in cointegrated systems. *Econometrica*, **59**, 283–306.

Phillips, P.C.B. 1991b. Spectral regression for cointegrated time series. In: Barnett, W. (ed), *Nonparametric and Semiparametric Methods in Economics and Statistics*. Cambridge: Cambridge University Press.

Phillips, P.C.B. 1991c. To criticize the critics: an objective Bayesian analysis of stochastic trends. *Journal of Applied Econometrics*, **6**, 333–364.

Phillips, P.C.B. 1998. Impulse response and forecast error variance asymptotics in nonstationary VARs. *Journal of Econometrics*, **83**, 21–56.

Phillips, P.C.B. 2006. A remark on bimodality and weak instrumentation in structural equation estimation. *Econometric Theory*, **22**, 947–960.

Phillips, P.C.B., and Hansen, B.E. 1990. Statistical inference in instrumental variables regressions with I(1) errors. *Review of Economic Studies*, **57**, 99–125.

Phillips, P.C.B., and Lee, C.C. 1995. Efficiency gains from quasi-differencing under nonstationarity. Pages 300–314 of: *Athens Conference on Applied Probability and Time Series Analysis*. Lecture Notes in Statistics, vol. 115. New York: Springer.

Phillips, P.C.B., and Perron, P. 1988. Testing for a unit root in time series regression. *Biometrika*, **75**, 335–346.

Poskitt, D.S. 2000. Strongly consistent determination of cointegrating rank via canonical correlations. *Journal of Business and Economic Statistics*, **18**, 77–90.

Poskitt, D.S., and Tremayne, A.R. 1980. Testing the specification of a fitted autoregressive-moving average model. *Biometrika*, **67**, 359 – 363.

Rice, J. 1984. Bandwidth choice for nonparametric regression. *Annals of Statistics*, **12**, 1215–1230.

Robinson, P.M. 1983. Nonparametric estimators for time series. *Journal of Time Series Analysis*, **4**, 185–207.

Robinson, P.M. 1988. Root-N-consistent semiparametric regression. *Econometrica*, **56**, 931–954.

Rudebusch, G.D. 2002. Term structure evidence on interest rate smoothing and monetary policy inertia. *Journal of Monetary Economics*, **49**, 1161–1187.

Saikkonen, P. 1991. Asymptotically efficient estimation of cointegration regressions. *Econometric Theory*, **7**, 1–21.

Sargan, J.D. 1964. Wages and prices in the United Kingdom: A study in econometric methodology. In: Hart, P.E., Mills, G., and Whitaker, J.K. (eds), *Econometric Analysis for National Economic Planning*. Colston Papers, vol. 16. London: Butterworth Co.

Sarkar, S., Kanto, A., and Martin, V.L. 2012. *Modelling nonlinearities in equity returns: The mean impact curve*. Tech. rept. Unpublished manuscript. Forthcoming in *Studies in Nonlinear Dynamics and Econometrics*.

Schmidt, P., and Phillips, P.C.B. 1992. LM tests for a unit root in the presence of deterministic trends. *Oxford Bulletin of Economics and Statistics*, **54**, 257–287.

Schwarz, G. 1978. Estimating the dimension of a model. *Annals of Statistics*, **6**(461–464).

Scott, D.W. 1992. *Multivariate Density Estimation Theory, Practice, and Visualization*. New York: John Wiley and Sons, Inc.

Severini, T.A. 2005. *Likelihood Methods in Statistics*. New York: Oxford University Press.

Shanno, D.F. 1970. Conditioning of quasi-Newton methods for function minimization. *Mathematics of Computation*, **24**, 647–657.

Shenton, L.R., and Johnson, W.L. 1975. Moments of a serial correlation coefficient. *Journal of the Royal Statistical Society (Series B)*, **27**, 308–320.

Shephard, N. 2005. *Stochastic Volatility: Selected Readings*. Oxford: Oxford University Press.

Sims, C.A. 1972. Money, income, and causality. *American Economic Review*, **62**, 540–552.

Sims, C.A. 1980. Macroeconomics and reality. *Econometrica*, **48**, 1–48.

Skalin, J., and Teräsvirta, T. 2002. Modelling asymmetries and moving equilibria in unemployment rates. *Macroeconomic Dynamics*, **6**, 202–241.

Smith, A.A. 1993. Estimating nonlinear time-series models using simulated vector autoregressions. *Journal of Applied Econometrics*, **8**, S63–S84.

Stachurski, J., and Martin, V.L. 2008. Computing the distributions of economic models via simulation. *Econometrica*, **76**, 443–450.

Steutel, F.W., and Van Harn, K. 1979. Discrete analogues of self-decomposability and stability. *Annals of Probability*, **7**, 893–899.

Stock, J.H. 1987. Asymptotic properties of least squares estimators of cointegrating vectors. *Econometrica*, **55**, 1035–1056.

Stock, J.H. 1994. Unit roots, structural breaks and trends. Pages 2739–2841 of: Engle, R.F., and McFadden, D.L. (eds), *Handbook of Econometrics, Volume 4*. Amsterdam: North Holland.

Stock, J.H. 1999. A class of tests for integration and cointegration. In: Engle, R.F., and White, H. (eds), *Cointegration, Causality, and Forecasting: Festschrift in Honour of Clive W. J. Granger*. Oxford: Oxford University Press.

Stock, J.H., and Watson, M.W. 1993. A simple estimator of cointegration vectors in higher order integrated systems. *Econometrica*, **61**, 783–820.

Stock, J.H., and Watson, M.W. 2002. Forecasting using principal components from a large number of predictors. *Journal of the American Statistical Association*, **97**, 1167–1179.

Stock, J.H., and Watson, M.W. 2005. *Implications of dynamic factor models for VAR analysis*. Working Paper 11467. NBER.

Stock, J.H., Wright, J.H., and Yogo, M. 2002. A survey of weak instruments and weak identification in generalized method of moments. *Journal of Business and Economic Statistics*, **20**, 518–529.

Stroud, J.R., Muller, P., and Polson, N.G. 2003. Nonlinear state-space models with state dependent variance. *Journal of the American Statistical Association*, **98**, 377–386.

Stuart, A., and Ord, J.K. 1994. *The Advanced Theory of Statistics, Volume 1 Distribution Theory, 6th Edition*. London: Hodder Arnold.

Stuart, A., Ord, J.K., and Arnold, S. 1999. *The Advanced Theory of Statistics, Volume 2A Classical Inference and the Linear Model, 6th Edition*. London: Hodder Arnold.

Subba Rao, T., and Gabr, M.M. 1984. *An Introduction to Bispectral Analysis and Bilinear Time Series Models*. Berlin: Springer-Verlag.

Taylor, J.B. 1993. Discretion versus policy rules in practice. *Carnegie-Rochester Conference Series on Public Policy*, **39**, 195–214.

Taylor, S.J. 1982. Financial returns modelled by the product of two stochastic processes — a study of daily sugar prices 1961–79. In: Anderson, O.D. (ed), *Time Series Analysis: Theory and Practice*. Amsterdam: North Holland.

Teräsvirta, T. 1994. Specification, estimation and evaluation of smooth transition autoregressive models. *Journal of the American Statistical Association*, **89**, 208–218.

Tong, H. 1983. *Threshold Models in Non-linear Time Series Analysis*. Lecture Notes in Statistics 21. Springer-Verlag.

Trenkler, C., Saikkonen, P., and Lütkephol, H. 2007. Testing for the cointegration rank of a VAR process with level shift and trend break. *Journal of Time Series Analysis*, **29**, 331–358.

Uhlig, H. 2005. What are the effects of monetary policy on output? *Journal of Monetary Economics*, **52**, 381–419.

Vasicek, O. 1977. An equilibrium characterization of the term structure. *Journal of Finance*, **5**, 177–188.

Vuong, Q.H. 1989. Likelihood ratio tests for model selection and non-nested hypotheses. *Econometrica*, **57**, 307–333.

Wald, A. 1949. Note on the consistency of the maximum likelihood estimate. *Annals of Mathematical Statistics*, **20**, 595–601.

Wand, M.P, and Jones, M.C. 1995. *Kernel Smoothing*. New York: Chapman and Hall.

Wang, Q., and Phillips, P.C.B. 2009. Asymptotic theory for local time density estimation and nonparametric cointegrating regression. *Econometric Theory*, **25**, 710–738.

White, H. 1980. A heteroskedasticity-consistent covariance matrix estimator and a direct test for heteroskedasticity. *Econometrica*, **48**(817–838).

White, H. 1982. Maximum likelihood estimation of misspecified models. *Econometrica*, **50**, 1–26.

White, H. 1984. *Asymptotic Theory for Econometricians*. Orlando: Academic Press.

White, H. 1989. Learning in artificial neural networks: A statistical perspective. *Neural Computation*, **1**, 425–464.

White, H. 1994. *Estimation, Inference and Specification Analysis*. New York: Cambridge University Press.

Yatchew, A. 2003. *Semiparametric Regression for the Applied Econometrician*. New York: Cambridge University Press.

Zhao, Z. 2010. Density estimation for nonlinear parametric models with conditional heterskedasticity. *Journal of Econometrics*, **155**, 71–82.

Author Index

Abramovitz, A., 111
Ahn, S.K., 682, 684
Aigner, D., 218
Aït-Sahalia, Y., 22, 109, 343, 351, 422
Akaike, H., 486
Al-Osh, M.A., 832, 833
Alzaid, A.A., 832, 833
Andel, J., 118
Andersen, T.G., xxxiii, 758
Anderson, A.P., 732
Anderson, H.M., 745, 746
Anderson, T.W., 250, 678
Andrews, D.W.K., 38, 658
Anthansopoulos G., 745, 746
Arnold, S., 86

Bai, J., 559, 564, 565
Baillie, R.T., 774
Banbura, M., 468
Banerjee, A., 603
Barro, R.J., 501
Barton, T., 118
Beach, C.M., 262
Beaumont, M.A., 435
Bera, A.K., 151
Bernanke, B.S., 523
Berndt, E., 92
Beveridge, S., 668
Billingsley, P., 601
Blanchard, O.J., 520, 541, 542
Blinder, A.S., 523
Bollerslev, T., xxxiii, 758, 774, 783
Boswijk, P., 683
Breitung, J., 658
Broyden, C.G., 97

Bu, R., 835
Butler, R.J., 216, 225

Campbell, J.Y., 502, 511, 688
Canova, F., 525
Carrion-i Silvestre, J.L., 651
Carter, C.K., 545
Cavaliere, G., 700
Chan, K.C., 342
Chang, Y., 643
Chapman, D.A., 419, 422
Chen, X., 739
Cheng, X., 700
Chib, S., 433, 456
Cochrane, J.H., 571
Conley, T.G., 422
Cornuet, J-M., 435
Cox, J.C., 24, 109, 111, 343
Craine, R., 571
Creedy, J., 717, 726

Davidson, J., 38, 49, 52, 601, 602, 683
de Nicolo, G., 525
Dickey, D.A., 619, 623, 626
Diebold, F.X., xxxiii, 456, 510, 758
DiNardo, J., 419
Dolado, J.J., 603
Drost, F.C., 785, 786, 807
Drovandi, C.C., 435
Duffie, D., 433, 444
Dungey, M., 567, 732
Durlauf, S.N., 612

Elliot, G., 622, 623, 640, 641, 652
Engel, C., 734

Engle, R.F., 662, 669, 710, 758, 785, 787, 797, 812, 836
Ericsson, N.R., 718, 749

Faddy, M.J., 435
Fan, Y., 739
Fletcher, R., 97
Forchini, G., 175
Fry, R., 522, 525, 526, 537
Frühwirth-Schnatter, S., 835
Fuller, W.A., 619, 623, 626

Gabr, M.M., 732
Galbraith, J.W., 603
Gallant, A.R., 433, 441, 444
Galli, J., 523
Getmansky, M., 261
Geweke, J., xxxiii, 433
Ghosh, A., 151
Ghysels, E., 758, 807
Giannone, G., 468
Gill, P.E., 100, 101
Goldfarb, D., 97
González-Rivera, G., 785, 786, 807
Gouriéroux, C., 433, 435, 461, 463
Granger, C.W.J., 662, 669, 710, 726, 731, 732, 739, 756
Greenberg, E., xxxiii, 433
Gurkaynak, R.S., 571

Hadri, K., 835
Hall, B., 92
Hall, P., 49
Hall, R., 92
Hamilton, J.D., 552, 734, 738, 752, 837, 844
Han, H., 775, 804
Hannan, E.J., 486
Hansen, B.E., 710, 723
Hansen, L.P., 368, 370, 373, 387, 422
Harding, D., 719
Harris, D., 651, 700
Harvey, A.C., 108, 271, 552, 558, 567, 570
Harvey, D.I., 651, 653
Hatanaka, M., 252
Hausman, J., 92
Heaton, J., 370
Hendry, D.F., 603, 718, 749
Heyde, C.C., 49
Hillier, G., 175
Hocking, J., 522, 537

Hodrick, R.J., 567
Horowitz, J.L., xxxiii
Hsiao, C., 683
Hurn, A.S., 111

Ingersoll, J.E., 24, 109, 111, 343

Jacquier, E., 456
Jaeger, A., 567, 570
Jeisman, J., 111
Johansen, S., 662, 672, 675, 683, 684, 688, 692, 697
Johnson, W.L., 508
Jones, M.C., 403
Jordà, Ò., 837, 844
Jung, R.C., 832, 833, 835, 840, 845
Juselius, K., 683

Kanto, A., 808
Karolyi, G.A., 342
Kelly, B., 787, 797
Kendall, M., 95
Kennan, J., 30, 845
Khouja, M.W., 224
Kim, C-J., 456, 735
Kim, D., 651
Kim, I-M., 619
Kim, S., 517
Klein, L.R., 184, 192
Klimko, L.A., 833, 845
Knez, P., 576
Kohn, R., 545
Konstas, P., 224
Koop, G., xxxiii, 468, 742, 743
Kroner, K.F., 787
Kuan, C.M., 726, 730
Kwiatkowski, D.P., 659

Lütkephol, H., 672
Labys, P., xxxiii, 758
Lee, C.C., 625
Lee, T-H., 701, 726, 731
Leybourne, S.J., 651, 653
Li, H., xxxiii
Lindsay, K.A., 111
Litterman, R., 576
Lo, A.W., 261
Longstaff, F.A., 342
Lorenz, H-W., 717
Lovell, C.A.K., 218
Luttmer, E.G.J., 422

Luukkonen, R., 723, 724, 725, 749
Lye, J., 757

MacKinnon, J.G., 262
Maddala, G.S., xxxiii, 619
Makarov, I., 261
Marin, J-M., 435
Marinucci, D., 711
Martin, G.M., 835
Martin, V.L., 404, 522, 537, 567, 571, 717, 726, 732, 757, 808, 835, 840
McCabe, B.P.M., 835
McDonald J.B., 216, 225
McFadden, D.L., 12, 61, 365
McKenzie, E., 832, 840
Mead, R., 100
Mehra, R., 391
Mikkelsen, H.O., 774
Monahan, J.C., 658
Monfort, A., 433, 435, 461, 463
Mosconi, R., 672
Muller, P., 545
Müller, U.K., 652
Murray, W., 100, 101

Nardari, F., 456
Nelder, J.A., 100
Nelsen, R.B., 152
Nelson, C.R., 583, 584, 613, 668
Nelson, D.B., 777
Nelson, P.I., 833, 845
Nelson, R.D., 216, 225
Nerlove, M., 456
Newey, W.K., 12, 61, 325, 335, 365
Neyman, J., 151
Ng, S., 559, 564, 565, 626, 643, 644
Nielsen, B., 672
Nowak, S, 837

Ord, J.K., 40, 68, 86, 138, 218

Pagan, A.R., 403, 411, 413, 419, 420, 525, 526, 531, 697, 719
Park, J.Y., 643, 710, 711, 775, 804
Pearson, N.D., 419, 422
Peersman, G., 525, 535
Perron, P., 626, 643, 644, 645, 649, 651, 658
Pesaran, M.H., 683, 684, 697, 742, 743
Pettitt, A.N., 435

Phillips, P.C.B., 175, 413, 596, 612, 623, 625, 626, 637, 644, 658, 659, 682, 684, 689, 697, 700, 710, 711
Piazzesi, M., 571
Plosser, C.I., 583, 584
Poirier, D.J., xxxiii
Polson, N.G., 456, 545
Poskitt, D.S., 507, 700
Potter, S.M., 742, 743
Prescott, E.C., 391, 567
Prestwich, K.M., 718, 749

Quah, D., 520, 541, 542
Quinn, B.G., 486

Rahbek, A., 700
Rapach, D.E., 521, 538
Reichlin, L., 468
Reinsel, G.C., 682, 684
Renault, E., 433, 435, 461, 463
Rice, J., 415
Robert, C.P., 435
Robertson, J.C., 531
Robinson, P.M., 413, 418, 711, 739
Rodriguez, G., 649
Ronning, G., 832, 833, 845
Ross, S.A., 24, 109, 111, 343
Rossi, P.E., 456
Rothenberg, T.J., 623, 640, 641
Roubini, N., 517
Rudebusch, G.D., 183, 456
Russell, J.R., 812, 836

Sack, B., 571
Saikkonen, P., 672, 689, 711, 723, 724, 725, 749
Sanders, A.B., 342
Santa-Clara, P., 758, 807
Sargan, J.D., 242
Sarkar, S., 808
Scheinkman, J.A., 422, 576
Schmidt, P., 218, 623, 659
Schwarz, G., 486
Scott, D.W., 401, 416
Severini, T.A., 69
Shanno, D.F., 97
Shenton, L.R., 508
Shephard, N., xxxiii, 456
Sheppard, K., 787
Shiller, R.J., 502, 511, 688
Shin, Y., 659, 683, 684

Sims, C.A., 467, 494, 504, 517
Singleton, K.J., 373, 387, 433, 444
Skalin, J., 744
Smith, A.A., 433
Stachurski, J., 404
Stegun, I.A., 111
Steutel, F.W., 812, 832
Stock, J.H., 189, 456, 561, 564, 565, 619, 623, 626, 640, 641, 644, 710, 711
Stroud, J.R., 545
Stuart, A., 40, 68, 86, 95, 138, 218
Subba Rao, T., 732
Susmel, R., 734
Swanson, E., 571

Tauchen, G., 433, 441, 444
Taylor, A.M.R., 651, 653, 700
Taylor, J.B., 183, 192
Taylor, S.J., 758
Teräsvirta, T., 723, 724, 725, 744, 749
Tobias, J.L., xxxiii, 419
Tong, H., 716
Tremayne, A.R., 507, 832, 833, 835, 840, 845
Trenkler, C., 672
Tse, Y., 701

Uhlig, H., 525
Ullah, A., 403, 411, 413, 419, 420

Vahid, F., 745, 746
Valkanov, R., 758, 807
Van Harn, K., 812, 832
Vasicek, O., 22
Vuong, Q.H., 212, 214

Wagner, H., 835
Wald, A., 61
Wand, M.P., 403
Wang, Q., 413
Watson, M.H., 711
Watson, M.W., 456, 561, 564, 565
West, K.D., 325, 335
White, H., 12, 38, 49, 52, 307, 333, 726, 729, 730, 731
White, S.B., 216, 225
Wooldridge, J.M., 783
Wright, J.H., 189
Wright, M.H., 100, 101

Xiao, Z., 151

Yaron, A., 370
Yatchew, A., 397, 415, 418
Yilmaz, K., 510
Yogo, M., 189

Zhao, Z., 118, 405

Subject Index

Akaike information criterion (AIC), 486, 779
AR(1) model
   Asymptotic distribution, 588–591
Artificial neural network, 726–731
   estimation, 728–730
   testing, 731
Asset returns
   statistical properties, 758–762
Asymmetry, 719
Asymptotic distribution
   super-consistency, 596
Asymptotic properties, 60–68
   consistency, 60–62
   efficiency, 65–68
   normality, 63–65
Augmented Dickey-Fuller test, 642–643
   lag length selection, 643
Autocorrelated regression model
   asymptotic distribution, 242–251
   estimation, 235–242
   lagged dependent variable, 251–253
   likelihood function, 230
   simultaneous systems, 258–261
   testing, 253–258
Autocorrelation function (ACF), 468
Autoregressive (AR) model, 228
   binary, 824–826
   relationship with moving-average (MA)
      model, 478, 481
Autoregressive conditional duration (ACD)
      model, 836
Autoregressive conditional hazard (ACH)
      model, 837
Autoregressive conditional heteroskedasticity
      (ARCH) model, 762–763

and leptokurtosis, 780–785
   ARCH(∞) model, 769
   diagnostics, 779–780
   estimation, 763–766
   news impact curve (NIC), 763
   nonstationary with nonlinear
      heteroskedasticity (ARCH-NNH),
      804
   testing, 767–769
   univariate extensions, 769–778
Autoregressive moving-average (ARMA)
      model, 228, 467, 471–472
   conditional maximum likelihood, 232–233
   estimation, 482–484
   testing, 489–491

Bandwidth, 394, 398–401, 413–415
Bartlett weighting scheme, 325
Beveridge-Nelson decomposition, 668
Bilinear time series model, 732–734
   estimation, 733
   testing, 734
Binomial thinning, 831–835
   conditional least squares (CLS), 833
   EMM estimation, 840
   maximum likelihood estimation, 833
Bollerslev-Wooldridge standard errors, 783
Bootstrapping, 742
Breusch-Pagan test of heteroskedasticity,
   287
Brownian motion, 446, 448
   estimation, 449–450
   standard, 598
Business cycle, 456
   Kaldorian nonlinear, 717

Capital asset pricing model (CAPM), 215, 261
  consumption (C-CAPM), 360
Censored regression model, 817
Central limit theorem
  functional (FCLT), 598–602
  Lindeberg-Feller, 47–49
  Lindeberg-Levy, 45
  martingale difference sequence, 49–51
  mixing, 51–52
Chi-square distribution, 133
Choleski decomposition, 289
CIR model, 109–112
CKLS model, 342, 381
Cochrane-Orcutt algorithm, 240–242
Cointegration, 668
  cointegrating rank, 668
  cointegrating vector, 668
  Engle-Granger two-step estimator, 674
  Granger representation theorem, 669–670
  testing, 689–696
    cointegrating vector, 693
    exogeneity, 695
    rank selection, 690, 698–700
Conditional maximum likelihood, 232–233
Conditional volatility, 456
Continuous Mapping Theorem, 602–603
Continuous-time models, 445–448
Convergence
  in probability, 40
Copula
  Gaussian copula, 152
Covariance matrix, 160
Cramér-Rao lower bound, 65–67
Curse of dimensionality, 397, 417
  overcoming, 545

Delta method, 102
Deterministic trend, 584
Deterministic trend model
  Sample moments, 594–596
Dickey-Fuller tests, 626–627
Difference stationary, 586
Discrete time series model, 812–818
  estimation, 819
  testing, 822–824
Double exponential distribution, 217
Downhill simplex algorithm, 100–101
Durations
  autoregressive conditional duration (ACD) model, 836

autoregressive conditional hazard (ACH) model, 837
  maximum likelihood estimation, 835

Edgeworth expansion, 68–69
Efficient method of moments (EMM), 441
  and instrumental variables, 442–444
  and SMM, 444
  estimation, 449–450
Exact maximum likelihood, 230–231
Exponential generalised autoregressive conditional heteroskedasticity (EGARCH) model, 777

Factor vector autoregressive (F-VAR) model, 559
Finite-sample properties, 68–72
  invariance, 71
  non-uniqueness, 72
  sufficiency, 70–71
  unbiasedness, 69–70
Full-information maximum likelihood (FIML), 167–171
  heteroskedasticity, 289–291
Functional Central Limit Theorem, 598–602

Gauss-Newton algorithm, 202–207, 235–237
  and Cochrane-Orcutt algorithm, 242
Generalised autoregressive conditional heteroskedasticity (GARCH) model, 769–771
  and leptokurtosis, 780–785
  asymmetry, 776–777
  Bollerslev-Wooldridge standard errors, 783
  diagnostics, 779–780
  estimation, 771
  fractional integrated GARCH (FIGARCH), 774
  GARCH-in-mean, 777–778
  integrated GARCH (IGARCH), 774–775
  testing, 771
Generalised method of moments (GMM), 352–353
  and maximum likelihood, 361–362
  asymptotics, 364–368
  conditional moments, 358–359
  empirical moments, 354–356
  estimation strategies, 369–372
  identification, 373–376
  objective function, 362–363

population moments, 353–354
  testing, 373–376, 380–381
Geometric Brownian motion, 451–452
  efficient method of moments (EMM)
      estimation, 453
  indirect inference, 452–453
Gradient
  definition, 17
  properties, 55–57
Granger causality, 492
Granger representation theorem, 669–670
Great Moderation, 294

Hadamard product, 499
Hannan information criterion (HIC),
      486
Hansen-Sargen J test, 375, 444
Hatanaka estimator, 252–253
Hessian matrix
  definition, 19–20
Heteroskedasticity, 272–276
  and autocorrelation, 292–293
  asymptotic distribution, 281–282
  estimation, 276–281
  simultaneous systems, 288–294
  testing, 282–288
Histogram, 393
Hodrick-Prescott filter, 567–570
Homoskedasticity, 272
Hypothesis testing
  asymptotic relationships, 136–137
  finite-sample relationships, 138–139
  linear, 122–123
  nonlinear, 123–124
  power, 140–141
  simple and composite, 121
  size, 139

Identification, 171–173
  in Kalman filters, 561–562
  in structural vector autoregressive (SVAR)
      model, 531–533
  in structural vector autoregressive (SVAR)
      models, 516
  test of over-identifying restrictions, 533–534
Impulse response function, 493–497
  standard errors, 498
  vector error correction model (VECM),
      696–697
Indirect inference, 435–440
  and indirect least squares, 439–440

Information criteria, 486–488
Information equality, 248–249
  misspecification, 317
Information matrix, 58–59
  information matrix equality, 58
Instrumental variables, 173–176
  and EMM, 442–444
  identification, 176
  weak instrument, 174
Integrated generalised autoregressive
      conditional heteroskedasticity
      (IGARCH) model, 774
Inverse cumulative density technique, 221
Invertibility, 481–484

Jacobian, 849
Jensen's inequality, 54
Johansen estimator, 675–679
Joint probability density function, 9–11

Kalman filter, 455–456, 544–546
  and vector autoregressive moving-average
      (VARMA) models, 566–567
  estimation, 561–565
  extensions, 557–560
  factor loadings, 545
  Hodrick-Prescott, 567–570
  initialisation, 552
  Kalman gain, 551
  latent factor extraction, 560
  measurement equation, 545
  multivariate, 554–555
  signal-to-noise ratio, 570
  state equation, 546
  state-space system, 546
  univariate, 548–552
Kernel density estimator, 393–397
  bandwith, 394
  Gaussian kernel, 394
  kernel functions, 394
  multivariate, 396–397
  optimal bandwidth, 398–401
  properties, 397–403
Kernel regression estimator
  multivariate, 416–418
  optimal bandwidth, 413–415
  properties
      asymptotic , 411–413
      finite-sample, 410
Klein model, 184
Kolmogorov-Smirnov test, 779

Lag operator, 850
Lagrange multiplier (LM) test, 120, 131–133
  asymptotic distribution, 133
  test for ARCH, 767–769
  test of linearity, 723
Lagrange multiplier (LM) tests
  autocorrelated regression model, 255–258
Laplace distribution, 217
Law of iterated expectations, 320, 340
Leptokurtosis, 761
Likelihood ratio (LR) test, 120, 124–125
  asymptotic distribution, 133
  test for ARCH, 767
Limit cycle, 716
Line searching, 98–99
Linear regression model
  and discrete time series model, 816
  estimation
    full-information maximum likelihood
      (FIML), 167–171
    instrumental variables, 173–176
    ordinary least squares, 162–166
  multivariate, 166
  reduced form, 160–161
  simultaneous system, 158–159
    identification, 171–173
    seemingly unrelated regression (SUR),
      176
  structural form, 160
  testing, 177–182
  univariate, 158
Linear time-series model
  asymptotic distribution, 488–489
Log-likelihood function
  defined, 12
  population, 54
  properties, 54–55
LST linearity test, 724–725
Lyapunov condition, 47

Marginal propensity to consume (MPC),
  210
Markov switching, 456
Markov switching model, 734–738
  estimation, 735–737
Martingale difference sequence (mds), 36
Matrix notation, 160
Maximum likelihood estimator, 12
  and generalised method of moments
    (GMM), 361–362

and ordinary least squares, 165, 247
  conditional, 232–233
  deterministic exogenous variables, 245
  exact, 230–231
  full-information, 167–171
  lagged dependent variable, 252
  misspecification, 307–311
  qualitative data, 818
  stochastic and independent exogenous
    variables, 245
Maximum likelihood principal
  motivating examples, 3–9
    AR(1) model, 6
    AR(1) model with heteroskedasticity,
      8
    ARCH model, 8
    Bilinear model, 7
    count model, 5
    exponential model, 6
    linear model, 6
    time invariant model, 4
Mixing, 38
  Central limit theorem, 51–52
Monte Carlo methods, 138
Moving-average (MA) model, 228
  relationship with autoregressive (AR)
    model, 478, 481
Multivariate GARCH models, 786–798
  BEKK, 788
  DCC, 791
  DECO, 797
  VECH, 787

Nadaraya-Watson kernel estimator, 392,
  406–408
Newey-West estimator, 334–335
  standard errors, 335
News impact curve (NIC), 763
  and asymmetry, 777
Newton methods, 88
  BHHH algorithm, 92–94
  method of scoring, 90–91
  Newton-Raphson, 89
Newton-Raphson algorithm, 230–237
Neyman's smooth goodness of fit test, 151
Nonlinear consumption function, 204
Nonlinear impulse responses, 740–743
Nonlinear least squares, 206–207
Nonlinear regression model, 194–195
  asymptotic distributions, 207–208

estimation, 196–203
testing, 208–214
Nonlinear time-series model
  autoregressive conditional
    heteroskedasticity (ARCH) model,
    762–763
    estimation, 763–766
    testing, 767–769
  generalised autoregressive conditional
    heteroskedasticity (GARCH) model,
    769–772
Nonparametric autoregression, 738–740
Nonparametric regression, 392, 407
Nonstationary process
  multivariate, 606
Normal distribution
  bivariate, 72–78
Numerical derivatives, 107–108

Okun's law, 542
Order condition, 171
Order of integration, 586
Ordinary least squares, 162–166
  deterministic exogenous variables,
    247–250
  Gauss-Newton algorithm, 207
  lagged dependent variable, 252
  stochastic and independent exogenous
    variables, 250–251
Ornstein–Uhlenbeck (OU) process, 454,
  637
Outer product of the gradients matrix, 92–93

Partial autocorrelation function (PACF),
  468
Parzen weighting scheme, 325
Poisson regression model, 830–831
Practical optimisation, 104–109
  choice of algorithm, 106
  concentrating the likelihood, 104
  convergence criteria, 108
  numerical derivatives, 107
  parameter constraints, 105
  starting values, 108
Present value model, 502
Probability limit (plim), 40–41
Probit regression model, 817
  ordered, 826–827
Profile log-likelihood function, 105
Purchasing power parity (PPP), 683

Quadratic spectral weighting scheme, 325
Quasi likelihood function, 312
Quasi-maximum likelihood estimator, 307,
  312–313
  and information equality, 317
  and linear regression, 326–331
  asymptotics, 314–316
    iid data, 320–322
    covariance matrix, 324–326
    dependent data, 322–323
  testing, 338
Quasi-Newton methods, 96–97
  BFGS algorithm, 96–97

Rank condition, 171
Rational expectations model, 501–502
Regularity conditions, 53–54
Risk behaviour, 777

Sandwich estimator, 324
Schwarz information criterion (SIC), 486, 779
Score
  definition, 17
Seasonality, 672
Semiparametric regression
  partial linear model, 418
Simulated generalised method of moments
    (SMM), 444–445
  and EMM, 444
Simultaneity bias, 531
Skewness, 47
Slutsky's theorem, 41
  and expectations operator, 70
  and probability limit, 70
Spurious regression problem, 617
Standard errors
  computing, 101–104
  Newey-West, 335
  White, 333
State-space model, 455–456
Stationarity
  definitions, 34–36
  examples, 476
  stationarity condition, 476
  strict, 35
  weak, 34
  Wold's representation theorem, 477–478
Stochastic frontier model, 218
Stochastic integral convergence, 607
Stochastic integral theorem, 604

Stochastic trend, 584
Stochastic trend model
  sample moments, 591–592
Stochastic volatility, 454–456
  indirect inference, 455
Strange attractor, 717
Structural breaks, 672
Structural vector autoregressive (SVAR)
    model, 468, 512–515
  estimation, 527–531
  identification, 531–533
    restrictions, 516–526
  non-recursive, 531
  partially recursive, 531
  recursive, 531
  test of over-identifying restrictions, 533–534
  testing, 533–534
  time-varying volatility, 799
Student t distribution
  multivariate, 809
Super-consistency, 596, 689

Taylor rule, 183
Threshold generalised autoregressive
    conditional heteroskedasticity
    (TARCH) model, 776
Threshold time series model, 719–726
  estimation, 722–723
  testing, 723–726
  weighting function, 719–722
Tobit model, 817
Trace statistic, 690
Trend stationary, 586
Truncated regression model, 818
Type-1 error, 139
Type-2 error, 140

Uncovered interest parity (UIP), 683
Unit root
  definition, 619
Unit root tests
  simulating critical values, 634–635
  asymptotic distributions, 629–630
  asymptotic local power, 636–642
  augmented Dickey-Fuller test, 642–643
  Dickey-Fuller tests, 626–627
  first-difference detrending, 624
  generalised least squares detrending, 625
  initial conditions, 652–653
  KPSS test, 659
  M tests, 627–629

M tests and autocorrelation, 643–644
  ordinary least squares detrending, 623–624
  Phillips-Perron test, 657
  point optimal tests, 639–641
  power
    asymptotic power envelope, 641
    structural break asymptotics, 647–650
    structural break critical values, 650
    structural breaks, 645–651
    union of rejections, 652
Unobserved-component model, 569

Variance decomposition, 498–499
Vasicek interest rate model, 22–27, 72
Vector autoregressive (VAR) model, 467–468,
    474
  dynamics of, 491–492
  relationship with vector moving-average
    (VMA) model, 479–480, 481
Vector autoregressive moving-average
    (VARMA) model, 467–468, 474
  estimation, 482–484
  likelihood function, 482
  testing, 489–491
Vector error correction model (VECM)
  and vector autoregression (VAR) model,
    666–667
  asymptotics, 684–689
  bivariate, 665–667
  deterministic components, 670–672
  estimation, 672–683
    Johansen estimator, 675–679
  identification, 682–683
    structural restrictions, 683
    triangular restrictions, 682
  impulse response function, 696–697
  multivariate, 667–668
  testing, 689–696
    effect of heteroskedasticity, 700–701
Vector moving-average (VMA) model, 475
  relationship with vector autoregressive
    (VAR) model, 479–480, 481
Vuong's non-nested test, 212–214

Wald test, 120, 128–129
  asymptotic distribution, 133–135
  aysymptotically equivalent forms, 129
  linear hypotheses, 129
  nonlinear hypotheses, 130–131
  test for ARCH, 767
  test of linearity, 723

Weak law of large numbers (WLLN),
38–40
Weighted least squares (WLS), 279–281
White estimator, 332–333
standard errors, 333
White test of heteroskedasticity, 287

White's theorem, 755
Wold's representation theorem, 477–478

Zellner-Revankar production function, 195,
199–200
Zig-zag algorithm, 238–240, 278–279

For EU product safety concerns, contact us at Calle de José Abascal, 56–1°,
28003 Madrid, Spain or eugpsr@cambridge.org.

www.ingramcontent.com/pod-product-compliance
Ingram Content Group UK Ltd.
Pitfield, Milton Keynes, MK11 3LW, UK
UKHW042210180425
457623UK00011B/131